American Economic Policy in the 1980s

A National Bureau
of Economic Research
Conference Report

American Economic Policy in the 1980s

Edited and with an Introductory Essay by

Martin Feldstein

 The University of Chicago Press

Chicago and London

MARTIN FELDSTEIN is George F. Baker Professor of Economics at Harvard University and president and chief executive officer of the National Bureau of Economic Research. He was chairman of the Council of Economic Advisers from 1982 to 1984.

338.973

The University of Chicago Press, Chicago 60637
The University of Chicago Press, Ltd., London
© 1994 by the National Bureau of Economic Research
All rights reserved. Published 1994
Printed in the United States of America
02 01 00 99 98 97 96 95 94 1 2 3 4 5
ISBN: 0-226-24093-2 (cloth)

Library of Congress Cataloging-in-Publication Data

American economic policy in the 1980s / edited by Martin Feldstein.
    p.   cm.—(A National Bureau of Economic Research conference
report)
    Includes bibliographical references and indexes.
    1. United States—Economic policy—1981–1993.   I. Feldstein,
Martin S.   II. Series: Conference report (National Bureau of Economic
Research)
    HC106.8.A439   1994
    338.973′009′048—dc20   93-27972
                                                                        CIP

⊗The paper used in this publication meets the minimum requirements of
the American National Standard for Information Sciences—Permanence
of Paper for Printed Library Materials, ANSI Z-39.48–1984.

Contents

Preface

This book examines the broad range of American economic policy in the 1980s. The eleven scholarly background studies presented trace the evolution of domestic and international policies, including developments in regulation and antitrust as well as monetary, trade, tax, and budget policies. These background papers are complemented by twenty-two personal essays by individuals who held key economic policy positions during those years or, in a few cases, in earlier administrations. I have written a long personal essay that discusses my own perceptions about those areas of economic policy with which I was most actively involved while I was in Washington and as an academic researcher.

The authors of the background papers and the policy officials met together to discuss these issues in Williamsburg, Virginia. A summary of the discussion at the conference also appears in this volume.

My goal in organizing this NBER project was to improve our understanding of how and why economic policy developed as it did in the 1980s and to create an authoritative record that others who study this period will want to consult. Like any study of history, this book discusses a combination of specific facts and general tendencies: the individual events, the personalities, and the critical moments that constitute the historic record as well as the broad evolving trends and intellectual forces that shaped those developments. As part of the analysis, I asked the authors of the background papers to consider explicitly the role that economists and economic ideas played in the policy developments that they studied. I also asked them specifically not to try to assess the effects of those policies or to prescribe directions for future policy.

The personal essays and the discussion remarks of the individuals who held senior policy positions during the 1980s provide an unusual and valuable source of information. They must, however, be read with caution. There is, of course, a natural tendency not to be too critical of one's own record or of the record of one's administration colleagues. But I was also struck by the excessive modesty of several of the participants, who appeared determined to avoid claiming the credit that they deserve for major intellectual and policy changes in the 1980s. Moreover, all the authors who look back in these chapters and essays to the 1980s have the advantage of knowing what followed, and that knowledge no doubt colors our interpretations of the events of the past.

I want to thank the authors of the eleven background papers for their efforts in combining economic analysis with an examination of the historic record that involved venturing beyond the usual methods of economic research to interview officials and former officials about the events of the 1980s. We are all grateful to those officials for their time and candor in contributing to this study.

Those former officials who prepared personal essays and who participated in the Williamsburg conference make this book a unique historic record and made the project an exceptionally interesting one for all the participants.

I am particularly indebted to my colleague Douglas Elmendorf for his help with this volume. He prepared the excellent record of the conference discussion in a way that captures both the substance of the issues and the very lively style of the meeting. He was assisted in this by Sheri Bittenbender, Karen Dynan, and Gina Raimondo. He was also responsible for all aspects of the preparation of the book itself.

My thanks go also to several people who provided helpful comments on my own essay: Geoffrey Carliner, Douglas Elmendorf, Kathleen Feldstein, Larry Lindsey, and James Poterba.

The Mellon Foundation provided financial support for this project. I am grateful to Jack Sawyer, former president of the Mellon Foundation, for encouraging and funding a series of NBER projects that have brought together academic economists and individuals who have played leading roles in government and business. The first of those projects, published in 1980 by the University of Chicago Press as *The American Economy in Transition,* established a style of research that has been repeated successfully in a number of areas since then.

As part of the current project on the political economy of the 1980s, I asked Alberto Alesina to organize an NBER project in which political scientists examined the forces influencing economic policy during that decade. The papers prepared in that project have been published in *Politics and Economics in the Eighties,* edited by Alberto Alesina and Geoffrey Carliner (University of Chicago Press, 1991).

I am also pleased to thank several members of the NBER staff for their assistance in the planning and execution of the meetings and in the preparation of these volumes, in particular Kirsten Foss Davis, Ilana Hardesty, Mark Fitz-Patrick, Norma MacKenzie, and Carolyn Terry.

This project has been particularly important to me both intellectually and personally. I am grateful to all those who participated and who helped bring it to a successful completion.

Martin Feldstein

1 American Economic Policy in the 1980s: A Personal View

Martin Feldstein

The decade of the 1980s was a time of fundamental changes in American economic policy. These changes were influenced by the economic conditions that prevailed as the decade began, by the style and political philosophy of President Ronald Reagan, and by the new intellectual climate among economists and policy officials. The unusually high rate of inflation in the late 1970s and the rapid increase of personal taxes and government spending in the 1960s and 1970s had caused widespread public discontent. Ronald Reagan's election in 1980 reflected this political mood and provided a president who was committed to achieving low inflation, to lowering tax rates, and to shrinking the role of government in the economy.

In our democracy, major changes in government policy generally do not occur without corresponding changes in the thinking of politicians, journalists, other opinion leaders, and the public at large. In the field of economic policy, those changes in thinking often reflect prior intellectual developments within the economics profession itself.

That was clearly true of the broad shape of economic policy in the 1980s. While there is certainly never unanimity among economists, by the late 1970s the combination of Keynesian macroeconomics and interventionist microeconomics that had been widely accepted in the postwar decades was clearly in retreat. In its place, the traditional market-oriented ideas that had previously characterized economics since the time of Adam Smith were having a greater influence on both research and policy conclusions.

Economists recognized that it was through improved incentives rather than through increased demand that a sustained increase in national income could be achieved. Research studies emphasized the adverse effects on incentives of high marginal tax rates and of the rules governing transfer programs like unemployment insurance and Social Security that penalized work and saving. An increasing number of economists recognized the complex adverse effects of inflation and the fact that the fundamental cause of inflation is excess demand rather than the monopolistic power of unions and businesses. New ideas on antitrust and on regulation replaced older thinking about the proper relation between the government and private businesses.[1]

I was privileged to have a front row seat on policy developments as chairman of the Council of Economic Advisers (CEA) from 1982 through 1984. In this chapter, I comment on those aspects of policy with which I was most closely involved during those years: monetary and exchange rate policy; tax policy; and budget issues. Of course, my interest in these subjects preceded my days in Washington and continued after I had returned to Harvard and the NBER. I have therefore commented on some aspects of the evolution of policy throughout the decade of the 1980s while generally giving much more detailed attention to the events during my time at the CEA.

This chapter is not intended as a detailed history of economic policy during the 1980s because that has been ably provided by the authors of the background papers in this book. Nor is it a collection of personal anecdotes aimed at capturing the spirit of the Reagan administration or the character of my administration colleagues. Rather it is an extensive essay that analyzes some of the reasons for the policy changes that occurred and that offers my judgments about some of those changes.[2]

I have not tried to summarize or comment on the other chapters of this book. I have also avoided references to the literature on economics and economic policy during those years. I do provide some bibliographic references to my own papers, particularly nontechnical ones, in order to incorporate their content into this chapter. It would, of course, be best to read the present introductory chapter in combination with both the academic background papers and the personal statements of the other contributors to this book.

Although I have avoided any discussion of personalities in these pages, I think it would be negligent of me to write so much about economic policy in the 1980s without saying something about my perception of President Reagan's personal views on economics and the role that he played in shaping economic policy during those years. I saw the president in small groups at least once a week over a two-year period and talked with him about every aspect of economic policy. I believe that he shaped economic policy significantly through his style of leadership and his consistent and well-communicated vision of what constituted good economic policy. In the sections that follow, I will comment more specifically on his attitudes about monetary policy and inflation, about taxes, about the budget deficit, and about particular major areas of government spending. Here I will make just some very general observations.

I never had any doubt during those years about the sincerity of Ronald

---

1. For more extensive discussion of these ideas, see Feldstein (1981c, 1982a, 1986c, 1988c).
2. For a discussion of the organization of policy-making during my time in Washington and the role of the Council of Economic Advisers in particular, see Feldstein (1989c, 1992b).

Reagan's basic goals for economic policy: smaller government, lower tax rates, and less inflation. He favored smaller government and less spending on domestic programs not only because he disliked the taxes needed to pay for large government programs but also because he believed that much of the money paid by the government went to those who were reasonably well off. He was clearly moved by poverty and individual hardship and wanted to avoid policy changes that would hurt such people. His concern in the area of taxation was high individual marginal tax rates; although he thought that the corporation tax was irrational and "should be abolished," it was not something that he understood or cared about in the way that he did about personal tax rates.

President Reagan delegated to the White House staff and the cabinet departments the responsibility for the specific designs of most domestic policies. He was most actively involved in shaping the details of those aspects of domestic policy that he had previously dealt with as governor of California, including issues like unemployment and welfare.[3]

I believe that Ronald Reagan was correctly described as a "great communicator," not just because he read prepared speeches very well, but because of his skill in less structured situations like press conferences and small meetings. He had the ability to convey a clear sense of policy direction without limiting his future flexibility. In that way, he was able to achieve more through negotiation and to make sacrifices on specific issues without changing the public's support for his overall program.

Although this chapter and the book as a whole focus on the experience of the United States, the shift of economic policy in the 1980s was part of a worldwide movement toward greater reliance on markets that included countries as different as England, Spain, Mexico, China, and the Soviet Union. Depending on national circumstances, strengthening the role of the market involved everything from lowering inflation and income taxes to reducing regulation and privatizing state industries.

The global shift in policy in the 1980s may have been nothing more than a collection of ephemeral national attempts to "try something different" in response to the widespread disappointment with the economic record of the previous decade: the rapidly rising unemployment in Europe, hyperinflations in Latin America, stagflation in the United States, and a total failure of Marxist central planning policies in Asia, Africa, Latin America, and the Soviet Union. It may, however, reflect a more long-lasting change based on a correct diagnosis of the specific causes of poor performance and on a more fundamental change in economic thinking around the world. Only time will tell. But a study of the changes that occurred in the United States and of the reasons for those changes may help us understand and anticipate events in other countries as well as in the United States.

3. On President Reagan's involvement in different aspects of domestic economic policy, see Feldstein (1984b).

The first part of this chapter discusses the important changes in monetary policy in the 1980s, particularly in the early part of the decade. The second and third parts deal with tax and budget issues. The final part discusses the fluctuations of the dollar and their relation to trade policy.

1.1 Monetary Policy and Inflation

1.1.1 Attitudes about Inflation

In 1980, opinion surveys identified inflation as the problem of greatest concern to the American public. The widely reported rate of consumer price inflation was over 12 percent in both 1979 and 1980, up from about 4 percent in the early 1970s and less than 2 percent in the first half of the 1960s. Many Americans felt that inflation was out of control and might spiral to higher and higher levels.

Two years later, after the deepest recession of the postwar period, inflation had been reduced to 4 percent. Except for fluctuations in the price of energy, the inflation rate remained at approximately that level for the remainder of the decade, while the economy enjoyed above-trend growth of real GNP and employment.

An analysis of this dramatic reversal of inflation can illustrate the complex way in which public opinion, politics, and technical economics interact in the shaping of monetary policy. The public's strong aversion to inflation contrasted with a rather widespread view among economists in the 1960s and 1970s that inflation was not a serious problem and that it was probably better to live with inflation than to pay the price—in terms of lost output—of reducing it. The oversimplified models used to analyze inflation indicated that the only cost of persistent inflation was that individuals would be induced to hold too little cash. No less an economist than James Tobin warned those economists who worried aloud about inflation that we would be embarrassed if the public ever discovered that the only real cost of inflation was the *de minimis* "shoe leather" cost of going too frequently to the bank to withdraw currency. Indeed, in a major address to the Econometric Society, Tobin went further and argued that a higher rate of inflation could be desirable because it raised real incomes by inducing people to substitute claims on real capital (bonds and stocks) for cash in their portfolios, thus reducing the yield required on investment in plant and equipment.

Nevertheless, the rising inflation of the 1970s increased the public's opposition to inflation and people's willingness to support a presidential candidate who promised tough action to reduce inflation. No doubt some people opposed inflation because of fallacious reasoning: they thought that they "deserved" the full real value of the nominal wage increases that they had received and resented having the purchasing power of those increases eroded by inflation. But the public's opposition cannot be attributed to this logical error alone.

People resented the fact that the combination of inflation and an unindexed tax system was pushing them into higher tax brackets, forcing them to pay a higher share of their real incomes in taxes. Many prospective home buyers knew that the rise in mortgage interest rates from less than 6 percent in the 1960s to more than 12 percent in 1980 prevented them from qualifying for a mortgage or being able to make the monthly payments even if they could find a willing lender. Pensioners saw the real value of their corporate pensions and personal savings eroding rapidly. Businessmen understood that the real value of depreciation allowances was sharply reduced by the high inflation rate, raising the effective rate of tax and discouraging investment in plant and equipment. And shareholders, who had been paying capital gains taxes on nominal gains even though the real value of their stocks had been declining, were shunning common stock, depressing the stock market and raising the cost of equity capital.[4]

Some economists might argue that these distortions were not inherent in inflation but reflected institutional details that could be corrected by indexing tax laws and pensions and redesigning mortgage payment schedules. But a decade and a half of rising inflation had occurred without such institutional corrections. By 1980, the public was ready for a tough anti-inflationary policy, and an increasing number of economists (although certainly not all economists) were becoming convinced of the high real costs of inflation.

The Federal Reserve had, of course, been aware of and unhappy about the rising rate of inflation throughout the decade of the 1970s but did not act forcefully enough to stop it. This may be because they underestimated its adverse effects or thought that it could be reversed at some future time at relatively low cost (Feldstein 1982b). But a significant part of the blame must also be attributed to the Fed's focus on nominal interest rates as a measure of the tightness of monetary policy.

As inflation rose, interest rates rose as well, although at a slower rate. Thus, real interest rates actually fell, while nominal interest rates were rising. Federal Reserve officials who saw nominal interest rates rise thought that they were increasing the cost of funds when in fact the real cost of those funds was declining. The mismeasurement was even worse when taxes were taken into account because nominal interest payments are deducted in calculating taxable income.

To see this effect of the interaction of inflation and tax rules, consider, for example, the effect on the real net cost of mortgage borrowing. Between 1965 and 1975, the interest rate on fixed rate mortgages rose from 5.8 percent to 9.0 percent, while inflation rose from 1.4 percent to 6.2 percent. The real interest rate thus fell from 4.4 percent to 2.8 percent. A taxpayer with a 30 percent marginal tax rate in both years would have paid a real after-tax rate of 2.7

---

4. I discussed these issues in a series of technical papers published in the late 1970s and collected in Feldstein (1983c).

percent in 1965 but 0.1 percent in 1975. Such calculations may be common-place now, but the logic eluded the Fed in the 1970s (see Feldstein 1980).

1.1.2   An Unsuccessful Disinflation

Paul Volcker became chairman of the Federal Reserve in August 1979. Two months later, he persuaded his colleagues on the Federal Open Market Committee (FOMC) that a strong commitment to reduce inflation and a radical change in the Fed's operating procedure were needed.

It could have been otherwise. The surge in inflation from 9 percent in 1978 to more than 12 percent in 1979 could have been attributed to the jump in oil prices rather than to excess demand. But Volcker seized the opportunity of an inflation surge to attack the inflation problem that had been festering for more than a decade.

The Federal Reserve announced in October 1979 that it would focus on slowing the growth of the money supply and would be willing to tolerate much greater movements in short-term interest rates. Interest rates then rose dramatically, and the economy slowed.

The interaction between the Federal Reserve and the Carter administration has not been fully documented. What is clear is that Paul Volcker had told CEA Chairman Charles Schultze and Treasury Secretary William Miller about his intentions in October and had presumably received at least the tacit consent of the Carter administration. But, when the short rates reached over 15 percent in March 1980, the Fed lost the support of the Carter administration. With less than nine months to the 1980 presidential election, President Carter authorized the Fed to use credit controls to constrain consumer spending and effectively forced them to do so by going on television to exhort consumer restraint in the use of credit.

During the next three months, the economy weakened dramatically. The Fed responded to a drop in the money stock by cutting short rates nearly in half. At the time, this looked like an attempt to reverse the recession during an election year rather than the inevitable interest rate effect of the Fed's new policy of targeting the monetary aggregates. The drop in interest rates was followed by an economic recovery in the third quarter of 1980. The very short period of tight monetary policy and weak economic activity was not enough to reduce the rate of inflation.

1.1.3   The Reagan-Volcker Disinflation Policy

Ronald Reagan's 1980 presidential campaign had emphasized the need to fight inflation and return to price stability. It was hoped that a gradual tightening of monetary policy combined with the fiscal stimulus of the 1981 tax cuts would permit inflation to be brought down slowly and without a recession.

To the extent that "credibility" of policy was thought to be helpful in accelerating the decline of inflation, the analysis was based on old commonsense propositions that had been put forward over the years by William Fellner and

Henry Wallich rather than on the more extreme version of those views embodied in the new rational expectations theories that claimed that even very tight money would not hurt the real economy at all if the policy change were correctly perceived. Nor was any credence given by either the Fed or the new administration to those extreme supply-siders who argued that reducing inflation did not require a contraction of demand since prices would fall once the supply-side policies had succeeded in increasing the supply of goods and services.

The Fed tightened monetary policy sharply immediately after the election, raising the Fed funds rate by 600 basis points in less than two months. This monetary contraction pushed the economy into a deep recession, a recession that was worsened by the very unusual drop of velocity in 1982. The unemployment rate rose from 7.5 percent in January 1981 to 10.2 percent in September 1982, when I joined the administration as chairman of the Council of Economic Advisers. On that occasion, my Harvard colleague Ken Galbraith commented to the *Boston Globe* that I had just signed on for a ride on the Titanic.

Despite the dramatic increase in interest rates and in unemployment, President Reagan supported the Fed's tough policy. A firm opposition to inflation was part of his overall conservative economic philosophy. Moreover, he believed that the public understood that the high interest rates and the recession were necessary to correct the inflation that he had inherited from the Carter years. It was indicative of his attitude, but nevertheless remarkable, that the president chose "Stay the Course" as the 1982 election campaign motto at a time when the unemployment rate was rising every month to higher levels than had been seen in the years since World War II.

It was also a remarkable indication of the public's concern with inflation that the president's "approval rating" in the opinion polls conducted by the White House turned up sharply in the second half of 1982 as it became clear that inflation had been brought down even though there was no sign of an economic upturn.

1.1.4   Monetary Easing and Recovery in 1982

Although the broadest measure of inflation (the GNP implicit price deflator) fell from nearly 9 percent in the final quarter of 1981 to only 4.5 percent in the first half of 1982, the Federal Reserve kept the Federal funds interest rate over 14 percent. The Federal funds interest rate was actually slightly higher in the first half of 1982 than it had been in the final quarter of 1981.

In a *Wall Street Journal* article in the summer of 1982 (Feldstein 1982c), I argued that a "one-time" increase in the money stock would, at least in theory, be appropriate at that time to reverse the recent rise of real interest rates. Without an injection of additional money, the increase in the real money stock required to return the interest rates to a sustainable equilibrium level could be achieved only by several years of depressed economic activity that kept the rise in prices below the rise in the nominal supply of money. But in that article I cautioned that injecting additional money would run the risk of frightening financial markets that the Fed was reverting to its old inflationary ways and that the "one-time" money supply increase was just the beginning of a new period of faster money growth. I hoped at the time that, if the rationale for a one-time injection of money could be communicated effectively to the financial markets, it might be possible to reduce short-term interest rates without arousing fears of renewed inflation.

Sometime after I wrote that article, and after my subsequent nomination as CEA chairman, but before I went to Washington in early September, I met with several people in the New York financial community to ask how they would respond to such an injection of liquidity by the Fed. There was virtual unanimity in this sophisticated financial group that the market would welcome a sign of easing by the Fed.

Paul Volcker and his colleagues dealt with the perception and credibility problem by easing without saying that they had done so. Interest rates fell sharply, with the Federal funds rate dropping from over 14 percent to below 9 percent by the end of the year. The Fed took no credit for easing but said only that the Fed funds rate was moving in parallel to other short-term market rates and that this general downward movement of rates reflected the fall of inflation. The sharp increase in the narrow money stock (M1) was explained away by references to the expiration of all-saver certificates, a technical factor that could probably account for only a very small part of the jump in the growth rate of M1 in late 1982.

In 1983 and 1984, the economy enjoyed stable inflation and rapidly increasing real GDP. The overall pace of nominal GDP growth was not in any way surprising in the wake of the Fed's substantial easing that had begun in mid-1982. The division of the nominal GDP rise between real growth and inflation was, however, more favorable than would have been expected on the basis of past statistical relations. The primary reason for this, I believe, was that the fiscal expansion caused the dollar to rise, reducing import prices and putting downward pressure on the prices of domestic products that must compete with foreign products. The result was lower inflation and therefore more room for faster real GDP growth within the same total nominal GDP (see Feldstein and Elmendorf 1989).

1.1.5   Presidential Support for the Fed

As the newly arrived CEA chairman in the fall of 1982, I heard loud complaints from businessmen and from members of Congress about the state of the economy and about the need for lower interest rates. Even with the easing of monetary policy that had begun during the summer of 1982, real short-term rates remained quite high. The real rate on six-month Treasury bills was more than 5.5 percent in the third quarter of 1982. Moreover, the prime rate charged to business borrowers came down more slowly than market rates; the gap between the prime rate and the six-month Treasury-bill rate widened from less than 3 percent at the start of 1982 to 4 percent in September. The unemployment rate was over 10 percent and was continuing to rise every month.

Although the NBER eventually identified November 1982 as the bottom of the recession, the fact that the economy had begun expanding was not clear until February 1983. During the months before the 1982 congressional election, the economy looked very weak, and Fed policy appeared unnecessarily tight to many observers. Some of the president's staunchest allies in Congress complained bitterly that excessively tight monetary policy was preventing the rapid growth that should have resulted from the supply-side tax cuts of 1981. On one occasion in October 1982, soon after I had joined the administration, a leading member of that group met with the president in the Oval Office. The president listened politely to his plea to lean on the Fed to achieve an easier monetary policy, but then explained that that would be wrong because it would jeopardize the progress on inflation. The president then added that it would in any case be inappropriate to interfere with the Fed's independence.

The president's comments in that meeting were quite consistent with his later actions and statements on monetary policy. On many occasions over the next two years, when the press reported that "the administration" was criticizing Federal Reserve policy, the criticisms were never coming from the president or being made at his request. The Fed's critics were either in the Treasury (Secretary Donald Regan or Undersecretary Beryl Sprinkel) or among the White House political staff. The White House officials who criticized the Fed wanted to protect the administration from any future criticism if the economy faltered by blaming the Fed in advance and distancing the president from Federal Reserve policy. On several occasions, when I thought that the criticism had gotten loud enough to worry about, I mentioned it to the president, who soon went out of his way at a news conference to express support for the Fed.

The ultimate measure of the president's support for the Fed's policies was his decision to reappoint Paul Volcker in 1983 for another four-year term as Fed chairman. Volcker's critics urged the president to dissociate himself from the 1981–82 recession by not reappointing the man most closely identified with the policy of high interest rates. They also urged him to "have his own man" at the Fed to assert his control of that institution. But the president accepted the advice of those who said that Volcker had done a good job in reducing inflation and that his reappointment at the Fed would be a sign of the president's continued commitment to low inflation.

1.1.6   The Determinants of Monetary Policy in the 1980s

It is difficult to generalize about the determinants of Federal Reserve monetary policy. Federal Reserve actions do not represent the views of the chairman alone but reflect a consensus among FOMC members or at least a majority of those voting at the FOMC meeting. Moreover, each FOMC member has his own implicit weights on a variety of considerations. I am nevertheless confident that Federal Reserve decision making in the 1980s was quite different than it had been in the 1970s or 1960s.

At a minimum, the difficulty and pain of reducing inflation in the early 1980s made the FOMC members more concerned about policies that could allow a resurgence of inflation. The emphasis was therefore on restraining the pace at which unemployment declined so that the recovery would not be fast enough to overheat the economy.

Monetary aggregates played a more central role in making and judging monetary policy than they had in the past, although probably not as substantial a role as the Fed's annual reports to Congress suggested. Nevertheless, it is surely more than a coincidence that M2 was within the target range in almost every year from 1983 through 1989. And, although the Federal Reserve paid more attention to the Federal funds rate after mid-1982 than it had in the previous two years, it did not go back to the narrow 50-basis-point range that it had used prior to 1989. Instead, it was common to have a wide range of 400 basis points for the Federal funds rate.

Monetarist critics accused the Fed in 1983 of abandoning monetary targets and allowing too rapid a growth of the monetary aggregates. In fact, however, the change in Fed rules permitting banks to pay interest on checking accounts that took effect in early 1983 changed the demand for money in two fundamental ways that temporarily made continuation of the previous money growth rates inappropriate. First, it made the difference between M1 and M2 much less meaningful, eventually forcing the Fed to abandon M1 targets and focus on M2. Second, the interest available on checking accounts caused a sharp increase in the demand for M2 relative to nominal GNP.[5]

The monetarist critics (including Treasury Undersecretary Beryl Sprinkel and many distinguished academic and business economists) were not convinced. They complained about the sharp acceleration of M2 in early 1983 and the deceleration that followed. They predicted that the spurt of money growth would cause inflation and that the subsequent sharp deceleration of money growth would cause an economic downturn. Since neither prediction materialized, the episode reduced the already weak support among economists and financial experts in general for focusing on monetary aggregates in deciding monetary policy, a case that had previously been undermined by the sharp decline of velocity in 1982.

In chapter 1 of the 1983 *Economic Report of the President,* I had previously argued that a strict policy of targeting monetary aggregates was less appropriate than one of targeting nominal GNP, using monetary aggregates as important intermediate targets or indicators in a way that reflected observed changes in velocity. I had tried to persuade Paul Volcker that an explicit state-

---

5. In the months before this regulatory change occurred, Paul Volcker told me privately that the Fed was expecting a substantial increase in the demand for M2 balances. The Fed staff had studied the experience in New England, where such interest-bearing checkable deposits had been introduced earlier, and concluded that for a few months the Fed should abandon the aggregate targets and stabilize nominal interest rates.

ment of such a policy would allow the Federal Reserve to vary the growth of monetary aggregates without causing financial markets to fear that the Fed had lost control or was returning to old inflationary ways. Volcker and his colleagues were never willing to be quite so explicit. Perhaps that was because they believed that the public and the Congress would not permit the Fed so much freedom of action if they understood the extent to which the Fed could actually influence nominal GNP and thus short-run movements in real economic growth. The Fed preferred to disguise its influence on both interest rates and nominal GNP, speaking instead about its policies to change "pressure on reserves."

In reality, of course, the FOMC members know that their policies affect aggregate demand and thus both real income and inflation in the short run so that any decision to change the level of interest rates is at least an indirect way of influencing real income and inflation. Indeed, because the staff presents model simulations of the effects of alternative policies on both the price level and real output, they are in effect inviting the FOMC to choose among alternative pairings of real GNP and inflation when they set the Federal funds rate and the targets for the monetary aggregates.

1.1.7   A Correct Strategy

In my judgment, the basic strategy of monetary policy in the 1980s was correct: tough medicine to reduce inflation quickly while the public's support permitted the necessary contractionary policy, followed by enough monetary easing to achieve a moderately paced recovery that would avoid overheating demand. The tough recession reduced inflation at substantially lower cost in terms of lost output than many critics of tight money had predicted at the start of the decade, and the restrained pace of expansion permitted a substantial decline of unemployment without any increase in inflation.

The Fed's reaction to the 1987 stock market crash was also appropriate—both in providing immediate liquidity and in rapidly withdrawing it once the markets had become calm. But, while I believe that the broad sweep of monetary policy was correct, there were many periods in the 1980s when the Fed's fine-tuning seemed to me inappropriate.

The Fed's unwillingness to focus on a nominal GNP goal may also have led at times to an inappropriate monetary policy. For example, monetary policy was tightened sharply in 1987, contributing to the collapse of the stock market. The Fed explained at the time that its policy was aimed at preventing a decline of the international value of the dollar. If this is an accurate description of the Fed's motivation, it shows the disadvantage of trying to target the exchange rate rather than the growth of nominal GDP.[6]

---

6. It is, of course, difficult to know whether the Fed's statements that monetary tightening in mid-1987 was designed to prevent a sharp fall of the dollar should be taken at face value. It is perhaps equally plausible that the Fed was using the international system as a way of obtaining administration support for a decision to restrain economic activity that the Fed judged was increasing too fast.

More generally, the problem that the Fed faced as the decade of the 1980s came to an end was that the economy had been expanding at too fast a rate for too long. A relatively easy monetary policy throughout the post-1982 period had cut the unemployment rate to 5.2 percent by the start of 1990. As a result of this policy, the rate of inflation (measured by the CPI excluding energy) rose from 3.9 percent in 1985–86 to 5.2 percent in 1990. The Fed then shifted to a pattern of tightening aimed at continuing the previous decline of inflation without an actual downturn of employment. Whether that strategy would have worked well will never be known because of Saddam Hussein's invasion of Kuwait.[7]

1.2   Tax Policy in the 1980s

The reforms of the personal income tax in the 1980s were the most substantial tax changes since the dramatic expansion of personal taxation during World War II. The top marginal tax rate for individuals was reduced from 70 percent in 1980 to less than 35 percent a decade later, median-income taxpayers saw their marginal tax rates reduced by a third, and millions of low-income individuals no longer paid any individual income tax. At the same time, the opportunity for middle- and upper-income individuals to reduce taxable income through a variety of special provisions was substantially reduced. Indexing of tax brackets meant that inflation would no longer increase effective tax rates.

The effective tax rate on investment income at both the personal and the corporate levels was also substantially reduced by the 1981 tax legislation. But, unlike the general reduction of personal tax rates, those changes in the taxation of investment income were reversed during the next five years.

These remarkable developments were driven by an unusual convergence of intellectual and political forces and shaped by the preferences of President Reagan and a few key administration officials. This paper begins by examining these general determinants of the tax reforms in the 1980s and then turns to a more detailed analysis of the sequence of specific tax legislation. Because Don Fullerton has provided an excellent analytic history of these tax changes in his chapter in this volume, my comments focus on my own interpretation of the causes of those changes and a personal perspective on the changes themselves. I provide only enough description of the legislative changes themselves to permit the reader to understand my comments.

---

7. For a detailed discussion of monetary policy actions through the entire decade, see Michael Mussa's excellent chapter in this volume. Feldstein (1992c) discusses monetary policy in the last few years of the decade and the early part of the 1990s.

1.2.1   The Determinants of Tax Reform in the 1980s

The Conceptual Foundations of Tax Reform

The tax reforms of the 1980s reflected ideas about taxation that public finance economists had been discussing for many years: combining base broadening with lower tax rates, substituting a "flat tax" for the finely graduated "progressive" rate structure, indexing tax brackets for inflation, using a "vanishing exemption" to increase the average tax rate of the highest-income taxpayers without raising their marginal rate, and restructuring depreciation rules to improve the efficiency of capital allocation. The "academic scribblers" who had written about these issues during previous decades may not have been in Washington when the changes occurred, but the influence of their ideas was very much present in the design of the tax legislation of the 1980s.

The intellectual roots of the tax reform went beyond the technical concepts of public finance specialists. They reflected a very fundamental retreat from the general Keynesian economic philosophy that had shaped economic policy throughout the postwar period. There were four interrelated aspects of this shift in thinking: attention to the effects of incentives on behavior; a concern with capital formation; an emphasis on the efficiency of resource use; and a negative attitude about budget deficits. None of these represented new ideas in economics; they were in fact a return to the earlier views that had dominated economics from the time of Adam Smith until the Depression of the 1930s ushered in the Keynesian revolution.[8]

Effects of incentives on behavior. The massive unemployment of the Great Depression had focused the economic profession's attention on the lack of demand as the cause of low output and employment. The Keynesian economics that was developed in the 1930s emphasized that an increase in demand through monetary or fiscal policy would raise national income. With one-third of the labor force out of work, there was no need to worry about the willingness of workers to supply labor.

The simple Keynesian models that shaped most economists' view of the world over the next several decades generally ignored incentives: labor supply was assumed to be a fixed, given quantity; household savings were assumed to depend only on income (and not on the rate of return to the saver); and business investment was assumed to depend on sales and capacity utilization rather than profitability. This was a dramatic reversal of the views that had been held by economists before the 1930s and the introduction of Keynesian economics. While sophisticated economists recognized that all the Keynesian assumptions were just analytic simplifications, this "demand-determined" worldview con-

---

8. On the retreat from Keynesian economics, see Feldstein (1981c). On the ways in which the policies of the 1980s reflected a return to older ideas, see Feldstein (1986c).

ditioned much of the economic thinking about practical policy problems in the 1950s, 1960s, and 1970s.

In the design of personal taxation, this emphasis on demand and disregard of supply incentives led to high marginal tax rates; at the end of the 1970s, marginal tax rates reached 49 percent for an individual with $25,000 of taxable income and exceeded 65 percent for taxpayers with incomes of $90,000 and above (although a maximum tax rate of 50 percent applied to personal services income). The interaction of inflation with tax rules that did not distinguish between real and nominal interest income or between real and nominal capital gains meant that many taxpayers faced marginal tax rates over 100 percent on real interest income and real capital gains.

The procedure of revenue estimating by the staffs of the Treasury and the Congress was symbolic of the disregard of the behavioral response of taxpayers to changes in tax rates. The revenue effect of any proposed tax change was always calculated on the assumption that it would have no effect on the behavior of taxpayers and therefore than an induced change in behavior could have no feedback effect on total tax revenue. Although the economists who managed these revenue-estimating calculations knew that the assumption of "no behavioral response" was not literally true, they regarded it as a good enough approximation on which to base policy decisions.

All this began to change in the 1970s. Academic economists began to focus research on the way in which tax rules and government transfers affected economic behavior. There were studies of the effects of taxation on labor supply, of the effects of Social Security on retirement behavior, and of the impact of unemployment insurance on the behavior of the unemployed. The common theme in all this research was that labor supply is responsive to incentives.

But it was the congressional consideration of changes in the tax treatment of capital gains that made Congress recognize the importance of taking the behavioral response of taxpayers into account in the analysis of tax reforms. In the context of the 1978 reduction of the capital gains tax rate, the members of the House Ways and Means Committee and the Senate Finance Committee focused on the fact that lower capital gains tax rates would cause taxpayers to realize more capital gains as they accrue. They recognized that this behavioral response would reduce and possibly eliminate the revenue loss that would otherwise result from lowering the tax rate on capital gains.

The logic of the capital gains response and the research on labor supply led some economists to note that cutting personal tax rates in general would also cause less revenue loss than the nonbehavioral (or *static,* to use the somewhat misleading label that became popular in Washington tax policy discussions) calculations implied. This idea, that tax cuts were not as expensive as they seemed because of taxpayers' positive supply response, was, of course, the basis for what came to be called *supply-side economics.* Economists like Art Laffer dramatized the importance of the supply-side response by claiming that it is so strong that a substantial across-the-board reduction in personal income tax rates would actually increase tax revenue.

I will return below to the experience with the capital gains tax reduction and to the claims of supply-side economists. But first I want to turn to another aspect of the retreat from Keynesian economics: the renewed interest in capital accumulation.

Capital formation. The 1970s saw a renewed interest in capital formation as an engine of economic growth. This too was a reversion from Keynesian economics to an idea that had been stressed by pre-Keynesian economists.

The accumulation of capital was understandably irrelevant in the economic conditions of the Depression years that shaped Keynesian economics. With vast amounts of unused capacity, additional investment was not needed to increase output. Increasing the propensity to save was even less important since the Keynesian "multiplier" analysis implied that an increased desire to invest in plant and equipment would automatically increase national saving by an equal amount. Indeed, textbook Keynesian theory stressed that an increase in the desire to save would actually reduce national income by decreasing the demand for output.

Although these ideas were developed for the economic conditions of the 1930s, they continued to have a powerful effect on economic thinking and policy in later decades. Various policies were adopted that would favor an increase in consumer spending rather than in saving: banking rules that limited interest paid to depositors and reduced the cost of mortgage borrowing, tax rules that reduced the return to saving and lowered the net cost of borrowing, a Social Security system that made private saving for retirement virtually unnecessary for a majority of households, and an acceptance of budget deficits as a useful tool of demand stimulus.

Ironically, the economic profession's development of "growth theory" in the 1960s did little to reverse the attitude that capital accumulation was unimportant. One reason is that the theory emphasized that a higher national saving rate does not increase the rate of economic growth in the very long run. This conclusion was reinforced by the implied calculation that a 1 percent increase in the saving rate would increase the rate of GNP growth in the short run only by about one-tenth of 1 percent.

Even when an investment tax credit was adopted in the early 1960s, it was conceived as a Keynesian cyclical stimulus rather than as a way of expanding productive capacity. The aversion to encouraging saving remained, reinforced perhaps by the fact that any plan that is likely to encourage substantial personal saving is likely to favor those with higher incomes or assets.

Nevertheless, the decline in unemployment throughout the 1960s turned attention from the Keynesian problem of increasing demand to the pre-Keynesian problem of raising output per worker. Economists in the 1970s began to focus again on the desirability of increasing national saving and investment in plant and equipment. Although growth theory implied that increased capital accumulation would have only a modest effect on per capita GNP, it was the only determinant of growth that seemed susceptible to changes in economic policy.

The emphasis on saving and investment played an important part in the tax reforms of 1981: strengthened incentives for business fixed investment through more rapid depreciation allowances; increased incentives to save through universal eligibility for individual retirement accounts; and an increased return on individual equity investments through lower rates of tax on capital gains. The reasons that these increased incentives were largely withdrawn later in the decade are discussed below.

Efficiency of resource use. Even before Adam Smith, economists like William Petty were concerned with making the best use of scarce resources. Much of the subsequent academic work in public finance—including the writings of David Ricardo, A. C. Pigou, Frank Ramsey, and Irving Fisher—was specifically concerned with levying taxes in a way that would raise the revenue required by the government with the least distortion to economic efficiency.

Once again, it was the experience of the Depression that diverted attention from this traditional economic concern with the efficiency of resource use. National income could be raised much more easily by putting unemployed resources to work than by increasing the efficiency with which already employed resources were used. During the early postwar decades, the attention of most economists who were concerned with economic policy was on policies to achieve and maintain full employment.

The pre-Keynesian tradition nevertheless continued within public finance with economists like Richard Musgrave and Arnold Harberger emphasizing the design of tax policies to reduce economic distortions. With the return to full employment in the postwar period, a wider group of economists eventually came to see the fundamental importance of these efficiency issues. The public finance economists of the 1960s and 1970s were concerned with efficiency questions rather than with the macroeconomic questions of achieving full employment. A substantial academic literature on the design of efficient capital income tax rules played a significant role in shaping the depreciation reforms in the Tax Reform Act of 1986.[9]

Adverse effects of budget deficits. Yet another of the Keynesian propositions that was rejected in the 1970s was the idea that an increased national debt would have no adverse effects because "we only owe it to ourselves." Analyses by James Meade, Franco Modigliani, and James Buchanan pointed out that, even when all the government debt is intranational, it is harmful to the extent

9. See, e.g., the NBER studies included in Feldstein (1983a, 1987c, 1987h).

that it substitutes for real capital formation and that it requires future interest payments that have to be financed by higher taxes that themselves involve distortions and therefore a loss of economic efficiency.

Ironically, it was Ronald Reagan, a longtime outspoken critic of budget deficits, who was president during the years when the United States amassed the largest increase in the national debt. But, despite this, as I emphasize in what follows, it was President Reagan's aversion to budget deficits that caused him to accept tax increases in 1982, 1983, and 1984.

Political Motivations for Tax Reform

The retreat from Keynesian economics in the 1970s and the growing influence of the technical ideas of public finance economists resulted in new tax legislation in the 1980s because they coincided with political forces that supported similar reforms.

Inflation and tax burdens. The inflation of the 1970s—a decade in which the level of consumer prices doubled—was in my judgment the primary political force driving the tax reforms of the 1980s.

The interaction of inflation and an unindexed tax system pushed middle-income individuals into sharply higher tax brackets. Between 1965 and 1980, a typical median-income family saw its marginal personal income tax rate double (from 22 percent to 43 percent), while a family at twice the median saw its tax rate jump from 38 percent to 54 percent.

The combined employer-employee Social Security tax also rose in these years from 7.25 percent in 1965 to 12.3 percent in 1980, and many states either introduced or increased their state income tax rates. A middle-class couple with about $40,000 of income in 1980 was shocked to find itself facing a combined marginal tax rate over 50 percent.

Average effective tax rates also rose sharply. A median-income family paid about 8 percent of its total income in federal income tax in 1965, but half again as much (12 percent) in 1980. And a family with income equal to twice the median saw its effective individual income tax rate rise from 13 percent to 21 percent over the same fifteen years.

While taxpayers always prefer lower taxes, the sharp rise in real tax burdens caused by inflationary bracket creep without any explicit legislation created a sense that the higher taxes were unfair, unjustified, and unnecessary.

Inflation also caused a sharp rise in the effective tax rates on the investment incomes of individuals and in the effective corporate tax rate.[10] The rise in inflation from 4 percent in the second half of the 1960s to 8 percent in the second half of the 1970s raised the short-term interest rates available to savers from 7 percent in 1969 to nearly 10 percent in 1979. Thus, the real interest

10. Several of my own papers on the interaction of inflation and tax rules that were written in the late 1970s and early 1980s are collected in Feldstein (1983c).

rate declined by 1 percentage point. This decline in the real interest rate (from 3 percent to 2 percent) was magnified by the fact that taxes are levied on nominal rather than real interest income. Even a taxpayer whose marginal tax rate remained unchanged at 40 percent would have seen his net real return decline from essentially zero (i.e., the 40 percent tax on the 7 percent nominal interest rate implies an after-tax return of 4.2 percent or only 0.2 percent above inflation) to *minus* 2 percent (i.e., the 10 percent nominal interest rate implied an after-tax return of 6.0 percent or 2 percent less than the rate of inflation).

In practice, the rise in the tax burden on interest income was compounded by the increase in marginal tax rates. Thus, for a median-income family whose marginal tax rate increased from 22 percent to 43 percent, the real after-tax return fell from about 1.5 percent to *minus* 2.3 percent, a decline of nearly 4 percentage points. For a family at twice the median income, the real after-tax rate fell from zero to *minus* 3.4 percent. Individuals resented this capital levy and felt justified in their demand for lower tax rates.

A similar distortion applied to the taxation of capital gains. An individual who had purchased a portfolio equivalent to the Standard and Poor's 500 in 1965 for $10,000 and sold it in 1980 would have realized a nominal gain of $3,520. But the rise in prices over that fifteen-year period meant that the individual needed $26,160 to buy the same volume of goods and services in 1980 that $10,000 bought in 1965. Thus, the taxpayer would pay a tax on $3,520 of gain even though he had incurred a real loss of nearly 50 percent of his initial investment (the $13,520 was only 52 percent of the $26,160 needed to maintain the purchasing power of the initial investment). Not surprisingly, individuals who invested in common stock felt that a dramatic cut in the capital gains tax rate was justified, and they found a sympathetic hearing among many members of Congress. That political pressure supported the capital gains tax reduction of 1978 and the subsequent reduction in 1981.

Finally, inflation grossly distorted the taxation of corporate income. Because the depreciation of plant and equipment for tax purposes is based on original cost with no adjustment for inflation, the rise in interest rates caused by inflation substantially reduced the present value of the depreciation deduction. Between 1965 and 1980, the rise in corporate bond rates reduced the present value of fifteen-year straight-line depreciation by more than 40 percent, a reduction equivalent to an increase of 20 percent in the initial cost of the investment.

Inflation also caused a sharp rise in artificial accounting profits for firms that used the first-in first-out method of accounting. Such artificial profits rose from a negligible $1 billion in 1965 to more than $40 billion in 1980.

These extra corporate taxes were partly offset by the deductibility of nominal net interest costs. Nevertheless, when Larry Summers and I put all the pieces together (Feldstein and Summers 1979), we concluded that the effect of inflation with the existing tax laws was to raise the 1977 tax burden on the capital income of the nonfinancial corporate sector by an amount equal to 69 percent of the real after-tax income of that sector (including retained earnings, dividends, and the real interest receipts of the corporations' creditors). Stated differently, the effect of inflation was to raise the effective tax rate on capital income of the nonfinancial corporate sector from 41 percent to 66 percent.

The greatly increased tax burden caused by inflation was a major engine of the tax reduction movement in the late 1970s that led to the 1981 tax cuts. It also helps explain why, once the idea of indexing tax brackets for inflation was explained to the public, it was politically unstoppable.

Personal incomes and public spending. The pressure for tax cuts reflected not only the increasing tax burden but also the combination of the stagnant pretax incomes of working families and increased government spending on transfer programs. Middle-income individuals felt that their own situations were deteriorating while the government taxed them more heavily in order to give money to an increasing number of transfer recipients. Between 1970 and 1980, median family income in constant dollars rose by less than 1 percent. A full-time year-round male worker earned $21,511 (in 1981 dollars) in 1970 and $21,162 in 1980 (in the same 1981 dollars). The corresponding figures for female workers showed a rise of $50 over the entire ten-year period. If per capita incomes rose, it was only because of the substantial rise in female labor force participation (from 43 percent in 1970 to 52 percent in 1980).

During the same decade, government nondefense spending rose rapidly. Nondefense outlays of the federal government increased from 11.2 percent of GDP in 1970 to 16.7 percent in 1980. Transfer payments and nondefense discretionary outlays rose 93 percent in real terms during the decade, jumping from 55 percent of total government outlays to 70 percent. Even when Social Security and Medicare outlays are set aside, nondefense spending rose by 82 percent in real terms between 1970 and 1980.

It is not surprising that voters were very receptive to the message that taxes and government spending should be sharply reduced to redress the distribution of income between wage earners and welfare recipients.

Political competition in 1981. Although the inflation-induced tax increases of the 1970s and the public's dissatisfaction with the shift of income to welfare recipients and other transfer beneficiaries provided the political impetus for a program to cut taxes and spending, the actual tax legislation in 1981 was shaped by a competition between Republicans and Democrats to get credit for tax cutting.

Ronald Reagan's presidential campaign had promised that he would seek 10 percent tax cuts for three successive years, a cumulative 27 percent reduction in marginal and average tax rates. When he presented this proposal to the Congress, the Democratic leadership responded with its own package of tax cuts that included such things as a tax credit for second earners and an expanded program of individual retirement accounts. A bipartisan coalition led by Republican Congressman Barber Conable and Democratic Congressman Jim Jones also supported sharp reductions in corporate tax liabilities through accelerated depreciation schedules; this Conable-Jones bill was known as 10–5–3 because structures would be depreciated for tax purposes in ten years, equipment in five years, and vehicles in three years. The final "compromise" legislation included virtually all these pieces (although the personal rate reductions were reduced from 10–10–10 to 5–10–10, or a cumulative 23 percent) plus an agreement to index tax brackets starting in 1985.

The political origins of the 1986 Tax Reform Act. The radical changes in tax rules and tax rates in the 1981 legislation would have been enough to characterize the 1980s as a decade of major tax reform. While it is perhaps not surprising that the 1981 legislation was followed by several small tax bills in succeeding years to reduce the budget deficit, it is quite remarkable that Congress enacted another change in tax rules in the Tax Reform Act of 1986 and did so as a piece of tax reform without any expected net revenue impact.

The specific features of the 1986 legislation reflected several of the intellectual developments that I have already discussed. It can be seen as a shift in emphasis from increasing the rate of investment to using the available investment dollars more efficiently. But the 1986 legislation owes its existence neither to the tax specialists' desire to increase allocative efficiency nor to strong public support for another round of tax changes.

Administration interest in a second round of tax reform originated in the White House as a political response to the initiative developed by Senator Bill Bradley and Congressman Dick Gephardt. The Bradley-Gephardt proposals called for a combination of lower rates and base broadening, appealing to traditional tax reform sentiments of fairness and more technical concerns about the efficiency of resource use. The influence of academic public finance economics in this design was very clear.

Jim Baker, then President Reagan's chief of staff, was concerned in early 1984 that the Democrats could seize the tax reform issue from the Republicans in the upcoming presidential election by building on the Bradley-Gephardt proposal. The president's 1984 State of the Union address therefore called for a new major tax reform that would reduce tax rates without increasing the deficit and ordered the Treasury to carry out the study and report after the election. What started as an attempt to preempt a political move became the most wide-ranging tax reform since the introduction of the income tax.

Presidential Preferences

It would be wrong to regard the tax reform of the 1980s as the product of intellectual fashions and political forces alone. President Reagan had strong convictions about tax policy that shaped the tax changes throughout his eight years as president.

President Reagan strongly opposed high rates of personal income taxation and particularly the very high level of the top marginal tax rate. He spoke privately of the personal disincentive and of the sense of frustration and unfairness created by tax rates of nearly 100 percent that he had experienced himself. Until the 1963 tax reductions, the maximum marginal rate was 91 percent, and the tax rate was 89 percent for income over $100,000. He had a visceral dislike of high maximum tax rates and wanted tax changes that would reduce them.

On the basis of his own experience and that of his friends, the president clearly believed that lower tax rates would increase work effort and reduce the use of accounting arrangements to shelter taxable income. This explains his enthusiasm not only for the initial 1981 rate cuts but also for the 1986 plan to combine even lower rates with a broader tax base. Although the president believed in the supply-side effect of lower taxes, I never thought that he accepted the extreme supply-side position that lower tax rates would actually increase tax revenue. He did make such statements in public announcements and press conferences,[11] but I never recall him saying that in private discussions with senior administration officials; perhaps, even if he once believed it, he no longer did by mid-1982 when I joined the administration.

When it came to deficit reduction, the president disliked any kind of tax increase but was less opposed to higher business taxes, especially when they took the form of "eliminating undeserved breaks and closing tax loopholes," a characterization that could be applied to the tax increases of 1982, 1983, and 1984 since the statutory tax rates were not increased. He strongly resisted the rise in the Social Security payroll tax that was proposed as part of the Social Security rescue package in 1983 but reconciled himself to this change by noting that it represented only advances in the dates of the increases that had been proposed and legislated by the Carter administration.

Although President Reagan's rhetoric always emphasized his opposition to increased taxes, he agreed grudgingly to the need for tax increases in 1982, 1983, and 1984 because he did not like the looming budget deficits. While projecting the image of a fierce opponent of taxes, in his prepared remarks and his press conferences he was always careful to avoid an outright promise that he would not raise taxes. Instead, he would say things like (my words) "I will not hurt the American economy by raising taxes" or "I will not raise taxes that penalize hard-working American men and women." It may have sounded like a promise not to raise taxes, but it was in fact a statement about the kinds of tax increases that he would accept. When pressed explicitly in a press conference, his favorite reply was of the form "A president should never say never."

The following excerpt from a 23 December 1981 press interview provides a good example of the president's ability to stress his opposition to higher taxes

---

11. See, e.g., his comments in a 7 July 1981 speech: "It's true, that I believe, as President Kennedy did, that our kind of tax cut will so stimulate our economy that we will actually increase government revenues, but the gross national product will be increased by even more so that government's excessive percentage will decline."

while keeping open all options for future tax increases. At that time there was already talk about the need for a tax increase that ultimately led to the enactment of the 1982 tax bill that raised a projected $100 billion over three years. When the president was asked about raising taxes, he replied as follows:

> Well, there certainly will be no change in taxes in 1982, I guarantee you. We have put a program in place that I believe will increase government's revenue simply by broadening the base of the economy, stimulating an increase in productivity, offering incentives that the program does offer.
>
> I learned a long time ago that putting your feet in concrete was dangerous, because I have among my mementos a round cement block with a pair of shoes embedded in it that was given me by the Capital Press Corps in Sacramento after I had put my feet in concrete and then, one day, had to stand before them and say the sound you hear is the sound of concrete breaking around my feet. So, they gave me that, but I would like to see what happens with this program.
>
> Of course there is one thing with regard to taxes that from the very first I did always speak of, and that was we continue to review where there are places where people are getting undeserved tax breaks, the so-called closing of loopholes. Now in that I do not include as loopholes the legitimate deductions that—without which the whole program would have failed a long time ago—but actual loopholes where, as I say, there is an unjust break. This we continue to review and I am not opposed to that.

A press interviewer then asked, "At what point will you make a decision?" and the president replied, "After I see what happens."

A subsequent questioner asked whether, even if there would be no tax increase in 1982 except for loophole closing, there might be a tax increase in 1983. The president replied that he would not "look kindly on anything that is contrary to the stimulative part of our tax program" but that "what I was trying to say with my story about the concrete block was that with the unexpected things that can happen I just feel that I'm in no position to comment on suggestions for a 1983 tax increase."

Later in the interview, the president was asked about excise taxes and replied that "I don't think that consumption taxes are in direct opposition to the tax program that we instituted."

It is clear from these remarks that the president was very eager to emphasize his opposition to higher taxes, and in fact to resist increases in marginal tax rates as such, but would not rule out any future tax increase if he felt it necessary and was more inclined to accept excise taxes than other forms of tax increase. This was not empty rhetoric since the president proposed and Congress enacted tax increases (by "closing loopholes") in 1982, 1983, and 1984 and a higher excise tax on gasoline in 1982.

1.2.2   The Sequence of Tax Changes in the 1980s

With these comments as a general background on the reasons—intellectual, political, and presidential—for the tax changes of the 1980s, I turn to some personal observations on the major tax changes themselves.

Reducing Capital Gains Taxes

The capital gains tax cut of 1978 is important as a precursor of the individual and corporate rate cuts enacted in 1981. By the late 1970s, the combination of inflation-induced increases in tax brackets and new additional taxes on capital gains (the add-on minimum tax and the reduced ability of taxpayers with capital gains to use the maximum tax on earned income) had raised the maximum tax rate on capital gains to more than 45 percent.

In 1978, the House Ways and Means Committee was considering legislation to reduce capital gains tax rates that would bring the top rate down to 28 percent. The staff at the Treasury and at the congressional Joint Tax Committee estimated the revenue consequences of the proposed changes on the assumption that the lower capital gains tax rates would have no effect on taxpayers' decisions to realize gains. The opponents of reducing the capital gains tax rate, including the Carter administration, charged that the projected revenue loss was too large to be acceptable. The supporters of lower capital gains taxes, who were generally unaware of the "no behavioral response" assumption used by the revenue estimators, argued that the projected loss of revenue was worth accepting because a lower capital gains tax would encourage venture capital and other activities that would contribute to economic growth.

Research that I was doing on the effect of capital gains taxation on shareholder behavior implied that the Treasury and congressional staff calculations were fundamentally wrong.[12] Since capital gains taxes are levied only when the individual actually sells an asset, the capital gains tax can be postponed indefinitely and thereby substantially reduced in present value. Moreover, the tax on accrued gains need never be paid if the asset is held until death and bequeathed to the taxpayer's heirs; their base for future capital gains taxation is the value of the property at the time that it is bequeathed. And since, under the tax rules of the 1970s, an individual could borrow against the appreciated asset to finance current consumption and deduct the interest paid in calculating taxable income, it was unnecessary to sell the asset in order to consume the value of the appreciation.

With these rules, capital gains realizations would be expected to be very sensitive to tax rates. The statistical analysis that I was doing of a very large random sample of individual tax returns appeared to confirm that. Indeed, tax-

---

12. This research, done with Joel Slemrod and Shlomo Yitzhaki, appeared in several papers that are reprinted in Feldstein (1983b).

payers appeared to be so sensitive in their decision to realize capital gains that a reduction in the capital gains tax would actually raise revenue.

The ink was hardly dry on my NBER working paper reporting these research findings when I was asked to testify about them to the Senate Finance Committee. Several senators made it clear that they had not previously understood the "static" nature of the staff's revenue estimates (i.e., the assumption that there would be no behavioral response to a cut in the capital gains tax rate) and that they did not believe that such static estimates were useful for evaluating the proposed tax changes. I had a receptive audience for my estimates of substantial feedback effects of taxpayer behavior on the revenue consequences of lower tax rates on capital gains.

The capital gains tax rules were changed in the 1978 legislation, reducing the effective tax on capital gains. The subsequent experience confirmed the conclusion that taxpayers are quite sensitive to the capital gains tax rate. The revenue-estimating procedure of the Treasury and Joint Tax Committee staffs was subsequently modified to take the behavioral effects of changes in capital gains tax rates into account in estimating revenue consequences.

Supply-Side Extremists and the 1981 Tax Reduction[13]

My advocacy of a capital gains tax cut and my emphasis on the favorable revenue effect of the induced increase in the tax base made me an early "supply-sider," probably before the term had been coined by former CEA chairman Herb Stein and certainly before I had heard the term.

I believed (and continue to believe) that the favorable feedback effects of tax cuts on revenue would not be limited to capital gains tax cuts, but I was also convinced that other kinds of economic behavior would be much less sensitive to taxes than capital gains realizations. I objected therefore to those supply-siders like Arthur Laffer who argued that a 30 percent across-the-board tax cut would also be self-financing because of the resulting increase in incentives to work. While lowering the very highest marginal tax rates might actually raise revenue, for most taxpayers a cut in the tax on wages and salaries would increase tax revenue only if the resulting increase in labor supply was much greater than either logic or previous experience suggested was at all likely.

I was not opposed to a substantial across-the-board rate reduction when the idea was debated in the late 1970s, although I thought and testified to Congress that the combination of a smaller rate cut and immediate bracket indexing was safer at a time when future inflation was uncertain. I recall discussing this with Senator Bill Roth, an early advocate of the 10–10–10 personal rate cut. He recognized the logic of the argument that indexing might be better but argued

13. Don Fullerton's chapter in this volume provides an excellent detailed survey of the evolution of the 1981 tax cuts. Since I was not then a member of the administration, I limit my remarks here to a recollection of my own views at the time.

that it would be harder to enact than a pure rate cut because it was more difficult for the public to understand.

While reasonable people could differ about just how big a tax cut was desirable, I had no doubt that a combination of a sizable tax cut and a reduction in spending would improve efficiency and was justified after a decade of increases in taxes and spending. I was convinced that there would be some favorable offsetting feedback effects of the lower tax rates on total revenue but that the tax cut would definitely not be self-financing.[14]

I was convinced, moreover, that the supply-side hyperbole about self-financing tax cuts was undesirable because it was discrediting what I thought was a good case for reducing tax rates. Critics of the tax cut could rightly argue that it was unlikely to be self-financing as its most ardent supporters were claiming and then jump to the wrong conclusion that such a tax cut would therefore be a mistake.

The rhetoric of self-financing tax cuts nevertheless continued during the 1980 presidential campaign and was later part of the administration's effort to sell the tax package to Congress and the nation. The implausibility of the claim that the tax cut would be self-financing clearly did not hamper the ability of the new Reagan administration to enact its package, but it did complicate my subsequent job as CEA chairman in defending the tax package as good economics despite its obvious failure to raise revenue. And just when an increasing number of mainstream economists were accepting the traditional "supply-side" view that incentives are important and that high tax rates do not raise correspondingly high revenues, the supply-side extremists gave supply-side arguments in general a bad name.

Within a few years, the surge in the budget deficit caused many of the original supply-side extremists to say that they had never claimed that the tax cut would raise revenue. For example, Martin Anderson, President Reagan's first domestic adviser, claimed in his 1988 book *Revolution* and in subsequent newspaper articles that the supply-siders had never said that the tax cut would be self-financing.[15] The record clearly points to the opposite conclusion. Writing about the proposed series of three 10 percent tax rate cuts, Arthur Laffer, the leading supply-sider, was quite explicit in saying that "each of the 10 percent reductions in tax rates would, in terms of overall tax revenues, be self-financing in less than two years. Thereafter, each installment would provide a positive contribution to overall tax receipts" (Laffer 1981, 201). This was not an isolated statement but part of a general line of argument that distinguished the self-styled "supply-siders" from the rest of the economics profession.

14. The actual size of the tax cut and the reasons for the increase of the budget deficit are discussed in the next section of this chapter.

15. I tried to be polite in my remarks on this subject to the 1985 meeting of the American Economic Association (Feldstein 1986c) by not identifying anyone by name when I said that the supply-siders had claimed that the tax cut would be self-financing, only to be accused by Anderson in his book of attributing views that the supply-siders never had.

Shrinking the Deficit: Tax Changes from 1982 through 1984

It became clear almost immediately after their enactment that the 1981 tax reductions would lead to deficit increases despite the administration's success in cutting many domestic spending programs. This led to a series of small tax increases in 1982, 1983, and 1984. Although President Reagan strongly opposed any increase in personal or corporate income tax rates, he accepted the increases in revenue that resulted from a variety of technical changes in business tax rules.[16]

The 1982 deficit reduction legislation The 1982 tax legislation was projected to raise $100 billion over three years by reducing the value of business depreciation allowances and by eliminating the "safe-harbor leasing" provisions. The "safe-harbor" rules allowed companies that had no taxable profits to take advantage of favorable depreciation rules and the investment tax credit when they made investments by transferring the tax benefits to companies that did have taxable profits.

The politics and economics of safe-harbor leasing contain an interesting lesson about the importance of the appearance of fairness in tax policy, even in an aspect as arcane as business depreciation rules. Safe-harbor leasing looked bad because it permitted companies with substantial taxable profits to pay little or no tax by buying the tax benefits from companies that had made investments. In reality, the transferable tax benefits were priced in such a way that almost all the value went to the firms that made the investments rather than to the firm that bought the resulting tax benefits. The safe-harbor leasing rules thus had the desirable effect of encouraging investment for new firms that lacked taxable profits and for established firms that were temporarily losing money as well as for established firms with taxable profits.

Although I was not in the administration at that time, my judgment, both then and in retrospect, is that the 1982 reversal of the favorable tax treatment of investment that had been enacted the year before was a mistake. A generous tax treatment of business investment is needed to balance the relatively favorable treatment of owner-occupied housing if a disproportionate share of national saving is not to flow into residential investment. Safe-harbor leasing was needed to allow all types of firms to face the same cost of investing. But the perception of firms buying the right to pay no tax made the safe-harbor approach politically unsustainable.

A further adverse effect of the 1982 tax legislation was that it was the first time that depreciation rules were changed retroactively on equipment that was already in use. This meant that, in the future, businesses would no longer count on the prevailing depreciation rules when they made investment decisions, a

---

16. The next section of this chapter discusses the policies and politics of deficit reduction in more detail. The current section focuses on the specific tax proposals in each year's budget.

factor that would made future investments riskier and would reduce the potency of changes in depreciation rules. I found that it also made it impossible in 1983 to interest businessmen in the idea of accepting indexed depreciation in exchange for a further lengthening of depreciation lives.

The 1983 contingent tax plan. The debate about taxes in the budget to be submitted in February 1983 (i.e., the fiscal year 1984 budget) provided a good lesson both about the difference between economic and political priorities and about the way that an internally divided administration worked in practice.

The preliminary estimates for that budget (the first that I participated in preparing as CEA chairman) implied that, without substantial changes in taxes or spending, there would be large deficits in each of the next five years. The sharp decline in inflation and the deep recession together meant that tax receipts would be low in 1983 and 1984, while the indexing of brackets scheduled to begin in 1985 meant that future revenue increases would be very modest. Even with the spending cuts that could be proposed (but not enacted), the projected deficits would remain unacceptably large.

At an informal dinner soon after Christmas 1982, Secretary of State George Shultz suggested that an energy tax on domestic and imported oil would be a good way to raise revenue. The combination of that energy tax and the proposed spending cuts would, on realistic economic projections, lead to substantial deficit reductions over the five-year budget horizon.

The "supply-siders" in the Treasury, the Congress, and elsewhere objected to any tax increase as economically counterproductive and argued that, once the recovery began, the revenue gains from the tax cuts enacted in 1981 would be so great that no further tax changes would be needed to eliminate the deficit. The White House political strategists, led by Chief of Staff Jim Baker, were concerned about the adverse political effects of any proposal to increase taxes. Baker was also aware that his leadership in achieving the 1982 tax increase may have weakened his relationship with the president and definitely had hurt his relations with those Republicans who were more concerned about keeping taxes low than about preventing large budget deficits.

In the White House budget discussion that followed, Ed Harper (the domestic policy adviser) and I suggested as a compromise that the energy tax could be legislated in 1983 but would take effect only in 1985 and then only if the deficit remained above some threshold level. Budget Director Dave Stockman, who was also skeptical of the supply-siders' claims and eager for a plan that would actually reduce the outyear deficits, supported the idea of a contingent tax.

Treasury Secretary Donald Regan, responding to the advice of the Treasury supply-siders and the White House political staff, opposed the idea of a tax increase and favored assuming that future economic growth would be fast enough to shrink the budget deficit. The CEA was responsible for the forecast, and my refusal to go along with the Treasury projections of five years of rapid growth made a tax increase necessary to achieve an acceptable projection of declining deficits.

Despite the opposition of Regan and others, the combination of spending cuts and the "conditional" energy tax increase was accepted by the president as part of the February 1983 budget plan for fiscal year 1984 and beyond. But getting presidential approval for a budget that combined a reasonable economic forecast and good policies for deficit reduction was far from getting those policies legislated.

The White House political strategists and Treasury Secretary Don Regan could not stop the president's adoption of a proposal for a contingent tax increase because they recognized the need to project declining deficits and an eventual budget balance. But they could make sure that it would not be enacted by asserting that the contingent tax increase would be acceptable to the president only if all the president's proposed spending cuts were also accepted by the Congress. Since the proposed spending cuts are at best only the first bid in a negotiation between the president and the Congress, it was easy for the White House staff and the Treasury to sink the entire budget by adopting a very tough no-compromise strategy and then to blame Congress for the continued deficits that the president had proposed to reduce. In the end, none of the administration budget was enacted that year.

Taxes for Social Security solvency. The tax changes that were actually enacted in 1983 were the result of a plan to protect the long-run solvency of the Social Security system. A bipartisan commission, headed by former CEA Chairman Alan Greenspan (who was then a private citizen), had been established in 1982 to find a way to deal with the projected gap between future Social Security benefits and taxes.[17] The report of the committee, released in 1983, called for raising the payroll tax and including half the benefits of higher-income individuals in income subject to personal taxation. The income level at which this inclusion began was fixed in nominal terms, permitting the tax to fall only on relatively high-income individuals in the near term, but gradually extending future taxation to all beneficiaries without the political pain of enacting additional legislation to increase taxes. The resulting rise in tax revenue made a substantial contribution to shrinking projected deficits over the next five years and beyond.

When the proposed Social Security changes were initially described to the president (before they were made public by the commission), he objected vehemently to the plan to close the Social Security funding gap by higher taxes alone with virtually no reductions in future benefits. He eventually reconciled himself to the higher payroll taxes on the grounds that this was essentially just advancing the date of changes that had already been proposed and enacted by

---

17. The 1983 decisions about Social Security are discussed more fully in Sec. 1.3.3, which deals with the budget and government spending.

President Carter. He accepted the inclusion of benefits in taxable income with the rationale that it was essentially equivalent to a reduction in the benefits paid to high-income beneficiaries. But the reality was that the Social Security financial crisis had been resolved without any fundamental changes in benefits, a subject to which I return below in the section of this chapter on government spending and the budget.

Raising taxes in 1984. When the forecasts were prepared for the budget to be enacted in 1984, the economy had already been in recovery for more than a year. Despite the relatively strong growth in the first year of the recovery, plausible estimates of the future path of expansion (estimates that subsequently proved to be essentially correct) left unacceptably high budget deficits for the indefinite future.

The spending cuts that could be proposed in an election year were not large enough to make a significant dent in the projected deficits. Once again, the Treasury supply-siders and their allies outside the administration argued that no tax increase was needed because growth would continue at a fast enough pace to provide the additional revenue. Some conservatives who didn't accept the supply-siders' optimism argued that it would nevertheless be better to hold out for further spending cuts since a tax rise would just lead to additional spending without shrinking the deficit. Not surprisingly, the White House political strategists were opposed to any tax increase in an election year.

David Stockman and I were convinced that the five-year deficit could be reduced significantly only with the help of a tax increase and that such an increase would achieve a net deficit reduction. I continued to favor some type of contingency tax increase. My preferred solution was a modification of indexing in which Social Security and other retirement benefits and personal tax brackets would be adjusted by 3 percent less than the inflation rate instead of by the full inflation rate. Such a modified indexing rule would still protect individuals completely against any unexpected rise in inflation. Although there would not literally be any tax increase (just a slowdown in future tax cuts) or any reduction of benefits (just a slowdown of future benefit increases), the modified indexing would raise a substantial amount of additional tax revenue and save roughly an equal amount in Social Security outlays.

In the end, such a raise in personal taxes and fall in personal benefits was politically too costly to be acceptable as part of the president's budget. Instead, the Treasury developed a series of technical changes in business tax rules that would over time raise a moderate amount of additional revenue. The president accepted that these were not real "tax increases" but just the closing of business loopholes, allowing the Treasury to collect the taxes that "should be paid."

I left the administration in the summer of 1984 hoping that, once the election was over, a political compromise could emerge that would combine a significant tax increase with reductions in entitlements and other spending (Feldstein 1984a, 1985b). But that was not to be. In the second Reagan term, there were no voices in the administration to support higher taxes as part of an overall budget compromise. Instead, budget deficit action shifted to the Gramm-Rudman initiative, while tax legislation turned from deficit reduction to revenue neutral tax reform.

The Tax Reform Act of 1986

The primary focus of the Tax Reform Act of 1986 was a dramatic reduction of personal income tax rates. The marginal tax rate on the highest incomes fell from 50 percent to 28 percent, and other rates were reduced to 15 percent. The challenge was to pay for these rate reductions with changes in tax rules that would be acceptable to voters as a trade-off for the rate cuts and to do all this in a way that appeared distributionally neutral, that is, that gave low- and middle-income taxpayers at least as large as percentage reduction in tax liabilities as the reduction given to high-income taxpayers.

The most difficult part of the distributional challenge was to limit the overall tax reduction of the highest-income taxpayers, whose statutory rate had been cut nearly in half. An early proposal to eliminate the personal deduction for state income taxes died because of the opposition of large states like New York with high state income taxes.[18] Raising the tax rate on long-term capital gains was then seized on as the way to show a substantial offsetting increase in taxes paid by high-income taxpayers. Although raising the capital gains rate for high-income taxpayers from the existing 20 percent maximum to 28 percent would substantially reduce realizations and therefore produce less revenue from these taxpayers that the "static" calculations implied, the reality was less important than the perception. What mattered was to show that taxing long-term gains like other income would offset the reduction in the top rate of personal income tax. The Treasury and congressional staff therefore ignored the behavioral effects of the proposed higher capital gains tax rate in their projections of tax changes by income bracket. Remarkably, they nevertheless took the reduced realizations into account when calculating the aggregate revenue effects of the proposed tax change!

A number of technical changes were also made in tax rules to discourage the use of tax shelter investments, particularly eliminating the use of so-called passive losses to reduce taxable income. As a practical matter, these changes were less important in discouraging the use of tax shelters than the publicity given them suggested. They were less important in practice because the other changes in tax rules—reducing the maximum personal rate to 28 percent, raising the capital gains rate to the same level as ordinary income, and cutting depreciation allowances—were sufficient by themselves to eliminate the advantage of tax shelter investments.

18. Eliminating the personal tax deduction might only have encouraged states to rely more heavily on corporate taxes, with a resulting larger revenue loss to the federal Treasury (see Feldstein 1985d; and Feldstein and Metcalf 1987).

The primary effect of eliminating the use of passive losses reflected the Treasury's decision to phase out these accounting losses on already existing tax shelter investments. This raised revenue from high-income taxpayers and did so quickly. However, just as with the 1982 retroactive changes in depreciation rules, it sent the message that depreciation tax rules could not be relied on in the future. It also encouraged tax-motivated investors in real estate to sell their properties immediately, exacerbating the collapse of real estate values and the problems of the banking system in the late 1980s.

Another change designed to limit the tax cut for the highest-income taxpayers was eliminating the personal exemptions and the use of the low bracket rates (the zero bracket and the 15 percent bracket) for high-income individuals. This feature, which had long been advocated by liberal tax reformers as a way of increasing the overall progressivity of the tax schedule, had the effect of creating a range in which the marginal tax rate exceeded 28 percent for taxpayers with moderately high incomes before dropping back to 28 percent. Although the average tax rate increased continuously with income, this "hump" or "bubble" in the marginal tax rate schedule was seen by many taxpayers as unfair. But, in practice, the pressure to remove the "bubble" led in the 1990 tax legislation to a modification of the rate schedule that raised tax rates at the top to 32 percent and that pushed the "bubble" to higher income levels.

But, even with all these changes, the high-income group appeared in 1986 to receive a proportionally larger tax cut than those at lower income levels. The designers of the tax reform therefore introduced a substantial increase in the personal exemption as a way of cutting taxes for lower-income taxpayers. An increase in the personal exemption leaves almost all marginal tax rates unchanged (except among those who no longer owed any tax as a result of the higher exemptions) and therefore has no favorable supply-side effect. Indeed, by increasing the after-tax income while leaving marginal tax rates unchanged, the increase in the personal exemption could be expected to increase the demand for leisure and reduce labor supply. Its justification was that it focuses tax cuts not only on those with lower incomes but also on large families who had been disproportionately hurt by the inflation-induced erosion of personal exemptions over the past decade.

The increased personal exemption was, however, very expensive, adding about $25 billion a year to the cost of the overall reform. To balance this, the administration and Congress agreed to increase corporate tax revenue by $25 billion a year. This was achieved despite a reduction of the corporate tax rate from 46 percent to 34 percent by lengthening depreciation lives and eliminating the investment tax credit.

The revenue estimators conveniently chose not to take the increased corporate tax revenue into account in calculating the effect of the overall reform on the taxes paid at each income level. This produced the politically convenient result of an apparent tax cut for each income class despite the aggregate estimate that the tax reform as a whole was revenue neutral.

A more accurate analysis might impute the additional corporate tax on the basis of the ownership of capital and would therefore indicate that the extra $25 billion of corporate tax was paid primarily by higher-income taxpayers.[19] If the corporate tax collections had been correctly imputed, it would not have been necessary to raise the capital gains tax rate in order to show that higher-income individuals were not receiving a disproportionately large tax cut.

Indeed, since little or no additional revenue would result from raising the tax rate on capital gains from 20 to 28 percent, that change was also unnecessary to make the tax package revenue neutral. The top rate on capital gains was raised by 40 percent to create an impression rather than to raise revenue or balance the distribution of tax changes. Once again, the content of tax reform was shaped by the desire for a perception of fairness rather than by the actual likely effects of the proposed changes on the distribution of taxes and the performance of the economy.

The Treasury staff took the tax reform legislation as an opportunity to redesign depreciation rules in a way that they thought would increase the efficiency of the allocation of the corporate capital stock. In order to achieve what was popularly described as a "level playing field," the Treasury staff carefully calculated the depreciation schedules for equipment and structures that they believed would achieve equal effective tax rates on investments in equipment, structures, and inventories.[20] In the process, the overall effective tax rate on capital in the corporate sector was increased. In my judgment, this attempt to achieve a "level playing field" for different types of investments was misguided in three ways.

First, the overall increase in the effective tax rate on the return to corporate capital as a whole increases the distortion between owner-occupied housing and business capital.

Second, the higher effective tax rates on investments in plant and equipment and in inventories increase the distortion within business investment between these forms of tangible investment that must be depreciated over time and intangible investments in such things as advertising, marketing, and price discounting that enjoy immediate expensing.

Finally, the Treasury calculations of equal effective tax rates as a standard of tax neutrality made no allowance for differences in the way that different types of investments are financed. Inventories can be financed by relatively low-cost short-term loans and real estate investments by somewhat more expensive mortgages and bonds, while equipment and research must rely more heavily on equity capital.

It is perhaps ironic that a Republican administration should have passed such

19. For an analysis of the distribution of the corporate tax increase by income class, see Feldstein (1988b).

20. For a discussion of the evolution of the tax changes proposed by the Treasury staff as part of the TRA86 legislative process, see the chapter in this volume by Fullerton.

an antibusiness tax reform bill. In part, this reflected the president's primary interest in personal rather than business taxes and his great desire to reduce the top tax rate. Increasing the corporate tax by $25 billion a year or approximately 25 percent was of course opposed by those businesses that would expect to pay higher taxes. The administration was very clever in defusing this opposition by seeking endorsements from those businesses that were not capital intensive and that would therefore gain more from the reduction in the corporate tax rate than they would lose from the less favorable treatment of capital investments. In addition, the administration promised a variety of corporations that had particular tax and nontax concerns that the Treasury would try to help them if they would publicly support the overall legislation. As a result, the business community as a whole did not offer any unified opposition to these tax changes. Since the total of the Treasury's promises was more than could be accommodated within the overall revenue target, the Treasury jettisoned some of these supporters during the final round of congressional negotiations when it was too late for them to reverse their support.

The general effect of the business tax changes was to reduce the reward to investment and therefore to saving, exacerbating the problem of a low national saving rate. The incentive to save was also reduced in the 1986 Tax Reform Act by narrowing the eligibility for IRAs, by reducing the allowable level of pension benefits, and by increasing the tax rate on capital gains.[21]

The decade ended with personal income tax rates much lower than they were when the decade began and with fewer opportunities for individuals to reduce tax liabilities by creative accounting or by investments that have large tax advantages but few economic profits. Although the lower rates should have supply-side advantages, the decline in the top marginal tax rate from 50 percent to 28 percent (now 32 percent) exaggerates the favorable change since many of those who had faced a marginal tax rate of 50 percent had previously used tax shelters to reduce the effective marginal tax rate on a substantial portion of their incomes. Whether the sharply reduced personal income tax rates of the 1980s will remain in the 1990s is now uncertain.

1.3   Government Spending and Budget Deficits

The budget deficit was the primary problem that concerned me during my two years as CEA chairman (from mid-1982 to mid-1984) and was a continuing source of controversy with some of the other members of the Reagan administration. Even now, a decade later, the deficit remains a major problem that I would regard as the significant negative legacy of a decade of otherwise generally favorable policy developments.

Long before the 1980 presidential campaign, Ronald Reagan had been an advocate of reducing both taxes and nondefense spending. Both these goals

---

21. For further comments that I made at the time, see Feldstein (1986a, 1986d).

were achieved to a surprising and unprecedented extent during the first two years of the Reagan presidency. The tax cuts turned out to be much greater than expected, while the spending cuts were much less than the president and his advisers had anticipated. The result was an enormous budget deficit that continues until the present.

The failure to correct the deficit reflects a complex mix of personal, political, and economic factors. Before trying to unravel them, I begin with a brief overview of the changes that occurred in the pattern of government spending. I then discuss the role of economic analysis in shaping the changes in the components of government spending. After that, I look in detail at two aspects of budget policy that were important during my years in Washington: Social Security reform and the attempted reform of Medicare and the tax treatment of health insurance. Finally, I discuss the budget deficit itself: its origins, the attempts to control it, and the reasons why it remains unresolved.

1.3.1 The Changing Structure of Government Spending

The broad structure of federal government spending changed dramatically during the 1960s and 1970s. The share devoted to defense fell rapidly, while nondefense spending rose even faster. These trends were halted and reversed in the 1980s. Table 1.1 presents the components of government outlays as percentages of gross domestic product.[22]

Spending for defense (including other international programs) fell from 10.5 percent of GDP in 1962 (a time before the increase in military spending associated with the Vietnam War) to 5.6 percent in 1980. The sharp decline was halted in the 1980s. A substantial investment in defense equipment and a significant rise in military pay raised the defense share of GDP during the first half of the decade to 6.9 percent of GDP in 1986 before it declined again to 5.8 percent of GDP in 1990.

Outlays on the Social Security and Medicare programs for the aged, together with other retirement and disability programs, more than doubled as a share of GDP from 3.0 percent in 1962 to 6.9 percent in 1980. The rapid growth continued during the first two years of the Reagan administration (to 7.8 percent of GDP in 1982) but then declined and stabilized at 7.6 percent of GDP as the very fast real GDP growth during the recovery outstripped the rise in Social Security spending by enough to offset the increases in Medicare costs.

The third major change in the structure of spending, and in many ways the most dramatic, was the sharp reversal of the rise in other nondefense outlays. Total domestic spending, other than Social Security and related programs (shown in row 3 of table 1.1), rose from 4.5 percent of GDP in 1962 to 7.9 percent in 1980. By 1984, it had been cut from 7.9 percent to 5.9 percent, a fall of more than one-fourth in the GDP share. It is, of course, always hard to

---

22. The figures begin with 1962 because that is the first year for which the Congressional Budget Office provides comparable data.

Table 1.1   **Government Outlays as a Percentage of GDP**

	1962	1970	1980	1982	1984	1985	1990
1. Defense and international	10.5	8.7	5.6	6.4	6.6	6.8	5.8
2. Social Security, Medicare and related retirement	3.0	4.4	6.9	7.8	7.6	7.6	7.6
3. Other domestic spending	4.5	5.2	7.9	6.9	5.9	6.1	6.1
3a. Domestic discretionary	3.0	3.9	4.9	4.1	3.7	3.7	3.3
3b. Entitlements[a]	2.8	2.6	4.1	4.1	3.4	3.7	2.8
3c. Offsetting receipts	−1.2	−1.2	−1.1	−1.2	−1.2	−1.2	−1.1
3d. Deposit insurance	−.1	−.1	0	−.1	0	−.1	1.1
4. Net interest	1.2	1.5	2.0	2.7	3.0	3.3	3.4
5. Total	19.3	19.9	22.3	23.9	23.0	23.8	22.9
6. Total without deposit insurance	19.4	20.0	22.3	24.0	23.0	23.9	21.8

Source: Congressional Budget Office.

Note: Totals may not equal the sum of individual components because of rounding errors.

[a]Excluding Social Security, Medicare, and related retirement.

know what would have happened without the determined effort of the Reagan administration to cut such spending. But, if spending had continued to grow relative to GDP during the 1980s as it had in the previous two decades, it would have reached 10.8 percent of GDP in 1990. The gap between that hypothetical projection and the actual 6.1 percent spending level represented more than $260 billion a year of outlays.

Despite the fall in total domestic spending relative to GDP, total government outlays relative to GDP showed little change in the 1980s. During the first half of the decade, this was due in equal measure to the rise in defense spending and in net interest payments. For the decade as a whole, the defense increase was only 0.2 percent of GDP. Social Security and related programs rose much more rapidly, increasing by 0.7 percent of GDP. Together these offset half the 1.8 percent fall in other domestic spending, leaving a net decline in spending of only 0.9 percent of GDP. However, the rise in net interest costs from 2.0 percent of GDP to 3.4 percent caused total government outlays to rise from 22.3 percent of GDP in 1980 to 22.9 percent in 1990.

These figures are somewhat misleading because of the large outlay for deposit insurance in 1990 (equal to 1.1 percent of GDP) after the deposit insurance program showed small surpluses over the previous decade. A more appropriate analysis would exclude deposit insurance outlays since these represent only the explicit recognition of losses that had accrued over a period of years.[23] When deposit insurance is excluded, the category "other domestic spending" declines from 7.9 percent of GDP in 1980 to 5.0 percent of GDP in 1990.

23. That procedure is followed by the Congressional Budget Office in many of their analytic comparisons. A further reason for excluding deposit insurance outlays is that some of those outlays are for the purchase of assets that will later be sold (see Feldstein 1989b).

Because of the 0.2 percent of GDP rise in defense spending and the 0.7 percent of GDP rise in Social Security and related programs, total noninterest spending was down 2.0 percent of GDP. Even after the 1.4 percent of GDP rise in net interest payments, total government spending was down by 0.5 percent of GDP.

Nevertheless, for many conservatives, the attempt to shrink government spending had failed. This hardened their opposition to tax increases to deal with the budget deficit. But, within the increased total outlays, there had been a dramatic and unprecedented reduction in domestic spending. The conservatives had achieved a greater budget victory than anyone could have anticipated in 1980. But, because many conservatives refused to recognize their own political success, they were not prepared to adjust the revenue side of the budget to shrink the deficit.

Before looking at the budget deficit debates in more detail, I will examine the impact of economists on the character of the spending changes that did occur.

1.3.2   The Role of Economic Analysis in Spending Reforms

Defense

Economic analysis and economists had little influence on the overall level of defense spending. I cannot judge the extent to which economists and defense analysts who criticized particular weapons systems did affect the shape of the defense budget. But the overall level of defense spending was not the result of adding up a series of individual decisions. The administration's target level for total defense spending was decided by the president and Defense Secretary Casper Weinberger and then negotiated with the Congress in similarly aggregate terms.

The national mood at the beginning of the 1980s favored increased defense spending. American military power and influence appeared to be eroding around the globe. The embarrassing failure of the attempted rescue of American hostages in Iran (when the military equipment failed in the desert and the entire mission had to be abandoned) was a symbol of declining capability. There was also a sense that the end of the draft and the erosion of military pay had led to a decline in the quality and morale of the armed forces.

In 1980, President Carter and candidate Reagan both promised that they would raise defense spending if elected for the next four years. During the last two years of his presidency, Jimmy Carter had actually increased defense outlays significantly, from $126 billion in fiscal year 1979 to $172 billion in fiscal year 1981. Even allowing for an approximately 23 percent rise in the price level during this time, real defense spending rose by 11 percent from 5.2 percent of GDP to 5.8 percent of GDP. President Reagan accelerated the increase in defense spending in order to put pressure on the Soviets, to enhance U.S. military capability, and to increase the morale and quality of the services through higher pay.

Cap Weinberger, himself a former Office of Management and Budget

(OMB) director, was able to keep defense spending outside the regular budget process. Although the OMB reviewed the details of the defense budget, the overall level of defense spending was decided by the president and the defense secretary alone, something without parallel in the other spending departments and a continuing source of frustration to OMB Director David Stockman.

After 1983, Congress tried to reduce the budget deficit by cutting the growth of defense spending. There was a growing public debate about whether the amount of defense spending requested by the administration was justified and about whether the rise in defense outlays was responsible for the budget deficit.

When I was CEA chairman, I recognized that as an economist I didn't have the expertise to judge the proper amount of defense spending. My view, which I repeatedly stated publicly, was that the nation could certainly afford the current and projected levels of defense spending if we were willing to pay for them by raising taxes or cutting other spending. Privately, I tried unsuccessfully to enlist Weinberger as an ally in the internal debate over raising taxes by arguing to him that, without higher taxes, Congress would cut the administration's defense requests more sharply than if there were the additional revenue to pay for the increased defense outlays. The president continued to ask for large spending increases for defense but eventually accepted Congress's demand for smaller increases rather than accede to larger tax rises.

Domestic Discretionary Spending and Entitlements Other than Social Security and Medicare

In contrast to the negligible role that economics played in shaping the size and composition of the defense budget, economic analysis did have a substantial impact on the myriad annually appropriated nondefense programs (the so-called domestic discretionary budget) and the smaller "entitlement" programs other than Social Security, Medicare, and related retirement programs. Although the economics profession as a whole pays relatively little attention to most of these programs, those economists who had studied them were often critical of individual programs. They criticized them for having costs that exceeded the resulting benefits, for transferring to the government things that could be better done in the private sector, and for creating adverse incentives for individuals and businesses. Such programs would have been worth cutting or eliminating even if there were not a large budget deficit.

Economists were generally not involved in the detailed legislative process dealing with these spending programs, but there is no doubt that economic reasoning set the framework for selecting appropriate spending cuts. Specific program cuts generally originated in the OMB. David Stockman was not only a brilliant budget director but also a "natural" economist who instinctively focused on programs that an economist would identify as suitable for cutting.[24]

---

24. Describing Stockman as a "natural" economist may be misleading. When I met Stockman at the beginning of his first term in Congress, he had done some systematic reading of economics and continued to read nontechnical economics during his years in Congress.

The budget ax fell heavily on such things as the Carter energy program, transfer programs that created adverse work incentives, wasteful intergovernmental grants, and similar activities.

Table 1.1 shows that, between 1980 and 1984, the combination of nondefense discretionary spending and the group of smaller entitlement programs was reduced from 9.0 percent of GDP to 7.1 percent of GDP, a drop of more than one-fifth of the former GDP share. Although some of the initial 1981 spending cuts were eventually restored, the decade ended with these programs down to only 6.1 percent of GDP. In contrast to this 32 percent decline in the GDP share in the 1980s, the corresponding spending share of GDP had risen by more than 12 percent in the 1960s and by 38 percent in the 1970s. David Stockman is undoubtedly too modest in his comments in this volume when he says that he and President Reagan had done little to reduce domestic spending.

Two things are striking about these cuts in nondefense discretionary spending. First, the major spending cuts were largely enacted during the first legislative year after President Reagan's inauguration.[25] Second, the political power of the aged allowed them to avoid cuts in the programs that specifically benefited them. Instead, the cuts fell primarily on small programs with changing groups of beneficiaries like unemployment insurance.

Net Interest Costs

Interest payments on the national debt increased from 2.0 percent of GDP in 1980 to 3.4 percent in 1990. The primary driving force in this increase was the growth of the national debt that resulted from the large budget deficits. The increase in the debt held by the public, from 26.8 percent of GDP in 1980 to 44.2 percent in 1990, accounts for nearly all the rise in the interest outlays.

Although the net interest payments on the government debt were a large and rising component of total government outlays in the 1980s, the Treasury Department failed to accept economic advice on how that debt service cost could be reduced. Throughout the decade, the administration issued forecasts that inflation and interest rates would continue to decline. These forecasts were sincerely believed and turned out to be correct. The Treasury nevertheless failed to accept the logic of their own forecasts by borrowing short in anticipation of the declining rates. Instead, the Treasury actually lengthened the maturity of the debt.

The national debt might instead have been managed in a way that significantly reduced the government's interest cost. Although interest rates were higher at the start of the decade than they had been in the 1970s, the level of

---

25. This reflected not only the substantial size of the early successes but also the loss of the effective control of the House of Representatives that occurred after the 1982 election. Although the Republicans were a minority in the House in 1981 and 1982, the coalition of Republicans and conservative Democrats supported the Reagan spending reforms. The Republicans suffered substantial losses in the 1982 congressional election because of the recession and the abortive attempt at cutting Social Security benefits, a subject to which I return later in this essay.

interest rates then fell sharply throughout the decade. The interest rate on ten-year bonds fell from 13.9 percent in 1981 to 7.7 percent in 1986 and then remained under 9 percent for the rest of the decade. Shorter-term rates fell even faster. The yield on a three-year Treasury security fell from 14.4 percent in 1981 to 7.1 percent in 1986 and then stayed below 9 percent.

In 1983, when the interest rates on ten-year bonds were still over 10 percent and the administration was forecasting a sharp fall in rates over the next five years, I suggested that the Treasury either borrow short (with the prospect of lengthening later when rates had declined), or use a floating-rate note, or link the interest rate to the rate of inflation.

Such suggestions were rejected by Treasury Secretary Don Regan for reasons that I could never understand. He argued, for example, that indexing the interest rate to inflation would indicate that we had lost confidence in our ability to reduce inflation in the future. I explained (to no avail) that the opposite was true. While the unwillingness of financial markets to lend to a government on a long-term fixed-rate basis is evidence that the market lacks confidence in that government's ability to control inflation, the United States was clearly able to issue long-term debt. Our decision to borrow with an interest rate that was linked to inflation or to Treasury-bill rates would show our confidence that rates would decline in the future.

But debt management is quite definitely a Treasury responsibility, and the CEA can only offer friendly advice. The Treasury not only failed to respond to its own interest rate forecasts but continued a policy, begun under the Nixon and Carter administrations, of deliberately lengthening the maturity of the debt. The average length of the privately held public debt rose from three years and nine months in 1980 to over six years in 1990.

1.3.3   Social Security Reform

The Social Security reforms enacted in 1983 were among the most remarkable domestic policy developments of the decade, not only in the magnitude of the changes that were made, but also in the procedure that was followed and in the incongruity of the reforms with the basic philosophical position of the president.

When I joined the administration in 1982, I had been studying Social Security for more than fifteen years since my days as a graduate student. I was (and remain) convinced that the provision of high Social Security benefits substantially reduces private saving and is a significant cause of our low national saving rate (Feldstein 1974, 1985c).

Social Security was on the administration's agenda from the start for two reasons. Such a large program (it represented 4.4 percent of GDP in 1980) could not be ignored in any attempt to reduce total government spending. Moreover, the Social Security program was itself in financial trouble with payroll taxes too low to cover current or projected benefits. The trust fund was shrinking and would soon be depleted unless some action was taken. This problem provided the opportunity for a serious consideration of Social Security reform.

In addition to containing detailed proposals for changing taxes and spending, the administration's original 1981 budget plan identified one major deficit reduction only by a set of asterisks and a promise that more detail would be given later. These asterisks actually denoted a major reduction in projected Social Security outlays that the administration had not yet designed in detail.

The president had been advocating a reduction of Social Security benefits for at least a decade. He objected to the payment of benefits to older individuals with high incomes and thought it wrong to have such high payroll taxes for a system not based on need. But he had gotten into political trouble himself once in proposing a change in Social Security in the 1976 presidential election primaries. He therefore instructed the OMB in 1981 to design a reduction of Social Security outlays without actually cutting benefits to any person sixty-five years old or older. Such a constraint need not have interfered with a long-term strategy for slowing the growth of Social Security, especially if the president's restriction could be interpreted to refer to nominal dollars so that a modification of the full benefit indexation was acceptable. But the need for substantial short-term budget cuts and for an immediate remedy of the Social Security program's financial problem caused OMB to formulate a short-term plan that satisfied the president's specific injunction against cutting benefits of those over age sixty-five but violated its spirit by proposing sharp benefit reductions for retirees between the ages of sixty-two and sixty-four. The OMB proposal called for an immediate and very substantial (20 percent) cut in the benefits of anyone who took early retirement at age sixty-two with pro rata reductions for those who retired between the ages of sixty-two and sixty-five.

The proposal for an abrupt reduction in benefits of individuals who were expecting to retire very soon caused a political uproar. The members of Congress were so opposed to the idea that none of them was prepared to introduce the administration's plan. Indeed, the Senate soon passed a unanimous sense-of-the-Senate motion putting themselves on record as opposed to any substantial cut in benefits.

A similar political fiasco occurred over the administration's plan to eliminate the floor on Social Security benefits.[26] Although the minimum benefit recipient conjures up the image of an individual with very low income, many of the minimum benefit recipients are retired government workers with substantial pensions who qualified for the minimum Social Security benefit by working in private industry for a few years after leaving government employment.[27] Retir-

26. Social security benefits are based on a formula that relates the level of benefits to the inflation-adjusted average monthly earnings during the individual's working life with a variety of adjustments to eliminate anomalous years. If this calculation results in a benefit below a prescribed minimum, the law provides that the individual will receive the minimum benefit.

27. Federal employees did not at that time participate in Social Security but could qualify for benefits by working in private employment before or after their years with the government.

ees who have very low Social Security benefits and no other income are entitled to means-tested Supplemental Security Income benefits. Nevertheless, the proposal to eliminate the minimum benefit was easily misinterpreted by its opponents and used to criticize the Reagan administration for denying Social Security to the "most needy" beneficiaries. The legislation repealing the minimum benefit was subsequently reversed by the Congress.

As a result of these two misjudged proposals, the Democrats were able to attack congressional Republicans who were running for reelection in 1982 as opponents of Social Security and of the aged. The Republicans eventually suffered substantial election defeats and lost effective control of the House of Representatives. The memory of those losses deterred congressional Republicans from supporting modifications of Social Security in future years.

Nevertheless, the financial gap in Social Security funding remained and had to be addressed. In an attempt to limit the damage to Republicans in the 1982 election, the president proposed that a solution to the financial problems of Social Security be worked out by a bipartisan committee headed by former CEA Chairman Alan Greenspan with members appointed by himself and by the Republican and Democratic congressional leaders. The committee would report in December 1982, after the election. The proposal was supported by the congressional leadership of both parties.

During the months before the election, the Greenspan Commission did work separately from the White House and other parts of the administration. There were, however, private discussions among the administration senior staff and with the president. In these private discussions, the president stressed his desire to see the financial problems of the Social Security program resolved by reducing the growth of future Social Security benefits. He recalled that the program began with a promise that the combined tax rate would never exceed 2 percent, and he resented the pressure to raise taxes from the existing 13.4 percent level. He wondered why the Social Security program could not be privatized and reluctantly accepted the explanation that continuation of the existing Social Security payroll taxes was needed to finance benefits of the current retirees.

Dave Stockman and I analyzed and discussed possible Social Security reforms. I favored a change in the indexing of Social Security benefits, shifting from the existing law that maintains postretirement benefits constant in real terms to indexing benefits by 3 percent less than the inflation rate. A 3 percent threshold would still protect beneficiaries fully from any increase in the inflation rate above 3 percent. Limiting the index modification to five years would mean that no individual's real benefit would be cut by more than 15 percent. The lowest 25 percent of benefits could be exempted from the adjustment without significantly altering the prospective savings. Stockman, who also wanted to shrink Social Security, focused on more opaque options, such as changing the "bend points" in the Social Security formula (i.e., the income levels at which the ratio of benefits to the individual's average previous earnings changes).

In December 1982, the Greenspan Commission announced that it was at a stalemate with Democratic and Republican members sharply divided on what should be done. The Democrats were unwilling to reduce benefits or postpone the retirement date. The Republican members did not want to close the Social Security financing gap by tax increases alone. But, without a unanimous report, Social Security would be thrown back into partisan controversy.

James Baker, then White House chief of staff, was having active discussions with commission member Alexander Trowbridge, a Democratic appointee, former Commerce Department secretary, and current head of the National Association of Manufacturers. It was never clear to me why Trowbridge was our negotiating contact with the commission. Baker reported to the White House Social Security group[28] the "compromise" that Trowbridge suggested for closing the Social Security financing gap: advance the date of a future payroll tax increase that had been enacted during the Carter years; subject half the Social Security benefits of married recipients with incomes over $32,000 and single recipients with incomes over $25,000 to personal income taxation (with the resulting revenue transferred from the Treasury to the Social Security trust fund); and require all employees of nonprofit institutions and new employees of state and local governments to participate in the Social Security program. There would be no reduction in benefits or postponement of the retirement age.

The president was clearly very unhappy with the proposed "compromise." The administration's group monitoring the Social Security issue discussed the option of encouraging the Republican members to remain firm. There would then be no commission plan, and the administration could propose a solution to the Social Security financial crisis that was more in keeping with the president's preferences.

I supported this strategy and advocated a change in benefit indexing as a way of achieving substantial outlay reduction over time without actually "reducing any checks in the mail." that is, without actually causing a decline in any individual's monthly Social Security check. I knew that the public opinion polls being conducted by the Chamber of Commerce and by the president's pollster (Dick Wirthlin) showed that the public favored limiting Social Security indexing to the same partial rules that prevailed in private industry. I described this to the president and made the case for a 3 percent threshold on benefit indexing.

The president talked about going on television, explaining to the viewers that high-income individuals should not be getting Social Security benefits from the government and that most retirees were getting much more in benefits than they had paid for. The only way to avoid higher taxes for younger families

---

28. The group that met with the president and vice-president to discuss these issues was David Stockman, Don Regan, White House Domestic Policy Adviser Ed Harper, Jim Baker, Presidential Counselor Ed Meese, Dick Darman (Jim Baker's deputy), Cabinet Secretary Craig Fuller, Legislative Affairs Director Ken Duberstein, Communications Director David Gergen, and myself.

was to slow the growth of benefits. It looked for a while as if the combination of a Social Security financing crisis and a conservative president would bring about the reduction in the size of the Social Security program that I thought was desirable for quite different reasons.

But, as the discussion continued, Jim Baker argued that that was too dangerous a strategy politically and that it would cause Republicans as a party to be stigmatized as being opposed to Social Security and to the aged. He argued that even if the polls currently implied that the public would support the president's ideas, that support would not persist after the Democrats mounted a campaign against the proposed changes. In any case, Baker argued, the Republicans in Congress had been hurt in the 1982 elections by the administration's Social Security proposals and would not support any proposal that could be characterized as a plan to shrink Social Security.

Although, as a general rule, I did not get involved in congressional negotiations, in this case I wanted to see for myself how much potential support the president would have if he proposed to modify Social Security indexing or some other aspect of Social Security benefits. My visits with congressional Republicans were not encouraging. While most of them spoke about the desirability of limiting benefit growth rather than raising taxes, almost every one of them explained why in his own particular case it would be much easier to vote for a bipartisan plan to raise payroll taxes than to support a controversial presidential initiative to slow benefit growth. The benefits of reducing the relative size of Social Security and thereby avoiding a 2 percentage point increase in the payroll tax seemed too small and the cost to Republicans of reducing Social Security benefits—even if only the growth of those benefits—politically too high for them to take on what would have become a partisan issue.

What would have happened if the president had decided to "go to the people" will never be known. He decided to follow Jim Baker's advice to accept a compromise plan proposed by the Greenspan Commission's Democrats. He indicated some modifications that he wanted and said that he would encourage the Republican members of the commission to accept the modified plan. He rationalized that the payroll tax increase was really just an advancing of the date of a tax increase that had been proposed by President Carter and therefore not really "his" tax increase. Similarly, he accepted the interpretation that subjecting half the benefits of the higher-income aged to the income tax was really equivalent to a reduction of benefits (ignoring the fact that it would be a reduction related to taxable income and therefore similar to a tax increase on higher-income taxpayers; although not indexing the income level at which such taxing begins would eventually make this a virtually universal tax, it would still be a greater tax on individuals in higher tax brackets). Expanding Social Security to currently uncovered workers could be regarded as closing an existing loophole.

Although the size of Social Security was not reduced, Social Security rules were changed in several ways that economists had long advocated to reduce the distortion in retirement behavior. First, the reduction of benefits for "retirees" with earnings above a threshold amount was reduced from fifty cents per dollar of extra earnings to thirty-three cents. Second, the increase in benefits for those who delayed retirement beyond age sixty-five was raised and scheduled to go on rising for future retirees until eventually the benefits would be actuarially equal regardless of the age of retirement. Finally, although the commission did not have the political courage to raise the retirement age, the Congress did modify the commission's proposal and enact a postponement of the retirement age at which full benefits would be payable from sixty-five to sixty-seven in the next century.

With these changes in taxes and future benefits, the Social Security actuaries could project that the system would remain solvent for the seventy-five-year Social Security forecast period. There would be a substantial Social Security surplus for several decades. This surplus would permit a fund to accumulate that could be used to meet the rising benefit obligation that would occur as the baby-boom generation retired after 2020 without increasing the payroll tax rate at that time. Surprisingly, this feature of the reform received relatively little attention in our discussions, which focused instead on the implications of the reforms for the Social Security finances in the 1980s and for the next few years of budget figures.

The Social Security reforms of the 1980s were one of the great ironies of the Reagan administration. Here was a president who wanted a substantial reduction in Social Security benefits. His OMB director and CEA chairman were also eager for such reductions. A substantial deficit in the Social Security program had forced a consideration of future benefits and taxes. Yet, when the dust settled, the Social Security program had not been reduced but had actually been given a more secure future. The 1983 legislative changes in Social Security thus removed the pressure for immediate benefit reductions, helped maintain confidence in the future benefit payments, and reduced the prospects of a substantial future benefit reform induced by a subsequent financial crisis as the total cost of benefits increased. The tax increases enacted in 1983 meant that, for the next seventy-five years, it would not be necessary to increase taxes again to meet the obligations that would result from the increased number of retirees. The size of the Social Security program was significantly enlarged by extending mandatory coverage to all employees of nonprofit institutions and eventually to all state and local government employees. The financing barrier between the proportional payroll tax earmarked for Social Security and the graduated personal income tax was broken by transferring funds from general revenue to the Social Security trust fund.

1.3.4   Reforming Medicare and the Health Insurance Tax Rules

In the fifteen years after it began, the Medicare program of health care for the aged grew from $3.2 billion in 1967 to $49 billion in 1982. Unlike Medicaid, which is means tested and financed in part by the individual state governments, Medicare is a program for all the aged, and it is fully financed by the federal government.

Health care was another area that I had been thinking about since my student days. By the early 1980s, experts agreed that Medicare's existing system of comprehensive insurance and cost-plus hospital reimbursements was a major contributor to the explosive rise in the cost of the Medicare program and more generally to the national rise in health care costs. My own research over the years had convinced me that greater out-of-pocket payments by patients at the time of care (i.e., increased deductibles and coinsurance) would make patients and their doctors more cost conscious and would thus improve the allocation of health care resources and reduce the excessive rise in health care costs.[29] I was also convinced (and remain convinced) that the exclusion of employer health insurance payments from taxable income caused health insurance to be much more complete and to have less cost sharing by patients at the time of care than would have been true without the implicit tax subsidy (Feldstein 1973; Feldstein and Allison 1974; Feldstein and Friedman 1977).

I was pleased, therefore, that the desire to limit the increase in Medicare costs and the search for ways to increase tax revenue by "closing loopholes" put health care reform on the agenda as we prepared the budget to be submitted in February 1984.

The basic tax reform idea was to limit employers' ability to provide tax-free income in the form of health insurance premiums. Political reality precluded including all employer-provided health benefits in taxable income. At most, the amount of tax-free income could be limited either by including in the employee's taxable income any employer payments over a certain level or by denying firms the usual business expense deduction for insurance premiums above a certain level. Either option would provide the correct incentive at the margin for employees with high levels of employer-provided health benefits. Indexing the tax-free limit to the general level of consumer prices would cause it to rise more slowly than medical care costs and therefore to become more significant over time.

The proposed change in the tax rule was described publicly as a way of raising tax revenue by closing a tax loophole that disproportionately favored high-income taxpayers. The idea that it would change the character of health insurance and therefore the patterns of health care was considered better left unsaid.

A parallel change was discussed for Medicare with an emphasis on increasing various deductibles and coinsurance payments to be paid by patients at the time that care is received. I favored this as a way of improving incentives in the choices of medical care. The budgeteers at OMB thought that it would be a good idea even if there were no behavioral response since it would reduce the cost of the Medicare program.

These tax changes and Medicare reforms were proposed by the president but died in the Congress. In retrospect, I believe that we set the limits on tax-

---

29. Several of my papers dealing with health insurance and hospital costs are collected in Feldstein (1981b).

free insurance premiums too low. Since many union contracts provided for benefits above the allowable level, the unions strongly opposed the proposed change on the basis of their members' immediate interests as well as on more general philosophical grounds. Similarly, too many Medicare recipients would see significant increases in their out-of-pocket costs. It would have been better to establish the principal of limiting the tax subsidy by setting much higher limits for tax-free employer payments and permitting the rise in medical care costs to make the limit binding for an increasing number of individuals over time. Similarly, it would have been better to introduce coinsurance payments at much higher levels of Medicare benefits and allow general medical care inflation to make these more broadly applicable over time. Because of the administration's eagerness for immediate revenue rather than structural reform, we got neither. In this way, the Medicare experience was very similar to our earlier experience with Social Security reform.

The analysts at the Department of Health and Human Services (HHS) were developing a different approach to Medicare reform. The HHS approach was to replace the existing system of reimbursing hospital costs with a system of paying specific fixed prices for patients in each of several hundred individual diagnostic groups. The HHS officials argued in interagency meetings that this would make the purchase of hospital care by the Medicare program similar to the market system by which the government procured other goods and services: setting a price and buying from vendors who would sell at that price. I argued unsuccessfully that this analogy was faulty because paying for the treatment of a patient with a particular diagnosis was very different from buying ordinary products and service. I was never certain whether the HHS officials really believed in the "market system" analogy of the proposed payment system or just regarded that as a useful way to sell their cost regulation plan to a market-oriented administration.

Although I liked the idea of ending the traditional cost-plus approach to reimbursing hospitals, I worried that the proposed HHS system would create an extensive bureaucracy to check that patients were correctly classified, to monitor the patients who were admitted to hospitals (to reduce unwarranted admissions), and to make certain that patients were not "undertreated" in order to keep costs down. It seemed ironic that a strongly market-oriented administration would not strengthen the market mechanism in medical care (by introducing copayments or competition among group providers) but should instead accept government price setting and detailed bureaucratic supervision for its largest domestic procurement.

1.3.5   Budget Deficits

Although the federal budget has been in deficit in all but nine years in the past half century, the deficit soared to new heights in the 1980s. These deficits absorbed more than half of net domestic saving, putting upward pressure on real interest rates and inducing a massive trade deficit in the 1980s.

But, unlike inflation and unemployment, the deficit is not visible to the general public, and its links to the future performance of the economy remain vague and poorly understood by almost everyone. The traditional association of deficits with inflation was clearly shown to be wrong by the U.S. experience of the 1980s. I regarded it as one of my important tasks to educate not only my administration colleagues but also the relevant members of Congress and the public at large about the long-run adverse effects of budget deficits. Only if they understood the serious long-run effects would they be willing to incur the short-run costs that would be needed to reduce the deficit.

Looking back on the decade of the 1980s, too little was done to cut the deficit and to restrain its future growth. The political costs of deficit reduction clearly and understandably exceed the political benefits of a smaller deficit and a higher national saving rate. That something was done in almost every year to shrink the deficit showed that the president and key congressional leaders did care about the problem. That more was not done showed that they did not care enough.

Sources of the Increased Deficit

In fiscal year 1984, more than a year after the start of a strong economic recovery, the deficit had reached 5.0 percent of GDP. The sharply rising deficit had generated a debate about its sources that sought to place blame and to justify alternative remedies. The administration's critics charged that this was due to excessive tax cuts and large increases in defense spending. The administration responded that much of the deficit was inherited from the Carter administration, that it had been enlarged by the recession, and that the real problem lay in rising entitlement costs and other so-called uncontrollables.

There were enough facts to support almost any conclusion. Debaters could prove almost anything by taking about nominal levels of taxes and spending: "How could tax cuts have caused the deficit since revenues actually rose from $517 billion in 1980 to $666 billion in 1988?" and "Despite the attempts to control domestic spending, nondefense outlays rose from $444 billion in 1980 to $607 billion in 1984; even if Social Security and Medicare outlays are excluded, domestic spending rose by nearly $80 billion."

The only way to make sensible comparisons is to look at ratios to GDP.[30] Between 1980 and 1984, the deficit rose from 2.8 percent of GDP to 5.0 percent of GDP, implying that more than half the deficit had been there when President Carter left office. The result is similar if we look at the cyclically adjusted structural deficit. The Congressional Budget Office estimates that the 1984 structural deficit (calculated at a 5.8 percent unemployment rate) was equivalent to 3.6 percent of GDP. Since the corresponding structural deficit for

30. The most recent figures from the Congressional Budget Office (*The Economic and Budget Outlook: Fiscal Years 1993–97* [1992]) now state ratios to GDP, and I use these figures even though we were looking at GNP ratios in the 1980s.

1980 was 1.8 percent of GDP, half the structural deficit was inherited from the Carter administration.

Roughly one-third of the 2.2 percent of GDP rise in the deficit between 1980 and 1984 can, in a purely arithmetic sense, be attributed to higher spending (total outlays rose by 0.6 percent of GDP) and the remaining two-thirds to lower taxes as a share of GDP. But the more one disaggregates the spending and tax totals, the more ambiguous the sources of the deficit become. For example, the "uncontrollable" outlays for Social Security and related programs and for net interest rose by 1.7 percent of GDP over the same four years, accounting for more than three-fourths of the increase in the deficit. Since "other domestic spending" fell relative to GDP by 2 percentage points (from 7.9 percent to 5.9 percent), this was more than enough to offset all the revenue decline (from 19.6 percent of GDP to 18.0 percent).

The most common view of the 2.2 percent of GDP increase in the deficit between 1980 and 1984 attributed it to a combination of the revenue decline (1.6 percent of GDP) plus the rise in defense outlays (an increase of 1.0 percent of GDP). But, to those who made this argument, it could reasonably be replied that the cut in "other domestic spending" paid for more than 75 percent of the combined effect of lower taxes and increased defense outlays.

For the decade of the 1980s as a whole, the combination of increased defense spending (from 5.6 percent of GDP to 5.8 percent) and the relative decline in revenue (from 19.6 percent of GDP to 18.9 percent) added only 0.9 percent of GDP to the deficit, less than one-third of the 2.9 percent of GDP decline of "other domestic spending" (excluding deposit insurance payments). The 2.0 percent of GDP rise of the deficit in the 1980s (0.9 percent if deposit insurance payments are excluded) can be more than accounted for by the combination of the increase in Social Security and related outlays (an increase of 0.7 percent of GDP) and in interest on the national debt (an increase of 1.4 percent of GDP).

No unambiguous resolution of the "sources of the deficit" is possible because the individual components can be combined in many different ways to support different points of view, each of which is true but incomplete.

The 1981 Tax Cuts

There is no ambiguity, however, about the fact that the tax cut enacted in 1981 provided a much larger decline in revenue than the administration had expected when that legislation was proposed or passed. The primary reason for this was that inflation declined much more rapidly than had originally been expected. A second but less powerful reason was that real economic growth was lower than projected in 1981. Finally, as Don Fullerton's chapter documents, the tax bill that emerged from the Congress was much more generous to business taxpayers than the original administration proposal.

A calculation that I made in January 1983 for discussion with the president and other members of the budget group[31] shows just how much greater the personal tax cuts were turning out to be than had originally been intended. The administration's original proposal for a series of three 10 percent cuts in personal tax rates ("10–10–10") was projected in the February 1981 budget calculations to reduce individual income tax collections to 11.3 percent of personal income in 1986. But, using the January 1983 economic forecast, individual income tax payments in 1986 would be only 10.1 percent of personal income.

This sharp decline in projected tax revenue was due almost completely to the revised economic outlook, particularly to the lower rate of inflation and therefore the reduced extent to which "bracket creep" would raise real tax liabilities. The extra tax breaks for individual taxpayers that Congress had voted in 1981 were just about offset by the effect of substituting a 5–10–10 schedule of rate cuts for the originally proposed 10–10–10 schedule of rate cuts. Substituting the actual 1981 tax legislation (the Economic Recovery Tax Act) for the proposed 10–10–10 plan, but retaining the 1981 economic forecasts, only reduced the projected revenue share of personal income from 11.3 percent of personal income to 11.2 percent.

I produced these numbers to support the case for a "mid-course correction," a revision of the third part of the 5–10–10 tax cut or a modification of the inflation indexing of personal tax brackets that had been enacted in 1981 and that was scheduled to begin in 1985. I argued that, if the president had been satisfied with the relative tax burden projected in 1981 (i.e., that individual income taxes would equal 11.3 percent of personal income in 1986), a modification of existing tax rules was now necessary to achieve those original targets.

The president was not persuaded by this argument. The original proposal for a 10–10–10 tax cut was aimed not at achieving a particular relative tax burden but at cutting taxes as much as feasible. Viewed from the perspective of 1980, the implied level of taxes hardly represented any decrease at all. The administration's 1981 projection that 10–10–10 would lower the ratio to 11.3 percent in 1986 was essentially only equivalent to maintaining the current tax share unchanged, not even seeking to return to the tax share of the middle of the 1970s. Individual income tax payments were 11.0 percent of personal income in 1979 and 1980 and 11.5 percent in 1981, up sharply from less than 10 percent of personal income in the mid-1970s.

The key reason for this very small decline in the projected level of individual taxes relative to personal income was the substantial "bracket creep" rise in effective tax rates that was expected to result from the combination of inflation and real income gains in the early 1980s. The February 1981 budget assumed that inflation would decline from over 10 percent in 1980 to 7.7 percent in

31. The small group that met intensively with the president in January to make decisions on all aspects of the budget consisted of Vice-President Bush, the three senior economic officials (Don Regan, Dave Stockman, and myself), and several White House staff members (Ed Harper, Jim Baker, Ed Meese, Dick Darman, Craig Fuller, Ken Duberstein, and Dave Gergen).

fiscal year 1982. The actual decline was to less than 5 percent. The forecast also projected strong real GNP growth of 5.2 percent for the coming year. This real growth projection might not have seemed unreasonable for an economy that was just coming out of the 1980 recession and that was then experiencing real GNP growth of more than 6 percent (in the fourth quarter of 1980 and the first quarter of 1981) and still had an unemployment rate of 7.5 percent. You didn't have to believe in supply-side miracles to anticipate such real growth, although there were some inside the administration who were expecting even stronger real growth before CEA Chairman Murray Weidenbaum persuaded them that such high real growth estimates were likely to be too optimistic.

Some of us outside the administration criticized this forecast as inconsistent with the Federal Reserve's very tight monetary policy (Feldstein 1981a). The interest rate on three-month Treasury bills was over 14 percent, and long-term government bonds had a 13 percent interest rate. The Fed had expressed a determination to slow the growth of nominal spending and bring down inflation.

In contrast to the administration's prediction of nominal GNP growth over 13 percent, the actual nominal GNP growth in the fiscal year that began in October 1981 was only 4.2 percent, with real GNP falling at a rate of nearly 2.0 percent. Although real GNP recovered and grew more rapidly over the next few years, inflation came down much more rapidly than either the administration or others had forecast, resulting in substantially less "bracket creep" and lower tax revenues than had been forecast.

Although the press joked that the administration's forecast had been prepared by Ms. Rosy Scenario, the big revenue error in the five-year budget forecast came not from overoptimism but from being too pessimistic about the speed with which inflation would be reduced. Nevertheless, the label "Rosy Scenario" stuck, and the administration's lack of credibility greatly increased the difficulty of the fiscal year 1983 budget negotiations in 1982 and reduced public support for the administration's policies.

The 1982 Tax Increase

The weakness of the economy and the rise of interest rates in 1981 quickly made it clear to careful analysts that the budget deficit would be more than the administration's initial projections. But it was the sharp decline of the stock market between March 1981 and a year later that, more than any other single thing, convinced the president that action was needed to reduce the deficit.[32]

32. The fall of the Dow Jones average from 1,000 in March 1981 to about 800 a year later reflected the combination of a weak economy, high interest rates, and the tax changes that reduced the market value of existing capital stock. (By making it less expensive to make new improvements in plant and equipment, the 1981 accelerated depreciation rules reduced the value of the existing capital stock and therefore of share prices that represented the ownership of that capital [see Feldstein 1981d].)

Many financial analysts blamed the stock market decline on the prospect that the fiscal policy would cause large budget deficits that would keep real interest rates high and that might prevent a decline in inflation. The president was persuaded (primarily by Jim Baker and Dave Stockman) that the stock market's decline was evidence that action to shrink the deficit was necessary. Formal negotiations with the Democratic and Republican congressional leadership produced a package of tax increases on business. These tax increases were achieved primarily by repealing some of the generous depreciation provisions of the 1981 tax legislation and the so-called safe-harbor leasing rules that permitted interfirm transfers of tax benefits. The package of tax changes would raise $17 billion in 1983, $38 billion in 1984, and higher amounts in subsequent years.[33]

Although I was not in the administration at the time, I gathered from subsequent conversations with some of those who were involved in the 1982 budget negotiation that the president was persuaded to accept the higher taxes by the assertions of the administration's negotiators (Jim Baker and Dave Stockman) that the congressional leadership had agreed to three dollars of outlay reductions for each dollar of additional tax revenue. Since a formal agreement between the administration and the congressional leaders was never completed, the "details" about the nature of the spending cuts were never spelled out for the president. In fact, the spending cuts that the negotiators were discussing involved little more than some dubious savings through management improvements and the projected reductions in interest on the national debt that the budgeteers assumed would follow from lower interest rates and a smaller debt.

The administration's negotiators knew that the spending reductions would never be achieved but preferred to maintain the fiction to get the president's support for the tax increase. During the years that I was in the administration, the president complained frequently that the Congress had failed to deliver on its promise to cut spending. Republican congressional leaders repeatedly told the president that this was not true since a final agreement had not been reached with the Congress in 1982. But, more important, the facts about the nature of the projected spending cuts themselves were never told to the president. As a result, the president always looked back on the 1982 tax legislation as unsatisfactory because he felt that he never got the spending cuts that he had been promised. That, in turn, made it difficult to get him to consider future budget deals with the Congress in which he would accept higher taxes in exchange for a congressional willingness to accept further cuts in nondefense spending.

The February 1983 Budget

I joined the administration in late August 1982 and immediately began to work on the deficit issue. The $49 billion increase in the budget deficit between

33. These tax changes are discussed on pp. 26–27.

1981 and 1982 was due almost completely to the deep recession.[34] But, although economic recovery would eventually eliminate the cyclical component of the deficit, the tax changes that had been enacted and the spending rules that were on the books implied that the deficit would continue to grow. Estimating the extent of that deficit growth was critical to planning the five-year budget to be submitted in February 1983.

It is politically true and economically desirable that substantial deficit reduction can be achieved only over a number of years. The 1983 budget would provide a suitable five-year policy horizon for implementing a deficit reduction plan. The necessary magnitude of the explicit deficit reduction (through new spending cuts or additional changes in tax rules) would depend critically on the extent to which economic growth (and inflation until the indexing of tax brackets became effective in 1985) would raise revenue without explicit legislative changes.

The medium-term economic forecast that would provide the framework for the budget was therefore crucial for deciding on the needed changes in spending and taxes. Since the budget was not to be used as a tool of short-run demand management, it seemed best to focus on estimating the overall rate of growth to the end of the five-year budget period and not on the year-to-year or quarter-to-quarter fluctuations along the way. Moreover, anything proposed in the February 1983 budget would not take effect before 1984.

With the help of Bill Poole (the CEA member with responsibility for macroeconomic forecasting) and Larry Summers (who was serving as special domestic policy economist on the CEA staff), I prepared a forecast that reflected what we regarded as consensus estimates of the likely changes in labor force and in productivity. We concluded that the most likely annual rate of real economic growth from the first quarter of 1983 to the final quarter of 1988 was 4.0 percent. This was clearly above the long-run potential growth rate of the economy but reflected the recovery from the very deep recession at the time of the forecast.

While I was quite happy to defend a 4 percent trend rate of real GNP growth for 1983–88, there was the awkward question of how to deal with the transition from recession to recovery. In the late fall of 1982, when the economic forecast had to be made final so that revenue and outlay estimates based on it could be calculated by the Treasury and the OMB, there was no clear evidence of an economic upturn (the November trough became clear only in the following year). Most private forecasters were predicting that the recession would end during the next twelve months, but there was no clear consensus on the likely time of the upturn or on the extent of further deterioration before the upturn began.

For the purpose of the five-year budget, however, this short-run uncertainty

---

34. According to Congressional Budget Office calculations, the structural deficit increased by only $6 billion between 1981 and 1982.

was not relevant. But, if we assumed 4 percent real growth for each quarter in 1983, there was a substantial risk that the entire budget would be dismissed by the Congress and serious private analysts as the work of Ms. Rosy Scenario if the first quarter of the year continued to show an economic decline.

It seemed better, therefore, to assume a lower rate of real growth for the first quarter and then to revert to a 4 percent rate for each quarter until the end of 1988, thereby emphasizing that, after the first quarter, we were using only the 4 percent average growth rate rather than trying to make short-term predictions. A 1 percent rate for the first quarter had the virtue of being greater than zero but low enough that it would not cast doubt on the forecast as a whole even if the economy was still in decline when the budget was presented.

With this assumption, our forecast implied a cumulative 3.9 percent of growth from the fourth quarter of 1982 to the fourth quarter of 1988.

This forecast was criticized inside the administration by those who said that it showed too little faith in the efficacy of the administration's program and who worried that it would imply a need for tax increases to achieve an acceptable deficit forecast. In fact, however, the real rate of economic growth during the five-year forecast period to the fourth quarter of 1988 eventually turned out to be 4.1 percent. The average error of 0.2 percent growth per year means that our forecast implied an underestimate of the fiscal year 1988 revenue of only about $20 billion, or 15 percent of the actual deficit in that year.

During the fall of 1982, I spent considerable time explaining publicly as well as inside the administration that the recent deficit surge was cyclical but that, as the economy recovered, we would still face a substantial structural deficit. I explained also that a persistent structural deficit would inevitably lead to reduced investment in plant and equipment and therefore to lower levels of future real incomes. In the shorter term, the crowding out of direct investment would be postponed by a capital inflow from abroad as the rise in the dollar (that had already begun) depressed net exports. But I was convinced that such a capital inflow would be only temporary and that a persistent decline in domestic saving caused by budget deficits would depress investment by a comparable amount.[35]

I stressed the long-run adverse effects of the deficit: reduced capital formation, lower productivity, and a need for higher taxes in the future just to keep up with the interest costs. But, while stressing the long-run effects, I also recognized the myopia of the political process and therefore discussed ways in which the deficit could hurt the economy in the nearer term. The crowding out of investment and the decline in net exported meant a lopsided recovery, with manufacturing and construction depressed relative to service industries. I ar-

---

35. My research with Charles Horioka (Feldstein and Horioka 1980) had persuaded me that chronically lower domestic savings rates depress domestic investment by a nearly equal amount. I gave no weight to the so-called Ricardian equivalence idea that larger deficits might induce equal increases in private saving.

gued that a lopsided recovery was inherently less stable than a recovery with a sustainable balance of activities. In addition, the projection of large future deficits could actually depress the overall current level of private spending by raising real long-term interest rates.[36]

I emphasized the desirability of a "backloaded" multiyear strategy for dealing with the deficit. I wanted to see a budget enacted in 1983 that would present a reliable and predictable reduction in the deficit over time, leading to a balanced budget at the end of five years. The ideal path of deficit reduction would be "backloaded" with just enough deficit reduction in the first year to reassure markets that the deficit would actually decline in the future.

I explained the rationale for such a "reliable and predictable backloaded multiyear plan" both during our internal budget deliberations and, after the president submitted his budget plan, in speeches and testimony. It would be wrong to have a large fiscal contraction just as the recovery was beginning. In contrast, a reliable multiyear deficit reduction plan leading to a balanced budget would cause a reduction in long-term real interest rates and in the dollar as financial markets became convinced that deficit reduction would actually occur as predicted. After a further lag of about a year, the lower real interest rate and lower dollar would result in higher levels of investment spending and net exports. The increased aggregate demand from this future spending would balance the contractionary effect of the future deficit reduction.

I emphasized that there was, of course, no way to coordinate the exact timing of the fiscal contraction and the private economic response. The shift from deficit stimulus to increases in investment and net exports involved risks of a "timing mismatch" that could cause the predicted expansion to stall temporarily. But the best strategy for avoiding the permanent damage of persistent large deficits would be to enact a reliable multiyear deficit reduction plan.

The preliminary estimates for the budget to be presented in February 1983 implied that, with no change in taxes or spending, there would be substantial deficits in each of the next five years. Even with the spending cuts that could politically be proposed in the budget (but probably not enacted), the projected deficits would remain unacceptably large. To show significantly declining deficits over the next five years, some kind of tax increase would be needed.

This conclusion, coming on the heels of the 1982 tax increase, was strongly resisted. The only alternative was to increase the projected rate of economic growth. The key White House staff dealing with this issue (Chief of Staff Jim Baker and his deputy, Dick Darman) argued that, even if 4 percent growth was the most likely estimate, it would be politically much better to project a 5 percent annual growth rate. Adding "just one point" to the real GNP growth

---

36. My views of the adverse effects of structural budget deficits appeared as chap. 1 of the *Economic Report of the President* for 1983 and for 1984 as well as in congressional testimony and public speeches.

rate for five years would reduce the projected budget deficit by about 2 percent of GNP. That stronger growth plus the spending cuts that could be proposed in the president's budget would eliminate the budget deficit as an immediate political problem.

I resisted, pointing out that 5 percent for five years was extremely unlikely. They countered that it might not be likely but that five consecutive years with an average growth rate over 5 percent had actually occurred in the 1960s. I reminded them of the Vietnam War, the subsequent rise in inflation after that expansion had driven the unemployment rate down to an unsustainable 3.7 percent, and our commitment to low inflation. Even if there was some chance that such growth might occur, it was sufficiently unlikely that it would be a mistake to base policy on that assumption. Moreover, a prediction of a 5 percent GNP growth rate for five years would deny credibility to the forecast and to the budget based on it.

None of this was particularly persuasive to those who saw the budget as a political statement rather than a fiscal planning tool and who wanted to avoid a forecast that would force a choice between large deficits and another tax increase. But I was not going to be pushed into a forecast that I thought was implausible or a budget plan that I thought hid the problem. In the end, the CEA forecast was accepted as the basis for the budget.

The "supply-siders" in the Treasury also called for projecting stronger growth on the grounds that, once the recovery began, the revenue gains from the tax cuts enacted in 1981 would be so great that no further tax changes would be needed to eliminate the deficit. They also argued that, even if the deficit persisted, it would be better to allow the deficit to continue than to raise taxes since higher taxes would hurt incentives while there was no evidence that deficits actually did any harm.

The Treasury staff never explicitly raised the so-called Ricardian equivalence argument (that large budget deficits did not matter because any increase in the government deficit would induce an equally large increase in private saving), presumably because it would be impossible to persuade noneconomists to take it seriously. Instead, the debate focused on whether deficits raised real interest rates. There was no doubt that real long-term interest rates were extremely high by past standards. Some argued that this was due to the investment incentives of the 1981 tax legislation. Others argued that it was because of the instability of monetary policy. Treasury Secretary Regan strongly resisted the idea that budget deficits were responsible for high interest rates but occasionally said that budget deficits might raise interest rates because people in financial markets thought they did even though they didn't.

A small group of senior administration officials met for dinner soon after Christmas 1982 for a preliminary, informal discussion of the budget plan. Secretary of State George Shultz, who generally did not get involved in detailed economic policies even though he had been an OMB director and Treasury secretary in the Nixon administration, joined the dinner and proposed an energy tax and an energy import fee. These were to become the centerpieces of the tax component of the 1983 budget.

To deal with the resistance to any tax increase, Ed Harper and I suggested that, as a compromise, the tax increase be made contingent on the future deficit: the tax increase would be legislated in 1983 but would take effect only in 1985 if the deficit remained above a relatively low threshold level. I had no doubt that the deficit would exceed that threshold and therefore expected that the contingent "standby tax" would be "triggered on." If the "supply-siders" and other optimists were right in their belief that growth would be so strong that the deficit would shrink rapidly, the contingent standby tax would be no tax at all. The contingent feature also gave the White House staff and others the ability to talk about their own personal belief that growth would be stronger than our projected 4 percent and therefore that there would be no tax increase.

Either way, the budget with a contingent tax would meet the need for a reliable multiyear deficit reduction plan. With the standby tax, the deficit would shrink to 1.6 percent of GNP by 1987–88. Dave Stockman, who was also skeptical of the supply-siders' claims and eager for a plan that would actually reduce the outyear deficits, supported the contingent tax idea.

The combination of spending cuts and the "conditional" tax increase was accepted by the president as part of the February 1983 budget plan for fiscal year 1984 and beyond. When the budget was first made public, there was a generally favorable reaction to the "realism" of the forecast and the "flexibility" of the president in including the standby tax. Our conversations with the Democratic congressional leadership suggested that there might be a basis for developing a compromise that would actually provide for multiyear declining deficits.

But that was not what either the White House political strategists or Treasury Secretary Don Regan, following their lead, wanted. They had accepted the proposal for a tax increase as part of the president's budget only because that was the only way to make significantly declining deficits compatible with the CEA forecast. But they didn't want Congress to enact another tax increase that would be attributed to President Reagan. They made certain that it would not be enacted by asserting that the contingent tax increase would be acceptable to the president only if all the president's proposed spending cuts were also accepted by the Congress. By adopting a very tough no-compromise strategy in discussing the budget with the Democrats, the White House and the Treasury were able to create a legislative stalemate and then blame Congress for the continued deficits that the president had proposed to reduce.

Although the tough position taken by the White House and the Treasury soon caused the press to declare the president's budget dead, it was never withdrawn. I continued to speak out loudly in favor of it, pointing out the harm of persistent deficits, stressing the president's desire to do something about them, and explaining the case for a multiyear reliable deficit reduction plan even if it had to include a tax increase. Moreover, even if the president's plan was dead for that year, I took the many opportunities that came along to educate the Congress and the pubic about the adverse effects of protracted deficits and the desirability of a backloaded multiyear strategy of deficit reduction.

My emphasis on the potential adverse effects of budget deficits and on the president's willingness to raise taxes as well as reduce spending made me unpopular with the White House political operatives, particularly with Jim Baker and Dick Darman. This led to a series of stories in the press about "the White House's" displeasure with my statements that many who were outside the administration incorrectly interpreted as reflecting the president's opinion.

I recognized that such "leaks" served many purposes. At the substantive political level, they positioned the administration on both sides of the budget issue: the president's chief economic adviser said that deficits are bad and taxes might be accepted as part of a program, while "the White House" said the opposite. Leaks also served as a potential form of intimidation, trying to stop my remarks or even to get me to resign. They never succeeded at either of those goals; indeed, when the press said I was being "silenced," I felt that I had no choice but to make further comments to show that I had not been silenced. Some of the White House staff also used leaks as "favors" to be given to friendly journalists in exchange for favorable press treatment for themselves.

When the leaks about me and the deficit got both loud and frequent, I eventually asked the president to review the parts of my "standard speech" that dealt with the deficit and the budget. He read the pages and gave his "OK" with only the suggestion that I mention the spending cuts in his budget plan before I talk about the proposed tax increases.

The February 1984 Budget

Although the Social Security legislation had improved the revenue outlook, the future deficit situation still looked very grim in the fall of 1983 when we began planning for the February 1984 budget. The economic forecast implied budget deficits of at least $200 billion a year for the next five years, despite steady economic growth and declines in interest rates on government debt that many outsiders considered to be too optimistic. Budget deficits of this magnitude would absorb more than two-thirds of net private saving, leaving a net national saving rate of only about 2 percent of GDP. We would either be dependent on substantial capital inflows from the rest of the world (with the associated massive trade deficit) or see a sharp decline in net investment in business plant and equipment and in housing.

The internal debate about this budget was in many ways a replay of the discussions of the previous year, but those who had opposed tax increases in 1983 were even less receptive to a serious deficit reduction plan now because of three developments: the strong economic growth of 1983; the failure of the budget discussions in 1983; and the upcoming 1984 election.

Real GNP had grown 7 percent from the fourth quarter of 1982 to the fourth quarter of 1983, more than twice the rate that we had projected. The Treasury supply-siders argued that the strong growth in 1983 was a harbinger of continued rapid growth that would generate much more revenue than we were projecting.

Dick Darman argued that the strong growth in 1983 justified assuming that we would grow at 5 percent for the next five years rather than at the 4 percent that we were projecting. The cumulative 5 percent of real GNP would mean additional tax revenue of about 2 percent of GNP by the end of the forecast period, making it unnecessary to propose any tax increase in the 1984 election-year budget.

While the very strong growth in 1983 made it harder to defend our five-year 4 percent forecast, I reiterated that our underestimate for 1983 was a matter of not knowing when the recovery would begin, that GNP growth in the first year of recoveries was generally in the 6 or 7 percent range, and that 4 percent was still the most likely growth over a five-year period. The only concession that I was prepared to make was to assume 4 percent for the next five years from the higher base at the end of 1983.

Despite the administration's seeming willingness to accept a tax increase as part of an overall package, the failure to reach any agreement on the previous budget proposal was also seen by some as an indication that there was no point in trying to compromise in the 1984 budget. In any case, we would be in an election year, when it would be politically attractive to argue that powerful economic growth would solve all problems.

Dave Stockman and I agreed that the deficit problem was too serious to ignore and that an effort had to be made to make some progress. Both of us had been very vocal over the past year about the need for budget action and did not want to go before Congress and the public in early January 1984 with a budget that called for no action and that projected that we would grow our way out of the problem.

I was also encouraged by several cabinet members, who agreed that the deficit had to be reduced and that a tax increase should be accepted as part of a plan for deficit reduction. This group included Special Trade Representative Bill Brock, Commerce Secretary Malcolm Baldrige, and Secretary of State George Shultz. Each had his own reason for not speaking out publicly about his views on this subject, but they all did make their position clear to the president on at least one occasion during the 1984 budget deliberations. Federal Reserve Chairman Paul Volcker urged deficit reduction both privately and publicly. Most of my academic economist friends also supported deficit reduction and agreed that the right tax increases were better than continued large deficits. There was no unanimity among businessmen, but the self-selecting group that spoke to me generally supported the view that deficit reduction, including higher taxes, was desirable. Too often, however, when a group of businessmen was given an opportunity to meet with the president, they would tell me privately how important the deficit reduction was and how they recognized that tax increases would have to be part of the package, but then not give the same message to the president. Instead, most of them would either settle for telling him what a fine job he was doing or say that they supported his call for deficit reduction without mentioning the need for higher taxes.

In my own meetings with the president during the fall of 1983, I tried to convince him of two things. The first was that he had already made dramatic reductions in nondefense spending (other than the Social Security and Medicare programs). After a political lifetime of campaigning against such spending, the president could hardly believe that he had actually succeeded in turning the trend around and cutting such spending by enough to bring the projected GDP share down to where it had been in the 1960s before the "Great Society" programs. I emphasized that just limiting such spending to the present real "current service level" that he had already achieved would bring the level of nondefense discretionary spending to about 3.2 percent of GDP by the end of his second term in 1988. There was no realistic scope for significantly reducing the projected budget deficit by further cuts in such programs.

My second major point was that we could not expect to grow our way out of the deficit through greater revenue associated with economic growth faster than the 4 percent a year that we were now projecting. With Social Security essentially off limits because of the 1983 Social Security agreement, some additional taxes would therefore be needed to shrink the deficit even if further progress could be made on discretionary programs and Medicare.

I think I did eventually persuade the president that he had succeeded in cutting nondefense discretionary spending and smaller entitlement programs substantially and that there was little scope for deficit reduction through additional cuts in those programs. But I don't think that I persuaded him that higher economic growth would not reduce the deficit by more than we were projecting. He accepted my economic projections as the basis for the budget and never tried to persuade me to change either the economic assumptions or the deficit implications, but I believe that he continued to hope that higher growth would come to his rescue.

I recall that on one occasion I said to him that, while economic growth at 5 percent a year for five years was "possible," it was very unlikely and it would not be prudent to base budget policy on such an unlikely event. When I reflected on that meeting later that day, I realized that saying that something was "unlikely" and "imprudent" was not a way of persuading Ronald Reagan. Such an argument might persuade a businessman who was accustomed to acting cautiously, but it was much less appealing to a politician, especially to someone with Ronald Reagan's life history. Here was a man who had gone from being a local sports announcer to a wealthy movie actor. When his acting career ended, he went on to become governor of the largest state in the nation, having never before held public office. And, after a resounding defeat in seeking the Republican presidential nomination a few years earlier, he won the

1980 nomination and went on to become president. And I was trying to tell him not to believe in something because it was unlikely!

Dave Stockman tried a different approach to persuading the president that it would not be possible to cut spending enough to bring the deficit down to an acceptable level without additional tax revenue. Stockman divided the overall budget into dozens of small parts and prepared three sets of options for each part: small cuts that would probably be acceptable to Congress but that would in the aggregate produce very little overall deficit reduction; moderate spending cuts that would be hard to get through Congress but that nevertheless would add up only to a small overall spending cut; and deep spending cuts that would be impossible to enact and that the president probably wouldn't want to propose in an election year. The budget group spent several afternoons reviewing these options one by one with the president so that he could in each case choose one option. Not surprisingly, the president chose the middle option in almost every case. At the end, Stockman announced that even if all these could be enacted, the overall spending cut would be relatively small.

Although Stockman had hoped that this would convince the president, from the time that he first described his plan to me I felt that it would not succeed. After all, in each budget area Stockman was showing the president only a small number of possible budget changes. The president continued to believe that there were possibilities that he was not being shown. He kept hoping that there was some general overhaul of the domestic programs that would permit major savings rather than the small savings that came from looking at each program in detail and in isolation.

Although he probably believed that the future tax revenue would be greater than we were projecting and that there were ways of cutting spending through reorganization that Stockman had not discovered, the president was locked by his own decisions on the individual spending programs into a budget that projected very large deficits for the next five years. The only way to reduce them was through changes in tax rules.

The Treasury's Office of Tax Analysis prepared a list of detailed tax reforms, primarily aimed at technical aspects of the measurement of business income. The president agreed to incorporate these "revenue raisers" into his budget with the explanation that they were not really "tax increases" but were essentially closing loopholes so that businesses would pay the taxes that they should.

The final budget also included reductions in the requested levels of future defense appropriations. When the president met with the entire cabinet to describe the proposed budget that would be released the next day, he noted that it was intended to be flexible and a basis for negotiating with the Congress since "everything was on the table" with "no restrictions in advance." He said that he expected that the Congress would be pleasantly surprised by his willingness to compromise on a revenue increase and smaller defense spending and that this time it would be possible to find a basis for an agreement with the Democrats.

The deficit reduction plan was certainly not as much as Dave Stockman and I had originally hoped for, but it was much better than it might have been. In addition, the deficit cuts in this election-year budget were to be described as a "down payment" on the additional deficit reduction measures to be proposed after the election.

The process of presenting this budget to the public taught me an interesting lesson in political communication. Since the economic forecast is released at the same time as the budget, I was called on to brief the White House press corps. As a teacher who always tried to explain things as clearly as possible, I explained that our forecast was unchanged with 4 percent growth rates, and that substantial harmful deficits would remain if no action was taken, but that the president's new budget would reduce the deficit substantially by a combination of tax increases and cuts in the growth of defense spending as well as by lower nondefense spending.

The statement that the president's budget would include "tax increases" and "lower defense spending" coming from the mouth of the CEA chairman was more newsworthy than I had imagined. What I said was perfectly accurate and in line with the details that would be released later that day by Dave Stockman and others. But my language was too unambiguous. At the same time that I was saying that we favored "tax increases" and "smaller increases in defense spending," the president was giving a speech saying that his budget "would not raise taxes on hardworking American families" or "threaten America's safety through reckless defense cuts."[37] The evening television news could pair our statements and make it look like the administration was in disarray and that, "once again," I was calling for tax increases and less defense spending while the president was not willing to yield on either.

Of course, there was no conflict between our statements. The administration's proposed tax increases on business "would not raise taxes on hardworking American families," and the lower level of defense spending was not "reckless" and would not "threaten our nation's safety." But by Washington's standards I had been too unambiguous in my statement, instead of hiding behind phrases like "the administration's budget puts everything on the table."

The Democrats responded to the president's budget with proposals for much lower defense spending and with attacks on his proposed reductions in domestic spending. In the end, defense spending was lower than the president had requested, and business taxes were raised, but nondefense spending was treated as might have been expected in an election year.

Deficit Reduction after 1984

The combination of higher tax revenue and lower spending, both relative to GDP, reduced the deficit by 1.0 percent of GDP between 1984 and 1990 (and 2.1 percent of GDP if the deposit insurance payments are excluded). Taxes rose

37. These are not precise quotes but my recollections of the type of language used at the time.

from 18.0 percent of GDP in 1984 to 18.9 percent in 1990. This reflected in part the delayed effects of the tax changes that had been enacted in 1982, 1983, and 1984. It also reflected the continuing economic recovery and the drift of individuals into higher tax brackets.

Spending on nondefense programs (other than net interest and the deposit insurance payments) fell by 1.0 percent of GDP during these same years. With no net change in the Social Security and Medicare programs as a percentage of GDP, the entire fall in saving was in the domestic discretionary and small entitlement programs, which together fell from 7.1 percent of GDP in 1984 to 6.1 percent in 1990.

Part of the reduction in spending was achieved with the help of the Gramm-Rudman legislation, which set explicit multiyear deficit reduction targets and provided for automatic spending reductions ("sequestrations") if the targets were not met. The law provided that these automatic spending cuts would be divided equally between defense outlays and certain nondefense programs. Since Social Security, Medicare, and certain other nondefense programs were excluded from the automatic spending cuts, the imposted cuts were concentrated on a relatively narrow range of the budget, requiring very substantial proportional cuts in the remaining programs if the deficit targets were not satisfied. Because such cuts would be politically too painful, Congress and the administration colluded to evade the spirit of the Gramm-Rudman legislation through a series of budget tricks—shifting things on and off budget, moving items between adjacent years, etc. Nevertheless, I believe that Gramm-Rudman did help reduce the deficit by focusing attention on the size of the deficit, by setting explicit targets, and by "requiring" across-the-board spending cuts in the first year after enactment that politicians would not have had the courage to propose and enact explicitly.

The decade ended with the 1990 structural deficit (excluding deposit insurance payments) at $150 billion, or 2.8 percent of gross domestic product. This was a significant improvement from the earlier peak of the structural deficit (4.4 percent of GDP in 1985) and substantially less than it would have been without the legislative initiatives that began in 1982.

In retrospect, the deficit did not do enough short-run harm to force the administration and the Congress to accept the political costs of deficit reduction. Despite the deficit, the economy continued to grow throughout the decade in the longest peacetime expansion, while tight monetary policy kept inflation under control. The nation's net saving rate was greatly depressed, but the inflow of capital from the rest of the world helped maintain net investment. The consequences of the high budget deficit and resulting low rate of national investment were beginning to be felt in slower real economic growth, but the decline in growth was so small and gradual and its link to budget deficits so unclear to the public that it failed to induce the tough political actions that would be needed to eliminate the budget deficit and raise national saving.

1.4   The Dollar and the Trade Deficit

The sharp gyrations of the dollar and of the trade deficit in the 1980s were among the most novel and least understood economic developments of the decade. The rise and fall of the dollar's international value reflected the major changes that were taking place in American monetary, tax, and budget policies. These fluctuations of the dollar altered the relative prices of American and foreign goods. The nation's international trade responded to these relative price changes, producing a massive trade deficit by the middle of the decade, followed by a return toward trade balance after the dollar began to decline.

1.4.1   The Rising Trade Deficit

In 1980, America's international trade was nearly in balance. Our imports of goods and services exceeded our exports by only $15 billion, about 0.5 percent of GDP. Our net earnings on overseas investments were nearly twice as large, leaving us with a positive current account balance and therefore an ability to add to our investments abroad.

Just seven years later, the trade deficit had increased nearly tenfold to $143 billion, or more than 3 percent of GDP. Our growing debt to the rest of the world increased our nation's payments on foreign assets in the United States to a point where they were nearly equal to what we were earning on American assets abroad. The current account deficit in 1987 was $160 billion, and foreign investors increased their net stake in the United States by that amount.

Economists recognized from the start that the deteriorating trade balance in the early 1980s was a natural reaction to the rising value of the dollar. When I arrived at the CEA in the fall of 1982, the real trade-weighted value of the dollar had increased 35 percent since 1980. Although the closely watched merchandise trade deficit had not yet begun to deteriorate, I was soon warning my administration colleagues that, because of the strong dollar, the trade deficit was about to surge. It subsequently rose from $36 billion in 1982 to $67 billion in 1983 and $113 billion in 1984.[38]

Manufacturing industries were particularly hard hit as manufactured exports slumped while the imports of manufactured products surged. A commonly expressed concern was that the Midwest manufacturing areas had become a "Rust Belt" and that our industrial sector was being "hollowed out." At the same time, the economy as a whole showed remarkable resiliency; because unemployed workers shifted from one industry to another and from one region

---

38. For the view of Council of Economic Advisers about the trade deficit and the dollar, see chap. 3 of the 1983 *Economic Report of the President* and chap. 2 of the 1984 *Economic Report of the President.* The CEA's senior staff international economist was Paul Krugman in 1982–83 and Jeffrey Frankel in 1983–84. For a less technical summary of the same views, see Feldstein (1983d, 1985a).

of the country to another, the overall economy expanded, and total employment increased continually from the end of 1982 until 1990.

The weakness of manufacturing and the expansion of imports caused a national self-examination and self-criticism. The list of criticisms included short-sighted management, a poorly educated labor force, confrontational labor relations, inadequate capital formation, and a lack of corporate concern about competing in world markets.

Unfortunately, this self-evaluation did not produce a program of self-improvement. Instead, the political response was to restrict access to American markets while blaming foreign governments for the inability of American firms to export.

As the trade deficit rose, some business executives and Commerce Department officials argued vehemently that the increased trade deficit was due to foreign practices that had to be stopped and that justified a more active U.S. trade policy. There was no doubt that some foreign markets were closed to American products, that some foreign governments were subsidizing export industries, and that some foreign firms were pursuing strategies designed to increase market share rather than to earn a return on capital similar to that sought by American firms. But none of this was new. If anything, foreign markets were becoming gradually more open and export promotion less common. Foreign practices could not account for the explosion of the U.S. trade deficit, and economists both in the government and elsewhere generally opposed any moves toward protectionalism and managed trade.

Similarly, although many of the criticisms of American industry were justified, these problems did not arise in the few years that it took the United States to shift from an approximate trade balance to a massive trade deficit. Moreover, even if there had been a recent decline in the overall level of American productivity relative to that in other countries, that would not have been a reason for a sharp rise in the trade deficit. Most countries of the world have much lower productivity than the United States but manage to achieve trade balance or surplus. As the British economist David Ricardo pointed out a century and a half ago, trade is governed not by overall productivity but by the differences in the relative productivity of different industries in different countries. Even if the United States were less productive in every industry than our foreign trading partners—something that is clearly not true—we would still be able to balance our trade (and raise our standard of living in the process) by exporting those things at which we are *relatively* more productive than our trading partners. Some serious problems undoubtedly did affect the competitiveness of particular American industries in the 1980s, but the source of our rapidly growing overall trade deficit was the dramatic rise of the dollar rather than a sudden fall in the productivity of American industry as a whole.

There were, of course, some special factors other than the strong dollar that did adversely affect our trade balance in the first half of the 1980s. The international debt crisis that began in 1982 forced the Latin American countries to shrink their imports from the United States as well as from other countries. A second important development of those years was the sharp improvement in Chinese agriculture as a result of Deng Xiaoping's economic reforms. Those reforms transformed China from a major food importer to a nation that was essentially self-sufficient in agricultural products. Since the United States is a major food exporter, the events in China reduced the demand for American agricultural exports. And there is no doubt that some of the newly industrialized nations in Asia had become much more formidable competitors in world markets for manufactured products.

But the primary reason for the sharp rise in U.S. imports and the stagnation of our exports was undoubtedly the dramatic rise of the dollar. According to the Federal Reserve, the trade-weighted value of the dollar relative to ten industrial currencies rose 73 percent between 1979 and the first quarter of 1985 after adjusting for differences in inflation. With a 73 percent rise in the price of American goods relative to the prices of foreign products, it was not surprising that American firms had a hard time exporting. And, even though some foreign firms selling in the United States took advantage of the exchange rate shift to increase their profit margins by raising their prices rather than just increasing the volume of their sales, it is easy to see why a 73 percent rise in the value of the dollar would lead to a surge in imports.

1.4.2 The Rise of the Dollar

The rise of the dollar began in 1980, reversing a decline that started in 1971 and that had accelerated in 1978 as a result of our increasingly rapid rate of inflation and the low real return on dollar assets. The initial impetus for the dollar's upturn was the tightening of Federal Reserve policy at the end of 1979. The increase in the real interest rate and the reduced risk of runaway inflation made dollar securities more attractive to international investors.

The election of Ronald Reagan reinforced the expectation that the Fed would pursue a tough anti-inflation policy. The Reagan plans for cutting taxes and increasing defense spending implied larger future budget deficits and caused real interest rates to rise further, thereby increasing the attractiveness of dollar investments and raising the value of the dollar.

The idea that larger budget deficits could increase the dollar's attractiveness and raise its value seemed paradoxical to many noneconomists, who resisted the notion that the budget deficit was responsible for the dollar's rise and the resulting loss of competitiveness of American products. History seemed to teach the opposite lesson: that a country that had a large budget deficit would see its currency decline in value. One had only to look at Latin America to see countries in which large budget deficits were associated with rapidly declining currency values.

The difference, of course, was that large budget deficits in those other countries were usually accompanied by rising inflation because in those countries the central banks bought the increased debt and thereby added equal amounts to the nations' money supplies. In many less developed countries, this link was an inevitable consequence of the lack of domestic capital markets in which budget deficits could be financed by selling government bonds to the public. In such cases, the rapidly rising inflation caused the nominal value of the currency to decline at a correspondingly rapid rate.

But in the United States in the early 1980s it was clear that the Federal Reserve would not alter its tough anti-inflationary policy in response to the increased budget deficit. The budget deficit would therefore mean higher real interest rates with no increase in inflation. The market's response was therefore a rising dollar. Each percentage point rise in the real long-term interest rate would raise the dollar's exchange value by several percentage points. Investors would be content to hold what was clearly an "overvalued" dollar that they knew would fall in the future because they would be compensated during that decline by the higher interest yield on dollar assets than on foreign securities.

The dollar continued to rise in 1982 and 1983 even after it was clear that inflation had stabilized and that the Fed had allowed short-term interest rates to decline. This made it clear that the dollar's continuing rise was due not to a very tight monetary policy (as some monetarists continued to claim) but rather to the increasing budget deficit in the context of a monetary policy that would prevent deficits from leading to higher inflation.

Although much of the budget deficit's initial surge was due to the deep recession, it gradually became clear that the structural deficit would grow even after the cyclical deficit declined. The structural deficit rose from about $49 billion in 1982 to $108 billion in 1983 and $134 billion in 1984 (according to 1992 estimates by the Congressional Budget Office). It reached a temporary peak of $177 billion in 1985 and $185 billion in 1986 before dropping to $120 billion in 1987. As investors adjusted up their projections of the future deficits during 1983 and 1984, real interest rates and the value of the dollar rose accordingly.

1.4.3 National Saving and the Twin Deficits

Although economists understood the links from budget deficit, to real interest rates, to the dollar, and finally to the trade deficit, the logic of this process seemed less plausible to noneconomists. During my time as CEA chairman, whenever I explained this chain linking the budget deficit with our trade problem, I could see that the skeptics thought that there were too many invisible links for the process as a whole to be plausible. Their skepticism was encouraged by the strict monetarists (including Treasury Undersecretary Beryl Sprinkel), who argued that the dollar's value is determined by monetary policy alone, and by the supply-side extremists, who argued that the budget deficit could do no harm. Others claimed that the dollar's rise was due to an increased attractiveness of the United States as a "safe haven" for funds, although it is hard to imagine why the United States had suddenly become so much safer than Switzerland or Germany.

A more plausible alternative explanation was that the 1981 tax changes raised the return on investments in equipment and buildings, bidding up real interest rates and the dollar. Although I accepted that that could in principle help explain the dollar's strength, my judgment was that the magnitude of the decline in national saving was substantially greater than the increased demand for investment. But assigning relative weights to these two components was not relevant to the two key policy questions that were debated within the administration as well as outside it: Would a lower budget deficit help bring down the dollar's value and ease the trade deficit? Did shrinking the trade deficit require government action to block imports, to open foreign markets, and to subsidize U.S. exporters? As long as the budget deficit was a major cause of the dollar's strength, the answer to the first question was a clear yes and to the second question a clear no.

Because of the difficulty of persuading noneconomists (and some of the administration's economists as well) of the links from the budget deficit to interest rates and then to the dollar and the trade balance, I frequently emphasized a more direct explanation: A country's trade balance is just equal to the difference between the amount that it saves and the amount that it invests. When a country saves more than it invests, it has a surplus of output that can be exported to the rest of the world. Conversely, when investment in plant and equipment, in housing, and in inventories exceeds the amount that is saved by households, businesses, and government, the extra investment requires an inflow of resources from abroad. The rise of the dollar was only the price mechanism by which the budget deficit caused the United States to go from trade surplus to trade deficit.

A larger budget deficit reduces national saving and therefore forces an increased trade deficit unless private saving rises or investment declines by sufficient amounts. In fact, net private saving declined relative to GDP in the first half of the 1980s, while net private investment increased slightly relative to GDP. Given these conditions, the rise in the trade deficit was inevitable.

The advantage of this explanation is that the basic relation—that national saving (net of the budget deficit) minus national investment equals exports minus imports—is neither an economic theory nor an empirical generalization but a basic accounting identity. Skeptics who doubted the more complex chain of reasoning or who resisted the idea that the budget deficit raised interest rates could accept that the budget deficit was nevertheless responsible for the increased trade deficit.

Not everyone was persuaded, however. In early 1984, when Treasury Secretary Don Regan was testifying to the Senate Budget Committee, one of the senators read him a passage from the CEA's recently released *Economic Report of the President* in which the link between the budget deficit and the trade deficit was explained. The source of the passage was not revealed, and the secretary was asked what he thought of the statement that he had just heard. He said that it was wrong and that it should be thrown in the garbage. When the senator revealed the source of the quote, the secretary, who seemed to enjoy public disputes with me, did not alter his view of its appropriate disposition.[39]

The episode would just be humorous if it were not indicative of the difficulty of achieving decent policy. The president could see for himself that, contrary to much of the conventional wisdom, the budget deficit was not raising the rate of inflation. The secretary of the Treasury, who claimed to speak not only with the authority of his Wall Street experience but also on the basis of the expert advice of the Treasury staff, repeatedly denied my assertions that the budget deficit was reducing investment and creating a trade deficit that hurt manufacturing industries. Fortunately, although Don Regan resisted efforts to create a realistic package of deficit reduction measures, he did not compound the problem by supporting the trade protectionists and did not favor currency intervention to lower the dollar.

1.4.4   Pressure to Reduce the Dollar

Although some people might dispute the role of the budget deficit in raising the dollar's value, there was no doubt that by 1983 the strong dollar was inflicting significant pain on American manufacturing firms and their employees. Manufacturing employment in 1983 was 11 percent lower than in 1979–80, and manufacturing profits were 33 percent lower.

The value of the dollar had increased from 1.81 marks per dollar in 1980 to 2.55 marks per dollar in 1983, a rise of 40 percent. The dollar also rose more than 50 percent relative to the British pound during this same brief interval. The secular trend in the dollar-yen ratio that had lowered the dollar by 37 percent relative to the yen in the 1970s had ended, and the dollar had instead risen relative to the yen in the early 1980s.

Not surprisingly, American exporters and those firms that competed directly with imported products appealed to Washington to adopt policies that would lower the dollar's value. They were joined by European governments that did not like the inflationary pressures caused by the relative decline in their own currencies, particularly the higher costs of dollar-denominated energy imports.[40] The Japanese government also worried that the bilateral trade imbalance caused by the overstrong dollar would exacerbate anti-Japanese protectionist pressures in the United States.

The obvious desirable policy response would have been a reduction in the

---

39. When I testified to the same committee the next day, I was asked about my reaction to the secretary's remark. I said that his comment was "just a throwaway line," and the hearing moved on to a more substantive discussion.

40. Some European politicians also claimed that the strong dollar was slowing the pace of recovery in Europe. Although this may have been a politically useful assertion for some European governments, it was certainly not correct (see Feldstein 1983d). The apparent paradox of European governments objecting to the rise of the dollar that was creating an export boom for their economies is discussed more fully in Feldstein (1986e).

U.S. budget deficit. But, as a participant in the budget process during those years, I can say with confidence that the administration's budget policy did not respond to the trade deficit and the high dollar. Since neither the president nor the Treasury secretary recognized the links between the budget deficit, the dollar, and the trade deficit, there was no way that the goal of reducing the dollar and the trade deficit could cause a willingness to accept tax increases or other budget changes that would not otherwise have been acceptable.

Without a reduction of the budget deficit, I argued that the case for trying to reduce the dollar was doubtful at best. The only practical way to have reduced the dollar would have been by an easier monetary policy. The resulting rise in the price level would have reduced the dollar's nominal value, but it would not have changed the real value of the dollar. Since the trade balance depends on the real value of the dollar, the net result would have been higher prices, higher inflation, and no improvement in the trade balance. Only to the extent that the easier monetary policy also increased the fear of even higher future inflation and thereby reduced the attractiveness of dollar securities to international investors would there have been a reduction in the real value of the dollar. Hardly an attractive option!

There were, of course, those who hoped that a policy of exchange market intervention could have lowered the dollar's value without any change in monetary or fiscal policy. But a careful analysis of past experience summarized in an official international study by the finance ministries of the G-7 countries that was released in April 1983 (the Jurgensen Report) confirmed the long-standing academic conclusion that sterilized intervention (i.e., intervention that does not alter national money supplies) would have no significant, lasting impact on exchange rates.

Moreover, even if the real value of the dollar could somehow have been reduced, I worried that lowering the dollar without shrinking the budget deficit would have been counterproductive. A lower dollar would have meant a smaller trade deficit, but that would have meant a smaller gap between saving and investment. With nothing done to increase saving, the level of domestic investment in the United States would have declined. Lowering the dollar without shrinking the budget deficit would have reduced the pain felt by exporters and by those who competed with imports but only by transferring the pain to other sectors of the economy that were directly sensitive to higher interest rates. If anything, without the trade deficit, the crowding out caused by the budget deficit would have been concentrated on a smaller number of industries and, therefore, even more painful. Moreover, the reduced level of investment in plant and equipment would have left the economy in a worse position for future years.

In short, the trade deficit was a safety valve by which the pressures caused by a massive budget deficit could be partly reduced through the resulting inflow of capital. The inflow of capital was the natural market response to the fall in national saving. There seemed no reason to believe that shrinking the trade deficit without lowering the budget deficit would represent an improved allocation of resources.[41]

Fortunately, despite the political pressures for currency intervention to drive down the dollar, the noninterventionists prevailed. Paul Volcker had an instinctive dislike for a lower dollar and understood that the Fed could lower the dollar's value only by returning to higher inflation. The Treasury also supported the view that intervention would be inappropriate. Treasury Secretary Regan liked to argue that the high value of the dollar was an indication of the strength of the U.S. economy and the high regard of investors worldwide for U.S. economic policies.

The issue was discussed with the president as part of the preparation for the Williamsburg summit. He had heard from many businessmen who were being hurt by the dollar's strong value, urging some action or international agreement to lower the dollar's value. We knew that President Mitterrand of France would argue at Williamsburg for an agreement to lower the dollar and to stabilize its exchange rate, leaving the details of how that might be accomplished to be worked out later. The president himself expressed a nostalgia for the days when exchange rates were fixed and worried about the damage that the dollar's rise was doing to the industrial sector of the economy. But, after a brief flirtation with the idea of a currency policy, the president was persuaded that the exchange rate is a price that, like other prices, was better left to the market without government interference. He went to Williamsburg prepared to argue this case to the French.

1.4.5   The Dollar's Decline

Economists recognized that the dollar would eventually decline. A rise in any country's real interest rates causes a temporary surge in the international value of its currency leading to a trade deficit and resulting capital inflow. In this process, the currency temporarily overshoots its long-term sustainable value. After this initial increase, if there are no further jumps in the country's real interest rate, the currency can then be expected to decline gradually at a speed that balances the higher interest rate, thereby eliminating both the desire of investors to flee the currency and the prospect for a new rise in the currency's value. As a result, the trade deficit itself could be expected to decline in the future.

My own research some years earlier had shown me that changes in domestic saving rates would temporarily be offset by international capital flows but that

---

41. I discussed these ideas within the administration and in testimony and talks. I also wrote an article for the *Economist* magazine spelling out these reasons for believing that, without a reduction of the budget deficit, it would be wrong to try to reduce the value of the dollar (see Feldstein 1983d).

for periods of a decade or longer the domestic rate of investment would adjust to domestic saving (Feldstein and Horioka 1980). I was convinced that that decline in the capital inflow would be brought about by a natural decline of the dollar leading to a smaller trade deficit.

There was much confusion in the early 1980s about the notion that the dollar was "overvalued." A currency can be willingly and rationally held by private investors even if it is overvalued in the sense that it leads to an unsustainable trade deficit and that everyone agrees that the currency's value will eventually fall. Investors are prepared to hold an "overvalued" dollar despite its expected decline if the interest rate on dollar bonds is high enough, relative to the interest rate on foreign bonds, to compensate the investors for the dollar's expected rate of decline.

The interest differential between dollar bonds and foreign bonds in the early 1980s implied an expected rate of dollar decline that might or might not be realized in practice. If the budget deficit were eliminated rapidly, the interest rate might fall quickly and bring with it a rapid fall of the dollar. Alternatively, if the budget deficit persisted, U.S. interest rates might remain high, with the dollar falling only as the risk to foreign investors associated with an increased share of dollar assets in foreign portfolios outweighed the interest differential. But, at each point in time, the actual level of the dollar was sustained by the market's belief that its expected rate of decline was balanced by the risk-adjusted interest differential.

In practice, the decline of the dollar was delayed by the rising levels of projected structural budget deficits and real interest rates. Each such reevaluation of the likely future budget deficit ratcheted the dollar higher through 1983 and 1984.

By early 1985, however, the dollar had reached a level relative to the Japanese yen and the deutsche mark that could not be reconciled with the existing interest differentials. Even if the dollar declined from that level at rates equal to the interest differentials between U.S. bonds and Japanese and German bonds, the U.S. current account deficits would grow explosively. While the dollar would eventually be low enough to eliminate the trade deficit, the amount of U.S. debt held by foreigners (and foreign investment in the United States) would by then cause our annual interest and dividend payments to foreigners to be rising faster than our GDP was growing.

Such an explosive growth of our current account deficit and our international debt was not possible. A speculative bubble had pushed the dollar too high at the end of 1984 and early 1985. Many private economists, as well as Fed Chairman Paul Volcker, recognized that the dollar was now overvalued in the more fundamental sense that a smooth decline at a rate of 3 or 4 percent a year (the interest differential) was no longer possible.

When the inevitable rates of decline of the dollar became greater than the interest differentials, some investors would lose money by being in dollar bonds rather than in Japanese or German bonds. As investors came to recognize that the dollar was irrationally overvalued in this sense, the speculative bubble burst, and a sharp decline in the dollar began in February 1985.

The change in the leadership at the Treasury from Don Regan to Jim Baker in early 1985 combined with the decline of the dollar to induce a change in the government's avowed policy. Baker would probably have wanted to have "his own policy" in this area and one that was more favorably regarded by foreign governments and the press. Moreover, the significant fall of the dollar between February 1985 and mid-summer (bringing the dollar down by 15 percent relative to the deutsche mark and nearly 10 percent relative to the yen) meant that the Treasury could no longer continue to claim that the dollar's value was a measure of the high international regard for the United States and its economic policies.

Baker and Volcker met with the finance ministers and central bank heads of the other G-5 countries (Germany, Japan, France, and Britain) at the Plaza Hotel in September 1985 and announced to the world that the G-5 had agreed that the dollar's value should decline. There was an immediate sharp drop of a few percentage points, followed by a resumption of the same overall rate of decline that had prevailed since February. Although the dollar's average rate of decline in the six months after the Plaza meeting was the same as in the prior six months (Feldstein 1986b), the world press persistently credited the Plaza meeting with causing the dollar's decline.

A falling currency is usually regarded as an indication of a finance minister's poor performance, but that was not so with Jim Baker. Baker was able not only to disregard the administration's previous rhetoric about the dollar as a measure of American virtue but even to turn the dollar's decline into a personal advantage by arguing that, if other countries did not do what the United States wanted (i.e., expand their domestic demand so that the U.S. trade deficit would decline), the U.S. dollar would be reduced. It was a relatively safe prediction— if foreign demand did not rise, the dollar would fall to shrink the trade deficit— but it gave the impression of a powerful U.S. Treasury secretary defending American interests. It was one of the unfortunate consequences of the apparent success of the Plaza meeting in lowering the dollar that it gave credibility to this type of claim.

Between the first quarter of 1985 and the first quarter of 1987, the real trade-weighted value of the dollar (as measured by the Federal Reserve's ten-country index) had fallen 36 percent, reversing more than 80 percent of the dollar's climb from 1979 to its peak in early 1985. Although it took about a year for importers and exporters to adjust their behavior, our trade balance then began to decline rapidly. Between the middle of 1986 and the middle of 1988, the real volume of U.S. exports rose by 35 percent, and the real trade deficit fell by nearly 40 percent.

1.4.6   Stabilizing the Dollar

A further decline of 15–20 percent in the value of the dollar during 1987 and 1988 might have eliminated the trade deficit before the end of the decade and saved the United States and the industrial world more generally from an increase in trade barriers and government-managed trade. If market forces had been left alone, the dollar might well have made that adjustment.

But that was not to be. The U.S. Treasury and the Federal Reserve worried that the falling dollar would substantially increase inflationary pressures in the United States. Foreign governments worried that the dollar's decline was undermining their ability to export to the United States and to compete with American imports in their domestic markets, thus increasing the risk of recession in their own countries. Instead of focusing on domestic monetary policies to achieve their desired macroeconomic goals, the finance ministers of the seven major industrial countries met at the French Finance Ministry in the Louvre in February 1987 and agreed to try to stabilize the dollar at approximately the then current level.[42] To do that, the United States raised short-term interest rates; the Federal funds rate rose from 6.1 percent in February 1987 to 7.3 percent in October 1987. Although the dollar did continue to decline for a few months, the finance ministers and central banks eventually persuaded the financial markets that they were serious about preventing a further slide of the dollar—even if that meant a substantial change in domestic monetary policy and, in the case of Japan, a backdoor purchase of dollar securities of the same magnitude as the U.S. current account deficit.

If there was ever an example of a sterilized intervention that was large enough to matter, it was the Japanese government's purchase of approximately $100 billion of dollar securities. I recall commenting to a Japanese Ministry of Finance official at the time that I thought that his government would lose a substantial amount on that "investment" since the dollar was then at 150 yen per dollar. He replied that his government did not mind the expectation of losing money since it would be cheaper than the cost of unemployment benefits and lost tax revenue that would result if the dollar were allowed to continue falling and weakening the ability of Japan to compete. Supporting the dollar would give Japanese industry time to develop new ways to be competitive at the higher yen-dollar rate that they knew was coming.

1.4.7   International Policy Coordination

On the basis of the apparent success of the Plaza meeting, Jim Baker pursued a policy of well-publicized "international policy coordination" meetings

---

42. I was and remain opposed to such attempts to target specific values of the dollar or to achieve "exchange rate stability" by diverting monetary policy from its task of managing domestic demand (see Feldstein 1987a, 1987b, 1987e, 1988a, 1989a).

among the G-7 finance ministers. Frequent meetings of those ministers after September 1985 produced communiqués promising to promote economic growth and currency stability with a variety of detailed promises for domestic policies, particularly in the United States and Japan.

In practice, discussion at the international policy coordination meetings focused on setting and revising exchange rate targets. Ironically, this was generally done without consulting the central banks and without any commitments on monetary policy among the finance ministers themselves.

I was (and remain) strongly critical of such public pursuit of policy coordination (see Feldstein 1987f, 1987g, 1988d, and 1988e). To the extent that such coordination meetings actually produced action to target exchange rates, it was necessary to sacrifice the domestic goals of monetary policy. These actions encouraged the tightening of monetary policy in the United States in 1987 that contributed to the 1987 stock market crash and to the easing of monetary policy in Japan that led to overvalued real estate and equity prices. The exchange rate targets themselves were also objectionable because they were generally set to achieve "stability" of whatever happened to be the current nominal rates rather than on any more objective basis.

In addition to their attempt to manage exchange rates, the international policy coordination meetings focused on encouraging macroeconomic expansion, emphasizing the interdependence among countries and the positive effect of expansion in one region on the level of GDP in the others. In fact, however, the degree of such interdependence among the United States, Europe, and Japan is quite limited. An extra dollar of GDP in one area has only a very small effect through trade flows on the GDPs in the other regions, an effect that could easily be achieved or offset by domestic fiscal or monetary policy.[43]

The highly publicized policy coordination meetings of the finance ministers unfortunately served as a substitute for much needed policy changes at home. They gave domestic voters the impression that "something was being done" and offered the promise that international coordination would achieve stronger economic growth, greater price stability, and a more stable environment for international trade.

European and Japanese promises to stimulate their economies were, of course, not commitments to particular actions. If stronger growth did not materialize, it could always be blamed on external forces. Because of the congressional form of government and the independence of the Fed, the U.S. Treasury could easily claim that it was powerless to make firm commitments. The undertakings of the U.S. Treasury at these meetings, which emphasized promises to reduce our budget deficit, simply corresponded to restatements of the budget requests that the administration had previously submitted to Congress.

Despite these problems in defining and enforcing agreements about macroeconomic coordination, it was convenient to blame any problems of domestic

43. See Feldstein (1983d) and Stanley Fischer's estimates in Feldstein (1987f).

economic performance on the failure of foreign governments to live up to their promises. International policy coordination not only failed to coordinate policy but actually created international tensions among the participants.

It was, of course, naive to expect that governments would sacrifice their own national interest in the spirit of international coordination. Unlike trade or arms negotiations, where the quid pro quo is explicit and tangible, macroeconomic coordination involves promises that are neither explicit nor tangible.

The frequent repetition of the theme of mutual interdependence eventually persuaded many in the United States that our economic performance depended more on decisions in Frankfurt and Tokyo than on decisions in Washington. This may have been a convenient excuse for U.S. officials, but it frightened the American public and financial investors in particular that an unwillingness of foreign governments to act in the American interest could do substantial damage to the American economy. The very public conflict between the United States and Germany in October 1987 over Germany's unwillingness to pursue a more expansionary policy was undoubtedly one of the factors that frightened financial markets and contributed to the stock market crash.

The stock market crash caused a temporary shift away from using monetary policy to target the dollar. Alan Greenspan, the recently appointed chairman of the Federal Reserve, announced at the time of the crash that the Fed would provide the liquidity needed to prevent the stock market collapse from becoming an economic downturn, and the Treasury secretary announced that economic policy would focus on the domestic economy, regardless of the consequences for the dollar. Interest rates were lowered, and the dollar declined. The public displays of international policy coordination and the attempts to target the dollar were over for a while (Feldstein 1987d).

But, by the middle of 1988, it was clear that the stock market crash would not precipitate a recession. The Federal Reserve began to raise interest rates and to withdraw the excess liquidity that had been provided after the crash. The Treasury resumed its old rhetoric about stabilizing the value of the dollar.

Having seen that the United States and other key countries were willing to use monetary policy to manage the dollar's exchange rate, many participants in the financial markets accepted the government's forecast that the dollar's value would remain in a relatively narrow range—generally assumed to be 120–40 yen to the dollar and 1.7–1.9 marks to the dollar. The combination of this expected dollar stability and the higher interest rates that prevailed on dollar bonds than on yen bonds or German bonds induced international financial investors to buy dollar bonds. Investors reckoned that, if a dollar bond paid 3 percent more than a yen bond, the extra yield of more than 20 percent over seven years would more than offset any minor fluctuations of the dollar-yen rate that might occur over that time.

Economists and other analysts who emphasized the fundamental determinants of the exchange rate warned that the higher rate of inflation in the United States than in Japan, our substantial remaining trade deficit, and Japan's massive trade surplus meant that the dollar-yen exchange rates would eventually shift and probably by much more than enough to outweigh the 3 percent a year interest differential. But the majority of market participants were prepared to go along with the implicit promise of the finance ministers to stabilize the dollar. And, as they bought dollar bonds, they bid up the value of the dollar. This rise in the dollar caused those portfolio investors who trade currencies on a so-called technical momentum basis rather than on the basis of "fundamentals" to be attracted to even further dollar buying.

By the early summer of 1989, the dollar had risen in value to more than two marks and 150 yen. The improvement in the U.S. trade deficit had run out of steam, and the outlook shifted to an increasing U.S. trade deficit in 1990. The attempt to use international coordination to stabilize the exchange rate had actually caused the exchange rate to move further from equilibrium and to worsen the U.S. trade deficit.

When the G-7 finance ministers met at the IMF–World Bank meeting in September 1989, they recognized publicly that the exchange value of the dollar had to decline. Although continuing to stress the desirability of stable exchange rates, their communiqué also noted (in the internally inconsistent manner not uncommon in such communiqués) that the dollar was then "too high to be consistent with long term fundamentals." To leave little doubt about their meaning, the central banks of the G-7 countries engaged in extensive exchange market intervention during the following weeks, selling dollars in exchange for other currencies. The Federal Reserve also continued to ease monetary policy and to lower U.S. interest rates while foreign central banks raised their interest rates.

By the late fall, the interest rates on U.S. Treasury bonds and on German government bonds had reached equality. Investors could no longer justify buying dollar bonds instead of deutsche mark bonds because of the higher yields. The U.S. current account deficit was at an annual rate of more than $100 billion, while Germany's current account surplus continued to exceed $50 billion. In that context, there was a sharp rise in the value of the deutsche mark, from 1.98 marks per dollar in June 1989 to 1.68 marks per dollar a year later.

Although the yen also appreciated from its low point during the summer of 1989, it only rose enough by the end of the following year to return to its level at the time of the Louvre agreement despite the fact that the prices of tradable manufactured products had increased by 15 percent in the United States during that interval and had not increased at all in Japan. By achieving nominal currency stability at the level prevailing at the time of the Louvre, Japanese policy, encouraged and assisted by the United States, had caused the yen to fall 15 percent in real terms, exacerbating the bilateral trade imbalance and the associated political friction.

1.4.8   No More Twin Deficits

By 1990, the dollar and the trade deficit had resumed their decline. The overall national income measure of the trade deficit in 1990 was less than 1.5 percent of GDP. The budget deficit had also declined from its peak but still represented 3 percent of GDP. This experience confirmed that the close parallel relation between the budget deficit and the trade deficit was only a temporary one (Feldstein 1992a). The decline in the dollar and the resulting decline in the trade deficit meant that the budget deficit was now crowding out domestic investment to a greater extent that it had before.

Experience thus confirmed that a country with a low national saving rate will eventually have a correspondingly low rate of domestic investment. The ability to raise our national saving rate will be an important determinant of our economic success in the 1990s and beyond.

References

Feldstein, Martin. 1992a. The budget and trade deficits aren't really twins. *Challenge* 35, no. 2 (March/April): 60–63.

———. 1992b. The Council of Economic Advisers and economic advising in the United States. *Economic Journal* 102 (September): 1223–34.

———. 1992c. The recent failure of U.S. monetary policy (the 1992 January Tinbergen Lecture of the Netherlands Royal Economic Society). Working Paper no. 4236. Cambridge, Mass: NBER. (Reprinted in the *Economist,* vol. 141, no. 1 [January 1993].)

———. 1989a. The case against trying to stabilize the dollar. *American Economic Review* 79, no. 2. (May): 108–12.

———. 1989b. FSLIC funding belongs off-budget. *Wall Street Journal,* 1 March.

———. 1989c. How the CEA advises presidents. *Challenge* 32, no. 6 (November/December): 51–55.

———. 1988a. Feldstein on the dollar. *Economist,* 3 December.

———. 1988b. Imputing corporate tax liabilities to individual taxpayers. *National Tax Journal* 41, no. 1. (March): 37–59.

———. 1988c. Keynesian economics at Harvard College. *Challenge* 31, no. 4 (July/August): 42–46.

———. 1988d. *Rethinking international economic coordination: A lecture on the occasion of the fiftieth anniversary of Nuffield College, Oxford.* Oxford Economic Papers, no. 40, pp. 205–19. Oxford: Oxford University Press.

———. 1988e. Thinking about international economic coordination. *Journal of Economic Perspectives* 2, no. 2 (Spring): 3–13.

———. 1987a. Correcting the trade deficit. *Foreign Affairs* 65, no. 4. (Spring): 795–806.

———. 1987b. The dollar must keep falling. *Wall Street Journal,* 18, February.

———, ed. 1987c. *The effects of taxation on capital accumulation.* Chicago: University of Chicago Press.

———. 1987d. The end of policy coordination. *Wall Street Journal,* 9 November.

———. 1987e. Fed policy shouldn't target the dollar. *Wall Street Journal,* 8 May.

————, ed. 1987f. *International economic cooperation.* Chicago: University of Chicago Press. (See also *International economic cooperation: A summary report.* Cambridge, Mass.: NBER, 1987.)

————. 1987g. A self-interested way to avoid death in Venice. *Financial Times,* 20 May.

————, ed. 1987h. *Taxes and capital formation.* Chicago: University of Chicago Press.

————. 1986a. A gamble with capital formation. *Wall Street Journal,* 19 May.

————. 1986b. New evidence on the effect of exchange rate intervention. Working Paper no. 2052. Cambridge, Mass.: NBER, October.

————. 1986c. Supply side economics: Old truths and new claims. *American Economic Review* 76, no. 2. (May): 26–30.

————. 1986d. Tax reform: Harmful if passed. *Wall Street Journal,* 14 February.

————. 1986e. U.S. budget deficits and the European economies: Resolving the political economy puzzle. *American Economic Review* 76, no. 2 (May): 342–46.

————. 1985a. American economic policy and the world economy. *Foreign Affairs* 63, no. 5 (Summer): 995–1008.

————. 1985b. How to get the deficit under $100 billion. *Time,* 4 February.

————. 1985c. The social security explosion. *Public Interest,* no. 81 (Fall): 94–106.

————. 1985d. A tax reform mirage. *Wall Street Journal,* 20 November.

————. 1984a. '85 is the year to correct the imbalance. *New York Times,* 18 November.

————. 1984b. Reagan is Reagan on the economy. *Wall Street Journal,* 12 September.

————, ed. 1983a. *Behavioral stimulation methods in tax policy analysis.* Chicago: University of Chicago Press.

————. 1983b. *Capital taxation.* Cambridge, Mass: Harvard University Press.

————. 1983c. *Inflation, tax rules, and capital formation.* Chicago: University of Chicago Press.

————. 1983d. The world economy today. *Economist,* 11 June.

————. 1982a. The conceptual foundations of supply side economics: Supply side economics in the 1980s. In *Proceedings of a conference sponsored by the Federal Reserve Bank of Atlanta and the Emory University Law and Economics Center, March 18, 1982.* New York: Dean Witter Reynolds.

————. 1982b. Inflation and the American economy. *Public Interest,* no. 67 (Spring): 63–76.

————. 1982c. Why short term interest rates are high. *Wall Street Journal,* 8 June.

————. 1981a. Budget policy without fine tuning. *Wall Street Journal,* 12 March.

————. 1981b. *Hospital costs and health insurance.* Cambridge, Mass.: Harvard University Press.

————. 1981c. The retreat from Keynesian economics. *Public Interest,* no. 64 (Summer): 92–105.

————. 1981d. The tax cut: Why the market dropped. *Wall Street Journal,* 11 November.

————. 1980. Tax rules as the mismanagement of monetary policy. *American Economic Review* 70, no. 2 (May): 182–86.

————. 1974. Social Security, induced retirement and aggregate capital accumulation. *Journal of Political Economy* 82, no. 5 (September/October): 905–26.

————. 1973. The welfare loss of excess health insurance. *Journal of Political Economy* 81, no. 2, pt. 1 (March–April): 251–80).

Feldstein, Martin, and E. Allison. 1974. Tax subsidies of private health insurance: Distribution, revenue loss and effects. *The economics of federal subsidy programs: A compendium of papers submitted to the Subcommittee on Priorities and Economy in Government of the Joint Economic Committee.* Pt. 8, *Selected subsidies.* 93rd Cong., 2d sess., Washington, D.C., 29 July.

Feldstein, Martin, and Douglas Elmendorf. 1989. Budget deficits, tax incentives and inflation: A surprising lesson from the 1983–84 recovery. *Tax Policy and the Economy* 3:1–23.

Feldstein, Martin, and B. Friedman. 1977. Tax subsidies, the rational demand for insurance and the health care crisis. *Journal of Public Economics* 7: 155–78.

Feldstein, Martin, and C. Horioka. 1980. Domestic savings and international capital flows: The 1979 W. A. Mackintosh Lecture at Queen's University. *Economic Journal* 90: 314–29.

Feldstein, Martin, and Gilbert Metcalf. 1987. The effect of federal tax deductibility on state and local taxes and spending. *Journal of Political Economy* 95, no. 4: 710–36.

Feldstein, Martin, and Lawrence Summers. 1979. Inflation and the taxation of capital income in the corporate sector. *National Tax Journal* 32, no. 4:445–70.

Laffer, Arthur. 1981. Government exactations and revenue deficiencies. *Supply Side Economics*. Cato Journal. Spring.

2 Monetary Policy

1. Michael Mussa
2. Paul A. Volcker
3. James Tobin

1. *Michael Mussa*

U.S. Monetary Policy in the 1980s

The story of U.S. monetary policy in the 1980s is fundamentally a tale of struggle and success, after a decade during which monetary policy contributed significantly to the poor performance of the U.S. economy. At the beginning of the 1980s, a great battle was waged against the demon of inflation that had damaged and distorted the U.S. economy since the late 1960s—a battle that was made necessary by the policies that nurtured the demon of inflation during the preceding fifteen years, especially during the late 1970s. In the recessions of 1980 and 1981–82, casualties from the battle ran high, with the unemployment rate rising to a postwar peak of 10.8 percent. In some areas, such as the savings and loan industry, the dead are still being counted, and the bill for their funerals is yet to be fully reckoned and paid. Nevertheless, despite the high costs of battle, a substantial and necessary victory over inflation was won in the early 1980s, and this success was sustained throughout the remainder of the decade.

Indeed, by the end of 1989, the economic expansion that began in November 1982 was already two years longer than any previous peacetime U.S. expansion. Real GNP had risen at a 4 percent annual rate from the recession trough and at a 3 percent annual rate from the preceding business-cycle peak. The unemployment rate had fallen to the lowest level since the early 1970s. Except for a temporary decline that was due to a fall in oil prices in 1986, the inflation rate ran at a steady rate close to 4 percent for the eight-year period beginning in December 1981. Judged by the objectives of the Employment Act of 1946— "maximum employment, production, and purchasing power"—the U.S. economy performed quite well after the costly victory over inflation in 1981–82, especially in comparison with its performance during the preceding decade.

Of course, economic performance was not solely determined by economic policy, and monetary policy was not the only policy to influence that performance significantly. Moreover, some aspects of U.S. economic performance and policy were not entirely satisfactory during the 1980s, including the persistence of relatively large budget and trade deficits and the failure to reduce inflation below a 4 percent annual rate. Nevertheless, an overall assessment of U.S. macroeconomic policy in the 1980s, in terms of the basic objectives of supporting sustainable growth while maintaining reasonable price stability, must be fundamentally favorable. The task of this essay is to analyze the significant contributions of monetary policy both to the macroeconomic problems confronting the U.S. economy at the beginning of the 1980s and to the generally successful record of dealing with those problems.

2.1   Assumptions and Qualifications

Monetary policy differs from most other elements of economic policy in the United States because it is under the control of a single institution—the Federal Reserve System. The most important decisions about monetary policy are made by the Federal Open Market Committee (FOMC), consisting of the seven governors of the Federal Reserve System and, on a rotating basis, five of the presidents of the twelve regional Federal Reserve banks (always including the president of the Federal Reserve Bank of New York). Since the members of the FOMC do not always share precisely the same views, the internal politics of the Federal Reserve occasionally have some importance for decisions about monetary policy.

However, within the Federal Reserve, there is general agreement about the primary goals of monetary policy—sustainable economic growth with low inflation. On the FOMC and on the Board of Governors, the chairman is usually able to shape a consensus supporting the policy that he favors. Unlike tax policy or expenditure policy or trade policy, authority over monetary policy is not divided between the legislative and the executive branches, with many powerful individuals, agencies, and interests affecting the ultimate outcome. For decisions about monetary policy, economic effects rather than political consequences are usually the dominant concern. Accordingly, this essay focuses primarily on the economic developments that influenced the conduct of monetary policy during the 1980s and on the economic effects of that policy.

Another important feature of monetary policy is that, like a military campaign, it is conducted on virtually a continual basis in real time. The FOMC meets about every six weeks to discuss the performance of the economy and to assess, and if necessary adjust, its monetary policy. In practice, the Federal Reserve tends to maintain the general stance of its policy—toward tightness or ease—for periods of many months. The analysis of monetary policy, therefore, can conveniently be divided into major episodes corresponding to the main thrust of the Federal Reserve's policy. However, within each major episode, decisions are continually made to adjust (or not to adjust) the degree of tightness or ease of monetary policy. The analysis of monetary policy must also be concerned with the reasons for and consequences of these adjustments.

Because of the way in which monetary policy is conducted, much of this essay is devoted to a chronological description of the main developments in the U.S. economy and in U.S. monetary policy from the late 1970s through the 1980s. This is combined with an effort to interpret the effects that monetary policy was having on the evolution of the economy and to assess critically the conduct of that policy. The interpretative effort is based not on a formally specified, statistically estimated econometric model, but rather on a broad, intuitively based understanding of how monetary policy influences the behavior of the economy. Three important presumptions underlie this assessment of monetary policy and should be explicitly stated. These presumptions are not "truths" that have been rigorously established by economic theory or empirical research. They represent my views about how monetary policy operates in the U.S. economy. They are widely shared by economic policymakers, especially at the Federal Reserve.

First is a modified version of the classic dichotomy: monetary policy exerts considerable influence on the behavior of the general level of prices (or the inflation rate) over the medium term but has only limited capacity to influence the medium or longer term behavior of real output and employment. Second, in the shorter run of a year or two years, a tighter monetary policy that tends to reduce inflation will also usually tend to reduce temporarily the growth of output and employment; but it is an unstable monetary policy, contributing to high and volatile inflation and to wide swings of economic activity, that impairs real growth in the longer term of five to ten years. Third, in the very short term, given the state of the economy, a tighter monetary policy usually means both an increase in short-term interest rates, especially the Federal funds rate, and a reduction in the rates of growth of monetary aggregates.

Several important qualifications should be noted to these general presumptions. Once monetary policy has allowed substantial inflationary pressures to build up in the economy, a determined effort to reduce inflation through a tighter monetary policy may well reduce the average real growth rate looking forward even over a medium-term period of three or four years. The presumption, however, is that, if monetary policy had more effectively resisted the rise of inflationary pressures in the first place, real growth would have been better (or, at least, no worse) in the longer term.

Monetary policy is not the only important factor influencing the behavior of the price level, especially in the short term. When the relative prices of some important commodities (such as oil) change suddenly and substantially, the general price level moves in the same direction, pretty much regardless of the stance of monetary policy. In the longer term, however, monetary policy can

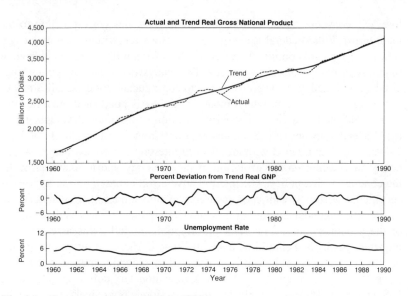

Fig. 2.1   Output measures, 1960:1–1990:1
Note: The actual and trend real GNP is the quarterly GNP in constant 1982 dollars. Logarithmic scale; trend calculated from Hodrick-Prescott filter ($L = 1,600$).

effectively resist a persistent rise in the rate of inflation, even if it is not the only influence on the general price level.

Monetary policy is also far from the only important factor that influences the course of economic activity. The general slowdown in the rate of real economic growth since the early 1970s, in the United States and other major industrial countries, is not plausibly the consequence of monetary policy. Even for business-cycle fluctuations in economic activity (as illustrated in fig. 2.1 by deviations of real GNP from its smoothed trend path), many factors other than monetary policy played important roles.[1] These factors include fluctuations in government spending associated with the Korean and Vietnam wars, other important fiscal policy actions of the U.S. government, the oil shocks and other commodity price disturbances of the early and late 1970s, some exogenous fluctuations in consumption and investment spending, and some important shifts in U.S. real net exports related to movements in foreign economic activity and in the foreign exchange value of the dollar. Indeed, even exogenous fluctuations in the rate of productivity growth—the central focus of "real"

---

1. The smoothed trend path of U.S. real GNP in fig. 2.1 is constructed by using the Hodrick-Prescott filter, which allows for some gradual change in the trend rate of growth or real GNP. There is nothing sacred about this particular filter, but it does give a generally reasonable basis for measuring business-cycle deviations of real GNP from its trend behavior. I would argue, however, that the trend line is probably a little low during 1980–83. The 1980 recession should push real GNP somewhat further below the trend line, and the 1981–82 recession should be reflected in a somewhat larger reduction of real GNP relative to trend.

business-cycle theories—probably played some meaningful role in postwar U.S. business cycles.

Monetary policy, however, was surely one important factor that influenced the course of economic activity during the recessions of 1957–58, 1960–61, 1969–70, 1974–75, 1980, and 1981–82, as well as during the growth slow-downs of 1966–67 and 1989–90. Given the longer-term movements in the trend rate of real economic growth, monetary policy also influenced the specific course of economic activity during postwar business-cycle expansions.

Discerning the effects of monetary policy on the price level and on economic activity is a difficult and somewhat imprecise task because these effects are not always stable from one episode to the next. Experience suggests that a tightening of monetary policy should be expected to slow real growth with a lag of a few months to a year or so and to slow the rate of inflation with a somewhat longer lag and conversely for an easing of monetary policy. However, a good deal depends on the context in which a monetary policy action is taken and on the effect of that action on expectations. In a strongly growing economy, monetary tightening may have little short-term effect on real economic activity, while, in an already weak economy or in combination with other negative shocks, a sharp monetary tightening may rapidly induce an economic downturn. If economic agents are highly sensitive to the risks of rising inflation, and if the central bank lacks credibility for its anti-inflation policy, a relatively minor action to ease monetary policy may stimulate a rapid and significant inflationary response. In contrast, if the monetary authority has established a high degree of credibility for its opposition to inflation, and if conditions in the economy are relatively slack, then even a substantial easing of monetary policy may take considerable time to generate significant inflationary results.

The interpretation of what constitutes a tightening or an easing of monetary policy also can be a complex and sensitive matter. An action to raise the Federal funds rate that would normally signify monetary tightening may not have this significance if increases in inflationary expectations or other pressures on market-determined interest rates are pushing rates up faster than the action of the monetary authority. Conversely, a sharp slowdown in money growth that would normally indicate monetary tightening (especially in a rapidly expanding economy) may not have quite the same significance if economic activity is falling in the initial stages of a recession. More generally, it should be recognized that changes in monetary growth rates and in the Federal funds rate reflect both policy actions of the Federal Reserve and endogenous responses to other developments in the economy.

With all these qualifications, it may be wondered whether it is possible to reach firm conclusions concerning the successes and failures of monetary policy during the 1980s. On the several important issues, I believe that reasonably clear answers can be given. Fortunately, these answers do not require precise estimates of the effects of monetary policy, and of the effects of all other factors, on the performance of the U.S. economy during the 1980s. Instead, it is a great advantage to assess the conduct of monetary policy qualitatively, by examining whether an alternative course of monetary policy would plausibly have improved the performance of the U.S. economy and whether the Federal Reserve ought reasonably to have had the sense and judgment to pursue such an alternative policy. Inevitably, of course, a significant degree of ambiguity will always remain in any such effort to assess fairly the complex and difficult task of conducting monetary policy in the U.S. economy.

2.2 Nurturing the Demon of Inflation

To analyze the most important issue in the conduct of monetary policy during the 1980s—the battle against and victory over high and volatile inflation—it is essential to review the development of the problem of inflation during the postwar era.

2.2.1 The Rise of Inflation

The inflation rate, measured by the annual rate of change in the Consumer Price Index (CPI), remained quite low from the early 1950s through the mid-1960s. Indeed, in 1956, the Federal Reserve became concerned when the inflation rate rose to 3 percent. The consequent tightening of monetary policy probably helped precipitate, deepen, or prolong the recession of 1957–58.

After remaining at or below 2 percent through 1965, the inflation rate rose to 3.4 percent during 1966. Concerned with possible overheating of the economy, the Federal Reserve tightened credit for about six months during 1966. There was a brief slowdown in economic growth in late 1966 and early 1967, but no recession. The inflation rate in 1967 leveled off at about 3 percent. However, with the resurgence of economic growth beginning in the second half of 1967 and the deepening U.S. military involvement in Vietnam, the inflation rate rose to 4.7 percent during 1968 and to 6.2 percent during 1969. Concern with high inflation brought a tightening of both monetary and fiscal policy beginning in late 1968—policy actions that surely contributed to the recession that started in late 1969. In contrast to the 1950s, however, the inflation rate reached 6 percent before effective policy measures began to operate against the inflationary menace.

Under the impact of rising unemployment and declining economic activity, the inflation rate (measured by the six-month annualized rate of change in the CPI) fell to 5.2 in late 1970 and continued down to about 3.5 percent during the first half of 1971. About six months into the recession, with evidence of no more than a partial victory over inflation, the Federal Reserve began to ease monetary policy fairly aggressively. Business activity began to expand in November 1970.

During the summer of 1971, monthly inflation rates began to edge upward. On 15 August, President Nixon imposed wage and price controls. For the next year and a half, these controls helped partially suppress a further rise of the inflation rate, despite a relatively easy monetary policy. As controls were phased out, however, the inflation rate began to rise. With the increase in world oil prices after the Arab-Israeli War of October 1973, the twelve-month inflation rate was pushed to 8.7 percent for 1973 and to 12.3 percent for 1974— inflation rates well above the 6.2 percent rate at the end of the long economic expansion of the 1960s.

The Federal Reserve began to raise the Federal funds rate in response to rising inflation in late 1972, but growth rates of monetary aggregates remained relatively robust until more aggressive actions to tighten monetary policy were undertaken beginning in mid-1973. These actions, together with other effects of the rise in world energy prices, helped bring an end to the expansion of the early 1970s. The cyclical peak for this expansion is officially placed at November 1973. However, owing partially to a speculative buildup of inventories, the sharp phase of economic downturn did not start until the late summer of 1974.

As economic activity plummeted during the final quarter of 1974 and the first quarter of 1975, the inflation rate also dropped sharply. The nearly complete absorption of the price level effects of the increase in world energy prices by early 1975 was presumably another important contributor to the decline of inflation. In any event, the inflation rates for 1975 and 1976 were 6.9 and 4.9 percent, respectively. This drop in inflation was a significant accomplishment relative to the high inflation of 1973–74. However, it still left the inflation rate at the end of the deep 1974–75 recession above the rates at the ends of earlier recessions.

2.2.2   Targets for Monetary Growth

In the spring of 1975, at the behest of Congress and over objections from the Federal Reserve, the FOMC began to announce its intentions for monetary policy by specifying growth rates for monetary aggregates. At the beginning of each year, target ranges were specified over the subsequent four quarters for the growth rates of three monetary aggregates: (old) M1, consisting of currency and demand deposits at commercial banks; (old) M2, consisting of (old) M1 plus time deposits at commercial banks; and (old) M3, consisting of (old) M2 plus deposits at savings banks, savings and loan associations, and credit unions. As a shorter-term guide for monetary policy, the FOMC also determined target growth rates for these three monetary aggregates during the coming quarter.

The target growth rates for monetary aggregates were not the operational guide to the actual conduct of monetary policy. At each meeting of the FOMC, operational guidance for monetary policy is provided in the directive to the manager of the Open Market Desk at the Federal Reserve Bank of New York. Since the early 1970s, this directive had made reference to growth rates of monetary aggregates as one of the concerns of the FOMC that should be taken into account by the manager of the Open Market Desk. However, the directive provided the critical guidance for the operational conduct of monetary policy by specifying a target range for the Federal funds rate.

The Federal funds rate is the interest rate on reserves lent between banks that are members of the Federal Reserve System and certain other participants in the market for "immediately available funds." The manager of the Open Market Desk at the Federal Reserve Bank of New York directly influences the Federal funds rates by open market operations that increase or reduce the supply of immediately available funds that may function as bank reserves. During the 1970s, the monetary policy directive from the FOMC usually instructed the manager of the Open Market Desk to maintain a specific value of the Federal funds rate provided that the monetary aggregates appeared to be growing within their desired short-term ranges. If the growth rates of monetary aggregates appeared likely to breach their desired short-term target ranges, the manager was usually authorized to make marginal adjustments to the Federal funds rate within a narrow tolerance range. This tolerance range was occasionally as wide as a percentage point, especially during 1975–76, but was usually limited to half a percentage point or less. Sometimes the language of the FOMC directive indicated a quite specific value for the Federal funds rate. At other times, the manager was instructed to use somewhat more discretion in adjusting the Federal funds rate in the light of economic developments.

The manager was generally instructed to seek further guidance from the FOMC if adjustments of the Federal funds rate outside its narrow tolerance band appeared necessary to contain monetary growth rates within their desired short-term target bands. In such situations, the FOMC might decide to alter (explicitly or implicitly) its monetary growth targets and avoid changes in the funds rate. Moreover, at any time, the FOMC could alter either its monetary growth targets or its prescription for the Federal funds rate if that appeared desirable in the light of information about the actual and prospective performance of the economy.

2.2.3   Recession and Recovery

During the recession of 1974–75, as the U.S. economy experienced sharp declines in both real output and inflation, the Federal funds rate was reduced rapidly from its peak of 13 percent in July 1974 to 5 percent in late May 1975. This decline in the funds rate both represented the normal monetary policy responses to developments in the economy and mirrored the substantial declines in other short-term interest rates. The sharp decline in market interest rates, in turn, reflected both the credit market effects of the drop in economic activity and the substantial decline in the actual and expected rate of inflation.

In the summer of 1975, as evidence of economic recovery accumulated, and as short-term interest rates moved modestly higher, the Federal funds rate was raised to 6.3 percent by late September.[2] Subsequently, as data indicated that

2. In this essay, the description of economic conditions that provided the context for decisions about monetary policy by the Federal Reserve is generally based on the official "Record of the

M1 and M2 were growing below the lower limits of their desired target ranges, the FOMC directed a series of reductions in the Federal funds rate down to 4.87 percent in January 1976. In May 1976, with indicators pointing to continued vigorous recovery, and with M1 and M2 now growing above their target ranges, the Federal funds rate was raised briefly to 5.5 percent and then held in the range between 5.25 and 5.5 percent through the summer months. During the autumn, amid signs of moderating real growth, with the monetary aggregates apparently growing within their short-term target ranges, the Federal funds rate was eased downward to 5 percent in early October and to 4.6 percent by late December. As the year ended, M1 was at the midpoint, and M2 and M3 were marginally above the upper limits, of the longer-term target ranges established a year earlier.

By the end of 1976, there was some evidence that inflation might be rising, while economic growth appeared sluggish. On balance, the evidence at this stage does not indicate that the Federal Reserve was knowingly fueling the resurgence of inflation. However, it may fairly be said that the Federal Reserve was not demonstrating much resolve to continue progress toward reducing inflation below the level that had led to the introduction of wage and price controls in August 1971.

2.2.4   Falling behind the Curve

During 1977, economic expansion proceeded rapidly, especially during the first half, while the twelve-month rate of consumer price inflation rose from 4.9 percent in December 1976 to 6.7 percent in December 1977. The Federal Reserve attempted to signal an effort to contain inflationary pressures by reducing, by half a percentage point, the upper and lower limits on the target growth ranges for monetary aggregates. The Federal funds rate was raised by three-quarters of a percentage point by mid-July and by an additional 1.25 percentage points by year's end.

The seriousness of these efforts to combat the rise of inflation during 1977, however, is open to question. The Carter administration's number one priority for economic policy was to maintain a vigorous expansion that would bring substantial reductions in the unemployment rate. The administration made clear that it did not favor a monetary policy that would interfere with this objective. On Capitol Hill, especially among Democrats, who dominated both

---

Policy Actions of the Federal Open Market Committee," which is published periodically in the *Federal Reserve Bulletin* and is reproduced each year in the *Annual Report* of the Board of Governors of the Federal Reserve System. Quite often, revised data provide a somewhat different picture of the performance of the economy than the Federal Reserve had at the time of its decisions. When this is a factor of substantial importance, it will usually be mentioned in the text. Where the issue is not important, revised data (rather than data available at the time) are sometimes used in this essay. The figures in this essay are all constructed with the most recent, revised data. It is important to recognize that the image presented by these figures does not always correspond to the information that the Federal Reserve had available at the time.

houses of Congress in the aftermath of Watergate, there was little sympathy for fighting inflation at the expense of progress in reducing unemployment.

In this political environment, the Federal Reserve authorized increases in the Federal funds rate only after evidence pointed to continued strong economic growth and only when the growth rates of monetary aggregates exceeded the shorter-term targets set by the FOMC. Despite a cumulative increase of 2 percentage points in the Federal funds rate, M1 grew by 7.8 percent from the fourth quarter of 1976 to the fourth quarter of 1977—2 percentage points higher than M1 growth for 1976 and 1 percentage above the upper limit of the target growth range for M1 for 1977. For M2 and M3, growth during 1977 was about 1 percentage point below growth during 1976, but at the upper limits of the target growth ranges for the aggregates.

In 1978, economic growth remained quite vigorous, while inflation worsened considerably. Specifically, real GNP rose by 6.3 percent on a fourth-quarter-to-fourth-quarter basis, while the twelve-month rate of consumer price inflation increased from 6.7 percent in December 1977 to 9.0 percent in December 1978. The target ranges for monetary growth in 1978 were set somewhat lower than for 1977, and the actual growth rates of M1, M2, and M3 were reduced from their 1977 growth rates. However, as in 1977, M1 grew above the upper limit of its target range, and M2 and M3 grew near the upper limits of their ranges.

On several occasions during 1978, the FOMC responded to the worsening inflation and to the rapid growth of monetary aggregates by raising the Federal funds rate, from around 6.5 percent in early January to 8.75 percent by late September, and ultimately to 10 percent by year's end. In April, the Carter administration signaled the increased priority that it assigned to curbing inflation when the president announced a variety of measures directed at that objective. At its meeting on 18 April 1978, the FOMC indicated the increased concern that it felt about rising inflation by reordering the official statement of its objectives in the directive to the manager of the Open Market Desk, placing "resisting inflationary pressures" ahead of "encouraging continued moderate economic expansion."

Despite the actions and statements of the administration and the Federal Reserve, by September 1978 it was clear that the efforts to combat rising inflation were not succeeding. At the end of the third quarter, virtually all measures of inflation were running significantly above their year-earlier levels. M1 was running well above the upper limit of its longer-term target range, and M2 and M3 were at the upper limits of their ranges. In October 1978, the U.S. dollar came under heavy downward pressure in foreign exchange markets, indicating a worldwide crisis of confidence in the ability and willingness of U.S. authorities to take effective action to control inflation.

2.2.5 A Failed Effort at Control

On 31 October and 1 November 1978, the administration and the Federal Reserve took action to deal with the crisis. The Treasury announced a variety of measures to acquire substantial amounts of foreign currencies with which to intervene in support of the dollar in foreign exchange markets. The Federal Reserve Board raised the discount rate by a full percentage point to 9.5 percent and established a supplementary reserve requirement for time deposits of over $100,000. The tolerance range for the Federal funds rate was raised from between 8.75 and 9.25 percent to between 9.25 and 9.75 percent. During the final two months of 1978, the growth rates of the monetary aggregates slowed considerably but remained above or near the upper limits of their longer-term growth ranges. The FOMC directed a marginal increase in the Federal funds rate to 10 percent, partly to support the dollar in foreign exchange markets and partly to enhance the credibility of its efforts to combat inflation.

The statement of Federal Reserve objectives for monetary policy in 1979 made it clear that reducing inflation was the number one priority. The target growth ranges for (old) M2 and (old) M3 were set at 5–8 percent and 6–9 percent, respectively—a 1 percentage point reduction in the maximum desired growth rate and a 1.5 percentage point reduction in the minimum desired growth rate from the 1978 monetary growth targets. Anticipating that the introduction of automatic transfer service (ATS) accounts would reduce the growth of demand for (old) M1 by 3 percentage points because of shifts from demand deposits to savings deposits, the target range for (old) M1 was set at 1.5–4.5 percent.

During 1979, inflationary pressures generally rose, while real economic activity followed an erratic and perplexing course. The increase in world oil prices, subsequent to the overthrow of the shah of Iran, contributed significantly to the increase in inflation. Specifically, the energy component of the CPI showed a 37.4 percent increase during 1979, compared with an 8.0 percent increase during 1978, and this helped raise the overall inflation rate from 9.0 to 13.3 percent. Even excluding energy prices, however, the rate of increase in the CPI escalated significantly from 9.2 percent during 1978 to 11.1 percent during 1979. Other measures of inflation, such as the rate of increase in the GNP price index or in average hourly earnings, also showed significant increases for 1979 over 1978. Moreover, most measures of inflation (except average hourly earnings) tended to show higher inflation rates as the year progressed—a disturbing development that surely increased fears of future inflation.

After registering an unexpectedly strong advance at the end of 1978, economic activity was believed (at the time) to have turned quite sluggish in early 1979. Specifically, it was estimated that real GNP grew at a rate of less than 1 percent during the first quarter. Incoming evidence during the spring and summer pointed increasingly to an economic downturn. By the 11 July meeting of the FOMC, it was clear that economic activity had declined during the second quarter, and further declines were widely anticipated. Indeed, the record of that meeting indicates that "no member of the Committee expressed disagreement with the staff appraisal . . . [suggesting] a further contraction in economic activity over the next few quarters."[3] Ultimately, revised data would show that economic activity was essentially flat during most of 1979, with moderate growth occurring during the summer quarter and again during the first quarter of 1980. However, as events unfolded during the course of 1979, it was generally believed, at the Federal Reserve and elsewhere, that a recession was either in progress or about to begin.

During the first half of 1979, monetary policy held the Federal funds rate nearly constant, in a narrow range between 10 and 10.5 percent. During the first quarter, (old) M1 declined, while (old) M2 and (old) M3 grew at rates below the lower limits of their target ranges. During the second quarter, growth of all the monetary aggregates picked up considerably, and, by early midsummer, each of these aggregates had reached or exceeded the upper bound of its target range. On 20 July, the Board of Governors raised the discount rate half a percentage point to 10 percent. On 27 July, the FOMC raised the upper limit of the Federal funds rate from 10.5 to 10.75 percent. On 14 August, the FOMC directed that the Federal funds rate be raised to an average of 11 percent and maintained within a band of 10.75–11.25 percent. On 16 September, the FOMC directed a "slight increase in the weekly average federal funds rate to about 11.5 percent."

This action raised the Federal funds rate in late September 1979 to 1.5 percentage points above the level it had reached just after the dollar stabilization crisis in November 1978. In the face of what was believed to be a very weak economy, most probably an economy already in recession, the FOMC believed that this was the appropriate degree of monetary tightening to combat clearly rising inflationary pressures.[4] The economy, however, was not as weak as was believed at the time. More important, while the Federal funds rate had been pushed up 1.5 percentage points during the ten months ending in September 1979, the inflation rate had risen by more than double that amount. Also, the monetary aggregates had risen from below the lower limits of their target ranges in March 1979 to or above the upper limits of those ranges by September. Once again, the Federal Reserve was falling behind the curve in its efforts to combat rising inflation. The foreign exchange market provided a further signal of this fact as the dollar once again came under severe downward pressure during the summer of 1979. Thus, eleven months after the administration and the Federal Reserve dramatically announced their new policies to curb inflation and strengthen the dollar, it was clear that those policies were not succeeding.

3. Unless otherwise indicated, most of the quotations in this essay are taken from the official "Record of the Policy Actions of the Federal Open Market Committee" (see no. 2 above). Several quotations, however, come from the semiannual "Monetary Policy Reports to Congress," which are also published in the *Federal Reserve Bulletin* and in the *Annual Report*.

4. A majority of the FOMC certainly may be said to have held this view. However, some members of the committee (especially Henry Wallich and, on one occasion, Paul Volcker) dissented and expressed their preference for a tighter monetary policy to combat inflation despite signs of economic weakness.

Of course, the acceleration of inflation during 1979 was partly the consequence of the second oil price shock that followed the overthrow of the shah of Iran. Had events developed differently, had the economy actually entered a recession in 1979, then perhaps the efforts to reduce inflation would have proved more successful. Moreover, it is understandable that the Federal Reserve was reluctant to take decisive action to tighten monetary policy when it faced the dreaded dilemma of rising inflation together with an economy that appeared to be in, or on the verge of, recession.

2.2.6   The Heritage of Rising Inflation

The dilemma that confronted the Federal Reserve in 1979 was not exclusively, or even primarily, the product of political upheaval in Iran and the second oil shock. In substantial measure, it was the consequence of failures to confront the rise of inflationary pressures more consistently and effectively at an earlier stage. Other countries, notably Switzerland and West Germany, that pursued more determined efforts to reduce inflation after the first oil shock in 1973 did not see their inflation rates rise as high in 1979 as in 1974–75. In contrast, the United States, which pursued a more laissez-faire policy toward inflation, confronted the second oil shock with inflation already rising through 9 percent and saw inflation jump to new peaks during 1979.

Moreover, the failure of U.S. monetary policy to curb the rise of inflation during the late 1970s cannot be explained away on the grounds that the Federal Reserve could not reasonably have understood the consequences of its actions. The failure is apparent not only in the persistent rise of inflation but also in the general tendency for monetary growth to exceed the targets set by the Federal Reserve. Specifically, as shown in figure 2.2, growth of M1 significantly exceeded the upper bound of its annual target range in 1977, 1978, and 1979. In 1975, M1 ended the year at the lower limit of its target range. This result, however, was largely the consequence of slow growth of M1 early in the year, attributable primarily to continued decline in economic activity and to the more rapid than anticipated decline in the rate of inflation. Only during 1976 was the growth of M1 close to the midpoint of the range set by the Federal Reserve.

For M2, as illustrated in figure 2.3, the story is worse. Only in 1978 was the growth of M2 close to the midpoint of its target range. In 1979, M2 growth was at the top of the target range, and, in 1975, 1976, and 1977, it was significantly above the upper limit of the target range. Moreover, for both M1 and M2, the Federal Reserve followed the practice of "rebasing" its monetary targets each year for the monetary growth that had actually occurred the preceding year. If the Federal Reserve had been effectively resisting the rise of inflation, this practice might have been defensible as a means of accounting for unanticipated shifts in money demand. In the circumstance of persistently rising inflation in the late 1970s, however, the practice of rebasing amounted to monetary accommodation of accelerating inflation.

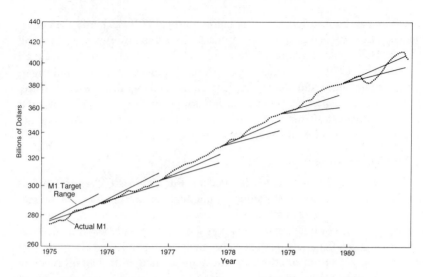

Fig. 2.2   M1 and growth target ranges, January 1975–December 1980
Note: The monetary targets are those established by the FOMC at the beginning of each year for
annual growth rates.

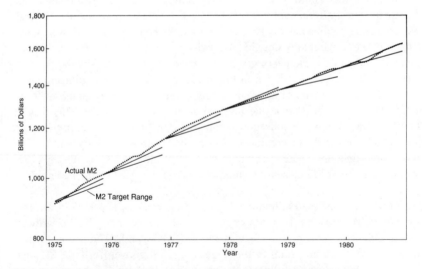

Fig 2.3   M2 and growth target ranges, January 1975–December 1980
Note: The monetary targets are those established by the FOMC at the beginning of each year for
annual growth rates.

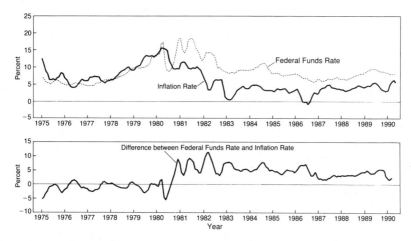

Fig. 2.4   Inflation rate and interest rate, January 1975–April 1990
Note: The inflation rate is a six-month moving average of the growth of the seasonally adjusted CPI, all items.

The inadequacy of the Federal Reserve's efforts to curb inflation during this period is also apparent in the behavior of the Federal funds rate, as illustrated in figure 2.4. The Federal funds rate was raised gradually from early 1977 through 1979. However, these increases in the Federal funds rate often lagged behind increases in the inflation rate, indicating fairly clearly that the Federal Reserve was "falling behind the curve" in its actions to combat rising inflation.

To observers outside the Federal Reserve, the developments of the late 1970s indicated that U.S. monetary policy was not deeply committed to resisting the rise of inflation. Most important, the actual inflation rate was rising persistently, even before the second oil price shock. Monetary growth was generally allowed to exceed announced targets. New targets were rebased to accommodate past inflation and past excessive monetary growth. Increases in the Federal funds rate often lagged behind increases in the inflation rate. Thus, while the Federal Reserve talked about a battle against the demon of inflation, it gave little evidence of much stomach for the fight.

2.3   The Demon Wins Another Round

Paul Volcker replaced G. William Miller as chairman of the Federal Reserve Board on 6 August 1979. For the preceding four years, Volcker had been president of the Federal Reserve Bank of New York and hence a member of the Federal Open Market Committee. Earlier, he had served in the Nixon administration as undersecretary of the Treasury for monetary affairs—traditionally a position of considerable responsibility for both domestic and international financial policy in the U.S. administration. Paul Volcker was very well known and highly regarded in the financial community and exceptionally well qualified to take command of the Federal Reserve at a time of economic turmoil and crisis.

2.3.1   New Operating Procedures

The appropriate starting date for the assessment of U.S. monetary policy in the 1980s is not the day of Paul Volcker's accession to the chairmanship of the Federal Reserve, however, but rather two months later, 6 October 1979. On that Saturday, the Federal Reserve announced a new effort to discipline the demon of rising inflation. The discount rate was raised a full percentage point to a new record of 12 percent. New reserve requirements were imposed on certain liabilities of member banks. Most important, the FOMC adopted new operating procedures for the conduct of monetary policy.

Under the new operating procedures, the Open Market Desk would no longer be directed to keep the Federal funds rate at a specified level or within a narrow tolerance range but rather to supply a volume of bank reserves consistent with desired rates of growth of monetary aggregates prescribed by the FOMC. Technically, the desk would operate by estimating the total volume of bank reserves needed to support the short-term monetary growth targets set by the FOMC. The amount of borrowed reserves likely to be supplied through the Federal Reserve discount window would also be estimated. Through open market operations, the desk manager would then supply the implied amount of nonborrowed reserves appropriate to meet the target for total bank reserves.

It was recognized that, under these new operating procedures, the short-term variability of the Federal funds rate was likely to increase substantially. A very broad tolerance range would be specified for the Federal funds rate for the periods between scheduled meetings of the FOMC. On 6 October the tolerance range for the Federal funds rate was set at 11.5–15.5 percent. Since the Federal funds rate had been running at about 11.5 percent during September, the new broad tolerance range gave wide latitude to the manager of the Open Market Desk to tighten reserve availability in order to reduce the growth rates of monetary aggregates as prescribed by the FOMC.

The shift to the new operating procedures was motivated by tactical, psychological, and political considerations and not by a profound religious experience that suddenly converted most members of the FOMC to the doctrine of "monetarism." Under the old operating procedures, the FOMC could have directed a large increase in the Federal funds rate in order to restrain monetary growth and resist rising inflation. Tactically, however, the FOMC did not know how large an increase in the Federal funds rate might be needed, and it recognized the virtue of significantly greater flexibility in adjusting the Federal funds rate to deal with ongoing developments. Psychologically, in attacking inflationary expectations, there appeared to be a gain from publicly announcing a more "monetarist approach" to the general conduct of monetary policy rather than just a change in the value of a particular policy instrument. Politically, the new operating procedures offered an important degree of cover for the highly unpopular action of sharply increasing interest rates and probably pushing the economy into recession. The necessary rise in interest rates would not be so visibly linked to Federal Reserve actions but could be blamed instead on market pressures arising from increased inflationary expectations and excess credit demands from the government and the private sector. The Federal Reserve could point to the generally agreed on need to resist inflation by restraining monetary growth as the essence of its policy.[5]

2.3.2   The Initial Assault on Inflation

The financial market response to the new Federal Reserve policy was immediate and dramatic. On the following Monday, the short-term interest rates leapt upward, and long-term bond prices tumbled. During the final two weeks of October, the Federal funds rate rose to 15.5 percent, before falling back to 13.5 percent in November and then edging up to 14 percent in late December. On average during the final quarter of 1979, short-term interest rates ran nearly 2 percentage points above late September levels, while long-term interest rates rose about a percentage point above their late September levels. During the final three months of 1979, growth of the monetary aggregates was slowed very substantially from the rapid pace of the preceding six months; M1, M2, and M3 recorded growth rates of 3, 7, and 6.25 percent, respectively.

Economic data reported during the first three months of 1980 indicated relatively sluggish real growth during the final quarter of 1979 but an apparent pickup of growth during January and February. Monetary growth remained subdued in January. In February, however, growth of the newly defined, narrow monetary aggregates, M1A and M1B, accelerated sufficiently to exceed the (relatively stingy) short-run target rates set by the FOMC. In response to this and other developments in the economy, the FOMC raised the upper limit of the tolerance range of the Federal funds rate (in a series of telephone conferences and at the regular meeting on 22 March) from 15.5 percent to 20 percent. The actual level of the funds rate jumped from 15 percent on 22 February to 19.4 percent by the end of March.

Despite the tightening of monetary policy, inflation continued to be very rapid during the final quarter of 1979 and accelerated further during the first quarter of 1980. Specifically, the (annualized) six-month inflation rate was recorded at 13.5, 13.3, and 13.4 percent in October, November, and December of 1979 and then at 14.2, 14.9, and 15.9 percent in January, February and March of 1980, respectively. Moreover, the remarkable surges in the prices of gold (to over $800 per ounce), silver (to over $50.00 per ounce), and other

---

5. William Greider (1987) provides a detailed (if not always sympathetic) discussion of the political and economic rationale underlying the shift in Federal Reserve operating procedures.

commodities by early February 1980 suggested growing hysteria about the possibility of runaway inflation.

In this environment, on 14 March 1980 President Carter acted to combat rising inflation. He announced a package of budget proposals to cut the projected federal deficit, and he authorized the imposition of controls on consumer credit by the Federal Reserve. The objective of these actions was to reduce pressures on interest rates arising from the federal deficit, to limit directly the growth of consumer credit that appeared to be fueling the inflationary process, and to attempt to break the psychological fear of uncontrolled inflation. As one high official of the Carter administration once explained it, "We decided to whack the donkey between the eyes with a two-by-four to make sure we had its attention."

2.3.3 Recession and Reversal

The budgetary proposals announced by President Carter were viewed with some disdain in financial markets and probably had little effect on the economy. The response to the credit controls, combined with the Fed's tight monetary policy, was virtually instantaneous—the economy nosedived into recession, with real GNP recording a spectacular 9 percent annualized rate of decline. Short-term interest rates tumbled, with the three-month Treasury-bill rate falling from 15.5 percent in March to 7 percent in June. The monthly inflation rate fell off somewhat in April, May, and June from the very high monthly rates in January, February, and March, but, on a six-month-average basis, the inflation rate remained very high.

After declining slightly in March, the narrow monetary aggregates, M1A and M1B, contracted sharply in April and then flattened out in May. The June rebounds in these aggregates largely offset the April declines but still left both M1A and M1B significantly below the lower limits of their longer-term target ranges. The broader aggregate M2 declined only modestly in April, and the strong rebound in June left it just above the lower limit of its target range. As evidence became available of the shortfall of monetary growth below the short-term targets set by the FOMC, and as other short-term interest rates dropped, the Federal funds rate plummeted to the 13 percent lower limit of its tolerance range by 6 May. The FOMC promptly reduced the lower limit of the tolerance range to 10.5 percent, and the actual funds rate fell almost to this limit by 14 May.

At the regularly scheduled FOMC meeting on 22 May, the desk manager was directed to provide reserves consistent with monetary growth rates "high enough to promote achievement of the Committee's objectives for monetary growth over the year, provided that in the period before the next regular meeting the weekly average federal funds rate remains within a range of 8.5 to 14 percent." Under this directive, the actual level of the Federal funds rate fell to 9.4 percent by the end of June. Thus, in three months, the Federal funds rate had been cut by 10 percentage points from its peak in late March. By this measure of monetary policy, all the tightening between the dollar stabilization program announced on 1 November 1978 and the extraordinary measures of March 1980 was effectively reversed.

Given the behavior of the monetary aggregates, the sharp decline of the Federal funds rate during the spring of 1980 was a natural consequence of the monetary operating procedures of the Federal Reserve. However, the FOMC knew that it had a choice about whether to permit a decline of quite such speed and magnitude. It was not required by law or by deep religious conviction to seek extremely rapid correction of all deviations of monetary growth from previously specified targets. The manager of the Open Market Desk could have been instructed to tolerate substantial shortfalls of M1A and M1B below their previously announced target ranges. The FOMC could have retargeted monetary growth in the second half of 1980 at the previously announced rates, but starting from the base established in the second quarter. This would have been consistent with the "rebasing" of the growth targets in earlier years, when the monetary aggregates had often grown near or even above the upper limits of the preceding year's growth targets.

The turmoil and uncertainty in the economy and financial markets provided good reason for the Federal Reserve to be cautious in its conduct of monetary policy. The virtually complete lack of experience with the Federal Reserve's new operating procedures provided additional reason for caution. Such caution clearly did not justify an incredible, 10 percentage point drop in the Federal funds rate in an effort to offset one or two months of negative growth of monetary aggregates. There was no precedent for such action. Only two or three months into a recession that was widely regarded as the necessary consequence of successful efforts to curb inflation, there was no credible reason to believe that quite such a large and rapid drop in the Federal funds rate was necessary to forestall a repeat of the Great Depression. Moreover, as illustrated in figure 2.4, the Federal funds rate fell much more sharply than any reasonable estimate of what was happening to the rate of inflation. This alone should have raised the caution sign that the Federal Reserve was being too aggressive in allowing such a large and rapid decline in the Federal funds rate.

As suggested at the time by Governor Wallich, the Federal Reserve could have resisted declines in the Federal funds rate below 12 or 13 percent while awaiting more information about economic developments. This would still have meant a very dramatic 6 or 7 percentage point easing of the cost of Federal Reserve credit in response to the downturn in the economy and in the monetary aggregates. Moreover, the record of the 22 April FOMC meeting reports that the committee was clearly apprised of the dangers that "aggressive efforts to promote monetary growth might have to be reversed before long, perhaps leading to significant increases in interest rates," and that "vigorous efforts in the short run to bring monetary growth into line with the Committee's longer-run objectives could result in excessive creation of money."

2.3.4   Rebound and Resurgence

Judged by the behavior of monetary aggregates, during the summer and early fall of 1980 monetary policy was very expansionary. From well below the lower limits of their target ranges in May, the narrow monetary aggregates M1A and M1B shot upward during the next five months, with M1A rising to near the upper limit of its range, and M1B rising above the upper limit of its range in October. (For the path of M1B, which was subsequently redefined, and M1, see fig. 2.2 above.) Meanwhile, M2 (as illustrated in fig. 2.3 above) rose from slightly below the lower limit of its target range to moderately above the upper limit. The Federal Reserve did not forcefully resist these monetary developments by rapidly reversing the spring decline in the Federal funds rate. The funds rate fell briefly below 9 percent in July and early August, generally remained below 11 percent through mid-September, and was pushed as high as 13 percent in the week before the 4 November presidential election.

Of course, in normal times, a 4 percentage point increase in the Federal funds rate in four months would represent a dramatic tightening of monetary policy. However, nothing about economic events in 1980 was very normal, and the Federal Reserve had no rational basis for believing that its actions to raise the Federal funds rate during the summer and early autumn of 1980 were in any way symmetrical with its actions to cut the Federal funds rate during the spring. In the spring, recognizing that a recession would probably be the necessary consequence of successful efforts to reduce inflation, two months of shortfall of the monetary aggregates below their target ranges had justified a 10 percentage point decline in the Federal funds rate. In the summer and early fall, with no firm reason to believe that substantial permanent progress had been made in reducing the inflation rate below about the 10 percent level, five months of very rapid growth of the monetary aggregates led to only a 4 percentage point increase in the Federal funds rate. Moreover, as illustrated in figure 2.5, not only did the interest rate of three-month Treasury bills fall significantly less than the Federal funds rate from late April to mid-June, but the Treasury-bill rate also began to move upward fairly sharply two months before the Federal Reserve began to push the Federal funds rate upward.

The recession of 1980 was sharp but very brief. By the summer of 1980, economic activity began to recover. Retail sales began to rise in June after four months of decline. Industrial production began to rise in August, having fallen 8.5 percent during the preceding six months. Employment, measured by the household survey, began to recover in July, while nonfarm payroll employment, measured by the establishment survey, began rising in August. Private housing starts began recovering strongly in June. After falling sharply in the second quarter, real GNP posted a slight gain during the summer. It then rose at a vigorous 5 percent annual rate in the autumn and at a very rapid 9 percent annual rate during the first quarter of 1981.

For one month, in July 1980, the CPI was nearly unchanged. The monthly

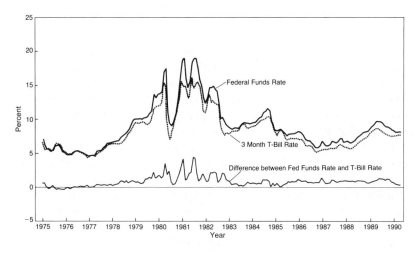

Fig. 2.5   Interest rates
Note: Federal funds rate and three-month Treasury-bill rate, January 1975–April 1990.

inflation rate, however, picked up to 8 percent in August and 12 percent in September. Even with the benefit of the July CPI result, the inflation rate for the last six months of 1980 was 9.7 percent. The December-to-December change in the CPI for 1980 was 12.4 percent, down only marginally from the 13.3 percent gain recorded for 1979. As measured by the GNP fixed-weight price index, there was no decline of inflation during the second half of 1980, and the inflation rate during all of 1980 was a percentage point higher than during 1979.

2.3.5   An Abortive Victory

In retrospect, especially knowing the price yet to be paid during the recession of 1981–82 to refight the battle against inflation, it is clear that the Federal Reserve accomplished only an abortive victory. Reducing inflation was the clearly stated, number one priority of monetary policy for 1980. The Federal Reserve clearly recognized that pursuit of this priority implied substantial short-term risks for business activity. It specifically pointed to the midpoints of its target ranges for monetary growth during 1980 as implying significant constraint on inflation. Early in the year, the Federal Reserve took decisive action to crush the bubble of inflationary hysteria. However, when the economy and the monetary aggregates turned sharply but briefly downward in the spring, and as the first glimmer of hope appeared in the long-proclaimed effort to reduce inflation, the Federal Reserve quickly and massively reversed the thrust of its policy. As year's end approached, the monetary aggregates were not at the midpoints of their target ranges but rather near or above the upper limits. Despite the pledges of forceful and persistent action to reduce inflation, and despite the recession of 1980, "inflation did not abate in 1980," as the

Federal Reserve conceded in its "Monetary Policy Report to Congress" in February 1981.

Of course, monetary policy is not made in retrospect. It is made in real time, without prescient knowledge of the future, and often without very accurate knowledge of what is currently happening. In this regard, 1980 certainly did not provide a congenial environment for the conduct of monetary policy. The economy shifted with unprecedented rapidity from inflation hysteria, to steep recession, and then back to expansion and accelerating inflation. There was little basis for assessing the impact on the economy of the imposition and subsequent removal of credit controls. Interest rates, usually a key indicator and instrument for the conduct of monetary policy, moved around with incredible volatility. The behavior of monetary aggregates was also extremely difficult to interpret and predict in the face of wide swings in interest rates and the deregulation of depository institutions.

Moreover, the Federal Reserve's new operating procedures seriously complicated the conduct of monetary policy during 1980. Partly, the problem was that neither the Federal Reserve nor the banking and financial system had any significant experience with the new operating procedures and certainly no experience relevant to the turbulent conditions of 1980. More important, many members of the FOMC apparently felt that it was important to demonstrate the seriousness and the symmetry of their commitment to the new operating procedures. The procedures served to justify the aggressive tightening of monetary policy in the autumn of 1979 and the extraordinary efforts to combat the inflationary hysteria of early 1980. When the economy tumbled into recession in the spring and the monetary aggregates fell well below their target ranges, symmetrical application of the new operating procedures demanded a very aggressive easing of monetary policy as measured by the Federal funds rate. Indeed, judged by the standard of achieving the monetary growth targets, the Federal Reserve failed to cut the funds sufficiently in the spring of 1980.

During 1980, the conduct of monetary policy was further complicated by the political environment of a presidential election. In the autumn of 1979 and the winter of 1980, despite the likely political costs of a recession, the Carter administration supported, or at least acquiesced in, the Federal Reserve's tight policy to combat rising inflation. When the economy fell steeply into recession, the administration approved the Federal Reserve's easing of monetary policy and surely would have been highly critical of the continuation of a very tight policy. It is unclear, however, that the administration actively sought quite the speed and extent of reductions in the Federal funds rate that occurred between late March and early June or that the administration could have effectively pressured a reluctant Federal Reserve to ease so dramatically.

During the summer and early autumn, as election day approached, administration officials understandably became increasingly unsympathetic toward any tightening of monetary policy. Nevertheless, the Federal Reserve began to nudge the Federal funds rate upward in September, and, on 25 September, the

Board of Governors authorized a full 1 percentage point increase in the discount rate—an unprecedented action so close to an election and one that elicited public criticism from President Carter. Despite this criticism, the Federal Reserve allowed or induced about a further 2 percentage point increase in the Federal funds rate before election day.

Market interest rates, however, began to move upward ten weeks in advance of upward movements in the Federal funds rate. In particular, the short-term Treasury-bill rate bottomed out by mid-June and had risen about 2 percentage points by mid-August—a fact that was known contemporaneously at the Federal Reserve. Also, an explosion of monetary growth began in June and continued through the summer and early autumn—developments that were known with only a brief delay at the Federal Reserve. Unquestionably, the Federal Reserve postponed actions to tighten monetary policy that were clearly called for by these developments under its own operating procedures. In all probability, political concerns about the consequences of a dramatic tightening of monetary policy shortly before a presidential election were an important reason for this delay.

It should be emphasized that the political concerns that influenced the Federal Reserve during the summer and early autumn of 1980 were not narrowly partisan—to aid in the reelection of President Carter. William Greider, who is not a great admirer of the Federal Reserve, makes this point in *Secrets of the Temple* (1987). He quotes Frederick Schultz, then vice chairman of the Federal Reserve Board, as expressing the views of many members of the FOMC: "Our attitude toward the election is that we'd like to dig a foxhole and crawl in until it's over." Greider's own conclusion is stated as follows:

> This disposition [to avoid political involvement] undoubtedly inhibited policy makers from executing sharp, stringent policy moves in the middle of a campaign if such decisions could be postponed. The majority of the FOMC, for instance, might have been more open to the arguments for tightening in the summer of 1980 if it had not been the season for presidential politics. Some governors, if pressed, would concede that during a campaign they would rather be easing than tightening if conditions permitted them to do so. Most of all, they wished for a smooth policy line that would avoid aggravating either political party. (p. 214)

These political difficulties, together with the other substantial problems of conducting monetary policy in the extraordinarily turbulent and uncertain environment of 1980, explain much of the erratic, seesaw course of monetary policy. They do not, however, entirely excuse the Federal Reserve's lack of persistence and determination in confronting the demon of inflation. To an important extent, the demon itself was the offspring both of the repeated failures to pursue sufficiently aggressive anti-inflation policies during the late 1970s and of the Federal Reserve's generally poor record of combating inflation since the mid-1960s. During the spring of 1980, the Federal Reserve was not compelled to ease as much as it chose to when the economy fell into recession. As the record of its own meetings indicates, the FOMC was warned about the possible need to reverse that policy if the recession proved short and inflation resurged. It could and should have recognized the difficulties that would be faced if such a reversal became necessary in the midst of the presidential election campaign.

Given the information available at the time, the Federal Reserve did not have a particularly sound basis for engineering the entire precipitous drop of the Federal funds rate during the spring of 1980, other than the desire to adhere to its own new and untested operating procedures. If the Federal Reserve sought to adhere to these operating procedures, it should and could have acted more quickly and aggressively to restrain the resurgence of rapid monetary growth during the summer and early autumn of 1980. The dismal record of the Federal Reserve in nurturing and tolerating the rise of inflation during the preceding three years justified and necessitated sustained action to combat inflation. In 1980, having summoned the courage to stand eyeball to eyeball with the demon of inflation, the Federal Reserve should not have blinked.

2.4   Bloodshed and Victory

The second and ultimately successful effort to combat inflation during the 1980s really began, appropriately enough, on 4 November 1980—two years after the dollar stabilization crisis of 1978 and on the day that Ronald Wilson Reagan was elected president of the United States. For twenty-one months, until August 1982, the Federal Reserve would consistently pursue a very tight monetary policy. As a consequence of this effort, the inflation rate would be driven down from 12.4 percent during 1980 to 3.9 percent during 1982. The U.S. economy would also be pushed into a deep and prolonged recession during which real GNP would fall absolutely by 3.3 percent and the unemployment rate would rise to a postwar peak of 10.8 percent.

During the seven weeks following the presidential election, the Federal funds rate was driven up 6 percentage points, to nearly 20 percent by mid-December 1980. The growth rates of the monetary aggregates fell off sharply in November and December. By year's end, the November–December slowdown in money growth pushed M1A back toward the midpoint of its target range and drove M1B and M2 down toward the upper limits of their ranges. Alternatively, adjusting for the larger than expected increase in NOW and ATS deposits, it could be said that both M1A and M1B ended the year just below the upper limits of their target ranges, after having shot from being well below these ranges in late May to above their upper limits in October.

2.4.1   Twelve Months of Tight Money

The slowdown of monetary growth that began in November and December 1980 continued into January and February 1981, placing the narrow monetary aggregates M1A and M1B (adjusted for shifts of deposits because of the nationwide introduction of NOW accounts) well below their target ranges. During this brief period in early 1981, M1A actually declined very sharply because interest-bearing checking accounts (not included in M1A) became widely available to individual households. In figure 2.6, which plots the six-month annualized growth rates of M1A and M1B, this development is reflected in the large negative growth rates of M1A during the first few months of 1981. For M1B, the six-month annualized growth rate declines sharply in late 1980 and early 1981 but does not become negative in early 1981. For M2, the six-month annualized growth rate, illustrated in figure 2.7, declines substantially from its relatively high level in the early autumn of 1980 but remains above the rate implied by the midpoint of the FOMC's target range for this aggregate.

As evidence of the substantial shortfall in the growth of the narrow monetary aggregates became available in late January and February 1981, the Federal funds rate fell from around 19 percent to the 15 percent lower limit of its tolerance range. This development probably reflected market anticipations of some easing by the Federal Reserve in pursuit of its monetary growth targets more than it did deliberate actions by the manager of the Open Market Desk. In any case, at its meeting on 2–3 February 1981, the FOMC decided that it would accept for some time a shortfall of the narrow aggregates below their short-term target ranges. Notably, at this juncture, the FOMC refused to authorize a further reduction in the lower tolerance limit for the funds rate.

At its meeting on the last day of March, the FOMC decided that, because of the confusion associated with shifts of deposits between the narrow aggregates, it would cease to make reference to M1A in its directive to the Open Market Desk. At this meeting, it also adjusted the tolerance range for the Federal funds rate to 13–18 percent. However, the funds rate fell below 15 percent only briefly during April, before preliminary data began to show more rapid growth of the monetary aggregates.

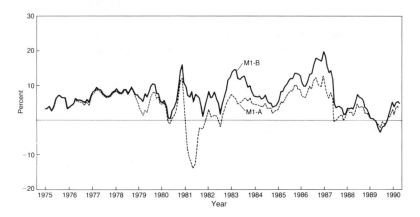

Fig. 2.6   M1 money supply growth, January 1975–April 1990
Note: The money growth rate is a six-month moving average of the respective M1 growth rate.

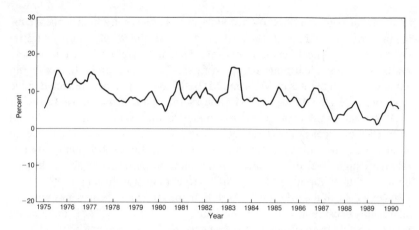

Fig. 2.7   M2 money supply growth, January 1975–April 1990
Note: The money growth rate is a six-month moving average of the M2 growth rate.

By early May 1981, monetary data showed M1B rising rapidly toward the midpoint of its target range and M2 growing above the upper limit of its target range. The Federal funds rate had already been pushed above the 18 percent upper limit of its tolerance range. In a telephone conference on 6 May, the FOMC authorized temporary excesses of the funds rate above this upper limit in order that "the reserve path should continue to be set on the basis of the short-run objectives for monetary growth." Two days earlier, the Board of Governors had raised the discount rate from 13 to 14 percent. At its regular meeting on 18 May, the FOMC formally raised the tolerance range for the funds rate to 16–22 percent. When these actions were taken, it was clear that economic activity had expanded rapidly during the first quarter—the final confirming echo of the rapid monetary growth of the summer and early autumn of 1980.

By the time of the FOMC meeting on 6–7 July 1981, it was apparent that economic activity had leveled out in the second quarter, following a revised estimate of a very strong growth during the first quarter. The large April increase in M1B had been reversed by sharp declines in May and June, and M1B (adjusted for deposit shifts into NOW accounts) was again well below the lower limit of its target range. M2 and M3 continued to grow above the upper limits of their ranges. Federal funds had generally been trading in the range of 18.5–19.5 percent during the preceding six weeks. The FOMC lowered the tolerance range for the funds rate to 15–21 percent in its directive of 7 July and maintained this range until its meeting on 5–6 October, when the range was reduced to 12–17 percent. Through mid-August, the actual level of the funds rate declined only marginally to about 18 percent. It then moved erratically downward, generally remaining above 15 percent through the end of October. From July through October, M1B grew very slowly and fell further below the lower limit of its target range, while M2 continued to skirt the upper limit of its range.

In retrospect, it is clear that monetary policy was really very tight during the twelve months from November 1980 through October 1981. For almost this entire twelve months, the Federal funds rate was kept above 15 percent, half the time in the range of 18–20 percent. On only two previous occasions had the Federal funds rate ever reached or exceeded 15 percent: very briefly in late October 1979 and for about two months from late February to late April 1980. Moreover, measured in real terms, subtracting the six-month annualized rate of change in the CPI, the Federal funds rate was exceptionally high from November 1980 through October 1981—generally in the range of 4–9 percent.[6]

The monetary aggregates also indicated a very tight policy. As illustrated in figure 2.6 above, after spiking upward in late 1980, the six-month annualized growth rate of M1B fell continuously during 1981 and reached almost zero in October. M1A registered sharply negative growth for most of 1981. M2 grew at an 8.7 percent annual rate between October 1980 and October 1981 but failed to keep pace with the 10.2 percent rise in the consumer price index.[7]

After twelve months of very tight monetary policy, information received during November and December 1981 indicated sharply declining economic activity during the fourth quarter, after a small gain in the third quarter and a small decline in the second. A recession was now clearly under way, and it was expected to be at least as deep as the average recession since the Second World War. Data on consumer and producer prices were generally showing inflation rates much reduced from their levels earlier in 1981 and in 1980. Reflecting both an actual and an expected slump in activity and decline of inflation, short-term interest rates began to move sharply downward in very late September, with yields on three-month Treasury bills registering more than a 4 percentage

6. There are several possible ways to measure the "real level of the Federal funds rate," and they yield somewhat different numerical answers. However, using any consistent method of measurement, this measure of monetary tightness was exceptionally high, relative to previous experience, for a very long time during 1981, and it continued to be very high until the summer of 1982. Subsequently during the 1980s, the real level of the Federal funds rate would generally remain very high by the standards of the 1960s and 1970s. For the measure of the real level of the Federal funds rate illustrated in fig. 2.4 above, this may be partly explained by the possibility that the average anticipated rate of inflation during much of the 1980s ran somewhat above the six-month annualized rate of change in the CPI and by the likelihood that the sharp declines in this measure of inflation during late 1982 through early 1983 and again during 1986 did not correspond to similar declines of the anticipated inflation rate. However, an important part of the continued high real level of the Federal funds rate (and other interest rates) during the 1980s remains very difficult to explain. It follows that this indicator of the stance of monetary policy needs to be interpreted with care.

7. The real quantity of any monetary aggregate may be measured by dividing the nominal quantity by a measure of the price level. Using the CPI to measure the price level, between October 1980 and October 1981, the real quantity of M2 was falling. In the context of the behavior of all the other indicators of monetary policy, this decline in the real quantity of M2 should be interpreted as further evidence of a tight monetary policy.

point drop by year's end. Long-term bond yields also dropped substantially from their peaks in late September, with yields on Treasury bonds falling 1.5–2 percentage points by year's end.

2.4.2   Nine More Months of Tight Money

The Federal Reserve responded to these developments by making monetary policy only modestly less tight. The discount rate was cut from 14 to 13 percent on 30 October and cut again to 12 percent on 3 December. The tolerance range for the Federal funds rate was reduced to 11–15 percent at the FOMC meeting on 21 November and then to 10–14 percent at the FOMC meeting a month later. The actual level of the funds rate declined from 15 percent at the end of October to 13.25 percent in mid-November and fell as low as 12 percent in early December before turning upward. Growth rates of the monetary aggregates picked up somewhat in the final two months of 1981, with M1B rising toward (but not quite to) the lower limit of its target range and M2 rising a modest further amount above the upper limit of its range. The FOMC, however, was not disposed to repeat the (never officially conceded) mistakes of 1979 and 1980 by directing a rapid acceleration of monetary growth at the first signs of real weakness in the economy. The official record of the 17 November meeting of the FOMC notes (in the usual dry and understated tone of these documents):

> Many members thought that an aggressive effort to stimulate M1B growth over November and December at a pace sufficiently rapid to compensate for the shortfall in October would interfere with achievement of longer-term economic goals and would risk overly rapid expansion of money and credit in later months, particularly if the effort were accompanied by a precipitous decline in short-term interest rates to levels that might not be sustainable.

In 1982, the Federal Reserve stopped reporting and announcing growth targets for M1A and relabeled M1B more simply as M1.[8] In January, M1 grew at a very rapid 21 percent annual rate, after increasing at an 11 percent rate in December 1981. This placed M1 significantly above the target range for that aggregate established by the FOMC. M2 grew at a 13 percent rate in January 1982 (originally estimated as 11 percent), after rising at an 11 percent rate the preceding December (originally estimated as 8 percent). These developments placed M2 slightly above its target range by the time of the FOMC meeting on 1–2 February 1982.

It was known at the time that most of the large January gain in M1, as well as much of the increase in this aggregate in November and December 1980, came from other checkable deposits (OCD). OCD consists of interest-bearing checkable deposits in NOW and ATS accounts at all depository institutions

---

8. The definitions of M2 and M3 were also modified. Money market funds held by institutions were removed from M2 (and remained in M3), and retail repurchase agreements of less than $100,000 (already in M3) were added to M2.

and small amounts of demand deposits at thrift institutions and credit unions. OCD is the part of M1 (previously M1B) that is not in M1A, the old concept of M1 consisting of currency plus non-interest-bearing demand deposits at commercial banks. It is now known that OCD has a much lower transactions velocity than ordinary demand deposits, indicating very strongly that the January 1982 increase in OCD and correspondingly in M1 did not signal that monetary expansion was exceedingly rapid. Even at the time, there was good reason to suspect that this was true and to pay heed to continuing signals from M1A that monetary policy remained quite tight. The Federal Reserve, however, had removed M1A from any direct role in the short-run operation of monetary policy in March 1981 and was committed to abandoning this aggregate altogether in February 1982.

Knowing the Federal Reserve's operating procedures, financial markets focused on the short-run behavior of M1 (= M1B) and M2, for which estimates were announced weekly. If the Federal Reserve was believed to be serious about achieving its monetary growth targets (as apparently it was in late 1981 and early 1982), then market forces would automatically tend to force the Federal funds rate and other short-term interest rates upward once it was reported that growth of M1 (= M1B) was accelerating above its presumed target in late December 1981 and January 1982. In any event, whether as an automatic result of market forces or with some additional push from the Open Market Desk, the Federal funds rate did rise from 12.25 percent around 20 December to 14 percent at the end of January.

At the FOMC meeting on 1–2 February 1982, it was recognized that the January rise in M1 resulting from the rapid growth of OCD was probably a deviation that should not be corrected by an effort to drive M1 rapidly back toward its target range. On the other hand, the FOMC was not prepared to ignore entirely the January increase in M1 or to alter its previously announced target ranges, or to reintroduce M1A into the monetary control procedures. Instead, to move M1 back toward its target range for 1982, the FOMC directed that no further growth should occur in M1 in the period January–March, and it raised the tolerance range for the Federal funds rate to 12–16 percent. It is noteworthy that this decision was taken in the knowledge that M1 (= M1B) had undershot its 1981 target range and that the rapid January growth had placed this aggregate only slightly above the lower limit of the extension of the 1981 target range. It was also taken in the knowledge that real GNP was estimated to have fallen at a 5.25 percent annual rate in the final quarter of 1981, that preliminary indicators suggested a further decline in output during the first quarter of 1982, and that inflation was continuing the clear trend of moderation that had begun in 1981. Clearly, something had changed since the spring of 1980 in the Federal Reserve's approach to dealing with the risks of recession and inflation.

On balance, M1 grew very little between January and the end of June. M2 grew sufficiently slowly to fall just below the 9 percent upper limit of its target growth range in March and subsequently ran essentially along this upper limit. After January, the Federal funds fluctuated generally between 14 and 15.5 percent and ended June at about 14.5 percent. Since the inflation rate (measured by the six-month annualized rate of change in the CPI) was running around 6 percent, the Federal funds rate in real terms generally exceeded 8 percent. Economic data during this period indicated, on balance, little change in output during the second quarter. Nonfarm payroll employment continued to decline, however, and the unemployment rate rose from 8.6 percent in January (already above the 7.8 percent peak reached during the brief 1980 recession) to 9.6 percent in June—at that point a record unemployment rate for the postwar era.

2.4.3   The Shift to Easier Money

By the end of June, the very slow growth of M1 for five months had erased the January bulge and brought this aggregate near to the upper limit of its 1982 target range. M2 continued to grow along the upper limit of its range. At this point, adherence to the monetary targets would have implied continuation of a tight monetary policy to bring both M1 and M2 toward the midpoints of their announced ranges. Some members of the FOMC (Governor Wallich and Reserve Bank Presidents Black and Ford) clearly favored this course. Alternatively, in view of the depressed level of business activity, the FOMC could have explicitly raised the targets for monetary growth. Governor Teeters, long a proponent of a somewhat less tight monetary policy, was an advocate of this latter option. The FOMC pursued neither of these courses. It did, however, raise the short-term growth targets for M1 and M2 by 2 and 1 percentage points, respectively, and it instructed the manager of the Open Market Desk that "somewhat more rapid growth would be acceptable."

With this decision, the FOMC effectively began fundamental change in the course of monetary policy in the direction of substantially greater ease. Initially, this change in policy was not apparent in the behavior of the monetary aggregates, as M1 declined slightly in July, while M2 growth increased modestly. In the face of a still deepening recession, however, the Federal funds rate dropped from 14.5 percent at the end of June to 15 percent by mid-July and to 11 percent by the end of July. The Federal Reserve Board cut the discount rate half a percentage point, to 11.5 percent on 19 July, by another half percentage point on 30 July, and by another half percentage point on 13 August. By late July, financial markets began to take the hint. The yield on three-month Treasury bills fell more than 4 percentage points between late July and the end of August, while longer-term bond yields declined more than 1.5 percentage points. Stock prices began what was to become the great bull market of the 1980s with a strong rally in August. The Federal funds rate fell to 10 percent by 18 August and to 9 percent just before the FOMC meeting on 24 August, at which time the tolerance range was reduced to 7–11 percent.

Monetary growth picked up considerably in August, with M1 and M2 rising at rates of 12 and 13 percent, respectively, and quite rapid monetary growth generally continued to the end of 1982 and throughout 1983. The Federal funds rate fell to 9 percent by the end of 1982 and generally ran in the range of 8.5–9.5 percent during 1983. The discount rate was cut five more times between 17 August and 17 December, down to a level of 8.5 percent, where it was held throughout 1983.

Thus, the very tight monetary policy that the Federal Reserve embarked on in November 1980 began to be reversed in July–August 1982—a year after the officially recognized starting date of the 1981–82 recession. Economic activity continued to decline until November 1982, with the unemployment rate rising ultimately to a peak of 10.8 percent. The demon of inflation, however, had finally been tamed. During the twelve months of 1982, the CPI rose only 3.8 percent, and the annual inflation rate would remain generally in the neighborhood of 4 percent through the rest of the decade.

2.4.4   The Rationale for Tight Money

In retrospect, it is clear that the prolonged tightening of monetary policy from late 1980 to mid-1982 was the most important action taken by the Federal Reserve during the 1980s and perhaps the most important monetary policy action since the catastrophic failure of the Federal Reserve to resist the monetary collapse of the early 1930s. Four important points should be discussed concerning the rationale for this policy.

First, an extended period of very tight money that would push the economy into deep and prolonged recession was not exactly the publicly announced intention of the Federal Reserve. Federal Reserve officials, especially Chairman Volcker, did indicate the need for a sustained and determined effort to combat inflation, even at the expense of considerable pain to the economy. However, in its semiannual "Monetary Reports to the Congress," the Federal Reserve usually suggested a more gradual approach to restoring stability to the general level of prices—an approach that was officially endorsed by the Reagan administration. In this regard, a passage from the "Monetary Policy Report" of 25 February 1981 is noteworthy:

> It is essential that monetary policy exert continuing resistance to inflationary forces. The growth of money and credit will need to be slowed to a rate consistent with the long-range growth of the nation's capacity to produce at reasonably stable prices. Realistically, given the structure of the economy, with the rigidities of contractual relationships and the natural lags in the adjustment process, that rate will have to be approached over a period of years if severe contractionary pressures on output and employment are to be avoided.

Second, while the Federal Reserve clearly did not pursue a policy that avoided severe contractionary pressures on the economy, it is arguable that no such policy would have achieved a substantial and sustained reduction of inflation. To succeed in the effort to reduce inflation, millions of private actors in the economy and in financial markets needed to be persuaded that inflation in the future would proceed at a substantially lower rate than in the past. Persuasion would be very difficult because, consistently for five years before 1981 and generally for the preceding ten years, people who had acted on the assumption that future inflation would be low turned out to be the economic losers whereas people who had acted on the assumption that future inflation would be high had been the economic winners.

Thus, to succeed in reducing inflation, the Federal Reserve had to establish its credibility as a consistent and effective warrior against the demon of inflation. Given the Federal Reserve's dismal record in restraining inflation since 1976, including the retreat of 1980, there was only one effective way for the Federal Reserve to demonstrate the anti-inflationary resolve of its monetary policy. The Federal Reserve had to show that, when faced with the painful choice between maintaining a tight monetary policy to fight inflation and easing monetary policy to combat recession, it would choose to fight inflation. In other words, to establish its credibility, the Federal Reserve had to demonstrate its willingness to spill blood, lots of blood, other people's blood.

Third, the Federal Reserve's tight monetary policy was partly the consequence of understandable and unavoidable miscalculation. The official record of the deliberations of the FOMC indicates that the likely depth and duration of the recession were consistently underestimated. To some extent, this tendency was probably a psychological correction for the FOMC's earlier errors in anticipating the 1979 recession that never quite materialized and in failing to appreciate the rapidity of the turnaround from recession to expansion in the summer of 1980. Outside the Federal Reserve, however, it was also widely believed that the 1981–82 recession would end five or six months sooner than it did—partly because of the expected expansionary effects of the Reagan administration's fiscal policy.

Moreover, judging the tightness or ease of monetary policy in the turbulent economic and financial conditions of 1981–82 was no easy task. There was a sharp downward shift in the velocities of circulation of various monetary aggregates that altered the significance of the growth rates of these aggregates as indicators of monetary policy. The occurrence and implications of substantial downward shifts in velocities were known and appreciated at the Federal Reserve. However, no one, including the Federal Reserve, had a firm basis for assessing precisely how much velocity shifted for different aggregates. In retrospect, knowing how much velocities did shift during 1981–82, the Federal Reserve's policy may now appear somewhat tighter than was reasonably understood or intended at the time. The Federal funds rate also became a less reliable indicator of monetary policy as market interest rates fluctuated with unprecedented volatility and as the anticipated inflation rate shifted downward to an extent that was extraordinarily difficult to evaluate. For understandable reasons, the Federal Reserve failed to appreciate how tight its policy really was,

in the context of a recession that turned out to be deeper and longer than originally anticipated.

Fourth, making due allowance for underestimates of the depth and duration
of the recession and for the difficulties in assessing the actual tightness of monetary policy, it is nevertheless clear that the Federal Reserve knowingly persisted in a very tight monetary policy for many months after the economy had
fallen into recession.[9] Indeed, as early as July 1981, with a year of tight monetary policy still in store, the forecasts presented to the FOMC pointed to a
deep and prolonged recession even under the most expansionary options for
monetary policy.[10] Having backed off from further monetary tightening during
much of 1979, and having reversed policy so rapidly and ignominiously in
1980, most members of the FOMC recognized that this time they had to hold
on to a tight policy until there was unmistakable evidence of real progress in
reducing inflation. The financial markets particularly, and the economy more
generally, were so sensitized by previous failures to control inflation that the
Federal Reserve perceived little latitude to ease monetary policy before the
summer of 1982.

2.4.5 An Excessively Tight Policy?

All things considered, it is still arguable that the Federal Reserve may have
kept monetary policy too tight for too long during 1982. Taking account of the
relatively high unemployment rate when the recession started and of the time
before recovery restored the economy to near its longer-term growth path, the
loss of output during the 1981–82 recession probably amounted to $200–$300
billion (in 1982 dollars), or possibly more.[11] As tends to be the case with long
and deep recessions, many workers and businesses never recovered an important part of the ground lost during this downturn. Other longer-term problems of the recession and the period of very high interest rates—notably the

9. The disparity between the Federal Reserve's rhetoric suggesting a gradualist approach to
combating inflation (discussed above) and its actual policy is not indicative of an effort to deceive
the public or the Congress. People well understood that the Federal Reserve's policy was very
tight, and it served the Federal Reserve's objectives to sustain this understanding. It was not polite
or politically astute, however, to be too explicit about the casualties that might result from the
Federal Reserve's policy or to contradict directly the administration's announced preference for a
gradualist approach.

10. At each meeting of the FOMC, analyses of the performance and prospects for the economy
are presented in the *Greenbook* and the *Bluebook*. The forecast presented to the FOMC at its
July 1981 meeting is discussed explicitly in Karamousis and Lombra (1989). The most optimistic
scenario presented for consideration by the FOMC envisioned an 8.3 percent average unemployment rate for 1982 and an 8.8 percent average unemployment rate for 1983.

11. The Hodrick-Prescott filter used to construct the smoothed trend path for real GNP in fig.
2.1 above indicates that real GNP barely fell below this trend during the recession of 1980 and
was significantly above this trend in mid-1981. Using deviations from the Hodrick-Prescott trend
to measure the output loss from the 1981–82 recession results in a comparatively small measured
loss—about $200 billion. If the loss is measured relative to a trend passing through the actual level
of real GNP during the second quarter of 1981, the loss is significantly larger—about $300 billion.

continuing problems of the savings and loan industry—are still of pressing importance in the United States. Other countries, particularly in Latin America, also felt and are still feeling the consequences of high interest rates and recession in the United States during the early 1980s. Moreover, given the fragile state of the U.S. financial system by the summer of 1982, avoidance of an even more serious economic downturn should be regarded as a fortunate outcome.

Of course, only a modest fraction of the cost of the recession of 1981–82 (and of associated economic problems) can be attributed to excessive and inappropriate tightness of monetary policy. Most of the cost is properly attributed to the necessity of combating the virulent inflation that was, in substantial measure, the consequence of previous laxity of monetary policy. Also, other factors such as the second oil price shock probably contributed in important ways to the length and depth of the recession. Nevertheless, if a somewhat less tight monetary policy during 1982 would have shortened the recession by even three or four months, without sacrificing a great deal of the progress in reducing inflation, it would have been a more desirable policy.

The difficulty is knowing at what point the Federal Reserve could have moved to a somewhat easier policy without provoking an adverse reaction by raising fears of future inflation. This problem clearly influenced the policy followed by the Federal Reserve, as expressed in the Federal Reserve's "Monetary Policy Report to the Congress" of 20 July 1982:

> Unfortunately, these stresses [of the recession] cannot be easily remedied through accelerated money growth. The immediate effect of encouraging faster growth in money might be lower interest rates, especially in short-term markets. In time, however, the attempt to drive interest rates lower through a substantial reacceleration of money growth would founder, for the result would be to embed inflation and expectations of inflation even more deeply into the nation's economic system. It would mean that this recession was another wasted painful episode instead of a transition to a sustained improvement in the economic environment.

Ironically, this statement is phrased as an expression of the Federal Reserve's future intentions rather than as a justification of its past actions. On the very day that this statement was released, the Federal Reserve cut the discount rate from 12 to 11.5 percent, signaling the beginning of what would become a four-and-a-half-year period of quite rapid monetary expansion. During this period, interest rates, both short and long term, would be driven significantly lower, and the U.S. economy would substantially recover from the devastation of both inflation and recession. By July 1982, enough blood had been spilled that the credibility of the Federal Reserve's anti-inflationary policy was established. Now, the economy generally, and the financial markets particularly, would sigh in relief or cheer in ecstasy, rather than shriek in terror, at the fact and prospect of a substantially easier monetary policy.

2.5 Savoring the Fruits of Victory

The victory over inflation and the obviously distressed state of the American economy were the key considerations leading to the Federal Reserve's shift to an easier monetary policy. Insofar as political considerations influenced the Federal Reserve's decision, these considerations all weighed in favor of the new policy. Concerned about the prolonged and deepening recession, many officials of the Reagan administration had been arguing for some time in favor of an easier monetary policy. On Capitol Hill, despite the upcoming congressional elections, monetary policy was not an issue of partisan dispute. Prominent legislators from both parties had been pressing for an easier policy since late 1981. Indeed, some Democrats were pushing legislation that would have limited the independence of the Federal Reserve and required the pursuit of an easier, lower-interest-rate monetary policy.[12]

As previously discussed, the Federal Reserve responded to criticism of its tight monetary policy by pointing to the necessity of maintaining a firm stance against the resurgence of inflation. In addition, Chairman Volcker and other members of the FOMC argued that the large and growing federal deficit was an important cause of high interest rates and that serious efforts to cut the deficit were essential to reduce interest rates without reigniting inflation. The evidence supporting this view was, and remains, somewhat ambiguous. Nevertheless, there is no doubt that the Federal Reserve's concern over the effect of the deficit on interest rates was genuine and that this concern was widely shared outside the Federal Reserve, especially in the financial community. The Tax Equity and Fiscal Responsibility Act (TEFRA) of 1982, which sought to reduce the federal deficit by partially reversing the tax cuts of 1981, was passed by Congress in mid-August. There is no clear evidence, however, that the passage of TEFRA was instrumental in persuading the Federal Reserve to ease monetary policy or that it played a particularly important role in the subsequent decline of interest rates.

2.5.1 Problems in the Financial System

In addition to concerns about the general health of the economy, it does appear that the Federal Reserve's shift to an easier monetary policy was influenced by specific concerns about the stability of the banking and financial system. In late June 1982, Federal Reserve officials learned that the Penn Square National Bank of Oklahoma City was on the verge of failure. The failure of Penn Square, with its prospective losses to depositors, was publicly announced on 5 July. It sent tremors through the banking system—tremors to which the Federal Reserve was very sensitive—as other banks and their uninsured depositors and other uninsured creditors worried who might be next.

---

12. As on other issues concerning political influences on the Federal Reserve, an excellent discussion of the events of 1981–82 is provided in Greider (1987).

Of even greater importance, Federal Reserve officials were aware at least as early as June 1982 that the government of Mexico was experiencing considerable difficulties in arranging new financing for a large volume of commercial bank loans coming due during the summer. Many of the largest banks in the country were important creditors of the Mexican government, and Mexico was not the only country with large loans from U.S. banks that was in obvious economic difficulty. Default by the Mexican government would be a financial bombshell that could easily provoke a nationwide banking and financial crisis. On the thirteenth of August—appropriately a Friday—the Mexican finance minister Jesus Silva Herzog arrived at the U.S. Treasury and at the Federal Reserve with the sad news that the Mexican government's coffers were empty and that default would occur the following week. A large bailout package was arranged over the weekend, and default was avoided. However, the message remained clear—the banking system was in serious jeopardy unless something substantial was done soon to stimulate economic recovery.

2.5.2   Full Speed Ahead

As previously discussed, the Federal Reserve began to ease monetary policy in July 1982 and pushed hard in the direction of easing from August through December 1982. With the shift to a much easier monetary policy, M2 and M3 rose from somewhat below to somewhat above the upper limits of their target ranges. M1 began to grow at about twice the maximum targeted rate and rose well above the upper limit of its target range by year's end. Since interest rates fell dramatically during this period, and since M2 and M3 contain more interest sensitive elements than M1, the relative behavior of these aggregates was not surprising. Nevertheless, during the fall of 1982, the behavior of M1 was becoming an embarrassment to the Federal Reserve; it was indicating far too clearly that the Federal Reserve had given up on the monetary targets announced in February (and reaffirmed in July) in order to pursue a much easier policy.

At the FOMC meeting on 5 October 1982, this problem was solved by deciding that, "because the behavior of M1 over the balance of the year is subject to unusually great uncertainties," a short-term target for growth of M1 would no longer be used as an operational guide for the execution of monetary policy. Instead, a short-term growth target for M2 (and M3) in the range of around 8.5–9.5 percent at an annual rate from September to December was the officially stated guide for the manager of the Open Market Desk. The expiration of all savers certificates in October and the introduction of money market demand accounts (MMDAs) in December were discussed as reasons for especially great uncertainty about the behavior of M1. It is noteworthy, however, that, when M1 grew unusually rapidly during January 1982 because of growth in its OCD component, the FOMC did not choose to ignore M1. At that time, the FOMC wanted to continue a quite tight monetary policy, and the behavior of M1 provided a plausible rationale for continuing such a policy. In October, when the behavior of M1 was becoming an impediment to the FOMC's desire to ease monetary policy, M1 got dumped as an effective monetary target.

During the autumn of 1982, not only was M1 dumped as a target for monetary policy, but the whole procedure of using monetary growth targets as the operational guide for monetary policy instituted in October 1979 was effectively abandoned. The Federal Reserve returned to operating procedures similar to those employed in the 1950s and 1960s, when monetary policy indirectly targeted the level of the Federal funds rate. Under the procedures used from October 1982 until the late 1980s, the FOMC determined the "degree of restraint" or "degree of pressure" to apply to the reserve position of banks, as calibrated by the extent to which banks needed to come to the Federal Reserve's discount window to borrow reserves.

Given the level of the discount rate and the policies of the Federal Reserve that control borrowing at the discount window, there is a relatively precise relation between the amount of borrowing and the level of the Federal funds rate. In the official language of the directive, "maintaining the existing degree of restraint (or pressure) on bank reserves" means holding the Federal funds rate constant, "increasing the degree of pressure" means raising the Federal funds rate, and "reducing the degree of pressure" means reducing the Federal funds rate. However, since the relation between the "pressure on reserves" and the Federal funds rate is not exact and constant, there is more room for the funds rate to move around under indirect targeting than was the case under the direct targeting procedures used in the late 1970s. (Recently, since 1987, the operating procedures appear to have moved back toward direct targeting of the funds rate, but there has been no official announcement of such a change.)

During 1983, the FOMC observed what was going on in the economy: a vigorous recovery of business activity with no sign of increasing inflation. With good reason, it liked what it saw. When the year was over, real GNP had risen by 6.5 percent (fourth quarter to fourth quarter), the unemployment rate had fallen 2.5 percentage points, and the twelve-month gain in the CPI was only 3.8 percent. On fifteen occasions, the Board of Governors turned down requests from Reserve banks for changes in the discount rate and held the discount rate constant at 8.5 percent. Throughout the year, the FOMC directed only slight changes in the degree of restraint on bank reserves, and the Federal funds rate moved narrowly (by the standards of recently preceding years) within the range of 8.5–9.5 percent.

The behavior of the monetary aggregates was monitored and discussed by the FOMC during 1983, but that behavior exerted little apparent influence on decisions concerning the degree of pressure on bank reserves. The deemphasis of the M2 growth target early in the year was officially rationalized by the instabilities created by the introduction of MMDAs. Rapid growth of MMDAs accounted for much of the very rapid growth of M2 during the first quarter of 1983. Following its decision of October 1982, the FOMC also ignored the very rapid growth of M1 throughout 1983, and it only "monitored" the behavior of this aggregate.

2.5.3   An Interval of Tightening

In January and February 1984, the Federal Reserve maintained the same policy stance that it had adopted in 1983. The degree of pressure on bank reserves kept the Federal funds rate close to 9.5 percent. In a telephone conference on 20 March 1984, the FOMC discussed recent increases in market interest rates and noted that "economic activity in most sectors was rising with considerable momentum, helping to generate strong demands for credit." The committee decided to relax informally the 10 percent upper limit of the tolerance range for the Federal funds rate. Subsequently, the tolerance range for the Federal funds rate was raised to 7.5–11.5 percent (at the FOMC meeting on 26–27 March) and to 8–12 percent (at the FOMC meeting on 16–17 July). The discount rate was raised from 8.5 to 9 percent on 6 April. The actual level of the funds rate was kept between 10 and 10.5 percent through June, then raised gradually to slightly over 11.5 percent in August, and then eased down to around 11 percent in late September.

The primary reason for the brief tightening of monetary policy from late March through September 1984 was the worry that continued rapid economic expansion was raising the risks of an acceleration of inflation. Estimates of real GNP growth indicated about a 9 percent real growth rate during the first quarter of 1984 and a still very rapid 7.5 percent rate of advance during the second quarter. When it became clear that the pace of expansion slowed considerably during the summer of 1984 and continued to be relatively sluggish during the fourth quarter, the Federal Reserve moved aggressively (but with some dissent within the FOMC) to reverse the monetary tightening of the period March–September. In October, the Federal funds rate was pushed down to 10 percent. In November, and again in December, the FOMC gave explicit directives to ease pressures on bank reserves, and the tolerance range for the Federal funds rate was reduced to 6–10 percent. The discount rate was cut to 8.5 percent on 21 November and then to 8 percent on 21 December. By year's end, the Federal funds rate had been pushed slightly below 8.5 percent.

In the official record of the FOMC's discussions of monetary policy during 1984, considerable attention is devoted to the behavior of monetary aggregates, with M1 being resurrected to a status of some importance. After a year and a half of rapid monetary growth and a full year of economic recovery, the Federal Reserve wished to maintain the hard-won credibility of its anti-inflation policy by indicating a more serious commitment to its monetary growth targets. When problems arose at the Continental Illinois National Bank during the spring and summer, the Federal Reserve sought to persuade financial markets that aid to Continental would not push the aggregates off target. Indeed, figures 2.2 and 2.3 above and figures 2.8 and 2.9 reveal that 1984 is the only year

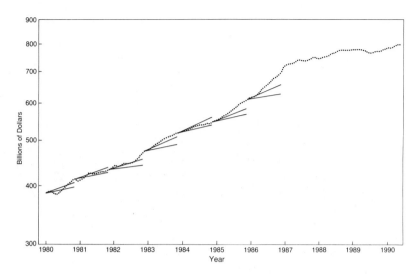

Fig. 2.8   M1 and growth target ranges, January 1980–April 1990
Note: The monetary targets are those established by the FOMC at the beginning of each year for annual growth rates.

in the entire history of monetary targeting by the Federal Reserve when both M1 and M2 ended the year near the midpoints of their respective target ranges.

During most of the 1980s, efforts to achieve the monetary growth targets, especially for M2, had some impact on the conduct of monetary policy. In fact, except for the aberration rationalized by introduction of MMDAs in early 1983, M2 ended each year of the 1980s within or very close to its announced target range. However, the target range was relatively broad, and the record indicates that achieving growth near to the midpoint of the range did not outweigh the actual and prospective performance of the economy as a dominant determinant of Federal Reserve policy.

Of course, 1984 was a presidential election year. Some in the administration were not particularly happy that the Federal Reserve embarked on a monetary tightening seven months before the election. Their concerns were more than narrowly political. Many monetarists believed that sharp changes in rates of growth of monetary aggregates were an important cause of economic instability. While they worried that the rapid money growth from October 1982 through 1983 might stimulate increased inflation, they also feared that too sharp a monetary slowdown might abort the economic recovery. Such concerns about changes in the rates of growth of monetary aggregates, however, were a bit too esoteric for most of the financial community and the press. By pursuing its announced monetary targets, the Federal Reserve probably helped insulate

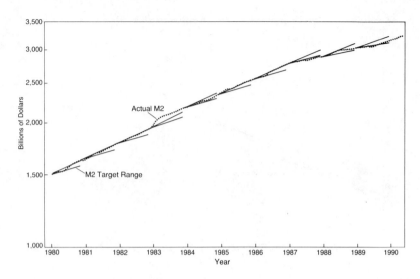

Fig. 2.9   M2 and growth target ranges, January 1980–April 1990

Note: The monetary targets are those established by the FOMC at the beginning of each year for annual growth rates.

itself from monetarist criticism. Thus, there was a marriage of convenience between the monetary tightening that the FOMC believed to be economically appropriate and the conscientious pursuit of its monetary growth targets.

In the latter part of 1984, an additional concern began to influence Federal Reserve policy: the extraordinary appreciation of the U.S. dollar against foreign currencies and the actual and prospective deterioration in the U.S. trade and current account balances. The dollar appreciated consistently, with only occasional small reversals, from the summer of 1980 until it reached its peak in early 1985. By late 1983, on a trade-weighted basis, adjusted for relative movements in national price levels, the real foreign exchange value of the dollar against other major currencies had risen about 45 percent from its low in the summer of 1980. At the Federal Reserve, and in the administration, most of this appreciation was regarded as a favorable development since a strong dollar helped reduce inflationary pressures. By the summer of 1984, the dollar had appreciated about another 10 percent in real terms, and it continued to appreciate in the autumn (rising a further 10 percent by the time of the peak in early 1985). At this point, the exceptionally strong dollar became a major concern in discussions about monetary policy, as indicated in the official record of the FOMC meeting on 21 December 1984:

> As they had at previous meetings, the members gave a good deal of attention to the effects of the continued strength of the dollar in foreign exchange markets. The related surge in imports was having a very negative impact on production in many domestic industries, while expansion of exports was be-

ing curbed by the appreciated value of the dollar as well as by relatively slow economic growth abroad.

The directive from this FOMC meeting specifically refers to "the continued strength of the dollar in foreign exchange markets" as a factor that should lead to further easing of monetary policy.

2.5.4   A Return to Easy Money

During 1985 and 1986, conditions in the economy, rather than the behavior of the monetary aggregates, continued to dominate Federal Reserve actions concerning the Federal funds rate and the discount rate. On balance, monetary policy was quite expansionary, in an environment of subdued inflation and moderate economic growth.

Specifically, in early 1985, concerns about the strong dollar and evidence that suggested a significant weakening of economic expansion (following a modest pickup in the fourth quarter of 1984) counterbalanced concerns about rapid expansion of the monetary aggregates. The Federal funds rate was kept in a relatively narrow range near 8.5 percent through the first four months of the year. As available evidence continued to indicate a very weak first quarter and a quite sluggish second quarter, the Federal funds rate was reduced to 8 percent in May and fell briefly to near 7 percent during June before returning to about 8 percent at the end of the month. The discount rate was cut from 8 to 7.5 percent on 17 May.

Nothing in the behavior of the monetary aggregates plausibly rationalized these adjustments. During the first half of 1985, M1 grew significantly above the upper limit of its target range, while M2 grew above and then along the upper limit of its target range. Moreover, revised data would ultimately show (years later) that economic growth had been considerably more vigorous during the first half of 1985, especially during the first quarter, than was believed at the time.

During the second half of 1985, the contemporaneously available evidence generally pointed to a moderate pace of economic expansion after a very slow first half. There were, however, mixed signals from different economic indicators, and there was some division among members of the FOMC concerning the prospects for future growth. Indicators of inflation generally showed the lowest rates of the 1980s, until modest upturns were reported in November and December. Despite persistent rapid growth of M1 above its target range and growth of M2 along the upper limit of its range, the FOMC decided not to increase the pressure on bank reserve positions from July through December and made one decision to ease slightly at its meeting in November. The Federal funds rate was maintained near 8 percent from July until December, when it rose briefly and marginally to about 8.25 percent.

International concern about the strong foreign exchange value of the dollar and its effects on payments imbalances and protectionist pressures led to the

Plaza Agreement of 22 September 1985. In this agreement, the finance ministers and central bank governors of the G-5 countries (France, Japan, the United Kingdom, the United States, and West Germany) announced their intention of seeking a somewhat lower foreign exchange value of the U.S. dollar and of pursuing other measures to reduce payments imbalances.

The Plaza Agreement, however, had little direct effect on U.S. monetary policy. In the months before the agreement, the FOMC had been concerned with the strong dollar, and this concern was one factor that probably contributed to decisions not to raise the degree of pressure on bank reserve positions despite rapid growth of the monetary aggregates (especially M1). After the Plaza, similar concerns contributed to similar decisions. On the other hand, throughout the period, the FOMC was alert to the danger that a precipitous drop in the dollar might contribute to inflationary pressures or erode the confidence of foreign investors whose capital was essential to finance the U.S. payments deficit. Especially late in 1985 and early in 1986, this concern provided a countervailing argument against efforts to ease the degree of pressure on bank reserves.

In early 1986, a division developed within the FOMC, and especially within the Board of Governors, concerning the advisability of further easing of monetary policy. Believing that the pace of expansion was becoming very sluggish and that dangers of a resurgence of inflation were remote, the four Reagan appointees to the Board of Governors favored some further easing. The three other governors, including Chairman Volcker, and most of the Federal Reserve bank presidents on the FOMC were unpersuaded of the need for further easing and feared the possible consequences for the dollar. On 24 February 1986, by a four-to-three vote, with Chairman Volcker in the minority, the Board of Governors approved the request of the Dallas Federal Reserve Bank to reduce its discount rate by half a percentage point.

At a meeting later the same day, this decision was rescinded by unanimous vote of the Board. The Board's *Annual Report* contains the following explanation of the shift: "Members who favored a reduction of the discount rate on domestic grounds decided that a delay of limited duration would be acceptable, given the outlook for easing actions by at least some other major central banks during the next couple of weeks, if not within the next few days." It should be added that a number of requests for discount rate cuts were made by Federal Reserve banks in January and February 1986 and were rejected by the Board of Governors. Acceptance of these requests would probably not have been enormously troubling to domestic or international financial markets. An open split of the Board of Governors that undercut the authority of the chairman, however, would have been quite a different matter.

The key economic event of 1986 was the dramatic drop in world oil prices and its impact on both inflation and economic activity. Reflecting the sharp decline in energy prices, the CPI fell in February, March, and April. For the twelve months of 1986, consumer prices rose only 1.1 percent, compared with

3.8 percent in 1985, 3.9 percent in 1984, and 3.8 percent in 1983. Economic activity in the energy-producing states was strongly negatively effected by the drop in oil prices. In addition, many U.S. manufacturing industries were continuing to feel the adverse impact of the strong dollar. As the data came in during the year, they indicated moderate real growth during the first quarter, a very sluggish second quarter, and then stronger but still relatively slow growth during the second half. Years later, revised estimates of real GNP would show a 6.6 percent growth rate for the first quarter, a −1.8 percent growth rate in the second quarter, a 0.8 percent growth rate in the third quarter, and a modest 2.3 percent growth rate in the fourth quarter. These figures, however, were not the estimates on which the Federal Reserve depended in deciding on monetary policy.

As evidence of the effects of the oil price decline became available, the Federal Reserve responded with actions to reduce interest rates. In coordination with other important central banks, the discount rate was cut half a percentage point to 7 percent on 6 March. Further half percentage point cuts were authorized on 18 April, 10 July, and 20 August, bringing the discount rate down ultimately to 5.5 percent—its lowest level for the decade. The FOMC directed or permitted substantial reductions in the Federal funds rate from slightly above 8 percent in January, to slightly below 7 percent in June, and then to 6 percent or slightly lower for July–November. Because of an extraordinary bulge of demand for transactions balances associated with provisions of the Tax Reform Act, the funds rate spiked up to nearly 9 percent for a few days in December but fell back to 6 percent in early January 1987.

In taking these actions, the Federal Reserve was often responding to developments in credit markets rather than leading market interest rates downward. In this regard, it is noteworthy that, between January and July, yields on longer-term Treasury bonds and notes fell more than either yields on three-month Treasury bills or the Federal funds rate. Except for the last downward step on 20 August, the reductions in the discount rate were clearly needed to catch up with developments that had already occurred in credit markets.

On the other hand, the Federal Reserve did not strongly resist declines in market interest rates during the first half of 1986 and did not act to push interest rates upward as the monetary growth accelerated in the second half. Specifically, except for a brief period early in the year, M1 consistently grew well above the upper limit of its target range, and it ended 1986 with more than double the maximum prescribed growth of 8 percent. M2 briefly fell slightly below the lower (6 percent) limit of its desired growth range during the first quarter but then accelerated to reach the (9 percent) upper limit of its range by year's end. M3 grew along the 9 percent upper limit of its desired range for essentially the entire year.

Judged either by growth rates of monetary aggregates or by the behavior of interest rates, monetary policy was quite expansionary during 1986—for the second year in a row. Thanks to the drop in oil prices, however, real economic growth slowed temporarily during 1986 (with a sharp downturn in energy-producing states), and the overall inflation rate (including energy prices) declined to the lowest level since the early 1960s. Thus, at the end of 1986, the U.S. economy had enjoyed four years of business expansion and five years with the annual inflation rate remaining at or below 4 percent.

It should be added that economic activity expanded very vigorously during 1987 and that, despite the stock market crash of October 1987, expansion continued at a fairly rapid pace during 1988. With the slowing of the growth of real consumption spending and real government spending, improvements in net exports and in investment were the keys to continued overall growth. Specifically, in late 1986, U.S. real exports, which had shown no net growth since 1980, began to expand rapidly, recording a 50 percent rise during the next four years. The gain in exports also helped spark significant increases in real business investment in plant and equipment. The expansionary monetary policy of 1985–86, operating through the exchange rate as well as through interest rates, was an important contributing cause to these developments. This same expansionary monetary policy was probably also a key underlying cause of the increase of inflationary pressures during the late 1980s.

2.5.5   A Flexible and Credible Policy

For four and a half years, beginning in the summer of 1982, the monetary aggregates grew, on average, quite rapidly—at rates that in the late 1970s would have implied very rapid inflation. Clearly, there were important shifts during this period in the relations between the growth of monetary aggregates and the growth of nominal GNP. To some extent, these shifts could be understood as responses of demands for various monetary aggregates to changes in interest rates or to changes in interest elasticities of demands for these aggregates arising from banking regulations and the introduction of new forms of deposits. In any event, on the whole, the Federal Reserve made appropriate judgments about the nature and magnitude of these shifts. It provided monetary growth sufficiently rapid to support vigorous economic expansion without generating increased inflationary pressures—at least not pressures that became apparent before the end of 1986.

Moreover, the Federal Reserve was able to sustain quite rapid monetary growth over an extended period without generating intense fears it was fueling a resurgence of rapid inflation—fears that might have necessitated a monetary tightening that would have cut short the business expansion. Thus, in the bloodbath of the 1981–82 recession, and in the brief monetary tightening during 1984, the Federal Reserve had firmly established its credibility as an inflation fighter. It was then able to utilize this credibility to pursue a more flexible monetary policy to promote economic expansion from late 1982 through 1986.

2.6 Keeping the Demon at Bay

During the final three years of the 1980s, with one brief interlude, the general stance of monetary policy shifted from fueling economic expansion to resisting the rise of inflation. The move to tighten monetary policy began early in 1987 and continued until the stock market crash on 19 October. For the next five months, monetary policy was primarily directed at reducing instability in financial markets and avoiding recession. Beginning in late March 1988, amid signs of continued economic expansion and with some indications of rising inflationary pressures, monetary policy became progressively tighter until June 1989. Subsequently, while the growth of monetary aggregates remained quite sluggish, the Federal Reserve eased the Federal funds rate gradually downward. During this three-year period, as was the case earlier, developments in the economy, rather than the behavior of the monetary aggregates, exerted the decisive influence on Federal Reserve decisions about the Federal funds rate and the discount rate.

2.6.1 A Move toward Tightening

More specifically, during the winter of 1987, the Federal funds rate remained at essentially the same level as during the fall of 1986. With the Louvre Accord on 22 February, resistance to further significant depreciation of the dollar became an officially stated policy of the U.S. government. At its meeting on 31 March, the FOMC devoted "a good deal of attention . . . to the implications of the currently strong downward pressure on the dollar in foreign exchange markets." The committee agreed that "the conduct of open market operations needed to be especially sensitive to any tendency for the dollar to weaken significantly further." During April, the Federal funds rate was pushed up about fifty basis points, apparently to support internationally coordinated efforts to resist further dollar depreciation. At the regular meeting on 19 May 1987, the FOMC agreed that "open market operations . . . would be directed toward some degree of reserve pressure beyond that sought in recent weeks (but not necessarily greater than that prevailing recently)." This action was motivated both by concern about the recent increase in inflation (the CPI rose at a 5.9 percent annual rate between December and March) and by continuing worries about the dollar.

During the first six months of 1987, growth of all the monetary aggregates slowed considerably from the rapid pace set in 1985 and 1986. The slowdown in January and February reflected the collapse of the year-end bulge of demand for transactions balances generated by the Tax Reform Act, but the slow growth in later months suggested significant tightening of monetary policy. Specifically, by the end of June, M2 was well below the lower limit of the 5.5–8.5 percent growth range established by the FOMC, and M3 was near to the lower limit of its 5.5–8.5 percent desired growth range. For the first half of 1987, M1 grew at a 5.1 percent annual rate, nearly 11 percentage points below its growth rate during 1986. For the FOMC, which had abandoned targets for M1 for 1987, this slowdown may have had little significance. However, for monetarists who focus on changes in the growth rates of monetary aggregates as a key indicator of shifts in the stance of monetary policy, it was important further evidence of a substantial tightening of monetary policy.

From June through mid-August, the dollar recovered slightly and then stabilized in foreign exchange markets, owing apparently to more favorable news about the U.S. trade balance. Available data showed that the U.S. economy was continuing to expand at a moderate pace. Recent price data showed that inflation had fallen off somewhat from the relatively high rates of the first quarter. Also, it became increasingly apparent that the federal deficit would register a large decline for the fiscal year ending on 30 September. Reflecting this good news on all fronts, stock prices continued to rise, with the Dow Jones industrial average recording a peak of 2,722 on 25 August. In this brief period of calm before the storm, on 11 August 1987, Alan Greenspan replaced Paul Volcker as chairman of the Federal Reserve Board.

2.6.2 The Crash

In late August, disappointing news about the U.S. trade balance, together with firming in foreign interest rates, brought the dollar under renewed downward pressure. Market interest rates in the United States moved up in sympathy with foreign interest rates and also (it appeared) in anticipation of tightening by the Federal Reserve. On 4 September, the Board of Governors raised the discount rate from 5.5 to 6 percent. Pressures on bank reserves were also increased at this time, and the Federal funds rate was pushed up about fifty basis points to slightly over 7 percent. At the FOMC meeting on 22 September, this increase in the funds rate was affirmed with a directive calling for maintenance of "the degree of pressure on reserve positions sought in recent weeks" and with an increase in the tolerance range for the Federal funds rate from 4–8 percent to 5–9 percent. These actions were taken with M2 substantially below the lower limit of its target range and with M3 slightly below the lower limit of its range. Available information indicated continued, moderately strong business expansion. There was no direct evidence of any significant acceleration of inflation, but recent declines in unemployment and increases in rates of capacity utilization raised worries that inflation might accelerate.

Short-term interest rates in Japan and West Germany moved further upward in late September and the first half of October. The Federal funds rate moved up to 7.26 percent for the week ending on Wednesday, 23 September, then up to 7.56 percent for the week ending on 30 September, then down to 7.43 percent for the week ending on 7 October, then up to 7.59 percent for the week ending on 14 October, and finally up to 7.76 percent on Thursday and Friday of that week. These increases in the Federal funds rate were not mandated by the FOMC directive of 22 September. The explanation given in the official record of the FOMC meeting of 3 November 1987 states that computer problems at a Reserve bank contributed to an exceptional increase in member bank borrowing (and hence in the funds rate) during the period from 22 September to 2 October. With respect to the behavior of the Federal funds for 5–16 October, the official record states, "Federal funds and other interest rates subsequently rose through mid-October as market participants appeared to anticipate monetary tightening in an environment of firmer policy abroad, concerns about the dollar, and pessimism about the prospects for domestic inflation."

Thus, the Federal Reserve claims to have done nothing explicit to tighten monetary policy further during the two weeks immediately before 19 October. Indisputably, however, the Federal Reserve allowed market participants "to anticipate monetary tightening" when it could surely have disabused them of such anticipations. Moreover, the actions of the Federal Reserve earlier in 1987 clearly made such anticipations of monetary tightening entirely rational.

The first paragraph of the lead story of the *Wall Street Journal* on Tuesday, 20 October 1987, succinctly and accurately describes the event of the preceding day: "The stock market crashed yesterday." Three months later, while serving as a member of the Council of Economic Advisers, I received a note from an able, intelligent, and normally sensible member of the White House staff suggesting that the word *crash,* which appeared many times in the description of the main macroeconomic events of 1987, be deleted entirely from the 1988 *Economic Report of the President.* Thus, while the Federal Reserve wished to deny (perhaps accurately) that it had done anything explicit to bring on the stock market crash, some in the administration wished to deny that the crash had occurred at all.

The apparent tightening of monetary policy in early October was surely one of several economic fundamentals that contributed to the 400-point slide in the Dow Jones Industrial Average during the two weeks before the crash, including the 108-point drop on Friday, 16 October. The 508-point drop in the Dow on Monday, 19 October, however, is not plausibly explained by economic fundamentals. It reflected pure panic.[13] Moreover, knowing now that the crash had a relatively benign outcome, it might even be argued that monetary tightening in the weeks before the crash helped restore a sense of reality to a stock market that had risen significantly beyond the level justified by economic fundamentals.

2.6.3 Aftermath

In any case, the response of monetary policy to the crash was massive, immediate, and appropriate. A terse public statement, released on the morning of Tuesday, 20 October, stated, "The Federal Reserve, consistent with its respon-

---

13. An opinion survey of financial market participants concerning the causes of the stock market crash was conducted for the Brady Commission. The results (summarized in the commission report) indicated that "economic fundamentals," including increases in interest rates, were key factors in generating the slide in stock prices during the two weeks before the crash. The crash itself, however, was attributed to panic in the marketplace.

sibilities as the nation's central bank, affirmed today its readiness to serve as a source of liquidity to support the economic and financial system." In the morning and early afternoon of 20 October, the Open Market Desk pumped $17 billion into the banking system—an amount equivalent to more than 25 percent of bank reserves and 7 percent of the monetary base. The Federal Reserve also let commercial banks know that it expected banks to continue to supply credit to other participants in the financial system, including loans to broker-dealers to carry their inventories of securities.

After a further, sickening decline on Tuesday morning, stock prices miraculously turned upward in the afternoon, and the Dow closed the day with a 102-point gain. Violent oscillations in stock prices continued through the week and, indeed, for the remainder of 1987. However, by Friday, 24 October, intense worry and nervousness replaced uncontrolled panic as the dominant mood in financial markets. As things calmed down and the crisis demand for liquidity subsided, the Federal Reserve withdrew most of the high-powered money that it had injected on 20 October. To avoid adding to turbulence in financial markets, it did so in a manner that kept the Federal funds rate very stable at about 6.75 percent—a drop of 1 percentage point from the level just before the crash.

The decline in stock market prices between August and late October reduced the value of marketable assets held by Americans by approximately $1 trillion. Since much of this wealth loss represented a reversal of gains made earlier during 1987 (and not yet fully incorporated in consumer spending), at the Council of Economic Advisers (CEA) we estimated that the direct negative effect of the decline in wealth on consumer demand would most probably be in the range of $25–$30 billion. The CEA projected that the effect on the economy would be about a 1 percent reduction of real GNP below the path that it would otherwise have followed during the next three or four quarters. With exports expected to contribute significantly to demand for U.S. products (the heritage of the decline in the dollar since early 1985), real GNP was officially forecast to rise by 2.4 percent during 1988. If achieved, such growth would be a not entirely unwelcome slowdown from the rapid pace of economic advance during 1987. However, at least at the CEA, two conditions were thought to be critical in order to achieve such a favorable outcome: avoidance of a further sharp drop in stock and bond prices and a monetary policy that was adequately supportive of economic expansion.

The FOMC anticipated that the lowering of pressures on bank reserves and the reduction in the Federal funds rate in the period immediately following the crash would lead to more rapid growth of the monetary aggregates. The operating procedures adopted by the Federal Reserve in the aftermath of the crash, however, placed little emphasis on achieving projected growth rates for monetary aggregates. Instead, they focused on maintaining stable conditions in money markets, which effectively amounted to pegging the Federal funds rate within a narrow range close to 6.75 percent.

In the event, the Federal Reserve's operating procedure delivered very slow growth of the monetary aggregates during the ten weeks following the crash. M1 actually declined at about a 4 percent annual rate during November and December, while M2 and M3 grew at rates of about 1.5 and 3 percent, respectively. At least at the CEA, there was considerable concern that monetary policy was not doing enough to forestall the possible negative effects of the crash on economic activity. The concern on the other side (as expressed in the "Record" of the FOMC) was that any visible move to ease monetary policy further by lowering the Federal funds rate "would not be desirable currently, especially in the light of the dollar's weakness and the risks to domestic financial markets and the economy that a sharp further decline in the dollar would incur."

The decline in U.S. interest rates relative to interest rates in Japan and West Germany after the crash did contribute to a modest decline of the dollar in late October. Disappointing news about the U.S. trade balance and the U.S. government's apparent laissez-faire attitude toward the dollar contributed to a further 8 percent decline in the dollar by year's end. Clearly, the Federal Reserve's intent was not to resist these declines in the dollar. Rather it was to avoid the risk of instigating an international financial crisis by permitting a reduction in the Federal funds rate that might be interpreted as an explicit attempt to drive down the dollar.

Since the Federal Reserve did not reduce the Federal funds rate further to stimulate modestly stronger monetary growth, we do not know whether there was really any serious danger that such a move would generate an international financial crisis. On the other hand, since a modest increase in inflationary pressures, rather than recession, turned out to be the main macroeconomic development of 1988, it does not appear that more rapid monetary growth was really essential during the weeks following the stock market crash. In retrospect, therefore, the Federal Reserve appears to have acted wisely in not pushing the Federal funds rate further downward in order to achieve more rapid monetary growth at the end of 1987.

Economic data available from late October through mid-December indicated that the economy was continuing to expand at a moderate pace during the period before the crash but provided little information about postcrash developments. Data for the automobile industry, however, did show a sharp downturn in sales and a buildup in inventories. When estimates of fourth-quarter GNP did become available in January 1988, they indicated that real GNP had continued to grow at a moderate pace but that much of this growth was accounted for by inventory accumulation rather than by growth of final sales—a signal of future weakness in business activity. Meanwhile, the growth rates of monetary aggregates picked up considerably in January, while the dollar recovered somewhat in foreign exchange markets. The Federal Reserve reacted to these developments by reducing the pressure on bank reserves and easing the Federal funds rate downward by about twenty-five basis points to just over 6.5 percent. Subsequently, the dollar declined slightly against some foreign currencies, but this appeared to be more in response to poorer-than-expected trade figures rather than to the slight easing in the funds rate.

2.6.4   A Return to Tighter Money

By the FOMC meeting on 29 March, recent data showed that the economy was growing more strongly than previously anticipated. Concern was expressed about prospects for prices and wages, but "aggregate measures of prices and wages had not yet shown any sustained tendency to accelerate." Monetary growth (except for M1) had remained relatively robust since January. In this environment, the FOMC directed "a slight increase in the degree of pressure on reserve positions." It also decided to continue the shift (begun in January) of the operating procedures toward achieving the desired degree of pressure on bank reserves rather than placing special emphasis on maintaining stable conditions in the money markets.

The trend of monetary policy established at the FOMC meeting on 29 March continued through the remainder of 1988 and the first half of 1989. Economic data indicated that the expansion was continuing, although generally at a somewhat slower pace as time passed. On balance, data on prices and wages indicated a gradual, mild increase of inflationary pressures, with the (six-month) annualized rate of increase in the CPI rising to 5.7 percent in June 1989. Growth of the monetary aggregates slowed progressively. Specifically, for the six months ending in June 1988, the annualized rates of growth of M1, M2, and M3 were 7.7, 7.9, and 8.2 percent, respectively. For the six months ending in December, these monetary growth rates were reduced to 2.2, 3.1, and 4.8 percent, respectively. Then, for the six months ending in June 1989, these monetary growth rates fell to -3.5, 1.9, and 3.4 percent, respectively.

Meanwhile, the Federal funds rate was pushed up progressively and substantially from 6.6 percent in March 1988, to 7.5 percent in June, then to 8.75 percent in December, and subsequently to 9.8 percent in March, April, and May 1989, before declining somewhat to 9.5 percent in June 1989. The discount rate was raised half a percentage point to 6.5 percent in August 1988 and by another half a percentage point to 7 percent in February 1989. The increase in the Federal funds rate by about double the increase in the inflation rate, together with the very slow monetary growth during the first half of 1989, indicates a very tight monetary policy. The Federal Reserve was clearly indicating its determination not to "fall behind the curve" in the effort to resist rising inflation—as it had with such disastrous consequences during the 1970s.

The 1988 presidential election occurred in the midst of these actions to tighten monetary policy. The presidential contenders, however, happily avoided any serious discussion of monetary policy. Republicans were relieved that the economy survived the crash without a recession and wished to avoid any criticism of the Federal Reserve that would only stir up needless controversy. The Democrats also saw nothing to gain from criticizing the Federal Reserve and sought to credit it, rather than the administration, with the success in reducing inflation and managing recovery. Thus, the Federal Reserve was left to do its job without the political pressures often associated with a presidential election.

By mid-May 1989, the available data began to show significant slowing in the pace of economic advance, and this was confirmed by information received in subsequent weeks and months. Also, owing primarily to a partial reversal of earlier increases in energy prices, measures of inflation generally showed significant moderation during the summer and autumn of 1989. In this environment, the Federal Reserve shifted to a somewhat less tight monetary policy. For the Federal funds rate, the small decline in June was followed by a fifty-basis-point decline in July and by a further drop to 8.5 percent in November. Growth of M3 remained quite sluggish during the second half of 1989, and M3 slipped slightly below the lower limit of its target range. In contrast, growth of M2 rose to nearly an 8 percent annual rate in the second half, moving M2 from below the lower limit of its target range in May to just below the midpoint of this range by year's end. M1 shifted from significantly negative growth during the first half of 1989 to positive growth at about a 5 percent rate and was essentially unchanged for the year as a whole.

It is noteworthy that, as the Federal Reserve moved to tighten monetary policy in the spring of 1988, the dollar began to rise in foreign exchange markets. The upward movement generally continued until June 1989, and the dollar remained quite strong for some time after monetary policy began to ease during the summer of 1989. Initially, the strengthening of the dollar was regarded as desirable both in terms of reducing inflationary pressures in the United States and in reference to internationally coordinated efforts to enhance exchange rate stability. By late 1988, however, the appreciation of the dollar reached the point where the U.S. Treasury and foreign governments intervened actively, but generally not successfully, to resist further dollar appreciation. The worry (at least at the U.S. Treasury) was that a stronger dollar might seriously impede further reductions in the U.S. trade and current account deficits. The Federal Reserve carried out the foreign exchange interventions directed by the Treasury and, as is traditional, intervened on its own account in support of Treasury operations. However, the Federal Reserve did not alter its monetary policy in order to resist appreciation of the dollar. Monetary policy remained directed toward its primary objectives of fostering price stability and promoting sustainable economic growth.

2.6.5 Looking Forward into the 1990s

The scope of this discussion of monetary policy properly finishes with the end of 1989. However, it is appropriate to mention two developments during 1990 that are relevant for assessing monetary policy in the 1980s. First, inflation accelerated briefly in early 1990 owing primarily (but not exclusively) to an extraordinary 2 percent bulge of consumer prices in January. This raised the six-month annualized rate of change in the CPI to 6 percent for the first half of 1990, providing further evidence that the Federal Reserve was not merely tilting at windmills in its efforts to resist the acceleration of inflation during the late 1980s. Second, economic expansion was very sluggish during the first half of 1990, and recently revised GNP data also show very sluggish growth during most of 1989. Specifically, for the five quarters starting with the spring of 1989, the most recent (July 1990) estimates of the annualized growth rates of real GNP are the following: 1.6, 1.7, 0.3, 1.7, and 1.2 percent, respectively. Preliminary evidence for the summer quarter of 1990, even before Saddam Hussein's invasion of Kuwait, indicates that, at best, economic expansion is continuing at a very slow pace.

No doubt, factors other than tight monetary policy contributed to this recent sluggishness in real economic growth. Nevertheless, it illustrates that determined efforts by the Federal Reserve to resist increases in inflation have a short-run cost in terms of the real growth of the economy. It also raises the question of whether the Federal Reserve was perhaps a little too forceful in its efforts to resist inflation during 1988–89 and a little tardy in its more recent actions to ease monetary policy. Any hope of providing a reasonably clean answer to that question, however, has probably become another victim of Saddam Hussein's aggression. If the U.S. economy falls into recession during the second half of 1990 or in early 1991, it will be extremely difficult to disentangle the effects of Federal Reserve policy before the 2 August invasion of Kuwait from the direct and indirect effects of the recent substantial rise in world oil prices. Moreover, the Federal Reserve now faces the delicate task of dealing both with negative output and employment effects of the rise in oil prices and with a short-term rise of inflationary pressures that is not the consequence of an excessively easy monetary policy.

2.7   Hail to the Chief

Since the Federal Reserve exercises very considerable independence in its conduct of monetary policy, this essay has focused primarily on the actions of the Federal Reserve. However, the Federal Reserve does not operate in a political vacuum, and its monetary policy must at least take some account of the economic policies of the administration and the Congress. In this regard, the key question for the 1980s is, What did Ronald Reagan do to win the great battle against inflation?

My answer may not be entirely unbiased. As a member of the Council of Economic Advisers for more than two years (from 1986 to 1988), it was part of my job to defend, as best as possible, the economic policies of the Reagan administration. However, I would identify the primary contributions of Ronald Reagan to the effort to reduce inflation as occurring much earlier in his administration.

2.7.1   Sending a Message

When the air traffic controllers went out on an illegal strike against the federal government in the spring of 1981, Ronald Reagan fired them. Beyond the federal workers who were directly affected, this action sent an important message that the climate of labor-management relations had changed. The general public support for the firing of the air traffic controllers, together with the results of the 1980 election, indicated forcefully that the American people wanted something serious done about the problem of inflation and would support tough measures to accomplish the task. The import of this message was not lost at the Federal Reserve or among those who exercised more direct influence over the setting of prices and wages.

There is no reliable way to estimate the extent to which the changed climate of labor-management relations may have diminished inflationary pressures in the early 1980s. It is noteworthy, however, that studies based on the experience of the 1960s and the 1970s generally suggested that a prolonged period of very high unemployment might be required in order to make substantial progress in reducing rates of nominal wage growth.[14] In the recession of 1981–82, the unemployment rate did rise to a postwar peak, and it remained relatively high through the initial stages of recovery. However, even given these high rates of unemployment, the drop in the rate of wage inflation during the early 1980s was surprisingly rapid.

2.7.2   Cutting Taxes

Along more traditional lines, but for reasons that are not widely appreciated, the Reagan administration's fiscal policy may have aided the effort to reduce inflation, or at least ameliorated the recessionary consequences of the tight monetary policy that was the essential weapon in the battle against inflation. From the perspective of Keynesian open-economy macroeconomics, the classic policy prescription to minimize the unemployment costs of reducing inflation is a tight monetary policy combined with an easy fiscal policy. This prescription is based on the presumption that monetary policy has a comparative advantage in influencing the price level while fiscal policy has a comparative advantage in affecting the level of output and employment. Moreover, in an open economy operating under a floating exchange rate, the combination of a tight monetary policy and an easy fiscal policy tends to appreciate the foreign exchange value of domestic currency, which assists in reducing inflation.[15]

Of course, given its generally anti-Keynesian bias, the administration would

---

14. A classic analysis of this issue is provided in Tobin (1980). Many other analyses also suggested that a prolonged period of high unemployment would be necessary to make much progress in reducing the core rate of wage inflation.

15. Even if an expansionary fiscal policy was desirable for macroeconomics stabilization purposes during the early 1980s, it does not necessarily follow that the Reagan administration's fiscal policy was entirely appropriate. On the supply side, the effects of the tax cuts may not have been as large as their advocates supposed. On the demand side, perhaps the tax cuts legislated in 1981 (and partially reversed in 1982) were too much of a good thing. Moreover, if the Reagan administration's fiscal policy was helpful from a Keynesian macroeconomic perspective, this should probably be regarded as a fortunate accident. It should not be taken as a lesson that fiscal policy can often be used, in a flexible manner, for macroeconomic stabilization purposes. On the other hand, the practical and political barriers to the flexible use of fiscal policy, and the serious problem of getting the timing right, do not obliterate the favorable effect of an important fiscal policy action that fortuitously occurs at about the right time.

not usually advance such arguments. Instead, it would point to the favorable "supply-side" effects of the Reagan tax cuts both in encouraging increased output and employment and in reducing inflationary pressures. Probably both lines of argument contain some element of truth. In any case, the inflation rate did come down more rapidly than was widely expected, the dollar did appreciate strongly in foreign exchange markets, and the U.S. economy did recover very rapidly from the recession of the early 1980s—generally more rapidly than other industrial countries that pursued different combinations of monetary and fiscal policy.[16]

At the Federal Reserve, the administration's fiscal policy was generally regarded as more of a problem for the conduct of monetary policy than as a benefit. During 1982, it was anticipated that the phasing in of the tax cuts legislated in 1981 would help propel the economy out of recession. However, the dominant view expressed by the Federal Reserve was that the large actual and prospective federal deficits pushed interest rates higher, eroded confidence in the government's anti-inflation program, and impaired the Federal Reserve's policy to curb inflation without excessive costs in terms of output and employment. This complaint about the budget deficit was repeated, almost as a religious incantation, in virtually every public statement by the Federal Reserve. In particular, the "Monetary Policy Report to Congress" of 20 July 1982 (quoted earlier) puts the issue as follows:

> The policy of firm restraint on monetary growth has contributed importantly to recent progress toward reducing inflation. But when inflationary cost trends becomes entrenched, the process of slowing monetary growth can entail economic and financial stresses, especially when so much of the burden of dealing with inflation rests on monetary policy. . . .
>
> The present and prospective pressures on financial markets urgently need to be eased not by relaxing discipline on money growth, but by adopting policies that will ensure a lower and declining federal deficit.

Thus, monetary policy gets the credit for reducing inflation, while entrenched inflationary cost trends and the federal deficit get the blame for the recession and high interest rates. Ironically, as previously noted, on the very day that this "Monetary Policy Report" was issued, the Federal Reserve began precisely the relaxation of monetary policy that it argues against in this statement. During the next five months, interest rates tumbled downward under the

---

16. The administration's easy fiscal policy may also have interacted with the Federal Reserve's tight monetary policy through their combined impact on the foreign exchange value of the dollar, which, in turn, influenced both inflation and economic activity. Martin Feldstein has long been a leading proponent of this view, arguing that the actual and expected fiscal deficit was a leading cause of dollar appreciation during the early 1980s—a development that helped bring down the inflation rate (see, e.g., Feldstein 1986). Feldstein has also argued that the Federal Reserve's monetary policy determined primarily the course of nominal GNP. In the face of this monetary policy, the administration's expansionary fiscal policy contributed to greater growth of real GNP and to less of an increase in the price level.

impact of a much easier monetary policy, despite continued expansion of the federal deficit.

Of course, the administration's fiscal policy (and the large deficits to which it contributed) did not push interest rates lower. Qualitatively, the effect must have been in the other direction.[17] The problem for the Federal Reserve was that it tended to be blamed for high interest rates, and, with some justification, it wanted to shift part of the blame to the administration and the Congress. However, from the perspective of the overall conduct of macroeconomic policy, in the circumstances of the early 1980s, an expansionary fiscal policy that may have put some upward pressure on interest rates was not necessarily inappropriate. In contrast, late in the 1980s, the key task for macroeconomic policy was to resist a rise of inflation, with an economy functioning relatively near to full capacity and with substantial continuing deficits in the trade and current accounts. In this situation, it might have made sense to rely somewhat less on a tightening of monetary policy to resist rising inflation. Certainly, it would have been desirable to make somewhat greater progress in reducing the federal deficit.[18]

2.7.3 Staying the Course

Probably the most important contribution of President Reagan to the fight against inflation was not something that he did but something that he did not do. During the critical period of 1981–82, he did not pressure the Federal Reserve to back off of its tight monetary policy before a convincing victory had been won over the demon of inflation. Despite its much vaunted "political independence," the Federal Reserve could not persist in a tight monetary policy during a deep recession against the determined opposition of a popular president. Nicholas Biddle and the Second Bank of the United States were taught that lesson by Andrew Jackson, and, for eighty years thereafter, the United States had no central bank. More recently, one can imagine what Lyndon John-

17. There are many papers dealing with the effects of the government budget deficits on interest rates. They do not all reach the same conclusion. For one view, see Blanchard and Summers (1984). For an alternative view, see Barro and Sala-i-Martin (1990). My reading of the evidence is that it is difficult to make a convincing case that movements in the federal deficit (either actual or anticipated) were the dominant cause of movements in nominal or real interest rates—the timing is just not right. The enormous swings in interest rates from the summer of 1979 through early 1981 are not associated with dramatic movements in fiscal policy. The large drop in interest rates after the summer of 1982 does not correspond to news about exceptionally favorable developments for the deficit. The rise in interest rates during 1984 does not correspond to unforeseen adverse developments for the deficit. The decline in interest rates during 1985–86 is not generally associated with favorable news on the deficit. During 1987, the rise in interest rates before the stock market crash was associated with an unexpectedly large decline in the deficit. The rise of interest rates from early 1988 through the spring of 1989 corresponds to no significant development concerning the deficit. In all these episodes, it is far easier to see the influence of monetary policy than of fiscal policy on the behavior of interest rates.

18. As discussed in chap. 2 of *Economic Report of the President, 1987,* many of the arguments for reducing the federal deficit do not depend on whether the deficit has a dominant effect on the behavior of interest rates.

son or Richard Nixon would have done had their personal political popularity dropped substantially and their party faced significant midterm electoral losses because of an excessively tight monetary policy directed by a group of appointed officials at the Federal Reserve.

In this connection, it should be emphasized that, while the Federal Reserve enjoyed some support for its tight policy in the financial community, it was not popular with the home builders and construction workers, with the automakers and autoworkers, with the farmers and farm implement makers, and with the whole array of business and labor that felt the pain of tight money, high interest rates, and recession. Congress generally pays attention to the financial community on financial matters. However, Congress always pays close attention to expressions of pain and complaint from constituents back home. Hence, tight money is rarely popular on Capitol Hill. In 1981–82, many members of Congress and congressional leaders from both parties were highly critical of the Federal Reserve's tight monetary policy. Senator Robert Byrd, leader of the Democratic minority, circulated draft legislation commanding the Federal Reserve to reduce interest rates. Senator Baker, leader of the Republican minority, did not support this legislation but was deeply concerned about the Federal Reserve's tight policy and reportedly expressed those concerns directly and repeatedly to Chairman Volcker.

Senior administration officials, both in the White House and at the Treasury, generally shared the view that the Federal Reserve was keeping monetary policy too tight for too long. A consensus to force the Federal Reserve to relax its policy never developed either among senior officials in the administration or in the Congress. However, there can be little doubt that, had Ronald Reagan pulled on his cowboy boots and led a lynch mob from the south lawn of the White House down to Federal Reserve headquarters on Constitution Avenue, he would have been joined not only by the members of his administration but also by majorities from both parties in both houses of Congress, by the Washington representatives of a vast array of American businesses, and by a fair number of foreign diplomats, particularly from heavily indebted countries.

For whatever reasons, Ronald Reagan did not do that. Instead, he campaigned through the dark and difficult days of the recession of 1981–82 on the slogan "Stay the Course."

2.8 Lessons from Defeat and Victory

In the early 1930s, the Federal Reserve made the Great Mistake. It failed to resist, as actively and effectively as it could, the massive contraction of the money supply between late 1929 and early 1933, thereby contributing to the financial and economic devastation of the Great Depression and to all the horrors it helped engender. In the late 1960s and the 1970s, the Federal Reserve made smaller but still important errors in the other direction. After contributing to the rise of inflation through an inappropriately easy monetary policy in the late 1960s, in the early 1970s, and again in the late 1970s, the Federal Reserve waited so long to take effective corrective action that the consequence was an unnecessarily deep and prolonged recession.

In particular, during 1977 and 1978, monetary policy helped fuel the resurgence of inflation. The initial efforts to combat rising inflation beginning in November 1978 were too timid. By the summer of 1979, in the face of the second oil price shock, it became clear that the timid initial efforts to combat rising inflation were ineffective and unpersuasive. Then, when the Federal Reserve finally did forcefully confront the inflationary demon in late 1979 and early 1980, it retreated at the first sign of significant casualties, before the battle had been won.

With its credibility badly damaged by its own past errors, the Federal Reserve rejoined the battle in November 1980 and, at the cost of a deep and prolonged recession, fought through to a convincing victory. Subsequently during the 1980s, the Federal Reserve successfully conducted a monetary policy that supported an exceptionally long and relatively vigorous economic expansion, without a substantial rise in the rate of inflation. Three important lessons can be learned, and apparently have been learned, from this experience.

2.8.1 Three Main Lessons

First, once the inflationary process has built substantial momentum and the credibility of the central bank has been impaired, it takes a determined tightening of monetary policy to reduce significantly the rate of inflation and restore confidence in a greater degree of future price stability. In principle, it might be hoped that a gradual, persistent tightening of monetary policy would control and ultimately diminish inflation without precipitating an economic downturn. However, experience indicates that a recession of significant depth and duration is the virtually inevitable consequence of a successful attack on deeply entrenched inflation. Efforts to avoid recession by stabilizing inflation once it has risen to a relatively high rate do not have a happy history. Under such a policy of monetary appeasement, the natural tendency is for the inflation rate to be ratcheted upward in a never-ending spiral toward hyperinflation.

Ultimately, there is no escape from the short-term economic damage of a determined effort to reduce inflation. The only option is postponement, which makes both the problem of inflation and the pain of its cure far worse. The Federal Reserve demonstrated that it learned this important lesson (perhaps too well) when it pursued a very tight policy for twenty-one months from November 1980 to August 1982. Implicitly, it accepted that a deep and prolonged recession was the necessary cost of gaining an important victory over the entrenched inflation that was largely the consequence of its own earlier policies.

Second, as a corollary of the first lesson, it is a serious mistake for monetary policy to allow the inflationary process to build substantial momentum before determined action is taken to curb the rise of inflation. Such action is likely to slow the pace of economic expansion and to raise the risk of recession. However, it is generally better to take moderate risks in this direction before inflationary pressures rise significantly than to delay action until a serious economic downturn becomes the likely consequence of necessary monetary tightening.

The Federal Reserve demonstrated its command of this lesson when it tightened monetary policy during 1984, during the first nine months of 1987, and again during most of 1988 and 1989. It remains, of course, an open issue whether the Federal Reserve went too far, or not quite far enough, in its recent tightening of monetary policy. Regardless of the outcome, however, it is apparent that the Federal Reserve is not disposed to repeat the same mistakes of the late 1960s and the 1970s.

Third, there is no *unique* quantitative guide to the monetary policy that best serves the generally agreed on and intrinsically related objectives of promoting maximum sustainable economic growth and assuring reasonable price stability. Instead, the central bank needs to examine a variety of indicators of the current and prospective performance of the economy and to assess several measures of the stance of its own monetary policy. This view—that the conduct of monetary policy requires judgment and discretion—has always governed the conduct of the Federal Reserve. Even during the period of relatively serious targeting of growth rates of monetary aggregates from October 1979 until the summer of 1982, the Federal Reserve was always looking at the performance of the economy and developments in financial markets in deciding on its policy.

The lesson of the late 1970s and the 1980s is that, in the turbulent and uncertain conditions likely to accompany a successful attack on entrenched inflation, there is no alternative to discretion in the conduct of monetary policy. There is also no escape from the responsibility to exercise that discretion wisely. On the basis of this experience, however, it remains an open question whether a more "rule-based" approach to the exercise of discretion in the conduct of monetary policy would more successfully avoid the problems of entrenched inflation or prolonged economic downturn.

2.8.2 The Meaning of Discretion

Economists have long disputed the virtues of "rules versus discretion" in the conduct of monetary policy—fundamentally a religious controversy, intrinsically related to the age-old dispute over free will versus predestination.[19] On

---

19. Following the work of Kydland and Prescott (1977) and of Robert Barro and David Gordon (1983), the recent academic literature has usually formulated the distinction between "rules and discretion" in terms of the ability of the monetary authority to precommit its policy in some specific and enforceable manner. In practice, it is questionable whether this distinction is very meaningful or useful. The economic variables that are really of interest to the public and their elected representatives (real economic growth, employment, and inflation) are not entirely under the control of monetary policy. The Federal Reserve could not realistically commit its policy to deliver specific outcomes for these variables. On the other hand, it is far from clear that the public would want specific commitments for those variables that the Federal Reserve can totally control if the outcome was unfortunate for the variables that really matter.

this issue, a highly relevant observation was made by Winston Churchill in his autobiography, *My Early Years*: "My conclusion upon Free Will and Predestination . . . , let the reader mark it, . . . they are identical."

Similarly, if there is a "rule" for monetary policy, then whoever writes it can revise it and whoever implements it must interpret it. Inevitably, some element of discretion infects every "monetary rule." Equally inevitably, the "discretionary" conduct of monetary policy is not whimsical and haphazard. The effort is always to achieve the desired outcome on the basis of what experience suggests to be the relation between actions taken and results achieved. Without some degree of consistency and regularity, there is no meaningful monetary policy. Thus, there is no sharp, clean distinction between "rules and discretion" but rather a muddy issue of the reliance to place on particular relations and indicators in guiding the actual conduct of monetary policy.

In this regard, the experience of the late 1970s and the 1980s powerfully illustrated the failure of interest rates to provide a continuously reliable guide for the conduct of monetary policy. From 1976 through 1979, the Federal funds rate was pushed up in a series of steps to levels that would have indicated a quite tight monetary policy in the context of the 1960s. However, during much of this period, the inflation rate was moving upward as fast as or faster than the Federal funds rate, and the Federal Reserve was falling behind the curve in its efforts to combat the rise of inflation. The level of the Federal funds rate, by itself, failed to provide a reliable indicator of the stance of monetary policy.

During the period of very tight monetary policy, from November 1980 until July 1982, the level of the Federal funds rate was generally very high both absolutely and in comparison with the rate of inflation. This fact, together with information about the performance of the economy and the slow growth of the narrow monetary aggregate M1A, correctly indicated a very tight monetary policy. However, for much of the period from the summer of 1982 through late 1986, the performance of the economy and the growth of the monetary aggregates indicated a relatively easy monetary policy. During this period, the Federal funds rate also generally remained well above the inflation rate. By the standards of the 1960s or 1970s, the level of the Federal funds rate, adjusted for inflation, would have suggested a very tight monetary policy. Thus, even in combination with the inflation rate, the Federal funds rate failed to provide a unique and completely reliable indicator of the stance of monetary policy.

On the basis of the experience of the late 1970s and the 1980s, similar con-

---

In the academic literature, there is also the notion that the problem with "discretion" is that the monetary authority cannot avoid the temptation to use it to surprise the public with greater than anticipated inflation in order to drive output and employment above their sustainable equilibrium levels. The practical relevance of this notion is also highly questionable. The Federal Reserve made mistakes in allowing inflation to build up momentum in the late 1960s and the 1970s. It was sometimes too timid in attacking inflation because of concern about the consequences for output and employment. However, there is little factual support for the accusation that the Federal Reserve actively sought to deceive the public by knowingly creating greater than anticipated inflation.

cerns apply to the use of monetary aggregates as the unique indicators of monetary policy. The key to the usefulness of monetary aggregates is a stable, highly predictable relation between the behavior of these aggregates and the behavior of economic variables of more fundamental interest, especially real GNP, the price level, and nominal GNP. As illustrated in figure 2.10, for the twenty years prior to 1980, the velocity of M1—the ratio of nominal GNP to M1—exhibited a relatively stable, 3 percent trend rate of growth. After 1980, this apparently stable relation between M1 (= M1B) and nominal GNP collapsed, with velocity declining sharply in the early 1980s and then remaining essentially flat, on balance, for the remainder of the decade. Clearly, a monetary policy that targeted the growth rate of M1 on the assumption of a 3 percent annual rate of increase in its velocity would have gone seriously, perhaps catastrophically, awry during the 1980s.

For M2, the trend behavior of velocity has remained essentially flat in the 1980s. However, there have been relatively large annual fluctuations in M2 velocity (i.e., fluctuations of 3 or 4 percent) that indicate that strict targeting of the growth rate of this aggregate would, on some occasions, have created serious difficulties.

Moreover, the usefulness of monetary aggregates as indicators of monetary policy is seriously impaired when the growth rates of these aggregates give disparate signals about the stance of monetary policy, as happened at several points during the 1980s. In particular, looking at the critical period of the battle against inflation from late 1980 through mid-1982, the growth rate of M2, illustrated in figure 2.6 above, does not by itself indicate a particularly tight monetary policy. Indeed, the growth rate of M2 during this period was marginally higher than the growth rate of M2 from early 1977 until October 1979, when, judged by the actual behavior of the price level, monetary policy was not firmly anti-inflationary. In comparison, the growth rates of M1 (= new

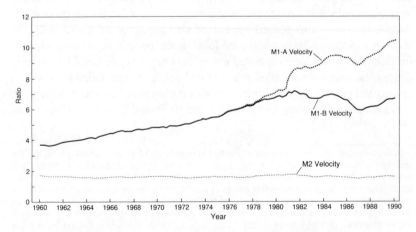

Fig 2.10   Velocity, various monetary aggregates, 1960:1–1990:1
Note: Velocity equals GNP divided by the respective monetary aggregate.

M1B) and especially of M1A ($=$ old M1), both illustrated in figure 2.5 above, indicate a significantly tighter monetary policy from late 1980 to mid-1982 than during the late 1970s. Another example of significant disparity in growth rates of different monetary aggregates occurs in 1985 and 1986. The growth rate of M2 during this two-year period is only marginally higher than during the period of tight monetary policy from late 1980 to mid-1982. In contrast, M1 grows at an exceptionally rapid pace during 1985–86, both in comparison with the period of tight monetary policy during 1981–82 and in comparison with the period of rising inflation during the late 1970s.

Of course, monetarists would argue that much of the disparity in the growth rates, and many of the movements in velocities, of different aggregates during the 1980s can be explained by movements in interest rates and by shifts into and out of newly created classes of deposits. Granted that this is correct, it does not controvert the fundamental lesson that some degree of discretion is required in the conduct of monetary policy. The only way to remove discretion completely would be to specify a precise and invariant definition of the monetary aggregate to be targeted and a rate at which this aggregate should be made to grow, month in and month out, regardless of virtually any condition or circumstance short of thermonuclear war. The experience of the 1980s indicates that there are situations in which this sort of discretionless monetary rule would perform rather poorly.

2.8.3   The Role of Monetary Aggregates

Given the inevitability of some degree of discretion in the conduct of U.S. monetary policy, it remains relevant to ask what emphasis should be given to monetary growth rates in guiding the Federal Reserve's policy. On this issue, the lessons of the 1970s and the 1980s are somewhat ambiguous. As previously discussed, strict targeting of monetary aggregates would have encountered severe difficulties in the turbulent economic and financial environment of the early 1980s. On the other hand, it is clear that the Federal Reserve would have avoided most of the error of contributing to the buildup of inflationary pressures during the late 1970s if it had been more assiduous in achieving its own announced monetary growth targets. Under those circumstances, much of the economic and financial turbulence associated with the determined effort to reduce inflation during the early 1980s might have been avoided, and monetary targeting might have proved more successful throughout the period.

More generally, it may be argued that, in conducting a discretionary monetary policy, the Federal Reserve generally needs to pay considerable attention, in a careful and sophisticated way, to the behavior of monetary aggregates. Some prominent monetarists have suggested that an "adjusted monetary growth rule" would provide an especially valuable guide for monetary policy.[20] The adjustments would take the form of a moving average correction for

---

20. Allan Meltzer and Bennett McCallum are leading advocates of some form of adjustable monetary rule. Meltzer's views are presented in several papers (see, e.g., Meltzer 1987, 1991). For McCallum's arguments, see McCallum (1988).

changes in the relation between monetary growth and the rate of growth of nominal GNP. The virtue of such a "rule" is that it would help prevent the big errors of monetary policy: avoiding the persistent declines in the money supply that contributed to the Great Depression of the early 1930s and avoiding the excessive monetary growth that contributed to the rise of inflation in the 1960s and 1970s.

At least in my view, the usefulness of such a monetary rule is not as the sole guide to the operational conduct of monetary policy but rather as a medium-term indicator that policy may be deviating from the desired course. The "rule" provides a warning signal against the danger of too much emphasis on interest rates and on shorter-term economic developments and forecasts in governing the conduct of monetary policy.

To illustrate the possible virtue of giving somewhat greater emphasis to monetary growth rates in guiding the medium-term conduct of monetary policy, it is relevant to examine, retrospectively, whether this might have improved economic performance. Because demand for the narrow monetary aggregate M1A (= old M1) is less sensitive to movements in interest rates than the broader aggregates, it is convenient to focus attention on this narrow aggregate. As was recognized at the time, it is necessary to adjust for the downward shift in demand for M1A when interest-bearing transactions accounts (not included in M1A) became widely available to households in 1980 and 1981. With these adjustments, M1 appears to provide useful indications that might have guided improvements in monetary policy.

In the late 1970s, M1A was growing at rates that indicated a relatively easy monetary policy, especially in light of the normal upward trend (for the preceding twenty-five years) in the velocity of this aggregate. Giving a little more weight to the growth of M1A in determining monetary policy in the late 1970s would have suggested a somewhat earlier and more vigorous attack on inflation. The slowdown in the growth of M1A in the autumn of 1979 and the winter of 1980 provided an appropriate indication of the necessary tightening of monetary policy to combat the surge of inflation at that time. The sharp upturn of growth of M1A during that summer and early autumn of 1980 provided an accurate indication of the Federal Reserve's unfortunate retreat from the battle against the demon of inflation. Making appropriate allowance for the shift of households out of traditional demand deposits, the very tight monetary policy from November 1980 to July–August 1982 is also clearly indicated by the behavior of M1A. Had the Federal Reserve taken this indicator more seriously, it would not perhaps have pursued quite such a tight policy for quite so long, and the recession of 1981–82 might not have been quite as deep and quite as long.

The sharp increase in the growth rate of M1A in late summer and autumn 1982 dramatically illustrated the shift to a much easier monetary policy. The gradually declining, but still moderately high, rate of growth of M1A until the spring of 1984 points to the continuation of a relatively easy monetary policy, while the sharp downturn in M1A growth later in the year indicates the brief period of monetary tightening. In retrospect, it seems that a modestly less easy monetary policy during late 1982 and 1983, which would have contributed somewhat less to the extraordinarily rapid pace of economic expansion from late 1982 to mid-1984, might have been appropriate. It might also have obviated the need for monetary tightening during 1984 that hit the economy at about the same time as the natural forces of economic recovery were abating.

During 1985 and especially 1986, the rapid growth of M1A indicated a substantial easing of monetary policy. Then, the sharp decline in the growth of M1A indicated an abrupt tightening of monetary policy during the first half of 1987, and the negative growth of M1A indicated further tightening just before the stock market crash. After a brief period of easing during the first few months of 1988, the growth rate of M1A indicated a very significant tightening of monetary policy from April 1988 through July 1989, followed by a modest degree of easing in the last quarter of 1989. Looking back at the very rapid real growth of the economy during 1987 (which is apparent especially in the revised data), it is relevant to ask whether a somewhat less expansionary monetary policy during 1986 might not have contributed to a more moderate pace of economic growth during 1987, thereby alleviating some of the need for monetary tightening in 1987 and conceivably in 1988–89. Again, taking more seriously the behavior of M1A as a guide for monetary policy might have contributed to a somewhat smoother, more sustainable course of economic expansion.

To avoid misunderstanding, it should be reemphasized that the issue is not whether the Federal Reserve should have set a specific target for the growth of M1A as the operational guide for monetary policy in the 1980s. Rather, the question is whether, at the margin, monetary policy might have been improved if somewhat more attention had been paid to the signals provided by the growth rate of M1A, within the context of the array of factors that guided Federal Reserve policy. Indeed, as previously discussed, rigid targeting of growth rates of monetary aggregates can lead to serious difficulties in the turbulent economic and financial environment of a determined assault on entrenched inflation. In these situations, the Federal Reserve faced tough decisions about how long to pursue a tight monetary policy in order to curb inflation, without highly reliable indicators of the actual tightness of its policy or of the likely future course of the economy. Careful judgment, rather than a mechanistic rule, was required to determine the most appropriate policy. Of course, with an appropriate monetary policy, difficult decisions about harsh actions to combat rising inflation should be an infrequent necessity. However, there is no guarantee, and no automatic rule, that assures that such decisions can always be avoided or that they will always be made wisely.

As the experience of the 1980s makes clear, real people and their elected representatives care a good deal about the growth of the economy, about the level of employment, about the rate of inflation, and about the level of interest rates. Intrinsically, they care little about growth rates of monetary aggregates. The only occasion on which the monetary growth rates became a subject of significant public interest was during the early 1980s, when the Federal Reserve was believed to be paying significant attention to these growth rates in determining its policy with respect to interest rates. Once the Federal Reserve effectively abandoned operating procedures that attempted to achieve targeted growth rates for monetary aggregates, general public interest in monetary growth rates waned rapidly. The implication is that, so long as monetary policy contributes to acceptable behavior of the economic variables that really matter to real people, the Federal Reserve is unlikely to be held publicly accountable for deviations of monetary growth rates from specified targets. Rather, such technical issues regarding the conduct of monetary policy—important as they may be—will remain primarily the domain of specialists who analyze and assess the Federal Reserve's performance.

Ultimately, it is the performance of monetary policy with respect to its influence on growth, employment, inflation, and other economic variables of real importance for which the Federal Reserve can and should be held responsible. The task of assessing the Federal Reserve's performance, however, is not simple—primarily because the Federal Reserve's job is not simple. Monetary policy is far from the only important influence on economic activity or even on inflation. The Federal Reserve must conduct its policy without precise information about the ongoing behavior of the economy or, especially, about its likely future behavior. On some occasions through no fault of its own, and on some occasions because of past errors of its own policy, the Federal Reserve will confront choices with no happy outcomes. Moreover, even when monetary policy is tuned appropriately, a tension always exists between good arguments that the policy should be a little tighter and good arguments that it should be a little easier. Almost inevitably, the Federal Reserve will get somewhat more than its fair share of praise when the economy performs well and somewhat more than its fair share of blame when the economy performs badly. Fortunately for us all, for most of the decade of the 1980s, the Federal Reserve has been more deserving of thankful applause than of harsh criticism.

References

Barro, Robert, and Robert Gordon. 1983. Rules, discretion, and reputation in a model of monetary policy. *Journal of Monetary Economics* 12, no. 1 (July): 101–21.

Barro, Robert, and Xavier Sala-i-Martin. 1990. World real interest rates. *NBER Macroeconomics Annual,* 15–61.

Blanchard, Olivier, and Lawrence Summers. 1984. Perpsectives on high world real interest rates. *Brookings Papers on Economic Activity,* no. 2:273–324.

Feldstein, Martin. 1986. The budget deficit and the dollar. *NBER Macroeconomics Annual,* 355–92.

Greider, William. 1987. *Secrets of the temple.* New York: Simon & Schuster.

Karamousis, Nicholas, and Ramond Lombra. 1989. Federal Reserve policy making: An overview and analysis of the policy process. *Carnegie-Rochester Conference Series on Public Policy* 30 (Spring): 7–62.

Kydland, Finn, and Edward Prescott. 1977. Rules rather than discretion: The inconsistency of optimal plans. *Journal of Political Economy* 85, no. 3 (June): 473–91.

McCallum, Bennett. 1988. Robustness properties of a rule for monetary policy. *Carnegie-Rochester Conference Series on Public Policy* 29 (Autumn): 179–203.

Meltzer, Allan. 1987. Limits of short-run stabilization policy. *Economic Inquiry* 25 (January): 1–14.

———. 1991. The Fed at seventy-five. In *Monetary policy on the 75th anniversary of the Federal Reserve System,* ed. M. Belongia, 3–65. Boston: Kluwer.

Tobin, James. 1980. Stabilization policy: Ten years after. *Brookings Papers on Economic Activity,* no. 1: 19–71.

2. Paul A. Volcker

Martin Feldstein asked me to comment on some of the significant events in monetary policy during my tenure as chairman of the Federal Reserve. I think that there are five periods that deserve particular comment: the Federal Reserve's adoption of a more monetarist approach to policy-making in 1979; the credit controls and recession of 1980; the relaxation of monetary policy beginning in late 1982; the Plaza Accord in September 1985; and the Louvre meeting in February 1987.

Let me begin in late 1979, when I went to Washington. Michael Mussa's background paper accurately describes the setting for monetary policy at that time. Inflationary expectations seemed to be rising, as there was little confidence in the financial markets that the Federal Reserve would effectively restrain an increase in inflation. One part of the problem, I believe, was that banks had lost any fear that they might ever be unable to raise funds for lending. The interest rate limit for large certificates of deposit had been removed in June 1979, and the banks thought that there was no constraint on their ability to obtain credit. Although the cost of funds to banks was high, the inflationary environment meant that the banks did not let this high cost deter them from continued lending.

Ironically, despite these inflationary expectations, there was also an expectation that a recession was starting. For several months before the summer of 1979, the Federal Reserve staff had been projecting that a recession would begin shortly.

Then the Federal Reserve raised the discount rate twice between July and September 1979. Unfortunately, although these discount rate increases raised short-term interest rates somewhat, they had virtually no effect on the psychological environment. In fact, and much to my surprise, the second increase was actually counterproductive. That increase was adopted by a four-to-three vote, and of course the votes are announced. The market interpreted the close vote as implying that the Federal Reserve was obviously not going to undertake any further tightening measures. Ordinarily, I might have been sensitive to that interpretation because one does like to have more of a consensus on shifts in policy. In this case, however, I was not concerned because I knew that I had three other votes if I wanted to tighten again. So it had not occurred to me in advance that the closeness of the vote would be a problem.

This event was one of the things that persuaded me that the Federal Reserve needed to pursue a strategy that would "shake up" the inflationary psychology and introduce some constructive uncertainty in financial markets. The strategy that we pursued—moving to a more monetarist approach to policy-making—had been the subject of endless analysis and debate at the Federal Reserve, and I had begun thinking about it earlier when I was still in New York. As I discussed the desirability of such a strategy as a means of dealing with expectations, there was enthusiastic support among both the Board members and the district bank presidents. I think that it is fair to say that the Carter administration was not enthusiastic. Members of the administration argued that the Federal Reserve should not launch this uncertain new approach, with unknown consequences, but should instead, if really necessary, tighten policy more severely in a more orthodox way.

Nevertheless, the change in policy was announced in early October 1979. I thought that there were two great advantages of the monetarist approach, which I had emphasized in some earlier speeches. First, it was a good way of disciplining ourselves. When we had announced that we were going to meet certain money supply targets, and not by manipulating interest rates but by working directly through the reserve base, we were committing a lot of prestige to that commitment, and it would have been very hard to rationalize a retreat. Second, it seemed to be a good device, given the spirit of the times, to convey what we were doing to the public. We said, in effect, that the United States was experiencing high inflation that needed to be dealt with and that inflation is a monetary phenomenon. Thus, we were not going to try to reduce inflation by manipulating interest rates but were instead going to go directly to the money supply. That seemed like a good way to explain what we were doing in a way that people could understand and support.

I did not expect at the time that interest rates would move as much as they did. Although we were working directly through reserves, we had established a wide band for the Federal funds rate and had agreed to reconsider our actions whenever the rate reached either end of this band. I thought that we should take this band seriously, but most members of the Open Market Committee were less conservative than I was on this point, and in the end the restriction was not very meaningful. Whenever the Federal funds rate reached the end of the band, there was a telephone meeting to ask whether the current policy should be continued, and the answer was always yes. As time passed, even less attention was paid to this band. So interest rates rose further and more rapidly than I had expected, and it was a disappointment that there were no favorable expectational effects on long-term interest rates. While the money supply itself behaved reasonably in line with our targets over the rest of 1979, it experienced a great deal of volatility. Also, there was little visible effect at that stage on either economic activity or inflation, the earlier projections of recession notwithstanding.

The next significant period for monetary policy was early in 1980. Inflation had been running at a double-digit rate for several months, creating a true sense of inflationary crisis. President Carter then proposed a budget with a deficit that by today's standards was small but was considered outrageously inadequate to the anti-inflationary challenge at the time. The budget was, in a sense, withdrawn. The Federal Reserve took some tightening measures but delayed others because we wanted to have a coordinated program with the new budget.

At this time, the president decided that consumer credit controls should be imposed. He realized that some restraint on spending was necessary, and he wanted the restraint to come not just from higher interest rates but also from direct control over consumer credit. He became convinced that such a step would send the message to the public that he was serious about reducing inflation.

We at the Federal Reserve resisted the imposition of consumer credit controls, partly because of the usual problems associated with rationing and partly because consumer credit was not rising very fast and did not seem to be the source of the inflationary pressures. There was a law on the books, however, that said that the president could, in effect, give the Federal Reserve the authority to impose consumer credit controls. I thought that it would be awkward, to say the least, for the president to give us the authority to impose controls and then for us to say that we were not going to impose them anyway. In the end, I felt that we could not talk the president out of the credit controls, and we had to recognize that he was taking politically difficult steps to cut government spending and was willing to accept and even support further monetary tightening without complaint.

So we agreed to impose controls on consumer credit, although we made those controls as mild as we possibly could. We exempted anything to do with housing and automobiles, which are by far the most important elements of consumer credit. In effect, we put a tax on credit cards, a psychological gesture that we thought would not amount to much. We were completely wrong, however, as the idea of cutting back on consumer credit apparently touched a guilty nerve in the American public. The country went immediately into recession, with the economy declining at a faster rate than we first realized.

Businesses selling consumer goods that were usually sold on credit faced huge sales declines even when their products were not actually covered by the credit controls. I recall some recreational vehicle dealers who had a two-thirds decline in sales from one week to the next. The result was that the economy dropped precipitously, and I realized in retrospect that I had never seen anything like it.

We soon discovered that the money supply was dropping precipitously at the same time. We were providing reserves at a rate that normally would have sustained a 3 or 4 percent annual increase in the money supply, but in fact the money supply actually declined for a month or two at a high annual rate. Only later could we hypothesize not only that consumers were refusing to take on additional credit, but also that they were repaying their outstanding credit card balances because they felt that it was the patriotic thing to do. The repayment was accomplished by a reduction in bank account balances, which created a totally artificial decline in the money supply.

This decline in the money supply provoked a chorus of comments from economists—monetarists and Keynesians alike—to the effect that the Federal Reserve needed to provide additional reserves to the banking system. At the same time, of course, there was a very steep decline in economic activity for one quarter. So we took off the credit controls as soon as we could because I thought that they were inappropriate when the economy was in a recession.

I think that there was no sense during the summer of 1980 that the economy was recovering. I remember meeting at that time with a group of leading bankers who were in Washington for some other purpose. I was starting to think that the sinking spell in the economy was ending, although I had no sense of a strong recovery. I asked the bankers whether they thought that they might look back in October or November and say that by the end of September the economy was reviving. Not one of those bankers said that they thought that that was at all possible. In fact, while we were having the meeting, the economy had already been expanding for a month or two, and quite a lot of momentum soon developed.

The money supply also began to increase during the summer, although from a very low level. Initially, we did not move to restrain the rebound in the money supply because the level remained well below our targets. We did take some action beginning in August, but many people argue in retrospect that we did not act aggressively enough to restrain the growth of money in the latter part of 1980. The fact is that, for some months, neither we nor our subsequent critics realized that the economy was rebounding as fast as it was. All the staff projections of the money supply were for modest increases; in fact, we ended up with very large increases. This put us in the awkward position of having to tighten money in the face of a presidential election campaign. Jimmy Carter was complaining (although in a very limited way, to his credit) about "monetarism" and rising interest rates, while Ronald Reagan was complaining about the wild expansion of the money supply. We did increase the discount rate around the end of September, which is historically the closest to an election that the discount rate has ever been increased.

In retrospect, however, monetary policy seems too expansionary during this short period. The money supply rose rapidly until October or November, when we tightened more aggressively and were able to get it under control. It was in a way a mostly wasted year restoring credibility in the attack on inflation. The main reason, it seems to me, was the complications introduced by the credit controls. This is a useful lesson. The unexpected psychological repercussions of that inherently mild action—the way the American public responded at that time to that gesture—were completely out of proportion to what we expected. We would not have had such a steep drop in the money supply or in the economy except for the controls.

The next interesting event was the easing of monetary policy in 1982. The recession had begun in mid-1981, but we did not adopt a strongly expansionary monetary policy until the summer of 1982. There were several reasons for our cautious stance in the first half of that year. First, there was a big jump in the money supply around the beginning of 1982 that carried it above our targets. Under the new approach and operating techniques, that development was not conducive to any aggressive moves to ease money. Second, although the economy was in a recession, inflation had not fallen very much by early 1982. Third, there were substantial expectations, generally shared within the Fed, that the economy would begin to expand in the second quarter of the year. I believe that the initial estimates of the second quarter did in fact show a small expansion, although that was later revised away. In studying the history of monetary policy, one must remember the difference between the revised figures available now and the unrevised figures available at the time. In the spring of 1982, we were operating in an environment in which we thought that the economy was probably beginning to recover, and the money supply remained somewhat above our targets.

However, this confidence in an imminent expansion became more and more questionable as the spring proceeded. The financial markets were under increasing pressure as well; this was an important background factor, although not the driving force, behind our eventual decision to ease. Sometime in July, as I recall, after the money supply had been stable for a long period, it finally fell back into our target ranges after its big jump at the beginning of the year. At this point, we decided that we could ease credibly, and we made some limited easing movements, the effects of which on interest rates were greatly amplified by market expectations, producing a solid decline. The stock market surged.

By the fall of 1982, the money supply began rising rapidly again. The money supply figures were clearly being distorted by the new money market accounts and other institutional changes, so this provided the occasion for an announcement that we were not going to follow M1 as religiously as we had been doing. In particular, we were not going to institute contractionary policy simply because the money supply figures were rising, and, in fact, we made another important easing move in the fall. By the end of the year, a strong recovery was under way.

Now let me turn to the Plaza Accord of 1985. This is an important event to discuss because the implications of the accord for monetary policy were the opposite of what is commonly thought to be the case.

The dollar had reached a peak in early 1985, and there was continuing debate both in the United States and overseas about exchange market intervention. Treasury Secretary James Baker and Deputy Secretary Richard Darman were more inclined to intervene than previous Treasury officials had been, and the meeting at the Plaza was largely at their initiative. I well understood the arguments for reducing the value of the dollar and had pleaded many times earlier for agreement on coordinated intervention. But I also held a good, traditional central banking view that countries deliberately depreciating their currencies often run afoul of inflation. I feared that the dollar decline might get out of hand, and I was simply not enthusiastic about an official doctrine that it is good to depreciate one's currency. So I wanted the decline in the dollar to be pursued without undue aggressiveness, and we had great arguments about how to do that. In the end, I think that my views about how to implement the intervention were largely accepted.

But the central question for today is, What were the implications of the accord for monetary policy? I read a lot of analysis that says that the Federal Reserve would have preferred to tighten policy for domestic purposes but was forced into a looser policy in order to help bring down the dollar. That is not true. By 1985, I was quite concerned that the U.S. economy was slowing down, and the Japanese and European economies were very sluggish as well. There was no doubt in my mind that it was not the right time to tighten policy. In fact, it was the absence of any need or desire to tighten that provided a "green light" for the Plaza Agreement. Indeed, there was substantial argument with the Fed in favor of loosened monetary policy for domestic purposes, but one reason that I opposed that action was because I did not want the dollar to fall in value too suddenly or confidence in our anti-inflationary resolve to be undercut. Thus, concern about the value of the dollar caused monetary policy to be shaded more on the tighter side during late 1985 than on the easier side, although that shading was evident in a refusal to ease rather than an actual tightening. I emphasize this point because it is just the opposite of what most commentators were saying at the time and have been saying more recently as well.

Finally, let me discuss the Louvre Accord of early 1987. During the summer of 1986, James Baker and I engaged in an ongoing public dialogue about the appropriate value of the dollar. He would say that he wanted the dollar to fall in value. My sense was that it had fallen enough, and I was afraid that it would be too weak, so I would testify the following day that I thought that its current value was just fine. We finally decided that he could say what he wanted and I could say what I wanted, and this was not particularly acrimonious because it had a favorable side effect—while the dollar continued to decline some, the contrasting approaches injected some uncertainty into the market, which prevented matters from getting out of hand. As the dollar remained weak, however, Treasury Department officials became more concerned about it. They arranged for the Louvre meeting, which was designed to reach an international consensus to stabilize exchange rates.

At neither the Louvre meeting nor the Plaza meeting was there any explicit discussion of monetary policy. This may be surprising from the standpoint of economic analysis, but it is not surprisingly bureaucratically or as a matter of international diplomacy. The central bankers had no desire to discuss monetary policy in that essentially political setting at the risk of tying their hands in the future. And the finance ministers felt that they could not press the point. The Germans in particular were very punctilious, with the people from the Finance Ministry believing that it was the Bundesbank's job to discuss monetary policy. The central bankers, quite naturally, preferred to discuss monetary policy issues "outside the room" and in other forums, but often they were not very explicit even then. In fact, big changes in monetary policy were not an issue at the Louvre. There was a lot of communication on a continuing basis afterward, but it was more in regard to intervention and exchange rates than to monetary policy per se. I think that everyone understood that the Plaza and Louvre agreements obviously had consequences for monetary policy, but that was all.

At both the Plaza meeting and the Louvre meeting, there were very explicit, painstakingly detailed discussions about who would intervene, in what amounts, and under what circumstances. Most of this discussion irritated me because I thought that it was very artificial—one cannot anticipate all the possible contingencies and determine who should do what in response. Nevertheless, there was a lot of discussion of that sort.

3. *James Tobin*

Speaking about Paul Volcker right after Paul Volcker, I am not in an enviable position. Imagine an academic critic following Douglas MacArthur in a retrospective discussion of the general's campaigns.

I shall discuss only briefly the three years from October 1979, the period of serious quantitative medium-run targets for monetary aggregates and of short-run operating targets for quantities of reserves. History will confirm the praise that Paul Volcker earned from his contemporaries for his resolute generalship of the war against the inflation of the late 1970s. The recessions did not reduce inflation to zero, but they did lower it to a comfortable rate, 4–5 percent, which proved to be stable during the subsequent cyclical expansion.

In 1979–80, many economists contended that the way monetary policymakers could bring about a relatively rapid and painless disinflation would be to announce strict monetarist targets and operating procedures and to commit themselves to stick with them regardless of what happened to business activity and employment. Thus, business managers and workers would be put on notice that their livelihoods and jobs depend on their own price and wage decisions— they must disinflate. This popular academic view may have influenced the climate of opinion in the Federal Reserve System and the financial markets. I gather that it was not as important in Volcker's own thinking as the need to obtain and display consensus in the system for a policy move appropriate to prevailing economic conditions.

If a "credible threat" was intended in the October 1979 revolution, it was attenuated by the policy roller coaster in 1980, severely criticized by Mike Mussa in his background paper and unapologetically reviewed by Paul in his remarks. Why Carter's credit controls were so powerful a restraint on aggregate demand and on money supplies remains a mystery. Evidently, their effects both on imposition and on removal greatly confused the Fed. Anyway, beginning in September 1980, a determined monetarist policy was followed for nearly two years. Did the policy make the disinflation faster and less painful than it would have been otherwise? The economic literature renders a mixed verdict. Certainly, it took substantial pain and suffering, not just threat, to get wage and price inflation rates down.

Was there any way to limit the cost? Some economists, myself included, had suggested combining the announcement of a firm disinflationary monetary policy with some variant of incomes policy, at least guideposts. There had been a stab at incomes policy in the Carter administration in 1979, but it was abandoned just at the crucial time. Rumor was that this decision was related to the contest for the Democratic presidential nomination, specifically to the position of organized labor. No incomes policy was conceivable in the new administration, although President Reagan's tough stand against the air traffic controllers in 1981 taught an exemplary lesson. One could say that the Fed itself was carrying out an incomes policy, albeit one that worked via actual pain and cost rather than by conjectural fears.

I hope that history will give Paul and his colleagues the praise that they deserve not only for fighting the war against inflation but also for knowing when to stop, when to declare victory. They reversed course in the summer of 1982, probably averting an accelerating contraction of economic activity in the United States and financial disasters worldwide. Many observers, knowing that the Fed takes seriously its responsibilities for financial stability, have assumed that the Mexican debt crisis and other financial threats were the main considerations in the Fed's decisions in 1982. According to Volcker, however, domestic nonfinancial business conditions were the main concern of the Federal Open Market Committee (FOMC).

I know that there are some hawks who thought then and think now that the anti-inflation crusade should have been pursued to the bitter end and that there are some who would resume now the push to zero inflation. I think that it was an act of genius, worth trillions of dollars of GNP—yes, real GNP—to have led the country to regard 5 percent inflation as zero, and I think that it is mischievous to rock the boat now.

The monetary management of the expansion of the last eight years—perhaps this record expansion has ended or is about to end—is my main topic.

For the management of aggregate demand, monetary policy has been the only game in town since 1981. The Reagan administration disabled fiscal policy as a tool of macroeconomic stabilization and dedicated it wholly to other goals, as discussed in other sessions of this conference. Structural budget deficits far beyond previous peacetime experience clouded the environment to which the Fed had to adapt. No doubt the economic and political implications of the federal budget complicated the Fed's decision problems. There were other new complexities and uncertainties: dramatically increasing international capital mobility; Latin American and other Third World debts; structural and regulatory changes in American banking and finance; insolvencies, threatened and actual, among American financial institutions.

Despite these handicaps, the Fed has been quite successful. Volcker and company, and then Greenspan and company, restored the reputation of fine-tuning and made it into a fine art. The proof is in the pudding. The economy grew steadily, if sometimes slowly, and eventually recovered the ground lost in the recessions. In 1988–89, unemployment was lowered well below what economists considered the lowest inflation-safe rates ten years earlier. Finally, after managing a "soft landing" at this new and lower nonaccelerating-inflation rate of unemployment (NAIRU), for the last two years the Fed has managed to steer the economy between the Scylla of price acceleration and the Charybdis of recession. I don't know how long that will be true, but it is true so far.

Demand management cannot take major credit for the improvement in the NAIRU, except that the previous deep recession may have helped discipline subsequent wage- and price-setting practices. Sharper foreign competition helped, a thin silver lining to the dark cloud of dollar appreciation. The decline in oil prices prior to August 1990 was a welcome contrast to the 1970s. Whatever cleared the path for expansion, the Fed does get credit for following the path into new territory, cautiously keeping the recovery going as long as inflation remained well behaved.

For the improved price performance of the 1980s, Mussa gives important weight to the new macroeconomic policy mix, loose fiscal policy and tight money. He echoes previous rationales for this combination. The argument is that the 1982–86 currency appreciation lowered the inflation rate associated with a given outcome in real output and employment. I am still skeptical. For the United States, the impact of appreciation on overall price indexes is small. Besides, it is temporary, essentially a loan from other countries that must be paid back. Later, the currency has to be depreciated, and the borrowed price reduction has to be reversed. Even in the short run, the gain from an appreciation is one shot; it lowers not the rate of inflation but the level of price indexes. The policy mix in question has serious costs in long-run growth and foreign indebtedness, costs that dwarf any small short-run macroeconomic advantages.

I have no inside information about how the Fed has done its fine-tuning. The interpretation that follows is simply inference from an outsider's observations.

The new Fed monetary regime, beginning in the fall of 1982, changed both medium-run targets of policy and operating procedures. Although target ranges for intermediate monetary aggregates are still voted on and announced, as required by law, they have lost importance, as the markets know very well (see Mussa's figs. 2.8 and 2.9).

The Federal Reserve recognized that intermediate monetary aggregates had lost whatever meaning they had because of regulatory and technological changes in the financial industries. Downgrading the monetary targets finessed at least one source of error in monetary policy, unexpected (or even systematic) changes in velocity. Mussa's figure 2.10 shows what happened to M1 and M2 velocities. Liberated from the Ms, the Fed is enabled to respond to shocks that change velocity but not the aggregates and is excused from responding to M changes that simply reflect velocity shocks. Tactically, in 1982, the changing and uncertain meanings of the Ms gave the Fed some cover for making changes in policy substance and operating procedure that Paul and his colleagues wanted to make anyway.

The Fed has aimed directly at observed and projected macroeconomic performance, as measured not by monetary aggregates but by variables that matter: real GNP growth; unemployment, excess capacity, and other indicators of slack; wage and price inflation. The weights on different measures of performance are not explicit; indeed, they doubtless differ among members of the Open Market Committee. The bottom line is likely to be some agreed on or compromise range for real GNP growth, higher or lower depending on the weights the committee is putting on the other variables.

Short-run operating instruments are no longer reserve quantities but, as in pre-1979 days, Federal funds rates. The differential between the funds rate and the discount rate reflects the pressure on the banks' reserve positions. Like most controllers, the Fed is a feedback mechanism, changing its instrument settings in response to discrepancies significant in size and duration between actual readings and projections of its target variables, on the one hand, and desired target paths, on the other.

Not surprisingly, Federal funds rates, and other interest rates as well, have been less volatile since 1982 than in the preceding monetarist regime. Paul admits that he was astounded by their volatility in 1980–82. Most of their recent volatility has been deliberate policy. When the Fed saw aggregate demand growing too slowly, the FOMC lowered the funds rate substantially (down 564 basis points in six months from July 1982). When demand was perceived to be growing too fast, the FOMC raised the rate (up 205 basis points in six months from February 1984). Likewise, the funds rate was lowered 163 points in the seven months from February 1986 and raised 210 points in the eight months from July 1988. Other interest rates moved in the same directions, longer rates of course by fewer points (see Mussa's fig. 2.4).

In retrospect, the tightening in 1984 looks excessive to me and too long maintained. The recovery was little more than a year old, and there was plenty of slack left in the economy. At the time of the February 1984 "Monetary Policy Report," the Board believed that real GNP had grown 6 percent from 1982:4, then thought to have been the recession bottom, to 1983:4 and that growth had slowed to 4.5 percent in 1983:4. The Fed reported that 1983 growth was in considerable measure due to rebuilding of inventories. The unemployment rate was said to be down 2.5 points, but it was still about 8 percent. Wage and price inflation was still abating. Yet the Fed was aiming for only 4.5 percent growth in 1984, fourth quarter to fourth quarter—they got it, now revised to 5 percent. (This is the only time that I found so explicit a target in a "Monetary Policy Report to Congress." Generally, the growth target is unstated or is implicit in the FOMC members' projections. In his remarks, Paul warned us against reading any policy intentions into those projections.)

In most postwar recoveries, growth was 6 percent or better in the first year. I have never found convincing the "speed limit" theory, which argues that high growth rates are dangerously inflationary even in very slack economies. Demand management, I think, should aim for high growth at the beginnings of recovery and gradually reduce stimulus as the margin of economic slack declines. The Fed's foot was a bit heavy on the brake.

I mention this episode because it did unintended and unexpected long-lasting damage. The return of double-digit short interest rates in mid-1984, raising long-term bond rates above 13 percent again, ratcheted the dollar up another big notch (20 percent nominal, 19 percent real, in the multilateral trade-weighted index). I realize that, as Paul Krugman convincingly argued, there must have been significant speculative content in the appreciation of the dollar. But U.S. interest rates had a lot to do with it. The merchandise trade deficit grew from $21.7 billion in 1983:4 to $29.3 four quarters later, the current account deficit from $18.3 to $30.0. Reversal of the deterioration proved to be a slow and difficult process, even after the dollar's exchange value fell.

By 1980, economists inside and outside the Federal Reserve and the Treasury understood the qualitative role of exchange rates, capital movements, and trade imbalances in the transmission of monetary measures—and fiscal measures too—to the economy in a world of floating exchange rates and mobile financial funds. Qualitatively, things happened the way our theory said they would. But I guess that no one, even in the Fed's international shop, foresaw how large these effects could be, how long they could persist, and how difficult they might be to reverse.

The drag of the import surplus was one reason that the recovery of real GNP proceeded even more slowly in the two years after 1984, 3.6 percent in 1985 and 1.9 in 1986, while unemployment hovered around 7.0 percent. Only in 1987–88, after the cautious easing of 1986 finally took effect, was the recovery completed, five and a half years after it had begun.

Real interest rates averaged 400 or 500 basis points higher in the 1980s recovery than in previous postwar expansions. This is the proximate cause of several well-known adverse developments in the U.S. economy and the symptom of others. Like most people in this room, I place most of the blame on federal fiscal policy. But the Fed could have lowered rates sooner and further in the period 1984–87.

I tell monetary policy skeptics like my friend Bob Eisner that we could have had—indeed, we would have had—the same recovery in the 1980s without the extraordinary fiscal stimulus, the same performance in GNP and employment without the negative by-products. I have based this claim on the generous interpretation of Fed policy that I have given above. Assuming that the Fed's targets for macroeconomic performance would have been the same had fiscal policy been pre-Reagan normal, I say that the Fed had plenty of room to lower interest rates in pursuit of those targets and would have used it. Maybe, in fact, sound fiscal policy would have made the Fed more expansionary. Maybe our central bankers held back at times in hopes of sending a message about fiscal policy to the president and Congress.

I am still saying these things, now to people who worry whether budget correction will cause recession. I hope I am right. The Fed might have to act faster, in larger steps, than they did in 1984–86. Twenty-five basis points every FOMC meeting would not be enough.

Sometimes, I am afraid, defense of the dollar has been given more weight than it deserves. I am not referring to the fall of 1979, when Paul tells us that the dollar's weakness and the complaints of major foreign central bankers simply reinforced the sufficient domestic reasons for a contractionary move. But supporting the dollar was a consideration in 1984 and again after the Group of Five agreed at the Louvre in early 1987 that the 1985–86 depreciation had gone far enough. (According to Paul, this was Treasury policy, not his preference. The idea that exchange rate policy is the province of the Treasury and that monetary policy is the province of the Federal Reserve seems dangerously anomalous, given that the two policies are essentially one and the same.) Interest rates to support the dollar contributed to the slowdown in 1987 and perhaps to the stock market crash in October. Following the crash, Greenspan and his colleagues eased decisively and let the dollar fall, with good macroeconomic results.

Dollar defense may be a consideration again now, when domestic demand expansions and tight monetary policies are raising interest rates in Japan and Europe. I see no good reason to oppose a depreciation of the dollar when lower interest rates are appropriate to domestic demand management, particularly when there is room in the economy for more net exports. How will we get the capital inflow that we need to "finance" our trade deficit if our interest rates are lower than those overseas? If it takes a dollar low enough to make investors around the world believe that it is going to rise, so be it.

As early as the spring of 1982, I suggested a tripartite accord—White House, Congress, and Fed—to shift the policy mix to tighter budget and easier money. It was a good idea then, and it has been a good idea ever since.

Summary of Discussion

Paul Volcker began the discussion by responding to several points made by Tobin. First, he addressed the extent to which the Federal Reserve worries about financial markets as well as about the economy. He thought that most people at the Fed focus on the economy, although in 1982 he had persuaded them to start thinking about the financial system as well. He and the president of the New York Federal Reserve Bank had worried more about the financial markets than other people had.

Next, Volcker agreed with Tobin that different members of the Federal Open Market Committee (FOMC) weigh various factors differently in choosing the appropriate monetary policy. This is why it is almost impossible to say what weights the Federal Reserve as a whole was giving to the money supply and to other indicators. Volcker thought that one reason that the FOMC keeps returning to interest rate targeting, which is what they seemed to be doing again, is simply that the rest of the committee never completely trusts the chairman. With a money supply target, some members of the FOMC might be suspicious that the chairman would use the small amount of leeway he has in week-to-week operations to produce a slightly different result than they want. With a Federal funds rate target, this problem does not exist.

Third, Volcker disagreed with Tobin's judgment about the degree to which there had been a problem with monetary policy in 1984. The general mind-set at the Federal Reserve had been that the Fed historically made the mistake of tightening monetary policy too late in an expansion and was then forced to tighten too abruptly. Perhaps that background contributed to the Fed sticking to a tighter policy in the summer of 1984 longer than it really intended or, in retrospect, than it should have. The lending market turned out to be tighter than expected because banks were reluctant to lend to each other as freely as they had in the past, and the result was double-digit interest rates. During July and August, there was much disagreement on the FOMC about how to respond, if at all, and it was not until September, when the economy began to look shakier, that monetary policy was finally relaxed.

Further, Volcker said that the Fed had paid attention to exchange rates in 1985 and 1986 and that he did not think that that had been a mistake. He added that Japan and Germany were growing even more slowly than the United States during that period and that he had felt that the burden was on them to expand in the interest of the world economy. So he had devoted considerable effort to encouraging them to expand so that the United States would not have to take inappropriately strong expansionary action itself.

Finally, Volcker remarked that he thought that there were signs that the Federal Reserve was going back to attempts to fine-tune the economy, deliberately or not.

Martin Feldstein asked whether the Federal Reserve expected a recession to occur in 1980 as a result of its change in monetary policy in late 1979.

Volcker responded that the Federal Reserve staff (like many others) had been projecting a recession for a long time but that it had not yet materialized. Thus, he thought that there was some risk of one occurring but that he was not at all certain, as the economy seemed to be expanding despite the expectations and people seemed to be willing to borrow and lend. Volcker said that he knew that a recession would occur sooner or later, regardless of the short-term stance of monetary policy, and that even now he is not sure whether the economy would have had a recession in March and April if credit controls had not been imposed. Volcker also noted that the White House had strongly urged (and authorized) the credit controls to make a political point as a supplement to the more traditional monetary restraint.

Feldstein questioned whether it was a natural thing that the economy had turned around so quickly after the very sharp downturn in 1980. As Volcker had described it, the credit controls induced a drop in money demand so that interest rates fell automatically without any explicit action by the Fed. In response to lower interest rates, money demand increased, and the economy recovered, with the Fed just a passive player. *Volcker* clarified that the Federal Reserve had taken the discretionary step of increasing nonborrowed reserves on several occasions.

Feldstein asked how effective the 1979 "regime shift" had been in convincing financial markets that the Federal Reserve was serious about reducing inflation.

Volcker believed that the outcome of the regime shift was not as favorable as he had expected or hoped. The Fed wanted to show banks that they did not have an inexhaustible supply of money, so they ought to take more care about the credit they were extending. This is the reason that the Fed put a special reserve requirement on time deposit accounts in October. Yet the policy was not as effective as hoped because of deep skepticism in the market. One indication was that people interpreted the fact that the Federal Reserve set monitoring ranges for the Federal funds rate as meaning that it was not really going to follow the new policy. Volcker added that this was why he was really not sure that there would have been a recession in March 1980 without the credit controls.

William Niskanen questioned the motivation of the Carter administration when it asked the Federal Reserve to impose credit controls in March 1980.

Charles Schultze replied that he had thought that the rationale for the policy was somewhat absurd. The Carter administration had been preparing an economic package that reduced the budget deficit by cutting social programs and encouraged the Fed to tighten monetary policy. But parts of the administration wanted a "liberal element" to combine with these conservative pieces, and the AFL-CIO was urging them to use credit controls to reduce the flow of credit without raising interest rates. So the Carter administration asked the Fed to impose the controls. Schultze added that no one had anticipated the public's response—people tore up their credit cards and mailed them back, and there was a 40 percent drop in the monthly sales of big-ticket items. What was, objectively, a relatively mild penalty on consumer loans unexpectedly turned into a massive reduction in borrowing.

Paul Krugman noted that, in the discussion of budget policy, both Stockman and Schultze concluded that the standard budget policy in the United States is essentially an equilibrating one but that there were unusual events at the beginning of the 1980s that changed matters. For monetary policy, most people would conclude that it normally has an inflationary bias, where the Federal Reserve fights recessions earnestly and responds to inflations somewhat late. But, in the early 1980s, monetary policy, like fiscal policy, was completely out of character. Krugman wondered why this was possible. One explanation might be the great intellectual confusion that was reigning in 1980. There was the monetarist/rational expectations belief, for example, that, if you strongly announced your willingness to suffer pain, you would not actually have to suffer it. Monetarism also gave the Fed the ability to say that it was simply targeting monetary aggregates and not actually planning on a recession.

Krugman also asked whether it was simply a "stealth tactic" for the Fed to use the trappings of monetarism to pursue an essentially orthodox disinflationary policy.

Volcker replied that he thought that monetarist theory had been important in shaping the monetary policy of the early 1980s, as the theory had gained respect from both the public and professionals. He thought that rational expectations theory had been much less important. Most crucial to the shaping of monetary policy, however, was the fact that the general public was very upset when inflation rates were 14–15 percent, and they realized that it had something to do with money. So they were more willing to tolerate measures to reduce inflation by reducing money growth than when inflation did not seem so troublesome.

Volcker asserted strongly that applying monetarist theory had not been a stealth tactic. He believed that the Fed had used monetarism partly to discipline itself and partly to take advantage of the public support for such a policy. It was much easier to explain a monetarist policy to the public because he could point out that money is related to inflation, so that, in order to restrain inflation, the Fed needed to restrain the money supply. It seemed common sense that too much money meant too much inflation—people had learned this in school and had read it in the daily press. Volcker felt that it had been a very simple message, important to the explanation and support of policy.

James Tobin stressed Krugman's question about the extent to which the Federal Open Market Committee had been influenced by the rational expectations/monetarist doctrine in the late 1970s and afterward. The theory says that, by making a credible threat that there will be pain and suffering about which the Fed will do nothing, the Fed can accelerate disinflation without as much pain and suffering. Had this theory been significant in the shift in policy during the period 1979–82?

Volcker responded that there had been a hope that the theory would work in a general way, but certainly no faith in the more extreme formulations. There was a view that, if the Fed was credible enough, then short-term interest rates might go up, but long-term rates would remain stable or even go down because everyone had so much faith in the new, powerful anti-inflation program. In fact, however, long-term rates went up.

William Poole said that one of the puzzles from the period 1979–82 is why both long- and short-term interest rates were so volatile. One answer could be that the markets did not gain confidence in the Federal Reserve's conviction to stick with its policy until the economy had suffered a considerable way through the recession. But Poole did not believe that this explanation completely solves the puzzle about why long rates were so volatile and followed short rates so closely.

Schultze commented that perhaps Volcker sold himself a little short by denying the use of stealth in 1979. Schultze said that Volcker had been right, and that he and William Miller [chairman of the Federal Reserve Board, 1978–79] had been wrong, about the tactic to be used when radically changing the stance of monetary policy. For twenty-five years, the public had perceived the Fed as sitting around deciding what interest rates were going to be the next month, and the politicians saw the Fed as directly responsible for every quarter of a percent rise in rates. In 1979, the Fed had to make massive moves in interest rates, which would have been impossible had they tried to do it directly. Now that the Fed no longer has to move interest rates a lot, they can go back to targeting them.

Volcker responded that the Federal Open Market Committee really had no idea that interest rates were going to rise to 19 percent. It was not as though they decided that they wanted interest rates to go 19 percent and just announced the money supply figure that they knew was going to result in those rates. Volcker had known that interest rates were going to go up, but, had he known in advance that they would increase so much, he did not think that he would have been able to convince the committee, or perhaps himself, to implement the same policy. He emphasized this point because he did not think that the Federal Reserve can survive as an institution if people become convinced that things are done by stealth. He felt that it is very dangerous for any institution that depends on people's confidence to adopt policies on the basis that they will fool people. He regretted the confusion on this point that had been sown by later comments of some on the Open Market Committee itself.

Feldstein repeated Tobin's statement that at some point the Federal Reserve had stopped targeting the monetary aggregates and had made the true target nominal GNP and the operating target the Federal funds rate. He asked Volcker if this were true.

Volcker replied that, as the chairman, he had looked at both the economy and the money supply figures and, as he had mentioned earlier, also at the exchange rate and at financial markets when that seemed important. He thought that the real shift in the operating target was in October 1982, when the Fed switched from total nonborrowed reserves to marginal borrowing. As time passed, there was a lot of debate in the Federal Open Market Committee (FOMC) between those who wanted to target interest rates directly and those who wanted to stick with borrowing. People may say that it amounts to the same thing because there is obviously a close relation, but it is not a perfect relation, and at times the two targets imply different operational approaches.

Volcker added that he had opposed returning to interest rate targeting because it induces a great reluctance to adjust policy, as Schultze said. When one is aiming directly at interest rates, it becomes a great decision to change them by a quarter of a percent, so, to avoid this inertia, Volcker did not want to target interest rates directly. Volcker said that it appears as though the Fed has gone back to targeting interest rates directly and that this has in fact created more inertia.

Volcker then addressed the issue of whether real GNP was the Fed's true target. He said that he was never confident that there was a close relation between Fed policy and nominal or real GNP over relevant time periods for operational decisions. So, even though he monitored the acceleration or deceleration of GNP, it was really very hard to target as a short-term operational matter. Volcker noted that the GNP numbers in the semiannual FOMC reports that Tobin mentioned were really projections, not targets.

Tobin pointed out that it seems logical to interpret those projections as implicit targets, given that they come from "the pilot of the boat." He went on to say that he did not mean to imply that the Fed was using real GNP as the target in any long-run sense but only that the Fed probably thinks of the economy in the old-fashioned terms of slack and catch-up in relation to normal full-employment growth. He noted that, although there are many economists in the world today who do not think of the economy in those terms, he thought that this is how the Fed was thinking of it during that period. So they based their real GNP goals on the implications for full employment as well as for inflation and the many other phenomena of concern.

Feldstein added that the Fed's nominal GNP projections seemed to be more or less consistent with traditional velocity relations and the Fed's monetary targets. Further, these nominal GNP projections were in line with the real GNP/inflation breakdowns forecast by the Fed. This suggests that, although the Fed may not literally have had nominal GNP targets, it did have a sense of the levels of nominal GNP, real GNP, and inflation that were consistent with its monetary policy. It seems as though the level of nominal GNP really was a central factor.

Volcker stated that the projections presented were not a set of forecasts that had been debated. They were the independent projections of nineteen voting and nonvoting members of the Federal Open Market Committee collected before the meetings, and the projections rarely changed after the meetings. Volcker added that people made projections of real GNP and of prices and then added them up to get nominal GNP. Occasionally, these projections of nominal GNP implied unusual velocity behavior when combined with the monetary targets, but the implied velocity was never completely unrealistic.

Fred Bergsten responded that, despite Volcker's description of the FOMC meetings, people have found a closer correlation of monetary policy with nominal GNP than with anything else.

Geoffrey Carliner asked how important President Reagan's support had been to the Fed in its efforts to fight inflation in 1981 and early 1982. He also wondered whether the Fed would have received similar support from President Carter.

Volcker said that he thought that the Federal Reserve had received fairly good support from Carter. Despite the surge in interest rates, Carter mentioned monetary policy only once during the 1980 campaign. The Reagan administration was very monetarist and did not care about interest rates, and it encouraged the Fed to pursue tight money in early 1981. The economy continued to grow for a while despite the very high interest rates, but, when the recession finally occurred, the administration stopped encouraging the restraint on money, and a certain amount of sniping developed. Volcker said that he thought that there were probably many people in the White House and at the Treasury who tried to get President Reagan to criticize the Federal Reserve at that point but that Reagan would not say anything bad about an anti-inflationary policy, which was important.

Feldstein agreed that there were many people within the administration who were taking every opportunity to criticize the Fed in 1983 and 1984, especially as more and more private forecasters were predicting another recession. Nevertheless, President Reagan often took the opportunity at news conferences to say that he was supporting the Fed.

Volcker added that, in his view, the most important single action of the administration in helping the anti-inflation fight was defeating the air traffic controllers' strike. He thought that this action had had a rather profound, and, from his standpoint, constructive, effect on the climate of labor-management relations, even though it had not been a wage issue at the time.

Charls Walker asked the role of the presidents of the Federal Reserve Banks in making policy. He wondered in particular whether they had supported or hindered Volcker's efforts from 1980 to 1982.

Volcker said that there had been a very harmonious board during that period. People knew each other well and did not have very divergent views. Without question, however, the most monetarist people were some of the bank presidents. So Volcker said that he instinctively knew that many of the bank presidents would be enthusiastic over the new policy because they had at times in the past promoted something like that themselves.

Volcker also remarked that, although he received supportive comments on monetary policy from the administration, their statements emphasized a gradual approach. After 1979, Volcker realized that it was not realistic to decrease the money supply gradually and expect that the economy would suffer no adverse effects. The Fed could not control the money supply that closely. Thus, Volcker tried to remove the word *gradual* from all statements after 1979.

Bergsten opened the subject of how external factors like the dollar had influenced Volcker's monetary policy. Although Tobin criticized Volcker for paying too much attention to the dollar, Bergsten thought that he had emphasized it much less than in the popular political view. In particular, Bergsten wondered about the role of external factors in Volcker's 1979 decision. The dollar had fallen sharply in late 1978 and remained precarious in 1979, and Volcker returned from the IMF meeting in Belgrade more quickly than had been scheduled. Had international events been, although not the cause of Volcker's decision, the trigger for deciding to move at that point?

Bergsten also asked about the role of external factors in 1982 when the Fed stopped targeting the monetary aggregates and went back to interest rate targeting. Some people suggested that the timing trigger had been the Mexico debt crisis because of its implications for the U.S. banking system.

Volcker said that the weakness of the dollar in 1979 had been just one factor in the whole inflationary expectations/lack of credibility picture. He had talked with some of his central banking colleagues at the Belgrade meeting to see how they would react to a strongly anti-inflationary monetary policy, and they had encouraged him. But he had returned from Belgrade not because of any great urgency caused by the meeting but because he felt that he should be back to work on this program. Even more important than the Belgrade meeting itself was a meeting with German Chancellor Helmut Schmidt during a stopover on the return flight. Schmidt had said that the U.S. economy was in trouble and that inflation was out of control. Shortly before that, Volcker had told Schultze and William Miller about the monetary policy he was considering, and the Schmidt visit may have been important in reinforcing the sense of urgency.

As for the change in policy in 1982, Volcker noted that the first signals of easing were in July, before the Mexican debt crisis erupted in the open. He did think that the precariousness of the international situation had been a factor but that domestic financial concerns had played a more important role.

On a related topic, *Poole* pointed out that the Plaza Agreement had committed the U.S. government to depreciate the exchange rate, requiring that interest rates be kept low. He felt that this had put a constraint on what the Federal Reserve could do. The market understood this constraint and took it as a signal that monetary policy was going to be biased in an easier direction than would otherwise have been the case.

Volcker recalled that he did discuss monetary policy with the secretary of the Treasury at the time of the Plaza Agreement but that, since he had thought that there was no reasonable prospect that the Fed would be tightening monetary policy for some months anyway, he had supported the agreement. Volcker said that, if he had thought that the Plaza Agreement would constrain the Fed's decision making, his discussion with the secretary of Treasury would have been different.

Feldstein asked if similar concerns were raised around the time of the Louvre Agreement and the period thereafter. *Volcker* said that there must have been some discussion at the time but that he did not remember it, probably because it had not been a problem. It had not been discussed at the Louvre itself.

Feldstein then asked why the Treasury changed its policy regarding the exchange rate between 1985 and 1987. In 1985, the Treasury seemed eager to push the value of the dollar down, whereas, in 1987, it wanted to keep the dollar from declining any further. He wondered how much the decision to stop the dollar from declining was due to Volcker's concerns about an increase in inflation.

Volcker said that, under Secretary Don Regan, the Treasury Department had taken it as a badge of national honor that the value of the dollar was high. They did not want to intervene, no matter how high the dollar climbed. On the other hand, Treasury Secretary James Baker and Deputy Secretary Richard Darman seemed to dislike the large trade deficit, and they were particularly concerned about the increasing protectionist pressures in Congress. Volcker thought that this concern was really what had triggered the Plaza Agreement.

As for the decision to stop the decline of the dollar in 1987, Volcker said that the Treasury was certainly aware of his concerns about inflation and more pointedly than about the implications of a continuing fall in the dollar. He thought that the Treasury had already become somewhat concerned about the implications of further dollar decline. Also, the Treasury was concerned about international cooperation from Japan, which it wanted to undertake an expansionary fiscal policy.

3   Tax Policy

1. Don Fullerton
2. Charls E. Walker
3. Russell B. Long

---

1. Don Fullerton

Inputs to Tax Policy-Making: The Supply-Side, the Deficit, and the Level Playing Field

Thousands of issues swirled in the whirlwind of tax policy-making in the Reagan era, and any effort to sort them out must inevitably be hampered by differences in perspective on their relative importance, their impacts, and even their definitions. Taxonomy and classifications can differ. After some reflection, however, it seems to me that most of the important issues can be categorized into three major forces that shaped the making of tax policy during the decade.

Financial support was provided by a grant from the Olin Foundation to the National Bureau of Economic Research. This paper would not have been possible without the generous time for interviews and comments provided by busy former and current policymakers such as J. Gregory Ballentine (deputy assistant secretary for tax analysis, Treasury Department, 1981–83, and associate director, Office of Management and Budget, 1983–85), David Brockway (chief of staff, Joint Tax Committee, 1983–87), Buck Chapoton (assistant secretary for tax policy, Treasury Department, 1981–84), Martin Feldstein (chairman of the Council of Economic Advisers, 1982–84), Representative Willis D. Gradison, Jr. (member, Committee on Ways and Means, 1975–1992), Larry Lindsey (associate director for domestic policy, the White House, 1989–1991), Mark McConaghy (chief of staff, Joint Tax Committee, 1981–83), Ronald A. Pearlman (assistant secretary for tax policy, Treasury Department, 1984–86, and chief of staff, Joint Tax Committee, 1987–1990), John Salmon (chief counsel, Committee on Ways and Means, 1981–84), Emil Sunley (deputy assistant secretary for tax analysis, Treasury Department, 1977–81), Randy Weiss (deputy chief of staff, Joint Tax Committee, 1983–88), and Jim Wetzler (deputy chief of staff, Joint Tax Committee, 1979–83). The author is also grateful for helpful suggestions from Larry Dildine, Drew Lyon, Charles McLure, Joe Minarik, and Jon Skinner. The research reported here is part of the NBER's research program in taxation. Any opinions expressed are those of the author and not those of the National Bureau of Economic Research.

First, tax policy in the 1980s was profoundly affected by the "supply-side" view popularized in the late 1970s by Arthur Laffer, Jude Wanniski, and Representative Jack Kemp. They pointed out that high personal marginal tax rates encourage taxpayers to stay home from work, enter the cash or barter economy, engage in tax shelters, or rearrange financial affairs to avoid paying tax. A reduction in the rate of tax would then have feedback effects that increase the tax base and mitigate the fall in revenue. Some define *supply-side* by the view that tax rate reductions have these advantageous feedback effects, and others define it by the extreme view that the tax base rises by more than the tax rate falls. In the latter case, the government could actually collect more revenue by lowering the rate of tax (see the papers in Meyer 1981). Whatever its definition, however, the supply-side clearly propelled policymakers into the Economic Recovery Tax Act of 1981 as well as the additional marginal rate reduction of the Tax Reform Act of 1986.

Second, the 1980s have been characterized by persistent large government deficits. Some point to the large tax cuts of 1981 as the "cause" of these deficits, while others condemn the failure to reduce spending. Whatever "caused" these persistent government deficits, however, they undoubtedly reshaped the making of tax policy after 1981. Up to this point, inflation in an unindexed tax system continually pushed taxpayers into higher brackets, increased real revenues automatically, and allowed Congress to enact successive tax "reduction" legislation. Tax policymakers simply did not have to worry about obtaining enough revenue (see, e.g., McLure 1990a). I will emphasize the importance of the indexing provisions of the 1981 act as the beginning of an era that instead has a perennial shortfall in revenue. The current process of tax policymaking is very different because of it.

Third, although I appeal to a rather broad definition, the *level playing field* evolved during this period to encompass notions of fairness, economic efficiency, and even simplicity. Some companies and individuals were observed to pay high effective tax rates, while others with the same income paid little or no tax at all. Economists pointed to these differences as a source of resource misallocation and economic inefficiency in production, a view that I call the *efficiency version* of the level playing field. Others simply viewed these differences as unfair, a view that I call the *equity version* of the level playing field. This view relates to *horizontal equity,* the equal treatment of those with the same income, in contrast to the *vertical equity* treatment of those with different incomes. Under either version of the level playing field, there was growing support for the idea that government should get out of the business of deciding which investments are most productive. This idea was certainly voiced earlier, but not until the 1980s was it assimilated, digested, and accepted.[1] It became a driving force in the tax increases of 1982–84, the Tax Reform Act of 1986, and beyond. (See, e.g., *The President's Tax Proposals* 1985.)

1. See the papers in the Summer 1987 issue of the *Journal of Economic Perspectives.*

I organize discussion around these three headings primarily because, as I will argue, they were wholly new forces in the field of tax policy-making. Certainly, other perennial issues were important during this period as well, and I take this opportunity to note topics *not* covered in this paper. Since I emphasize the domestic economy, readers interested primarily in foreign repercussions should see Grubert and Mutti (1987) or McLure (1990b). Those interested in the politics of tax reform should see Witte (1985), Stewart (1991), or Conlan, Wrightson, and Beam (1990). For the effects of the budget process on tax policy, see Rudder (1983) or Merrill, Collender, and Cook (1990). On issues of complexity, see McLure (1990a).

Also, since I emphasize the economic thinking of policymakers during debates about proposals, I do not discuss the actual effects of tax changes. For the effects of the 1981 act on the distribution of tax burdens, see U.S. Congressional Budget Office (1987), U.S. House of Representatives (1990), and Lindsey (1990). For many other economic effects of the 1986 act, see U.S. Department of the Treasury (1987) and all the papers in Slemrod (1990).

Details of the tax laws themselves can be found in various publications of the U.S. Congress and the Commerce Clearing House. Details of the arduous process toward just one piece of legislation, the 1986 act, can be found in Birnbaum and Murray (1987) and Conlan, Wrightson, and Beam (1990). Since this one chapter must cover legislation throughout the 1980s, it cannot do justice to these details. Instead, I will discuss selected issues, especially as they relate to the supply-side, the deficit, and the level playing field. Primarily, however, I will argue that it is most unusual to have the phenomenon of three such wholly novel developments shaping policy in one decade.

3.1 Some Relevant Background

To imagine the debate around the turn of the century about the proposed Sixteenth Amendment's direct tax on incomes, one only need consider the current debate about a possible tax on value added: the new tax would be a powerful source of revenue even at low rates and might allow considerable growth of government if imposed at higher rates. Table 3.1 outlines a history of just the top marginal income tax rate, the additional tax paid if a person in the highest income bracket were to earn one more dollar. This top rate starts at only 7 and then 15 percent, but it jumps significantly at the First World War and again near the Second World War. Remarkably, the table shows that the top personal marginal tax rate from 1944 until 1964 was over 90 percent.

Since this paper is supposed to discuss what prompted tax policy changes since 1980, it will address the specific question, What prompted the dramatic reduction in personal marginal tax rates from a top 70 percent rate in 1980 to a top 33 percent rate by 1988? One easy, and probably correct, answer is to point out the increasing popularity around 1980 of the supply-side view that high marginal tax rates can stifle incentives to work and invest. This review of

Table 3.1   **The Top Federal Marginal Personal Income Tax Rate in the
                        United States**

Years	Top Rate (%)	Years	Top Rate (%)
1913–15	7	1946–51	91
1916	15	1952–53	92
1917	67	1954–63	91
1918	77	1964	77
1919–21	73	1965–67	70
1922–23	58	1968	75.25
1925–31	25	1969	77
1932–35	63	1970	71.75
1936–39	79	1971–81	70
1940–41	81	1982–86	50
1942–43	88	1987	38
1944–45	94	1988–	33

Source: Tax Foundation (1988, table C36). For some surcharges and special rules, see the notes to Tax Foundation (1988).

Note: From 1944 to 1963, when the top marginal rate exceeded 90 percent, maximum effective rate limitations kept the total tax as a fraction of taxable income (the average tax) below 90 percent. This cap varied between 77 percent (1948–49) and 88 percent (1952–53). Also, these top bracket rates include surcharges of 7.5 percent in 1968, 10 percent in 1969, and 2.5 percent in 1970. They exclude the minimum tax (enacted in 1969) and the 50 percent maximum rate on earned income (enacted in 1971).

prior history, however, turns the question on its head. The inverted question is much more difficult, and perhaps unanswerable. What in the world prompted tax policymakers during the twenty-year period from 1944 until 1964 to enact personal marginal tax rates *over 90 percent?*

For two reasons, the top rate is a misleading indicator of the overall impact of the tax. First, the revenue impact of the income tax depends much more on the taxation of middle brackets than on the taxation of just the top bracket. Pechman (1987, 375) shows that 96.7 percent of tax returns in 1980 (paying 68.7 percent of the tax) were in brackets below $50,000 of adjusted gross income. Second, the link between rates and revenues is broken by exemptions, deductions, and a host of special provisions. Pechman estimates that "in 1947 only about 40 percent of personal income was subject to tax; this rose to 50 percent in 1969 and then declined to 45–47 percent between 1971 and 1984" (p. 66). For both these reasons, the total federal individual income tax after 1947 was never more than 11.3 percent of personal income, a high that it reached in 1981.

Table 3.2 shows more detailed information about the personal income tax between 1947 and 1985. The first column repeats the top bracket rate, from table 3.1 above, and the second column shows the tax as a percentage of personal income. For the years shown, this ratio hit a low of 7.0 percent in 1949, rose to 10.2 percent in 1952, and fell below that level for the next fifteen years. It then reached highs of 11.2 in 1969 and 11.3 in 1981. The third column shows

Table 3.2   **Personal Income Tax Rates and Revenues**

Year	Top Bracket Rate %	Tax as % of Personal Income	Tax as % of Federal Receipts
1947	91	9.5	46.5
1948	91	7.4	44.0
1949	91	7.0	42.8
1950	91	8.1	36.7
1951	91	9.4	41.5
1952	92	10.2	46.7
1953	92	10.1	46.5
1954	91	9.1	45.7
1955	91	9.4	43.9
1956	91	9.7	43.2
1957	91	9.7	44.5
1958	91	9.3	43.6
1959	91	9.9	46.3
1960	91	9.6	44.0
1961	91	9.9	43.8
1962	91	9.9	45.7
1963	91	10.1	44.7
1964	77	9.3	43.2
1965	70	9.0	41.8
1966	70	9.3	42.4
1967	70	9.8	41.3
1968	75.25	10.8	44.9
1969	77	11.2	46.7
1970	71.75	10.1	46.9
1971	70	9.6	46.1
1972	70	9.5	45.7
1973	70	9.8	44.7
1974	70	10.2	45.2
1975	70	9.5	43.9
1976	70	9.8	44.2
1977	70	9.9	44.3
1978	70	10.4	45.3
1979	70	10.6	47.0
1980	70	11.1	47.2
1981	70	11.3	47.7
1982	50	10.4	48.2
1983	50	9.7	48.1
1984	50	9.7	44.8
1985	50	9.8	45.6

Source: Pechman (1987, 313–14, 346, 370) and Steuerle and Hartzmark (1981, 160).

Note: From 1944 to 1963, when the top marginal rate exceeded 90 percent, maximum effective rate limitations kept the total tax as a fraction of taxable income (the average tax) below 90 percent. This cap varied between 77 percent (1948–49) and 88 percent (1952–53). Also, these top bracket rates include surcharges of 7.5 percent in 1968, 10 percent in 1969, and 2.5 percent in 1970. They exclude the minimum tax (enacted in 1969) and the 50 percent maximum rate on earned income (enacted in 1971).

the personal income tax as a percentage of total federal receipts. For virtually all the years shown, this fraction varied only between 41 and 48 percent, reaching its high in 1982. The relative stability of the personal tax, however, masks the falling corporate tax share and the rising payroll tax share of federal receipts.

Thus, the top 90 percent personal rate was perhaps not viewed as such a problem: it was good for the perception that rich people paid plenty of tax, but less than one-tenth of 1 percent of taxpayers ever had to pay at that rate. Virtually anyone with that much income would be doing something to avoid that bracket. With the benefit of hindsight, however, this logic dovetails perfectly with the supply-side view that high rates are counterproductive by inducing changes in behavior. Incentives clearly were stifled for those allowed to keep less than a dime out of a dollar's extra effort. In particular, Ronald Reagan tells of making movies during this period with over a 90 percent top bracket: "So we all quit working after four pictures and went off to the country" (Stockman 1987, 11). The perceived success of the Kennedy-Johnson cut in the top rate from 91 to 70 percent in 1964 was a major factor in the subsequent effort in 1980 to cut the top rate to 50 percent.

Another important feature of the prior tax code was that inflation and not just real growth would push poor households onto the tax roles and middle-income taxpayers into higher brackets. Minarik (1985, 37) shows that, from 1965 to 1980, the marginal rate on a family with the median income increased from 17 to 24 percent while that on a family with twice the median income increased from 22 to 43 percent. Inflation did not increase the marginal rate of those already in the top bracket, but it did increase their tax as a fraction of income (see Steuerle and Hartzmark 1981). As a result, legislators always seemed to find themselves with surplus revenue that could be used for some combination of increased spending or decreased taxes: "In the seven-year period from 1975 through 1981, eight of the eleven major revenue measures (73 percent) enacted by Congress were estimated by the Treasury Department to lose revenues in the first three fiscal years after enactment, with an average revenue loss of $27 billion" (Merrill, Collender, and Cook 1990, 37).

Very little rate reduction occurred from 1965 to 1980, so the primary form of tax reduction was through additional credits or deductions. Special Analysis G of the U.S. Budget documents the growth of "tax expenditures," the revenues lost from special tax provisions that might have been direct expenditures instead. Without these tax expenditures, personal tax revenues would have been 50 percent higher in 1974, almost twice as high in 1984, and over twice as high in 1986. Tax expenditures sometimes exceeded 45 percent of direct federal outlays (but the 1986 act cut them to 34 percent of those outlays).

This is not to say that the government often had a surplus, for the money was most often spent or returned to taxpayers before it was ever collected. The point is that revenues were always projected to rise until a future year in which a surplus was expected. Table 3.3 shows, from 1976 to 1989, the deficit or

Table 3.3   **CBO Baseline Budget Deficit (−) or Surplus (+) for Fiscal Years, as a Percentage of GNP**

Report Date	Prior Year	Current Year	First Year	Second Year	Third Year	Fourth Year	Fifth Year
1976[a,c]	−2.9	−4.7	−2.8	−1.6	1.6	1.8	1.8
1977[c]	−3.9	−2.8	−2.2	−.7	.5	1.7	2.7
1978[c]	N.A.	N.A.	−1.7	−.4	.9	2.0	2.8
1979[d]	−2.4	−1.8	−1.9	−1.1	.2	1.2	2.4
1980	−1.2	−1.8	−.8	−.6	.0	.0	.1
1981[b,d]	−2.2	−2.1	−2.2	N.A.	N.A.	N.A.	N.A.
1982	−2.7	−4.2	−5.1	−5.4	−5.4	−5.6	−5.4
1983	−4.2	−6.6	−6.1	−6.0	−6.0	−6.0	−5.9
1984	−6.4	−5.7	−5.3	−5.4	−5.7	−5.9	−6.3
1985	−5.2	−5.6	−5.2	−5.2	−5.1	−5.2	−5.3
1986	−5.4	−5.0	−4.0	−3.4	−2.8	−2.1	−1.7
1987	−5.3	−4.0	−3.6	−3.2	−2.5	−1.9	−1.4
1988	−3.4	−3.4	−3.5	−3.1	−2.8	−2.5	−2.1
1989	−3.2	−3.0	−2.6	−2.4	−2.2	−2.0	−1.7

Source: Merrill, Collender, and Cook (1990). For their source, Merrill et al. refer to various issues of the CBO's *Economic and Budget Outlook.* Total deficit includes off-budget items.

Note: NA = not available.

[a]Average of path A and B forecasts (5 and 6 percent GNP growth assumptions).

[b]Calendar year 1981–82 GNP estimated as average of published range.

[c]Fiscal year GNP estimated as 25 percent of prior and 75 percent of future calendar year GNP forecasts (50 percent of prior and future calendar years used for fiscal year 1976).

[d]Calculated by subtracting outlays from revenues, both as a percentage of GNP.

surplus from the past year and the current year and the projected deficit or surplus for the next five years. In the late 1970s, the current deficit was always projected to turn into a surplus within those five years. The quote given above makes clear that a tax reduction such as the 1981 act was not necessarily unusual, except perhaps for the extent of the rate cut. The act included indexing after 1985, however, so that inflation would no longer push taxpayers into higher brackets. The result is a fundamental shift in the nature of the policy problem, as shown in table 3.3: after 1981, the budget is always projected to remain in deficit. Until the row for 1986 (the 1987–91 projection), those deficits were even expected to rise as a fraction of GNP. As a consequence, "in the following seven years of 1982 through 1988, fourteen of the seventeen major revenue measures (82 percent) were estimated to raise revenue in the first three years after enactment, with an average revenue gain of $15 billion" (Merrill, Collender, and Cook 1990, 37). Thus, 1981 represents a watershed year in the making of tax policy, from an era of constantly projected surpluses to one of constantly projected deficits. As discussed below, the making of tax policy would never be the same.

Policymakers used the excess revenue during the postwar period, not just to offset bracket creep in the personal tax system, but to provide additional investment incentives in the corporate tax system. In 1954, Congress first introduced accelerated methods of depreciation such as double-declining-balance or sum-of-the-years'-digits. Then, in 1962, the Treasury issued "Guidelines" with a 30–40 percent shortening of previously suggested Bulletin F lives, and the Congress enacted the first investment tax credit (ITC) for equipment. In 1971, the Asset Depreciation Range (ADR) permitted a 20 percent reduction from the Guideline lifetimes. Some acceleration was perhaps intended to offset the reduction in real allowances caused by increasing inflation, but still the corporate income tax fell from 30.3 percent of federal revenue in 1954 to 12.5 percent in 1980. The 1981 act further reduced depreciation lifetimes with the Accelerated Cost Recovery System (ACRS), and the corporate income tax fell to 10, 8, and 6 percent of federal revenues in 1981, 82, and 83, respectively (Pechman 1987, 370).[2] Thus, the postwar period reflects a falling ratio of observed corporate taxes to profits, or the "average effective tax rate," from 51 percent in 1960 to 24 percent in 1985 (Auerbach and Poterba 1987, 6).

A more forward-looking measure of investment incentives is the "marginal effective tax rate," the ratio of expected future taxes to expected future income from a hypothetical marginal investment. One such measure, shown in the bottom row of table 3.4, fell from 48 percent under 1960 law, to 37 percent under 1980 law, to 26 percent under the 1981 act. This measure includes *all* taxes on the expected income from the investment, such as corporate taxes, property taxes, and personal income taxes. However, other calculations from King and Fullerton (1984) indicate that the effective rate from just property taxes and personal taxes in 1981 would be 35 percent. In other words, the corporate tax system under 1981 law provides a net *subsidy* in the sense that its elimination would cause an *increase* in this total effective tax rate from 26 to 35 percent. This subsidy results from the combination of accelerated depreciation, the investment tax credit, and interest deductions at a statutory corporate rate that exceeds the average of the rates at which recipients are taxes on interest income.[3]

Of course, this subsidy is not uniform across all investments of all firms, and therein lies an important problem. The 1960 calculations, before the investment tax credit was enacted, show effective tax rates of 59 percent for equipment and 45 percent for buildings or inventories. By 1980, with the ITC, these were 18 percent for machinery, 41 percent for buildings and 47 percent for inventories. In the calculations of King and Fullerton (1984, 252) for just prop-

2. Note that the 1981 act did not reduce the statutory corporate tax rate. Also, Auerbach and Poterba (1987) show that accelerated depreciation and other legislated changes account for less than half the decline in corporate tax revenues since the mid-1960s while reduced profitability and other factors account for the rest.

3. King and Fullerton (1984) also show how inflation raises this effective tax rate through depreciation allowances based on historical cost and through taxation of nominal capital gains and lowers the effective tax rate through deductions for nominal interest at a rate that exceeds the average rate of recipients. The net effect of inflation is mixed.

Table 3.4	Marginal Effective Tax Rates in the United States (%)			
	1960 Law	1980 Law	1981 Act	1986 Act
Asset:				
Machinery	59.3	17.6	−5.5	38.9
Buildings	45.0	41.1	30.2	43.1
Inventories	45.6	47.0	47.0	42.8
Industry:				
Manufacturing	58.8	52.7	43.5	51.1
Other industry	38.4	14.6	.7	31.3
Commerce	42.4	38.2	27.5	39.5
Source of finance:				
Debt	−3.6	−16.3	−31.9	5.5
New share issues	96.5	91.2	84.9	74.7
Retained earnings	73.1	62.4	53.4	59.6
Owner:				
Households	65.3	57.5	48.2	54.4
Tax-exempt institutions	−.9	−21.5	−37.6	5.5
Insurance companies	37.6	23.4	11.2	36.3
Overall	48.4	37.2	26.2	42.1

Source: King and Fullerton (1984, 244, 255, and 261). Column 4 is from Fullerton and Karayannis (1993). Calculations assume a 10 percent pretax rate of return, a 6.77 percent rate of inflation, and sufficient tax liability for the firm to use all available credits and deductions. These rates include the net effect of all corporate taxes, property taxes, and personal taxes on the income from a marginal investment in the corporate sector.

erty taxes and personal taxes in 1980, the effective rate for machinery is 34 percent. Thus, even by 1980, the corporate tax system was providing a net subsidy for machinery. Under the fully phased-in version of the 1981 act, assuming enough tax liability that all credits and deductions could be used, the total effective tax rate on machinery was a *negative* 5.5 percent (table 3.4). The corporate subsidy was so large that it more than offset positive property taxes and personal taxes on corporate-source income.[4]

As discussed more fully below, the 1981 act was intended to provide more investment incentives for capital formation that, in turn, would enhance future productivity. The familiar course for such incentives was to apply them primarily to equipment. But the 1981 act carried this logic to such an extreme that the effective tax rate on machinery was −5.5 percent, the rate on buildings was +30 percent, and that on inventories or land was still +47 percent. Averaged over these assets, as shown in table 3.4, an investment financed by new share issues faced a marginal effective tax rate of +85 percent, and one financed by debt faced −32 percent. As a consequence, some equipment-

4. Even if the firm did not have enough tax liability to use all credits itself, the "safe-harbor leasing" feature of the 1981 law allowed it to lease equipment from another firm that could use the credit, at a rental price that passed through the benefit of the credit.

intensive or debt-intensive firms were paying little or no tax in the early 1980s, while other firms such as retailers were paying high effective tax rates.[5]

Many economists pointed out that these differences would lead to misallocations of resources and a lower value of output than if the same amount of tax were collected in a more uniform manner. Others simply thought it unfair that some firms with positive income were paying no tax. These investment incentives were the building blocks of tax shelters, and they were sometimes used by high-income firms and individuals to avoid paying any tax at all. Calls were heard for a "level playing field" that would subject all firms and all types of investment to more similar effective tax rates. The development and impact of such ideas will be examined below.

3.2   The Supply-Side

It was 1974 when Arthur Laffer first drew his famous curve on a napkin in a Washington restaurant.[6] Its logic is amazingly simple. Government revenue must be zero at a tax rate of 0 percent, and revenue must also be zero at a tax rate of 100 percent since nobody would bother to work or earn other forms of income subject to tax. If any revenue is raised between tax rates of 0 and 100 percent, there must be an intermediate rate at which revenue is maximized. The counterintuitive implication is that there must also be a range over which a higher tax rate reduces revenue. Even more surprising, perhaps, is that this result was not already well known and well understood by everyone interested in tax policy.

The principle economic reason given for this result was that taxpayers react by changing their *supply* of taxable labor or capital, a terminology that was useful in distinguishing this microeconomic orientation from the previous macroeconomic orientation of tax cuts designed to stimulate aggregate *demand*. To academic economists, however, the presentation of the idea had a number of problems. First, of course, the idea was not exactly new: "High taxes, sometimes by diminishing the consumption of the taxed commodities, and sometimes by encouraging smuggling, frequently afford a smaller revenue to government than what might be drawn from more moderate taxes" (Adam Smith [1776] 1975, bk. 5, chap. 2). Second, economists were quite familiar

5. If the corporate investment is financed by stocks and bonds sold to a tax-exempt institution, the total effective rate in table 3.4 is -37 percent. Presuming that the corporation can use all excess credits and deductions on the marginal investment against its tax liability on intramarginal investments, the positive corporate tax is more than offset by the ITC, accelerated depreciation allowances, and interest deductions at the statutory corporate rate, with no subsequent tax on the exempt recipient of the interest and dividends.

6. "Dining with Wanniski and Richard Cheney, Rumsfeld's deputy, Laffer tried to explain how higher tax rates can produce less revenue. . . . When Cheney seem mystified, Laffer impulsively grabbed a napkin and drew a curve, demonstrating the variable relationship between tax rates and revenues. Thus was born what Wanniski popularized in his writings as the Laffer Curve" (Evans and Novak 1981, 63).

with the idea that economic outcomes were determined by the interaction of both supply and demand. Third, Laffer and other early champions did not just point out the existence of the downward-sloping range of the curve but also claimed that "we are well within this range at present" (Laffer 1977, 79). Fourth, they emphasized the effect of lower tax rates on actual labor and capital supply, at least initially,[7] rather than on financial arrangements and other tax avoidance behavior that can be used to reduce one's tax base.[8]

An unfortunate result was that these surface issues were easily attacked. It was quickly shown that the curve did indeed exist within preexisting economic models with both demand and supply behavior but that "reasonable estimates of an aggregate labor supply elasticity and of an overall marginal tax rate are both low enough to suggest that broad-based cuts in labor tax rates would not increase revenues" (Fullerton 1982, 20). Use of this preexisting model found that the revenue-maximizing tax rate was in the 70–80 percent range. Such responses address the extreme claims, perhaps, but not the more subtle and important points of the supply-side movement. What we learned ultimately from this movement is that tax rate reductions may have large effects on the tax base through means other than actual labor or capital supply.[9]

Indeed, the quote from Adam Smith should be suggestive. Two hundred years ago, when most government revenue was obtained from tariffs, a particularly high rate would not necessarily discourage imports; it would just shift them to an untaxed form. Similarly, high rates of tax may do little to actual labor supply, but they may shift it to an untaxed form such as "receiving income as fringe benefits, devoting expenditures to tax deductible items, and participating in the underground economy" (Browning 1989, 52). Use of a model with these three behaviors found that the revenue-maximizing tax rate was in the 50–60 percent range.

Tax avoidance can take additional forms as well. In 1985, the president's Council of Economic Advisers called for lower marginal tax rates that would reduce the incentive to hold tax-free municipal bonds, to take advantage of the deductibility of state and local taxes by shifting more activity into that govern-

---

7. Representative Jack Kemp, e.g., said, "The case that I'm making is that this tax system is biased against innovation, against investment, against savings, against work. There's such a tax on labor and capital that it's causing in part the deficit" (*New York Times,* 30 November 1980).

8. In addition, some of the initial jargon was simply wrong, suggesting that the peak of the curve is "the point at which the electorate desires to be taxed" and where "revenues plus production are maximized" (Wanniski 1978, 98).

9. Another lesson from more recent literature is that the effect of a tax rate change depends greatly on what is done with the revenue. If extra revenue is used to provide cash or the equivalent back to taxpayers, then work effort necessarily falls. The taxpayer does not really lose any income, so the change in relative price makes him substitute from work into leisure. True supply-siders believe that most government programs *do* provide cash or private goods. Instead, however, the revenue may be spent on something that bears no relation to choices about private goods and leisure (where economists say that the public good is "separable" in utility). The relative price of leisure falls, so the substitution effect makes an individual work less, but he has less income to spend on private goods and leisure, so the income effect makes him work more. On net, labor may either rise or fall.

ment sector, to take business deductions for travel, meals, and entertainment, to use fringe benefits as a form of compensation, to take deductible charitable contributions, to use interest-deductible debt rather than equity to finance an investment, to earn tax-free "imputed" net rents from owner-occupied housing, to search out legal tax shelters, and to engage in illegal tax evasion (see U.S. Council of Economic Advisers 1985).

After some rate reduction was completed, Lindsey (1990) found that tax cuts for lower brackets had positive feedback effects on revenue but did not pay for themselves. However, he found that high-bracket taxpayers (those earning more than $200,000) brought so much more activity into the tax base that they ended up paying more tax rather than less. In other words, the use of his model found that the revenue-maximizing tax rate was in the 40–50 percent range.

For these reasons, and with the value of hindsight, it might be said that the *supply-side* movement was entirely mislabeled. This terminology emphasizes actual labor supply, which for most people is not very adjustable, and it thus gave traditional thinkers an easy target. Supply-siders were branded as extremists even before they got a chance to list these other more adjustable behaviors as additional reasons that a tax cut could raise revenue. Moreover, the *supply-side* label did not convey their more central message, namely, that economic growth would be aided by shrinking the size of government.

It did not help that the supply-siders themselves were ambiguous. In intellectual circles, they tried to explain the myriad ways in which rate reduction can have positive feedback effects on revenue, but, in the popular press, these complex arguments always seemed to get reduced to the claim that people work more and revenues rise. Others besides Laffer and Wanniski helped feed this misunderstanding, partly in order to bring attention to their cause. A "wake-up call" was needed to put the issue before the people and convince policymakers that taxes had any such incentive effects at all. Jack Kemp was quoted as saying, "Frankly, it is my belief that at lower, more efficient rates of taxation, we'll get more revenue" (*New York Times,* 30 November 1980), and candidate Reagan said, "Even the government winds up getting more money at the lower rates."[10] As Murray Weidenbaum (1988, 19) wrote, "Supply-side economics has made a useful positive contribution in moving the issue of incentives . . . to the front page of our newspapers." The problem with this ambiguity was that then they had to deal with the consequences:

> Journalists and academics continued to declare that there was not a scrap of evidence for supply-side economics. When pressed on this matter of evidence, it always turned out that they meant there was no evidence that tax-rate reductions would pay for themselves in each bracket. Since Reaganomics was not based on the Laffer Curve, they either did not know what

10. This quote was used on a 1981 broadcast of "All Things Considered," on National Public Radio, entitled "Tax Less, Work More" (no. 81311).

they were criticizing or pretended not to know in order to hold on to their strawman. (Roberts 1984, 133)

As noted above, the cut in the top rate might have paid for itself, but not across-the-board cuts in all marginal rate brackets.

These problems with the initial presentation of supply-side ideas may have been the source of weak academic support, but problems with inflation were definitely the source of strong public support. Increases in the Consumer Price Index (CPI) were substantial:

Year	% Change CPI	Year	% Change CPI
1976	5.8	1979	11.3
1977	6.5	1980	13.5
1978	7.6		

Source: U.S. Council of Economic Advisers (1990, 363).

In fact, inflation was a factor in two supply-side precursors of 1978. In California, inflation had been increasing nominal assessed values, with the result that property taxes would rise even with no change in the tax rate, until a popular uprising passed Proposition 13 to limit these automatic tax increases. In addition, inflation had been increasing nominal selling prices and therefore taxes on capital gains. President Carter did not recognize the shifting political winds, perhaps, until a popular uprising passed the Steiger Amendment to convert his proposed capital gains rate *increase* into a capital gains rate *decrease*.[11]

Inflation was having at least two other important effects on taxes. First, it was pushing taxpayers into higher brackets, increasing personal marginal tax rates through "bracket creep." One response was the Kemp-Roth plan of 1977, H.R. 8333, also known as "10–10–10" to summarize its three successive years of 10 percent cuts in all marginal tax rates. However, rate reduction would not offset the effect of inflation on low-income households that had become taxable. Second, inflation was reducing the real value of depreciation allowances, increasing the cost of capital, and decreasing investment incentives. The response to this problem was the Conable-Jones plan, H.R. 4646, also known as "10–5–3" to summarize its three depreciation lifetime categories for all assets: ten years for structures, five years for equipment, and three years for light vehicles.

These proposals each represented massive tax reductions, at least relative to the then current unindexed tax system that was projected to turn a 2.4 percent of GNP deficit into a 2.4 percent of GNP *surplus* (in table 3.3 above, the row

11. At the time, the top bracket was 70 percent, and the capital gains exclusion was 50 percent, but the "alternative tax on capital gains" allowed a 25 percent rate on the first $50,000 of net capital gains. In January, the *President's 1978 Tax Program* (U.S. Department of the Treasury 1978) proposed repealing the alternative tax and thus raising the top capital gains rate to 35 percent. The enacted legislation instead raised the exclusion, to 60 percent.

for 1979). Each was motivated in part by supply-side considerations. For different reasons, however, each was actually a very traditional piece of legislation.

As described above, the entire postwar period had seen frequent income tax "reduction" legislation.[12] The Kemp-Roth plan was a bit larger, perhaps, and it provided rate reduction in contrast to the more common practice of adding new credits and deductions. But inflation was greater than normal, and bracket creep had sent marginal rates to all-time highs. Thus, despite supply-side rhetoric, even 10–10–10 could be viewed as another ad hoc offset to inflation. In particular, it was traditional legislation in that it did not propose indexing to *end* the continuing cycle of bracket creep and tax "reduction."

Similarly, as described above, depreciation had been accelerated in 1954, 1962, and 1971. In 1980, inflation was higher than usual, so the proposed acceleration in allowances was higher than usual. Again, the Conable-Jones 10–5–3 plan was traditional legislation in that it did not propose to index depreciation allowances in a way that would guarantee a certain real value of depreciation whatever the rate of inflation. According to David Stockman (1987, 62), it did not even arrive with any supply-side rhetoric: "Conable and his Ways and Means Committee Republicans had consolidated their own coalition. It was an awesome assembly of business lobbies and trade associations representing everything from autos to real estate, steel, and zinc smelters. . . . The old guard was much more comfortable with this approach than with the supply-side marginal rate reduction plan." For related reasons, this business tax cut did not jibe with the populist message of the personal tax cuts: "Kemp and the supply-side purists did not like it, viewing it as just another tax shelter for established big corporations that would be little or no help to up-and-coming entrepreneurs, the future hope of the capitalist system who above all wanted a quick drop in taxation of 'unearned' income" (Evans and Novak 1981, 99).

In addition, these proposals were not designed according to any particular careful theory, supply-side or otherwise. There was no special reason for three successive 10 percent rate cuts, except that it spread out the cost, and no special reason for that particular total percentage cut, except that it was big. The special appeal was the simplicity of the numbers, 10–10–10. It was something that the man on the street could understand. Even for an area as arcane as business depreciation provisions, the simplicity of 10–5–3 had appeal.[13]

Thus, the proposals had several things going for them. Inflation was at an all-time high, the budget was projected to go into surplus, the simplicity was appealing, there was a popular antitax uprising, *and* a new supply-side theory

---

12. In contrast, the postwar period also saw frequent Social Security tax *increase* legislation.

13. As David Brockway pointed out to me, "10–10–10 is not something you generate out of a computer." Also, "they were running out of corporate tax base, so eventually the bubble would burst. . . . If anything is devoid of intellectual content, it's 10–5–3."

provided some intellectual (if ambiguous) underpinnings. For many traditional legislators, however, the extreme version of the supply-side view may have worked against the proposal. Few in Congress gave any credence at all to the idea that the rate cut would pay for itself.

The proposals had much more going for them in 1980, however, when candidate Reagan came on board. Ronald Reagan was a natural opponent of high taxes and big government, and his campaign pushed the populist message of the supply-side. He garnered populist support with 10–10–10 and courted business support with 10–5–3. Despite their differences, both these proposals were tax cuts, both would help offset inflation, and both were proposed by Republicans. Why choose between them? Reagan was more interested in the personal rate cut, but both these odd bedfellows were adopted by the Republican platform. The landslide election of 1980 certainly appeared to be a strong mandate for tax reduction.

After the election, Ronald Reagan collected into his administration several different kinds of appointments. The White House was dominated by moderate Republicans such as James Baker and Richard Darman, while the Treasury Department included some extreme supply-siders such as Norman Ture and Paul Craig Roberts. The budget director, David Stockman, was a bit of a halfbreed. He professed to be an ardent supply-sider, but he never believed that the tax cuts would pay for themselves. Rather, he believed in the importance of smaller government for greater productivity and economic growth. He quickly calculated that the cost of the two tax cuts together was "staggering" (Stockman 1987, 64), but he had a two-part plan. First, since the proposal still did not include indexing, a few years of inflation would help undo some of the cost. Second, "the prospect of needing well over $100 billion in domestic spending cuts to keep the Republican budget in equilibrium appeared more as an opportunity than as a roadblock" (p. 74).

As we shall see, indexing was added to the proposal before it was passed, and actual spending cuts were small compared to the remaining deficit. The more immediate problem, however, was the administration's February 1981 economic forecast: "When you added the supply siders' assumption of 5.2 percent real growth [for 1982] to Weidenbaum's 7.7 percent inflation, you got a mountain of money GNP—and phantom tax revenues" (Stockman 1987, 106–7). Thus, it was "Rosy Scenario" who convinced policymakers that they could afford the big tax cut.

Although the Senate had gone Republican in 1980, the tax cuts were still far from a sure thing. Many legislators viewed the size of the personal tax cut as irresponsible. In the first place, Democrats were naturally opposed to the tax and spending cuts, and, in the second place, traditional Republicans agreed with George Bush's campaign quote that supply-side was "voodoo economics." Both these groups were more inclined toward the business tax cuts, and Democrat Lloyd Bentsen even had his own similar accelerated depreciation scheme in the Senate Finance Committee. The personal rate cuts were of no interest to business leaders and lobbyists but of great interest to the new president still in his honeymoon period. The two proposals were married in the White House, as corporate executives agreed to support Kemp-Roth in exchange for White House support of the Accelerated Cost Recovery System (ACRS), a modified version of Conable-Jones that reduced structure lifetimes from thirty to forty years to fifteen years, equipment lifetimes to five years, and light vehicles to three years.

Democrats were still balking, and the White House eventually agreed to cut the first year of the personal rate reduction from 10 to 5 percent, delay it for a year, and add a couple of "ornaments" designed to attract support from particular sources.[14] Many observers said afterward, however, that such compromises were not necessary. The Democrats were reeling not only from electoral defeats but also from successive legislative defeats on Stockman's spending cuts. Southern "Boll-Weevil" Democrats had formed a viable coalition with Republicans, and other Democrats were shrinking in fear of the next election. One insider told me that "the Republicans could have crammed in twice the cuts and still got the vote, but they only bit off as much as they thought they could chew." When the president was shot on 30 March, anything he wanted could have sailed right through. The Democratic leadership promised a tax bill by July.

Meanwhile, the professional tax staffs in both the Treasury Department and the Joint Tax Committee were analyzing the proposals, and it was soon clear that the combination of the investment tax credit and accelerated depreciation allowances would be even more generous than simply allowing businesses to "expense" immediately the full cost of the investment. In my interviews, these insiders said that they knew that the outcome would be a host of administrative problems related to tax shelters, the leasing of equipment, the churning of real estate, and corporations without enough tax liability even to make use of the allowable credits and deductions. Besides, in their judgment, it just seemed "wrong." Among other issues, it raised the specter of providing more investment incentive to an older taxable firm than to a struggling new high-tech firm that was not yet taxable.

The Treasury had two responses. First, they designed "safe-harbor leasing" so that a taxable firm could buy the equipment, lease it to an untaxed firm that had really wanted to make the investment in the first place, and then charge a rent that passes the tax benefits through to the untaxed firm. The result, we would see later, was that many large profitable corporations could zero-out their tax liability, which caused significant perception problems even if these firms were passing through the tax advantages by receiving reduced rents for the equipment. Second, in June, the Treasury proposed a reduction in the gen-

---

14. Up to this point, the administration was trying to keep "clean" a bill that would balance the budget by 1983 (using the "Rosy Scenario"). Although these changes started them down the road toward a "dirty" bill, the cost of the ornaments was offset by the lower first-year rate cut.

erosity of ACRS.[15] The result in this case was "Lear-Jet Weekend." Corporate executives flew to Washington from all over the country to point out that their support of the personal rate cuts was dependent on full White House support of their business tax cuts. By Monday, the full depreciation plan was restored.[16]

Along the way, the administration's tax plan had been named after Barber Conable (R., New York) and Kent Hance (D., Texas). It has been amended by a second-earner's deduction, an estate and gift tax reduction, a higher ceiling on Individual Retirement Accounts (IRAs), and a credit for oil royalty owners. But the Democrats were not just sitting on their hands. All tax legislation is required by the Constitution to begin in the House of Representatives, and the House was still controlled by the Democrats. The new chairman of the House Ways and Means Committee, Dan Rostenkowski, wanted to put his own stamp on the bill. Democrats were nervous about the third year of 10 percent personal rate cuts, so they came up with an alternative of their own. They saw enough of the supply-side argument that they viewed as sensible the cut in the top rate from 70 to 50 percent, so they made it immediate rather than phased over three years. To try to rationalize the depreciation scheme, they offered straight expensing of equipment. To attract particular other constituencies, they added significant cuts in the estate and gift tax, a larger oil royalty credit, an IRA for those who already have pension plans, a cut in the corporate tax rate from 46 to 34 percent, and other sweeteners. The Republicans countered by adding several of these ornaments plus additional provisions for indexing and for all-savers' certificates. The result was the "bidding war" of summer 1981 (see Rudder 1983; and Witte 1985). Sweeteners were added *both* to the administration's bill and to the Democratic alternative in attempts to bid support away from the other. The bills were fundamentally very similar, so the struggle really amounted to whose name would be on the bill to win. At this point, all semblance of responsible policy-making went out the window. Several observers thought that the result was nothing other than a "feeding frenzy."[17]

The resulting bill, passed in August, had not just three years of personal rate cuts and the Accelerated Cost Recovery System (ACRS). It had safe-harbor leasing, expanded IRAs and Keogh accounts, all-savers' certificates, estate and gift tax cuts, a second-earner deduction, an incentive stock option, a larger employee stock option plan (ESOP), an oil royalty owner's credit, a research and development (R&D) incremental tax credit, a child-care credit, deductions for charitable contributions of nonitemizers, an increase in the homeowners'

15. Double-declining-balance was reduced to 150 percent declining balance, while utilities and industrial structures were given longer lives.

16. Although double-declining-balance was restored, it was delayed until after 1985. Lives would be shortened immediately, but depreciation would be 150 percent of declining balance in 1981–84, 175 percent in 1985, and 200 percent thereafter. Each depreciation schedule is laid out in a table, and each involves switching to straight line or sum-of-the-year's-digits at the optimal point in the life of the asset.

17. The logic "was that of the alcoholic: One more couldn't hurt, given all that had gone down already" (Stockman 1987, 248). See also McLure (1990a).

capital gains exclusion, a deduction for adoption expenses, a new exclusion of foreign earned income, and many other special provisions.

To be sure, many of these proposals had been kicking around for some time and had good tax policy arguments supporting them. Many did not. The point here is not to debate the arguments for and against each provision but to note the process by which they were all combined in one bill. No attention was paid to the long-run revenue consequences of the two main provisions, let alone all these additional provisions. Especially given the nature of the bidding war, all observers thought that the bill was pure politics. There was virtually no economic input to the process. Stockman (1987, 278) notes that "supply side theory was, well, as relevant as love at an orgy."

Of the professional economists I interviewed who were involved in this process, almost all said that economic analysis may have had an impact only on some small aspects of the legislation. They pointed out that certain assets were moved from one depreciation category to another on the basis of economic estimates of useful service lives. Also, safe-harbor leasing was suggested as a way to provide the same economic incentives to both taxable and untaxed firms. And the second-earner deduction had been suggested by economist Joe Pechman years before as a way to lessen the perverse incentive effects of the marriage penalty. Here was a modest proposal that was targeted directly at the logic of the supply-side. Given the higher earnings of the family's primary worker, the secondary worker faced a high initial marginal tax rate *and* a more adjustable labor supply decision. Since the second-earner deduction cuts the tax of just the more responsive secondary worker, it is more likely to have a large positive feedback effect on revenue.

These economists all agreed with the noneconomists that the big decisions were pure politics, however. First of all, if the peak of the Laffer curve were really as low as 40 percent, then a pure supply-side rate cut would apply only to the top brackets. No supply-side response would be expected from a low-income taxpayer's reduction in rate from 14 to 11 percent. In addition, the depreciation scheme was pushed by the business lobby, while economists were pushing alternatives such as expensing or the "first-year-recovery" proposal of Auerbach and Jorgenson (1980).[18] Moreover, the ideas that *had* been put forward by economists were ignored. Economists had pushed the value-added tax (VAT), a proposal that spelled electoral defeat for Al Ullman, the former chairman of the House Ways and Means Committee. Economists had pushed the idea of a consumed-income tax, a proposal that was ignored by all politicians except Gary Hart.[19] Economists had pushed the integration of corporate and

18. Instead of indexing later depreciation allowances, this proposal would avoid the effects of inflation by providing a deduction in the first year of the life of each asset that would be equivalent in present value to real economic depreciation.

19. Under a consumed-income tax, each taxpayer would file an annual return that measures consumption by including all forms of income and then deducting all forms of savings. As discussed below, a deduction for net saving means the inclusion of net borrowing.

personal income taxes, another idea that was totally ignored in the political process.[20]

Despite these arguments, I think that it is possible to take the exact opposite position, namely, that economic considerations determined the big issues while politics decided relatively small issues such as the provisions added during the bidding war. These staff economists are correct that they had more impact on the details of this legislation than on its fundamental form. In several important respects, however, *other* economists from the academic and private sectors had a *prior* impact on the nature of the legislation. It is more difficult to see the indirect role of economists whose writings get sifted through colleagues and the media before entering the political marketplace of ideas, but these impacts were crucial nonetheless.

First, whatever the validity of particular claims made at the time, the supply-side is inherently an economic concept. The main point of the supply-side is that incentives matter, and that point was ignored or forgotten as previous politics had raised marginal tax rates to over 90 percent. It was economic ideas that first suggested these rates be brought back down again. The Kemp-Roth bill might not have been available for consideration but for supply-side economics.

Second, economic analysis deals not only with incentives but also with the distribution of tax burdens. While incentive considerations suggested reducing the top marginal tax rate, distributional considerations suggested reducing rates for low-income taxpayers as well. Here, economists and politicians were in agreement that the tax cut should not be only for high-income households. In fact, bracket creep had been raising the taxes of low- and middle-income taxpayers more than it had been raising the taxes of those already in the top bracket.

Third, many economists had been pointing out the perverse effects of inflation not only through bracket creep but also in reducing the real value of depreciation allowances, raising capital gains taxes, and exaggerating the real effects of interest paid and received. Although most economists might have preferred to index depreciation allowances for inflation, Feldstein (1981, 38) supported 10–5–3 by noting that, "for moderate rate of inflation and real discount rates, the acceleration proposal and full indexation are quite similar." Much economic analysis was devoted to the problem of insufficient savings and investment, and this analysis provided much impetus to the final bill's expanded IRA, reduced capital gains rate, and R&D credit. Politics merely determined the right time to insert these provisions, some aspects of their form, and a few other provisions like ESOPs.

---

20. Businessmen like to talk about double taxation, but not integration. Yet Ullman wanted to pay for integration by imposing a VAT. As David Brockway, talking with me, remembered it, "Politically, this is ludicrous: impose a sales tax in order to cut tax for business. It just reflects the haywire political compass of the Democrats. At least the supply side had a focus."

Finally, it is an economic argument that underlies the indexation of tax brackets for inflation, the provision that perhaps unexpectedly turns out to have the biggest effect of all.

3.3   The Deficit

Concern about the revenue impact of the Economic Recovery Tax Act of 1981 (ERTA) began "immediately if not sooner." Some legislators knew even as they voted for the bill that it would soon have to be fixed.[21] For example, on 14 September 1981, the *New York Times* reported that

> Mr. Moynihan, a Democrat and New York's senior Senator, voted for the Administration's tax legislation this summer—both in committee and on the Senate floor—but maintained in an interview that he really supported only certain parts of that bill. He gave it his vote, he explained, "because it was that or nothing."
>
> Asked to specify how he would revise the tax bill, Mr. Moynihan said he was not ready to provide details, other than to say he would cut the $750 billion, five-year cost of the Administration's bill by approximately $250 billion, or one-third.

Even the administration, as part of the "September offensive" directed primarily at spending cuts, proposed $22 billion of what was for the first time euphemistically called "revenue enhancement." But the primary problem developing during this period was the deepening recession. The "Rosy Scenario" of February 1981 may or may not have been overly optimistic from the beginning, but now the economic forecasts repeatedly had to be revised downward. According to David Stockman's mea culpa (1987, 369), "The failed September Offensive had been aimed at reducing the 1984 deficit by $75 billion. Now the deficit estimate had increased by an order of magnitude—to $150 billion. We were suddenly faced with the stark reality of what had been hidden from the beginning. Our sweeping fiscal plan had led straight into the jaws of triple-digit deficits."

Because the budget plan covered only the years through 1985, the apparent problem was still simply the size of the ERTA tax cut. Much discussion ensued about whether to delay the second year's 10 percent rate cut or to abort the third year's additional 10 percent cut. Policymakers still had not recognized the long-run implications of bracket indexing, scheduled to start after 1985. Without indexing, they could have avoided any legislation to raise taxes. By just waiting a bit longer, inflation would have raised taxes for them. The budget problem, although severe, would have been only temporary.

Since supply-side theory recommended that marginal tax rates be reduced,

---

21. The Economic Recovery Tax Act of 1981 passed by a vote of 238 to 195 in the House and 89 to 11 in the Senate.

it might also be thought to recommend that rates stay reduced. Yet indexing was not put into the 1981 legislation by any supply-sider such as Arthur Laffer, Jude Wanniski, Jack Kemp, or even Ronald Reagan. It was inserted late in the summer of 1981 by Republicans Bill Gradison in the House and Bill Armstrong in the Senate. The administration did not even want indexing. As Congressman Gradison remembers it, the administration tried to renege on a deal that indexing would be added to Conable-Hance, the administration's bill in the House, if Armstrong managed to get it into the other version of the bill in the Senate.[22]

Then, at the height of the bidding war, despite his administration's earlier opposition, President Reagan used indexing to great advantage in selling his "bipartisan" package (since Conable-Hance was named after members of both parties) over the "Ways and Means" (Democratic) plan. On 27 July, he went on national television with an oversize chart (reproduced here as figure 3.1) showing that, although the "Ways and Means" plan gave larger cuts initially, taxes would subsequently rise. With indexing, the "bipartisan" tax cut would remain a tax cut.

This figure demonstrates vividly the single most unusual feature of the 1981 legislation. Prior tax cuts were temporary. Not only was the 1981 tax cut the biggest in U.S. history; it was permanent.[23] It was not the size of the deficit as much as this permanence that so greatly affected all subsequent tax policy-making.

During the course of the next year, additional policymakers came to realize that revenue must be raised. Within the administration, some began seriously to discuss a $100 billion tax increase, and others began to resign.[24] The form of the tax increase, however, was still subject to debate. Democrats favored repeal of the third year's rate cut; as Rostenkowski said, "I see it as repealing something that taxpayers have never enjoyed—as opposed to taking money right out of their pockets with heavy consumer taxes" (*Washington Post*, 10 May 1982). The Republicans leaned toward excise taxes, user fees, greater enforcement, and generally anything that appeared less as a tax. Asked whether the new tax bill represented a turnaround from the philosophy of last year's supply-side tax cut, Senate Finance Chairman Bob Dole said, "We're

22. As Stockman tells it, "'Armstrong doesn't have the votes on the Senate floor,' the Senate's best vote-counter told Jim Baker. 'We'll bury indexing in an hour'" (1987, 275). Then, after indexing was voted into the Senate bill by 57 to 40, "Conable insisted that tax indexing be incorporated in Conable-Hance II. Both Don Regan and I fought that one, but Conable and his GOP colleagues persisted. We solved the impasse by delaying the effective date of tax indexing until 1985" (p. 281). While true supply-siders would favor both the rate cut and indexing, fiscal conservatives in the administration may have feared the sheer size of the rate cut and viewed bracket creep as a way to reduce it. The budget was defined as a three-year problem (1982–84), however, so any cost after 1985 was irrelevant.

23. Policymakers at the time used nominal terms to describe the 1981 act as the biggest tax cut in U.S. history and the 1982 act as the biggest tax increase in U.S. history.

24. Paul Craig Roberts resigned as assistant secretary of the Treasury in January 1982, and Norman Ture resigned as undersecretary in June (see also Regan 1988, 184).

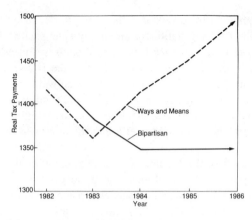

Fig. 3.1   Keeping taxes down—$15,000 wages
Source: Roberts (1984).

not trying to make a U-turn; we're just trying to avoid going over the cliff" (*Washington Post,* 16 August 1982).

One unusual feature of this bill is that, instead of beginning in the House of Representatives, as is required by the Constitution, it essentially began in the Senate Finance Committee. Chairman Dole circumvented the constitutional restriction by latching onto a minor tariff bill that *had* passed the House. His committee could then produce a virtually new bill and go straight to a conference with House members to work out the "differences." An immediate question is why Rostenkowski did not cry bloody murder at this constitutional outrage. After all, one might think that the Democrats would want to help undo the Republican tax cut of 1981. The answer is that Rostenkowski was in on the plan. He wanted a bill in 1982, but many on his Ways and Means Committee did not. In many ways, the House was more supply-side oriented than the Senate. Since its members faced election more often, the House was more susceptible to swings in the public mood such as the ongoing antitax revolt. Rostenkowski could simply pick conferees that agreed with him, negotiate with the Senate, and avoid ever taking on his full committee (see also McLure 1990a).

In its final form, the Tax Equity and Fiscal Responsibility Act of 1982 (TEFRA) raised $98.3 billion over three years. Given the flap over news accounts of major corporations that were paying no tax, it repealed the safe-harbor leasing provision of the 1981 act. Mostly, it took little nicks at many features of the law. It added to the individual alternative minimum tax (AMT), increased the floor for deductible medical expenses and casualty losses, taxed more of unemployment benefits, reduced deductions for some mineral companies, required capitalization and amortization of construction period interest and property taxes, amended the completed contract method of accounting, accelerated corporate estimated tax payments, limited the use of tax-exempt industrial development bonds, restricted allowable pension contributions and benefits, and amended provisions for foreign income, life insurance companies, and unemployment taxes. It added excise taxes on airport use, communication, and cigarettes.[25]

Its two largest provisions, however, were modifications to depreciation and compliance. Calculations such as those in table 3.4 above began to show that the combination of ACRS and ITC was considerably more generous than expensing, especially since the rate of inflation had fallen. Inefficiencies and inequities would result from high effective tax rates for some assets and negative effective tax rates for others. Thus began the development of the "level playing field." In this case, tax increases had some political appeal by targeting those receiving extra benefits. Note that the calculations in table 3.4 reflect the fully phased-in version of the law, with double-declining-balance, scheduled to begin after 1985. The 1982 act simply made permanent the 150 percent method that ERTA had specified for 1981–84. It also decreased the basis for depreciation deductions by half the investment tax credit. According to economists doing the calculations, these changes were designed to leave benefits approximately on par with expensing.

The compliance provisions included various income reporting responsibilities and increased penalties, but also the first withholding on interest and dividends, at a 10 percent rate. Wages and salaries had been subject to withholding for years, so it might be natural to think that interest and dividends could be subject to similar rules. Wages and salaries were no longer a major compliance problem, while interest and dividends were often not reported. Any significant administrative problems had been considerably reduced by the coming of computers to the banking and brokerage industries. But this provision raised a terrific outcry from banks and depositors, largely through Senator Bob Kasten's write-in campaign. It was repealed the next year.

Perhaps most striking about TEFRA and other subsequent efforts to raise revenue is not the provisions that they included but one possibility that they excluded. They did not repeal bracket indexing. Another look back at table 3.3 above reveals that, whereas the 1979 five-year projection showed a surplus as large as 2.4 percent of GNP, the 1982 projection showed a deficit as large as 5.4 percent of GNP. The result is that tax increase legislation took the hard road, with bills every year from 1982 to 1985.

At the time of passage, the revenue effects of each bill were projected a few years ahead. More recently, however, the Office of Management and Budget (OMB) has estimated the past effects of each bill through 1990, relative to the law in effect before ERTA. These "static" estimates ignore possible behavioral responses. As shown in table 3.5, prior law would have increased revenues dramatically throughout the 1980s, but the 1981 bill reduced revenues by at

---

25. Commerce Clearing House (1981, 1982, and 1984) publications provide details and explanation of the three tax bills enacted in those years.

Table 3.5   Changes in Budget Receipts, Fiscal Years 1982–90

	1982	1983	1984	1985	1986	1987	1988	1989	1990
Receipts under laws in effect 1/1/81	650.8	656.0	749.4	821.3	822.5	873.9	1,002.6	1,088.2	1,167.3
Changes due to:									
ERTA (1981)	−35.6	−82.6	−136.8	−168.5	−170.3	−207.5	−264.4	−290.9	−322.8
TEFRA (1982)		17.3	36.0	40.7	39.2	49.2	57.3	55.7	57.2
Social Security (1983)		5.3	15.5	31.2	30.5	39.7	70.3	85.2	105.1
DEFRA (1984)			.9	9.3	9.3	16.0	25.4	27.7	31.0
TRA (1986)							−8.9	−24.4	−20.3
Technical corrections (1987)							11.4	16.9	18.7
Total receipts	617.8	597.5	666.4	736.8	734.0	776.4	908.7	975.8	1,057.6

Note: These figures are taken from selected rows of table 3 in Stewart (1991). Rows for administrative action and other small legislative changes are omitted here, but they are reflected in the last row for total receipts.

Stewart's explanation: "The first row of figures is an estimate of the amount of revenue that would have been generated in each fiscal year if no change to tax law had been made in the 1980s. Other rows gives estimates of the revenue gains or losses for that fiscal year attributable to the relevant change in tax law. For instance, if there had been no changes to federal tax law during the decade, then the federal government is estimated to have received $1167.3 billion in revenues during FY 1990. The net effect of the 1981 ERTA is estimated to be a loss of revenues during FY 1990 to the order of $322.8 billion. The net effects of changes to the 1981 ERTA itself are reflected in the estimates for the relevant subsequent tax laws; for example, the effects of rolling back the accelerated depreciation provisions of the ERTA that occurred in 1982 are reflected in figures for TEFRA."

Stewart's source: "Budget of the United States, FY 1982–1990. These are estimates provided in the annual budget documents, therefore they are subject to frequent revision. Therefore, these figures should be taken to represent ballpark figures, rather than hard-and-fast estimates."

least $200 billion per year after 1987. Then the Tax Equity and Fiscal Responsibility Act of 1982 (TEFRA) raised revenue, by $50 billion per year after 1987.

Later sections of this paper discuss how ambiguities in prospective revenue estimates cause problems for debate about proposed tax changes, but these ambiguities apply even to retrospective estimates for past tax changes. Since nobody really knows how the economy would have evolved under prior tax law, the OMB estimates in table 3.5 simply apply the old law to actual economic magnitudes to get prior law baseline revenues for comparison with actual revenues. In contrast, Lindsey provides one attempt to estimate how various economic magnitudes would have been different under prior law. Without some of the incentive-induced increases in the tax base, revenues under old law would not have been as high as in these OMB estimates. Thus, "ERTA cost less than one-third as much as implied by the naively calculated direct effect estimate" (Lindsey 1990, 74).

Meanwhile, demographic trends were playing havoc with the pay-as-you-go Social Security system. Payroll tax receipts would be sufficient to cover retirement benefit payouts while the baby-boom generation was still working but might not be sufficient after that population bulge was retired. In 1983, a "bipartisan" commission reached an agreement to restore the long-run health of the beleaguered system, through moderate increases in current payroll taxes and transfers from general revenue to build a temporary "surplus" in the trust fund. The effect starts small, as shown in table 3.5, but grows to $100 billion per year by 1990.

The next large tax increase was the Deficit Reduction Act of 1984 (DEFRA, to rhyme with TEFRA). It was raising only $25 billion per year by 1988, but it required many more pages than any of the previous bills. Just a list of the table of contents gives some idea of its breadth: tax changes affecting individuals, tax provisions affecting business, foreign sales corporations and foreign tax provisions, private foundations and exempt organizations, leasing, retirement plans and other employee benefits, tax shelters and related transactions, straddles, life insurance provisions, estate and gift taxes, tax-exempt obligations, administration and compliance, and excise taxes. Each of these chapters has twenty or thirty subheadings.

Among other changes, DEFRA raised the depreciation lifetime for structures from fifteen to eighteen years. Another bill the next year raised this life to nineteen years.

Legislators during this period were forced by the deficit to raise taxes, and they were forced by political realities to raise taxes on somebody who was "hiding" some special deal buried in the tax law. The general approach was to scour the tax code for provisions that were obscure rather than blatant. Policymakers could not increase rates or hit a popular personal deduction, but they could hit a "loose" provision that had been allowing some rich person to avoid paying tax (see Minarik 1897, 1359). Thus, tax policy came to be made in a fashion that is the *exact opposite* from the previous era. Up until 1981, Congress could return excess tax revenue, and undo the projected surplus, by granting new special exemptions or deductions. After the rate cuts and indexing of ERTA, Congress needed to undo the projected deficit by deleting such special provisions. Thus, deficit reduction also leveled the playing field.

Tax reformers such as Stanley Surrey and Joe Pechman had for years decried the practice of opening new loopholes that erode the tax base and create unfair disparities in the taxation of otherwise similar individuals. The basic political and economic forces were not in their favor, however, until the 1981 bill provided the logical extreme of such practices. It was the reductio ad absurdum of opening loopholes. But the sleeper was the indexing provision, as it would force policymakers thereafter to close loopholes instead.

This deficit-driven policy-making has advantages and disadvantages. Many of those interviewed think that it puts far too much emphasis on revenue considerations rather than other policy considerations. Some "good" tax policy changes might actually lose revenue. If so, they can't get enacted. On the other hand, given all the "good policy" reasons of Surrey and Pechman for closing various loopholes, deficit-driven policy-making might well create better policy. Indeed, the whole point of the indexing provision was to put fiscal discipline into the tax policy-making process. Congress should be run like a corporation for which raising funds must be recognized as costly and spending funds must be demonstrated as worthwhile.

At least two books and many articles have been written in attempts to explain how the Tax Reform Act of 1986 was able to reverse previous practice, take on the special interests, close loopholes, and provide true reform (see, e.g., Birnbaum and Murray 1987; and Conlan, Wrightson, and Beam 1990). It was indeed important legislation. But the direction of tax policy-making had really changed by 1981. As we shall see in the next section, the many diverse and arcane base-broadening provisions of the 1986 act were very similar in nature to the earlier revenue-raising provisions of 1982–85.

3.4   The Level Playing Field

Various political and economic forces were still coming at the tax code from different directions, to be sure, but they were beginning to push it together instead of pulling it apart. Perhaps four developments were most important. First, supply-side theory continued to affect tax policy. Calls were heard for a "flat tax" that would put all taxpayers together in the same low tax bracket with absolutely no deductions other than those needed to define income. Since total federal individual tax revenues were about 11 percent of personal income, one naive approach would simply define a broad tax base equal to personal income, tax it at 11 percent, and get at least the same revenue. The low rate would be a tremendous boost for incentives to work and to save. A problem, of course, is that some components of personal income would be difficult to tax. Also, this extreme version of a flat tax would greatly increase the burden on poor and low-income taxpayers while greatly reducing that on high-income taxpayers. A "modified flat tax" (on consumed income) with a large personal exemption and a single tax bracket of 19 percent is fully described in Hall and Rabushka (1983).

Second, the tax system had become inordinately complex. In addition to complaints from taxpayers in all kinds of situations, there were estimates from economists that

> the average compliance time comes to 21.7 hours, valued at $231, and $44 in additional expenses, for a total of $275 per household. Applying the re-weighted averages to an estimated 97 million taxpaying units in 1982 yields aggregate estimates of 2.13 billion hours and a total resource cost of $26.7 billion. This cost is approximately 1.4 percent of aggregate adjusted gross income, and more than seven percent of total federal and state income tax revenue. (Slemrod and Sorum 1984, 465)

This is only an average. Since most taxpayers took less than twenty-one hours to fill out the short form for a return with the standard deduction, other tax-payers must have had to take much more than twenty-one hours. Many had to fill out ten or twenty forms just for one return. In contrast, a modified flat tax such as that in Hall and Rabushka could be filed once a year on a postcard.

Third, public confidence in the tax system was further undermined by re-ports about corporations and high-income individuals paying no tax. In Octo-ber 1984, Robert McIntyre and his Citizens for Tax Justice calculated the aver-age effective tax rate for 250 large profitable corporations in years 1981–83. He found that 128 paid *no* federal income taxes in at least one of these three years and that seventeen paid no taxes in all three years. For example, "The single biggest gainer from the 1981 legislation was Ronald Reagan's former employer, General Electric. GE earned $6.5 billion in pre-tax domestic profits over the three years, paid not one cent in federal income taxes, and claimed tax refunds of $283 million in taxes paid before Reagan took office" (McIntyre 1984, 2). Many of these companies used safe-harbor leasing to avoid paying tax, but the repeal of safe-harbor leasing in 1982 did not come fast enough to avoid the attention to other problems with the corporate tax brought by the intense media coverage of this report.

For individuals, the U.S. Department of the Treasury (1985) examined the 1983 returns of taxpayers with "total positive income" over $250,000 per year and found that 64 percent reported "losses" from partnerships, subchapter S corporations, rental and royalty activities, farms, and businesses. Of this entire high-income group, 11.4 percent had tax liability that was less than 5 percent of income. Another 9.8 percent had effective tax rates between 5 and 10 per-cent, and 32.0 percent had tax rates between 10 and 20 percent. The public decided, correctly, that such a system was just not fair. Thus, the "horizontal equity" version of the level playing field meant that taxpayers in the same economic circumstances ought to have to pay the same tax.

Fourth, economists both in and out of academe were calculating marginal effective tax rates of the sort shown above in table 3.4, with huge disparities between different types of assets or financing. Perhaps the major source of these differences was the investment tax credit (ITC) that was available for equipment but not for other investments of the firm. To economists, these disparities did not present a problem of equity, for no one ought to be concerned with the "fair" treatment of a machine relative to a building. Equity is an issue only among individuals. In equilibrium, individuals must be earning the same net-of-tax rate of return on a machine as on a building because otherwise they would invest more in the favorable asset until net returns *were* equalized. Instead, the problem was one of economic efficiency. If net returns were equal and effective tax rates were not, then the differences must show up in gross rates of return on these assets. Thus, some assets must be more productive, to cover a high effective tax rate, while other assets could be less productive and still yield the same net rate of return to the investor. The tax system was "distorting" the allocation of resources, as it encouraged *more* investment in the asset that was *less* productive.

Even with a fixed total stock of capital, according to this argument, total output would increase by taking investment away from the asset with the low gross rate of return and putting it into the asset with the high gross rate of return. Moreover, just such a reallocation would be induced by leveling the relative tax treatment of different assets. It was sometimes difficult for economists to explain this efficiency version of the level playing field, however, so they did not always object to the perception of inequity created by disparate treatments of different assets or firms.[26]

This efficiency argument rejects implicit industrial policy, the notion that government knows better than private firms what assets are the most productive. But the investment tax credit was not always conceived as industrial policy. In 1964, it was primarily a temporary macroeconomic tool used to stimulate aggregate demand. The ITC was repealed in 1969 and reintroduced in 1971. Perhaps it made sense to limit a temporary ITC to equipment, where stimulus could have immediate effect, and to exclude buildings, where lags might delay the effect of the stimulus until after the need was long gone. This logic was lost, however, when the ITC became permanent in 1975. It then

26. The confusion of these two concepts is interesting in itself. I would have expected economists to emphasize efficiency arguments for a level playing field and others to voice the equity arguments. Certainly members of Congress were heard discussing the equitable treatment of different assets or firms. But these comments may have been directed at the lay public. In the interviews for this paper, a surprising number of noneconomist policy-makers described very accurately in their own words the economic efficiency argument for a level playing field.

became a microeconomic tool that influenced not just the amount but also the type of investment.

This free-market approach of economists should not be oversold as a driving force for tax reform. At best, the gains in economic efficiency would be small for all taxpayers. More certainly, the cost of lost credits would be large for particular taxpayers. Also, the playing field could never be completely level as long as owner-occupied housing retained its untaxed treatment. Besides, Congress was not about to reject the government's influence over the allocation of resources. Provisions of the tax code were *intended* to influence home-ownership, charitable contributions, retirement savings, corporate research and development, pollution control, and other worthy causes. Instead, the point is simply that such provisions had been overextended through the years. Shelter organizers were able to attract investors to projects that had little or no economic return, only tax advantages. It was merely a happy coincidence for economists that their view about the inefficiency of disparate effective tax rates seemed to mesh with the more populist view about the inequity of disparate effective tax rates. It was clear that investments were misallocated, simply because so many high-income individuals and corporations were paying no tax.

Several issues of perennial interest to tax reformers are distinctly absent from the list given above of developments affecting this new climate for tax reform. In particular, this list excludes the classic argument that loopholes for the rich should be closed in order to restore the "intended" degree of progressivity given by the graduated marginal rate structure (see Musgrave 1987; and Pechman 1990). The list excludes consideration of revenue. It excludes perennial (and therefore "traditional") arguments about the remaining effects of inflation on the measurement of taxable income and the double taxation of corporate-source income. Senator Bill Bradley was probably the first member of Congress to grasp the new climate for tax reform. In his first term as senator, he devoted considerable energies to fashioning a comprehensive tax reform plan, cosponsored with Representative Dick Gephardt and introduced as the Fair Tax Act of 1982. He considered the classic arguments for tax reform and rejected them. He did not propose further indexation for inflation or integration of corporate and personal taxes. He decided not to try to close loopholes in a way that would raise the aggregate burden of high-income taxpayers. Indeed, he decided not to raise revenues at all or even to change the distribution of tax burdens. The reasons for such a strategy may seem obvious now, namely, lower marginal rates, less complexity, more similar tax burdens for those in the same income group, and a more efficient allocation of resources. But consider how his colleagues must have wondered at the time. If this proposal does not change the amount of tax paid in total or by any particular income group, then why bother? Put bluntly, "Simplification for the sake of simplification is to beat your brains out and go through the whole process and then end up without a dime's dent in the deficit" (Senator Packwood, quoted in the *Washington Post,* 30 November 1984).

The Bradley-Gephardt proposal was a modified flat tax in the sense that it would eliminate a long list of "loopholes," broaden the base, and reduce marginal tax rates to only three tax brackets of 14, 26, and 30 percent. Major personal deductions were retained, such as home mortgage interest, charitable contributions, and state and local income and property taxes, but they applied only against the 14 percent rate. The return would not fit on a postcard, but filing would be simpler because many taxpayers would use the enlarged standard deduction. Other forms were eliminated altogether. Taxes would rise for shelter abusers and fall for others. The plan would repeal the ITC and reduce the corporate rate to 30 percent but leave corporate taxes unchanged.

There seemed to be much discussion of modified flat rate proposals, but nobody seemed to know quite how to forge the right coalition. The Bradley-Gephardt plan was not taken too seriously. Yet the Reagan reelection campaign was apparently afraid that Walter Mondale would endorse Bradley-Gephardt and steal the issue for the Democrats. Given the president's long-standing desire to reduce marginal tax rates, they decided to preempt the Democrats in the February 1984 State of the Union address by having him order the Treasury Department to conduct a "study" that would not be due until after the election. Then, as it turns out, Mondale never got close to endorsing Bradley-Gephardt.

The ensuing debate involved several years, many interesting personalities, and umpteen versions of tax reform. Besides Bradley-Gephardt and the Republican plan called Kemp-Kasten, the public had opportunities to examine the Treasury proposal, the President's proposal, Rostenkowski's "staff option," the House bill, Senate Finance Committee Chairman Bob Packwood's staff option, and the Senate bill as well as the final conference agreement signed as the Tax Reform Act of 1986. The political interactions of these policymakers and their various proposals have been fully described elsewhere (see Birnbaum and Murray 1987; and Conlan, Wrightson, and Beam 1990), so I will try to touch on a few issues of particular interest.

Because of the political ploy of ordering a "study" to be completed after the election, tax experts at the Treasury Department were given a rare opportunity to craft a very apolitical document. White House officials did not even want to know what was in it. Within this ivory tower environment, economists had an unusual say in the formulation of the plan. For this reason, many other economists were surprised that Treasury economists did not propose a consumed-income tax that would allow a deduction for all savings and expensing of all investment. It would reduce the cost of capital, set all marginal effective tax rates to zero, and remove problems measuring real income. McLure and Zodrow (1987, 40–41) list several reasons for rejecting a consumed-income tax, but the most compelling is that it would have to include all borrowing in the tax base.[27] The public was simply not ready to accept the idea of paying a tax on borrowed funds that did not even represent income to the taxpayer (see Regan 1988, 206). Instead of including all borrowed funds, a consumed-income tax could disallow all interest deductions, but public acceptance of this idea was no easier.

Even within an income tax, some economists in the Treasury wanted to allow expensing for investment. Without including borrowing in the tax base or disallowing interest deductions, however, expensing would make marginal effective tax rates negative: for a debt-financed investment, the firm would get to deduct both the value of the asset and the normal return on it. Expensing by itself would cost considerable revenue and not fix problems with shelters.

Thus, the decision was made to design a more comprehensive income tax base. The Treasury followed the new logic of tax reform insofar as it wanted a plan that was revenue neutral, distributionally neutral, and simpler, one that would equalize the tax treatment of individuals in the same income group (the equity version of the level playing field) and equalize the tax treatment of different types of investment (the efficiency version of the level playing field). Among other provisions, the Treasury proposal would have eliminated percentage depletion, expensing of intangible drilling costs for oil and gas, expensing of many expenditures in multiyear production, the exclusion for most employee fringe benefits, the deduction for state and local taxes, and the entire minimum tax. It would have substantially increased the personal exemption.

As in Bradley-Gephardt, the original idea was to be revenue neutral for individuals and for corporations considered separately. When all the tough choices were made about which credits and deductions to eliminate, these constraints initially led to three personal rate brackets of 16, 28, and 37 percent. This result was a bit of a disappointment since lower rates had been hoped for. When the same process of base broadening was conducted on the corporate side, enough new revenue was generated to reduce the corporate rate all the way to 28 percent. This base broadening included the repeal of the investment tax credit and a depreciation scheme that was based on economists' estimates of real economic depreciation (Hulten and Wykoff 1981).

Officials in the Treasury had two major problems with this outcome. First, Secretary Don Regan had an aesthetic problem. He thought that the personal rates of 16, 28, and 37 percent were cumbersome. He wanted something simple and catchy like the earlier Kemp-Roth 10–10–10 or the Conable-Jones 10–5–3. "Give me 15–25–35," he ordered. Second, attorneys in the Treasury had a legal problem. With a rate as low as 28 percent, the corporate tax might become a shelter that allowed high-income individuals to incorporate them-

---

27. See n. 19 above. The taxpayer must be consuming all income and all borrowed funds, minus any monies put into various forms of savings and investment. Thus, the inclusion of borrowed funds would be offset immediately by a deduction if they were used to make an investment.

selves, pay the 28 percent rate, and avoid the higher 37 percent personal rate. The corporate rate and the top personal rate needed to be closer together. The obvious solution to both problems was to lower the personal rates to 15–25–35 and make up the revenue by raising the corporate rate to 33 percent.[28]

Thus was born the proposal to shift $150 billion of burden over five years from individuals to corporations. The Treasury had an aesthetic problem and a legal problem, operating in a relatively apolitical environment. The solution was a political master stroke. All subsequent versions of tax reform retained a similar shift of at least $100 billion over five years, for good political reasons. It allowed tables of estimated distributional effects to show a tax cut for *every* personal income group, even in the revenue-neutral bill. Otherwise, the table would have to show some tax increases to offset any group that received even a small net tax cut. Everybody knew that individuals somewhere bear the ultimate burden of corporate income taxes, but most simply ignored it.[29] Besides, as pointed out earlier, the corporate tax had fallen from 30 percent of federal revenue in 1954 to 6 percent of federal revenue in 1983. Perhaps this trend had gone too far.

Would President Reagan recommend a corporate tax increase of this magnitude, after just pushing the largest corporate tax decrease in history? For the success of tax reform, the device was brilliant, like Nixon going to China. On the other hand, it is not clear whether Reagan confused the cut in the corporate rate with the increase in the corporate burden. The day after praising the Treasury plan in his 1985 State of the Union address, Reagan was interviewed by the *Wall Street Journal* (8 February 1985): "The president said he hadn't studied the plan in sufficient detail to realize that it sought an increase in the relative tax burden on business. Moreover, he suggested that taxes on corporations are merely passed on to individuals anyway. 'Someday,' he said, 'I would hope that we could arrive at a tax structure that would recognize that you can't tax things, you only tax people.'"

Following Bradley-Gephardt, the U.S. Department of the Treasury (1984) proposal adopted the new logic of tax reform. It was revenue neutral, distributionally neutral, and leveled the playing field. Unlike Bradley-Gephardt, however, it did not eschew traditional tax reform issues. It addressed the integration of corporate and personal taxes by providing firms with a deduction for 50 percent of dividends paid. It addressed the problem of inflation in measuring real income by providing indexation of interest, depreciation, and capital gains.

---

28. Note that the corporate rate could have been raised without affecting the overall corporate burden, e.g., by allowing more accelerated depreciation. By this time, the Treasury experts were wedded to the idea of a tax on comprehensive economic income, however. Given the "ideal" tax base, a higher rate necessarily meant a higher burden. For more discussion of the reasons for this shift, see McLure (1986, 1643).

29. The distributional burdens of corporate tax changes are estimated by Feldstein (1988).

Some of these provisions made the proposed law more complex rather than simpler.

Moreover, these problems with inflation simply do not have the same kind of effect as bracket creep. With fixed nominal tax brackets, *any* rate of inflation would keep raising taxes as a percentage of income by continuously pushing individuals into ever higher brackets. Thus, the indexing of brackets in the 1981 bill was crucial to the subsequent making of tax policy in the era of deficits. These other problems are different. Inflation does reduce the real value of depreciation deductions, and it thus takes the effective tax rate to a new higher level. However, a constant rate of inflation does not *keep* raising the effective tax rate beyond that level. Similarly, the taxation of purely nominal capital gains and nominal interest raises real taxes to a higher level. In these cases, an increase in the rate of inflation will increase the tax, but a decrease in the rate of inflation will decrease the tax. Any given level of inflation could be offset by ad hoc adjustments such as accelerated depreciation or an exclusion for part of capital gains.

Thus, the point of these additional forms of indexing in the Treasury proposal was to account automatically for variations in the rate of inflation. The effective tax rate would be invariant to the rate of inflation, only with indexing for depreciation, interest, and capital gains. It was a traditional economist's type of reform, of no interest to Congress or constituents.

In fact, economists have long wondered why businesses do not show more interest in these forms of indexation. After all, the increase in later years' depreciation deductions to account for inflation would raise the present value of allowances and thus reduce the cost of capital. While businesses would rather have indexation than nothing, the relevant choice is usually between indexation and acceleration. For a given revenue cost, acceleration provides deductions that are earlier and more certain. Businesses see indexation as a provision that could subsequently be repealed by Congress, thus providing lower benefits than were expected at the time of investment. Moreover, traditional accounting practices are dominated by nominal magnitudes. Accountants are uncomfortable with deductions that are uncertain in nominal terms, even if they are more certain in real terms. Similarly, businesses showed little interest in the deduction for dividends paid.

For better or worse, these traditional reform provisions for indexing and integration did not survive the new climate for reform. The 50 percent dividend deduction was cut to 10 percent by the president's proposal, delayed by the House bill, and dropped by the Senate bill. Interest indexing was deemed unworkable and did not appear in any version beyond the Treasury plan. Capital gains indexing was modified by the president's proposal and dropped thereafter. Finally, depreciation indexing was retained by the president's proposal, cut by the House, and dropped by the Senate (see the details given in exhibit 3.1).

The Treasury proposal was also criticized for raising the cost of capital. Even though the corporate rate was reduced from 46 to 33 percent and allow-

Exhibit 3.1

Depreciation indexing, a case study in policy-making

The basic economic argument for depreciation indexing is that policy should decide the level of tax revenue and investment incentives, without interference from changes in the rate of inflation. The Accelerated Cost Recovery System enacted in 1981 was intended, in part, to offset the extraordinarily high rates of inflation at the time. But, when inflation fell dramatically, accelerated allowances were *more* generous than required to offset inflation. Indexing would maintain the real value of deductions whatever the rate of inflation.

At the Treasury in 1985, I might have expected noneconomist policymakers to reject these arguments, but I did not expect trouble from economists as well. Once interest indexing was rejected as unworkable, economists at the Joint Tax Committee argued that the system would be unbalanced with one and not the other. The advantage of deducting inflation-bloated interest payments was approximately offset by the disadvantage of deducting inflation-eroded depreciation allowances. The Treasury countered that, if they were in the same tax bracket, the lender's extra tax would exactly offset the borrower's benefit, so depreciation should be considered separately. The economists responded that lenders were generally in lower tax brackets than borrowers.

Rostenkowski's staff option ignored depreciation indexing, but the Treasury came up with a partial plan that indexed allowances for 80 percent of the extent to which the rate of inflation exceeded 5 percent. It had no estimated revenue implications since projected inflation was less than 5 percent, but Congress was still uninterested. We prepared all the economic arguments for indexing, with all the charts and graphs, and drove to Capitol Hill to meet with the Ways and Means task force on depreciation headed by Richard Gephardt. We never got to discuss it. When the issue arose, Gephardt simply said that Rostenkowski had talked on the phone with James Baker while we were driving over. Baker had made a plea for this partial indexing plan, and Rostenkowski had agreed to 50 percent of inflation over 5 percent. It was a done deal.

The Treasury Department worked more closely, in some ways, with the Republican Senate and managed to get depreciation indexing into Packwood's staff options. Senator Danforth, a Republican on the Finance Committee, got it taken out altogether. Even later, the issue had some appeal to Deputy Treasury Secretary Richard Darman, but not for economic reasons. He simply saw it as a way to reduce the cost of capital with most of the revenue cost outside the five-year budget window. Darman had become known for a certain sleight of hand, so I even tried suggesting to him that we support the right policy for the wrong reason: by slowing down allowances but indexing at the same time, we could *reduce* the cost of capital and *raise* revenue in the five-year budget period. Still it didn't fly.

ances were indexed, the ITC was repealed and asset lives lengthened.[30] Typical were the comments of the Chamber of Commerce (1984, 1): "This increased tax wedge on capital income would reduce capital investment and, consequently, harm economic growth rates, reduce U.S. international competitiveness and exacerbate the federal deficit. . . . [It] constitutes a reversal of the pro-growth policies inaugurated in 1981."

Finally, all these "modified flat tax" proposals could be criticized for offering false rate reduction. Consider, for example, a world where all compensation is always paid 80 percent as wages and 20 percent as fringe benefits and where wages are subject to a tax rate of 50 percent. A revenue neutral reform could then broaden the tax base to include all fringes and reduce the tax rate to 40 percent. Yet it would have absolutely no effect. If the ratio of fringes to wages is fixed, as assumed, then 40 percent of compensation is paid in tax before the reform as well as after. The rate reduction is more effective if fringes are fixed as work effort responds. The overall effect depends on the flexibility of all tax advantages such as fringe benefits, interest deductions, and charitable contributions.

Thus, the release of the Treasury proposal in November 1984 was accompanied by acclaim from many economists and traditional reform advocates, alarm from businesses and capital formation advocates, and yawns from the general public. Senator Bob Packwood, the chairman of the Finance Committee, said, "I sort of like the tax code the way it is" (*Washington Post,* 30 November 1984). Secretary Regan quickly noted that his proposal "was written on a word processor. It can be changed" (*Washington Post,* 8 December 1984).

The next most crucial step in the progress toward tax reform was the January 1985 job switch by Donald Regan and James Baker. It put an advocate of tax reform next to the ear of the president and a savvy politician in charge of the main tax reform effort. The president did not really need to be convinced, however, as he was always in favor of lower tax rates. With some misgivings, the administration decided to make tax reform the primary domestic policy initiative of Reagan's second term. So the new Treasury secretary Baker and Deputy Secretary Richard Darman set about trying to make the proposal more acceptable. Besides reducing the traditional reform provisions for indexing and integration, they provided better investment incentives through acceleration of depreciation allowances. They restored tax breaks for oil and gas, fringes, and some other popular benefits. In order to keep the personal rates at 15–25–35,

---

30. The marginal effective tax rate in the corporate sector was 29 percent under 1985 law and would rise to 43 percent under the Treasury proposal, as estimated by Fullerton (1987). Considering components separately, the 29 percent rate would rise to 41 percent with just interest indexing, would rise to 40 percent with just repeal of the ITC, would fall less than 1 percent with just the full taxation of real capital gains, would fall to 28 percent with just the deduction for half of dividends, and would fall to 27 percent with just the personal rate cuts. It would *rise* to 30 percent with just the corporate rate cut because the reduced tax on equity is more than offset by the reduced advantage of nominal interest deductions. Under the same assumptions, this effective tax rate is 34 percent under the president's proposal.

they recouped some revenue through a tough additional minimum tax. Then a last-minute computer snag left the new proposal still significantly short of revenue. Thus was born the "windfall recapture tax" proposal to raise $56 billion over the five-year budget period. The logic was that firms had already made investments to earn income that they had expected would be taxed at the 46 percent rate, so the reduction to a 33 percent rate provided an unexpected windfall that could be recaptured. On the release of the president's proposal in May 1985, this provision caused the biggest stir. It was viewed as a retroactive tax and therefore unfair.

When I was asked to speak to various groups about the tax reform process, I used to bring with me a balloon that I would underinflate to fit in the palm of my hand. "The revenue needed for neutrality with current law is like the air in this balloon," I would say, "and each of the other demands on the tax system is a constraint, like pressing on one part of the balloon." When I pressed one part of the balloon, I got a bulge sticking out somewhere else. The pressure to reduce rates to 15–25–35 created in the Treasury proposal a bulge in the form of "economic" depreciation allowances that were viewed as inadequate to provide basic incentives for capital formation and competitiveness. The pressure to accelerate those allowances in the president's proposal just pushed the bulge somewhere else, primarily in the form of the windfall recapture tax.

Dan Rostenkowski, chairman of the House Ways and Means Committee, accepted the president's challenge to push tax reform. Actually, he thought that it was based on solid Democratic principles of fairness: it would take the poor off the tax roles, remove shelters for the rich, and raise corporate taxes. Democrats could hardly reject such suggestions. Then, in the committee markup during the fall of 1985, Rostenkowski was under considerable pressure to restore several tax breaks, primarily state and local tax deductions. He also dropped the recapture tax. The result was a major bulge in personal tax rates, with the top bracket reduced only to a 38 percent rate. The House bill also did not provide the full $2,000 exemption that was viewed as important to take those below the poverty line off the tax roles. Finally, it shifted $140 billion over five years from individual to corporate taxes.

House Republicans objected, and they managed to stop the entire bill on a procedural rule. The primary domestic policy initiative of the president's second term was killed by lawmakers in his own party. It was resurrected only when President Reagan traveled to Capitol Hill. He encouraged Republicans to keep tax reform alive and vote for this bill by promising to *veto* it if adequate changes were not made in the Senate. H.R. 3838 limped through on a voice vote in December.

Robert Packwood, Republican chairman of the Senate Finance Committee, had no real interest in taking up tax reform at all. Quotes given above indicate that he liked the existing tax code, saw no point in simplification for its own sake, and had greater concern about the deficit. However, he could not let the Republican president's major domestic policy initiative die on his doorstep. He made up yet another set of staff options for the Finance Committee deliberations. In order to suppress the personal rate bulge and the corporate tax bulge, Packwood's staff options suggested disallowing deductions for business payments of excise taxes. But the air of the balloon was simply pushed out into a new bulge. This veiled increase in excise taxes was preferred to the increase in corporate taxes by some lawmakers, but it violated accepted practices of measuring net income by the difference between gross income and legitimate business expenses such as excise taxes paid. It did not survive the markup. Moreover, senators on the committee were quick to restore many tax breaks that they themselves had devised in past years, from municipal bonds to natural resources. The coup de grâce was an accelerated depreciation scheme for "productivity property" that allowed lawmakers to pick and choose which assets in which industries were to be deemed "productive" enough to warrant special treatment. The revenue cost was not as big a problem as the symbol: this concept flew in the face of the entire spirit of tax reform that would level the playing field and leave profit-maximizing firms with the task of deciding which were the best investments. It was business as usual, a depreciation scheme written by Charls Walker and Ernest Christian, the same corporate lobbyists who had devised the earlier ACRS in 1981 and even ADR in 1971.

With a revenue hemorrhage on his hands, Chairman Packwood decided to stop the markup. On Friday, 18 April, Packwood had his famous two-pitcher lunch with Chief of Staff Bill Diefenderfer at the Irish Times. They discussed the impending death of tax reform, a possible minimalist strategy of closing a few loopholes to get some rate reduction, and an alternative, more dramatic strategy. What would really make tax reform attractive, they reasoned, would be *very* low rates. If the top rate were only 25 percent, for example, then maybe taxpayers would not mind losing a few deductions. What would it take to get rates that low? Joint Tax Committee Chief of Staff David Brockway was asked to devise a new plan altogether. He returned with no state and local tax deduction, no mortgage interest deduction, and no charitable contribution deduction but a top rate of 25 percent.

This plan became the starting point for a "core" group of seven senators who showed some interest. They "spent" a point or two of rate reduction to add back most of those key, popular personal deductions. Since the low top rate created a huge tax cut for high-income brackets, and since the bill was intended to be approximately distributionally neutral, they accepted other changes that would raise the tax on high-income individuals such as the full taxation of nominal capital gains and the disallowance of some "passive losses." These hits were not easy to take, but finally the balloon was starting to assume a round shape.

The Finance Committee ended up with a 27 percent rate, an income range over which the benefits of exemptions and the lower 15 percent rate bracket were phased out by a 5 percent surcharge, and a unanimous 20 to 0 vote for tax reform. The full Senate passed it 97 to 3. The conference with the House required enough revenue-losing modifications to require a top rate of 28 percent. With the 5 percent surcharge over the phase-out range, the maximum marginal rate was actually 33 percent. The president signed the bill on 22 October 1986.

3.5   Some Final Remarks

The Tax Reform Act of 1986 was a very intricately constructed package of provisions, each of which depended on the others. The original "supply-side" idea of greater incentives gave the motivation for lower rates, but the era of "deficits" implied that these rate reductions must be paid by base broadening and a "level playing field."

Plenty of criticisms were leveled at the legislation, but mostly they were attempts to take some of the interwoven provisions without others. "We like the lower corporate rate, but we don't like the slower allowances." As this over-simplified example makes clear, you can't have one without the other. In particular, many complaints were heard about the full taxation of nominal capital gains. Certainly, there are good reasons for a capital gains exclusion or at least for indexing in order to tax only the real capital gain. But this imperfect provision was a necessary price of the package since it was the only way to keep the percentage tax cut in the top income group *down* to one digit. Even then, lower-income groups received smaller cuts. Similarly, neither the minimum tax nor the passive loss rule would be needed in a perfect system, but they were needed to achieve this reform. They raised revenue from existing shelters of high-income taxpayers, and they help prevent new shelters, as discussed below.

Others point to the anomaly that the marginal tax rate increases from 15 percent, to 28 percent, to 33 percent, but then falls back to 28 percent for the highest-income taxpayers. It does not seem fair to tax the richest at a lower rate than those less rich. However, while the marginal tax rate is important for the incentive to earn one more dollar, it has little to do with equity. Fairness is best measured by taxes paid as a fraction of income, the average tax rate. Since the first block of income is untaxed, someone in the 15 percent marginal rate bracket has a tax that is less than 15 percent of total income, and someone in the next 28 percent bracket has a tax that is less than 28 percent of total income. The stated purpose of the 5 percent surcharge in the penultimate income group is to "phase out" the benefits of the untaxed block of income and the 15 percent rate block of income, bringing the total tax *up* to 28 percent of total income. As soon as the average tax rate hits 28 percent, the 5 percent surcharge ends, and the taxpayer is back down to a 28 percent marginal rate. In other words, the average tax rate is always less than 28 percent until reaching the highest income level, where every dollar is taxed at 28 percent.[31]

---

31. This provision is similar to the maximum effective rate limitation of 1944–63, which capped the average tax rate below the 90+ percent top marginal tax rate (see table 3.1 above).

Still, why try to claim that the top rate is 28 percent instead of admitting the 33 percent rate and just extending it out to all taxpayers above a certain income level? In the first place, senators did *not* grant that the top rate was really 33 percent. Yes or no, they would ask, is it possible for anyone's tax to exceed 28 percent of their taxable income? No. In the second place, when senators were trading off key deductions against each percentage point of tax rate, as it increased from 26 to 27 and then to 28 percent, they were told that a 1 percent increase in the top bracket would raise about $30 billion over five years. In contrast, extending an official 33 percent rate bracket to those few taxpayers above the phase-out range would raise only about $25 billion over five years. It made no sense to these senators to enact a 5 percentage point increase in the top rate to raise $25 billion when a 1 point increase in the top rate would raise $30 billion.[32]

Another question is whether Congress went too far in attacking shelters, the "whipping boy" of tax reform. First, rate cuts would make shelters less attractive simply by reducing the tax saving from sheltering a dollar at the margin. Second, longer lives for both equipment and structures would chip away at the basic building blocks of which shelters are constructed. Third, the capital gains rate hike would make the conversion of ordinary income into capital gains income irrelevant. Fourth, at-risk rules were tightened. Fifth, the passive loss rule was designed specifically with shelters in mind. Finally, the tough new alternative minimum tax would keep any taxpayer from overusing what was left of any tax shelter arrangement. Was this overkill? In combination, these features are guaranteed to stop pure shelter arrangements.[33] And, once a shelter is stopped, each additional hit is no longer relevant. The passive loss rule may be important in preventing pure shelter arrangements, but it acquires little long-run revenue because virtually nobody goes so far as to pay it.

Although more taxpayers were induced to use the standard deduction instead of itemizing, these antishelter and other provisions helped keep the final bill far from a "simplification." But that goal was a bit of a red herring anyway. (For an opposing view, see McLure [1990a]). Uninformed taxpayers thought that simplification meant having two rate brackets instead of eleven, although calculating taxable income is a much tougher job than using taxable income in the rate tables to figure the tax. Also, the media used "simplification" to summarize *other* aspects of tax reform.[34] Simplification was primarily important to the extent that the average taxpayer thought that high-income individuals

32. Current estimates of the U.S. Congressional Budget Office (1990) suggest that a 1 percentage point increase in the 28 percent rate would raise $50 billion over five years while the extension of the 33 percent rate would raise $40 billion over five years.

33. McLure (1990a, 92) calls this the "vampire approach" to dealing with tax shelters: "In order to be safe when dealing with a vampire, one drives a stake through the heart, hangs a cross around the neck, places a mirror over the eyes, and fills the coffin with wolfsbane."

34. For example, the *Wall Street Journal* of 8 February 1985 repeatedly refers to the "Treasury's tax-simplification plan" and then defines the concept as "drastic tax-rate reduction for individuals and businesses coupled with elimination of a host of tax preferences."

were *using* complexity to avoid their fair share of tax. With nice simple digits like 10–10–10, 10–5–3, or 15–25–35 appearing throughout the decade, one might think that a reform needs to be, not simplification, but simple minded.

The first theme of this paper is the supply-side logic of personal marginal rate reductions. Rates were reduced not just in 1981 but again in 1986. President Reagan was able to leave office with the top marginal rate less than half what it was when he started. Some economic effects of these changes are analyzed in papers appearing in Slemrod (1990). Important associated effects on the distribution of tax burdens are not discussed much here, but evidence on the 1981 changes is debated in U.S. Congressional Budget Office (1987), U.S. House of Representatives (1990), and Lindsey (1990).

The second theme of this paper is the impact of deficits on the process of tax policy-making. Lawmakers now pay much attention to estimates of revenue impact. For a number of reasons, it seems like too much attention. First, each revenue estimate is only an estimate. It is an imperfect best guess made by an arbitrarily assigned estimator who uses old data, a set of arbitrary assumptions, and error-prone computer calculations. A different estimator could easily make other reasonable assumptions and get a different answer. Second, these revenue estimates are always relative to existing law, as if that were some valuable standard against which to judge all changes. There is *nothing* absolute about current law, for that is why changes are being considered in the first place. An example is the way that any indexing proposal appears to lose billions of dollars, relative to the tyranny of current law, when in fact inflation under current law might be *raising* billions of dollars of revenue more than was intended (see McLure 1986, 1645). Third, other good reasons to enact some tax change may be overwhelmed by the estimate of a revenue loss, given the difficulty of reducing each dollar of deficit. Fourth, the process has established five-year budget periods of absolute importance. Four years doesn't matter, or six years, or any kind of present value calculation. The process becomes incredible when minute details of several small provisions that each add $200 million of revenue are combined to pay for a big provision that costs tens of billions, with a reasonable error of plus or minus one or two billion.

These criticisms are quite valid, but what is the alternative? The process absolutely needs some kind of discipline. As Senator Pat Moynihan of the Finance Committee puts it, "Everyone is entitled to his own opinion, but not his own facts" (Birnbaum and Murray 1987, 275). There is no free lunch, and policymakers need a common language for communicating about the necessary trade-offs among alternatives. Indeed, the tax reform process really started working properly only when the "core" group of senators came out of their closed room not just with a new low-rate proposal but with a rule that amendments themselves must each be revenue neutral. Any lawmaker who wants some tax break must, for the first time, recognize its cost in terms of some other added tax. For another example, consider the differences in legitimate estimates of the revenue impact of a change in the capital gains rate. These estimates are not even the same sign, let alone the same magnitude. When the rate was raised in 1986, the revenue estimate was positive. Later, other estimates showed that a reduction in the capital gains rate would raise revenue. Either is possible, but not both. The government cannot raise revenue by raising the capital gains rate and then raise more revenue by lowering it again. The procedures to provide and use revenue estimates can undoubtedly be improved, but, in the era of deficits, their importance is here to stay.

The last theme of this paper is the level playing field. Certainly, the equity version of the level playing field had a role in making sure that individuals in the same income group could not end up with very different tax burdens owing to shelters. This more populist version just happened to support the efficiency version that called for more equal marginal effective tax rates on different assets. Such calculations were popular in the early 1980s, but Merrill (1987) discusses several reasons that these economic models were of only limited importance to the actual policy debate. One such model, however, was used not only in academic research to evaluate alternative proposals in the early 1980s (see Fullerton and Henderson 1984) but also within the Treasury department to evaluate successive reform options in 1985–86 and later as the basis for calculations appearing in the *Economic Report of the President* in 1987 (pp. 87–90) and again in 1989 (pp. 92–93).

Looking over the decade of tax policy in the making, a question frequently asked is whether the Tax Reform Act of 1986 (TRA) was a reversal of the Economic Recovery Tax Act of 1981. When asked this very question, most interviewees responded immediately, "Yes, it was a reversal." Where ERTA accelerated depreciation and expanded the ITC, the 1986 act slowed down depreciation and repealed the ITC. One bill greatly reduced corporate taxes; the other greatly increased them. Then, after further reflection, or prompting from the interviewer, most added, "Well, I suppose that personal rate reduction was one aspect similar in the two bills." A significant minority of interviewees responded immediately, "No, it was not a reversal." Some thought that debates about both ERTA and TRA had an unusual concern with the structure of taxation (e.g., indexing) and not just revenues.[35] Others pointed immediately to the similarity of the rate reduction.[36]

To the extent that TRA did reverse ERTA, via depreciation allowances and corporate taxes, the reversal did not start with the 1986 bill. The more im-

35. Before Congress on 18 February 1981, in support of ERTA, Reagan said that "the taxing power of government . . . must not be used to regulate the economy or bring about social change." The same logic applied to TRA and the level playing field.

36. This question is addressed specifically by Fullerton and Mackie (1989). They measure the efficiency effects of both ERTA and TRA by using a simulation model that incorporates the intertemporal distortion of higher taxes on capital and the interasset distortion of differing effective tax rates. They find that, if one adopts the "new view" (that personal taxes on dividends are unimportant disincentives), then the reduced tax on capital in ERTA is more important for overall efficiency. But, if one adopts the "old view" (that personal taxes on dividends are important investment disincentives), then the level playing field and additional rate reduction in TRA are more important.

portant bill as a watershed in tax policy-making was the Economic Recovery Tax Act of 1981. The powerful forces of "supply-side" thoughts about incentives and rate reduction began with the 1981 bill. Indexing of brackets and the resulting "era of deficits" started with the 1981 bill. And the process of using the tax code to encourage or reward particular economic activities through various tax provisions culminated in the 1981 bill. Forever after, projected deficits (shown in table 3.3 above) required that these provisions be cut back or repealed. This new era of tax policy was in effect as of August 1981, but its first products were not evident until TEFRA in 1982 and DEFRA in 1984. These bills closed loopholes, slowed depreciation, and started to level the playing field. By 1986, in these respects, the Tax Reform Act of 1986 was simply more of the same.

References

Auerbach, Alan J., and Dale W. Jorgenson. 1980. Inflation-proof depreciation of assets. *Harvard Business Review* 58:113–18.

Auerbach, Alan J., and James M. Poterba. 1987. Why have corporate tax revenues declined? In *Tax policy and the economy,* ed. Lawrence H. Summers. Cambridge, Mass.: MIT Press.

Birnbaum, Jeffrey H., and Alan S. Murray. 1987. *Showdown at Gucci Gulch: Lawmakers, lobbyists, and the unlikely triumph of tax reform.* New York: Random House.

Browning, Edgar K. 1989. Elasticities, tax rates, and tax revenue. *National Tax Journal* 42 (March): 45–58.

Chamber of Commerce. 1984. *The effect of the Treasury proposal on capital formation and economic growth.* Washington, D.C.

Commerce Clearing House. 1981. *Economic Recovery Tax Act of 1981: Law and explanation.* Chicago.

———. 1982. *Explanation of Tax Equity and Fiscal Responsibility Act of 1982.* Chicago.

———. 1984. *Explanation of Tax Reform Act of 1984.* Chicago.

Conlan, Timothy J., Margaret T. Wrightson, and David R. Beam. 1990. *Taxing choices: The politics of tax reform.* Washington, D.C.: Congressional Quarterly Press.

Evans, Rowland, and Robert Novak. 1981. *The Reagan revolution.* New York: Dutton.

Feldstein, Martin. 1981. Adjusting depreciation in an inflationary economy: Indexing versus acceleration. *National Tax Journal* 34 (March): 29–43.

———. 1988. Imputing corporate tax liabilities to individual taxpayers. *National Tax Journal* 41 (March): 37–59.

Fullerton, Don. 1982. On the possibility of an inverse relationship between tax rates and government revenues. *Journal of Public Economics* 19 (October) 3–22.

———. 1987. The indexation of interest, depreciation, and capital gains and tax reform in the United States. *Journal of Public Economics* 32 (February): 25–51.

Fullerton, Don, and Yolanda K. Henderson. 1984. Incentive effects of taxes on income from capital: Alternative policies in the 1980s. In *The legacy of Reaganomics,* ed. Charles R. Hulten and Isabel V. Sawhill. Washington, D.C.: Urban Institute Press.

Fullerton, Don, and Marios Karayannis. 1993. The taxation of income from capital in the United States, 1980–1990. In *Tax reform and the cost of capital: An international comparison,* ed. Dale W. Jorgenson and Ralph Landau. Washington, D.C.: Brookings.

Fullerton, Don, and James B. Mackie. 1989. Economic efficiency in recent tax reform history: Policy reversals or consistent improvements? *National Tax Journal* 42 (March): 1–13.

Grubert, Harry, and John Mutti. 1987. The impact of the Tax Reform Act of 1986 on trade and capital flows. In *Compendium of tax research, 1987.* Washington, D.C.: Treasury Department.

Hall, Robert E., and Alvin Rabushka. 1983. *Low tax, simple tax, flat tax.* New York: McGraw-Hill.

Hulten, Charles R., and Frank C. Wykoff. 1981. The measurement of economic depreciation. In *Depreciation, inflation, and the taxation of income from capital,* ed. Charles R. Hulten. Washington, D.C.: Urban Institute Press.

King, Mervyn A., and Don Fullerton, eds. 1984. *The taxation of income from capital: A comparative study of the United States, the United Kingdom, Sweden, and West Germany.* Chicago: University of Chicago Press.

Laffer, Arthur B. 1977. Statement prepared for the Joint Economic Committee, May 20. In *The economics of the tax revolt: A reader,* ed. Arthur B. Laffer and Jan P. Seymour. New York: Harcourt Brace Jovanovich.

Lindsey, Lawrence B. 1990. *The growth experiment: How the new tax policy is transforming the U.S. economy.* New York: Basic.

McIntyre, Robert S. 1984. *Corporate income taxes in the Reagan years.* Washington, D.C.: Citizens for Tax Justice.

McLure, Charles E. 1986. Where tax reform went astray. *Villanova Law Review* 31, no. 6:1619–66.

———. 1990a. The budget process and tax simplification/complication. *Tax Law Review* 45, no. 1 (Fall): 25–95.

———. 1990b. International considerations in United States tax reform. In *Influence of tax differentials on international competitiveness: Proceedings of the VIIIth Munich Symposium on International Taxation.* Deventer: Kluwer Law and Taxation.

McLure, Charles E., and George R. Zodrow. 1987. Treasury I and the Tax Reform Act of 1986: The economics and politics of tax reform. *Journal of Economic Perspectives* 1 (Summer): 37–58.

Merrill, Peter R. 1987. Economic analysis and the Tax Reform Act of 1986. Working paper. Joint Committee on Taxation.

Merrill, Peter R., Stanley E. Collender, and Eric W. Cook. 1990. Tax legislation and the budget in the 1980s. In *National Tax Association—Proceedings of the Eighty-second Annual Conference, 1989, Atlanta, Georgia.* Columbus, Ohio: National Tax Association.

Meyer, Laurence H., ed. 1981. *The supply-side effects of economic policy.* St. Louis: Center for the Study of American Business and Federal Reserve Bank of St. Louis.

Minarik, Joseph J. 1985. *Making tax choices.* Washington, D.C.: Urban Institute Press.

———. 1987. How tax reform came about. *Tax Notes* 37, no. 13 (December): 1359–73.

Musgrave, Richard A. 1987. Short of euphoria. *Journal of Economic Perspectives* 1 (Summer): 59–71.

Pechman, Joseph A. 1987. *Federal tax policy.* 5th ed. Washington, D.C.: Brookings.

———. 1990. The future of the income tax. *American Economic Review* 80 (March): 1–20.

The president's tax proposals to the Congress for fairness, growth, and simplicity. 1985. Washington, D.C.: U.S. Government Printing Office.

Regan, Donald T. 1988. *For the record: From Wall Street to Washington.* New York: Harcourt Brace Jovanovich.

Roberts, Paul Craig. 1984. *The supply-side revolution: An insider's account of poli-cymaking in Washington.* Cambridge, Mass.: Harvard University Press.

Rudder, Catherine E. 1983. Tax policy: Structure and choice. In *Making economic pol-icy in Congress,* ed. Allen Schick. Washington, D.C.: American Enterprise Institute.

Slemrod, Joel, ed. 1990. *The economic impact of tax reform.* Cambridge, Mass.: MIT Press.

Slemrod, Joel, and Nikki Sorum. 1984. The compliance cost of the U.S. individual income tax system. *National Tax Journal* 37 (December): 461–74.

Smith, Adam. [1776] 1975. *The wealth of nations.* London: Dent.

Steuerle, Eugene, and Michael Hartzmark. 1981. Individual income taxation, 1947–79. *National Tax Journal* 34 (June): 145–66.

Stewart, Charles H. 1991. The politics of tax reform in the 1980s. In *Politics and eco-nomics in the eighties,* ed. Alberto Alesina and Geoffrey Carliner. Chicago: Univer-sity of Chicago Press.

Stockman, David A. 1987. *The triumph of politics: The inside story of the Reagan Revo-lution.* New York: Avon.

Tax Foundation. 1988. *Facts and figures on government finance.* Baltimore: Johns Hop-kins University Press.

U.S. Congressional Budget Office. 1987. *The changing distribution of federal taxes: 1975–1990.* Washington, D.C.: Congress of the United States.

———. 1990. *Reducing the deficit: Spending and revenue options.* Washington, D.C.: Congress of the United States.

U.S. Council of Economic Advisers. 1985. *The economic case for tax reform.* Washing-ton, D.C.: Executive Office of the President.

———. 1987, 1989, 1990. *Economic report of the president.* Washington, D.C.: U.S. Government Printing Office.

U.S. Department of the Treasury. 1978. *The president's 1978 tax program.* Washington, D.C.: U.S. Government Printing Office.

———. 1984. *Tax reform for fairness, simplicity, and economic growth.* Washington, D.C.: Office of the Secretary.

———. 1985. *Taxes paid by high-income taxpayers and the growth of partnerships.* Washington, D.C.: Office of Tax Policy.

———. 1987. *Compendium of tax research, 1987.* Washington, D.C.: U.S. Government Printing Office.

U.S. House of Representatives. 1990. *Tax progressivity and income distribution.* Wash-ington, D.C.: Committee on Ways and Means.

Wanniski, Jude. 1978. *The way the world works.* New York: Simon & Schuster.

Weidenbaum, Murray. 1988. *Rendezvous with reality: The American economy after Reagan.* New York: Basic.

Witte, John F. 1985. *The politics and development of the federal income tax.* Madison: University of Wisconsin Press.

2. *Charls E. Walker*

I believe that the "why" (or the politics) of federal tax policy in the 1980s can best be explained in terms of three fundamental factors: (1) significant swings in what I call the *pendulum* of U.S. tax policy; (2) still another demonstration of the convention political science wisdom that presidents of one party can often achieve policy goals that presidents of the other party cannot, goals that appear on the surface at least to be contradictory to the party's philosophy, culture, and/or constituencies; and (3) the emergence of a huge, politically intransigent federal deficit.

I shall deal with these factors out of order, starting first with the budget crunch. Don Fullerton has provided a good discussion of this factor in his background paper, so my remarks shall be supplemental and deal primarily with the politics of tax policy.

Tax Policy to Raise Revenue

Inasmuch as the fundamental purpose of a nation's tax system is to provide revenue, it may seem strange to single out this factor for special treatment with respect to the 1980s. The point is not that revenue raising is not essential but rather that it came largely to drive tax policy in the United States after 1981. The (misnamed) Tax Equity and Fiscal Responsibility Act of 1982 (TEFRA) was a valiant if only partially successful effort to bring down the mounting federal deficit that emerged as a result of the spending and tax policies of the early Reagan years. Fullerton has given us a good blow by blow on TEFRA.

Perhaps the most important aspect of the emergence of revenue impact as the major driving force in tax policy—at least to "outsiders" (both outside and *within* the Congress) trying to affect policy—was that the professional revenue estimators on the staff of the Joint Committee on Taxation (JCT) (and, to a lesser extent, at the Treasury's Office of Tax Analysis [OTA]), and the members to whom they responded, became of overwhelming importance in any debate over specific tax provisions.

In one instance involving a Walker Associates client during the debate on and markup of TEFRA, we were almost certain that our proposed substitution for a very tough provision (from the client's standpoint) would at least be revenue neutral. The JCT reported otherwise, and we were not allowed to look into the staff's "little black box" and examine the assumptions and analysis that blew our proposal out of the water. The fundamental merit of our proposal was not even debated; we were killed by a staff revenue estimate. That is *not* good tax policy, and it is *not* fair.[1]

Is there an answer to this problem? In my judgment, the revenue estimators have much more power than they should have in our democratic system. It is the members who legally possess final power over revenue estimates (as my friend Russell Long demonstrated in the capital gains fight of 1978). One solution would be to emulate public policy in other difficult, technical areas and

---

1. The JCT staff has finally been more forthcoming—at least on one issue. It recently shared with the world at large its assumptions and analysis on revenue estimates during the recent capital gains debate. That's progress—although I think that the JCT staff estimates of the revenue impact of a capital gains cut are still too conservative, especially if scored on an overall macroeconomic basis.

transfer revenue estimating to an outside panel of carefully selected nongovernment economists—short of that, to set up a "National Academy of Science"–type nonpartisan panel of experts to review and critique the JCT and OTA revenue-estimating procedures. Neither of these steps seems to be even remotely close to the horizon.

Three other political points about tax policy and the budget crunch should be noted before I turn to the other two factors affecting tax policy in the 1980s. One involves decision making in Congress, the second relates to the basic forces to which Congress was responding, and the third shows how a voter uprising can quickly force Congress to reverse an earlier unpopular tax decision.

During his years as chairman of the Senate Finance Committee, Russell Long did all that he could to promote tax decisions on a collegial, consensus basis. This approach had a great deal going for it, especially during years in which, more often than not, we operated under divided government, with all its inherent difficulties. Partisan factors tend to be minimized under this approach.

But, when the new chairman of the committee, Bob Dole, began his effort to push through TEFRA in 1982, collegiality was thrown out the window. I don't say this to be critical of Bob Dole. I haven't talked to him about it, but I suppose that he simply wanted to get the job done, quickly, and without a lot of talk—perhaps Russell can enlighten us on that. In any event, the eleven Republicans on the committee would meet in private caucus, Dole would cut a deal, and the group would emerge (in most instances) as a solid phalanx, in effect telling the Democratic members, "Take it or else." It worked. But, not only did it make tax legislation less "fun," it also probably helped move us toward the excessive partisanship that finally emerged this fall in the efforts to construct an effective deficit-reduction package. If that's so, it's too bad. We direly need ways to make divided government work well today, as it did during the years of Eisenhower and even Nixon.[2]

My second political point involves the frequently made statement that the passage of TEFRA in a congressional election year proves that the need to bring down a mounting deficit can be a driving force in tax policy, causing members to vote against their constituents' desires. Not so. TEFRA passed, not because of the emerging deficit per se, but because the media convinced

2. This is neither the time nor the place to discuss the basic factors that have led to the budget fiasco of 1990. But I must note that the *Economist* seemed to me to be on the right track when it recently noted (after calling the summit agreement a "mouse") that one of the basic problems is that the U.S. system of government was invented 200 years ago and might not be quite suitable for the present—or at least need some significant changes. I strongly agree. The Founding Fathers, for good reasons at the time, insisted on checks and balances and a weak executive. Now that we have moved so far toward that type of plebiscite democracy that the Founding Fathers distrusted, with members voting more and more their constituents' desires even when they know they're wrong, the chief executive needs more power in the budget arena. Once he sends up his budget, he's technically "out of play" (unless he can motivate voters directly through his bully pulpit and congressmen through persuasion or political pressure), until what might be one final continuing

the voting public that the sky-high interest rates and collapsing stock market of 1981–82 were *caused by* the deficit—staunch the red ink, and the pain of ultra high borrowing costs and shrinking net worth would disappear.

If this view is correct—and you know that it is—then we can understand why nothing other than an inadequate weapon known as Gramm-Rudman-Hollings was used to attack the deficit until 1990, when George Bush decided (too late?) that he had better reconfigure his lips and get deficit reduction moving or else he would seriously injure his prospects for reelection in 1992. And, sad to state, when he made that move last May, and since that time, the "non-pain" federal deficit has continued to rise, thus dooming the chance to get a solid deficit-reduction plan voted by Congress only shortly before the 1990 election. As one member said in speaking against the first package, "Are we supposed to vote for legislation which includes our own death warrants?" Good question.

A second reason that TEFRA passed Congress in an election year is that it primarily hit corporations, not individuals. The biggest individual revenue raiser in the legislation was mandatory withholding of income taxes on interest and dividends—a provision on which, as noted below, Congress quickly turned tail. To be sure, everyone "knows" that people, not institutions, ultimately bear all taxes, but that knowledge seems to count for little in the political arena. In Russell's famous dictum of tax reform—"Don't tax you; don't tax me; tax that fellow behind that tree!"—the "fellow behind that tree" is frequently a faceless corporation.

My third political point about TEFRA is the just-noted and, to some, astonishing reversal of Congress on the TEFRA provision to force withholding of taxes on interest and dividends. That reversal didn't surprise me at all, and I doubt that it surprised Russell; we had gone through almost exactly the same thing in 1962. Withholding had passed the House as part of John Kennedy's "tax reform" efforts, but it went down the tube in the Senate (and Congress) as a result of a very effective (but dishonest) publicity campaign mounted by the U.S. Savings and Loan League. As executive vice president of the American Bankers Association at the time, and fresh out of the Treasury, I refused to join the league in the campaign—partly because the ads were dishonest, partly

---

resolution appears before him—a measure that he must sign or literally bring the government to a halt.

I'm not sure that I favor the line-item veto; it will not help in the crucial area of entitlements, could give an LBJ-type president huge power in bringing congressmen "around," and might impair national security policy when and if an overly "dovish" man or woman (e.g., George McGovern) occupies the presidency at a time when new weapons systems need to be developed. At the least, however, the president should have restored to him the recession and impoundment powers taken away in the Budget Control Act of 1974. Furthermore, can we not come up with some innovative but politically acceptable methods for the president, representing all the people, to exercise at least some control over growth of entitlements? I refer that tough question to Charles Schultze and David Stockman.

because I knew that they would kill withholding without the presence of organized banking's fingerprints.[3]

There are millions upon millions of voters who own savings accounts, receive dividends, and so on, and they detest the idea of withholding. The sponsors of withholding in 1982 like to blame the bankers and savings and loans (S&Ls) for the repeal of the provision in 1983. The banks and S&Ls might have speeded the process, but permanent withholding was not in the cards from the start. In fact, the banks and S&Ls did the politicians a favor by helping force its repeal *before* it could go into effect.

Events in 1989 demonstrate that powerful taxpayer uprisings can still carry the day and force reversals of earlier legislation. Cases in point are the provision of the Tax Reform Act of 1986 (TRA) that affected employee benefit programs (sec. 89), reversed as a result of a voter uprising (mainly small businesses), and the catastrophic health provisions enacted in 1988, shot down in flames by the elderly only a year later.

All in all, a revenue-driven tax policy can make life miserable for almost all parties—legislators, Treasury officials, interest groups, lobbyists, the whole crowd. Only the revenue estimators seem to prosper and perhaps be happy at such times.

The Tax Policy Pendulum

Let me begin to illustrate what I mean by the tax policy pendulum by quoting the final examination question on tax policy for my graduate students at the University of Texas at Austin last semester:

In enacting the Tax Reform Act of 1976, Congress tried to move the tax system toward its image of "fairness" by raising taxes on business and on high-income individuals who enjoyed large capital gains. Only two years later, Congress passed the Revenue Act of 1978, which did just the opposite by cutting corporate tax rates, making "permanent" the investment tax credit, and—by means of the Bill Steiger/Russell Long amendment—slashing taxes on capital gains.

Less than a year later, in the summer of 1979, Representatives James R. Jones (who had authored the House version of the 1978 bill) and Barber Conable, accompanied by such Senate worthies as Lloyd Bentsen, Gaylord Nelson, Bob Packwood, Jack Danforth, and Jack Heinz, introduced the "10–5–3" capital cost recovery bill, which, if passed, would cut corporate tax

---

3. Those of us who like to think of ourselves as politically astute frequently quote taxi drivers to make our points—and, indeed, it was a New York taxi driver who made the telling comment on withholding to me in 1962. When he found that I spent considerable time in Washington on legislative matters, he said, "Do you know what that damn John Kennedy is trying to do to me— and, to think, I voted for the guy?" "No," I replied. "What is that damn Kennedy trying to do to you?" "He's trying to pass a law that will take some of my money out of my savings account." "But don't you realize that you owe that money as taxes to Uncle Sam?" His response was short and telling: "Like hell I do!"

liabilities in half within five years. In less than six weeks, over 300 House members and some seventy-five senators had signed onto the legislation. Its significant features were enacted in 1981 as part of President Reagan's Economic Recovery Tax Act.

Finally, in 1986, Congress passed a Tax Reform Act, which repealed the investment tax credit; lengthened depreciation guidelines; eliminated the preferential tax on capital gains; sharply limited the individual retirement account provisions passed originally in 1981; and greatly reduced the attractiveness of "tax shelters."

Explain.

(Oh, how I hated that type of question in my graduate days. "Explain," indeed!)

What were student answers that I did not accept? That federal tax policy is simply and for no good reason unpredictable, swinging erratically with no discernible pattern. Or that Congress acted with uncharacteristic good sense and courage in 1976 and again in 1986, repulsing the greedy "Gucci Gulch" lobbyists in order to make the tax system "fair." Or, vice versa, that the good sense and courage was demonstrated in the 1978 and 1981 bills. None of these answers gained a passing grade.

The answer that I did accept was that the "pendulum" of U.S. tax policy had repeated past performance, making a one and a half swing from the "fairness" objective, which is fueled by voters' unhappiness with what they view as an unfair and oppressive federal income tax—to tax policy oriented toward economic goals—and back to "fairness" again. Let me explain in terms of my personal experience with U.S. tax policy.

Although my presence on the Washington scene runs back almost four decades, my direct concern with taxes began only in 1961, when the Treasury moved administratively to liberalize certain depreciation guidelines and John Kennedy proposed the investment tax credit (ITC) to Congress. Interestingly, JFK's call for the ITC "to get the country moving again" (one of his major campaign themes) and to enhance U.S. "international competitiveness" (yes, even then) was opposed by both the labor and the business communities. The American Bankers Association was a major exception; we applauded and worked for the ITC; I personally testified for it before Congress. Congress somewhat reluctantly approved it in 1962.

These first steps toward what I would call a *pro-capital formation* tax policy (which might now be called *supply-side*), strongly oriented toward economic goals, were followed by what was surely a major "supply-side" proposal in early 1963, when JFK called for slashes in both business and individual taxes, the latter closely resembling the Kemp-Roth tax cut of the late 1970s. The tax measure was bogged down in the Senate Finance Committee at the time of JFK's assassination, but LBJ broke it loose, and Congress enacted the bill in 1964.

The point here, as related to the pendulum of tax policy, is that the original JFK macro tax cut had also included a large number of "tax reform" measures (defined solely in terms of "fairness"), in the image of, and prepared by, the dean of all such "reformers," Treasury Assistant Secretary Stanley Surrey.[4] The "reform" portion of JFK's proposal collided with the growth section, and, not surprisingly, growth won. After all, JFK had indeed promised "to get the country moving again." Add to that the skill and pragmatism of his Treasury team of Doug Dillon and Joe Fowler and the recognition by Council of Economic Advisers (CEA) Chairman Walter Heller and his associates that tax policy for growth was indeed important—well, economics won, and "reform" lost. As Russell will recall, JFK promptly dropped the reform elements from his package when they showed signs of dragging the whole bill down.

JFK could do this, without major political damage, because the "tax reform" crowd at the AFL-CIO, along with Stan Surrey and his disciples, would doubtless be sullen, but not really mutinous. Here we get close to the final factor in 1980s tax policy that I shall discuss below—what a president of one party can do that a president of the other cannot. More important in this instance, however, was the fact that, in 1963–64, the public was not nearly so unhappy with the federal income tax system as it later became. Bracket creep was still far down the road, tax shelters had not become a national scandal, and stories about big corporations or millionaires paying little or no federal taxes were not as yet front-page news.

By the time I took my second seat at the Treasury in January 1969—indeed, I should say that at almost *precisely* the time I took it—public unhappiness with the income tax almost exploded. Outgoing Democratic Treasury Secretary Joe Barr had done his successors the "favor" of telling Congress that many multimillionaires or even billionaires were paying little or no federal income taxes. At the same time, Stan Surrey's comprehensive swan song tax reform proposal was publicly released (rather than privately handed to us).[5]

The news of millionaires paying little or no federal income taxes rocketed around the country. A staffer told me that the Treasury received more gripe mail about income taxes in February 1969, following the Barr revelations in January, than in all of 1968. The ranking Republican on the House Ways and

---

4. I use quotation marks when referring to "tax reform" because, as Webster tells us, "reform" means "to amend or improve by change of form or removal of faults." "Tax reform" that makes a system "fairer" (in someone's image) by, e.g., raising taxes on saving and investment may cause the economy to falter and unemployment to rise—a policy that can surely be viewed as "unfair." Unfortunately, in my view, the "fairness" gang captured the high rhetorical ground a long time ago. When those in the media speak of "tax reform," they are almost always buying "fairness" as reform's sole ingredient. A strong case can be made that, in a fundamental sense, the Kennedy-Johnson tax measures of 1961–1964, the Jones-Steiger-Long bill of 1978, and the Economic Recovery Tax Act of 1981—all strongly pro–capital formation, pro-jobs, pro-growth, and pro-competitiveness—deserve the label *reform* no less than the 1969, 1976, and 1986 tax acts.

5. LBJ, who could be devious, had promised AFL-CIO head George Meany that, if organized labor would support his proposal for a 10 percent income surtax in the spring of 1968, he would send a true "tax reform" proposal to Congress before he left office in January 1969. Surrey worked hard and long and brought forth an ambitious plan, but LBJ kept it bottled up—until only a few days before Richard Nixon was sworn in.

Means Committee, a fine politician and wonderful human being named John Byrnes, prepared a hard-hitting, pro-"tax reform" speech for delivery about that time, but shared it in advance with Committee Chairman Wilbur Mills—only to find that Wilbur in effect stole his speech and gave it first!

I believed all along that the "tax reform" pressure might die out, as it usually had in the past—until 15 April. When the typical taxpayer got to the bottom of his return and saw that he had to add LBJ's surtax to what he already considered a tax bill much too high—he exploded again. As a result, during 1969, Treasury officials and staff, tax committees and staff, and many others worked night and day to produce the Tax Reform Act of 1969, up to that time the shining example of "tax reform" defined in terms of fairness.

Wonder of wonders—that bill was largely put together in a Republican treasury (drawing, of course, from Stan Surrey's plan) and was signed by none other than Richard Nixon. Nixon could succeed where JFK could not—another example of my third element of tax policy, discussed below.

Tax policy swung back toward the goal of economic growth only two years later, a move ushered in by the recession of 1970. With the economy weak, inflation mounting, and convertibility of the dollar into gold becoming harder to maintain, Nixon announced his New Economic Policy in August 1971. In addition to cutting the link between gold and the dollar and a wage-price freeze, the president asked Congress for restoration of the ITC, which had been repealed in the "tax reform" flurry of 1969, and statutory approval of a new depreciation system known as the Asset Depreciation Range (ADR).[6] These two actions, both of which Congress approved, provided the United States with a creditable and fairly competitive capital cost recovery system.[7]

The tax policy pendulum moved little in the first half of the 1970s, but, by

6. Earlier, in 1965, the ITC had been "suspended." Congress quickly reactivated it in 1966 as investment spending dropped sharply.

7. Once in a very long while, a tough legislative goal can be achieved with a single argument presented on a single piece of paper; such was the case with the restoration of the ITC and the enactment of ADR in the fall of 1971. Sophisticated financial/political reporters had told me, "Walker, you'll never get both ITC and ADR. Which will you settle for?" Sounding perhaps more optimistic than I really felt, I simply said, "Just you watch—it's a piece of cake!"

Educating Congress with respect to international competitiveness was the key (just as it is likely to be a big part of the next swing of the tax policy pendulum back to economic goals). Treasury tax staff had prepared what was in effect a "present value" table of the capital cost recovery systems in Japan, Western Europe, and the United States. The AFL-CIO, then very powerful in Congress, had swung from its traditional free trade position toward protectionism, and Congress was uptight about foreign competition and the "export of jobs." Our capital cost recovery table showed that, even if both the ITC and ADR were approved, our system, in competitive terms, would still fall far short of the Japanese and Western European systems. Representative James Burke, who had been the AFL-CIO stalking horse in introducing a blatantly protectionist tax bill known as the Burke-Hartke Act, said in executive session of the Ways and Means Committee, "I'm with Charly on this. He's convinced me that we need both of these measures." Russell may recall our successful use of the table later in his committee.

Nothing at all was said about whether these business tax cuts were or were not fair. The members, reflecting their constituents concerns, were much more interested in jobs, growth, and competitiveness.

1976, "tax reform" was again center stage, culminating in the Tax Reform Act of 1976. Work on the measure began in the summer of 1975, under new Ways and Means Committee Chairman Al Ullman and before a much-expanded group. According to reports from reliable sources, AFL-CIO President George Meany had insisted that the House Democrats "stack" the Ways and Means Committee by adding some eleven or twelve members, from the traditional twenty-five to thirty-six or thirty-seven. The goal was to get a comprehensive "tax reform" bill. The main result was agony for Al Ullman, for the expanded committee was ideologically split right down the middle. Consensus, or even near consensus, was impossible.

Nevertheless, Al Ullman pushed ahead and ultimately succeeded in obtaining passage a year later of the Tax Reform Act of 1976. Perhaps its most spectacular "reform" was to attack the alleged problem of nontaxation of capital gains at death by requiring the original basis of inherited property to be carried over to the heir. Once middle America's farmers and small businessmen found out about this action, they rose up (as with withholding in 1962), and the provision was repealed even before it went into effect.

Then came the first of two spectacular swings in the tax policy pendulum: the passage of the Jim Jones–Bill Steiger–Russell Long–devised Revenue Act in 1978; the overwhelming congressional endorsement of "10–5–3" when introduced in the summer of 1979; and the ultimate passage of the Economic Recovery Tax Act of 1981 (ERTA), which gave the United States one of the most competitive capital cost recovery systems in the industrial world.

How to explain this swing of the pendulum? There were several factors. Business groups and some academics in the early 1970s had begun to warn that the United States faced a capital shortage, and various studies tended to point in that direction. Senators Lloyd Bentsen and Bill Brock mounted hearings to study the issue, concluding that a problem did indeed exist. Brookings undertook such a study, and it is with the reporting of that study to the House Ways and Means Committee that I began to feel that the tide was beginning to turn in the direction of a pro-capital formation policy.

At a hearing in July 1975, the late Joe Pechman told Ways and Means that Brookings—where Joe was then director of economic studies—had engaged a distinguished panel of experts, which had concluded that the United States would have no capital shortage problem in the future provided that we do two things: restore full employment and convert the federal deficit into a surplus. Whereupon Representative Bill Frenzel, a "legislator's legislator," all-around fine person, and world-class "doodler," dropped his pencil and exclaimed, "What did you just say?" Joe repeated his statement and asked, "Does that conclusion surprise you, Congressman?" Frenzel replied, "Surprised? I'm flabbergasted. You have just convinced me that we have a very big capital formation problem!"

By 1975, when Joe testified, the various studies and discussions of a capital shortage were having a decided impact on public opinion. Seventy-eight percent of the nation's "thought leaders" polled by the Opinion Research Corporation (ORC) believed that there was a looming investment shortage and that, "over the next ten years or so," it would be "somewhat serious" (30 percent), or "very serious" (8 percent). Even more significantly, an identical 78 percent of the federal legislators polled by the ORC came to the same conclusion. Moreover, by a ratio of 50 to 38 percent, federal legislators stated that existing tax laws hurt capital formation. By 1976, according to the Cambridge Report, 60 percent of the general public believed that there was "a problem with raising the dollars needed for business investment."

So, understandably and inevitably, the tax policy pendulum began to swing from "tax reform for fairness" to "tax reform for jobs, growth, and competitiveness." The American people, and therefore Congress, had concluded that the U.S. economy was not performing up to snuff and that the tax system had a great deal to do with that. The result was the strongly pro-capital formation tax bills of 1978 and 1981. And, since pro–capital formation tax legislation means reducing the hit on saving and investment, tax "benefits" (as scored by the Joint Tax Committee) can be said to flow to the upper-income rather than to the lower-income citizens. The answer on this to the "tax reform by fairness" crowd is that there is nothing "fair" about rising unemployment and lagging growth in living standards. What "tax reformers" refer to in pejorative terms as *trickle-down* economics (still a favorite of the *Washington Post*) can also be called *capital formation* economics, which almost everybody agrees is essential to achieving higher per capita income and thus expanding living standards.

In speaking to groups about this phenomenon, I was prone to say that, in the 1970s, capital formation became "as American as apple pie"—until my friend George Will returned from a trip to California and told me of a sign on a fast-food place advertising "kosher burritos." Now what, asked George, could be more American than kosher burritos? What indeed! I changed my line. In the 1980s, capital formation became as American as kosher burritos. But, alas and alack, the pendulum was soon to swing back again, and with great vigor, culminating in the Tax Reform Act of 1986 (TRA).

I have a love-hate relationship with that legislation. I "love" the low individual and corporate rates, something I never thought I would see in my lifetime. But I "hate" the more than $150 billion, five-year "hit" on capital formation that in effect paid for those low rates (plus other "goodies" distributed by this "revenue-neutral" legislation). Worst of all, of course, was repeal of the ITC. That action, coupled with lengthening of depreciation guidelines, raised the capital cost of investing in new equipment by 41 percent, when viewed from the standpoint of the investor, and by 13 percent, when viewed from the standpoint of the user, which includes depreciation. For the entire period after 1981, the relevant figures are 90 percent and 23 percent, respectively.[8]

8. See the testimony of Mark Bloomfield before the House Ways and Means Committee (101st Cong., 2d sess., 5 March 1990).

From an economic standpoint, worse tax action for a nation whose capital costs had already been driven too high by the upward pressure of the huge federal deficit on domestic real interest rates can hardly be imagined. John Paulus, then chief economist for Goldman Sachs, wrote in the *Washington Post* that the tax bill would have been near perfect—for Japan. Martin Feldstein was also very critical of the anti-capital formation parts of the legislation. Our purpose today, however, is to discuss not the wisdom of the decade's tax policy but how it happened.[9]

The 1986 TRA was partly the result of the tax policy pendulum swinging back toward "tax reform for fairness," for the American people by 1985 had become very angry with the federal income tax. Not only did they crave simplicity in order better to understand the system as a whole as well as to stay away from the tax preparer, but they were also furious with reports of rich individuals and big corporations who paid little or no taxes. Still, such unhap-

---

9. Still, I cannot resist taking substantive issue with Fullerton. I believe that his statement that "Treasury I" would have "leveled the playing field" of tax policy for business investment omits an aspect of tax neutrality that is crucial to promoting capital formation. While it is indeed true that equality of tax rates on the income from all three types of business investment (structures, equipment, and inventories) will tend to result in what the economists call *efficient* allocation of resources *in the present,* the existence of an income tax inherently promotes misallocation of resources *over time.* We know that the personal income tax is in effect a double tax on saving; it taxes the income from which saving is generated and at the same time taxes the proceeds of such saving. And we add to this double tax on saving still a third layer, a tax on corporations. The result—as is widely recognized—is a tax system that promotes consumption and is biased against saving and investment.

By raising taxes on the latter, TRA in fact made the playing field more uneven. The bias of the income tax can be eliminated by substituting a consumption tax, such as a value-added tax (VAT), for the business income tax or by moving the latter toward a consumed income tax by cutting back on the taxation of saving and investment. Given the political inevitability of the corporate income tax, this was the policy route that we took with ERTA in 1981—and, from the standpoint of economic progress, a very good route in my book.

When we "corporate lobbyists" conceived of "10–5–3" in 1979 (actually, it was more the creation of Representative Jim Jones, based on an earlier business group proposal known as "10–5"), we wanted to bring the tax treatment of investment on equipment as close to theoretical expensing as possible, as under a neutral VAT. Given the high discount rates that existed at the time, we hit very close to our target period. As interest rates fell, however, the combination of short depreciation lives and a 10 percent ITC shifted the rate to a theoretically negative level, to what might be called a "subsidy" for tax-paying corporations (or those who temporarily took advantage of "safe-harbor leasing").

But I do not apologize for this "subsidy." As DeLong and Summers (1991) tell us so convincingly in a study covering a cross section of nations, investment in equipment is indeed the key to stronger economic growth in mature economies and to more rapid development in less-advanced economies. DeLong and Summers conclude that investment of 1 percent of gross domestic product (GDP) in equipment is associated with a third of a percentage point increase in the overall growth rate of overall GDP—a very substantial rate of return.

To me, the case for expensing all business investment is strong, and it is even stronger for expensing investment in *productive* equipment—and I would risk a theoretical "tax subsidy" to that end. If that is industrial policy, then so be it.

Incidentally, Fullerton is dead wrong when he says that JFK's original ITC was not conceived as industrial policy but was intended as a temporary macroeconomic tool used to stimulate aggregate demand. Just the opposite was true (if the public statements of JFK and his aides are to be believed—as well as private statements to me and others).

piness had not in the past broken out so strongly as to support so massive a revision of the tax law (a trillion-dollar crap shoot, as Dave Stockman said to me). Indispensable to the whole process was the presence in the White House of a popular *Republican* president who was really dedicated to getting individual tax rates down, even at the cost of raising the very corporate tax burden that for many years he had condemned as an unnecessary and unwise appendage to our federal tax system.[10]

This, of course, brings us to the final factor conditioning U.S. tax policy in the 1980s.

What Presidents of One Party Can Do That Those of the Other Cannot

The most often cited example of a president of one party leading the effort to achieve a difficult and perhaps politically divisive policy goal is, of course, Nixon's successful effort to establish relations with Communist China during his first term. Conventional political wisdom—and I think it is correct—is that liberal Democrat Hubert Humphrey, if victorious in 1968, would have faced a difficult if not impossible task in that regard. The probability is that he would have been roundly attacked and solidly opposed by the Republican Right, a group that had "no place else to go" when Nixon moved and—to repeat the phrase—became sullen but not mutinous. What has not been sufficiently recognized is that this same U.S. political characteristic applies to other politically divisive policies, including tax policy.

For example, in the late 1950s, we Republicans in the Eisenhower Treasury wanted to mount a campaign in Congress for a pro-growth, pro-capital formation, "supply-side" cut in income taxes of individuals and corporations. But the Democratic leadership in Congress said, in effect, *"no way"*—in no way

10. As late as February 1983, Ronald Reagan told a group of businessmen in Boston that the corporate tax was (my words) a dumb, lousy tax and ought to be eliminated. As both he and I have said thousands of times, "Corporations don't pay taxes; people do. And the fact is that the corporate tax is a hidden tax of the worst type, for nobody knows who really pays it. We ought to get rid of it." The press responded to this statement with great relish. But the tempest died quickly when (as George Will put it) Reagan's aides made it crystal clear that he was *not* speaking for his administration. Fullerton has noted Regan's statement in 1985 that reflected his earlier position—but this was before Don Regan had much of an opportunity, as the new chief of staff, to convince the president that "the higher business taxes would just hit those companies paying too little now."

Interestingly enough, Ronald Reagan has some pretty heavy academics backing him up. My favorite quote in this respect comes from Arnold Harberger, viewed by many as the foremost academic expert on the corporate income tax. At a conference in 1983, he said, "There is no sound *economic* underpinning for the corporation income tax. The tax originated because corporations are legal persons—but so too are three-year-olds, eighty-five-year-olds, manic depressives, blonds, and idiots. Why select out this particular class of legal person as the object of special (and harsh) taxation? There is no respectable *economic* answer to this question." The conclusion must be that the corporate income tax is a bad tax. I am therefore puzzled as to why so many economists (and lawyers) devote many hours of study and effort to bringing internal "rationality" to the tax. Even if *all* rates were equalized on *all* investment *all* the time, it would still be a bad tax that exists almost solely for political reasons.

was it possible for a Democratic Congress to agree to the tax reductions on upper-income individuals and corporations that such a proposal would have to include. But, lo and behold, that's precisely what John F. Kennedy proposed in 1961–63 and a Democratic Congress approved in 1962 and 1964.

Even so, as already noted, JFK had to drop "tax reform" from his proposal; even a Democratic Congress was not going to buy that. Eight years later, however, a Republican Treasury devised—and a reluctant Nixon approved—what up to that time was the high-water mark in "tax reform." To be sure, the Tax Reform Act of 1976 was enacted by a Democratic Congress, and I cannot for the life of me remember why Gerald Ford did not veto the legislation. But, by the "tax reform" standards of 1969 and, later, 1986, it was pretty weak tea.

There is little doubt that the 1986 act would not have had a snowball's chance in you-know-where if it had not been conceived by a Republican Treasury and accepted and pushed by a popular and highly articulate Republican president. Not that the Reagan imprimatur was enough—each of what I call the "four horsemen" of the TRA could be said to have been indispensable to success: Reagan; Baker/Darman at the Treasury (together they make up one horseman); Ways and Means Chairman Danny Rostenkowski; and Senate Finance Chairman Bob Packwood, who, with his top aide, pulled it all together (as Fullerton points out) over a bucket of beer.

The indispensability of these other three horsemen notwithstanding, it was a Ronald Reagan production from beginning to end. To drive this point home, can anyone conceive of Jimmy Carter pulling off the same victory? Indeed, Carter entered the White House declaiming that the U.S. income tax system was a disgrace and that he would do something about it. When he finally sent up his "tax reform" proposals in 1978, they were decidedly weak, with the major recommendation to raise taxes on capital gains. Congress did precisely the opposite, and very little of Carter's "tax reform" passed.

Conclusion

Martin has told us not to look at the future, and, although I have taken a peek or two, I have largely abided by his wish. But there are of course important lessons to be learned from the 1980s experience as we proceed through the 1990s. But I supposed that's another subject for another conference.

Reference

DeLong, J. Bradford, and Lawrence H. Summers. 1991. Equipment investment and economic growth. *Quarterly Journal of Economics* 106, no. 2 (May): 445–502.

3. *Russell B. Long*

The late John F. Kennedy used to keep a chart in the Oval Office of the White House. It showed the decline of the national debt as a percentage of the gross national product under Truman and Eisenhower. Then, during my years as chairman of the Senate Committee on Finance, I insisted on obtaining from the Treasury an updating of that information.

Here is what it showed. Our net federal debt was 118 percent of the gross national product in 1945. Under Truman and Eisenhower, it declined to 46 percent, less than half. Then, under Kennedy, Johnson, and Nixon, it declined to 25 percent, less than one-quarter of what it was in 1945.

To be sure, the debt grew in terms of dollars. But, in terms of its relation to the gross national product (which represents what we have with which to pay both the debt and the interest), it was cut to less than one-quarter. What had caused that?—(1) economic growth, which included (2) increased productivity, (3) high employment, (4) population increase, and (5) inflation. The increases in those factors greatly offset the small annual increase in the national debt to cause the ratio to go steadily down.

During the Kennedy-Johnson years, we saw how fiscal policy—using tax cuts and tax credits along with lower rates—could be used to promote economic growth. Then, during the Carter administration, Senator Bill Roth started making speeches advocating a 30 percent cut in tax rates—10 percent a year each year for three years. In those speeches, he emphasized the experience of the Kennedy-Johnson tax cut. Toward the end of the Carter administration, Republicans began to coalesce behind the Kemp-Roth 30 percent tax cut proposal.

When President Reagan came into office, he recommended a first-year tax cut of about 5 percent (the same magnitude as the Finance Committee bill we had recommended in 1980). But he went far beyond that to recommend a further tax cut of another 10 percent in rates to take effect in 1982 and a third tax cut of still another 10 percent to take effect in 1983. All this was to be incorporated into one gigantic tax cut bill, known as ERTA, the Economic Recovery Tax Act.

Why did he recommend such huge tax cuts? We need go no further than to note that, in his campaign, he had recommended a 30 percent across-the-board cut in rates, spread evenly across three years—the Kemp-Roth bill.

As the former chairman of the Committee on Finance, I was proud of the part I played in passing the Kennedy-Johnson tax cut, which had been the largest tax cut up to that time and had worked very well. At a minimum, I felt that I had to vote to give President Reagan's bill a try.

As the bill progressed through the committees and the floor of both Houses, it picked up amendments to make it an even greater tax cut than the president had advocated. Why were the add-on amendments accepted?

Well, it is rather difficult for an administration (asking for the largest tax cut in history) to insist that other suggestions, such as indexing the tax code to eliminate the so-called bracket creep, should not also be tried. That is especially the case with regard to items that the president has been known to endorse in previous years.

Part of the income tax package leveled the top rate on personal income taxation to 50 percent, and we provided that 60 percent of a long-term capital gain would be excluded from taxation. Thus, the top rate for a "long-term" capital gain was reduced to an overall rate of 20 percent.

Did it bother me that we might be cutting taxes too deeply? Not particularly.

In previous years, I had voted for large tax cuts and for needed tax increases. On two different occasions, I had gone to sitting presidents, President Johnson as well as President Nixon, and urged them to recommend suspending or repealing the investment tax credit (ITC) because it appeared to be overheating the economy. At the presidents' recommendation, we had twice repealed and subsequently reenacted the investment tax credit.

But I was not prepared for the series of events that transpired during the next few weeks. When the first stage—the 5 percent tax cut—went into effect in October 1981, the stock market started going down rather than up. The economy—which had been booming since Ronald Reagan took office—turned downward.

The economy was on its way into a recession. Why? It was explained to me this way. First, various gurus and economic thinkers on Wall Street such as Henry Kaufman thought that the massive tax cuts would lead to huge deficits. Second, they believed that the huge deficits would be inflationary. Third, they reasoned that the inflation would require high interest rates. And, fourth, they concluded that the high interest rates would make it impractical to build the new plants and equipment on which we were relying.

This would prevent the economic boom that we had predicted. Their logic was compelling. By my lights, that was not a difficult problem to overcome. It was my view that the president should be persuaded to "stretch out" the tax cuts as long as need be. That should restore confidence and achieve the desired degree of economic expansion.

When I explained my theory to Republican Senator Bob Dole, the new chairman of the Finance Committee, he suggested that the two of us should call on President Reagan so that I could explain my suggestion. (Incidentally, I was not alone in this thinking. Charls Walker was reported to be thinking along the same lines. He will tell you that there were a lot of other highly regarded advisers of President Reagan's who agreed.)

The president received us graciously, but, when I tried to explain my recommendation, Ronald Reagan took over the conversation, and I hardly had a chance to get more than a few words in edgewise. Ronald Reagan was determined to stay the course. And he did.

Then, after a few months, we saw the deficit getting out of hand. I was invited to sit with what was later known as "the Gang of Seventeen." We were asked to recommend revenue increases and spending cuts that could lead us to a balanced budget. The Gang of Seventeen failed because then Speaker "Tip" O'Neill (ably represented by Dick Boland) would not agree to cut back on Social Security—not even the cost-of-living adjustment (commonly referred to as the COLA).

If you were not going to cut in the area of Social Security, then it made no sense to cut in the smaller entitlement areas like government retirement, railroad retirement, and other lesser entitlement programs. For lack of savings in the entitlement areas, the Reagan administration was not interested in pushing for a "budget-balancing" package that had no hope of balancing the budget.

Without the spending cuts, Ronald Reagan was not willing to advocate—or sign into law—the tax increases that he would have considered under other circumstances. So the tax suggestions went down the drain with the spending cuts.

Thereafter, as responsible Americans far and wide spoke out for a tax increase, Bob Dole seized the initiative and put together TEFRA, the Tax Equity and Fiscal Responsibility Act. This was heralded as a measure to close tax loopholes and achieve greater tax uniformity.

It was a significant tax increase, and it became law. Bob Dole's TEFRA took away from business about half the benefit of Ronald Reagan's ERTA bill.

Meanwhile, we passed a five-cent tax increase on gasoline. Then came the Social Security Rescue Package. This measure found ways to shift more general revenues into the Social Security fund. It made the Social Security fund solvent temporarily by adding to the national debt.

The more logical part of the Social Security package was that, in future years, the Social Security taxes were to be increased to bring in more revenue. A couple of years later, the deficit-reduction package repealed most of what was left for business in ERTA. Neither of those bills touched the rates. Now add all that together, and you have a lot of tax increases.

Then came the so-called Tax Reform Act of 1986. It took away a great number of deductions and used the revenue to reduce the rates. Much was said about the fact that 7 million relatively low-income taxpayers were removed from the rolls. However, the big item of controversy was the repeal of capital gains.

In general terms, we reduced taxes for about 70 percent of individual taxpayers and sought to make it back by raising taxes on corporations. That latter objective, paying for the individual tax reductions by increasing taxes on corporations, was not achieved—not in full at least.

The reason was that corporations found ways to reduce tax liabilities—such as obtaining capital by borrowing money rather than by selling stock. This led to very thin margins of equity in some corporations. That, in turn, made companies more vulnerable in the case of temporary adversity.

The lower rates had to do a lot of good. But much of that good was merely by terminating the stifling effect of income tax rates that were too high.

Well, here we are. We are still stuck with a capital gains tax on transactions many of which are not income at all in a real sense. We have had very large deficits for every year after the ERTA tax cut went into effect.

And, after ten years under Presidents Reagan and Bush, the debt, as a percentage of the GNP, is now back to where it was toward the end of the Eisenhower administration. In terms of fiscal and monetary prudence, America has lost the ground it gained under Kennedy, Johnson, and Nixon.

We have a situation that must be turned around. It will take time. But eventually the people will learn that to put our income tax rates much higher than we have now is self-defeating. It stifles the economy and retards economic growth.

If large amounts of additional revenue are needed, we should turn to a tax on consumption, as our friends in Europe have done. That may take several years to do, but it will happen because it makes sense.

Summary of Discussion

Murray Weidenbaum began the discussion by agreeing with Walker that politicians of one party can change policy in a way that politicians of the other party often cannot. He recalled that President Reagan was considering whether to include in his initial tax proposal a recommendation to lower the top tax bracket from 70 to 50 percent, and he asked what the response to that recommendation would be. His advisers said that the Democrats would lambaste them as the party of the rich, but, if this recommendation were not included in the administration proposal, then they likely would put it in themselves because it is a good idea. Reagan said that he would let the Democrats twist his arm and then reluctantly go along with it, which is what Weidenbaum believed had actually happened. Weidenbaum added that one fundamental flaw with the Joint Tax Committee's revenue estimates is that they were static; in other words, a tax change designed to quicken the growth rate is estimated to have no effect on revenue through a faster growth rate.

Rudolph Penner thought it was interesting that neither Walker nor Long made any mention of the journalistic crusade of the supply-siders in the late 1970s and early 1980s as an important factor in the original tax cuts.

Charls Walker responded that the role of the extreme supply-siders was overplayed by the press. The basic economic policy group around Ronald Reagan during the 1980 campaign was not economists Arthur Laffer and Jude Wanniski but rather George Shultz [former secretary of the treasury and later secretary of state], Arthur Burns [former chairman of the Federal Reserve Board], Alan Greenspan [former chairman of the Council of Economic Advisers and later chairman of the Federal Reserve Board], economist Milton Friedman, Walter Wriston [chairman of Citicorp], Jim Lynn [former director of the Office of Management and Budget], Representative Jack Kemp, and Walker himself. This team felt "almost to a man" (Kemp excluded) that the Kemp-Roth tax cut of "10–10–10" should be extended at least over a five-year period instead of a three-year period. Someone wrote Reagan's speech at the Republican convention to include the phrase "three-year cut." But the economic policy group met less than three weeks later in Los Angeles, and Greenspan told Reagan that it would be much easier to reach the goal of reducing both spending and taxes to 18–20 percent of GNP after five years if they could extend the Kemp-Roth plan from three years to five years. Reagan said, "I don't care," and they all "nearly fell out of their chairs."

Thereafter there was debate within the group, with Kemp on one side and most of the other members on the other side. They were moving toward backing away from the three-year approach when Reagan got into trouble talking about some other issues, and the economic policy group decided (in putting together an economic policy speech after Labor Day) that they couldn't back away. But the basic idea of the economic plan constructed by this group was *not* that the tax cuts would pay for themselves but that there had to be a concomitant cut in the rate of growth of federal spending. The press played it up as purely a "supply-side off a napkin thing," even though Laffer was not even a participant in the deliberations.

Weidenbaum noted that Laffer was on the economic policy group, but *Walker* stated that Laffer either did not attend or did not say anything. *Martin Feldstein* added that William Roth had been talking about a "10–10–10" tax cut for quite a number of years before Roth had ever heard of Laffer or supply-side economics.

Robert Litan said his understanding was that Laffer and other supply-siders had had a major intellectual influence on Kemp. Since Walker indicated that Kemp was on the panel and was staunchly defending the three-year rather than the five-year program, the role of the suppler-siders should not be understated. *Walker* confirmed that it was Kemp who had the reference to a three-year plan included in Reagan's speech.

Russell Long addressed the question of President Reagan's political motivation for supporting tax reform in the mid-1980s. Long felt that Senator Bill Bradley and others were attracting a lot of publicity by talking about tax fairness and tax reform and that it looked as though it might be a problem for the Republican party if the Democrats made much headway on the issue. Also, some of the Republicans on the Senate Finance Committee were interested in tax reform, so it seemed to Long that Reagan decided that he ought to "get out front" on the issue. Long believed that, when a politician thinks some legislation is going to pass, it is often better to "bend with the wind and go along" because then one has some influence on what happens. If one tries to stop the law, then things could happen that would hurt the people one is representing. He always felt that, after the storm had passed, people would decide to restore special capital gains tax provisions in order to encourage economic growth.

Weidenbaum said that the decision made in January 1984 to encourage tax reform was a political decision based on fear on the part of James Baker [White House chief of staff] and others that Democratic presidential candidate Walter Mondale would join the flat tax bandwagon of Bradley and Representative Dick Gephardt. Thus, the president said a few lines in his State of the Union message that directed the secretary of the Treasury to undertake a study and report back in December 1984. In fact, Reagan had no great relish for tax reform except for lower tax rates.

David Stockman discussed several crucial facts that he believed ruled tax policy for most of the 1980s. First, as late as early 1981, a 30 percent tax rate cut had a very small constituency in Congress. There was no great support for it in the Democratic party, and, even in the Republican party, only a minority of the "backbenchers" like Kemp and Stockman were in favor of it. Nevertheless, the policy was being developed at a time when the inflation rate was running at 10 or 11 percent, and there was a group of more orthodox members of Congress who saw the 10–10–10 tax cut as simply a politically attractive form of temporary indexing. Stockman remembered Alan Greenspan making the argument strongly to the skeptical middle-of-the-road Republicans that a 10 percent rate cut in this environment was basically going to keep the real tax rates constant, so they would not be taking a major fiscal risk.

What happened in reality was that the monetary policy being implemented at the same time lowered inflation dramatically faster than anybody expected, so that, by the fall of 1983, the inflation rate was running about 3 percent on an annual basis. As a result, the 10–10–10 tax cut became a far deeper fiscal cut in terms of the real revenue base of government.

Second, since there was not a strong constituency for this tax change in the Republican party, when the fight really got serious in committee, a compromise had to be made between the middle-of-the-road tax indexers and the supply-side rate cutters. To get the tax bill out of the Senate Finance Committee, it had to be agreed that there would be a vote on the Senate floor about indexing. Stockman remembered Senator Bob Dole saying that the indexing provision would be easily defeated on the floor and that this is the way we can get an 18-to-3 committee vote in favor of the bill before it went to the floor. However, indexing passed, and the unexpectedly large real rate cut in 1981–83 was locked in permanently in 1985 by the indexing.

The revenue impact of indexing was far beyond what anybody expected. Today, people are always looking at five-year budget projections, and the natural question is why didn't anybody think about the long-term revenue impact at the time. That was in the early days of long-term budgeting, however, and almost everybody looked at one-year budget projections, and nobody took five-year projections seriously.

The third crucial fact is that, even with indexing and the rate cut, the tax bill would not have passed in 1981 unless all the other tax policy constituencies were accommodated. So the 10–5–3 capital depreciation schedule was married to the bill, the estate tax was dismantled over four or five years, there were huge savings and IRA incentives included, anything that the oil and gas industry could imagine was added, and so on. The tax bill that was signed into law in 1981, under the economic conditions that actually materialized by 1986, cut the revenue base by 5 percent of GNP when the back-loaded features of the bill were fully in force. So, in August 1981, the government cut a gaping 5 percent of GNP hole in its revenue base, bringing it down to 17 percent of GNP. This was relative to spending of 23 or 24 percent of GNP under the defense and domestic policy conditions of the time.

Stockman recapitulated his view that everything that happened to tax policy after 1981 was driven by the near impossibility of our political system coping with a 5 percent of GNP hole in the fiscal balance. The hole was slowly closed in the 1982 act, the 1983 act, and the 1984 act, so, by the time they got to 1986, the hole was only 4 percent rather than 5 percent. However, it was that fundamental, shocking imbalance that drove almost the whole economic and fiscal policy story, in Stockman's view, in the 1980s.

Feldstein noted that Stockman's calculation of a revenue loss of 5 percent of GNP was a static estimate with no behavioral response because it was based on the economy as it actually worked out. The supply-siders would argue that, without that tax cut, there would have been less GNP growth and thus less revenue, so the actual cut is smaller than the 5 percent. *Stockman* and *Feldstein* agreed that the actual cut was not much smaller, however.

William Poole commented that the unexpectedly rapid decline in inflation was importantly affected by the unexpected appreciation of the dollar. He thought that this appreciation had been a result of three separate factors. First, monetary policy became substantially more disciplined, and expectations of inflation and actual inflation came down. Second, economies abroad turned much weaker than expected. Most people did not foresee the Latin American debt crisis a couple of years in advance, and the European economies turned soft as well. Finally, the investment incentives in the 1981 tax law increased the attractiveness of investment in the United States by increasing the after-tax rate of return, and this brought capital to the United States, which aided in the appreciation of the dollar.

Penner questioned the emphasis on indexing as the cause of so much lost revenue. Before indexing was in force, Congress regularly offset the extra inflation tax by cutting tax rates, although not always the rates that affected the people who were hurt by inflation. He thought that one of the remarkable things about the last twenty-five years is that, through all the swings of the tax pendulum that Walker discussed, the overall federal tax burden had been almost a divine constant of between 18 and 20 percent of GNP. Every time the ratio had risen to 20 percent, there had been a reaction, and it had gone back down.

Feldstein said that Penner's point raised the question of whether there would have been discretionary tax cuts in the mid-1980s, despite the increasingly large budget deficits, if the indexing had not been in place.

Feldstein recalled that he had debated the merits of the 10–10–10 tax cut as an approximation to indexing with Walker and others back in the late 1970s and had argued very much against it. There was no question that, given the inflation forecast of the time, the two proposals were approximately equal, but Feldstein thought that there was too much uncertainty about that forecast. He also liked the idea of indexing per se and instituting a permanently indexed system rather than accomplishing a one-time tax cut and then having inflation push people up into higher brackets again.

Feldstein asked the group how indexing came to be an accepted idea. He remembered trying to persuade Representative Barber Conable of the virtue of indexing, and Conable visited Canada to see how indexing was working there and came back to say that it was terrible and that he was firmly opposed to the idea. Eventually, Conable was a big advocate of indexing, and Feldstein wondered how that pendulum on indexing shifted and why it did not include capital gains or depreciation.

Weidenbaum thought that William Fellner at the American Enterprise Institute was instrumental in starting the discussion, not by directly influencing the media or Capitol Hill, but by influencing the people who influence both the media and the Hill.

Feldstein said that he and Fellner and a few others were part of a group that met with Conable occasionally when he was the ranking minority member of the Ways and Means Committee. When that group advocated indexing, however, Conable was very resistant, and there was no general support for the idea.

Stockman said that the more cynical explanation of the increased interest in indexing is the political fight in the Republican party between the young backbenchers and the middle-of-the-road traditional Republicans. People like Conable and Representative Bill Gradison repaired to indexing as an alternative to a "radical, experimental, dangerous" 30 percent rate cut. The idea for indexing had been around for a long time, but this was the source of the political momentum. *Long* said that, once people started asking about bracket creep before civic clubs and in similar settings, it was very hard to defend the other side.

Feldstein asked why the indexing of capital gains was never accepted, even though it should be subject to the same kinds of arguments. *Walker* responded that the people who were pushing capital gains tax changes from the outside believed that they could get indexation almost any time because both sides of the aisle in Congress think it is a good idea. Thus, they have not pushed for indexing as the centerpiece of capital gains tax changes to the exclusion of a "real" differential capital gains cut.

Feldstein returned to another topic raised by Stockman, the reason that so many additional items were added to the basic 10–10–10 tax cut. Feldstein contrasted Stockman's argument that the only way to pass the tax cut was to add 10–5–3 depreciation and so on with Long's argument that people felt that the tax cut would be approved so they might as well add a lot of other ideas that had been around.

Long responded that there had been a similar situation about add-on arguments when they were working on the Kennedy tax cut bill in 1963 and 1964. At one point, they realized that they had added so much extra baggage on top of the investment tax credit that they had to kill some of these extra provisions or abandon the bill. He thought that, if someone in the Reagan administration had "read the riot act" to the right group in Congress, much of the objectionable language could have been dumped out.

Stockman explained that, while the administration bill was being considered, there was an alternative bill emerging in the House (the Conable-Hance bill) that was an attempt to avoid a "competitive political auction" on tax cuts. That was going to be a consensus bill that did not have all the cuts that the administration wanted but that would also not lead to a competitive bidding contest between the Democrats and the Republicans in the House. The White House was trying to decide whether to support the consensus bill, but they had just won the big fight on the budget on the House side (the Gramm-Latta bill), and they felt that they had the ability to push through their own bill and therefore did not have to compromise. The Democrats were smarting badly at that point because they had just lost the first strategic level domestic policy fight in the Congress in thirty years (again, Gramm-Latta), so they were not overly interested in compromising either. On 4 June 1981, the decision was made by the White House not to embrace the bipartisan Conable-Hance bill but to go for their own bill. The bill was loaded up in the House Ways and Means Committee, and, by the time it got to the floor, "everything that had ever been thought of by any tax constituency in the last thirty years" was in the bill. Because it happened in the House first, the Senate couldn't help carrying the junk across the Capitol from the House into the Senate bill.

Stockman felt that he had misspoken earlier by saying that these additions were needed to get a bill passed. The real explanation is that the process turned into a competitive political auction, both bills were loaded with extra features, and there were "no shuckers to do the shucking" when the conference bill was put together because all the steps had been endorsed with huge votes in both houses. There are times when strategic decisions are made that affect the course of events, and to go for a competitive bill rather than a compromise in the House was the key decision made in early June 1981.

Harry Reasoner argued that one of the most disastrous features of the 1981 tax act was the subsidization of real estate investment. That contributed to misallocation of capital, to vast overbuilding, to the savings and loan crisis, and to other adverse economic impacts throughout our economy. He wondered whether anyone at the time the legislation was passed believed there was an economic justification for it or whether anyone expressed concerns.

Weidenbaum answered that the 1982 *Economic Report of the President* included a table that showed the combined effects of the investment tax credit and 10–5–3 depreciation rules producing negative tax rates on some assets, but that was after the fact.

Stockman argued that there was a strong case for encouraging plant and equipment investment and that the powerful real estate lobby simply jumped into the action. So 10–5–3 was really a marriage of convenience between a powerful real estate lobby and the original case for accelerated depreciation of plant and equipment.

Feldstein added that most public finance economists did not understand at the time how much the tax shelter industry could accomplish with the new tax law. Only after the fact did economists learn what the combination of extreme leverage (no cash in the deal) and those kinds of depreciation rates could produce.

Walker thought that the revenue impact of these add-on provisions for the 1981 tax act was being overstated. He thought that the three big revenue impacts were the personal income rate cut (10–10–10), the new depreciation schedule (10–5–3), and the indexing of personal tax rates. The 10–5–3 cut was married to the 10–10–10 cuts as a compromise between those who defined supply-side tax cuts solely in terms of individual tax cuts and those who said that capital cost recovery is important in the business community. So those two items were what the Reagan task force recommended and basically what the Treasury Department eventually proposed.

Geoffrey Carliner asked why the political system was unable to solve the problems in the 1980s that it had been able to solve before. In other words, why was it unable to restore the rough fiscal balance of previous decades?

Feldstein responded that an important difference in the 1980s was indexing. Once indexing was on the books, there were not the automatic tax increases that had occurred in past decades.

Long felt that, since President Reagan had led the charge for the big tax cut, he did not relish the idea of working to repeal some of the things he had proudly signed into law. Long understood that, commenting that Reagan had not had as much experience as Long had at reversing his position. Long joked that he had voted *for* the investment tax credit three times and *against* it three times. He felt that flexibility is not a bad thing when the situation requires it.

Weidenbaum said that he, Baker, and others had constructed a package of excise tax increases that Dole was going to introduce in early 1982.

Stockman confirmed that the package was arranged in January 1982 because the administration was about to have to present the first $100 billion deficit in history and nobody wanted to send that up to Capitol Hill. They were about to print the budget, but the Chamber of Commerce and the business lobbies fought the taxes, and they "died by noon." The budget had to be printed that same afternoon, so they invented prospective management savings to reduce the budget deficit. Today, a triple-digit deficit is nothing, but in those days it was close to fiscal treason.

The management savings were made up on the spot, but they had an important legacy. They were ridiculed on the Hill until it came time to put the TEFRA (Tax Equity and Fiscal Responsibility Act) package and budget together later in 1982. Then those savings were adopted as part of the "three-for-one" deal, in which there was supposed to be three dollars in spending cuts for every dollar in taxes raised by TEFRA. Those management savings were "out of this world" and could not have been achieved by anybody, but, two years later, the president and the Republican right wing decided that Congress had engaged in a great act of treachery by adopting the TEFRA tax increases and not producing the expected spending cuts. These particular spending cuts were never real cuts anyway. This was another aspect of why the government could not deal with the 7 percent fiscal hole: after a while, people began to believe things that were not true about the opportunities for change that existed.

William Niskanen said that, in the spring of 1981, many economists testified that the tax cuts would be wildly inflationary. This was the basis of the charge that the Reagan program was incoherent because, while monetary policy was presumed to reduce inflation, the tax cuts were presumed by economists of both parties to be inflationary.

Niskanen asked the group about two contingent tax proposals that did not pass. In June 1981, Representative Jim Jones, then head of the House Budget Committee, proposed that the third year of the tax cut be made contingent on Stockman delivering on his $44 billion "magic asterisk." Niskanen felt that this proposal was appealing from a public choice point of view because it provided a continuing incentive to both the administration and Congress to agree on $44 billion of further spending cuts. Why did the administration reject this idea so abruptly?

A different contingent tax proposal was suggested by the administration in the winter of 1983, in which they proposed a contingent tax increase if Congress made spending cuts. Niskanen thought that that was a bizarre proposal and wondered what its origin was.

Feldstein responded that the conditional tax increase with which he was involved was in the budget that was submitted in early 1983. The supply-siders and others were forecasting so much economic growth that the deficit was going to go away, and they argued that, if taxes were raised in 1983, that would kill the recovery. So the president's budget in the beginning of 1983 said that there would be a tax increase if there was not sufficient growth in 1984 to shrink the deficit to whatever the targets were. But this proposal never had the support of Baker in the White House or of the Treasury, so it was never pushed in Congress and died along the way.

Stockman said that the conditional tax increase was proposed because it seemed unacceptable within the administration to propose a budget that pointed the country toward the first permanent $200 billion budget deficit policy. It was easy to describe the idea internally in the administration, but, when the budget became public and reporters started asking about the contingent tax, nobody knew what it was. Sooner or later, someone said, maybe it's a flat tax, and that became part of the vocabulary of the fiscal debate over the course of the year, and eventually, as Bradley and the flat-taxers turned up the heat, there was the Treasury study in early 1984. The administration became hooked on the idea as a result of having to describe a contingent tax that was put in to help clean up the numbers but really had no content.

Walker thought that Jim Baker and Richard Darman [deputy White House chief of staff] were deeply concerned about the deficit in the summer of 1984 and earlier and wanted to do something about it. He said that Darman was accused in the campaign of 1984 of having a secret tax plan in the closet, and Walker believed that it was true. Walker believed that, if Baker and Darman had stayed in the White House in the first year of Reagan's second term, then there would have been serious consideration given to what Darman called a "big fix" on fiscal policy. However, Donald Regan was chief of staff in the White House by then, and he did not have a very good understanding of either the political or the economic issues involved. So the personality changes made a large increase in taxes (say 2 percent of GNP) absolutely impossible. Such an increase is not possible through nickel-and-dime tax changes or through the income tax because the revenue from the income tax comes mainly at the expense of the middle class, which is the driving political force in the country. The remaining possibility is a broad-based consumption tax, not just because it is a consumption tax, but because it raises so much revenue.

Walker said that the politics of tax increases started to change when Walter Mondale told the Democratic Convention in August 1984 that both he and Reagan knew that taxes would have to be increased but that Mondale would say so and that Reagan would not. At his next press conference, Reagan said that he was against raising taxes until federal spending was down to the lowest possible level relative to GNP. In other words, he did not close the door to the idea. However, it became clear that Mondale had made a big political mistake, so, by the time the campaign ended, "no tax increase" had become dogma as far as the president, and later Regan, was concerned. Over the next several years, it became basic Republican policy. Walker felt that the United States now has a plebiscite democracy that is giving the people exactly what they want—low taxes *and* high spending.

James Poterba shifted the discussion to the distributional politics of the tax burden. Looking back over the decade, he was struck that the 1981 changes were very beneficial to those at the top of the income distribution and that the 1983 Social Security reform moved in the same direction by putting higher tax burdens on low-income earners. However, if one consolidates the corporation tax changes into the 1986 tax reform, that represents a reversal by putting higher burdens on those at the top of the income distribution. And the 1990 discussions of taxes on yachts, planes, and millionaires suggest that we have come full circle on this topic.

Walker felt that the Democrats were now considering a strong populist approach as a political strategy, in contrast with Stockman's remark after the 1978 tax act passed that the country is no longer concerned with how income is distributed but with how it is created. This partisan debate had received a big push in the previous three or four months as a result of the debate on the budget and the capital gains proposal. Walker also cited David Broder's recent column on the Op-Ed page of the *Washington Post* in which Broder said that the "fairness" issue would not work politically because the real concern of the American people is not the taxes that rich people pay but the taxes that they pay themselves.

Long agreed that tax rates should not be so high as to be counterproductive. He held that view in terms of the personal income tax as well as the corporate income tax, and he felt that the tax code should not go beyond the point at which it will really reduce economic activity. He believed that, as long as low-income people are doing better, middle-income people are doing better, and those in all walks of life are doing better, it is very important to keep accumulating capital and making investments. At some point we have to be in favor of creating more wealth even if it doesn't come in with quite the distributional pattern we would like.

4 Budget Policy

1. *James M. Poterba*
2. *David Stockman*
3. *Charles Schultze*

1. *James M. Poterba*

Federal Budget Policy in the 1980s

The 1980s began without a hint of extraordinary budget deficits that would emerge later in the decade. In his January 1980 State of the Union message, President Carter labeled deficit reduction his "top budgetary priority." Although his initial fiscal 1981 budget projected a $16 billion deficit, rising inflation in early 1980 coupled with bipartisan pressure for fiscal restraint led President Carter to modify his budget plans. In March 1980, he proposed an anti-inflation fiscal program with a balanced budget.

Five years later, President Reagan proposed a budget with a $180 billion deficit, and actual deficits exceeded $200 billion. His aggressive tax reductions, the military buildup of the early 1980s, and changing economic circumstances combined to produce the largest peacetime deficits in U.S. history. The rapid growth in deficits occurred despite calls for fiscal responsibility and budget balance throughout the decade. Measured as a share of GNP, the federal deficit rose from 2.8 percent in fiscal 1980 to a peak of 6.3 percent for fiscal 1983. To provide some perspective on these deficits, the federal deficit averaged 0.8 percent of GNP in the 1960s and 2.1 percent in the 1970s.

A series of deficit-reduction measures as well as an extraordinary period of economic growth lowered the deficits throughout the latter part of the 1980s. The federal deficit was 2.9 percent of GNP for fiscal 1989, although it increased to 4.1 percent of GNP in fiscal 1990. Much of the late-decade deficit reduction was due to off-budget surpluses in the Social Security Trust Fund. The 1990s opened with renewed uncertainty regarding the future course of

U.S. deficits, as some Social Security reform plans called for payroll tax cuts that would widen federal deficits by as much as 1 percent of GNP per year.

This paper surveys the tumultuous economic history of federal budget policy in the 1980s. It summarizes the central economic trends, quantifies the sources and magnitudes of changes in the federal deficit, and discusses the political forces that supported these developments. The paper is divided into seven sections. The first presents statistical measures of federal deficits and describes the role of tax cuts and spending growth in the widening and then contracting federal deficits of the last decade.

Sections 4.2–4.4 focus on particular policy actions that affected the federal deficit. Section 4.2 concentrates on the Economic Recovery Tax Act of 1981 and the associated spending reductions that composed President Reagan's economic program. The third section analyzes the piecemeal attempts at deficit reduction in the aftermath of the 1981 reforms, notably the revenue-raising tax acts and budget cuts of 1982 and 1984 and the "revenue-neutral" Tax Reform Act of 1986. Section 4.4 examines the Social Security Amendments of 1983, the single most important factor in narrowing the federal deficit during the second half of the 1980s.

Section 4.5 discusses various attempts to reduce or eliminate deficits by altering the budget process. These include the Balanced Budget Amendment, which, while frequently discussed, never achieved political viability, and the various Gramm-Rudman-Hollings deficit limitation bills. Section 4.6 provides a brief discussion of deficit patterns in the late 1980s and the forecasts for the early 1990s. A concluding section distills several lessons in federal budget policy from the experience of the last decade. The final section also summarizes the political trends that accounted for the deficit expansion of the early 1980s and the contraction later in the decade.

4.1   Deficits and Debt in the 1980s

The 1980s were a decade of unprecedented peacetime federal budget deficits, when the federal government borrowed more than $6,000 for each U.S. citizen. This section chronicles the growth and subsequent reduction in federal deficits and provides some historical perspective on these events. In particular, it addresses the relative importance of tax and spending changes in explaining the changing federal deficit.

4.1.1   Changing Federal Deficits

Table 4.1 reports annual federal deficits for the fiscal years between 1970 and 1990, with average deficits for selected earlier time periods. The first three columns present federal outlays, revenues, and the deficit in nominal dollars, while the last three columns report each of these variables as a fraction of gross

Table 4.1   **Federal Receipts, Outlays, and Deficits, 1950–89**

	Billions of Dollars			Percentage of GNP		
Years	Outlays	Receipts	Deficit	Outlays	Receipts	Deficit
1950–59	69.3	67.5	1.8	18.0	17.6	.4
1960–69	129.9	124.2	5.7	19.0	18.2	.8
1970–79	324.2	288.6	35.6	20.5	18.3	2.1
1980–89	882.2	725.8	156.4	23.1	19.0	4.1
1970	195.6	192.8	2.8	19.8	19.5	.3
1971	210.2	187.1	23.0	19.9	17.7	2.2
1972	230.7	207.3	23.4	20.0	18.0	2.0
1973	245.7	230.8	14.9	19.2	18.0	1.2
1974	269.4	263.1	6.1	19.0	18.6	.4
1975	332.3	279.1	53.2	21.8	18.3	3.5
1976	371.8	298.1	73.7	21.9	17.6	4.3
TQ[a]	96.0	81.2	14.7	21.4	18.1	3.3
1977	409.2	355.6	53.6	21.2	18.4	2.8
1978	458.7	399.6	59.2	21.1	18.4	2.7
1979	503.5	463.3	40.2	20.6	18.9	1.6
1980	590.9	517.1	73.8	22.1	19.4	2.8
1981	678.2	599.3	78.9	22.7	20.1	2.6
1982	745.7	617.8	127.9	23.8	19.7	4.1
1983	808.3	600.6	207.8	24.3	18.1	6.3
1984	851.8	666.5	185.3	23.1	18.1	5.0
1985	946.3	734.1	212.3	23.9	18.6	5.4
1986	990.3	769.1	221.2	23.7	18.4	5.3
1987	1,003.8	854.1	149.7	22.7	19.3	3.4
1988	1,064.0	909.0	155.1	22.2	19.0	3.2
1989	1,142.6	990.7	152.0	22.2	19.2	2.9
1990	1,251.9	1,031.5	220.4	23.2	19.1	4.1

Source: OMB, *Budget of the United States Government: Fiscal Year 1991*, historical tables 1.1 and 1.2.

[a] Transition quarter.

national product. In each case, the expenditure statistics reflect actual outlays, not the budget authority amounts that are appropriated by Congress.[1]

Table 4.1 and the associated graph presented in figure 4.1 demonstrate the pronounced expansion of the federal deficit during the 1980s. From an average of 2.1 percent of GNP during the 1970s, the federal deficit grew to 4.1 percent of GNP during the 1980s. The deficit rose most rapidly at the beginning of the 1980s. Between 1980 and 1983, the federal deficit expanded by 3.5 percent of

---

1. Budget authority is the amount that an agency is authorized to spend; outlays measure actual spending in a given fiscal year. For so-called slow-spending programs, e.g. public housing, it can take five years or more for the sum of outlays to equal budget authority.

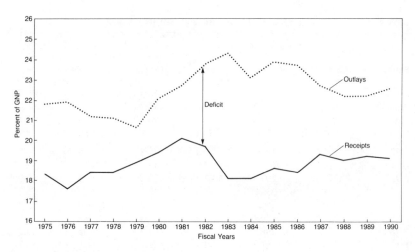

Fig. 4.1   Receipts and outlays of the U.S. government

GNP. This change in the budget deficit was the largest two-year movement since 1969, when the enactment of the federal income surtax reduced the deficit from 3.0 percent in fiscal 1968 to a 0.3 percent surplus in 1969. The deficits of the early 1980s, twice as large as the deficits in all but two other postwar years, are small by comparison to wartime deficits. In 1943, for example, the U.S. federal deficit was 31 percent of GNP.

The second half of the 1980s was characterized by gradual deficit reduction. The federal deficit was only a slightly larger share of GNP at the end of the decade than at the beginning. Federal revenues accounted for 19.4 percent of GNP in 1980, compared with 19.1 percent in fiscal 1990. The similarity of these shares does not reflect the significant changes within the decade, from 20.1 percent in 1981 to 18.1 percent in 1983 and 1984. Similarly, although outlays of 23.2 percent of GNP in 1990 were higher than the 22.1 percent in 1980, this in part reflects the weak economy of 1990. In 1989, outlays were only 22.2 percent of GNP. Moreover, even 1989 outlays are below those in years such as 1983 (24 percent of GNP).

4.1.2   Where Did Deficits Come From?

The information in table 4.1 provides a simple answer to the question of where the deficits came from. Between 1980 and 1983, federal revenues fell by 1.3 percent of GNP, expenditures rose 2.2 percent, and the deficit increased by 3.5 percent. Thus, tax cuts would appear responsible for approximately one-third of the deficit change in the early 1980s.[2] Between 1983 and 1989, as

---

2. Federal receipts grew by 0.7 percent of GNP between fiscal 1980 and fiscal 1981, and outlays rose 0.6 percent. Relative to a fiscal 1981 benchmark, the tax cuts are therefore more important factors in the deficit increase.

deficits narrowed, outlays fell by 2.1 percent of GNP, while receipts climbed by 1.1 percent, once again suggesting that the expenditure changes were roughly twice as important as tax policy actions.

The changes in federal receipts and outlays are characterized by substantial heterogeneity across revenue source and program type. Table 4.2 disaggregates the two sides of the federal deficit into major tax and expenditure categories for each fiscal year since 1980. The increase in expenditures between the two decades can be traced primarily to an increase in transfer payments to individuals, which includes both direct payments and those channeled through state government, sharp growth in net interest payments due to both increased federal borrowing and higher real interest rates, and an expansion of federal military spending in the early 1980s. Net interest payments were nearly twice as large in the early 1980s, relative to GNP, as in the 1970s; this corresponded to an absolute increase of more than 1.5 percent of GNP. Transfers increased by more than 2 percent of GNP between the 1970s and the first four years of the 1980s. The increase in defense spending is less dramatic; in part owing to the Vietnam conflict, military spending for the 1970s averaged 5.7 percent of GNP, well above the 5.0 percent in fiscal 1980. The Reagan defense buildup raised this spending level by nearly 1.5 percent, to 6.5 percent of GNP, by 1986.

One category of expenditure that is not shown separately in table 4.2, but that has declined during the last decade, is federal spending for nondefense

Table 4.2   **Composition of Federal Outlays and Receipts, Fiscal Years 1980–89**

	1970s	1980	1981	1982	1983	1984	1985	1986	1987	1988	1989
Outlays											
Military	5.7	5.0	5.3	5.9	6.3	6.2	6.4	6.5	6.4	6.1	5.9
Net interest	1.5	2.0	2.3	2.7	2.7	3.0	3.3	3.3	3.1	3.2	3.3
Payments for individuals	9.2	10.4	10.8	11.4	11.9	10.8	10.8	10.7	10.6	10.4	10.4
Other	4.1	4.7	4.3	3.8	3.4	3.1	3.4	3.2	2.6	2.5	19.6
Total	20.5	22.1	22.7	23.8	24.3	23.1	23.9	23.7	22.7	22.2	22.2
Receipts											
Individual income tax	8.3	9.1	9.6	9.5	8.7	8.1	8.5	8.3	8.9	8.4	8.7
Corporate income tax	2.8	2.4	2.0	1.6	1.1	1.5	1.6	1.5	1.9	2.0	2.0
Social insurance taxes	5.2	5.9	6.1	6.4	6.3	6.5	6.7	6.8	6.8	7.0	7.0
Excise taxes	1.2	.9	1.4	1.2	1.1	1.0	.9	.8	.7	.7	.7
Other receipts	1.0	1.0	1.0	1.1	.9	.9	.9	1.0	.9	.9	.9
Total	18.3	19.4	20.1	19.7	18.1	18.1	18.6	18.4	19.3	19.0	19.2

Source: Data are drawn from OMB, *Budget of the United States Government: Fiscal Year 1991*, A–302, A–287.

Note: Entries are percentages of GNP. The 1970s data for outlays correspond to averages for the period 1971–79; those for revenues correspond to 1970–79.

capital, or "infrastructure." Real net federal investment declined from an average of $16.1 billion (1982 dollars) in the last five years of the 1970s to $11.7 billion in the last five years of the 1980s. As a share of GNP, the decline is even more striking, from 0.5 to 0.3 percent during a ten-year period. This includes some reduction in water and power projects, a decline in community development outlays, and cuts in various other capital programs.

The lower panel of table 4.2 shows receipts and tracks the important rise of social insurance taxes as well as the decline of the corporate income tax. Corporate tax revenues as a share of GNP fell by 1.7 percent between the 1970s and the early 1980s, in part the result of legislative changes and in part because of falling corporate profits.[3] Individual income taxes fell by 1.5 percent of GNP during the first two fiscal years of the Reagan administration. Payroll taxes are the most important growth category with respect to federal receipts. The combined collections from employers and employees increased by more than 1 percent of GNP during the 1980s, and the average of these taxes in GNP was 1.8 percent higher at the end of the decade than in the 1970s. The legislative changes in individual and corporate income tax receipts were due to the various tax reform acts of the 1980s; the payroll tax increase, however, was the result of the 1983 Social Security compromise.

4.1.3   Debt Accumulation in the 1980s

Deficits measure the flow of government spending relative to receipts. The government debt is a stock that equals the accumulation (with interest) of past deficits and that therefore changes only slowly in response to budget deficits. Table 4.3 presents information on the evolution of the federal debt over the last half century. The first column shows the stock of debt, measured in 1989 dollars, at the end of each year. Real privately held federal debt grew from a total of $884 billion (1989 dollars) in 1980 to $1,990 billion at the end of 1989.

A more informative measure of the debt burden is the debt-to-GNP ratio, which is shown in the second column of table 4.3. These entries provide some perspective on the recent debt accumulation: federal debt at the end of 1989 was only one-third as large, relative to GNP, as in 1945. Nevertheless, the debt-to-GNP level rose by 15 percentage points during the 1980s, a far larger increase than that in any other peacetime decade. More important, the accumulation of debt reverses the usual historical pattern of *reduction* in the debt-to-GNP ratio during periods of peace and rapid economic growth.[4]

---

3. Auerbach and Poterba (1986) show that falling corporate tax revenues are due both to lower corporate profit rates during the 1980s and to the corporate tax reductions in the Economic Recovery Tax Act of 1981.

4. Barro (1986) estimates the relation between debt accumulation and economic conditions from U.S. experience before 1980. His results would have predicted real debt growth of 31 percent during the period 1983–88, when in fact real debt increased by 80 percent. The predictions for 1987–88 would be a 1.7 percent growth of real debt, but the actual growth was 8 percent. Poterba and Summers (1987) provide further detail on these calculations.

Table 4.3   **U.S. Public Debt, 1940–89**

Year	Real Debt ($billions 1989)	Debt/GNP (%)	Real Debt per Capita ($thousands 1989)
1940	387.5	35.9	2.9
1945	1,644.4	105.7	11.7
1950	1,031.0	64.1	6.8
1955	952.2	48.9	5.7
1960	852.4	40.3	4.7
1965	810.5	29.5	4.2
1970	662.0	21.4	3.2
1975	730.5	20.8	3.4
1980	883.9	21.6	3.9
1981	916.7	22.3	4.0
1982	1,065.0	26.4	4.6
1983	1,229.0	28.6	5.2
1984	1,420.0	31.4	6.0
1985	1,612.7	34.4	6.7
1986	1,777.0	37.2	7.3
1987	1,879.0	37.3	7.7
1988	1,899.8	36.5	7.7
1989	1,989.8	37.3	8.0

Source: Debt is interest-bearing privately held U.S. Treasury debt excluding that held by the U.S. government and the Federal Reserve System from the *Federal Reserve Bulletin*. real debt computed using fourth-quarter GNP deflator for each year. Per capita debt computed from fourth-quarter population from the national income and product accounts.

Table 4.3 also reports yet another measure of debt burdens, real federal debt per capita. At the beginning of the 1980s, the government's debt averaged $3,900 (1989 dollars) for each U.S. citizen. By 1989, it had grown to over $8,000. During the 1980s, real per capita government borrowing doubled, and the federal government borrowed the equivalent of $16,000 for each family of four.[5] The burden of repaying this debt will be allocated among future generations by future government fiscal policies.

4.1.4   Caveats Regarding Deficit Measurement

Although the deficit statistics presented in table 4.1 above are the standard basis for budget discussions in both Washington and the media, they are not ideal deficit measures for several reasons.[6] Two important criticisms, that the deficits ignore economic conditions and do not capture the effects of inflation,

5. One introspective test of the effects of government deficits on economic activity is to ask whether households have responded, e.g., by reducing their consumption outlays, in the same fashion that they would have if this debt had been accumulated on personal account. A negative answer suggests that government deficits depress national saving, contrary to the "Ricardian equivalence" doctrine.

6. Eisner (1986) discusses a number of these issues in greater detail.

can be remedied with statistical adjustments. Other difficulties are harder to remedy but may also make reported deficits a misleading fiscal indicator.

The first deficit criticism is that accounting-based deficits do not reflect the influence of changing economic conditions on federal receipts and outlays. Tax receipts rise in periods of strong economic expansion and contract during slack times. Federal outlays, however, *expand* during periods of weak economic activity as payouts for various transfer programs increase. The *full employment deficit,* which describes the net federal deficit or surplus that would be observed if current tax and spending programs remained in force but the economy was at full employment, adjusts reported deficit statistics for cyclical changes by standardizing revenues and outlays to a single point in the business cycle.[7]

The second problem is that standard deficit measures fail to capture the effects of inflation on the government's fiscal position. Federal debt is a nominal liability. Inflation therefore improves the government's real balance sheet by reducing the value of outstanding debt. The *inflation-adjusted deficit* adds a measure of the inflationary gain on nominal government liabilities, including long-term government bonds, Treasury bills, and currency, to the conventional deficit measure.

Table 4.4 presents time-series information on the cycle- and inflation-corrected budget deficits, in each case as a share of GNP.[8] The first column shows the unadjusted deficit as a share of GNP. The second column reports the cycle-corrected deficit. It shows a larger change in the deficit within the 1980s, and a smaller change between the 1970s and the 1980s, than the standard deficit measure. During the 1970s, a decade with a deep recession, the cycle-adjusted deficit averaged 1.6 percent of GNP, compared with 2.7 percent during the 1980s. The unadjusted deficit averaged 1.6 percent of GNP, compared with 2.7 percent during the 1980s. The unadjusted deficits averaged 1.7 and 3.7 percent of GNP, respectively. The full-employment deficit also shows much smaller reduction in deficits between the mid-1980s and the latter part of the decade than the unadjusted data. The unadjusted deficit, in this case measured on the national income and product accounts basis, peaks at 5.2 percent of GNP in 1983 and declines to 2.6 percent of GNP in 1989. The cycle-adjusted series shows a peak of 4.3 percent in 1986, with a smaller decline to 3.7 percent in 1989. This pattern reflects the strong economic expansion of the mid-1980s as well as the weak economic conditions in 1983. Deficit reduction when the

7. Full employment is a convenient base on which to standardize the deficit, but it is not unique. Similar comparative measures of government deficits could be based at other points in the business cycle.

8. Both the unadjusted deficits, in the first column of the table, and the adjusted deficits are measured for *calendar* years, not the fiscal years of standard budget documents, because the cycle-adjusted data are provided from the Commerce Department and are linked to national income and product account (NIPA) data. There are also difference in the accounting conventions used in the NIPAs and in federal budget documents that make it difficult to compare the data in table 4.4 with the budget data in other tables.

Table 4.4   **Federal Deficits Corrected for Cyclical Fluctuations and Inflation**

| Years | Reported Deficit | Deficit Adjusted for: | |
		Business Cycle	Cycle and Inflation
1950–59	−.1	N.A.	N.A.
1960–69	.3	N.A.	N.A.
1970–79	1.7	1.6	.0
1980–89	3.7	2.7	1.4
1970	1.2	1.6	.4
1971	2.0	2.0	1.3
1972	1.4	1.9	1.2
1973	.4	1.4	−.4
1974	.8	.7	−1.5
1975	4.3	2.6	1.1
1976	3.0	1.8	.7
1977	2.3	1.7	.2
1978	1.3	1.5	−.5
1979	.6	.8	−2.1
1980	2.2	1.3	−1.4
1981	2.1	.8	−1.1
1982	4.6	1.7	.7
1983	5.2	2.6	1.5
1984	4.5	3.4	2.2
1985	4.9	4.2	2.9
1986	4.9	4.3	3.9
1987	3.5	3.5	1.8
1988	2.9	3.6	2.0
1989	2.6	3.7	1.8

Source: The first column is from the national income and product accounts, table 3.2. The cyclically adjusted deficit is from the Bureau of Economic Analysis and is based on a trend GNP series associated with a constant 6 percent unemployment rate. The inflation adjustment multiplies the ex post inflation rate within the year by the stock of government debt outstanding at the end of the previous year.
Note: Figures are given in terms of percentage of GNP. N.A. = not available.

economy is near full employment (as in 1988) does not imply tightening of fiscal stance, and large deficits in a deep recession do not necessarily signal a loose fiscal policy.

The third column of table 4.4 shows the combined effect of inflation and cycle correction. Recognizing the effects of inflation widens the apparent difference in fiscal policy between the 1970s and the 1980s, although it does not fully offset the earlier cyclical correction. In the 1970s, inflation rates were significantly higher than in the 1980s. This implied larger inflationary gains on the federal debt, in effect raising federal receipts. Declining inflation thus lowers the federal government's gain on outstanding liabilities and exacerbates the deficit. Correcting for both the cycle and the role of inflation, the data suggest a shift from approximate budget balance in the 1970s to a deficit of 1.4 percent of GNP in the 1980s.

Although corrections for the business cycle and inflation are the two most common adjustments to reported deficits, one other accounting omission is at least as important. This is the problem of measuring the federal government's implicit liabilities. The savings and loan crisis of the late 1980s illustrates that such implicit liabilities can exert an important influence on the federal fiscal position. Loan guarantees of various kinds, for example, federally guaranteed mortgages through the Federal Housing Administration and the Veterans Administration, Guaranteed Student Loans, and subsidies for export sales through the Commodity Credit Corporation, commit the federal government to make lenders whole in the event of borrower default. Because defaults often occur decades after the loans were guaranteed, the flow of new guarantees is not very helpful in assessing the federal government's loan exposure. In fiscal 1988, the outstanding stock of federally guaranteed debt was $527.8 billion, or nearly one-quarter of the federal debt held by the public.

Proper accounting for implicit liabilities would debit the federal government for the value of the insurance that it provides when a loan is written and subsequently keep track of the changes in the value of outstanding guarantees and consider these as either gains or losses on federal account. The data on default and repayment profiles that are needed to measure the value of insurance have not been well analyzed, however. Thus, while there is a clear consensus that implicit liabilities are a very important part of the federal budget, there is little consensus on how to measure them.

4.2   The Reagan Revolution and Supply-Side Economics

Restraining the growth of government spending and closing the budget deficit were central issues in the 1980 presidential campaign. Republican candidate Ronald Reagan, riding the wave of antigovernment sentiment that had resulted in California's Proposition 13 and touting his record of expenditure cutbacks in California, supported a general rollback in federal spending. The precise nature of his proposals did not become clear, however, until the last few months of the campaign.

Incumbent president Carter adopted various budget policies as the election year unfolded, in part dictated by rapidly worsening U.S. inflation forecasts during 1980. President Carter's initial budget message, in January 1980, called for a $16 billion deficit. When rising inflation rates catalyzed bipartisan support for deficit reduction, however, the president revised his fiscal 1981 budget. His second budget message, in April 1980, called for a $16.5 billion *surplus* in fiscal year 1981 and included 17 billion in new taxes. The most important tax changes were a gasoline conservation tax and a new withholding tax on interest and dividends, neither of which enjoyed widespread congressional support.

The specter of a fiscal 1981 deficit reemerged during congressional budget debate. The House did not approve the president's proposed oil import fee, and Democrats in both houses lobbied for increased spending on social programs. At the same time, rising unemployment lowered federal receipts in fiscal 1980 and suggested a revenue shortfall in 1981. By mid-July 1980, less than four months after President Carter had called for a budget surplus, Treasury Secretary G. William Miller acknowledged (see *New York Times,* 15 July 1980, 1) that the fiscal 1980 deficit could be $60 billion and that the fiscal 1981 deficit was likely to be near $30 billion.

Large and growing federal deficits provided a campaign issue for the Republican presidential candidates. Both George Bush and Ronald Reagan called for spending cuts. Beginning in late June, however, the Reagan campaign also promised substantial tax reduction, along with budget cuts.[9] In part, this reflected Reagan's conversion to various supply-side economic doctrines, such as Arthur Laffer's argument that cutting tax rates could raise revenue and thereby help stem the tide of federal red ink. As the election neared, GOP candidates were pointing to President Carter's 1976 promise to balance the federal budget as a prime example of his unkept promises. During the last two months of the election campaign, the ultimately victorious Republican candidates promised that, if their proposed program cuts and tax reductions were enacted, they would balance the budget by 1983 and deliver a $121 billion *surplus* by 1983.[10]

4.2.1   1981: Tax Cuts and Expenditure Restraint

Ronald Reagan's electoral victory in November 1980, coupled with Republican victories that gave the GOP control of the Senate for the first time since 1954, provided an electoral mandate for the dramatic fiscal experiment that unfolded in the early 1980s. President Reagan's campaign rhetoric described a three-part fiscal agenda: significant tax rate reductions to restore incentives, deep cuts in government entitlements and direct expenditures, and a balanced budget. A countervailing set of promises suggested significant growth in military outlays.

Immediately after Election Day, the new administration began designing policies directed at these three objectives. Just after the election, for example, Edwin Meese announced that President Reagan would issue an executive order calling for 2 percent cutbacks in all federal outlays within a week of taking office. In late 1980, the president-elect's economic advisers, particularly future Office of Management and Budget (OMB) Director David Stockman, began a program-by-program analysis designed to generate a plan of spending cuts.

9. Candidate Reagan proposed a $36 billion tax cut, which would cost 22 billion in fiscal 1981. Details may be found in the *New York Times,* 26 June 1980, 1.

10. Press reports regarding these proposals, such as that in the *New York Times* (10 September 1980, 4), noted, however, the lack of specific plans regarding some reductions in "wasteful expenditures."

After taking office in January, the president began lobbying in earnest for these cuts as well as for a three-year, 25 percent reduction in federal tax rates.

The president's tax and expenditure proposals were nothing short of revolutionary, changing broad trends in recent fiscal policy. An unusual constellation of circumstances gave the proposals a chance of success, however. First, there was broad public dissatisfaction with economic policy. Inflation in 1979 and 1980 had been 13.3 and 12.5 percent, respectively, and the Federal Reserve Board's efforts to squelch inflation had combined with inflationary expectations to drive up interest rates. Unemployment was also rising, from 5.8 percent in 1979 to 7.6 percent in 1981. Although there was no consensus in early 1981 regarding what should be done, there was a consensus that *something* had to be done.

Second, President Reagan's gospel of limited government had received striking affirmation in the November elections. Several liberal Democratic senators, for example, Birch Bayh of Indiana and George McGovern of South Dakota, had been defeated by conservative challengers preaching small government and the supply-side doctrine of lower tax rates. This lesson was not lost on other members of Congress, many of whom feared constituent revolt if they did not deliver a change in economic and fiscal policy.

Finally, President Reagan and his White House staff proved masterful at Capitol Hill political lobbying.[11] On the expenditure side, the administration focused its attention on the omnibus appropriations bill, on the grounds that passing a low enough spending level would force restraint on each of the various speciality committees when they considered their appropriations. With respect to revenues, the president unveiled a tax reform package that promised rate reductions across the board. In this case, fear of constituent reactions to a vote against such a tax bill quieted the opposition to such a tax change and facilitated the administration's lobbying.

President Reagan's February 1981 budget proposal called for a fiscal 1982 tax reduction of $53.9 billion, coupled with spending cuts of $41.4 billion. The proposed deficit was $45 billion (*Congressional Quarterly Weekly Report* [*CQWR*], 21 February 1981, 331). The legislative package that emerged from Congress included smaller spending cuts but followed the broad outline of the president's tax cut proposals. Actual expenditure cutbacks in the omnibus reconciliation bill were estimated to reduce fiscal 1982 outlays by $35.1 billion. House Budget Chairman James Jones described the bill as "clearly the most monumental and historic turnaround in fiscal policy that has ever occurred," and the *CQWR* labeled it "the most abrupt and far-reaching change in . . . federal program directions since the advent of the New Deal" (1 August 1981, 1371).

---

11. Several examples of the tools of persuasion used by the White House—ranging from presidential telephone calls to agreeing to save particular pet programs from the budget ax—are described in the *Congressional Quarterly Weekly Report* (*CQWR*), 1 August 1981, 1372–3.

Spending cuts fell across a wide range of entitlements and other federal programs. Cutbacks in the Food Stamp Program, Comprehensive Employment and Training Act (CETA) programs, the Energy Department, and many other programs were combined in the legislation. The only program area that was exempt from the stringent budget tightening was defense. From 23.2 percent of the fiscal 1980 budget, military spending rose to 24.9 percent in 1982, 26 percent in 1983, and 26.7 percent in 1984 and 1985. Measured as a share of GNP, defense outlays rose from 5.3 percent in fiscal 1981 to 6.3 percent in 1983 and 6.4 percent in 1985. Budget authority grew even more quickly than these changes in outlays. The difficulty in obtaining the proposed budget cuts, along with the president's clear commitment to higher defense spending, foreshadowed difficulties in future rounds of expenditure reduction.

The president's tax bill also marked a dramatic departure from past policy. The Economic Recovery Tax Act of 1981 (ERTA) called for a 5 percent across-the-board reduction in tax rates in October 1981 and successive 10 percent cuts on 1 July 1982 and 1 July 1983.[12] ERTA reduced the top tax rate on unearned income from 70 to 50 percent, called for inflation indexing of all personal income tax brackets for years after 1985 (a provision not in previous legislative proposals such as Kemp-Roth), and expanded eligibility for tax-favored investment instruments such as Individual Retirement Accounts (IRAs). The bill also changed business taxation, notably by introducing the Accelerated Cost Recovery System (ACRS) of depreciation allowances, which provided significantly greater investment incentives than previous law.[13]

Significant legislative controversy surrounded both the budget and the tax bills. Because the president viewed the tax reduction as a critical part of delivering on his campaign promise to get the government "off the backs" of ordinary households, administration officials were willing to negotiate with legislators, in some cases on a vote-by-vote basis. In many circumstances, the *quid pro quo* for a congressman supporting the tax cut was administration support for an expenditure program that affected the congressman's district. The result was near-complete success in passing the tax reform but more limited achievement regarding spending cuts. More important, there was little prospect for further significant reductions in nondefense spending in later years. Given the administration's commitment to continued growth in defense outlays, tax reductions beyond the fiscal 1982 level were likely to result in high deficits.

A central feature of the 1981 tax reduction was its multiyear phase in, with large outyear tax reductions. Had the first-year tax changes in ERTA taken effect but later changes been scrapped, the deficit for fiscal 1983 would still

12. These provisions bore a strong resemblance to those in the 1977 Kemp-Roth tax proposal, which called for a three-year reduction in average tax rates by approximately 27 percent (10 percent reductions in each of three consecutive years). In part, this reflected Congressman Jack Kemp's central role in designing the Reagan economic program.

13. Fullerton's chapter in this volume provides a more detailed discussion of the tax reform provisions.

Table 4.5   **Effects of Tax Law Changes on the Federal Deficit**

Year	ERTA (1981)	TEFRA (1982)	DEFRA (1984)	TRA (1986)	OBRA (1987)
1981	−8.9				
1982	−35.6	2.5			
1983	−91.1	16.6			
1984	−136.8	36.0	.9		
1985	−170.3	39.2	9.3		
1986	−209.8	46.7	16.1		
1987	−241.7	56.9	22.0	21.5	
1988	−264.4	57.3	25.4	−8.9	8.6
1989	−290.9	55.7	27.7	−24.4	13.9
1990	−322.8	57.2	31.0	−20.3	16.1
1991	−352.7	61.2	33.8	−16.4	15.7

Source: Entries are reported in current dollars for each fiscal year and are based on estimates as reported in various issues of the OMB's *Budget of the United States Government.* Estimates in the first row are drawn from the fiscal year 1983 budget, those in the second row from the fiscal 1984 budget, etc. The eighth through eleventh rows are all drawn from the fiscal 1990 budget.

Note: Figures are given in terms of billions of current dollars. OBRA (1987) is the Omnibus Budget Reconciliation Act.

have risen as a result of the deteriorating economy and a slowing inflation rate. The actual structure of ERTA, however, placed significant deficit pressure on the budgets for fiscal 1983 and 1984. The tax bills' revenue cuts were exacerbated by the Federal Reserve Board's success in taming inflation. When the tax system is not indexed (even under the 1981 law indexing did not take effect until 1985), inflation inexorably pushes taxpayers with a given real income into higher nominal tax brackets, thereby raising revenue. The revenue effects of a given tax rate reduction are therefore dependent on the rate at which prices and wages are rising.

Table 4.5 shows the estimated effects of the 1981 tax changes on revenues in the fiscal years since 1981.[14] Although the ERTA-induced revenue loss in fiscal 1982 was only $36 billion and that in fiscal 1983 was $91 billion, the estimated effect by 1985 was nearly $170 billion. The links between future tax rate reductions, inflation, and the deficit were clear to sophisticated budget analysts,[15] who began forecasting future deficits of more than $100 billion in the months after passage of the tax reform. These forecasts ignited concerns on Capitol Hill, and particularly in the Senate, that the Reagan fiscal program would be feasible only with somewhat higher revenues.

The deficit projections of both the Congressional Budget Office (CBO) and

14. The estimates assume no behavioral responses to tax changes. If, as Lindsey (1989) e.g., argues, the rate reductions generated a larger tax base, then these estimates overstate the revenue loss.

15. For example, in *The Triumph of Politics,* David Stockman writes that "a 30% rate reduction spread over three years in a 10% inflation per annum economy amounts to a zero reduction in real tax rates. . . . The same 30% tax reduction in an inflationless . . . economy would amount to a 30% reduction in real tax rates. You would therefore need whopping big expenditure cuts to make the budget balance." (1986, 67).

Table 4.6   Deficit Forecasts by the CBO and the OMB, 1981–85

		Deficit Projections							
		1981		1982		1983		1984	
Year	Actual Deficit	CBO	OMB	CBO	OMB	CBO	OMB	CBO	OMB
1981	79	48	78						
1982	128	30	46	129	118				
1983	208	−18	23	176	107	210	225		
1984	185	−76	−17	206	97	212	203	203	200
1985	212	−138	−69	226	83	231	205	208	195

Source: Various issues of the OMB's *Budget of the United States Government* and the CBO's *Economic and Budget Outlook.*

Note: Figures are given in terms of billions of current dollars.

Office of Management and Budget (OMB) are shown in table 4.6. In each case, the forecasts are made roughly at the same time as the president's budget message, that is, in January or February. In early 1981, both organizations forecast deficits of less than $50 billion for fiscal 1982. By early 1982, however, the effect of the Reagan economic program and rising unemployment had swelled budget forecasts to $118 billion (OMB) and $129 billion (CBO) for fiscal 1982. While the forecasts agreed reasonably well for the short term, there were substantial differences in the forecasts of long-term deficit prospects. The CBO called for a rising deficit profile reaching $226 billion by 1984, while the OMB, assuming that as-yet-unspecified budget cuts would be enacted in 1982, projected average deficits of just below $100 billion for the period 1983–85. The OMB also assumed more favorable economic conditions than the CBO. In the 1982 projections, for example, the OMB assumed real economic growth of 5.2, 5.0, and 4.7 percent in fiscal 1983, 1984, and 1985, respectively, compared with 4.4, 3.6, and 3.5 percent in the analogous CBO forecasts. By the beginning of 1983, however, both the economic and the budgetary assumptions of the CBO and the OMB were again in reasonable agreement, and each organization reported deficit forecasts of more than $200 billion in *each* of the fiscal years 1983–85.

    Early in the Reagan presidency, both the CBO and the OMB underpredicted the fiscal 1983 deficit, while OMB forecasts were well below the 1984 and 1985 deficits as well. Misestimates of future revenues were the single most important factor in these errors, as table 4.7 indicates. The OMB's error in forecasting the fiscal 1983 deficit, $101 billion, consisted of a $65 billion overestimate of revenues and a $36 billion underestimate of outlays. The relative importance of revenue and outlay errors was similar for the OMB's 1984 deficit underestimate. The more accurate CBO forecasts, in contrast, overpredicted revenues by smaller absolute amounts and in some cases (1984 and 1985) actually overpredicted outlays.

    Although tax analysts debated the magnitude of the projected deficits by

Table 4.7   **Revenue and Expenditure Projection Errors, Early 1982**

Forecast Date	1982	1983	1984	1985
1982 OMB forecast:				
Deficit error	10	101	88	129
Revenue error	9	65	57	63
1982 CBO forecast:				
Deficit error	−1	32	−21	−14
Revenue error	13	51	35	29

Source: Author's tabulations based on various issues of the OMB's *Budget of the United States Government* and the CBO's *Economic and Budget Outlook.*

Note: Figures are given in terms of billions of current dollars.

quibbling with some of the OMB's and the CBO's economic assumptions,[16] the central message of the multiyear deficit projections being made in late 1981 and early 1982 was that the 1981 tax and expenditure changes had not solved the deficit problem; if anything, they had exacerbated it. The prospect of $200 billion deficits before the end of President Reagan's first term galvanized congressional Republicans, and some administration officials, to begin searching for further fiscal reforms that would narrow the deficit. This search ushered in the era of piecemeal deficit reduction between 1982 and 1985.

4.3   Piecemeal Deficit Reduction: The Aftermath of ERTA

Supporters of the 1981 tax and spending cuts believed that their new policies would stimulate the economy, eliminating the federal deficit in a few years. The preliminary evidence in the two months after the passage of ERTA did not confirm this. Interest rates were at all-time highs, with the prime rate above 20 percent and mortgage interest rates topping 17 percent. The stock market declined in the month after passage of ERTA, and popular accounts attributed the general financial malaise to expectations of large and rising budget deficits. In an effort to reassure financial markets that runaway deficits would not emerge in the "outyears" of the 1981 tax cut, in the fall of 1981 both Congress and the administration began to consider further spending cuts.

From the administration's perspective, this was an opportunity to consolidate earlier political victories and reduce government outlays. For many in Congress, however, it was an effort to reassess the budgetary priorities of the Reagan economic program and to consider delaying or abandoning the multiyear aspects of the 1981 tax reform.

16. In the early 1982 forecasts, e.g., the CBO assumed higher inflation rates (6.9 percent for fiscal 1983 and 1984 and 6.4 percent for fiscal 1985) than did the OMB (6.0, 4.6 and 4.8 percent, respectively).

4.3.1 The Tax Equity and Financial Responsibility Act of 1982

In September 1981, President Reagan called for fiscal 1982 cutbacks of $13 billion, including a controversial delay in the cost-of-living adjustment for Social Security recipients. He also requested $3 billion of additional tax revenue, although none of the proposed changes involved modifying the basic structure of the 1981 tax act. The administration tax plan was billed largely as a change in tax administration, a tightening of tax enforcement to raise revenue. At the same time, congressional Democrats suggested modifying the recently enacted tax reform bill to avoid major revenue shortfalls.

Budget action in late 1981 was hamstrung by disagreement within the Republican party concerning the appropriate strategy for deficit reduction. OMB Director David Stockman, along with Senate Republicans, favored higher taxes in fiscal 1983 and 1984, while House Republicans (including several ardent followers of supply-side economics, such as Phil Gramm and Jack Kemp), Treasury Secretary Regan, and the president were committed to further expenditure cuts.[17] Although Senate Republicans passed a budget resolution calling for deficit reduction, the House Budget Committee reacted to the lack of White House leadership by deferring any serious budget-cutting initiative until early 1982.

When Congress returned in early 1982 to reconsider the deficit issue, the economy showed clear signs of deep recession. Standard cyclical forces therefore contributed to an expanding federal deficit. In January, President Reagan called for a substantial tax increase for fiscal years 1983–85, including energy taxes and a controversial withholding tax on interest and dividends to improve taxpayer compliance. The Senate Finance Committee followed the administration's lead and, in an unusual departure from standard practice, with tax bills originating in the House, the Finance Committee took the lead in formulating a tax-increase package by attaching a deficit-reduction plan to a minor tax bill that had already cleared the House. The Democrat-controlled House was not willing to initiate a major tax increase in an election year or even to risk constituents isolating their congressman's vote on such a bill. Thus, when the final deficit-reduction bill cleared the Senate, the House voted to send the measure immediately to conference.

The bill that emerged from this unusual legislative process was the Tax Equity and Fiscal Responsibility Act of 1982 (TEFRA). It called for dividend and interest withholding, rescission of some of the generous asset depreciation provisions of the previous year's tax bill,[18] a stronger individual minimum tax,

---

17. At the same time, House and Senate conferees were discussing the restoration of the Social Security minimum benefit, which had been eliminated in the Omnibus Reconciliation Act earlier in 1981. This conference, which some hoped would address the broader question of Social Security's financial future, was inconclusive on the broad issues. This set the stage for the Greenspan Commission and the sweeping 1983 Social Security reforms.

18. Changes to capital cost recovery were part of the Senate bill, not that passed by the House, but they were retained in the conference bill.

a faster payment schedule for corporate tax payments, increases in telephone, airport, and cigarette excise taxes, and changes in a variety of intricate corporate tax provisions related to leasing and the accounting for profits in multiyear contracts. The president's budget for fiscal 1984 forecast that TEFRA would raise fiscal 1983 revenues by $17.3 billion and fiscal 1984 revenues by $38.3 billion. By comparison, the same budget estimated that ERTA had reduced revenues in fiscal 1982, 1983, and 1984 by $35.6, $82.6, and $103.3 billion, respectively.

The budget agreement also included a projected $17.5 billion of spending cuts, drawn mainly from new limitations on hospital payments under Medicare. The notable omission from the expenditure reductions was defense. The president's support for expanding the military, coupled with Defense Secretary Weinberger's within–the–White House budgetary politics,[19] protected defense outlays during this period of budget tightening. Early in the Reagan presidency, targets for the growth in defense outlays had been specified in nominal terms. Although the inflation rate by early 1983 was several percent per year below the rate assumed in setting the nominal outlay targets, the secretary of Defense argued for, and largely received, the nominal budget allocations that had been set in 1981. This contributed to rapid expansion of the military budget, with total military spending rising by 1 percent of GNP between fiscal 1981 and fiscal 1983. This is particularly remarkable given the tight fiscal environment throughout this period.

The most important budgetary lesson of the first two years of the Reagan presidency is that it is easier to cut taxes than to cut spending. The difficulty of paring nondefense discretionary outlays, the significant share of the budget that consisted of nondiscretionary outlays, and the president's commitment to a larger military made it extraordinarily difficult to envision expenditure reduction large enough to counterbalance the multiyear tax reduction passed in 1981. TEFRA did reduce federal deficits; the OMB estimates in table 4.5 above suggest revenue gains of between $40 and $50 billion per year. However, this was only a partial offset to the already large and growing federal deficits.

4.3.2   The 1984 Deficit Reduction Act

The eighteen months following the passage of TEFRA were marked by improving economic news, leading some to hope that economic expansion could trim the large deficits then being forecast by the CBO and the OMB, and by a major Social Security reform that is discussed in a later section. There was even some backsliding on deficit reduction: the Interest and Dividends Tax Compliance Act of 1983 extended the deadline for the start of interest and dividend withholding; this was the first stage in a legislative campaign that eventually led to the elimination of his provision.

---

19. David Stockman (1987) provides a number of examples of Weinberger's tenacious defense of the military budget.

The prospect of an economic miracle eradicating significant deficits had been dashed by early 1984. Consensus forecasts continued to suggest unprecedented budget deficits, and financial markets remained disturbed by the absence of progress in limiting the deficits. This provided the backdrop for President Reagan's call in his 1984 State of the Union address for renewed bipartisan effort to reduce the deficit. In March, the president introduced a plan with the backing of Senate Republicans that for the first time countenanced defense cutbacks, as well as higher taxes, to tame the deficit. The proposal involved cutting defense budget authority by $57 billion from the prior request level and reducing outlays by $40 billion over the fiscal years 1985–87. It also called for an across-the-board freeze on discretionary domestic spending cutbacks in health and farm programs that would reduce spending by $43 billion, and a $48 billion tax increase, although, again, the changes would not affect the individual income tax.

Shortly after the president's budget was sent to Congress, leading administration officials, notably Council of Economic Advisers (CEA) Chairman Martin Feldstein and David Stockman, made it clear that achieving significant progress in deficit reduction would require budget cuts in excess of those proposed by the president. A nontrivial fraction of the Democrat-controlled House sought deficit reduction perhaps twice as large as the "down payment" proposed by the president, in part to underscore the need for higher taxes to finance the ongoing military buildup, and in part to generate larger defense cuts. The congressional Democrats sought to emphasize, at the beginning of an election year, that the Republican economic program had left the federal fiscal house in disarray.

Although motivated by different considerations, support for deficit reduction was clear in both houses of Congress. There were differences nevertheless between Senate and House proposals. The GOP-backed Senate plan called for $45 billion in extra revenues, $30 billion in entitlement cuts, and $41 billion in defense cuts over three fiscal years. The House Democrats' proposal, however, included nearly $50 billion of higher taxes, only $10 billion in entitlement cuts, and $96 billion in defense cutbacks. Both plans promised total deficit reduction ($149 billion in the Senate, $182 billion in the House) well in excess of the initial administration proposals.

The conference committee had difficulty merging the spending cuts of the House and Senate bills and consequently reported a much smaller spending cut then either bill had called for. The resulting legislation, the Deficit Reduction Act of 1984 (DEFRA), called for roughly $50 billion in additional taxes and spending cuts of $13 billion targeted at the health sector once again. The costs of health care to beneficiaries was increased, and the bill also incorporated a fifteen-month freeze on doctors' fees. Defense cutbacks were largely deferred by the conference committee because of substantial differences between the House and the Senate proposals.

Just as the passage of TEFRA had been marked by unusual parliamentary practices, standard budgetary procedures were disregarded in 1984 as both houses of Congress struggled with the deficit-reduction measures. The Senate, for example, debated and passed legislation on deficit reduction before action on the revenue or expenditure targets for the year had been approved. In the House, the reconciliation bill was the vehicle for deficit reduction. It was debated and considered before the appropriate reports from the various committees. In this way, the budget was being determined first by setting the bottom line, then by filling in program totals. Historically, the practice worked in the opposite direction, with each committee appropriating funds for a given purpose and the budget committee then aggregating these requests. The departures from standard practice in both 1982 and 1984 were an important factor in the success of balanced-budget and budget-reform legislation in the next congressional session.

4.3.3   The Tax Reform Act of 1986

By the end of 1984, the sluggish economic growth of the early 1980s had given way to a sustained recovery, with real GNP growth of 1.7 percent in the four quarters ending in December 1984 and 3.0 percent for the period ending in December 1985. The improving economy reduced the urgency for Congress to heed continued calls for deficit reduction from financial markets, and deficit reduction became a less salient economic and political issue.

Ronald Reagan's top priorities in this first term were reducing the growth of federal nondefense spending, along with the taxes to finance it, and restoring U.S. military capabilities. In his second term, the priority shifted to reforming the structure of the federal tax system by lowering marginal tax rates. In early 1984, President Reagan asked the Treasury Department to design a tax overhaul plan. The Treasury's report, which was released shortly after Reagan's overwhelming reelection in November 1984, called for sweeping changes in the structure of tax rates for individuals and corporations. On Capitol Hill, although most tax writers were skeptical of the prospects for a far-reaching reform, there was a sentiment that the era of "loophole closing" revenue bills such as DEFRA and TEFRA had passed. The *CQWR* explained, "A 'cats and dogs' revenue raising bill, like [the] measures enacted in 1982 and 1984 making hundreds of miscellaneous tax changes, will be difficult to pass again. 'There are only big cats and dogs left, and they bite' says John Salmon, Ways and Means Chief Counsel" (27 October 1984, 2787).

In both 1982 and 1984, the rationale for tax reform was raising revenue. The tax reform process that began in late 1984, however, was descended from the flat-tax discussions that had circulated in Washington for nearly a decade. This tax reform debate was different: virtually all the proposed plans were revenue neutral. The nineteen months between the Treasury Department report and the ultimate passage of the Tax Reform Act of 1986 (TRA) involved many of the same curious parliamentary and lobbying practices that had characterized the major budget debates earlier in the decade. When the process concluded with passage of TRA, the outcome (as in 1981) was nothing short of remarkable. The reform represented the single most important change in the U.S. tax code in decades, placed the United States in the vanguard of a worldwide movement toward cutting marginal tax rates, and radically altered the tax disincentive to work at higher incomes.

Despite its important role for tax structure, the 1986 reform was not as important for the course of the federal budget as the tax reforms earlier in the decade. It was not designed to affect the deficit, but most estimates suggest that the TRA did reduce federal revenues. The OMB estimates in table 4.5 above suggest a favorable revenue effect in fiscal 1987, as a result of the transition rules in the new legislation. In subsequent years, however, the TRA generated revenue losses of approximately $20 billion per year. While the precise magnitude of the timing effects from TRA are not clear, their direction is that they helped narrow the deficit in 1987 and contributed to larger deficits in later years.[20]

4.3.4   Summarizing the Effects of Tax Changes

The net effect of the various tax reforms during the first six years of the 1980s, described in table 4.5, indicates that deficits by fiscal 1986 were approximately $150 billion higher than they would have been without these tax changes. The piecemeal reforms of 1982 and 1984 were just that: they did not reverse even half the deficit increase built into the 1981 Economic Recovery Tax Act. Nevertheless, total federal tax revenues do not show this large a decline. Lawrence Lindsey's (1989) study of the tax changes in this period attributes at most half the deficit increase to the effects of tax reform and attributes a significant part of the remaining increase to higher military outlays. The OMB estimates in table 4.5 are not necessarily inconsistent with Lindsey's view, however, because the income tax changes were only part of the tax reform landscape in the early 1980s. The other important feature was the reform of Social Security, which raised payroll taxes and changed the future benefit structure for the federal government's most important transfer program. Although often neglected in federal tax policy discussions, the payroll tax was a critical source of federal revenue growth during the 1980s. Receipts from this tax rose from 6.1 percent of GNP in fiscal 1981 to 6.7 percent in fiscal 1985 to 7.0 percent in fiscal 1990. The next section considers the major changes in the Social Security system during the 1980s, with particular attention to their significance for the federal budget.

4.4   Social Security and the Federal Deficit

Federal deficits and the Social Security system are inherently interlinked policies since both transfer resources between generations. Because the central

20. Analyses of how tax changes affect revenues are notoriously difficult because key assumptions about household and firm responses to tax reform are often controversial. The OMB estimates presented here assume *no* behavioral responses. They consequently neglect, e.g., the retiming in capital gain realizations as a result of the Tax Reform Act.

issue of economic concern is the net transfer between generations, not its components such as income taxes, payroll taxes, government spending, or transfers, it is important to consolidate the two in analyzing the government's evolving fiscal position. The budgeting conventions of the late 1980s combined the surplus or deficit from the Social Security Trust Fund, part of the "off-budget" surplus, with the "on-budget" surplus or deficit from other federal operations in calculating the total budget deficit. Trust fund surpluses were a central factor in the apparent improvement in the federal deficit during the late 1980s.

Although there were numerous changes during the 1980s in federal tax and on-budget expenditure policy, there was only one important change in Social Security policy: the Social Security Amendments of 1983. This landmark legislation, however, introduced significant changes in both the financing and the prospective benefits of the Social Security system. One direct consequence of this legislation was that the Social Security Trust Fund ran surpluses, rather than deficits, beginning in 1985 and thereby helped offset the on-budget federal deficit.

4.4.1   The 1983 Social Security Compromise

The 1983 Social Security Amendments are the anomaly of U.S. budgetary history in the 1980s. They combined a tax *increase* and a reduction in the level of government transfer payments, at a time when the tax reductions of 1981 were still being phased in. They also represent an important political compromise, in many ways the most significant such compromise of the decade.

The stage for Social Security reform in the early 1980s was set in the previous decade. Real Social Security benefits increased more than 25 percent in the early 1970s, generating greater program costs. The reduction in labor force activity among the aged, notably the growth of early retirement, also contributed to higher outlays. At roughly the same time, the rate of economic growth slowed, reducing the expansion of the payroll tax base that finances the system. These factors led to a payroll tax increase in 1977, which was viewed at the time as ensuring Social Security's solvency well into the next century. Long-range forecasts regarding the Social Security Trust Fund are necessarily quite uncertain, however. Even by 1980, continued benefit growth in part due to overindexation of benefits for inflation and a sluggish economy led to new forecasts of insolvency.

In May 1981, President Reagan proposed radical changes in the Social Security system, including lower benefits for early retirees and reduced rates of real benefit growth. After two weeks of outcry from various pro–Social Security lobbies such as the American Association of Retired People (AARP), discussion of serious reform was tabled by a Senate resolution promising no precipitous cuts in benefits. Although the administration continued to seek abolition of the $122 Social Security minimum benefit and this provision was included in the 1981 budget conference committee's report, both houses of Congress voted in December to restore the minimum benefit. This illustrated the political difficulty of addressing the Social Security problem: no legislator would survive a reelection campaign if he or she were known as the architect of a Social Security benefit reduction. This suggested that a political compromise on Social Security could not be fashioned through usual legislative channels.

The political stalemate led President Reagan to appoint a fifteen-member National Commission on Social Security Reform, chaired by Alan Greenspan, to study the fiscal problems of the system and propose solutions. The commission was charged to report at the end of December 1982 and, by early December, had reached no consensus on how to proceed. Chairman Greenspan requested a two-week extension of the reporting deadline, however, and during this time worked with small groups of commission members to reach a compromise proposal. This plan, which was announced in mid-January, formed the basis for the 1983 Social Security Amendments.

The Amendments had four central features: (i) acceleration of payroll tax increases scheduled for the late 1980s; (ii) partial taxation of Social Security benefits for elderly households with substantial non–Social Security income; (iii) a six-month postponement of the cost-of-living adjustment originally scheduled for July 1983; and (iv) a gradual increase in the Social Security retirement age from sixty-five to sixty-six in 2007 and sixty-seven in 2027. The third and fourth provision were particularly controversial because they seemed to some to violate the basic spirit of the Social Security program. Senator Claude Pepper, for example, long a champion of Social Security, recognized proposals ii and iii as tantamount to benefit reductions but was unsuccessful in persuading his fellow senators to block the plan.[21]

4.4.2 Deficit Accounting and Social Security

The net effect of these changes is that, for the next twenty-five years, Social Security taxes are projected to exceed benefit outflows and to result in accumulation of a substantial Social Security Trust Fund. In fiscal 1989, Social Security Trust Fund revenues exceeded outlays by $52 billion.[22] This surplus, combined with a deficit of $205 billion from other federal operations, implied a reported deficit of $152 billion. More than half the deficit reduction since 1986, when the combined deficit peaked at $221 billion, is due to the growth of payroll tax receipts. Table 4.8 and figure 4.2 show the net effect of the Social

21. The retirement age changes, although legislated for the distant future, caused substantial changes in the present discounted value of the Social Security transfers to and from different generations. The principal "losers" were those born into, and slightly after, the baby-boom generation. The gainers are the children of the baby boom, who will not be required to finance heavy outlays for their parents' retirement. A systematic treatment of the gains and losses from the 1983 reforms is provided in Pellechio and Goodfellow (1983).

22. The reported off-budget Social Security surplus overstates the excess of taxes over benefits for the trust fund. In 1989, the trust fund tax receipts were $267 billion, while benefit payments were $227 billion. The trust fund also spent $5 billion on administration, so the net surplus, measured as taxes less outlays, was $35 billion. However, the trust fund received $10 billion in net interest payments from the Treasury and collected $12 billion in transfers from other federal agencies.

Table 4.8   Social Security Surpluses and the Budget Deficit, 1980–89

Year	Deficit Excluding Social Security	Social Security Surplus	Total Deficit
1980	73	−1	74
1981	74	−5	79
1982	120	−8	128
1983	108	0	108
1984	186	0	185
1985	222	9	212
1986	238	17	221
1987	169	20	150
1988	194	39	155
1989	205	52	152
1990	277	57	220

Source: Congressional Budget Office (1990) and the December 1990 *U.S. Treasury Bulletin.*
Note: Figures are given in terms of billions of current dollars.

Security surplus on federal deficits during the 1980s. The figure demonstrates the central role of the Social Security surpluses in narrowing the federal deficit.

The growing surplus in the Social Security accounts is also the key factor in the narrowing deficits projected for the early 1990s. While the Congressional Budget Office forecasts in July 1990 (see Congressional Budget Office 1990, 36) call for a combined deficit of $146 billion in 1994, this reflects a $255 billion deficit for on-budget federal activities, substantially offset by a $109 billion Social security surplus. The real on-budget deficit, which is not shown in the table, is projected to grow by $6 billion 1989 dollars between fiscal 1989 and fiscal 1994, compared with a projected decline of $32 billion (1989 dollars) in the unified deficit.

4.4.3 The Future of Social Security

The 1983 Social Security reform is important, not just because it altered the federal budget deficit during the latter part of the 1980s, but also because it represented a basic shift in budget policy with respect to transfer payments. Until 1983, the Social Security system operated on a pay-as-you-go (PAYG) basis, with revenues collected solely from the payroll tax used to finance current outlays. The difficulty with this approach, and a central factor behind the 1983 reform, was that maintaining a solvent PAYG system would place high tax burdens on working households in the next century. Aaron, Bosworth, and Burtless (1989) estimate that, to finance Social Security benefits in the next century under a PAYG system, the payroll tax rate would rise from 12.1 percent in 1990 to 16.8 percent in 2040. Including the taxes needed to maintain a PAYG Medicare program, the payroll tax rate in 2040 would be over 23 percent.[23] The decision to raise taxes during the next three decades by enough to

23. This estimate is drawn from Aaron, Bosworth, and Burtless (1989, 51).

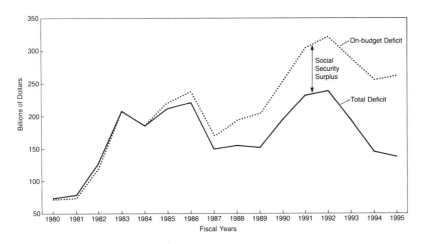

Fig. 4.2   U.S. federal budget deficit

accumulate a significant trust fund surplus is a rare example of a government deciding, in the face of a large future expenditure burden, to raise taxes. As the shape of the Social Security compromise became clear, House Speaker Thomas P. O'Neill, Jr., explained that "we are changing the tradition of this country. In America, each generation has always paid for the generation that has gone before them"(*CQWR,* 12 March 1983, 488).

The 1983 reforms rejected the rising pattern of tax rates implied by this approach as unacceptable fiscal policy. This may reflect a judgment about the appropriateness of large burdens on future generations or a concern among the current work force that such tax rates would never be enacted but rather would be avoided through benefit cutbacks during their retirement. The current policy calls for accumulating a sizable Social Security trust fund in the early part of the next century. Table 4.9 shows the evolution of trust fund assets as a share of GNP during the next century. By 2020, the projections call for assets of $9.4 trillion, or nearly 30 percent of GNP.

The high budget deficits resulting from the economic policies early in the Reagan administration may in some ways have facilitated the Social Security compromise. The apparent inability of Congress and the administration to grapple with the short-run deficits in fiscal 1983–84 may have undermined public confidence in the long-run fiscal health of the Social Security system, making it necessary to take decisive action and discourage any further discussions of potentially bankrupt Social Security system. The general climate of tax reduction in the two years prior to this historic reform may also have contributed to public willingness to accept a set of tax changes that raised payroll taxes and reduced future benefits.

By the end of the 1980s, there were signs that the consensus for using higher payroll taxes to reduce federal budget deficits was eroding. In late December 1989, Senator Moynihan, the chairman of the Senate Finance Subcommittee

Table 4.9   **Social Security Trust Fund Accumulation, 1990–2050**

Year	Current-Dollar OASDI Trust Fund Assets	Trust Fund Assets/GNP (%)
1990	200	3.7
2000	1,290	12.7
2010	4,490	24.5
2020	9,390	29.7
2030	12,410	22.8
2040	10,680	11.2
2050	780	.5

Source: Hambor (1987, 14).

Note: Trust fund assets are reported in billions of current dollars.

on Social Security, proposed to roll back the increase in the payroll tax that took effect on 1 January 1990 and to continue rollbacks in future years. Supporters of such a proposal cite two arguments. First, the large Social Security surpluses are masking the true magnitude of the federal budget problem, thereby forestalling the needed fundamental action to raise taxes or reduce spending. Although it is difficult to marshall a convincing economic argument along these lines since virtually all the policymakers involved in the deficit process recognize the key role of Social Security, there may be a political justification for such a view. The statistic reported as the budget deficit may have some focal value in attracting the public's attention to the status of fiscal policy. Larger deficit numbers may therefore generate increased pressure for deficit reduction.

The second argument supporting payroll tax reduction is concerned with tax structure. The payroll tax does not tax wage income above a cap level ($51,300 in 1990). It is a flat rate tax, and it is levied on wage but not capital income. These factors make the tax less progressive than the federal income tax. Part of Senator Moynihan's strategy in proposing the Social Security tax reduction was presumably to focus renewed attention on the structure of the entire federal tax system, not simply the income tax, which received a major renovation in 1986. Although at this writing there is little active discussion of the Moynihan proposal, one important lesson of the 1980s is that budgetary politics can change rapidly and in unexpected directions.

4.5 Budget Balance Initiatives

Social Security reform and radical marginal tax rate reductions are the two most lasting fiscal legacies of the 1980s. They were not the most significant reforms to receive active discussion, however. At several junctures, various balanced-budget amendments received serious congressional consideration, although they never received sufficient support to send them to the president for his signature. The Gramm-Rudman deficit targets and the associated reforms in the federal budget process, however, have the potential to influence federal budget policy far into the future.

Beginning in 1982, each Congress considered adopting legislation that would *mandate* balanced budgets. The definition of *balance,* the date when such balance was required, and other provisions varied in the proposals. The two most important initiatives were the 1982 drive for the Balanced Budget Amendment (BBA) to the Constitution and the multiyear budget limitation debate that culminated in the Gramm-Rudman-Hollings legislation in 1986.

4.5.1   The Campaign for a Balanced-Budget Amendment

The most serious discussion of a balanced-budget amendment occurred in early 1982, when previously unthinkable deficits of more than $200 billion were being forecast and there seemed little prospect of achieving adequate spending cuts to balance the budget. In this environment, the notion of a rule that would bind the budget process to yield zero-deficit outcomes attracted a following, although the discussion of precisely how this would occur was always somewhat vague.

The notion of a balanced-budget amendment was not original to the lawmakers of the early 1980s. In September 1978, for example, a bill concerned with the International Monetary Fund was amended to require that annual budget outlays of the federal government could not exceed receipts for fiscal years beginning in 1981, although the bill allowed that the requirement "may be superseded by the action of future Congresses." Congress reaffirmed its attention to balance the fiscal 1981 budget in separate 1980 legislation (see *CQWR,* 12 October 1985, 2038). These strictures were summarily ignored in the actual budgetary process.

There are two ways to amend the Constitution: thirty-four states can pass legislation calling for a constitutional convention, or Congress can pass a proposed amendment and then send it to the states for ratification. Proponents of the BBA operated on both fronts. In January 1982, the Alaska legislature passed a resolution calling for a constitutional convention; it was the thirty-first state to pass such legislation. Simultaneously, Congress considered BBA legislation.

The GOP's Senate victories in 1980, which shifted control of the Senate to the Republican party, were a central factor in advancing the BBA in the early 1980s. The shift made Senator Strom Thurmond of South Carolina, an active supporter of the BBA, the chairman of the Senate Judiciary Committee. Throughout the decade, the Democrat-controlled House was less enthusiastic about budget-limitation measures than the Senate. The BBA debates of 1982 illustrate this.

In August 1982, the Senate passed a balanced-budget amendment by a 69 to 31 margin, two more than the two-thirds majority needed for constitutional amendments. The legislation required Congress to adopt a balanced budget before the start of each fiscal year, although it incorporated limited override provisions for deficits in wartime or if approved by 60 percent of Congress. During the Senate debate on the BBA, proponents fought back amendments to allow overrides related to economic conditions. The legislation thus ran afoul of the standard concern of macroeconomists, that the BBA straitjackets fiscal policy and makes it impossible to use deficit finance to counteract adverse fiscal developments.

Despite support from the White House, the BBA did not pass the House by the required two-thirds majority. House Judiciary Chairman Peter Rodino was strongly opposed to the BBA on the grounds that it introduced matters of economic policy that did not belong in the Constitution into an otherwise legal document. His efforts to bottle up the BBA in committee were overruled, however, when Barber Conable, the chief House sponsor, collected signatures from more than half the House and forced action by the full House. Supporters of the BBA were optimistic about the chances of passage, arguing that, in an election year, it was extremely difficult for any House member to vote against the BBA, and thus for budget deficits, and to explain their action to constituents.

The House Democratic leadership nevertheless worked to defeat the proposal by calling the bill for full House action more quickly than GOP supporters had expected, leaving relatively little time to organize the pro-BBA lobbying effort. The full House voted for the BBA by a 236 to 187 majority, nearly fifty votes short of the necessary two-thirds majority. President Reagan ironically explained that "this vote makes clear who supports a balanced budget and who does not. Voters across America should count heads and take names" (*CQWR*, 2 October 1982, 2420). Although the Senate considered balanced-budget amendment legislation again in early 1985, the measure never achieved the same level of support that it did in 1982.[24]

The debate over the Balanced Budget Amendment highlights one of the paradoxical features of budgetary politics in the United States. Table 4.10 presents data from Gallup polls of the American people at various times during the 1980s, in each case showing that more than half, and, early in the decade, nearly three-fourths, of the population supported a balanced-budget amendment. Support for tax increases, however, rarely exceeded 25 percent, and that for entitlement cuts was rarely above 10 percent. The only program category that the electorate seemed willing to cut was defense, precisely the area where the administration felt its strongest mandate for increased outlays.

4.5.2   The Gramm-Rudman-Hollings Deficit Limitation Measures

Even though the BBA could not command sufficient legislative support for passage, Congress retained a desire to alter the budget process in ways that

---

24. The administration's budget proposal for fiscal 1984, presented in early 1983, contained an innovative provision for a "trigger tax increase," which would take effect if the deficit exceeded certain targets. Although this provision never became law, it was a precursor to the Gramm-Rudman legislation later in the decade.

Table 4.10   **Gallup Polls on the Federal Budget Deficit**

Date of Poll	Deficit a Very Serious Problem	Deficit Reduction Measures			
		Support Balanced Budget Amendment	Support Tax Increases	Support Military Cuts	Support Entitlements Cuts
1980 March		75			
1982:					
May		74		43	
November			18	57	12
1983 June		71			
1984 December			23	61	11
1985:					
April	58		18	66	9
August	57		25		
August		54			
November	61		29		
1986 January			22	59	9
1987 July			16	58	9

Source: George Gallup, *The Gallup Poll: Public Opinion* (Wilmington, Del.: Scholarly Resources), various annual editions, 1980–87.

would reduce the chance of future deficits. In late 1985, the Senate took up legislation to raise the federal debt limit from $1.8 trillion to $2.1 trillion. The expansion in debt authority was needed to avoid a federal financial crisis since increased borrowing was required to make federal interest payments. During the debate on the debt ceiling bill, Senators Phil Gramm, Ernest Hollings, and Warren Rudman took the initiative on broad deficit issues and introduced a bill requiring a phased-in program of deficit reduction, leading to budget balance in fiscal 1991. The proponents of Gramm-Rudman-Hollings (GRH) relied on blitzkrieg legislative tactics to advance their bill; the *CQWR* described this as "breach[ing] Congressional custom in a manner not seen since the landmark budget- and tax-cutting bills of 1981" (12 October 1985, 2035). The resulting bill passed the Senate by a wide majority (75 to 24) and led to frustration among Democratic congressmen at the GOP's seizing of the high ground on the deficit problem, which the Republicans had in many ways created.

The Senate GRH bill had two components. The first altered the timing of the federal budget process, accelerating budget discussions and placing deadlines earlier in the calendar year in an effort to permit more deliberation before the start of the fiscal year. The second objective was to introduce a set of deficit targets and a mechanism for ensuring that actual deficits did not exceed them. The key provisions were as follows. (i) The president would be required to submit budgets with forecast deficits no greater than the maximum for a given year. (ii) The OMB and the CBO would prepare estimates of the projected deficit from the enacted budget and tax legislation. (iii) If the average of the CBO and the OMB deficit computations exceeded the maximum allowed, the president would have two weeks to issue a "sequester" order, requiring permanent reductions in budget authority for all outlays other than Social Security, interest on the federal debt, and existing contractual obligations. (iv) Half the sequester cuts would come from entitlement programs with automatic spending increases, such as Medicaid, AFDC, and food stamps, while the other half would come from other discretionary programs. (v) A suspension clause rendered the need for spending cuts inoperative if the economy was in recession, defined as two consecutive quarters of real decline in GNP, or in a war declared by Congress, or whenever a three-fifths majority of Congress voted for such suspension. These provisions represented a total alteration in the ground rules of budgetary politics in the United States.

The Senate took the lead in this round of deficit reduction, but the House also passed a deficit-limitation bill requiring declining deficits in future years and making automatic cuts in nearly half the federal budget if the Congress and the president could not reach a suitable budget agreement. The House Democrats, however, supported tighter deficit targets in 1986, hoping to drive home the magnitude of the budget crisis before the 1986 midterm elections in which twenty-two Republican senators would stand for reelection. The House and Senate versions also differed in the nature of the automatic cuts required if the deficit target was not achieved. The House bill exempted Medicare from mandatory cuts and generally placed more of the cuts on the defense budget than the Senate plan.[25]

After nearly two months of deliberation, in December 1985 a conference committee reached agreement on a compromise deficit-limitation bill, which President Reagan signed. The bill called for a deficit target of $171.9 billion in fiscal 1986, nearly the midpoint of the earlier House and Senate levels, declining to zero by fiscal 1991. The intervening deficit targets are shown in table 4.11. Half the automatic cuts would come from defense and half from nonexempt nonmilitary programs.[26] All programs would have to be cut *by the same percentage;* this limited the president's flexibility, which had been built into the Senate bill. A key provision required the General Accounting Office (GAO) to calculate the average of the OMB and the CBO deficit estimates and transmit an estimate of the needed sequester to the president.

The GAO provision was critical because it was the basis for a constitutional challenge to GRH by Representative Mike Synar. Because Congress can dismiss the head of the GAO, Synar argued that the bill provided executive authority to an organization that was under legislative control. Although GRH included a fall-back provision requiring both houses of Congress to approve the sequester plan and send it to the president, this would negate the all-important inevitability of the budget cuts that the GAO procedure provided. In

25. The House and Senate plans also differed in the nature of the target specified. The House bill required cuts in budget authority, while the Senate targets were set in terms of budget outlays, which meant harsher cuts in programs with long outlay horizons.

26. Exempt programs included AFDC, Medicaid, food stamps, Social Security, and veterans programs.

Table 4.11   Deficit Reduction Targets in Gramm-Rudman I and II

	Gramm-Rudman I	Gramm-Rudman II
1988	108	154
1989	72	146
1990	36	110
1991	0	74
1992	0	38
1993	0	0

Source: Congressional Quarterly Weekly Report (various issues).
Note: Figures are given in terms of billions of current dollars.

July 1986, the Supreme Court found for Synar and declared GRH unconstitutional. Chief Justice Warren Burger wrote that "to permit an officer controlled by the Congress to execute the laws would be, in essence, to permit a Congressional veto." (*CQWR,* 12 July 1986, 1561).

The Supreme Court decision derailed the first Gramm-Rudman-Hollings deficit-limitation plan. A year later, when the Senate was again debating an increase in the debt ceiling, proponents of deficit limits again attached a proposal for gradual deficit elimination to the debt legislation. The key difference between the new legislation, sponsored by Senators Gramm, Chiles, and Domenici but frequently referred to as Gramm-Rudman (hereafter GR), and the previous bill was a final step in the sequester process that required the GAO to submit its report to the OMB, an executive agency. The OMB would review the GAO report, and the president would then issue an order based on it to enforce spending cuts. Many of the other provisions were similar to those in the 1985 legislation, but the deficit targets were loosened from levels in the original legislation to require a deficit of $144 billion in fiscal 1988, declining to zero in fiscal 1993. In addition, the law permitted a $10 billion margin of error in all years until 1993. The intervening deficit targets are shown in table 4.11.

The president signed the new legislation on 29 September 1987, ushering in a new era of deficit politics. The remainder of the 1980s would be marked by various forms of brinkmanship, as Congress tried to force the president to raise taxes or face defense cutbacks and the president tried to force cuts in discretionary programs.

The evidence is still accumulating on the effects of deficit targets. One can debate on a priori grounds whether such targets could ever affect spending outcomes. Since Congress and the president can always agree to modify the targets, they represent a weak form of budgetary restraint. Various budgeting gimmicks, such as the postponement of some expenditures until the first day of the next fiscal year or the acceleration of some receipts, also provide opportunities to reduce the stringency of the effective targets.

There are two reasons, however, for suspecting that deficit targets *do* affect budgetary outcomes. First, they provide a benchmark for budget deliberations, an objective standard against which the president's budget proposal or congressional modifications can be evaluated. Media discussions of whether particular proposals meet the deficit targets appear to "score" different proposals and may encourage frugality by both the president and the legislature. Second, the sequestration procedures through which cutbacks occur enable current legislators to shirk some responsibility for spending reductions, blaming the cuts on the previous Congress that enacted the budget targets. While Congress and the president may opt to circumvent this process if the cuts are too painful, a sequester that is perceived as an equitable reduction in expenditures might be allowed to take effect. In any case, the threat of a painful sequester probably does provide some pressure for budget compromise.[27]

Ultimately, deficit targets cannot avoid the need for fundamental political compromise on the appropriate mix and level of taxes and expenditures. Legislation such as Gramm-Rudman may, however, help focus the process of budget negotiation.

4.6   The Quiet Years: Deficits in the Late 1980s and Early 1990s

After constant change in the first six years of the 1980s, the federal fiscal scene was remarkably calm in the final years of the decade. A period of continuing economic growth helped reduce the federal deficit from 5.3 percent of GNP in 1986 to 2.9 percent of GNP in fiscal 1989. A slowing economy in fiscal 1990, however, combined with growing outlays for the thrift bailout, raised the deficit to 4.1 percent of GNP in fiscal 1990. Roughly one-third of the deficit reduction between 1986 and 1989 occurred through increases in tax receipts, in this case largely the payroll tax, as total federal receipts rose from 18.4 to 19.2 percent of GNP. This growth in receipts occurred largely as a result of economic growth rather than changes in the tax code. At the same time, the level of federal outlays relative to the economy declined from 23.7 percent of GNP to 22.2 percent.

President Bush's campaign promise "No New Taxes" effectively prevented any serious discussion of tax hikes during the first eighteen months of his administration. Just before the midterm elections of 1990, however, the president agreed to renege on this promise. Administration support was crucial to passage of the multiyear deficit-reduction package of 1990, which should lead to several hundred billion dollars of deficit reduction during the first half of the 1990s.

The federal budget process is currently anchored by the deficit-reduction targets in the Balanced Budget Act. These targets are $136 billion for fiscal

---

27. At this writing, a major test of the workings of the Gramm-Rudman targets is under way. If the targets are suspended on account of military action in the Persian Gulf, the case for their providing an effective break on deficit outlays will be weakened.

1989, followed by $100 billion, $64 billion, and $28 billion for fiscal 1990, 1991, and 1992, respectively. The deficit target for 1993 is *zero,* and the act does not specify targets for subsequent years.

Current forecasts call for continued gradual reduction in federal deficits, in the tradition of the late 1980s. The most widely cited forecasts are provided by the Congressional Budget Office, which assumes that no new spending programs are enacted between now and 1995. A similar assumption is embodied in the CBO's revenue forecasts. Given assumptions about economic growth, however, revenues are allowed to rise as they would if future incomes were taxed according to the current rate schedules. Table 4.12 shows the forecast federal deficit declining from 2.9 percent of GNP in 1989 to 1.8 percent in 1995. Since 1.8 percent is below the forecast growth rate of nominal GNP, these projections imply a declining ratio of debt to GNP during the period 1990–94.

Table 4.12 reports the deficit projections as well as several components of the deficit. The off-budget surplus, primarily the result of payroll taxes in ex-

Table 4.12   **Deficit Forecasts, Fiscal Years 1989–95**

		Projections					
	Actual 1989	1990	1991	1992	1993	1994	1995
Billions of current dollars							
Revenues	991	1,044	1,123	1,188	1,260	1,337	1,417
Outlays	1,143	1,238	1,355	1,426	1,455	1,483	1,555
Total deficit	152	195	232	239	194	146	138
GRH targets	136	100	64	28	0	. . .	. . .
Social Security surplus	52	59	73	83	95	109	124
On-budget deficit	204	254	305	322	289	255	262
Deficit excluding RTC outlays	143	159	162	179	182	177	157
Publicly held debt	2,189	2,378	2,607	2,844	3,038	3,183	3,321
Percentage of GNP							
Revenues	19.2	19.1	19.3	19.1	19.0	19.0	18.9
Outlays	22.2	22.6	23.2	23.0	22.0	21.0	20.7
Total deficit	2.9	3.6	4.0	3.8	2.9	2.1	1.8
Social Security surplus	1.0	1.1	1.3	1.3	1.4	1.5	1.7
On-budget deficit	4.0	4.6	5.2	5.2	4.4	3.6	3.5
Deficit excluding RTC outlays	2.8	2.9	2.8	2.9	2.7	2.5	2.1
Publicly held debt	42.5	43.5	44.7	45.8	45.9	45.1	44.2

Source: Congressional Budget Office (1990).

cess of Social Security outlays, was discussed above. One other important change during this period, however, was the rise of federal outlays to rescue savings and loan institutions. These outlays, which are denoted by the RTC (Resolution Trust Corp.), are also noted in the table. They increase the estimated federal deficit by more than 1 percent of GNP for fiscal years 1991 and 1992 but reduce the deficit in fiscal years beginning with 1994.

The time-varying effect of RTC outlays on federal deficits reflects the nature of these expenditures. Much of the cost of liquidating the thrifts involves working capital, loans that the RTC will take out from the federal government at the beginning of the decade when it takes over assets but will repay later in the decade. Although the interest on such working capital is a real cost from the federal government's perspective, the capital itself is a loan rather than an outlay. The government acquires the assets of thrift institutions in return for extending these loans, so the net effect on the federal balance sheet depends on the net worth of the rescued thrifts, not their gross asset value.

The most appropriate measure of federal deficits for the period 1990–95 is the deficit excluding the noninterest, nonadministrative costs of the RTC. This is shown in the second-to-last row in each panel of table 4.12. The table shows a continuing reduction in federal deficits from 2.8 percent of GNP in 1989 to 2.1 percent in 1995, although the deficits in the early years of the 1990s are well in excess of the deficit targets imposed by Gramm-Rudman. Resolving this disparity is a fundamentally political problem.

4.7   Lessons and Conclusions

The 1980s witnessed more dramatic changes in peacetime federal budget policy than any decade since the Second World War. These changes were the result of major shifts in federal tax and spending policy, reflecting a large military buildup and sweeping reductions in federal taxes. A unique constellation of political forces was needed to prompt such changes.

The experience of the 1980s suggests several preliminary lessons, some of which are not surprising, about the political economy of budget policy. First, it is harder to cut spending and raise taxes than to do the opposite. The central thesis of David Stockman's *The Triumph of Politics* (1986) is that politics eventually prevailed over the ideological zeal of the Reagan reformers. It was more difficult to pare spending than President Reagan had anticipated, but there was widespread support for tax reduction. The Reagan economic program of tax cuts and spending reduction was therefore tilted toward deficit finance from the outset. This was a catalyst to the large budget deficits of the 1980s.

Second, inflation can whipsaw fiscal policy when the tax system is progressive but not indexed. Such a tax system can yield both revenue gains and unexpected revenue shortfalls. The essence of budget balance in the 1970s, a decade of rising federal outlays, was the built-in revenue gains from bracket creep in the federal income tax. When budget forecasts at the beginning of the 1980s counted on the continuation of these gains, however, and the Federal Reserve was unexpectedly successful in curbing inflation, unexpected deficits materialized quickly. With indexation of the federal income tax code in the Tax Reform Act of 1986, the period of significant bracket creep is behind us.

Third, mechanical budget targets may provide a useful focus for fiscal policy debates, but they are unlikely to replace the fundamentally political process of tax and spending negotiation. It is simply not possible, short of a constitutional amendment, for one Congress and administration to commit future legislators or executives to particular actions. This perennial ability to override budget targets, by creating a national emergency or other extenuating circumstances, limits the intrinsic power of balanced-budget rules. Even a constitutional change might fail, as the opportunities to alter accounting rules or other aspects of the budget process might provide latitude for future policymakers. Nevertheless, these rules may focus the budget debate in useful ways, and they can have real effects on budget outcomes. They may also be useful in specifying a benchmark set of budget cuts that can form the basis for debate and discussion. If the prespecified cuts are perceived as fair and equitable, they may set the stage for similar outcomes in budget negotiations.

Fourth, the off-budget outlays and implicit liabilities that economists have long warned are a central part of the federal deficit picture have emerged as controversial topics of policy debate. The Social Security Trust Fund and the Resolution Trust Corporation are at the heart of the policy debates regarding deficit policy at the beginning of the 1990s. Phantom attempts to achieve deficit targets by camouflaging spending as loan guarantees, by instituting tax policies that yield short-term revenue gains but long-term losses, and by invoking accounting tricks to balance one budget at the expense of the next only make the problem of budgetary balance more difficult. Real progress in deficit control requires political consensus to live with tax levels that are commensurate with expenditure demand. One lesson that the 1980s have not taught is how this can be achieved.

References

Aaron, H. J., B. P. Bosworth, and G. Burtless. 1989. *Can America afford to grow old?* Washington, D.C.: Brookings.

Auerbach, A. J., and J. M. Poterba. 1986. Why have corporate taxes declined? In *Tax policy and the economy,* vol. 1, ed. L. Summers. Cambridge, Mass.: MIT Press.

Barro, R. 1986. The behavior of United States deficits. In *The American business cycle: Continuity and change,* ed. R. J. Gordon. Chicago: University of Chicago Press.

Congressional Budget Office. 1990. *The economic and budget outlook: Fiscal years 1991–1995: An update.* Wasington, D.C., July.

Eisner, R. 1986. *How real is the federal deficit?* New York: Free Press.

Hambor, John C. 1987. Economic policy, intergenerational equity, and the Social Security Trust Fund buildup. *Social Security Bulletin* 50 (October): 13–18.

Lindsey, L. B. 1989. *The growth experiment.* New York: Basic.

Pellechio, A., and G. Goodfellow. 1983. Individual gains and losses from Social Security before and after the 1983 amendments. *Cato Journal* 3 (Fall): 417–42.

Poterba, J. M., and L. H. Summers. 1987. Finite lifetimes and the effects of budget deficits on national saving. *Journal of Monetary Economics* 20 (September): 369–92.

Stockman, D. A. 1986. *The triumph of politics.* New York: Harper & Row.

2. *David Stockman*

It occurred to me that to address the topic of budget policy in the 1980s is to be reminded of the words of Gandhi, when he was asked what he thought about Western civilization: "It would be a good idea," replied he.

Well, budget policy in the 1980s would have been a good idea too. But instead what we got was $1.5 trillion worth of cumulative deficits, radical deterioration of our internal and external financial health, and a political system that became so impaired, damaged, fatigued, and bloodied by coping with it year after year that it now functions like the parliament of a banana republic.

Now, my point of departure is that, for the thirty prior postwar period years leading to 1980, there was no real hint that this kind of fiscal carnage was possible in the American political system. Deficits tended to average about 1–2 percent of GNP. They ebbed and flowed with short-term economic and political cycles, and policy was relentlessly incrementalist in the sense that Senator Long invoked earlier when he said, "I voted for the ITC six times, three times for it and three agin." Policy continuously oscillated in a narrow channel, resulting in long-run fiscal equilibrium over three decades.

The contrasting radical breakdown in the 1980s will doubtless spawn decades of academic diagnosis, but, as a thoroughly biased, and therefore unreliable, participant, let me offer a four-point theory of what I think happened. The breakdown came in about four equal doses. One was a huge case of mistaken belief by the GOP in terms of its attitudes toward domestic spending (or toward what for shorthand purposes I'll designate in the rest of this presentation as its attitudes toward the welfare state). The second part of this breakdown was ideological mischief begotten by the supply-siders, particularly as they shaped and sized the original package.

The third part of the breakdown I would describe as a one-time, sixty-day breakdown in the normal partisan checks and balances of the fiscal process that led to the tax bidding war in June 1981, the auctioning off of a massive chunk of the revenue base in July, and the consequent 7 percent of GNP "hole in the budget" that became the defining condition of the 1980s.

The fourth part of the equation I would call the *steel wool effect* of a Madisonian (divided, fragmented) constitutional system. When major, polarizing domestic policy action is discretionary (e.g., national health insurance), the Madisonian system is conservative (i.e., it delays action and wears down the activist proponents). But, where such mega–policy actions are necessary and unavoidable (as in the 1980s budget breakdown), it generates an escalating level of friction and frustration. In the context of the 1980s deficit saga, it thus had the effect of rubbing raw, injuring, and debilitating the two political parties as they struggled year after year with the near impossible task of assembling majorities for the allocation and distribution of fiscal pain that was orders of magnitude larger than could be coped with in a single sitting or act of governance. Consequently, the fixing of this giant budget hole became a multiact ordeal that generated an accumulating level of mistrust, conflict, and demoralization within the system that paralyzes the process still today.

To understand these four factors, I found it useful to dial in on them through the lens of my ex-mentor (or, I should say, one of my ex-mentors since it seems I've had a fair number over the years) John Anderson and his penultimate question as an independent presidential candidate in 1980. "How could you slash taxes, pump up defense, and balance the budget all at the same time?" His answer was, "With mirrors." In hindsight, it seems that he was right. But I believe that that would be too easy and too ahistorical an explanation for the 1980s fiscal breakdown, one that ignores much of the important flavor and moods of early 1981 that actually shaped this process.

The reason that sane adults even entertained the Reagan macro budget proposition was that, until it was designed, sized, and executed into law, as a matter of mood, preference, and policy direction, it sounded right to much of the newly ascendant Republican government. So we introduce factor number one. The Republican party had become self-intoxicated by decades of its own chicken-dinner speeches and fulminations against big government. By 1981, it therefore had a willingness to believe that substantial blocks of domestic outlays could be excised from the budget and therefore that spending reduction would compose a viable part of a big sweeping change in the fiscal equation. Now, I will not dwell here on any war stories but just offer three facts and an obvious interpretation.

The facts have to do with the great center block of the budget, and I call this *the old people's budget* and *the poor people's budget*. The former consists of Social Security, Medicare, and the related retirement programs, the latter of AFDC, food stamps, Medicaid, the other means-tested income transfer programs, and a few social service programs.

Here are the three facts. First, in the early 1960s, the combination of the poor people's budget and the old people's budget cost 4 percent of GNP. Second, on the eve of this 1981 change in policy, the old people's budget and the poor people's budget cost 10 percent of GNP (1980). So, in a sense, in the intervening two decades there had been a series of policy decisions to allocate 6 percent of GNP away from the productive population of the country toward the old and poor, a policy decision that was obviously valid for a democratic government to make if it wished.

My third fact is that by 1986, after the Reagan revolution was all over except for the shouting, the old people's budget and the poor people's budget cost precisely 10 percent of GNP, exactly the same as it cost in 1980. There was no net change, just some minor reallocations on the margin from the poor to the old.

The meaning is that, after six years on the wrestling mat of big, real, painful fiscal choices, as opposed to twenty years on the chicken circuit of costless rhetoric, the Republican party, collectively, got up from the mat, dusted itself off, ran to the opposite corner, and embraced the status quo in the big fiscal center block programs—lock, stock, and barrel. This outcome of validating the domestic center block of the budget obviously destroyed the whole Reagan fiscal equation, period. But I think that the interesting question is why, in the heat of real-time politics, the Republican party collectively ate its rhetorical hymnbook, so to speak. Well, by 1984–85, I didn't really have much to do any more, so I undertook an exhaustive study, brick by brick, of the political process by which this 6 percent reallocation in the center block—from 4 to 10 percent of GNP to the old people's budget and the poor people's budget—had occurred over the preceding twenty years. The result, I think, was quite interesting.

Most of that reallocation occurred in the old people's budget, as you can imagine, and, in fact, it was the result of thirteen major legislative acts between the late 1950s and the late 1970s. So I analyzed the voting record on these major acts—Medicare, Medicaid, the 1972 Social Security Amendments, the expansion of disability insurance, and so forth. Collectively over the period, the Republican vote in the Senate on these thirteen major acts was 90 percent yes, 10 percent no. The House Republicans were a little more conservative— the collective vote over the twenty-one-year period was 80 percent yes, 20 percent no. In short, the Republican party had been the coarchitects over the previous twenty years of this massive and permanent change in the center block of the domestic budget. Now that was on the social insurance or old people's budget side.

If you look at the record on the poor people's budget, it was even more interesting. In 1962, all these programs that are included in this heading cost $15 billion (in 1986 dollars). By 1980, they had increased nearly eightfold to $112 billion, and that was the other piece of the center block that had to be confronted when the new policy was put into place. I thought that it would be interesting to see when this growth had occurred—a $100 billion change from $15 billion to $112 billion over those eighteen years—and here are the answers. Of this growth, $16 billion occurred during the big spending wave of the Carter administration and $27 billion during the runaway spending period of Kennedy-Johnson, leaving a mere $54 billion, or well over half, to have occurred in the Nixon-Ford watch.

So again, the Republican party, both as to the administrations and as to the ranking members of most of the relevant committees of jurisdiction in the House and the Senate, had been coarchitects of the other piece of the center block.

I think that this is significant because, in 1980, the entire remainder of the budget, other than this 10 percent old people's and poor people's budget, was 13.2 percent of GNP, and interest and defense were 7 percent. Thus, there was 6 percent left for all other domestic programs. And, of that 6 percent, most of it consisted either of what all of us would agree were legitimate functions of government, such as lighthouses or the FBI, or of what I would call the discretionary pocket change that is necessary to lubricate a political democracy.

As a matter of fact, if you look at that 6 percent residual and just take one major piece, the agriculture, veterans, education, transportation, public works, and local economic development programs at 1986 prices, you will find the following. Under the Carter or pre-Reagan policy that was in effect in January 1981, had these policies and programs remained unchanged, they would have cost $150 billion (in consistent 1986 budget prices). In 1986, when the Reagan "cutting" was all over, the Reagan actual policy—when the dollars were totaled up at the end of 1986 for the same set of agriculture, veterans, education, transportation, and public works program—was not $150 billion; it was $140 billion. So, in these programs, partisan differences as to funding and policy over the period 1981–86 were microscopic.

Now, I'm not trying to gainsay $10 billion in budget savings. That was not easy to get. But, from a fiscal policy viewpoint, when you have knocked a $200 billion hole in the revenue side of the equation, also at 1986 prices, a $10 billion spending cut in the secondary part of the budget and no change in the center block are really not a lot to write home about.

This is apparently what the public wanted, so I'm not reciting all this to moralize or even condemn the special interest groups. In fact, I think that the result was a legitimate referendum, in a sense, on all these programs year after year, as they were set up, debated, and left mostly intact in the legislative process. My point is that part of the reason that we set off down what turned out to be an imprudent course in 1980 was that the Republican party at that moment in time was suffering from a kind of cumulative, cognitive dissonance about "runaway spending" that in early 1981 gave an implausible fiscal equation and air of plausibility.

The second factor, the ideological mischief, I can cover very quickly. And here I'm not arguing with the content of the supply-side economics because it was pretty obvious and unobjectionable. But I do take issue with its militant rejection of incrementalism as an approach to policy, the militant rejection of one-year-at-a-time fine-tuning and its attempted replacement with radical multiyear structural change in the major revenue, defense, and domestic components of the budget.

The problem with radical, structural, multiyear change was that it required the policy process to undertake an impossible act. And that was to forecast this massive hunk of GNP called the U.S. economy that floats around in an open world financial system three to five years into the distant future with some precision. This, of course, gets us to "Rosy Scenario," the most fabulous forecasting error in human history, in which, for the relevant period in which these sweeping changes were being made, fiscal 1982–86, we overpredicted GNP by the precise sum of $2.145 trillion. Now, that was cumulative, but, on a final year basis, 1986, it meant that the forecast of money GNP was $660 billion higher than what actually turned out. Now, you remember that, in a pre-Reagan unindexed tax system, we took in about 30 percent of the marginal dollar of money GNP in revenue. So, when we overpriced the GNP by $660 billion, we overestimated the revenue base by over $200 billion. This had two effects. First, it gave the illusion, as this architecture was being constructed, that we were cutting prospective surpluses, and that didn't seem like such a dangerous thing.

Second, the administration was not alone in the $2.1 trillion massive overshoot of where the outyear GNP and revenue base would be. The far more realistic and sober Congressional Budget Office (CBO) forecast of March 1981—and they had a month more to think about this—overestimated the five-year GNP by only $1.7 trillion rather than $2 trillion. But the effect on the revenue base of all this massive overforecasting of long-run money GNP was basically to disconnect the alarm systems in the political and fiscal process and lead to a course of events that should not have happened.

Specifically, if you go back to Rosy Scenario and price out the pre-Reagan tax policy to 1986—and this is in the documents from February 1981—you will see that, under that forecast of the GNP, the projected "old law" tax take was going to be 24 percent of GNP. Then, if you priced out the pure proposed Reagan tax cuts, 10–10–10 and 10–5–3, it was going to reduce the tax base by 4.5 percent of GNP. Twenty-four minus 4.5 was going to get you to 19.5 percent—when it was all done. And a 19.5 percent tax take was, in turn, the golden mean of the previous thirty years of fiscal history in the United States. So the outcome as then projected, with these faulty views of the future, was not crazy but more or less in line with where we had been.

My point here is that, if you do some reverse fiscal engineering, and take the world that actually occurred, and look backward and price out the pre-Reagan tax policy from a 1986 vantage point looking back—because the money GNP was massively lower (as to both output and prices)—the pre-Reagan policy generated less than 22 percent of GNP in taxes in the world that actually occurred. If you then expanded the tax cut that resulted from the bidding war that we discussed, from 4.5 to nearly 6 percent of GNP, you ended up, not at the gold mean (19.5 percent), but with a outyear revenue base by fiscal year 1986 that amounted to 16.9 percent of GNP, the lowest level since 1939!

Then, if you bump the spending side, which had been about 20 percent over the postwar period, by 1 percent for defense (a little that we were going to restore), and if you add to that a 2 percent bump in interest expense as these massive deficits materialize, both actually and prospectively, you end up with a budget equation in which the outlay side is locked at 24 percent and the revenue side at 17 percent. There was a 7 percent "hole" that became the whole history thereafter.

The third factor was how the bidding war got so out of hand. Well, I think that the fatal act probably occurred on 12 January 1981, if you want to be precise. On that particular night, there was a meeting of what we then euphemistically called the "College of Cardinals." Those were the long-standing, middle-of-the-road, incrementalist Republican leaders—Senators Howard Baker, Peter Domenici, Mark Hatfield, and Bob Dole, Representative Bob Michel, and so forth—who basically had great fears and uneasiness about the whole plan. They couldn't quantify it, but they knew in their bones that radical multi-year tax cuts were a dangerous thing. As a matter of fact, because of that, 10–10–10 didn't have a snowball's chance.

It was in this context that a major, once-in-a-decade kind of political bargain was struck in Senator Baker's library. It was agreed that supply-side was the right policy direction: the marginal rates were too high, the economy needed supply-side stimulus, but—and here is the key point—the *size of the tax cut* would have to be earned by the prior enactment of a *multiyear spending cut package*. Once the latter was done, then we would see how much tax cut we could afford. Would it be a 15 percent, a 20 percent, or a 25 percent rate cut? The size of the spending cut success would drive the shape of the executed tax plan, as opposed to the paper document.

Now again, this seemed utterly plausible. I heartily embraced that formula myself and sold it in the White House because I was only a half-breed supply-sider anyway. The other half was kind of recidivist Hooverite.

Now, this sensible formula led to a derailment in May 1981, in my judgment, when, against all odds, the Gramm-Latta or White House Republican Dixiecrat version of the spending cut piece, the first proposition, which had to be shaped and sized, passed the House despite the Democrats having a majority. This had two powerful effects. First, it further anesthetized the "College of Cardinals" as to the incipient fiscal dangers. The experience of real budget cutting was novel and alien—after all, they had been distributing goodies for twenty years. What was recorded by the CBO as $35 billion in cuts felt politically to them like it was $50 billion or $100 billion, so bruised and battered were they when the smoke cleared on the budget resolutions and reconciliation bills. In fact, the permanent cut turned out to be less than $20 billion (after it could all be measured a few years later). Some of it was pure legerdemain at the time, such as taking SPRO (the Strategic Petroleum Reserve) off budget, a big $3 billion savings, and a lot of it got incrementally repealed and put back into the budget in a process of hostage taking over the next three or four years. We couldn't and didn't know at the time that the rule of multiyear budgeting is that, for every dollar you cut, at best sixty cents is permanently saved.

So my point is that what felt like a $50 billion cut politically ended up a $20 billion cut in reality—not very much, but it came at the crucial moment in late May when we were about ready to launch the tax process. The feeling of accomplishment on the budget-cutting package became a vast exaggeration of reality mainly because the legislative experience had been so jarring and so traumatic. Consequently, the guard came down even further among the "College of Cardinals."

The second consequence was that the House Democrats lost control of the House on something really important for the first time in twenty-seven years. In fact, they had been crushed and humiliated in a political sense. And, as we went into the next phase of this logical process—spending first, size the tax cut, do the latter later—the Democrats turned out to have one and only one objective in mind, and that was recouping their manhood and political power in the House. Thus, on the crucial date of 4 June, when the choice came down to bipartisan compromise or an auction on the tax bill, both sides were brittle, recalcitrant, and breathing partisan fire. The irony is that, once the auction route was chosen, rather than compromise, the congressional Democrats spent the next thirty days savaging the tax code, which was totally against their long-run interest, and then spent the thirty days of July passing out hundreds of billions in tax goodies to Republican interest groups, which, in retrospect, was nothing short of insane.

This leads to my fourth point. There we were with a 7 percent of GNP hole in the budget, spending at 24 percent, revenue at 17 percent, and there was only one thing to do—spend the next decade raising taxes and restoring and replenishing the revenue base, since there was no spending left to cut, as history subsequently proved. Now, for the next thirty months (after August 1981), the restoration of the revenue base turned out to be a quite heroic chapter in U.S. history. The center of both parties rallied to the unpleasant job of raising taxes. Almost everyone in the White House joined in the work of tax raising, except for the guys who wore the Adam Smith ties and, unfortunately, the guy who had to sign the tax bills. But, in any event, over this thirty-month period, we passed the Tax Equity and Fiscal Responsibility Act (TEFRA); something like $50 billion in revenue replenishment in the outyears; a Social Security tax bill that had a lot of revenue, direct and indirect, in it, including the upper income recapture of taxes; the Deficit Reduction Act (DEFRA) in 1984; and so forth.

By July 1984, we had replenished the revenue base on a 1986 price basis, back to 19.5 percent of GNP, the golden mean, where we had started way back in 1980. But then, the 22 percent policy spending level that was built into the budget had ballooned to 24 percent because of the accumulating interest, and we still had a huge hole. Moreover, Mr. Madison's contraption, the constitutional system that absolutely frustrates the assembly of governing majorities, had taken its toll.

From a conservative viewpoint, the great virtue of our system is that it prevents governments from acting and therefore prevents a great deal of mischief. And that is OK under ordinary conditions of balance. But we needed majorities to rectify a massive, artificial imbalance, and, in a sense, the political process became impaled on the mechanism.

As a result, there was only one way to get these year-after-year tax bills through the labyrinth of our process, and that was a combination of browbeating and furious wheeling and dealing. But after two and a half years of forced march back up the unpleasant political hill of tax raising, the collective system was seething with grievances, bruises, irritations, and a sense of huge unfairness because much of what had been done at the policy level on tax restoration had absolutely no rhyme or reason. The justification for most of it was that we had to put something in the collection plate, and we did whatever was possible.

Now, in this context, after July 1984, the system went into full paralysis owing to one blunder and one big lie. The first blunder was obviously Mondale and his error of speaking the truth out loud in public early in the campaign in 1984. But what compounded and put the system into paralysis from that point forward was a second factor, what I call the *big lie:* the last destructive act of the supply-siders before they faded into the dustbin of history.

In about July 1984, they convinced Meese and the president that they had been badly double-crossed in the "three-for-one" spending and tax-raising deal in the 1982 TEFRA. This claim is not even debatable. It was a blatant lie. But it split the Republican party into two camps, with one camp under Mr. Vladimir Ilyich Gingrich [a reference to Representative Newt Gingrich], leading the Republican backbench true believers off on a partisan stab-in-the-back campaign that had nothing to do with reality.

But, in any event, over the next five years, the Democratic tax raisers that the system needed went deep into their bunkers, while Gingrichites, posing as the fiscal equivalent of Whittaker Chambers, stood outside the door with their antitax M-16s at the ready. Now, in my judgment, incalculable damage was done by these fiscal gunslingers because the entire remainder of this long business expansion of five years was squandered and the remainder of the problem didn't get fixed.

As the draftsman and the accountant for the three-to-one deal that gave rise to the "big lie" and the ultimate paralysis and the fix that we are in today, I would like to conclude by setting the record straight. There was $300 billion in multiyear spending cuts planned against $100 billion in tax increases. But, of the $300 billion, $100 billion of that was debt service savings, half legitimate and half a little artifact or expedient that was manufactured at the time. A debt service savings of $50 billion would occur if you closed the policy gap by raising revenues or cutting spending—it was legitimate.

The other $50 billion was a result of a convention adopted in the bipartisan negotiating process that, if we were to make this fundamental change in course and fix this huge gap, interest rates would drop 2 percent over a period of time, and the deficit would be $50 billion lower.

Now, by the time we got to 1984, the latter had already occurred and would continue to occur over the remainder of the three or four years. The supply-siders chose not to count that fact. Much of the other $50 billion also occurred because most of the policy changes were actually made. That's the first $100 billion: most of the debt service savings actually occurred. The next $50 billion was "management savings." That could not possibly have happened because, on a full-year, fully effective basis, it would have required firing one of every two non–Department of Defense civilian employees in the federal govern-ment—and, at that particular time, we were fighting drug wars and crime wars and a lot of other things, and we needed more people rather than fewer. That $50 billion did not happen, but it got put in the package because it had been in the administration's January 1982 budget—and had been invented twelve hours before the printing deadline to avoid sending the first $100 billion deficit rec-ommendation in history to Congress. And that had occurred, in turn, because, at the last minute, the president and Meese had gotten religion from the Cham-ber of Commerce and dropped a $50 billion package of excise tax increases.

The third $50 billion was defense. Every dime of this happened, except Cap Weinberger did not want to count it or acknowledge it, so therefore it was believed by the White House that that part of the spending deal had been lost as well.

The next $70 billion of that cut consisted of discretionary domestic appro-priated programs that were supposed to be cut over a three-year period. Most of this did not occur, but one of the reasons was that every single appropriations bill from TEFRA through the 1984 campaign was *signed* by the president be-cause the White House believed that it might not be good for the reelection campaign not to sign. As a consequence, that $70 billion probably didn't hap-pen, but it didn't want to happen in terms of the posture that the White House took on all the bills.

The other tiny remainder was $30 billion in entitlements cuts, of which $19 billion was actually enacted. So, if you go through all this, you end up with $11 billion slippage of the $300 billion target. Not bad. And it seems to me that to call this some grave stab in the back is indeed nothing less than a "big lie."

From that point forward, the Democrats were in the bunkers, and back-benchers from the Republican party in the House were on the outside, so we had paralysis, in effect, for five years. I think that, in this whole sad chapter, there is a positive outcome here. It ended on 14 June 1990, when Bush finally moved his lips. I think it constituted the first step in the Republican return to adulthood as far as fiscal policy matters are concerned. Undoubtedly, there will be some misfires along the way. But, with both parties out of the bunkers or the closet on the fundamental problem of restoring the tax base, rational dis-course was once again recommenced, a process of adult negotiation is slowly resuming, and, over a period of a few years in my judgment, the remaining correction will eventually be made.

The 1980s fiscal breakdown, therefore, constitutes a detour in history. It does not require any change in the process. It does not say that there's a fundamental disease in our political democracy. It says that there were a series of accidents and incidents that were unfortunate but that are now, even as we meet here, in the process of being remedied.

3. *Charles Schultze*

After listening to David Stockman, I don't know where to start. He already said many of the same things I was prepared to say, and with greater insider's knowledge. It appears that a recidivist Stevensonian and a recidivist Hooverite interpret the same facts the same way.

The letter of invitation suggested that I give my impressions of what drove policy decisions during the 1980s, what options were chosen, and why certain policies were followed rather than others. But, while it may surprise and amaze you, I was not consulted very much by the Reagan policymakers. What inside information I do have comes from reading the same leaks in the *Post,* the *Times,* and the *Wall Street Journal* and from the memoirs to which all of you have had access, spiced only occasionally by a few tidbits of gossip from friends on the Hill. I decided, therefore, to concentrate primarily on an attempt to put the 1980s budget policy into a historical and institutional context. By coincidence, this also happens to provide additional background and further support for some of Dave Stockman's observations.

In stark outline, my major thesis is simple. The American political system has tremendous inertia. It is terribly hard to get things done. And the budget-making component of that political system shares the inertia. Contrary to popular myth and public choice theory, the budget system does not have a bias that tends routinely to produce excessively large expenditures, taxes, or deficits. One characteristic of an inertial political system like ours, however, is that, while it is very hard to make a big mistake, once you make a large one, the inertia also works against correcting it. And 1981 was one big mistake! Since 1982 we have been fighting the inertia. This systemic problem was compounded by the particular beliefs of two presidents. The first one believed that, next to nuclear war, the worst thing that could ever happen to a country was a tax increase (and he wasn't quite sure about the ranking). The second one, at least up until 14 June 1990, appeared to have inherited a paler version of the same belief.

Let me fill in a little of this outline. The American political system of divided powers shares with the Japanese and the Swiss the characteristic that it takes a large degree of consensus to get anything substantial done, compared to other major industrial countries, whose parliamentary systems can move much more rapidly and without the need for as wide a consensus. In fact, the inertia of our system is usually a virtue. The great majority of what elected officials, and often a majority of the population, would like to do in the first flush of enthusiasm is almost always wrong. It is not a coincidence that the United States and Japan have by far the lowest share of government spending in GNP among the major industrial countries. From table 4.13, you can see that government spending in the United States and Japan is 10–30 percent lower than in other countries. If we exclude defense, the Untied States is lower than Japan. And the U.S. growth in the government spending share over the past fifteen to twenty years has been the lowest of all the other countries.

The political and institutional inertia that I noted above clearly applies to the budget process. Contrary to the public choice literature, it is a myth that the democratic majoritarian process of making budgets through congressional processes biases the government toward spending too much and borrowing excessively to do so. Table 4.14 provides additional evidence. It divides the budget into two parts: (i) outlays and revenues of the Social Security Trust Fund (including hospital insurance) and (ii) everything else, which for simplicity let's call "the general operating budget." The postwar years were indeed marked by a very large increase in Social Security expenditures and revenues relative to

Table 4.13   **Six Countries' Government Spending as a Share of GNP, Selected Years, 1965–86[a] (%)**

	1965	1970	1980	1986
United States				
Total	27.8	32.2	34.1	37.2
Excluding defense	20.7	24.9	28.8	30.5
Japan				
Total	19.1	19.1	32.1	33.0
Excluding defense	N.A.	18.3	31.2	32.1
France				
Total	N.A.	44.5	47.0	52.9
Excluding defense	N.A.	41.2	43.7	49.7
Germany				
Total	36.9	39.0	48.8	47.2
Excluding defense	N.A.	36.1	46.0	44.5
Sweden				
Total	N.A.	43.7	62.0	64.9
Excluding defense	N.A.	40.4	58.9	62.3
United Kingdom				
Total	35.9	39.5	45.2	46.0
Excluding defense	N.A.	N.A.	40.3	41.2

Note: N.A. = Not available.

[a]All levels of government.

Table 4.14   **Budget Outlays and Revenues as a Share of GNP, Fiscal Years, 1955–90 (%)**

Budget Components	1955	1960	1965	1970	1975	1980	1985	1990
Total budget[a]								
Outlays	17.7	18.2	17.6	19.8	21.8	22.1	23.9	21.9
Revenues	16.9	18.3	17.4	19.5	18.3	19.4	18.6	19.6
Of which:								
Social Security[b]								
Outlays	1.1	2.2	2.5	3.5	4.7	5.3	5.9	5.7
Revenues	1.4	2.1	2.6	4.2	5.1	5.3	6.2	7.2
General operating								
Outlays	16.7	16.2	15.2	16.5	17.4	17.0	18.2	16.8
Revenues	15.6	16.3	14.9	15.6	13.5	14.2	12.7	12.9

[a]Total outlays and revenues are smaller than the sum of the two components because intrafund transactions such as payments from the general fund to the Social Security fund are netted out in the total.
[b]Includes outlays and revenues of the old age and survivors, disability, and hospital insurance trust funds.

the size of the economy and, of course, far in excess of what would have been required simply by a maturing of the system in effect forty years ago. But, rightly or wrongly, wisely or unwisely, the American people have overwhelmingly approved this expansion and have been willing to pay the full tax burden of supporting the system. Look, for example, at public acceptance of the changes legislated in 1983. Voters did not rebel against the bipartisan decision to adopt a payroll tax schedule sufficient to begin accumulating substantial surpluses in the fund. The Social Security and Medicare system is overwhelmingly popular, and its expansion appears to reflect pretty accurately the will of the electorate rather than some defect in the political system à la public choice theory.

Social Security and Medicare apart, the general operating budget of the federal government, as shown in table 4.14, has remained a virtually stable share of GNP since at least 1955 (the major exception, ironically, being the large increase in the first five years of the Reagan administration). Similarly, the share of general revenues in GNP did not rise in the postwar years: indeed, it fell.

If you now look at table 4.15 you can see that, within the totals of the general operating budget, there appears to be another rule of thumb that governs long-run budget outcomes—the share of GNP taken by civilian program spending rises to absorb any major decreases in the defense share but does not rise in the absence of such defense reductions. In particular, sustained rises in the civilian budget share were not financed through tax increases or deficits. Even when the unexpected occurred—for example, large increases in Part B of Medicare and in Medicaid over their projected levels—the response was to

Table 4.15   **Federal Government General Operating Outlays as a Share of GNP, Selected Fiscal Years, 1955–90 (%)**

Category	1955	1960	1965	1970	1975	1980	1985	1990
Total	16.7	16.2	15.2	16.5	17.4	17.0	18.2	16.8
Defense	11.1	9.5	7.5	8.3	5.7	5.0	6.4	5.4
Nondefense	5.6	6.7	7.7	8.2	11.7	12.0	11.8	11.3
Net interest	1.4	1.5	1.4	1.6	1.8	2.1	3.4	3.7
. Civilian programs	4.2	5.2	6.3	6.6	9.9	9.9	8.4	7.6

squeeze these overruns out of the other spending. The application of this general rule by Congress and the administration kept the total operating budget at a roughly constant percentage of GNP.

The popular view that Congress traditionally tended to outspend presidentially requested budgets is principally a myth. In a 1985 article, Paul Peterson analyzed appropriation requests and enactments (including supplementals) from 1947 through 1984. He found that, over the thirty-eight years, the Congress, on average, *cut* $800 million from the president's budget requests. Interestingly, the Congress increased defense appropriations on average while cutting civilian by enough to achieve an overall reduction.

Peterson notes some limitations to his conclusions. Conceivably, the Congress might have spent a lot more, had it not been for the threat of a presidential veto. The Congress does have a nice habit of initiating new projects, and, once projects are started, presidents feel obliged to request appropriations to complete them. Water resource projects are a good case in point.

The Peterson analysis does not include entitlements. But it is far from obvious how that omission affects the conclusion. For example, as Peterson pointed out, the Congress turned down both Nixon and Carter's welfare reform programs, and, as I noted above, it forced the rest of the budget to eat Medicaid and supplemental medical insurance (SMI) overruns. So, despite some qualifications, I think the conclusion stands. In the aggregate, Congress did not increase the president's budget, at least not by enough to make any macroeconomic difference.

There is also the popular view that, in the absence of an indexed tax system before 1985, the bracket creep caused by nominal GNP growth produced a continuing rise in the average effective rate of the personal income tax, which the Congress then spent. That is also a myth. Periodically, those revenues were given back in tax cuts. Indeed, if anything, the tax cuts were somewhat too generous. As you can see, going back to table 4.14, general revenues as a share of GNP actually declined slightly over the thirty-five years prior to 1980 and would show a long-run decline even if we had corrected for the recessions of 1975 and 1981. The average effective tax rates of the federal personal income tax fluctuated closely around a mean of 10 percent of personal income from 1947 to 1980. From 1976 to 1980, it averaged a little above that, at 10.5 percent. But, in essence, the average personal income tax rate did not drift upward as alleged; potential creep was offset by periodic rate cuts. Now, clearly, the country was due for another rate cut in 1980 because the average rate had begun to move up. And, within the long-term stability of the average rate, the marginal rate had risen. But, about the magnitude of the 1981 tax cut, one can only apply the remark alleged to have been made by John Jacob Astor, standing in the lounge of the Titanic when ice from the iceberg began cascading on deck: "Bartender, I know I asked for ice, but this is ridiculous!"

In sum, prior to the 1980s the United States had a political and budget-making system under which there had been a large, and apparently quite popular, parallel expansion in Social Security outlays and revenues but that had been quite effective in holding all other budget outlays to a remarkably stable and, by international standards at least, modest fraction of the nation's GNP. Adjusted for the business cycle, budget deficits were seldom a major problem. From a macroeconomic standpoint, the budget process was quite workable. There were micro problems that we all know about, problems that existed then and have continued: pork barrel allocation of projects, parochialism, and unwillingness to call a halt to projects that prove wanting. But, in the aggregate, the system has been quite successful in keeping a lid on the fraction of the economy claimed by the government. The sins of the budget and of the Congress were mainly micro sins, not macro sins.

In 1981, that macro inertia was broken through by the Reagan revolution. And, as David Stockman so nicely put it, the largest impact came in the first two months—the 1981 tax cut, combined with the launching of a massive four-year buildup in defense spending. The root of the error was not simply a bad forecast within the limits of the optimism typically displayed by those proposing policy changes. I have in my files a March 1981 Treasury release, outlining all the great things that were going to happen were the tax cut realized. What it promised was that gross private domestic investment, as a share of GNP, would rise from 15.7 percent to 19.9 percent over the next five years. The share (measured in current dollars) actually remained constant until 1986, and then fell, to less than 15 percent. The release projected that business fixed investment would rise from 11.5 to 15 percent and promised other aspects of performance well outside the range of historical experience. (Mind you, this was not the initial rosy scenario; this was the result after Murray Wiedenbaum and other people had cut back the even more ambitious promises of the initial projections.) The essential mistake was the reliance on the absolutely unwarranted hype of supply-side ideologues rather than on the failure to achieve a reasonable target for budget-cutting.

Once the mistake had been made—in response to an unusually charismatic president with a large electoral margin—the inertia of the system worked against correcting the mistake. And, as I said, the inertia was coupled with the fact of having had two presidents who were adamantly opposed to the tax increase needed to deal with the problem.

Let me make one final set of comments about the budget history of the 1980s. If you look at table 4.15 again, you will see that the 1980s did succeed in reducing significantly the GNP share of civilian spending programs (outside Social Security). As a share of GNP, that spending was reduced from 9.9 percent of GNP in 1980 to 7.6 in 1990, a drop of 2.3 percentage points. A small part of the drop may be due to the fact that 1980 was a year of minirecession, but the decline adjusted for that fact is still some 2 percentage points. About 60 percent of that decline in the civilian spending share was achieved by huge cuts in a limited number of programs. I had thought until recently that the cuts in the share of civilian spending in GNP were principally the result of penny-pinching everywhere with little selectivity. But, as can be seen in table 4.16, there were indeed some very substantial selective cuts in programs that we might label the "losers." And, of the 2 percentage point reduction in the share of non–Social Security civilian spending in GNP, about 60 percent came from these losers. A number of large programs were, if not eliminated, virtually eliminated or cut back very substantially.

Some may look at these data and conclude that, at least in one respect, the Reagan revolution and the large deficits it produced were successful; they forced the inertial system into sharp reductions in low-priority programs. So, you might conclude, we got something for the deficits, even if the revolution did not deliver on its other promises. But think again. Look back at table 4.15. You will notice that interest on the public debt expanded to fill two-thirds of the decline in civilian operating programs. Not all of that expansion in interest payments was directly and indirectly due to the deficits, but a large fraction was. So, to the extent that the large deficits can be seen as a strategy, forcing a decline in civilian spending, it was an incredibly expensive one. It ended up replacing program spending, the benefits of which may indeed have been smaller than its costs, with interest payments on the debt, which provide no benefits whatsoever.

Table 4.16   Major "Losers" in the Budget

	1980	1990
Total losers[a]	1.5	.3
Total "losers"[b]	63.4	13.8
Energy (excluding R&D)	10.9	.1
Community and regional development	17.8	6.4
Training and employment	16.2	5.3
General revenue sharing	13.6	1.8
International financial programs	3.8	−.3
Education and training of health care workers	1.1	.5

[a]Percentage of GNP.
[b]Billions of 1992 dollars.

Summary of Discussion

Martin Feldstein initiated the discussion by describing how nondefense discretionary spending by the federal government has changed over time. This category of spending, which excludes Social Security and other entitlement programs, grew steadily as a share of national output over several decades and reached almost 6 percent of GNP in 1980. But the trend was sharply reversed during the Reagan administration, and, by the mid-1980s, this type of spending had fallen to less than 4 percent of GNP. In light of this turnaround, Feldstein thought that Stockman had understated his achievements as budget director when he said that it had been impossible to achieve significant spending reductions.

Feldstein wondered what had changed in public attitudes and in the Congress that had made such a dramatic shift politically acceptable. It was not, he believed, a fear of budget deficits because the spending reductions had begun with the Gramm-Latta law, which predated the rise in the deficit.

David Stockman disagreed with Feldstein's interpretation of the spending numbers. He argued that it was not appropriate just to compare overall spending before and during the Reagan administration. Rather, the appropriate comparison was between actual spending under the Reagan administration and an estimate of how much pre-Reagan policies would have cost in that same year. He gave one example of such a comparison—the cost of a large set of programs that included almost everything in the discretionary budget was $150 billion in 1980 and $140 billion, adjusted for inflation, in 1986. This was clearly not a big decline.

Stockman also said that a few programs had been introduced in 1979 and 1980 that had temporarily ballooned 1980 spending. These included countercyclical assistance through general revenue sharing, a large public service jobs program, and a surge of research funded by the Energy Department. Because these programs were not part of the "settled, long-standing consensus" about domestic spending, they were easily excised in the 1981 budget and did not reemerge. Although Stockman thought that it had been important to eliminate these temporary items, this should not obscure the fact that the core of domestic spending—the items he had termed the "old people's and poor people's" budget—had not been reduced in the 1980s.

Michael Mussa disagreed, saying that political pressures had in fact produced significant changes in spending during the 1980s. He said that one could always *claim* that the increases in spending on Social Security and Medicare and other programs in the 1960s and 1970s were a permanent part of the budget, while the programs that had been enacted later in the 1970s were temporary because they had been scheduled to disappear. But it seemed to Mussa that one could prove almost anything with that sort of analysis. He argued that, if one looked carefully at programs for the poor and at many discretionary components of spending, there had been very substantial cuts in those programs as a share of GNP and that there had been substantial pain associated with the cuts.

Two large programs had not been restrained in the 1980s, however. First, it had proved to be impossible to alter Social Security substantially. The Democrats had fought any change, and President Reagan and the Republicans had decided not to pay the political cost of addressing the issue. Second, Medicare was taking an exploding share of the budget, although the need to reduce the budget deficit had finally resulted in pressure on doctors and hospitals to contain that spending. Mussa believed that this action might augur future attempts to decrease the contribution of the working-age population in support of the elderly population.

Mussa added that every president for over twenty years had campaigned on a platform of reducing government spending. Although it is politically very hard to cut spending, it is also politically hard to raise taxes, so it is difficult to know how large a government the public truly wants.

Feldstein stressed Mussa's point that the "temporary" spending of the later 1970s could easily have become a permanent part of the budget. Further, whenever temporary spending programs had expired in the past, new programs had been introduced that continued the overall increases in discretionary spending.

Stockman argued that there had been no reason for discretionary spending to continue growing in the 1980s. In particular, the caseloads of most discretionary programs were not growing, so there was no reason that this spending should have grown in absolute terms and maintained its share of GNP. The appropriate measure of policy change is whether the absolute dollars being spent in 1980 changed in real terms by 1986. And the answer is not very much. Stockman also emphasized his view that there are no significant reductions in domestic spending that anybody in Congress would even talk about now in public, much less vote for. He had knocked on many doors of tiny and obscure programs over eight years, and even the Republicans did not want to cut any of them. In the recent budget package, the only domestic spending reductions were based on "beating up on the doctors," which is just a game because they raise the expected prices under Medicare every year before cutting them.

Feldstein reiterated that one could look at any five-year historical period and say that there was no reason for discretionary spending to have increased, but it had consistently increased anyway.

Stockman repeated his view that the chief source of growth in nondefense spending from 1960 to 1980 was in the "old people's budget and the poor people's budget." Even apart from Social Security, the big growth was in Medicare and Medicaid. Stockman said that Schultze's table 4.16 showed all the significant spending reductions in the 1980s, and they were in a very limited list of programs amounting to about 1.5 percent of GNP.

Charles Schultze added that he believed that the administration had reduced spending by an additional 1 percent of GNP by "penny-pinching" in other programs, meaning that the growth in spending was held to inflation or a little less while the real economy was growing.

Schultze then returned to Feldstein's opening comment that a fear of deficits had not been the driving force in reducing spending. Schultze believed that, to the contrary, the existence of huge budget deficits for eight years had prevented even the big spenders in Congress from calling for new programs or additional spending. This had been a bad way to reduce spending because the resulting deficits meant that the country simply spent more now on interest.

Feldstein asked Stockman to comment on the theory that the administration had deliberately created large deficits in order to apply the pressure on spending of which Schultze had spoken.

Stockman said that the theory is not correct and is not supported by the evidence. First, the "rosy scenario" that had projected shrinking deficits under the administration's budget plan had been publicly debated for months before the plan was enacted. Second, Congress had not based its actions on the administration's rosy scenario but had used the Congressional Budget Office (CBO) forecast instead. So it was ridiculous to argue that the administration's plan had been pushed through Congress "by stealth." Stockman did not think that anybody had had the idea that they were creating a huge deficit that would be a great disciplining mechanism for Congress; he agreed with Schultze, however, that the 1981 fiscal changes did have that effect.

Stockman also reiterated his view that there had been no fundamental change in public or congressional attitudes about the core of government spending. He said that the spending numbers overwhelmingly proved this point.

Feldstein asked Schultze whether he knew why the CBO had aided and abetted the rosy scenario. *Schultze* responded that it is human nature in that kind of job not to fly too much against the proposals of a popular president. One comes to believe that there is something to the proposals, and one does not want to lose credibility by opposing them entirely. *Feldstein* noted that a large part of the error in projecting the deficit was due to an inflation forecast that was actually too *pessimistic.* The forecasters greatly overestimated nominal GNP, and thus tax revenue, because nobody believed that the Fed was going to bring inflation down so quickly.

Stockman added that nobody in government ever predicts a recession, although *Rudolph Penner* said that the CBO had predicted a recession for 1979 and that, because they had been wrong at the time, they were more reluctant to be pessimistic in the early 1980s. *Feldstein* said that the Council of Economic Advisers (CEA) had projected a 1 percent GNP growth rate for the first quarter of 1983 because they did not want to forecast negative growth and one was the smallest integer. Then the recovery began, and the "true supply-siders" disparaged the "gloom and doomers" in the CEA for not appreciating the economy's true growth potential.

Schultze described five theories that had evolved in support of the tax cuts of the early 1980s. The first was a pure supply-side theory: the economic growth that would result from a substantial reduction in taxes will not make up the lost revenue entirely but will come close. In other words, the country could "grow out of" the deficit. Schultze recalled that, as a presidential candidate, Ronald Reagan had once said that the country could finance the defense buildup with the extra revenue gained from the tax cuts. The second theory, of which Stockman had spoken, was that spending could be reduced to match the lower tax revenue. The third theory, introduced when the first two did not work, was that deficits do not matter anyway. Then the fourth theory was that, even if deficits did matter, they were still very useful in holding down spending. At some point, President Reagan had said that the way to reduce your kids' spending is to give them a smaller allowance—and Congress was the kids. And the final theory was that, even if the other four theories are not right, the deficits are less harmful than the tax increases that would be necessary to eliminate them.

James Poterba noted another feature of budget policy in the early 1980s, which was that, despite the burgeoning deficits, there had also been a growth in political support for various kinds of budget-balancing initiatives. The Balanced Budget Amendment probably reached its highest level of support in 1982, and, although it was not approved by Congress, the country did end up with the Gramm-Rudman law in its various forms, institutionalizing a form of budgetary brinksmanship that the country was still living through.

Poterba wondered what set of political expectations had generated this support for balanced budget rules. Was it a view that the government would not actually follow through on the budget targets being enacted? Was it a view that the government would at some point substantially reduce spending? Or was it a reluctant recognition even in the early 1980s that the government would at some point need to undo the big tax cuts and that this was just a way of precommiting to do so?

Penner said that he had been fairly involved in the drafting of the Gramm-Rudman law and that it had clearly been a bipartisan initiative. Penner did not discuss the Republicans' motivations for supporting the law, but he said that the Democrats had believed that the law "was a wonderful device for smoking out the president" and forcing him to raise taxes in order to protect his defense buildup. Unfortunately, as it turned out, the president was quite willing to sacrifice defense programs in order to avoid major tax increases. In any case, it proved to be quite easy to cheat on the law so that the targets would not be binding, and, on those rare occasions that they had been binding, of course they were changed.

On a broader issue, Penner expressed his disagreement with Stockman's view that there was no fundamental problem with the U.S. budget process. He believed that it had been easier in the past to make big changes in the direction of fiscal restraint because the political leadership had had much more influence over their followers. When Eisenhower was embarrassed by a $13 billion deficit, there was a shift in fiscal policy between 1959 and 1960 that was three times as big as the changes embodied in the recent budget agreement. The Vietnam surtax package was four times as big as the recent budget agreement when measured by the change in the full employment surplus. But, today, each member of Congress is an individual entrepreneur, and it is very hard to get the members to agree on anything. Penner could not imagine a Representative Newt Gingrich thwarting his president in the past without having some horrible sanction applied against him.

Charls Walker strongly supported Penner's comments and believed that Schultze and Stockman had been much too optimistic in their presentations. Walker said that the United States has become more and more of a plebiscite democracy, where the members respond very quickly to what the public wants. But the public today seems to be either schizoid or wily because they have sent people to Congress to support spending and then elected a conservative president to restrain that spending. Walker believed that this type of divided government had worked in the past because of strong congressional leadership but that the rise in congressional entrepreneurship that Penner described had made divided government unworkable today. Walker concluded that the president should be given more authority in the budget process than simply sending a budget up to Congress and being forced either to accept the final bill or to veto it and stop the government.

William Niskanen described two notions of fiscal responsibility, only one of which he said had been raised so far in the discussion. The notion on the table was that the government should build a revenue base that supports the level of spending that the politicians seem to want. The alternative notion is that the government should reduce spending to the level of taxes that voters seem prepared to support. Niskanen remembered Stockman as an aggressive and maybe naive younger man who had thought that the responsibility of the Office of Management and Budget was to cut spending to the level of taxes that people are willing to pay. Stockman's comments at the conference were saddening because he seemed to have switched to the view that the only responsible fiscal behavior is to increase revenues to match the current level of spending.

Niskanen believed that there are two important fiscal facts. One is that voters clearly react against increases in taxes. He had studied a century of presidential elections, and, even prior to the New Deal, increases in taxes reduce the percentage of the popular vote for the candidate of the incumbent party. Economist Sam Peltzman had recently completed a much more comprehensive analysis of senatorial elections, congressional elections, and gubernatorial elections, and the evidence is overwhelming that people have consistently voted against the candidate from the party that has raised taxes. All the voting data imply that voters do not believe that marginal spending is worth as much as the taxes that pay for it. The second important fiscal fact, faced by the budget director and by everyone in the executive branch, is that it is difficult to cut spending.

But which of these fiscal realities should be taken as given? The clear signals coming from the electorate or the difficulties faced by conscientious, hard-working budget directors like Stockman in persuading the Congress to cut spending? Niskanen believed that there is a massive agency problem in the U.S. political system, in which political representatives who favor high spending are elected and reelected even though the voters have been sending a consistent signal for at least a hundred years about the size of the government they want.

Stockman responded that Niskanen had raised the fundamental question in deciding whether institutional reform is needed in the national budget process. Does the permanent and rigid consensus about spending reflect the political machinations of elected officials, or does it reflect the views of an electorate that is saying that it wants most of these programs? Stockman believed that there is no case for the existence of an agency problem. When politicians refused, time after time, to reduce spending on Social Security, Medicare, and related social insurance programs, it was clear that "this was the public speaking through the voice of fear-ridden elected officials." And "it was the public speaking when the most conservative president likely to be elected in modern history" vowed in a debate with Democratic presidential candidate Walter Mondale that he would never touch Social Security. Stockman believed that the same public consensus holds for the current programs designed to aid poor people.

Feldstein asked Stockman how he would respond to the argument that Social Security recipients and near recipients have strong positive feelings for the program while the rest of the public does not care enough to express its opposition. *Stockman* said that the existence of constituencies with concentrated interests is not an agency problem but rather an inherent feature of democracies.

Schultze suggested two pieces of evidence against Niskanen's hypothesis of a severe agency problem. The first is that government spending is higher in many affluent countries whose parliamentary systems force their governments to respond more quickly than the U.S. government to shifts in public opinion. The second is the public support in the United States for increases in Social Security; Social Security provides an excellent test of Niskanen's hypothesis because taxes are increased along with benefits.

Niskanen responded that what is regarded as reality inside the Beltway is very different from what is regarded as reality outside the Beltway. Many politicians vote for increases in spending and give speeches to special interest groups in favor of spending, but the speeches they give "on the rubber chicken circuit" are not supportive of big government. Niskanen thought that the catastrophic health insurance episode of 1988 and 1989 provided an interesting lesson. This is the one major welfare program that had been reversed in his lifetime, and its dominating characteristic was that the population group that was supposed to benefit from the program was the same group that bore the taxes. This is not true of Social Security or Medicare or most other programs.

Feldstein said that a large part of the public does not agree with either of Niskanen's conceptions of responsible fiscal policy. Despite the efforts of many economists, many people believe that the budget deficit is not a big problem, so there is no urgent need either to raise taxes *or* to reduce spending.

Stockman said that the public had been deliberately miseducated for a long time because of a "reign of terror in the political system" in which "one side went into the bunkers and the other side postured and told lies." Slowly the country is coming out of this hole, and the political debate is reemerging in mature form. The public will start to be educated again, but it takes time to repair the damage that was done.

Paul Krugman summarized the Schultze/Stockman view of budget policy as the view that the United States has a basically sound political process that spent the 1980s trying to recover from two months of craziness in early 1981. Krugman disputed this view, arguing that what happened in Washington in early 1981 had not been just an accident in the political process or an operational failure of a few people inside the Beltway. Instead, Krugman believed that a mass movement had arisen in the United States that demanded impossible things from the government. This led to tax cuts and budget problems at the state and local level as well as at the federal level.

Krugman said that he had been doing some informal and painful research about public opinion by appearing on some radio talk shows. He had concluded that the public view of the country's fiscal problems is dominated by two false ideas. First, people believe that the United States has a crushing burden of taxes, by both historical and international standards. Second, they believe that most government spending goes to vast armies of unproductive bureaucrats. Mythical figures—like bureaucrats looking after their one Indian or welfare queens driving Cadillacs—loom very large in the public perception. Krugman hypothesized that this mass movement of impossible demands had arisen largely from the stagnation of American living standards in the 1970s and had nothing to do with the government per se.

William Poole commented that, over the past fifty years, U.S. government spending relative to GNP has been rising by an average of roughly 5 percentage points per decade. In Europe, this process has gone much further; Sweden may be at a level of spending and taxes that is past the top of the Laffer curve. This process cannot be continued indefinitely, and Poole thought that, even if government spending had not been reduced by much in the 1980s, the appropriate role of that spending had at least been addressed in a way that it had not been addressed before.

Stockman agreed that the rhetorical propositions about the expansion of government had become more negative and skeptical during the 1980s, which was an accomplishment. But he took issue again with the notion that the Reagan era had stopped an ongoing expansion of government that would otherwise have continued forever. In fact, he argued, the massive expansion of the welfare state had exhausted itself—or completed its task, depending on one's view—

in the late 1970s in nearly every Western country. The expansion had stopped in Britain under Prime Minister Thatcher and had stopped in the United States under President Carter. Three big projects that could have maintained the momentum of expansion in the United States—a guaranteed family income, national health insurance, and significant federal aid to education—were all killed by the Democrats. Social Democratic parties around the Western world had concluded in the late 1970s that their work was done. President Reagan had solidified this position in the United States, but the forces were already in motion in the body politic.

Stockman responded to Krugman's comments as well, saying that the public's mistaken notions about what is in the budget and how money can be saved had originated with or at least been reinforced by President Reagan. Reagan had believed in these ideas and had repeated them incessantly in speeches. As a specific example, Stockman recalled a discussion that he had had with Reagan about ways to reduce spending on Social Security. Stockman had proposed either a reduction in the cost-of-living adjustment or a targeted program to reduce certain types of benefits. But Reagan had said that he did not want to cut any benefits that people had earned; he just wanted to eliminate the waste in the program. The specific waste that he had mentioned was from people who had died but were still receiving benefit checks. So the administration had studied this issue and had made an administrative change that eliminated this waste—which amounted to $20 million in a $250 billion system. Because the public had been so miseducated, the political system was unable to restore revenue when it was needed.

Schultze agreed that there had been a gradual disenchantment with the welfare state around the world and a desire to stop its expansion. But the United States had responded by cutting taxes, and other countries had responded by cutting spending.

Feldstein noted another remarkable difference between the restraint of the welfare state in the United States and its restraint in other countries. Although the same forces had taken hold at the same time around the world, this had occurred at very different levels of spending in different countries.

5   Exchange Rate Policy

1. Jeffrey A. Frankel
2. C. Fred Bergsten
3. Michael Mussa

1. Jeffrey A. Frankel

The Making of Exchange Rate Policy in the 1980s

Although the 1970s were the decade when foreign exchange rates broke free of the confines of the Bretton Woods system, under which governments since 1944 had been committed to keeping them fixed, the 1980s were the decade when large movements in exchange rates first became a serious issue in the political arena. For the first time, currencies claimed their share of space on the editorial and front pages of American newspapers. For the first time, congressmen expostulated on such arcane issues as the difference between sterilized and unsterilized intervention in the foreign exchange market and proposed bills to take some of the responsibility for exchange rate policy away from the historical Treasury-Fed duopoly.

The history of the dollar during the decade breaks up fairly neatly into three phases: 1981–84, when the currency appreciated sharply against trading partners' currencies; 1985–86, when the dollar peaked and reversed the entire distance of its ascent; and 1987–90, when the exchange rate fluctuated within a range that—compared to the preceding roller coaster—seemed relatively stable (see fig. 5.1). It was of course the unprecedented magnitude of the upswing from 1980 to February 1985, 59 percent in the Fed's trade-weighted index, that made the exchange rate such a potent issue. U.S. exporters lost

The author would like to thank I. M. Destler, C. Randall Henning, Wendy Dobson, Martin Feldstein, Edwin Truman, Paul Volcker, J. David Richardson, Michael Mussa, William Niskanen, C. Fred Bergsten and a few anonymous sources for providing information, comments on earlier drafts, or both. The author would also like to thank Menzie Chinn for efficient research assistance.

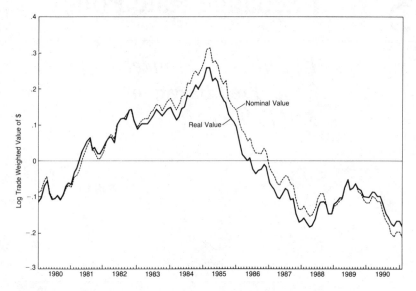

Fig. 5.1   Nominal and real value of the dollar, Morgan Guaranty indices (1980–82 = 0)

price competitiveness on world markets, and other U.S. firms faced intense competition from cheaper imports. Most analysts considered the appreciation of the dollar (allowing for the usual lag of at least two years in trade effects) to be the primary cause of the subsequent deterioration of the U.S. merchandise trade deficit, which rose $123 billion from 1982 to 1987.

This paper begins with a review of the history of exchange rate policy during the 1980s. It then proceeds to discuss the competing philosophical views, proposals, and economic theories and the competing objectives, interest groups, and policymakers that went into the determination of policy. The paper concludes with some thoughts on possible generalizations regarding the political economy of exchange rates.

It must be acknowledged from the outset that the topic of exchange rate policy differs in at least one fundamental respect from such topics as regulatory or trade policy: many economists believe that there is no such thing as exchange rate policy or, to be more precise, that there is no independent scope for the government to affect the exchange rate after taking into account monetary policy (and perhaps fiscal policy or some of the microeconomic policies that are considered by other papers in this volume).

There are, on the other hand, many who believe that such tools as foreign exchange intervention and capital controls *can* have independent effects on the exchange rate. Everyone agrees, furthermore, that an announcement by government officials regarding a desired path for the exchange rate or regarding possible changes in exchange rate *regimes* (e.g., fixed vs. pure floating, vs. managed floating, or vs. target zones) can have important effects via market participants' perceptions of its implications for future monetary policy.

If this were a paper on the economics of exchange rate determination, then it would be central to try to settle the issue of whether the money-supply process and a stable money-demand relationship can together explain the exchange rate. But the assignment here concerns the political process of policy determination rather than the economic process of exchange rate determination. There is no question that the exchange rate is a distinct subject for concern, debate, deliberation, and attempted influence.

In exchange rate policy, as in regulatory policy, "do nothing" is one of the options for the government. Indeed, as we shall see, this was the option officially adopted during the first Reagan administration, 1981–84. Nevertheless, it is by no means a foregone conclusion that this option is the one that is most desirable from an economic standpoint or that it is the one that is likely to prevail for long from a political standpoint.

5.1 The Chronology of U.S. Exchange Rate Policy in the 1980s

5.1.1 The First Phase of Dollar Appreciation, 1980–82

The dollar ended the 1970s in the same fashion that it had started it, by falling in value. The devaluations of 1971 and 1973 had been deliberate attempts to eliminate the accumulating disequilibrium of the Bretton Woods years. The depreciation of 1977–78 also began with a deliberate attempt by Treasury Secretary Michael Blumenthal and others in the Carter administration to "talk down" the dollar. In the absence of a willingness among trading partners to expand at as rapid a rate as the United States, a depreciation of the dollar was at the time viewed as the natural way of staving off the then-record U.S. trade deficits that were beginning to emerge. But the decline soon got out of control. The depreciation of the late 1970s is now usually thought of, in the economic arena, as a symptom of excessive U.S. monetary expansion and, in the political arena, as one of many symbols of the "malaise" that is popularly associated with the Carter administration.

The reversal of this down phase in the dollar began, not with the coming of Ronald Reagan, but rather with the monetary tightening by Federal Reserve Chairman Paul Volcker. In October 1979, the Fed announced a change in its open market procedures, designed to combat inflation and motivated partly by the need to restore the dollar to international respectability. For the subsequent several years, Volcker showed his determination to let interest rates rise however far they had to rise to defeat the inflation of the 1970s. During the period 1981–82, the U.S. long-term government bond rate averaged 13.3 percent, a two-point increase relative to 1980. Interest rates among a weighted average of trading partners rose as well, but not by as much: the U.S. differential averaged 1.9 percent over 1981–82, compared to 0.6 percent in 1979–80. The real (i.e., inflation-adjusted) interest rate differential rose even more, by between two and three points, depending on the measure of expected inflation used (Frankel 1985). The increase in the relative attractiveness of dollar assets in the eyes of global investors brought about between 1980 and 1982 an appreciation of the U.S. dollar by 29 percent in nominal terms and 28 percent in real terms. Evidence of the textbook-perfect effects of the monetary contraction was seen, not only in the rise of the dollar, but also more broadly in the recessions of 1980 and 1981–82. The traditional channel of monetary transmission to the real economy, the negative effect of an increase in interest rates on the construction industry and other interest rate–sensitive sectors, was subsequently joined by the modern channel of transmission, the negative effect of an increase in the value of the dollar on export industries and other exchange rate–sensitive sectors.

5.1.2   The Second Phase of Dollar Appreciation, 1983–84

The trough of the recession came at the end of 1982; a recovery began in 1983 that was both vigorous and destined to be long lived. The dollar continued on its previous upward path. Between 1982 and 1984, it appreciated another 17 percent in nominal terms and 14 percent in real terms. The textbooks had no trouble explaining why global investors continued to find dollar assets increasingly attractive: the U.S. long-term real interest rate continued to rise until its peak in mid-1984. The differential vis-à-vis trading partners during 1983–84 averaged about 1 percentage point higher than in the previous two years. Nor did the textbooks have much trouble explaining the source of this increase in U.S. real interest rates. As the Reagan administration cut income tax rates, indexed tax brackets for inflation, and began a massive buildup of military spending, the budget deficit rose from 2 percent of GNP in the 1970s to 5 percent of GNP in the mid-1980s. (The sharp increase in the budget deficit in 1982 could be blamed largely on the recession. But, by 1985, the increase was mostly structural.) The increased demand for funds that these deficits represented readily explains the increase in U.S. interest rates, the inflow of capital from abroad, and the associated appreciation of the dollar.

At the same time, the effects of the ever-loftier dollar began to be felt in earnest among those U.S. industries that rely on exports for customers or that compete with imports. The affected sectors on the export side included particularly agriculture, capital goods, and aircraft and other transportation equipment; on the import side they included textiles, steel, motorcycles, and consumer electronics; and on both sides they included semiconductors and automobiles. Overall, the effects on exports and imports added up to a $67 billion trade deficit in 1983, double the record levels of 1977–78. This too was a prediction of the standard textbook model. The fiscal expansion was essentially "crowding out" private spending on American goods, not only in the interest rate–sensitive sectors through the traditional route, but also in the exchange rate–sensitive sectors through the modern route.

5.1.3   The Noninterventionist Policy of the First Reagan Administration

Throughout this period, 1981–84, the Reagan administration had an explicitly laissez-faire (or benign neglect) policy toward the foreign exchange market. The policy was noninterventionist in the general sense that the movement of the dollar was not seen as requiring any sort of government response or, indeed, as a problem. It was also noninterventionist in the narrower sense that the authorities refrained from intervening in the foreign exchange market, that is, from the selling (or buying) of dollars in exchange for marks, yen, or other foreign currencies. The undersecretary for monetary affairs, Beryl Sprinkel, announced in the third month of the administration that its intention was not to undertake such intervention except in the case of "disorderly markets." Lest anyone think that the qualifying phrase was sufficiently elastic to include common fluctuations in the exchange rate, he explained that the sort of example of disorderly markets that the administration had in mind was the occasion of the March 1981 shooting and wounding of the president.[1] The historical data reveal that this date was in fact almost the only occasion between 1981 and 1984 when the U.S. authorities intervened in the market.

I shall discuss in sections 5.2 and 5.3 the various philosophies that gave rise to the laissez-faire stance of the first Reagan administration. For the moment, let us note that the matter is somewhat more complicated than a simple case of government regulation versus the free market.

For Sprinkel, a longtime member of the monetarist "Shadow Open Market Committee" and follower of Milton Friedman, the matter *was* a simple case of the virtues of the free market. Under floating exchange rates, the price of foreign currency is whatever it has to be to equilibrate the demand and supply of foreign currency in the market; it is, virtually by definition, the "correct price." Attempts by the monetary authorities to intervene in the foreign exchange market to keep the value of the currency artificially high or artificially low are unsound gambles with the taxpayers' money, as likely to be counterproductive as attempts by the Department of Agriculture to intervene in the market for grain to keep the price of grain artificially high or artificially low.

But there were other free market conservatives in the starting team at Treasury, the supply-siders, who believed in the need to stabilize the exchange rate just as firmly as the monetarists believed in the desirability of leaving it to be determined by the market. The issue was settled firmly on the side of nonintervention by the secretary, Donald Regan. He had neither a monetarist nor a supply-sider philosophy (nor, indeed, much of an economic or philosophic framework of any sort). Regan, rather, saw the issue more in terms of politics and personalities. In the absence of any guidance from the White House (and, on exchange rate policy even more than on other areas of policy, there was in

---

1. The source here, as for many other points in this paper, is the authoritative study by Destler and Henning (1989, 20).

fact no guidance forthcoming from the White House [see Regan 1988]), Regan saw his role as defending himself and the president from any suggestions that the status quo with respect to the dollar was a bad thing or that it required a response. He subscribed to the "safe-haven" view that the pattern of capital inflow, dollar appreciation, and trade deficit was the result of the favorable investment climate created by the Reagan tax cuts and regulatory changes, in opposition to the textbook view that it was the result of a fiscal expansion and an increase in real interest rates.

When the heads of state of the G-7 countries met at Williamsburg, Virginia, 28–30 May 1983, the Europeans complained to Reagan about America's budget deficit and its effects such as high interest rates. But Reagan and Regan responded that the strong dollar and U.S. trade deficits were not problems and, in any case, were not due to high interest rates and fiscal expansion (Putnam and Bayne 1987, 179).

Within the first Reagan administration, the view that the strong dollar was the result of the differential in real interest rates was put forward early and often by Martin Feldstein, the chairman of the Council of Economic Advisers from 1982 to 1984.[2] His view was that the source of the increase in real interest rates was the increase in the federal structural budget deficit and the consequent shortfall of national saving. This explanation was increasingly accepted as the correct one for the appreciating dollar and widening trade deficit by other members of the president's cabinet. Representatives of trading partners' governments also tended to share this view. But it was rejected by the Treasury and some White House aides, principally on the grounds that the emphasis on the "twin deficits" amounted to "selling short" America and the president's policies. Regan and Feldstein were frequently described in the press as embattled over the issue.

In February 1984, the annual *Economic Report of the President,* the main text of which is in fact always the report of the Council of Economic Advisers, was submitted to the Congress. It contained an estimate that the market considered the dollar to be "overvalued" by more than 30 percent and a forecast that, as a consequence, the trade deficit would almost double to approximately $110 billion in 1984 and that the borrowing to finance these deficits would in 1985 convert the United States from a net creditor to a net debtor in the international accounts. In Senate testimony, when asked to reconcile this pessimistic outlook with his own, more rosy, forecasts, Regan was quoted as saying that, as far as he was concerned, the senators could throw the report of the Council of Economic Advisers into the waste basket.[3]

---

2. After the Williamsburg Summit, Feldstein told the press that he hoped that the meeting had increased awareness of the dangers of the dollar appreciation (Putnam and Bayne 1987, 179).

3. As part of the interagency review process in January, Don Regan had (unsuccessfully) threatened Feldstein that he would tell the president not to sign the *Report* if it did not adopt a more upbeat tone than the existing draft, abandoning its emphasis on the bad outlook for the trade deficit and its analysis of the dollar as the major cause of the problem. The text was not altered in substance. Needless to say, the deficit predictions subsequently came true.

5.1.4   The Yen/Dollar Agreement of 1984

Complaints about the strong dollar and the effect it was having on trade were heard increasingly, however, and administration policymakers became increasingly aware of two (related) risks: that trade would be a potent weapon that the Democrats would use in the November 1984 presidential election and that such complaints would result in protectionist legislation on Capitol Hill. In October 1983, therefore, Regan launched the yen/dollar campaign, an attempt to respond to the political issue of the appreciating dollar and widening trade deficit, without abandoning the administration's free market orientation. (As was also true later, the Treasury continued to resist the characterization that the dollar was "too high" and preferred to say that *other* currencies—in this case the yen—were "too low.") In subcabinet and cabinet meetings, Regan succeeded in setting the request for liberalization as a top U.S. priority in President Reagan's visit to Japan and his meeting with Prime Minister Nakasone in November 1983. As a result, a working group of Treasury and Ministry of Finance representatives was formed, and its work culminated in the Yen/Dollar Agreement of May 1984.

I described in my 1984 study how the impetus behind the U.S. campaign for Japanese liberalization was rooted in what I considered questionable economic logic on the part of Treasury Secretary Don Regan.[4] This was the notion that Japanese financial liberalization would help promote capital flow from the United States to Japan, rather than the reverse, and would help reduce the corresponding U.S. trade deficit, through an appreciation of the yen against the dollar. Regan acquired this theory from an American businessman, Caterpillar Tractor Chairman Lee Morgan, in late September 1983.[5] It was not a theory that had previously had many adherents in the U.S. government.[6]

The questionable component of the argument adopted by Regan was the proposition that the Japanese authorities at the time were using capital controls or administrative guidance to discourage the flow of capital into Japan and to depress the value of the yen. Prohibitions against foreign acquisition of most Japanese assets did in fact exist in the 1970s, but they were formally eliminated in the Foreign Exchange Law of December 1980. The de facto liberalization dated from April 1979. It is evident from a comparison of the Euroyen and

---

4. My study was published four months after I left the staff of the Council of Economic Advisers.

5. Morgan based his analysis and recommendations on Murchison and Solomon (1983). It is quite clear that their goal was promoting the flow of capital from the United States to Japan, rather than the reverse; their list of suggested measures for Reagan to urge on Nakasone included, e.g., "an increase in the Government of Japan's overseas borrowing with the proceeds converted immediately into yen to assist Japan in financing its substantial budget deficits" (pp. 25–27).

6. Undersecretary Sprinkel had testified as recently as the preceding April that there was no merit to the theory that the Ministry of Finance was using capital controls to keep the yen undervalued. A study by the General Accounting Office released the same month found the same thing. On the other hand, Secretary of State George Shultz did in private propose something very much like the yen/dollar campaign in the summer of 1983. But he recognized that the State Department was obliged to leave exchange rate matters to the Treasury.

Tokyo short-term interest rates that arbitrage was able to eliminate the onshore-offshore differential that existed prior to that date. In the early 1980s, the objective of the Japanese authorities was, if anything, to *dampen* the depreciation of the yen, not to promote it.[7] Thus, it could have been predicted—and was predicted (Bergsten 1984; CEA 1984; and Frankel 1984)—that, if the Ministry of Finance were to agree to U.S. demands to avoid any remaining interference with international financial flows, the impact would be an acceleration of capital outflow attracted by higher interest rates in the United States, rather than the reverse.

To be sure, other motives for the liberalization campaign were very relevant as well. From the beginning, the appeal of the idea to Don Regan and others in the administration lay in the political need to be seen beginning to respond to public and congressional concerns over the rising U.S. trade deficit (particularly in a presidential election year) and the desire to do so in a way consistent with free market ideology. As the first instance of the Treasury attempting to respond to the trade deficit issue via exchange rate policy, in order to fend off protectionist pressures, the yen/dollar campaign anticipated the Plaza Accord by almost two years. To this extent, the plan made perfect sense politically.[8]

Two varieties of the free market argument are potentially quite sensible. One is that the point of the exercise was to promote the internal efficiency of the Japanese economy. This is apparently one of the things that U.S. officials had in mind later when they spoke of the Yen/Dollar Agreement as having been a success and cited it as a model for the 1990 Structural Impediments Initiative with Japan or won/dollar talks with Korea. The typical reaction of an outsider, however, is that the Japanese would not appear to need any advice from the United States on how to run their economy, while the typical reaction of an American would be that the goal of U.S. policy should be to promote the competitiveness of the American economy relative to Japan, rather than the reverse.

The remaining argument is that the point of the campaign was to promote better treatment in Japan of U.S. banks, securities companies, and other providers of financial services. Several measures of this sort indeed appeared on the list that Regan discussed with Finance Minister Noboru Takeshita on 10 November 1983, on the occasion of President Reagan's visit to Japan, and in the May 1984 agreement. This component of the campaign is perfectly analogous to Reagan administration pressure on Japan at that time to allow, for example, the free import of beef and citrus products. There is no question that the initiation of the yen/dollar campaign in October 1983 gained political momentum when New York financial institutions responded to a Treasury invitation to

7. For evidence that the Japanese government in the early 1980s sought to resist the depreciation of the yen against the dollar, not to exacerbate it, see CEA (1984), Frankel (1984, 16–25), Funabashi (1988, 89–92), GAO (1984), and Haynes, Hutchison, and Mikesell (1986).

8. I describe below the switch in Treasury emphasis toward bringing down the dollar after James Baker succeeded Don Regan as secretary in January 1985 (see also Funabashi 1988, 75ff.).

contribute a wish list of proposed measures. There is also little question that the measures that were adopted worked on U.S. service exports in the desired direction.[9] But my claim is that the objective of helping U.S. providers of financial services was secondary to the objective of affecting capital flows and the exchange rate.

5.1.5   The "Bubble," June 1984–February 1985

From mid-1984 to February 1985, the dollar appreciated another 20 percent. This final phase of the currency's ascent differed from the earlier phases, not only in that the appreciation was at an accelerated rate, but also in that it could not readily be explained on the basis of economic fundamentals, whether by means of the textbook theories or otherwise. The interest rate differential peaked in June and thereafter moved in the wrong direction to explain the remainder of the upswing. Two influential studies were written, to the effect that the foreign exchange market had been carried away by an irrational "speculative bubble" (Krugman 1985; Marris 1985; Cooper 1985).[10] The trade deficit reached $112 billion in 1984 and continued to widen. Many who had hitherto supported freely floating exchange rates began to change their minds.

Attitudes in the administration began to shift subtly in one respect. Treasury officials (both in public and in private) had previously denied that the large federal budget deficit and the trade deficit were problems or that the United States was becoming dependent on the foreign capital inflow to make up the shortfall in national saving.[11] But, toward the end of the first Reagan administration, these officials began (explicitly) to admit that the budget deficit *was* a problem and (implicitly) to admit that the country did indeed need to borrow

9. Several qualifications can be noted. First, measures to help U.S. financial institutions were not in the interest of U.S. manufacturing (and, for this reason, did not appear in the original Murchison-Solomon [1983] report). Second, in contrast to recent U.S. efforts to include services in the Uruguay Round of GATT negotiations, these measures may not have been in the interest of promoting the existing liberal international trade regime, as they were negotiated bilaterally and the benefits (such as the decision by the Tokyo Stock Exchange to make seats available) often accrued more to U.S. financial institutions than those of third countries. Third, one variety of the "Yanks hoodwinked again" school argues that the wily Japanese somehow used liberalization to attain more benefits for *their* banks in the United States and Europe than they granted to U.S. banks operating in Japan. Of course, standard theories of the "gains from trade" say that both countries can benefit simultaneously from liberalization.

10. Contemporaneous statements by economists that the dollar was greatly overvalued included presentations by Krugman, Bergsten, and Richard Cooper to a prominent Federal Reserve System conference in Jackson Hole, Wyoming, just one month before the Plaza meeting. Another reference on "the dollar as an irrational speculative bubble" that dates from this year is Frankel and Froot (1990).

11. Some, particularly Destler and Henning (1989, 29), attribute the May Yen/Dollar Agreement to a desire on the part of Treasury officials to make it easier for Americans to borrow from Japan. But this argument dates the borrowing motivation too early and attributes too much consistency to Treasury behavior. As of the spring of 1984, these officials were still claiming that the United States did not need to borrow from abroad to finance a shortfall of saving. The motivation in the Yen/Dollar Agreement was, rather, the one noted above: to try to decrease the yen/dollar exchange rate and reduce the U.S. trade deficit, which is diametrically opposed to the motivation of increasing the net flow of capital from Japan to the United States.

from abroad to finance the deficits, and they took steps to facilitate such borrowing. In July 1984, Assistant Secretary David Mulford moved to make it easier for U.S. corporations to borrow from abroad, by eliminating the withholding tax on payment of interest to foreign residents, and allowed bearer bonds to be issued in the Euromarket. In September 1984, the Treasury created a new kind of bond that was specially targeted so as to appeal to foreign investors and sent Undersecretary Sprinkel to Tokyo and various European capitals to help drum up customers for these bonds. But these measures did not constitute a decision that the strong dollar and trade deficit presented a problem. When it was no longer possible to postpone the choice between allowing the saving shortfall to keep interest rates high (thereby crowding out the interest-sensitive components of U.S. demand, so as to protect the exchange rate–sensitive components) and allowing it to keep the dollar high (thereby crowding out net exports, so as to protect the interest-sensitive sectors), in late 1984 the Regan-Sprinkel team finally opted for the latter alternative de facto. Indeed, the increase in attractiveness of U.S. assets that was brought about by the July policy changes by Treasury furnishes virtually the only change in economic fundamentals that could conceivably help explain the appreciation of the dollar over this period when interest rates were falling.

5.1.6   The Plaza Sea Change, 1985

The pivotal event in the making of exchange rate policy in the 1980s was the shift from a relatively doctrinaire laissez-faire policy during the first Reagan administration to a more flexible policy of activism during the second administration. In later sections, I will consider the extent to which economics, politics, and personalities combined to produce this shift and the extent to which the shift in policy was in turn responsible for the reversal of the dollar's appreciation.

An obvious point from which to date the switch is 22 September 1985, when finance ministers and central bank governors from the G-5 countries met at the Plaza Hotel in New York and agreed to try to bring the dollar down.[12] The Plaza Accord was certainly the embodiment of the new regime. But I would prefer to date the start of the new era from the beginning of that year. With the inauguration of the second Reagan administration, Don Regan and Beryl Sprinkel left the Treasury (for the White House and the Council of Economic Advisers, respectively). James Baker became secretary of the Treasury, and his aide Richard Darman became deputy secretary.[13] Both men had already

12. The story of the Plaza is described in detail in Funabashi (1988, 9–41).
13. The deputy secretary job that Darman took had previously been occupied by Tim McNamar. (McNamar did not quite have either Sprinkel's zeal for free market ideology or Regan's zeal for the exercising of power and in any case did not play a central role in exchange rate policy.) The position of undersecretary for monetary affairs was not filled after Sprinkel's departure. Thus, Darman de facto succeeded Sprinkel in the area of exchange rate policy. David Mulford continued in the next-lower rank as assistant secretary for international affairs throughout the remainder of the second Reagan administration and was eventually promoted to a new position of undersecretary for international affairs in the Bush administration.

developed at the White House a reputation for greater pragmatism than other, more ideological members of the administration. In January confirmation hearings, Baker explicitly showed signs of the departure with respect to exchange rate policy, stating at one point that the Treasury's previous stance against intervention was "obviously something that should be looked at" (Destler and Henning 1989, 41–42).

Another reason to date the change from early in the year is that the dollar peaked in February and had already depreciated by 13 percent by the time of the Plaza meeting. Some, such as Feldstein (1986), would argue that the gap in timing shows that exchange rate "policy" had in fact little connection with the actual decline of the dollar, which was instead determined in the private marketplace regardless of what efforts governments made to influence it. But, notwithstanding that official policy did not change until September,[14] there are two respects in which the bursting of the bubble at the end of February may have been in part caused by policy change.

First, it was widely anticipated that Baker and Darman would probably be more receptive to the idea of trying to bring down the dollar than their predecessors had been. If market participants have reason to believe that policy changes to reduce the value of the dollar will be made in the future, they will move to sell dollars today in order to protect themselves against future losses, which will have the effect of causing the dollar to depreciate today.

Second, some intervention was agreed on at a G-5 meeting attended by Baker and Darman on 17 January and did take place subsequently (see Funabashi 1988, 10).[15] The U.S. intervention was small in magnitude.[16] But the German monetary authorities, in particular, intervened heavily to sell dollars in foreign exchange markets in February and March.[17] The February intervention was reported in the newspapers and, by virtue of timing, appears a likely candidate for the instrument that pricked the bubble. It is in turn likely that the accession of Baker to the Treasury in January and the G-5 meeting were the developments that encouraged the Germans to renew their intervention efforts at that time.

The German authorities could claim credit for the reversal of policy. (So, for that matter, could the French, who had long and consistently been arguing in favor of foreign exchange intervention.) Looking back, Baker instead got the

14. A June 1985 meeting of G-10 deputies in Tokyo, e.g., concluded that there was no need for international monetary reform and also endorsed the 1983 finding of the Jurgensen Report (*Report of the Working Group* 1983) that intervention did not offer a very useful tool to affect exchange rates (Obstfeld 1990; and Dobson 1991).

15. Surprisingly, the G-5 public announcement on 17 January used language that, on the surface at least, sounds more prointervention than was used later in the Plaza announcement: "in light of recent developments in foreign exchange markets," the G-5 "reaffirmed their commitment made at the Williamsburg Summit to undertake coordinated intervention in the markets as necessary."

16. A total of $659 million in foreign exchange purchases from 21 January to 1 March, as compared to $10 billion by the major central banks in total (*Federal Reserve Bank of New York Quarterly Review* 10 [Spring 1985]: 60; and 10 [Autumn 1985]: 52).

17. Intervention was particularly strong on 27 February and appeared to have an impact on the market (e.g., *Wall Street Journal,* 23 September 1985, 26).

credit in public, perhaps because of his skill at receiving favorable coverage from the U.S. media and the extent to which political perceptions in the 1980s asymmetrically tended to radiate from Washington, D.C., out to the rest of the world, rather than vice versa.

In April, at an Organization of Economic Cooperation and Development (OECD) meeting, Baker said, "The US is prepared to consider the possible value of hosting a high-level meeting of the major industrial countries" on the subject of international monetary reform. This trial balloon never went much further, despite similar proposals in the Congress (Putnam and Bayne 1987, 199). Monetary issues were not extensively discussed at the Bonn Summit of G-7 leaders in May.[18]

On 22 September, however, the G-5 ministers, meeting at the Plaza, agreed on an announcement that "some further orderly appreciation of the non-dollar currencies is desirable" and that they "stand ready to cooperate more closely to encourage this when to do so would be helpful," language that by the standards of such communiqués is considered (at least in retrospect) to have constituted strong support for concerted intervention, even though the word *intervention* did not appear. A figure of 10–12 percent depreciation of the dollar over the near term had been specified as the aim in a never-released "nonpaper" drafted by Mulford for a secret preparatory meeting of G-5 deputies in London on 15 September and (according to American government sources) was accepted as the aim by the G-5 ministers at the Plaza.[19] There was, apparently, little discussion among the participants as to whether changes in monetary policy would be required to achieve the aim of depreciating the dollar.

On the Monday that the Plaza announcement was made public, the dollar fell a sudden 4 percent against a weighted average of other currencies (slightly more against the mark and the yen). Subsequently, it resumed a gradual depreciation at a rate similar to that of the preceding seven months.[20] Interest rates continued to decline gradually, despite fears of Volcker and many others that a

18. History records that the G-7 summit of May 1985 was overshadowed by the public relations disaster of Bitburg, which arose when President Reagan embarrassingly found himself committed to visiting a German cemetery that contained graves of Nazi SS soldiers (Putnam and Bayne 1987, 200–201). History will neither confirm nor deny the report that this mistake on the part of the White House advance team was an indirect consequence of the strong dollar. On the afternoon when aide Michael Deaver should have been inspecting the Bitburg cemetery, he and other White House aides reportedly were instead out buying BMWs (Bovard 1991, 316), which at the time could be had in Germany for half the U.S. price as the result of the appreciation of the dollar against the mark.

19. The "nonpaper" also specified the total scale of intervention to be undertaken over the subsequent six weeks (up to $18 billion) and the allocation among the five countries (Funabashi 1988, 16–21). Intervention actually undertaken by the end of October turned out to be $3.2 billion on the part of the United States and $5 billion on the part of the other four countries, plus over $2 billion on the part of G-10 countries that were not represented at the Plaza, particularly Italy (*Federal Reserve Bank of New York Quarterly Review* 10 [Winter 1985–86]: 47).

20. Because the rate of depreciation in the six months after the Plaza was no greater than in the six months before the Plaza, Feldstein (1986) argued that the change in policy had no effect. This logic is far from conclusive, however.

depreciation might discourage international investors from holding dollars and thereby force interest rates up.[21] Before long, the Plaza had widely become considered a great public success.

5.1.7 The Apotheosis of International Coordination, 1986

Baker's ambitions for joint international policy-making concerned more than just exchange rates. His efforts to get Japan, Germany, and other trading partners to agree to expand their economies go back to negotiations leading up to the Plaza (Funabashi 1988, 11–12, 36–38; Putnam and Bayne 1987, 205; *Wall Street Journal,* 23 September 1985, 1, 25). At the next summit of G-7 heads of state, held in Tokyo in May 1986, the United States persuaded the others to adopt a system of so-called objective indicators. The list of indicators included the growth rate of GNP, the interest rate, the inflation rate, the unemployment rate, the ratio of the fiscal deficit to GNP, the current account and trade balances, the money growth rate, and international reserve holdings, in addition to the exchange rate. The plan was to expand the existing G-5 finance ministers' meetings to include Italy and Canada and to agree in each meeting on a set of quantitative predictions/goals for each of the indicator variables. At subsequent meetings, each of the seven economies' performances would be judged against those goals. In the words of the Tokyo Economic Declaration, the finance ministers and central bankers would "make their best efforts to reach an understanding on appropriate remedial measures whenever there are significant deviations from an intended course."

Mulford, as an unnamed Treasury source, indicated to the press that G-7 members were supposed to feel substantive "peer pressure" to modify their policies so as to meet the agreed-on goals. The other countries suspected that the U.S. Treasury's aim in setting up this system was to pressure them into greater economic expansion, as a way for the United States to reduce its trade deficit without itself having to undertake unpleasant fiscal retrenchment. The Germans spoke out against the "robotization" of international policy-making.

The maneuvering that went on outside G-7 meetings in 1986 was more substantive than the maneuvering that went on inside. Baker was repeatedly quoted in the press as "talking the dollar down," in large part as a weapon to induce the trading partners to cut interest rates. This was a tack very much reminiscent of an earlier Treasury secretary, Blumenthal. The pitch went something like this: "We would prefer that you expand your economies and thereby import more from us so that reduction of the U.S. deficit can be achieved in a way consistent with growth for all parties. But, if you are not willing to go along, then I am afraid we are just going to have to let the dollar depreciate more, in which case your exports to us will fall."

The Germans and Japanese intervened in the foreign exchange market to try to support the dollar but complained that "these efforts were in vain, not least

---

21. The role of Volcker and monetary policy during this period is discussed in sec. 5.6 below.

because statements by U.S. officials repeatedly aroused the impression on the markets that the U.S. authorities wanted the dollar to depreciate further. More-over, until then [the Louvre Accord in late January 1987] the Americans hardly participated in the operations to support their currency" (*Report of the Deutsche Bundesbank for the Year 1984,* quoted in Obstfeld 1990, 227). Mean-while, Fed Chairman Volcker was also being quoted as favoring the current level for the exchange rate, in apparent opposition to Baker.

By September 1986, the yen/dollar rate had declined from its peak of 260 to about 154. Japanese exporters were feeling heavily squeezed. At an unan-nounced rendezvous in San Francisco, Japanese Finance Minister Kiichi Miya-zawa met with Baker. They made a deal under which the exchange rate would be stabilized in its current range, and in return the Japanese would undertake greater fiscal expansion. The agreement was not announced until October. In the interim, the yen had depreciated back to about 162 yen/dollar. The Ameri-cans suspected the Japanese of deliberate manipulation so as to lock in a more favorable rate and returned to talking down the dollar. This episode is an ex-ample of the difficulty of enforcing an international cooperative agreement if its terms are not made explicit and public from the beginning to allow partici-pants and outside observers to judge compliance.

5.1.8   The Louvre Accord and the Return of Dollar Stability

The next meeting of G-7 finance ministers was held at the Louvre in Paris on 21–22 February 1987. The Baker-Miyazawa agreement proved to be some-thing of a dry run for the Louvre Agreement. The ensuing communiqué showed that the United States had agreed that the dollar should be stabilized "around current levels," and in return Japan had agreed to expand domestic demand in general, and Germany and some of the others had agreed more narrowly to cut taxes. One interpretation as to why Germany and the others were willing to participate at the Louvre when they had not been earlier is that the Baker-Miyazawa agreement demonstrated the readiness of the United States and Japan to proceed with a "G-2," and the Germans and the others did not want to be left out.[22]

Two questions of importance for evaluating the Louvre Agreement concern quantitative bands and intervention. The communiqué that was released after the meeting, as with all G-7 meetings, contained little hard information and conveyed the major policy change with a few understated words: "The Minis-ters and Governors agreed that the substantial exchange rate changes since the

---

22. Standard economic theories of the gains from coordination do not explain why a country should necessarily mind if other countries enter into an agreement without it. (Indeed, in many cases, the excluded countries should in theory be able to reap the benefits from worldwide eco-nomic expansion, enhanced monetary stability, or some other "public good," without having to bear any of the burden.) But there must be some loss of power or prestige from being left out, because it is a commonly expressed subject of concern. Italy, which at the Tokyo Summit of May 1986 had won an expansion of the G-5 ministers group to the G-7 (Putnam and Bayne 1987, 208–9), refused to join in the Louvre communiqué, in protest against its exclusion from an infor-mal G-5 meeting that had already worked out the Louvre Accord.

Plaza Agreement will increasingly contribute to reducing external imbalances and have now brought their currencies within ranges broadly consistent with underlying economic fundamentals. . . . Further substantial exchange rate shifts among their currencies could damage growth and adjustment prospects in their countries." As with the Plaza Accord, participants denied to the press that any specific quantitative target range had been set (*Wall Street Journal*, 23 February 1987, 3). Subsequent newspaper reports spoke of the range or target zone that had been set at the Louvre and made guesses as to what it might be. Most knowledgeable observers surmised that probably no explicit quantitative range had in fact been agreed on. This view was overturned, however, when Funabashi (1988, 183–87) reported that the Louvre participants had after all set a "reference range" of 5 percent around the current level.[23]

The advantage of having kept the target range secret was borne out when the dollar broke out of the lower end of the range. By April 1987, the scheduled time of a G-7 meeting, the yen-dollar rate had fallen 7 percent from the Louvre baseline. The Japanese finance minister, Miyazawa, was forced to accept Baker's proposal to "rebase" at the current level of 146 yen/dollar, with the same width of the reference range bands as before.

The U.S. commitment at the Louvre to oppose further depreciation of the dollar might be supposed to show up in three ways, besides the announcement of the agreement itself: an absence of statements by the secretary of the Treasury "talking down the dollar," purchases of dollars in foreign exchange intervention operations, and a tighter monetary policy. From then on, Baker did indeed refrain, for the most part, from talking down the dollar. For the first time since the heavy dollar sales of 1985, the United States also did indeed intervene substantially in the foreign exchange market in the aftermath of the Louvre, buying dollars to discourage further depreciation. Finally, U.S. interest rates did indeed begin a gradual rise in February (reversing a three-year downward trend), although the Federal Reserve was motivated more by a desire to choke off inflation, which was beginning to edge up slightly again, than by a feeling of commitment to support the value of the dollar. Perhaps as a result of these three steps, the dollar appreciated, particularly against the mark, from the date of the Louvre until mid-March (at one point inducing a small amount of Fed intervention in March to dampen the appreciation).

5.1.9   The Financial Markets Fear a Dollar Plunge, 1987

Many analysts had been warning for some time of the possibility of a "hard landing," which could be defined as a fall in the dollar that, because it is caused by a sudden portfolio shift out of dollar assets, is accompanied by a sharp

23. More precisely, a narrower margin of ± 2.5 percent, after which point intervention would be called for on a voluntary basis, and a wider margin of ± 5 percent, at which point a collaborative policy response would be obligatory. Such meetings are notorious for each country emerging with its own view as to what was agreed on, and there is always the possibility that the 5 percent target range was a U.S. proposal about which some countries, such as Germany, were unenthusiastic. No legal or quasi-legal documents are signed at such meetings.

increase in interest rates that have a contractionary effect on economic activity (e.g., Marris 1985).[24] Two events shook financial markets in 1987; each of them began with markings of such a portfolio shift. First, in the spring, a fall in demand for U.S. bonds, perhaps led by nervous foreign investors, led to a depreciation of the dollar (despite concerted intervention in support of the dollar) and an abrupt decline in bond prices and increase in interest rates.

Second, world stock markets crashed on 19 October 1987. Of the various possible causes that have been proposed for the bursting of the apparent bubble, several are international in nature. By the fall of 1987, the U.S. trade deficit still had not improved,[25] and Jim Baker was again hoping to convince the largest trading partners to expand their economies. On 15 October, the Commerce Department reported an unexpectedly large August trade deficit, and the New York stock market reacted with a then-record ninety-five-point fall.[26] On 18 October, Baker again called on the German minister, Stoltenberg, to undertake expansion, with renewed dollar depreciation as the threatened alternative. When the U.S. and other stock markets crashed on the next day (508 points in the case of New York), two possible causes that were identified were the 14 October trade deficit announcement and Baker's threat to the Germans to let the dollar fall. A third hypothesis is that the markets feared that the Fed would deliberately raise interest rates to try to keep the dollar from falling through a floor set at the Louvre (Feldstein 1988a; Obstfeld 1990).[27]

On 19 October, many observers at first feared that the hard landing was at hand. But, in large part owing to the rapid reaction of the Federal Reserve, interest rates fell rather than rose, and there was no subsequent slowdown in economic activity. The Fed was prepared to allow a sharp decline in the dollar if the alternative were insufficient liquidity to avert a financial crisis; although the dollar, surprisingly, did not depreciate on 19 October.

Consultations among the various governments began immediately, but, in the absence of a clear idea as to what macroeconomic policy commitments could be made, with respect to U.S. fiscal policy in particular, no G-7 meeting was scheduled. Dollar depreciation was again a concern, with frequent intervention in support of the dollar having little apparent effect. Two months after the stock market crash, G-7 representatives decided in a "Telephone Accord" to try to breathe new life into the Louvre Agreement. Paragraph 8 of their 22

24. This was also a major concern of Paul Volcker's.

25. In retrospect, the trough in the dollar trade deficit occurred in the third quarter of 1987 (and the trough in the "real trade deficit," i.e., the quantity of exports minus the quantity of imports, in the third quarter of 1986).

26. Other immediate market reactions that day included a decline in the dollar and an increase in short-term interest rates, precisely as in the portfolio-shift/hard-landing scenario (*Wall Street Journal,* 5 November 1987, 22).

27. This explanation was partly inspired by Chairman Greenspan's move to raise interest rates earlier in the year. But Greenspan's motivation was probably to respond to incipient signs of re-emerging inflation, particularly to demonstrate his independence from the administration and to earn his tough-guy credentials in the eyes of the market soon after his appointment to replace Paul Volcker, more than to meet any exchange rate commitment made by Baker at the Louvre.

December 1987 communiqué (which the G-7 leaders were later to repeat word for word in the communiqué of the Toronto Summit in June 1988) modified slightly earlier statements in favor of exchange rate stability. It included new wording: "Either excessive fluctuation of exchange rates, a further decline of the dollar or a rise in the dollar to an extent that becomes destabilizing to the adjustment process, could be counterproductive (Dobson 1991, table 4.8, p. 65; *New York Times,* 8 January 1988, 26). The asymmetry of the language, describing the undesirability of a rise in a more qualified way than the undesirability of a fall, was a deliberate signal that the group wanted to put a floor under the dollar at its current level. The markets were initially unimpressed, but heavy around-the-clock intervention in support of the dollar[28] in January 1988 was apparently quite effective at combating dollar weakness.

Periodically in 1987 and 1988, Japan's Ministry of Finance used administrative guidance to encourage Japanese institutional investors to hold more U.S. assets than they might choose on profit-maximizing grounds, in order to keep the dollar from depreciating further than it already had by then. This happened, in particular, in response to the U.S. bond market fall in the spring of 1987. Koo (1988, 8) tells us, "Even though the imposition of such quasi-capital controls [reporting requirements for Japanese banks handling foreign exchange— and an implicit threat behind them—imposed in May 1987 to head off a dollar collapse] was against the spirit of the Yen/Dollar Committee sponsored jointly by the Japanese Ministry of Finance and the US Treasury to deregulate Japanese financial markets, no complaints were heard from the US" (see also Hale 1989, 2–4).

5.1.10   Dollar Rallies, 1988 and 1989

The dollar began to appreciate after the intervention of January 1988. Its strength in mid-1988, leading up to the November presidential election, led some observers to suggest that the authorities in Japan and Germany were supporting the U.S. currency in order to help candidate George Bush win the election and thus head off the danger of protectionist trade policies under the Democrats.

A new dollar rally followed in 1989. For the first time since 1985–86, the official message switched from a desire for "exchange rate stability around recent levels" back to an implication that the current strength of the dollar was not justified (Dobson 1991, table 4.8, p. 66): in the communiqué of a Washington meeting in September 1989, the G-7 "considered the rise in recent months of the dollar inconsistent with longer run fundamentals."

The yen, in particular, weakened against the dollar at the end of the decade,

---

28. Called the "G-7 bear trap" by Destler and Henning (1989, 66). The intent of the intervention was to "bridge" until substantial improvements in the U.S. trade deficit materialized, at which time market sentiment in favor of the dollar could take over. In the event, this plan worked quite well (Dobson 1991).

in association with political scandals in Japan in 1989 and an investor shift out of Japanese security markets in early 1990. Japanese officials apparently thought that, having supported the U.S. currency earlier, the Americans should now return the favor and support the yen. U.S. authorities had bought yen and marks in 1988 and 1989 to dampen the appreciation of the dollar. But a Paris G-7 meeting in early April 1990 produced no support for Japan (beyond a statement that the ministers had "discussed . . . the decline of the yen against other currencies, and its undesirable consequences for the global adjustment process" [Dobson 1991, table 4.8, p. 66]).

5.1.11   Exchange Rates Policies in Other Parts of the World

Most political discussion of "the dollar" does not bother to distinguish what partner currencies are intended or what their relative weight is in the basket. Some standard weighted average of the major industrialized countries is usually used when precise numbers are needed, while the mark and—especially—the yen often come in for extra attention, by virtue of the importance of Germany and Japan in international trade and finance. The lack of American concern with other currencies stems in part because the various dollar exchange rates are highly correlated and in part because the less-important currencies are considered esoteric in the U.S. political sphere.[29] Nevertheless, some specific issues concerning other currencies did arise in the 1980s and are worth mentioning both as they relate to the dollar and to the extent that they shed light on American thinking regarding foreign exchange markets in general.

First, after the LDC debt crisis surfaced in August 1982, it became necessary for many countries in Latin America and elsewhere to take policy steps to convert their existing trade deficits into trade surpluses and thereby earn the foreign exchange to service their international debts. High on the usual list of such policy steps is the devaluation of the currency. The Mexican peso, Brazilian cruzeiro, Argentine peso, and many others underwent repeated large nominal and real devaluations. For the most part these devaluations were components of policy packages taken under the guidance, indeed insistence, of the International Monetary Fund and with the full support of the U.S. government. But demurs were occasionally heard from two different sources within the U.S. political galaxy. A few U.S. industries that faced competition from these countries charged that the devaluations represented subsidies or other unfair trading practices and were sometimes supported in these charges by protectors in the Commerce Department or in the Congress. An example was charges by the U.S. copper industry that they faced unfair competition from Chile in the form of a devaluation of the Chilean peso.

The other source of protest was more philosophical than political: the "supply-siders" argued that devaluation, like fiscal austerity (the twin officially

---

29. Recall the famous quote from the Nixon tapes, "I don't give a ——— about the lira."

sanctioned policy for problem debtors), was not an effective or desirable way to improve the trade balance because it had no real effects. The supply-sider viewpoint deserves attention—if for no other reason than that it was represented in the Reagan administration, especially at the beginning, with sufficient vigor, for example, to produce the 1981–83 tax cuts.

Another major nondollar currency development of the 1980s was the movement toward enhanced monetary and financial unification within Europe. The founding of the European Monetary System (EMS) by Giscard and Schmidt in 1979 had been portrayed at the time as something of a challenge to the primacy of the dollar, and policy toward the EMS at the U.S. Treasury had been at best neutral.[30] But, when "Europe 1992" frenzy caught fire in Europe in 1988 and generated some fears of a "Fortress Europe" in the American Congress, media, and business communities, the attitude of the administration ranged from indifferent to benign. This benign indifference particularly characterized the decade's developments on the monetary side: France's retreat from the go-it-alone expansion and controls on capital outflow that the Socialists had instituted in 1981, the agreement by EMS members to phase out all capital controls by July 1990, and the completely unanticipated decision by East and West Germany in 1990 to undertake monetary unification.[31] All three events tended to be welcomed as further signs of the worldwide free market revolution that Ronald Reagan had helped start.

The Europeans, however, often feel that the U.S. policymakers are insufficiently appreciative of EMS concerns, for example, of the way that the long-awaited depreciation of the dollar in 1985 might put strains on the cross-rates between the deutsche mark and the weaker currencies in the EMS. After the Plaza Accord, Treasury officials thought that the Germans had not done their agreed-on share of intervention. This view was expressed by Mulford at a G-5 deputies meeting in Paris in November 1985. The Germans explained that the Bank of Italy had sold over $2 billion in place of the Bundesbank so as to avoid putting upward pressure on the lira/mark cross-rate. They considered American reluctance to accept this explanation to be a sign of indifference to the EMS (Funabashi 1988, 27–30).

A third area of the world that featured interesting exchange rate developments was the East Asian newly industrialized countries (NICs): Korea, Taiwan, Hong Kong, and Singapore. Here U.S. policy played a determining role. In 1986 and 1987, there became fashionable the view that the explanation for the lack of improvement in the U.S. trade balance since February 1985 was that the traditional indices of the U.S. "effective exchange rate" vastly overstated the depreciation of the dollar that had taken place, by giving excessive

---

30. Funabashi (1988, 31) explains views within the Treasury.
31. One striking development of 1990 that was presumably in large part a consequence of the fall of Communism in Central Europe was the appreciation of the mark and other European currencies.

weight to the yen and European currencies: that such trading partners as the East Asian NICs, Brazil and Mexico (newly important competitors in manufactures) and Argentina, Australia and Canada (traditional competitors in wheat and beef in third-country markets), had little or no representation in the indices and that their currencies had *not* appreciated against the dollar.[32]

The two countries that came in for particular attention were Korea and Taiwan. (Singapore and Hong Kong were relatively exempt from criticism because both follow free trade policies. The Latin American countries had the excuse of difficult debts to service.). As of 1986, the new Taiwan dollar had only begun to appreciate against the U.S. dollar, and the Korean won still had not begun to do so, even though both countries had large trade surpluses. The U.S. government soon began to apply pressure on the two (as Fred Bergsten first urged in Seoul in July 1986), and the currencies were in fact allowed to appreciate relatively strongly. In the periodic reports to Congress required by the Omnibus Trade Bill of 1988, the Treasury focused heavily on Korea and Taiwan. In the October 1989 report, the Treasury announced the beginning of negotiations that went beyond simply pressuring Korea to appreciate the won, to push for a general liberalization of Korean financial markets and conversion to a market-oriented foreign exchange system, presumably meaning a regime of free floating.[33] There was a general appeal to the superiority of free market principles and a citation of the precedent of the yen/dollar talks.

5.2 Competing Economic Theories

Policies that are adopted are naturally the outcome of the positions held by various interest groups and policymakers and their interactions through the political process and their relative power. Secs. 5.4 and 5.5 of the paper discuss the competing interest groups and policymakers. Sec. 5.3 discusses the various possible positions regarding exchange rate policy among which they choose. In the area of exchange rates, the links from policy tools to the determination of the exchange rate, and even the links from the exchange rate to the economic welfare of various groups, are not entirely certain. For this reason, the differing models or views as to how the foreign exchange market (and the rest of the economy) operates can be as relevant as differing economic interests in determining the positions taken by various actors. Thus, in this section I begin with a brief discussion of alternative exchange rate theories.

32. A few economists at regional Federal Reserve banks initially overstated the case by including the Latin American countries in a comprehensive *nominal* exchange rate index and proclaiming that the depreciation of the dollar had in fact not taken place! A properly computed comprehensive *real* exchange rate index shows that the 1985–87 depreciation of the dollar was less than one would think if the other countries were not included but that the difference was not large.

33. Korea agreed to move to a so-called Market Average Rate system in March 1990 (see Frankel 1993).

5.2.1   Trade Balance Equilibration

A regime of purely floating exchange rates has held roughly for the United States since 1973 and held precisely in the early 1980s. Under such a regime, the exchange rate is determined in the private market and adjusts to clear supply and demand for foreign exchange without any intervention by the monetary authority. An old-fashioned view of exchange rate determination is that the supply and demand for foreign exchange are dominated by exports and imports (respectively) so that under floating rates the exchange rate adjusts so as to clear the trade balance. What makes this view old-fashioned is that foreign exchange markets today are dominated by financial transactions, rather than by trade, and have been ever since the major industrialized countries removed their major controls on the international flow of capital. The importance of international capital flows explains why the record U.S. trade deficits of the mid-1980s did not immediately produce an equilibrating depreciation of the dollar: the deficits were easily financed by massive borrowing from abroad. Some observers, however, professed to be surprised by this development and argued that the magnitude of the U.S. trade deficit in itself was evidence that floating exchange rates were not operating "as they were supposed to" and that some reform was therefore called for (Murchison and Solomon 1983).

One consequence of the trade balance equilibration view is the implication that, if one country adopts a policy change that differs from that of its neighbors (e.g., the fiscal expansion adopted by the United States in the 1980s), under a floating exchange rates the effects are felt entirely within the domestic economy, rather than being in part transmitted abroad, for example, via a domestic trade deficit and foreign trade surplus. It would in turn follow that, under floating rates, there is little need for international coordination of macroeconomic policy of the sort agreed on at the Louvre.

Large international capital flows are the most important of several ways in which this old-fashioned "insulation" result can be invalidated. Nevertheless, for the case of changes in monetary policy, leading multicountry econometric models suggest that it is in practice not far wrong to think that the exchange rate adjusts so as to produce little effect on the trade balance and little international transmission (Frankel 1988a). For fiscal policy, on the other hand, the trade balance and transmission effects are typically even greater under floating exchange rates than under fixed rates. Thus, it is no surprise that record U.S. trade deficits and European trade surpluses emerged beginning in 1983 or that calls for international coordination of policy followed.

5.2.2   Monetarism

For many, the most commonsensical modern view of international monetary economics was that of the monetarists. Among the relevant tenets of monetarism are (i) a belief in the central role of the money supply, particularly for determining the price level and exchange rate; (ii) a strong preference for low and stable growth in the money supply, so as to give price stability; (iii) suspicion of the motives and abilities of the Federal Reserve Board and an axiomatic belief that the country is more likely to get the proper sort of monetary policy if the Fed is brought more directly under the control of the political process (i.e., Congress or the Treasury); (iv) faith in free markets in general; and (v) extension of the free market philosophy to include the virtues of a freely floating exchange rate so that any country that prints too much money has to bear the burden itself in terms of inflation and currency depreciation. This last, the belief in floating exchange rates, was a position that Milton Friedman (1953) had advanced almost alone, at a time when such a change in the exchange rate regime seemed a remote pipe dream.

The monetarists entered the 1980s riding high. Largely as a response to the inflation of the 1970s and the other failures of Keynesian economics, the views of Milton Friedman and his followers had gone from those of an outlandish minority to wide acceptance and had supposedly been adopted as official policy by the Federal Reserve Board. At long last, a member of the Shadow Open Market Committee, Beryl Sprinkel, was appointed undersecretary for monetary affairs (1981–84), the position in the Treasury that traditionally has had responsibility not only for monetary affairs but for the exchange rate and other matters of international finance as well, and another, William Poole, was appointed to the President's Council of Economic Advisers (1982–85).

It was downhill from there. Intellectually, the monetarists were soon faced with the breakdown of their most cherished relation, that between money and prices. The big fall in velocity in the early 1980s caused the Federal Reserve Board to abandon its monetarist rule (in mid-1982 de facto, and several years later explicitly). Politically, their champion Sprinkel, who duly lectured the Fed from 1983 to 1986 that its rapid rate of money growth would soon produce a resurgence of inflation, was overruled by the secretary of the Treasury, who sought to pressure the Fed for *faster* growth, for the usual reasons of political expediency, particularly in the election year, 1984. This spectacle must have been an edifying lesson for the monetarists on the political economy of monetary policy. (Refer back to tenet iii above.)

In interagency meetings and public appearances, Sprinkel tried to explain the appreciation of the dollar as due to the administration's success at bringing down the rate of inflation. Such a factor could explain a *nominal* appreciation but not the *real* appreciation of the dollar in the early 1980s, which was almost as big as the nominal appreciation (as is readily apparent in fig. 5.1 above). Nor, for that matter, could the monetarist view explain the clear observed increase in real interest rates. With both the relation between money and prices and the relation between the price level and the exchange rate breaking down, the monetarists were in heavy retreat by the latter part of the decade. Sprinkel was not happy with the Treasury's 1985 conversion to managed exchange rates, but by then he was not in a position to affect policy on that topic.

5.2.3 Overshooting

The theory that *could* readily explain an increase in the real interest rate and a real appreciation of the dollar was the mainstream textbook macroeconomic view subscribed to by Feldstein and Volcker, among others. As explained in sec. 5.1 above, the two variables are closely associated: the increase in the real interest differential signals an increase in the expected rate of return on dollar securities; international investors respond to the enhanced attractiveness of dollar securities by increasing their demand for them, which causes the dollar to appreciate. The elegant seminal statement of this process was the overshooting model of Dornbusch (1976). In the overshooting equilibrium, everyone in the market agrees that the dollar has become "overvalued" in the sense that its current value is greater than its long-run value and that it will have to depreciate in the future; the market's expectation that the dollar will depreciate in the future is just sufficient to offset the higher interest rate that dollar assets pay, with the result that investors view dollar and nondollar securities as equally attractive in this equilibrium.

The overshooting model had some major difficulties of its own. Although the model could account for the *fact* of the dollar appreciation and for the *magnitude* (at least as of early 1984), it could not explain the *duration* of the appreciation, a long, drawn-out process that lasted until February 1985. In theory, the appreciation should have occurred in one jump (e.g., when the magnitude of the budget deficits became known), or in two jumps (e.g., beginning with the monetary contraction of 1980), or at most in four or five jumps (as bits of information on the monetary/fiscal policy mix came out). It should then have begun its gradual return to long-run equilibrium. As described in section 5.1.5 above, from mid-1984 on, far from beginning its return to long-run equilibrium, the dollar continued to appreciate at an accelerated rate, in the face not only of an ever-worsening trade balance but of a real interest differential that had begun to diminish as well. It appeared that the dollar was "overshooting the overshooting equilibrium." This was definitely *not* how floating exchange rates were supposed to behave, and observers increasingly began considering alternatives.

5.2.4 New Classical Macroeconomics

It was clear that the last 20 percent real appreciation of the dollar up to February 1985 could not be correlated with readily observable, standard, macroeconomic fundamentals. That left two possibilities. The first theory, coming from the new classical macroeconomic school, says that movements in the real exchange rate come from fundamental shifts in "tastes and technology" that may not be observable. Although most proponents of the new classical school are notorious for omitting to suggest what the specific fundamental shifts might be in any particular episode, others have suggested that Reagan reductions in tax rates, especially on capital income, could be the explanation behind the appreciation of the dollar in the early 1980s (e.g., Dooley and Isard 1985; Bovenberg 1989).[34]

This school of thought provides the most respectable intellectual foundation for the "safe-haven" view of the strong dollar that was so prevalent in the first Reagan administration. But many observers find it implausible that there could have been a shift in taste toward American goods or an increase in U.S. productivity, or tax effects, sufficiently large to explain an upswing in the value of the dollar as large as that from mid-1984 to February 1985, only to be reversed rapidly thereafter. At the Plaza in September 1985, the Treasury abandoned the previous line that the value of the dollar was an indicator of American economic strength. One obvious motivation was the awareness that the downward trend that had appeared over the preceding six months would, under this theory, be interpreted as evidence of American economic weakness.[35]

5.2.5   Speculative Bubbles

The second possibility is that the final stage of appreciation of the dollar in February 1985 was an example of a speculative bubble: a self-confirming increase in the value of the dollar arising from purchases of dollars by speculators who think that it will appreciate. The standard theory of speculative bubbles has the advantage that it can be perfectly consistent with rational expectations: a speculator cannot necessarily expect to make money from the knowledge that the market is in a bubble because he does not know when the bubble will burst. But the standard version of the theory has the disadvantage that it has nothing to say about what gets such speculative bubbles started.

Recent formulations of fads and speculative bubbles that are not necessarily rational focus on the existence of different classes of speculators: one class that forecasts on the basis of macroeconomic fundamentals and another that just tries to guess which way the rest of the market is going. The apparently perverse increase in the demand for dollars in 1984–85, for example, might be explained by the decreased confidence that speculators were placing in fundamentalists' forecasts of future depreciation and the increased confidence that they were placing in the extrapolations of "technical analysts" (Frankel and Froot 1990; Krugman 1985; Marris 1985).[36]

5.2.6   Portfolio Balance

For present purposes, the most important aspect of the portfolio-balance model is that it adds a policy tool: its says that even *sterilized* foreign exchange

---

34. This view was also put forward by CEA members Niskanen and Poole in the 1985 *Economic Report of the President.*

35. In this sense, Secretary Baker was jumping on the bandwagon rather than leading it.

36. Technical analysts, also known as "chartists," use such atheoretical techniques as extrapolating past trends in the exchange rate by noting whenever the short-run moving average crosses the long-run moving average.

intervention, that is, intervention that does not change money supplies, can affect the exchange rate. The reason is that investors are assumed to view long positions taken in various currencies as imperfect substitutes for each other, even if they are not holding actual foreign currency. Other approaches, such as the monetarist model, by contrast, are quite firm that only to the extent that intervention changes money supplies (in which case it is just a species of monetary policy) can it have an effect. This is the position Beryl Sprinkel took, for example, when his French counterpart Michel Camdessus tried to argue the desirability of foreign exchange intervention in preparations for the 1982 summit of G-7 heads of state at Versailles (Putnam and Bayne 1987, 133).

Another aspect of the portfolio balance approach is that it implies that, although trade balance equilibration is not operative in the short run, it is operative in the long run. Because a deficit country must borrow to finance its deficit, the accumulation of international indebtedness over time will eventually force its currency to depreciate. Some would say that mounting indebtedness is what finally forced the dollar down during the period 1985–87.

5.3   Competing Views on Desirable Exchange Rate Arrangements

Differing models as to how the foreign exchange market operates translate into different views as to the appropriate government response. But it is not a one-to-one correspondence.

5.3.1   Leave the Foreign Exchange Market Alone

There are four principal variants of the school of thought that says that the government should allow the foreign exchange market to function freely on its own. The most extreme position, held by monetarists and the new classical school, says that there is no need to be concerned about exchange rate fluctuations because they have no real effects. The simplest form of this argument claims that movements in the real exchange rate are nonexistent because movements in the nominal exchange rate serve only to offset differences in inflation rates. But this view steadily lost adherents as the 1980s progressed because it was evident that the nominal appreciation of the dollar was almost fully reflected as a real appreciation of the dollar. The more sophisticated form of the argument (the new classical view, mentioned above) holds that, although there clearly are real fluctuations in the exchange rate, these are fluctuations due to real changes in productivity or tastes and would have taken place anyway, even if the exchange rate had not been freely floating. An increasing number of observers also found this view harder to swallow in 1984–85, but the vote was far from unanimous.

Even among the large majority who agree that exchange rate movements have real effects on the trade deficit and other important variables, there are other viewpoints that lead to the conclusion that the government should refrain from interfering. One is the view that exchange rate movements are the natural result of changes in macroeconomic policy and may actually be desirable if one takes the changes in policy as given. In the case of the 1982–84 dollar appreciation, attributed to the widening federal budget deficit, the question was whether the dollar appreciation was desirable if one took the budget deficit as a given political constraint.

CEA Chairman Feldstein argued that it was. The strong dollar acted as a "safety valve" to distribute the crowding-out effects of the budget deficit more evenly among sectors of the private economy. The Feldstein doctrine (so christened by Fred Bergsten) held that, even if policymakers were somehow able to force the dollar down without changing fiscal (or monetary) policy—for example, by sterilized foreign exchange intervention or capital controls—the favorable effects on the export- and import-competing sectors would be more than offset by unfavorable effects: the lost capital inflow would result in real interest rates even higher than those prevailing at the time, which would hurt those sectors of the economy (such as capital goods) where demand is sensitive to the real interest rate. The result would be a "lopsided recovery" (CEA 1984; Feldstein 1984).

One related viewpoint refuses to take fiscal and monetary policy as given. It argues that exchange rate targets or other financial gimmickry can deflect political resolve to deal with budget deficits and other domestic objectives that ultimately may be more important than the exchange rate or the trade balance.[37] Another argues that, if central banks are encouraged to intervene in the foreign exchange market, they will gamble away the taxpayers' money, to little avail.[38] A final viewpoint is that floating rates allow a greater degree of policy independence among countries that do fixed rates or managed floating (even if they do not allow complete insulation as held by the trade balance equilibration view) and that such decentralization of national policy-making is best because each country is the best judge of its own needs (Corden 1983).

5.3.2 Commit Monetary or Fiscal Policy to Helping Stabilize the Exchange Rate

The argument that allowing the full effect of the mix of monetary and fiscal policies to be reflected in the exchange rate maximizes the chance that those policies will be adjusted appropriately has a mirror-image argument on the other side: committing countries to exchange rate targets maximizes the chance that monetary and fiscal policy will be appropriate.

Many believe that the government should commit to some degree of stabilization of the exchange rate. One of the more prominent and practical proposals is the Williamson proposal for target zones. Part of the argument for making

37. A counterargument that places more weight on the exchange rate and trade balance objectives is based on the political economy point that Congress tends to adopt damaging protectionist policies when a dollar appreciation increases the trade deficit. Bergsten (1982, 1984), e.g., argued that, for such reasons, the exchange rate objective should be given increased weight.

38. This concern is common among the monetarists.

such a commitment is that, even though macroeconomic policies will ultimately have to be adjusted in order to keep the exchange rate within the band,
such adjustment is desirable. Williamson (1983, 1987) has argued, for example, that, if target zones had been in place in the early 1980s, the Reagan
administration would have been forced to abandon its policies that were producing excessive budget deficits.[39]

5.3.3   Attempt to Decouple the Exchange Rate from Other Macroeconomic Policies

For anyone aware simultaneously of the trade costs of an overly strong dollar, the inflationary consequences of an expansionary monetary policy to depreciate the dollar, and the political difficulties in cutting the U.S. budget deficit, any sort of policy instrument that could bring about a depreciation of the
dollar *without* changing monetary or fiscal policy would be a godsend. A few
such instruments have been proposed.

Although *sterilized intervention* has no effect on the exchange rate in the
view of many because by definition it does not change money supplies, it *can*
have an effect if it changes expectations regarding future money supplies *or* if
the portfolio-balance model is correct. At the Versailles Summit of 1982, the
French argued that foreign exchange intervention did provide an independent
and useful tool; the Americans agreed to form an intergovernmental working
group to study the question (and to enact a process of "multilateral surveillance" by the Group of 5). The findings of the working group, known as the
Jurgensen Report (*Report of the Working Group* 1983), were submitted to the
G-7 leaders at the Williamsburg Summit of 1983.

Although the Plaza Accord is widely perceived as having strikingly reversed
the position of the G-7, particularly the United States, on the question of the
effectiveness of intervention, there was in fact no discussion in the Plaza deliberations or in the communiqué as to whether the intervention undertaken
should be sterilized or not. Indeed, there was not much discussion at the major
meetings as to what sort of monetary policies would be appropriate to support
exchange rate objectives. The exception is that the Plaza Accord called for
Japanese monetary policy to "exercise flexible management with due attention
to the yen exchange rate" (Funabashi 1988, 265; Dobson 1991, table 5.1, p.
82). When the Bank of Japan raised its discount rate soon after the Plaza, it
claimed a reduction in the yen/dollar rate as its objective, although others were
less sure that this was truly its motive.

Concerted intervention, that is, by all or most of the G-7 central banks simultaneously, is reported to be more effective. There is indeed some evidence
that the whole may be greater than the sum of the parts, especially if the inter-

---

39. Feldstein, on the other hand, has countered that, if a serious target zone had been in place
in the early 1980s, the government would not have reacted to the dollar appreciation by cutting
the budget deficit but would have shifted to an inflationary monetary policy sooner.

vention is *announced* to the public and if it reinforces a movement that is already under way (Dominguez and Frankel 1991; see also Mussa 1981).

Capital controls were used by the United States to lessen downward pressure on the dollar before 1973 and by Germany and Japan to stem upward pressure on their currencies. Some, such as Tobin (1978), Bergsten (1984), and Dornbusch (1986), proposed in the early 1980s that the U.S. reimpose controls to stem capital inflow or that Japan be urged to strengthen its controls on capital outflow (rather than being pressured to remove them). It was also suggested that the Japanese government could and did use *administrative guidance* to discourage Japanese investors from holding dollar assets in the early 1980s or to encourage them to hold dollar assets in 1987–88.

Most economists viewed these various instruments as unlikely to be very effective, in the absence of changes in monetary or fiscal policy. Many practitioners, however, believed that they could have an effect, at least in the short run.

5.3.4   Fix the Exchange Rate

For some countries (small and open), a fixed exchange rate may be a practical option. Here one of the major arguments for fixing the rate is to commit monetary policy to a noninflationary policy in a way that is sufficiently credible to workers and financial markets that reduced expectations of inflation help eliminate actual inflation. For a country like the United States, a fixed exchange rate is no longer a very viable option.[40]

Nevertheless, a special case of a fixed exchange rate system, the gold standard, was frequently proposed by a certain influential group, the supply-siders. The same *Wall Street Journal* editorial writers who brought us the Laffer curve in the area of tax policy also brought us the Mundell-Laffer hypothesis (which claimed that changes in the nominal exchange rate were one for one and instantly offset by changes in price levels so that devaluations had no real effects) and the proposal that monetary stability could be restored only by returning to a regime where the central bank made a commitment to peg the price of gold. This view had important adherents in the starting team at the Treasury in 1981. But, in March 1982, the Gold Commission that had been appointed to investigate such proposals submitted a negative report. By 1983, only the moderate Manuel Johnson, at the assistant secretary level, was left among the original supply-siders at Treasury. When Johnson was appointed vice-chairman of the Federal Reserve Board at the beginning of 1986, joining other recent appointees perceived as favoring easier money, some feared that gold standard proponents had taken over. But, like Thomas à Becket after he was appointed archbishop of Canterbury, the historical integrity of the institutional prevailed, and Johnson became a model of central banker rectitude.

---

40. McKinnon (1988), however, continued to offer specific versions of his proposal for a return to fixed exchange rates (among the United States, Germany, and Japan).

The administration continued to be susceptible to penetration by a minority of gold bugs, however. Laffer came to meetings of an academic advisory group in the White House, gold-bug think tanks like Jude Wanniski's firm Polyconomics and the Lehrman Institute were heard from frequently, and Congressman Jack Kemp was always a rival for the attentions of Conservative Republican supporters. At the October 1987 annual meeting of the IMF, Baker proposed that the G-7 add to its list of indicators the price of "a basket of commodities, including gold." This proposal was accepted by the G-7 at the Toronto Summit in June 1988, although without the explicit reference to gold, which Baker had included in his speech to outflank congressional gold bug Kemp.

5.4   Competing Interest Groups

In this section, I consider some of the major economic interest groups affected by the exchange rate.

5.4.1   Manufacturing

U.S. manufacturers were clearly hurt by the appreciation of the dollar in the early 1980s, losing export customers around the world and losing domestic customers to competition from a flood of imports.[41] In contrast to smaller, more open countries, exchange rate policy in the United States had not traditionally been a high priority in the list of issues on which the manufacturing sector would lobby in national politics. But, during the period 1983–85, as the value of the dollar continued to climb to new heights and the trade balance continued to sink to new lows, an increasing number of business groups and chief executives from large corporations lodged complaints in Washington and urged action.

Lee Morgan, chairman of Caterpillar Tractor in the early 1980s, stands out as an example of activism on the exchange rate issue, both in terms of the consistency and the earliness (starting as early as December 1981 [testimony before a House committee cited in Funabashi 1988, 70]) of his efforts and in terms of their policy payoff. The Illinois maker of construction equipment was engaged in intense competition for customers around the world with a Japanese rival, Komatsu. Morgan realized that, as a major American exporter, his interest lay with outward-oriented trade policies rather than protectionism. But he also realized that taking measures to reduce costs at Caterpillar would not be sufficient to maintain international competitiveness if they were offset by appreciation of the dollar.

Morgan's influence went far beyond that of the CEO of a typical large corporation. He could claim to be a spokesman for the business community, heading

---

41. Branson and Love (1988) provide statistical evidence on the sectoral effects of the strong dollar.

a task force of the influential Business Roundtable, which took a strong position on the exchange rate beginning in 1983. Furthermore, he personally had a degree of access to top policymakers that went beyond that of a typical political supporter.[42] In repeated meetings with administration cabinet members (the first one was in the White House in October 1982), Morgan argued for an activist exchange rate policy.

For the first two years, such lobbying by the Business Roundtable and others (the National Association of Manufacturers [NAM] was also vocal on the need for policies to bring down the dollar) appeared to have little or no effect on policy. But, as described in section 5.1.4 above, Lee Morgan's visit to the White House and Treasury in late September 1983 (with Murchison and Solomon) was the impetus for Don Regan's entire yen/dollar campaign. By the beginning of 1985, the number of voices from the U.S. manufacturing sector protesting the administration's neglect of the dollar and the trade deficit had multiplied greatly. This was certainly a major influence on the thinking of Baker and Darman when they finally shifted the administration to an activist position on the exchange rate.

The Business Roundtable was usually careful to say that measures to try to bring down the dollar should not be taken in isolation, that measures to reduce the federal budget deficit were an important part of the package. An interesting question was whether the economic interest of American manufacturing lay on the side of efforts to bring down the dollar, if one took the budget deficit as a fixed political constraint. In the widely accepted analysis of Feldstein, measures that did not try to work through macroeconomic policies (say, capital controls, foreign exchange intervention, or public statements)—even if effective at bringing down the dollar and reducing the trade deficit—would reduce the capital inflow and raise U.S. interest rates. The crowding out would be borne less by exchange rate–sensitive industries and more by interest rate–sensitive industries.

Neat theoretical distinctions regarding sector sensitivities tend to break down, however, as soon as one recognizes that many of the industries that are most sensitive to the exchange rate are the same as the ones that are the most sensitive to the interest rate: autos, aircraft, and capital goods in general. This may explain—if one is willing to attribute enough sophistication to business leaders—why many of them did not devote much energy to the exchange rate issue until the bubble period of late 1984 and 1985, when the dollar seemed divorced from economic fundamentals: until then, the trade-off between high

---

42. The Reagan administration was said by insiders to owe a large political favor to Morgan and his company, as one of three American suppliers that had heavily lost business when the government instituted an embargo on equipment being used in the construction of the USSR-Europe gas pipeline beginning in December 1981. (Caterpillar lost sales of two hundred pipe layers [Nollen 1987, 7]). It was also relevant that Caterpillar's hometown (Peoria) had House Minority Leader Robert Michel as its congressman.

interest rates and a high dollar had been regarded as inexorable, given the budget deficit.

The manufacturing leaders who had been complaining about administration neglect of the dollar all praised the Plaza Agreement of September 1985. Some, like NAM, continued to call for a weaker dollar in 1986 and 1987 and in particular to call for appreciation by Taiwan, Korea, and other NICs. But, in the late 1980s, the exchange rate was no longer a salient enough issue to rouse most of the business community to political action (Destler and Henning 1989, 130–31).

5.4.2   Agriculture

The agricultural sector is quite sensitive to the exchange rate. In theory, the effect on the farmer comes directly through the price that he or she receives for his or her product: a 10 percent increase in the value of the dollar causes an immediate 10 percent fall in the world price of the crop when expressed in dollars. In practice, subsidies and other distortions in almost every country partially insulate farmers from the international market. But inflationary monetary policies, together with specific agricultural policies, encouraged American agriculture to expand output and exports in the 1970s, with the result that, by the 1980s, they had indeed become quite dependent on exports.

The switch in the monetary/fiscal policy mix in the early 1980s and the appreciation of the dollar put strong downward pressure on dollar commodity prices. Existing farm support programs reduced the impact on the farmer by buying up large quantities of unwanted crops and making support payments that in some years were as large as total net farm income. But the existence of the large accumulated government holdings of commodities kept prices depressed for some years after the macroeconomic situation began to reverse in the mid-1980s, with the result that the effect of the programs was to spread the negative effect out over time (not to mention inflict high costs on consumers) rather than just to dampen it. The rural sector considered the 1980s a disastrous decade for it, and there was much talk of a bifurcated economy, with service-oriented California and the Northeast doing well and everybody in between (both the Rust Belt and the Farm Belt) doing poorly.

Farm lobbies came out in favor of a depreciation of the dollar, and Agriculture Secretary Block was one of the voices in cabinet meetings in 1983–85 who were concerned about the policy mix, the dollar, and the trade deficit. Agrarian populists consistently favor easier money, lower interest rates, and a weaker dollar. Ninety years ago they were championed by presidential candidate William Jennings Bryan, who campaigned against the "cross of gold," the commitment to the gold standard that was keeping money tight. In the early 1980s, a *return* to the gold standard was seen as a way of getting easier money by supply-siders like 1984 presidential candidate Jack Kemp (Frankel 1986). At the beginning of 1986, agrarian populism got a champion appointed to the

Federal Reserve Board: Wayne Angell, who, at the time, was considered to be in favor of easy money. One observer has included the Farm Aid movement as one of the pressure groups that in 1985–86 successfully protested the high dollar and trade deficit, leading to a switch to policies of intervention in the foreign exchange market and easier money.[43]

Although the agricultural sector was clearly in the camp opposed to the strong dollar, it did not expend a great deal of lobbying time or expense on this particular issue. Obvious explanations include that lobbying resources expended directly on farm legislation had a greater payoff, and that a serious attack on the macroeconomic source of the appreciation (the budget deficit) would likely include cut-backs on farm subsidies (Destler and Henning 1989, 124). But there is another possible reason why efforts to bring down the dollar, even taking the budget deficit as given, may not have been clearly in the farm sector's interest: interest rates. The high real interest rates that resulted from the 1980s switch in macro policy mix were as much a source of negative pressure on commodity prices (via low inventory demand) and of financial distress for farmers (many of whom were heavily in debt) as the high dollar. Thus, the commodity sector faced the same trade-off between interest rates and the dollar as such industries as capital goods, autos, and aircraft: an effort to bring down the dollar *without* changing macro policies—even if successful—would be a mixed blessing in that it would probably lead to even higher interest rates.

5.4.3   Labor

In classic Hecksher-Ohlin-Samuelson trade theory, the interests of labor and capital (or land) should line up on opposite sides, according to whether the manufacture of exports and imports is intensive in their use. In practice, their interests seem to fit better the "specific-factor" model. Auto workers and auto capitalists, for example, both have a lot invested in the auto industry and thus ally themselves more closely with each other in questions of trade than with workers or capitalists, respectively, in other industries.[44] In the case of the strong 1980s dollar, this means that labor in the manufacturing sector was opposed to the strong dollar in the same way as managers and owners in that sector.

Relative to the agricultural sector, labor had a head start in the sense that the trade deficit had already been a priority concern for some time (particularly in the sectors badly hurt by import competition in the 1970s: auto, steel, and textiles). The AFL-CIO, for example, came out against the administration's neglect of the dollar and its implications for the trade deficit in early 1984. But labor representatives gave less priority to the exchange rate issue than the business community did, in part because they tended to be more enamored of

43. See Havrilesky (1990, 57), who sees this episode as fitting a "public choice" theory of how monetary expansion follows after a period of redistributive policies.

44. See Frieden (1990, 13–19), who argues that the steadily increasing degree of international capital mobility is detaching the interests of the "capitalist class" from sector-specific policies.

industrial policy as an alternative antidote for the trade deficit (Destler and Henning 1989, 122–24).

5.4.4   Sectors That Benefit from a Strong Dollar

There are a number of actors in the economy who benefit from a strong dollar, most obviously consumers, firms that import inputs (such as oil and semiconductors), and the importers themselves (including shipping, marketing, and retail). The entire segment of the economy composed of goods and services that are not traded internationally clearly benefits from an increase in the price of their output in terms of the price of the internationally traded segment of the economy. The strongest case, in theory, is the construction industry. In the first place, the tradable component there is close to zero. In the second, measures to force down the dollar at the expense of a cutoff in capital flows and an increase in real interest rates would hurt the construction sector more clearly than any other.[45]

All the sectors just named during the strong-dollar period were in fact silent on the exchange rate issue. Part of the explanation is that constituents with grievances tend to speak louder in the political process than constituents who are benefiting from the current state of affairs. Much of the explanation is that the links from the exchange rate to their economic welfare are less tangible, certain, and well understood than is the case for the sectors hurt by the strong dollar. American consumers are notoriously unaware of their own fondness for imports.

In the case of interest-sensitive industries like construction, even though their lobbying representatives did not focus on international factors, they always favored a reversal of the early 1980s pattern of monetary contraction, fiscal expansion, and high real interest rates. Furthermore, the monetary authorities were fully aware that they would become a source of political pressure in the event that a cutoff of foreign capital inflows forced up interest rates.

5.4.5   Banks and Other Financial Institutions

Henning (1990, 41) argues that many U.S. banks were "unsympathetic to industry's problems in the early 1980s. With far less leverage over the management of industrial enterprises than their foreign counterparts, some bank CEOs hoped, with the Federal Reserve, that the appreciation of the dollar would force rationalization and cost-saving upon what they perceived to be a spendthrift and undisciplined manufacturing sector."

At a large 1985 meeting sponsored by Congressman Jack Kemp and Senator Bill Bradley, some representatives of the banking and financial community were among the few defenders of a laissez-faire exchange rate regime, against

---

45. Frieden (1991, 448) argues that the Reagan administration's polices may have been a deliberate response to the interests of its "principal bases of support in the defense community, in real estate and related sectors, and in the international investors group, [where] pressures were for increased spending on nontradables."

the many industrial executives and other participants who had gathered to rally around efforts to bring the dollar down. Lester Thurow declared that the issue was a syndrome familiar from the United Kingdom, in which the financial community in the City of London supports a strong currency while the manufacturing cities support a weak currency. In American terms, it would be "Wall Street" versus "Main Street." But John Bilson, a self-described Chicago currency speculator, responded that the issue is not a strong dollar versus a weak one but rather a highly variable dollar, from which currency traders profit, versus a stable dollar, which industry finds more conducive.

Foreign exchange trading is big business for banks, in terms of both volume (over $110 billion a day in 1989) and profit. Econometric causality tests suggest that higher exchange rate volatility leads to higher dispersion of opinion across market participants (as reflected in survey data) and that higher dispersion in turn leads to a higher volume of trading (Frankel and Froot 1990). Exchange rate volatility is also clearly in the interest of those who make their living trading foreign exchange futures and options on the Philadelphia and Chicago Mercantile Exchanges; these instruments did not even exist under the fixed exchange rate system that ended in 1973. In short, one could explain on simple self-interest grounds a tendency for the financial community to be more supportive of floating rates than the rest of the country.

Two representatives of the financial community, in particular, spoke out against the government's 1985 switch toward trying to stabilize exchange rates. In 1986, the Chicago Mercantile Exchange formed a group called the American Coalition for Flexible Exchange Rates to lobby against exchange rate management. In 1987 and 1988, the Economic Advisory Committee of the American Bankers' Association also offered public statements against interfering with floating rates (Destler and Henning 1989, 131–36).

The large New York banks, however, for the most part stayed away from this sort of activity, and there is no reason to believe it had much impact (Destler and Henning 1989).[46] Even though exchange rate volatility is a boon to the foreign exchange trading room, it can be a headache to bank divisions that deal with international borrowing and lending, in the same way as it is to the international operations of nonfinancial corporations.[47] In any case, lobbying the government in favor of volatility would be too antisocial a mode of behavior for most financial institutions to engage in. Henning (1990 p. 41) concludes that most bankers "neither actively opposed nor supported those corporate of-

46. Destler and Henning explain that one reason that much of the banking community viewed with concern Baker's attempt to manage exchange rates (at the Louvre, in particular) is that it would threaten the independence of the Fed in setting monetary policy.

47. One view is that there is a relevant split *within* the financial community, between Chicago-based traders of futures and options, who profit from volatility, and the New York–based investment bankers, who—exercising influence through the secretary of the Treasury and Washington regulatory agencies—have sought in recent years to reign in the freewheeling ways of the Midwesterners.

ficials from the real sector who called for a depreciation of the dollar in 1982–85."

One place where the New York financial community has secured the help of the government is in putting pressure on countries in East Asia and elsewhere to open their financial markets to greater participation by U.S. firms. Such issues would properly fall in the sphere of trade policy rather than exchange rate policy, but for the Treasury's linking them to the campaign to appreciate the yen in 1984 and the won in 1988–90. In the yen/dollar talks, Don Regan put high priority, for example, on the Tokyo Stock Exchange making some seats available to American securities companies.[48]

5.5 Competing Policymakers

A policy-making agency determines its stand on an issue on the basis in part of the ultimate goals of its constituents (e.g., low interest rates or a low dollar) and its perceptions of the link between policy instruments and economic goals. Actual policy is then determined by the interaction of the agencies with each other and with the media.

5.5.1 The Federal Reserve Board

In the United States, the Treasury has primary responsibility for intervention, while the Fed has official responsibility for monetary policy. Indeed, in practice the Treasury usually determines intervention in the foreign exchange market, even though the Federal Reserve Bank of New York is the agent that undertakes all intervention in a mechanical sense, and even though the foreign exchange reserves that are used are the Fed's own as often as the Treasury's.[49] Economic theory says that it should be virtually impossible to determine exchange rate policy separately from monetary policy. But the politics of this attempt at decentralized responsibility have their own logic.

In 1984 and 1985, Volcker, concerned about the trade deficit, supported the idea of some amount of foreign exchange intervention to try to bring the dollar down. This put him in conflict with the Treasury, particularly with Regan and Sprinkel in 1984. There was little question of the Fed chairman trying to overcome Treasury objections to intervention; Volcker was well advised to save most of his ammunition to protect Fed independence on monetary policy and a bit to snipe at the fiscal policies that were at the root of the trade deficit. But

48. The first beneficiary turned out to be Merrill-Lynch, the company of which Regan had previously been chairman (Frankel 1984, 47).

49. Over the years, some Treasury officials have taken the position that the secretary of the Treasury, as the chief financial officer of the government, has the ultimate legal authority over intervention even when it is conducted with the Federal Reserve's own money. Fed officials like Paul Volcker point out that such claims are not based in any legal statute, such as the Federal Reserve Act, which gives the central bank its independence, but agree that the Fed has never challenged Treasury supremacy in this area in practice and is unlikely to do so in the future.

Volcker clearly welcomed Baker's 1985 abandonment of the position that the strong dollar was a good thing. He did not view the Plaza as putting undesirable constraints on monetary policy.

Soon after the Plaza, the positions had switched, with the Treasury in favor of further depreciation of the dollar and Volcker warning of the dangers of a speculative run. The Fed had no choice but to go along when the Treasury wanted to intervene. But, during the remainder of the decade, the central bank played the traditional role of the party more concerned about the dangers of a free-fall of the currency and an increase in inflation.

By 24 February 1986, the balance of power at the Federal Reserve Board had swung away from Volcker in favor of the recent easy-money Reagan appointees, who voted a reduction in the discount rate against the opposition of the chairman in a famous "palace coup." Volcker then managed to persuade Governors Preston Martin and Wayne Angell to defer the discount rate cut until he could arrange similar coordinated cuts by the Bundesbank and the Bank of Japan. The explanation offered by Volcker was that a unilateral U.S. monetary expansion would cause the Plaza depreciation to turn into an uncontrolled free-fall of the dollar.[50] But it appears clear that Volcker was also looking for a way to avoid having been outvoted by his Board, a way to save face and thereby retain the effective leadership. The chairman retreated into the complexities of international finance, knowing that this was unfamiliar territory to the others. One lesson here is that the bonds of fraternity that existed between Volcker and his counterparts at the German and Japanese central banks were stronger than the relationship between him and the recent Reagan appointees. It was not long thereafter that Vice-Governor Martin resigned from the Board.

In 1987 Greenspan inherited Volcker's concern that a weak dollar policy would be an inflationary policy, while in 1988 Nicholas Brady inherited Baker's concern that a strong dollar policy would be bad for growth and bad for the trade balance. Indeed, these actors were playing out the age-old conflict between central bankers and treasury ministers over whether money should be tight.

Vice-Chairman Manuel Johnson had responsibility at the Fed for dealing with other countries' central banks (after the death of Henry Wallich and especially after the resignation of Wallich's replacement, Robert Heller). Johnson and Mulford reportedly came into more open conflict over the dollar than did Greenspan and Brady. One story has it that, after a failure of Johnson and Mulford to iron out differences in 1989 (Redburn 1990, 63), Johnson in protest registered a technical objection to the way the Treasury was running exchange rate policy: a disproportionately large share of the intervention was being conducted with the Fed's reserves fund rather than with the Treasury's own ex-

---

50. Funabashi (1988, 48–49) accepts the explanation that Volcker both knew more and cared more about the exchange rate implications of such actions than did the other, more domestically oriented governors.

change stabilization fund. Later, in the aftermath of the Japanese stock market crash of early 1990, the Johnson-Mulford conflict resurfaced over whether the Fed or the Bank of Japan should be the one to ease. Johnson resigned in mid-1990, however.

Most other countries, to a greater extent than the United States, vest responsibility for exchange rate policy and monetary policy with the same authority. But, when it comes to international discussions, the U.S. "schizophrenia" seems to prevail. As noted above, the G-5 ministers, at the Plaza and subsequently, did not discuss sterilization of intervention, or even monetary policy, when deciding to take action to try to affect the exchange rate. Whether or not intervention in reality offers a tool for affecting the exchange rate that is independent of monetary policy, the policy-making apparatus is set up as if it does: exchange rate policy is discussed by the G-5 and G-7 finance ministers, while monetary policy is discussed by central bankers, for example, at G-10 meetings ten times a year at the Bank for International Settlements in Basel. Although the G-7 meetings would probably benefit from the attendance of the central bankers, the latter are not entirely sure that they want to be included. A system in which the politicians can be seen engaging in international economic diplomacy in the public eye, without binding the monetary authorities to the policies that would logically be required if the commitments to manage exchange rates were interpreted literally, is a system that has attractions for both sets of actors.

5.5.2   The Rest of the Administration

In the years 1983–84, the press contained many reports to the effect that CEA Chairman Feldstein was a lone voice of dissent within the administration, that the White House and the rest of the cabinet sided with the Treasury in maintaining that the deficit dollar problem was not a problem. In reality, Secretary of Commerce Malcolm Baldrige, Secretary of Agriculture John Block, Special Trade Representative (later Labor Secretary) William Brock, and Budget Director David Stockman were all by 1984 speaking in cabinet and subcabinet meetings on the damage done by the strong dollar.[51] The president did not himself deal with policy issues as detailed as the value of the dollar, in the sense of running or attending cabinet meetings on the subject.

Secretary of State Shultz occasionally expressed a view in private, based on his own background as an economist. In a very low-key way, he argued within the administration for dollar depreciation as early as July 1983, including even investigation of a possible "interest equalization tax" on capital in-

---

51. Nor did the president ever "discipline" Feldstein in any way for failing to toe the line. This would simply not have been consistent with Reagan's temperament. (Stockman [1986], e.g., reveals that his own celebrated "trip to the woodshed" for speaking out on the budget deficit never in fact took place.) This allowed Feldstein to claim, truthfully, that he had as much right to claim to be speaking for the administration as Regan did.

flow.[52] But Undersecretary for International Affairs Allen Wallis, the State Department representative at cabinet-level meetings on the dollar and the trade deficit, sided with the Treasury position that the strong dollar was good rather than bad. In any case, as already noted, Shultz recognized that dollar issues were the Treasury's turf, not his. After 1985, with the depreciation under way, the tendency for other agencies to cede primacy on this issue to the Treasury was reinforced.

5.5.3   Congress

Throughout the 1980s, Congress evinced far more concern with the U.S. trade deficit than did the White House. In the political environment of Capitol Hill, denying that a problem like the trade deficit or the strong dollar is really a problem provokes strong attacks. Many hearings were held to underscore that these were in fact serious problems. Studies were commissioned.[53] The 11–13 November 1985 conferences on the dollar organized by Congressman Jack Kemp and Senator Bill Bradley (or, more accurately, entrepreneured by their former staffers Smick and Medley) was billed as a "U.S. Congressional Summit" and had pretentions even more far reaching in scope: legislators and other representatives from foreign countries were invited, and the organizers also sought to associate Baker and Darman with the conference's views on world monetary reform. Such activities had the effect of raising public consciousness of the exchange rate as an issue.

The Congress was much more limited in the specific policy actions it could take, however. The one relevant sphere in which the Congress did have primacy was trade legislation. Although this alternative (perceived) means of addressing the trade deficit was not directly relevant to the exchange rate, there were important political links. In April 1985, Senators John Danforth (R) and Lloyd Bentsen (D) took the position that the Congress should insist on plans for addressing the exchange rate problem as a prerequisite for granting the administration the "fast-track authority" it had requested for (what was to become) the Uruguay Round of multilateral trade negotiations (Destler and Henning 1989, 104–5).

This case of specifically tying trade policy to the exchange rate issue was relatively rare. More often, congressmen simply responded to the record trade deficits by proposing trade legislation that free traders in the administration found unpalatable, unintentionally exerting pressure on the Treasury to try to bring down the dollar and thereby the trade deficit. The threat of mounting

52. Shultz gave a speech at Princeton in the spring of 1985 that some considered an important public reversal of the benign neglect policy of the first Reagan administration, setting the stage for the Plaza.

53. As was hinted at in sec. 5.1.4 above, some of Caterpillar Tractor Chairman Lee Morgan's impact on exchange rate issues was exercised via his congressmen. For example, he persuaded Senator Charles Percy to ask the GAO to investigate charges of exchange rate manipulation on the part of Japan's Ministry of Finance.

protectionism on Capitol Hill was certainly one of the major motivations for the Treasury's 1985 turnaround on the dollar. The success of the Plaza initiative at forestalling protectionist legislation is the major respect in which Baker deserves credit for a political triumph, notwithstanding the open question whether the Plaza was in fact responsible for the dollar depreciation, and notwithstanding that the trade deficit did not in fact improve in dollar terms until 1988 (and did not fall below its 1985 level until 1989).

The Congress also began to pass resolutions and consider bills that required specific action on exchange rate policy. Of several bills submitted in mid-1985, a proposal by Senator Bradley was the most specific. It would have required the creation of a "warchest" of intervention funds to be used according to the following rule: every time four consecutive quarters show a current account deficit in excess of 1.5 percent of GNP and a dollar at least 15 percent above the level corresponding to current account balance, the Treasury would be required to purchase at least \$3 billion in foreign currency over the subsequent quarter. Needless to say, the Treasury was disturbed by these open assaults on its right to make exchange rate policy. This threat from the Congress was another of the factors that contributed to Baker's reversal of policy in 1985.

Even after the Plaza, skeptical congressmen continued to press for systematic reform of exchange rate policy. More bills were proposed by others, including Representative Stan Lundine (D), who, in the original version of his bill, proposed an explicit link between the exchange rate and negotiating authority for the Uruguay Round. In December 1985, the House Banking Committee passed a compromise bill that did not quantitatively mandate intervention, like the Bradley proposal, but did require the secretary of the Treasury to report to Congress twice a year on exchange rates, among other provisions. As Congress debated various bills to deal with the still-widening trade deficit over the subsequent three years, with the twist of increasing emphasis on the East Asian NICs rather than just Japan, proposals regarding exchange rates remained part of the debate (Destler and Henning 1989, 99–111).

The outcome, the Omnibus Trade and Competitiveness Act of 1988, included a large subsection on exchange rate policy. In four areas, it called for Treasury activism and, as in the House Banking Committee bill, required regular Treasury reports to the Congress: "An assessment of the impact of the exchange rate on the current account and trade balance, overall economic performance, competitive position, and indebtedness of the United States; recommendations for policy changes necessary to achieve a 'more appropriate and sustainable' current account balance; reporting of the results of bilateral negotiations with countries that manipulated their currencies; and analyses of exchange-market developments and their causes, including capital flows, and of intervention, among other things (Destler and Henning 1989, 111–13). In the first four reports submitted subsequently, the Treasury understandably evaded as much as possible the injunction to specify exchange rate and current account targets. But it took up with relish the mandate regarding countries that "manipulate" their exchange rate, spending a very high percentage of the reports on Korea and Taiwan.[54]

5.5.4   The IMF and Other International Agencies

The International Monetary Fund has always conducted reviews of U.S. policy in annual "Article IV" consultations, as it does for any country. But the United States pays no attention whatsoever to these reviews.[55]

The IMF did in the 1980s become involved in the G-7 process. When the G-7 leaders at the 1982 Versailles Summit instructed the G-5 finance ministers to undertake at their regular meetings multilateral surveillance of the international implications of the member countries' policies, the managing director of the IMF was invited to participate.

Previously, the OECD had been the body that had seen itself as providing the technical background for G-7 economic summits. This input in theory took place through a succession of meetings of country officials that began with Working Party 3 (WP 3). In WP 3 in 1981–84, and as Economic Policy Committee (EPC) chairman in 1985–88, Beryl Sprinkel patiently explained to other countries' finance vice-ministers and central bank governors (as well as to his own country's delegation) the errors in their view of the chain of causality that ran budget–interest rate–capital flow–dollar–trade deficit. WP 3 reported to the Economic Policy Committee (EPC) which normally designated as its chair the U.S. chairman of the Council of Economic Advisors, in a mostly futile attempt to get the American team interested in the deliberations. The EPC in turn reported to ministerial meetings, which reported to the G-7 summit leaders.[56]

The Americans (as well as the British) were reportedly unhappy with "Keynesian" tendencies at the OECD and so began to place more emphasis on the IMF (Putnam and Bayne 1987, 161). Since 1986, when the G-7 leaders formalized surveillance with a system of indicators at the Tokyo Summit, the IMF Research Department has been entrusted with compiling the countries' numbers. The G-7 ministers' meetings begin with a presentation by the IMF managing director, providing an overview of the issues and his recommendations. Exchange rate issues, however, are mostly treated outside this "surveillance" context (Dobson 1991, chap. 3).

54. The results are described in Frankel (1993) and more briefly in sec. 5.1.11 above.

55. In the 1984 consultation, when the IMF staff wrote a report that subscribed to the widely accepted view that the strong dollar and the trade deficit were problems caused by the budget deficit and high real interest rates, Sprinkel responded in terms that suggested that it was the report, rather than U.S. policies, that needed to be evaluated.

56. As CEA chairman in 1982–84, Feldstein was chairman of the Economic Policy Committee. He shared with many of the other countries a belief in the deficit-dollar chain of causality, in opposition to Regan and Sprinkel. But Feldstein did not view the apparatus of international cooperation (the OECD, the G-5 or the G-7, and summit meetings) as a particularly useful forum in which to mobilize support for correction of the U.S. fiscal deficit. He may have thought that, within the U.S. policy debate, allying with other countries' governments was more likely to undermine one's stance politically than to reinforce it. (On reasons to be skeptical of coordination, see also Feldstein 1988a, 1988b.)

As noted above, the Bank for International Settlements (BIS) in Basel is the venue for regular meetings among the G-10 central bankers. While the tightly knit group of central bankers operates at a distance from the bright lights of macroeconomic policy coordination and public pronouncements on exchange rates, they are able by telephone to coordinate the timing of intervention operations or changes in the discount rate more precisely than the finance ministers are able to coordinate anything.

5.6 Theories of the Political Economy of Exchange Rate Policy-Making

A number of generalizations have been, or can be, hazarded regarding the making of exchange rate policy.

5.6.1 The Switch from Benign Neglect to Activism as a Political Cycle

The 1985 switch in Reagan administration attitudes toward the dollar was a complete about-face. (Administration spokesmen initially denied that there had been such a 180-degree change in course, but, as public approval of the Plaza grew, Baker accepted credit for it as a new policy initiative.) It would be good to have an explanation for such a shift in policy that went beyond the specifics of the change in personnel.

A benign view of the switch has been offered by Cohen (1988, 218): the political system worked in the way it should, as the administration eventually responded to Congress and the grievances of groups adversely affected, by adopting policies to bring down the dollar. A less benign view would ask, first, whether the administration should not have recognized the dollar as a problem much sooner and, second, whether even the Plaza switch was indeed an adequate way to address the trade deficit, given the lack of simultaneous progress on the budget deficit and national saving.

It has been suggested by others that there is a regular cycle within the term of a given political leader, for many countries, but especially large countries like the United States for which international trade historically makes up a relatively small proportion of GNP. In his initial vision for the country, the leader ignores concerns of international trade, finance, and exchange rates. In part this is because he has usually won his office by courting exclusively domestic constituencies. In part it is because he is not fully aware of economic relations such as that between excessive spending and trade deficits or such as constraints placed on his country by the need to maintain the confidence of international financial markets. Later in his term, problems develop, and he switches to international activism, either because unpleasant international deficits demand a response or because the prospect of international economic diplomacy offers a pleasant diversion of popular attention from domestic problems. Bergsten (1986) has argued that, when the Reagan administration switched abruptly from benign neglect of the dollar to activism in 1985, it was following a pattern traced by Johnson in the late 1960s, Nixon in 1971, and Carter in 1978.

5.6.2   Market-Based versus Credit-Based Financial Systems

Henning (1990) puts forward an interesting hypothesis to explain why the constellation of domestic political forces does not prevent large currency over-valuations such as that experienced by the dollar in the early 1980s (or by the pound in 1980), in contrast to Japan, Germany, and France, where the interests of industry are represented with sufficient strength that exchange rate stability is a major goal of policy. The explanation essentially consists of two proposi-tions. First, in all countries, the banking community enjoys a special access to policymakers that industry may not. Second, the financial system in the United States (and the United Kingdom) is "capital market based," meaning that in-dustry obtains most of its external finance by issuing securities, while the fi-nancial system in the other three countries is "credit based," meaning that most corporations borrow from one or more large banks with which they are closely associated. In Japan, Germany, and France, then, the financial community can speak powerfully on behalf of private-sector interests that are unified in sup-porting a competitively valued and stable currency. In the United States and the United Kingdom, by contrast, bankers do not necessarily have the same incentives as industry. Furthermore, argues Henning, it is natural that the market-based financial system that exists in the two Anglo-Saxon countries creates a constituency for the dollar and pound to be international currencies while the private sector in Japan, Germany, and France resists any measures that would widen the international use of—and add to the demand for—their currencies.

5.6.3   Proposals for Reform of the Policy-Making Structure

For those who think that the difficulties stemming from the large swings in the dollar in the 1980s could have been handled better by policymakers, it is natural to ask if there are not some inherent flaws in the structure of the policy-making process that could be addressed by institutional reform.

One view is that the difficulty with the 1981–85 dollar appreciation, indeed, the difficulty with the overall macroeconomic policy mix of the decade, was lack of coordination between the United States and its trading partners. In this view, the U.S. government deliberately chose a policy mix that would give high real interest rates and a strong dollar, in order to reduce import prices, thereby "exporting inflation" to its neighbors. In technical terms, the noncooperative equilibrium is characterized by competitive appreciation, each country afraid to lower real interest rates on its own because of the inflationary consequences of currency depreciation. If this diagnosis is correct, the solution would simply be to strengthen the G-7 coordination process and use it to agree to simultaneous reductions in real interest rates (Sachs 1985).[57] The difficulty with this theory as an interpretation of the 1980s is that (1) only the United States, not its major trading partners, adopted a policy mix featuring fiscal expansion and (2), if currency appreciation is such an advantageous means of reducing inflation, then the U.S. policy of the early 1980s was optimal (from a selfish viewpoint), which would tend to undercut the case for reform.

A second view is that the difficulty with the 1981–85 dollar appreciation, and the overall U.S. macroeconomic policy mix, was lack of coordination between the *Treasury* and the *Fed*. The Fed refused to expand the money supply in the absence of a commitment on the part of the administration to raise taxes and cut the budget deficit because it would be inflationary. The administration (together with Congress) refused to raise taxes and cut the budget deficit in the absence of a commitment on the part of the Fed to allow interest rates to fall sufficiently because it would be recessionary. In this view, the high real interest rates and high dollar occurred simply because the two sides never could get together on the policy mix.

The relevance of this view to actual events is doubtful. It is true that Fed officials tended to be included in interagency meetings on international economic topics less often in the Reagan administration than in previous administrations. Paul Volcker and Don Regan, in particular, were often at odds in the press. Nevertheless, communication was regular, and there is no evidence that, but for the right institutional arrangement to promote cooperation, a deal could have been struck. Rather, disagreements stemmed either from differing priorities (the Fed more concerned about inflation, the Treasury about growth) or from differing perceptions as to the right model.[58]

The leading recent proposal for systematic reform of the U.S. institutional structure of exchange rate policy-making is that of Destler and Henning (1989). They argue that exchange rate policy is made by a very small circle of senior government officials in the Treasury and the Fed, is dangerously divorced from fiscal and monetary policy, and is frequently unresponsive to the legitimate concerns of private economic actors. They recommend a broadening of the process, particularly through three important changes: (1) the creation in both the House and the Senate of new select oversight committees on the dollar and the national economy; (2) the establishment of a new private-sector advisory group on exchange rates to counsel the secretary of the Treasury; and

57. Another version of the view that the problem is a lack of international coordination involves beggar-thy-neighbor "competitive depreciation," just the reverse of competitive appreciation. Here the problem with the Nash noncooperative equilibrium is that each country is tempted to follow an overly expansionary monetary policy in order to depreciate its currency and improve its trade balance, thereby exporting unemployment to its trading partners. One could view the Louvre Accord as an attempt by U.S. trading partners to address this problem.

58. If the monetary authority believes that an increase in government spending would appreciate the dollar while the fiscal authority believes that it would not, the two agencies may seek to cooperate optimally and yet still end up with a harmful policy mix (Frankel 1988b).

(3) more active involvement of agencies such as the CEA, the office of the U.S. Trade Representative (USTR), and the Agriculture and Commerce Departments (Destler and Henning 1989, 145–64).[59]

The view of this author is that, during the period July 1984–February 1985, the dollar had appreciated so far that some action such as foreign exchange intervention to try to bring it down was indeed warranted, even taking the budget deficit as given. Since all the groups that Destler and Henning would like to bring in to the policy-making process were more worried about the dollar and the trade deficit at this time than the Regan Treasury, it follows that exchange rate policy during this eight-month period might have been better had their proposed institutional reforms already been in place. Under most other circumstances, however, a broadening of the policy process in this way, in the sensitive and relatively technical area of exchange rates, could make things worse rather than better.

Exchange rate policy, like monetary and fiscal policy, is potentially vulnerable to populist pressures. Policymakers in the public eye—lacking forebearance and sometimes lacking awareness—might succumb to the temptation to tinker with international financial gimmickry so as to seem to be addressing the exchange rate issue, in place of making hard macroeconomic policy decisions. Sometimes they will refuse to devalue a currency that needs to be devalued, out of a stubborn unwillingness to admit publicly that their past policies have failed. Other times they will seek to devalue a currency that should not be, in order to gain the short-term advantage of higher output and employment, figuring that the costs in terms of higher inflation will not show up until after the next election. For such reasons, I am skeptical of proposals to democratize the policy-making process for exchange rates and would, if anything, prefer to see more power concentrated with the Federal Reserve. The Fed tends to have more of the historical memory, technical expertise, and insulation from politics that are so lacking elsewhere.

5.6.4   The Bandwagon as Paradigm

I would like to propose a common paradigm to fit the markets, the media, and the makers of policy. The paradigm is the bandwagon, by which I mean that the typical resident of each of the three worlds bases his or her actions more on what seems to be "in" at the moment than on what makes the most sense viewed in a longer-term perspective.

Consider first the markets. In theory, speculators should base their actions on an evaluation of the true worth of the currency as determined by macroeconomic fundamentals. In practice, by 1985, only five of twenty-four foreign exchange forecasting services were relying on fundamentals. (Fifteen relied on

---

59. One of their (quite valid) purposes in making the proposals was to make the exchange rate a deliberate policy instrument consistent with macroeconomic policy, rather than treating it as a residual.

technical analysis, three used both, and one did not specify.) This is as compared to 1978, when nineteen of twenty-three services surveyed relied on fundamentals (three on technical analysis). This lack of attention to long-term fundamentals and increasing reliance on time-series extrapolations may explain the apparent speculative bubble of 1984–85.[60]

A speculative bubble would seem to offer some scope for useful intervention by policy-makers. It is for this reason that the Plaza and other 1985 policy moves to try to bring down the dollar could be viewed as a success. But, to favor government intervention as a regular matter of course, one would have to believe that the policy-making process is systematically less liable to bandwagons than the markets, and this may not be the case.

Historical memory in both the Treasury and the Congress is notoriously short. Official views do not evolve gradually over time as more information becomes available. Rather, views change sharply with the personnel, who turn over every few years, and with their economic philosophy or perception of political advantage. The noninterventionist dogmatism of Beryl Sprinkel has come in for much criticism; the political pragmatism of a Jim Baker will usually win out in a popularity contest among journalists or congressmen, and in 1985 it happened to give what may have been the right answer as economic policy as well. But pragmatism can often give the wrong answer. Trade policy is an example where the stubbornness of the Treasury and the White House in the 1980s was fortunate and where greater accommodation to the Congress or outside interests would have given a less satisfactory outcome, from an economic viewpoint.

It may sound undemocratic to reserve exchange rate policy-making for a small elite like the Federal Reserve Board. But democracy does not mean putting every issue up for a vote every day. Our system places some policymakers under the relatively frequent and direct control of the electorate, such as the two-year-termed House of Representatives, and others farther removed, such as the members of the Supreme Count. The question is whether exchange rate policy is a more fitting topic for the former approach or the latter. Exchange rate policy would seem to be the sort of topic that is best reserved for specialists removed from political pressures.

Although the media were not considered above as a separate interest group or policymaker, they are in fact the ultimate arbiter of policy (until the historians get their turn). Most critics of the tremendous power of the media phrase their criticism in terms of the particular bias that they think the media has. But the real problem with the media is that, in its efforts to escape charges of bias, it does not undertake enough analysis. Journalists cover the stories that other

---

60. One could explain the continued appreciation of the dollar simply by international investors putting less weight on the fundamentalist forecasts of dollar depreciation and consequently becoming increasingly attracted to the high rates of return offered on dollar assets (Frankel and Froot 1990).

journalists are covering (so-called pack journalism). The goal is to describe current trends rather than to give opinions. The arbiters of policy can end up being arbitrary in their evaluations.

Success in Washington is often judged in a rather superficial way. The system in the aggregate works a bit like trial by fire or water in medieval times. A policy operation is a success if it is a political success, it is a political success if it is a media success, and it is a media success if it is a success in the public opinion polls. The opinion polls often resemble coin tosses because the respondents are not well acquainted with the issues that the questions concern.

It is of course true that the dollar began to depreciate in 1985, as desired. But the policymakers may just have been lucky. The initiatives taken by Jim Baker at the Plaza and other G-7 meetings were, at the time, so tentative that he could, and would, have disavowed that there had been any change in policy had they not been received well. These initiatives *were* received well, in large part because Baker's style was such a welcome relief (especially to the press) after Don Regan. Regardless of whether one believes that the dollar would have come down in 1985–87 even without the initiatives, it is certain that favorable reviews, such as those in newspaper editorials and congressional testimony, made them a political success.

The enhanced stature of Baker and the G-7 in turn meant that their pronouncements carried more weight with the markets. In 1986 and 1987, foreign exchange traders would leap for their terminals every time a report came out that Baker had said something. After 1985, G-7 meetings replaced trade balance announcements (or, in the early 1980s, money supply announcements) as the current fad variable that the markets followed.

By 1984, the market bandwagon had carried the dollar far away from a sensible equilibrium. In 1985, the interdependent bandwagons ridden by the media and the makers of policy carried the dollar back. Next time, the media/policymaker bandwagons could as easily be the ones to carry the dollar away from equilibrium.

References

Bergsten, C. Fred. 1982. What to do about the U.S.-Japan economic conflict. *Foreign Affairs* (Summer), 1059–75.

———. 1984. The United States trade deficit and the dollar. Statement before the Senate Committee on Banking, Housing and Urban Affairs, Subcommittee on International Finance and Monetary Policy. Washington, D.C., 6 June.

———. 1986. America's unilateralism. In *Conditions for partnership in international economic management,* by C. F. Bergsten, E. Davignon, and I. Miyazaki. Report no. 32. New York: Trilateral Commission.

Bovard, James. 1991. *The fair trade fraud.* New York: St. Martin's.

Bovenberg, A. Lans. 1989. The effects of capital income taxation on international competitiveness and trade flows. *American Economic Review* 79, no. 5 (December): 1045–64.

Branson, William, and James Love. 1988. U.S. manufacturing and the real exchange rate. In *Misalignment of exchange rates: Effects on trade and industry,* ed. Richard C. Marston. Chicago: University of Chicago Press.

Cohen, Stephen. 1988. *The making of United States international economic policy.* 3d ed. New York: Praeger.

Cooper, Richard. 1985. The U.S. payments deficit and the strong dollar: Policy options. In *The U.S. dollar—recent developments, outlook, and policy options.* Kansas City: Federal Reserve Bank of Kansas City.

Corden, W. Maxwell. 1983. The logic of the international monetary non-system. In *Reflections on a troubled world economy,* ed. F. Machlup et al. London: Macmillan.

Council of Economic Advisers (CEA). 1984. *Economic report of the president.* Washington, D.C., February.

Department of the Treasury. 1989. Report to the Congress on international economic and exchange rate policy. Washington, D.C., October.

Destler, I. Mac, and C. Randall Henning. 1989. *Dollar politics: Exchange rate policymaking in the United States.* Washington, D.C.: Institute for International Economics.

Dobson, Wendy. 1991. *Economic policy coordination: Requiem or first step?* Policy Analyses in International Economics, no. 30. Washington, D.C.: Institute for International Economics, May.

Dominguez, Kathryn, and Jeffrey Frankel. 1991. Does foreign exchange intervention matter? Disentangling the portfolio and expectation effects for the mark. Working Paper no. 3299. Cambridge, Mass.: NBER. (Revised as Foreign exchange intervention: An empirical assessment. In *On exchange rates,* ed. Jeffrey Frankel. Cambridge, Mass.: MIT Press, 1993.)

Dooley, Michael, and Peter Isard. 1985. Tax avoidance and exchange rate determination. Washington, D.C.: International Monetary Fund, Research Department, November.

Dornbusch, Rudiger. 1976. Expectations and exchange rate dynamics. *Journal of Political Economy* 84 (December): 1161–74.

———. 1986. Flexible exchange rates and excess capital mobility. *Brookings Papers on Economic Activity,* no. 1:209–26.

Feldstein, Martin. 1984. The dollar exchange rate. Remarks before the World Affairs Council of Philadelphia, 29 February.

———. 1986. New evidence on the effects of exchange rate intervention. Working Paper no. 2052. Cambridge, Mass.: NBER, October.

———. 1988a. Distinguished Lecture on Economics in Government: Thinking about international economic coordination. *Journal of Economic Perspectives* 2 (Spring): 3–13.

———. 1988b. International economic cooperation: Introduction. In *International economic cooperation,* ed. Martin Feldstein. Chicago: University of Chicago Press.

Frankel, Jeffrey. 1984. *The Yen/Dollar Agreement: Liberalizing Japanese financial markets.* Policy Analyses in International Economics, no. 9. Washington, D.C.: Institute for International Economics.

———. 1985. *Six possible meanings of 'overvaluation': The 1981–85 dollar.* Essays in International Finance, no. 159. Princeton, N.J.: International Finance Section, Princeton University, December.

———. 1986. Comments on overshooting, agricultural commodity markets, and public policy. *American Journal of Agricultural Economics* 68, no. 2 (May): 418–19.

———. 1988a. Ambiguous macroeconomic policy multipliers in theory and in twelve econometric models. In *Empirical macroeconomics for interdependent economies,* ed. Ralph Bryant et al. Washington, D.C.: Brookings.

————. 1988b. The implications of conflicting models for coordination between monetary and fiscal policy-makers. In *Empirical macroeconomics for interdependent economies,* ed. Ralph Bryant et al. Washington, D.C.: Brookings.

————. 1993. Liberalization of Korea's foreign exchange markets and the role of U.S. trade relations. Working Paper no. 93-008. University of California, Berkeley, Institute of Business and Economic Research, Center for International Development and Economic Research, January. (Also forthcoming in *Building a new economic relationship: Republic of Korea and United States economic relations,* ed. J. Mo and R. Myers. Stanford, Calif.: Hoover Institution Press.)

Frankel, Jeffrey, and Kenneth Froot. 1990. Exchange rate forecasting techniques, survey data, and implications for the foreign exchange market. Working Paper no. 90/43. Washington, D.C.: International Monetary Fund, May. (Greatly abridged in *American Economic Review* 80, no. 2 [May]: 181–85.)

Frieden, Jeffry. 1990. International finance, national governments, and economic interest groups: Can they co-exist? Department of Political Science, University of California, Los Angeles. Typescript.

————. 1991. Invested interests: The politics of national economic policies in a world of global finance. *International Organization* 45, no. 4 (Autumn): 425–51.

Friedman, Milton. 1953. The case for flexible exchange rates. In *Essays in positive economics,* ed. Milton Friedman. Chicago: University of Chicago Press.

Funabashi, Yoichi. 1988. *Managing the dollar: From the Plaza to the Louvre.* Washington, D.C.: Institute for International Economics.

Hale, David. 1989. The Japanese Ministry of Finance and dollar diplomacy during the late 1980's; or, How the University of Tokyo Law School saved America from the University of Chicago Economics Department. Chicago: Kemper Financial Services, Inc., July.

Havrilesky, Thomas. 1990. Distributive conflict and monetary policy. *Contemporary Policy Issues,* 50–61.

Haynes, Steven, Michael Hutchinson, and Raymond Mikesell. 1986. *Japanese financial policies and the U.S. trade deficit.* Essays in International Finance, no. 162. Princeton University, International Finance Section, April.

Henning, C. Randall. 1990. International monetary policymaking within the countries of the Group of Five. Washington, D.C.: Institute for International Economics, August.

Koo, Richard. 1988. Japanese investment in dollar securities after the Plaza Accord. Statement submitted to the Joint Economic Committee of the U.S. Congress, 17 October. (Published by the Nomura Research Institute, Tokyo, March 1989.)

Krugman, Paul. 1985. Is the strong dollar sustainable? In *The U.S. dollar—recent developments, outlook, and policy options.* Kansas City: Federal Reserve Bank of Kansas City.

McKinnon, Ronald. 1988. Monetary and exchange rate policies for international financial stability: A proposal. *Journal of Economic Perspectives* 2 (Winter): 83–103.

Marris, Stephen. 1985. *Deficits and the dollar: The world economy at risk.* Policy Analyses in International Economics, no. 14. Washington, D.C.: Institute for International Economics, December.

Murchison, David, and Ezra Solomon. 1983. The misalignment of the United States dollar and the Japanese yen: The problem and its solution. Howrey & Simon, 1730 Pennsylvania Ave., Washington, D.C.; Stanford University, 19 September.

Mussa, Michael. 1981. The role of official intervention. Occasional Paper no. 6. New York: Group of Thirty.

Nollen, Stanley. 1987. Business costs and business policy for export controls. *Journal of International Business Studies* 18 (Spring).

Obstfeld, Maurice. 1990. The effectiveness of foreign-exchange intervention: Recent experience. In *International policy coordination and exchange rate fluctuations,* ed. W. Branson, J. Frenkel, and M. Goldstein. Chicago: University of Chicago Press.

Putnam, Robert, and Nicholas Bayne. 1987. *Hanging together: The seven-power summits.* 2d ed. Cambridge, Mass.: Harvard University Press.

Redburn, Tom. 1990. The Fed has the edge on the economic policy front. *International Economy* 4, no. 3 (June/July): 61–63.

Regan, Donald. 1988. *For the record: From Wall Street to Washington.* New York: St. Martin's.

Report of the Working Group on Exchange Market Intervention ("Jurgensen Report"). 1983. Washington, D.C.: U.S. Department of the Treasury, March.

Sachs, Jeffrey. 1985. The dollar and the policy mix: 1985. *Brookings Papers on Economic Activity,* no. 1:117–86.

Stockman, David. 1986. *The triumph of politics: Why the Reagan revolution failed.* New York: Harper & Row.

Tobin, James. 1978. A proposal for monetary reform. *Eastern Economic Journal* 4, nos. 3–4:153–59.

U.S. General Accounting Office. 1984. *Floating exchange rates in an interdependent world: No simple solutions to the problems.* Washington, D.C., 20 April.

Williamson, John. 1983. *The exchange rate system.* Policy Analyses in International Economics, no. 5. Washington, D.C.: Institute for International Economics.

Williamson, John, and Marcus Miller. 1987. *Targets and indicators: A blueprint for the international coordination of economic policy.* Policy Analyses in International Economics, no. 22. Washington, D.C.: Institute for International Economics, September.

---

2. C. Fred Bergsten

The Issue

Exchange rate policy has two dimensions for the United States: national management of the dollar and, to a large extent, determination of the international monetary regime.[1] The United States reversed or sharply modified its policy in both respects on three separate occasions during the 1980s. Hence, whatever one thinks of its substantive importance, the issue area is of unusual interest in an assessment of economic policy in the past decade.

As the 1980s began, the Carter administration and the Volcker Fed were successfully attempting to *strengthen* the dollar (from its free-fall of late 1978) in part through *managed floating.* From the outset of 1981, the new Reagan administration reversed that policy: it studiously *ignored* the dollar ("benign

1. Destler and Henning (1989, 10–11) usefully define, and distinguish between, *direct* and *indirect* exchange rate policy. I address both in this statement.

neglect") and aggressively espoused *pure floating* (Reagan I). In September 1985, the administration reversed its own policy and sought to *drive down* the dollar through, among other things, renewed *managed floating* (Reagan II). In early 1987, the third shift targeted dollar *stability* and installed a new system of *reference ranges* (Reagan III).

Jeffrey Frankel's superb background paper accurately and cogently describes these changes and their economic impact. As requested by our chairman, I will focus on the decisions that were made at each key turning point, the alternatives that might have been considered at the time, and the consequences for the economy of the paths that were taken and—obviously more speculatively—those that were rejected.

Reagan I (or Regan-Sprinkel)

Despite all the well-advertised shortcomings of economic policy in the Carter administration, the Reagan administration inherited a healthy international economic position. The current account was in balance for the third straight year despite the second oil shock. The United States was the world's largest creditor country. The exchange rate of the dollar was virtually at fundamental equilibrium (in terms of trade competitiveness).[2] Trade liberalization had resumed with the successful conclusion of the Tokyo Round of the GATT.

The new administration regarded all these variables as irrelevant. It came into office with a series of extremely strong (and, as events revealed, internally inconsistent) views on how the domestic economy should be managed. No thought was given to the external consequences of its new policies or to how those external effects might in turn feed back on the domestic economy. The best evidence of this total neglect was the administration's initial projection of the current account balance for 1983: it got the level just about right, at $70 billion, but had the sign wrong.[3]

Hence, the exchange rate (and the entire external position) was viewed as a residual rather than as a policy instrument or even as an intermediate variable. An ideological aversion to governmental interference in markets reinforced this outcome, as did the view—widely shared internationally at the time—that sterilized intervention in the exchange markets had no lasting impact anyway.[4] Total laissez-faire prevailed for over four years. Indeed, by extolling the virtues of a strong dollar, the stance of Reagan I toward the exchange rate added to the overvaluation and resulting trade deficits that were fundamentally generated by the mix of very loose fiscal policy and very tight monetary policy.

From my point of view as one of the few early and vocal critics of Reagan I (see Bergsten 1981a, 1981b), the enormous irony is that the policy worked

2. As calculated three years later by Williamson (1983, fig. A-7).
3. As reported to the author by David Stockman, director of the Office of Management and Budget at the time.
4. That view has subsequently been effectively challenged by Dominguez and Frankel (1991).

for an extended period. The "riverboat gamble" of Reaganomics was that its huge budget deficits would not sustain (or even accelerate) the high rates of inflation that it inherited or, given a resolute inflation-fighting Federal Reserve, push interest rates sky high and crowd out so much domestic investment that growth would be impossible. But foreign capital inflows and the soaring dollar helped cut inflation and held real interest rates down by as much as 5 percentage points (crowding out the tradables sector instead) (see Marris 1987, 44). Benign neglect of the dollar contributed to the "victory" over inflation, permitted recovery from the recession of 1982, and facilitated the expansion of the 1980s.[5]

The *alternative* to benign neglect in 1981 was continuation of the dollar policy of the late 1970s—an effort to maintain the currency at a level that would achieve rough balance in the current account, mainly via coordinated intervention in the exchange markets (with accompanying rhetoric) and through pushing the surplus countries to grow faster (the "locomotive approach"). The cardinal question is the impact that that strategy would have had on the domestic economy: would it have "forced" the Fed to ease money to hold the dollar down, weakening the battle against inflation (although easing the recession of 1982), or would it have "forced" a tightening of fiscal policy and thus lessened the problems that plague us to this day?

Such an "alternative" policy could have made some difference on the external variables. The dollar would have risen a bit less had the United States and the G-5 sold dollars (as in 1980) and the administration displayed less enthusiasm for its climb; in particular, the last 20 percent or so of the dollar's climb in late 1984/early 1985, which then and now defies any logical explanation except as a speculative bubble, might well have been prevented by official intervention and jawboning. Less diplomatic crockery would have been broken had the United States maintained a willingness to cooperate meaningfully and benign neglect been less aggressive. Less protectionist pressure would have been stimulated in the Congress had the administrative at least tried "to defend American trade interests."

But the dollar and the trade deficit would still have soared and become Feldstein's "safety valve" for the economy.[6] I suspect that the Fed would have

---

5. Reagan I also "worked" in the sense that its extreme antipathy to any action on the dollar enhanced the drama, and thus probably the market impact, of the shift to Reagan II at the Plaza, as described below. However, the policy also contributed in important ways to the adoption by the administration, as Secretary Baker later admitted (in remarks to the Institute for International Economics on 14 September 1987), that "no administration . . . has granted more import relief to U.S. industry than any of its predecessors in more than half a century." The macro/monetary/dollar policy of Reagan I made it impossible for that administration to achieve its own objective of maintaining open markets at home and promoting liberalization abroad, as indicated in Paula Stern's contribution to this volume.

6. I subdivide the period Reagan I into Feldstein I and Feldstein II: the chairman of the Council of Economic Advisers touted the virtues of the strong dollar and the trade deficit as a "safety valve" in the former but switched in the latter to citing their costs as a key reason to deal seriously with the budget.

hung tough against inflation. It is hard to imagine much effect on fiscal policy.

Hence, the major impact of the alternative policy would have been, as in 1977–78 and 1986–87, on America's economic relations with its key allies. Unable and unwilling to change course at home, but concerned in this alternative scenario about incipient dollar overvaluation and trade deficits and the resulting protectionist pressures, such an administration would have strongly opposed the tightening of fiscal policy in Japan and Germany that contributed in important ways to the buildup of their surpluses (and our deficit). Both might have budged a bit, Germany because it was fighting "Eurosclerosis," and Japan to limit renewed "trade conflict." But any results would probably have been quite marginal here too: only slightly faster growth (and perhaps inflation) abroad, a slightly smaller buildup in the American trade deficit with a little less recession in 1982 and a smaller decline in the inflation rate.

The only *effective* alternative to Reagan I would have been for the foreigners to take draconian measures to restrict their capital outflows in an effort to force a reversal of America's policy mix, as proposed by a few European and American economists at the time. Given the openness of international capital flows and the markets' zeal for Reaganomics during this period, however, it would have been extremely difficult to implement such a policy. Moreover, the other countries would have choked off their own export booms (although, with less inflation from currency depreciation, it would then have been easier for them to stimulate domestic demand). They would have frontally attacked an American administration that was riding high and done so during a period of considerable East-West tension. The bottom line is that, although an active exchange rate policy might have modestly limited the costs of Reagan I, it was probably an inevitable casualty of the policy mix adopted during that period.

Reagan II (or Baker-Darman I)

The two unsustainabilities of Reagan I exchange rate policy, although slow to arrive, did occur as predicted. The *internal* unsustainability hit most clearly: incensed by record trade deficits and the administration's total neglect thereof, and goaded by a tradables sector, which finally found its political tongue after the election of 1984, the Congress threatened to pass highly protectionist trade legislation.[7] Fear of the *external* unsustainability, that is, a "hard landing" of the dollar and the economy, suddenly seemed real as well if the current account deficit continued to soar because the dollar bubble had burst in early 1985 and considerable depreciation had already occurred.[8]

---

7. Congressman Bill Frenzel commented to me at the time that "the Smoot Hawley tariff itself would have passed overwhelmingly had it come to the House floor in the fall of 1985."

8. The publication of Marris (1987) may have had a significant effect on thinking about this aspect of the problem. Marris's goal was of course to write a self-denying prophecy, which so far looks to have been successful to an important extent.

Hence, Baker-Darman reversed Regan-Sprinkel. They won G-5 agreement both to drive the dollar down and to resume coordinated intervention in the currency markets (à la 1978–80) to do so.[9] There was little disagreement with the new policy either at home or abroad, although questions soon arose about how *far* and how *fast* the realignment should occur.

Two alternatives might have been chosen: *earlier* adoption of the Plaza strategy and greater reliance on *domestic* policies (especially in the United States) to achieve the desired current account adjustments. The timing, however, was dictated by American politics: only after the election of 1984 did Regan and Sprinkel leave the Treasury, and only then did the domestic tradables sector muster the political courage to attack the administration's dollar policy and take its case to the Congress.[10] Given Reagan I, it would have been difficult to move to Reagan II much sooner (although the G-5 ministerial in January 1985 started the process of driving the dollar down, with much less publicity than the Plaza and much less active U.S. participation).

A *more meaningful* alternative would have been serious cooperation on "the fundamentals" as well as on exchange rates—which turned out to bear most of the burden of pursuing smaller current account imbalances. The monumental failure of Baker-Darman was their unwillingness or inability to use the external threat to convince the president to launch a serious effort to correct the problem at its source: the budget deficit. At just about the same time, Congress was launching the Gramm-Rudman-Hollings initiative, and the Senate Republican leadership developed a major budget package. But the president backed away, leaving the flip-flop on dollar policy—plus renewed exhortations to the Japanese and the Germans (à la 1977–78) to grow faster—to achieve the adjustment and avert new protectionism.

A *subalternative* would have been for the Federal Reserve to let the dollar fall much faster during this period in an effort to force the administration to make such a change in fiscal policy. The Fed had considerable leeway to pursue such a strategy throughout 1986 because of the sharp fall in oil prices and the virtual absence of inflation pressure and some incentive to do so because lower dollar interest rates would have further eased Third World debt and strengthened American banks. However, Chairman Volcker chose instead to talk down the efforts to talk down the dollar and to resist any declines in U.S. interest rates—paradoxically reducing fears of the "hard landing" and thus limiting pressure on the administration to get serious on the fiscal front.[11]

Nevertheless, Reagan II also worked to a considerable extent. Congress eventually passed the Omnibus Trade and Competitiveness Act of 1988, but it

---

9. The full story is in Funabashi (1988).

10. The full story is in Destler and Henning (1989).

11. On that front, "benign neglect" arose again despite the Plaza strategy: 1986 was the year of tax reform rather than fiscal contraction. And one (unexpected and unintended) result of tax reform was a sharp decline in the budget deficit in fiscal year 1987, permitting the illusion of progress on "the fundamentals," although very little had in fact been achieved.

was shorn of most of the blatantly protectionist proposals of 1985–86—due in important ways to the Plaza strategy and the clear improvement in American competitiveness from the lower dollar. On the financial side, the sharp dollar depreciation of 1985–86 was accompanied by continued large inflows of foreign capital despite lower U.S. interest rates—achieving considerable adjustment without the "hard landing." But this problem finally erupted and triggered the shift to Reagan III.

Reagan III (or Baker-Darman II)

The "hard landing" seemed to be at hand in 1987. The dollar plunged at the start of the year, while interest rates rose. Private capital inflows dried up, and foreign central banks had to finance the bulk of America's massive external deficit ($163 billion, 3.5 percent of GNP) throughout the year. The bond market dropped sharply in the spring. Black Monday hit in October.

Hence, the administration again reversed course on the dollar. Building on a yen-dollar stabilization agreement reached at the behest of the Japanese in September–October 1986, the G-5/G-7 adopted the Louvre Accord in February 1987 to try to stop the fall of the dollar and stabilize currencies within unannounced reference ranges (of ±5 percent). They maintained the stabilization effort throughout the year, rebasing the yen-dollar range downward in April 1987 and engineering the "Telephone Accord" in December that finally succeeded in stabilizing the dollar in early 1988.

The shift to stabilization at the Louvre was the closest call of the three Reagan shifts on the dollar. The move was understandable because there *was* a serious risk of a "hard landing." From the Treasury's standpoint, the Fed's unwillingness to try to counter the rise of interest rates triggered early in the year by the plunging dollar raised the prospect of heavy domestic costs if it continued the Plaza depreciation strategy. Hence, Baker-Darman decided to try to negotiate an alternative adjustment strategy with the G-7 that included throwing in the exchange rate towel.

However, there were *at least* two alternatives in 1987. The trade deficit was still rising (in nominal terms) at the time of the Louvre Accord and did not peak until the third quarter of that year. Hence, in terms of the agreed adjustment strategy and the continuing threat of both unsustainabilities, it was arguably quite premature to halt the depreciation. Indeed, stabilization around the Louvre level left the dollar overvalued and invited further trouble later—as occurred in the fall and played a major role in triggering Black Monday.

It must be recalled that the administration itself triggered the renewed dollar slide in early 1987, and letting it go further was a real alternative—which could have been chosen either by the United States or, via an unwillingness to support the dollar in an effort to (again) prompt American budget correction, by the foreign monetary authorities. Given the shift in market sentiments against the dollar and the stance of the Fed, however, seeking additional trade adjustment via further dollar depreciation or "forced" fiscal action could have brought still higher interest rates and considerable financial disruption. It would have taken enormous nerve to let the dollar continue falling.

The better option was for the administration and the G-7 to do the Louvre but to realize that those rates could not hold for long. Hence, they should have quietly worked out a second "rebasing" to depreciate the dollar quickly and cooperatively by another 10 percent or so during the summer vacation period in August. The G-7 could thus have led the markets to a sustainable level rather than fighting additional dollar decline once past the crisis atmosphere of the spring.[12]

I believe that this course would have *avoided* Black Monday. It would have obviated the need to drive the dollar back up in the aftermath thereof. It would thus have promoted more trade adjustment and less protectionism. It would have enhanced the credibility of both the administration and the G-5/G-7. My impression is that such a strategy was rejected because of a politically inspired focus on trying to maintain stability until November 1988 and an erroneous belief that the "Louvre levels" would hold until then.

This was the one major episode of the 1980s where, *given* the basic course of fiscal and monetary policy, exchange rate policy erred and triggered events that could have levied significant costs on the American economy.[13] The basic lesson of the decade in this area, however, is that dollar policy under current institutional arrangements—in both senses cited at the outset—is largely determined by the macroeconomic policy context (both at home and abroad). As noted, different exchange rate policies—particularly regarding intervention and rhetoric—could have limited the damage to a moderate degree on several occasions, especially during Reagan I and again in 1988–89, when the United States and the G-7 failed to resist a renewed rise in the dollar that further delayed the needed adjustment. The only alternatives that would have had major effects at the critical decision points, however, would have been Machiavellian strategies to deliberately worsen the situation in the short run in an effort to force the political process to take actions that were needed in the long run— a risky course that few governments would want to pursue and that no policy regime should require to produce sustainable results.

I believe that we need a systemic change under which a regime is installed that is sufficiently oriented toward the exchange rate, such as target zones, for macroeconomic policy to be *affected by* the external outlook on an ongoing basis.[14] The European Community has done this with its European Monetary

---

12. Williamson's (1992) latest estimates conclude that the dollar was still overvalued by about 10 percent at the Louvre level.

13. The stock market would probably have corrected from its sharp runup earlier in 1987 in any event, and Black Monday turned out to have modestly positive effects on the economy by producing lower interest rates and some action on the budget deficit. Nevertheless, the outcome could have been much less benign, and policy should obviously seek to avoid triggering such huge market disruptions.

14. My preferred model is in Williamson and Miller (1987).

System, as demonstrated most dramatically in the case of France in 1983. If such a global system had been in place for some time before 1981, operating effectively and credibly, might it have tilted the United States away from adopting at least the extreme version of Reaganomics? If so, we could have still experienced economic success in the 1980s with fewer adverse legacies for the 1990s and beyond.

Moreover, the absence of systemic arrangements—along with the relative lack of attention paid to the exchange rate in the United States—virtually guarantees that policy in this area will continue to flip-flop as it did the 1980s. Indeed, similar reversals can be observed in the Nixon administration (from its original "benign neglect" to Treasury Secretary Connally's aggressive pursuit of devaluation in 1971) and the Carter administration (from seeking a lower dollar in 1977–78 to seeking a stable or stronger dollar in 1979–80) (see Bergsten 1986). The United States needs to pursue a new exchange rate approach, both domestically and internationally, to stabilize and strengthen the utility of this policy instrument.

References

Bergsten, C. Fred. 1981a. The costs of Reaganomics. *Foreign Policy* 44 (Fall): 24–36.
———. 1981b. U.S. international economic policy in the 1980s. Statement before the Subcommittee on International Economic Policy and Trade, House Foreign Affairs Committee. 97th Cong., 1st sess. 24 February.
———. 1986. America's unilateralism. In *Conditions for partnership in international economic management,* by C. F. Bergsten, E. Davignon, and I. Miyazaki. Trilateral Papers, no. 32. New York: Trilateral Commission.
Destler, I. M., and C. Randall Henning. 1989. *Dollar politics: Exchange rate policymaking in the United States.* Washington, D.C.: Institute for International Economics.
Dominguez, Kathryn, and Jeffrey Frankel. 1991. *The effects of foreign exchange intervention.* Washington, D.C.: Institute for International Economics.
Funabashi, Yoichi. 1988. *Managing the dollar: From the Plaza to the Louvre.* Washington, D.C.: Institute for International Economics, May.
Marris, Stephen. 1987. *Deficits and the dollar: The world economy at risk.* Policy Analyses in International Economics, no. 14. Washington, D.C.: Institute for International Economics.
Williamson, John. 1983. *The exchange rate system.* Policy Analyses in International Economics, no. 5. Washington, D.C.: Institute for International Economics, September.
———. 1992. *Equilibrium exchange rates: An update.* Washington, D.C.: Institute for International Economics.
Williamson, John, and Marcus H. Miller. 1987. *Targets and indicators: A blueprint for the international coordination of economic policy.* Policy Analyses in International Economics, no. 22. Washington, D.C.: Institute for International Economics, September.

3. *Michael Mussa*

The 1980s witnessed extraordinarily large swings in the foreign exchange value of the dollar and in the U.S. current account. During President Reagan's first term, these international macroeconomic developments exerted little influence on U.S. economic policy. After 1984, however, in the face of large and expanding international imbalances and growing protectionist sentiment, and with a shift in the team of key administration officials, U.S. economic policy moved to a more active and visible concern with management of the exchange rate and the balance of payments. In discussing these critical international macroeconomic developments, and in assessing the policy responses to them, three main points deserve particular emphasis.

First, much of the movement in the foreign exchange value of the dollar and in the U.S. current account was an understandable response to other important macroeconomic developments, including especially the monetary and fiscal policies of the U.S. government.

Second, in the circumstances of the 1980s, much of the movement in the dollar in the U.S. current account was desirable from the perspective of the macroeconomic performance of the United States and other countries. This is a reasonable judgment despite the many significant problems attributable to, or manifest in, the movements of the dollar and in the U.S. current account.

Third, for the United States, operating in a system of market-determined exchange rates, there is some useful role for "exchange rate policy" that is separate from monetary and fiscal policy. Moreover, influencing the exchange rate or the current account is occasionally a significant concern of general macroeconomic policy. However, the independent influence of exchange rate policy is quite limited, and key domestic economic objectives usually dominate the conduct of monetary and fiscal policy.

These issues are discussed or alluded to in Jeffrey Frankel's excellent paper and are considered in Fred Bergsten's thoughtful remarks. Somewhat surprisingly, I find myself in close agreement with most of Fred's comments, and I have only modest differences with Jeff's discussion and analysis. These remarks will focus primarily on those issues where we have some disagreement or meaningful difference of emphasis or interpretation.

Causes of Exchange Rate Adjustments and Payments Imbalances

Since the collapse of the Bretton Woods system in early 1973, market forces have played the dominant role in determining the foreign exchange value of the dollar. These market forces, however, are sensitive to perceptions concerning the actual and expected future conduct of economic policies. After all, if economic policies kept exchange rates pegged for long periods under the Bretton Woods system, it stands to reason that these policies ought to be important determinants of exchange rate behavior under a floating rate system. The influence of these policies, especially U.S. monetary policy, is apparent in the major movements of the foreign exchange value of the dollar during the 1980s. Major movements in the U.S. current account, in turn, can be explained to a significant extent (with a lag) by movements in the value of the dollar.

The Important Role of Monetary Policy

In the late 1970s, the real foreign exchange value of the U.S. dollar fell to the lowest level in the postwar era. In my view, the apparent incapacity of U.S. economic policy, especially monetary policy, to restrain and reverse the persistent rise of the U.S. inflation rate was the key reason for this dollar depreciation. Nominal depreciation was required to match the excess of U.S. inflation over that of other countries, and real depreciation reflected the "overshooting" response to progressively greater disappointment about the inability to contain the rise of inflationary pressures.

After an abortive effort to combat inflation through monetary tightening during late 1979 and early 1980, the Federal Reserve embarked on a determined and ultimately successful effort beginning in late 1980. For twenty months, despite a deepening recession, a tight monetary policy was maintained until the summer of 1982. The inflation rate was brought down from 13 percent during 1980 to 4 percent during 1982, where it remained for most of the rest of the decade. Unquestionably, this successful effort to control inflation dramatically altered expectations concerning both the likely future course of inflation and the willingness of the U.S. policy authorities to undertake determined and costly actions to combat rising inflation.

In a world where national price levels adjust relatively slowly in comparison with exchange rates and other asset prices, the modern theory of exchange rate determination predicts the response of the exchange rate to such a change in expectations. There should have been a strong real appreciation of the dollar as the "overshooting" response to the dramatic shift from growing fears of policies that tolerated a persistently rising inflation rate to a growing conviction that policies would deliver a much more moderate inflation rate. This response should not have occurred all at once, with the initial tightening of monetary policy, but only gradually, as people became increasingly persuaded that the reduction in inflation would prove enduring.

Indeed, it is entirely possible that real appreciation of the dollar in response to changing expectations of the longer-term inflation rate continued well after the Federal Reserve's shift to an easier monetary policy in the late summer of 1982. As the economic activity recovered vigorously during 1983, the inflation rate nevertheless remained slightly below 4 percent. This development provided reassurance that there would not be a rapid rebound of inflation with the onset of economic recovery, as had occurred after the abortive attack on inflation during 1980. Moreover, when some indication of rising inflationary pressures appeared in early 1984, the Federal Reserve retightened monetary policy during the spring and summer. This important action, taken in a presidential election year and at some risk to the continuation of the recovery, demonstrated the durability of the Federal Reserve's resolve to resist increases in inflation.

Thus, in explaining the enormous upswing in the foreign exchange value of the dollar between the summer of 1980 and early 1985, I would assign somewhat greater importance than Jeffrey Frankel does to the shift in the perceived stance of U.S. monetary policy. There remains, however, an important part of the upswing of the dollar that is difficult to attribute to monetary policy or to any other identifiable change in economic fundamentals. This is especially so for the last 10 or 15 percent of dollar appreciation in late 1984 and early 1985.

While the decline of the dollar during 1985 and 1986 is associated with a substantial easing of U.S. monetary policy, this factor alone appears inadequate to explain the nearly complete reversal of the dollar's earlier appreciation. The U.S. inflation rate remained about 4 percent during 1985 and, under the impact of falling world oil prices, dropped to barely 1 percent during 1986. Thus, despite monetary easing, there was no substantial reason to fear that the Federal Reserve had again reversed course and would tolerate a substantial increase in the longer-term inflation rate. Accordingly, there should not have been a strong overshooting effect toward dollar depreciation in response to the easing of monetary policy.

On the other hand, the theory of exchange rate determination does imply a gradual unwinding of the overshooting effect of the earlier shift in expectations concerning U.S. monetary policy. Real dollar appreciation attributable to rising confidence about the anti-inflationary stance of U.S. monetary policy during the early 1980s should have been gradually reversed during the mid-1980s. In addition, the persistent deterioration of the U.S. trade and current account balance during 1985–86 apparently provided information suggesting that a lower real exchange rate for the dollar was needed to achieve a sustainable balance of payments position for the United States. Nevertheless, as Jeffrey Frankel suggests, when account is taken of all the "fundamental" factors, there remains room for a spontaneous reversal of earlier market enthusiasm, or for exchange rate policy, to have played a significant role in bringing down the dollar.

The firming of U.S. monetary policy from early 1987 until the stock market crash on 19 October probably helped forestall further declines in the dollar, especially during the spring, when Japanese and German monetary policy was moving toward greater ease. After the crash, the apparent concern of the Federal Reserve with combating possible recession contributed to dollar weakness. Subsequently, from March 1988 through June 1989, U.S. monetary policy was progressively and substantially tightened in response to concerns about rising inflation. This monetary tightening was surely an important cause of dollar appreciation during this period, despite the wishes of the G-7 finance ministers to avoid much of this appreciation.

The Influence of Fiscal Policy

In addition to monetary policy, U.S. fiscal policy is also often cited as a key determinant of major swings in the foreign exchange value of the dollar. The standard analysis, as described by Jeffrey Frankel, is that the expansionary fiscal policy of the first Reagan administration helped push up U.S. real interest rates (relative to foreign real interest rates) and through that mechanism contributed substantially to the real appreciation of the dollar from 1980 through 1984. By making U.S. goods relatively more expensive in comparison with foreign goods, the real appreciation of the dollar was, in turn, the proximate cause of the massive deterioration of the U.S. current account balance. Symmetrically, the increased demand for capital implied by the fiscal deficit and reflected in high U.S. interest rates induced a massive inflow of foreign capital that was the financial counterpart of the current account deficit.

On these issues, I would argue that the emphasis on the interest rate mechanism as the channel through which fiscal policy influenced the exchange rate and the current account has been somewhat overdone. In the circumstances of the early 1980s, the Reagan tax cuts and defense buildup probably did put some upward pressure on U.S. interest rates. However, the empirical evidence that fiscal policy has consistent and powerful effects on interest rates is not compelling. Moreover, there are other channels through which expansionary fiscal policy might have affected the real exchange rate and the current account.

During the first six quarters of economic recovery, from the end of 1982 through the middle of 1984, real domestic demand in the U.S. economy rose at a phenomenal 9 percent average annual rate. The usual Keynesian effects of expansionary fiscal policy are part of the explanation of this growth of domestic demand. So too are the supply-side, incentive effects of substantial reductions in tax rates on business investment and (perhaps) also the favorable incentives of lower individual taxes on labor effort. In addition, the restoration of consumer confidence and the gain in household wealth occasioned by rising stock and bond prices provided a powerful stimulus to consumption spending.

During the same period, real domestic demand rose very sluggishly in other industrial countries and was generally falling in developing countries affected by the debt crisis. On the basis of a very simple economic theory, without complications involving interest rates, the pattern of the growth of domestic demand around the world should have had important effects on the real foreign exchange value of the dollar. The price of U.S. output, for which demand was growing rapidly, should have risen relative to the price of the outputs of nations where domestic demand was growing slowly. In addition, as emphasized by many "supply-side" economists, the increased attractiveness of owning U.S. capital (partly resulting from the Reagan tax cuts) may have stimulated a flow of foreign investment, which tended to appreciate the dollar. Also, concerns about economic and military security in Western Europe during the early 1980s may have contributed a "safe-haven effect" to dollar appreciation.

After the middle of 1984, the rate of growth of real domestic demand slackened in the United States and began to pick up in other industrial countries. From late 1986 through the end of the decade, the growth of real domestic demand in the United States often fell below that of other industrial countries. Again, a simple theory suggests that these developments should have implied a weakening in the real foreign exchange value of the dollar.

For the current account, there is also a simple story. When real domestic demand dropped sharply during the recession of 1981–82, part of that decline fell on imports of foreign goods, and the U.S. current account improved. When U.S. real domestic demand expanded very rapidly during the initial stages of recovery, part of that expansion fell on increased imports of foreign goods, and the U.S. current account deteriorated. This deterioration was accentuated both by the slow growth of demand in other countries, which retarded the growth of U.S. exports, and by the real appreciation of the dollar, which shifted a larger fraction of world demand growth toward foreign goods and away from U.S. goods. In the mid-1980s, deterioration of the U.S. current account continued because of the lagged effects of the strong dollar.

In late 1987, for a variety of reasons, the U.S. current account began to improve. Most important, the effects of the huge real dollar depreciation since early 1985 started to take hold, stimulating rapid growth of U.S. exports and retarding growth of U.S. imports. At the same time, moderating growth of consumer spending and reduction of the U.S. fiscal deficit significantly diminished growth of real domestic demand in the United States. In other industrial countries, strong gains in real incomes and some stimulative fiscal policy actions were simultaneously generating stronger growth of real demand. The combined effect of all these forces was a 60 percent increase in U.S. real exports (in the GNP accounts) over the four years beginning with the fourth quarter of 1986 and a more than one-third reduction of the nominal U.S. current account deficit by 1990 from its peak in 1987.

Of course, movements in U.S. interest rates were not totally unrelated to movements in the dollar, in the U.S. current account, in U.S. monetary policy, or in U.S. fiscal policy. The point is that the interest rate mechanism is not the only plausible channel through which U.S. fiscal policy might have exerted some influence on the evolution of the dollar and the current account. For economic policy, the bottom-line issue is whether large and persistent fiscal deficits tended to contribute to the large U.S. current account deficit or, equivalently, whether actions to reduce the fiscal deficit might contribute to reductions in the current account deficit. On this issue, broad agreement was ultimately reached within the administration, despite skepticism about the interest rate effects of fiscal policy. The proviso, of course, was that deficit reduction be achieved through economic growth and spending restraint rather than through tax increases.

Virtues of Exchange Rate Adjustments and Payments Imbalances

Many discussions of U.S. economic policy lament the wide swings of the dollar exchange rate and the deterioration of the U.S. current account as critical problems of the 1980s. Clearly, many individuals and enterprises did suffer significant hardships from the intense pressure of foreign competition. Nevertheless, it is important to recognize that, from a broad macroeconomic perspective, much of the movement in the foreign exchange value of the dollar and in the U.S. current account during the 1980s was a necessary and often desirable concomitant of generally favorable economic developments.

Benefits from the Dollar's Upswing

At the beginning of the 1980s, U.S. economic policy fought a necessary and successful battle against the evils of persistently rising inflation. After a deep recession that was the inevitable consequence of this struggle, the U.S. economy enjoyed nearly eight years of relatively vigorous economic expansion during which the annual inflation rate generally remained close to 4 percent. Growth of productivity and of real per capita GNP was not as strong as during the period of exceptional economic progress in the 1950s and 1960s. However, taking account of the need to combat inflation inherited from the 1970s and of the success of that effort, the overall record of U.S. macroeconomic performance during the 1980s was a significant improvement over recent years.

Concerning specifically the upswing of the dollar during the early 1980s, there should be no doubt that the successful assault on inflation during 1981–82 was a key reason for substantial real dollar appreciation. Only a failure to confront this critical problem effectively would have kept the dollar at the depressed level to which it had fallen in the late 1970s.

As previously discussed, further real appreciation of the dollar during 1983 and early 1984 was partly due to the same economic forces that generated the very strong initial recovery of the U.S. economy from the recession of 1981–82, especially as reflected in the phenomenally rapid growth of real domestic demand. Moreover, dollar appreciation during this period clearly helped diminish inflationary pressures in the United States, both directly, by reducing import prices, and indirectly, by putting pressure on producers of internationally tradable goods to control costs and keep their prices from rising.

Dollar appreciation during 1983 and early 1984 also helped spread the impetus of strong demand growth in the United States to other countries where economic recovery would otherwise have been anemic or virtually nonexistent. Deterioration of the U.S. current account was the manifestation of this desirable leakage of demand growth from the United States to other countries, especially to developing countries that were struggling to improve their own current accounts.

On the other hand, given the usual lag in the impact of exchange rate changes on trade flows, the final year of dollar appreciation was probably not reflected in the U.S. current account until 1986. By this time, further deterioration of the U.S. current account was not particularly a blessing for the United States or the rest of the world. Nevertheless, dollar appreciation during the spring and summer of 1984 did help restrain inflationary pressures in the United States and was partly attributable to a timely action to retighten U.S. monetary policy to provide reassurance of the Federal Reserve's resistance to any resurgence of inflation. Thus, only for the last three or four months of dollar appreciation, in late 1984 and early 1985, is it possible to find neither a plausible economic rationale or a meaningful macroeconomic benefit.

Avoidance of the Hard Landing

In the mid-1980s, many economic commentators expressed concern about the dangers of a "hard landing"—a sharp drop in the dollar that would frighten foreign investors and cut off the flow of foreign capital essential to finance much of U.S. net investment. For the United States, the predicted result was both high inflation (due to rising import prices) and deep recession (resulting from higher interest rates and the collapse of investment). For other countries, the prospect was recession resulting from a sharp decline in U.S. demand for their exports.

In the event, there was no hard landing. Although the dollar did drop precipitously from early 1985 until early 1987, there was no marked acceleration of inflation in the United States, no sharp cutback in the inflow of foreign capital, no sudden upsurge in interest rates, and no U.S. recession. Indeed, the stimulus to U.S. export growth and to investment by export-oriented industries contributed substantially to economic growth beginning in late 1986 and helped forestall a possible recession in the aftermath of the stock market crash of October 1987. In Japan, there was a brief pause in growth as export industries felt the impact of a sharply stronger yen, but there was no general economic downturn among countries whose currencies appreciated strongly against the dollar. Thus, all things considered, not only did the world economy adjust remarkably smoothly to the large decline of the dollar in the mid-1980s, but the effects of this exchange rate adjustment probably also contributed to a more satisfactory macroeconomic performance during the second half of the decade.

Of course, it cannot reasonably be argued that all of the wide swing in the foreign exchange value of the dollar or in the U.S. current account during the 1980s was necessary and desirable, even leaving aside the bizarre appreciation of late 1984 and early 1985. In the early 1980s, a less tight U.S. monetary policy and a less easy fiscal policy might have avoided some of the enormous appreciation of the dollar, without sacrificing much progress in reducing inflation or in speeding economic recovery. Later in the decade, a more vigorous attack on the U.S. fiscal deficit and a more even course of U.S. monetary policy (less easing in 1985–86 and less tightening in 1988–89) might have achieved superior results for growth and inflation while also smoothing the course for the dollar and generating larger reductions in the U.S. current account deficit.

In other leading countries, monetary and fiscal policies supporting some-what stronger growth of domestic demand early in the decade might also have limited the extent of dollar appreciation and the need for subsequent correc-tion, without exacerbating domestic inflation or impairing economic growth. Nevertheless, while improvements in economic policies both at home and abroad might have produced a somewhat smoother course for the dollar, there is little doubt that substantial swings in the foreign exchange value of the dollar and in the U.S. current account played an essential and desirable role in achiev-ing the relatively favorable macroeconomic performance of the 1980s.

The Limited Role of Exchange Rate Policy

Monetary policy and fiscal policy are the primary tools through which the U.S. government may affect the foreign exchange value of the dollar and the current account balance. The issues of exchange rate policy, therefore, are pri-marily questions of the degree to which the behavior of the exchange rate or the current account should influence monetary and fiscal policy. In addition, there is the question of the extent to which the U.S. government can conduct an exchange rate policy that is separate from its monetary and fiscal policy.

The Exchange Rate as a Concern of Monetary Policy

During the 1980s, concerns about the exchange rate and the current account rarely exerted significant influence on the Federal Reserve's conduct of U.S. monetary policy. The record of the meetings of the Federal Open Market Com-mittee (FOMC) indicates that, except for a few occasions in 1985, 1986, and 1987, relatively little attention was paid to international economic develop-ments in decisions about monetary policy. A detailed analysis of the Federal Reserve's actions reveals that concerns about inflation and about output and employment growth were almost always the critical determinants of U.S. mon-etary policy. Moreover, as Jeffrey Frankel points out, in the formulation of both the Plaza Agreement and the Louvre Accord (the two most important policy actions explicitly directed at affecting the value of the dollar), no explicit con-sideration was given to monetary policy.

With regard to the appropriate influence of the exchange rate on U.S. mone-tary policy, it would seem peculiar—even outrageous—to argue that the Fed-eral Reserve should have avoided or aborted its determined effort to combat inflation in 1981–82 because of concern about possibly excessive appreciation of the dollar. Similarly, few would argue that the Federal Reserve should have risked reigniting rapid inflation by running a highly expansionary monetary policy throughout 1984 in order to induce dollar depreciation.

Perhaps most revealing is the episode of monetary tightening from early 1988 to mid-1989. Initially, this U.S. monetary tightening helped firm the dol-lar in a manner consistent with the preferences of exchange rate policy, as ex-pressed by the G-7 finance ministers. By late 1988, however, it was feared that further dollar appreciation might impede progress in reducing international payments imbalances. While finance ministries, including the U.S. Treasury, ordered intervention to combat the rise of the dollar, U.S. monetary policy remained targeted to resisting inflation. The dollar continued to appreciate.

The issue posed by this episode is whether U.S. monetary policy should have given much greater emphasis to the exchange rate in late 1988 and the first half of 1989. For those who believe that the inflationary danger was exaggerated and that monetary policy was too tight for purely domestic economic purposes, this is not a challenging question. However, granting that the danger of rising inflation was real, can it persuasively be argued that monetary policy should have ignored this danger in favor of stabilizing the exchange rate? The bitter experience of the late 1970s and early 1980s demonstrated the costs of allowing inflation to build momentum before taking effective action. Would the late 1980s have begun a repeat of this sad experience had the Federal Reserve ignored the inflationary danger and focused more attention on stabilizing the dollar?

International Influences on U.S. Fiscal Policy

For U.S. fiscal policy, there is no question that concerns about the exchange rate or the current account have rarely, if ever, been determining factors. During President Reagan's first term, the administration's fiscal policy was dominated by the supply-side tax cuts, by cuts in domestic spending programs, and by the defense buildup—all of which were key policy priorities. Strong dollar appreciation was not an officially anticipated result of this fiscal policy but was welcomed as a sign of the administration's overall success. Some officials, notably Council of Economic Advisers (CEA) Chairman Martin Feldstein, expressed skepticism. However, in the political environment of Ronald Reagan's reelection campaign, there could be no room for doubt about the virtues of a strong dollar, whatever its cause and whatever future difficulties it might portend.

In President Reagan's second term, the initial priority for fiscal policy was not deficit reduction but tax reform. However, by early 1985, the rising U.S. current account deficit and increasing protectionist sentiment did become serious concerns of administration policymakers. The response was to seek dollar depreciation and stronger growth of foreign demand for U.S. exports rather than to mount a determined assault on the federal deficit. Even under the pressure of the Gramm-Rudman-Hollings (GRH) deficit reduction targets, there was little effective action to reduce the federal deficit until late 1986. The president supported domestic spending restraint but would not agree to tax increases or military spending cuts. The Congress talked about deficit reduction and criticized the president's budget but exhibited little willingness to cut any spending programs or propose any specific tax increases. In the political debate over the budget, there was vague recognition that the fiscal deficit might be related to the current account deficit. However, this relation was not sufficiently compelling, and concern over the current account was not sufficiently great, to stimulate much action to reduce the fiscal deficit.

In fiscal year 1987, the federal deficit fell to 3 percent of GNP, from 5 percent in the preceding fiscal year. This accomplishment partly reflected political pressures to do something to meet the GRH deficit targets in the congressional session that ended just before the 1986 midterm elections. In part, it was the accidental consequence of the revenue bulge from the onset of tax reform and from the exceptionally and unexpectedly strong performance of the U.S. economy. The budget agreement pounded out after the stock market crash achieved enough to lock in the accidental gains of fiscal 1987 and hold the budget deficit to 3 percent of GNP for the remainder of the decade.

From the perspective of international economic policy, the key fact about the deficit reduction accomplished during the final three years of the 1980s is that it was no more than marginally affected by concerns about the exchange rate and the current account. For years, foreign government officials had been berating U.S. officials, including President Reagan, about the need to cut the U.S. fiscal deficit. When significant deficit reduction was achieved, U.S. officials were happy to take credit for their contribution to "international economic policy coordination" (while foreign officials expressed skepticism about the size and permanence of the accomplishment). Nevertheless, viewing the process as a member of the Council of Economic Advisers, I have no doubt that domestic political and economic concerns, rather than efforts at international policy coordination, were the driving force behind any accomplishments in the area of fiscal deficit reduction.

In the future, of course, it is possible that international economic concerns may weigh more heavily in the conduct of U.S. fiscal policy. However, long experience before, during, and after the 1980s suggests that such concerns will rarely exert much influence on U.S. fiscal policy. The powerful interests at play in any significant issue of fiscal policy and the division of power and the nature of the policy-making process dictate that vague concerns about the exchange rate and the current account will be given little weight in politically determined outcomes. The notion that U.S. fiscal policy will be actively manipulated to affect the exchange rate or the balance of payments is an economist's dream— or nightmare. It is not a practical issue of economic policy.

Official Intervention and Exchange Rate Policy

Finally, there is the question of exchange rate policy that is separate from monetary and fiscal policy. Such policy consists of sterilized official intervention in foreign exchange markets and public statements (and background rumors) of high government officials directed toward altering the behavior of exchange rates. In the first Reagan administration, there was no such policy— or, as Jeffrey Frankel describes it, there was Treasury Undersecretary for Monetary Affairs Beryl Sprinkel's policy of benign neglect. In the second Reagan administration, Treasury Secretary James Baker, Deputy Secretary Richard

Darman, Undersecretary David Mulford, and (later) Nicholas Brady pursued more active and publicly visible policy to influence the exchange rate.

In my view, the early policy of "benign neglect" was 80 or 90 percent correct, and the subsequent policy was more of a political and public relations success than a substantive accomplishment. As previously discussed, much of the appreciation of the dollar during the early 1980s was the inevitable and, to a substantial extent, desirable consequence of the macroeconomic events and policies of that period. Exchange rate policy that did not alter monetary or fiscal policy could not have done much to avoid most of the appreciation of the dollar, and it would probably have been a mistake to try.

The important exception (and one of the few issues on which I have a significant disagreement with Beryl Sprinkel) is the last 10 or 15 percent of dollar appreciation in late 1984 and early 1985. Given the enormous run-up of the dollar by the summer of 1984, there was no plausible economic rationale for further appreciation. In retrospect, and even at the time, it seems clear that avoiding the final lunge of appreciation would have been worthwhile. An official statement that too much dollar appreciation was undesirable—backed by substantial, coordinated intervention against the dollar—might have turned the tide. If ever there was an occasion for using exchange rate policy to correct a fundamental disequilibrium, this was such an occasion. Surely, there was little harm in trying.

The occasional usefulness of exchange rate policy was illustrated in February 1985, when the dollar finally began its long downward correction. At this time, there was publicly reported intervention against the dollar by leading central banks, including (for the first time since 1981) the Federal Reserve. In the Plaza Agreement of 22 September 1985, the finance ministers of the G-5 countries publicly declared that "some further orderly appreciation of non-dollar currencies is desirable," and this declaration was subsequently backed by coordinated intervention.

It is difficult to know how much these efforts at exchange rate policy contributed to the dollar's actual decline during 1985. The easing of U.S. monetary policy, together with the implications of large and growing U.S. current account deficits, was surely an important fundamental force for a lower dollar. Moreover, as Martin Feldstein and others have emphasized, the dollar headed downward throughout most of 1985, even when there were no official announcements or intervention pushing in that direction. On the other hand, there were large drops in the dollar simultaneously with major interventions and immediately after the announcement of the Plaza Agreement. On balance, the lesson from this experience appears to be that exchange rate policy can enjoy success when it is reinforcing rather than resisting the basic trend in the market and when it is supported by, or at least consistent with, more fundamental economic forces.

The limits on the effectiveness of exchange rate policy are powerfully illustrated by events later in the decade. By the spring of 1986, although the U.S.

Treasury remained favorably disposed toward further dollar depreciation, the Japanese and German governments began to intervene against what they perceived as excessive appreciation of their currencies. Despite quite a large intervention, the yen and the deutsche mark continued to appreciate. In the Louvre Accord of February 1987, the G-7 finance ministers proclaimed that the dollar had depreciated sufficiently and that further depreciation would be resisted. Within weeks, market pressures forced an upward rebasing of the implicit target range for the yen. Late in 1987, in the aftermath of the stock market crash, the dollar began to move sharply downward, despite substantial intervention by foreign central banks, but with the perception that U.S. authorities were not unhappy with further dollar depreciation. During 1988–89, the progressive tightening of U.S. monetary policy overwhelmed the internationally coordinated, publicly announced efforts to resist dollar appreciation through the limited tools of exchange rate policy.

It is not surprising that exchange rate policy, unsupported by more fundamental forces, often exhibited little influence on the value of the dollar. Even if portfolio-balance models of exchange rate determination (referred to by Jeffrey Frankel) are correct, it would presumably take hundreds of billions of dollars of sterilized intervention to affect significantly the foreign exchange value of the dollar by altering the relative supplies of assets denominated in different national currencies. When more modest official intervention succeeds in influencing exchange rates—as it sometimes does—it is because intervention signals something about official intentions concerning more fundamental policies that markets are more prepared to believe rather than to contradict.

Finally, some of the dangers of an excessively active exchange rate policy should be noted. Large-scale official intervention can become expensive to the taxpayer if the authorities consistently fail to outguess the market. In practice, however, losses from official intervention are usually not large, except when authorities persist in futile attempts to defend an unsustainable exchange rate. Perhaps of greater concern is the possibility that excessive and unsuccessful use of exchange rate policy will diminish its effectiveness on those few occasions when it can be helpful. The signaling effect of official intervention ought to depend on the quality of the signal, and a record of misguided intervention presumably impairs signal quality. Probably of greatest concern is the risk that exchange rate policy may pervert the conduct of other, more important policies, especially monetary policy. For example, it has been suggested that the recent increase of inflation in the United Kingdom has been the consequence of rapid money creation resulting from efforts to stabilize the sterling/deutsche mark exchange rate during the late 1980s. In the United States, where monetary policy is institutionally separated and insulated from exchange rate policy, this danger may not be acute. However, in the political environment where government officials occasionally become attached to the success of their pet policies, this danger should not be entirely ignored.

Summary of Discussion

Paul Volcker began the discussion by stating some of his views on exchange rate policy. First, he expressed his agreement with Mussa on the topic of sterilized intervention—there is not much cost to it, and it is sometimes helpful as a signaling device. So he thought that sterilized intervention should not be abandoned as a policy tool, but he would not expect too much from it. He disagreed entirely with the description in Frankel's paper of the Federal Reserve's legal authority for exchange market intervention. Although the Treasury Department may apply pressure on the Fed to intervene in certain ways (or more likely *not* to intervene), the Fed is clearly entitled legally to intervene (or not to intervene) on its own. It boils down to the practical need for coordination and the Treasury's general claim to executive leadership in international economic policy.

Next, Volcker said that he instinctively likes a strong dollar. He thought that the dollar had been too strong during the period 1983–85, but he gets nervous when people are too relaxed about the dollar depreciating. Also, he thought that it would have been dangerous and ineffective to try to manipulate the value of the dollar by monetary policy, in the absence of the president and Congress making the changes that we have seen as necessary in fiscal policy.

Finally, Volcker said that the United States should be trying to achieve more stable exchange rates and that monetary policy would need to play a role in that.

Martin Feldstein asked whether the policymakers who met at the Louvre and the Plaza had distinguished between sterilized and unsterilized intervention. *Volcker* responded that people assumed that the intervention would be sterilized, although there was no explicit discussion of this point.

Feldstein then asked why the policymakers had pursued a course of action that the Jurgensen Report had declared to be useless. Did the policymakers think that sterilized intervention might work in some instances? Did they intend the policy to be a signal of something and, if so, of what?

Volcker said that, although the tone of the Jurgensen Report had been extremely skeptical, it had not said that sterilized intervention was ineffective under all circumstances. He added that he had indicated to the Treasury Department prior to the Plaza Agreement that monetary policy was unlikely to be tightened soon, which would have defeated the effort to depreciate the dollar. *Feldstein* supposed that the sterilized intervention had thus sent a signal that the Fed was not going to tighten monetary policy soon.

It seemed peculiar to *William Poole* that many people want to continue to use sterilized intervention, even though they seem to agree that it is not very effective. He thought that the danger of retaining sterilized intervention as a policy instrument is that it would be used in circumstances where it is inappropriate and potentially harmful. Poole drew an analogy to credit controls; he thought that the economy would have been better off if the Federal Reserve had not had the authority to impose credit controls in 1980, even though there are, conceivably, some circumstances under which such controls might be useful. Poole doubted that the marginal signaling value of exchange market intervention was worth the possible misuse of the tool.

Volcker replied that he thought that exchange rate intervention could be quite effective as a signaling device *if* it is believed that more fundamental policies will be changed if needed to back up that signal. In this case, one might avoid the need, for instance, of a change in fiscal or monetary policy that might cut across the grain of other objectives as long as markets are confident that the government would be willing to do it if required in the end to back up the stability of the currency. What is involved is expectations. Nevertheless, he agreed with Poole that intervention can be abused, and he said that the chairman of the Federal Reserve Board should take care to use it constructively.

Fred Bergsten asked whether fundamental macroeconomic policy in the United States would have been different at the time of the Plaza agreement had exchange rate intervention been ruled out. Would fiscal policy have been tightened, for example?

Feldstein answered that he thought that macroeconomic policy would not have been any different. *Volcker* agreed, saying that, although Treasury Secretary James Baker probably acknowledged that there was a connection between the budget deficit and the trade deficit, he was unwilling to bear the political costs that he thought would be incurred by proposing any change in fiscal policy.

Bergsten said that, if Feldstein and Volcker were correct that fiscal policy would not have changed under any circumstances, then it was good to use exchange rate intervention at least to try to lower the value of the dollar.

Poole responded that it is not clear that the Plaza Agreement had much effect on the value of the dollar anyway. The dollar had depreciated a lot before the Plaza Agreement, and, although it continued to decline steadily, its decline was actually slowed by the actions of foreign central banks. Official capital flowed into the United States after the agreement because the Japanese, German, and British central banks were trying, Poole thought, to prevent their own currencies from appreciating too rapidly.

Feldstein agreed, noting that, if one studies the movement of the exchange rate over this period, there is no significant change at the time of the Plaza Agreement.

Jeffrey Frankel said that he disagreed with Poole and Feldstein that one cannot see the effects of sterilized intervention by looking at exchange rate patterns in 1985. Frankel argued that, although people generally date the intervention from the time of the Plaza meeting, it actually began in January or February 1985 after the G-5 meeting in London. At both meetings, the participants agreed to roughly $10 billion worth of intervention, although a greater fraction of that intervention was undertaken by the United States after the Plaza meeting.

Frankel added that he and economist Kathryn Dominguez had studied the sterilized intervention by the German Bundesbank and the Federal Reserve for 1985–88, and they had found a statistically significant effect on the value of the dollar. The estimated effect was very small, however, except when the intervention was publicly announced. Thus, one might say that sterilized intervention is effective because it is signaling future monetary policy, but Frankel did not know if this was the correct conclusion to draw.

Frankel concluded that he had been quite skeptical in the early 1980s that sterilized intervention could be effective, but, when the dollar had become so strong by late 1984, he had begun to think that it was a good time to try it. He thought now that a good case can be made that the intervention pricked the speculative exchange rate bubble, starting at the beginning of 1985.

Geoffrey Carliner wondered why it was necessary to use sterilized intervention as a signal that the U.S. government wanted the dollar to depreciate when Volcker and Baker could simply have stated their desire for this to happen.

Volcker said that Baker wanted to use this issue as a negotiating tool, by threatening other countries that, unless they took action to strengthen their currencies, the United States would take action to depreciate the dollar.

Feldstein pointed out that, had Baker wanted only to threaten other countries, he could have contacted his counterparts in Bonn and Tokyo and delivered the message privately. Feldstein thought that, by making a public announcement, Baker had placed himself in a no-lose position in the United States. If the dollar did not fall, that would have been because foreigners had taken the policy steps that the United States desired. If the dollar did fall, that would have shown how powerful Baker was. Essentially, Baker had been able to convince the U.S. public that a falling dollar would be a virtue and a sign of U.S. strength.

Bergsten said that the policy became much riskier for Baker as U.S. interest rates started to increase in early 1987. To continue the depreciation of the dollar, Baker needed to persuade Volcker to combat the rising interest rates with expansionary monetary policy. Yet Volcker did not seem to accede to Baker's requests, and Bergsten asked Volcker if this had been a problem.

Volcker responded that there really had not been much of a conflict. The Federal Reserve had not tightened monetary policy to a point that was disturbing to Baker, and it was not clear that even tighter policy would have prompted Baker to publicize their differences.

Bergsten believed that Baker had been more committed to expansionary monetary policy and further depreciation of the dollar than Volcker admitted. The trade deficit was still increasing, and many in Congress continued to call for protectionist measures. Further, the Treasury wanted the dollar to continue falling so as to apply additional pressure on the Germans and Japanese to expand their own economies.

Michael Mussa returned to Poole's point about the dangers of exchange market intervention. He thought that the danger was that a country would try to defend a particular exchange rate that was really indefensible. This would cost the taxpayers large amounts of money, and, in an effort to save both money and prestige, the government might change fundamental economic policy in a way that could be detrimental to more important policy objectives.

Feldstein asked whether there was any evidence that this had happened in the 1980s. In particular, he wondered whether the Federal Reserve had kept interest rates higher in 1987 than they would otherwise have been, in order to defend the value of the dollar under the Louvre Agreement.

Mussa replied that the record of the Federal Open Market Committee indicated that the Federal Reserve had in fact been concerned with the exchange rate at that time. It was not clear, however, whether they were concerned because of the exchange rate itself or because of the inflationary implications of further depreciation. Mussa thought that there was really no way to separate these issues.

Mussa added that Federal Reserve Governor Manuel Johnson had dissented from a later Fed decision regarding intervention, arguing that the Fed should not support the Treasury's decision to intervene. Johnson expressed concern that the Treasury was trying to resist a clearly rising trend of the dollar, rather than intervening as a signal or to smooth market developments. This was another instance in which one might argue that exchange market intervention was inappropriate.

Thomas Enders said that he thought that the Federal Reserve had not been entirely responsible for the rise in interest rates in 1987. In fact, the yield curve tilted upward, in addition to shifting upward, which is hard to attribute to tighter monetary policy. The real cause of the rise in interest rates was probably an increasing lack of long-term foreign capital.

Mussa agreed and pointed out that, while the Germans and Japanese had been lowering interest rates in the spring of 1987, by the summer they were raising them. The Federal Reserve must have felt that, if it did not allow U.S. interest rates to rise along with foreign interest rates, it would have faced a significant depreciation of the dollar.

William Niskanen offered two comments about sterilized intervention. First, he argued that there is no evidence that the Federal Reserve had subordinated its concern about stabilizing domestic demand to any concern about the exchange rate during the entire period 1984–88. In particular, although the Fed may have accommodated policy to exchange rate concerns for very brief periods of time, it did not do so over any period as long as three months. Second, Niskanen did not know of any argument that suggested that the Fed's single policy tool should be directed toward stabilizing exchange rates rather than stabilizing nominal domestic demand. The Federal Reserve cannot stabilize both, so it must pick one, and Niskanen did not see any reason why the Fed should focus on exchange rates. It seemed clear that directing monetary policy toward domestic economic goals had been the right thing for the Federal Reserve to do.

Niskanen added that he thought that the primary objective of the Plaza and Louvre agreements had been to place constraints on the Fed's behavior. Then Baker had timed his speeches about the dollar so that it had looked as though he had a lot of influence over the Federal Reserve. In fact, Federal Reserve policy had not been affected by either the international agreements or Baker's speeches.

Bergsten responded that Niskanen's argument goes back to the basic question of whether the Plaza Agreement had any effect on the dollar exchange rate. It was clear that there were differences among the conference participants on this subject. Frankel argued that intervention can make a difference, and Bergsten supported this view. He believed that sterilized intervention can affect the exchange rate by influencing market psychology and expectations and by signaling future policy. He said that, if one could use rational economic analysis to explain the rapid appreciation of the dollar in late 1984 and early 1985, then one could say that the decline was purely rational as well. But, in fact, there was no rational economic theory that explained the final 20 percent of the dollar's rise, so one cannot dismiss the idea that the Plaza Agreement was effective through psychological channels.

Mussa maintained that the basic path of the foreign exchange value of the dollar is determined by fundamental monetary and fiscal policy and that exchange rate policy, meaning sterilized intervention, has little influence on it. But he thought that it was plausible that exchange rate policy could have some small effect, as Frankel and Bergsten were arguing.

Feldstein claimed that 1987 had been very different from earlier periods because the exchange market intervention had been accompanied by changes in U.S. monetary policy and by massive purchases of dollar securities by the Japanese. Both the monetary policy changes and the asset purchases showed the markets that the countries were prepared to sacrifice their domestic monetary policy goals in order to reach their exchange rate goals. This willingness to change fundamental policies on the basis of exchange rate considerations had greatly increased the power of the sterilized intervention signal. So Feldstein concluded that intervention had mattered during this period, although not for the standard reasons.

Returning to an earlier comment, Feldstein asked Mussa to explain the mechanism by which a budget deficit can produce a current account deficit without affecting either interest rates or the dollar.

Mussa responded that interest rates probably did rise in response to the expansionary fiscal policy but that the budget deficit was not the primary force affecting those rates. He said that it is very difficult to find correlations between the budget deficit, interest rates, and the dollar. Mussa added that the existence of a budget deficit may mean that domestic spending exceeds income, which directly produces a current account deficit. If the economy has nontraded goods, then the real exchange rate reacts to the current account deficit, without requiring any link to interest rates.

Bergsten returned to the issue of whether sterilized intervention was costly for taxpayers. He argued that, in fact, the United States had made money over time through various interventions. When the Carter administration had intervened, for example, it had made over $1 billion.

David Richardson remarked that short-term expediency can sometimes lead to bad long-term policies. He emphasized the point in Frankel's paper that the temporarily large trade deficits in the early 1980s had resulted in a 1988 trade bill that may do long-term damage to U.S. trade policy.

6 Economic Regulation

1. *Paul L. Joskow and Roger G. Noll*
2. *William A. Niskanen*
3. *Elizabeth Bailey*

1. *Paul L. Joskow and Roger G. Noll*

Deregulation and Regulatory Reform during the 1980s

According to political and journalistic rhetoric, the United States relies on a market economy to allocate economic resources. Thus, the forces of supply and demand, largely unfettered by government intervention, are regarded as determining the quantities, qualities, and prices of goods and services that are produced in the domestic economy. The roots of this belief probably lie in two distinctive features of the U.S. economy: (i) the extent of private ownership of capital combined with relatively little public (nationalized) enterprise and (ii) the absence of strong, centralized economic planning. Nonetheless, this common belief is largely a myth.

Through civil law and regulation, federal, state, and local governments have a substantial effect on almost all industries. Civil law limits property rights, defines contractual obligations, and sets quality standards for goods and services through tort law. Regulatory policy takes two general forms. "Economic" regulation controls profits, sets prices, and determines who can participate in a market or use a particular resource. "Social" regulation controls polluting by-products of production, sets health and safety standards for products and workplaces, restricts the content of information provided by sellers through advertising and other means of describing products to consumers, and establishes requirements to protect buyers from fraudulent, discriminatory, or incompetent behavior by sellers. All these policies profoundly affect prices, costs, product quality, the dynamics of business competition, and the allocation of resources in the economy.

From approximately 1970 through 1990,[1] federal regulatory policy in the United States experienced profound and far-reaching change. The period is defined by the passage of perhaps the two most economically significant regulatory statutes in the nation's history: the Clean Air Acts of 1970 and 1990. The 1970 act was quickly followed by a five-year succession of bills regulating workplace safety and health, water quality, product safety, the price of oil, the environmental effect of all construction projects requiring federal approval or expending federal funds, the safety of consumer products, the management of employee retirement funds, and the operation of futures markets. The cumulative effect of these acts was to expand regulation dramatically—a change in policy that is comparable to, or perhaps even exceeds, the regulatory policies enacted during the mid-1930s under the administration of Franklin Roosevelt but that was accomplished under the putatively conservative administration of Richard Nixon. After a decade of no significant new social regulatory statutes, the Clean Air Act of 1990 again substantially expanded environmental regulation by enacting strict new policies regarding acid rain, auto emissions, and airborne toxics.

As the ink dried on the expansive environmental, health, and safety regulatory statutes of the 1970s, the scope of economic regulation began to recede. Price, profit, and entry controls in transportation, communications, energy, and finance were either eliminated or dramatically relaxed. By the early 1980s, much of the Roosevelt-era system of economic regulation was gone; however, the Nixon-era reforms in social regulation remained largely in place. By the late 1980s, considerable experience with relaxed price, profit, and entry controls had accumulated. The specter of reregulation loomed over some industries.

The rationales, causes, and consequences of "microeconomic" regulatory interventions have always been the subject of considerable political and intellectual controversy. The dramatic policy changes of the period reflect these disputes. This chapter examines the nature, causes, and consequences of changes in economic regulation during the 1980s. (Kip Viscusi's essay in this volume covers environmental, health, and safety regulation.)

We begin with a discussion of the economic and political theories of economic regulation. We then summarize the major changes in economic regulation during this period. Finally, we offer our conclusions about which economic and political variables appear to be responsible for stimulating economic regulatory change during this period. The industries affected by the regulatory reform movement have diverse characteristics, so the fact that changes occurred in so many industries at about the same time is almost certainly more

---

1. All choices of dates to demarcate an era are somewhat arbitrary.

than mere coincidence. Yet simple explanations for the question, "Why now?" are elusive.

6.1 Economic and Political Theories of Price and Entry Regulation

The task of theories of economic regulation is to explain and predict which markets will be regulated and with what effect. Any such theory must deal with both the economic and the political spheres of human behavior. Presumably, the performance of a market generates the desire to change the behavior of those who participate in it. The actions that change market interventions are taken by political actors: civil service bureaucrats, political appointees (who manage regulatory agencies), Congress and the president (who collaborate on regulatory legislation and budgets), and the courts (which interpret statutes and determine the legality of regulatory agency decisions). Thus, a theory of economic regulation must account for why the events in a market lead to the political act of policy change.

Economics and political science offer several explanations of changes in regulatory policy. Each discipline has a purely normative or "public interest" version, which starts with the proposition that regulatory policy is designed to advance public welfare. Likewise, the two disciplines contain several "positive" theories (i.e., purely predictive and free of normative motivation, although not free of normative implications). We will begin with the normative theories and then describe the positive ones (for a more complete discussion, see Noll [1989]).

6.1.1 Normative Economic Theory

The traditional economic "public interest" rationale for price and entry regulation turns on perceived failures of unregulated markets to yield reasonably competitive behavior and performance in certain circumstances. Although markets can fail if consumers are poorly informed, historically "natural monopoly" or "natural oligopoly" has been the most important rationale for introducing price and entry regulation (Schmalensee 1979). Specifically, when production is characterized by significant economies of scale and sunk costs, market structure, behavior, and performance may depart significantly from the perfectly competitive ideal. Industries with these characteristics will "naturally" evolve toward monopolies or oligopolies, with adverse efficiency and distributional consequences. Dynamically, in the absence of price and entry regulation, industries with these characteristics are said to be characterized by at least one of several problems: excessive entry, costly duplication of facilities, either monopoly exploitation or unstable prices and "destructive competition," excessive investments to deter competitive entry, and a variety of other performance failures.

Several distinguished nineteenth- and early twentieth-century economists argued that, in industries with these characteristics, performance would be improved by having a single firm supply the service and subjecting its prices to government regulation (Sharkey 1982, 12–28). It was argued that entry restrictions would ensure that the efficiencies associated with economies of scale were achieved and that cost-based price regulation would pass on the efficiency gains to consumers.

Since the seminal article by George Stigler (1961), economists have developed a comparably rich literature on the performance of markets in which consumers are poorly informed. Even when such markets are structurally competitive, some firms may be able to sustain monopoly prices, and firms may be inefficiently small. Normally, informational requirements are the recommended solution, but complex products with arcane characteristics may require price regulation to prevent monopoly pricing.

These market failure stories have several flaws as either a normative or a positive theory of regulation. First, once any significant degree of informational imperfection or economies of scale and sunk costs is incorporated in market models, market outcomes will depart from the perfectly competitive ideal. But these models provide no clear way to identify industries where, in the absence of regulation, industry performance will be sufficiently poor to justify price and entry controls. Because most real markets are in some way imperfectly competitive, the market failure approach can provide a rationalization for regulating almost any industry, if one assumes that regulation can in fact ameliorate market imperfections costlessly.

Second, price and entry regulation is also imperfect. Regulators can be imperfectly informed only about the "efficient costs" and the "optimal" prices of services. Price and entry regulation can increase costs, retard productivity growth, and promote cross-subsidization, harming at least some consumers. Furthermore, regulatory procedures aimed at identifying the right costs, setting the right prices, and determining the optimal number of firms create incentives to produce inefficiently and may discourage or distort technological changes that would benefit consumers. As a result, from a normative perspective, decisions regarding the nature and extent of government regulation should balance the costs of imperfect competition against the costs of imperfect regulation.

Third, even when imperfect regulation is less costly than imperfect competition, subsequent changes in supply and demand conditions may lead to a different conclusion. Sensible regulation today does not necessarily mean that regulation and prevailing industry structures should be cemented in place for all time. In most cases, regulatory statutes do not ask regulators to identify only markets that are substantially imperfectly competitive and to regulate them only temporarily until competition can be relied on. Instead, statutes normally presume a permanent state of comprehensive regulation. Significant deregulation, therefore, normally requires a new law if it is to escape judicial reversal.

Finally, market failure rationales do not explain the incidence, persistence, or nature of economic regulation in many industries. One would be hard pressed to support an efficiency argument for price regulation of trucking, buses, airlines, property/casualty insurance, or natural gas wells. Moreover, regulatory procedures and outcomes typically are not consistent with the notion that the purpose of the regulatory process is to simulate hypothetical competitive market outcomes. Rather than protecting consumers generally from exploitation, government regulation often protects incumbent producers from competition and is used to redistribute income from one group of customers to another (Stigler 1971; Posner 1971).

The failure of normative economic theory to explain regulatory policy has given rise to several theories of the politics of regulation. Some assign a role to economic efficiency effects, but others ignore them entirely. Here we review some of the more influential of these theories.

6.1.2   Ideological Shift

It has become common, especially in the popular press, to refer broadly to the changes in economic regulation as *deregulation,* which is then held to be synonymous with a kind of libertarian ideology, "to get government off the backs of the people." These changes are often attributed to the Reagan administration, the implication being that they were a consequence primarily of an ideological shift in the executive branch of the federal government. In a sense, this is a political "public interest" account. Citizens changed their views about the role of government, adopting a more conservative, free market ideology and in 1980 elected a president to carry out the implied policy change. This view is at best simplistic and more likely simply wrong.

The changes in economic regulation in the recent past include some examples of virtually complete deregulation of prices, entry, and the quality of service (e.g., airlines, trucking, railroads). But other changes have taken the form of a peculiar mixture of regulation and competition (e.g., telecommunications and natural gas production and transportation) or of preliminary steps to encourage competition on the fringes of the market and in vertically or horizontally associated industry (e.g., electric power). In only one case was a regulatory agency eliminated (airlines); in all cases (even airlines) the industry is still regulated in some way, although typically according to different criteria from those used prior to the late 1970s. Resources devoted to economic regulation by the federal government have declined in some areas (primarily transportation) but have been relatively stable or increased in others, as shown in table 6.1.

Many of the changes in economic regulation were launched prior to the Reagan administration. Moreover, the causes of these changes reflect the actions of regulators, legislators, judges, and presidents of both parties and all ideological types in both federal and state government. Thus, these changes simply do not reflect a sudden ideological change in federal executive branch views about the strengths and weaknesses of price and entry regulation generally. Indeed, many of the most significant changes in economic regulation be-

Table 6.1   **Staffing of Selected Regulatory Agencies (full-time equivalents)**

Agency	1970	1980	1985	1990
Civil Aeronautics Board (CAB) (airlines)	686	753	0	0
Interstate Commerce Commission (ICC) (railroads, trucks)	1,912	1,940	839	661
Federal Communications Commission (FCC) (telecommunication, broadcasting)	1,645	2,156	1,828	1,839
Federal Energy Regulatory Commission (FERC) (natural gas, electric power)	1,164	1,605	1,533	1,500
Federal Deposit Insurance Corporation (FDIC)	2,669	3,691	3,554	3,065
Comptroller of Currency	1,920	3,331	3,250	3,730
Securities and Exchange Commission (SEC)	1,436	2,100	2,046	2,451
Antitrust Division (DOJ)	595	939	649	623

Source: Warren and Chilton (1990).

gan during the Carter administration and were initiated by liberal Democrats appointed by Carter to economic regulatory agencies. Moreover, Carter's principal rival for the presidency within the Democratic party was Senator Edward Kennedy of Massachusetts, whose advocacy of airline deregulation in the mid-1970s is regarded as an important milestone in achieving reforms in economic regulation. Thus, it is not particularly productive to refer to a generic *deregulation* movement or to think of it primarily as a consequence of the election of Ronald Reagan. The causes are far broader than ideology or party and far more pragmatic and complex than a simple desire to reduce the scope of government. An important implication of this fact is that Ronald Reagan's departure from the presidency per se is not likely to cause these reforms to be rescinded.

6.1.3   Ideas and Garbage Cans

A second political explanation having far more impressive scholarly credentials attributes causal influence to the way the intellectual establishment thinks about government policy. Although a political account, the "ideas theory" assigns only a minor role to electoral politics. Elections simply force political officials to take visible actions to solve salient national problems. Unlike in the "ideology theory," the electorate is not assumed to care very much about exactly how the problem is solved or what political philosophy the solution reflects. Instead, it wants actions and, later, visible improvements.

The role of the intellectual elite—academics, scholars at think tanks, and journalists who write for newspaper editorial pages and policy-oriented periodicals—is to provide explanations and solutions for what is wrong. In the case of economic regulation, the specific contribution of intellectual gadflies was scholarly and popular literature that found regulated industries to be inefficient and protective of certain special interests. With a few important exceptions, the source of this new perception about economic regulation was economists, who, from about 1960 until about 1975, produced the first serious empirical and theoretical studies examining what regulation actually does, as opposed to what normative economic theory says it ought to do. Nonetheless, it is not economists who have attributed much importance to this literature in actually causing policy change but political scientists (Derthick and Quirk 1985) and lawyers (Breyer 1982; Levine 1981).

The causal link between the intellectual elite and political action can take two forms: pure ideas or garbage cans. The pure ideas theory is essentially congruent to the normative economic theory of regulation. It argues that somehow political actors were unaware of the extent to which economic regulation had drifted from the norm of protecting consumers against market imperfections. Hence, once political actors came to believe that the economics literature was correct, they responded by changing policy. This version of the ideas story has basically the same infirmity as the normative economic theory, in that it either fails to explain much of regulation at the time regulatory statutes were passed or assumes substantial ignorance on the part of the political officials who enacted these statutes. Moreover, if the real point of regulation is to cure market failures in the interests of consumers, why did it take so long to change statutes that were patently inconsistent with this objective? The theory leaves unexplained the very long gap between the publication of the research findings and the actual reform of policy. Richard Caves's (1962) critical study of airline regulation and the similar study by John Meyer et al. (1959) of truck and rail regulation predated significant deregulation of these industries by more than fifteen years. Indeed, in 1936, in the midst of the era when many economic regulatory statutes were being passed, Pendleton Herring, one of the most distinguished political scientists of his generation, observed that, in the regulatory process, "the milieu is distinctly one of special interest" (1936, 183).

The "garbage can" version of the causal link between ideas and policy change is borrowed from a theory proposed by Michael Cohen, James March, and Johan Olson (1972) as a way to understand all nonmarket organizations. The premise is that leaders of these organizations are unlikely to be very skilled at understanding the causes of substantial changes in their organizational environment because, most of the time, they are supposed to be managing a relatively stable, even inflexible, institution. More specifically, elected officials are unlikely to know much about the effects of economic regulation or, for that matter, about the consequences of any other relatively technical policy—or about the causes of a new social problem. Thus, most of the time elected officials are not thinking seriously about any given policy, and agency officials are appointed to maintain the status quo.

When an external shock occurs, government officials seek a solution but are uncertain about how to identify it. Meanwhile, back at the think tank, intellectuals have been creating a variety of new ideas about all significant policies or social problems. The *garbage can* is a metaphor for the variety of idea products that are available should political actors need them. In the case at hand, the garbage can called *economic policy* was filled with research findings concerning the operation of the domestic economy, but one especially large and impressive piece of garbage was the work on economic regulation. The instigating events were the economic stagflation of the 1970s or economic shocks particular to specific industries. The initial response was traditional remedies (fiscal and monetary stimulation and price controls), but, when these did not work, political leaders dipped into the garbage can. They found that economic regulation was causing inefficiency in basic infrastructural industries, so they asked some producers of the garbage to reform the system. The fact that economic regulation could not possibly have been the cause of stagflation was in a sense beside the point: it was time to take actions that would improve economic efficiency, and the relevant experts were virtually united in predicting that reforming economic regulation would have this effect.

The obvious criticism of the garbage can model is that economists' views about microeconomic policy generally (agriculture, energy, trade, medical care, etc.) usually involve a proposal for greater liberalization, yet only in economic regulation—not even in social regulation—were the economists' prescriptions seriously considered. The theory has a response to this criticism: other ideas were pulled out of the garbage can when crises emerged in the trade deficit, agriculture, energy, and the environment. But this explanation is not very satisfying, even if true, because it implies an irrational unpredictability to policy change. Indeed, the explanation is tautological, for any policy change must have been somebody's idea and so confirms the theory. It also implies that political decision makers are incapable of learning from past experience by generalizing from successes and failures, even if initially the selection of policies was random.

Nonetheless, we cannot deny that, had the research about economic regulation reached more benign conclusions, the history of policy change would have been different. Nor can we escape the fact that many contributors to the scholarly literature on economic regulation went on to serve in regulatory agencies and were in positions to provide the stimulus for regulatory reform.

6.1.4 Interest Group Bias

The predominant positive (nonnormative) theory of regulation is based on the dominance of organized special interests in the political process. The focal point of the theory is factors that cause citizens to become mobilized to try to influence public policy. The theory assumes that politicians are motivated to win reelection and in order to do so adopt policies that either will cause their constituents to vote for them or will generate campaign contributions. One problem for a politician is that a voter is virtually powerless and so has little incentive to vote or even to know what policies an official advocates (Downs 1957). But groups of citizens are organized for various nonpolitical purposes, notably into firms, trade associations, labor unions, and other groupings according to economic interests (Olson 1965; Moe 1980). Economic groupings can easily and cheaply form the basis for bargaining with politicians for favorable public policies in return for political support. Because a person's income is a very important part of life, and because government has a substantial effect on the distribution of income, economic organizations have an incentive to participate in politics. Moreover, when organized as economic interest groups, citizens are no longer powerless because their votes and contributions can become a significant factor in an election. Of course, economic interest groups are not the only organizations that might be influential; other institutions such as churches, avocational affinity groups (e.g., the Sierra Club or Ducks Unlimited), and state and local government are also potential parties to political bargains with politicians.

The interest group theory predicts that economic regulation is instituted in response to demands among organized interests for changes in market rules that will confer economic benefits on them, at the expense of the groups that are affected by the market rules but that are not sufficiently well organized to have a countervailing influence on policy (Stigler 1971; and Peltzman 1976). Thus, economic regulation should benefit the regulated industry (both profits and employment conditions for unionized labor), the supplier industries, and certain groups of customers who are organized according to their economic interests, at the expense of suppliers (e.g., nonunion labor) and customers (e.g., the prototypical consumer), who are not well organized.

Interest group theory has several predictions about the nature of regulation. First, it predicts cross-subsidies among regulated services and products, generally working to favor organized customers at the expense of unorganized ones. Second, relatively competitive industries offer greater opportunities for the creation and redistribution of rents than do monopolies. In the former case, regulation can retard entry and enforce collusive prices, creating greater profits for incumbent firms. It can also dissipate some of these profits by setting highly favorable prices for organized consumer groups. Monopoly regulation, then, should be rare, arising only when the monopolist is not natural and therefore faces the prospect of competitive entry or when regulation is demanded by organized buyer and/or supplier interests that seek to restrain the power of the monopoly. The latter case differs from the normative economic account, however, because it does not predict that ordinary consumers will benefit from regulation.

According to the theory, the causes of deregulation are factors that make regulation sufficiently less beneficial to some organized interests that, considering the costs of participating in the regulatory and political processes, these interests come to believe that they are better off without regulation (Peltzman

1989). For example, if the demand for regulated services becomes more elastic, there is less monopoly rent to extract and so less net benefit to confer on organized interests. Alternatively, owing to change in technology, supplier or buyer groups may prefer to become vertically integrated rather than to buy regulated services but are prevented from doing so by regulatory entry barriers. Or, owing to changes in income and the pattern of demand, all participants in the regulated market may become organized, leaving no remaining source of benefits to be distributed among the organized interests. Then costly regulation will generate no compensating benefits to organized groups, and they will favor eliminating it. Finally, again owing to changes in technology or demand, an industry that once feared entry may have become a natural monopoly. If so, regulation is no longer necessary to sustain monopoly profits and so will no longer be favored by the incumbent firm. Thus, if economic regulatory reform is largely consistent with interest group theory, some quite explicit facts ought to be observable about who supported and opposed deregulation and who benefited and who lost when liberalization took place.

There are reasons to doubt that interest group theory is a complete explanation for changes in economic policy. Most apparently, a great deal of political participation is not accounted for by the activities of organized interests. Despite the obvious and growing importance of political action committees in campaign finance, which quite likely does reflect organized special interests, the majority of campaign contributions still come from individuals. Likewise, campaign volunteers are primarily highly motivated individuals, not organized groups. In addition, economic special interest is hardly the motivation behind numerous political organizations, ranging from the League of Women Voters to grass-roots organizations within political parties. Thus, at least some citizens seem to care about policy in ways other than economic self-interest and are not dissuaded from active political participation by individual powerlessness. It remains to be seen, however, if any of these influences play a substantial role in economic regulatory reform.

6.1.5   Political Entrepreneurship

The theory of political entrepreneurs focuses on candidates for office, rather than interest groups, as the vehicle for organizing citizens to participate in the political system. If an unorganized group of citizens is harmed by a policy, the politician can provide resources to motivate the group to express its policy choices in the political process. Political candidates, and especially incumbent politicians, command considerable resources for communicating with constituents and, in addition, receive free publicity in the mass media. If politicians can package a message in an attractive and comprehensible way and thereby convince some unorganized voters that a policy is harmful, they may succeed in obtaining additional political support.

Unfortunately, the theory of political entrepreneurship does not predict exactly which unorganized groups will be the focus of a politician's activities.

Indeed, the primary prediction is unpredictability. The theory of majority-rule democracy, beginning with the seminal work of Kenneth Arrow (1951) and culminating in the depressing results of Linda Cohen and Steven Matthews (1980), states that, in general, a series of majority-rule votes can produce literally any technically feasible policy. Whatever existing policy is, another policy can obtain majority-rule support. Indeed, no matter what today's policy is, a sequence of majority-rule votes can produce any other policy. Thus, a political entrepreneur can select from among a very large number of strategies for defeating the status quo. Consequently, the targets of the entrepreneurial skills of a politician are predictable, if at all, only from the personal policy preferences of the politician and the relative costs of organizing different opposing coalitions.

In contrast to the organization of economic interests, political entrepreneurship does not leave unorganized consumers (or nonunion labor) without effective representation. In the case of economic regulation, the political entrepreneur theory is consistent with (if it does not predict) a populist base for the regulatory reform movement.[2] One might observe deregulation being led by self-appointed spokespersons for consumers who suffer the costs of a regulatory policy that has been captured by organized economic interests. Moreover, the political entrepreneurship theory is also consistent with unstable regulatory policy, alternating between protecting organized interests and the pursuit of economic efficiency, since either policy, with the right twist, can defeat the other when the other is the status quo.

A major criticism of this line of theorizing is that it is flatly contradicted by the stability of policy. After all, economic regulation was in place for decades before it was liberalized. The answer to this critique is that, knowing that majority rule is unstable, politicians build in institutional impediments to change in order to make policy unresponsive to the kinds of attacks described above. The idea, called *structure-induced equilibrium,* is that agencies and Congress are organized to give each partner in a winning coalition a veto over future policy changes (Shepsle and Weingast 1981). Thus, a policy can change only if a member of its enacting coalition ceases to be represented in Congress or before an agency that was created to be responsive to its interests or if it changes policy preferences in ways that other coalition members would approve. Thus, organizing a new interest in economic regulatory policy will not produce policy change unless circumstances have changed so that the new organization can avoid some veto points.

In Congress, the veto points are created by committee rights. All legislation is referred to committees, which are responsible for particular policy domains. Usually a bill will not be passed until its relevant committee has approved it; however, this process can be circumvented by referral to another committee or

---

2. For an interpretation of the rise of political opposition to slavery as an example of political entrepreneurship, see Riker (1982, chaps. 8, 9).

by a discharge petition to force the issue to the entire legislative body. In economic regulation, the relevant committees are often the House and Senate Commerce Committees. One form that destabilizing political entrepreneurship could take is to bypass Commerce or so threaten to bypass it that the committee reports a bill that it does not favor but prefers to what might emerge if it were bypassed. These alternatives are, however, costly. They require that Congress ignore committee specialization, which diminishes the incentive of specialized committees to be expert in a particular area of policy. Similarly, if one committee bypasses another, it can be subject to retaliation. Because members of Congress typically are assigned to committees on the basis of their expressed preferences, bypassing another committee generally means risking a position of greater value in order to influence a policy of lesser value. Consequently, bypassing a committee ought to be rare and ought to occur only when there is a relatively high level of dissatisfaction with a policy. Likewise, no politician would have an incentive to organize a new group to attack a policy unless these conditions were satisfied. Hence, one would expect a "political entrepreneurship" model to explain regulatory reform only if the level of public discontent with regulatory policy was quite high.

6.1.6 Function of the Theories

The principal purpose in summarizing the main theories of regulatory policy is to structure our review of how change took place and what consequences flowed from it. Together these theories tell us where to look for political support for liberalization of economic regulation and alternative predictions about how liberalization should have affected prices, costs, and service quality in regulated sectors. With these ideas in mind, we now turn to a description of the origins and effects of the changes in economic regulation.

6.2 Overview of Economic Regulation and Its Reform

Virtually every sector of the economy that was subject to economic regulation before 1975 has experienced very significant changes in the nature and extent of regulation. These changes have had significant effects on industry structures, price levels and structures, costs, and productivity. The industries in which changes in economic regulation occurred are airlines, trucking, buses, railroads, telecommunications, natural gas production and transmission, cable television, banking and financial services, electric power, and property and liability insurance. These industries vary widely in structure, performance, the nature of regulation, and the distribution of regulatory responsibilities between federal and state authorities. There are also wide variations in the rationales, causes, and consequences of regulatory change across these industries. Table 6.2 provides some general information about the major industries affected by changes in economic regulation. A necessarily brief review of regulatory changes that took place in the airline, trucking, telecommunications, insurance,

Table 6.2   **Deregulation and Regulatory Reform during the 1980s**

Industry	Primary Regulatory Agencies	Regulatory Changes	Source of Regulatory Change
1. Airlines	CAB	Deregulation of prices and entry	a) CAB initiatives b) Airline Deregulation Act of 1980 c) Antitrust enforcement
2. Trucking	ICC, state agencies	Deregulation of prices and entry	a) ICC initiatives b) Motor Carrier Act of 1980
3. Railroads	ICC	Price flexibility, ease of exit, mergers	a) ICC initiatives b) 4R Act of 1976 c) Staggers Rail Act of 1980 d) Economic and competitive pressures
4. Telephones	FCC, stage agencies	Industry restructuring, price flexibility, ease entry, incentives regulation	a) Agency initiatives b) Federal antitrust case c) Competitive pressures
5. Natural gas	FERC, state agencies	Unbundling of gas supplies, deregulation of field prices, contractural revisions	a) Natural Gas Policy Act of 1978 b) Fuel Use Act of 1978 c) Exogenous shocks d) FERC Initiatives e) State commission initiatives
6. Electric power	FERC, state agencies	Entry into wholesale generation, competition in wholesale power, procurement policies	a) Public Utility Regulatory Policy Act of 1978 b) Regulatory-induced economic pressures c) Competitive pressures d) Environmental pressures
7. Property/liability insurance	State agencies	More price regulation	a) State legislative/regulatory initiatives
8. Cable television	Municipalities, FCC	Deregulation of prices	a) Cable Television Act of 1984 b) FCC initiatives
9. Banking	FSLIC, FDIC, Comptroller of the Currency, Federal Reserve	Partial deregulation of investment portfolios, deposits services, and interest rates	a) Depository Institutions Deregulation Act of 1980 b) Garn–St. Germain Depository Act of 1982 c) Financial Institutions Reform, Recovery, and Enforcement Act of 1989

banking, and natural gas industries demonstrates just how diverse are the rationales, causes, and consequences associated with these changes.

6.2.1 Airlines and Trucking

The airline and trucking industries are the classic cases of virtually complete deregulation of prices and entry. (The airline industry is discussed in more detail below.) Until about 1977, airline prices and route structures were heavily regulated by the Civil Aeronautics Board (CAB), and interstate trucking was similarly regulated by the Interstate Commerce Commission (ICC) (Joskow and Rose 1989, 1469–73). Frequently, competing suppliers were certificated to provide service on particular routes, but price competition was largely precluded by price regulation based on industry-wide average costs. Scholarly research on regulation in these industries performed in the 1960s and early 1970s concluded that regulation increased costs and prices, distorted technological change, led to excessive service quality as a consequence of nonprice competition in conjunction with excessive prices, and involved significant cross-subsidization among classes of customers (Joskow and Noll 1981, 4–10; Joskow and Rose 1989, 1469–73, 1480–86). Furthermore, research suggested that these industries did not have pervasive market failures, were or could be structurally competitive, and, absent regulatory constraints, would behave and perform at least as well as many industries that are not subject to price and entry regulation.

The origin and persistence of economic regulation in these industries was widely attributed by students of regulation to serving special interests. Incumbent firms were protected from competition. Organized labor could make use of protective regulation to prevent competition from new nonunionized suppliers and to achieve supracompetitive wages and attractive work rules. Some consumer groups obtained subsidies through their political influence over the regulatory process.

Most economists viewed complete deregulation of prices and entry, along with the application of conventional antitrust sanctions, as desirable from an efficiency perspective (Joskow and Noll 1981, 4–10). Nevertheless, economists also believed that, because of the substantial financial stake of well-organized interests in the status quo and the diffuse nature of the costs imposed on many consumers by deregulation, neither industry was a likely candidate for deregulation (Kahn 1983). Nevertheless, regulators appointed to the CAB and the ICC during the Carter administration moved aggressively to use existing statutory authority to relax price and entry regulation substantially (Bailey, Graham, and Kaplan 1985; Kahn 1979; Keeler 1983). Congress subsequently enacted statutes that clarified the legality of the efforts of the CAB and the ICC to relax or remove price and entry regulation and encouraged these agencies to proceed with deregulation initiatives. The Airline Deregulation Act of 1978 established statutory transition arrangements that eventually led to complete deregulation of prices and entry and the demise of the CAB. The

Motor Carrier Act of 1980 gave the ICC clear statutory authority to relax price and entry restrictions and to encourage competition in trucking, although the ICC retained authority to regulate prices and entry under a public interest standard that is more consistent with promoting competition than protecting incumbent competitors.

The deregulation initiatives in airlines and trucking were not part of a general ideological package that promoted less government regulation and more reliance on unregulated markets. They took place during a period of rapid inflation and instability in world energy markets and were promoted as components of a whip-inflation strategy. Deregulation was opposed by the industries subject to regulation and by organized labor. The initial regulatory initiatives came about through the appointment of CAB and ICC commissioners already oriented toward deregulation and the use of the administrative process to relax price and entry regulation. Administrative deregulation was followed quickly by legislation that not only provided clear statutory authority for more flexible pricing and entry rules but clearly articulated a congressional preference for less regulation and more competition. The major actors at the regulatory agencies in the Carter administration viewed deregulation as being desirable because the *specific* economic characteristics of these markets made effective competition a likely outcome. They believed that price and entry regulation not only was unnecessary but was the cause of demonstrably worse performance than under competition. The fact that both airlines and trucking were largely regulated by federal agencies, with little state involvement in price and entry regulation (more for trucking), also meant that deregulation could proceed as a national initiative without requiring fifty states to implement complementary policies.

Airline and trucking regulation differed considerably in the years before deregulation. The changes in the late 1970s at the ICC were cataclysmic, in that the agency had clung tenaciously to the need for detailed, heavy-handed regulation of trucking until the very end. The Carter appointees truly revolutionized the agency. At the CAB, change was somewhat more evolutionary. In the early 1970s, the agency tried to reform pricing rules within the context of continued economic regulation in a major rule-making proceeding, the Domestic Passenger Fare Inquiry (DPFI). The DPFI tried to bring fares more in line with costs and allowed some off-peak fares to go into effect (Breyer 1982, 211–12). However, between 1970 and 1974, the CAB administered a "route moratorium" under which it refused to hear applications even by existing airlines to serve new routes. It also encouraged airlines to make agreements to limit the number of flights on each route (Breyer 1982, 208–9). Additional price flexibility was introduced during the Ford administration by allowing airlines to engage in a variety of special discounts. In Senate hearings in 1976, the chairman of the CAB testified that the Board unanimously supported substantial reduction in its control over prices and entry. Although real deregulation did not occur until after President Carter was elected, Carter appointees entered an agency that had already begun some initiatives to liberalize the prevailing rigid system of regulation.

The differences between the ICC and the CAB obviously do not reflect any consistent view toward economic regulation in structurally competitive industries. The CAB experience predates any conceivable emergence of an ideological deregulation fervor. Sentiment for airline deregulation began to crystalize after President Ford asked Congress to establish a National Commission on Regulatory Reform in 1974. It was strengthened by the famous Kennedy hearings, in which the junior senator from Massachusetts presided over a highly critical review of the agency's anticompetitive policies (U.S. Senate 1975; Breyer 1982). But, according to Derthick and Quirk (1985), one reason for the CAB's modest reforms in the early 1970s was an effort to respond to the criticism of the agency in the economics literature. Moreover, as described by George Douglas and James Miller (1974), who participated in the DPFI, economic analysis played a significant role in shaping the resulting pricing reforms. Why the CAB, but not the ICC, apparently was influenced by economics so early in the game remains a mystery.

6.2.2   Telecommunications

While airlines and trucking were regulated primarily by federal agencies, the telephone industry has been subject to pervasive regulation by both federal (the Federal Communications Commission [FCC]) and state agencies. In principal, the division between state and federal responsibilities in telecommunications turns on distinctions between intrastate and interstate utilization of the telecommunications network. This distinction is often rather blurry in practice; hence, the division of policy into state and federal issues for purposes of regulating prices, entry, and the availability of service confronts special problems.

First, the telecommunications network is characterized by joint and common costs. Interstate and intrastate calls use the same switching and transmission equipment that constitute the local exchange network. As a result, the allocation of costs between state and federal jurisdictions is inherently arbitrary and creates a natural opportunity for rent-seeking behavior.

Second, until the 1980s, the telephone industry was dominated by a single vertically and horizontally integrated company (AT&T). As a result, its activities spanned all regulatory jurisdictions, and its size, sophistication, and complexity were enormous compared to the resources of any of its regulators. As a result, AT&T was difficult to regulate by any single agency.

Third, after World War II, significant technological changes took place in switching, transmission, and customer equipment. These changes caused telecommunications technology to converge with microelectronic and computer technologies and hence gave firms in these industries potential competitive opportunities in telecommunications. Moreover, technological change also worked to reduce the importance of scale economies in the industry. This caused outsiders to believe that a somewhat different system design, with a somewhat different form of management, could provide better or less costly products than were being supplied by AT&T. For the most part, these changes had a greater effect on the parts of the industry in the federal jurisdiction. Until about 1980, the slowest progress took place in the lines connecting customers to the local switch, which accounts for more than 60 percent of the costs of local telephone companies.

Fourth, state and federal regulators encouraged some entry by setting prices to effectuate cross-subsidies. Some competitive entry may have been attracted, not because alternative suppliers could provide service at a lower cost or of a better quality than AT&T, but because regulators set some prices too high.[3] Likewise, by pricing other services too low, regulators may have discouraged entry where it was warranted. The net effect of the pricing structure was that, on balance, federal services subsidized state services.

Fifth, when reform began, it was widely believed that broad, efficiency-enhancing regulatory reform would require more than simple deregulation of prices and entry. The local exchange continues to be a state-regulated monopoly, at least for residential and small business customers. In long distance, the most plausible permanent market structure is a natural oligopoly, but for at least several years it was expected to remain dominated by a single firm, AT&T. Hence, at least for a while, complete economic deregulation of long distance was implausible, although it may be attractive in the 1990s. Competitive behavior is more likely in other segments of the telephone industry, but, because of AT&T's size, a transition period was needed to allow sufficient competitive constraints to develop.

Finally, promoting competition in segments where it can be effective—equipment and long-distance services—was thought by some to be substantially inhibited by the vertically integrated structure of the telephone industry, especially one in which a single supplier provided almost all local exchange service. According to this view, promoting competition required fundamental structural changes in the industry, in part because coordinated state and federal regulatory reform of a resistent, vertically integrated monopoly would be slow and difficult.

Because the structural view prevailed, regulatory reform in telecommunications was affected by both regulatory initiatives and a federal antitrust suit that led to a complete restructuring of the telephone industry in 1984. New entrants and customer groups that benefited from these policies became an important political force for continuing reform within the regulatory process, the courts, and the legislative and executive branches.

Meanwhile, most state regulatory authorities played a small, sometimes

---

3. In the early days of long-distance competition, specialized common carriers did not pay local telephone companies part of their revenues, as did AT&T. Eventually, the FCC adopted a complicated and quite arbitrary pricing system for local access for all carriers. These prices depended on the form of access enjoyed by a carrier and were lower for AT&T's competitors because their access was worse. Today, all carriers pay the same prices for the same quality of access.

counterproductive role in regulatory reform efforts in this industry. The single most important beneficiaries of cross-subsidy in telecommunications were basic access customers in small towns and rural areas—a service that is regulated by the states (Noll and Smart 1990). Competition threatened these cross-subsidies and so threatened to cause state regulators to have to raise these highly visible prices. Not surprisingly, most state regulators did not rejoice at this prospect and fought liberalization.

The key point about developments in telecommunications policy is that it is difficult to point to any single decision that introduced competition. More than anything else, FCC decisions seem to be driven by technological progress— and by the fact that much of this progress has come from outside the industry, from companies willing and able to go head to head against AT&T in some market. And, more than other agencies, throughout most of its history the FCC has been a relatively reluctant regulator. Unlike in transportation and energy regulation, economists had not undertaken extensive empirical studies of telecommunications regulation.[4] And, unlike airlines and trucking, regulatory reform in telecommunications took place without any legislative action. Indeed, the primary legislative threat has been to reverse both FCC liberalization and the antitrust case. In both 1976 and 1981, AT&T, with some support from executive branch officials who disapproved of events at the FCC and the Department of Justice, almost succeeded in obtaining legislation to establish in law its monopoly status (see Temin and Galombos 1987). Then, in 1986, Congress fell only one vote short in the Senate from reversing the FCC's move toward eliminating cross-subsidies in AT&T's price structure. Although one should not read too much into near misses on legislation, it is apparent that regulatory reform in telecommunications has been on far shakier political ground than was deregulation of airlines and trucking.

6.2.3   Natural Gas

Like telephones, the natural gas industry has been subject to pervasive regulation by both federal and state regulators. And, as with telephones, federal regulators (the Federal Energy Regulatory Commission [FERC] and its predecessor, the Federal Power Commission [FPC]), the courts, and the U.S. Congress have played the dominant role in changing regulatory policy and industry structure. Unlike the telephone industry, natural gas was not extensively integrated either horizontally or vertically.

Natural gas is produced by numerous firms, most of which sell to independent interstate natural gas pipelines. These pipelines sell gas to independent distribution utilities, which have de facto exclusive geographic franchises to resell gas to residential, commercial, and industrial customers other than large industrial and electric utility customers that purchase gas directly from pipe-

---

4. Nearly all the research focused on measuring the magnitude of scale economies in the industry, and this work produced largely inconclusive results (see Fuss 1983).

lines. Because of this structure, the costs of natural gas production, pipeline transportation, and retail distribution are readily separable.[5]

Federal regulation encompasses (since 1954) the prices that interstate pipelines pay for natural gas in the field and the prices that pipelines charge to local distribution companies for gas and pipeline transportation (since 1938). State regulation covers the prices charged to retail customers by local gas distribution utilities. Federal regulators are responsible for certificating the construction (entry) of new natural gas pipelines and the expansion of existing pipelines, while state regulators are responsible for certificating extensions of local gas distribution systems. Of course, since a large fraction of the costs of a local distribution company is accounted for by the costs of the gas it purchases, federal regulation of field prices and pipeline charges has important implications for the ultimate prices paid by retail customers.

Initially, the Federal Power Commission was also a reluctant regulator, refusing to regulate the field prices of natural gas because the industry was structurally competitive. But, in 1954, the Supreme Court ruled that the Natural Gas Act of 1938 required the agency to regulate the price paid by interstate pipelines for gas in the field, despite the fact that a plain reading of the statute suggested otherwise. After several years of experimentation with cost of service regulation on a producer-by-producer basis, the FPC introduced field price regulation in the early 1960s, setting separate ceiling prices for "old gas" and "new gas" in each of five gas-producing areas on the basis of the average historical cost of discovery, development, and extraction in that area. This system of historical average cost pricing could lead to prices that equated supply and demand only by accident. Within a decade, field price regulation had produced the predictable result: excess demand for gas and prices insensitive to trends in substitute fuel prices and their impact on the demand for natural gas (MacAvoy 1971, 1973; MacAvoy and Pindyck 1973). The problem was vastly exacerbated by the first oil price shock of 1973, causing substantial increases in demand at regulated prices, but no opportunities for gas prices to adjust to clear the market. Shortages and administrative rationing of natural gas became major problems for the industry and its regulators during the 1970s.

After years of bitter debate, Congress finally passed the Natural Gas Policy Act of 1978 (NGPA), surely the most complicated economic regulatory statue yet enacted. The basic idea of the statute was to let the price of gas gradually rise to market clearing levels and to provide a means whereby higher-cost wells could be profitably exploited. The mechanism was an incredibly elaborate classification scheme for gas wells, combined with a separate regulatory pricing procedure for each category. Eventually, as old, cheap wells played out and new, expensive wells replaced them, gas prices would increase, and regulatory price constraints would no longer be binding. Unfortunately, the price adjust-

---

5. The costs of natural gas production are not readily separable from the costs of producing oil, however.

ment mechanisms contained in the NGPA were based on specific assumptions about the future price of oil, a close substitute for natural gas for many end users. Just as the NGPA was passed, oil prices rose sharply as a consequence of the Iranian revolution (1979–81). At first it appeared that the gas price trajectory contained in the NGPA was too low and that gas shortages would continue until prices for many categories of gas were to be deregulated in 1985. But, after 1981, oil prices began to fall and then collapsed in 1986. The recession of 1981–83, and a restructuring of the economy that adversely affected industries that used large quantities of natural gas, made the situation even worse. A gas shortage quickly became a gas glut.

During the mid- and late 1980s, the combination of historical regulatory practices and changed economic conditions caused the natural gas industry to plunge into economic turmoil. Before the gas glut, pipelines had signed long-term contracts for future gas supplies that anticipated high oil prices and a growing demand for natural gas. They had also signed contracts with local distribution companies to provide bundled gas and transportation services at the average cost of service. When oil prices fell and the demand for gas declined, the supplies of gas that pipelines had contracted for could no longer be sold to end users at prices that recovered the costs of these contracts. As a result, major changes ensued in federal and state economic regulation and in the structure of the industry.

Three significant changes took place in the way gas is sold. Rather than being required to purchase bundled gas and transportation services, pipeline customers could purchase at least some gas directly from field producers and contract with gas pipelines for transportation services only. Thus, many gas pipelines now act as common carriers, charging customers only for pipeline transportation services that continue to be regulated by the FERC, using traditional rate-of-return procedures. Because of the unbundling of gas supplies from transportation services, gas pipelines, gas distribution companies, and large direct service customers increasingly compete directly for field gas, and a large brokering industry has emerged to arrange for gas supplies for local distributors and direct service customers who choose not to rely on pipelines for bundled gas supplies and transportation services.

During the late 1980s, gas prices were significantly below the prices that would have emerged had the old system of bundled sales and long-term contracts been retained. Contract prices and quantities negotiated in the late 1970s and 1980s generally reflected the expectation that oil prices would continue to rise and gas demand to increase. Many of these contracts were breached, voluntarily renegotiated, or renegotiated as a consequence of regulatory pressures during the mid- and late 1980s as oil prices and the demand for natural gas declined. Gas distributors and pipelines sustained large financial losses through the renegotiation of these contracts (on the order of $10 billion). Furthermore, the difference in gas prices appears to have widened between customers who can readily turn to substitute fuels and customers who do not have good fuel switching capabilities.

For the last few years, the FERC has actively embraced the unbundling of pipeline transportation from pipeline provision of gas supplies and has promoted competition for field gas by pipelines, distributors, and end users. These policies appear to reflect more a response to the problems caused by changing economic conditions and the historical legacy of price regulation than an exogenous regulatory reform initiative. Unbundled pipeline transportation was initially instituted by the pipelines themselves in an effort to respond to declining gas demand and their contractual obligations to producers. The primary impetus for these changes was the unanticipated reduction in the price of oil after 1981 and the associated effects on gas demand of relatively high prices and quantities for gas that were specific in rigid long-term contracts written after 1978 and before the recession of 1981–83. These changes in energy markets made it impossible to sustain the complex regulatory and contractual status quo.

6.2.4   Property and Liability Insurance

Many economists and other scholars view liberalization in transportation, communications, and energy as a triumph of sound economic analysis over interest groups who used the regulatory process to feather their own nests. It is important to recognize, however, that, just because scholarly research concludes that an industry is structurally competitive and would perform better without costly and inefficient price and entry controls, it does not follow that public policy will quickly move to remove or relax regulation. The property/liability insurance industry is a case in point.

The property/liability industry is structurally competitive (Joskow 1973; Joskow and McLaughlin 1991; Joskow and Rose 1989, 1473–75). Concentration ratios are low, entry is easy, and there is no evidence of excess profits or inefficiency in states that do not regulate insurance rates. To the extent that a market imperfection exists, its cause is consumers who are not fully informed about the financial strength of insurers. Hence, all states set minimum standards for the capitalization of insurance companies and place restrictions on their investments to protect purchasers of insurance (and insurance guarantee funds) from bankruptcy risks. While there may be very good reasons to subject insurance firms to financial regulations, especially given the presence of an insurance guarantee fund in each state, one is hard pressed to find a rationale for subjecting insurance to either maximum or minimum price regulation.

Yet insurance rates, especially personal lines (auto, homeowners), have been heavily regulated by the states since World War II. For many years, both the insurance industry and its regulators relied heavily on collective price setting and actively discouraged competitive pricing (Joskow 1973; Joskow and McLaughlin 1991). Insurance rate making has led to significant cross-subsidization, typically shifting costs from urban to rural drivers (Rottenberg 1989). The industry and its regulators were particularly hostile to competitive pricing by low-cost direct writers like State Farm and Allstate. During the late 1960s and 1970s, many states relaxed or eliminated prior approval rate regulation and encouraged independent rate making and deviations from the advisory rates filed by rating bureaus (Joskow and McLaughlin 1991). However, complete deregulation of insurance rates (along with the application of the antitrust laws)[6] occurred in only a single state, Illinois. Then, during the 1980s, the movement toward less price regulation ground to a halt, and many states began increasing the scope of price regulation.

Changes in insurance rate regulation have been heavily influenced by changes in the costs of providing insurance. During the period of liberalization, rates were stable or falling, reflecting stable or falling loss costs and/or underwriting costs, and low cost competitors were seeking to expand their businesses by offering lower rates or innovative products (Harrington 1984). During this period, the regulatory debate tended to focus on minimum rather than maximum rate regulation and "excessive" competition, reflecting the aversion of some firms to competition. When insurance rates rose rapidly, as occurred in many lines of insurance during the late 1980s, political pressures for maximum rate regulation were more intense. In one case—California—extensive rate regulation was enacted, not by the legislature, but by citizen initiative. Ironically, swings in insurance rates depend largely on loss costs. These in turn depend heavily on the costs of accidents as determined by prices for repairs and liability rules as determined by the tort system, neither of which is subject to significant control by the insurance industry.

Despite competitive opportunities in property/liability insurance, an administration in Washington supposedly committed to removing unnecessary regulations, and pricing and availability problems, the regulatory reform movement of the 1980s passed the insurance industry by. There was no meaningful national policy regarding insurance, and many states responded to economic shocks by stopping and then reversing a trend toward less rate regulation and cross-subsidization that had begun during the 1970s.

6.2.5 Banks

The first American industry to be regulated was the banking industry, largely because a nation must control banking at least minimally in order to control its money supply and macroeconomic performance. But economic regulation of banks is largely a creature of the Great Depression, when widespread bank failures caused massive losses of personal savings among American citizens and contributed to deepening and lengthening the Depression.

In some ways, bank regulation is similar to the regulation of insurance com-

---

6. The McCarran-Ferguson Act provides insurance firms with a limited exemption of the antitrust laws to the extent that they are regulated by state law.

panies. Regulators control the investment portfolio of a bank to assure its financial health and to protect depositors against fraud. But, unlike insurance, bank regulation also segmented the market, imposing geographic limits on lending activities and focusing lending by savings and loan institutions on real estate mortgages. The government also insures depositors against financial loss should the bank fail. In the past, regulators controlled the interest rates that banks could pay depositors and the types of deposits that a bank could offer. Finally, regulators specify the accounting practices that are used to measure the financial health of a bank and regularly examine bank records to assure that the bank is sound and in compliance with regulations. Unlike insurance regulation, the federal government is the dominant player in the banking industry.

Certainly, the single biggest scandal during the era of liberalization of economic regulation is the massive increase in bank failures during the 1980s.[7] First, some large commercial banks failed, owing to the abrogation of loans by several foreign countries and massive default on agricultural loans during the farm crisis of the early 1980s. Then came the savings and loan debacle, in which a very large fraction (estimates range around one-third) of the nation's savings and loans either went bankrupt or are "zombies"—walking-dead institutions that are technically bankrupt but have not yet closed down because they still have a positive cash flow.

The essence of the banking problem is that banks of all kinds—commercial, savings and loan, mutual savings associations, credit unions—make a large number of long-term loans but rely heavily on short-term deposits to finance them. An important component of public policy toward banks is to provide a means for banks to shed long-term loans by selling them to others, leaving the bank as a collection agent for the source of long-term funds. Nonetheless, banks still hold a considerable amount of long-term debt and so can be seriously squeezed when interest rates go up significantly. The regulation of interest rates and investment portfolios was intended to ameliorate this problem.

A second important element of banking regulation was the segmentation of the industry. Commercial banks were the source of loans to business and checking account services without interest on the deposits. Savings and loans were primarily in the business of financing real estate activities, especially housing, and obtained funds through savings accounts paying interest rates subject to regulatory ceilings. The major liberalizing reforms of the past decade have been to reduce substantially the distinctions between these institutions and to relax the regulation of interests rates paid on deposits. All banks now offer checking accounts bearing interest, and all have varieties of savings accounts with restrictions on short-term withdrawal but higher interest rates. Likewise, investment portfolios of all institutions can now contain commercial

7. For more details about the turmoil in financial regulation during the 1980s, see the companion essay in this volume by Robert Litan.

paper (even junk bonds) as well as loans to finance all forms of physical capital investments. The last step in deregulation was the Garn–St. Germain Act of 1982, which essentially freed the savings and loan industry from nearly all the restrictions that distinguished it from commercial banks. These reforms made economic sense, for they improved the efficiency of capital markets by eliminating artificial distinctions among sources and uses of funds. Moreover, they should have reduced banking risks by allowing all banks to have more diversified loan portfolios.

The underlying problem with the banking sector is that many of its investment turned bad, with the result that the liabilities of some banks (deposits) exceeded the assets (collectable loans). But the relaxation of regulation exacerbated the problem, for it took place at precisely the same time as the 1980s oil glut, agricultural depression, Latin American loan defaults, and real estate boom and bust. Meanwhile, because of deposit insurance, customers had little incentive to seek out banks with strong portfolios as the place to make deposits. Moreover, banks are very highly leveraged institutions because regulators have established quite low equity requirements. This means that banks have more funds to lend (and hence charge lower rates of interest), but it also means that they are vulnerable to a general rise in loan default rates.

All these factors conspired to make the conditions of many banks, and especially savings and loans, quite precarious. Then another effect kicked in—the "pending bankruptcy effect." An owner of a bank can lose no more than the amount of equity invested, no matter the magnitude of the bank's excess liabilities. Hence, when a bank (or any other corporation) nears bankruptcy, owners have an incentive to take very large risks—to make loans with a high probability of default but at very high interest rates. If the loans prove good, the bank is saved; otherwise, the federal government through deposit insurance simply takes a bigger loss. This is still another reason why bank portfolios had been regulated in the past. In fact, financial soundness reviews of banks were *not* deregulated. Bank audits continued and should have nipped the pending bankruptcy effect in the bud.

To an important degree, the problems in banking were exacerbated by the fact that, in the 1980s, banks were allowed to invest in riskier loans. But, as explained by Romer and Weingast (1990), the magnitude of the debacle was not caused by deregulation. Even with more relaxed rules, bank regulators detected the problem and sought to cure it in 1985 and 1986, when its magnitude was still rather small. But the political leadership intervened to prevent it, pressuring the agency not to close down failing banks before the losses mounted and not to impose more rigid financial management on banks that were in trouble but still viable. And, as Romer and Weingast and many lurid press stories report, the reasons behind these political interventions had very little to do with the ideology of deregulation or the ideas of economic liberals. Instead, these political interventions were constituency service for generous contributors to political campaigns and other important supporters.

As with insurance, one faces a serious challenge in producing a convincing argument that banking markets are not structurally competitive and that economic regulation of prices (interest rates) and entry (types of services each category of bank can offer) has any hope of improving on the market. But, like insurance, one *can* argue that banks ought to be subject to scrutiny of their financial management, especially if deposits are insured by the government. The problems in banking arose because the attempt to relax price and entry controls, and so improve the efficiency of capital markets, was erroneously accompanied by *less*, not *more*, scrutiny of financial management, primarily because the industry wanted to be left alone and was able to convince political leaders to let it be. The result was a perverse incentive structure for banks and depositors that turned unlucky events in financial markets into a national economic catastrophe.

6.2.6 Implications from Six Industries

Our brief review of six industries subject to economic regulation in the 1970s and subsequent regulatory change should make clear that we will not find a simple explanation for the significant changes in regulatory institutions that occurred between the mid-1970s and the mid-1980s. The potential for a reasonably competitive market structure (airlines, trucking, banking, telephone equipment) appears to be a necessary, but certainly not a sufficient, condition to explain deregulation. The insurance industry has not been deregulated, and the airline, trucking, and banking industries were not more structurally competitive in 1978 than they were in 1960. Changing economic and technological conditions can play an important role in stimulating regulatory change (telecommunications, natural gas), but dramatic economic changes do not appear to be necessary (airlines, trucks), and economic shocks can just as easily stimulate more regulation as less (insurance in the 1980s [Joskow 1973; Joskow and McLaughlin 1991], banks in the 1990s). The performance of a regulated industry may be so poor that some change is necessary to enable the industry to provide service of a reasonable quality, although institutional response to poor performance may take place very slowly (airlines, trucks). Modest regulatory reforms can lead to results and create constituencies that lead to further regulatory changes (telecommunications), some of which are undesirable (banks). Regulatory changes may be affected by the implementation of other public policies, especially antitrust (telecommunications). Political interventions can be helpful (airlines and trucking), disastrous (banks), or inconclusive (telephones). Actions by the executive, legislative, and judicial branches, and by state and federal authorities, can interact with one another in complex ways.

6.3 Domestic Airlines: Deregulation of a Structurally Competitive Industry

The airline industry is the cleanest example of virtually complete deregulation of prices and entry and, along with the trucking industry, the only one where it makes sense to speak simply about *deregulation*. It is also the sector in which we have the most experience with deregulation and is (too) often used as a model for deregulation and regulatory reform in other industries. From roughly 1938 until 1977, the U.S. domestic airline industry was subject to heavy *economic* regulation by the Civil Aeronautics Board (CAB).[8] Regulation of airline *safety* and the operation of the air traffic control system and commercial airports were, and still are, the responsibility of a separate federal agency, the Federal Aviation Administration (FAA).

The CAB determined which companies were permitted to provide commercial airline service, decided which city-pair routes they were permitted to serve, set ticket prices, and, near the end, controlled many details of service quality. Airlines serving the same route all charged the same fares, and most passengers could take advantage of one of two fares—coach or first class. These fares were determined by a simple formula based on the average cost per passenger mile incurred by all airlines providing domestic air service, only partially taking into account cost differences associated with distance, passenger volume, and other factors affecting route-specific costs.

Beginning in the early 1960s and continuing into the 1970s, numerous economists studied the consequences of CAB regulation of airlines (Caves 1962; Levine 1965; Eads 1972, 1975; Douglas and Miller 1974). In a departure from historical precedent, economists were in virtually complete agreement—Democrats and Republicans—about the consequences of CAB regulation. Specifically, economists generally agreed that CAB regulation was undesirable and unnecessary for three reasons.

First, regulated prices were too high on average, were too inflexible, and did not reflect the relative costs of providing service on different routes and at different times of the day, week, and year. Prices on long-distance and densely traveled routes were set especially high in an attempt to generate subsidies for high-cost service to small cities. An economically rational pricing structure not only would reduce prices generally but would also reallocate passengers to improve the industry's performance.

Second, the costs incurred by domestic airlines were too high, and air service was provided inefficiently. These inefficiencies emerged because inefficient airlines were protected from competition, because CAB route allocations led to a route structure that did not use aircraft efficiently, and because regulatory rules enhanced the bargaining power of unions, leading to excessive wages and inefficient work rules. In addition, because airlines could not compete on

---

8. In the United States, regulatory responsibilities are shared between the federal government and the various state governments. In general, the provision of *interstate* services is subject to federal regulatory jurisdiction, while the provision of *intrastate* services is subject to state regulatory jurisdiction. Because most U.S. airlines are engaged in interstate commerce, they have been regulated almost exclusively by the federal government. The exceptions were a small number of *intrastate* airlines that provided service within the states of Alaska, California, Florida, and Texas. The pre-deregulation history of CAB regulation can be found in Breyer (1982, chap. 11), Bailey, Graham, and Kaplan (1985, chap. 1), and Keeler (1983).

the basis of price, they competed in service quality, causing the average quality of service to be *too high*. Service quality is measured by the fraction of seats that are filled, the probability of finding an empty seat available on short notice, the provision of various amenities, and the frequency of flights between cities (given the total number of passengers carried). Although passengers may enjoy having an empty seat next to them on which to put a briefcase, regulated fares reflected the cost of providing seats for briefcases. Passengers were forced to pay for seats regardless of whether or not they wanted to provide their brief-cases with a comfortable ride.

Third, scholarly studies also concluded that there was no good economic reason to regulate prices, the number of firms allowed to enter the industry, or the number of firms allowed to provide service on specific city-pair routes. Students of the airline industry argued that price and entry restrictions should be removed because unregulated competition would yield a more efficient air-line system. Among other things, they argued that airline service is not a natu-ral monopoly, that many routes could support multiple competing airlines, and that the U.S. industry could support several large national carriers. Further, they argued that, although few airlines might compete on any given route, the threat of entry would hold fares down and constrain monopoly pricing.

Despite the consensus among professional economists about the infirmities of airline regulation, deregulation and regulatory reform lacked political sup-port until the early 1970s. Then the CAB initiated some modest rate-making reforms that brought prices more in line with costs and recognized the prob-lems of costly excess capacity resulting from excessive prices and nonprice competition. Although these changes responded to some of the economists' criticisms, they did so in a way that preserved the basic regulatory structure. Moreover, by continuing to prohibit entry and to set minimum prices that were above those that would prevail under competition, the agency continued to protect incumbents and to impose cross-subsidies.

Executive branch support for airline deregulation first emerged during the Ford administration, although it led to little change. The first important source of congressional political support for airline deregulation came from an un-expected source—liberal Democratic Senator Edward Kennedy. Assisted by then-professor and regulatory critic Stephen Breyer, Kennedy poached on the turf of the Senate Commerce Committee by launching a much-publicized hear-ing on the CAB that was orchestrated to embarrass the agency. The authors of studies of the CAB were dutifully paraded before the Senate Judiciary Committee to report their findings and conclusions. But, although Kennedy continued to support airline deregulation (an action that may well have in-fluenced then-candidate Jimmy Carter), nothing much came of the Kennedy initiative.

Interest in regulatory reform in general, and airline deregulation in particu-lar, gained political momentum during the Carter administration, stimulated in part by concerns about rapid inflation and stagnant productivity growth in the

U.S. economy. Administrative deregulation[9] of the airline industry began to take place during the first year of the Carter administration with the appointment of deregulation-minded commissioners (Alfred Kahn and Elizabeth Bailey) and with some support from Congress, especially from Senator Kennedy and Senator Abraham Ribicoff. Senator Ribicoff chaired the Senate Governmental Affairs Committee, and soon after Kennedy completed his airline hearings Ribicoff launched a massive, critical review of economic regulation, eventually producing a multivolume series of studies and reform proposals (see U.S. Senate 1977–78). Whereas Kennedy and Ribicoff could not force Congress to take the lead, which would have stripped the Commerce Committee of its jurisdiction, they could, in turn, stop Commerce from slowing administrative deregulation. Kennedy's Judiciary Committee and Ribicoff's Governmental Affairs Committee were responsible for administrative procedures and operating methods in regulatory agencies, giving at least one of them a veto over laws changing regulatory procedures should they choose to exercise it. Eventually, facing a fait accompli, Commerce capitulated, and the chair of the subcommittee of Senate Commerce that had authority over airlines, Senator Robert Cannon, actually became an advocate of deregulation. In late 1978, the CAB's administrative deregulation was codified into law along with a sunset provision for the agency with the passage of the Airline Deregulation Act.

The Airline Deregulation Act provided for the gradual removal over a six-year period extending well into the 1980s of virtually all restrictions on entry into the airline industry, all restrictions on which airlines could fly which routes, and all restrictions on pricing. The Reagan administration supported continued deregulation when it took office and appointed CAB commissioners committed to deregulation, with the result that by 1984 the domestic airline industry was freed from virtually all the old economic regulations that it had been subject to for forty years.

What have been the effects of airline deregulation to date?

6.3.1   Price Level

The evidence on the effects of airline deregulation on average air fares is clear: average fares are lower than they would have been if CAB rate making had continued. The vast majority of passengers pay fares that carry substantial discounts from the fares that would have resulted from applying the old CAB pricing formula. Average fares rose in the late 1980s, owing to growing demand for air service, capacity constraints in aircraft, scarce landing slots at the

---

9. *Administrative deregulation* refers to changes in regulatory policies instituted by the CAB itself without any formal statutory authorization by the U.S. Congress. The 1938 act establishing the CAB did not require restrictive price and entry regulation but gave the CAB broad authority to supervise the development of the commercial airline industry. Regulatory procedures that evolved after 1938 led to virtually complete restrictions on entry and rigid price regulation. The regulators appointed by President Carter simply endeavored to reinterpret the statute to allow for more competition.

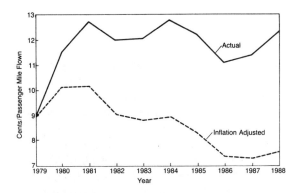

Fig. 6.1 Average domestic passenger fare per mile
Source: U.S. Department of Transportation (1990a, 7).

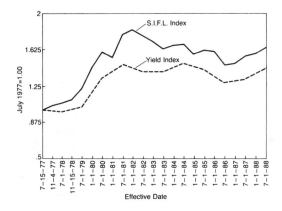

Fig. 6.2 SIFL and yield indices, July 1977 = 1.00
Source: U.S. Department of Transportation (1990c, *Executive Summary,* 8).

busiest airports, rising fuel costs, and the diminution of competition in some markets. Nevertheless, consumers still save billions of dollars each year in lower air fares as a consequence of deregulation (Morrison and Winston 1986, 1989). Figure 6.1 displays the average fare per passenger mile from 1979 through 1988. Inflation-adjusted prices are far below what they were in 1979. Of more interest is a comparison of actual fares with those that would have existed if pre-deregulation pricing policies had continued. Figure 6.2 displays an index of actual prices and an index that roughly measures the prices that would have been charged had the pre-1978 fare formulas (SIFL, or standard industry fare level) continued to be used over the period 1979–88. It is clear that deregulated fares are, on average, lower. Morrison and Winston perform a more sophisticated analysis that is consistent with this comparison.

6.3.2   Price Structure

To say that fares are more complicated now than before deregulation is an understatement. A wide variety of discount fares is now available in addition to standard coach and first class fares. Average fares vary widely from route to route, reflecting differences in travel density, distance, the number of competing airlines, when passengers fly, how far in advance passengers can make a reservation, and whether passengers on particular routes are primarily business or tourist travelers (Bailey, Graham, and Kaplan 1985; Morrison and Winston 1986; Borenstein 1989). Other things being equal (distance, density, etc.), prices are higher on airline routes involving a hub dominated by one or two carriers at one end and on routes with only one or two competing carriers (see fig. 6.3). Competitive entry leads to significantly lower postentry prices (Bailey, Graham, and Kaplan 1985, 61; Morrison and Winston 1986, 1989; Keeler 1983). Fares on shorter low-density routes have risen relative to fares on other routes reflecting cross-subsidies built into regulated rates (see fig. 6.4).

6.3.3   Airline Costs

The average cost of providing airline service has declined substantially in the last decade (holding various input prices constant); airline productivity has risen significantly. Deregulation of routes caused airlines to change their route structures dramatically. Typically, airlines have selected a few cities (hubs) in which to concentrate maintenance and to base flight crews. Except for long-distance flights between many large cities, routes typically consist of flights out of hubs, with aircraft and crew returning at night to their point of origin. The movement to hub and spoke systems led to more efficient utilization of aircraft and crews. Price competition and the threat of hostile takeovers have also encouraged greater efficiency. The average fraction of seats sold has in-

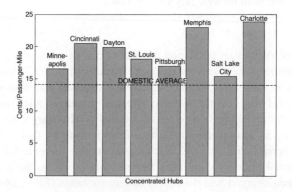

Fig. 6.3   Average fare per mile at concentrated hubs compared to domestic average
Source: U.S. Department of Transportation (1990a, 8).

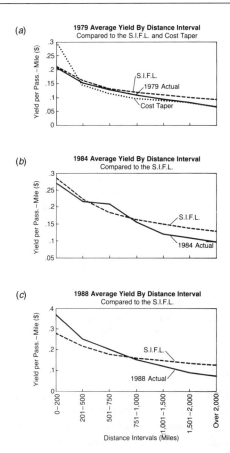

Fig. 6.4 (*a*) **1979 average yield by distance interval compared to the SIFL and cost taper;** (*b*) **1984 average yield by distance interval compared to the SIFL** (*c*) **1988 average yield by distance interval compared to the SIFL**
Source: U.S. Department of Transportation (1990c, 1:12).

creased from less than 55 percent in 1976 to over 62 percent in 1988. Competition, including the emergence of nonunion carriers, has also broken the power of airline labor unions, leading to lower wages and more flexible work rules (Bailey, Graham, and Kaplan 1985, chaps. 4, 5, 8; Morrison and Winston 1986).

6.3.4 Quality of Service

The quality of service has clearly declined in some dimensions and, perhaps less obviously, increased in others. Not all the changes in service quality are the direct consequence of deregulation, however. Let us look first at the ways in which the quality of service has declined.

Table 6.3   Changes in Frequency at Domestic Points, July 1979–July 1988

% Increase	N	40 Seats and Under	Over 40 Seats
Points with an increase in frequency:			
Less than 10 percent[a]	38	20	18
10.0–50.0 percent	101	42	59
50.1–100.0 percent	79	36	43
100.1 percent and over	52	35	17
Total	270	133	137
Points with a decrease in frequency:			
Less than 10 percent	27	18	9
10.0–50.0 percent	140	110	30
50.1–99.9 percent	60	53	7
Total	227	181	46
All points	497	314	183

Source: U.S. Department of Transportation (1990b, 1:57).

[a]Includes points with no change in frequency. Classification of points by average seating capacity is based on July 1988. Includes only points served in both parts.

Reduced Service Quality

Since deregulation, air travel has increased, and planes and airports are more crowded. Because of the increase in travel, delays have increased. Some passengers have lost service. Jet service has been cut back or eliminated in many small communities, and a few have lost all airline service. Decreases in flight frequency have been concentrated in small communities (see table 6.3), especially those within an hour's drive of a larger airport. Owing to hubbing, the fraction of passengers traveling on nonstop flights has declined. Average trip time has increased slightly (Morrison and Winston 1986). The average age of the commercial fleet has increased as airlines have extended the life of older aircraft. Initially, the purpose of this strategy was to control costs by deferring purchases of new, more costly aircraft; however, in the late 1980s airlines replaced old planes and expanded their fleets as fast as manufacturers could produce new aircraft. Then in the early 1990s the recession forced airlines to cut costs by keeping old planes in service.

Many of these reductions in the quality of service were anticipated by students of airline regulation (although not advertised heavily). The most severe problems—crowded airports, air traffic control problems, and associated delays—are primarily a consequence of the failure of government to expand airport capacity and air traffic control capabilities in response to the surge in passenger volume and flights since deregulation. The lower fares and new routes created by deregulation substantially increased air travel (see fig. 6.5),

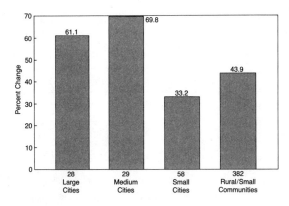

Fig. 6.5   Growth in weekly flights, 1978–89
Source: U.S. Department of Transportation (1990a, 2).

but in 1990 the number of air traffic control personnel was about the same as it was in 1980. President Reagan exacerbated the air congestion problem by firing air traffic controllers in 1981, after a strike, and again in 1987. Likewise, the trust fund from airline ticket taxes has been in surplus during the 1980s, and airport capacity in most cities has remained unchanged for nearly twenty years. Finally, scarce airport capacity is not allocated sensibly. In short, the parts of national air transport policy other than economic regulation have not responded to the increased demands being placed on the system. One *cause* is deregulation, which increased travel, but the *fault* is a failure of other policies.

Increased Service Quality

The number of weekly flights has increased dramatically, and most of the population is served by airports at which flight frequency has increased (see fig. 6.5). The number of markets served by major carriers with hub and spoke systems has increased dramatically. As a result, many travelers can reach most destinations more easily (see table 6.4). While the fraction of passengers traveling on nonstop flights has declined, the fraction of passengers who travel with more convenient on-line connections has increased owing to hubbing (see fig. 6.6).

6.3.5   Industry Structure and Intensity of Competition

Conventional wisdom appears to be that airline deregulation has caused a reduction in competition, but the changes in market structure since 1978 are more complicated than first meets the eye. Three interdependent structural changes have taken place: entry, exit, and consolidation of new and existing airlines; the movement to hub and spoke systems; and the expansion of existing airlines to serve new routes.

Immediately after deregulation began, several new, low-cost airlines entered

Table 6.4   **Number of Points Served, Major Carriers, Month of July 1979, 1984, and 1988**

Carrier	Number of Points Served		
	1979	1984	1988
American	50	75	173
Continental	32	64	137
Delta	69	107	190
Eastern	63	84	142
Northwest	34	42	167
Pan American	25	40	35
Piedmont	48	70	123
Trans World	49	59	94
United	80	112	169
USAir	81	92	131
Total stations (duplicated)	531	745	1,361

Source: U.S. Department of Transportation (1990b, 1:24).

Note: Includes service provided by code-sharing commuters. Data limited to the forty-eight contiguous states.

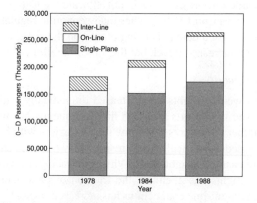

Fig. 6.6   Origin–destination passengers, by routing
Source: U.S. Department of Transportation (1990b, *Executive Summary,* 12).

the industry, and several more small, regional carriers expanded into larger, national airlines. In addition, numerous independent commuter airlines entered or expanded to provide many small communities with more frequent service. One effect of entry and expansion was intense price competition (Bailey, Graham, and Kaplan 1985, chap. 5). After initial success, made possible, in part, by the inefficiency of the existing airlines, virtually all the new "major" entrants and many of the expanded regional carriers either failed financially, were absorbed by larger airlines because of financial difficulties, or simply merged with other airlines. The number of commuter carriers also declined from its peak in the early 1980s, and most commuter carriers are now affiliated with a major airline.

The dramatic rise and fall in the number of airlines had many causes. Some airlines failed as an inevitable consequence of the dramatic change in the competitive environment created by deregulation. Some failed because of poor management decisions. Some failures were due to the failure of government authorities to expand the air traffic control system and airport capacity to accommodate the huge increase in the number of passengers and flights that was induced by lower fares and competitive entry. Some were due to bad merger policies applied by the Department of Transportation, which permitted several airline mergers that reduced rather than enhanced competition (Borenstein 1990). Still other airlines failed as fuel prices rose and recession reduced the demand for air travel in 1990 and 1991.

The rise and fall in the number of airlines left the industry somewhat more concentrated in the late 1980s than it was before deregulation. In 1978, the top ten airlines accounted for roughly 90 percent of domestic revenue passenger miles (RPM). Owing to the entry and the expansion of smaller airlines, the share of the top five and the top ten airlines declined until about 1985. Mergers and airline failures subsequently led to greater concentration among the five and ten largest airlines than had existed prior to deregulation (see fig. 6.7). There was further consolidation in response to fuel price increases and recession in the early 1990s.

The expansion of hub and spoke operations had two significant effects (Borenstein 1989). First, at many large and medium hubs, the market shares of the dominant carriers increased significantly (see table 6.5). Second, all major airlines increased the number of hubs at which they provided service (see table

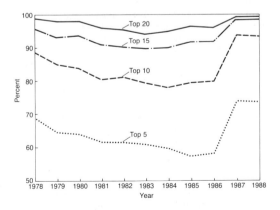

Fig. 6.7 Percentage of domestic RPMs by carrier rank, calendar year 1978–88
Source: U.S. Department of Transportation (1990b, 1:22).

Table 6.5   **Point Concentration, Cumulative Percentage Distribution of Total Enplacements[a] (starting with *most* concentrated points)**

Hub Size and Year	90% or More	80% or More	70% or More	60% or More	50% or More	40% or More	30% or More
Large hubs:							
1988	2.1	10.7	13.3	13.3	33.9	54.3	67.5
1984	. . .	. . .	5.7	5.7	24.3	50.1	55.1
1979	. . .	. . .	.7	.7	13.1	26.6	38.9
Medium hubs:							
1988	. . .	. . .	8.0	17.5	28.5	43.3	63.8
1984	. . .	. . .	. . .	5.1	11.8	26.7	50.7
1979	. . .	. . .	.8	2.8	14.5	42.7	77.6
Small hubs:							
1988	. . .	.8	1.4	7.5	22.0	48.2	80.3
1984	.9	3.0	8.6	16.2	36.4	66.6	88.2
1979	10.2	10.2	.7	30.2	53.0	81.6	96.3
Nonhubs:							
1988	32.1	38.7	52.9	64.8	82.9	92.2	100.0
1984	40.6	51.9	63.2	67.3	77.7	91.1	100.0
1979	42.4	49.4	57.6	67.7	91.5	97.3	99.3
Total:							
1988	2.3	8.9	12.5	14.8	33.3	52.9	68.5
1984	1.1	1.5	6.5	7.9	24.6	48.7	57.9
1979	2.8	3.1	5.0	6.6	20.2	36.8	52.3

Source: U.S. Department of Transportation (1990b, 1:47).

[a]Although distributed on the basis of dominant carrier share, these data reflect total enplacements for all carriers.

Table 6.6   **Number of Large, Medium, and Small Hubs Served, Major Carriers, Month of July 1979, 1984, and 1988**

Carrier	Large Hubs			Medium Hubs			Small Hubs		
	1979	1984	1988	1979	1984	1988	1979	1984	1988
American	21	26	27	22	28	31	7	19	44
Continental	14	21	25	11	11	28	4	8	25
Delta	23	27	27	17	21	28	17	30	43
Eastern	21	26	26	18	26	24	20	21	32
Northwest	18	22	26	4	8	25	4	5	32
Pan American	8	23	20	0	14	14	0	2	2
Piedmont	13	18	24	5	10	17	9	21	28
Trans World	22	25	27	15	25	26	9	9	17
United	23	27	27	17	31	31	22	37	45
USAir	15	23	26	15	17	27	12	17	25
Total stations	178	238	255	124	191	251	104	169	293

Source: Official Airline Guide (July 1979, July 1984, and July 1988).

Note: Includes services provided by code-sharing commuters. Data are limited to the forty-eight contiguous states.

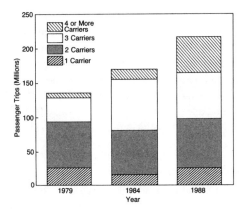

Fig. 6.8   Passenger trips by competitive status
Source: U.S. Department of Transportation (1990a, 4).

6.6). Thus, the large airlines were increasing their market shares at individual hubs, and they were also expanding the number of hubs to which they provided at least some service.

The cumulative effect of these changes is an increase in the number of competing airlines serving the average route. Whereas fewer domestic airlines serve the nation, more serve any given route owing to the growth in hubs and routes by the major carriers. In 1988, a much larger fraction of travelers flew on routes with three or more competing carriers than was the case in 1979 (see fig. 6.8).

6.3.6   Airline Safety

The most significant concern about airline deregulation has been that it would lead to a significant deterioration in airline safety. The standard argument goes something like the following. Intense competition will force airlines to cut costs in order to compete effectively and to provide satisfactory earnings to stockholders. In the process of cutting costs, airlines will cut maintenance expenditures excessively or unwisely defer the replacement of older aircraft. Especially during economic downturns, when pressures on earnings are most severe, maintenance and investment in safety may suffer as airlines try to maintain earnings. The most detailed empirical evidence regarding the validity of this theory, produced by Nancy Rose, is inconclusive. Rose (1990) finds no relation between fatalities and financial performance, but she does find a small, weak effect on nonfatal accident rates.

The concerns about the effects of *economic* deregulation on airline safety are worthy of careful consideration, but several observations about the relation between these concerns and actual experience are in order. First, although many argue that the margin of airline safety has declined, by all objective measures safety has not declined since deregulation (Morrison and Winston 1986,

1989). Second, airline safety regulation was never the responsibility of the CAB and has not been deregulated. The Federal Aviation Administration regulates safety. Deregulation has made the FAA's job more demanding, but the FAA has not grown in proportion to the number of flights and aircraft in service. If safety is inadequate since deregulation, the policy error is the failure to provide the FAA with adequate resources to do its job. Third, above all, airline safety is good business. Passengers are sensitive to airline fatalities and will avoid an airline for several months after a fatal crash (Borenstein and Zimmerman 1988).

6.3.7 Overall Assessment

Students of the airline industry broadly agree that deregulation has been a success from an efficiency perspective. But not all interest groups have benefited from deregulation. Smaller communities have a different type of service, and fares have increased on the shortest and least dense routes. The competitive pressures since deregulation have led to lower wages and less attractive work rules for airline employees. Many airlines have lost significant amounts of money, and several have gone bankrupt. Deregulation has given some airlines market power in some routes.

Public policy toward the U.S. afrline industry in the near future is likely to emphasize three things. First is to remove barriers to competition created by dominant carriers at certain hub airports. The competitive effects of future mergers will be examined more carefully. Efforts will be made to free entry at hub airports that are dominated by a single airline. The second policy concern is to increase airport capacity and to use capacity more efficiently. Because the lead time for new airports is long and local opposition to expansion often intense, increasing the efficiency with which existing capacity is utilized is a very high priority. The third policy emphasis is to intensify safety regulation and to improve the air traffic control system.

6.4 Railroads: Regulatory Reform for a Sick "Natural Monopoly"

The causes and consequences of regulatory reform in the railroad industry cannot be understood without an appreciation of the history of railroad regulation and its effects. The Interstate Commerce Commission (ICC) was the first "modern" independent federal economic regulatory agency. The Act to Regulate Commerce of 1887 created the ICC as an independent federal regulatory agency to supervise the pricing behavior of the railroads for freight shipped in interstate commerce. The initial act gave the ICC relatively broad but vague authority to enforce a variety of common carrier obligations that were already covered, but difficult to enforce, by common law (Keeler 1983, 22–23). The primary focus of the act was to give the ICC the authority to prohibit railroads from charging rates that were unduly "discriminatory." The railroads were in principle prohibited from charging a higher price per ton for transporting any given commodity on individual "short-haul" segments of a specific "long-haul" route. Charging different prices per ton mile for different *commodities* was not prohibited. As a result, to maximize profits, the railroads used "value of service" or "value of commodity" rate structures that involved relatively high prices for (then) high-valued commodities and relatively low prices for (then) low-valued commodities. Commodity price discrimination has been the norm throughout the hundred-year history of federal regulation of freight transportation.

As interpreted by the courts, the 1887 act did not specifically give the ICC authority to set minimum or maximum rates based on cost of service principles, require regulatory approval for rate changes, or provide for penalties for charging prices that the ICC found to be discriminatory. Nor did the ICC have any authority over entry or exit. Entry and exit were regulated by the states through railroad charters or via common law obligations placed on common carriers (Keeler 1983, 19–24). The ICC could only reject rates and request that railroads file new ones if it determined that existing rates were unjust, unreasonable, or discriminatory.

The rate-making authority of the ICC was expanded significantly by a series of amendments to the Act to Regulate Commerce passed between 1903 and 1910. These amendments gave the ICC the authority to set maximum rates and to suspend rate changes pending an investigation of their reasonableness, provided penalties for discriminatory pricing, and plugged loopholes in the provisions barring short-haul versus long-haul rate discrimination. These same amendments also extended the jurisdiction of the ICC to interstate telecommunications, which was governed by the same regulatory system as railroads until the FCC was created in 1934.

ICC regulatory decisions preceding World War I and during the initial years of the war, a period of rapid inflation, placed burdensome financial constraints on many railroads. Several railroads went bankrupt or were forced to reorganize between 1906 and the entry of the United States into the war in Europe, and the railroads were accused of making inadequate investments in right of way and rolling stock to provide reliable service to shippers.[10] Soon after the United States entered the war, the railroad system was taken over by the federal government, and significant rate increases were put into effect. In 1920, the railroad industry was returned to private management in conjunction with the passage of the Transportation Act of 1920. The 1920 act gave the ICC pervasive regulatory authority to set minimum and maximum rates and rate structures, to certify railroads to provide transportation services for specific commodities on specific routes, to determine whether railroads could cease

10. The poor financial performance of the railroads during the Progressive Era has largely been ignored by students of the political economy of railroad regulation. This is especially true of revisionists who seek to argue that the legislation passed by Congress between 1903 and 1910 and ICC actions implementing the associated statutory authority were designed to benefit the railroads (see Kolko 1965).

providing service on specific routes (abandonment), and to encourage rationalization of the railroad industry through mergers. The 1920 act preempted state authority over entry, exit, and reorganization of railroads. The ICC regulatory umbrella was extended to the trucking industry in 1935 and to certain types of barge transportation in 1940. These acts had the effect of almost entirely suppressing price competition among railroads and between railroads and competing modes.

A great deal has been written about the economic motivation for federal regulation of the railroads. One view is that railroad regulation is motivated by the need to constrain monopoly power. Railroad monopolies supposedly arose because of the economies of scale and sunk costs associated with railroad rights of way, terminals, and networks, combined with the limited competitive alternatives that many shippers faced in the late 1800s and early 1900s. Others argue that regulation was introduced to protect the railroads from competition. Here the argument is that price regulation was first sought to limit cheating on collusive pricing agreements by railroad cartels. According to this view, regulation would be used to place a floor rather than a ceiling on prices. The producer protection motivation is associated with the subsequent extension of ICC regulation to trucking in 1935 and to certain barge transportation in 1940. Still another view associates changes in railroad regulation with more complex interest group politics, finding winners and losers among both railroads and shippers (Gilligan, Marshall, and Weingast 1989).

Whatever one's views about the origins of regulation, by the 1950s regulatory constraints on rates, combined with growing competition from alternative transport modes, began to place severe financial burdens on the railroads. The first severe financial problem emerged in passenger service. It then spread to freight transportation, as modern trucks traveling on an expanding interstate highway system siphoned off more and more of the railroads' highest-valued freight. The railroads were propped up with loans and rate adjustments and eventually were allowed to abandon passenger service entirely. By the early 1970s, many Eastern and some Midwestern railroads were bankrupt, and others faced deteriorating financial performance. Maintenance and investments in tracks, rights of way, and rolling stock were inadequate, and the quality of railroad freight transportation was deteriorating rapidly.

In the mid-1950s, the railroads began to recognize that the existing regulatory structure was increasingly disadvantageous to them and increasingly advantageous to their competitors (Keeler 1983, 29). They sought more pricing freedom from the ICC and Congress to adjust rates to reflect changing cost and competitive conditions. The railroads' efforts met with very limited success. Efforts to raise rates on commodities where railroads had a competitive advantage over trucks and barges (coal and other bulk commodities and long-haul traffic) were resisted by shippers. Efforts to abandon service where railroads could not compete economically with trucks were resisted by those affected. Efforts to reduce railroad rates for services where railroads could compete more effectively with trucks and barges (manufactured commodities, shorter hauls) were opposed by competing truckers. The railroads also had agreed to union wage and work rules that were excessively costly and blocked improvements in efficiency. Basically, the railroads found themselves stuck with price structures, route structures, and labor relations that reflected the economic conditions of the 1920s and 1930s (Hilton 1969). Because of regulatory (and court) restrictions on the ability of the railroads to respond to changing economic conditions, reflecting opposition from competitors and customers who benefited from the status quo, the railroad industry was rapidly self-destructing by the 1970s.

The problems faced by the railroad industry were widely recognized by the 1960s (Friedlaender 1969) and grew progressively worse during the 1970s. Yet regulators and legislators did relatively little to ameliorate them until well into the Carter administration. Many students of the railroads and their regulation recognized that a financially viable and efficient railroad industry required rate adjustments, route rationalization, and industry reorganization (mergers). Some argued that competition among railroads and between railroads and other modes would provide adequate competitive constraints on prices for most routes and commodities so that regulation of railroad rates could be limited to situations where shippers did not have good competitive alternatives (captive shippers).

In 1976, Congress passed the Railroad Revitalization and Regulatory Reform Act (4R Act), which gave the ICC greater freedom to permit necessary mergers, rate flexibility, and the abandonment of unprofitable routes. But the ICC, responding to competitor and shipper opposition, interpreted the 4R Act narrowly, and it led to little change. During the Carter administration, the new ICC commissioners who favored price and entry competition for trucking also adopted a more expansive interpretation of the 4R Act. They allowed increased price flexibility and expedited route abandonment and merger applications.

In 1980, Congress passed the Staggers Rail Act, which gave the ICC expanded authority to give the railroads considerably more pricing flexibility and to allow abandonments of uneconomic routes. As with similar legislation enacted for the airline and trucking industries, the Staggers Act expressed a clear congressional intent to change the underlying rationale for railroad regulatory policy. Rather than working under the assumption that price competition needed to be suppressed, the new legislation adopted the view that railroads should be given substantial freedom to set prices and to enter or exit markets and that price regulation should be limited to situations where the railroads had monopoly power. It also recognized that, because many shippers had competitive alternatives, stringent enforcement of historical railroad service obligations was no longer necessary. Proponents of railroad deregulation no doubt benefited here from contemporaneous changes affecting airlines and trucking.

The Staggers Act did not technically deregulate the railroads. Opponents of deregulation, especially shippers and consumers of coal, were successful in getting regulatory protections written into the 1980 statute. Nevertheless, the Reagan-era ICC used its new statutory authority to give the railroads almost complete freedom to set rates and to abandon routes. The consequences of these reforms have not been studied nearly as intensively as has deregulation of the airlines. Nevertheless, regulatory reform appears to have had dramatic effects on the railroad industry (Rose 1988; Moore 1986, 1988; Barnekov 1987; Keeler 1983). Railroads have cut costs, reduced track mileage, expanded combined rail/truck and rail/barge services, renegotiated union agreements, restructured rates, and increasingly relied on confidential contracts with shippers rather than filed tariffs. There has also been significant consolidation of the industry through end-to-end and parallel line mergers, although the ICC drew the line on parallel mergers when it rejected the proposed merger of the Sante Fe and the Southern Pacific railroads. Conrail, formed by the federal government out of pieces of the bankrupt Eastern railroads, was returned to the private sector.

Perhaps the most controversial issue associated with the debate about railroad pricing flexibility was its effects on average rates. Opponents of deregulation argued that railroads had monopoly power and that rates would rise after deregulation; however, average real and nominal rail freight transport rates have fallen since 1980 (see fig. 6.9). While the rates for some commodities over some routes have risen, real rail freight rates have declined at least slightly for every commodity group since 1980 (using the GNP deflator). The feared dramatic increases in coal transportation rates have been limited to situations where shippers are served by a single railroad and have also been constrained by the depressed state of the coal market since the mid-1980s (Joskow 1990). Despite the decline in rail rates, railroad profitability has increased (see fig. 6.10). The railroad industry has been able both to reduce rates and to increase profitability by cutting costs, abandoning unprofitable routes, consolidating

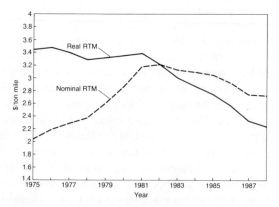

Fig. 6.9   Railroad revenue per ton mile (RTM)
Source: Association of American Railroads (1989, 30).

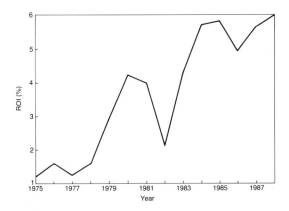

Fig. 6.10   Net return on investment, class I railroads
Source: Association of American Railroads (1989, 18).

operations, and increasing productivity. Railroad employment has declined dramatically since 1980 (see fig. 6.11), and worker productivity (as measured by revenue ton miles per employee) has increased (see fig. 6.12). Although the careful study of the effects of deregulation on truck drivers' wages done by Nancy Rose (1987) has not been performed for railroad workers, real wages appear to have stabilized since the early 1980s (see fig. 6.13). Overall, railroad deregulation in the 1980s achieved most of what proponents of deregulation had promised. We began the 1990s with a healthy railroad industry that looks very different from the one that existed in 1980.

6.5   Telecommunications: Restructuring and Regulatory Reform to Encourage Competition

Until the early 1970s, the American Telephone and Telegraph Company (AT&T) had a monopoly over almost all segments of the U.S. telecommunications industry. Through full or partial stock ownership, AT&T controlled roughly two dozen Bell operating companies (BOCs—New York Telephone, New England Telephone, Pacific Telephone, etc.), which provided local service to approximately 85 percent of Americans and intrastate long-distance telephone services to virtually all residential and business customers in the United States. These local operating companies were (and are) subject to price regulation by state regulatory agencies.[11] AT&T Long Lines had a de facto monopoly over commercial interstate long-distance service. Its rates and services were (and are) regulated by the Federal Communications Commission

---

11. Whereas regulation of the airline and railroad industries involved primarily federal regulatory agencies, the evolution of public policy in telecommunications involves an important role for both state and federal regulators.

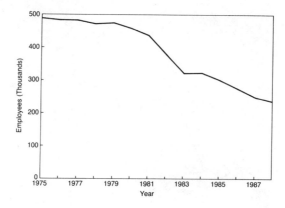

Fig. 6.11   Railroad employees
Source: Association of American Railroads (1989, 56).

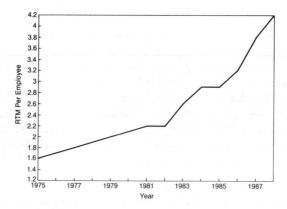

Fig 6.12   RTM per employee
Source: Association of American Railroads (1989, 41).

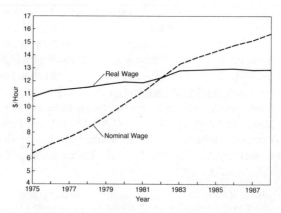

Fig. 6.13   Railroad employee wages
Source: Association of American Railroads (1989, 56).

(FCC), which also has jurisdiction over the radio spectrum, including broadcast television, microwave systems, and radio telephony.

Western Electric, a wholly owned, unregulated subsidiary of AT&T, produced virtually all the telephone transmission and switching equipment used by AT&T affiliates and the customer premises equipment (i.e., telephones) offered to the BOCs' customers. Because AT&T was a virtual monopoly supplier of telephone service, Western Electric effectively had a virtual monopoly over the supply of telephone transmission and switching equipment. Because AT&T generally required customers to use customer premises equipment (CPE) provided by AT&T and bundled the sale of telephone service and CPE together, Western Electric had a virtually complete monopoly on customer premises equipment as well.

The FCC was never as protective of AT&T as the CAB had been of airlines or the ICC had been of trucking. During the 1960s and 1970s, the FCC began to open two key components of the telecommunications industry to competition. In particular, it first grudgingly allowed, and eventually encouraged, competitors to provide terminal equipment (e.g., telephones and switchboards) to AT&T consumers. It also allowed competing long-distance service companies like MCI and Sprint to enter the market. The political and economic pressures that led to these changes in regulatory policies are complex. We will focus on technological changes that played an important role in stimulating competitive pressures and regulatory reform.

6.5.1   Structural Issues

As with railroads, an understanding of contemporary issues in telecommunications policy requires an understanding of the history of the industry and its regulation. The proper scope of competition has been a continuing source of controversy throughout the twentieth century. AT&T became a ubiquitous telecommunications monopoly because it used its control over the only viable long-distance technology to force independent local telephone companies to merge with it. At the turn of the century, local telephone companies competed directly for customers. The controversy of the day was how best to deal with the long-distance monopoly: by creating a matching local service monopoly (the solution proposed by AT&T) or by requiring mandatory interconnection of AT&T's long-distance system to all local telephone companies (the solution advanced by independent telephone companies).

AT&T achieved its monopoly but was also subject to economic regulation. In 1910, regulation of interstate telephone service was given to the ICC. But the structure of AT&T continued to be controversial into the 1930s. During the debate over the Communications Act of 1934, which established the FCC, the ownership of Western Electric by AT&T became a major issue. Some drafts of the act contained strong language favoring competition and even instructed the agency to restructure the industry; however, the act as passed simply listed competition as a consideration and ordered the FCC to study the issue and report back later.

By the time the FCC finished its study, World War II had begun, and Congress and the president were otherwise occupied. But, as soon as the war ended, the controversy reemerged. Developments in microwave technology during the war created new opportunities for business users to construct their own private intracorporate telecommunications systems rather than relying on AT&T and its affiliates. Hence, both potential competitors to AT&T's monopoly and large businesses petitioned the FCC to allow them to use this new technology. After a decade of investigation and debate, the FCC issued the Above 890 decision, allowing the construction of private microwave systems to enable large firms to bypass AT&T for their internal telecommunications requirements.

Meanwhile, AT&T's ownership of Western Electric continued to be an issue. During the war, the computer industry had been born, and electronics had grown substantially. Firms in these industries saw a lucrative prospect in selling equipment to telephone companies but could not owing to their vertical integration into manufacturing. In 1949, the Truman administration filed an antitrust suit against AT&T that sought divestiture of Western Electric, which the Eisenhower administration quickly settled at virtually no cost to AT&T.

The Above 890 decision led naturally to a desire by owners and builders of private microwave systems to sell services to others. Likewise, satellite technology offered still another basis for competitive entry. Responding to these developments, the FCC began issuing a steady stream of decisions that gradually introduced competition into all aspects of telecommunications—even to a limited extent in local access. In long distance, the FCC decided in 1969 to allow MCI to compete with AT&T in offering private line common carrier service between St. Louis and Chicago. A year later, in the Specialized Common Carrier decision, the FCC opened private lines generally to competitive entry. In 1968, in the Carterfone decision, the FCC established technical rules that permitted some customer equipment that was not owned by the telephone company to be interconnected to the network; five years later, it generalized this decision by completely opening the customer equipment market to competition. The FCC also adopted the "open skies" policy for communications satellites, allowing anyone (except AT&T, which was initially barred) to launch domestic telecommunications satellites for any purpose. All these monumental decisions occurred before any generic deregulation movement and industry restructuring resulting from antitrust litigation and before much had been published by economists on the economics of the industry.

The FCC took a major retrograde step in its general move toward liberalization at about the time deregulation started to become popular elsewhere. In the 1976 Execunet decision, the FCC decided to draw the line on how far competition would be stretched. Execunet was MCI's conventional long-distance service. The FCC ruled that MCI could not enter this market, concluding that AT&T ought to have a protected monopoly in ordinary toll service. MCI appealed, and the D.C. Court of Appeals ruled in its favor, stating that the Communications Act (unlike many regulatory statutes) contained a presumption in favor of competition and that the agency bore a burden of proof to show that long-distance competition was not in the public interest. By the time this decision was rendered, Carter appointees controlled the FCC and, as elsewhere, were ardently pursuing liberalization in all aspects of communications regulation. These officials decided not to try to establish an evidentiary record that would sustain the original decision.

Despite the generally procompetitive policies of the FCC, AT&T's control over the local switched telephone exchange gave it the power to block or slow down these competitive developments. Competing suppliers of long-distance service needed access to the local exchange system to make their services available to most customers. AT&T first denied them access and then provided an inferior type.[12] Competing suppliers of customer premises equipment had to be able to connect their equipment to the local loop and to be able to market their equipment on a "level playing field" with AT&T equipment. AT&T enforced stringent interconnection conditions that made it costly for competing equipment to be used by customers and, through bundling of telephone and equipment services, forced customers to pay AT&T for customer premises equipment even if they did not use AT&T's equipment. New data and information services required upgrading of the local and long-distance network. AT&T was slow to facilitate these services' availability. To do so meant retiring equipment that, according to the regulatory rules, would have continued to earn a profit for AT&T. Moreover, it meant forgoing the possibility that AT&T could monopolize these services when Bell was ready to provide them. State regulators were also concerned that AT&T was overcharging itself for Western Electric equipment, then passing these inflated costs through in regulated rates charged to customers. This behavior, it was argued, made it possible for AT&T to evade state rate regulation by shifting profits back to its unregulated subsidiary via excessive transfer prices.[13]

AT&T's monopoly had attracted the attention of the antitrust authorities at the U.S. Department of Justice since the turn of the century.[14] In 1974, the

12. A still controversial issue is whether the entry of long-distance carriers occurred simply because the regulated price structure forced AT&T's long-distance prices to be far above costs. On the one hand, competitors paid far less to local telephone companies. On the other hand, they were provided a distinctly inferior form of local access. Eventually, when BOCs were forced to provide equal access at the same price charged to AT&T, *all* the competitive long-distance carriers chose equal access rather than continued inferior access at a lower price. This suggests that the cost of inferior access exceeded the benefit of a lower price.

13. The evidence on this point is weak. Western Electric did cut prices after divestiture, but only after radically restructuring the company to cut costs. A more plausible story is that AT&T had simply grown fat from lack of competitive pressures. The evidence that AT&T delayed the introduction of new products and services to protect its "rate base" equipment and services monopoly was much stronger.

14. Antitrust concerns and challenges arising from AT&T's relation with Western Electric were first raised in 1908 and were serious at the time of the passage of the Communications Act of 1934, which transferred regulation of AT&T from the ICC to the FCC and ordered the new commission to study these relations. That study identified a variety of problems. The government then

Department of Justice brought an antitrust suit against AT&T.[15] The government charged that AT&T had violated Section 2 of the Sherman Act by monopolizing or attempting to monopolize a variety of telecommunications markets. The basic theory underlying the relief sought by the Justice Department was that the only portion of the telecommunications business that was likely to remain a monopoly was the local switched exchange system.[16] Long-distance interexchange service was conducive to competition, as was the provision of telephone switching equipment, customer premises equipment, and information services. As a firm that operated at all levels of the telephone business, AT&T had a conflict of interest. It had incentives to use its control over the monopoly segment of the business—the local loop—to protect itself from competition in the other segments of the business. It was argued further that the FCC was unable to regulate access to the local loop effectively, given the conflict of interest that existed between AT&T affiliates and even between state and federal regulation. As a result, the Department of Justice argued that the only way that competition could flourish in potentially competitive segments of the business was to prevent AT&T from using its control over the local exchanges to thwart competition in these other markets.

The antitrust suit against AT&T was settled in 1982 with the government getting most of the remedies that it sought. The settlement separated AT&T from its local operating companies (BOCs). The local operating companies were organized into seven separate, independent holding companies. Each provides local exchange and intrastate interexchange services in a specific region of the country. They were also required to provide "equal access" to competing long-distance companies. The local exchange networks could remain legal monopolies, subject to state rate regulation, at the discretion of the states. AT&T was allowed to retain Western Electric and most of Bell Labs. The local operating companies were given part of Bell Labs, now called Bell Communications Research, as a jointly owned research-and-development facility but were forbidden to manufacture telephone switching, transmission, and customer premises equipment, to offer long-distance service, or to offer certain information services within their franchise areas. These restrictions are subject to review every three years by the federal court administering the 1982 consent

---

brought an antitrust suit against AT&T after World War II seeking divestiture of Western Electric. This suit was settled in 1956 without requiring AT&T to divest Western Electric as the antitrust authorities had initially requested.

15. For more details on the contentions of both sides of the case, see Noll and Owen (1988).

16. A common claim is that Justice accepted the view that local service was a natural monopoly. In fact, Justice actually assumed that, regardless of the technical facts, state regulation and an incumbency advantage were likely to make local service a monopoly for the foreseeable future. But radio technology could prove this to be a poor forecast. By 1988, William Baxter, the assistant attorney general for antitrust, who negotiated the divestiture agreement, opined that the biggest mistake in the restructuring of telecommunications was letting the BOCs, rather than AT&T, inherit the rights to radio telephone service.

decree that accompanied the settlement of the government's antitrust case. The reorganization officially took effect in 1984.

The final irony of the history of structural controversy in telecommunications is the reversal of field by the Reagan administration Department of Justice on the basic theory of the AT&T divestiture. AT&T was formally broken apart in 1984; by 1986, the Department of Justice was advocating permitting the Bell operating companies to reintegrate into nearly all the prohibited competitive markets: manufacturing, information services, and long distance (except in their own service territories). The antitrust authorities argued that they now believed that regulatory authorities could prevent local telephone companies from making use of their local franchised monopolies for anticompetitive purposes in other parts of the industry. The fact that the late Reagan administration would propose undoing most of the early Reagan administration's single most important policy accomplishments in telecommunications is testimony to the enduring nature of the controversy over the structure of the industry.

Major liberalizing decisions by federal regulators took place in the 1980s regarding radio telephone services. Historically, the FCC assigned mobile telephone frequencies to specific industries for specific purposes. But, during the 1980s, the FCC has moved to a general first-come, first-served system that encourages joint and multiple uses. As a result, the spectrum allocated for mobile radio telecommunications is becoming less Balkanized and more like a traditional common carrier service—only in this case with multiple competitors. Second, in permitting the use of cellular telephone technology, the FCC rejected AT&T's proposal to create a single monopoly supplier and instead created a duopoly. This assured that at least one cellular operator in each city is not the local telephone company and therefore has no interest in making certain that cellular does not compete with the traditional local telephone network as a means of basic access. Moreover, because of policies liberalizing other mobile services, radio access to the telephone network is slowly growing among other radio licensees, notably so-called specialized mobile telecommunications. Today radio technology is too expensive and too inefficient in its use of the radio spectrum to be a viable competitor for local telephone access. But digital technology already developed but not deployed solves the spectrum problem, and the next technical generation down the line is expected to lower radio telephone costs to approximately 150–200 percent of wireline access. At this level, with its added valuable feature of mobility, radio telephone service holds the promise of becoming a viable competitor to local telephone companies.

6.5.2 Pricing Issues

Historically, pricing in telecommunications has been extremely inefficient. Prices bore little relation to the costs of corresponding services and carried a heavy burden of cross-subsidy. In general, these subsidies ran from long distance to local service, with about half the costs of local service being paid by long-distance tolls. The cornerstone of the system was and is the basic monthly access charge for residents and businesses to connect to the telecommunications network through the nearest switch of the company that has the monopoly franchise to provide local service. Basic access is priced substantially lower for residences than for businesses; however, businesses have a second access possibility that reduces their costs substantially. If a business uses a large number of access lines, it can buy Centrex. The primary feature of Centrex is that it enables one person in an office to call another by dialing fewer numbers, but all such calls are routed through the local telephone company's nearest central office switch, just as if they were local calls. By purchasing Centrex, a company pays the high business access price only for a portion (10–20 percent) of its access lines. The rest are priced much lower—even lower than residential access.

The purpose of Centrex pricing is to induce companies not to buy their own small switch for handling their own intraoffice calls. This not only keeps the customer buying lots of lines but also eliminates some "bypass" possibilities for long distance, as explained below. Of course, whether Centrex is simply a reasonable competitive offering or a classic example of regulated monopolies engaging in cross-subsidization is a matter of continuing controversy. Competitors claim that Centrex must be subsidized if residential local access is subsidized because the former rate is lower than the latter. Local telephone companies respond that Centrex customers are, on average, less than half as far from the central office switch as other customers and so require less investment. Competitors respond that no other access prices are based on distance to the switch and that, in any case, telephone companies decide where to locate switches and can select these locations strategically to make Centrex costs lower but residential access more expensive. The debate is endless and proves mainly that regulatory cost allocation procedures rarely can resolve a dispute about whether a telephone company is setting anticompetitive or procompetitive prices.

Long-distance prices do not distinguish between residences and businesses, but they do come in three general types: interexchange toll calls, intrastate inter-LATA toll calls, and interstate toll calls. Interexchange service is a call within the local service territory of a local telephone company that must be transported from one central office switch to another. Often adjacent central office switches are connected by dedicated trunks, and companies usually impose no toll charge for such a call. But some calls within a local service territory—called a local access and transport area (LATA)—travel hundreds of miles and are indistinguishable from other forms of long distance. Nevertheless, in most states, local telephone companies have a legal, franchised monopoly in these intra-LATA toll calls as well. In these states, carriers such as AT&T or MCI either are barred altogether from permitting such calls on their network or, if they make them, are required to pay the local telephone company all or most of the charges it would have collected had the call gone over its network. In general, intra-LATA toll prices are extremely high in relation to cost. Long-distance calls within LATAs by local telephone companies account for approximately 25 percent of all long-distance revenues and cover almost as large a share of local exchange costs as did interstate long distance prior to the regulatory changes of the 1980s.

The second category of long-distance service is calling between LATAs— or between the service territories of a local company (or two local companies)—within the same state. The prices for these intrastate inter-LATA toll calls, as well as entry conditions, are regulated by states, except that, since 1984, the divestiture agreement has barred Bell operating companies from providing this service. States could hand this service entirely to a single long-distance carrier, and a few small states did so after divestiture. But, in general, this market contains numerous firms. States sometimes regulate the price of intrastate inter-LATA long distance; however, because long distance is becoming substantially competitive, the most important regulated price is the charge the long-distance carriers pay to reach their customers through the local telephone network. Most states set usage-based carrier access charges—that is, they tack on a charge per minute of use to long-distance calling that is given to local telephone companies. In some cases, this charge equals or exceeds the charge for the long-distance portion of the call, despite the fact that the latter can be for hundreds of miles but the former is for only a few miles.

Finally, the federal government (i.e., the FCC) regulates long-distance calling between states. Divestiture barred Bell operating companies, but not other providers of local service, from the interstate long-distance market. The federal government regulates only AT&T's prices and even here has been a passive player, for AT&T annually or more frequently initiates proposals to lower its rates. In addition to AT&T, MCI, and Sprint, the market contains a few additional national companies and many regional companies. The latter normally offer their customers the opportunity to call anywhere, but all or most of their network is simply leased space on the networks of the three larger players. The small facilities-based carriers design their routes to minimize costs in a particular region, focusing their marketing on customers whose long-distance calling is predominantly to a few cities.

The most important price that federal regulators control is the access charge by local telephone companies for interstate long-distance origination and termination in a local exchange. Until the mid-1980s, all access charges were carrier use charges, and approximately half the costs of the three major long-distance carriers were payments to local telephone companies. In 1985, the FCC began to transfer the federal share of local cost responsibility—about 25 percent of the total cost of local exchange service—to a monthly subscriber line charge. To a subscriber, this charge is indistinguishable from the monthly access price set by the state. By 1990, the FCC had transferred about half the federal share of local costs to subscriber line charges; this, in turn, meant approximately a 25 percent reduction in interstate long-distance rates during the first five years after the policy was adopted but also about a 20 percent increase in residential access prices and a 10 percent increase in business access prices.

The last important aspect of the telephone system is the pricing of so-called bypass services. A customer can avoid paying carrier access charges in the originating local telephone area by connecting directly to a long-distance network. Local telephone companies and long-distance carriers both sell "private line" service that enables a customer to do this. A private line can connect the customer to the entire network of a long-distance carrier, to a specific office in another city, or to another local calling area. The second is the business that MCI initially entered in 1969, but it quickly began offering the first and third as well. The Execunet case arose when MCI offered long distance without a private line.

Because carrier usage charges are still a significant part of long-distance charges and were half of them before 1985, usage fees create an incentive for large customers to use bypass—even if it is actually more costly (in terms of actual costs, not prices). Seeing this irrationality in pricing, MCI and Sprint picked bypass (private lines) as their point of entry for precisely this reason. They could offer large business customers massive savings in long-distance charges, inducing them to try these upstart competitors against Ma Bell.

From an efficiency perspective, the problem is paying for a fixed cost (the local access connection) with a usage-based charge. This prevents the price of usage from equaling its cost and thereby discourages use. The compensating price change is lower lump sum access charges for connections to the local exchange. The justification given for this practice is to encourage "universal service," that is, telephone subscription by every household. But, in an advanced economy like the that of United States, lower access charges for connection to the local loop do not encourage much increase in the penetration of telephone service. In the United States, the demand for access is almost perfectly inelastic for all business and all but the poorest households. Virtually everyone has a telephone and would continue to have one if the price went up a few dollars. Hence, carrier usage charges reduce long-distance calling but produce almost no offsetting increase in basic access subscription. This constitutes almost a total net loss from a societal perspective.

The importance of carrier access charges goes beyond their distorting effect on ordinary long-distance telephone calls; it also distorts the development of new information services. Most of these services use a large, centralized data base and are most efficiently used by accessing them for a large area—perhaps the entire country—by long distance. For smaller customers without bypass alternatives, carrier use charges discourage use. Meanwhile, purely local services are encouraged because local usage charges are either zero (most residences) or small (businesses) compared to long distance. Hence, the price structure tends to distort the types of information services that are offered to small users.

The FCC's pricing policy since divestiture has been to lower usage charges to the small actual costs of usage and to increase monthly access prices to cover the rest of the federal share of local service costs. From an economic efficiency standpoint, this is an excellent policy. From a political standpoint, it is extremely controversial. Indeed, in January 1986, Congress fell one Senate vote short of overturning this policy (it had already passed the House). This is a very puzzling circumstance. The explanation probably lies in two facts about the economics and politics of telephones. First, many people make very few interstate long-distance calls. One study by Texas regulators found that most customers make one or zero interstate calls per month, but, of course, Texas is a very big state. A large part of long-distance calling is for business and so is not paid by individuals directly; instead, it is buried in the costs of business products and services. Second, the monthly basic charge for access is a visible price faced by almost all Americans; long-distance charges, by contrast, are less visible and far more complex. It is far easier to see and to become aware of a change in access prices than a change in long-distance prices. Thus, the FCC's policy initiative increases a visible, widely shared price in return for lowering a large number of largely invisible ones. Political leaders most likely were not so much voting against efficiency or in favor of a local telephone company special interest as they were simply fearing that voters would react negatively to this particular kind of change. Nonetheless, in the closest congressional vote in the regulatory reform era, efficiency won—but only after the FCC had trimmed its sails by promising to phase in subscriber line charges over several years. Thus, the efficiency benefits of the plan will accrue gradually in hopes that it will minimize the chance of political backlash against increases in basic access prices.

6.5.3   Postreform Performance

What have been the effects of the dramatic change in the structure and regulation of the telecommunications industry? It is useful to examine what has happened in each of the segments of the telecommunications business since AT&T was reorganized in 1984 (for more details, see Noll and Owen 1989).

Customer Premises Equipment (CPE)

Now that customer premises equipment has been unbundled from telephone service, interconnection restrictions removed, and self-dealing conflicts largely eliminated, a vigorously competitive market has emerged. Equipment prices have fallen, and the kinds of equipment that are available have increased. Despite Western Electric's historical claims that it was an efficient equipment supplier, offering customers what they needed at a fair price, it has not been successful as a CPE supplier in this new competitive environment. Western's market share has fallen from 85 to 20 percent. This fall began before divestiture, owing to FCC policies to unbundle CPE and to promote competition among suppliers.

Telephone Transmission and Switching Equipment (TSE)

The evolution of competition in telephone switching equipment has been slower. Competition has increased as the BOCs have turned to some suppliers other than AT&T/Western. AT&T is still the major player, with a national market share of about 60 percent (down from 85 percent before divestiture). Northern Telecom, the manufacturing arm of Bell Canada, is second. Contrary to common belief, European and Japanese firms have not been particularly successful in the market, although, by buying U.S. production facilities, Siemens appears well positioned to become a third significant supplier. Competitive pressures have stimulated more rapid diffusion of new TSE technology, especially fiber optic transmission lines, computerized switching equipment, and digital networks. Much of this equipment is provided by computer and microelectronic firms that were not in the industry in the early 1980s.

Long-Distance Service

Three strong players compete in the long-distance market offering voice and data services throughout the entire United States. Prices for a wide variety of long-distance voice, data, and video services have fallen dramatically. A wide array of specialized services are available to business and residential customers. The major issue remaining with regard to competition in long-distance markets is when competition will permit complete deregulation. AT&T still has about 60 percent of the market, although its market share understates the intensity of competition. In 1989, the FCC took a step in the direction of regulation by abandoning traditional cost of service regulation of AT&T's rates in favor of a simplified "rate cap" system. The new procedure gives AT&T more flexibility to meet competition and provides strong incentives for AT&T to reduce costs and increase productivity yet still provides safeguards against monopoly abuses. The new procedure is a natural transition state to complete deregulation of long-distance rates sometime in the 1990s.

Local Service

An important change in FCC policy during the 1980s has been to reduce substantially—and eventually to eliminate—the subsidies of local service from overpricing long distance. While the new FCC policy has stopped the growth of subsidies from long distance to local service and improved efficiency, in doing so it has put pressures on local prices (Noll 1985). Table 6.7 shows the average price to residential customers for unlimited local service during the past fifty years. Beginning in 1985, these figures also include the FCC's subscriber line charge (SLC). Since divestiture, residential local service has increased $5.00 per month, or about 45 percent, about half of which is SLC. In the five years prior to divestiture, local rates rose by about $3.40, an increase of 40 percent. This comparison, however, understates the effects of FCC-led rate reform, for the earlier period was one of rapid inflation and high

Table 6.7   **Charge for Unlimited Local Service (dollars)**

January		January		January		October	
1940	3.44	1955	5.29	1970	5.87	1983	11.58
1941	3.63	1956	5.34	1971	6.16	1984	13.35
1942	3.70	1957	5.37	1972	6.51	1985	14.54
1943	3.83	1958	5.44	1973	6.79	1986	16.13
1944	3.84	1959	5.60	1974	7.14	1987	16.66
1945	3.84	1960	5.64	1975	7.31	1988	16.59
1946	3.84	1961	5.70	1976	7.77		
1947	3.87	1962	5.71	1977	7.98		
1948	4.09	1963	5.75	1978	8.16		
1949	4.20	1964	5.76	1979	8.19		
1950	4.47	1965	5.78	1980	8.32		
1951	4.69	1966	5.77	1981	8.82		
1952	4.83	1967	5.71	1982	9.73		
1953	5.18	1968	5.72	1983	11.14		
1954	5.18	1969	5.79				

Source: Lande (1989, 16).

Note: Data exclude equipment rental but include estimates of state and local taxes. Data for 1983–88 do not include maintenance of inside wiring. Data for 1940–83 (January) are from AT&T; remaining data are from FCC survey of ninety-five cities.

interest rates, both of which can be expected to increase local telephone rates. As is apparent from the table, before the stagflation problems of the 1970s, local rates were highly stable.

The prices in table 6.7 are averages over cities and states having very different price structures. Table 6.8 shows the trends in local service prices for businesses and residences during the 1980s. These figures do not include the SLC but instead show the rates established by state regulators. As is apparent from the table, two major features of telephone pricing are the differences between rural and urban rates and the spread between business and residential rates. In 1980, before either divestiture or long-distance competition had any substantial effect on the industry, residential rates in smaller communities were about two-thirds the prices charged in the large cities, while small town business rates were less than half the prices charged to big city businesses. During the postdivestiture era, these differences have fallen, especially the differences in business rates (for more details, see Noll and Smart 1990).

Basic access prices bear little relation to the cost of service. The cost of local access service is extremely dependent on the size of the community. Nationwide, the average monthly cost of local exchange service is approximately $20.00; however, in large cities it is in the mid-teens, whereas in some rural areas it can approach $100 per month. The marginal cost of service is lower, with recent estimates varying from $10.00 to $13.00 in larger cities.

Together, the price and cost data shed interesting light on the system of cross-subsidies in telephone sources. If the FCC's subscriber line charges are

Table 6.8   Rates for Single-Line Service: Average for all Companies (years)

Size of Locality (no. of terminals)	Predivestiture		Divestiture Plans		Postdivestiture				Change		
	1980	1981	1982	1983	1985	1986	1987	1988	1980–86	1983–86	1986–88
Business											
Smallest	14.33	15.23	17.04	19.98	25.18	26.04	25.83	25.63	11.71	6.06	−.41
1,000	14.71	15.62	17.44	20.31	25.45	26.29	26.08	25.87	11.58	5.98	−.42
5,000	16.33	17.26	19.02	21.80	26.68	27.41	27.19	26.99	11.08	5.61	−.42
25,000	19.23	20.23	22.08	25.33	29.69	30.34	30.00	29.77	11.11	5.01	−.57
50,000	20.97	22.14	24.39	27.54	32.32	32.78	31.99	31.74	11.81	5.24	−1.04
100,000	22.93	24.11	26.27	29.64	34.47	34.72	34.22	34.04	11.79	5.08	−.60
250,000	25.29	26.96	29.25	32.52	37.66	38.05	37.55	37.27	12.76	5.53	−.78
500,000	27.82	29.54	30.78	34.43	39.08	38.86	38.74	38.33	11.04	4.43	−.53
750,000	27.91	29.20	33.43	35.23	38.61	37.69	37.49	36.95	9.78	2.46	−.74
1,000,000	31.55	34.21	34.06	37.56	38.40	37.34	37.22	36.33	5.79	−.22	−1.01
Difference	17.22	18.98	17.02	17.58	13.22	11.30	111.39	10.70	−5.92	−6.28	−.60
No. of companies	50	50	51	50	48	48	48	48			
Residential											
Smallest	6.49	6.69	7.42	8.64	10.68	10.92	10.78	10.67	4.43	2.28	−.25
1,000	6.60	6.82	7.54	8.76	10.78	11.01	10.86	10.76	4.41	2.25	−.25
5,000	7.05	7.25	7.97	9.20	11.15	11.36	11.21	11.11	4.31	2.16	−.25
25,000	7.84	8.05	8.82	10.11	11.95	12.13	11.96	11.85	4.29	2.02	−.28
50,000	8.26	8.54	9.43	10.73	12.60	12.71	12.52	12.40	4.45	1.98	−.31
100,000	8.70	9.02	9.92	11.21	12.94	13.07	12.86	12.78	4.37	1.86	−.29
250,000	9.38	9.72	10.56	11.76	13.64	13.76	13.54	13.44	4.38	2.00	−.32
500,000	9.87	10.31	10.97	12.27	13.99	13.95	13.68	13.56	4.08	1.68	−.39
750,000	9.74	10.02	11.33	11.95	13.12	13.11	12.94	12.76	3.37	1.16	−.35
1,000,000	9.56	9.94	10.37	11.41	13.08	13.28	13.27	12.98	3.72	1.87	−.30
Difference	3.07	3.25	2.95	2.77	2.40	2.36	2.49	2.31	−.71	−.41	−.05
No. of companies	52	53	54	54	51	51	51	51			

Source: National Association of Regulatory Utility Commissioners, *Exchange Service Telephone Rates*, 1980–83, and *Bell Operating Companies Exchange Service Telephone Rates*, 1985–88.

added to the figures in table 6.8, in cities with more than about 50,000 terminals (about 100,000 people), residential customers pay more than $15.00, which exceeds the marginal cost and approaches the average cost. Meanwhile, businesses in these cities are paying $40.00 a month, which is approximately double the nationwide average cost and triple the marginal cost. Obviously, in large cities, business access is a major *source* of subsidy, and residential access is not subsidized significantly, if at all. In smaller towns and rural areas, residential prices and probably business prices are well below average and marginal cost. Clearly, small towns and rural areas are the primary recipients of the subsidy. Thus, the generalization that long distance subsidizes local service is misleading. It would be more accurate to say that long-distance service and business access service in larger cities subsidize residential and business access in less populated areas. The cross-subsidy is targeted not at residences but at less densely populated areas.

One important implication of these facts it that the "universal service" justification for price regulation is largely a hoax. Even in small towns, businesses do not need subsidies to be telephone subscribers, and subscribers in larger cities are not subsidized. In fact, cross-subsidization in telecommunications resembles the scheme in transportation before deregulation—subsidization of small communities. Moreover, while the cross-subsidy in the telephone industry is reduced after the reforms of the 1970s and 1980s, it is still present. In contrast, deregulation of trucks, rails, and airlines has, through competition, eliminated cross-subsidies.

Productivity Growth and Cost Savings

The former AT&T companies have been able to achieve enormous cost savings and have demonstrated an extraordinarily high rate of productivity growth since the divestiture in 1984. Despite substantial growth in the volume of business, aggregate employment among the former AT&T subsidiaries has declined substantially. The pressures of competition and the removal of structural and regulatory distortions have led to cost savings far beyond what anyone had anticipated. This raises serious questions about whether AT&T was as efficient as many people used to think it was.

Overall Results

The overall consequences of reforms in telecommunications regulation is difficult to assess by a single measure. Table 6.9 contains one relevant piece of information, the annual rates of change in prices for telephone services and a number of other items. The figures compare the past fifty years to the ten years after the Execunet decision, letting MCI into the message toll long-distance business. It is clearly difficult to detect any trend after 1978; telephones have always performed about 2 percent better than the CPI and continue to do so. Telephone prices also perform better than prices of other regulated utilities, and this spread increased after 1978; however, this is due to the greater impor-

Table 6.9   Annual Rates of Change for Various Price Indexes (%)

	1935–88	1978–88
CPI, all goods and services	4.2	6.1
CPI, all services	4.6	7.5
CPI, telephone services	2.2	4.3
CPI, piped gas	3.8	7.1
CPI, electricity	2.4	6.2

Source: Industry Analysis Division (1989, 4).

tance of fuel costs in the other industries rather than to some fundamental change in productivity treads. These figures do not include either customer equipment or new communications services that use the telecommunications network. Were these included, the performance of the sector since 1978 would be substantially better than the fifty-year trend.

Table 6.10 contains more details about telecommunications pricing since 1978. It clearly shows the divergence between local service and long-distance price trends. It also reveals an interesting pattern between the CPI and the overall telephone price index. Telephones did much worse in the early 1980s than since 1986. The price increases in the early period reflect regulatory lag from the inflation of 1978–80; by 1983, this adjustment was over. Then, for three years after divestiture, telecommunications prices rose more rapidly than the CPI. The most plausible explanation is the disrupting effect of divestiture and accommodating changes in price regulation. But, since 1987, the price performance in telecommunications has been far better.

While difficult regulatory issues remain to be resolved and the transition to competition is not complete, as the data show, the telecommunications industry is more efficient, more flexible, and more competitive than it would have been without the dramatic and controversial changes of the 1970s and 1980s. The rough adjustment period apparently is largely over; the future holds promise for mounting benefits from these changes. Nevertheless, structure and prices in telecommunications are still issues engendering great political controversy. In the 1990s, as states attempt to assert more authority and the BOCs seek approval to reintegrate, further upheavals certainly cannot be ruled out.

6.6   The Natural Gas Industry: A Saga of Rent Control[17]

Natural gas price regulation can be understood only in the context of the bizarre evolution of regulatory policy in this industry. Many of the industry's problems were caused by federal regulation of the price of natural gas in the field, which sought to capture scarcity rents associated with competitive gas

17. With apologies to Stephen Breyer (1982, chap. 13). See also Braeutigam and Hubbard (1986), Broadman and Montgomery (1983), and Lyon (1990).

Table 6.10   **Changes in Telephone Price Indexes, 1978–88 (%)**

Year	CPI	All Telephone Services	All Local Charges	Monthly Residential Service	Interstate Toll	Intrastate Toll
1978	9.0	.9	1.4	3.1	−.8	1.3
1979	13.3	.7	1.7	1.6	−.7	.1
1980	12.5	4.6	7.0	7.1	3.4	−.6
1981	8.9	11.7	12.6	15.6	14.6	6.2
1982	3.8	7.2	10.8	9.0	2.6	4.2
1983	3.8	3.6	3.1	.2	1.5	7.4
1984	3.9	9.2	17.2	10.4	−4.3	3.6
1985	3.8	4.7	8.9	12.4	−3.7	.6
1986	1.1	2.7	7.1	8.9	−9.5	.3
1987	4.4	−1.3	3.3	2.6	−12.4	−3.0
1988	4.4	1.3	4.5	4.5	−4.2	−4.2

Source: Industry Analysis Division (1989, 5–7).

supplies rather than to control monopoly or oligopoly pricing.[18] The structure and regulation of the natural gas industry, especially the changing regulatory environment, are complex. Figure 6.14 contains a diagram depicting the structure of the industry and the relation between different segments. Figure 6.15 contains a diagram depicting the regulatory environment. These figures will be useful in understanding the discussion that follows.

Municipal and state regulation of local gas distribution goes back to the mid-nineteenth century. The economic rationale for price and entry regulation of gas distribution companies was (and is) that gas distribution is a natural monopoly and that costs could therefore be minimized if distribution services were provided by a single firm within a single geographic area. Price and entry regulation was regarded as necessary to promote reliability, safety, and least-cost supply and to prevent monopoly prices.

Regulation of prices and entry into local gas distribution began prior to the development of large natural gas reserves and an extensive long-distance pipeline network to move the gas from where it was found to where it was consumed. Originally, local gas distributors produced gas themselves from coal and coke. Because of its relatively high cost and low thermal content, manufactured gas was used primarily for lighting and cooking, although the lighting market was rapidly captured by electricity in the early part of the twentieth century.

In the 1920s, "waste" natural gas became available in conjunction with the growth of petroleum extraction, and technological progress made possible economical long-distance transportation of natural gas. These developments led

18. Some gas is sure to be cheaper to extract than other gas. Hence, in a competitive world, the owner of cheap gas will make far higher profits than the owner of more expensive but economically worthwhile gas. The higher profits in cheap gas are called *scarcity rents.*

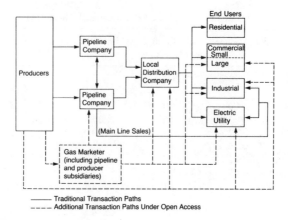

Fig. 6.14   **Principal buyer/seller transaction paths for natural gas marketing**
Source: U.S. Department of Energy (1989, 2).

to fundamental changes in the natural gas industry. Beginning in the 1930s, and accelerating after World War II, cheap natural gas became available in many cities remote from oil- and gas-producing areas. Manufactured gas plants were closed, and the market for gas expanded rapidly as less costly natural gas was used for healing and as an industrial and electric utility boiler fuel. Local distributors relied on independent interstate pipelines to acquire gas and to transport it to them.[19]

For over fifty years, interstate natural gas pipelines provided gas supplies and transportation services as a bundled product at a single price pursuant to long-term contracts between the gas distributor and the pipeline. Gas pipelines were not common carriers, and gas distributors did not purchase directly from gas producers. Gas pipelines purchased gas under long-term contract from gas producers to fulfill their obligations to local gas distribution companies (LDCs). Federal regulation of interstate pipelines was introduced with the passage of the Natural Gas Act of 1938. The economic rationale for pipeline regulation was that pipelines had natural monopoly or oligopoly characteristics. The states sought federal regulation of interstate pipelines because state regulation of interstate pipeline charges was preempted by the commerce clause of the Constitution. Most cities were and are served by a small number of pipeline companies, and, in the absence of price regulation, it was thought that pipelines would be in a position to charge monopoly prices for gas delivered to the city gate. The Natural Gas Act of 1938 gave the FPC (now the FERC) authority to regulate the price of gas delivered by interstate pipelines to gas distribution

---

19. Although it has not been studied in any detail, we suspect that the combination of state laws regarding public utility corporations and restrictions provided for in the Public Utility Holding Company Act of 1935 may have constrained the incentive and ability of interstate gas pipelines to integrate forward into gas distribution. Pipeline regulation made integration of interstate gas pipelines upstream into gas production financially unattractive as well.

MARKET	DATE	PRODUCTION		TRANSPORTATION	SALE FOR RESALE	FINAL SALES
		DRILLING, PRO RATIONING, ETC.	WELLHEAD PRICING			
INTRASTATE	1978	STATE	STATE	STATE	STATE	STATE
			Federal Price Ceilings (FERC) NGPA			
	1985		Federal Price Ceilings, Many Categories Decontrolled (FERC), NGPA			
INTERSTATE		STATE	NOT REGULATED	NOT REGULATED Public Utility Commission of Rhode Island v. Attleboro Steam and Electric Co. 1927 Missouri v. Kansas, Natural Gas Co. 1924		STATE (for rates)
	1938 1954	Except for Federal Lands and Federal Offshore. Subject to Department of Interior	Philips Petroleum Co. v. Wisconsin, 1954 Federal Rate Regulation (FERC), NGA	Federal Rate Regulation (FERC), NGA		Pennsylvania Gas Co. v. Public Service Commission of New York, 1920
	1978		Federal Price Ceilings (FERC) NGPA			FEDERAL (FERC) (for certification)
	1985		Federal Price Ceilings, Many Categories Decontrolled (FERC), NGPA			

Fig. 6.15   Regulatory jurisdiction of the natural gas industry
Source: U.S. Department of Energy (1989, 3).

companies and direct service customers. The associated prices were based on both the average cost of gas purchased from producers and the average historical cost of transporting it. Pipelines also took on a long-term obligation to provide gas supplies to local gas distributors at rates regulated by the FPC. That is, the FPC forced the industry to rely on regulated long-term contracts between pipelines and local distributors. The FPC also endeavored to get the pipelines to secure long-term contracts for adequate supplies of gas to meet the needs of downstream distributors.

Prior to 1954, natural gas production was not subject to price or entry regulation. The production of natural gas is a highly competitive industry, and there is no natural monopoly rationale for regulating the field price of natural gas. If market power is present in the relation between pipelines and gas producers, it is a monopsony problem. However, after World War II, gas distributors and their state regulators sought to force the FPC to extend price regulation to gas producers. The distributors' motivation for seeking the extension of federal regulation to the price of natural gas purchased by pipelines in the field had nothing to do with monopoly prices. Rather, it simply reflected the desire of distributors to extract a share of the scarcity rents associated with existing natural gas reserves and the costs of extracting gas from them. Much of the gas being sold to interstate pipelines after World War II was developed in conjunction with oil many years earlier. It was originally a "waste" product for which there was little demand and was sold at a very low price to consumers located close to gas-producing areas. As the demand for natural gas grew after World War II, field prices under new contracts soon began to rise significantly. In response to the demand for field price regulation, the FPC claimed that it lacked the statutory authority to regulate natural gas production. In 1954, in response to a lawsuit brought by the state of Wisconsin, the Supreme Court determined that the Natural Gas Act of 1938 required the FPC to regulate the prices that interstate pipelines paid for natural gas. Congress subsequently passed legislation exempting gas production from price regulation, but the bill was vetoed by President Eisenhower.

Since the 1954 decision, the natural gas industry has been in almost continual regulatory and political turmoil resulting largely from the efforts of the FPC, the FERC, and later Congress to regulate the price of natural gas in the field.[20] The FPC's initial efforts to set prices on a producer-by-producer basis using conventional public utility cost of service principles quickly became a regulatory morass (Breyer 1982, 248–50). In the 1960s, the FPC began to set ceiling prices for "old" gas and "new" gas in each of five producing areas, based on the average cost of finding and producing natural gas discovered at different times in each area (Breyer 1982, 250–52).

Areawide field prices that were too low combined with average cost pricing for gas delivered to distributors (the average cost of gas purchased by a pipeline pursuant to all its contracts) led to severe supply shortages first in the market for new gas reserves in the late 1960s and then in the market for flowing gas beginning in the early 1970s (Breyer 1982, 244–47). This in turn led to a complex set of rules to allocate the shortages among different customer classes, with existing residential customers getting the highest priority and industrial and utility customers who could switch to oil getting the lowest priority. Dislocations in world oil markets in the mid-1970s made the growing shortages of natural gas even worse. Oil and gas are close substitutes in many end uses. As the price of oil rose, the demand for natural gas increased, and the price of natural gas in unregulated intrastate markets rose along with the price of oil. Although the FPC increased natural gas prices in 1974, in 1976 the price of intrastate gas was twice the price of interstate gas (Carpenter, Jacoby, and Write 1987).

Policymakers faced a classic regulatory dilemma during the 1970s. The price of natural gas sold in interstate markets was being held far below market clearing levels. Since the historical average cost of natural gas, the foundation for FPC field price regulatory policy, had not risen with market values, traditional rate-making methods could not possibly yield market clearing prices. The large unregulated intrastate market caused producers to bypass the interstate market to supply gas where the price was highest, making the shortages in the interstate market even worse. Deregulation of field prices was an obvious

---

20. Until 1979, natural gas that was produced and sold to an intrastate pipeline for resale within the same state was exempt from federal regulation. Separate intrastate markets emerged in Texas and Louisiana. Field prices for intrastate natural gas eventually climbed far above field prices for natural gas dedicated to interstate pipelines. Shortages did not develop in the intrastate markets.

alternative; however, deregulation would transfer an enormous amount of income from consumers and consuming regions of the nation to producers and producing regions. Although the "natural gas problem" was hotly debated in Congress during the 1970s, regulators spent most of the decade trying to allocate gas shortages.

Soon after President Carter was elected, his administration sought to have new, comprehensive energy legislation passed by Congress. The proposed National Energy Act eventually was broken into several different parts dealing individually with oil, natural gas pricing, natural gas allocations, electric utility regulation, conservation, and research and development. After bitter debate, Congress passed the Natural Gas Policy Act (NGPA) in late 1978 (the intense lobbying over the NGPA was well captured in a piece produced by PBS soon afterward). The NGPA was designed to provide for a transition from relatively low regulated prices to higher market clearing prices by moderating the short-run impact of higher prices on natural gas consumers. A companion piece of legislation (the Fuel Use Act) sought to erase the allocation problem by restricting the use of natural gas to generate electricity and as a boiler fuel in industry, which it was argued involved "inefficient" uses for natural gas.

The NGPA sought to achieve its objectives by extending federal regulation of field prices to intrastate natural gas and by establishing a complex set of rules for determining the prices of different "vintages" of natural gas. The base price of "old" gas (reserves from which gas was flowing before April 1977) was fixed at prevailing levels, with automatic adjustments in the base price for inflation as measured by the GNP deflator. The price of "new" gas was set higher, but below what was then thought to be the market clearing level. The legislation contained adjustment provisions that allowed the ceiling price for new gas to increase gradually to the projected market clearing price in 1985. The latter was based primarily on projections of the price of oil (the 1985 gas price target was based on the assumption that, in 1985, the price of oil would be $15.00 per barrel in 1979 dollars). "New" gas prices were scheduled to be deregulated in 1985 as they reached projected market clearing levels, while certain categories of "high-cost" gas were deregulated immediately.

The result of these regulations was that, by 1981, gas in the field was selling at anywhere between $1.00 and $11.00 per thousand cubic feet, depending on the regulatory category into which it fell. Each pipeline held a portfolio of contracts, each of which carried different prices. Pipelines sold gas to local distribution companies and direct service customers at the average price of the gas associated with this portfolio of contracts.

The NGPA also contained provisions that explicitly allowed the FERC (the successor agency to the FPC) to authorize interstate pipelines to provide unbundled transportation service to transport gas owned by intrastate pipelines or local distribution companies. The intent of this legislation appears to have been to provide a mechanism for distributors to acquire gas in the intrastate market to alleviate shortages in the interstate market. While interstate pipelines had traditionally sold gas and transportation service bundled together, the FPC had approved some transportation-only service for selected high-priority customers whose gas supplies in the interstate market had been curtailed. This section of the NGPA appears to have been inserted to provide a limited mechanism to help the FERC deal with shortages affecting certain priority users.

President Carter barely had time to sign the NGPA when the Iranian revolution led to another major dislocation in world oil markets. The average refiner acquisition cost of crude oil rose from $12.50 in 1978 to $35.00 in 1981. Oil prices once again rose dramatically relative to the price of natural gas specified in the NGPA (fig. 6.16). Almost as soon as it was written, the assumptions on which the NGPA's natural gas price adjustment provisions were based became invalid as market conditions changed dramatically. In particular, it appeared that gas prices would be too low through 1985 and then "fly up" to market clearing levels as "new" gas supplies were deregulated.

The unification of the interstate and intrastate markets made it possible for interstate pipelines to acquire gas reserves again. However, because the NGPA had fixed prices at what appeared to be levels below their market clearing values (at least until 1985), gas pipelines engaged in intense nonprice competition for gas by offering to contract for gas supplies pursuant to terms and conditions that had very favorable provisions from the producers' perspective. In particular, gas pipelines signed long-term contracts with very high (80–95 percent) minimum take or pay provisions. These contracts were based on projections of growing natural gas demand and rising prices and caused pipelines to bear the risks of changes in natural gas prices after 1985. It didn't seem to occur to the pipelines or policymakers that not all the contracted gas could be sold. After all, for thirty-five years, the major problem that gas pipelines faced was getting enough gas supplies to meet the needs of their customers.

After the initial run-up in oil prices in 1979–81, two events disrupted the

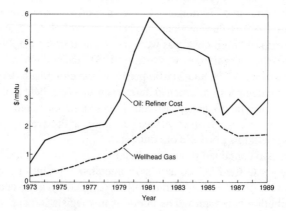

Fig. 6.16   Gas vs. oil prices
Source: U.S. Department of Energy, *Monthly Energy Review* (various issues).

institutional arrangements induced by the NGPA. First, oil prices began to decline after 1981. At first, the decline was gradual, but, in 1986, the oil market collapsed (see fig. 6.16). Second, the economy experienced a severe recession in 1981–83. The recession was particularly severe in some industrial sectors that consumed significant quantities of natural gas (e.g., steel and autos). Moreover, structural changes in the economy that were accelerated by the recession had a permanent adverse impact on these sectors, resulting in a permanent reduction in natural gas demand. Natural gas consumption fell by nearly 20 percent between 1980 and 1983.

Of course, as these changes took place, NGPA field price regulations and long-term contracts between gas producers and pipelines kept operating. As oil prices fell, gas prices rose (see fig. 6.16), and natural gas consumption fell. The long-term take or pay contracts became increasingly onerous to the pipelines as the rising regulated/contract prices and minimum take obligations reinforced one another. If gas pipelines could not sell all the gas they had contracted for, they tried to pass along the full cost of minimum take obligations as higher prices to local gas distributors. Local distributors also had minimum bill contracts with pipelines and tried to pass the price increases along to retail customers. Furthermore, since gas pipelines could not sell all the gas they had contracted for, a surplus of natural gas began to emerge by 1983, and field production was curtailed. Spot gas was available in the field at prices substantially less than the prices pipelines were paying in long-term contracts and passing along to consumers. In a few short years, a serious gas shortage had been transformed into a serious gas glut.

Gas pipelines faced a serious problem. They had contracted for gas that they could not sell at uniform regulated prices that would allow them to recover the costs of al their contractual obligations. As oil prices collapsed after 1985, the retention of their largest price-sensitive customers with fuel-switching capabilities became increasingly difficult. Pipelines faced three choices. They could swallow tens of billions of dollars in excess take or pay liabilities and continue to market and price gas according to prevailing regulatory procedures, recovering as much as they could from their LDC and direct service customers on the basis of prices determined by traditional average cost pricing principles. They could breach their contracts with producers, trying to prevail in court on the basis of the force majeure provisions in contracts, or ultimately to renegotiate the contracts. They could try to sell more gas by offering lower prices for gas to new customers and to price-sensitive old customers who would otherwise switch to oil while continuing to charge captive customers higher rates.

The pipelines initially tried to do a little of each. First, pipelines sought to pass as much of their purchased power costs on to local distributors as they could; however, local distributors also served price-sensitive customers and had to deal with state regulators who pressured them to minimize their minimum bill obligations. They resisted paying for take or pay liabilities associated with gas supplies in excess of what they could sell and sought protections in pipeline rate proceedings at the FERC. Gas pipelines also began to breach some contracts and to insist on renegotiating others. Finally, gas pipelines began to utilize new marketing methods to obtain new customers and retain existing customers who might otherwise have switched to oil.

Of particular interest was the decision of some pipelines to offer brokering packages through which they would acquire specific quantities of low-priced spot gas in the field for specific LDC or direct service customers and then transport it to them using an unbundled transportation rate. The brokered gas could be gas that the pipeline would otherwise be obligated to take under its contracts with producers. By limiting these special marketing programs to new customers and customers with fuel switching capabilities, the pipelines could sell more gas at smaller margins without cutting into the revenues that they were able to earn from captive customers. In short, they engaged in classic third-degree price discrimination.

This "unbundling" response by some pipelines to the economic crisis resulting from historical regulatory rules, contractual arrangements, and changing economic conditions ultimately led to profound changes in the way natural gas is contracted for in the field and transported by pipelines. While the provision of unbundled transportation service had once been an exception, used in special cases to cope with shortages, it is now the norm. Local distributors and direct service customers now routinely contract directly with producers for a significant fraction of their gas, relying on pipelines for unbundled transportation service to move this gas. However, LDCs continue to rely on pipelines for traditional bundled gas supplies for a significant fraction of their needs, especially during the winter when spot gas supplies are more costly and less reliable.

The FERC initially supported the pipeline's efforts to increase gas sales by using unbundled transportation arrangements to engage in price discrimination and welcomed the associated net revenues that could be applied to their fixed costs, thereby reducing costs attributable to captive or core customers (FERC Orders 319 and 234-B). The resulting price and access discrimination was justified as providing benefits to captive customers who might otherwise be stuck with paying for the pipeline's fixed costs. Then, in 1985, the D.C. Circuit held that these programs were illegal under the statutes governing the FERC's regulation of natural gas pipelines. The rejection of the new program came just as the world oil market was collapsing, reducing further the maximum prices that pipelines could profitably charge for gas on standard tariffs. While average field prices had begun to decline by 1985 in response to contract renegotiations and deregulation of new gas prices in 1985, they did not fall nearly as much as the price of oil (see fig. 6.16). Furthermore, responding to complaints from local gas distributors, in 1984 the FERC eliminated gas costs from minimum bills in pipeline tariffs (Order 380), reducing the exposure of local distribution companies to take or pay obligations and shifting the burden entirely to the pipelines. These developments provided further incentives for pipelines to breach their contracts with producers.

In 1985, the FERC recognized that it needed to implement a more affirmative policy to resolve the contractual crisis in the industry and to cope with the inefficiencies caused by regulated pipeline prices that greatly exceeded the price of spot gas in the field and that distorted gas production decisions. The FERC used the crisis to "encourage" the gas pipeline industry permanently to change the way it does business. Specifically, the FERC began to pursue a long-term policy of requiring pipelines to provide open nondiscriminatory unbundled transportation service for gas purchased in the field by distributor and end-use customers in competition with one another and with pipelines (Order 436 and Order 500). While providing transportation to all on a nondiscriminatory basis is technically voluntary, the FERC provided a substantial incentive to participate by discouraging contract carriage certificates that are not tied to open access rules and by trying to tie the resolution of the rate-making treatment of pipeline take or pay liabilities to participation in the general open access regulations.

Because pipelines needed to find alternative ways of marketing gas, and because the FERC channeled these needs to create a common carrier gas transportation system, virtually all major interstate pipelines now provide unbundled transportation service. The proportion of the gas transported by pipelines that is owned by third parties purchasing unbundled transportation service has grown enormously and by 1990 accounted for roughly 70 percent of the gas moved by interstate pipelines (see figs. 6.17 and 6.18). By purchas-

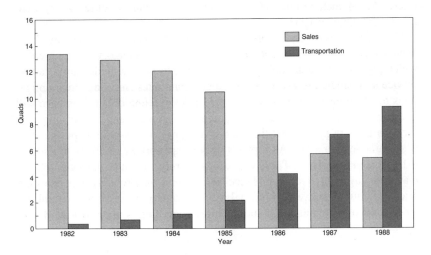

Fig. 6.17   Transportation to market vs. system sales
Source: "Carriage Through 1988," INGAA, Issue Analysis 89-2, May 1989.

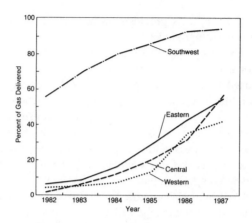

Fig. 6.18   Percentage of gas delivered by twenty major interstate pipeline companies to LDCs and end users in transportation programs, by major market area, 1982–87
Source: U.S. Department of Energy (1989, 45).

ing gas directly from producers or through gas brokers, local gas distributors and large customers have kept their gas costs lower than if they had to buy exclusively from pipelines based on standard tariffs. Most contractual disputes between gas producers and gas pipelines have been resolved (just as oil prices rose significantly again!), and the demand for gas, especially to generate electricity, is increasing. In 1990, the field price of over 90 percent of the gas produced in the United States was either unregulated or below regulated ceiling prices. Amendments to the NGPA passed in 1989 remove all remaining field price regulations in 1993.

Not all the regulatory problems that plague the natural gas industry have been solved (Teece 1990). The FERC has created a regulatory environment in which pipelines have an ambiguous obligation to provide both transportation service and bundled gas service. The appropriate rates and contractual obligations to place on buyers consistent with these pipeline obligations have still not been fully resolved. Furthermore, enthusiasm for unbundled transportation services must in part reflect the abundant supply of low-priced spot gas that was available after 1985. As supplies tighten, spot prices are likely to rise and to become more volatile. Those who choose to rely too much on spot purchases may someday learn to regret it (Teece 1990)—and will probably seek new field price regulations actively. Nevertheless, the primary cause of the natural gas mess, field price regulation, is now almost gone. Let us hope that we do not try it again.

6.7   The Causes of Reform

The preceding review should leave the reader convinced that no simple explanation accounts for the reforms in economic regulation that took place after 1975. Nonetheless, some general forces appear to be at work.

The prior wave of regulatory reform occurred in the 1930s, a period of great economic turmoil. Whereas the 1970s and 1980s were hardly as tumultuous as the 1930s, in comparison with the first twenty-five years after World War II they were certainly no picnic either. The economy generally performed poorly during most of the past two decades, and this gave added salience to proposals that could improve efficiency by a politically visible amount. In the immortal words of Everett Dirksen, "a billion dollars here and a billion dollars there, pretty soon you are talking real money."

Nonetheless, economic hardship alone would not have been sufficient had regulation been working reasonably well. Here the academic scholars deserve a role in the story. The numerous studies of economic regulatory policies, along with the cynical interpretation of them that emerged as the economist's political theory of regulation, could hardly have escaped official Washington. The real message of this work was that the market failure rationale for economic regulation had been vastly oversold across the board. In no case could one categorically state that the natural monopoly clearly encompassed all facets of a regulated industry. And one could readily show that attempts to regulate markets having little or no natural monopoly characteristics were costly.

But, we might ask, so what? Why did protected erstwhile competitors fail to defend their turf? Is interest group theory dead? Obviously not—the savings and loan debacle is testimony to the proposition that the special interest view of regulation is not devoid of merit. And, if we look more deeply, in no case did regulatory reform occur with *no* significant organized support. The railroads had wanted to be less regulated since the 1950s. They were successfully opposed by competing modes until the industry essentially went belly up. Because railroads really are an extremely efficient and important means of transporting many types of goods, it would have been cosmically foolish to let them disappear. So the truckers lost—and, while Congress was at work, it deregulated the truckers as well.

In telecommunications, AT&T can blind us by its predivestiture size. Surely, AT&T did not want either divestiture or deregulation. But, since the invention of the telephone in 1876, AT&T has not been the only significant player in telecommunications, and its structure has always been controversial. Even so, technology probably forced the issue. Hughes Aircraft, not AT&T, invented the geosynchronous satellite; immediately thereafter, AT&T was frozen out of satellite communications for more than a decade. Numerous players in the electronics industry (radio, computers, semiconductors) also produced technologies that made use of communications—and they sought part of the action. Technology proceeded to make transmission costs in telecommunications so low that large-scale users sacrificed very little in unit costs by abandoning the scale economies of the public network and going it alone. MCI, of course, was a peanut company, an unlikely candidate to overcome AT&T. But much groundwork had already been laid by much larger companies in bringing about Above 890 and "open skies" in satellites.

Airlines pose a difficult case. Until the very end, when the die was cast, no major carrier wanted deregulation, nor did any other organized interest. Aircraft manufacturers have been a major beneficiary of deregulation, but they played no role in the deregulation debate. Here the most plausible explanation is political entrepreneurship by Senator Kennedy and then-president Carter. We find no plausible interest group account of their advocacy of deregulation or of Carter's great care in seeking out CAB appointees who would carry out the deed. In choosing between political entrepreneurship and the force of economic ideas, we simply cannot bring ourselves to choose the latter because ideas did not work elsewhere in the same period.

The general economic troubles of the 1970s were especially centered in the energy sector. Here the case that regulatory reform might actually address the economic problems associated with stagflation—the part associated with wildly fluctuating energy prices—was not the stretch that it was in the other regulated industries. In the late 1970s, Congress and the president believed that their political futures were at stake in doing something about energy. Gradual natural gas deregulation was surely a plausible move—deregulation because the economic disruption of the oil crisis had been exacerbated by the regulation-induced gas shortage, gradual because politicians naturally sought to avoid cataclysmic disruptions, even if gradualism is itself costly. Note that, a decade later, gradualism was also pursued in rationalizing telephone pricing.

In sum, our account is forced to give some role to almost all the theories discussed in section 6.1. Economics research seems to have played a role in most, but not all (i.e., telecommunications), of the reforms that we have reviewed. In most cases, some organized interests favored reform, but there are exceptions here as well (airlines and trucks). More important, the biggest interests rarely won. A minimal degree of organized support may be necessary, but, once the game has strong players on both sides, the winner does not usually seem to be the one that ought to have the most clout. Maybe this is when ideas matter. Indeed, while normative principles of efficiency are not sufficient for reform, they seem to have influenced the form that reform took once a policy change was at hand. Whereas the ultimate result was never the first-best solution from the economics textbooks, in every case economics had an important role in structuring the reform. Yet, in every case, the desire to avoid disruptive change and to protect some identifiable interest constrained the design of the reform in ways that reduced economic efficiency.

Certainly, the main question in the 1990s is whether these reforms are here to stay. Were it the case that they were largely the result of Reaganism, we would be skeptical of their durability, for Reaganism did not really survive even into Ronald Reagan's second term. But relaxation of economic regulation was not a Reagan reform, although parts of it were surely broadly in step with Reagan ideology and the Reagan administration aggressively pursued the regulatory liberalization reforms that began in the late 1970s. If anything, however, the Reagan administration *reduced* the chance that these reforms would endure: by refusing to let FAA programs expand in pace with airline growth after deregulation, by permitting several anticompetitive airline mergers, by failing to stop the banking debacle when the cost was still in the tens of billions, by allowing federal devolution to have priority over regulatory reform and so to be too deferential to states that seek to increase regulation (insurance, telecommunications), and by generally ignoring economic regulatory issues in the second term. The cost is likely to be increased regulation of an undesirable form in banking (rather than more rigorous financial scrutiny) and perhaps even a return to airline regulation. Nonetheless, most of the changes since 1975 seem to have proceeded too far and created too many interests to protect them to make reversal plausible. For the most part, these policy changes did improve the performance of regulated industries and did make consumers better off in ways that are clearly visible. In this sense, the "ideas" account again has some force. Relaxation of economic regulation *was* a good idea, and in most cases it has worked reasonably well.

References

Arrow, K. 1951. *Social Choice and Individual Values.* New York: Wiley.

Association of American Railroads. 1989. *Railroad facts.* Washington, D.C.

Bailey, E. E., D. R. Graham, and D. P. Kaplan. 1985. *Deregulating the airlines.* Cambridge, Mass.: MIT Press.

Barnekov, C. 1987. Railroad deregulation: The track record. *Regulation* 1:19–27.

Borenstein, S. 1989. Hubs and high fares: Dominance and market power in the U.S. airline industry. *Rand Journal of Economics* 20 (Autumn): 344–65.

———. 1990. Airline mergers, airport dominance, and market power. *American Economic Review* 80, no. 2:400–404.

Borenstein, S., and M. Zimmerman. 1988. Market incentives for safe commercial airline operation. *American Economic Review* 78, no. 5:913–35.

Braeutigam, R., and R. G. Hubbard. 1986. Natural gas: The regulatory transition. In *Regulatory reform: What actually happened,* ed. L. W. Weiss and M. W. Klass. Boston: Little, Brown.

Breyer, S. 1982. *Regulation and its reform.* Cambridge, Mass.: Harvard University Press.

Broadman, H., and D. Montgomery. 1983. *Natural gas markets after deregulation.* Washington, D.C.: Resources for the Future.

Carpenter, P., H. Jacoby, and A. Write. 1987. Adapting to change in natural gas markets. In *Energy: Markets and regulation,* ed. R. Gordon et al. Cambridge, Mass.: MIT Press.

Caves, R. 1962. *Air transport and its regulators.* Cambridge, Mass.: Harvard University Press.

Cohen, L. R., and S. A. Matthews. 1980. Constrained Plott equilibria, directorial equilibria, and global cycling sets. *Review of Economic Studies* 47:975–86.

Cohen, M. D., J. G. March, and J. P. Olson. 1972. A garbage can model of organizational choice. *Administrative Science Quarterly* 17:1–25.

Derthick, M., and P. Quirk. 1985. *The politics of deregulation.* Washington, D.C.: Brookings.

Douglas, G., and J. Miller III. 1974. *Economic regulation of domestic air transport.* Washington, D.C.: Brookings.

Downs, A. 1957. *An economic theory of democracy.* New York: Harper & Row.

Eads, G. C. 1972. *The local service airline experiment.* Washington, D.C.: Brookings.

———. 1975. Competition in the domestic trunk airline industry: Too much or too little. In *Promoting competition in regulated markets,* ed. A. Phillips. Washington, D.C.: Brookings.

Friedlaender, A. 1969. *The dilemma of freight transport regulation.* Washington, D.C.: Brookings.

Fuss, M. A. 1983. A survey of recent results in the analysis of production conditions in telecommunications. In *Economic analysis of telecommunications,* ed. L. Courville, A. de Fontenay, and R. Dobell. New York: North-Holland.

Gilligan, T. W., W. J. Marshall, and B. R. Weingast. 1989. Regulation and the theory of legislative choice: The interstate commerce act of 1887. *Journal of Law and Economics* 32 (April): 35–62.

Harrington, S. 1984. The impact of rate regulation on prices and underwriting results in the property-liability insurance industry: A survey. *Journal of Risk and Insurance* 51:577–623.

Herring, E. P. 1936. *Public administration and the public interest.* New York: McGraw-Hill.

Hilton, G. W. 1969. *The Transportation Act of 1958: A decade of experience.* Bloomington: Indiana University Press.

Industry Analysis Division. Common Carrier Bureau. Federal Communications Commission. 1989. Trends in telephone service, Washington, D.C., 15 February.

Interstate Natural Gas Association of America. 1989. Carriage through 1988. Issue Analysis no. 89–2. Washington, D.C., May.

Joskow, P. L. 1973. Cartels, competition and regulation in the property-liability insurance industry. *Bell Journal of Economics* 4:375–427.

———. 1990. The performance of long-term coal contracts: Further evidence from coal markets. *Rand Journal of Economics* 21, no. 2 (Summer): 251–74.

Joskow, P. L., and L. McLaughlin. 1991. McCarran-Ferguson Act reform: More competition or more regulation. *Journal of Risk and Uncertainty* 4:373–401.

Joskow, P. L., and R. G. Noll. 1981. Regulation in theory and practice: An overview. In *Studies in public regulation,* ed. Gary Fromm. Cambridge, Mass.: MIT Press.

Joskow, P. L., and N. L. Rose. 1989. The effects of economic regulation. In *The handbook of industrial organization.* vol. 2, ed. R. Schmalensee and R. D. Willig. New York: Elsevier Science.

Kahn, A. 1979. Applications of economics in an imperfect world. *American Economic Review* 69:1–13.

———. 1983. Deregulation and vested interests: The case of airlines. In *The political economy of deregulation: Interest groups in the regulatory process,* ed. R. Noll and B. Owen. Washington, D.C.: American Enterprise Institute.

Keeler, T. E. 1983. *Railroads, freight, and public policy.* Washington, D.C.: Brookings.

Kolko, G. 1965. *Railroads and regulation, 1877–1916.* Princeton, N.J.: Princeton University Press.

Lande, J. L. 1989. Telephone rates update. Washington, D.C.: Industry Analysis Division, Common Carrier Bureau, Federal Communications Commission, 3 February.

Levine, M. 1965. Is regulation necessary? California air transportation and national regulatory policy. *Yale Law Journal* 74:1416–47.

———. 1981. Revisionism revisited? Airline deregulation and the public interest. *Journal of Law and Contemporary Problems* 44:179–95.

Lyon, T. 1990. Natural gas policy: The unresolved issues. *Energy Journal* 11:23–49.

MacAvoy, P. W. 1971. The regulation-induced shortage of natural gas. *Journal of Law and Economics* 14:167–99.

———. 1973. The regulation-induced shortage of natural gas. *Bell Journal of Economics* 4:454–98.

MacAvoy, P. W., and R. S. Pindyck. 1973. Alternative regulatory policies for dealing with the natural gas shortage. *Bell Journal of Economics* 4:454–98.

Meyer, J. R., M. Peck, J. Stenason, and C. Zwick. 1959. *The economics of competition in the transport industries.* Cambridge, Mass.: Harvard University Press.

Moe, T. 1980. *The organization of interest.* Chicago: University of Chicago Press.

Moore, T. 1986. Rail and trucking deregulation. In *Regulatory reform: What actually happened,* ed. L. W. Weiss and M. W. Klass. Boston: Little, Brown.

———. 1988. Transportation policy. *Regulation* 3:57–62.

Morrison, S., and C. Winston. 1986. *The economic effects of airline deregulation.* Washington, D.C.: Brookings.

———. 1989. Enhancing the performance of the deregulated air transportation system. *Brookings Papers on Economic Activity: Microeconomics,* 61–112.

National Association of Regulatory Utility Commissioners. Various years. *Bell operating companies exchange service telephone rates.* Washington, D.C.

———. Various years. *Exchange service telephone rates.* Washington, D.C.

Noll, R. 1985. Let them make toll calls: A state regulators lament. *American Economic Review* 75:52–56.

———. 1989. Economic perspectives on the politics of regulation. In *Handbooks of industrial organization,* vol. 2, ed. R. Schmalensee and R. D. Willig. New York: Elsevier Science.

Noll, R. G., and Bruce Owen. 1988. The anticompetitive use of regulation: *U.S. v. AT&T.* In *The antitrust revolution,* ed. John Kwoka and Laurence White. New York: Scott Foresman.

———. 1989. United States vs. AT&T: An interim assessment. In *New competition in telecommunications,* ed. Stephen Bradley and Jerry Hausman. Boston: Harvard Business School Press.

Noll, R. G., and S. R. Smart. 1990. State telephone pricing after divestiture and federal deregulation. In *After the breakup,* ed. B. Cole. New York: Columbia University Press.

Official Airline Guide. Various issues. Oakbrook, Ill.: Official Airline Guides.

Olson, M. 1965. *The logic of collective action.* Cambridge, Mass.: Harvard University Press.

Peltzman, S. 1976. Toward a more general theory of regulation. *Journal of Law and Economics* 14:109–48.

———. 1989. The economic theory of regulation after a decade of deregulation. *Brookings Papers on Economic Activity: Microeconomics,* 1–41.

Posner, R. A. 1971. Taxation by regulation. *Bell Journal of Economics* 2:22–50.

Riker, W. H. 1982. *Liberalism against populism.* Prospect Heights, Ill.: Waveland.

Romer, T., and B. R. Weingast. 1990. The political foundations of the thrift debacle. Working paper. Cambridge, Mass.: NBER.

Rose, N. 1987. Labor rent-sharing and regulation: Evidence from the trucking industry. *Journal of Political Economy* 95:1146–78.

———. 1988. An economic assessment of surface freight transportation regulation. In *Economic deregulation: Promise and performance.* Proceedings of the 1987 Donald S. MacNaughton Symposium. Syracuse University.

———. 1990. Profitability and product quality: Economic determinants of airline safety performance. *Journal of Political Economy* 98, no. 5, pt. 1 (October): 944–64.

Rottenberg, S. 1989. *The cost of regulated pricing: A critical analysis of auto insurance premium rate-setting in Massachusetts.* Boston: Pioneer Institute.

Schmalensee, R. 1979. *The control of natural monopolies.* Lexington, Mass.: Lexington.

Sharkey, W. 1982. *The theory of natural monopoly.* Cambridge: Cambridge University Press.

Shepsle, K. A., and B. R. Weingast. 1981. Structure induced equilibrium and legislative choice. *Public Choice* 37:503–20.

Stigler, G. 1961. The economics of information. *Journal of Political Economy* 69:213–25.

———. 1971. The theory of economic regulation. *Bell Journal of Economics and Management Science* 2:3–21.

Teece, D. 1990. Structuring and regulation of the natural gas industry. *Energy Journal* 11, no. 1:1–36.

Temin, P., and L. Galambos. 1987. *The fall of the Bell system.* Cambridge: Cambridge University Press.

U.S. Department of Energy. Energy Information Administration. 1989. *Growth in unbundled natural gas transportation services: 1982–1987.* DOE/EIA-0525. Washington, D.C.

———. Various issues. *Monthly Energy Review.* Washington, D.C.

U.S. Department of Transportation. 1990a. *Executive Summary.* Washington, D.C., February. (This is a summary of U.S. Department of Transportation [1990d].)

———. 1990b. *Industry and Route Structure.* 2 vols. and *Executive Summary.* Washington, D.C., February. (Published in conjunction with U.S. Department of Transportation [1990d].)

———. 1990c. *Pricing.* 1 vol. and *Executive Summary.* Washington, D.C., February. (Published in conjunction with U.S. Department of Transportation [1990d].)

———. 1990d. *Secretary's task force on competition in the U.S. domestic airline industry.* Washington, D.C., February. (This is the umbrella study under which U.S. Department of Transportation [1990a, 1990b, and 1990c] are published.)

U.S. Senate. Committee on the Judiciary. 1975. *Oversight of civil aeronautics board practices and procedures.* Washington, D.C.: U.S. Government Printing Office.

———. Governmental Affairs Committee. 1977–78. *Study on federal regulation,* vols. 1–2. Washington, D.C.: U.S. Government Printing Office.

Warren, M., and K. Chilton. 1990. Regulation's rebound: Bush budget gives regulation a boost. Occasional Paper no. 81. Center for the Study of American Business, Washington University, May.

2. *William A. Niskanen*

One of the four "key elements" of Reagan's program of economic recovery was "a far-reaching program of regulatory relief." Despite that initial commitment, the Reagan administration made few proposals for new deregulatory legislation, and it did not manage the deregulation that had been previously approved especially well. My remarks today summarize the reasons for this outcome and, consistent with the structure of this conference, focus on the traditional subjects of economic regulation—leaving others to address the interesting issues involving the regulation of financial institutions; health, safety, and the environment; antitrust; and trade.[1]

Policies and People

The initial and continuing focus of the Reagan regulatory program was relief, not reform. In his December 1980 "economic Dunkirk" memo, David Stockman summarized the rationale for this approach: "A dramatic, substantial *recession* of the regulatory burden is needed for the short term cash flow it will provide to business firms and [for] the long term signal that it will provide to corporate investment planners. A major 'regulatory ventilation' will do as much to boost business confidence as tax or fiscal measures."[2] Most of this regulatory relief was to be accomplished by administrative rulings rather than by new legislation.

The new administration moved quickly to implement this approach during its first month in office. A Task Force on Regulatory Relief, chaired by Vice President George Bush, was established to provide general policy guidance. A large number of pending regulations were suspended for sixty days to permit review by the new administration, and the remaining price controls on oil and Carter's voluntary price and wage controls were terminated. The regulatory review was centralized under the Office of Information and Regulatory Affairs (OIRA), which was part of the Office of Management and Budget (OMB). The most important of these initial measures was a new executive order that instructed the executive agencies, to the extent permitted by law, to use the maximum net benefit criterion to choose among regulatory options. This executive order also established a special procedure for major regulations and authorized the OIRA to review all proposed rules prior to their publication in the *Federal Register.*

Most of the new appointees to regulatory positions had a strong commitment to deregulation. Two economists who had designed the initial regulatory agenda were soon appointed to key positions—Murray Weidenbaum as chair-

---

1. For obvious reasons, most of this summary is taken from Niskanen (1988, 115–54).
2. The "economic Dunkirk" memo is reproduced in Greider (1982, 137–59).

man of the Council of Economic Advisers (CEA) and James Miller as head of the OIRA. The most important other initial appointments included William Baxter as assistant attorney general for antitrust and Mark Fowler as chairman of the Federal Communications Commission (FCC). Many of the subsequent appointments also reaffirmed this commitment. I and Tom Moore each served four years as the microeconomic member of the CEA. Miller's successors as head of the OIRA were Chris DeMuth, Douglas Ginsburg, and Wendy Gramm. Miller later served as chairman of the Federal Trade Commission and Ginsburg as assistant attorney general for antitrust. The later appointment of Heather Gradison as chairman of the Interstate Commerce Commission proved important to forestall pressures to reregulate railroads and trucking. For the most part, the disappointing regulatory record of the Reagan administration cannot be blamed on a lack of skills or commitment on the part of those with the most direct responsibility.

The Record of Economic Regulation

A brief review of major developments in economic regulation illustrates the patterns of the Reagan record.

Agriculture

Two early reviews of agricultural marketing orders were aborted without substantial change. In 1979, a consumer group had innocently asked the Department of Agriculture to review the federal milk marketing orders. In April 1981, however, the department denied this request on the basis of estimates that a more efficient distribution of milk production would increase the federal budget costs of supporting milk prices. A major review of the broader set of marketing orders led to a preliminary 1982 decision to eliminate the restrictions on entry and to increase substantially the limits on the rules of fresh products. A storm of protest from California citrus growers, however, led the administration to modify the final 1983 guidelines, which phased out the entry restrictions on two small crops and only slightly increased the sales limits on the major crops. Congress locked up this decision by one of the first of many new "muzzling laws" that prohibited any further expenditure of funds to study this issue.

Communications

The major changes in the regulation of communications were the result of forceful early initiatives by two individuals, Mark Fowler and Bill Baxter. In 1981, the FCC deregulated most radio broadcasting restrictions, implemented a simplified system for renewing radio licenses, and induced Congress to extend the license period for both radio and television stations and to authorize a lottery system for the award of new licenses. The later record, however, was mixed. A 1983 initiative to relax the "financial interest and syndication rules," which restrict the right of television networks to develop original programming and to syndicate reruns, was stopped by "the California mafia" in the White House responding to pressures from Hollywood. In 1984, Congress approved the full deregulation of cable rates but did not approve any new entry into the monopoly cable markets. After the sharp subsequent increase in cable rates, Congress may soon compound this error by reregulating cable rates, again without permitting new entry. And the major missed opportunity was the failure to change the system for allocating the electronic frequency spectrum, a system that corresponds roughly to the way the Soviets run their economy. As a consequence, some new technologies have been delayed even though large parts of the spectrum are underutilized.

The major change in communications regulation was the result of Baxter's January 1982 resolution of the long-standing antitrust case against AT&T. Under the threat of a court decision imposing a divestiture plan, Baxter and AT&T worked out a plan, effective in 1984, that allowed AT&T to maintain its long-distance services, its unregulated communications services, and its manufacturing company but required it to divest its twenty-two local operating companies. As expected, this decision led to a substantial reduction in long-distance rates and a substantial increase in the (state-regulated) local rates. This decision was not broadly popular, and Congress considered more than a dozen bills to stop or limit the increase in subscriber charges. After a considerable amount of populist posturing, Congress forced the FCC to delay the access charge ruling but did not reverse this basic change in the structure of the telecommunications service industry.

Energy

After the important early decision to terminate the price controls on oil, the administration's later record on energy regulation was disappointing. A simple bill to deregulate the wellhead prices of natural gas was approved by the cabinet council in 1982 but was deferred by the White House as part of a general strategy of avoiding any more controversial issues prior to the election. A more complicated 1983 proposal by the Department of Energy received no support in Congress. The reaction by both the White House and Congress was based on a broadly shared but incorrect expectation that decontrol of natural gas would have increased retail gas prices.[3] In the end, the Federal Energy Regulatory Commission effectively decontrolled gas prices by setting price caps that, until this summer, were above market prices. And, in 1988, Congress quietly terminated the Fuel Use Act, which had restricted the use of oil and natural gas in new power plants. The administration also equivocated on other energy issues. For example, the required corporate average fuel economy on new cars was administratively reduced by one mile per gallon, but the administration

3. For my own analysis of the effects of controls on the wellhead prices of natural gas, see Niskanen (1986).

would not propose the termination of this absurd law; Congress is now considering a large proportionate increase in the required fuel economy—a measure that, not incidentally, would be biased against Japanese cars.

Labor

The Department of Labor made several administrative changes in the regulations affecting work under federal construction contracts and on work at home but would not propose a change in the laws authorizing these regulations. The only major legislative proposal was to authorize a lower minimum wage for teenage summer employment, a proposal that was strongly rejected by Congress.

Transportation

The Reagan administration and Congress made only small changes to extend or complement the major transportation deregulation measures instituted during the Carter administration. In 1982, the administration concluded an agreement with the major European nations to permit greater flexibility in the fares on transatlantic flights. Also in 1982, Congress approved the full deregulation of intercity bus travel—a measure that provoked little controversy because there never was a basis for regulating that industry and the demand for bus service had slowly declined in response to rising income and airline deregulation. And, in 1984, Congress approved the Shipping Act to enable ocean shipping companies to offer lower rates and better services than permitted by the shipping conferences. The administration's proposal to terminate the Interstate Commerce Commission on its centennial in 1987, however, fell on deaf ears, and the ICC still maintains considerable authority that could be used to reregulate trucking and the railroads.

The major missed opportunity was the failure to reform, expand, or privatize the airports and airways systems in response to the large increase in commercial flights induced by airline deregulation. For example, the number of air traffic controllers is now about the same as before the 1981 strike, and the system for allocating landing slots at congested airports has yet to be rationalized as no new major airport has been built for fifteen years. In late 1985, after several years of pressure from the OIRA and the CEA, the Department of Transportation approved the resale of landing slots at the four most crowded airports, but this action was later challenged by Congress. In 1988, the department even overruled an increase in landing fees on light aircraft using Logan Airport. And the administration showed no interest in several proposals to subcontract or privatize parts of the airports and airways systems. The failure to follow airline deregulation with complementary changes in the airports and airways system is the primary reason for the increased airport congestion and airline delays and the background rumbles, primarily from business travelers, for some reregulation.

Patterns and Lessons

The major pattern of the Reagan record on economic regulation was the attempt to rely primarily on administrative deregulation and the reluctance to propose changes in legislation that would extend or lock in prior deregulation. The primary reason for this pattern is that regulatory relief was clearly the lowest priority of the four key elements of the Reagan economic program. This should not be surprising. The other key elements were more ambitious and promised clearer benefits. Deregulation usually leads to diffused benefits and concentrated costs. Some types of deregulation were checked by campaign commitments that Reagan had made to the construction, trucking, and maritime unions and by business interests, especially in California, to which the administration was responsive.

The major lesson from this record is that the potential for administrative deregulation is quite limited. The able people who led the OIRA probably pushed the White House regulatory review process as much as possible, given the limited change in regulatory legislation. Their aggressive actions to review, modify, or delay regulatory proposals initiated by the executive agencies, however, were ultimately checked by both Congress and the courts. On several occasions, Congress threatened to constrain the authority of the OIRA or to eliminate its funding, a controversy that has not yet been resolved. (For example, the position of the head of the OIRA has not been filled for over a year, and Congress is again bargaining with the administration over measures that would reduce the authority of the OIRA.) A more explicit construct was the application of a "hard look" doctrine by the federal court of appeals for the District of Columbia to proposals for both regulation and deregulation. The primary effect of this doctrine is to require a more explicit rationale, based on the criteria in the regulatory legislation, for regulatory changes of any kind. This role of the courts, a position generally endorsed by the Reagan administration, increases the importance of changing the regulatory legislation if the momentum for deregulation is to be revived.

Another lesson is that budget policy sometime got in the way of good regulatory policy. This was first apparent when David Stockman agreed to the egregious sugar program in exchange for a few votes on the fiscal year 1982 budget. Our budget accounting conventions are also a problem. Since user fees are treated as an offsetting receipt, for example, both the deposit insurance funds and the airports and airways fund showed negative net outlays for most of the Reagan years, despite a rapid increase in liabilities and investment backlogs. The objective of any budget director to limit measured budget outlays was part of the reason why the administration was slow to address both the deposit insurance disaster and the increased airline delays. The major current threat of mandated benefits of several kinds, in turn, is primarily a consequence of the perception that it is difficult to expand the welfare state through the federal fisc. We still need a system that forces a review of the costs of proposed and recurring federal actions of all kinds.

For all these problems, the Reagan regulatory record was probably better than average. The total costs of regulation, as measured by several indirect indices, increased at a slower rate than at any time since the 1950s. For those of us who were directly involved, however, this record was very disappointing. Some mistakes and, more important, the missed opportunities failed to sustain the momentum for deregulation initiated in the 1970s and set the stage for what portends to be a regulatory explosion in the 1990s.

References

Greider, William. 1982. *The education of David Stockman and other Americans.* New York: Dutton.
Niskanen, William A. 1986. Natural gas price controls: An alternative view. *Regulation* 10 (November/December): 46–50.
———. 1988. *Reaganomics: An insider's account of the policies and the people.* New York: Oxford University Press.

3. *Elizabeth Bailey*

I agree that much of the momentum for deregulation was set in the 1970s. But I am more upbeat than Bill Niskanen because I see a lot of progress in the evolution of decontrol policies during the 1980s. The airline industry went the farthest. Its regulatory agency, the Civil Aeronautics Board (CAB), was fully dismantled in the 1980s. This was a major achievement.

Moreover, a number of effective policies for dismantling economic regulation were designed in the 1980s for trucks and rail. True, their regulatory agency, the Interstate Commerce Commission, continues to exist. But the actual fact, I think, is that most goods are now moving largely by contract and therefore largely outside the regulatory web.

For other industries, like electric utilities, gas pipelines, and telecommunications, the 1980s ushered in what economist Alfred Kahn calls a "half regulated, half free" system. Yet, even here, I see evolution. I see some coherent direction in the design of decontrol policy.

While I agree with Paul Joskow and Roger Noll that policy implementation across industries has been imperfect and sometimes reflects political (rather than economic) influence, nevertheless I see more of a unifying policy theme than they do. Moreover, the theme relates very much to economic ideas. Decontrol policies of the 1980s have been influenced by the ideas, not of defunct economists, but of economists who are living today and who have participated as deregulators and as witnesses before Congress and the courts.

Public intervention is still undertaken. But, now, the preference is to seek policies that move in the direction of the market economy, of competition. Policies are designed to promote actual and potential competition instead of to preclude it by preventing entry. The focus is now on figuring out in a much more systematic way how markets can be successful.

Alfred Kahn recently expressed a similar view about the evolution of regulatory policy. He says that evolution "is the path not of a full circle or pendulum which would take us back to where we started," as was discussed by Charls Walker this morning with tax policy. Instead, the path is that "of a spiral, which has a direction. That direction is an expression of a preference for seeking consistently to move in the direction of the first-best functioning of a market economy, rather than the second- or third-best world of centralized command and control" (Kahn 1990, 353–54).

Let me go back in history a little bit and outline how this shift of people's attitudes from detailed regulation to a preference for market freedom took place. When economic regulation was first designed in the late nineteenth century, both transportation and communications were inconvenient and costly. So it made economic sense to encourage industry-wide natural monopolies and oligopolies to promote efficiency in supply.

I think the government had other motivations as well. Economic development was considered extremely important, and there was a criterion of equity. Service was needed to all parts of the United States at a reasonable cost as we underwent western expansion. Over time, however, economic development goals were largely satisfied. Services were universally available and at reasonable prices. There was also technological change that was lowering cost and bringing new modes of transportation and communications into being. Increasingly, rules that were designed for railroads were extended inappropriately to more competitive modes, like air and truck. The government started to maintain equity, not just for rural consumers, but between modes of transportation and between different carriers and players within industries. Regulations became even more cumbersome, and scholars began to discover and to highlight regulatory failures as being worse than the market failures that regulation was meant to address. Hearings in aviation in the early 1970s were the most dramatic example of bringing these regulatory failures to public attention (see Breyer 1982).

The Kennedy hearings dramatized the fact that the CAB was holding air fares at a high level that prevented many ordinary citizens from using them. Citizens were offered much lower prices in states, such as California and Texas, that had decontrolled interstate prices. It was demonstrated that the market worked much better for consumers than did regulation.

So the attitude that favored regulation began to change. The imperfections of competition were deemed to be preferable to the imperfections of regulation. The new decontrol policy has been codified in a modern, more refined version of workable competition, known as contestability theory or contestability-enhancing principles (see Baumol, Panzer, and Willig 1982; and Bailey 1991).[1] These principles dictate removing regulatory and antitrust barriers that prevent the access of competition or that prevent competitive pricing or contracting. They include making an effort to free markets that can be competitive. Similarly, they include examining markets to see whether potential competition is workable before actual share of market is taken to be a sign of monopoly power.

Even when sunk costs are significant, traditional rate and entry regulation may not be necessary: where possible, government should intervene to ensure equal access to the sunk facility. If the facility is privately owned, government should require equal access by all users at equal prices. If the facility is owned by a public authority, then that authority should have open access among its users. If it is not possible to ensure equal access, sunk investments should be isolated. That portion of the industry should continue to be regulated. Even here, however, a form of regulation should be adopted that permits as much freedom of contracting and other operating flexibility as possible.

These prescriptions are displayed to a remarkable degree in the U.S. decontrol movement of the 1970s and early 1980s. They provide a unifying theme for otherwise quite diverse industry situations.

In aviation, open entry into city-pair routes was seen as providing multiple competing airlines in most traffic markets. The threat of potential competitors was thought to offer an acceptable constraint on monopoly pricing in thin traffic markets. Thus, the Airline Deregulation Act of 1978 opened entry fully in all markets. One year later, full upward pricing freedom was to be conferred. The industry thought to be the most contestable was thus the most fully deregulated.

In railroads, the 1976 Railroad Revitalization and Regulatory Reform Act (the 4R Act) offered price freedom when shippers had competitive alternatives from competing railroads or more broadly from trucks and barges. Regulation was continued in situations, such as coal transport, where a particular railroad holds a position of market dominance. So that was a very appropriate way, from the contestability stance, of sorting out what needed to be done in that industry.

In telecommunications, technological change meant that competition was now possible in long-distance services. Contestability theory would say that these markets should be deregulated. The Department of Justice (DOJ) reasoned that, for this deregulation to succeed, it was necessary to divest AT&T of its local exchange services. Then AT&T would be unable to use its geo-

---

1. The philosophy that competition is the preferred policy as long as the free market can achieve a level of performance at least as high as can be enjoyed under government regulation or ownership dates its origins to Clark (1940).

graphical control at the local exchange level to thwart competition in long-distance markets. The divested local exchange companies were deemed not to be competitive given today's technology. So price regulation was continued for local exchange services. Equipment manufacturing is competitive structurally and therefore was opened for the most part to competitive forces. So the broad framework of divestiture was consistent with the theory.

In gas transport, the Federal Energy Regulatory Commission (FERC) opened competition by changing the rules of supply. Now distributors and end-use customers can purchase gas directly in the field in competition with one another and with pipelines. Pipelines are constrained to transport this gas at nondiscriminatory rates. So the logic of decontrol is evident here as well.

In the electric utility industry, beginning efforts are being made to recognize that the generation layer of the industry has the potential for competitiveness. Thus, there has been some deregulation of wholesale bulk power sales. The distribution function, where sunk costs are still substantial, continues to be regulated.

Therefore, despite the variety of different interest groups, from legislators to bureaucrats to academicians to executives, who were involved in policy setting for these industries in 1970s and 1980s, I believe that there was implicit consensus on the central ideas that guided the control movement.

It is as though the same energies were tapped into by the various protagonists in this period. The shared flow of thought had coalesced during the preceding decades of regulatory oversight. The switch from the focus on market failure was necessitated by the dynamics of competitors trying to gain access to markets. Economists, regulators, and antitrust administrators became used to dialogues in which parties actively spent more and more of their time not thinking about natural monopoly but instead thinking about why entry should be permitted in markets that previously had been shielded from entry. A new entrant desiring to participate in long-distance telecommunications services would force one expert witness into developing the idea that such services were no longer natural monopolies. A responding witness would develop a test to show that a low price response to competitive entry was acceptable since it did not place an unwarranted burden on the consumers of the firm's monopoly services.

And so was forged, by a process of conflict, a framework of consensus.

The transition to the freer environment has been dynamic and turbulent. Certain groups have gained, such as customers in dense markets. Other groups have both gained and lost, such as customers in thin markets where service has improved but price has risen. Other groups have lost, such as organized labor, whose pay is declining to competitive levels. So there has been controversy. There has also been further evolution in decontrol policy as some of the performance results have been analyzed and understood. Some degree of experimentation continues to take place.

The railroad industry has experimented with price caps and stand-alone cost concepts in dealing with continued regulation of captive markets, such as coal transport to public utilities. These ideas have been most efficacious for they offer the protection of regulation in setting overall price ceilings while encouraging freedom of contracting. Most of the coal movements now operate not under the regulatory tariffs but instead under very sophisticated contracts that set a number of conditions on investment and performance as well as price. These ideas could beneficially be spread to other deregulatory settings, especially telecommunications and gas pipelines.

In telecommunications, decontrol policy could be made much more bold. Because of the price distortions of state regulation, the prices of long-distance services have been held way above costs in order that prices of local, particularly rural, services can be low. This structure has encouraged massive entry and investment in duplicative switches and fiber optic cable during the decontrol period. While costly, there is the benefit that full deregulation of long-distance services could now be justified, and this may happen soon. So, even though AT&T still has a very big market share, several other firms now have the potential to serve the entire market. Similarly, total deregulation of telephone equipment is warranted, including lifting the restriction that prevents local operating companies from entering this business.

In airlines, it is now recognized that the industry is imperfectly contestable. Fortress hubs and computer reservations systems have sunk cost characteristics. Hubs, involving a whole system of routes that need simultaneously to be offered, constitute an entry barrier and hence afford geographic rents to carriers. In addition, few carriers now have the resources to construct and deploy computer reservations systems. Competition is working reasonably well, but there is a balance between quite low prices in competitive city-pair markets and higher prices on monopoly routes and at concentrated airports. The DOJ realizes that both hubs and reservations systems have brought service benefits to consumers even as they have reinforced the oligopolistic characteristics of the industry. Rather than reregulate, however, DOJ intervention is being undertaken on a case-by-case basis to keep the degree of these rents reasonable. Other important issues in aviation are the need to find airport polices that address airport congestion issues now and for the future and the need for policies that preserve an adequate number of competitors in the industry.

Perhaps the industry most in need of systematic application of contestability-enhancing decontrol policies is the electric utility industry. Just as railroad rates of return were set too low by regulators in past decades, so today state regulators are allowing electric utilities rates that are insufficient to finance new plant construction, both in terms of transmission facilities and generation. Moreover, in both electric and gas utilities, partial deregulation has introduced price distortions that encourage uneconomic bypass. For example, private firms are finding it cheaper to construct billions of dollars of direct pipelines rather than pay the high cross-subsidy prices set for common carrier services.

To conclude, I will say that I am confident that deregulation is the right policy for the long run, but I know that it continues to present difficulties today. However, I do not believe that we are going to backslide, as Bill Niskanen is concerned. Full economic regulation just does not make sense at a time when the pressures for market economies are manifesting themselves throughout the world. Indeed, I think that the momentum from U.S. decontrol policies is responsible in no small measure for the move toward privatization and market economies in other countries. So the United States must continue to evolve policies that spiral in the direction of economic freedom, adopting a philosophy of minimalistic interventions.

References

Bailey, Elizabeth E. 1991. Contestability and the design of regulatory and antitrust policy. *American Economic Review* 71 (May): 178–83.
Baumol, William J., John C. Panzer, and Robert D. Willig. 1982. *Contestable markets and the theory of industry structure.* New York: Harcourt Brace Jovanovich.
Breyer, Steven. 1982. *A regulation and its reform.* Cambridge, Mass.: Harvard University Press.
Clark, J. M. 1940. Toward a concept of workable competition. *American Economic Review* 30 (June): 241–56.
Kahn, Alfred E. 1990. Deregulation: Looking backward and looking forward. *Yale Journal on Regulation* 7 (Summer): 325–54.

Summary of Discussion

Paul Joskow believed that people may underrate the actions of the Reagan administration regarding economic regulation. Joskow thought that this is partly because the administration had a very tough act to follow. In the late 1970s, there was both administrative deregulation and significant statutory changes, while there were fewer statutory changes in the 1980s.

Joskow argued, however, that the administration had prevented the regulatory situation from worsening in the 1980s, which had been a real threat. The Interstate Commerce Commission (ICC), for example, went beyond what the Carter administration had been willing to do. This was especially true in the case of railroads, where the ICC interpreted the law in such a way as to prevent the captive shippers from capturing the regulatory process again. Joskow wished that there had been a sunset provision for the ICC, like that for the Civil Aeronautics Board, but going through Congress to obtain that provision might have had greater costs than benefits.

The appointment of Mark Fowler to the Federal Communications Commission was also a good decision, according to Joskow. Fowler dealt very effectively with congressional concerns about changes in the telecommunications system after 1984, and, despite criticism, he maintained the system of adding access charges to local telephone bills.

Finally, with regard to natural gas, no one wanted to raise the issue of natural gas policy in the early 1980s, given what had happened in 1978. By 1983, it was probably not worth spending a lot of political capital in order to revise regulations that were scheduled to expire in 1985 anyway. By 1986, when the oil and gas markets collapsed, the regulations were no longer binding. Overall, Joskow felt that a fair appraisal of economic regulatory policy in the 1980s is between a B+ and an A−.

Robert Litan argued that there is tremendous latent demand on the part of the public for reregulation of prices whenever the price of a particular commodity begins to soar. Examples at the state level include attempts to regulate the prices of insurance and cable television. At the federal level, the move for reregulation of airlines is partly due to the high prices in St. Louis and Minneapolis and also partly due to a concern for safety and a widespread feeling that deregulation caused the whole mess. It is interesting, Litan added, that this demand for reregulation has not applied to oil prices. One reason may be that the Reagan administration dismantled oil price controls right at the beginning—the United States has not had controls on oil prices for ten years. The other reason is that most people remember the long lines in 1973–74 and associate them with the price controls. This may be one case in which latent demand for reregulation will not arise precisely because people draw the connection between price regulation and its adverse effects.

David Stockman asserted that the Reagan administration believed that economic regulation was wrong as a matter of first principles. He said that, if one looked at the economy in 1979, perhaps $400–$500 billion of GNP was regulated: oil, gas, trucking, railroads, even airlines were just coming out of regulation. Now all that regulation is gone, and there is very little likelihood that the political system could build it back up again—there are too many players who benefit from an open market. Thus, Stockman believed that the battle of first principles had been won and further, had diffused throughout the entire world. Deregulation was not only a domestic success but also a global victory that will have huge consequences for a long time to come.

7 Health and Safety Regulation

1. W. Kip Viscusi
2. Christopher DeMuth
3. James Burnley

1. W. Kip Viscusi

The Misspecified Agenda: The 1980s Reforms of
Health, Safety, and Environmental Regulation

7.1 The Agenda for Regulatory Reform

The 1970s marked the advent of a new wave of regulation of health, safety, and the environment.[1] Congress created a series of new agencies with broad responsibilities, including the Occupational Safety and Health Administration (OSHA), the Environmental Protection Agency (EPA), the National Highway Traffic Safety Administration (NHTSA), the Consumer Product Safety Commission (CPSC), and the Nuclear Regulatory Commission (NRC). Although some of these agencies consolidated the functions previously dispersed among other smaller agencies, the sweeping legislative mandates given to these agencies marked a dramatic increase in the level of regulation of the American economy. Congress directed these agencies to promote health, safety, and environmental quality almost without compromise.

Expectations were high. One of the principal authors of OSHA's enabling

A variety of individuals read the draft manuscript and provided helpful comments, including Robert Crandall (Brookings), John F. Morrall and Arthur Fraas (OMB), James Kallenborn and Frank Frodyma (OSHA), and Christopher Schroeder and Henry Grabowski (Duke). Since none of these individuals shared all my views and some expressed specific disagreements, they should not be held responsible for any of my conclusions.

1. For history of the development of these regulatory agencies, see the discussions in MacAvoy (1979) and Cornell, Noll, and Weingast (1976).

legislation predicted that the agency would cut workplace injuries in half.[2] Engineering studies of traffic safety claimed automobile safety belts would dramatically reduce the carnage on the highways.[3]

This initial optimism was coupled with substantial resistance on the part of firms. These government regulations represented an intrusion into previously unregulated decisions. Enterprises no longer had the freedom to select the most profitable technology. Instead they had to meet often quite explicit guidelines regarding the character and performance of these technologies. To make matters worse, there were also widespread suggestions that the regulations were ineffective in promoting their intended objectives.

It quickly became clear that these efforts were quite costly and that their economic impacts had to be monitored. These concerns provided the impetus for establishing White House regulatory oversight efforts.

The second general reaction to the new wave of regulation was that of dissatisfaction. Supporters of regulation demanded greater achievements that were commensurate with these agencies' responsibilities, and critics placed great emphasis on the low benefits relative to the dollars being expended. Regulatory reform for health, safety, and environmental regulation had become a prominent political issue less than one decade after the establishment of these agencies.

Although there was not unanimous agreement on the direction that these agencies should take, there were a number of central themes to these calls for reform.[4] Here I will review these guidelines for reform that emerged in the economic literature and policy debates of the 1970s. These guidelines will serve as the reference point for assessing the regulatory reforms of the 1980s.

First, economists recognized that there were often legitimate market failures that needed to be addressed. Environmental problems involve a classic case of externalities. Moreover, imperfect consumer and worker information may impede market provision of safety. Market forces involving risk are not, however, completely absent. A series of studies in the 1970s documented labor market compensation for risk on the order of several hundred thousand dollars per statistical death for workers who had selected themselves into very high-risk jobs to as much as several million dollars per death for the more typical blue-collar worker (see Thaler and Rosen 1976; Smith 1976; and Viscusi 1979). Because of these constructive market forces, it is essential to ascertain that there is a legitimate market failure before determining that a regulation is warranted.

The second general principle is that one should obtain an assessment of

---

2. More specifically, Representative William Steiger predicted that injuries would be reduced by "50 percent or something like that." See his statement in U.S. Congress (1972, 274–78). See also Nichols and Zeckhauser (1981).

3. For a description of the optimistic projections, see the discussion in Peltzman (1975).

4. Perhaps the most comprehensive statement of the general principles that should guide regulatory reform appears in the U.S. Office of Management and Budget (1988).

the costs and benefits of the regulatory policy. Initially, the concern was with regulatory costs. The steel and automobile industries, for example, were hit particularly hard. Since these basic industries were in decline and threatened by foreign competition, ensuring that excessive government regulation was not the causal factor in their demise became a prominent concern.

Regulatory impacts should, however, be measured correctly. In assessing these costs and benefits, what matters is the value of the expected payoffs that will accrue to society. One should use the mean of the probability distribution rather than focusing on worst-case scenarios or, as many agencies do, the upper end of the 95 percent confidence interval for the risk level.[5]

Although assessing the impacts of policies is an essential prerequisite to sound policy choice, one must then utilize this information to select among policy alternatives. The third regulatory principle is that policy choices should be cost effective. Available policy alternatives that can achieve the same benefits at less cost are preferable. Another example of an inefficient regulatory alternative was the imposition of a requirement for a technological solution to air pollution problems by mandating the installation of scrubbers, whereas a lower-cost method of achieving the same benefits by altering the type of coal used would have been sufficient.[6]

A class of regulatory options viewed as being superior to existing regulations on cost-effectiveness grounds is that of performance-oriented alternatives.[7] Performance standards for the guarding of machines, for example, would not only be less costly than OSHA specification standards but would also pertain to more types of machine designs, thus reducing machine guarding risks for a larger number of workers. Similarly, use of protective equipment to avert hearing loss resulting from excessive noise exposure would impose considerably lower compliance costs than changing the workplace environment. Although there are legitimate debates regarding the feasibility of such performance-oriented alternatives, owing to the difficulties of monitoring compliance, the economic critics of regulatory agencies have urged these agencies at least to assess the merits of performance-oriented alternatives.

A fourth regulatory reform principle is that there should be an appropriate balancing of the benefits and costs of policies. Strict adherence to efficiency guidelines suggests that a benefit-cost test would be applicable, but the oversight process did not formally adopt this criterion until the 1980s. Even where a precise calculation of benefits and costs is not feasible, agencies should con-

5. In some instances, as in the case of EPA policy, the conservatism bias may be less scientifically based since there is an effort to ensure a "margin of safety" beyond the no-risk level. From an economic standpoint, the aversion of society to incurring risks should be reflected in the valuation of the payoffs rather than a misrepresentation of the probabilities that influence these payoffs (see Zeckhauser and Viscusi 1990; and Nichols and Zeckhauser 1986).

6. Lobbyists from the coal-producing areas likely to be most affected by a regulation permitting the choice of coal and focusing on the overall pollution level rather than on the means of attaining pollution control exerted substantial influence in determining this policy (see Crandall 1983).

7. See, e.g., the discussions in MacAvoy (1977) and Viscusi (1983).

sider the overall merits of the policy and pursue only those policies that they judge to be in society's best interests.

Although the degree to which economists adhere to strict compliance with a benefit-cost test varies, the importance of addressing efficiency concerns is widely accepted as an important role for economists active in these policy debates.[8] As the Carter administration's chairman of the Council of Economic Advisers, Charles L. Schultze, (1982, 62), observed:

> For this reason, I strongly believe that economists in government have a particular role to play in the area of micro policy, not merely as disinterested purveyors of technical advice, but as advocates. I am not merely offering the pious statement that the economists ought to favor efficiency. What I am saying is that in matters of specific micro policy, and within reasonable bounds, his role is to be the partisan advocate for efficiency *even when the result is significant income losses for particular groups*—which it almost always is.

Emphasis on the role of balancing of benefits and costs also leads to support for market-oriented alternatives. For example, one can achieve the efficient outcome with respect to environmental risks by appropriate pricing of pollution. Although there has been no effort to establish large-scale markets for pollution rights, under the Carter administration EPA introduced a number of innovative market-oriented options,[9] such as the bubble policy introduced in December 1979 (*Federal Register* 44 [11 December 1979]: 71779). The bubble policy was introduced only on a very limited basis just before the turn of the decade, but its originators hoped that this policy could be extended to enable firms to meet their pollution control objectives at less cost.

Even if these regulations were well designed, effective enforcement would be needed to ensure compliance. OSHA promulgated thousands of standards for health and safety, but it coupled these detailed requirements with very weak enforcement. The prospect that a firm would see an OSHA inspector was remote, as these inspectors visited firms with roughly the same frequency as the passage of Halley's comet. If an inspector did arrive, the penalties assessed were very low. Greater financial penalties were needed if firms were to have the proper safety investment incentives.

The final and perhaps most important theme that emerged was that there was a need for broad-based reform. The legislative mandates established by

8. For example, some economists such as Lave (1981) indicate a variety of decision criteria that can be applied other than simply benefit-cost analysis in its traditional form. However, even these modifications of the traditional benefit-cost framework provide for a greater degree of balancing than is achieved by the decisions of regulatory agencies.

9. EPA also introduced related efforts called *netting* and *banking*. The netting policy begun in 1976 enabled firms to achieve compliance even though one part of the plant was being modernized, thus avoiding the entire plant being held to the new source requirements. The banking policy enables firms to store their pollution rights if they are in compliance. See Crandall (1983) and, for a recent discussion of such policies, Hahn and Noll (1990).

Congress were overly restrictive and did not adequately recognize the economic trade-offs. All the enabling legislation for the risk and environmental agencies required that the agency promote the health or environmental objective, but none required that there be an explicit balancing of the costs and benefits of these efforts. Moreover, many of these pieces of legislation explicitly prohibited such trade-offs. The U.S. Supreme Court's interpretation of the Occupational Safety and Health Act is that the agency could not base its regulations on a formal benefit-cost test. Moreover, the Clean Air Act even more explicitly prohibits the consideration of costs of any kind in setting ambient air quality standards, much less utilizing benefit-cost analysis.

By far the most important need was for fundamental legislative reform to incorporate the opportunity for such balancing of cost and benefit considerations in the design of regulatory policy. Such changes are fundamental to any reform effort since the legislative mandates will limit the degree to which regulatory oversight activities will be able to influence the policies of the regulatory agencies. Short-term efforts to alter regulatory policies by slowing the pace of regulation or altering the enforcement effort will not yield long-run changes in the regulatory approach. Ultimately, the agency's enabling legislation will determine the shape of these policies.

A major failure of the Reagan regulatory reform effort is not just that such reforms were never achieved but that they were never even attempted. The legislative energies of the Reagan administration were devoted to tax reform rather than rewriting the legislative mandates of regulatory agencies. Although regulatory reform was one of the four key pillars of the Reagan economic program, it was generally viewed as meriting the lowest priority of the four major areas of concern. As a result, the reform measures that were introduced would necessarily have a short-term impact. Indeed, the deregulation effort did not even last through the first Reagan term.

My analysis begins with a discussion of the changes in institutional structure, notably the budgetary and staffing allocations of the regulatory agencies and the strengthening of the regulatory oversight mechanism. I then turn to the performance of the regulatory reform effort in altering the structure of regulation, promoting the balancing of benefits and costs, revamping existing regulations, and modifying the structure of new regulatory initiatives. I then examine changes in regulatory enforcement policy and the overall impact of health, safety, and environmental regulation in the 1980s.

The principal theme of this assessment is that there were two quite distinctive regulatory agendas during the two Reagan administrations. The first period, which covered most of the first Reagan term, was one of deregulation. There were a number of constructive changes, including the strengthening of the regulatory oversight mechanism, an improvement in the balancing of costs and benefits of regulatory policies, and selected new regulatory initiatives. These reform efforts failed to achieve their full potential because of the absence of fundamental legislative reform and, more generally, the absence of meaningful regulatory reform as contrasted with regulatory relief.

After the enthusiasm for the initial deregulation agenda waned, the regulatory approach came to resemble that of the pre-Reagan era. The pace of regulation and the implementation of these regulations became more vigorous, and there was little evidence that the character of the regulatory policies had undergone much more than a temporary interruption during the short-lived period of deregulation. The opportunity for sound regulatory reform through an appropriately specified reform agenda had been missed.

7.2   Budgetary and Staffing Trends

7.2.1   The Rationale for Cutbacks

For the usual economic process in which there are diminishing marginal benefits and rising marginal costs, economists would recommend a decrease in such activities once the incremental burdens exceed the benefits. This maxim also applies to regulatory policy if scaling back the degree of regulation will eliminate regulations whose net effects are adverse.

Straightforward application of this principle assumes that the policy mix is efficient. If we are not on the efficient frontier, then the main reform that is needed is to alter the character of the regulation. Although some regulations were excessively stringent, there is little evidence that the number and scope of safety and environmental regulations promulgated was too great. In contrast, for rate and entry regulation, there was a widespread consensus that regulatory restrictions of all kinds were unnecessary, as they impeded the efficient operation of markets. In these contexts, sound regulatory reform was synonymous with deregulation. Unfortunately, deregulation is not an appropriate objective for all classes of regulatory activity.

The need for better risk regulation rather than deregulation was also stressed by leading economists in Reagan's regulatory reform effort. Shortly after Reagan's election, the future chairman of the Council of Economic Advisers, Murray Weidenbaum (1980, 15), observed: "In the case of the newer social regulation, which typically attempts to correct imperfections in the market (so-called externalities, meaning the costs imposed by one segment of the economy on another), the approach should be to seek out the most effective and the least burdensome methods of achieving the desired objectives."

The distinctions made by other administration spokesmen were less refined. Office of Management and Budget Director David Stockman called for a "substantial rescission of the regulatory burden," with a need for a major "regulatory ventilation" to assist American business.[10] President Reagan subsequently

---

10. Stockman's comments are based on his December 1980 memorandum "Avoiding a GOP Economic Dunkirk," which is reproduced in Greider (1982, 137–59).

established the Presidential Task Force on Regulatory Relief headed by Vice-President Bush, with a notable emphasis on relief rather than reform. In reflecting on the regulatory achievements of the Reagan administration, President Reagan observed,

> Over the last 7 1/2 years, we have substantially reduced that burden, cutting red tape and slowing the pace of new regulation.
> When I became President in 1981, I directed that Federal agencies, within the scope afforded by law, should reduce the excess burden of government regulation that is borne by every worker, consumer, business, and state and local government in this Nation. Under the guidance of the Presidential Task Force on Regulatory Relief, Federal agencies have eliminated unnecessary regulatory costs ranging in the tens of billions of dollars.[11]

Achieving a balance between regulatory costs and risk reductions had become a subsidiary concern. Deregulation had become the fundamental policy objective during the initial years of the Reagan administration.

7.2.2   Shifts in Budgets and Staffing

One mechanism for scaling back the role of government regulation is to cut back on an agency's budget and staff. In the extreme case, one could eliminate an agency altogether.

A prominent target for elimination was the Consumer Product Safety Commission. This small-scale product safety agency had a disappointing performance record from the standpoint of both supporters and opponents of the overall function of the agency. Short of abolition, another possibility was to move this independent commission into the executive branch by making it an agency under an existing cabinet member, thus increasing the potential for executive oversight. Although there were suggestions that such options were under consideration, no serious efforts were made to achieve a restructuring. The policy option chosen instead was to cut back on the agency's activities. From 1980 to 1989, the CPSC budget dropped by one-fourth (table 7.1), and its staffing declined by over 40 percent.

These extreme cutbacks are not the only instance of increasing budgetary stringency. In terms of staffing, the summary statistics at the bottom of table 7.2 indicate that there was an overall drop of personnel in all the risk agencies listed in this table. The fringe advisory groups—the Council on Environmental Quality and the Occupational Safety and Health Review Commission—experienced particularly dramatic declines in their staff.

For most agencies, the general pattern from 1980 to 1985 was one of fairly stable nominal budgets but declining personnel. From 1985 to 1989, there was a stabilization and in some cases an expansion of the regulatory agencies. The case of OSHA is particularly noteworthy. OSHA's staff in 1980 was almost one

---

11. See the statement by Ronald Reagan in the U.S. Office of Management and Budget (1988, viii).

Table 7.1   **Budgetary Trends for Principal Health, Safety, and**
Environmental Agencies

	Obligations ($millions) by Fiscal Year			
	1975	1980	1985	1989
Environmental Protection Agency	794	1,360	1,928	3,309
Council on Environmental Quality	4	8	1	1
Occupational Safety and Health Adm. (DOL)	97	191	220	248
Mine Safety and Health Adm. (DOL)	67	144	150	162
Food and Drug Adm. (HHS)	207	334	437	530
Nat'l Highway Traffic Safety Adm. (DOT)	104	136	114	133
Federal Aviation Adm. (DOT)	196	281	294	424
Consumer Product Safety Commission	37	43	36	34
Nuclear Regulatory Commission	148	396	445	421
National Transportation Safety Board	10	17	22	25
Food Safety and Inspection Service (DOA)	. . .	381	405	457
Occupational Safety and Health Review Commission	5	7	6	6
Total	1,669	3,298	4,058	5,750

Source: Warren and Chilton (1990, table A-1). Agency selection and totals calculated by the author.
Note: DOL = Department of Labor; HHS = Department of Health and Human Services; DOT = Department of Transportation; DOA = Department of Agriculture.

Table 7.2   **Staffing Trends for Principal Health, Safety, and**
Environmental Agencies

	Permanent Full-Time Positions by Fiscal Year			
	1975	1980	1985	1989
Environmental Protection Agency	11,004	11,615	13,978	15,321
Council on Environmental Quality	50	32	11	9
Occupational Safety and Health Adm. (DOL)	2,435	3,015	2,176	2,415
Mine Safety and Health Adm. (DOL)	2,940	3,857	2,829	2,671
Food and Drug Adm. (HHS)	6,441	7,419	7,104	7,226
Nat'l Highway Traffic Safety Adm. (DOT)	881	874	640	652
Federal Aviation Adm. (DOT)	6,947	6,692	6,358	4,556
Consumer Product Safety Commission	884	871	502	487
Nuclear Regulatory Commission	2,006	3,041	3,318	3,078
National Transportation Safety Board	310	388	357	324
Food Safety and Inspection Service (DOA)	. . .	13,213	9,839	8,962
Occupational Safety and Health Review Commission	172	165	94	74
Total	34,070	51,182	47,206	45,775

Source: Warren and Chilton (1990, table A-2). Agency selection and totals calculated by the author.
Note: See table 7.1.

and a half times greater than it was in 1985. These cutbacks primarily affected the OSHA inspection personnel, as there was a dramatic decrease in the OSHA enforcement staff. By decreasing the enforcement effort, the government could reduce the burden on business imposed by government regulation. Decreasing the enforcement stringency did not, however, address the long-term reform need, which was a restructuring of the standards that would be enforced. The extent of the decreased inspection effort may not have been of major consequence, however, since the probability of inspection was already quite low and did not change much in the early 1980s. By 1989, the OSHA staff and budget had increased substantially from its 1985 level, but in terms of personnel OSHA remained below its level in 1980.

The principal exception to these adverse trends was EPA. Although there were cutbacks at EPA during the Gorsuch era, these cuts were quickly reversed. Because of the increased responsibilities of EPA over an increasingly broad range of hazards including unconventional pollutants, such as hazardous wastes and toxic substances, both the budget and the number of personnel of this agency rose considerably in the 1980s. Indeed, the total EPA budget in 1989 was more than double its 1980 level.

Altering budgetary allotments and personnel in the manner indicated in tables 7.1 and 7.2 is much easier to achieve than a fundamental shift in the character of policy. Overhauling an agency's regulatory structure is a daunting task, as the performance record considered below will indicate. However, reducing an agency's expenditures and staffing within the context of broadly based cutbacks in taxes and government programs simultaneously achieves regulatory relief as well as economic savings.

In some cases, the loss in safety from these cutbacks was not great. The Occupational Safety and Health Review Commission, for example, plays only a minor advisory role. Moreover, the overall emphasis of the cutbacks was correct. EPA merited the greatest increases since it had the fastest-growing regulatory agenda. New classes of environmental risks emerged to augment the traditional concerns of the agency with air pollution, water pollution, and pesticides as well as the increased concern with long-term hazards such as acid rain and global warming. Although the overall cutback strategy appears to have been ill chosen, the realignment of the relative degrees of responsibility among these agencies appears to have been correct.

7.3   The Regulatory Oversight Process

Although appointments to regulatory agencies are an important mechanism for influencing policy, the incentives of the agencies' career staff and the pressures exerted by the traditional constituencies lead to the need for some form of executive branch oversight. Unlike legislative initiatives, regulations do not require congressional action. Judicial review will also not be sufficient since the agency generally has broad leeway subject to its legislative mandate and the provisions of the Constitution.

7.3.1   Regulatory Oversight in Previous Administrations

To address the costs imposed by regulations, President Nixon introduced informal quality of life reviews. This framework took on more structure within the Ford administration, as President Ford established a formal oversight process whereby regulatory agencies were required to prepare an inflationary impact statement assessing the effect of major regulations on productivity and costs (Executive Order 11821, 24 November 1974). In addition, the Ford administration established the Council on Wage and Price Stability in 1974 to oversee this oversight effort. The Council's legislation enabled it to "intervene and otherwise participate on its own behalf in rulemaking, ratemaking, licensing, and other proceedings before any of the departments and agencies of the United States, in order to present its views as to the inflationary impact that might result from the possible outcomes of such proceedings." The agency's authority was advisory in nature, and it covered independent and executive branch regulatory agencies.

President Carter bolstered the structure of this review process by requiring that regulatory analyses show that "alternative approaches have been considered and the least burdensome of the acceptable alternatives have been chosen" (Executive Order 12044, 24 March 1978). This requirement was tantamount to a cost-effectiveness test. The Council on Wage and Price Stability remained the main oversight group responsible for overseeing this effort. Carter also established a Regulatory Council to track agencies' upcoming regulatory agenda in its regulatory calendar. These activities were supplemented by a new body within the executive office of the president—the Regulatory Analysis Review Group (RARG). RARG consisted of representatives from the Council of Economic Advisers, various branches of the White House (domestic policy staff, Council on Wage and Price Stability, and Office of Management and Budget), and various executive branch agencies that served on a rotating basis. This interagency group prepared assessments of selected major regulatory activities that were then filed in the rule-making proceedings by the Council on Wage and Price Stability. These advisory efforts laid the substantive groundwork for lobbying by leading White House officials—the chairman of the Council of Economic Advisers and the inflation advisor to the president, Alfred E. Kahn.

Although these advisory efforts sometimes influenced the structure of regulations and, perhaps more important, educated the regulatory agencies concerning the appropriate perspective they should take in assessing prospective regulations, there was general agreement that the process needed to be strengthened. So long as the oversight activities remained advisory in nature, their ultimate impact would be modest. Second, the economic tests applied to new regulations did not require that agencies strike any balance between the benefits and the costs of regulations, only that they attempt to achieve a particular objective as cheaply as possible, however ill chosen that objective might be.

7.3.2   Reagan's Oversight Process

The Reagan administration quickly restructured the oversight process. First, it abolished the Council on Wage and Price Stability so as to eliminate the wage and price standards role of the council that had emerged during the Carter administration. The council's regulatory oversight staff then moved to the Office of Management and Budget. From an institutional standpoint, this change enhanced the leverage that the regulatory oversight process could exert since it was more closely involved with budgetary and staffing decisions. The only disadvantage is that the abolition of the council also eliminated the legislative authority to intervene in the rule-making proceedings of independent agencies, such as the FTC and CPSC.

The leading economic participants in the development of the initial oversight effort were CEA Chairman Murray Weidenbaum and James C. Miller III, the administrator of the Office of Information and Regulatory Affairs (OIRA) at the Office of Management and Budget (OMB). Miller was an experienced regulatory reformer, having served as an official at the Council on Wage and Price Stability during the Ford administration.[12] The day after his inauguration, President Reagan established the Presidential Task Force on Regulatory Relief chaired by Vice President Bush, with Miller serving as the executive director. Shortly thereafter, on 17 February 1981, President Reagan promulgated Executive Order 12291, which established the major ingredients of the new regulatory oversight structure.

This executive order instituted two major changes. First, agencies were required to show that the benefits of regulations exceeded their costs and that they had chosen the policy option that maximized the net benefits to society. Although agencies were exempted from this requirement when it violated their legislative mandate, even in these situations the agency was required to assess, but not necessarily compare, benefits and costs. Unfortunately, the exemption pertaining to conflicts with legislative mandates is the central provision, not a minor nuance. Since all health, safety, and environmental agencies are governed by restrictive legislative mandates that limit benefit-cost trade-offs, in practice OMB cannot require that these regulations satisfy a benefit-cost test.

The second component of Executive Order 12291 is that approval by the regulatory oversight group was no longer an advisory process. The agency was required to submit the proposal to OMB for approval before it could move forward. It could appeal any adverse decision to the President's Task Force on

---

12. For a selection of the regulatory analyses prepared by President Ford's oversight group, see Miller and Yandle (1979).

Regulatory Relief. This executive order continues to be regarded as "the backbone of executive regulatory oversight activities" (see U.S. Office of Management and Budget 1988, 13–14).

The oversight process also added an earlier review procedure through the institution of regulatory planning provisions in 1985.[13] President Reagan issued Executive Order 12498, which required regulatory agencies to submit to OMB a draft regulatory program, thus expanding the regulatory calendar concept of the Carter administration. Oversight activities address regulations in their final stages. By that point, the agencies have already established a major commitment to a regulatory policy, making their positions difficult to alter. Moreover, agencies have also generated substantial political support for regulations soon to be issued, limiting the ability of OMB to alter the regulatory structure. By influencing the regulatory program of an agency at an earlier stage, OMB could better alter the direction of regulatory policy.

A controversial component of the regulatory oversight agenda was the principle of federalism: "Federal regulation should not preempt state laws or regulations, except to guarantee rights of national citizenship or to avoid significant burdens on interstate commerce" (U.S. Office of Management and Budget 1988, 20). The economic rationale is that the costs and benefits of regulations may differ by area and that regulations should reflect this heterogeneity.

Rigid application of this approach, however, ignores some of the benefits of uniform national standards. If firms must invest in technologies to comply with a variety of different regulations, regulatory compliance costs may escalate.

One such situation is with respect to hazard warnings. Uniform national standards are desirable since they provide individuals with a common warnings vocabulary. Right-to-know movements with differing requirements have, however, proliferated at the local level. A chief example is California Proposition 65, passed in 1986, which requires firms selling products that pose risks of cancer or birth defects (e.g., wine manufacturers) or that expose their workers or customers to carcinogens (e.g., gas stations) to provide appropriate warnings. Beginning in 1986, the food industry sought federal preemption of these local warning efforts, urging the FDA to adopt a uniform national warning standard. The worst-case outcome for industry involves packaging foods with different warnings for different states. Application of the federalism principles suggested that there is no reason for the government to intervene, and the government did not. Although the national government should not attempt to establish uniform national regulations that adopt unattractive state regulations on a broader scale, national uniformity may benefit firms through reduced compliance costs.

13. This was undertaken under Executive Order 12498, 4 January 1985.

7.3.3   The Regulatory Budget Alternative

Although the Reagan oversight mechanism included many of the ingredients needed to make oversight more effective, it did not undertake the radical transformation of the oversight process that some individuals had advocated. There had been several proposals in the late 1970s and early 1980s that the government establish a regulatory budget, not unlike its budget for actual allocations.[14] In its simplest version, the regulatory budget concept involves OMB establishing a budgetary limit for each regulatory agency, where this budget pertains to the total cost that these regulations can impose on society. Imposing such limits clearly would provide regulatory discipline.

There are, however, several factors that limit the attractiveness and feasibility of this proposal. First, the regulatory budget proposal is responsive to the regulatory relief objective, but it does not directly alter the character of regulations. Second, whereas budgets for agencies have an automatic validating process in that an agency will know at the end of the year whether it has exceeded the budget, there is no such internal check for a regulatory budget. Agencies must rely on cost estimates that may not accurately reflect the actual impacts. In some cases, even calculating costs will be a substantial object of controversy. What, for example, is the cost of affirmative action requirements?

Finally, establishing a regulatory budget requires that an agency know in advance what the appropriate budgetary levels should be. Moreover, that calculation requires a detailed assessment of the benefits and costs of regulations. For prospective regulations, benefits and costs can be assessed most easily within the context of the type of oversight mechanism that OMB adopted. Since an agency would always wish to pursue an effort with a positive benefit-cost balance irrespective of previous budgetary decisions, there seems then to be no rationale for proceeding on other than a piecemeal basis for new regulations. If existing regulations were to count with respect to the budget, difficult problems arise with respect to establishing the cost of regulations promulgated many years earlier. Moreover, achieving changes in existing regulatory policies for which many firms have already invested billions of dollars in compliance expenditures will create substantial political opposition. One cannot simply replace a regulation from the 1970s with an unfavorable benefit-cost balance by a new regulation with a more favorable benefit-cost balance. The substantial vested interests in the earlier regulatory regime will resist such changes.

Overall, the regulatory budget does not appear to be compelling conceptually, and, more important, it would impose a degree of discipline on the regulatory agencies that would far exceed what could be achieved. In practice, OMB encountered substantial opposition in promoting a benefit-cost requirement for

---

14. For advocacy of this budget concept, see DeMuth (1980a, 1980b, 1984) and Litan and Nordhaus (1983). In Viscusi (1983), I provide a detailed critique of the regulatory budget approach.

new regulatory policies. Implementing an overall regulatory budget concept would have required much more political support than the oversight group had.

7.3.4   Performance of the Reagan Oversight Effort

An assessment of the overall performance of the regulatory oversight process cannot be divorced from an evaluation of substantive changes in regulatory policy, which is the subject of the subsequent sections. However, it is useful to highlight a few of the most distinctive aspects of this process.

First, the change in the oversight test to include a benefit-cost requirement was consistent with most reform agendas. The regulatory analysis filings during the Ford and Carter administrations often advocated such balancing even though the executive orders empowering these efforts did not require a benefit-cost test.

The benefit-cost analysis requirement often led to exemplary studies of this type. A prominent example of a well-executed benefit-cost assessment is the Department of Transportation's analysis of the merits of center-high-mounted stop-lamps, which analyzed the comparative efficacy of different types of stop-lamps in reducing collision damage and compared these reduced damage savings with the lamps' costs. EPA's assessment of the gasoline lead phase-down rule similarly was accompanied by an excellent regulatory analysis, as was the analysis of the construction fall protection standard carried out by OSHA.[15] These improvements in the quality of regulatory analyses represented a substantial advance from earlier years.

What is less clear is that the extent to which these improved analyses altered the policy choices or simply verified the good choices being made. Although many of the benefit-cost analyses carried out by the agencies were of high quality, it would be naive to assume that regulatory policies in the 1980s were dictated by strict adherence to a benefit-cost test.

The second major advance of the Reagan regulatory oversight process was the increased leverage given to the oversight effort. The requirement that the agency submit the regulatory proposal to OMB for prior approval gave the oversight group more binding authority than it had had in the past. Indeed, many supporters of the efforts of regulatory agencies feared that OMB would now dictate regulatory policy. The substantially increased authority of the regulatory oversight process was noted by James C. Miller III, whom the press designated the "regulatory czar": "If you are the toughest kid on the block, most kids won't pick a fight with you. The Executive Order establishes things quite clearly" ("Deregulation HQ" 1981, 19).

After the initial wave of regulatory reform efforts, the political support for deregulation began to wane. This shift was reflected in Vice President Bush's

---

15. For a review of these analyses, see the Office of Management and Budget (1988, esp. 16–17).

decision to abolish the Presidential Task Force on Regulatory Relief in August 1983. Agencies also began to challenge this authority.

The extent of the decreased impetus for regulatory reform is reflected in several events. During the debate over the 1986 reauthorization of the oversight group, Representative Dingell led an effort to eliminate the OIRA group. The compromise ultimately reached provided for more disclosures of OMB's review efforts.

A 1986 court decision (*Environmental Defense Fund v. Lee Thomas*) required that OMB not delay rule makings if the agency faced a statutory deadline. EPA subsequently used this ruling to curtail OMB's review ability by delaying proposals until near the legislative deadline. Whereas the deadline was reached only once before 1986, after the court decision EPA ran up against the constraint six to seven times per year. Labor unions have also adopted this strategy on behalf of OSHA, as they have obtained court orders to force regulation of formaldehyde, ethylene oxide, asbestos, and lead. The courts required that OSHA examine these issues, not that it necessarily issue regulations. The OSHA health standards staff, however, used these orders to push for stringent regulations.

Finally, Representative Dingell wrote a letter to Lee Thomas in 1987 expressing concern with respect to OMB review before EPA had made its regulatory decision. This congressional concern has also been utilized by EPA to curtail the role of OMB.

The result has been a substantial expansion of regulatory activity. Whereas EPA proposed an average of three to five major rules in the early 1980s, under Lee Thomas EPA's major rules proposals averaged twenty per year. The decrease in the regulatory initiatives in the early 1980s proved to be only temporary, as OMB had little ability to alter the structure of this expanded regulatory regime in a fundamental way. By the end of the 1980s, the OMB oversight group was no longer Miller's "biggest kid on the block." Instead, it was influential only on the margin.

The success of the components of the OMB effort had also differed. The basic Executive Order 12291 providing for benefit-cost analyses and establishing the character of regulatory reviews has proved to be most consequential. The subsequent Executive Order 12498 requiring OMB review of the regulatory agendas has proved less successful. The thumbnail sketches of regulatory options being considered provide OMB with some indication of future regulatory policies, but these projected agendas have been sufficiently fragmentary, and OMB's leverage has been sufficiently weak that there has been little influence on the future direction of regulatory policies.

Although the strengthening of the regulatory oversight process represents a prominent but limited achievement, the transformation in the character of the oversight mechanism also has deficiencies. Whereas regulatory oversight in earlier administrations entailed comprehensive analyses of regulations that would be filed in the public record for the rule-making proceeding, OMB's review is an internal procedure. In situations in which oversight officials do not have to compile comprehensive analyses and make public the results of these analyses, the oversight mechanism may not serve as an advocate of the most attractive option from an economic standpoint. Moreover, until the benefit-cost assessment is undertaken, the optimal regulatory alternative may not be clear. The danger of mistaken decisions is particularly great when leading political actors in the White House believe that they know the answer in advance and do not feel the need to be guided by a precise analysis of the merits of the regulatory option.

The absence of a more public regulatory debate has other possible drawbacks as well. Although the secretive nature of the negotiation process with agencies has advantages in terms of enabling parties to modify their stance without incurring the costs of altering their positions in a public confrontation, disclosure of OMB's reasoning would foster public understanding and provide guidance to other agencies regarding proper criteria for policy design. In many situations, OMB was attacked, perhaps needlessly, for delaying regulations or blocking regulations.

OMB's record in reforming regulation suggests that, in most cases, the review process has little effect on the regulation (see table 7.3). Almost three-fourths of all regulations in 1987 were approved by OMB in their initial form, and almost one-quarter were approved after revision. Only 3 percent of the proposals were rejected. In the absence of a public record of the manner in which the proposals were altered either in anticipation of the review or as part of the review, a more precise assessment of the impact of oversight is not possible.

7.4   Establishing an Appropriate Price for Risk

7.4.1   Agency Practices in Establishing Risk-Dollar Trade-Offs

The essential ingredient of benefit-cost trade-offs in the context of risk and environmental regulations is to establish the risk-dollar trade-off. Before the Reagan administration, agencies erred in two competing directions. First, in monetizing the benefits of health risks, agencies typically assessed the lost earnings and medical costs associated with the risk. Some agencies, such as the CPSC, had more detailed injury cost models, but these were not based on individuals' willingness to pay for risk reduction. Nonpecuniary health impacts and, more generally, society's willingness to pay to avoid small risks were not recognized.

An opposite bias is that the legislative mandates of the risk regulation agencies were absolute in character. The Clean Air Act requires EPA to set ambient air quality standards independent of cost considerations. In other instances, trade-offs are possible, but these trade-offs must fall short of a full-blown benefit-cost test. Agencies such as OSHA and EPA consequently focused on

Table 7.3   **Nature of Regulatory Oversight Actions, 1987**

	USDA	EPA	DOT	DOL	All Agencies	% of Total
Total reviews	420	205	202	64	2,314	100
Consistent without change	345	123	127	31	1,631	71
Consistent with change	58	60	64	31	549	24
Withdrawn by agency	5	9	7	0	59	3
Returned for consideration	2	0	4	0	10	0
Returned sent improperly	0	1	0	0	5	0
Emergency	6	0	0	1	15	1
Statutory or judicial deadline	4	12	0	1	45	2

Source: U.S. Office of Management and Budget (1988, 552).
Note: See table 7.1.

affordability. Indeed, OSHA's legislative mandate requires that it follow this approach. The general consensus is that the net effect of these biases led most risk regulation agencies to err on the side of excessive stringency, judged from the standpoint of economic efficiency.

The obvious solution is to rewrite the legislative mandates of these agencies. Ultimately, no meaningful regulatory reform can be achieved without some explicit attempt to balance the competing effects of regulation. Because legislative reform was not undertaken to achieve this end, the regulatory reform efforts could have only a modest and short-term impact.

7.4.2   Valuing Life: The Hazard Communication Debate

Perhaps the most noteworthy change in the nature of the regulatory debate is that the appropriate government expenditure per statistical life saved became an explicit object of concern. In earlier administrations, the regulatory oversight staff raised issues dealing with the value of life, with the principal reaction of agency economists being that such calculations were politically infeasible. Since lives were too sacred to value, agencies calculated the "costs of death." These costs consisted of the present value of the lost earnings and medical expenses. Although this concept may be appropriate from a tort liability compensation perspective, it abstracts from the value that individuals place on their welfare above and beyond their financial well-being. Moreover, it neglects the fact that attitudes toward risk-dollar trade-offs involving small probabilities may entail quite different terms of trade than if one were faced with the prospect of certain death. In this as in other policy contexts, the appropriate benefits value is society's willingness to pay for the risk reduction.

Agencies ultimately adopted the value of life approach, but not because of its compelling intellectual foundation. In the 1980s, OSHA undertook a regulatory analysis for its hazard communication standard, which would have required labeling and other forms of risk communication for all risky chemicals used in manufacturing. OSHA's regulatory analysis indicated that the benefits exceeded the costs. Armed with this favorable result, OSHA submitted the regulation to OMB for approval. OMB correctly observed that the risk effects had been misassessed by OSHA, leading to a substantial upward bias in the benefits. OMB concluded that a more accurate assessment implied that costs exceeded benefits. After OMB rejected the regulation in 1982, OSHA appealed its case to the Presidential Task Force on Regulatory Relief.

To see how value of life considerations entered this debate, consider the statistics in the summary table 7.4. All figures in this table have been discounted to reflect the appropriate time lags involved for diseases such as cancer that have long latency periods. Although the hazard communication regulation would affect lives, it would also affect other health impacts, chiefly nonfatal job injuries and disabilities. At the time of the analysis, statistics were available on the implicit dollar value that workers attached to nonfatal injuries and fatalities, but there were no comparable values for disabling injuries. The approach that I used was to assess the sensitivity of the results, taking as fixed the estimated trade-off between fatalities and lost workday injuries (estimated to be at a ratio of 20:1) and varying the rate of trade-off between lost workday injuries and disabling injuries from a situation in which both receive equal value to one in which disabling injuries have a value five times as great as a lost workday injury. The other major assumption needed pertains to the efficiency of the regulation in reducing risk. OMB indicated that the risk reduction that would be experienced would be on the order of 5 percent, whereas OSHA estimated the impact of the regulation as reducing injuries by 10 percent.

Table 7.4 includes each of these benefit-weighting assumptions and provides calculations for both the OMB and the OSHA risk assessments. The first row of statistics in table 7.4 consists of the net discounted costs minus all mone-

Table 7.4   Summary of Benefit and Cost Effects of the OSHA Hazard Communication Regulation

| | Lost Workday Equivalents | | | |
| | Weights, 1,1,20:[a] Effectiveness | | Weights, 1,5,20:[a] Effectiveness | |
	5%	10%	5%	10%
Net discounted costs less monetized benefits ($)	2.632×10^9	2.616×10^9	2.632×10^9	2.616×10^9
Total lost workday case equivalents (discounted)	9.5×10^4	18.9×10^4	24.7×10^4	49.7×10^4
Net discounted cost/lost workday case equivalent ($)	27,900	14,000	10,700	5,300

Source: Viscusi (1982).

[a]These are the relative weights placed on lost workday cases (always 1), disabling illnesses (1 or 5), and cancers (always 20) in constructing a measure of lost workday case equivalents.

tized benefits, thus providing a net financial impact figure that can be used in calculating the new cost per unit of health impact. The second row provides the estimated discounted total lost workday case equivalents for the regulation using the weights given at the top of the table. The bottom row of table 7.4 presents the estimated discounted cost per lost workday case equivalent injury prevented.

Whether the regulation should be pursued depends on whether this cost-effectiveness measure is greater than the estimated value of nonfatal injuries. My past estimates indicated an implicit value of injuries on the order of $23,000–$35,000 (in 1982 dollars) so that, for three of the four sets of assumptions listed, the regulation clearly passes a benefit-cost test. In one instance, the benefits exceed the cost except for the lowest end of the range of estimates of the implicit values that workers attach to injuries.

Secretary of Labor Donovan indicated that he viewed this analysis as providing support for the regulation, but OMB regulation head Christopher DeMuth maintains that he was not fully persuaded (see Earley 1985). The ultimate decision to issue the regulation may reflect in part the increased strength of the regulatory agencies after the initial period of deregulation. Moreover, the regulation had the strong support of labor as well as of chemical industry groups, who sought to avoid the costs associated with a variety of different state warnings regulations by having a uniform national regulation.

The policy outcome was not as consequential as the process that took place. The terms of the debate had changed dramatically since the 1970s. Regulatory agencies and the White House oversight group focused their attention on whether the benefits of the regulation exceeded the costs, whereas in earlier administrations such concerns were subsidiary. Agencies had viewed their role as being governed by a higher-level agenda in which formal trade-offs of this type were not permitted.

The new enthusiasm of agencies for the value-of-life approach can be traced primarily to its effect on the attractiveness of policies. This methodology boosts the monetized value of health benefits by a factor of ten, which is approximately the ratio of the estimated implicit value of life to the present value of the earnings of workers for whom these values are estimated. Although agency decisions are seldom dictated solely by benefit-cost concerns, the preparation of proper benefit assessments represents a substantial dividend of the OMB oversight effort.

7.4.3 The Value of Life Regulatory Record

The net effect of the effort to strike a balance between benefits and costs is shown in the cost per life saved statistics in table 7.5. Since these figures pertain to average costs per life saved rather than marginal costs, the tests indicate whether the regulation is preferable to no regulation, not whether the level of stringency is optimal. An appropriate reference point for assessing how far we should move down this table in terms of policy acceptability is the value of life

Table 7.5   **The Cost of Various Risk-Reducing Regulations per Life Saved**

	Year and Status	Agency	Initial Annual Risk[a]	Annual Lives Saved	Cost per Life Saved (millions of 1984 $)
Pass benefit-cost test					
Unvented space heaters	1980 F	CPSC	2.7 in 10^5	63.000	.10
Oil and gas well service	1983 P	OSHA-S	1.1 in 10^3	50.000	.10
Cabin fire protection	1985 F	FAA	6.5 in 10^8	15.000	.20
Passive restraints/belts	1984 F	NHTSA	9.1 in 10^5	1,850.000	.30
Underground construction	1989 F	OSHA-S	1.6 in 10^3	8.100	.30
Alcohol and drug control	1985 F	FRA	1.8 in 10^6	4.200	.50
Servicing wheel rims	1984 F	OSHA-S	1.4 in 10^5	2.300	.50
Seat cushion flammability	1984 F	FAA	1.6 in 10^7	37.000	.60
Floor emergency lighting	1984 F	FAA	2.2 in 10^8	5.000	.70
Concrete and masonry construction	1988 F	OSHA-S	1.4 in 10^5	6.500	1.40
Hazard communication	1983 F	OSHA-S	4.0 in 10^5	200.000	1.80
Benzene/fugitive emissions	1984 F	EPA	2.1 in 10^5	.310	2.80
Fail benefit-cost test					
Grain dust	1987 F	OSHA-S	2.1 in 10^4	4.000	5.30
Radionuclides/uranium mines	1984 F	EPA	1.4 in 10^4	1.100	6.90
Benzene	1987 F	OSHA-H	8.8 in 10^4	3.800	17.10
Arsenic/glass plant	1986 F	EPA	8.0 in 10^4	.110	19.20
Ethylene oxide	1984 F	OSHA-H	4.4 in 10^5	2.800	25.60
Arsenic/copper smelter	1986 F	EPA	9.0 in 10^4	.060	26.50
Uranium mill tailings inactive	1983 F	EPA	4.3 in 10^4	2.100	27.60
Uranium mill tailings active	1983 F	EPA	4.3 in 10^4	2.100	53.00
Asbestos	1986 F	OSHA-H	6.7 in 10^5	74.700	89.30
Asbestos	1989 F	EPA	2.9 in 10^5	10.000	104.20
Arsenic/glass manufacturing	1986 R	EPA	3.8 in 10^5	.250	142.00
Benzene/storage	1984 R	EPA	6.0 in 10^7	.043	202.00
Radionuclides/DOE facilities	1984 R	EPA	4.3 in 10^6	.001	210.00
Radionuclides/elem. phosphorous	1984 R	EPA	1.4 in 10^5	.046	270.00
Benzene/ethylbenzenol styrene	1984 R	EPA	2.0 in 10^6	.006	483.00
Arsenic/low-arsenic copper	1986 R	EPA	2.6 in 10^4	.090	764.00
Benzene/maleic anhydride	1984 R	EPA	1.1 in 10^6	.029	820.00
Land disposal	1988 F	EPA	2.3 in 10^8	2.520	3,500.00
EDB	1989 R	OSHA-H	2.5 in 10^4	.002	15,600.00
Formaldehyde	1987 F	OSHA-H	6.8 in 10^7	.010	72,000.00

Source: Morrall (1986, 30). These statistics were updated by John F. Morrall III via unpublished communication with the author, 10 July 1990.

Note: P, F, or R: proposed, final rule, or rejected, respectively.
OSHA-S = OSHA safety regulations.
OSHA-H = OSHA health regulations.
FRA = Federal Railroad Administration.
EDB = Ethylene dibromide.

[a]Annual deaths per exposed population. An exposed population of 10^3 is 1,000, 10^4 is 10,000, etc.

estimates in the literature at that time (see Thaler and Rosen 1976; Smith 1976; Viscusi 1979, 1983). Workers in high-risk jobs value each expected death at under $1 million, the value of life of workers in typical blue-collar risk jobs was on the order of $3 million, and the value of life of individuals in very high-income positions may be $7 million or more, but these last estimates are the least reliable.

Judged by these standards, many of the regulations in the 1980s clearly pass a benefit-cost test. The policies of the FAA appear to be outstanding bargains. Their low costs per life saved figures should not, however, be viewed as a regulatory success. A main contributor to this low figure is that the FAA valued the lives saved in airplane crashes using the present value of the lost earnings of the accident victims. This approach underestimates the value of life of airplane passengers by more than an order of magnitude. In one case, the FAA dismissed repairs of the DC-10 as being not worthwhile because of the low level of the risk, whereas a proper benefit-cost calculation indicates that the risk reductions were clearly desirable.[16] Application of value of life principles and benefit-cost analysis would have led an agency to be more aggressive.

The cutoff in table 7.5 for policies with benefits in excess of their costs is probably just below the regulation of benzene/fugitive emissions, with a cost per life saved of $2.8 million. Policies below that regulation in the table would not pass a benefit-cost test unless they protect populations with comparatively high values per life. OMB rejected none of the policies with lower costs per life, whereas they rejected eight policies with higher costs per life. OMB blocked some of the particularly inefficient regulations, although several regulations with very low efficacy were enacted. Indeed, the minimum threshold for OMB to reject a regulation is quite high. None of the regulations in table 7.5 with costs per life saved below $142 million were rejected. OMB's efficacy is apparently limited to the most extreme instances of regulatory excess.

Given the uncertainties involved with benefit-cost analysis, the character of the agency's legislative mandates, and the continued ability of regulatory agencies to wield substantial influence, the most that could have been hoped for is an elimination of the most unattractive policies from a benefit-cost standpoint. By that criterion, substantial progress was made.

7.5 Sunset Actions and Regulatory Reforms

7.5.1 The Reform Record

The widespread dissatisfaction with the character of regulatory standards has long led regulatory reformers to urge modification of these regulations. President Ford's Task Force on Regulatory Reform proposed that OSHA's standards be replaced by more performance-oriented alternatives. More generally,

16. For a review of these calculations, see Viscusi (1983).

since the original regulations had seldom been based on benefit-cost grounds, there was always a potential gain from altering previous policies.

The major sunset action of the Carter administration was the decision by OSHA director Eula Bingham to eliminate or modify 928 OSHA regulations in October 1978. Although many of the changes that she instituted were only editorial and did not alter the substantive focus of the regulation, this regulatory pruning eliminated the "nitpicking" aspects of OSHA regulation, which were the source of widespread ridicule of OSHA's efforts.

A potentially ambitious effort at deregulation occurred in 1980, as Carter administration economists developed an automobile industry relief package. The auto industry bore the brunt of a substantial body of regulatory costs, including emissions requirements, safety standards, and fuel economy standards. Some regulatory critics believed these costs contributed to the economic decline of the automobile industry. However, the timing of the main cost increases—the late 1960s, the early 1970s, and 1980–81—does not coincide with the economic decline of the auto industry. A more influential factor was the rise in fuel prices in the 1970s and the shift to small cars. Substantive action to support a pivotal industry in an election year did, however, offer political benefits.

The Carter administration developed a reform package that provided only very limited relief. Its principal component was a proposal to reduce the stringency of high-altitude emissions requirements, which offered a payoff of $500 million over a three-year period. The rest of the package had little substance because policy changes were opposed by the EPA and NHTSA administrators.[17]

7.5.2 Reagan's Auto Industry Relief Package

The advent of the Reagan administration marked a change in the regulatory climate. Shortly after taking office, the Reagan administration suspended the "midnight regulations" issued by the Carter administration in its closing days and ordered a reexamination of their merits. This effort yielded some partial dividends. As Council of Economic Advisers member William Niskanen (1988, 118) observed, "Of the 172 proposed rules that were suspended, for example, 112 were approved without change, and only eighteen were withdrawn. OIRA's batting average would never again be as high."

The Reagan administration's most comprehensive deregulation effort was its automobile industry relief package. The agenda for this reform effort was not a product of the Reagan administration efforts alone. Many of the regulations included in this group had previously been opposed at the time of their promulgation by the White House economists, many of whom were now at OMB. In addition, some of the components of the relief package had previously been

17. For a detailed recounting of the Carter administration experience, see Eads and Fix (1984, esp. 125–32).

advocated by the Carter administration economists for inclusion in the 1980 relief package but were not included because of opposition from the affected agencies.

The impetus for reform stemmed in part from the rise in regulatory costs in 1980 and 1981. The estimates by White (1982) indicate that the total costs of emission regulations per automobile mushroomed from $559 in 1979 to $906 in 1980 and then to $1,551 in 1981. Safety regulation costs were in addition to this amount. Estimates by Crandall et al. (1986) suggest that the additional equipment cost per automobile rose from $431–$641 in 1979 to $512–$822 in 1981 and that the fuel penalty increased from $116 in 1979 to $159 in 1981. The Reagan package for relief of the automobile industry consequently had been developed in an environment of rapid cost escalation for automobiles that could be traced to the influence of government standards.

Table 7.6 summarizes the components of the package, their status as of mid-1983, and the cost savings that the administration claimed for them.[18] The measures with the greatest savings for industry included the delay of the paint shop standard, the elimination of the driver vision standard, the delay of the tougher hydrocarbon solution standards, the scrapping of the safety standards for explosive multipiece tire rims, and the delay of the passenger restraint requirements. Overall, this reform package provides a very comprehensive program of regulatory relief.

The success of this reform effort stemmed not only from the White House regulatory reformers' zeal but also from the nature of the Reagan appointments to regulatory agencies. The NHTSA head, Raymond Peck, has been justifiably termed "an expert deregulator" (see Graham 1989, 145), and EPA administrator Anne Gorsuch developed a well-established reputation for scaling back the efforts of her agency.

Although some of the items in table 7.6 represent attractive reforms, others may not pass the usual economic tests. The paint shop requirement, for example, may represent the most cost-effective way of meeting hydrocarbon emissions standards. Abolition of this regulation would lead to more costly controls being required for other establishments near automobile paint shops, such as gasoline stations (see Eads and Fix 1984, 132). The costs of the regulation were, however, quite high, particularly in the short run. By delaying the regulation, OMB gave firms additional opportunity to change over to the new technologies required, greatly reducing the ultimate costs of the regulation. The merits of passive restraints are also much debated, even by economists.

Some of these deregulation efforts ultimately were viewed as constituting

---

18. One of the most expensive components is the high-altitude emissions standard that was adopted earlier as part of the Carter administration reforms but for which the estimated savings were $500 million as opposed to $1.3 billion. It should also be noted that the legitimacy of the "public" cost calculation and the "industry" cost calculation is questionable because of the complicated way in which costs affect prices. These calculations often assume, e.g., that the safety measures are not valued by consumers but are simply a deadweight loss.

Table 7.6   **The Reagan Administration's Auto Reform Package**

Issue	Action (date of completion)	5-Year Savings ($millions)	
		Industry	Public
Rules Acted on:			
Gas-tank vapors	Declined to order new controls on cars (Apr. 1981)	103	1,300
Emissions tests	Streamlined certification of industry tests on vehicles (Oct. 1981, Nov. 1982)	5	. . .
	Raised allowable "failure rate" for test of light trucks and heavy-duty engines from 10 to 40 percent (Jan. 1983)	19	129
	Reduced spot checks of emissions of vehicles on assembly lines by 42 percent; delayed assembly-line tests of heavy-duty trucks until 1986 (Jan. 1983)	1	1
High-altitude autos	Ended assembly-line tests at high altitude, relying instead on industry data (Apr. 1981)	.2	. . .
	Allowed industry to self-certify vehicles as meeting high-altitude emission standards (Apr. 1981)	1	1
Pollution waivers	Consolidated industry applications for temporary exemptions from tougher emissions standards for nitrogen oxide and carbon monoxide (Sep. 1981)	. . .	. . .
Paint shops	Delayed until 1983 tougher hydrocarbon pollution standards for auto paint shops (Oct. 1981)	300	. . .
Test vehicles	Cut paperwork required to exempt prototype vehicles from environmental standards (July 1982)	. . .	. . .
Driver vision	Scrapped existing 1981 rule and second proposed rule setting standards for driver's field of view (June 1982)	10	. . .
Fuel economy	Decided not to set stiffer fuel economy standards to replace those expiring in 1985 (Apr. 1981)	. . .	. . .
Speedometers	Revoked rule-setting standards for speedometers and tamper-resistant odometers (Feb. 1982)	. . .	20
Tire rims	Scrapped proposal to set safety standards for explosive multipiece tire rims (Feb. 1982)	300	75
Brake tests	Eased from 30 to 20 percent the steepness of grades on which post-1984 truck and bus brakes must hold (Dec. 1981)	. . .	1.8
Tire pressure	Scrapped proposal to equip vehicles with low-tire-pressure indicators (Aug. 1981)	. . .	130
Battery safety	Scrapped proposal to set standards to prevent auto battery explosions (Aug. 1981)	. . .	. . .
Tire safety	Revoked requirement that consumers be told of reserve load capacity of tires; eased tire makers' reporting requirements (June 1982)	. . .	. . .

Table 7.6   (continued)

Issue	Action (date of completion)	5-Year Savings ($millions)	
		Industry	Public
Antitheft protection	Eased antitheft and locking steering wheel standards for open-body vehicles (June 1981)	. . .	. . .
Fuel economy	Streamlined semiannual reports of automakers on their progress in meeting fuel economy goals (Aug. 1982)	. . .	.1
Tire ratings	Suspended rule requiring industry to rate tires according to tread wear, traction, and heat resistance (Feb. 1983)	. . .	10
Vehicle IDs	Downgraded from standard to administrative rule the requirement that all vehicles have ID numbers as an aid to police (May 1983)	. . .	. . .
Seat belt comfort	Scrapped proposal to set standards for seat belt comfort and convenience (June 1983)	. . .	. . .
Rules with Uncertain Futures:			
High-altitude emissions	Failed to revise Clean Air Act order ending weaker high-altitude emissions standards in 1984; eased through regulatory changes	38	1,300
Emissions reductions	Failed to revise Clean Air Act order to cut large trucks' hydrocarbon and carbon monoxide emissions by 90 percent by 1984; standard was delayed until 1985	105	536
	Failed to ease Clean Air Act order reducing nitrogen oxide emissions from light trucks and heavy-duty engines by 75 percent by 1984; regulatory changes under study	150	563
Particulate pollution	Delayed a proposal to scrap specific particulate standards for some diesels in favor of an average standard for all diesels; stiffer standards delayed from 1985 to 1987	40	523
Methane standards	Shelved because of "serious" costs; questions a plan to drop methane as a regulated hydrocarbon	. . .	. . .
Passive restraints	Delayed and then revoked requirement that post-1982 autos be equipped with passive restraints; revocation overturned by Supreme Court in June 1983	428	981
Bumper damage	Cut from 5 to 2.5 MPH the speed at which bumpers must resist damage; change is on appeal	. . .	308

Source: Wines (1983, 1534–35).

regulatory relief rather than regulatory reform. The Supreme Court eventually overturned NHTSA's rescission of the air bag rule.

There are likely to be some disagreements regarding the particular components of the program as well as the permanence of the regulatory reforms. On balance, however, these auto industry relief measures primarily delayed regulatory costs. They did not alter the long-term structure of auto regulations in any fundamental manner.

Perhaps the main reason that there was a failure to restructure the regulations rather than simply reducing their cost is that the overriding objective was not regulatory reform but auto industry relief. OMB Director Stockman (1986) viewed these policies with some disapproval, as he considered them to be a thinly veiled policy of protectionism.[19] The overriding objective of cost reduction rather than meaningful reform limited the degree to which this political success was also a beneficial reform measure.

7.5.3   Other Reforms and Sunset Actions

Other reform efforts met with less success. OSHA, for example, reexamined its cotton dust regulation that had been bitterly opposed by both the textile industry and Carter administration economists in a dispute that ultimately led to a battle in the U.S. Supreme Court. OSHA's reassessment of the regulation indicated that the original regulatory analysis was wildly inaccurate and that the standard could be profitably altered in several ways. For example, a policy of low-cost environmental controls (e.g., taping leaks in duct work) coupled with testing and rotating workers would achieve most of the health gains of the original standard. One could also question whether a cost of several hundred thousand dollars for each case of partial or total disability prevented was reasonable. The Supreme Court's decision to explicitly rule out a benefit-cost test in the cotton dust case and to require that the agencies set the lowest "feasible" standard did not preclude performance-oriented alternatives or some balancing of competing interests. However, by the time of the Reagan administration review, the largest textile manufacturers were already in compliance with the cotton dust regulation, leading them to join with labor in advocating retention of the status quo.

The lack of enthusiasm for altering a regulatory regime that was once bitterly opposed is likely to be a more general phenomenon whenever firms incur fixed costs of compliance. The regulatory reforms that OSHA did undertake were largely of a piecemeal variety. For example, OSHA revised its electrical

---

19. As Stockman (1986, 155) observed, "Lewis and the others had cooked up a theory that the auto industry had been so overregulated and crippled by air bags, pollution control devices, safety standards, and other government-imposed Ralph Naderite schemes that it was now up to the government to undo the damage. . . . This cover-up for protectionism really frosted me."

standards for the construction industry to be in conformance with new industry standards (29 CFR sec. 1926.800 [1] [1985]).[20]

The overall performance of the Reagan administration's deregulation and sunset actions is mixed. Of 119 regulations reviewed by the President's Task Force on Regulatory Relief, seventy-six regulations were revised, in twenty-seven cases revisions were proposed, and in sixteen cases revisions by the task force were still under way when this group issued its final regulatory report (Presidential Task Force 1983, 68).

The extent of the various revisions cited in the report card that the Presidential Task Force issued on its performance is not indicated, but particularly in the early years it is evident that some progress was made. The fact that the task force was disbanded in 1983 is a reflection of the decreasing prospects over time for altering the structure of regulation. The climate for regulatory reform had clearly changed, and there would soon be a return to the previous regulatory environment.

Sunset actions and other changes in the structure of existing regulation are difficult to achieve. With regulations already in place, industry's interest in altering these regulations is divided. Moreover, shifting the character of regulations over time may impose additional adjustment costs. The initial wave of deregulation efforts under the Reagan administration isolated some promising candidates for change. The greatest subsequent gains could be achieved by focusing on new regulation proposals.

7.6   New Regulatory Initiatives

7.6.1   Environmental Policy

The major regulatory innovation sought by economists in the environmental area has been the greater utilization of market-based policies. Notwithstanding the widespread enthusiasm of economists and reformers for various forms of emissions trading options, such measures remain the exception rather than the rule.

Table 7.7 summarizes the performance of these policies through 1984. The most popular market-oriented trading system is that of netting, whereby a firm can modify its existing plant and equipment in a manner that increases the level of pollution from one source, provided that it also decreases pollution emissions from other sources in such a manner that the *net* increase does equal that of a major source. The netting policy is restricted to internal trading for a particular firm. By its very design, this effort should have little effect on

20. Through this standards reform, OSHA attempted to bring its regulation into conformance with the National Electrical Code, which had undergone its last major revision in 1981—four years before the final OSHA standard was promulgated.

Table 7.7   **Summary of Emissions Trading Activity**

Activity	Estimated No. of Internal Transactions	Estimated No. of External Transactions	Estimated Cost Savings ($millions)	Environmental Quality Impact
Netting	5,000–12,000	None	25–300 in permitting costs; 500–12,000 in emission control costs	Insignificant in individual cases; probably insignificant in aggregate
Offsets	1,800	200	Probably large, but not easily measured	Probably insignificant
Bubbles:				
Federally approved	40	2	300	Insignificant
State approved	89	0	135	Insignificant
Banking	< 100	< 20	Small	Insignificant

Source: Hahn and Hester (1989, 138).

environmental quality. Table 7.7 indicates that the emission control cost savings from netting are substantial.

The second most frequent emissions trading option is that of offsets. This option introduced in 1976 permits construction of new facilities that will create pollution in areas of the country that exceed maximum allowable concentration for pollutants. Companies must, however, purchase offsets from existing facilities that provide for more than equivalent reduction of the same pollutant from pollution sources that are already in compliance. By 1984, most of the offset transactions were internal rather than involving external trades, and the cost savings are not believed to be substantial.

The third trading concept in table 7.7 is the bubble policy. The Carter administration introduced the bubble policy in December 1979. By envisioning an artificial bubble around a firm for which a firm must be in compliance in terms of its total level of pollution, rather than having to meet a particular requirement for each pollution source, a firm can establish the most cost-effective mechanism for achieving the pollution reduction within its "bubble." By 1984, bubbles had been adopted in fewer than 200 instances, with cost savings believed to be under $500 million.

The final trading option—banking—enables firms to store rights to pollution over time if they are in compliance with their standards and then use these compliance rights as offsets against pollution. This policy enables firms to avoid sacrificing pollution rights should they choose to replace their current high-polluting plant and equipment with a more efficient lower-pollution technology. The use of banking policies has, however, been infrequent.

These market-oriented systems have generated nontrivial financial benefits, without any substantially detrimental environmental consequences. The small scale of these efforts reflects the extent to which the EPA has viewed these market systems as experimental options rather than as an integral part of agency policy.

Firms must obtain EPA approval to utilize these trading options, and the costs of this approval are often substantial. Approval of the applications is not always forthcoming, as there has been long-term suspicion by most EPA officials and environmentalists more generally of market options. Pollution rights trading policies involve costs in locating a seller of emissions credits and in establishing the terms of trade. Firms also face substantial uncertainties when they embark on the emissions trading path since there is no guarantee that these experimental EPA policies will continue for the duration of the investment that they must make.

Although Carter administration and Reagan administration economists had long advocated such market approaches, it was not until the Bush administration that such efforts became a prominent part of the nation's declared economic agenda (CEA 1990, 193–97). The degree to which these efforts will become a central component of EPA policy is not yet apparent.

Although EPA expanded the role of market-oriented systems very little in

the 1980s, it did undertake other initiatives. Its air pollution efforts were particularly active, especially with respect to the continuing phase down of the use
of lead in gasoline. In 1985, the permissible lead content in gasoline was reduced from 1.0 grams per gallon to 0.5 grams per gallon, and, in 1986, the
permissible level dropped to 0.1 grams per gallon. What was particularly noteworthy about this increasing stringency of the lead standard is that it was also
supported by sound regulatory analysis demonstrating the excess of benefits
over costs (U.S. Office of Management and Budget 1988, 16). EPA also expanded its efforts against airborne toxins in the 1980s, and it undertook substantial efforts to reduce indoor air pollution stemming from asbestos and
radon.

As will be discussed below within the context of enforcement, implementation of the Superfund legislation (CERCLA, 1980) was also a new concern of
the agency in the 1980s. The 1984 Resource Conservation and Recovery Act
(RCRA) amendments were also a major legislative initiative through which
Congress imposed a series of deadlines for EPA actions, thus limiting the
agency's discretion.

Two other major additions to EPA's agenda were the long-range problems of
acid rain and the greenhouse effect. In each case, EPA identified major problems meriting national attention, but it failed to justify the economic merits of
these efforts. The result has been a delay for greater study of these problems
and symbolic efforts as part of the international dialogue on these issues.[21]
With respect to the global environmental problems, the United States participated in the 1985 Vienna Convention and the 1987 Montreal Protocol, which
led to the freezing of chlorofluorocarbon production levels, and in 1989 the
United States participated in the Paris Summit focusing on global environmental concerns. To the extent that the United States has been an activist member
of these groups, it has been through fostering recognition of the economic
costs involved.

The desirability of particular global warming and acid rain policies remains
in doubt. Portney (1990) estimates that the acid rain provisions of the 1990
Clean Air Act amendments will provide $5 billion in benefits with costs in the
$2–$9 billion range. These acid rain provisions are desirable only if the costs
are not much above the midpoint of the cost range. The exploratory analysis of
global warming policies by Nordhaus (1990) likewise indicated mixed results
regarding the attractiveness of the policy measures that have been proposed.
Actions such as control of chlorofluorocarbons are economically desirable, but
very ambitious policies may not be worthwhile. The main shortcoming of EPA
policies with respect to these long-run environmental issues is the continuing
need to identify the specific policies that merit adoption in terms of the net
benefits that they offer society.

---

21. Niskanen (1988) reports that David Stockman blocked the acid rain initiative developed by
William Ruckelshaus.

Table 7.8   **Trends in EPA Regulation Costs**

		Present Value of Costs ($billions) of EPA Regulations	
	Year	Proposed Rules	Final Rules
	1987	70	14
	1988	21	84
	1989	17	6
	1990	250	95

Source: Estimates prepared by U.S. Office of Management and Budget, August 1990. Figures for 1989 and 1990 are preliminary.

Although EPA was not successful in winning approval for these policies, overall the late 1980s marked a dramatic resurgence in EPA regulatory activity. Table 7.8 summarizes the present value of costs for major EPA rules proposed or finalized from 1987 to 1990. These cost levels are quite impressive, including proposed regulations with costs of $70 billion in 1987 and $250 billion in 1990 and final regulations with costs of $84 billion in 1988 and $95 billion in 1990. To put these levels in perspective, note that, during the expansionary period of EPA regulation before Reagan, the costs associated with proposed EPA regulations were $26–$29 billion in 1979 and for the entire period 1975–80 were only $218–$296 billion.[22]

EPA had not simply returned to its earlier degree of regulatory activity; by the late 1980s and the early 1990s, EPA was undertaking more costly regulatory initiatives than at any time in its history.

7.6.2   Pharmaceutical Regulation

One of the most highly publicized areas of successful new regulatory initiatives was for pharmaceuticals. Critics of the FDA had long charged that the agency erred on the side of preventing adverse effects of newly approved drugs as opposed to taking into consideration the benefits that new drugs may offer.[23] One FDA official remarked that no one was going to blame him for slow approval of a beneficial drug, but he would be blamed for approving the next Thalidomide.[24]

Throughout the 1980s, the OMB regulatory oversight group sought to expedite the FDA drug approval process. The political leverage for achieving an accelerated approval time for new drugs was increased by the AIDS constituency. Since the prospects of patients suffering from life-threatening diseases

22. These estimates are provided in Viscusi (1983, p. 143, table 8.2).

23. For an extensive assessment of the FDA's drug approval policies, see Grabowski and Vernon (1983).

24. This comment was made to me by an FDA official in a training session on the use of economic analysis presented at the FDA in 1982.

such as AIDS were very poor, a policy of giving expedited approval to these drugs offered potential benefits with little apparent mortality risk.

FDA adopted a general regulatory commitment to trying to accelerate the drug approval process without compromising its quality, and it established a special commitment to expediting the approval of drugs for diseases such as AIDS.

The statistics in table 7.9 present the total number of new chemical entities approved and their approval time. Drugs that are ranked 1A are believed to be of substantial importance, and the 1AA drugs are generally drugs for diseases such as AIDS. If we contrast the patterns before and after the FDA policy change in 1987, there is no striking departure from earlier trends. The number of new drug approvals increased somewhat from the earlier years, particularly given the low drug approval rates in 1980 and 1983. The number of approvals given to the 1A and 1AA drugs increased in 1988 and 1989 from the level in the mid-1980s, but the total number of such approvals was almost identical to the rate of approval in 1982–83. The speed of the drug approvals also did not change markedly. The average drug approval time in the late 1980s is not substantially different from that in earlier years. The rate of approval for the 1A and 1AA drugs was particularly rapid in 1987 and 1989 but comparatively slow in 1988.

The most that can be concluded from this evidence is that there has been some modest effort to target more drugs as being 1A or 1AA and to avoid the long lag time of over three and a half years that was present in 1984. Since many of the drugs involved in this approval process have been in the FDA pipeline for several years, the ultimate effects of a shift in FDA drug approval policy will not be fully apparent until the 1990s. The changes that have been

Table 7.9   **New Drug Approvals and Time to Approval**

	No. of NCEs Approvals		Avg. Lag Time (months) from Submission to Approval	
Year	All Drugs	1AA/1A Drugs	All Drugs	1AA/1A Drugs
1980	11	2	35.18	26.38
1981	23	2	31.03	14.25
1982	22	4	26.02	9.81
1983	12	4	28.67	21.44
1984	21	2	43.44	27.75
1985	26	3	32.08	32.67
1986	18	1	34.19	17.50
1987	18	2	32.76	12.00
1988	16	4	36.39	41.00
1989	21	5	35.61	22.05

Source: All figures are based on calculations by the author using chronology of new chemical entities (NCEs) developed by the University of Rochester Center for Study of Drug Development, 10 July 1990 (computer printout).

made are consistent with the principles being advocated by most economists, and the extent of the changes evinced in FDA activities has been modest.

7.6.3 Occupational Safety Regulation

The literature on OSHA has long stressed the need to go beyond the technology-forcing nature of the initial era of OSHA regulation. One such performance-oriented mechanism is the 1980 OSHA proposed hazard communication regulation included as part of Carter's "midnight regulations" package. This regulation established chemical labeling in the manufacturing industry.

The ultimate regulation issued by the Reagan administration expanded on the original Carter proposal by adding material safety data sheets. Chemical suppliers were required to provide downstream firms with information regarding the chemical ingredients. Although potentially attractive in theory, the material safety data component of the regulation has been of little benefit because of the overly technical nature of the information provided. In addition to being the most costly new regulatory initiative in the risk area during the first Reagan term, this regulation was also innovative in many respects. This informational regulation represented a shift in the domain of regulatory activity that occurred throughout the 1980s. Right-to-know measures at the federal and local level proliferated in an effort to inform individuals of the risks from exposures on the job, exposures from the environment, and exposures from products.

The other major innovation in OSHA's regulatory structure was the adoption of the permissible exposure limits of the American Conference of Governmental Industrial Hygienists (ACGIH). OSHA's original standards for health risk exposures were based on approximately 400 exposure limits that had been recommended by the ACGIH, which is an industry advisory group. Each year a committee of fifteen individuals, chiefly hygienists and toxicologists from industry, meets to set threshold limit values for chemical exposures, where the objective is to achieve levels for which "no injurious effect will result no matter how often the exposure is repeated" (see Stokinger 1984). Although a zero-risk exposure is not necessarily optimal, this industry group informally incorporates concerns of feasibility.[25] The ACGIH had developed 200 standards for new health hazard exposures as well as 100 revisions of the exposure limits for existing OSHA standards that had been based on the earlier ACGIH exposure limits. Adopting all these revisions through a generic regulation rather than through a substance-by-substance rule-making approach enabled OSHA to expand its efforts in the health area, which had been given insufficient attention compared to safety concerns.

Although this regulation appears to be attractive on balance, its main short-

---

25. For the permissible exposure limits advocated by the ACGIH for which there is evidence on the benefit-cost trade-offs, the cost per case of cancer prevented appears to be generally in the reasonable range (see Broder and Morrall 1983; and Mendeloff 1988).

coming is that the process for generating such broadly based standards did not originate within the agency but was instead devised by an industry group. This process raises the long-term possibility that the function of such industry-designed standards will be to restrain competition and to promote the vested interests of the particular firms represented in the industry organization rather than to advance the interests of society at large. This type of capture theory has been offered by Stigler (1971) in the case of economic regulation. If OSHA were to continue to base its regulations on guidelines recommended by industry, then this procedure would all but ensure the long-run capture of OSHA. These dangers are also apparent in other areas of OSHA regulation, as the lobbying of the large textile firms in support of the retention of the cotton dust standard illustrated.

The other innovations in OSHA's regulatory agenda were more incremental. A collaborative effort of OSHA and the OMB regulatory oversight group led to an innovative OSHA grain-handling standard.[26] Grain dust levels in grain-handling facilities often lead to explosions involving the deaths of dozens of workers. In 1984, OSHA proposed to reduce the risks posed by such exposures by decreasing the permissible grain dust level. The outcome that resulted from the collaboration by OSHA and OMB offered firms a series of several performance-oriented alternatives that they could choose in order to achieve compliance: (i) clean up the dust whenever it exceeds one-eighth of an inch; (ii) clean up the dust at least once per shift; or (iii) use pneumatic dust control equipment.[27]

The flexibility offered by these various alternatives enables firms to choose the most cost-effective mechanism for achieving the desired safety objective. Although the introduction of flexibility of this type did not become a prevalent characteristic of new OSHA standards, it did mark the introduction of a greater degree of diversity in the regulatory approach than had been reflected in previous OSHA efforts.

Perhaps most important is the trend in the level of OSHA regulation. As in the case of EPA, there was a resurgence of regulation in the late 1980s. As indicated by the present value of the costs of proposed and final rules summarized in table 7.10, new OSHA regulations were generating substantial costs. Major regulations proposed in 1988 and 1989 would impose costs of $12 billion and $10.5 billion, respectively. If we exclude the OSHA carcinogen policy that was proposed in 1978 but never adopted, proposed OSHA standards imposed costs of only $35–$44 billion for the entire period 1975–80.[28] The level

26. A description of the activities and views of the oversight group is provided by the Office of Management and Budget's 1984 unpublished memorandum "OSHA's Proposed Standards for Grain Handling Facilities." See also the letter from Christopher DeMuth, administrator for information and regulatory affairs, OMB, to the solicitor of the U.S. Department of Labor, Francis X. Lilly.

27. Office of Management and Budget, "OSHA's Proposed Standards," 5–6.

28. For supporting data, see Viscusi (1983, 143–44).

Table 7.10   **Trends in OSHA Regulation Costs**

	Year	Present Value of Costs ($billions) of OSHA Regulations	
		Proposed Rules	Final Rules
	1987	2.8	2.7
	1988	12	.2
	1989	10.5	12.7

Source: Estimates prepared by U.S. Office of Management and Budget, August 1990.

of OSHA policy initiatives at the end of the second Reagan term had surpassed that of the pre-Reagan era.

7.6.4   Traffic Safety Regulation

One of NHTSA's early success stories in the 1980s that promoted safety in an effective manner was the promulgation of the regulation for rear-window brake lights (*Federal Register* 49, no. 97 [17 May 1984] 20818ff.). The installation of such brake lights reduces the reaction time of drivers of following vehicles because of the greater visibility of the single center high-mounted stop-lamp.

The Department of Transportation regulations with the broadest potential impact on fatalities were its safety belt standards. The Department of Transportation issued regulations requiring the enactment of mandatory safety belt laws. If this condition was not met, the federal government would require phased installation of passive restraint systems.

This compromise measure was a response to the U.S. Supreme Court decision to overturn the automobile industry relief package's rescission of the passive restraint requirements. Since many of the benefits of passive restraints could be achieved through use of seat belts, this measure represents an effort to utilize the ability of the individual to reduce his or her own risk rather than always relying on a technological solution. The decision to leave the ultimate decision of whether mandatory safety belt laws would be enacted to the states is consistent with the Reagan administration's principle of federalism.

In this case, there is no apparent heterogeneity in the benefits or the costs of a mandatory seat belt requirement to warrant leaving this matter up to the states. Since most economic studies indicate that the benefits of seat belt use far exceed the costs, the case for making the standard nationwide seems quite strong, if a mandatory requirement overruling individual choice is sensible.[29]

29. For a review of the benefits and costs of seat belt use, see Arnould and Grabowski (1981).

7.6.5   Smoking and Individual Responsibility for Risk

Perhaps the most aggressive new area of risk regulation in the 1980s was with respect to smoking behavior. Surgeon General C. Everett Koop issued increasingly strident attacks against cigarette smoking, designating smoking as more addictive than heroin and calling for a smoke-free society by the year 2000. Even the Council of Economic Advisers joined in the chorus of attacks against smoking, calling it the "greatest avoidable risk" (CEA 1987, 184).

The governmental policy efforts against smoking took two forms. The first consisted of public attacks against cigarettes that usually accompanied the issuance of the annual report of the surgeon general on smoking. Such reports ideally inform individuals regarding the risks of smoking, thus promoting a greater balancing of risks and benefits in individuals' decision making. The surgeon general's reports, however, went beyond information provision. They became advocacy documents against smoking behavior.

The second form of policy action consisted of a change in the warnings accompanying cigarettes. In 1984, Congress mandated a series of rotating cigarette warnings alerting consumers to a diverse set of risks pertaining to cigarettes. These warnings replaced the single warning in place since 1969 that indicated that "cigarette smoking is dangerous to your health."

Changes in hazard warning programs and public information campaigns can be easily undertaken by a policymaker wishing to pursue antismoking policies. These measures are more feasible than changes in the cigarette tax or national regulations pertaining to smoking behavior. However, as the percentage of smokers in society declined in the 1980s, the pressures against smoking increased.

Table 7.11 summarizes several key smoking trends. The total cigarette consumption per capita dropped considerably in the 1980s. As cigarette companies began to market their product to an increasingly smaller group, the price of cigarettes rose, which in turn also influences the number of people who will purchase the product. Cigarette taxes as a percentage of the retail price have dropped over the past twenty years, but the absolute level of this tax is much higher than before because of the rapid increase in the price of cigarettes. As the final columns in table 7.11 indicate, since the 1970s the percentage of the population smoking has been on the decline, and the percentage of former smokers has been on the rise.

Efforts by the surgeon general to publicize the potential risks of secondhand smoke contributed to widespread restrictions on cigarette smoking throughout the country. These have included regulations limiting smoking on airline flights as well as a diverse set of local smoking standards, particularly for restaurants. Although the main effect of the antismoking efforts has been to accentuate an already declining smoking trend and to increase the prevalence of restrictions on smoking, the shift in the acceptability of this particular product risk has been dramatic.

Table 7.11   **Principal Aspects of Smoking Behavior**

	Cigarettes per Capita	Cigarette Price per Pkg. ($avg.)	Cigarette Taxes as a % of Retail Price (median)	Present Smoker (%)	Former Smoker (%)
1970	2,534	.39	46.8	36.7	17.9
1980	2,821	.63	33.1	32.6	20.6
1985	2,501	1.05	30.8	29.8	24.4
1989	2,156	1.44	26.4	N.A.	N.A.

Source: Tobacco Institute, *The Tax Burden on Tobacco:* for cigarettes per capita, see *1989,* vol. 24 (1990), p. 6; for price per package and tax percentage, see *1970,* vol. 5 (1971), p. 83, and *1980,* vol. 15 (1981), p. 93. U.S. Dept. of Commerce (1989, 119 [smoking percentages]).

Note: N.A. = not available.

Particularly surprising is the nature of the discussion of smoking by government economists (CEA 1987, 184–86). In its extensive discussion of smoking, the 1987 *Economic Report of the President* did little to address any of the economics issues at stake. To what extent is there a market failure? Do individuals have knowledge of the risks that smoking may pose? How substantial are the costs of changing smoking, and what is the welfare loss from this "addiction" phenomenon? For all these risks to individuals from their own decisions, do the discouraging effects of taxes eliminate any market failure? If current taxes do not eliminate the market failure, what level of taxes is needed? Finally, in the case of secondhand smoke, for which smoking restrictions do the benefits of regulation exceed the costs? Are we going to treat passive smoking risks as a trump card that dominates other concerns that might be present regardless of their magnitude? What is most striking is not the fact that society has undertaken such initiatives, largely through the personal energy of the surgeon general, but rather the fact that the oversight economists have offered virtually unqualified support of these efforts in the absence of any regulatory analysis.

Perhaps the main point that economists are making by highlighting these antismoking efforts is that risks are not always the responsibility of a corporation. Responsibility for risk taking must be shared by the individual as well. This theme pervades much of the Reagan administration's efforts, and it provides a counterpoint to the view that controlling risk is simply a responsibility of government and industry. However, the government has not yet distinguished situations where it is appropriate to rely on personal responsibility for making decisions and contexts in which we should interfere with this responsibility by establishing regulations to overrule these choices.

7.6.6   The Overall Record on New Regulations

The early 1980s was not a period of major activity in terms of new regulations, but this hiatus was short lived. By the mid-1980s, the earlier pace of regulation had returned.

The chief new additions to the regulatory agenda marked a shift in the emphasis on taking advantage of individual safety-enhancing actions to promote safety. The OSHA hazard communication regulation and the increased emphasis on mandatory seat belt usage were examples of this policy direction. The antismoking crusade also marked an emphasis on the role of individual risk behavior, as did the risk communication component of EPA's radon policy. The increases in states' penalties against drunken driving were in a similar vein. The 1970s era of risk regulation was characterized by an emphasis on engineering controls and technological solutions to safety, whereas the 1980s attempted to incorporate more recognition of individual actions.

The extent of new regulatory activity was now, however, great. The most prominent administrators of major risk regulation agencies with a strong commitment to their agency's agenda were William Ruckelshaus and Lee Thomas. However, since these individuals succeeded Anne Gorsuch, their successful performance could do little more than reverse the damage that had already been done. Moreover, none of the appointees demonstrated a commitment to their agencies' objectives coupled with a sound economic agenda for regulatory reform.

7.7   Strategies for Regulatory Enforcement

In some contexts, regulatory enforcement is not a major concern. NHTSA can readily monitor whether firms are in compliance with automobile design standards since cars are a mass-produced product. Even an agency with a very small staff such as the CPSC has little difficulty in ascertaining whether firms are in compliance with its narrowly prescribed standards, such as safety cap requirements.

In some cases, however, effective enforcement design and targeting is an integral part of ensuring an effective regulatory program. The early OSHA enforcement efforts were characterized by infrequent inspections and low levels of penalties for violations, thus providing little incentive for firms to invest in safety. In contrast, EPA targets major sources of air and water pollution with at least one inspection annually. Nevertheless, a General Accounting Office (GAO) study in the early 1980s suggested that noncompliance rates for air and water pollution regulations might be as high as 80 percent.[30] Internal EPA studies indicate that enforcement for conventional pollutants is more effective than for unconventional pollutants. Enforcement problems for asbestos, toxic pollutants, and hazardous waste sites are much more difficult.

One widely espoused recommendation by economists is to replace the reliance on a fleet of inspectors by an injury tax or a pollution tax, such as a marketable pollution permit scheme. Environmentalists have never supported

30. See the discussion in Stanfield (1984, 1034).

such market-oriented policies because they have the appearance of enabling firms to buy their way out of safety and environmental improvements. Industry has provided little support for such a penalty system since creating effective incentives involves the imposition of nontrivial costs, thus increasing the stakes above the current regime.

Concern with effective enforcement presupposes, of course, that the agency's regulations are well designed. Unfortunately, standards for agencies such as OSHA and EPA are often excessively stringent. Lax enforcement is not necessarily the solution since exempting firms from any safety or environmental requirements is also not the ideal. In many cases, however, there is an effort to strike an appropriate balance by establishing phased compliance schedules to accommodate the substantial economic costs that a firm may face. Because of the difficulties of adjusting for ill-designed regulations through diminished enforcement, I will use the effective enforcement reference point as the policy objective.

7.7.1   OSHA's Enforcement Efforts

Under the Carter administration, OSHA's emphasis was on increasing the degree to which inspections focused on consequential hazards. The number of inspections undertaken declined, but the emphasis on serious violations and the level of penalties increased. This strategy complemented the standards reform effort to eliminate the less consequential regulations.

Thorne Auchter, Reagan's first head of OSHA, sought to decrease the confrontational role of OSHA by making inspections more of a consultative activity. This low-key inspection effort was coupled with a decrease in the inspection staff. To maintain any impact from inspections with a diminished number of full-scale inspections, one must increase their output.

The innovation that Auchter made was to introduce what OSHA termed "records check inspections" (see U.S. Department of Labor 1984, ii–iii). Auchter introduced a new, more cursory type of inspection so that the total number of inspections rose while the number of comprehensive inspections declined. Beginning in October 1981, OSHA inspectors at a firm examined the firm's lost workday accident rate for the past two years (or three years in the case of very small employers). Firms with injury rates below the national manufacturing average were exempted from inspections, and firms with injury rates in excess of the national average received a detailed inspection. This procedure established a mechanism for targeting inspections to enhance their productivity and contributed to Auchter's reputation as a "well-informed and effective manager" (see Niskanen 1988, 130). By fiscal 1983, records check inspections exceeded 10,000 per year, more than one of every six OSHA inspections.

One can view the records checks as being a mechanism for obtaining current information on firms' safety performance in a relatively low-cost manner, enabling OSHA to target its efforts better. One might, of course, modify the records checks approach by making the inspection exemption threshold industry specific.

The adoption of records check inspections came under substantial fire by outside critics since the procedure completely exempted from inspection firms that might violate OSHA standards (see Simon 1983). Falsification of accident records to obtain the exemption was also a potential problem, but no studies have documented any change in injury-reporting practices.

Had such inspections been introduced as an additional component of the enforcement effort rather than as part of a general policy of reduced enforcement, they might have been better received. Since the total change in OSHA policies reflected a drop in the number of inspections coupled with a replacement of full-scale inspections by more cursory records check inspections, the overall appearance was that of diminishing the enforcement effort.

The other component of OSHA's enforcement effort—penalties—had increased gradually under the Carter administration, but penalties were still at very low levels. To decrease OSHA's confrontational character, Auchter imposed a dramatic reduction in penalties and, in particular, required that any penalty in excess of $10,000 must be formally approved by the OSHA director. The chilling effect of this policy is reflected in an 80 percent reduction in the frequency of penalties above the $10,000 threshold (see Simon 1983). Company appeals of inspection decisions also became viewed as a negative index of an inspector's job performance, as the emphasis was on negotiated solutions rather than confrontations.

The statistics in table 7.12 indicate the character of these changes. The early years of the Reagan administration marked a decline in the number of inspections. The actual decline is ever greater since a substantial portion of these inspections are records check inspections. The average safety inspection time dropped from sixteen hours per inspection in 1980 to ten hours per inspection in 1983, and the average case hours per health inspection declined from forty-four hours per inspection in 1980 to thirty-three hours per inspection in 1983. The citations issued per hour of safety and health inspections increased so that the productivity of these inspections per unit time rose over that period.

The dramatic shift in the financial incentives created by OSHA is indicated by the data in the final column of table 7.12. The drop in penalties began in fiscal year 1981, for which the Carter and Reagan administrations overlapped. By fiscal year 1982, total OSHA penalties had dropped to $5.6 million, a figure that is far less than the $80 billion in wage compensation that workers received in that time period for job risks (see Viscusi 1983).

This period of deregulation subsequently gave way to a reversal in OSHA's emphasis. There was a resurgence in the penalty levels by 1987 and 1988, with considerably more penalties being levied in 1988 than in any year in OSHA's history. The extent of the change in enforcement stringency is borne out in the data presented in table 7.13 on the number of OSHA penalties in excess of $1

Table 7.12   **Summary of Federal OSHA Inspection Activity**

Fiscal year	Inspections (thousands)	Violations (thousands)	Proposed Penalties ($millions)
1972	28.9	89.6	2.1
1973	47.6	153.2	4.2
1974	78.1	292.0	7.0
1975	80.9	318.8	8.2
1976	90.3	380.3	12.4
1977	59.9	181.9	11.6
1978	57.2	134.5	19.9
1979	57.9	128.5	23.0
1980	63.4	132.4	25.5
1981	57.0	111.4	10.8
1982	61.2	97.1	5.6
1983	68.9	111.7	6.4
1984	72.0	111.6	8.1
1985	71.3	119.7	9.2
1986	64.1	129.0	12.5
1987	61.5	137.0	24.5
1988	58.4	154.9	45.0

Source: OSHA computer printouts and data published in U.S. Department of Labor, *Report of the President to Congress on Occupational Safety and Health* (various years).

Table 7.13   **Trends in Large OSHA Penalty Levels**

Year	No. of Penalties above $1 Million	Year	No. of Penalties above $1 Million
1972–85	0	1988	6
1986	1	1989	9
1987	4		

Source: Based on data provided in U.S. Department of Labor (1990).

million. Until 1986, OSHA had never penalized a firm by that great an amount on the basis of a single set of citations. However, in the late 1980s, Secretary of Labor Brock introduced a severe penalty structure for egregious violations. A substantial and increasing number of such penalties were levied, ranging as high as the 1989 penalty of $7.3 million against USX. This single firm's penalty exceeded the total penalties levied for the entire country for 1982 or 1983. Moreover, the fines imposed by OSHA attracted widespread attention to the enforcement effort, altering the public's perception of its stringency.

Consequently, the decade of the 1980s was one of enforcement extremes. By most criteria, the enforcement effort in the early 1980s was the most lax in OSHA history, whereas by the end of the decade OSHA had become more vigorous in its enforcement than ever before. The strategy of deregulation through regulatory neglect had been abandoned.

7.7.2   The EPA Enforcement Effort

The enforcement strategy at EPA bore some similarities to that at OSHA, with the principal exception being that the initial EPA head Anne Gorsuch was generally regarded as a poor manager (see Niskanen 1988, 128). Environmental critics charged that Gorsuch had abandoned EPA's mission: "There is a massive regulatory resistance going on in this administration. . . . This administration is massively disobeying these laws because they don't like them. In this context, the only mechanism we have for enforcement is the courts."[31]

Anne Gorsuch had shifted substantial enforcement authority to the states, decreasing federal technical support for the enforcement effort as well as federal financing of it. Organizations such as the National Governor's Association expressed dismay at the shift in EPA policy: "The perception within the regulating community was that there would be no enforcement. . . . That made the states' job so much harder."[32]

For the politically prominent Superfund program, Gorsuch also erred by appointing personnel who had no apparent regulatory commitment or expertise. Rita Lavelle's management of the Superfund program attracted criticism for managerial incompetence and alleged sweetheart deals with industry.

Gorsuch was succeeded in March 1983 by William Ruckelshaus after Gorsuch's highly contentious and weak performance. Ruckelshaus was the initial head of EPA in 1970, and his selection reflected the need to restore the credibility of the agency. The successor to Ruckelshaus, Lee Thomas, was a career administrator who continued the policies of Ruckelshaus.

Table 7.14 provides a quantitative perspective on the enforcement effort by summarizing EPA's civil referrals to the U.S. Department of Justice—EPA's principal enforcement sanction. During the Gorsuch era, referrals to the Justice Department for violations of air and water regulation declined substantially, as did total referrals. Perhaps most striking was the drop in referrals for hazardous waste violations. Since these violations pertain to regulations that had been established only recently and should have been the major growth area for new EPA initiatives, the reversal in these referrals to less than half their level in 1980 is a substantial departure. The hazards posed by toxins and pesticides, which would eventually compose an increasingly important part of the EPA's agenda in the 1980s, received almost no attention whatsoever.

The data in table 7.15 on administrative actions undertaken by EPA provide a similar perspective. The lowest number of administrative actions was in 1982, but by the late 1980s administrative enforcement actions had returned to the higher levels of the Carter administration.

The restoration of the enforcement effort in fiscal 1984 and 1985 marks the

31. This statement was made by Jonathan Lash, senior staff attorney at the Natural Resources Defense Council (see Mosher 1981, 2233).
32. Statement by Edward A. Helme, director of the National Governors' Association Natural Resources Group, quoted in Stanfield (1984, 1035).

Table 7.14   **EPA Civil Referrals to the Department of Justice**

Fiscal Year	Air	Water	Hazardous Waste	Toxics, Pesticides	Total
1972	0	1	0	0	1
1973	4	0	0	0	4
1974	3	0	0	0	3
1975	5	20	0	0	25
1976	15	67	0	0	82
1977	50	93	0	0	143
1978	123	137	2	0	262
1979	149	81	9	3	242
1980	100	56	53	1	210
1981	66	37	14	1	118
1982	36	45	29	2	112
1983	69	56	33	7	165
1984	82	95	60	14	251
1985	116	93	48	19	276
1986	115	119	84	24	342
1987	122	92	77	13	304
1988	86	123	143	20	372

Source: Based on Russell (1990, table 7-6), using data from *Mealey's Litigation Reports: Superfund* 1, no. 18 (28 December 1988): C-1.

Table 7.15   **EPA Administrative Actions Initiated (by act), Fiscal Years 1972–88**

	Clean Air Act (1970)	Clean Water and Safe Drinking Water Acts (1972/1974)	Resource Conservation and Recovery (1976)	Superfund (CERCLA) (1980)	FIFRA[a] (1947)	Toxic Substances Control Act (1976)	Totals
1972	0	0	0	0	860	0	860
1973	0	0	0	0	1,274	0	1,274
1974	0	0	0	0	1,387	0	1,387
1975	0	738	0	0	1,641	0	2,352
1976	210	915	0	0	2,488	0	3,613
1977	297	1,128	0	0	1,219	0	2,644
1978	129	730	0	0	762	1	1,622
1979	404	506	0	0	253	22	1,185
1980	86	569	0	0	176	101	864
1981	112	562	159	0	154	70	901
1982	21	329	237	0	176	101	864
1983	41	781	436	0	296	294	1,848
1984	141	1,644	554	137	272	376	3,124
1985	122	1,031	327	160	236	733	2,609
1986	143	990	235	139	338	781	2,626
1987	191	1,214	243	135	360	1,051	3,194
1988	224	1,345	309	224	376	607	3,085

Source: Based on Russell (1990, table 7-7), using data from *Mealey's Litigation Reports: Superfund* 1, no. 18 (28 December 1988): C-5.

[a]FIFRA = Federal Insecticide, Fungicide, and Rodenticide Act.

impact of the Ruckelshaus reforms on EPA's enforcement credibility. In a January speech at EPA, Ruckelshaus observed, "Unless [the states] have a gorilla in the closet, they can't do the job. And the gorilla is EPA (Stanfield 1984, 1034).

The reality of the gorilla in the closet became reflected in the actions that EPA undertook. Enforcement patterns for particular EPA programs often changed dramatically. Under the Superfund program established in 1980, EPA undertook no administrative actions whatsoever before the Ruckelshaus era. In fiscal year 1984, the number of administrative actions that EPA initiated jumped to 137 per year, climbing eventually to 224 per year (*Mealey's Litigation Report: Superfund* 1, no. 18 [28 December 1988]: C-5).

The main contribution of the Gorsuch era at the EPA was to scale back the enforcement effort and slow down the implementation of the newly emerging programs for hazardous wastes and toxic substances. The contribution of the Ruckelshaus and Thomas era was twofold. First, the enforcement capabilities of EPA were restored to their levels at the start of the decade. Second, Ruckelshaus and Thomas fostered the development of enforcement efforts in the newly emerging areas of EPA's agenda.

7.8 The Impact of Regulation on Health, Safety, and Environmental Quality

The ultimate objective of social regulation policies is to influence health, safety, and environmental outcomes. Assessing the impact of the regulatory activities of the 1980s is not straightforward. Some of the ultimate costs of these regulations have not been fully transmitted throughout the economy. This is particularly true for situations involving noncompliance, phased schedules for compliance to accommodate industries in economic hardship, and regulations promulgated in the 1980s but with increasingly stringent requirements being imposed over time. A second complicating factor is that regulation is not the only influence on safety and environmental outcomes. Safety risk levels of all kinds have been declining throughout the century.[33] As society has become wealthier, our preferences for safety are enhanced. Ideally, we would like to distinguish the effects of government regulation from the trends that would otherwise have taken place in the absence of regulation.

Table 7.16 provides a summary of several death risk trends. One can view 1970 as marking the beginning of the decade of safety and environmental regulation. All three sets of death rates in table 7.16 have been in decline since the 1930s. The rate of decline for work accidents was somewhat greater in the 1980s than in previous decades, while the rate of decline in motor vehicle accidents is a bit higher than in the 1970s. The 1980s rate of decline in home accidents, which reflects the activities of the CPSC and the FDA, was almost

33. The only exception to this pattern is that of automobile fatalities, which are also in decline if one recognizes the changing age distribution and the change in the miles driven.

Table 7.16   **Principal Death Risk Rates**

| | Annual Rate of Increase in Death Rates | | |
	Work	Home	Motor Vehicle
1930–40	−1.8	−.2	−3.3
1940–50	−2.3	−2.2	−4.0
1950–60	−2.8	−2.1	−3.5
1960–70	−1.2	−1.7	−.8
1970–80	−1.6	−2.7	−3.3
1980–90	−3.2	−2.4	−4.3

Source: Calculations by the author using death rate data from National Safety Council (1988, 14–15, 70–71).

Note: All figures are given per 100,000 population.

identical to that in the 1970s. Overall, death rates continued to drop in the 1980s at roughly the same pace as in previous decades.

7.8.1   Job Risk Trends

Other job risk measures suggest somewhat different risk trends. Table 7.17 reports four different measures of workplace risk levels that capture injuries other than death risks. The bottom panel of table 7.17 presents the percentage annual growth rates for these four different risk measures: the rates of decline for total injuries, lost workday injuries, nonfatal injuries without lost workdays, and the total rate of lost workdays. The patterns for these four measures indicate a slowing in the rate of decline or, in the case of total lost workdays, a lower rate of increase.

Since cyclical factors and other influences are at work, one needs a more detailed econometric analysis to isolate the independent influence of regulatory policy. The findings in Viscusi (1986) for 1973–83 indicate that the effect of the previous year's OSHA inspections on injury rates in the current year ranges from a low value of 2.6 percent for total injury rates, to an intermediate value of 3.6 percent for lost workday case rates, to a high value of 6.1 percent for the rate of total lost workdays. Moreover, there is no evidence of a dropoff in the impact of these inspections on injuries with the advent of the records check inspections. A more detailed examination of the performance of OSHA records check inspections by Ruser and Smith (1988) indicates that, for plants potentially subject to the records check procedure, the reported injury rates declined by 5–14 percent. There was, however, underreporting of job injuries during that period.[34] What we do not know is whether there was any change in the extent of underreporting. On balance, however, there is no evidence that the institution of records check inspections decreased the overall efficacy of the typical OSHA inspection.

---

34. For a discussion of the underreporting problem, see Ruser and Smith (1988).

Table 7.17   **Occupational Injury and Illness Incidence Rates per 100
                   Full-Time Workers**

| | | Injuries and Illnesses | | |
Year	Total Cases	Lost Workday Cases	Without Lost Workdays	Lost Workdays
1973	11.0	3.4	7.5	53.3
1974	10.4	3.5	6.9	54.6
1975	9.1	3.3	5.8	56.1
1976	9.2	3.5	5.7	60.5
1977	9.3	3.8	5.5	61.6
1978	9.4	4.1	5.3	63.5
1979	9.5	4.3	5.2	67.7
1980	8.7	4.0	4.7	65.2
1981	8.3	3.8	4.5	61.7
1982	7.7	3.5	4.2	58.7
1983	7.6	3.4	4.2	58.5
1984	8.0	3.7	4.3	63.4
1985	7.9	3.6	4.3	64.9
1986	7.9	3.6	4.3	65.8
1987	8.3	3.8	4.4	69.9
1988	8.6	4.0	4.6	76.1
% annual rate of increase				
1973–80	−2.9	+2.3	−6.3	+2.9
1980–90	−.1	0	−.3	+2.0

Source: Calculations by the author and data from U.S. Bureau of Labor Statistics (1989, table 6) and U.S. Bureau of Labor Statistics, *Occupational Injuries and Illness by Industry* (various years).
Note: Data for 1976–88 exclude farms with fewer than eleven employees.

7.8.2   Auto Safety Effects

Analysis of the impact of automobile safety regulation is also complicated by the role of competing influences that affect the safety trend, such as the character of highway construction and the age composition of the population. There is substantial controversy in the literature over the effect of automobile safety regulations on highway accident rates because of the possibly counterproductive effect of safety belt regulations on driver behavior.[35] Drivers wearing safety belts faced lower expected accident costs and as a result will have a reduced incentive to exercise care.[36] The general consensus in the literature is

35. The initial paper in this area is that of Peltzman (1975). For further discussion of these issues and the controversy over this line of research, see Blomquist (1988), Crandall et al. (1986), and Graham (1989).
36. To obtain a status report on this debate, see Crandall et al. (1986), which advocates the safety-enhancing viewpoint. For the most recent perspective from the school of thought that places substantial weight on the counterproductive impacts of safety policies, see Blomquist (1988).

that automobiles have become much safer for passengers, but there has been an apparent increase in the risk posed to pedestrians and bicyclists. The competing magnitudes of these effects has long been debated.

The performance of the other aspects of automobile regulation is mixed. Automobile emissions standards have lowered the pollution levels for new cars, but the penalty levels on the cars that fail to comply with the standards have led motorists to keep old, high emission vehicles on the road (see Crandall et al. 1986). Fuel economy standards are also a binding constraint, but most economists would prefer market-based incentives, such as a gasoline tax, so that motorists can respond to the changing terms of trade rather than be constrained by specific fuel economy standards on corporate fleets.

7.8.3   Pollution Trends

The net effect of automobile and other pollution regulations on environmental outcomes is summarized by the pollution trends in table 7.18. The data in this table provide information on emissions, which are correlated with air quality but are not an exact measure of it. Moreover, the monitoring data involve substantial error, where the direction and magnitude of the error are unknown. Perhaps the most striking aspect of the table is that the wave of deregulation efforts and lax environmental enforcement that characterized the period 1981–

Table 7.18   **National Pollution Emissions Trends**

		Pollutant (teragrams/year)			
Year	Particulates	Sulfur Oxides	Nitrogen Oxides	Carbon Monoxide	Lead (gigagrams)
1960	21.6	19.7	13.0	89.7	N.A.
1970	18.5	28.3	18.5	101.4	203.8
1975	10.6	25.8	19.5	84.1	147.0
1980	8.5	23.4	20.9	79.6	70.6
1981	8.0	22.6	20.9	77.4	56.4
1982	7.1	21.4	20.0	72.4	54.4
1983	7.1	20.7	19.3	74.5	46.4
1984	7.4	21.5	19.8	71.8	40.1
1985	7.1	21.1	19.8	67.0	21.1
1986	6.8	20.9	19.0	63.1	8.6
1987	7.0	20.6	19.3	64.1	8.0
1988	6.9	20.7	19.8	61.2	7.6
% annual growth rate					
1960–70	−1.5	+3.7	+3.6	+1.2	. . .
1970–80	−7.5	−1.9	+1.2	−2.4	−10.1
1980–88	−2.6	−1.5	−.5	−3.2	−20.0

Source: U.S. Environmental Protection Agency (1990, 2).

Note: N.A. = not available.

82 did not lead to a rapid deterioration of environmental quality. The improvements in environmental quality took place at a slower pace than in earlier years, but there is no evidence of worsening air quality for the five different measures of pollution listed.

The first type of air pollution emission listed in table 7.18 is that of particulates, which arise primarily from fuel combustion (e.g., coal combustion by railroads), forest fires, industrial processes, and highway motor vehicles. The rate of decline in particulate emissions in the 1980s was 2.6 percent annually. This rate is much less than during the 1970s, when tremendous progress was made against this class of emission.

The second type of emission, sulphur dioxide, arises from stationary fuel combustion and industrial processes. The principal contributor to this type of pollution is fuel combustion involving sulphur-bearing coal. After an increase in sulphur oxides in the 1960s, there was a decline in these emissions through both the 1970s and the 1980s at roughly comparable rates, primarily because of increased controls of emissions by nonferrous smelters and sulfuric acid plants.

The third class of emission in table 7.18, nitrogen oxides, arises from both highway motor vehicles and stationary sources, such as coal-fired electric utility boilers. After an increase in these emissions during the 1960s and 1970s, there was a slight decline in such emissions during the 1980s. Automobile emissions controls are among the policies that have contributed to this trend.

The fourth class of emission included in table 7.18 is that of carbon monoxide, for which highway motor vehicle emissions are the largest contributors. The rate of decline in carbon monoxide emissions increased in the 1980s.

Of the sets of statistics in table 7.18, the lead statistics in the final column provide the strongest evidence of improvements in environmental quality. These gains can also be traced to specific regulatory policies. The primary sources of these lead emissions are motor vehicles and industrial processes. The impact of EPA's successive reductions in the allowable lead content of gasoline in 1985 and 1986 was dramatic. Lead emissions were cut almost in half between 1984 and 1985, and between 1985 and 1986 they were reduced by more than half again. Within a two-year period, 80 percent of all lead emissions were eliminated. Moreover, on the basis of the OMB review of the regulatory impact analysis, this environmental improvement also represents a situation in which the benefits to society of the improved environmental quality exceed the costs. This decrease in lead emissions is perhaps the major environmental success story of the 1980s.

For other EPA efforts that were central to the environmental policy in the 1980s, there are no comparable measures of environmental pollution levels, but there are some indices of policy achievements.

For the Superfund program established by legislation in 1980,[37] the 1980s

---

37. The statistics presented below are based on the discussion in Acton (1989), particularly the material in app. A.

marked a significant environmental cleanup effort. By 1989, EPA had identified over 30,000 Superfund sites and had inspected almost 10,000 of them. In over 12,000 cases, EPA concluded that no further action was warranted. In terms of actual cleanup activities, EPA had initiated removal actions in 1,347 cases, although it has completed only a small fraction of these removal efforts. These removal actions pertained to 274 of the 1,063 sites that EPA put on its national priority list. If one views this listing as comprehensive, EPA had begun to address roughly one-fourth of its high-priority waste sites in the 1980s. The extent of the risk that was reduced and the extent that it should have been reduced given the costs and benefits of cleanup are not known. Moreover, without any comparable efforts in the 1970s, there is no good reference point for assessing the pace of the cleanup.

7.9   The Regulatory Record of the 1980s

The 1980s record in terms of influencing the structure of safety and environmental policies is very mixed. The initial efforts of the Reagan administration emphasized deregulation and budgetary cutbacks rather than changes in the structure of regulation. This approach reflected an antiregulation approach rather than meaningful regulatory reform. This misplaced emphasis dissipated much of the political momentum for regulatory reform at the start of the Reagan administration. Because of the disappointing performance of prominent officials such as Reagan's first head of EPA, much of the 1980s was spent restoring the credibility of the agencies rather than making substantive advances. There were also some regulatory achievements—the phase down of lead in gasoline, the introduction of the OSHA hazard communication policy proposed by Carter and enacted by Reagan, and expediting the approval of drugs for life-threatening diseases.

By the mid-1980s, the regulatory reform effort had ended. Vice President Bush terminated his Task Force on Regulatory Relief. Regulatory agencies proposed regulations with greater costs than ever before. OMB became less influential in altering the structure of regulation, and regulatory enforcement became more vigorous than before the onset of deregulation.

The window of opportunity for regulatory reform was not great, and this opportunity had been squandered on a misguided deregulation agenda. There was no attempt whatsoever to address the fundamental long-term problems arising from agencies' restrictive legislative mandates. At a more modest level, there was not even a broad-based effort to adopt market-based approaches to controlling risk or to emphasize more performance-oriented regulations. By the mid-1980s, regulatory policy returned to the same patterns as in earlier administrations, except that OMB appears to have had some limited influence in eliminating some of the most inefficient regulations.

In effect, there were two Reagan regulation agendas—the deregulation agenda that pertained from 1981 to 1983 and the return to the traditional regulatory agenda from 1984 to 1989. The Bush administration has continued the policies of the second Reagan agenda. In retrospect, the deregulation efforts will be viewed as a temporary policy aberration rather than as an effort with any lasting impact.

The extent to which this record should be viewed negatively depends in large part on the reference point used for the assessment. Advocates of meaningful regulatory reform will be disappointed in this performance because of the forgone opportunity for fundamental change. The widespread consensus on the direction for reform reflected in the economics literature contrasts with the very mixed nature of the reform efforts. The impetus for meaningful regulatory reform and effective oversight appears to have been lost, as the task of undertaking the unfulfilled risk and environmental agenda of the 1980s had taken precedence.

References

Acton, J. P. 1989. *Understanding superfund.* Santa Monica, Calif.: Rand Corp., Institute for Civil Justice.

Arnould, R., and H. G. Grabowski. 1981. Auto safety regulation: An analysis of market failure. *Bell Journal of Economics* 12:27–45.

Blomquist, G. C. 1988. *The regulation of motor vehicle and traffic safety.* Boston, Mass.: Kluwer Academic.

Broder, I., and J. F. Morrall III. 1983. The economic basis for OSHA's and EPA's generic carcinogen regulations. In *What role for the government?* ed. R. Zeckhauser and D. Leebaert. Durham, N.C.: Duke University Press.

Cornell, N., R. Noll, and B. Weingast. 1976. Safety regulation. In *Setting national priorities,* ed. H. Owen and C. Schultze. Washington, D.C.: Brookings.

Council of Economic Advisers (CEA). 1987. *Economic report of the president.* Washington, D.C.: U.S. Government Printing Office, January.

———. 1990. *Economic report of the president.* Washington, D.C.: U.S. Government Printing Office, February.

Crandall, R. W. 1983. *Controlling industrial pollution: The economics and politics of clean air.* Washington, D.C.: Brookings.

Crandall, R. W., H. K. Gruenspecht, T. E. Keeler, and L. B. Lave. 1986. *Regulating the automobile.* Washington, D.C.: Brookings.

DeMuth, C. 1980a. Constraining regulatory costs: I. The White House review programs. *Regulation* 4:13–26.

———. 1980b. The regulatory budget. *Regulation* 4:29–43.

———. 1984. A strategy of regulatory reform. *Regulation* 8:25–30.

Deregulation HQ: An interview on a new executive order with Murray L. Weidenbaum and James C. Miller III. 1981. *Regulation* 5, no. 2:14–23.

Eads, G., and M. Fix. 1984. *Relief or reform? Reagan's regulatory dilemma.* Washington, D.C.: Urban Institute.

Earley, Pete. 1985. What's a life worth? *Washington Post Magazine,* 9 June 1985, 13, 36–41.

Grabowski, H. G., and J. M. Vernon. 1983. *The regulation of pharmaceuticals: Balancing the benefits and risks.* Washington, D.C.: American Enterprise Institute.

Graham, J. D. 1989. *Auto safety: Assessing America's performance.* Dover, Mass.: Auburn House.

Greider, W. 1982. *The education of David Stockman and other Americans.* New York: Dutton.

Hahn, R. W., and G. L. Hester. 1989. Where did all the markets go? *Yale Journal on Regulation* 6, no. 1:109–54.

Hahn, R. W., and R. Noll. 1990. Environmental markets in the year 2000. *Journal of Risk and Uncertainty* 3, no. 4 (December): 351–68.

Lave, L. B. 1981. *The strategy of social regulation: Decision frameworks for policy.* Washington, D.C.: Brookings.

Litan, R., and W. Nordhaus. 1983. *Reforming federal regulation.* New Haven, Conn.: Yale University Press.

MacAvoy, P., ed. 1977. *OSHA safety regulation: Report of the presidential task force.* Washington, D.C.: American Enterprise Institute.

———. 1979. *The regulated industries and the economy.* New York: Norton.

Mendeloff, J. M. 1988. *The dilemma of toxic substance regulation.* Cambridge, Mass.: MIT Press.

Miller, J. C., and B. Yandle. 1979. *Benefit-cost analyses of social regulation.* Washington, D.C.: American Enterprise Institute.

Morrall, J. F., III. 1986. A review of the record. *Regulation* 10, no. 2:13–24, 30.

Mosher, Lawrence. 1981. Environmentalists sue to put an end to "regulatory massive resistance." *National Journal,* 19 December, 2233–34.

National Safety Council. 1988. *National Safety Council accident facts.* Chicago.

Nichols, A., and R. J. Zeckhauser. 1981. OSHA after a decade: A time for reason. In *Case studies in regulation: Revolution and reform,* ed. L. W. Weiss and M. W. Klass. Boston: Little, Brown.

———. 1986. The perils of prudence. *Regulation* 10, no. 2:11–24.

Niskanen, W. A. 1988. *Reaganomics: An insider's account of the policies and the people.* New York: Oxford University Press.

Nordhaus, W. D. 1990. Global warming: Slowing the greenhouse express. In *Setting national priorities,* ed. H. Aaron. Washington, D.C.: Brookings.

Peltzman, S. 1975. The effects of automobile safety regulation. *Journal of Political Economy* 83:677–725.

Portney, P. R. 1990. Economics and the clean air act. *Journal of Economic Perspectives* 4, no. 4 (Fall): 173–81.

Presidential Task Force on Regulatory Relief. 1983. Reagan administration regulatory achievements. Washington, D.C.: U.S. Office of Management and Budget, 11 August.

Ruser, J. W., and R. S. Smith 1988. The effect of OSHA records-check inspections on reported occupational injuries in manufacturing establishments. *Journal of Risk and Uncertainty* 1, no. 4:415–35.

Russell, C. 1990. Monitoring and enforcement. In *Public policies for environmental protection,* ed. P. Portney. Washington, D.C.: Resources for the Future.

Schultze, C. L. 1982. The role and responsibility of the economist in government. *American Economic Review* 72:62–66.

Simon, P. 1983. *Reagan in the workplace: Unraveling the health and safety net.* Washington, D.C.: Center for Study of Responsive Law.

Smith, R. S. 1976. *The Occupational Safety and Health Act: Its goals and achievements.* Washington, D.C.: American Enterprise Institute.

Stanfield, Rochelle. 1984. Ruckelshaus casts EPA as "gorilla" in states' enforcement closet. *National Journal,* 26 May, 1034–38.

Stigler, G. 1971. The theory of economic regulation. *Bell Journal of Economics and Management Science* 2:3–21.

Stockman, D. A. 1986. *The triumph of politics.* New York: Harper & Row.

Stokinger, H. 1984. Modus operandi of Threshold Limits Committee of ACGIH. *Annals of the American Conference of Industrial Hygiene* 9:133.

Thaler, R., and S. Rosen, 1976. The value of saving a life: Evidence from the labor market. In *Household production and consumption,* ed. N. Terleckyz. NBER Studies in Income and Wealth, no. 40. New York: Columbia University Press.

Tobacco Institute. Various years. *The tax burden on tobacco.* Washington, D.C.

U.S. Bureau of Labor Statistics. 1989. BLS reports on survey of occupational injuries and illnesses in 1988. USDL-89-548. Washington, D.C., 15 November.

———. Various years. *Occupational injuries and illness by industry.* Washington, D.C.: U.S. Government Printing Office.

U.S. Congress. Committee on Education and Labor. Select Committee on Labor. 1972. *Occupational Safety and Health Act of 1970: Oversight and proposed amendments.* Washington, D.C.: U.S. Government Printing Office.

U.S. Department of Commerce. 1989. *Statistical abstract of the United States, 1989.* Washington, D.C.: U.S. Government Printing Office.

U.S. Department of Labor. 1984. *OSHA revised field operations manual.* Washington, D.C.

———. Occupational Safety and Health Administration. 1990. Penalties proposed. Internal OSHA computer printout. Washington, D.C., 16 July.

———. Occupational Safety and Health Administration. Various years. *Report of the president to Congress on occupational safety and health.* Washington, D.C.

U.S. Environmental Protection Agency. Office of Air Quality. 1990. *National air pollutant emission estimates, 1940–1988.* EPA-450/4-90-001. Washington, D.C., March.

U.S. Office of Management and Budget. 1988. *Regulatory program of the United States government, April 1, 1988–March 21, 1989.* Washington, D.C.: U.S. Government Printing Office.

Viscusi, W. K. 1979. *Employment hazards: An investigation of market performance.* Harvard Economic Studies, no. 148. Cambridge, Mass.: Harvard University Press.

———. 1982. Analysis of OMB and OSHA evaluations of the hazard communications proposal. Statement prepared for Secretary of Labor Raymond Donovan, 15 March.

———. 1983. *Risk by choice: Regulating health and safety in the workplace.* Cambridge, Mass.: Harvard University Press.

———. 1986. The impact of occupational safety and health regulation, 1973–1983. *Rand Journal of Economics* 17, no. 4:567–80.

Warren, M., and K. Chilton. 1990. *Regulation's rebound: Bush budget gives regulation a boost.* Report no. OP81. St. Louis: Center for Study of American Business, April.

Weidenbaum, M. L. 1980. Reforming government regulation. *Regulation* 4, no. 6:15–18.

White, L. J. 1982. *The regulation of air pollutant emissions from motor vehicles.* Washington, D.C.: American Enterprise Institute.

Wines, Michael. 1983. Reagan plan to relieve auto industry of regulatory burden gets mixed grades. *National Journal,* 23 July, 1532–37.

Zeckhauser, R. J., and W. K. Viscusi. 1990. Risk within reason. *Science* 248:559–64.

2. *Christopher DeMuth*

As Kip Viscusi stated in his fine paper, the primary goal of the Reagan administration in the area of regulation was to improve the efficiency of regulatory programs by hewing to economic thinking as much as possible. Thus, this area of economic policy provides a good occasion to address the questions with which Martin Feldstein opened this conference, namely, Where was economic thinking influential in policy-making, Where was it not, and, Why?

Let me begin by mentioning three reasons why regulatory policy represented a fruitful area in which to increase the role of economic reasoning in policy-making. First, the regulatory agencies have an enormous amount of discretion in interpreting the laws, despite a common belief that statutory standards are very strict (and often so uneconomic as to make almost any economist shrink in horror). In truth, the agencies are usually told in general terms to promote occupational safety, or pollution reduction, or whatever, and are then given great discretion in how they do so through particular regulations.

Second, as a sort of constitutional price for this discretion, regulatory agencies are required to be highly, and I think almost uniquely, rationalistic about what they do. They must give public notice about their intended policies and draw a coherent connection between those policies and their legislated objectives. Further, both the agencies' decisions and the rationales that they offer for those decisions are subject to some degree of review by the courts. Clearly, rule making can be a contentious and politicized process, and the rationales that the agencies give may disguise narrower or unworthy goals, but, nevertheless, there is an obligation to justify what is being done in regulatory policy that is greater than that for monetary or fiscal policy.

Third, a series of executive orders beginning in the Nixon administration has created a progressively more aggressive and formal review of regulatory policy by the Office of Management and Budget (OMB) and other White House offices. Although these orders began with rather vague and ad hoc standards—"quality of life" in the Nixon administration and "inflation impact" in the Ford administration—they have been expressed increasingly in economic or at least cost-benefit terms. That progression culminated in an executive order signed by President Reagan shortly after he came into office that set forth a series of net social benefit standards that are reported below in section A of the appendix.

Many of the people supporting regulatory reform, including many colleagues and allies around this table, had academic backgrounds and were very sympathetic to the notion of using economics in regulatory policy. During the time that I administered President Reagan's regulatory review program at OMB, roughly sixty regulations came in for review every week, and I think that everyone there tried to push the economic standard as thoroughly as possible in that review process. Indeed, I tried to some extent to codify our approach to regulation through a kind of common law of review of individual rules. By applying economics to a variety of types of regulatory action, I tried to give the agencies and the outside world a sense of how we interpreted and were applying the executive order. Eventually, a set of regulatory policy guidelines was established in another executive order; they are reported below in section B of the appendix. Someone recently described these guidelines as the most relentless application of microeconomic theory to regulatory policy ever attempted.

In the rest of these remarks, I want to discuss the extent to which we succeeded or failed in our attempt to push economic thinking. I think that the best framework for this discussion is to consider three types or classes of regulatory policy where the executive branch has broad legal discretion. In the first case, corresponding to guideline 2 in section B of the appendix, economics provides a clear prior indication of what the right policy is. The second situation is at the other extreme, where determining the correct policy is not a matter of theory but requires a lot of empirical work as well; this situation corresponds to guideline 4 in section B. The third situation is an intermediate one, corresponding to guideline 3 in Section B. My conclusion will be that the attempt to apply economic thinking in the regulatory review process was most successful where the policy implications of economic analysis were most widely understood and accepted by policy officials who were not themselves economists—in other words, where economic thinking had already suffused the thinking of regulators who were not professional economists.

The first class of regulation that I want to consider is agricultural marketing orders, which might involve removing 25 percent of the almonds from the market for the coming year or denying certain people the permission to plant hops on their underutilized cropland. Many people at the White House had thought that the executive order on regulation would affect primarily the regulation of transportation, occupational health and safety, and the environment and were surprised to discover a spate of these egregious agricultural marketing orders coming in for review. In some ways, I wished that I could ignore these orders because, although they were offensive, I suspected that their economic impact was not nearly as great as the impact of the health, safety, and environmental regulations. At the same time, many people outside the administration believed that the executive order on regulation was simply a way to provide relief for industry rather than sound economic policy. So, in that situation, we simply could not ignore these marketing orders.

The analysts at the Agriculture Department were shocked when I told them that I did not even want to see their cost-benefit analyses demonstrating the marketing orders to be beneficial. I knew without looking at the facts that the rules could not be beneficial, that price controls and entry controls in thoroughly competitive markets were empirically uninteresting. I started rejecting these rules left and right, including one Michigan cherry order the rejection of which put an end to any prospects that Dave Stockman had for a future political career, for which he has been, I hope, deeply grateful to me.

Dealing with these marketing orders absorbed a lot of time and attention, and, as Bill Niskanen pointed out, eventually there was an appropriations rider that prevented OMB from reviewing the orders in the future. As I look back on this issue, however, I am surprised at how much change we were able to make, given the political opposition based on the highly concentrated nature of the benefits of these orders. We abolished the two marketing orders that contained outright entry controls; we greatly reduced the use of "set asides" in a variety of other orders; and for the two largest and most harmful marketing orders, affecting California citrus crops, we greatly truncated the growing season to which the orders applied and allowed free marketing at the beginning and the end. Further, the people in the Agricultural Marketing Service gradually assimilated an economic way of thinking about the effects of entry and price controls. Thus, although we had no allies in the beginning, by the end it did not even matter very much when Congress passed the appropriations rider. My understanding is that these agricultural marketing orders are continuing to come unraveled, and I think that eventually they will fade away.

The second class of regulation deals with environmental protection. This regulation applies to situations where there are no markets, where there are large externalities, and where regulation is clearly justified. But, in contrast with the agricultural marketing orders, there is nothing in economic theory to decide what the appropriate extent of that regulation should be. Let me focus on the example of effluent guidelines under the Clean Water Act, where the Environmental Protection Agency (EPA) sets industry-by-industry standards for the amounts of various sorts of pollutants that can be discharged. This is an area of regulation where the *use* of cost-benefit analysis itself was not particularly controversial—we were not arguing that economics says you cannot control water pollution, and almost everybody at EPA acknowledged that cost-benefit analysis was an appropriate way to gauge pollution control measure. Significant controversies arose in the *application* of cost-benefit analysis, however.

To start, it was difficult to measure the benefits of reducing water pollution. We usually had a pretty good estimate of the costs of reducing pollution, but many of the benefits were recreational or aesthetic, which are very hard to measure or assess in any quantitative way. We noticed, however, that the effluent guidelines produced enormous discrepancies across industries in the per-unit cost of reducing pollution. EPA had developed a fairly helpful metric for comparing the pollution effects of different kinds of discharge, so we could calculate the cost per pound of reduction of this average pollution equivalent. What we found were differences across industries that were often of several orders of magnitude! Clearly, although we might have disagreed about exactly what the benefits of pollution reduction were, all those rules could not be correct. Some rules must be too costly, or some must not be costly enough.

It turned out that the explanation for these massive discrepancies was that many people at EPA believed that cost-benefit analysis meant financial analysis. That is, they would impose a much tougher standard on a particular industry if it were much more profitable than other industries. Their idea of cost-benefit analysis was to turn the screws on the pulp and paper industry, the pharmaceutical industry, and other highly profitable industries and to ease way back in steel and other industries that were experiencing commercial difficulties. This astounded us because it fit so neatly into many political economy theories of rent seeking and regulation. In fact, I believe that it has provided fodder for some subsequent academic articles.

As I look back on this class of regulations, I believe that we made very substantial headway in increasing the role of economics in policy-making. First, the range of pollution reduction costs in the effluent guidelines was much narrower at the end of the Reagan administration than at the beginning. Second, the people who were working on these matters at EPA came to take a very different approach toward effluent guidelines. Finally, the administration made similar progress in other areas of regulation involving health risks. When one rule imposed a cost of $900,000 at the margin per life saved and the next rule imposed a cost of $245 million at the margin per life saved, there was a problem. At $245 million we were clearly well above what anybody in the United States would ever spend for risk avoidance in their private lives. So we were able to eliminate a lot of harmful regulations at the top while maintaining a good deal of disagreement on what the appropriate level of spending should be lower down. In particular, I think we did a good job at putting an end to a large number of extraordinarily harmful and silly regulations in the area of hazardous air pollutants.

I want to mention also the lead phase-down regulation, which was a substantial victory for economic analysis and a case where OMB and the White House were reversed rather than EPA. One of our early targets for elimination was the lead phase-down regulation, which required that lead be removed from gasoline refining at a faster rate than would be dictated by the phasing in of new cars that required no-lead gasoline. A very fine piece of analysis persuaded everyone that the health harms of leaded gasoline were far greater than we had thought, and we ended up adopting a much tighter program than the one we had inherited. At the same time, the introduction of marketable lead permits saved many hundreds of millions of dollars from the cost of that regulation.

The third class of regulation that I want to address represents an intermediate case between price and entry controls, on the one hand, and externality regulation, on the other. The case that I have in mind is product standardization, which may be a component of health and safety regulation but often concerns a normal economic good. In particular, it often pertains to a new good or an innovation in an older good that somebody wants to have adopted uniformly.

This is the area of regulation where cost-benefit analysis is the most problematic in my view. Consider an innovation that increases people's safety. It is easy to assume a certain level of effectiveness for this innovation and show that it would be cost beneficial to make every product conform to this new standard. But such an analysis ignores the fact that the optimal rate of diffusion of a new technology is not instantaneous but involves a learning process. Some individuals will gain more from this innovation than other people, and they will purchase the innovation at the price at which it will initially come on the market. As the innovation diffuses through the market, it will be improved much more, in terms of both quality and price, than if a government rule had universalized the initial innovation.

Consider the issue of passive restraints, which is bureaucratic argot for airbags in cars. When I was in the administration, economist Bill Nordhaus presented a very persuasive cost-benefit analysis showing that the airbag rule supported by the insurance companies would have substantial positive net benefits. This did not surprise me, but it did not show that it was desirable for the government to impose this technology on all consumers at once. I argued at the time that the most effective national airbag rule, in terms of promoting automobile passenger safety, would be a constitutional amendment forbidding the federal government from making any rule having to do with airbags. My rationale was simply that airbags were a normal economic good with which we had very little practical experience. If the government made no rule about airbags, it seemed clear to me that they would be introduced and would diffuse through the market in about the way that car radios or sunroofs did. I never doubted that an affluent couple living in downtown Boston with three teenage sons would be foolish not to purchase a car with an airbag at the initial design and price or that a thirty-five-year-old single woman who always fastened her three-point seatbelt, had a modest income, and lived in a rural part of Kansas would be foolish to purchase an airbag at the price at which it would first appear on the market. In fact, if one looks at the history of automobile manufacturers' experiments with airbags, there is a good deal of evidence that they were seriously interested in the technology at an early stage. They turned away from airbags only when it became clear that, if this were a promising technology, they would be forced to install it instantly on every new car they sold.

Yet these arguments, which seemed highly persuasive to me and to the economists I was working with at OMB, seemed strange and irrelevant not only to program officials at the Transportation Department but also to political officials at the White House. They never became part of the administration's public argument in the airbag controversy, and we eventually issued a complex rule that phased in airbags according to the pace of state legislation requiring the use of seat belts. And, as a general matter, I discovered that the executive order had much less practical effect in the intermediate case of product standardization than in the polar cases of price and entry controls and pollution controls.

Although it would be academically fashionable to attribute this difference to the large rents to be obtained by producer groups from product standardization, my casual impression is that the extent of political pressure brought to bear in this class of regulations was not much different than in the agricultural marketing orders and the EPA pollution controls. Instead, I attribute the difference to differences in the diffusion of economic thinking. The harms of government price and entry controls are widely understood and accepted and are bolstered by popular tales of farmers denied permission to farm their own land and of oranges left to rot in the fields. The notions of cost effectiveness and of the wastefulness of treating two identical pollution problems differently are also easy for noneconomists to grasp and apply. But the idea that the government should refrain from standardizing a product or a production process in a way that is abstractly "good" is more complicated—accepting it requires not only particular facts (as in the case of pollution controls) but also assumptions about the operation of private markets that laymen are often less willing to make than economists. It is an interesting puzzle that economists have been much more successful in persuading others of the evils of price fixing than of the evils of quality fixing.

Appendix

A. Regulatory Principles

Executive Order 12291 provides in section 2 that, "to the extent permitted by law,

(a) Administrative decisions shall be based on adequate information concerning the need for and consequences of proposed government action;
(b) Regulatory action shall not be undertaken unless the potential benefits to society for the regulation outweigh the potential costs to society;
(c) Regulatory objectives shall be chosen to maximize the net benefits to society;
(d) Among alternative approaches to any given regulatory objective, the alternative involving the least net cost to society shall be chosen; and
(e) Agencies shall set regulatory priorities with the aim of maximizing the aggregate net benefits to society, taking into account the condition of the particular industries affected by regulations, the condition of the national economy, and other regulatory actions contemplated for the future."

B. Regulatory Policy Guidelines

Section 1 of Executive Order 12498 reaffirmed the following guidelines for rulemaking agencies originally set forth in 1983:

1. Regulations should be issued only on evidence that their potential benefits exceed their potential costs. Regulatory objectives, and the methods for achieving these objectives, should be chosen to maximize the net benefits to society.

2. Regulation of prices and production in competitive markets should be avoided. Entry into private markets should be regulated only where necessary to protect health or safety or to manage public resources efficiently.

3. Federal regulations should not prescribe uniform quality standards for private goods or services, except where these products are needlessly unsafe or product variations are wasteful, and voluntary private standards have failed to correct the problem.

4. Regulations that seek to reduce health or safety risks should be based upon scientific risk-assessment procedures, and should address risks that are real and significant rather than hypothetical or remote.

5. Health, safety, and environmental regulations should address ends rather than means.

6. Licensing and permitting decisions and reviews of new products should be made swiftly and should be based on standards that are clearly defined in advance.

7. Qualifications for receiving government licenses should be the minimum necessary. Where there are more qualified applicants than available licenses, the licenses should be allocated by auction or random lottery rather than by administrative procedures.

8. Where regulations create private rights or obligations, unrestricted exchange of these rights or obligations should be encouraged.

9. Federal regulations should not preempt State laws or regulations, except to guarantee rights of national citizenship or to avoid significant burdens on interstate commerce.

10. Regulations establishing terms or conditions of Federal grants, contracts, or financial assistance should be limited to the minimum necessary to achieving the purposes for which the funds were authorized and appropriated."

C.   Sources

The text of Executive Order 12291 is taken from *Regulatory Program of the United States Government* (Washington, D.C.: Executive Office of the President, Office of Management and Budget, March 1986), xiii. The "Regulatory Policy Guidelines" were first set forth and elaborated in *Reagan Administration Regulatory Achievements* (Washington, D.C.: The White House, Presidential Task Force on Regulatory Relief, 11 August 1983). Executive Order 12291 was issued on 17 February 1981 and Executive Order 12498 on 4 January 1985.

---

3. *James Burnley*

When I arrived at the U.S. Department of Transportation from elsewhere in the Reagan administration in early 1983, first to be general counsel and then, after a few months, deputy secretary, I did not come in with a well-formulated notion of how the regulatory processes of the department should be administered. I certainly shared the basic impulse of the administration that we needed both regulatory reform and regulatory relief, but I had not been required by my previous government responsibilities to consider regulatory issues beyond this elementary level. I found that the department faced quite a few regulatory issues that had to be addressed forthwith, in both macro and micro terms. Thus, some major catching up had to occur immediately in my own analytic processes.

What we were in fact doing in the 1980s in the transportation area was consolidating economic deregulation since we came into office following a liberal Democratic administration that had nonetheless been successful in economic deregulation of most modes of transportation. All that we had left to attempt to deregulate were the interstate bus industry and the maritime industry. Deregulation of the trucking industry needed—and still needs—to be completed. But it quickly became apparent that, whether you are in a consolidation process or whether you wish, for example, to extend deregulation by sunsetting the Interstate Commerce Commission (ICC), which is a wonderful idea, the best way to undercut efforts to move toward a completely free market system is to be insensitive to the clear differences that exist between economic regulatory activities and safety regulatory activities.

Let me hasten to observe that there is a massive gray area in the middle. However, when it comes to purely economic regulatory activity, such as what the fare shall be when you fly between Washington and New York, there really is no safety dimension to that decision-making process. If you believe in free markets, you can quickly conclude that the government should not be in that business.

If, on the other hand, you are insensitive to this distinction or, worse still, consciously believe that the government should not regulate the maintenance of commercial aircraft and that you can leave that to the marketplace, then you will very quickly find that your agenda on economic regulatory issues is caught in a tremendous backwash. Again I emphasize that there is a massive gray area. I am describing two ends of a spectrum, and there are numerous decisions that do not lend themselves to a neat dichotomy.

Thus, when we talk about whether the Reagan administration should have gone further in a particular instance to deregulate a particular facet of transportation, I would suggest that the discussion must occur within the proper context. It should begin by considering the impact of a given regulatory decision on safety and the extent to which safety can be preserved or enhanced while deregulating economic activity. In many instances, aggressive safety regulation is a prerequisite to progress on economic deregulation. Understanding that there is a relation is critical if you wish to have the spiral that Elizabeth Bailey alluded to instead of having a pendulum that swings first one way and then the other on economic regulatory matters.

Second, we learned that, in addition to the need to be vigorous in safety-related rule-making activities, economic deregulation can be undermined by the perception of lax enforcement. Let me be very specific about that. The Reagan administration's first Federal Aviation Administration (FAA) administrator, a very able man with many years of experience in aviation, sincerely believed that we could carry out aviation safety regulatory enforcement with

25 percent fewer safety inspectors than were employed the day President Reagan was sworn in. Now, you may argue endlessly about whether he was right or wrong in that judgment. However, soon after joining the Treasury Department, I did conclude and, more important, Secretary Elizabeth Dole also concluded and persuaded OMB Director David Stockman that, on the whole, we were going to have a tougher time defending and perhaps even someday extending aviation economic deregulation if we continued down a path of ever fewer safety inspectors.

There are many issues that lend themselves very neatly to a cost-benefit analysis. However, I would suggest that another lesson to be learned from the 1980s, at least at the Department of Transportation (DOT), is that, if you let cost-benefit analyses drive all regulatory decision making, you will sometimes get outcomes that trample other equally important values. For example, it cannot be the case for the true Reaganite that federalism is an empty concept. In fact, President Reagan signed an executive order on federalism late in his second term that required agencies explicitly to take into account the impact on federal/state relations of each new regulatory proposal.

Yet, if you wish significantly to expand the capacity of the aviation system in this country virtually overnight, there is a neat, simple way to do it. You could preempt all local decision making on airport noise issues—an idea that has great appeal in many aviation circles. And, if you did a cost-benefit analysis of absolute preemption of all local decision making, I have a high level of confidence that the economic benefits would be calculated to greatly outweigh the costs. However. if cost-benefit analysis is conducted in a vacuum, there are other equally important values, in this case the right to recognize at least some local decision-making role, that will get lost. Therefore, even while assuring that benefits outweigh costs for each rule making, other values must be weighed as well.

We also learned that, if you are to be successful in deregulating administratively, it is terribly important that you work hard at it and that you do it well. Perhaps the premier example is found in the regulatory war over passive restraints in automobiles. Now, I do not mean to criticize those who went before me at DOT, but it was my judgment—and I think that it was a judgment that Chris DeMuth shared, and it certainly was a judgment that all nine members of the U.S. Supreme Court shared—that the decision made at the beginning of the Reagan administration to rescind the regulations requiring passive restraints (automatic seat belts or air bags in cars) was not as well justified as it could have been. And, while there was a five to four decision of the Supreme Court as to some aspects of that rescission, all nine justices did agree that there were certain very important issues that simply had not been properly or fully analyzed.

The result of that Supreme Court decision in 1983 was that we had to revisit the issue, and we were extremely constrained by the Court's specific guidance on how much weight we were to give various competing factors. While it left us some discretion, it went so far as to cite in a footnote its own understanding of the cost-benefit ratio on 1980 Chevettes. This was based on National Highway Traffic Safety Administration (NHTSA) figures, but the Court chose to send us a clear signal. It noted that NHTSA had found that, with these automatic detachable seat belts, there was 70 percent usage in 1980 Chevettes compared to 31 percent usage for manual seat belts in such cars. It was clear that we would have to carry a very heavy burden of proof if we decided not to require passive restraint systems.

There were clearly missed opportunities for further economic deregulation, in the sense that there is always more that could have been done. However, I believe that, at least in transportation, the Reagan administration does not need to apologize. As I noted at the outset, we were in a period of consolidation. For example, in 1978, Congress passed legislation to sunset the Civil Aeronautics Board (CAB). A successor act was passed in 1984 that included much more specific instructions about how the CAB was to go out of business. One of the issues that, believe it or not, senior DOT officials had to spend a lot of time on was whether the residual functions of the CAB being transferred to the department would be spread out among existing offices of DOT or be handled by a little CAB within the department, staffed by that agency's remaining employees. The latter approach would have simply changed the CAB's address on the bureaucratic plan of organization of the U.S. government. It would have been an arm of the department, like the FAA or the U.S. Coast Guard.

Now, this may appear to be a fairly easy decision. However, the Reagan appointee who was chairman of the CAB believed very, very strongly that it should move intact to DOT and that it should open up for business the next day just like the day before. He lobbied Congress aggressively, despite signals from the White House to the contrary. Thus, we had to put a lot of time and energy into defending the idea that the sunset of an agency ought to mean that it ceases to exist.

I would suggest to you that, while, on the one hand, it may seem the sort of issue that does not drive this country in one fundamental direction or another, it had perhaps more significance than even we realized at the time. In the summer of 1987, we had one of the periodic waves of hysteria concerning aviation safety that seems to sweep over this country every few years. This occurs regardless of whether the economics of aviation are regulated or deregulated and regardless of the actual safety record of commercial aviation. When that wave hit in 1987, had the CAB been intact and performing its residual functions as an identifiable entity within the Department, it would have been far easier for those in Congress who wished to reregulate the economics of the industry to have done so. All that would have been required was legislation to put the same people back in charge of economic regulation who were in charge of it before. In fact, 300 of them were transferred to DOT when the CAB closed. Because both the people and the residual functions were dispersed and fragmented among our various existing offices, there was no agency "in waiting" for restoration to its former "glory."

So I would suggest to you that, in looking both at what we did and at how best to reduce economic regulatory activities in the future, there are a number of contexts that are relevant. Economic regulatory issues cannot be intelligently discussed in isolation. You cannot, for example, discuss the extraordinarily good idea of privatizing the air traffic control system (an idea, by the way, that the airline industry has now embraced in large measure) without extensive consideration of actual and perceived safety effects. You cannot escape the interrelation between what people who fly on aircraft, or who drive the interstates beside big trucks, feel in their guts about the safety of those activities and how this country ultimately will come out on economic deregulation of those industries. It is terribly important to keep in mind at all times that they are inextricably intertwined.

Summary of Discussion

Murray Weidenbaum began the discussion by expressing his agreement with much of what the panelists had said. He believed that Secretary James Watt and Ann Gorsuch at the Interior Department had initiated the regulatory backlash because Gorsuch thought that she could undo regulations without going through the legal system. In the end, regulatory reform was a considerable disappointment, although cost-benefit analysis did become institutionalized at the Office of Management and Budget (OMB), as the reformers had wanted.

Kip Viscusi commented that there is a strong consensus in the academic literature regarding health and safety regulation and that this consensus was reflected in the appointments to the Council of Economic Advisers and the OMB. But some actions, like the appointment of Ann Gorsuch, reflected a confusion between regulatory reform and deregulation; these actions were motivated by a nonacademic agenda and were not consistent with any branch of the economics literature. Viscusi also noted that, because economists possess a very clear vision of what ought to be done in this area of policy, they tend to give any results that are achieved lower marks than they deserve.

Robert Litan argued that the Reagan administration had made a big mistake in choosing the airbag rule to rescind first. There had been tension at the beginning of the administration between the people who wanted regulatory relief and the people who wanted cost reform and the institutionalization of cost-benefit analysis. The repeal of the airbag rule fueled the fears of those who thought that cost-benefit analysis would be applied everywhere merely for the purpose of cutting costs. It would have been more effective to begin with other

policy issues, such as tradable emission rights, for which one can clearly demonstrate the preservation of a certain level of benefits at reduced cost. Opening
with the passive restraint rule aroused unnecessary opposition and poisoned
the waters.

William Poole raised the question of how economists can more effectively
make their case for policy changes in a regulatory arena heavily influenced by
public pressure groups who are aggressively unreceptive to cost-based
analysis.

Phillip Areeda echoed Poole's curiosity about why what economists know
so clearly is ignored by Congress and special interest pressure groups. When
Congress legislates that cost cannot play a role in certain regulatory decisions,
something very strange is going on. The explanation must be one of two things.
Possibly the authors of such legislation are absolutists and believe that life,
clean water, or whatever must be protected with no regard for the costs. This
is unlikely. Their theory, instead, appears to be that they need to push their case
in an exaggerated fashion in order to get even slight movement in the direction
they want. The result is bad legislation and regulation.

Christopher DeMuth pointed out that no one individual had made the decision criticized by Litan, the decision to pursue the issue of airbags prior to that
of marketable pollution permits. An administration is a group of disagreeing,
contentious people with their own agendas, and this sequence of actions just
happened that way. Further, the administration had taken several actions prior
to the airbag decision that were part of an economically consistent program.
These actions involved removing bad regulations regardless of the size of the
business constituency involved.

Returning to Areeda's and Poole's questions, DeMuth argued that the politics of environmentalism is radically different from that of consumerism and
product safety. Areeda's explanation gets at part of the problem, but another
part is that an important goal of many environmental and consumer groups is
to promote membership. When these groups are impervious to economic logic
that demonstrates that the policy they favor is not going to promote consumer
welfare or occupational safety or environmental quality, it is because they do
not particularly care about these goals. Their extreme positions promote their
own institutional maintenance and enhancement needs. Twenty years ago they
might have felt the need to take extreme positions as a bargaining tactic with
more powerful business interests, but, given their relative strength compared
to regulated businesses today, this no longer seems necessary.

David Stockman claimed responsibility for making the airbag regulation a
high priority in February 1981. He repeated his earlier observation that the
Reagan administration believed that economic regulation was wrong as a matter of first principles, and this rule was selected because it was highly illustra-
tive of that point. Consequently, on its first day in office, the administration
rescinded oil price controls and announced that it would rescind the airbag
rule. The reasoning was simply that this rule did not involve any damage to

third parties—it merely dictated that it would be good for the American public if they were to spend $800 per car for a feature that saved lives at a cost of $300,000 per life. The regulatory agenda was to get such "fundamentally wrong" items off the table first so that the focus could be turned to legitimate externalities that were in need of better decision-making mechanisms.

William Niskanen agreed with Stockman's reason for making the airbag regulation a high-priority issue. He felt, however, that the administration did not follow through on making the distinction between measures that affect only one's own safety and measures that affect the safety of others. The government has *not* accepted this distinction, as applied to smoking, internal car measures, or anything else. Since that principle was not applied, the airbag decision was made, ultimately, on a cost-benefit basis and not on a matter of principles. The first principle that Stockman cited has not, in fact, stuck.

As for the future, Niskanen did not expect much reregulation of areas that have been successfully deregulated. The only area in which there has been significant reregulation is in the asset portfolios of banks; this was a mistake, but an understandable mistake given the collapse of the insurance funds. There is some threat of reregulation in railroads and airlines, but he did not expect this to matter very much. On the other hand, Niskanen did expect a regulatory explosion in the 1990s in two new areas. First is the environment, where the Clean Air Act alone may cost $40 billion per year, and many other things, like Big Green, will play important roles as well. The second area is mandated benefits, where mandated medical insurance may cost another $40 billion a year. One major benefit was passed in 1990, and several others are in the works. Niskanen believed that these areas will see new and extended forms of regulation that will be quite costly in the 1990s.

8 Financial Regulation

1. *Robert E. Litan*
2. *William M. Isaac*
3. *William Taylor*

1. *Robert E. Litan*

U.S. Financial Markets and Institutions in the 1980s: A Decade of Turbulence

The U.S. financial system suffered its greatest shocks in the 1980s since the Depression. Not since the 1930s did so many commercial banks and savings and loan associations fail. Because most of the deposits at these institutions were federally insured, the federal government will spend hundreds of billions of dollars during the next several decades cleaning up the wreckage.

The securities markets, too, experienced their share of turmoil. After rising more or less consistently for five straight years, the stock market plunged deeply between August and October 1987 and then dropped sharply again in October 1989. As the decade came to a close, the newly developed junk bond market collapsed, although at this writing it has substantially recovered.

The 1980s were not marked solely by disaster, however. The decade saw many innovations and success stories. Whole new financial instruments and markets developed at an almost breathtaking pace: asset-backed securities, variable rate mortgages, financial futures, to name just a few. While at the beginning of the decade many of the nation's largest banks were struggling, by the end new "superregional" banks seemingly came from nowhere to challenge the once dominant "money centers" for U.S. banking supremacy. Perhaps most surprising, all the financial troubles had little impact on the "real" economy. Indeed, as bank and thrift failures mounted, and despite the October 1987 crash, the economy marched upward, finishing the decade by marking the longest peacetime economic expansion in the nation's history.

As in earlier eras, policy-making toward financial markets and institutions in the 1980s was driven largely by crisis. Nevertheless, the remedies that put out the immediate fires, especially those that raged among depository institutions, have had significant longer-run consequences.

Not all crises during the decade triggered a policy response. For example, Congress took no action on "reform" suggestions advanced by a special administration task force convened to study the causes of the October 1987 stock market crash.

In addition, not all policy actions during the decade responded to crises. While Congress was deadlocked over the issues of interstate banking and financial product-line deregulation (or "restructuring"), many states filled the vacuum by legislating in each of these areas. Similarly, federal regulators took various steps under existing law to better adapt the financial framework to ongoing market developments. Finally, toward the end of the decade, bank regulators in the major industrialized countries launched an ambitious effort to put bank regulation in these countries on a common footing, a step that may foreshadow future international cooperative regulatory initiatives on other financial and, perhaps, nonfinancial issues.

This chapter attempts to make some sense out of these and other events and developments. Given the broad scope of the U.S. financial services industry and the limited space here in which to consider it, it concentrates only on depository institutions and securities markets. This limited focus means that other important developments affecting financial markets or institutions, such as the crisis in property-casualty insurance in the mid-1980s, must be ignored.

The discussion begins with some brief background information on the U.S. financial system that is relevant for understanding the important developments in financial markets and institutions during the 1980s. The chapter then describes those developments, both episodic and structural, noting how federal policy-makers responded (or didn't respond) to each. Specifically, why did Congress react to at least some of the crises in the depository industry but take no action following the stock market crashes of 1987 and 1989? Similarly, what accounts for the failure by Congress to address in a meaningful fashion the important structural weaknesses in the U.S. financial system, despite several opportunities to do so?

Answers to these questions provide a useful transition to the third section of the chapter, which identifies what alternative courses of action could have been taken and why they weren't. The concluding section briefly draws out several implications and lessons from the earlier analysis. To be sure, the policy discussions on financial institutions and markets in the 1990s are likely to be focused on a different set of questions than those that preoccupied policy-makers' attention in the 1980s; one key difference is that policymakers will be paying more attention to international issues in this decade than they did in the one just past. However, precisely for this reason, there should be opportunities in the 1990s for breaking many of the policy stalemates of the 1980s.

8.1 Background

Depository institutions and securities markets carry out the same important function in a market economy: both channel the surplus funds of savers to deficit-spending consumers and to firms that have investment opportunities in excess of their retained earnings. Commercial banks and thrift institutions accomplish intermediation directly by collecting deposits, some used for transactional purposes (checking accounts) and most for savings, and lending the funds to businesses and individuals. By exploiting economies of scale in evaluating and monitoring borrowers, both types of depositories direct funds between large classes of savers and borrowers far more cheaply than if these individuals and firms attempted to find each other themselves.

Securities markets perform intermediation services more cheaply still, but, until recently, only for commercial borrowers of sufficient size and creditworthiness to be able to sell their debt and equity on the open market. Unlike individual loans provided by depositories, securities are commodities and can be readily traded as such. Securities markets, whether organized exchanges or informal trading networks, provide the settings that allow these trades to take place. Accordingly, they make it possible not only for individuals to participate directly in the intermediation process but also for other financial institutions— insurance companies, pension funds, and mutual funds—to purchase and sell securities and thus to perform intermediation services as well.

As the nation entered the 1980s, most of the regulatory apparatus that governed the depository and securities industries was inherited, and little changed, from the 1930s. Depression-era legislation created the Securities and Exchange Commission (SEC), registration requirements for securities dealers, and regular reporting and disclosure requirements for companies whose stocks and bonds are traded in public markets. In 1940, Congress added legislation governing the operation of investment companies, now commonly known as mutual funds. The securities acts were designed principally to ensure that buyers and sellers of securities are fully informed of all relevant information at the time they make their trades.

The Depression-era legislation for depository institutions had different purposes. At the time, of course, the principal national concern was restoring confidence in a banking system that experienced approximately 9,000 failures between 1930 and 1933 and a series of deposit runs. Perhaps the most important response was the creation of federal deposit insurance, first for bank accounts up to $2,500 (1933), then for thrift accounts up to $5,000 (in 1934, with the ceiling for bank accounts raised at the same time). The deposit insurance ceilings were raised intermittently in succeeding decades, reaching $40,000 by the end of the 1970s. Significantly, there has been no nationwide deposit run since federal insurance was introduced, although, as I discuss below, many experts believe that federal insurance in turn led to a whole new set of problems during the 1980s.

Congress also responded to the banking crisis of the 1930s by segmenting depository institutions from the securities markets and other financial intermediaries. In particular, the Glass-Steagall Act of 1933 separated commercial and investment banking largely in response to allegations at the time that banks had abused their securities powers to cause undue losses to other banks and customers.[1] A little more than two decades later, Congress extended the segmentation of depositories by enacting the Bank Holding Company Act of 1956 (amended in 1970), which limited organizations that own banks to a narrow range of nonbanking activities that are "closely related to banking." Similar provisions were enacted during the 1960s for companies that own more than one thrift institution.[2]

The bank and thrift holding company restrictions have been justified, in part, as a means for insulating depositories and the federal insurance funds from nonbanking risks. But fear of "bigness" has also played a significant role in bank and thrift regulation. Congress traditionally has not been willing to permit the development of Japanese-style *zaibatsu* bank/nonbank conglomerates in the United States. Quite the contrary, Congress has endeavored to protect small depository institutions from competitors within the same industry. In legislation enacted before and since the Depression, Congress has prohibited depositories and their parent companies from crossing state lines without the permission of individual states (permission that no state granted until the 1970s). The Banking Act of 1933 (of which the Glass-Steagall Act was a part) also established ceilings (Regulation Q) on interest rates payable on bank deposits (which were extended to thrift deposits in 1966) largely in order to limit competition among banks. Indeed, although deposit insurance was justified primarily as a means of protecting the banking system from runs, it was strongly advocated by small banks in particular, which saw insurance as a crucial vehicle for preventing their depositors from migrating to larger banks.

Depository institutions have been segmented not only from other types of financial intermediaries but also from each other. Different charters and regulatory systems for commercial banks and thrifts, for example, have traditionally separated bank lending for businesses, and more recently for consumers, from thrift lending for residential mortgages. Although the different types of depositories responded to very different needs and thus arose in response to market developments (Litan 1987b, 12–19), legislation dating from the Depression has encouraged the development of thrift institutions in particular (through tax incentives and a government-backed secondary market for mortgage loans, among other things) in order to promote home ownership.

---

1. Recent scholarship, however, has discredited the validity of many of the allegations about bank abuses in the securities business before the Glass-Steagall Act was passed (see Benston 1990a).

2. Unitary thrift holding companies—those owning a single thrift—have been exempt from the affiliation limitations applicable to multithrift holding companies. During the 1980s, a number of nonfinancial firms exploited this "loophole" to acquire thrifts.

Although it was not free from difficulty, by at least several measures the Depression-era financial structure worked reasonably well through the 1970s. The bank and thrift failure rate fell dramatically after deposit insurance was introduced. For example, from the end of World War II through 1979, rarely did more than 10 banks rail in any single year. Indeed, as shown in table 8.1, even during the volatile 1970s, marked especially by the 1973 and 1979 "oil price shocks," the bank and thrift failure rate was remarkably low.

By other measures, the securities markets were also performing as could reasonably be expected. Despite many ups and downs in price movements, the nation's securities markets steadily became more efficient in processing transactions. Between 1960 and 1979, for example, annual stock trading volume on the New York Stock Exchange (NYSE) jumped more than tenfold, from 766 million to 8.3 billion. Similarly, a whole new over-the-counter market linked by computers—NASDAQ—developed to handle trades in companies

Table 8.1   Financial Health of U.S. Depository Institutions, 1970–89

	Thrift Institutions			Commercial Banks			Economywide Data	
Year	Failures[a]	Failures/ 1,000	ROE	Failures	Failures/ 1,000	ROE	Failures/ 1,000	ROE Manufacturing
1970	10	2.2	N.A.	8	.6	N.A.	4.4	9.3
1971	4	.9	N.A.	6	.4	N.A.	4.2	9.7
1972	2	.5	N.A.	3	.2	N.A.	3.8	10.6
1973	5	1.2	N.A.	6	.4	N.A.	3.6	12.8
1974	1	.2	N.A.	4	.3	N.A.	3.8	14.9
1975	11	2.2	7.3	14	1.0	11.3	4.3	11.6
1976	12	2.5	10.3	17	1.2	11.0	3.5	13.9
1977	10	2.1	13.1	6	.4	11.5	2.8	14.2
1978	4	.9	13.9	7	.5	13.1	2.4	15.0
1979	4	.9	11.4	10	.7	14.3	2.8	16.4
1980	32	6.9	2.5	10	.7	13.7	4.2	13.9
1981	82	19.1	−16.6	10	.7	13.1	6.1	13.6
1982	247	64.6	−16.7	42	2.9	12.1	8.9	9.2
1983	70	20.0	6.1	48	3.3	10.7	11.0	10.6
1984	36	10.6	2.9	79	5.5	10.5	10.7	12.5
1985	64	20.0	7.9	120	8.3	11.2	11.5	10.1
1986	80	26.0	.2	138	9.7	10.0	12.0	9.5
1987	77	26.5	−16.8	184	13.4	1.5	10.2	12.8
1988	233	92.2	−24.3	200	15.2	13.4	9.8	16.1
1989	39[b]	122.3	N.A.	207	15.5	N.A.	N.A.	N.A.

Sources: Kane (1989); *Statistical Abstract of the United States* (various years); *Economic Report of the President* (1990); Office of Thrift Supervision; Resolution Trust Corporation; FDIC (1988).

Note: ROE = return on equity. N.A. = not available.

[a]Only those failures resolved by the FSLIC or RTC. Data for the years 1970–74 and 1989 provided by the Office for Thrift Supervision; 1976–88 data taken from Kane (1989).

[b]Includes only failed thrifts resolved during the year. At year end 1989, another 281 thrifts were in conservatorship, and hundreds more were waiting to be placed in conservatorship.

Table 8.2   **Share of Financial Assets Held by Major Intermediaries**

Intermediary	1946	1950	1960	1970	1980	1985	1989
Commercial banks	57.3	51.2	38.2	38.6	36.8	33.3	30.9
Savings and loans	4.3	5.7	11.8	12.8	15.2	14.9	11.8
Mutual savings banks	8.0	7.7	6.9	5.9	4.3	3.1	2.8
Credit unions	.2	.3	1.1	1.3	1.7	1.9	2.1
Life insurance	20.3	21.4	19.4	15.0	11.5	11.1	12.1
Private pension	1.5	2.4	6.4	8.4	11.7	11.9	12.0
State and local govt. pension	1.2	1.7	3.3	4.5	4.9	5.7	7.0
Other insurance	3.0	4.0	4.4	3.7	4.3	4.1	4.7
Finance companies	2.1	3.2	4.6	4.8	5.0	5.0	5.0
Mutual funds	.6	1.1	2.9	3.5	3.4	6.8	9.4
Other	1.5	1.4	1.1	1.5	1.2	2.3	2.3

Source: Board of Governors of the Federal Reserve System, flow of funds accounts

not listed on either the NYSE or other major stock exchanges. Trading in the securities markets was given a strong boost in the early and mid-1970s when, after vigorous prodding by the Justice Department's antitrust division, the SEC and the Congress dismantled the system of fixed brokerage commissions established by the NYSE. This step was also encouraged by the growing importance of institutional investors and traders in the markets who were gradually deserting the NYSE and instead trading directly among themselves or on regional exchanges. In turn, the growth in the securities markets facilitated the rise of certain nonbank financial intermediaries—notably pension funds, finance companies, and mutual funds—which, as table 8.2 demonstrates, substantially increased their share of the nation's financial assets.

Nevertheless, several cracks in the post-Depression financial system had already become evident by the 1970s, if not before, and were to become much more visible during the 1980s. Dating from the 1950s, the FDIC consistently arranged mergers of failed banks instead of paying off their depositors and thus effectively guaranteed in full deposit accounts above the statutory insurance ceilings. This policy became explicit when the FDIC protected all deposits at Franklin National Bank in 1974, the largest bank failure up to that time since World War II. By stretching the federal safety net on an ad hoc basis in response to various crises, bank regulators undermined depositor discipline against excessive risk taking by banks and thrifts, a development the consequences of which would show up vividly in the 1980s.[3]

By the end of the 1970s, market developments also were adding strain to the compartmentalized financial structure (Pierce 1991). Advances in computer

---

3. For an excellent history of the FDIC's response to bank crises in the postwar period, see Sprague (1985).

technology in the 1960s and 1970s permitted competition to develop in the core depository and lending services provided by banks and thrifts, which, as discussed later, had powerful effects in the following decade. For example, the new processing technologies made it possible for money market mutual funds to offer individuals limited transaction services on accounts yielding higher rates of interest than the Regulation Q interest ceilings that applied to bank and thrift deposits. In response, during the 1970s, regulators began lifting the interest ceilings for large depositors, a trend that was to accelerate in the 1980s.

Similarly, on the lending side, computer technology facilitated the growth of the commercial paper market, which highly rated corporations used to raise funds directly rather than borrowing from banks. Ultimately more significant, advances in data processing made it possible for quasi-governmental financing agencies and private investment banks to "securitize" mortgage instruments by packaging them into bundles and then to distribute units of the resulting trusts to individual investors, nonbank financial institutions (pension funds, mutual funds, and insurance companies), as well as to depositories. By turning formerly illiquid loans into tradable commodities, the securitization process was gradually undermining the economic rationale for depository institutions as specialized evaluators and monitors of credit; markets instead were performing that role.[4]

Finally, the 1970s were the last years when it could be safely said that U.S. financial institutions and markets were dominant in global financial markets. As the decade ended, corporate shares traded on U.S. stock markets still accounted for over half of market capitalization of shares traded on worldwide stock markets; European and Japanese stock markets were far behind (OTA 1990, 25). Similarly, although U.S. banks had been steadily losing ground in the international size rankings, table 8.3 illustrates that, by the end of the 1970s, the United States still had two of the world's top ten banks and six of the top fifty. Most of these larger banks were active competitors in foreign markets.

All this was to change in the 1980s. That the federal safety net extended to all bank and thrift deposits—at least those at the largest depositories—was to be made even more explicit. The franchise values of commercial bank and thrift charters were to be much further diminished by nonbank competition, securitization in particular. More important, solvency problems among depositories, especially among thrifts, were to become more severe than at any time since the Depression and the costs imposed on the federal government of resolving them were to reach unparalleled heights. U.S. security markets would be further revolutionized by new markets and instruments. And U.S. financial institutions and markets would find themselves under much greater competitive pressure from foreign institutions both at home and abroad.

---

4. The impact of securitization on the thrift and banking industries is also discussed in greater detail below.

Table 8.3   Nationality of the World's Largest Banks by Deposit Size

	Number of Banks in Top 10					Number of Banks in Top 50				
Country	1956	1960	1970	1979	1988	1956	1960	1970	1979	1988
United States	5	6	4	2	0	25	19	13	6	2
United Kingdom	3	3	2	2	0	7	5	4	4	4
Canada	2	1	1	0	0	6	5	5	4	1
France	0	0	1	4	0	3	3	3	4	4
Germany	0	0	1	2	0	0	3	4	7	7
Italy	0	0	1	0	0	3	5	4	2	1
Japan					10	3	8	11	16	25
Australia						1	1	1	0	0
Netherlands						0	0	1	3	2
Switzerland						0	0	3	3	3
Belgium						0	0	0	1	0
Other						2	1	1	0	1

Source: Benston (1990b).

8.2   Key Events and Policies of the 1980s

The reaction of policymakers to the varied events of the 1980s was highly uneven. As in earlier periods, federal authorities tended to move only when a crisis forced them to do so. This was not the case, however, with certain state legislatures, which reacted (perhaps without knowing so) to basic structural developments. Accordingly, in reviewing the key financial events and policies of the 1980s, it is essential to distinguish the crises from the important, but less well-recognized, structural trends.

8.2.1   The Crises

All three segments of the U.S. financial system reviewed in this chapter—thrift institutions, banks, and securities markets—experienced severe shocks during the 1980s. Table 8.4 lists the key crises in chronological order, together with a brief description of the policy responses. As highlighted in the table, Congress reacted only to certain crises; regulators (principally the Federal Reserve) handled the others. In all cases, however, the immediate responses have had significant longer-run consequences.

Thrifts

The three crises that rocked the thrift industry during the 1980s had the most significant immediate (if not permanent) economic impact and thus deserve the most attention.

The initial thrift crisis occurred as the decade opened. Its origins are well known and stem from the Federal Reserve's vigorous program of monetary restraint launched in late 1979 to attack double-digit inflation. The Fed's efforts

Table 8.4   **Financial Crisis of the 1980s**

Year	Crisis	Response
1980–82	Market value insolvency among thrifts	Deposit interest deregulation; broader thrift powers; higher deposit insurance ceiling; relaxed supervision
1982	LDC debt crisis	Fed-coordinated new bank lending
1984	Continental Illinois failure	Regulatory protection of uninsured depositors ("too big to fail")
1985	Thrift deposit runs in Ohio and Maryland	Freezing of accounts; Fed discount window lending
1987	Stock market crash	Fed discount window lending
1988–89	Second stage of thrift disaster	Federal cleanup effort launched; tighter capital standards
1989	A lesser stock market decline	No response
1989	Collapse of junk bond market	No response

in the short run produced some of the highest nominal interest rates in the nation's history. By March 1980, short-term Treasury bills were yielding more than 15 percent, providing depositors with strong incentives to move funds from their regulated bank and thrift accounts paying interest no higher than 5.5 percent to money market mutual funds (MMFs), which invested principally in U.S. government obligations.[5] With little chance that interest rates would soon fall dramatically, the nation's banks and thrifts faced a dangerous threat to the stability of their deposit bases that both the administration and the Congress clearly recognized.

But one obvious solution—instant and complete deregulation of deposit interest rate ceilings—also posed a danger of its own, especially for thrift institutions whose assets consisted primarily of fixed-rate, long-term mortgages but whose liabilities could be repriced within a much shorter period. For these institutions, deregulation of deposit interest rates when market rates were well above the prevailing ceilings would increase funding costs much more rapidly than earnings from investments. Since thrifts were locked into earning low-interest rates on their existing stock of mortgage loans, deregulation could expose them to many years of losses until they acquired a sufficient volume of new, higher-yielding mortgage loans.[6]

Congress and the administration attempted in 1980 to avoid both dangers—deposit runs under the current regulatory regime and continuing losses under

5. In fact, assets held in MMFs jumped from just $12 billion in January 1979 to $61 billion in March 1980 (*Economic Report of the President,* 1981 and 1982).

6. Of course, this would not have occurred had Congress deregulated deposit interest rates in the early 1970s when urged to do so by the Hunt Commission. If deregulation had been implemented much earlier, thrifts would have had much higher-yielding mortgages in their portfolios in the early 1980s when interest rates soared.

deregulation—by compromising. In March 1980, the president signed into law the Depository Institutions Deregulation and Monetary Control Act (DIDMCA) of 1980, which established a committee to phase out deposit interest ceilings over the next six years. To encourage depositors not to leave their institutions in the interim, and to mollify thrifts concerned about the adverse impact of interest deregulation on their costs of funds, during a conference committee session Congress added provisions increasing the deposit insurance ceiling on thrift and bank accounts from $40,000 to $100,000.[7] In addition, to provide other revenue sources for thrifts beyond fixed-rate mortgages, the DIDMCA also permitted federally chartered thrifts to invest a limited portion of their assets in consumer loans.[8]

Federal thrift regulators also took advantage of several other features of DIDMCA to enhance the economic viability of the thrift industry in an environment of partial deposit interest deregulation. In 1981, the Federal Home Loan Bank Board authorized federal thrifts to offer the equivalent of interest-paying checking accounts, or negotiable-order-of-withdrawal (NOW) accounts, which by then a number of states had already authorized for their thrifts. In an effort to reduce the industry's exposure to wide swings in interest rates, the Board permitted federally chartered thrifts to extend adjustable-rate mortgages.

Although well intentioned, these various measures could not stop either the hemorrhaging of deposits or red ink from the thrift industry, given continued double-digit market interest rates. Thus, with only modest deregulation of interest rates on larger deposit accounts, thrifts continued to lose smaller deposits to money market funds; in 1981 and 1982, deposit withdrawals at thrifts exceeded new deposits by $32 billion (Brumbaugh 1988, 39).[9] At the same time, by paying higher interest rates to keep their large-dollar deregulated deposits, most thrifts had no choice but to suffer continued operating losses. As shown in table 5, 85 percent of all thrifts operating in 1981 lost money; that figure fell to "only" 68 percent in 1982.

As thrift deposit outflows and operating losses mounted, Congress acted again.[10] In December 1982, Congress enacted the Garn–St Germain Deposi-

---

7. Although the increase in the insurance ceiling has since been criticized as an example of "midnight" congressional decision making, according to one knowledgeable source who was present at the critical conference committee session, the FDIC's authorized representative reported that the FDIC's acting chairman, Irvine Sprague, did not object to the increase during a telephone conversation at the time. Sprague has not since explicitly refuted these events, but he also claims to have communicated that his agency had consistently been against the $100,000 figure (Sprague 1990, 19).

8. The DIDMCA had many other provisions. Among them were provisions extending reserve requirements to banks and thrifts that were not formal members of the Federal Reserve System.

9. Total deposits at thrifts nevertheless rose, owing solely to interest credited on accounts that remained in thrifts (Brumbaugh 1988, 40).

10. By the end of 1982, assets at the MMFs had grown to more than $200 billion—nearly ten times larger than just three years before—and threatened to draw still more deposits from both thrifts and banks.

Table 8.5   **Profitability of the Thrift Industry, 1980–89**

	Number as a % of All Thrifts	Assets as a % of All Thrift Assets
1978	97.3	98.7
1979	93.5	95.9
1980	64.4	67.0
1981	15.2	8.7
1982	32.2	39.4
1983	64.8	66.8
1984	72.1	73.3
1985	78.8	84.9
1986	73.0	72.4
1987	64.8	66.2
1988	69.7	68.2
1989	63.0	60.1

Source: White (1991).

tory Institutions Act, which accelerated deposit interest deregulation by authorizing banks and thrifts to offer deposit instruments directly competitive with the MMFs: "money market deposit accounts" with minimum balances of only $2,500. The act also enhanced thrifts' asset diversification authority by increasing the asset limit for consumer loans and by allowing federally chartered thrifts to extend commercial real estate mortgages as well as ordinary business loans.

Regulators moved as well, principally by weakening the financial requirements for new entrants and existing owners. This process began in 1980 when the Board lowered the minimum capital requirement for thrifts from 5 percent of assets to 4 percent, a step that was authorized by DIDMCA. The Board effectively diluted capital requirements much further the following year by adopting various changes in thrift accounting for regulatory purposes to make thrifts look healthier than they appeared under "generally accepted accounting principles" (GAAP).[11]

The seemingly technical differences in accounting treatment had very significant impacts. As shown in table 8.6, the industry's capital-to-asset ratio during the early 1980s (and later) was consistently higher under the Board's "regulatory accounting principles" (RAP) than it was under GAAP. However, even GAAP overstated the industry's true financial condition. If goodwill and other intangible assets were properly excluded from net worth, the industry barely had any "tangible" capital. And, when the industry's assets and liabilities were valued at their *market value,* the industry was clearly insolvent—by

11. Among other things, thrifts were allowed to spread their losses when they sold low interest-bearing mortgages over the remaining lives of those mortgages; to book as income large up-front fees for originating new mortgages; and to count as capital for regulatory purposes the "net worth certificates" that the Board issued to many thrifts in exchange for offsetting promissory notes.

Table 8.6   Thrift Capital-to-Asset Ratios under Alternative Accounting Measures, 1980–86

Year	RAP Net Worth as a % of Total Assets	GAAP Net Worth as a % of Total Assets*	Tangible Net Worth as a % of Total Assets	Market-Value Net Worth as a % of Total Assets
1980	5.26	5.26	5.23	−12.47
1981	4.27	4.15	3.91	−17.32
1982	3.69	2.95	.54	−12.03
1983	4.02	3.14	.47	−5.64
1984	3.80	2.86	.41	−2.74
1985	4.36	3.15	.81	N.A.
1986	4.56	3.41	1.33	N.A.

Source: Brumbaugh (1988, 50).
Note: N.A. = not available.

more than $100 billion, even according to the chairman of the Bank Board at the time (Pratt 1989; see also Carron 1982b).

Why would regulators deliberately go to such lengths in effect to hide and ignore the financial condition of the institutions they supervised? One important answer lies in the limited resources of the thrift insurance fund, the Federal Savings and Loan Insurance Corporation (FSLIC). As illustrated in table 8.7, with less than $7 billion in reserves in the early 1980s, the FSLIC could close only a relative handful of the insolvent thrifts, which it in fact did (see table 8.1 above). However, as table 8.8 indicates, the number of RAP-insolvent thrifts, and the assets that they controlled, was substantially less than the number of insolvent institutions measured on a more realistic tangible capital basis.

Regulators had another reason for adopting and encouraging the use of more liberal thrift accounting methods. Even as market interest rates headed toward record levels, it was widely expected among policymakers and legislators that the high-interest environment would be temporary: rates eventually would come down and thus restore the thrifts to their pre-1980 healthy condition. On this view, RAP could be (and was) justified as a temporary device to tide the industry over until it (inevitably) recovered.

The prevailing optimism was as convenient as it was necessary. Faced with steeply rising federal deficits at the time, neither the Reagan administration nor the Congress was willing to authorize the more than $100 billion that would then have been required to close all thrifts insolvent on a market-value basis. Not only would such a radical step have been extraordinarily expensive, but it almost certainly would have been politically infeasible, given the political power at the time of the thrift industry and its allies (primarily the housing industry) in Congress. Clearly, if the industry could be restored to health sim-

Table 8.7   **Reserves of FSLIC and FDIC (Millions of Dollars and Percents)**

	FSLIC		FDIC	
Year	Reserves	% of Insured Deposits	Reserves	% of Insured Deposits
1970	2,903	2.05	4,380	1.25
1971	2,987	1.77	4,740	1.27
1972	3,142	1.56	5,159	1.23
1973	3,454	1.56	5,615	1.21
1974	3,791	1.60	6,124	1.18
1975	4,120	1.48	6,716	1.18
1976	4,480	1.37	7,269	1.16
1977	4,873	1.29	7,993	1.15
1978	5,328	1.26	8,796	1.16
1979	5,848	1.27	9,793	1.21
1980	6,462	1.28	11,020	1.16
1981	6,156	1.18	12,246	1.24
1982	6,307	1.13	13,771	1.21
1983	6,425	.96	15,429	1.22
1984	5,600	.71	16,529	1.19
1985	4,600	.54	17,957	1.19
1986	−6,300	−.71	18,253	1.12
1987	−13,700	−1.47	18,302	1.10
1988	N.A.	N.A.	14,061	.80

Sources: Kane (1989); FDIC (1988).

Note: N.A. = not available.

Table 8.8   **Numbers and Assets of Insolvent and Weakly Capitalized Thrifts, 1981–87**

	RAP-Insolvent Thrifts[a]		Tangible-Insolvent Thrifts[b]		Thrifts with Tangible Capital below 3% of Assets	
	No.	Assets ($billion)	No.	Assets ($billion)	No.	Assets ($billion)
1981	33	3	112	29	702	163
1982	71	13	415	220	783	217
1983	48	13	515	234	879	273
1984	71	15	695	336	853	321
1985	130	26	705	335	726	437
1986	255	66	672	324	581	335
1987	351	99	672	336	471	339

Sources: White (1991) and Barth and Bartholomew (1990), both based on Federal Home Loan Bank Board (FHLBB) data.

[a]Thrifts that were insolvent on the basis of regulatory accounting principles (RAP).

[b]Thrifts that were solvent on a RAP basis but insolvent on a tangible net worth basis.

ply with a drop in interest rates and an end to the economic downturn, why then shut most of it down? Moreover, Congress took action in 1980 and 1982 to facilitate the industry's recovery by broadening its investment powers. The administration was so optimistic that the industry would indeed bounce back that it felt comfortable reducing the examination and supervisory staff at the Bank Board and thus the frequency of thrift examinations, as shown in table 8.9.

In fact, some part of the optimistic outlook for the industry proved correct. Beginning in 1983, the economy started to grow again, and interest rates fell markedly. As expected (and hoped), a good portion of the industry returned to profitability, and the industry's capital improved by all measures (table 8.6 above).

In 1985, however, the industry was jolted again by its second crisis of the 1980s: the deposit runs on state-chartered thrifts in Ohio and Maryland following the failures of Home State Savings (Ohio) and Old Court Savings and Loan (Maryland). The runs affected only the thrifts in these states that were *not* federally insured but instead insured by state-sponsored funds. The runs were stopped in both states by a combination of actions: state-imposed limits on depositor withdrawals coupled with discount window lending by the Federal Reserve to solvent thrifts with liquidity problems. For these reasons, Congress saw no need to get involved.

Still, outside Maryland and Ohio, substantial troubles remained. As reflected in table 8.8 above, the decline in interest rates did not cure the tangible capital insolvency of hundreds of thrifts that collectively held more than $300 billion in assets. In addition, the table indicates that hundreds more institutions with even more assets were thinly capitalized. The owners and managers of both classes of institutions had strong incentives to take risks at the expense of the FSLIC by gambling with federally insured funds; if their strategies were wrong, the owners and managers had little or nothing to lose (the FSLIC would

Table 8.9   **FSLIC-Insured Thrift Examinations and Examination Resources, 1980–84**

	Examinations and Supervision Staff	Examinations	No. of FSLIC-Insured Thrifts	Thrift Industry Assets[a]	Examinations per Thrift	Examinations per Billion Dollars of Assets
1980	1,308	3,210	3,993	593.8	0.80	5.41
1981	1,385	3,171	3,751	639.8	0.85	4.96
1982	1,379	2,800	3,287	686.2	0.85	4.08
1983	1,361	2,131	3,146	813.8	0.68	2.62
1984[b]	1,337	2,347	3,136	976.9	0.75	2.40

Sources: Barth and Bradley (1989) and Barth, Bartholomew, and Bradley (1989); both based on Federal Home Loan Bank Board (FHLBB) data.

[a]In billions of dollars.

[b]Includes special, limited-scope examinations.

bear all remaining losses); but, if they were right, they (and not the FSLIC) would reap all the gains.[12] Various experts inside and outside government called attention to the effective insolvency of the FSLIC and its exposure to still additional losses if insolvent thrifts then open were not closed quickly, but their warnings went unheeded.[13] The prevailing attitude throughout Congress and most of the administration was that the industry's health would continue to improve with declining interest rates and a growing economy.

By 1986, however, the administration recognized that the FSLIC did not have sufficient resources to close all insolvent thrifts (table 8.7 above). In an effort to replenish the FSLIC's reserves, the administration requested Congress to authorize a capital "infusion" of $15 billion, financed "off budget" with bonds issued by a new agency to be created solely for that purpose. In fact, the "infusion" was primarily a borrowing by the FSLIC against future premium revenues. The administration's proposal was opposed by many thrift institutions and by various elected officials who argued that the money was both unnecessary and likely to be wasted by the FSLIC. Eventually, in 1987, Congress agreed on a lower recapitalization figure of $10.8 billion as part of broader banking legislation.

The ink on the 1987 funding legislation was barely dry when outside analysts warned that much more money would be necessary fully to resolve the thrift problem.[14] As the year ended and through 1988, the cost estimates moved upward. By summer of 1988, the chairman of the Bank Board, M. Danny Wall, conceded to Congress that almost $40 billion over a ten-year period would be required, a figure that by then was far below private estimates. Yet, despite the mounting cost projections, the thrift issue was barely mentioned during the 1988 presidential campaign, largely because it was a political liability for both parties.[15]

The third thrift crisis of the 1980s emerged after the 1988 election and was more political than economic. Although roughly one-third of the industry then was unprofitable (table 8.5 above), there was no imminent danger of a deposit run. Nevertheless, this last crisis was precipitated after the election by the Fed-

---

12. This "moral hazard" in federal deposit insurance has been so frequently noted by so many economists that it is inappropriate to single out any group of scholars who have pointed it out.

13. Economists at the Bank Board, e.g., pointed out in internal analyses in 1985 that the FSLIC was effectively insolvent. The chairman of the Bank Board, Edwin Gray, made the same point to Congress in the same year.

14. For example, in their thorough analysis of the situation through 1986, Brumbaugh and Carron (1987) estimated that $30 billion would have been required to close all insolvent thrifts. In addition, Bert Ely (a well-known independent financial consultant) repeatedly issued cost estimates in the mid to late 1980s indicating that the FSLIC had insufficient resources to rid the thrift industry of all its insolvent institutions.

15. That the problem could have grown so large during a Republican administration was clearly a political liability for the party's standard bearer, George Bush. The Democrats, however, could be blamed for helping lower the administration's original $15 billion request for additional funding for the FSLIC. In addition, the speaker of the House, Jim Wright, was under heavy attack for, among other things, his close involvement with several executives and owners of insolvent thrifts.

eral Home Loan Bank Board, which disposed of many insolvent thrifts by providing purchasers with extensive guarantees against future losses. The guarantees enabled the Board to complete these transactions without cash, of which the FSLIC had very little.[16] In part, the Board rushed through its late 1988 transactions because certain tax benefits to acquirers of thrifts were scheduled to expire at the end of that year, and the presidential elections were over.

Whether or not the rush of deals was so intended, it certainly had the effect of provoking both the next administration and Congress to address the thrift insolvency problems in a much more comprehensive and systematic fashion. As its first order of business, the incoming Bush administration proposed a far-reaching plan to close down approximately 500 clearly insolvent thrifts over three years and another 200 marginal thrifts through 1999. It asked Congress for $50 billion, again in off-budget financing, to carry out the job; the remaining $24 billion in estimated cleanup costs were to be paid by the thrift industry in the form of higher deposit insurance premiums (the plan proposed that banks, too, would pay higher premiums to cover the rising cost of bank failures). In addition, the plan proposed that a new agency (the Resolution Trust Corporation, or RTC) be created to dispose of the insolvent thrifts and their assets; that capital standards for thrifts be raised to the equivalent of bank standards and that thrifts be required to return to their original mission (housing finance) by investing at least 70 percent (up from 60 percent) to their assets in mortgage and consumer loans; and that the federal supervisory and regulatory structure for the industry be brought inside the executive branch (the Treasury Department) rather than remain in the independent Bank Board. The administration's plan left for the future—the 1990s—the controversial questions surrounding the future separation of the thrift and bank industries (and the regulatory apparatus that governs them) as well as the redesign of the deposit insurance system for both banks and thrifts. In August 1989, the Congress approved most of the administration's original proposal in the Financial Institutions Reform, Recovery, and Enforcement Act of 1989 (FIRREA).

Since FIRREA's passage, the estimated costs of resolving the third thrift crisis of the 1980s has risen substantially. In May 1990, the Treasury Department revised upward the total cost of the post-FIRREA thrift closures and assisted sales from the original present discounted cost of $74 billion to a range of $90–$130 billion.[17] Both the Congressional Budget Office and the General Accounting Office have projected even higher costs.

---

16. In all, the Board disposed of 205 thrifts—179 by funding acquisitions and twenty-six through liquidations—in 1988, estimating at the time that the eventual present discounted cost to the federal government (including another eighteen "stabilizations") would be $38.6 billion.

17. The FDIC has since estimated that the present discounted cost of the pre-1989 guarantees on thrift disposals will exceed $50 billion, up from the $38.6 billion originally estimated by the Bank Board.

Banks

The two major banking crises of the 1980s, fortunately, have proved to be far less costly than the thrift crises, at least thus far. However, unlike the thrift affairs, each banking crisis was viewed at the time as a serious threat to the stability of the entire U.S. financial system.

As shown earlier in table 8.4, the initial bank crisis arose in 1982 when what would later be a regular occurrence throughout the decade, a developing country with major debts to U.S. and other banks—in this case, Mexico—found itself unable to make interest payments on its debt.[18] At the time, the nine "money center" banks in the United States had loans outstanding to Latin American countries in the aggregate almost double their equity capital (Sachs and Huizinga 1987, 558). If Mexico defaulted on its debt, then these banks faced the possibility of defaults by other developing country borrowers as well—a circumstance that could have easily imperiled many, if not all, of the largest U.S. banking organizations.

Federal regulators—principally the Federal Reserve—had to take this threat seriously. At the time, a toppling of one or more major banks in the midst of a recession (even in an expansion) could have threatened the entire banking system if uninsured depositors began to run from many other banks. Even the free market–oriented officials inside the administration eventually grew concerned about such an outcome. In addition, the Federal Reserve no doubt felt some moral obligation to find some solution to the Mexican debt crisis and the threat it imposed to the U.S. banking system because, through much of the 1970s, it had encouraged the banks to recycle the "petrodollars" deposited by oil-exporting nations in U.S. banks to oil-importing countries in the developing world, principally in Latin America.

Initially, the Federal Reserve intervened directly in April 1982 by itself lending dollars to Mexico in a series of currency swaps (dollars for pesos) (Greider 1987, 485–86). By August, however, Mexico's economic situation had deteriorated much further, and the threat of default became immediate. This time the Treasury joined the Fed in developing a larger financing plan to tide Mexico over until it could receive lending support from the International Monetary Fund (conditional on structural economic changes within Mexico to improve its ability to service its debt). Under the new plan, the U.S. government agreed to pay in advance for $2 billion of oil and food sold by Mexico, while the Fed and other major central banks agreed to lend an additional $1.85 billion (Greider 1987, 517–18).

Although the rescue plan devised by the Federal Reserve and the Treasury Department averted the immediate threat posed by the Mexican debt situation

18. For a complete discussion of developing country debt problems in the 1980s, see the chapter by Paul Krugman in this volume.

to the U.S. banking system, Congress was not content to forget the matter. Directly responding to that crisis, in November 1983 Congress enacted the International Lending Supervision Act, which for the first time required the federal bank regulatory agencies to set and enforce minimum capital standards. Two years earlier, the agencies had announced minimum capital guidelines but had done so purely as a matter of discretion, not in response to a specific statutory instruction.

The new standards were not sufficient, however, to prevent the decade's second major banking crisis: the failure of Continental Illinois Bank in 1984. Ranked at the beginning of the 1980s as one of the best-managed banks in the country, Continental ran into difficulties early in the decade when it purchased what proved to be sour energy loans from a then little-known bank in Oklahoma, Penn Square, which failed in 1982. As Continental's loan losses mounted, institutional depositors at the bank—principally other banks from around the world—grew increasingly concerned about the bank's ability to survive and thus to honor in full the uninsured funds deposited with it. In May 1984, these depositors began to run, threatening to bring down what was then the nation's sixth-largest bank with over $40 billion in assets.

Federal bank regulators—the Comptroller, the FDIC, and the Fed—initially attempted to avert the crisis by cajoling other large U.S. banks to provide emergency credit to Continental. But, as with the early attempts to address the Mexican debt crisis, this early effort, too, proved insufficient. By midsummer, the deposit run had worsened and threatened to exhaust the credit extended by Continental's would-be rescuers. Eventually, the FDIC decided to take over Continental and its holding company, extending full guarantees to all the bank's depositors, both insured and uninsured.

The regulators' actions in the Continental crisis explicitly confirmed that, in fact, there were banks in the United States that were "too big to fail" (TBTF)— or, more precisely, too big for the regulators to permit uninsured depositors to lose (Kaufman 1989). Four years later, regulators would demonstrate that banks and even thrift institutions not as large as Continental would also qualify for TBTF status. In each of these cases, uninsured depositors were explicitly protected in full: First Republic Banks of Texas (over $25 billion in assets); MCorp Banks of Texas (approximately $15 billion in assets); and American Savings and Loan of California ($31 billion in assets). As discussed below, TBTF has since become one of the most controversial and troubling of all banking policies adopted in the 1980s.

Securities Markets

Finally, the 1980s were marked by three significant crises in U.S. securities markets, all occurring toward the end of the decade when the economy was in the midst of an economic expansion. For many, the surprising feature of each crisis was that none caused the expansion to end.

The first and most noteworthy securities crisis, of course, was the stock mar-

Table 8.10   **Largest One-Day Percentage Stock Market Declines**

1. 19 October 1987	−20.39
2. 28 October 1929	−12.34
3. 29 October 1929	−10.16
4. 6 November 1929	−9.92
5. 18 October 1937	−9.27
6. 20 July 1933	−8.88
7. 21 July 1933	−8.70
8. 20 December 1985	−8.52
9. 26 October 1987	−8.28
10. 5 October 1932	−8.20
11. 12 August 1932	−8.02
12. 31 May 1932	−7.84
13. 26 July 1934	−7.83
14. 14 March 1907	−7.59
15. 14 May 1940	−7.47
16. 26 July 1893	−7.39
17. 24 September 1931	−7.29
18. 12 September 1932	−7.18
19. 9 May 1901	−7.02
20. 15 June 1933	−6.97
21. 16 October 1933	−6.78
22. 8 January 1988	−6.76
23. 3 September 1946	−6.73
24. 28 May 1962	−6.68
25. 21 May 1940	−6.64

Source: Schwert (1990).

Note: Based on the Dow Jones Industrial and Railroad Indexes from 1928–62 and 1988–89 and the CRSP value-weighted index of New York Stock Exchange and American Stock Exchange stocks from 1962–87, all including dividends.

ket crash of 19 October 1987, which, as shown in table 8.10, was the largest one-day percentage drop in stock prices since official stock indexes have been computed. In addition, the 508-point drop in the Dow Jones Industrial Average (DJIA) on 19 October was preceded by a decline of roughly 500 points dating from late August 1987. In the two-month period, investors in U.S. stocks lost over $1 trillion.

The October 1987 crash created a crisis for several reasons. Most immediately, the steep decline in stock prices threatened the liquidity, if not the solvency, of any securities firms that were faced with potentially huge losses on securities they held in portfolio, either on their own account or as security for their margin customers, many of whom were unable to meet their margin calls. With securities firms imperiled, major banks began calling in their loans, further drying up liquidity and threatening the clearing of trades. At the larger, macroeconomic level, policymakers obviously were concerned that the crash would seriously damage investor and consumer confidence and thereby trigger a decline in spending sufficient to plunge the economy into recession.

As in the banking crises, the Federal Reserve was the lead agency most able and willing to take action. Fortunately, just weeks before the crash, on the order of its new chairman, Alan Greenspan, the Fed had completed a contingency plan to deal with precisely the events that unfolded in October. Accordingly, the Fed was ready to provide liquidity through open market operations (purchasing Treasury securities, thereby increasing the money supply and reducing short-term market interest rates). In addition, Fed officials reportedly urged leading banks to lend freely to securities firms experiencing liquidity problems; in turn, the Fed reportedly promised open access to its discount window if the banks themselves then had liquidity difficulties (*Wall Street Journal,* 20 November 1987, 1, 23).[19]

The Fed's interventions worked. The stock market quickly bounced back and over the next two years marched steadily upward. By October 1989, the DJIA had returned to its pre–October 1987 level. Although at the time many economists predicted that the crash would significantly reduce GNP growth, that didn't occur. Real GNP advanced at a 6.1 percent annual rate in the fourth quarter of 1987 and continued its upward climb thereafter, which permitted the Fed gradually to withdraw some of the liquidity that it had pumped into the markets immediately after the crash.

Nevertheless, as summarized in table 8.11, the severe market jolt unleashed a torrent of government- and privately sponsored analyses of why it happened and what, if anything, could be done to prevent a recurrence in the future. As illustrated in the table, however, the studies reached no consensus on either the causes or the cures, if any. Much attention was paid in the media and in Congress to the role played by computer program trading strategies and stock index arbitrage, trading techniques that arose in the 1980s with the growth of the financial futures and options markets. Critics of these strategies argued that, precisely because the "derivative" instruments were cheaper to trade than the underlying stocks (primarily because the cash deposits on futures were far lower than the margin requirements for stocks), they fueled the speculative behavior that ultimately led to the crash. Defenders of the derivative markets, principally the futures and options exchanges, argued that the derivatives and the underlying stocks were necessarily linked and that there was no evidence that, although futures and option trading had exploded in volume—indeed, by the late 1980s, future trading volume (in dollar value) exceeded that on the stock market itself—it had enhanced speculation.

Whatever the merits of these respective positions, the various studies did not decide the outcome of this debate. In the end, the only significant actions taken in the wake of the crash were voluntary measures by the NYSE and the Chi-

---

19. The *Wall Street Journal* account of the crash noted above in the text also suggested that various brokerage firms may have manipulated the Major Market Index (a basket of approximately twenty stocks) on 20 October to induce a stock market rally on that day. However, as reported in table 8.11 below, one of the studies that examined this allegation found no evidence to support it.

Table 8.11   **Major Studies of the October 1987 Stock Market Crash**

Study	Major Findings/Recommendations
The "Brady" Commission	The crash was caused by external factors (high trade deficit; proposed tax legislation)
	Recommended that a single regulatory agency be responsible for market regulation; that margin requirements on stocks/futures be coordinated; and that trading be halted during large price drops
Securities and Exchange Commission	Institutional selling the largest direct factor in causing the crash; no evidence of manipulation of the Major Market Index on 20 October
	Criticized use of "front running" by various brokerage firms
	Recommended margin requirements on futures to combat liquidity
Commodity Futures Trading Commission	Also found no evidence that Major Market Index had been manipulated; concluded that money managers used portfolio insurance more than index arbitrage
New York Stock Exchange	Recommended that stock index futures be traded on the floor
Chicago Mercantile Exchange	Rejected tighter regulation of trading strategies and or margins
National Association of Securities Dealers	Found that retail investors were net sellers of stock while institutional investors were net buyers
General Accounting Office	Found that crisis was exacerbated by inability of the NYSE computer system to handle orders; recommended increased supervision of the computer sytem
Investment Company Institute	Mutual fund managers were able to meet nearly two-thirds of customer redemption demands during the crisis

cago Mercantile Exchange (the "Merc") to introduce "circuit breakers" when stock or index prices dropped by certain amounts during a trading day.[20] Given the lack of consensus among the studies, coupled with these private initiatives, it is hardly surprising that Congress did not legislate in this area.

Still, the stock market was again to crash at the very end of the decade on 13 October 1989, or almost exactly two years after the October 1987 plunge.

20. The Merc imposed a temporary trading halt during the morning of 24 July 1990 after the DJIA fell by more than 100 points during the first hour of trading; the halt was credited with helping break the price decline. Later that week, the SEC approved a parallel proposal by the NYSE that required all stock index trades to be made on upticks following fifty-point declines in the DJIA.

The second time around, however, the DJIA dropped "only" 191 points, a 6.1 percentage point decline. With the benefit of its successful experience following the October 1987 crash, the Federal Reserve had relatively little trouble reacting to the 1989 episode: it pumped additional reserves into the financial system, which lowered the interest rate on Federal funds (overnight borrowings by banks), and announced during the following week its readiness to provide needed liquidity. Again, the decisive action worked; the market quickly calmed and later resumed its upward climb into 1990.

The final securities market crisis of the 1980s—the collapse of the "junk bond" market—also occurred at roughly the same time, with similarly benign macroeconomic consequences. The rise of the junk bond market, of course, was one of the major success stories of the decade. Pioneered largely by one individual (Michael Milken) and one brokerage house (Drexel Burnham Lambert), this market was created by matching institutional buyers hungry for higher-yielding instruments with noninvestment grade corporate issuers. Although most junk bonds (by dollar volume) were issued in connection with corporate restructurings (leveraged buyouts, other mergers and acquisitions, divestitures, and other restructurings), many were also issued by new companies without a long track record to earn an investment grade ranking from the private rating agencies (Crabbe, Pickering, and Prowse 1990, 596). By the end of 1989, over $200 billion in junk bonds were outstanding, virtually all of which had been issued during the 1980s.

The junk bond market weakened in 1988 when Michael Milken and his (by then former) brokerage firm were indicted for violating various securities laws. In the late summer of 1989, however, several events combined to force the market's collapse—sharp price declines of outstanding bonds and a virtual halt to new issues. The market began to unravel when a number of large, visible issuers of the bonds (Robert Campeau, Southland, and Integrated Resources, to name a few) defaulted. It was then severely shocked with the passage of FIRREA, which included provisions requiring thrift institutions to divest all their junk bond holdings by 1994. Although in the aggregate the thrift industry held only 7 percent of all junk bonds outstanding and nearly 80 percent of thrift investments in these bonds were concentrated in just ten savings institutions (GAO 1988), junk bond investments became one of the visible symbols of excessive risk taking in the thrift industry that many members of Congress believed necessary to attack. Enacted at precisely the time when several junk bond issuers were already in trouble and confidence in the market tenuous, the divestiture provisions (whatever their merits) cast a long shadow over the entire market and propelled it down further.

Ultimately, the junk bond market's fall was so deep that its principal creator, Drexel Burnham, was forced to declare bankruptcy early in 1990. Significantly, in contrast with the rescues of uninsured depositors of major failed banks during the 1980s, neither the Federal Reserve nor the Securities and Exchange Commission lifted a finger to prevent Drexel's demise, which caused barely a ripple in the financial markets when it happened.

Summary

Several themes run through the various financial crises of the 1980s. First, and perhaps most important, none of them led to macroeconomic disaster, largely because of successful crisis intervention by the Federal Reserve, in conjunction with other banking regulators, when necessary.

Second, certain of the interventions had significant longer-run consequences. In particular, by protecting uninsured depositors at large banks out of fear of the destabilizing consequences of large-scale bank runs, the banking authorities removed some of the market discipline against undesirable risk taking by large insured depositories. Much of the debate on financial reform in the 1990s will be aimed (indeed, it already has been) at finding ways to restore some of that discipline, whether by the market or by regulation.

Third, congressional intervention occurred only where it was required or when there was a clear consensus about what needed to be done. The various pieces of thrift legislation were examples of the first type: in each case, regulators or administration officials could not resolve the crisis without legislative authorization (deposit interest and asset deregulation or funds required for resolution of failed thrifts). In the case of the 1983 legislation requiring regulators to set and enforce bank capital standards, the Mexican debt crisis had already passed, but consensus was possible largely because regulators had already voluntarily set out to do the same thing. In areas where there was no consensus among either the expert community or the relevant interest groups—for example, securities market reforms or more the more basic structural financial issues discussed in the next section—it was not surprising that Congress took no action.

Finally, as indicated at the outset of the chapter, much of the financial policy-making in the 1980s was reactive in nature. In the thrift area in particular, the relevant policy-making institutions—the Congress, the executive, and the independent regulator (the Bank Board)—took few, if any, measures that could have mitigated, let alone prevented, the costly crises that eventually developed in the 1980s. The reasons for this inaction will be explored in later sections.

8.2.2   Structural Trends

The various financial crises of the 1980s obscured for policymakers and the public several significant structural developments that are likely to be at the top of the policy agenda in the 1990s. However, for reasons to be spelled out below, these developments attracted much less attention during the 1980s.

Thrifts

Again, it is appropriate to begin with thrift institutions because the fundamental economic forces at work in this industry were perhaps most poorly understood or recognized by policymakers.

Savings institutions developed in the early nineteenth century because no other intermediaries were then willing to originate and hold residential mort-

gage loans. The federal government has since promoted their growth by providing thrifts with special tax benefits and by creating a series of federal agencies to purchase mortgages and thus to generate liquidity for the institutions
that originate them.

Beginning in the early 1970s, however, these same agencies—notably the
Government National Mortgage Association (Ginnie Mae), the Federal National Mortgage Agency (Fannie Mae), and the Federal Home Loan Mortgage
Corporation (Freddie Mac)—embarked on a process that, as suggested earlier,
has undermined the economic rationale for and the long-run profitability of
the thrift industry. In the jargon of Wall Street, these agencies "securitized"
mortgages by pooling them (or providing guarantees on pools arranged by private investment firms) and then issuing securities backed by these pools (formally mortgage trusts). As shown in table 8.12, in just the thirteen years between 1975 and 1988, the volume of mortgage securities grew by more than a
factor of forty, reaching nearly $770 billion in 1988, representing more than
35 percent of all outstanding mortgages.

Securitization has had revolutionary consequences for the thrift industry,
which through the 1980s were barely appreciated in Congress. By converting
formerly illiquid mortgage instruments into liquid securities, the securitization
process has substantially increased the demand for mortgage instruments.
Now, pension funds, insurance companies, mutual funds, and even commercial

Table 8.12   **Securitized Mortgage Investments Outstanding ($billion)**

Year	Securitized Residential Mortgages	% Securitized	GNMA Passthroughs	FNMA MBS	FHLMC MBS and PC	Conventional Passthroughs
1975	17.8	3.7	16.2	. . .	1.6	. . .
1976	28.4	5.3	25.6	. . .	2.8	. . .
1977	49.7	7.9	42.9	. . .	6.8	. . .
1978	65.7	8.8	53.0	. . .	12.0	.7
1979	92.1	10.7	75.8	. . .	15.3	1.0
1980	112.2	11.7	93.9	. . .	17.0	1.3
1981	127.9	12.4	105.8	.7	19.9	1.5
1982	178.0	16.6	118.9	14.5	42.9	1.7
1983	246.2	20.7	159.8	25.1	58.0	3.3
1984	290.7	22.1	180.0	36.2	70.9	3.6
1985	372.0	25.3	212.1	55.0	100.5	4.4
1986	537.6	31.2[a]	262.7	97.2	171.4	6.3
1987	684.2	35.2	317.6	140.0	212.6	14.0
1988	768.9	35.4	340.5	178.3	225.0	25.1

Sources: Jaffee and Rosen (1990); *Federal Reserve Bulletin* (October 1989); Board of Governors of the
Federal Reserve System, flow of funds accounts.

Note: MBS = mortgage = backed securities. PC = participation certificates.

[a]Values after 1985 are securitized residential mortgages as a percentage of home mortgages owed by
nonfinancial sectors.

banks are major holders of mortgage instruments. In turn, the larger demand has lowered mortgage yields, by some estimates by as much as a full percentage point (Rosenthal and Ocampo 1988, 12), from what they would be otherwise.

While this has been good news for consumers, it has been devastating for thrifts. With lower yields available on mortgages, thrifts have had to absorb a reduction in the "spread" that they have been accustomed to earning between their cost of funds and yields on mortgage investments. Indeed, the decline in the spread has been so substantial that, unless a thrift has a stable pool of low-cost deposits or happens to be in a high-growth market where mortgage yields command a premium, it can no longer earn a market rate of return on its capital by primarily holding long-term fixed-rate mortgages (Carron and Brumbaugh 1991)—except by doing what thrifts traditionally did, gambling on interest rates by funding long-term mortgages with short-term deposits (the maturity mismatching that caused the decade's first thrift crisis). While profits may still be available from investing in adjustable-rate mortgages (ARMs), which thus far have not yet been securitized in substantial volumes, eventually the spreads in this line of business will also narrow considerably as ARMs are standardized and securitized.

The message for the thrift industry is hardly pleasant: it has no long-run future in the American financial system. Eventually, currently health thrifts must become banks, or they will steadily join the list of casualties that the government is already trying to bury.

Although the implications of securitization for the future of the thrift industry are widely recognized among policy analysts who specialize in this area, there is little or no evidence that they have thus far been understood in Congress or the administration, for that matter. FIRREA contains contradictory provisions relating to this subject. On the one hand, Congress demonstrated no appreciation for the implications of securitization by requiring thrifts to increase from 60 percent to 70 percent of assets their investments in mortgage and related consumer loans; this measure has only worsened the profitability problem that thrifts already confronted by further limiting their diversification opportunities. On the other hand, FIRREA also permitted thrifts eventually (by 1994) to convert to bank charters and thus to escape the 70 percent "qualified thrift lender" requirement (although, unless they pay a large one-time fee, the converted entities must still pay the higher insurance premiums required of all thrifts).

As the costs of the thrift rescue effort continue to mount, it is increasingly likely that Congress and the administration will reconsider whether to maintain separate bank and thrift charters and regulatory systems. Three factors have prevented a melding of the two industries thus far: the continuing (but weakening) political influence of many savings and loans and the widespread perception that the last thrift crisis of the decade was "caused" by provisions in the Garn–St. Germain Act allowing thrifts into nonmortgage investments. The first factor is becoming less important as the remaining healthy thrifts realize that the only way that they will be able to survive as depositories is with a bank charter (but without the higher insurance premiums). The second factor should continue to have more lasting influence even if it is misplaced. Although it is clear that insolvent thrifts invested more of their assets in nontraditional investments (White 1991; and Barth and Bradley 1989), they were encouraged to do so by lax enforcement of capital standards, which invited precisely the kind of risk taking with nontraditional investments that later led to higher losses (Brumbaugh, Carron, and Litan 1989). A key question for the 1990s is when policymakers—legislators in particular—will realize what really caused the thrift crises of the 1980s so that they can properly address the devastating implications that securitization is having for the thrift industry as it is presently structured.

Finally, Congress has thus far been reluctant to meld the thrift and bank charters because of a seemingly innocuous, but critically important, distinction between the laws governing bank and thrift holding companies. In brief, the Bank Holding Company (BHC) Act limits the businesses with which any bank can be affiliated (by virtue of its common parent holding company) to those that are "closely related to banking." The Savings and Loan Holding Company Act contains a similar provision for thrift holding companies, but only for those that own *two or more thrifts*. Accordingly, an organization owning only one thrift—such as Sears or the Ford Motor Company—can be engaged in any other activities it desires.

If the distinction between thrift and bank charters were eliminated, how would these unitary thrift holding companies be treated? If thrifts were treated like banks, then clearly the BHC Act would require the conglomerates to divest themselves of any businesses "not closely related to banking." Of course, many other financial enterprises would argue against divestiture and instead for changing the activity restrictions in the BHC Act. They would be opposed by those who believe that mixing "banking" and "commerce" could unwisely stretch the federal safety net to protect nonbanking enterprises.

In the 1990s, it is likely that the questions surrounding the mixing of banking and commerce will be addressed. If they are not, then it will be difficult, if not impossible, to meld the bank and thrift industries together (unless current unitary thrift holding companies are "grandfathered").

Banks

Even less noticed is the fact the securitization is likely to have the same effects on the banking industry as it has had on thrifts. However, for banks, the securitization process started differently.

Beginning in the 1970s, well-rated corporations that previously borrowed from banks found it cheaper and more convenient to issue their own commercial paper (generally backed, however, by a standby bank letter of credit). This process accelerated markedly during the 1980s: commercial paper issued by nonfinancial companies grew from $28 billion in 1980 to $85 billion in 1988. In addition, the growth of the junk bond market allowed many lesser-rated (or nonrated) companies to raise money more cheaply than by borrowing from banks. The banks, of course, had only themselves to blame for losing their best borrowers to the markets. As a result of mounting loan losses—initially on loans to developing countries but by the end of the decade losses on real estate loans and for highly leveraged transactions—most large banks suffered erosions in their credit ratings, which in turn made it more expensive for them to attract uninsured deposits. When bankers added even a slim spread to their higher cost of funds, they discovered that they could no longer profitably lend to their lowest-risk (and even medium-risk) corporate customers.

The securitization of bank loans will have similar effects on many other banks throughout the system. Although banks traditionally have not been as important sources of residential mortgage finance as thrifts, they nevertheless have suffered the same loss of maturity-matched spreads in mortgages due to securitization as have thrifts. More important for the future, banks are increasingly securitizing their bread-and-butter consumer loans (auto and credit card). It is widely expected that, eventually, they will do the same for many ordinary commercial loans. While individual banks that pioneer in the development and marketing of these securitization techniques will no doubt profit from their efforts, the implications for the future of the banking industry as a whole are disturbing. With spreads reduced on their highest-quality assets, banks will increasingly hold on their balance sheets only their higher-risk, nonliquid loans, posing future risks to the bank insurance fund, if not to the banking system generally.

Indeed, these risks have been mounting throughout the past three decades. Figure 8.1 illustrates that, since 1960, net loan losses have been rising as a percentage of total bank loans outstanding,[21] a trend that is reflected in the rising number and rate of bank failures (see table 8.1 above). Similarly, as illustrated in table 8.13, the composition of bank lending has been shifting away from traditional commercial and industrial loans to real estate loans, which can be especially high risk, as events in Texas in the mid-1980s and at the end of the decade in New England have demonstrated. Finally, the additional risks show up in a dramatic increase during the 1980s in the numbers of "problem banks," or those designated by bank examiners to have two of the poorest bank ratings (of five possible rankings). Although the number of problem banks declined at the end of the decade from a 1987 peak of 1,575, the 1,093 problem banks at the end of 1989 were nearly three times the previous

---

21. A regression in logarithmic form of the net loan loss ratio against the unemployment rate and a time trend suggests that, over the period 1960–89, the loss ratio has been rising at roughly 6 percent (not percentage points) per year; the ratio also rises by an estimated 79 percent for each percentage point of unemployment. Both coefficient estimates are statistically significant at the 95 percent confidence level; the equation (with a correction for serial correlation) explains 93 percent of the variance of the net loan loss ratio (in logarithmic form) over the period.

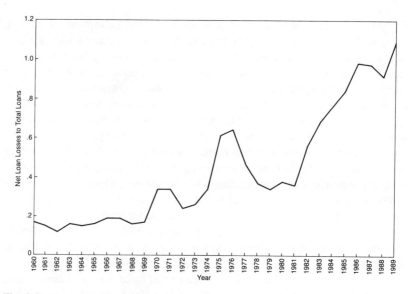

Fig. 8.1   Net loan charge-offs to average total loans (%)
Sources: Statistical Abstract of the United States (various years); FDIC published reports and data base.

Table 8.13		Composition of Commercial Bank Loan Portfolios (% share of total loans)					
Type of Loan	1972	1975	1978	1981	1984	1987	1989
Commercial and							
industrial	35.1	36.6	32.9	36.7	35.8	32.9	31.7
Real estate	25.2	26.0	28.2	29.4	28.5	34.5	37.8
Individual	22.1	20.3	22.0	18.9	19.2	19.3	18.9
Security	4.0	2.6	2.6	2.2	2.6	2.0	1.9
Nonbank financial	5.6	5.6	3.5	3.1	2.4	1.9	1.6
Agricultural	3.7	3.9	3.8	3.4	3.0	1.7	1.5
State and subdivisions	.0	.0	.0	.0	3.5	3.1	2.1
Foreign banks and official							
institutions	1.4	2.2	3.5	2.6	1.4	.8	.7
Lease financing,							
receivables	.4	.8	1.0	1.0	1.2	1.4	1.6
Other	2.6	2.1	2.4	2.4	2.4	2.5	2.3

Source: Economic Report of the President (1990).

postwar peak of 385 in 1976. Moreover, at the end of the decade many banks were still thinly capitalized by conventional, historical–cost accounting standards, which the thrift experience teaches can significantly overstate the true condition of financial intermediaries (Brumbaugh and Litan 1990).

Given the implications of securitization for banks as well as thrifts, what could policymakers do? Clearly, one step urged by virtually all academic specialists in this area is to permit banks to diversify geographically by expanding into all states, not only through holding companies, but also directly through additional branches. The largest banks that could best profit from this consolidation attempted to interest Congress in this reform early in the 1980s, but the move was strongly resisted by the thousands of smaller banks who feared they could not compete with the larger banks, the "money centers" in particular. In the absence of a consensus among the interests most immediately affected, Congress was not inclined to act. In any event, the issue was rendered moot in 1985 when the Supreme Court ratified the constitutionality of the reciprocal interstate banking arrangements legislated by various states in the early 1980s designed to permit large banks outside New York to grow into major regional institutions. By the end of the decade, all but a handful of states would have such arrangements; several were already allowing or scheduled to permit banking organizations from anywhere in the country (including New York) into their states.

Another potential remedy to the rising risks of traditional banking is to permit banks or their holding companies to engage in a broader range of activities. However, given the poor name that thrifts gave "asset diversification" in the 1980s, it was unlikely that Congress would take this approach. Moreover, the efforts by banks to expand into other businesses—notably securities, insurance, and real estate—were vigorously opposed, quite predictably, by firms in those other lines of activity. This was the case even though nonbanking and even nonfinancial) firms had found their way into banking during the 1980s by exploiting several provisions in the laws governing bank and thrift affiliations. One particularly ingenious device used by a variety of firms was to acquire or open a bank that invested its federally insured deposits only in consumer, but not commercial, loans. Such a "nonbank" bank (as it was called) could circumvent the business affiliation (as well as the geographic) restrictions in the Bank Holding Company Act. Congress closed this loophole in 1987 (in the same legislation that authorized an additional $15 billion for the FSLIC).

Nevertheless, during the 1980s and continuing into the 1990s, a number of states have been sympathetic with the banks' arguments and have allowed their state-chartered banks into various activities (principally securities brokerage and underwriting and insurance agencies) that national banks cannot lawfully enjoy (Litan 1987a). In these states, the interest-group gridlock that stalemated congressional action either was not as strong as it was on the federal level (because banking interests in the states had substantially greater political influence than their rivals) or was superseded by state legislators eager to attract additional banking business to their states.

In addition, even federal regulators were sympathetic with the banks. Late in the decade, the Federal Reserve exploited a loophole in the Glass-Steagall Act's requiring separation of commercial and investment banking by authorizing bank holding companies to establish separate securities underwriting affiliates as long as they were not "principally engaged" in otherwise impermissible securities underwriting. By 1989, the Fed allowed these affiliates of banks to earn up to 10 percent of their revenues from underwriting a wide range of non-Treasury securities. Similarly, the Comptroller fo the Currency authorized national banks themselves to underwrite their own asset-backed securities without going through investment banking companies. All these decisions were upheld by the courts in the face of legal challenges by the securities industry.

Yet another policy option is to increase bank capital requirements, a step that Chairman of the Federal Reserve Alan Greenspan suggested in July 1990 before the Senate Banking Committee (Greenspan 1990). The rationale for rising capital requirements is that, if the banking system is experiencing increasing risk, then it ought to match the additional risk with additional capital. Coming on the heels of the new capital standards negotiated as part of the Basle Accord (discussed below), Greenspan's suggestion not surprisingly has concerned the U.S. banking community, especially the larger banks now increasingly worried about their slipping international competitiveness. Indeed, some have argued that, if the banks have to meet higher capital standards, they will take additional risks to do so, precisely the opposite of what the Fed intends. Whether or not this is correct, the notion that banks meet even higher capital standards than those negotiated as part of the Basle Accord was not on the public policy agenda at any time during the 1980s.

Finally, there is a question whether the deposit insurance system can be redesigned to discourage some of the additional risk taking that banks clearly have evinced. Among the alternatives are to enhance depositor discipline by lowering or restricting current insurance coverage of $100,000 per deposit account or to increase discipline by other interested parties—shareholders, holders of uninsured (subordinated) debt, and regulators. In the Garn–St. Germain Act of 1982, Congress instructed each of the major insurance funds (the FDIC, the FSLIC, and the National Credit Union Association) to report back with suggestions for reforming deposit insurance. Yet, as would be the case with the securities market studies later in the decade, these reports reached no consensus. In addition, in 1984 the problems with Continental Illinois and the weaknesses at several other major banks made many in Congress hesitant to tamper with the deposit insurance system in any way that might destabilize deposits at large banks in particular. Not surprisingly, therefore, Congress took no action.

When the third thrift crisis of the decade struck in 1988–89, Congress again directed that a study of deposit insurance be made (as part of FIRREA), this time by the Treasury Department, which is scheduled to report its recommendations in early 1991. At this writing, it is not clear how Congress will respond, if at all, to the Treasury's study (nor is it known what the Treasury will recommend).

Securities Markets

Although the nation's securities markets also experienced revolutionary changes during the 1980s, there was (and still is) much less agreement within the expert community, let along among policymakers, about the policy implications of these structural developments than about the market trends affecting the depository industries. Two particular developments deserve mention.

First, and perhaps most important, the 1980s witnessed a growing institutionalization of the securities markets. For example, the share of block trading at the New York Stock Exchange rose from about 29 percent in 1980 to almost 55 percent in 1988 (GAO 1990, 23). As noted earlier, institutionalization was facilitated by the deregulation of fixed brokerage commissions in the 1970s, but it was also fueled by the growth of pension funds and by the increasing desire of individuals to diversify their stock holdings through mutual funds rather than on their own.

As the markets have grown more institutionalized, policymakers have begun to consider how to modify securities regulation and disclosure, most of which rests on the Depression-era premise that individual investors must be protected. Yet regulation, registration, and disclosure requirements can be expensive and raise capital costs for corporations issuing stocks and bonds here. In recognition of these costs and the changes in market participation, the SEC introduced "shelf registration" in the 1980s for corporations that make repeated use of the capital markets, streamlining the previous (often duplicative) registration requirements for individual securities issues. In addition, in 1990 the agency adopted Rule 144a to allow corporate issuers to take advantage of a lower-cost method of raising capital if their securities were issued first only to institutional investors.[22] Such action portends possible two-tiered securities regulation in the future: one set of rules for securities issued to individuals, another for securities bought and traded by institutions.

Second, the institutionalization of the securities markets was a principal driving force behind the explosive growth of the derivatives markets in the 1980s—principally, financial futures and options (on bonds, stocks, and stock and bond indexes).[23] The derivative instruments allowed institutions to trade their large blocks of securities (whether for hedging, arbitrage, or speculation) more cheaply in derivative form than as stocks or bonds directly for two reasons. The derivatives markets offered lower margin requirements. In addition, as their dollar volume surpassed trading volume on the stock exchanges, the futures markets offered deeper and more liquid markets for institutional traders than the markets for the underlying securities (where prices could be significantly moved by large institutional trades).

The rise of the derivatives markets, however, led to one of the most heated financial policy debates of the 1980s: whether financial futures increased the volatility of prices of the underlying securities and/or contributed to excessive speculative behavior. On the first question, there appears little room for argu-

22. Specifically, the rule exempts U.S. and foreign corporations from registration requirements for bonds and stock sold to institutional investors with investment assets of $100 million or more and, in the case of banks and thrift institutions, with net worth of at least $25 million. In addition, the rule permits the resale of these private securities to other qualified institutions at any time.

23. Trading on options on individual stocks had been authorized in the 1970s by the Commodity Futures Trading Commission.

ment. Whether measured by variations within a month or within a day, stock market returns show no trend increase in volatility since the mid-nineteenth century; there are major exceptions, of course, surrounding various market crashes (29 October 1989, 19 October 1987, etc.), but erratic price movements on these occasions have been temporary (Schwert 1990, C-8–C-15). On the second question, however, there is no clear consensus among the experts, and thus, not surprisingly, Congress has not imposed higher margins on futures or consolidated futures regulation within one agency, as the SEC has suggested but the Commodity Futures Trading Commission has strongly opposed.

Globalization and Competitiveness

Finally, and perhaps most important for the 1990s, the U.S. financial system, like the underlying real economy, was shocked in the 1980s by global forces, a trend that has since spawned concerns about the "competitiveness" of U.S. financial institutions and markets.

Table 8.3 above indicates that, by one commonly cited benchmark, size rankings of banks, U.S. depositories slipped badly during the 1980s. By the end of the decade, no U.S. bank ranked in the top ten in the world; only two made the top 50. The banks at the top of the list were all Japanese.

In an age of securitization and financial innovation, however, asset size can be misleading since increasingly the largest profits are made in trading and fees. By profitability, U.S. banks even at the end of the decade looked much better: three of the five most profitable banks in the world (measured by returns on equity, adjusted for differences in capital ratios, inflation, and tax rates) were American and the other two European; Japanese banks ranked far down the list (*Business Week,* 2 July 1990, 80–85).

Still, U.S. bankers could hardly take comfort from the fact that, during the 1980s, they lost significant ground to foreign-based institutions. At home, where the competition is probably more important and certainly more evident, U.S. banks lost market share in commercial lending to foreign banks, dropping from 86 percent of the market in 1980 to 72 percent by 1988 ("Foreign Bank Growth" 1990). And, weakened by their problem loans and shortage of capital, through much of the decade American banks withdrew from foreign markets (*New York Times,* 5 July 1990, A1, D9).

Ironically, the deteriorating competitive position of U.S. banks led to one of the most important policy developments of the 1980s—one with potentially far-reaching implications for future financial regulation. As they grew increasingly concerned about their loss of market share, U.S. banks complained to their regulators that foreign banks, those from Japan in particular, were permitted by their authorities to operate with lower capital ratios and thus were able to leverage their limited capital into faster growth, both in their home markets and in the United States. Accordingly, they urged U.S. regulators to negotiate a common international bank capital requirement among the major industrialized countries.

The banks' request was received favorably by the regulators, not just because of their similar concern about a "level playing field," but also because of their desire to raise capital standards for prudential reasons as well. By 1987, the Federal Reserve joined with its counterparts from ten other major countries in the Basle Capital Accord, which set common "risk-based" capital rules for banks in all these countries. The standards were risk based since different categories of assets were weighted differently.[24] The regulators recognized that the new system failed to account for various other risks (related to portfolio composition, susceptibility to interest rate movements, and liquidity), but they argued that the new common standards were still better than the previous dissimilar rules in different countries. At this writing, the major central banks are working to refine the risk standards to account for these additional risk factors.

Securities markets around the world also grew more globalized during the 1980s, and simultaneously the U.S. markets became less dominant. For example, by the end of the decade, the share of worldwide market capitalization represented by U.S. corporations had fallen from more than 50 percent in 1980 to below 30 percent in 1988; Japanese stocks, in contrast, had vaulted into first place, with 45 percent (Hale 1990, 154).[25] Although most stocks are still traded only in their country of origin, the shares of foreign stocks traded on the major exchanges around the world have been rising rapidly: by early 1990, trading in foreign stocks accounted for approximately 6 percent of the trading volume on the NYSE, 7 percent on the Tokyo Stock Exchange, over 20 percent on the London Stock Exchange, and above 30 percent on the other major European markets (OTA 1990, 29–30). Ultimately, the organized exchanges may give way to private international trading networks (such as GLOBEX, operated jointly by the Chicago Mercantile Exchange and Reuters) that will allow round-the-clock/round-the-world trading.

A critical question for the 1990s and beyond will be whether, and if so how, securities regulation will be coordinated internationally. In global markets, no country can exert its regulatory will without risking the transfer of its corporations and/or its markets overseas. Indeed, critics of proposals to tax securities and financial instruments transactions—as a way of reducing speculation— rest their opposition primarily on the risk that such a tax would drive much current trading off shore. Still, however, there is no consensus as to what degree, if any, U.S. securities authorities should be ready to yield their sovereign control over U.S. securities markets to a wider international body of regulators, as their bank regulatory counterparts have already done.

---

24. At one extreme, government securities carried 0 risk weight and thus no capital requirement; at the other extreme, commercial and most other nonmortgage loans carried a 100 percent risk weight and thus the full capital requirement.

25. At this writing, however, U.S. markets have reportedly regained the top ranking worldwide owing to the major drop in Japanese share prices during 1990.

8.3   Roads Not Taken

With so many seemingly adverse developments affecting the U.S. financial markets and institutions during the 1980s, two natural questions are whether policymakers could have made better choices and, if so, why they didn't. With respect to the structural developments in the financial arena just reviewed, the answers to these questions have already been suggested. Only in the case of interstate banking was there a clear consensus among independent experts on what should be done; neither Congress nor the administration acted because of the deep split in views between large and small banks. On the need for additional bank product diversification and deposit insurance reform there was also a fair degree of consensus; however, among the experts, let alone the policymakers, there was little agreement about the forms that these efforts should take. Finally, with respect to the developments in securities markets, there was no consensus either among the experts or among relevant interests on the proper policy reaction.

Accordingly, the more interesting questions center on the alternative policy measures that could have been taken to avert or respond to the various crises of the decade. In the case of thrifts, starting the inquiry with the 1980s is too late, for several actions could have been taken in the 1970s that probably would have prevented most, if not all, of the damage that occurred the following decade. The Hunt Commission, for example, recommended in 1971 that deposit interest controls be phased out and that banks and thrifts be allowed to offer ARMs. At that time, however, most depositories were not enthusiastic about the lifting of interest controls, which would have raised their cost of funds. Only by the early 1980s, when market interest rates were so high above the Regulation Q ceilings that depositors were rapidly fleeing their banks and thrifts for money market funds, was the industry, and thus Congress, receptive to accelerated removal of the remaining interest rate controls.

Lenders were more supportive of ARM authority in the 1970s, but powerful forces in Congress were not. In particular, ranking members of the banking committees feared that, in an environment of rising interest rates, ARMs would be detrimental to the interests of consumers. This attitude, too, would change by 1980, when the thrift industry was in serious trouble.

Given, therefore, the inevitability of the 1981–82 thrift crisis, was there any other course of action that policymakers could have adopted to avoid, or minimize, the subsequent asset quality crisis among thrifts? In theory, of course, policymakers could have shut down all thrifts with negative net worths measured at market value—or most of the industry. But, as suggested earlier, this option would not have been politically realistic.

The more feasible course would have been to impose growth limits on all thrifts with inadequate (or negative) capital and to have *strengthened* supervision of weak thrifts, rather than weaken it as actually occurred. Clearly, in retrospect, this would have prevented much of the asset gambling that poorly capitalized thrifts were permitted to engage in with virtually unlimited quantities of federally insured funds (White 1991, chaps. 5–7).

The Bank Board, in fact, tried variations of this approach in the mid-1980s. It attempted to prohibit "brokered deposits" (deposit accounts just under the $100,000 ceiling placed by brokerage firms in generally weak or insolvent thrifts offering high rates of interest), but this effort was rebuffed by the courts as outside the Board's statutory authority. In 1984, the Board also limited direct investments by thrifts (equity positions in stocks, physical assets, or nonthrift businesses that various states allowed their state-chartered thrifts).

However, in each case, the Board received little encouragement and, in some quarters, outright hostility. The deregulation-minded Treasury Department, as well as its former secretary and current White House chief of staff, opposed limits on the thrift industry, believing that, as the economic expansion continued, insolvent thrifts would be lifted to health.[26] The same attitude prevailed in the banking committees of both congressional chambers, where many members were beneficiaries of political donations from thrifts, their owners, and their trade associations. Accordingly, by the time the Board was able substantially to increase the thrift supervisory force (by transferring thrift examiners to the independent Federal Home Loan Bank System, which was free from civil service salary caps and control by the Office of Management and Budget), it was too late. Many weak or insolvent thrifts had grown enormously and had already gambled (or defrauded) their way to big losses.

The major "road not taken" during the two major banking crises, of course, would have been for the Federal Reserve not to have intervened and let market developments take their natural course. Of course, even with perfect hindsight, it is impossible to know how events otherwise would have played out. All that is known is that in each case—the Mexican debt crisis of 1982, Continental Illinois in 1984, and the several large bank failures in 1988—policymakers feared that, if they did not intervene, not only would one or more banks fail, but uninsured depositors at other solvent banks would panic and run from them, too.

Whether this concern was well grounded and, even if so, whether the consequences of a major deposit run would have been as devastating as policymakers apparently feared continue to be debated among legislators, administration officials, and academic experts. Critics of what has become known as TBTF argue that systemwide runs will not occur because uninsured depositors are capable of distinguishing solvent from insolvent depositories but that, even if a wider run started, it would not affect real economic activity since depositors would merely shift their funds from one bank to another, leaving the money supply in the banking system unchanged (Kaufman 1989). Furthermore, by

26. Former Secretary Regan also tried during the mid-1980s to force the resignation of the Bank chairman, Ed Gray. Eventually, Gray's term expired in 1987, and he was replaced with M. Danny Wall, formerly a top aide to the minority members of the Senate Banking Committee.

protecting all depositors at large banks, policymakers not only disadvantage smaller banks (whose depositors may not get the same treatment) but undermine market discipline against risky bank behavior.

Defenders of TBTF (very few openly "support" the concept) counter principally by pointing to the disruptive effects that a contagious deposit run can have, even if eventually all the funds are merely shifted around the banking system. In the interim, markets can become very unsettled, and interest rates can "spike" upward, as they have in previous financial crises (Carron 1982a). Even though temporary, the negative macroeconomic consequences may be too great for policymakers to risk, especially in the midst of a recession, as was the case during the Mexican debt crisis in 1982.

For these reasons, it is not surprising that, even today, the Federal Reserve continues to be skeptical about depositor discipline, especially for larger banks (Greenspan 1990, 13). One of the interesting questions for the 1990s is whether Congress will nevertheless restrict the Fed's ability to implement TBTF, as the American Bankers Association urged in 1990, or whether it will look elsewhere for additional discipline against excessive risk taking by banks.

Finally, whatever one may believe about the wisdom of the Federal Reserve's effective protection of uninsured depositors at large banks, it is universally agreed that the Fed took appropriate action in response to both stock market crashes of the late 1980s. Without the assurances of liquidity that the Fed provided immediately after both events, trading on the stock exchanges could have ground to halt, shattering not only the confidence of securities investors but of firms and consumers as well.

8.4   Concluding Thoughts: Outlook for the Future

In the 1980s, policy toward financial institutions and markets was driven largely by crisis. Interest group deadlock on a variety of structural issues—interstate banking, financial product restructuring, deposit insurance reform, and securities markets reforms—thwarted at least Congress from taking any major initiatives.

As the 1990s opened, however, the globalization of financial markets and the growing intensity of foreign competition in the financial services industry has shifted the political balance. As part of its 1992 initiative, the European Economic Community is permitting the development of major integrated financial service firms. Japan has been gradually liberalizing its financial markets and constraints on activities of its banks and securities firms. With American financial institutions no longer dominant in the global market, policymakers are paying increasing attention to how they can reform the nation's financial structure to enhance the "competitiveness" of U.S.-based financial institutions. In this environment, policymakers are likely to grow more receptive to breaking the stalemate that has thus far persisted on many of the important structural issues affecting the financial marketplace.

An open question is to what extent, and at what pace, policymakers in the United States will join with their counterparts abroad to harmonize regulation and supervision of financial institutions and markets. The Basle bank capital standards set an important precedent that may eventually be followed for other aspects of bank regulation (e.g., deposit insurance and bank affiliations with nonbanking enterprises), if not during the 1990s, then conceivably after the year 2000. In addition, as already noted, as securities trading becomes more internationalized, the prospects for international cooperation in securities regulation also improve.

Whatever policy decisions in the financial arena are made in the 1990s, Americans in this decade and beyond will be paying for the costly policy mistakes of the previous two decades that led to the thrift debacle. The resolution of the thrift crisis is likely to cast a shadow over financial policy-making in the 1990s.

Finally, those who provide economic advice to policymakers can take away some valuable lessons from the 1980s. Perhaps the most important result from the decade is that the real economy proved to be far more resistant to the many financial upheavals than many would have predicted. This is largely because the Federal Reserve intervened to prevent each crisis from generating adverse macroeconomic effects. But, in the case of the stock market crashes in particular, it appears that both consumers and firms were (and arguably still are) much less influenced by short-term stock price movements than may have been commonly believed.

Economists who advise policymakers on financial matters also, somewhat surprisingly, can take heart that their efforts ultimately will have some use. Although policymakers largely ignored the advice of many banking specialists throughout the 1980s by failing to rationalize the regulation of financial institutions and to reform the deposit insurance system, these issues are likely to be at the top of the agenda in the 1990s, and policymakers are already looking to the accumulated wisdom of the academic community for guidance. One hopes that the 1990s will have fewer crises to distract attention from the important structural issues in financial markets that should be addressed.

References

Barth, J. R., and P. F. Bartholomew. 1990. The thrift-industry crisis: Revealed weaknesses in the federal deposit insurance system. Paper presented to a Stanford University conference, Washington, D.C., 18–19 May.

Barth, J. R., P. F. Bartholomew, and M. G. Bradley. 1989. Reforming federal deposit insurance: What can be learned from private insurance practices? Reserve Paper no. 161. Washington, D.C.: Office of Policy and Economic Research, Federal Home Loan Bank Board, June.

Barth, J. R., and M. G. Bradley. 1989. Thrift deregulation and federal deposit insurance. *Journal of Financial Services Research* (September), 231–59.

Benston, G. J. 1990a. *The separation of commercial and investment banking: The Glass-Steagall Act revisited and reconsidered.* Oxford: Oxford University Press.

———. 1990b. U.S. banking in an increasingly integrated and competitive world economy. Paper presented at the American Enterprise Institute conference "International Competitiveness in Financial Services," Washington, D.C.

Brumbaugh, R. D., Jr. 1988. *Thrifts under siege.* Cambridge, Mass.: Ballinger.

Brumbaugh, R. D., Jr., and A. S. Carron. 1987. Thrift industry crisis: Causes and solutions. *Brookings Papers on Economic Activity,* no. 2:349–77.

Brumbaugh, R. D., Jr., A. S. Carron, and R. E. Litan. 1989. Cleaning up the depository institutions mess. *Brookings Papers on Economic Activity,* no. 1:243–83.

Brumbaugh, R. D., Jr., and R. E. Litan. 1990. The banks are weaker than you think. *Challenge* (January–February), 4–12.

Carron, A. S. 1982a. Financial crises: Recent experience in U.S. and international markets. *Brookings Papers on Economic Activity,* no. 2:395–422.

———. 1982b. *Plight of the thrift institutions.* Washington, D.C.: Brookings.

Carron, A. S., and R. D. Brumbaugh, Jr. 1991. Viability of the thrift industry. *Housing Policy Debates* 2:1–24.

Crabbe, L. E., M. H. Pickering, and S. D. Prowse. 1990. Recent developments in corporate finance. *Federal Reserve Bulletin* (August), 593–603.

Federal Deposit Insurance Corporation (FDIC). 1988. *FDIC annual report.* Washington, D.C.

Foreign bank growth: Are U.S. fears justified? 1990. *Washington Post,* 24 June, H1.

General Accounting Office (GAO). 1988. *Financial markets: Issuers, purchasers and purposes of high yield, non-investment grade bonds.* Washington, D.C., February.

———. 1990. *Securities trading: SEC action needed to address national market system issues.* March.

Greenspan, A. 1990. Testimony before the Committee on Banking, Housing, and Urban Affairs of the U.S. Senate. 12 July.

Greider, W. 1987. *Secrets of the temple: How the federal reserve runs the country.* New York: Simon & Schuster.

Hale, D. 1990. Global finance and the retreat to managed trade. *Harvard Business Review* (January–February), 150–62.

Jaffee, D. M., and K. P. Rosen. 1990. Mortgage securitization trends. *Journal of Housing Research* 1:117–37.

Kane, E. J. 1989. *The S&L insurance mess: How did it happen?* Washington, D.C.: Urban Institute.

Kaufman, G. 1989. Are some banks too large to fail? Myth and reality. Working paper. Federal Reserve Bank of Chicago, June.

Litan, R. E. 1987a. Financial restructuring: Which way for Congress. *Challenge* (November–December), 36–43.

———. 1987b. *What should banks do?* Washington, D.C.: Brookings.

Office of Technology Assessment (OTA). 1990. *Trading around the clock: Global securities markets and information technology.* Washington, D.C.: Congress of the United States.

Pierce, J. L. 1991. *The future of banking.* New Haven, Conn.: Yale University Press.

Pratt, R. 1989. Discussion comments. In *The future of the thrift industry.* Proceedings of the fourteenth annual conference of the Federal Home Loan Bank of San Francisco.

Rosenthal, J. A., and J. M. Ocampo. 1988. *Securitization of credit: Inside the new technology of finance.* New York: Wiley.

Sachs, J., and H. Huizinga. 1987. U.S. commercial banks and the developing-country debt crisis. *Brookings Papers on Economic Activity,* no. 2:555–601.

Schwert, G. W. 1990. Stock market volatility. App. C in *Market volatility and investor confidence.* Report to the Board of Directors of the New York Stock Exchange, 24 May.

Sprague, I. 1985. *Bailout: An insider's account of bank failures and rescues.* New York: Basic.

———. 1990. Finger pointers rewriting history of S&L crisis. *American Banker,* 22 August, 5, 19, 26–27.

White, L. J. 1991. *The S&L debacle: Public policy lessons for banks and thrifts.* Oxford: Oxford University Press.

2. *William M. Isaac*

It is a distinct honor and privilege for me to be invited to appear before such a distinguished group of scholars. My friend Marty Feldstein has asked that I address the collapse of the savings and loan (S&L) industry.

I guess I'm in a rather unique position to comment on the collapse of the S&L industry in that I served as chairman of the Federal Deposit Insurance Corporation (FDIC) from 1981 through 1985 when the seeds of the S&L disaster were sown. Some of you might not be aware that the FDIC insures the deposits in the savings bank industry and that the savings banks were suffering the same kinds of problems as the S&Ls in the early 1980s. It's an interesting case study to compare the widely divergent ways in which the FDIC and the Federal Savings and Loan Insurance Corporation (FSLIC) responded to these problems.

Before I get into that subject, I need to go back in time to set the stage. Thrifts were created in the nineteenth century in response to a market need. Banks were not satisfying the desire of consumers for a safe haven for their savings dollars and for a vehicle to finance their most basic and expensive need: housing. Thrifts were formed, initially as philanthropic organizations, to fill the void.

Across the span of a century, market conditions changed dramatically. Not only banks, but also many other financial intermediaries, recognized the opportunities for profit in serving consumers and developed the products to do so.

In the meantime, in response to the banking collapse of the 1930s, the government had intervened with a series of measures designed to limit competition. Interest rate controls were put in place to restrict price competition. A rate differential was established to encourage the flow of funds to thrifts. A deposit insurance system was created to maintain stability and to preserve a diverse (and uneconomic) banking structure. Laws were passed mandating that thrifts function as nondiversified lenders. Branching restrictions severely curtailed geographic expansion and diversification. And other fences, such as the Glass-Steagall Act, were erected to keep the various types of financial intermediaries on their own distinct playing fields.

The first signs of tension in this rather comfortable scheme began to appear in the 1960s. The Johnson administration's "guns and butter" fiscal policy in the mid-1960s set off inflationary pressures that led to higher and more volatile interest rates, which impaired the viability of long-term lenders such as thrifts.

Largely in response to these pressures, in 1971 the Hunt Commission recommended that deposit interest rate controls be phased out, that thrifts and other lenders be allowed to offer variable-rate mortgages, and that mutual thrifts be permitted to convert to stock form of ownership. The recommendations were ignored by the administration and Congress.

My old agency—the FDIC—committed what I believe was a major public policy mistake in 1972 when it greatly expanded the scope of coverage of the deposit insurance system: rather than allowing the Bank of the Commonwealth in Detroit to fail, the FDIC infused capital into it. All creditors were also bailed out by the FDIC at U.S. National in San Diego in 1973 and Franklin National in New York in 1974.

President Roosevelt had been opposed to a federal deposit insurance system when it was proposed in the 1930s. He believed that it would be unduly expensive and doomed to fail because it would force the well-managed banks to subsidize the high flyers. A compromise was reached calling for very limited depositor protection plan—initially only $2,500 per account. Amounts above the insurance limits were to be exposed to the risk of loss. The FDIC's actions in 1972, 1973, and 1974 represented a vast expansion of the scope of the deposit insurance program and, I'm convinced, began the process of undermining discipline in our financial system.

The Federal Reserve Board committed a significant mistake in 1977 when it ruled that bank holding companies could not acquire healthy thrifts. Somehow the Fed managed to find that the operation of a thrift was not sufficiently related to banking to allow bank holding companies to enter the business. The real reasons were political: the Fed did not want to offend the thrift industry or the smaller banks, which viewed bank holding company acquisitions of thrifts with alarm because they would permit the larger banks to bypass the restraints on geographic expansion. This decision by the Fed was critically important because it prevented the thrifts from becoming part of diversified financial institutions.

Inflation raged during the Carter administration, with the prime rate soaring above 21 percent. Thrifts—both S&Ls and savings banks—suffered massive disintermediation and began to hemorrhage red ink owing to their long-term, fixed-rate loan portfolios.

Congress belatedly authorized deregulation of interest rates in 1980. But, by then, much damage had already been done. Thrifts had amassed huge portfolios of long-term, fixed-rate loans, and banks and thrifts alike had invested heavily in staffs and bricks and mortar to enable them to engage in the only form of competition previously allowed: nonprice competition. Banks and thrifts should have been provided a lengthy phase-in period to adjust to interest rate deregulation, as would have been the case if Congress had acted in the early 1970s when the Hunt Commission made its recommendations. Instead, they were thrust into a deregulated environment virtually overnight.

When the Reagan administration entered office in 1981, it was faced with an overwhelming number of failing thrifts. It's important to note that the problem at this point was an interest rate spread problem, not asset quality, and it affected both S&Ls insured by the FSLIC and savings banks insured by the FDIC.

At the FDIC, we formed a savings bank project team in early 1981 to study the problems and come up with a program for dealing with them. We concluded that our regulatory response needed to be relatively stringent in order to prevent the problems of the weaker savings banks from contaminating the stronger ones. We decided that we would merge savings banks that were insolvent on a book or liquidity basis into relatively strong institutions with FDIC financial assistance. Because the insolvencies were being caused by what we hoped were extraordinarily high interest rates that would eventually recede, we decided that, in most cases, our financial assistance should take the form of income maintenance agreements. These agreements called for the FDIC to guarantee the acquiror a positive interest rate spread on the acquired asset portfolio. The deals were structured so that the acquiror's assumed cost of funds was the average cost of funds for the region rather than the actual cost. This gave the acquiror an incentive to hold down the interest rates paid on deposits. The agreements assumed that the composition of an acquired asset portfolio did not change from the date of acquisition except for an assumed runoff of the portfolio due to principal repayments. This gave the acquiror the incentive to restructure the asset portfolio as interest rate conditions warranted.

It was our belief that these types of agreements would enable the FDIC to resolve the savings bank problems at the lowest possible cost. When interest rates receded, payments under the agreements would cease. Acquirors would receive whatever amount of money was needed to carry them through the high interest rate period and no more.

We ran projections on the cost of resolving the savings bank problems under a variety of interest rate scenarios, including a worst-case scenario that assumed that rates would continue to rise almost indefinitely. We could envision the possibility that the FDIC fund would be depleted. We made a conscious decision that we would not allow the finite nature of our financial resources to dictate our regulatory response. We would do what we felt we needed to do, and, if we ran out of money, we would go to the Congress and ask for more.

For savings banks that were technically solvent but failed to meet our normal capital standards, we decided that we would allow them to continue in operation so long as they did not do anything to increase the FDIC's exposure to risk. In short, this meant that we would not allow them to grow by more than a nominal amount, engage in new activities, or pay above-market rates for deposits. So long as a marginally capitalized savings bank behaved itself and did not increase its risk profile, it made financial sense for the FDIC to deal with it later, after interest rates receded, rather than sooner. If it began to increase its risk profile, the FDIC would deal with it immediately, as the Bowery Savings Bank in New York and a couple of others learned.

Over at our sister agency, the FSLIC, a different approach was taken. Weak S&Ls were merged into other weak S&Ls. The asset portfolios were marked to market in the merger, and the resulting goodwill was allowed to be counted as capital to support future growth. Capital standards were lowered, and regulatory accounting techniques, such as loss deferral and appraised equity capital, were authorized to enable insolvent S&Ls to continue in operation and even grow.

On the basis of conversations that I had at the time with the top officials of the FSLIC and its parent, the Federal Home Loan Bank Board, it was felt that the FSLIC did not have sufficient funds to deal with the S&L problems and that the proper response was therefore to defer dealing with the problems as long as possible. It was felt that one solution was to allow S&Ls to grow their way out of the interest rate mismatch—to bury their old portfolios of low-yielding assets with newly booked assets carrying much higher yields.

I must say that, at the time, the FSLIC's policies received a far more favorable response within the industry and in political circles than the FDIC's policies did. Loss-deferral accounting is a case in point. That accounting technique allowed a thrift to sell its underwater assets at a loss, book the loss as goodwill to be amortized over a period of years, and reinvest the proceeds in assets earning higher yields. The thrift industry, many state banking departments, and many members of Congress favored loss-deferral accounting. The FDIC felt that booking the goodwill as capital would only lead to greater problems in the future, so it refused to permit the technique even after the state of New York adopted rules allowing savings banks in New York to use loss-deferral accounting.

In 1982, Congress, with the support of the Reagan administration, passed the Garn–St. Germain Act. That law sanctioned the policies being pursued by the Bank Board and the FSLIC. It broadened the lending and investment authorities of S&Ls and reduced capital standards for thrifts by mandating a net worth certificate program. From this point forward, S&Ls began a tremendous growth spurt, with much of the growth in higher-risk activities.

In 1983, the FDIC issued a study calling for significant reforms in the deposit insurance system to instill greater depositor discipline in an environment of deregulated interest rates. The study, which was ignored by the Congress and the administration, concluded that the de facto system of full depositor protection, to which we had evolved, was fundamentally inconsistent with interest rate deregulation. If changes were not made to put depositors at risk, a disproportionate amount of the funds would flow to the marginal institutions willing to pay the highest rates.

Ed Gray took office as chairman of the Bank Board in 1983. After serving about a year, Gray became concerned about the rapid growth and risky investments in the S&L industry. Much of the growth was being funded by fully insured brokered funds, so Gray joined me in causing the FDIC and the FSLIC to adopt regulations curtailing deposit insurance coverage on brokered funds. The money brokers challenged the regulations, and the federal court ruled that the agencies lacked statutory authority. The battle moved to Capitol Hill, but the agencies' position was opposed by the administration and key members of Congress. This defeat suffered by the FDIC and the FSLIC would ultimately prove to be extraordinarily expensive to the American taxpayers.

The Bank Board's examination force was grossly understaffed to keep pace with the rapid growth and mounting problems in the S&L industry. Ed Gray sought permission from the administration to increase examiners' salaries and increase the work force. While he ultimately prevailed, it was only after much delay and considerable infighting.

In 1985, Gray proposed to limit the investment authority of S&Ls. He met with stiff opposition from the S&L industry, the administration, and key members of Congress, so he had to trim his proposal.

The administration finally began to pay some attention to the S&L problems in 1986 and proposed to recapitalize the FSLIC to the tune of $15 billion. The measure was strongly opposed by the U.S. League of Savings Institutions and by key members of Congress, such as the then speaker of the House, Jim Wright, and was cut back to $5 billion.

Ed Gray left office in 1987, discredited and under attack by the administration, the industry, and the Hill. Danny Wall became chairman of the Bank Board, determined to improve the S&L industry's tarnished image. He consistently understated the industry's problems and steadfastly maintained that the FSLIC had enough money to handle things. This allowed the politicians to continue ignoring the situation until after the 1988 elections. By this time, the losses had grown to unfathomable proportions.

In extending me the invitation to speak today, Marty asked that I focus on the development of the problem, not on future solutions. So I will endeavor to be true to his charge. But I believe that it is essential that we learn some lessons from what is clearly the sorriest episode in American financial history. In my judgment, the foremost lesson is that attempts by the government to interfere with the operation of the markets are doomed to fail, no matter how well intended. Government interference with the markets—the restraints on geographic and product diversification, the controls on interest rates paid on deposits and charged on loans, the refusal to allow thrifts and banks to combine, and the overly broad protection of depositors—was without question the direct and proximate cause of the thrift debacle.

The second lesson is that there is a critical role for the government to play in supervising the financial system. The government needs to play the role of the traffic cop, whose duty is to establish and enforce the rules of the road. Certain basic rules of safety—such as capital standards and risk diversification requirements—must be established.

If the government is to enforce these rules properly, we must ensure that the regulatory agencies are as free as possible from political interference and that there are proper checks and balances in the system. I am convinced that the savings bank problems were better contained than the S&L problems because the insurer—the FDIC—was able to function as an independent watchdog and was relatively free of political pressures. The FDIC was independent of the primary regulator of savings banks and was relatively independent of the political process. It did not need, for example, approval of its budget or staffing levels from Congress or the administration. The FSLIC, in contrast, was organized as a subsidiary of the Bank Board, which was the primary regulator of S&Ls. Moreover, it needed approval of its budget and staffing levels from both the administration and the Congress. This almost forced the agency into an incestuous relationship with the industry it was supposed to be regulating in order to garner the political support it needed.

3. *William Taylor*

I am in general agreement with Litan and Isaac on the factors they have cited this morning as being responsible for the crisis in the savings and loan industry and the strains in banking and other sectors of the financial system. If we have differences, they are to be found in the degree of importance to be assigned to particular factors. Accordingly, I will use my time to indicate which factors I think deserve greatest emphasis.

The impact of the increasingly competitive market conditions that evolved during the 1980s cannot be overemphasized. There is an old saying that, left to compete to the death, many will die. So it has been with financial institutions. Increased competition led to a narrowing of revenue/cost margins and a loss of customers with consequent effects on profitability. In response, institutions increasingly turned to risky loans and to risky ventures in an effort to maintain profitability and, indeed, in some cases viability.

The intensified competition can be traced to many factors. Financial and technological innovation added greatly to competitive pressures coming from outside the industry. The development of money market mutual funds by non-bank financial firms constituted a particularly important challenge to the funding activities of banks, large and small.

Banks also became subject to major new competitive pressures in their lending activities. Banks traditionally had a special access to comprehensive, and somewhat exclusive, credit information and special expertise in analyzing that information. Enhanced technology made the information more readily accessible to everyone in the marketplace, thereby limiting the uniqueness of banks in this regard. Technological innovation also enhanced opportunities to achieve economies within the industry through merger and consolidation, thus adding to competitive pressures on high-cost, inefficient firms.

These developments, moreover, produced strong pressures to dismantle an array of legal and regulatory restrictions so that depositories would be able to compete more effectively and take advantage of the new profit opportunities. The resulting removal of these restrictions, however, proved to be a double-edged sword because the dismantling of arrangements that had long protected depositories from competition was also involved. Proponents of dismantling the restrictions and the protections offer that a more efficient system will develop to better serve the public. This may indeed be true, but, in the meantime, the process can be painful, as has been dramatically demonstrated.

Of the host of public policy decisions that affected competitive conditions in the banking business in the decade of the 1980s, some were more heralded than others and some more significant than others. Early in the decade much was made of the deregulation of interest rates as banks clamored for the opportunity to compete with money market mutual funds. As the rate deregulation took hold, there was an increasing call for increases in the services that banks could offer. It was said that banks and thrifts must be deregulated on both sides of the balance sheet if they were to be effective competitors in the new world. And, indeed, to some degree the powers of banks were expanded and those of thrifts maybe a bit more.

As the focus of attention was riveted on expanded powers at the national level, a public policy impact at least as dynamic in my view was occurring at the state level, for states were not only liberalizing the powers of banking organizations but also easing intrastate and interstate geographic restrictions. The country entered the 1980s with only one state that would allow holding companies located outside the state to buy a bank within its borders, the state of Maine. It ended the decade with forty-seven states having laws that allow the interstate expansion of bank holding companies, albeit some more restrictive than others. And the degree of intrastate liberalization of branching laws was almost as extensive.

Another significant area of public policy in the 1980s involved the question of who could merge with whom. At the beginning of the decade, there was a whole apparatus in place in the government to see that competition within a geographic area was carefully monitored and maintained. In considering a proposed merger or acquisition, great effort was made to determine whether one market circle intersected with another market circle to the detriment of current competition, or future competition, or future potential competition. Concern with such questions waned as the decade proceeded, reflecting the influence of the combination of a few court cases and a new set of antitrust guidelines as well as the advent of interstate banking. The result has been the removal of barriers to entry of companies from "outside" a geographic region and the general encouragement of the merger, acquisition, and consolidation process. Occasionally, a proposed merger will raise competitive issues, such as the recent case in Hawaii, but for the most part opposition to concentrating and consolidating the banking industry is now considerably diminished from what it was at the start of the 1980s.

For example, prior to 1980, the Federal Reserve approved no more than a few mergers or acquisitions by bank holding companies where the target company or bank had more than $1 billion dollars in assets. In the 1980s, on the other hand, almost 100 such mergers or acquisitions were approved. As a result, the number of banking organizations in the country, as measured by the sum of bank holding companies plus the number of independent banks, was reduced by almost 25 percent. So, while many view the deregulation of interest rates and the liberalization of powers as the big developments of the 1980s, I would offer that at least as much impact resulted from the policy decisions pertaining to structure and competition.

In addition to policy decisions that affected the competitive positions of depositories, there were also others that had significant effects on the course of developments over the decade. Two in particular require mention because of the adverse impact that they have had. First, it seems logical that a bank or thrift institution that cannot compete effectively in the marketplace and becomes insolvent should be closed promptly and sold or liquidated as soon thereafter as practical. Yet to do so in an insured system requires having enough in the insurance fund to pay depositors. In the 1980s, there was not enough money in the thrift insurance fund and therefore various artificial measures were taken to keep troubled institutions open. This approach has proved to be very costly.

The second policy decision deserving special mention was what I call adoption of the desupervision principle. We, the supervisors, some more aggressively than others, reacting to our own budgetary problems of the mid-1970s, decided to alter the manner in which banks were examined and supervised. The "top-down" approach became popular. In place of labor-intensive on-site audit and evaluation procedures, the bank examination process became more off-site and consultative in nature. Off-site surveillance systems were developed from financial reports submitted by the banks. Policies and procedures at banks were reviewed with less emphasis on specific assets. The time between on-site exams was extended materially, and in general there was less comprehensive and independently developed information on each bank.

Without denying the benefits of surveillance systems or the need for policy review, let me state my view that the extent of the shift to this less hands-on and less often approach to supervision must be questioned. It seems essential that a good supervision program include annual on-site examinations that have as their purpose the determination of whether assets are of good enough quality to generate the cash flow required to meet obligations due to the bank's depositors and creditors and whether the bank's books need to be adjusted to reflect reasonable values. I think that the experience of the 1980s demonstrates clearly the wisdom of the annual, full-scope examinations, and I believe that all agencies responsible for supervision will adhere to this approach in the coming decade.

In summary, the problems of depositories and the financial system more generally that developed in the 1980s can be attributed primarily to the intensification of competitive conditions, resulting from financial and technological innovation and from changes in public policies—the deregulation of deposit interest rates, new and sometimes riskier powers, liberalized antitrust policies, and the loosening of restrictions on geographic expansion. All these promise net benefits to society in the long run in the form of a more efficient delivery of services to the public at lower cost, but they create or intensify difficulties for firms competing in these markets during the transition period. Compounding the effects of intensified competition were shortfalls in the execution of two public policies in particular—the manner in which distressed institutions were resolved and the reduced emphasis given to "hands-on" on-site examinations in the supervision process.

Summary of Discussion

Robert Litan praised Isaac's management of the financial problems in the savings bank industry and agreed with Isaac's assessment that the FDIC had been more successful dealing with savings banks than the FSLIC had been with thrift institutions. He noted, however, that the FSLIC's thrift problem had been of much greater magnitude. In the early 1980s, roughly 70–85 percent of the thrifts were losing money; on a market-value basis, the thrift industry was over $100 billion in the red. The problem in the savings bank industry was not nearly as large, so Litan asked Isaac whether he would have made similar policy decisions had he been handling the thrift crisis instead. Would he have requested more money with which to resolve the problem directly, or would he first have pursued a policy of shrinkage or at least containment of growth?

As a second point, Litan responded to Isaac's suggestion that banks should have been given permission back in 1977 to buy healthy thrifts. He agreed that many bank organizations would have bought healthy thrifts as a way of circumventing the interstate restrictions. Had this happened, however, it would not have eliminated the thrift crisis. Although separately capitalized, the failing thrifts would have been affiliates of banks through their holding companies, and these holding companies would have been facing a large insolvency problem. Further, the bank holding companies might have experienced greater difficulty dealing with the LDC debt problem when it arose. On the other hand, had there been many banks in such difficulty, Volcker would have had at least partial jurisdiction over the resolution of the thrift crisis. Would that have improved the outcome?

Litan also argued that one should not become obsessed by the crises in the financial industry and forget that both the savings banks and the thrifts suffered from underlying structural problems. In the long run, securitization would have eliminated the need for a separate thrift industry even without the crisis in the 1980s: thrifts simply would have become less and less profitable as separate institutions. In a slower way, the same thing is happening to the banking industry. Over the last thirty years, loan losses have been steadily rising in the banking industry as banks have taken greater and greater risks in response to some systemic pressure. The increased risk creates a need, as Taylor suggested, for more capital in the banking system.

William Isaac responded that he would not have handled the savings and loan crisis differently than he had handled the savings bank problem. The policies that he pursued were those suggested by professional bank supervisors; his role was protecting the professional staff from political pressure, and he had been willing to take the heat from Congress if there were objections to the policies.

The excuse that the FSLIC had bigger problems relative to its capital than did the FDIC is not a new one. The problem that the FDIC faced with the savings bank industry, however, was actually quite large—there was no certainty that they had enough money to deal with the problem. As it turned out, interest rates came down, and the problem was solved at a cost of several billion dollars. But, under other projected scenarios, the fund could easily have gone broke. Even so, the agency made the decision that it would spend whatever it took to do the job right and would go to Congress and ask for more money if it were needed. The agency believed that the alternative was to create an even bigger problem in the future, which would have required even more money to resolve. This same logic would have pertained to the savings and loan industry, and Isaac would have followed the same path. He would not have encouraged expansion, as the FSLIC chose to do, but would have curtailed growth and asked Congress for more money if necessary.

Charls Walker submitted two corrections to earlier comments. First, the Treasury Department during the first Nixon administration wanted to institute financial reform before problems grew into crises. It was drawn off track, however, because the first task to which it was directed was the one-bank holding company legislation. Walker noted that he had tried to prevent the Federal Reserve from becoming the regulator of bank holding companies, but had been unsuccessful.

Second, with respect to the Hunt Commission, everyone had agreed that reforms were needed with respect to deposit interest rates and other issues. Walker had argued, however, that, in order to get through Congress, the proposal needed to come from a blue-ribbon commission of leaders in the affected industries. A commission was formed, and it developed an excellent report, but in 1971 and 1972 the Treasury sponsored a great deal of legislation on other issues. This meant that action on the Hunt Commission report was postponed until just before Walker left the Treasury, and by that time no one was very interested anymore. Walker felt that both these points show that there were efforts to solve some financial regulation problems in other than a crisis situation but that the turn of events prevented their success.

Elizabeth Bailey highlighted Isaac's comment that Roosevelt had worried about levying deposit insurance premiums on the basis of average risk in the industry so that banks that had not made risky loans would end up subsidizing banks that had made risky loans. She observed that the policies in the late 1980s have set up exactly that kind of system, resulting in enormous premiums on deposit insurance in exactly the way that Roosevelt had feared. *Isaac* responded that he too is very concerned about the current deposit insurance system, which requires very basic reform.

Rudolph Penner returned to an ongoing conference theme regarding the influence of policy analysts on different issues. He believed that the analysts had been particularly ineffective with regard to the deposit insurance fiasco. One reason was the work of lobbyists and the flow of campaign funds to Congress. Another reason was colossal ignorance on the part of legislators—analysts simply had no credibility relative to a local thrift owner who was decrying his troubles. Thrifts really had a wonderful image in the 1980s.

There was one aspect of analysis, however, on which a lack of credibility was deserved, and that was the estimates of the cost of the problem. In January 1986, the Congressional Budget Office (CBO) was suggesting that the problem could have costs as high as $25 billion. By the summer of 1988, Litan's paper quotes Danny Wall [chairman of the Federal Home Loan Bank Board] as estimating $40 billion, and the CBO was projecting nearly $100 billion. What went wrong with the estimates technically that made them so misleading?

Litan responded that he spends a lot of time doing cost estimates, and one of the key problems is that the estimates must rely on the financial statements of the institutions themselves. Roughly speaking, the estimates are calculated by taking the financial statistics, projecting how many institutions holding which types of assets will fail, and then applying cost ratios to the different types of assets. The problem that arose in making cost estimates for thrifts was that, as each new year's data arrived, the cost ratios were skyrocketing. The total assets of failing institutions were in fact relatively stable between 1984 and 1988—there were roughly $300 billion of assets held by 600–700 institutions. The FSLIC could resolve only the worst of them every year, however, and, whereas the costs were initially about ten to fifteen cents per dollar, by 1986 and 1987 the institutions that they were resolving cost thirty to forty cents per dollar. When that is the tip of the iceberg, it is hard to predict the costs for the rest of the iceberg.

In a way, this is a problem still faced by the Resolution Trust Corporation today, as many of the assets that it considers are undeveloped properties or partially completed buildings. It is impossible to determine their net worth.

William Taylor expanded on Litan's explanation. In his experience doing cost estimates with the Federal Reserve staff, they had found that, if one strips out the accounting devices, such as deferred losses and goodwill, and then sums the resulting net worth over all institutions for which the number is negative, one gets a figure of approximately $30 billion. That is, before any assets are discounted, the cost is already about $30 billion. When the discounting is applied, the numbers just go up.

Martin Feldstein posed the question of why the administration chose to oppose legislation that would have restricted insurance on brokered deposits since that decision clearly contributed to the growth of thrifts in the second half of the 1980s.

Isaac said that the administration claimed that it was in favor of brokered funds because they allowed markets to work by letting money be transported around the country more freely. The real reason may have been the political pressure being applied by Merrill Lynch and other major houses that were making a lot of money on brokered funds. In the midst of the battle over this legislation, a senior official at Merrill Lynch had said to Isaac, "What kind of reaction did you expect you were going to get from us? This is a 'no brainer' business: we go around the country sweeping up the money, putting it in institutions. No risk, no effort, and we're making $30 million a year. And you expect that we're going to lie down and play dead when you decide you don't like that anymore?" That was almost a verbatim quote, Isaac said.

In keeping with the market-oriented style of the Reagan administration, Isaac had suggested that they remove the federal subsidy from the brokered funds market—money brokers should put money into institutions that they believed would pay it back *without* the benefit of a federal guarantee. The administration did not accept Isaac's argument, and the legislation was defeated. Had the subsidy been removed, the savings and loan loss might have been much less; as a rough estimate, the money brokers' continued business probably cost the government about $50 billion.

Taylor suggested that the problem was even wider than brokered deposits. Some banks sent people to metropolitan areas all over the country, where they would run advertisements encouraging people to come to a designated location and receive insured deposits paying well above the market rates. Thus, there were many egregious transactions that were not handled through brokers.

William Poole noted that there are some reasonable uses of brokering and that it is difficult to write legislation that distinguishes the improper uses from the proper ones. Also, it is very easy for a brokerage firm to accomplish the same thing in a different way if it is proscribed from direct brokering activity. The emphasis on brokered funds is entirely misplaced because it is so easy to get around any rules on the subject.

Isaac agreed that there are other ways to raise funds but argued that brokered funds were, by far, the most egregious form of abuse. It does not make sense to knock down a rule that is correcting 90 percent of the abuse out of fear that there might be 10 percent leakage anyway. *Poole* concurred but held that, if the rule had been passed, people would have immediately shifted to the indirect methods for raising funds. *Isaac* responded that he did not doubt the ingenuity of markets to find ways to get around the government or to take advantage of subsidies. Had these indirect methods become a significant problem, he would have found a way to deal with that, but he had wanted simply to handle the 90 percent portion of the problem first.

Litan agreed with Taylor's point that brokered deposits were more a symptom than the underlying problem. The underlying problem was growth. Isaac said that he had constrained the growth of savings institutions that were insured by the FDIC and had coordinated the broker deposit rule with Ed Gray [chairman of the Federal Home Loan Bank Board]. Had they considered simply imposing a growth restriction in lieu of a brokered deposit rule?

Isaac answered that the FDIC had been reasonably vigilant about trying to contain growth. Growth restrictions are generally applied, however, to institutions that are already in trouble. The regulators issue a cease-and-desist order telling them not to grow, and, if they do, they can be fined or punished in some other way. But the problem with brokered deposits is that they can grow very, very fast. The money brokers were going to institutions that did not have problems and dumping hundreds of millions of dollars of funds into them virtually overnight. Suddenly, a good institution would have problems, and it was too late to stop it with simple growth restrictions: the growth had already occurred. Generally, one would need "ten times as many bank examiners" as they had to control that kind of growth with regulation.

Feldstein asked whether Congress had not thought that growth was the desired solution to the problem?

Taylor noted that, during 1984 and 1985, the growth rates at some savings and loans were fantastically large. A 20 percent growth rate in the assets of a bank or financial institution is very difficult to absorb, and 100 percent is unthought of, but they saw some growth rates of 2,300 percent. To use the funds, these banks were frantically seeking real estate investments, and, even though many of these investments were called "loans," they were really straight equity investments in real estate.

Thomas Enders asked whether the federal insurance agencies had considered how insurance should be priced and whether they believed that the price adequately reflected the overall risk.

Taylor believed that the issue had not received much consideration. The change from insuring $40,000 per account to insuring $100,000 per account received very little debate overall, and he remembered no discussion about pricing.

Isaac said that pricing had been given some consideration at the FDIC. They had focused on risk-based premiums: charging riskier banks more rather than raising the overall level of the premium. Ninety percent of bankers favored this policy in principle, but there was no consensus on how such a system should be implemented.

On the question of the overall level of premiums, the FDIC had not believed that deposit insurance coverage was underpriced. There seemed to be enough premium income to deal with the problems that arose. Isaac believed that one reason that the FDIC is running short of money now is that they are not handling failures as efficiently as they should. In 1984, the FDIC had handled Continental Illinois's $40 billion failure with an $800 million expenditure; the way that failures are being resolved now, a $40 billion failure would probably cost the FDIC $4 or $5 billion. Another reason that the FDIC is running short of money is the aftereffects of the savings and loan crisis. Many real estate loans that went sour for commercial banks did so because so much overbuilding had been funded by poorly run savings and loans.

Feldstein asked Isaac to speak about the Continental Illinois decision. How is the decision made that a bank is "too big to fail"?

Isaac said that the decision was both abhorrent and the right thing to do under the circumstances. He gave three explanations for the decision to save Continental. The first was the likely repercussions on the savings and loan industry. If Continental had failed, several large thrifts would have fallen with it, the FSLIC would have toppled immediately, and the entire thrift industry might have collapsed. In retrospect, a collapse in 1984 might have cost $20 billion to clean up instead of the $200 billion six or seven years later, but no one dreamed that the problem would reach this scale. Second, several other large banks were in trouble as well. There would have been chaos throughout the banking system and a number of big bank failures had Continental failed, and the FDIC did not have the money or the people to handle that. A third reason was that 2,500 small banks in the Midwest carried over $6 billion in uninsured deposits at Continental, so the chaos following a Continental collapse would have extended quite widely.

But, although the Continental Illinois decision seemed right to Isaac at the time, he continued to believe that "too big to fail" is an inappropriate concept. The notion can be avoided if the country develops rules that impose discipline on the financial system in advance of crisis.

Taylor agreed with the decision to save Continental Illinois, but he believed that it could have been done in such a way as to avoid spreading the doctrine of "too big to fail." The rescue had started as a managed liquidation, but then the government essentially became the owner. It would have been much better had the liquidation been continued until the assets were reduced to a fairly insignificant level and then this residue been sold to another party. Taylor added that the decision to bail out the holding company's creditors had actually saved the government money because the holding company's assets outside the bank were clearly greater than its liabilities. By bailing out the creditors, this extra value went to the FDIC, not to the creditors.

Poole suggested that the risk of bank runs makes the notion of "too big to fail" a sensible one for large banks. Although these banks might behave with more discipline if they thought that they would be allowed to fail, even the most disciplined bank has a lot of short-dated liabilities and can run into unforeseeable problems. Allowing uninsured depositors to lose their deposits does not get to the problem of disruption of the overall monetary system. So a policy of letting large banks fail poses too big a risk to the system to be very credible in advance.

Poole argued that deposit insurance should be extended to all liabilities called deposits but that there should also be more uninsured capital at banks, particularly long-dated capital such as equity or ten-year subordinated notes.

Isaac clarified his views of the proper role of insurance: he thought that demand accounts should be insured in full and other accounts up to $100,000. Deposits greater than $100,000, however, should be exposed to some loss when a bank fails; this will not seriously undermine the financial system. If it were announced now that this policy will be implemented in five years, bank capital ratios would rise substantially, balance sheets would be handled more conservatively, and banks would maintain more liquidity. These rules would allow the market to do the job of disciplining these institutions.

Poole noted that, before deposit insurance was instituted, there had been recurrent banking panics that involved some of the very largest banks. It is not clear why the environment would be permanently different under Isaac's policy; in fact, the whole history of banking since deposit insurance was instituted makes it likely that many banks will believe that, when push comes to shove, the authorities will not allow them to fail.

Isaac said that the biggest banking panic was in 1929–33 and that there were not a lot of failures at the big banks. Most of the banks that failed were small, and deposit insurance was created so that the small depositor would continue to do business at uneconomically small banks. The big banks were opposed to deposit insurance; they wanted nationwide branching and a restructuring of the industry instead.

William Rhodes observed that most senior bankers have strong opinions today about the "too big to fail" doctrine but that, when deposit insurance was increased to the $100,000 level, most of them were indifferent. That is to say, the banking community cares about the issue now but did not focus on it when relevant policies were being established several years ago.

Michael Mussa said that the country has a general problem with letting an enterprise fail. This arises not only with the thrifts and with Continental and other banks but also with the Pension Benefit Guarantee Corporation. When a firm that has a pension plan gets in trouble and can no longer make the payments, it receives a dispensation allowing it to stop paying its pension insurance premiums—an insane way to run an insurance system in Mussa's view. The same rationale prevented effective action on the thrifts at an earlier time, and it is a difficulty that we have with all the disguised liabilities of the government. It is tough to decide just to kill an institution off.

Taylor closed by saying that the government's will should be strengthened to kill off these organizations. It may not be possible to do so at the expense of the depositors, but, if a firm cannot survive in the marketplace, it should be taken out of the marketplace.

9   Antitrust Policy

1. *Phillip Areeda*
2. *William F. Baxter*
3. *Harry M. Reasoner*

1. *Phillip Areeda*

Antitrust Policy in the 1980s

Antitrust law influences the structure of markets as well as the conduct of business firms vis-à-vis their competitors, suppliers, and customers—for example, by breaking up AT&T, jailing price fixers, limiting the way products and services are distributed, or questioning competitors' joint research. The primary objective is low-cost production, competitive rather than monopoly or cartel levels of output and price, and advanced innovation and productivity.[1] Of course, "undue" pursuit of competitive price levels today might obstruct innovations that would benefit consumers much more tomorrow, and overly zealous or otherwise misguided policy could defeat all these objectives.

By the 1980s, antitrust interventions in the economy had reached that misguided state, in the view of Reagan administration, which set about to redress the matter. The chief antitrust administrator lectured Congress and the profession on the errors of the past, stated the government's intention not to enforce "foolish" doctrines, although they were "the law" as pronounced by the courts, and issued various policy statements and guidelines with that effect. The number of lawyers in the Justice Department's Antitrust Division was reduced by half over the decade, and its appropriations reflected a 30 percent decline in

---

1. Few actual cases turn on the further question much discussed by antitrust commentators: are the economic objectives just stated the "exclusive" objective of antitrust law, or should those laws be used to promote "fairness" in, say, manufacturer-dealer relationships or deconcentration for its own sake? Similarly, few cases present a clear choice between transferring income from consumers to producers and, on the other hand, reducing resource use, making resource allocation more efficient, and promoting innovation. Compare Areeda (1983) with Lande (1982) and Schwartz (1979).

1980 dollars.[2] Federal Trade Commission (FTC) personnel and antitrust activities also declined over the decade.[3]

As will appear in more detail below, the main current was efficiency. Today, few would use antitrust law to prevent the achievement of clear efficiencies (in any of the senses of that term), the importance of which has been driven home by international competition.

In addition, many practices once regarded as generally sinister (such as tie-ins) are now seen to serve legitimate functions, at least in many circumstances. Indeed, the innocent explanation may predominate when greater economic sophistication persuades us that the practice in question can increase market power only rarely. Furthermore, markets may become concentrated, even down to a single firm, because large scale minimizes costs; nor will such markets exploit consumers when relatively easy entry makes the market "contestable." The administration seemed to believe that substantial and durable barriers to entry were rare and that competition would generally prevail in the absence of naked price-fixing cartels or ill-advised government policies.

While extensive private enforcement of the antitrust laws continued, the courts also felt some of the same intellectual currents underlying the administration's position, although not to the same degree or with any consistency. Since the late 1970s, the courts have qualified antitrust law's "per se" prohibitions, tolerated more joint ventures among competitors and more restraints in buyer-seller arrangements, required clearer proof before characterizing price competition as "predatory," recognized that antitrust suits could be used by some plaintiffs to chill competition, and increasingly understood that antitrust suits do raise general policy questions that should not be left to juries in the guise of finding the facts about who did what with what intention. Of course, any such broad statement of direction oversimplifies somewhat.

We shall see that courts are key players in antitrust policy and that they seldom state policy alternatives clearly. Indeed, judicial methods and techniques often focus on rulings about litigation procedures or the meaning of precedent, deemphasizing conscious policy choice. Moreover, the choices are the product of hundreds of judges, acting individually and not always consistently, notwithstanding a single Supreme Court atop the judicial pyramid. Nevertheless, trends do emerge. This paper will describe some of them, generally praising the antitrust developments of the 1980s.

Section 9.1 describes the antitrust players. Section 9.2 deals with the elimi-

2. See *Report of the American Bar Association Section of Antitrust Law Task Force on the Antitrust Division of the U.S. Department of Justice* (1989), pp. 7, A2.

3. See *Report of the ABA Section of Antitrust Law Special Committee to Study the Role of the Federal Trade Commission* (1989), p. 28. Although the FTC has concurrent jurisdiction to enforce the antitrust laws (except for criminal prosecutions), this paper speaks of "the government" or "the administration" in terms of the Antitrust Division of the Justice Department because it simplifies the presentation without distorting the story of antitrust policy in the 1980s. Although the FTC is an independent agency, its decisions during the decade have been largely congruent with those of the Justice Department.

nation of competition through price-fixing conspiracies, the limited ability of antitrust law to cope with the cartel-like results that sometimes emerge in concentrated markets, and the key antitrust policy of preventing mergers that so consolidate competitors as to create market concentration. Section 9.3 briefly treats other forms of cooperation among competitors that are allowed when "reasonable." Section 9.4 discusses the ferment in buyer-seller agreements, and section 9.5 considers the individual practices of actual or prospective monopolists, especially vertical integration and predatory pricing.

Two related topics are not treated: regulated industries and the policies of the several states. Regulation might seem to occupy a separate domain in which competition is not possible to protect consumers and promote innovation, while antitrust law prevails elsewhere. In fact, some markets without effective competition are unregulated, and the two regimes often cohabit a market in which competition is partly possible and partly not. This paper does not discuss the degree to which regulation displaces antitrust policy or the degree to which antitrust principles influence regulators, although both were substantially affected by deregulation during the 1980s.

Nor have I space for the role of the fifty states in antitrust policy, although that role is significant. First, each state is largely free to displace national competitive policy if it then supervises the private parties involved.[4] Second, each state may enact its own antitrust law. Federal antitrust law is not understood to preempt the field to the exclusion of state law, as federal labor law does, and the Supreme Court has not yet been ready to see specific conflicts that would oust state law.[5] Third, state attorneys general may enforce the federal antitrust laws in federal court on behalf of their citizens. They became much more active during the 1980s in response to what they perceived as the antitrust laxity of the Justice Department—in what has been called a "Balkanization" of antitrust policy.[6]

9.1 The Players

It is not Congress or the administration but the courts that primarily develop, articulate, and enforce antitrust policy. Because their training, procedures, and methods differ greatly from those of other governmental organs, judges make

---

4. See my *Antitrust Law* (Areeda 1978–), chaps. 2B, 2B′. There are currently nine volumes in this work, with D. Turner on vols. 1–3 (1978) and on vols. 4–5 (1980). Volumes 6–7 were published in 1986, vol. 8 in 1989, and vol. 9 in 1991. References marked by a prime (′) or a decimal point in the number are to the 1992 supplement (with H. Hovencampe). (Hereafter all references will be simply to *Antitrust Law* and will be mostly by paragraph numbers, which run sequentially through all volumes.)

5. See, e.g., California v. ARC America, 490 US 93 (1989) (dealers buying from manufacturer cartel may recover, under federal law, three times the overcharge they paid even if they passed it all on to consumers; consumers recover nothing under federal law, but state law may allow them to recover from the same manufacturers thrice the overcharge they paid the innocent dealers).

6. *ABA Report* (n. 3 above), p. viii.

policy with less economic or market knowledge. They are not always aware that they are creating national economic policy when they allow vaguely instructed juries to decide key antitrust issues or when they review jury or lower court decisions in the light of prior judicial decisions. Let me explain briefly why courts have this preeminent antitrust role relative to legislators or administrators and how judicial procedures and methods secrete industrial policy, often unconsciously. The curiosity is that it works as well as it does.

American antitrust law is almost entirely a creature of the judges who gave content to the few vague words of the Sherman Act of 1890.[7] The substantive provisions of that statute merely forbid "conspiracies in restraint of trade" and actual or attempted "monopolization."[8] The Justice Department can initiate civil and criminal suits to enforce the antitrust laws, but its views do not bind the courts, whose jurisdiction can also be invoked by private parties seeking to forbid antitrust violations or recover treble damages for resulting injuries. With few exceptions, moreover, government officials have no power to immunize private conduct from the antitrust laws.[9]

Nevertheless, the Justice Department has an important educational function. As an expert agency presumably motivated solely by the public interest, its arguments influence the courts, both when it sues and when it files an advisory brief in private litigation. It also influences business choices directly. Only a small fraction of business decisions affecting competition are ever litigated. In common with most laws, the antitrust laws are self-enforcing in that firms often consult their lawyers before acting and follow the advice they receive. That advice, in turn, reflects the lawyers' estimate of the likelihood that the government or private parties will sue and their understanding of what the courts have done in the past and are expected to do in the future. Government policy statements thus affect the lawyers' judgment on these questions as well as the degree to which businesses choose to consult their lawyers or to follow the advice they receive. Stern warnings by the Justice Department reinforce this self-policing and voluntary compliance with the law, while publicly debunking past excesses tends to do the opposite.[10]

Of course, Congress has the last word on the scope and application of the antitrust laws, but its amendments over the years have largely been confined to

7. 26 Stat. 209 (1890), as amended, 15 U.S.C.A. §§ 1–7 (1990).

8. Even the somewhat more specific Clayton Act of 1914 applies only where the effects may be "substantially to lessen competition"—again, an undefined concept. 38 Stat. 730 (1914), as amended, 15 U.S.C.A. §§ 12–27 (1990). The third relevant statute authorizes the Federal Trade Commission to forbid "unfair methods of competition." 38 Stat. 717 (1914), as amended 15 U.S.C.A. §§ 41–58 (1990). This undefined term has mainly been applied congruently with the Sherman Act. See *Antitrust Law,* ¶ 307.

9. In practice, however, a government decision not to attack a merger may amount to immunity, as explained later in this paper.

10. See *ABA Report* (n. 3 above), p. viii, expressing concern that the Department's "non-enforcement rhetoric" during the 1980s may have gone too far and threatened to "undermine self-policing and voluntary compliance with the law."

procedural matters.[11] Congressional diffidence in antitrust matters reflects the usual difficulties of mustering a sufficient consensus to "interfere" in what the courts do. Second, legislators may fear that pervasive antitrust legislation could open Pandora's box, unleashing unknown expansions or contractions. In addition, there is no agreement on what more detailed legislation would say. After all, the Sherman Act already speaks in those vague and general terms in which Congress so often legislates today (at least when it is not taxing or controlling Defense Department procurement). Finally, there is an astonishing degree of confidence in the courts as developers of antitrust law. In many respects, judicial rulings are icons that administrators flout at their peril.[12] These reasons may explain why supplemental legislation has usually been very narrow.

This preeminent judicial role complicates writing about antitrust policy in the 1980s. The readily dated legislative and executive players, who articulate their policy choices with relative clarity, tell only a portion of the story. The remainder is an undated mosaic of inferences drawn from many judicial decisions, which are not entirely consistent and which seldom articulate their implicit policy choices. Nevertheless, the judicial story connects to that of the political branches in three ways. At the most general level, the economic conditions influencing political choices also come to the attention of judges in several forms: general reading, legal articles and treatises, expert witnesses, and arguments of the litigants. Second, judges sometimes accept the guidelines and other general pronouncements of the Justice Department's Antitrust Division. Third, judges as well as administrators tend to reflect the general outlook of the president who chooses them. Although antitrust attitudes have not themselves determined the judicial selection process, more of the "liberal" judges appointed by President Carter sympathized with antitrust plaintiffs, left issues to ultimate disposition by juries, and found more antitrust violations than the "conservative" judges appointed by President Reagan. While any such correlation is loose indeed, one could expect to see less intrusive antitrust rulings over the Reagan years.[13]

Although these forces tend to push administrative and judicial developments in similar directions, very important differences remain: information penetrates litigation more slowly than the political branches; judicial lawmaking is highly decentralized and thus develops slowly and inconsistently;[14] judicial

---

11. New legislation with respect to mergers, joint research ventures, and resale price maintenance is discussed below. We shall also see later that antitrust procedures have substantive significance.

12. See, e.g., *ABA Report* (n. 3 above), pp. 19–21.

13. In addition to his Supreme Court appointments, President Reagan made seventy-eight appointments to the Court of Appeals and 290 to federal district courts, accounting for some 47 percent of active federal judges in courts of general jurisdiction (see Goldman 1989).

14. Although the Supreme Court can resolve differences among the lower courts, its own heavy caseload generally allows it to speak only after clear differences emerge in the lower courts, only episodically, and often only in delphic terms.

procedures often obscure policy issues and choices by emphasizing the facts of the particular case and vague jury instructions; and, of course, change is slowed by such judicial values as following prior decisions and refusing to decide more than the narrowest issue that will dispose of a case.

I now ask how these forces played out in and among the three branches for several antitrust areas.

9.2   Price Fixing, Conspiracy, and Mergers

Agreement on buying or selling prices among competitors has long been the central prohibition of every nation's antitrust law, including our own.[15] Nor has there been any change in this policy. Price fixers are consistently prosecuted. Unlike most antitrust offenders, moreover, price fixers suffer imprisonment and fines as well as treble damage liability to their victims.[16] In dispute is not this principle but the kinds of arrangements that should be classified as "price fixing" (as discussed in sec. 9.3 below) and the circumstances in which a conspiracy (or "agreement") among competitors can be inferred. It turns out that price leadership and related forms of tacit coordination among oligopolists are not considered "agreements" and thus are not prohibited by the Sherman Act even when cartel-like pricing results. However, antitrust law does address the mergers among competitors that create or reinforce oligopoly. Significant developments have occurred on each of these subsidiary topics.

9.2.1   Conspiracy Generally and in Oligopoly

Because competitors agreeing on price seldom do so openly, antitrust law must often infer the existence of an agreement from circumstantial evidence. Whether the evidence warrants that inference is the most frequently litigated question in antitrust cases.[17] An agreement is readily inferred when it alone explains the parties' conduct—as when they simultaneously bid the same

15. Monopoly prices charged by a single firm are sometimes addressed by foreign laws, which authorize some administrative agency to forbid the "abuse of a dominant position" (e.g., Article 86 of the treaty creating the European Economic Community). By contrast, Section 2 of our Sherman Act forbids "monopolization," which has been construed to address improprieties in obtaining or maintaining monopoly power but not the "mere" enjoyment of the fruits of a lawfully obtained monopoly. See *Antitrust Law*, ¶¶ 710, 710'.

16. United States Sentencing Commission Guidelines, 7 Trade Reg. Rep. ¶ 50,010 (1989). Criminal Fines Enforcement Act of 1984, 98 Stat. 3136, 18 U.S.C.A. § 3623 (1987), was the most recent increase of the fines under Section 1 of the Sherman Act. The fines now are up to $250,000 for violations committed by individuals and up to $1 million for violations committed by corporations. The act also states that fines may exceed the stated limits up to the extent of twice the gross gain derived by the defendant from the offense or twice the gross loss resulting to others, unless this "would unduly complicate or prolong the sentencing process." There have also been recent proposals to raise the maximum fines for violations of Section 1 to $10 million for corporations and to $350,000 for individuals. Antitrust Criminal Penalties Amendments of 1989, H.R. 3341, 101st Cong., 1st Sess., 135 Cong. Rec. H7089 (daily ed. 17 October 1989).

17. See also sec. 9.4 on agreements between a manufacturer and its dealers.

amount on a novel, made-to-order product.[18] In less clear cases, three kinds of policy choices arise.

The first, illustrating the connection between judicial procedures and substantive policy, is the standard for allowing juries to find agreements. The procedural question is whether the judge rules the evidence insufficient to go to the jury and therefore either grants "summary judgment" for the alleged conspirators, dismissing the case before trial, or later "directs a verdict" of no agreement. If not, the economy bears the heavier costs of lengthier trials, and juries are more likely than judges to indulge extralegal sympathy for the plaintiff or antipathy to defendants and find agreements that did not really exist. The resulting treble damages impose heavy, unnecessary, and unproductive costs on doing business. On the other hand, undue generosity in granting summary judgments or directed verdicts could immunize actual conspirators and reduce the deterrence of antitrust prohibitions, thereby burdening the economy with more illegal agreements than would otherwise occur.

During the 1980s, the Supreme Court chose fewer jury trials, as illustrated by the contrast between the Poller case of 1962 and the Matsushita decision of 1986. The later case disowned the former's view that summary judgment was disfavored in antitrust cases and ruled that "conduct as consistent with permissible competition as with illegal conspiracy does not, standing alone, support an inference of antitrust conspiracy."[19] In effect, the Court emphasized that the plaintiff must show not only that the evidence is consistent with conspiracy but also that a reasonable juror could find that conspiracy was more likely than not.[20]

The second policy choice, also indirect if not unaware, is suggested by the phrase "standing alone" in the last quotation. Some courts allowed inferences of a price-fixing agreement when the defendants have not only charged the same prices but also engaged in some other joint, or even separate, conduct—such as disseminating past prices,[21] telephoning each other to verify a buyer's claim that a rival offered a lower price,[22] agreeing to exchange the product with each other in kind (with adjustments for different qualities) while they simultaneously purchase that product from others,[23] or even separately publicizing price increases more widely than necessary to inform immediate customers.[24] Because there is no way by which one can reason from the existence

18. See *Antitrust Law,* ¶ 1425.

19. Poller v. Columbia Broadcasting System, 368 U.S. 464 (1962); Matsushita Elec. Indus. Co. v. Zenith Radio Corp., 475 U.S. 574, 588 (1986).

20. See *Antitrust Law,* ¶ 1405'. The Supreme Court has not yet ruled on the suggestion by some lower courts that cases may be removed from the jury when too complex for them (see ibid., ¶ 315.1).

21. American Column and Lumber Co. v. United States, 257 U.S. 377 (1921).

22. United States v. Container Corp. of America, 393 U.S. 333 (1969).

23. City of Long Beach v. Standard Oil Co. (Cal.), 872 F. 2d 1401 (9th Cir. 1989), cert. denied, 110 S. Ct. 1126 (1990).

24. Coordinated Pretrial Proceedings in Petroleum Prods. Antitrust Litigation, 906 F. 2d 432 (9th Cir. 1990), cert. denied, 111 S. Ct. 2274 (1991).

of such activities to the presence of a price-fixing agreement, such rulings in effect delegate to the jury or some other fact finder the policy choice that such activities should themselves be prohibited. Perhaps such activities should be prohibited because they unnecessarily help oligopolists to coordinate their prices without agreeing on any price, and one might see a growing tendency to do so.[25] However, it is unwise to leave that policy choice to be made inconsistently by juries in each case.

The third policy choice concerns oligopolistic markets inhabited by only a few firms. Unlike more competitive markets, where each firm is too small to influence market prices by increasing its output until its marginal costs reach the market price, an oligopolist cannot increase its sales significantly except at lower prices. Its few rivals would then see the price cut or feel its impact and might be expected to match it. Nor will an oligopolist suffer by leading a price increase—especially by an advance announcement of a future increase—that can be quickly reversed if rivals do not follow. Such reversals mean that rivals cannot win greater volume by remaining low and thus will follow when they conclude that higher industry prices will increase profits. Through such recognition of their mutual interdependence, oligopolists may "tacitly coordinate" at the same supracompetitive level that would result from a clearly illegal cartel agreement. When cartel-like prices prevail,[26] antitrust law asks whether such tacit coordination involves the agreement or "conspiracy" that triggers Section 1 of the Sherman Act.[27] Although wise antitrust policy might choose to address such oligopolies,[28] the courts are constrained by the requirement in Section 1 of the Sherman Act of an agreement that has not been satisfied by mere tacit coordination (notwithstanding occasional Supreme Court language pointing the other way).[29] The 1890 Congress hardly had oligopolistic coordination in mind. Although the Sherman Act has been extended far beyond the assumptions of the original legislators, tacit coordination differs significantly from traditional agreements and may be less effective and therefore less dangerous. In addition, we must hesitate to impose the Sherman Act's criminal or treble damage punishments on each oligopolist who independently sets his price in the light of actual or anticipated reactions of rivals and who can hardly do otherwise unless the judges administer prices or break up the firms.[30] Antitrust

25. See *Antitrust Law,* ¶¶ 1406–7, 1435–36.

26. They need not. For example, entry may be so easy that incumbents know that they cannot successfully maintain supracompetitive prices. Or each may suppose that it can win incremental volume with discounts hidden from rivals; if so, prices will fall to competitive levels. Or a price increase may be so risky that no one firm can afford to lead unilaterally—as where "lumpy" orders are few but large and awarded on secret bids. For additional factors, see *Antitrust Law,* ¶¶ 1425d–e, 1430.

27. The economist's term, *tacit collusion,* is best avoided here, for *collusion* connotes agreement to the layman and thus obscures the very legal question in issue.

28. For a brief discussion of typical legislative proposals to break up highly concentrated markets, see Areeda and Kaplow (1988, ¶¶ 329–32).

29. See Interstate Circuit v. United States, 306 U.S. 208 (1939), which is explained in *Antitrust Law,* ¶ 1426.

30. For conflicting arguments on this point, see *Antitrust Law,* ¶ 1432d–e.

courts rightly abjure such day-to-day regulation, and an expansive reading of the agreement concept hardly seems a compelling mandate for wholesale restructuring of the many oligopolistic markets by the courts.

During the 1970s, the Antitrust Division threatened to bring cases urging the courts to reach mere oligopolistic pricing.[31] But nothing came of this initiative, which was abandoned during the 1980s. Instead, we have what might be called a two-step *containment policy.* One step limits certain practices that "facilitate" tacit coordination by existing oligopolies.[32] The other prevents mergers concentrating markets in the first place.

9.2.2   Mergers among Competitors

A short history will illuminate the important merger policy decisions of the 1980s.[33] Because a merger necessarily embodies an agreement among the merging firms, Section 1 of the Sherman Act applies. The Justice Department used that statute to prevent a number of railroad mergers but little else. Section 7 of the Clayton Act of 1914 specifically proscribed mergers whose effect may be substantially lessened competition, but narrow judicial constructions made it largely ineffective. Believing that many markets had become oligopolistic as a result of mergers, Congress amended Section 7 in 1950. Although the amendments were rather technical in character, the courts perceived a mandate hostile to mergers. The Supreme Court condemned every merger that came before it during the 1960s, including those with postmerger shares of as little as 7.5 percent of an unconcentrated market in which entry was relatively easy. The cases were consistent, a dissenting Justice commented, only in that "the Government always wins."[34] The only Supreme Court case upholding a merger among competitors was a 1974 decision resting on the peculiarity in the coal industry that one of the merging firms had trivial reserves while virtually all its present sales merely implemented existing long-term contracts.[35] But even that case recognized that the number of significant firms in the market appeared to be the single best predictor of the likelihood of oligopolistic coordination.

All those cases were suits by the Justice Department. Although private parties can also attack mergers, they seldom do. If a merger created or reinforced oligopoly pricing, competitors would be benefited rather than injured. If a merger, instead or in addition, created a more efficient firm that could injure rivals through more aggressive competition, they would be injured. Because

31. See Department of Justice Budget Authorization (Antitrust Division): Hearing before Committee on the Judiciary of U.S. Senate to Consider Authorization of FY79 Appropriations for Justice Department, 95th Cong., 2d Sess., pp. 77–129 (1978) (Statement of John H. Shenefield, assistant attorney general, Antitrust Division).

32. For a few examples, see the fourth paragraph of this section. For a comprehensive analysis, see *Antitrust Law,* ¶¶ 1435–36.

33. See ibid., ¶¶ 902–3.

34. United States v. Von's Grocery Co., 384 U.S. 270, 301 (1966).

35. United States v. General Dynamics Corp., 415 U.S. 486 (1974).

that injury is not the kind that antitrust law is designed to prevent,[36] however, rivals are not allowed to attack such a merger.[37] Consumers are allowed to sue mergers injuring them, but the prospect of such injury is usually too remote to give rise to any immediate damages. That is, illegality usually rests not on any demonstrable present impact but on the prophylactic concern that substantially increased concentration might lead to tacit price coordination in the future.

Thus, however hostile the courts may be, most mergers will not be prevented unless the Justice Department chooses to sue.[38] Prospective merger partners usually abandon projects to which the Justice Department objects or modify them to eliminate government objections, consummating only those that are not likely to be attacked. Hence, Justice Department policy largely determines the number and character of mergers.

The Justice Department recognized its preeminent role in this area by promulgating "guidelines" indicating how it will exercise its discretion to sue. Its 1968 guidelines declared that the government would ordinarily sue where the merging parties accounted for as little as 8 percent of a concentrated market in which the leading four firms had 75 percent of the business; combined shares of 10 percent would suffice in less concentrated markets. Factors other than market shares would be considered only in "exceptional circumstances." Not surprisingly, competitors seldom merged during the 1970s. The Reagan years brought a major change with the issuance of new guidelines that were much more hospitable to mergers through wider market definitions, higher thresholds of concern, and openness to many nonstructural factors.[39]

Many antitrust issues, including mergers, turn on market power. Monopolization under Section 2 of the Sherman Act implicates *monopoly,* which is understood to be substantial market power. Productive joint ventures among competitors are usually ignored when the collaborators lack market power. Similarly, a merger concerns us when it creates a monopoly for the merging firms[40] or, more commonly, creates or reinforces the potential for tacit price coordination with rival firms. To make all these assessments, we need to iden-

36. The requirement of so-called antitrust injury is an important, and largely unheralded, recent judicial development. It forces the courts to articulate the rationale for the antitrust prohibition allegedly violated by the defendant and thereby forces judges to go behind antitrust jargon, giving more conscious attention to the antitrust policies implicated by a suit. See, e.g., *Antitrust Law,* ¶ 1640.

37. Cargill v. Monfort, 479 U.S. 104 (1986). The lower courts are divided as to the standing of a target firm to challenge a hostile takeover bid that would allegedly injure consumers. See *Antitrust Law,* ¶ 340.2i.

38. The Federal Trade Commission Act can also institute its own proceedings to prevent mergers, although it has generally followed the same policies as the Justice Department. See FTC Statement Concerning Horizontal Mergers, 4 Trade Reg. Rep. ¶13, 200 (1988).

39. As issued in 1982 and refined in 1984, the guidelines are reprinted in 4 Trade Reg. Rep. ¶ 13, 103 (1992). The guidelines were further refined in 1992. See id. at ¶ 13, 104.

40. Although rare today, monopoly-creating mergers were the turn-of-the-century (and later) objects of Standard Oil, American Tobacco, U.S. Steel, and others. See, e.g., Standard Oil Co. v. United States, 221 U.S. 1 (1911); United States v. American Tobacco Co., 221 U.S. 106 (1911); United States v. United States Steel Corp., 251 U.S. 417 (1920).

tify the relevant rivals—that is, the "relevant market"—and its structure. Market definition is superfluous when exercised market power has been revealed by persistently excessive price-cost margins or profits. However, such direct measurements of exercised market power have usually seemed too elusive for antitrust litigation, and, in any event, past prices or profits do not tell us whether a merger or some other development creates a new potential for individual power or tacit coordination. Accordingly, the courts usually rely on large market shares as the indicator of power and on market structure as the indicator of oligopolistic coordination.

The new merger guidelines clarify the government's market definition methodology and also offer quantitative benchmarks. As a first cut, the government groups all geographically proximate producers of the merging firms' product into a hypothetical cartel and asks whether it could profitably maintain significantly higher prices for a significant time period—defined ordinarily as 5 percent for one year—without losing too many sales to other producers. If so, the first-cut market is the relevant market for antitrust purposes. If not, the hypothetical cartel is expanded to the next most similar product (or adjacent region), and the same question is asked until an affirmative answer is obtained. This generally sensible methodology probably defines broader markets than more intuitive practices found in many antitrust cases and would make even more transparent the obviously gerrymandered markets seen in some antitrust cases.[41] Working in the same direction are the 5 percent and one-year specifications. Although arbitrary, they offer greater certainty to planners and courts,[42] notwithstanding the customary absence of sufficient data for clear results. Finally, the guidelines always generate an unduly wide market when the firm(s) producing a particular product in a particular region already charge a profit-maximizing monopoly price. In that event, any price increment would necessarily be unprofitable, with the result that the government would widen the market.[43] The effect of widening a market beyond product X, of course, is to increase the number of firms and to reduce the shares of all X producers and thus ordinarily to allow mergers.[44]

The new guidelines are also more tolerant in their numerical thresholds. The government and the courts traditionally looked at the shares of the merging

41. See, e.g., United States v. Aluminum Co. of America (Rome Cable), 377 U.S. 271 (1964); United States v. Continental Can Co., 378 U.S. 441 (1964).

42. The courts have not generally adopted these guidelines. See, e.g., Marathon Oil Co. v. Mobil Corp., 530 F. Supp. 315 (N.D. Ohio), aff'd, 669 F. 2d 378 (6th Cir. 1981), cert. denied, 455 U.S. 982 (1982) (local area is relevant market even though prices differ only by 1 percent from those nearby).

43. The implied indifference to mergers reinforcing preexisting tacit coordination is not, I believe, sound merger policy, although the guidelines are supported by the practical difficulty of learning whether premerger prices were competitive or monopolistic.

44. Of course, widening a market to $X + Y$ would transform a merger of X and Y producers into one of competitors. Second, widening a market could bring in a relatively large firm (although not one of the merging parties), which is greatly emphasized by the government's concentration measure, to which I now turn.

parties and at an aggregation of the leading four (or eight or more) firms. Because that aggregation might be shared equally by the leading firms or held almost entirely by one, and because it tells nothing about the remaining firms, the government now uses the Herfindahl-Hirschman Index (HHI) measure, which expresses market concentration as the sum of the squares of each firm's market share.[45] Including every firm is desirable but requires more data than are usually available. Squaring shares emphasizes differences among firms— perhaps too much so—and magnifies errors in measuring each firm's share.

The guidelines profess indifference apart from extraordinary circumstances to markets in which a postmerger HHI remains below 1,000, concern above that level, and great concern above 1,800.[46] However, neither concern nor great concern triggers further consideration unless the merger raises the index 100 or 50 points, respectively.[47] For example, merging two 7 percent firms does not trigger these guidelines even though the market has only five other equally sized firms.[48]

In a substantial retreat from earlier cases and guidelines, exceeding these numerical thresholds "provide[s] only the starting point for analyzing the competitive impact of a merger."[49] Unless the HHI exceeds 1,800 and rises by more than 100 points, the Justice Department will weigh several additional factors diminishing the dangers to competition: the likelihood of significant entry within two years, the expansion potential of efficient fringe firms, worldwide excess capacity that could supply us, the quality of the next best substitute or region not included within the relevant market, extreme product heterogeneity, or impaired resources or financial condition suggesting that a firm's market share overstates its competitive significance.[50] In all events, the government will tolerate otherwise anticompetitive mergers that are shown by clear and convincing evidence to be reasonably necessary to achieve significant net efficiencies.[51] Notwithstanding some expansion in the scope of antimerger legislation,[52] the government allowed many mergers during the 1980s that it would

45. Dropping decimal points, as the government does, a 10 percent firm enters the HHI index as $10 \times 10 = 100$. So a market with ten 10 percent firms has an HHI of 1,000. A one-firm market has 10,000.

46. These numbers correspond roughly to four-firm concentration ratios of 50 and 75 percent, respectively (see Weinstock 1984).

47. Additional concern arises under the guidelines when any market's leading firm with at least a 35 percent share acquires even a 1 percent firm.

48. The postmerger HHI would be 1,675, raised 98 points ($[14 \times 14] - 49 - 49$) by the merger.

49. Guidelines, § 3.11.

50. The guidelines also note several factors that would exacerbate the threat to competition: restraints on expansion of foreign exports (if included within the relevant market); product homogeneity; ready information about rivals; orders frequent, regular, and small rather than lumpy; past collusion; mandatory delivered pricing and other standardized transactions; stable market shares; or acquisition of any unusually disruptive and competitive firm. Guidelines, §§ 3.2–3.45.

51. The guidelines also allow otherwise forbidden acquisitions of failing companies or divisions, as did the cases and earlier guidelines. Guidelines, §§ 5.

52. Amendments in 1980 covered more local acquisitions as well as those involving partnerships and proprietorships in addition to corporations. 94 Stat. 1154, 1157–58 (1980). Congress did not enact narrowing administration proposals to (1) require a "significant probability" of anticompeti-

have challenged in preceding decades.[53] Of the more than 10,000 merger proposals reported to the enforcement agencies from 1982 to 1986, the Justice Department announced an intention to challenge eighty-one, and twenty-five more were abandoned after the FTC requested additional information or authorized further enforcement.[54] Mergers not involving competitors appear not to have been challenged at all—another departure from the 1960s.

With few government suits, the courts had little occasion to decide the legality of mergers during the 1980s. In one private suit, a court condemned a merger on the conventional ground that it increased concentration unduly, raising the postmerger share to around 20 percent where the largest four firms held about half the rather narrow market defined by the court.[55] And several FTC condemnations of mergers were upheld.[56] A few decisions, however, were even more tolerant than the government and refused to condemn mergers because the court believed that entry was relatively easy.[57]

Speaking generally, these developments reflect the view that mergers are both less dangerous and more beneficial than they had seemed. Unless government itself blocks entry, the enforcement agencies came to believe that competitive forces are too robust to be defeated by most mergers. Even with substantial concentration, it was far from clear that concentration was closely correlated with high profits throughout the market, which would presumably be the result of supracompetitive prices. Indeed, suggestions that only the leading firms earned higher profits in concentrated markets might imply that enhanced efficiency was the object and result of growth, whether by internal expansion or by merger.[58]

---

tive effects rather than a tendency in that direction, (2) forbid only those mergers that "substantially increase the ability to exercise market power" rather than those that may "substantially lessen competition" or tend to create a monopoly, and (3) direct courts to consider six economic factors such as the number and size distribution of firms, conditions of entry, and, notably, efficiencies.

53. Of ninety-four mergers condemned by the courts during the 1960s and 1970s (as set forth in *Antitrust Law*, ¶ 909) at least twenty-nine would not have been challenged under the new guidelines, according to Kauper (1984, 174, n. 8).

54. 54 Antitr. & Trade Reg. Rep. 476–77 (1988). See also Conference Board Seminar Examines Enforcement, Restructuring Trends, 52 Antitr. & Trade Reg. Rep. 535, 541 (1987) (as of 1987, apparently no suits challenging mergers with an HHI below 1,800 and perhaps not even below 2,000 or even 2,200); Scherer (1989, 91) ("Many mergers that almost surely would have drawn a challenge from past administrations were let through; and the number of challenges issued per year by the two enforcement agencies declined by half relative to 1960–1980 averages despite all-time peak levels of merger activity").

55. Monfort v. Cargill, 761 F. 2d 570 (10th Cir. 1985), rev'd on other grounds, 479 U.S. 104 (1986).

56. See, e.g., Hospital Corp. of America v. FTC, 807 F. 2d 1381 (7th Cir. 1986), cert. denied, 481 U.S. 1038 (1987) (approving condemnation of merger where regulation limited entry); FTC v. Warner Communic., 742 F. 2d 1156 (9th Cir. 1984) (using concentration ratios rather than HHI and emphasizing a trend toward concentration); FTC v. Coca-Cola, 641 F. Supp. 1128 (D.D.C. 1986), vacated after merger abandoned, 829 F. 2d 191 (D.C. Cir. 1987).

57. United States v. Syufy, 903 F. 2d 659 (9th Cir. 1990); United States v. Waste Management, 743 F. 2d 976, 981–84 (2d Cir. 1984).

58. A significant portion of the literature on the connection between structure and performance is effectively summarized by Scherer and Ross (1990, chap. 9).

9.3   Other Cooperation among Competitors

The courts have long condemned "price fixing" as illegal *per se*—that is, without proof of detrimental effects or actual market power and without considering justifications. This category came to include competitors who, although setting no price, agreed to divide markets, to buy at market prices the "excess" supply offered by weaker rivals unable to store it, to rotate bids, to charge only one's published prices (although free to publish a new price list at any time), or to eliminate certain discounts or bidding practices.[59]

Once such practices were identified as *per se* illegal "price fixing," private plaintiffs and occasionally the government attempted so to label almost any agreement that could eliminate price competition among competitors. Even the most procompetitive joint venture between two tiny firms could eliminate price competition among them and, if they became more efficient and expanded, might even come to have some impact on the market; although the latter impact seems desirable, the law purports to forbid price-fixing agreements regardless of whether higher or lower prices result.[60]

Because so inclusive a definition of *price fixing* would condemn arrangements that had little in common with the traditionally unjustified cartels, the courts have never defined *per se* illegal price fixing as broadly as plaintiffs desire. Yet only recently did the Supreme Court expressly say that the categorical condemnation of "price fixing" does not actually cover all " 'price fixing' in the literal sense." "Literalness is overly simplistic and often overbroad," the Court explained, and does not dispense with the need to examine potential harms and benefits in order "to characterize the challenged conduct as falling within or without that category of behavior to which we apply the label '*per se* price fixing.' "[61] Thus, except where they have already considered and rejected claimed justifications—such as a cartel's claim that "cutthroat" competition deprives its members of deserved returns—the courts remain ready to consider appropriate justifications. Where the challenged conduct is of a kind that can benefit the economy, the courts turn from *per se* rules to the so-called rule of reason, which declines to interfere with minor restraints and which allows more significant restraints to be "redeemed" by lower costs, greater innovation, corrections of market failures, and the like.

Speaking broadly, I perceive a greater receptivity, both in the courts and in the administration, to claims of redeeming virtue—especially cost savings and innovation potential. Collaborators have themselves become readier to offer affirmative justifications rather than merely rest on an objector's failure to prove a significant threat to competition. More important, our attitudes have changed pervasively since mid-century. Once overwhelmingly dominant in the

59. See *Antitrust Analysis*, ¶¶ 227–28.
60. Arizona v. Maricopa County Medical Society, 457 U.S. 332 (1982).
61. Broadcast Music v. Columbia Broadcasting System, 441 U.S. 1, 9 (1979). See also Northwest Wholesale Stationers v. Pacific Stationery & Printing Co., 472 U.S. 284, 290–91 (1985).

world, our industries seemed invulnerable and the primary suppliers of American consumers, with continued productivity growth inevitable. If antitrust law then erred on the side of preserving rivalry at the expense of efficiency, the possible sacrifice might appear minor and short lived. More recently, growing imports challenged many basic industries, creating the specter of industrial decline and demonstrating that efficiency and innovation are not inevitable but must be achieved.

Although the cases are too few and their language too oblique for clear proof without a more detailed presentation than this paper allows, most commentators would agree that the courts have become more hospitable to claims of efficiency. And Congress favored cooperation both on research and on exports. Responding in 1984 to suggestions that the antitrust laws impeded the joint research needed to maintain the competitiveness of U.S. industry against increasing foreign competition, Congress passed the National Cooperative Research Act with three features.[62] Although largely declaratory of existing law, it eliminated any doubt that joint research and development ventures were to be judged under the rule of reason, "taking into account all relevant facts affecting competition." In addition, any such venture that was ultimately held to be unlawful would give rise only to actual damages rather than the usual treble damages for antitrust violations if the venturers had promptly notified the Justice Department and the Federal Trade Commission of their identities and of the nature and objectives of the venture. Finally, contrary applications of state law were forbidden.[63]

On the export front, the Webb-Pomerene Act long exempted from the antitrust laws agreements or acts in the course of export trade by associations entered into for the sole purpose of engaging in such trade.[64] Congress went further with the Export Trading Company Act of 1982 to favor expanded cooperation to promote exports.[65] It eliminated any doubt that our antitrust laws served to protect U.S. consumers and exporters rather than foreign consumers or producers. Those laws were declared inapplicable to "conduct involving . . . commerce (other than import trade . . .) with foreign nations—unless such conduct has a direct, substantial, and reasonably foreseeable effect" (1) on domestic or import trade or (2) "on export . . . commerce . . . of a person . . . in the United States."[66]

The act also allows the secretary of commerce, with the concurrence of the attorney general, to certify that specific export trade or activities or methods of

---

62. 98 Stat. 1815 (1984), 15 U.S.C.A. §§ 4301–5 (1990).

63. Additional legislative proposals favoring certain joint production as well as joint research ventures are currently pending. See, e.g., National Cooperative Production Amendments of 1990, H.R. 4611, 101st Cong., 2d Sess., 136 Cong. Rec. H3099 (daily ed. 5 June 1990); Defense Production Act reauthorization for four years, S. 1379, 101st Cong., 1st Sess., 135 Cong. Rec. S8602 (daily ed. 24 July 1989).

64. 40 Stat. 516 (1918), as amended, 15 U.S.C.A. §§ 61–65 (1990).

65. 96 Stat. 1233 (1982).

66. In the latter event, only "injury to export business in the United States" is cognizable.

operation will not (1) lessen competition with the United States; (2) restrain any competitors' export trade; (3) unreasonably enhance, stabilize, or depress prices within the United States of goods of the class exported; (4) constitute unfair methods of competition against export competitors; or (5) "include any act that may reasonably be expected to result in the sale for consumption or resale within the U.S. of the goods . . . or services exported." Such a certificate immunized the recipient from criminal or civil antitrust liability under state or federal law, except that an injured person may obtain injunctive relief or single damages for violation of the listed standards (other than the last). In such a suit, it will be presumed that "conduct which is specified in and complies with a certificate . . . does comply with [those] standards."

9.4 "Vertical" Relationships between Buyer and Seller

Although "horizontal" collaboration among rivals can harm or benefit the economy more substantially than "vertical" restraints involving buyers and sellers, the latter have been litigated more often and discussed more passionately. Entrenched doctrine opposing such restraints continued to weaken during the 1980s with the growing perception that suppliers can seldom increase their market power through vertical restraints and, hence, must often adopt them to make distribution more efficient. More vocal reformers say "never" rather than "seldom" and "always" rather than "often." In their view, minor exceptions for readily observed facts take care of such anticompetitive vertical agreements as those that a manufacturer adopted only because compelled to do so by a cartel of its dealers themselves. Others doubt that the exceptions are minor or that their occurrence can be easily seen. Vocal traditionalists doubt that genuine efficiencies are often involved, insist that any efficiencies can usually be obtained in other ways, and, in any event, favor antitrust protection of "small" dealer autonomy against "oppressive" manufacturers.[67] To illustrate these forces more concretely, let us turn to restraints on a dealer's resale and to tie-ins—conduct that the Reagan administration largely blessed, decrying earlier overenforcement.

9.4.1   Resale Limitations

Still in force is the 1911 Dr. Miles ruling that categorically condemned manufacturer-dealer agreements specifying dealers' resale prices.[68] Seeing no legitimate manufacturer interest beyond the wholesale price, the Supreme Court equated the vertical agreement's elimination of intrabrand price competition among dealers with the clearly illegal horizontal agreement among dealers themselves to eliminate such competition. Of course, manufacturer interests in

---

67. For extensive analysis of these themes in the context of vertical agreements limiting a dealer's resale prices, customers, or territories, see *Antitrust Law,* chap. 16A.
68. Dr. Miles Medical Co. v. John D. Park & Sons Co., 220 U.S. 373 (1911).

distribution do not end at the wholesale level. Resale price maintenance might induce dealers to provide greater services than otherwise and thereby expand sales volume more than lower resale prices.[69] Moreover, horizontal and vertical price-fixing agreements differ. A dealer cartel seeks maximum profits for its members, while greater dealer profit than required for effective distribution injures the manufacturer.[70] Nevertheless, much actual resale price maintenance has apparently resulted from dealer pressure.[71]

During the 1980s, the Justice Department unsuccessfully urged the Supreme Court to reconsider the *per se* prohibition[72] and later issued guidelines indicating that it would seldom attack resale price maintenance.[73] Congressional forces, on the other hand, have sought to legislate continued *per se* prohibition.[74] In all events, the categorical prohibition of 1911 endures.[75]

However, the Supreme Court recently ameliorated that prohibition by expanding the more lawful "nonprice" category in Business Electronics[76] and by returning to a narrower definition of vertical "agreement" in Monsanto.[77]

Price or Nonprice Restraints

Vertical agreements confining dealers to certain territories or customers— so-called nonprice restraints[78]—also reduce or eliminate intrabrand competition, and not just on price, but on service as well. Moving toward *per se* illegality in the mid-1960s, the Supreme Court abruptly changed course in the late 1970s, ruling in Sylvania that such restraints did not appear so pernicious and

---

69. For circumstances bearing on whether dealers themselves would provide such services without vertical price fixing, see *Antitrust Law,* ¶¶ 1611ff.

70. See id. at ¶ 1603

71. Although this has never been true of agreements imposing a ceiling on resale prices, the Supreme Court has unwisely condemned those agreements as well. Albrecht v. Herald Co., 390 U.S. 145 (1968). Nevertheless, it has refused to allow challenges of ceiling-price agreements by competitors of the restrained dealers. Atlantic Richfield Co. v. USA Petrol. Co., 110 S. Ct. 1884 (1990). Moreover, the lower courts have narrowed the concept of forbidden maximum price agreements. See *Antitrust Law,* ¶ 1639.

72. See Monsanto Co. v. Spray-Rite Serv. Corp., 465 U.S. 752, 761–62 n.7 (1984). Curiously, an appropriations rider forbade the Department of Justice from pursuing that argument. Departments of Commerce, Justice, and State, the Judiciary, and Related Agencies Appropriations Act of 1984, Pub. L. No. 98–116, § 510, 97 Stat. 1071, 1102–3 (1983).

73. Justice Department, Guidelines for Vertical Restraints (1985), 4 Trade Reg. Rep. ¶ 13, 105 (1990).

74. Price Fixing Prevention Act of 1989, H.R. 1236, 101st Cong., 2d Sess., 136 Cong. Rec. H1538 (daily ed. 18 April 1990).

75. During the Great Depression, Congress responded to lobbying by dealers against severe retail price competition by enacting an antitrust exemption for resale price maintenance in states that chose to permit it. 50 Stat. 673, 693 (1937). When Congress repealed that exemption in 1975, it assumed—but did not enact—continued *per se* prohibition. 89 Stat. 801 (1975). For an analysis of that legislation, see *Antitrust Law,* ¶ 1629.

76. Business Elec. Corp. v. Sharp Elec. Corp., 485 U.S. 717 (1988). For other exclusions from the vertical price-fixing concept, see *Antitrust Law,* pars. 1473–74, 1622–27.

77. See n. 72 above.

78. This category also includes agreements prescribing dealer hours, inventories, services, etc.

so lacking in redeeming virtue to warrant categorical prohibition.[79] After all, limiting intrabrand competition might facilitate new entry or services strengthening competition with other brands. Of course, such restraints are unlawful when unreasonable, but few plaintiffs have been willing or able so to prove.[80]

The Sylvania Court acknowledged that resale price maintenance might also strengthen intrabrand competition but expressly disclaimed any retreat from Dr. Miles because price restrictions might impede interbrand price competition (by preventing dealers from cutting retail price in competition with other brands or by helping rival manufacturers monitor each other's pricing and thereby facilitating their tacit price coordination) and because *per se* prohibition here was assumed by Congress[81] and was so venerable.[82] This reluctance to overrule old precedents is obviously less potent in the legislative and executive branches.

In all events, this sharp distinction between price and nonprice restraints—condemning the former *per se* while usually allowing the latter as reasonable—makes the classification of actual restraints critical. For example, one dealer complains that a rival has disobeyed an express territorial restriction by selling in the complainer's region. The manufacturer's subsequent steps to discipline this invader have readily been classified as nonprice restraints even though the complaint emphasized the invader's low prices. In the absence of an express nonprice restraint, however, how should we classify the termination of a price cutter in response to complaints of another dealer? Assuming that the manufacturer had agreed with the complainer to terminate the plaintiff because of the plaintiff's low prices, the Supreme Court nevertheless classified the restraint as nonprice in the absence of an agreement prescribing some dealer's resale price.[83]

Refusals to Deal as Agreements

Vertical restraints not involving an actual or prospective monopolist are not covered by the Sherman Act in the absence of an agreement. The core concept is relatively clear in the horizontal area where cooperation among competitors creates power that did not otherwise exist. In the vertical area, by contrast, a manufacturer needs no promise or commitment from a dealer but might simply announce publicly that dealers reselling for less than list price would no longer be supplied. Recognizing the absence of any commitment by dealers and seeing only the manufacturer's choice of customers, the Colgate case found no agreement.[84] Recognizing the resulting toleration of resale price control by manufacturers, the courts retreated from Colgate and condemned threats or termination based on resale prices, allowing only suggestions or persuasion.

---

79. Continental T.V. v. GTE Sylvania, 433 U.S. 36 (1977).
80. See *Antitrust Law,* ¶ 1645.
81. See n. 75 above.
82. 433 U.S. (n. 79 above) at 51 n.18.
83. Business Elec., n. 76 above.
84. United States v. Colgate & Co., 250 U.S. 300 (1919).

In 1984, Monsanto forbade the inference of agreement merely from a manufacturer's termination of a discounter in response to a rival dealer's price complaint and used language resurrecting Colgate,[85] although the Court actually upheld a jury finding of agreement based on rather weak evidence.

Congressional response has been no better. Proposed legislation insists that mere termination of a price cutter after complaint of a rival dealer prevents summary judgment for suppliers and would sustain any jury verdict of illegal vertical price fixing.[86] It seems shameful to rule or legislate in terms of the procedural issue of when or what juries may decide without defining the agreement concept suitable for these vertical cases. Neither Congress nor the courts have focused on that policy choice.[87]

9.4.2   Tie-ins

The courts first encountered tie-ins in the course of defining patent infringement. Use of a patented machine without license from the patent holder is, of course, an infringement. When a patent holder licensed use of his patented machine only in connection with approved materials, he claimed that any other use of the machine was unlicensed and therefore an infringement. The courts typically upheld such restrictions until the 1917 Motion Picture Patents case considered a monopolist of motion picture projectors who allowed use of those machines only to project films approved by the monopolist; there was no doubt that these restrictions were part of an effort by established machine and movie makers to exclude rival movie makers from the market.[88]

The Court held that violation of the license restriction did not infringe the patent. Indeed, during the pendency of such a "misuse," the courts refuse to enforce a patent against an undoubted infringer.[89] Believing that tie-ins typically disrupted competition in the tied product without any offsetting legitimate function, the courts also came to condemn them as *per se* antitrust violations.[90] Moreover, the courts expressed hostility to possible justifications, for tie-ins "serve hardly any purpose beyond the suppression of competition."[91]

The law might have rested there in the absence of a typical overextension. To win treble damages without having to demonstrate any real power or effect, inventive plaintiffs succeeded in sweeping an ever larger number and type of

---

85. 465 U.S. at 764, 763, and n.9.

86. Price Fixing Prevention Act of 1989, H.R. 1236, 101st Cong., 2d Sess., 136 Cong. Rec. H1538 (daily ed. 18 April 1990).

87. For an extensive analysis of these several issues, see *Antitrust Law,* chap. 14D.

88. Motion Picture Patents Co. v. Universal Film Mfg. Co., 243 U.S. 502 (1917). See *Antitrust Law* ¶ 1701.

89. Morton Salt Co. v. Suppiger Co., 314 U.S. 488 (1942).

90. Although the customary verbal formula seemed to require some power in the tying-product market and some effect in the tied market, the former was inferred from the tie itself, and the latter was satisfied by a nontrivial dollar volume of trade, no matter how small the percentage of trade affected.

91. United States v. Loew's, 371 U.S. 38, 44 (1962), citing Standard Oil Co. of California v. United States, 337 U.S. 293, 305–6 (1949).

business arrangements into the tying category, such as a fast-food franchise coupled with ready-to-operate premises or an automobile from a manufacturer with delivery arranged by the seller.[92] Such cases illustrate how far tying law strayed from any intelligible concern with the preservation of competition. Not only do these examples stretch the core idea of a two-product tie-in, but they involve antitrust intervention without any noticeable threat to the health of competition in any market.

With this thoughtless expansion, many courts came to see that arguable tie-ins are to be found everywhere, that many of them actually serve legitimate objectives without threatening competitive vitality in the second market or anywhere else and without even harming the plaintiff buyer. So the retreat began. A few courts allowed "business justifications" as affirmative defenses to tie-ins, notwithstanding the language of *per se* illegality.[93] Others held that the alleged tying and tied products were really a single product, which then fell entirely outside tying law. While many of those "single-product" rulings reflected genuine doubt about a product's metaphysical boundaries, others reflected a belief that antitrust law should remain aloof, either because the arrangement was justified[94] or surely without harmful impact on the market.[95] The Supreme Court came to require actual proof of power with respect to the tying product rather than simply inferring it from the existence of the tie.[96] Finally, some lower courts have moved slightly toward requiring plaintiffs to show that the tie could bring the defendant market power in the tied market,[97] and a growing number of them realize that the injuries claimed by the typical plaintiff—buyers forced to take a second product—are usually an illusion.[98]

Although the Supreme Court insists that tie-ins are unlawful *per se,* it demands real proof of power over the tying product and does not preclude proof of redeeming virtues. Its *per se* rule thus precludes examination of the only factor that matters—namely, whether there is any substantial impact on the health of competition in the tied market. A minority of the Justices recognize that this *per se* rule does not simplify antitrust administration.[99] Indeed, a sensible law of tie-ins would focus primarily, if not solely, on effects in the tied market and redeeming virtues, ignoring complex characterizations of one

---

92. Northern v. McGraw-Edison Co., 542 F. 2d 1336, 1347 (8th Cir. 1976), cert. denied, 429 U.S. 1097 (1977). Anderson Foreign Motors v. New England Toyota Distrib., 475 F. Supp. 973 (D. Mass. 1979).

93. For example, United States v. Jerrold Elec. Corp., 187 F. Supp. 545 (E.D. Pa. 1960), aff'd *per curiam,* 365 U.S. 567 (1961).

94. For example, Principe v. McDonald's Corp., 631 F. 2d 303 (4th Cir. 1980), cert. denied, 451 U.S. 970 (1981).

95. For example, Coniglio v. Highland Servs., 495 F. 2d 1286 (2d Cir.), cert. denied, 419 U.S. 1022 (1974).

96. Jefferson Parish Hospital District No. 2 v. Hyde, 466 U.S. 2 (1984).

97. For example, Carl Sandburg Village Condominium Assn. v. First Condominium Devel. Co., 758 F. 2d 203, 210 (7th Cir. 1985). See *Antitrust Law* ch. 17B-2.

98. See *Antitrust Law,* ¶ 340.4a.

99. See Jefferson Parish (n. 96 above) at 32 (concurring opinion).

product or two and ignoring power in the tying product. This is a likely course of development, toward which the 1980s decisions demanding real proof of power are only a minor step.

Although the Justice Department of the 1980s would largely agree with these sentiments, it had relatively little impact on the law. To be sure, it issued policy statements withdrawing earlier objections to various patent license restrictions,[100] and it did not institute suit, but private suits in this area are numerous.

9.5 One Firm's Low Prices or Vertical Integration

The actual or prospective monopolist is my final substantive topic, one with significant administrative and judicial developments during the 1980s, particularly as to vertical integration and allegedly predatory pricing.

9.5.1 Vertical Integration and the Bell System

The most notorious antitrust policy decision of the decade was the breakup of the Bell telephone system, separating AT&T's research, equipment manufacture, and long-distance operations from its Bell operating company (BOC) monopolies of local telephone exchanges and the organization of the latter into seven regional monopolies, which made no equipment and affiliated with no long-distance firm.[101] The players were the Antitrust Division, which initiated the suit against AT&T in the mid-1970s; the district judge, whose preliminary opinion indicated that AT&T would be found guilty of illegal monopolization;[102] and, of course, AT&T, which consented to the breakup without a full trial and appeals to higher courts. Let me summarize briefly the theory of the government's AT&T suit and hypothesize rationales for each player's position. For simplicity, I will focus on the equipment issue.

AT&T supplied the BOCs with equipment. They "purchased over eighty percent of the nation's central office switches and transmission equipment and nearly always purchased that equipment from AT&T's Western Electric affiliate, even when those products were more expensive or of lesser quality than equipment available from competing vendors."[103] The potential anticompetitive effect was twofold: consumers would pay higher prices and use telephones less, and new competition in the equipment business would be retarded.

In unregulated areas, vertical integration has few price-output effects because a lawful monopolist is legally free to charge the monopoly price for its product whether or not it purchased supplies from itself upstream.[104] Without

---

100. Antitrust Division Reappraisal of 1981, 4 Trade Reg. Rep. ¶ 13, 129 (1988).
101. U.S. v. AT&T, 552 F. Supp. 131 (D.D.C. 1982), aff'd sub nom., Maryland v. United States, 460 U.S. 1001 (1983).
102. United States v. AT&T, 524 F. Supp. 1336 (D.D.C. 1981).
103. United States v. Western Electric Co., 900 F. 2d 283, 290 (D.C. Cir. 1990).
104. See *Antitrust Law,* ¶¶ 710, 725.

any need to justify an inflated downstream price, such a monopolist has every incentive to buy from the cheapest source. By contrast, a rate-regulated BOC has an economic incentive to pay an inflated price to AT&T and thereby earn excess profits for the supplying arm. Since the regulators normally take a utility's costs as given, the inflated equipment prices are passed on to consumers. In effect, consumers come to pay the monopoly price for telephone service "notwithstanding the FCC's best efforts to stop it."[105] Moreover, with few buyers other than self-supplying AT&T, independent equipment makers had relatively little ability or incentive to enter or remain in the business or to engage in research or development looking toward better equipment or telephone service. The Justice Department's theory of the case was that AT&T's incentives and ability to prefer itself and thereby foreclose competition from other sources themselves operated as an entry barrier. Potential equipment rivals believed that they would not have open and competitive access to the patronage of the telephone monopolies and thus would not enter the market.

What made the AT&T case far from simple was the Bell system's claim that integration generated substantial efficiencies that would be lost if the equipment business were separated from the local BOCs. Speaking generally, efficiencies appeared to result from network uniformity[106] and from joint engineering of the network and the products designed for it.[107] Centralizing these activities in Bell Labs allowed efficiencies that are not equally available when independent firms deal through the market.[108]

Ironically, the close relationships that could create efficiencies could also lead to preferences for Western Electric and discrimination against independent equipment manufacturers. The latter repeatedly alleged that the Bell system maintained those close relationships to ensure that the BOCs would buy equipment from Western Electric at inflated prices and pass those on to con-

---

105. Western Electric (n. 103 above) at 290.

106. By setting standards and engineering an integrated national telephone network, AT&T presumably assured that everything connected optimally with everything else, that an appropriate degree of redundancy was built into the network to cope with natural calamities, and that this could all be done without incessant negotiations and frequent contractual revisions among independent parties.

107. Through its basic and applied research, Bell Labs determined the functions to be performed by the telephone network and developed and disseminated generic specifications for new equipment needed to perform these functions. To satisfy these generic requirements, Bell Labs (and occasionally others) then designed and developed specific products, which would be fabricated by Western Electric. Bell Labs then evaluated the products that had been manufactured by Western Electric or others to decide which products best met the Bell system's needs.

108. For example, although network engineers worked in groups different from product designers, they could consult together at various preliminary stages. Before completing network specifications, network engineers could solicit the cooperation of product designers in assessing the practical feasibility at acceptable cost levels of various products and features. Because judgments on such matters could change as product design followed adoption and release of generic specifications, the designers could return to the network engineers with suggested revisions in those specifications. Although unrelated firms could cooperate in the same way, their partially adversarial relationship obstructs such cooperation. Each might fear that the other seeks selfish advantage rather than the good of "the whole"; indeed, there is no "whole" among unrelated firms.

sumers. This incentive for self-dealing meant that Bell Labs had an inherent conflict of interest that led it, according to critics, to choose its own designs and Western Electric products over better or cheaper designs or products of other manufacturers. Moreover, competing manufacturers saw themselves as victims of an inherent or intentional informational disadvantage as well the victims of price-cost manipulation. Product designers within the Bell system enjoyed superior access to essential network information.[109] Furthermore, rival equipment manufacturers alleged that AT&T misallocated product design expenses (that should have been allocated to Western Electric products) to network engineering (and its associated research and development). By thus escaping some of its true costs, Western Electric could appear to offer prices at or below rival prices, although its true costs and profits were no lower and perhaps even higher.

The Justice Department either doubted that such efficiencies existed or shared AT&T's apparent view that any efficiencies of integration were destined to be lost anyway. Legislative and regulation proposals would have (1) imposed restrictions on the sharing of information between the Bell system's telephone engineers and product designers, allowing them to communicate with each other only in much the same way as totally unrelated firms,[110] and (2) required "competitive bidding" or market tests that would have prevented the Bell companies from buying Western Electric products even when they were the best or cheapest way to provide desired services.[111] Such "safeguards" seemed likely to deprive society of the benefits of integration without saving it the social

109. Consultations by network engineers before publication of generic product specifications gave them a headstart. Later revision of published specifications at the suggestion of affiliated product designers could make obsolete the work and expenditures that independent manufacturers had based on the published generic specifications. Thus, publication of network information was bound to seem to independents to be either too late (after Bell system designers' headstart) or too early (before the generic specifications became truly final and beyond subsequent alteration).

110. See, e.g., Second Computer Inquiry, 77 F.C.C. 2d 384, 457–87 (1980) (requiring that separate subsidiaries be established to provide equipment on consumer premises that is connected to the network and prohibiting disclosure of network information to subsidiaries before it is made public); Computer and Business Equipment Manufacturers Assn., 93 F.C.C. 2d 1226 (1983) (interpreting Computer II rules to require disclosure of network information to manufacturers at make/buy decision point, even when there is no communication between subsidiaries); H.R. 5158, 97th Cong., 1st Sess. §§ 251–54 (1981) (requiring that certain products and services be provided through separate subsidiaries and prohibiting disclosure of certain information to such subsidiaries unless it had been made public); proposed amendment to S. 898, 97th Cong. 1st Sess. (1981) (allowing results of research and engineering studies to be made available to affiliates only if simultaneously made public). Such proposals were also incorporated into the "regulatory" decree that AT&T attempted to negotiate with the Justice Department.

111. See, e.g., S. 898, 97th Cong. 1st Sess. (1981) ("Baxter I" amendment containing market test dictating that Western Electric could have no greater market share of Bell system business than it had of other business); H.R. 5158, 97th Cong., 1st Sess. § 243 (requiring "dominant carrier" to purchase increasing percentages of products from unaffiliated manufacturers); AT&T, Charges for Interstate Telephone Service (Docket 19129 Phase II), 64 F.C.C. 2d 1, 44–45 (1977) (requiring plan for separation of procurement and manufacturing functions, including procedures for competitive bidding).

costs of continued antitrust litigation, for antitrust immunity was not proposed, and someone would always claim that the "safeguards" had not worked.

The basic rationale of the decree was very simple: the natural monopoly of local telephone service (where competition was not possible) was isolated from "adjacent markets" (where competition was fully possible but likely to be compromised if affiliated with the monopoly).[112] The decree separated the regional monopolies into seven regional Bell operating companies and separated those BOCs from equipment manufacture and long-distance and certain other services.[113]

Outside the regulated area, the government remained largely indifferent to vertical integration, although many private suits challenged an integrated firm's refusal to supply its competitors. The rulings are too various for coverage here,[114] although they illustrate the general theme of this paper that the courts have been reluctant to interfere with the individual firm's internal efficiency-creating arrangements.[115]

9.5.2   Predatory Pricing[116]

Finding a rival's price cut unwelcome, a firm may label it "predatory"[117] and seek to enjoin it or to recover treble damages based on the profits that would have been earned at higher prices. Recent dispositions in the lower courts—without significant input from Congress, the administration, or the Supreme Court—illustrate one path by which economic policy emerges from the legal system.

Until a decade or so ago, courts left juries free to label prices as predatory on the basis of vague instructions inviting consideration of the defendant's intention to capture the market, the "reasonableness" of the challenged price, the depth and duration of the cut, the impact on rivals, and similar factors. Obviously, however, an intention to prevail and even to gain a monopoly is the essence of competition, not its antithesis, as the courts increasingly realized. Indeed, without a more disciplined test for predation, the risk of antitrust dam-

---

112. The settlement also ended a previous consent decree preventing AT&T from competing in any noncommunication business, such as computers.

113. In a few respects, the final decree did not completely isolate the operating monopoly from adjacent markets. For example, the BOCs were allowed to publish "yellow pages," in the hope that "excess profits" from the yellow pages would subsidize local telephone service and keep rates down. AT&T (n. 101 above) at 193–94.

114. See *Antitrust Law,* chap. 7D'.

115. See ibid., ¶¶ 729.2, 736.2f.

116. This nondetailed and nontechnical summary omits citations to the particular cases and commentaries, which are discussed at length in *Antitrust Law,* chaps. 7C, 7C'.

117. A monopolist violates Section 2 of the Sherman Act by obtaining or maintaining its monopoly through predatory pricing. Moreover, such pricing would normally be seen as an illegal attempt to monopolize by any firm with a large or dominant market share. In addition, the Robinson-Patman Act's prohibition of price discriminations injuring the discriminator's rivals is now largely understood to require predatory pricing.

ages or even litigation may chill the impulse, perhaps already weak, toward price competition in oligopoly markets.

A suggestion in the legal literature for a cost-based test of predation appealed to the courts and stimulated an outpouring of legal and economic commentary. There was general agreement that what maximizes consumer welfare in the short run does not necessarily do so in the long run, especially when dealing with strategic activity designed to benefit the predator, and harm the public, in the long run. Although the judges have not quite known how to choose among various proposals for dealing with the long run, this uncertainty has had remarkably little impact on the cases that now emphasize price-cost comparisons, approving prices above full costs with few qualms, approving prices above variable costs (as a rough surrogate for marginal costs), although with more qualms, and disapproving prices below variable costs.[118] Some courts make these price-cost comparisons determinative, seeing no readily administrable way to deal with long-run strategic possibilities. Other courts refuse to make such comparisons determinative but usually end up approving prices above variable (or other) costs because nothing else clearly indicates long-run actual or intended harm.

Second, the courts have become more sensitive to the prerequisites for successful predation—both the ability to outlast rivals and the ability later to win enough monopoly profit long enough greatly to offset diminished revenues while destroying rivals. With many rivals, weakening one would not enable the alleged predator to earn monopoly profits. With easy entry, the prospective payoff from ruining rivals would be short lived at best. Hence, consumers would not be injured. With insufficient gains in prospect, moreover, the rational defendant would not sacrifice available short-run profits in the first place. Where successful predation is impossible, it probably has not occurred.

Regarding predation as widespread, some criticize these developments as promonopoly rather than antitrust. Regarding successful predation as virtually impossible, others argue that any antipredation inquiry wastes resources at best and probably chills price competition as well. By contrast, it seems remarkable that mere judges have done as well as they have in this complex area.

9.5.3 Monopolization Generally

Monopolies are not unlawful unless acquired or maintained "willfully." The quoted term does not mean intentionally—for building the better mousetrap that brings an intended monopoly is assuredly lawful—but improperly. Unfortunately, the courts often let the jury decide what is improper. In the Aspen case, the defendant Ski Co. operated ski lifts on three mountains in the Aspen

---

118. The present account bypasses such obvious questions as who measures variable costs, when, by what definition, and with what adjustment for circumstances affecting the closeness of variable to marginal costs.

area and was found (incorrectly) to have monopoly power. It had previously offered a discounted weekly four-mountain lift ticket with the other operator (Highlands) in the area but stopped doing so, apparently in the belief that its discounted, weekly, three-mountain ticket would outcompete a weekly one-mountain ticket from Highlands. The latter sued and prevailed after the jury was instructed that, although Ski had no unqualified duty to cooperate with Highlands, it was nevertheless liable if it acted "by anticompetitive or exclusionary means or for anticompetitive or exclusionary purposes."[119]

Such a verbal formula is potentially mischievous, for a jury could see any conduct as "exclusionary" or "anticompetitive" as long as it is not obliged to say that a defendant must always market its product jointly with rivals. For example, Western Union (WU) supplied Telex service and decided to cease supplying the terminals on which messages were typed. It instructed its salespeople to try to sell its machines and to inform customers of machines made by others, including the plaintiff.[120] Its commission schedule encouraged salesmen to peddle others' terminals—to the great benefit of the plaintiff, which had no salesmen of its own. Liquidating its own machines too slowly, Western Union altered its commission schedule to encourage salesman to push its own terminals, and plaintiffs' sales fell. Plaintiff won a monopolization verdict on the ground that WU's change in its practice of aiding the plaintiff was motivated by exclusionary purposes—a desire later stated internally as one to "flush these turkeys." The change was said to be unjustified by efficiency; peddling plaintiff's machines as well as its own would maximize buyer choice.

The appeals court wisely reversed. It reasoned that WU's withdrawal from the machine market could hardly monopolize it, that punishing withdrawals of assistance to competitors would discourage such aid in the first place, and that rivals were presumably able to peddle their own machines. WU's intention to "flush these turkeys" was irrelevant once the court decided that a firm is not obliged to promote rival products. After all, long-run efficiency is generally promoted by encouraging each firm to try its best to sell its own products. That was the national policy question at stake, and the court understood that it, not the jury, should make that policy choice.[121]

---

119. Aspen Skiing Co. v. Aspen Highlands Skiing Corp., 472 U.S. 585, 596 (1985).

120. Olympia Equip. Leasing Co. v. Western Union Telegr. Co., 797 F. 2d 370 (7th Cir. 1986), cert. denied, 480 U.S. 934 (1987).

121. To similar effect was Berkey Photo v. Eastman Kodak, 603 F. 2d 263 (2d Cir. 1979), cert. denied, 444 U.S. 1093 (1980), in which Kodak was judged to be a monopolist. When Kodak introduced a new camera and distinctive film to accompany it, Berkey successfully claimed in the trial court that Kodak acted with exclusionary intent by introducing the new products without predisclosing them to Berkey. The appeals court correctly reversed, holding that requiring predisclosure was bad antitrust policy because it would reduce the return from and thus the incentive for innovation. Rather than leaving the jury to adopt the policy that innovators should share their discoveries with rivals in the guise of finding exclusionary intention, the court decided that policy question.

9.6 Conclusion

Antitrust law rests on general and vague legislation. Congress decided in 1890 that competition should be promoted but did not decide how or to what extent, delegating that task to the courts. Although it has occasionally amended the antitrust laws and retains the last word, antitrust policy is largely the product of the federal courts, supplemented in the merger area by the administration's choices as to which transactions to attack. Judicial policy-making differs from that of the other branches. Courts rule only episodically in the peculiar procedural context of the specific facts, issues, and arguments that happen to be presented to them by the government as plaintiff or by private parties promoting their own interests. Moreover, judges are further constrained by their own competence as lawyers rather than as economists framing industrial policy and by legal methods that submerge policy choices in procedural rulings and language emphasizing legal doctrine and appealing to precedent and "established law."

Yet policy choices do emerge from this stew of precedent, legal technicalities, procedural rulings, different degrees of economic sophistication, accidents of opinion writing, and occasionally clearly understood policy. It may seem remarkable that sensible policy appears so often. It would appear more often if the judges focused more consciously on the truth that many procedural rulings allowing a jury to impose liability on certain conduct amount to a policy against such conduct, and vice versa. Getting more of the policy choices out in the open would improve the process.

References

Areeda, P. 1978–. *Antitrust law.* 9 vols. to date. Boston: Little, Brown.
———. 1983. Introduction to antitrust economics. *Antitrust Law Journal* 52:523ff. (Reprinted in *Antitrust policy in transition: The convergence of law and economics,* ed. E. Fox and J. Halverson. Chicago: American Bar Association, 1984.)
Areeda, P., and L. Kaplow. 1988. *Antitrust analysis.* 4th ed. Boston: Little, Brown.
Goldman, S. 1989. Reagan's judicial legacy: Completing the puzzle and summing up. *Judicature* 72:318ff.
Kauper, R. 1984. The 1982 horizontal merger guidelines: Of collusion, efficiency, and failure. In *Antitrust policy in transition: The convergence of law and economics,* ed. E. Fox and J. Halverson. Chicago: American Bar Association.
Lande, W. 1982. Wealth transfers as the original and primary concern of antitrust: The Efficiency interpretation challenged. *Hastings Law Journal* 34:65ff.
Scherer, F. M. 1989. Merger policy in the 1970s and 1980s. In *Economics and antitrust policy,* ed. R. Larner and J. Meehan. Westport, Conn.: Greenwood.
Scherer, F. M., and D. Ross. 1990. *Industrial market structure and economic performance.* 3d ed. Boston: Houghton Mifflin.

Schwartz, L. 1979. "Justice" and the non-economic goals of antitrust. *University of Pennsylvania Law Review* 127:1076ff.

Weinstock, D. 1984. Some little known properties of the Herfindahl-Hirschman Index: Problems of translation and specification. *Antitrust Bulletin* 29:705ff.

2. *William F. Baxter*

In thinking about antitrust policy during the first Reagan administration, or any other period of time, it is important to recognize the inherent limitations that the Justice Department faces in establishing policy. I do not refer to the fact that policy is largely determined by statutes passed by Congress and by their interpretation in federal courts, although that circumstance is of course a significant constraint. Nevertheless, the statutes and their interpretation are often very vague, and ample room is left in which to move. Rather, I refer to the fact that the Antitrust Division can only bring cases and hence is only well suited to achieving changes in the direction of more, rather than less, government intervention in the marketplace. For a variety of institutional reasons, it is quite inconceivable to bring cases for the purpose of losing them.

I had thought a fair amount about these factors and the sense in which they establish a one-way ratchet that, in my opinion, has contributed substantially over the years to a pattern of meddlesome, interventionist antitrust policy, sometimes petty and mechanical as in the tie-in area, sometimes discretionary and potentially disastrous as in the concept of no-fault monopoly that characterized the old Alcoa decision and underlay the attack on IBM.

Recognizing those constraints, I was less than wildly enthusiastic when I was called by Ed Schmults [then deputy attorney general designate] in January of 1981 and asked whether I would come to Washington to discuss the possibility of becoming the next Antitrust chief.

I called back after several days, soon thereafter went East to talk with Ed and with William French Smith [then attorney general designate], and was quite forthright about my concerns and about my intentions. After describing the one-way ratchet problem, I indicated that I planned to counteract that pressure by being aggressively noisy and confrontationally critical of existing antitrust doctrine in every forum that I could get to, particularly including the congressional committees, thereby attempting to build a backfire against an ever more interventionist antitrust policy by giving the business community a glimpse of a future far less encumbered by pointless rules and roulettes. I told Schmults and Smith, neither of whom I had ever talked to before, that my immediate objectives would include the following: expeditious disposition one way or the other of both the AT&T case and the IBM case; promulgating new merger guidelines; improving the general understanding in the business community of the importance of intellectual property, trade secrets, and patents and copyrights; and increasing the alienability, and hence the value, of such property by getting rid of a variety of the absurd antitrust restrictions having to do with licensing and with ownership transfers. Finally, I indicated that I would devote substantial resources to developing an amicus program in which the Justice Department would file supporting briefs on the side of antitrust defendants in private antitrust litigation and attempt to persuade the courts, when we perceived it to be the case, that the rules being advocated by the plaintiff were in fact destructive of rather than supportive of competition. This last program, I predicted during that first interview, would be highly controversial. I emphasized that I had no interest in coming to Washington to be an assistant attorney general in the tradition of my predecessors. I asked them to find someone else unless they felt they would be comfortable with the execution of the agenda I had suggested. And I told them that I would stay as long but no longer than the moment that further progress on that agenda was possible.

Only a few days passed after my return from Washington to Stanford before Bill Smith called and asked me to come on. I moved quickly and was sitting in the office by late January, although I did not complete the relocation of my shell-shocked family until late March and was not officially confirmed until early April.

I will deal with the AT&T case first because it was the very first item to which I turned. Some of you will recall that a tentative consent decree had been negotiated between the Department of Justice (DOJ) and AT&T late in 1980. I will refer to it as the "December decree." Judge Green had declined to accept it, in view of the then-impending change in administration, unless the new administration expressed satisfaction with it. I studied that proposed consent decree in my first weeks at the Justice Department. I rejected it.

I have not gone back, proximate to the time of this presentation, to review the terms of the December decree. I remember that my reaction to it then was that it was more nearly punitive and symbolic than sensibly addressed to the underlying structural problem of the telecommunications industry. The decree would have divested some but not all of Western Electric from AT&T. It required the divestiture of a few, but only a few, of the Bell operating companies (BOCs). But it failed to take the one step that I regarded as structurally crucial, namely, to separate the inescapably regulated local exchange activity, a natural monopoly resting on the pervasive scale economies present in the local loops, from every other species of activity save only those activities functionally proximate to the local loops that had to be included in the basic operating companies to achieve efficient operation. Assuming that there had been a violation of Section 2 of the Sherman Act, it was clear to me that a sensible remedy called for divestiture of the local exchange portion of the network, with the cut being made above the level of a class 5 switch and no higher in the switching hierarchy than the class 4 switch. But I wanted to review the evidence on the merits with respect to the question of substantive violation before making any response if I could. Judge Green had insisted that he have an answer to the acceptability of the December consent decree by the end of March and that litigation was to resume the first week in April unless he had an affirmative answer. My request for additional time was denied. I then communicated a negative answer regarding the decree, and we went back to trial.

I reviewed the evidence bearing on the merits as quickly as I could, although more and more distractions were consuming my time. In particular, intracabinet warfare was being waged by Secretary of Defense Caspar Weinberger and Secretary of Commerce Malcolm Baldrige against my stated intention to go forward with the trial in the AT&T case. I will never be certain whether I was helped or hurt by the fact, but both the assistant attorney general and the deputy attorney general had found it necessary to recuse themselves in the AT&T case and thus were completely out of the loop in the running battle between me, Weinberger, and Baldrige, a battle that continued through the summer and autumn of 1981. Basically, they wanted me to drop or delay the case, ostensibly so that the Congress could "work its will." My position was that there was no reasonable prospect that the Congress was ever going to get together on any legislation, that the judge would not permit delay, and that, if I were to drop the case, it would cause a political stink that would damage the credibility of the administration at its outset. I concurred in the proposition that the call was properly one for the White House and told them that I was quite willing to drop the case if they would simply persuade the president of the rightness of their views and have him instruct me in writing to dismiss the case. No such written instruction ever arrived. They wanted me to take the political heat for their policy call, and I made it clear that I was not going to do that. This fencing went on through the summer of 1981. In response to pressure from those two departments, and in an effort to strike a cooperative posture toward the Congress, I submitted two proposed amendments to the pending legislation, amendments that because known in Washington as "Baxter One" and "Baxter Two." That performance, I confess, was rather disingenuous: I had absolutely no expectation that the Congress would ever find either of the two amendments acceptable. And I intended the amendments more as a tutorial on what the AT&T problem really was than as serious legislative proposals.

As early as April 1981, I had told AT&T, in response to an inquiry from its general counsel, Howard Trienens, what I would regard as a satisfactory consent decree on the basis of which I would be willing to settle and dismiss the case. I told them that my terms were the surgical separation of the local exchange activity as described in the preceding paragraph. He smiled and confessed that he would not even bother carrying that answer back to his client because his client would find it totally unacceptable. I smiled and told him that my proposal had one enormous advantage to AT&T: I proposed to let AT&T work out all business and financial aspects of its own reorganization subject to the basic architectural constraints that I had enumerated. I said that I thought that AT&T would find that far preferable to having Judge Green dictate the reorganization as he surely would when the government won the case, as I expected we would.

In September, Judge Green ruled on a motion to dismiss at the end of the government's case, and his opinion made it clear that, in his view, the government was winning the factual battle hands down. AT&T and the government prepared to resume litigation in January 1982, hearing AT&T's evidence. As those preparations went on, my proposed consent decree apparently began to look better to AT&T, and, in December, Howard phoned to ask whether we might talk about it once more. We started drafting a decree. Negotiations continued furiously for several weeks over the question of the precise point in the network hierarchy where the cut between local and long distance would be made. AT&T wanted to make the cut immediately above the class 5 switch. That would dictate that rival long-distance carriers interface with the local exchange carriers at tens of thousands of nodes all over the United States. I wanted a greater concentration of traffic to occur while it remained in the hands of the local exchange carriers (LECs) and wanted the cut to occur closer to the class 4 switch. We eventually arrived at a compromise that neither of us thought very satisfactory. The agreement was announced on 8 January 1982.

Before dropping the topic of AT&T, I would like to explain that there are two distinct forms of misbehavior in which the predivestiture AT&T had the capacity and the incentive to engage and, in my view, had in fact engaged. One of the two operates through self-dealing. It is the pattern of cross-subsidization that Phillip Areeda outlines nicely in his background paper. In the context of central office switches, prototypically, AT&T charges the regulated local exchange carrier too much for the switch, raises local telephone rates to cover those costs, and banks the profit outside the scope of state regulation at the switch manufacturing level of Western Electric. If the local regulator is sufficiently obtuse, the effectiveness of regulation is totally subverted as the integrated company syphons all consumer surplus out from under the demand curve for local telephone service. If the local regulator is somewhat more astute, it insists on regulating the rate of return for Western Electric as well as for the local exchange carrier. Many states had taken this course. The result is to extend the span of incentive deadening regulation to a much greater slice of GNP than is dictated by the natural monopoly circumstance that gives rise to the need for regulation.

The second form of misbehavior is rather more subtle and causes the dollars to flow in the opposite direction. For example, it might occur when there is a substantial demand for a technologically new application: for example, the airlines need a real-time, on-line, semiprivate network connecting airline offices and travel agencies all over the United States to operate a reservation system that is capable of yielding instant information on a seat-by-seat basis as to what is vacant and what is sold. For the long-distance segments of this proposed network, the airlines might be able to go to several competing carriers. But, in order to reach the local airlines sales offices and the thousands of travel agents, the network must terminate through the local exchange in every city in the United States. If the local exchange will not interface with any long-distance carrier except an affiliated carrier, justifying its refusal with a complicated story about interface intricacies and economies of vertical integration, then the integrated enterprise is able to construct entry barriers at the potentially competitive long-distance level, and it is able to charge monopoly prices for the service to the airlines, thereby causing the airline ticket prices to be too high. The monopoly profits are now flowed *to* the local exchange entities, where they serve to subsidize residential phone rates. Since most members of the local Public Utilities Commission will in fact be running for attorney general if not governor of their states, this is a very popular maneuver. Unlike the first mode of misbehavior, to which the local Public Utilities Commission will be hostile although not necessarily effectively so, this second form of misbehavior will reliably enlist the local PUC as an ally. Although, in my judgment, both forms of misbehavior were being carried on by AT&T, in quantitative terms the second was vastly more significant and involved billions of dollars of misallocation. A very substantial part of local exchange costs was being born by potential competitive, but entry blocked areas of activity, primarily long-distance services.

One could, of course, regard this as a matter of common costs to which Ramsey pricing would be an appropriate reaction. But the patterns of pricing that were observable were nowhere near Ramsey. Quite the contrary, the least elastic demands were present at the local loop level.

The AT&T case consumed perhaps 35 percent of my time during the year 1981. The IBM case consumed another 35 percent. As soon as I had determined that I was unwilling to accept the December decree in AT&T and that the factual evidence made the case substantively sound, I sent the AT&T litigators off to battle and turned to a substantive review of the IBM case. I found the records and the documents that had been assembled totally intimidating. There was no reasonable prospect that I could get through any substantial fraction of that material, however long I remained in Washington. A few meetings with the government litigation team revealed that it was infused with inappropriate zeal and exhibited total insensitivity to the problem of antitrust inhibition of vigorous competition. It could not be relied on for objective evaluation. I decided to approach substantive evaluation by scheduling a series of seminars on particular issues. Friday afternoons were set aside for the purpose, or perhaps it was every second Friday afternoon. The government litigation team and the IBM litigation team (Cravath, Swaine & Moore) each were to submit, by the immediately preceding Wednesday, a memorandum containing references to documents and to the trial record regarding some major fact issue: for example, what was the relevant market, what was IBM's share, did IBM misbehave in the pricing of the 360–90 machine, did IBM misbehave in modifying its CPU interface to accommodate a new IBM disc drive when the consequence was greatly to complicate the interface problems of a competitive disc drive, etc.

I am no longer able to recall and to report the precise factual conclusions that I reached on these various issues. My basic conclusion was that the government was right on only a few of them and that a few was not enough. The government was probably correct that the relevant market during the complaint period was something like "large size, general business purpose, data-processing machines," although one did not have to look very far forward to see the contours of that market being effectively assailed. And surely IBM did have, and had had for a long time, a very large fraction of that market. But unless Section 2 was to be regarded as creating a status offense, there was no violation unless significant instances of socially undesirable behavior could be proved. And instances of such misbehavior by IBM were not supported by the trial record. I take as an example one fact episode that was regarded by the government as one of its most damning: predatory pricing of the 360–90 machine. Yes, IBM had lost money on the 360–90 machine, but it did not follow, as the government seemed to think it did, that IBM pricing of that machine was predatory. The 360–90 was by conscious design a highly experimental machine through which IBM hoped to enter the supercomputer market. Its costs were in major part research and development costs, with substantial transferability to other existing machines and to machines unbuilt. Most important, IBM never succeeded in selling more than a handful of the machines, even at the low prices to which government objection was taken. Meanwhile, the supposed victims of the predatory scheme were successfully selling machines in vastly greater numbers. As an example of predation, it was pathetic.

When the series of seminars had come to an end and I had reviewed my notes, it was quite clear to me that the case was substantially at its end and should be dismissed. The only litigation step that remained was to submit proposed findings of fact to the judge. One approach that I might have taken was to let the case run its course in the hopes that the judge would reach the same conclusion I had, namely, that the case should be dismissed because the government had not proved what it had to prove.

Had I thought that outcome a reasonable prospect, I probably would have followed that path. As chief of the government effort, I could have accepted the outcome gracefully and given an endless series of speeches on why the judge was really right and why good competition policy required the government to prove far more than it had proved.

But I was dreadfully confident that that was not to be the outcome. The record revealed with unmistakable clarity that the judge, already well past retirement age, planned to run out his career managing the IBM case; furthermore, he had developed an intense and often quite undisguised hatred for at least one member of the IBM trial team. The problem was not that the government was about to lose the IBM case but that it was about to win it at the trial level, a result that would be followed by an appeal by IBM to the Second Circuit, an appeal I thought almost certainly successful. Then, in 1984 or 1985, the parties would find themselves back in the federal district court, before the same judge, if he was then still alive, dealing with a remand order from the Second Circuit, at which point the record in the case would be absolutely irrelevant to the current status of the data-processing industry. I dismissed it myself on 8 January 1982.

I am painfully conscious of the frequency with which I have been using the first-person singular. That usage is verbally economical but quite unjustified. I had three magnificent assistants whom I had brought to the Antitrust Division with me, two of whom had been my own students, a third the student of one of my closest friends, a professor at the University of Chicago, who had recommended each of us to the other. Tad Lipsky, a Stanford Ph.D. candidate in economics and a law school graduate who had been my teaching assistant and on whose dissertation committee I had served, was with me and helped me at each step of the way through the entire IBM matter. Ron Carr, a graduate of the Chicago Law School and one of the most intelligent and sensible lawyers with whom I have ever worked, was largely responsible for the result in the AT&T case and took the laboring oar in overseeing the corporate reorganization. Tyler Baker, another of my research assistants at Stanford, was the principal draftsman of the Merger Guidelines, to which I will eventually come.

A third matter to which I gave some attention in the early months of 1981 was the problem posed by antitrust subversion of the value of intellectual property. One of the most intellectually arid, judicially irresponsible, and, in my view, quantitatively significant of antitrust errors has been its treatment of the competition/intellectual property interface. Intellectual property, and the legislative decision to confer exclusivity on owners of intellectual property, represents a judgment where the long-run dynamic gains from rewarding its creation exceed the short-run static losses that are associated with the time-limited phenomenon of exclusivity. That there is a trade-off between these long-run and short-run phenomena is sufficiently obvious that one would suppose the courts would not have regarded as cosmic perception their own discovery of a tension between antitrust and the short-run dynamic characteristics of intellectual property; but they did, and they deduced from their perception the conclusion that intellectual property must be narrowly confined. Especially in the hands of the Warren Court and Justices Black and Douglas in particular, narrow confinement often meant total emasculation. And one particular line of emasculation involved the elimination of practicable licensing possibilities.

Intellectual property, like any other information, is inherently intangible. Once the information is developed and comprehended, an incremental application of the information in one more useful context to produce one more unit of output has a marginal cost approaching zero, and, typically, it is not an observable event. For these reasons, the problem of drafting royalty clauses in intellectual property licenses is a difficult one. If the licensor is to capture some reasonable proportion of the surplus under the demand curve for his property, he must be able to charge more to those who use the idea in applications having lofty derived demand curves and less in applications where the derived demand curves are more modest. And, in any particular application, appropriation is significantly enhanced if the owner is able to charge more to those who use the idea more intensely and achieve with it greater value added than he charges to those who use it less intensely and achieve less.

These objectives require metering devices of one kind or another. If the invention is a new machine, royalties based on the revolutions the machine makes each month may be an entirely satisfactory device. Of course, it requires a tamper-proof revolution counter and a monthly visit by the meter reader and thus is an expensive counting device. The social costs of metering may be greatly reduced if the patentee can require that the user of a patented stapling machine buy all his staples from the patentee (or the patentee's nominee). Standard judicial doctrine looks at such an instance and leaps to the absurd conclusion that the patentee is attempting to monopolize staples. It matters not whether the number of staples demanded for use in conjunction with the machine is orders of magnitude smaller than the total number of staples produced and sold in the relative market.

There are a variety of contexts, particularly involving process patents and combination patents, in which identification of a satisfactory counting device is, at best, challenging. By holding that the licensor of a process patent "is attempting to extend the patent beyond the legal boundaries of his monopoly," the courts have held that he may not base his royalty on the output of the process because, it is said, the output is not subject to the exclusivity feature patent. It is quite sensible for the courts to be alert to reject any effort by a patentee to extend the scope of exclusivity to products or activities not covered by the claims of the patent. But no such extension of claims of exclusivity are involved in the cases to which I refer; rather, there is a confusion between the problem of extending claims of exclusivity and the problem of basing the royalty on a product or activity admittedly not within the realm of exclusivity. There can be no conceivable objection to using, as a royalty counting device, some palpable object or operation that is a strong complement to the exclusively held abstract idea.

It is sometimes said with a straight face that we should insist that the patentee base his royalty obligation as narrowly as possible on the patented idea because this will facilitate substitution in the production process of other resources for incremental uses of the exclusively held idea and thus increase the elasticity of demand for the idea itself. It is not clear why anyone would advocate substituting resources with positive marginal social costs for resources without marginal social costs or why, in the face of legislative creation of an intellectual property system, it is thought to be a good idea to minimize the returns to creativity.

In the 1970s, the Justice Department had industriously gathered up nine instances of these enfeebling inanities and bundled them into a policy statement that became known in the industry as the "nine no-nos." The DOJ announced that it would proudly bring antitrust actions against intellectual property licenses that contained one or more of these nine perfectly benign practices; DOJ declared that each of the practices was illegal per se. In the spring of 1981, we issued a policy statement repudiating the "nine no-nos" and attempted to explain why such devices were frequently useful and efficient devices for minimizing transaction costs and maximizing returns to creativity, usually without any increase in the static deadweight loss associated with the claim to exclusivity.

But it was not clear then, and it is not clear now, how much good the repudiation did. It is one thing to promise that the Justice Department will not proceed against licenses that have those characteristics; it is quite another to be able to give assurances that private parties will not do so. Although I think that the analysis is now understood by most attorneys who practice in intellectual property areas, many of them, probably most of them, still abide by the "nine no-nos" for entirely sensible reasons. Some thirteenth-best royalty-counting device is available, and its use carries assurance that corporate counsel (substantially all patent licenses are drafted by in-house counsel) will not be embarrassed by a subsequent judicial decision holding that his license constitutes an antitrust violation or, at best, a "misuse" of the intellectual property. The impact of the inferior revenue mechanism on returns may be substantial, but at least it is a great deal less obvious. And, of course, if returns are too greatly diminished, there is always the alternative of abandoning the practice of licensing entirely.

This problem is an extreme instance of the one-way-ratchet limit on influence.

Yet another undertaking on which we started in the months immediately after our arrival at the Justice Department was the drafting of the Merger Guidelines. I viewed this task as one of exceptional importance. But I also knew that, because of the other problems then on my desk, I probably would not turn to it for a year or more. Accordingly, I decided to appoint a committee chaired by Tyler Baker to create an initial draft and to solicit comment on it. I told Tyler that the draft was to spell out the process of market definition, to use a measure of concentration that had a richer content than the four-firm concentration ratio, to deal with the problem of entry, and to deal with the problem of efficiencies. In my view, the document produced by Tyler and his colleagues represents the most important contribution to the general welfare by the Antitrust Division in recent history.

Prior to the Celler-Kefauver Amendments of 1950, there was no merger control law in the United States. Mergers could be reached, it is true, under Section 1 of the Sherman Act as "agreements in restraint of trade," but the courts used that power with great restraint during the first half century of the Sherman Act's existence. It is sometimes said that Section 7 of the 1914 Clayton Act was intended by the Congress to be a merger control law, but it was not; it was intended, for reasons that are obscure, to limit the use of the holding company structure. (I take particular note of this fact because the error, which is widespread, has crept into the background paper prepared by Areeda, although I know from his other writings that he does not disagree with the judgment that I have expressed in the text.) It is entirely clear that the Congress, in passing the 1950 amendments to Section 7, was articulating a policy preference that a merger control regime both more restrictive and more encompassing in its scope of inquiry be executed by the enforcement agencies and by the courts.

Congress got what it asked for, in spades. The Antitrust Division brought a sequence of absurd cases starting with the Brown Shoe decision, where a vertical acquisition by a 4 percent manufacturer of a 1½ percent distributor was held unlawful notwithstanding that the market at each functional level was wholly without concentration. The Supreme Court opinion left the lower courts without effective guidance as to relevant criteria.

The Philadelphia Bank case halted a merger that probably should have been stopped, and the opinion articulated a somewhat more reasonable standard, suggesting that a merger between two firms whose market shares in any relevant market summed to 30 percent was presumptively illegal. But, although we learned that a sum of 30 percent was too much, there was no suggestion of what was not too much, and Brown Shoe was cited with approval. The Philadelphia Bank case was shortly followed by a series of intellectually dishonest opinions that manipulated market definition so as to produce market shares that summed to 30 percent, and they, in turn, were followed finally by the Von's Grocery case, involving the merger of two 4 percent grocery chains. That merger was held illegal because the market was exhibiting a "trend toward concentration," the number of firms having fallen over a period of eleven years from 5,365 to 3,818.

These developments occurred in the twenty-five years immediately subsequent to the Second World War. The U.S. economy was unchallenged by rivals. Western Europe and Japan were rebuilding from wartime devastation. Eastern Europe and the Soviet Union faced not only the rebuilding problem but also the overwhelming handicap of command-and-control modes of economic organization. If this line of merger cases was imposing substantial inefficiency on the U.S. economy, and I believe that it was and continued to do so well into the 1980s, there was not, at the date of the cases I have mentioned, any standard that would furnish objective support for that proposition. At least in retrospect it seems clear that we were saddled with an absurdly restrictive merger policy, toward horizontal mergers in particular but toward vertical mergers to a lesser degree, from the mid-1960s onward.

During those same years, the corporate community became convinced that management was a science transcending the industrial characteristic of that which was to be managed. If one could run a steel company, one could run a violin company. No doubt a variety of nonlegal forces contributed to this mind-set: the rapidly increasing utility of the computer, given the development of a general operating system that allowed applications programs to be written in higher-level languages; the enormous increase in the efficiency of communications and the availability of semiprivate networks; and perhaps the infusion into corporate ranks of tens of thousands of M.B.A.s who had never seen a factory floor.

The excessively restrictive merger laws combined with the previously mentioned forces to produce an enormous wave of conglomeration in the U.S. economy. It became clear eventually that management skills were not as ubiquitously transferable as had been supposed. The conglomerates, as a group, did rather badly. As international competition from Western Europe and Japan intensified, this conclusion became ever more dramatically evident in corporate financial reports. We are still emerging from the conglomeration wave, and deconglomeration implies respecialization and hence horizontal mergers. My immediate purpose in writing the Merger Guidelines was to facilitate the movement in the direction of deconglomeration. I had no particular preconception as to how loose merger standards should be beyond a tutored intuition that one generally need not worry about structure in a market that had eight or ten or more firms of roughly comparable size.

The Merger Guidelines have been criticized for being too permissive and for being too restrictive. I fully expected the first line of criticism. The Guidelines were substantially more permissive than the body of case law that I was attempting to alter. They were more permissive not primarily in the size of the market shares that were permitted to combine: a change in the Herfindahl-Hirschman Index (HHI) of 100 points corresponds to a merger between two 7 percent firms, and 7 percent is only 175 percent as large as the "two 4 percent firms" standard that appeared in the 1968 Justice Department Guidelines. The sense in which the new Guidelines were dramatically more permissive lay rather in the level of market concentration prerequisite to viewing a merger as a problem at all. The prerequisite of a relatively highly concentrated industry was a point that the Brown Shoe line of cases had missed almost entirely. Anticipating that the criticism would come from that side of the spectrum, the safe-harbor threshold of 1,000 points on the HHI was selected as much as a political anchorage to windward as because anyone thought that nicely round number was just right. I will comment on criticism from the opposite side, mostly unanticipated, hereafter.

For me, the two most difficult problems posed by the Merger Guidelines were the provisions dealing with recognition of efficiencies and with the failing firm problem. The efficiencies problem was primarily an empirical one. I was convinced that a little bit of efficiency outweighs a whole lot of market power. But, if the Department took the position that an expectation of cost savings could offset an expectation that market power was being created—note that the analytic structure of Section 7 is inherently ex ante—the cost savings would be promised in every individual case. I expected the Justice Department's error rate in evaluating those claims to be very high. Selecting the substantive rule that will result in minimizing the sum of type one and type two errors in a context such as this one is very difficult. My own judgment as to how that might best be done was to adopt a permissive merger standard so that one worried about the generation of market power only when concentration was substantial and market shares were large, thus permitting efficiencies to be attained without ever addressing their presence or magnitude and, having done that, to deny recognition of claims of efficiency in the remaining cases except when the claim was of substantial magnitude and, atypically, could be shown clearly and convincingly. Hence, the initial version of the efficiency provision was, on its face, relatively hostile to such claims. The efficiencies provision is one of several in the 1982 Guidelines that was substantially rewritten in the 1984 Guidelines, but it seems doubtful to me that the substantive change is as great as the verbal change.

A failing firm defense is necessary because it is obvious that it is never desirable, as a matter of economic policy, to cause productive assets to be consigned to the scrap heap or to be moved to new areas of activity where their value is significantly less than the value in their initial activity. If a firm is truly failing in the sense that it is about to abandon a field of activity, then, provided that the assets will be used for some level of production in the hands of new owners, it is better that they be acquired and used even if their acquirors, post-merger, have a 100 percent market share. Prices cannot be higher or output lower in the market if, instead, the assets are removed from production entirely.

The more difficult problem arises not when there is one potential buyer but when there are several, who offer a range of prices. One must then entertain the hypothesis that the high bidder sees incremental value in the assets not because of their productive potential but because, secure from the hands of others who might use them intensively, the assets create market power. What substantive rules can channel assets, under those circumstances, into the hands of the bidder who would use them to produce the largest output?

The obvious difficulty of that factual question and the institutional unsuitability of the Antitrust Division to provide the answer have deterred any serious suggestion that the problem be approached directly. Rather, the law has attempted to cope with the problem by asking whether, with respect to any particular bidder for such assets, there is some other "less competitively offensive" potential buyer; and, to advance that inquiry, it has imposed the procedural requirement that the seller attempt to shop the assets to competitively less offensive buyers.

But one cannot seriously suppose that these issues would be satisfactorily resolved by requiring that assets be transferred to that bidder who has the smallest market share so long as his bid exceeds scrap value by a dollar. If the industry is sufficiently concentrated to pose a merger problem, and if market shares are sufficiently substantial to cross the size of transaction safe harbor, it does not seem tenable to insist that the seller accept the lowest bid on the basis of the presumption that all higher bids reflect not productivity but market power aspirations.

The problem is further compounded by the great difficulty in knowing whether the seller has really shopped the assets to "less competitively offensive buyers" in good faith. If the seller has an offer he regards as satisfactory from one company, he has a strong incentive to assure that no lower bid be forthcoming from any other. The seller's investment banker perceives his client's objective without receiving detailed instructions, and, when the assets are placed with him for sale, it would be an incompetent investment banker indeed who could not go through the motions of contacting potential buyers without success. The value to the investment banker of the patronage of the seller will almost invariably exceed any "success premium" that the Justice Department insists be made a part of the investment banker's reward structure. If the Justice Department attempts vertical integration into investment banking, it is not likely to be a successful peddler: he who receives a cold call from the Justice Department has every reason to expect that he is being asked to buy a role in a lawsuit as well as a bundle of assets.

No Guideline change was in the 1984 version, but I do not believe that that fact reflects satisfaction with the current resolution of the problem.

The only other policy initiative that seems to me to deserve mention is one particular offshoot of the amicus program. We did indeed intrude ourselves into a number of private lawsuits, and we filed briefs in opposition to one party or the other who was asserting a position that we regarded as seriously wrong but nevertheless had some prospect of succeeding, either because it was supported by precedent or because it had enough superficial plausibility to bedazzle the district judge involved. One particular theme in that general campaign of law purification was an effort to harmonize the rules with respect to resale price maintenance, or vertical price fixing, with the rest of the law of vertical arrangements.

After the Supreme Court's decision in the Sylvania case, substantially all vertical arrangements, but not resale price maintenance, were held to be subject to a rule of reason. That, as a practical matter, meant that they were OK unless someone was able to show that, because of the market context, the vertical arrangement had the potential for aggravating a horizontal problem in a concentrated market. That rarely was the case.

But, as to resale price maintenance, the situation was more complex. The Supreme Court had held, back in 1911, that vertical price arrangements had precisely the same consequences and were objectionable for precisely the same reasons as horizontal price fixing. Hence, they were subject to the same *per se* restrictions. And the courts have repeated this nonsense over the intervening years.

During the Depression, Congress legalized resale price maintenance (RPM) under certain circumstances, and that legalization remained in effect until the mid-1970s. In 1975, Congress repealed that conditional legalization, and resale price maintenance was understood by all to be restored to the state of the law reflected in the old Dr. Miles case. It was illegal *per se.*

But, until Sylvania, vertical market divisions and vertical customer allocations were also illegal *per se;* and no one seriously doubted that the court had the power to move them into the rule of reason category pursuant to its generally recognized authority to invent and refurbish competition law within the gaping interstices of existing legislation.

Was the power of courts to reinterpret the law as it pertained to vertical price fixing any less? Yes, some argued, it was less. In 1975, Congress eliminated the conditional legalization and quite clearly intended to put the practice back into *per se* illegality from whence it had come. Yes, all conceded that. But that didn't really answer the question. Nothing in the 1975 legislation indicated that Congress intended both to put RPM back in the *per se* illegal category and to freeze its status, removing this particular feature of antitrust law from the interpretive freedom of the courts. For some reason, the distinction between returning resale price maintenance to a *per se* status over which courts retained discretionary interpretive freedom and freezing it in a category with respect to which there was no interpretive freedom was a distinction that proved difficult to explain to a large number of politicians.

Spray-Rite v. Monsanto was one of the private cases into which we intruded. Monsanto manufactured an agricultural herbicide that had to be applied just so in order to work properly, and it had placed a great deal of emphasis in its own marketing efforts on equipping its dealers to give tutorials to the ultimate farmer users. Monsanto also clearly discouraged price competition among its dealers, perhaps in an effort to force them to compete along a more service-oriented parameter of rivalry. In any event, it refused to renew Spray-Rite's dealership after competitive dealers had complained of Spray-Rite's price cutting. The court of appeals affirmed a poorly supported jury finding that the refusal to renew was pursuant to a conspiracy with the reporting dealers to set resale prices. In doing so, it announced a new evidentiary rule: if there are complaints by competitive dealers about the plaintiff dealer's price cutting, and if, subsequent to such complaints, the manufacturer terminates the dealer, that constitutes sufficient evidence of a vertical price fixing agreement. Unhappy with this *post hoc ergo propter hoc* approach to the problem, we seized on the case as a vehicle to attack the *per se* rule of Dr. Miles.

Elimination of the old *per se* rule is important for several reasons. Most obviously, there are a variety of circumstances under which a manufacturer will find it cost effective to freeze price at the distribution level in order to stimulate rivalry among its distributors on some other parameter, usually service related. Second, the continued existence of the rule seriously interferes with the free flow of communication between a manufacturer and his distributors. A manufacturer's distributors serve as his eyes and ears in the marketplace, and he is dependent in important ways on the information that flows back from him. If the dealers must be cautioned that they cannot discuss competitive circumstances such as price behavior by other dealers, the value of that flow is impaired. And, since the individuals who will be party to these conversations are not legally trained, the scope of prohibition must be considerably broader than the scope of the problem for prophylactic reasons. Third, because resale price does not differ in principle from other forms of vertical restraint, and because it produces very much the same objective consequences at the downstream level, manufacturers often find it necessary to obdure the use of lawful vertical constraints out of a concern that they will give rise to circumstances that will constitute circumstantial evidence of resale price maintenance. Thus, the rule against RPM impairs the value of practices legalized in theory but not in operation by the Sylvania case.

We won at most half a victory in the Monsanto case. The court, quite properly on legal grounds, declined to address the issue of whether Dr. Miles should be overruled, finding that it had not been properly raised in the courts below. Although we did not win with respect to the holding, we won with respect to the opinion. The court recited at great length the importance of free information flows and, to protect them, articulated an evidentiary standard for showing the existence of *agreement* that, in the great majority of cases, will be difficult for plaintiffs to meet.

The final "policy effort" of my tenure was one of more symbolic than real importance, and our efforts encountered total failure. This was the effort to persuade the Federal Communications Commission (FCC) to abandon regulations adopted pursuant to motion picture industry lobbying that fenced the television networks out of the syndication market, the so-called financial syndication restriction rules. In a benighted effort of the late 1970s, the Justice Department also obtained judicial consent decrees that parallel the FCC regulations in their terms. We were fully prepared to seek the termination of the consent decrees and were fairly confident that we could have been successful in that. But there was no point in making the effort if the FCC could not be persuaded to take parallel action. Formal contacts with the FCC made it clear that that agency was prepared to end the restrictions if the administration took a clear position in favor of that course. The motion picture industry intervened at the White House, and the question was eventually decided there. To put the matter bluntly, I was invited to debate the question before the president in the Oval Office against Charlton Heston. I have lost many arguments that I should have won, but never one to so vacuous an opponent. That episode was one of several that convinced me that it was time to go home.

3. Harry M. Reasoner

Phillip Areeda has done a splendid job of describing antitrust policies in the 1980s. With that background, I have been asked to address briefly the factors that shaped antitrust policy in the 1980s from the perspective of a practitioner. My practice during the 1980s involved antitrust counseling, the trial of antitrust cases for both plaintiffs and defendants, and active participation in the American Bar Association Section of Antitrust Law, of which I served as chair in 1989–90.

In addressing this topic, I want to treat antitrust as a national competition policy to produce and protect efficient markets—a definition comprehending significantly more than the topics we often pigeonhole under the rubric of antitrust policy. I will discuss briefly what I perceive in broad terms to be the five most significant factors that shaped policy in the Reagan Era.

The Compartmentalized Approach to Competition Policy

Modern American politics is marked by compartmentalized thinking. For example, many see no intellectual tension between blanket condemnation of welfare policies and support of agricultural subsidies. This same type of compartmentalized thinking has driven our approach to competition policy and our definition of the proper sphere of antitrust. Thus, while the Reagan administration proclaimed the importance of free markets and competition, it simultaneously promoted market-distorting and anticompetitive policies. For example, so heavily did the administration's 1981 tax bill subsidize real estate investment that the Treasury would have realized a net gain if all real estate taxes had simply been abolished. Capital was diverted from productive uses. The tremendous overbuilding in real estate, the collapse of those markets, and the resultant impact on financial institutions illustrate vividly the costs of economically unsound distortion of capital markets. Yet so cabined is our approach to competition policy that no input was sought, considered, or proffered from the federal agencies responsible for competition policy (see Reasoner 1990, 65–67).[1]

Similarly, "antitrust" merger analysis is usually conducted as if the tax laws did not exist rather than often being the most important factor involved (Reasoner 1990, 66–67). Some would suggest that, viewing competition across the entire range of governmental activity, our economy ended the 1980s more circumscribed by governmental intervention than it began, particularly when the amount of trade subject to international restraints, such as "voluntary" quotas, is considered (Muris 1989, 56–57).

1. Our comparative advantage for a number of years after World War II was so great that we were not compelled to develop a sound competition policy in order to be prosperous (see *Global Competition* 1985).

The Greater Role of Economic Learning

Beginning in the late 1970s, the courts, which make much of our antitrust policy, have become increasingly receptive to economic learning.[2] The Chicago School, of course, has been an enormous influence. This has occurred both because the Chicago School espouses an intellectually elegant and coherent system and because some of its proponents have matched Saint Paul in zeal and output (see, e.g., Posner and Easterbrook 1980; and Posner 1976).[3]

Further, and perhaps most important, Chicago School adherents have expressed their views in ways that lawyers and judges think they can understand. Economic theory is persuasive to courts and lawyers only when it is accessible from their intellectual framework. Prior to the growth of a persuasive body of economic writings accessible to lawyers and judges, courts and practitioners were often prey to arguments based on the mechanical use of precedents that made no sense either in economic theory or, for that matter, from the perspective of any logical policy.

One of the most significant developments in the acceptance of economic analysis has been the publication of Areeda's great treatise, *Antitrust Law,* (1978–). It provides a comprehensive theoretical treatment of antitrust law. Its genius is that it melds economic theory with a legal analysis of cases that lawyers and judges can follow and convert into briefs and opinions. Much as Scott (1989) has informed the law of trusts and Wigmore (1985) the law of evidence, *Antitrust Law* has informed the thinking of antitrust lawyers and the courts.

The Reagan Administration's Minimalist Approach to Antitrust Policy

The 1980s began with a consensus that antitrust policy had developed a number of economically irrational excesses. In the 1960s and 1970s, terminating inefficient distributors had become a hazardous business with a spurious antitrust suit often part of the transaction costs; the tying doctrine had been taken to absurd conceptual extremes;[4] trivial mergers were attacked;[5] predatory pricing cases could be made against the price competition of new competitors with no market power;[6] conspiracy charges could be made against a single firm and its own subsidiaries.[7]

William Baxter, as the first head of the Reagan administration's Antitrust

2. See Continental T.V., Inc. v. GTE Sylvania Inc., 433 U.S. 36 (1977); and Calvani (1990).

3. Easterbrook and Posner alone are cited some 145 times in the *Index to Legal Periodicals* during the 1980s. I do not address the question of how completely Chicago School theory captures the real factors that drive behavior in our markets. For example, tax policy, which is often a critical determinant, is not often addressed. Our ability to verify empirically theories in this area is still very limited (see Bok 1960, 228, 240–47).

4. United States Steel Corp. v. Fortner Enterprises, 429 U.S. 610 (1977).

5. United States v. Von's Grocery Co., 384 U.S. 270 (1966).

6. Utah Pie Co. v. Continental Baking Co., 386 U.S. 685 (1967).

7. Perma Life Mufflers, Inc. v. International Parts Corp., 392 U.S. 134, 141–42 (1968).

Division, in a brilliant series of speeches and amicus briefs (Baxter 1984) accomplished splendid successes in antitrust reform contributing to the mitigation or elimination of many of these flaws in the law.

Unfortunately, the administration's efforts at remaking antitrust law were not limited to Assistant Attorney General Baxter's elegantly reasoned efforts. After Baxter and Attorney General William French Smith left Washington, Secretary of Commerce Malcolm Baldrige and Attorney General Ed Meese, apparently in the belief that antitrust enforcement was not important to the functioning of competitive markets, sought to diminish dramatically the role of the antitrust laws. Antitrust bashing—incredibly ignoring tax policy, monetary policy, and relative capital costs and blaming the antitrust laws for our problems in international competition—was fashionable rhetoric for administration officials throughout the remainder of the 1980s. Both the Antitrust Division and the Federal Trade Commission were reduced to approximately half their former size and resources during the 1980s (see "Report . . . on the Antitrust Division" 1990, 750, n. 2; and "Kirkpatrick Committee Report" 1989, 105).

Critical to compliance with our antitrust laws is the belief of businessmen that these laws are important and will be enforced. As with the tax laws, we depend on voluntary observance. At the end of the 1980s, most antitrust practitioners felt that the importance of antitrust compliance had been dangerously reduced in the eyes of businessmen (see "Report . . . on the Antitrust Division" 1990, 749). When divorced from populism, antitrust has no natural political constituency. Few businessmen want competition for themselves. In general, they are pleased to receive tax breaks, subsidies, quotas, and tariffs and to enjoy minimal competition. Businessmen read, not the Antitrust Division's reasoned arguments for reform, but the hyperbolic antienforcement rhetoric of Meese and Baldrige, reinforced by the cheerleading of the *Wall Street Journal.* The perceived administration hostility toward antitrust enforcement, the slashing of the enforcement agencies' budgets, and the diminution in private enforcement led many to believe that they could basically ignore the antitrust laws.[8]

The Decline of Private Enforcement of the Antitrust Laws

The effect of a perceived decline of government enforcement of the antitrust laws was accentuated by a diminution in the ability of private plaintiffs to bring suits to enforce the antitrust laws. One of the consequences of economic learning was that the courts started to move away from bright line *per se* rules of illegality and to apply economic analysis under the "rule of reason" (see Crane 1987, 16–19). When courts apply a sophisticated economic analysis in assessing practices, those that are not competitively harmful or that are even

---

8. Thus, the Conference Board thought it appropriate to hold a conference entitled "Is Antitrust Dead?" The answer, on balance, was no, but note that the question was considered worth asking.

competitively beneficial may be saved. The arguably greater precision achieved was expensive from the viewpoint of the administration of justice. A court is a very difficult, costly, and uncertain place to conduct an economic analysis. It is costly and risky for a plaintiff to try a rule of reason case, so there is a real disincentive for plaintiffs to attack any practice where the rule of reason will be applied.

Further, the standing rules were modified to narrow the class of those who can bring suit to enforce the antitrust laws.[9] Competitors, who ordinarily might be the only ones who could afford to attack a merger, were held not to have standing to do so in most circumstances.[10] Assume a merger that we can be positive will hurt consumers. Merger litigation is very resource intensive, and the resources of the Antitrust Division are limited. The Antitrust Division must carefully limit the cases it brings. It cannot begin to attack every merger. Since consumers cannot normally afford to attack mergers, restricting the ability of competitors to sue results in a serious diminution in those who are in a position to enforce the antitrust laws (see Hovenkamp 1989).

The Emphasis on Federalism

As the federal government was being perceived to leave a lacuna in antitrust enforcement, state attorneys general moved into it. The only natural political constituency of antitrust is a kind of populism. Many of these state attorneys general made emotional appeals to this constituency. It is difficult to say how much difference the increased state activity will make. Bringing traditional price-fixing suits will not make a great difference because the resources of the states are limited. However, they have moved into more significant areas. For example, seventeen states have sued in federal court in California attacking the casualty insurance industry for allegedly conspiring to eliminate pollution coverage and occurrence policies.[11] They seek to reform the way that a segment of the insurance industry is operating worldwide. The case could be very significant. Because the seventeen states have filed within the federal system, in theory at least any adjudicated result will be consistent with federal policy.

But Texas has taken the next step and done what a sophisticated result-oriented plaintiff would do. Texas did not file in federal court in California. It filed in state court in Texas.[12] If the states routinely begin to use their state court systems to bring cases of potentially national structural significance,

9. Atlantic Richfield Co. v. USA Petroleum Co., 495 U.S. 328, 110 S. Ct. 1884 (1990); ABA Antitrust Section (1984, 1988).
10. Cargill, Inc. v. Monfort of Colorado, Inc. 479 U.S. 104 (1986).
11. In re Insurance Antitrust Litigation, 723 F. Supp. 464 (N.D. Cal. 1989), appeal docketed, No. C-88–1688-WWF (9th Cir. 2 December 1989).
12. See Texas v. Insurance Services Office, Inc., 699 F. Supp. 601 (W.D. Tex. 1988) (remanding to state court).

there could be a real problem of a Balkanized competitive policy. The Supreme Court's bias is toward federalism. The Sherman Act is not broadly preemptive ("Report . . . to Review" 1990). A fractionated national policy could be particularly troublesome in the merger area. States could be motivated to attack mergers to protect local employment, local corporate headquarters, and other reasons inconsistent with efficient national markets.

As the states have become more aggressive, conflicts have developed between state and federal policy. First, and most serious, is the manipulation of state and municipal governments to create regulatory schemes that insulate industries from competition. Businesses can get immunity from the federal antitrust laws by going to the state legislature and, for example, having it create a state board of hairdressers that regulates the hairdressing market. Prices can then be raised, using the board as an effective barrier to entry and protection against antitrust attack.[13] This type of costly anticompetitive conduct has proliferated in the states. Perhaps constrained by political pressure, the state attorneys general have not shown initiative in opposing it.

Another problem is that, theoretically, if we return to an era of national litigation in the price-fixing area, a producer could be held liable both under the federal laws to the direct purchaser of the goods and under the state laws to the indirect purchaser (who purchased the same goods from the direct purchaser), so a company could wind up paying six times for damages caused by one overcharge.[14] It would be very difficult for a company to get a fair defense if faced with the *in terrorem* possibility of sextuple damages.

From a broad perspective, these five factors—compartmentalization, the ascendance of economic theory, the administration's minimalist approach, the decline of private enforcement, and the emphasis on federalism—begin to explain what developed in the area of antitrust law during the Reagan administration. In antitrust, however, as in other areas of the law, Holmes's dictum remains valid: The life of the law is not logic.

References

Areeda, P. 1978–. *Antitrust law.* 8 vols. to date. Boston: Little, Brown.

Baxter, W. 1984. A review of Antitrust Division briefs. *Journal of Reprints for Antitrust Law and Economics* 15:541ff.

Bok, D. 1960. Section 7 of the Clayton Act and the merging of law and economics. *Harvard Law Review* 74:226ff.

Calvani, T. 1990. Future direction of antitrust law enforcement. *Washburn Law Journal* 29:364ff.

Crane, M. 1987. The future direction of antitrust. *Antitrust Law Journal* 56:3ff.

---

13. Southern Motor Carriers Rate Conference v. United States, 471 U.S. 48, 62–64 (1985).
14. See California v. ARC America Corp. 490 U.S. 93, 109 S. Ct. 1661 (1989).

Global competition: The new reality. 1985. Report of the President's Commission on Industrial Competitiveness. Washington, D.C., January.

Hovenkamp, H. 1989. Antitrust's protected classes. *Records* 44:483ff.

Kirkpatrick Committee report—report of the American Bar Association Section of Antitrust Law Special Committee to Study the Role of the Federal Trade Commission. 1989. *Antitrust Law Journal* 58:43ff.

Muris. 1989. Antitrust's next decade. In *Is antitrust dead?* Research Report no. 928. New York: Conference Board.

Posner, R. 1976. *Antitrust law: An economic perspective.* Chicago: University of Chicago Press.

Posner, R., and F. Easterbrook. 1980. *Antitrust—cases, economic notes, and other materials.* 2d ed. Saint Paul: West.

Reasoner, H. 1990. The state of antitrust. *Antitrust Law Journal* 59:63ff.

Report of the ABA Antitrust Law Section Task Force on the Antitrust Division of the U.S. Department of Justice. 1990. *Antitrust Law Journal* 58:737ff.

Report of the ABA Section of Antitrust Law Task Force to Review the Supreme Court's Decision California v. ARC America Corp. 1990. *Antitrust Law Journal* 59:273ff.

Scott, A. 1989. *The law of trusts.* 6 vols. 4th ed. Boston: Little, Brown.

Wigmore, J. 1985. *Evidence in trials at common law.* 11 vols. 4th ed. Boston: Little, Brown.

Summary of Discussion

William Baxter agreed with Reasoner that Reagan administration policy had shifted to an extreme position against antitrust enforcement, but he believed that this shift did not occur under Doug Ginsburg, Baxter's successor as head of the Justice Department's Antitrust Division. He suggested that the change in tone was initiated by a separate group during the time of Ginsburg's successor. *Harry Reasoner* agreed with Baxter. *Baxter* also pointed out that the antitrust bar had *not* supported his efforts, perhaps because antitrust enforcement had made millionaires of many of them.

Phillip Areeda raised three issues. First, he said that the interaction of state and federal antitrust law is going to become an important issue in the 1990s. The Supreme Court has ducked this problem so far, but, with more intensive enforcement of State antitrust law, the question of whether state or federal antitrust law should dictate national policy will have to be faced. Second, he said that the role of economists in the development and improvement of antitrust law has become very significant and that their contributions will no doubt be enduring. Finally, he repeated the concern in his paper that so much policy-making in antitrust is left to judges, who seem often unqualified for the task. But, considering the tax policy-making process discussed in another session of the conference, he felt that turning antitrust policy back to the president and Congress might *not* be a good idea after all.

Paul Joskow thought that there had been dramatic changes in antitrust policy in the 1980s and that Baxter's three-year term had set a standard that still applies. Effectively, Baxter put up a sign in his office reading, "No More Mush." His approach to mergers, vertical restraints, and predation demonstrated that the Justice Department's role in antitrust enforcement was to look for business practices that created and enhanced market power, *not* to stomp on business behavior and organizational forms that enhanced efficiency and led to lower prices but might simultaneously have hurt some individual competitors.

Joskow's sense was that economists' role in the Justice Department increased greatly during the 1980s, perhaps at the expense of the lawyers—the lawyers were even required to take an economics course. Also, the Merger Guidelines developed by Baxter in 1982 and revised in 1984 have been influential beyond merger policy: they have refined the questions asked by the courts in antitrust analysis more generally, especially in terms of defining markets and market power.

The courts changed as well in the 1980s. As Areeda emphasized in his paper, President Reagan appointed a large number of judges, several of whom were law professors specializing in antitrust: Richard Posner, Frank Easterbrook, and Stephen Breyer. Their decisions have been very influential because they state clearly what the economic issue is and how to address it. It has been very important to other judges, for whom antitrust cases can be confusing and difficult to understand, to have some clear decisions to guide them.

Joskow thought that these changes in the courts were also important to keep in mind when evaluating the effect of Justice Department antitrust policy in the 1980s. Although the Justice Department is often criticized for not having vigorously enforced Section 7 of the Clayton Act, people do not usually mention that, while in the 1960s and 1970s the Justice Department never lost in court, now it almost never wins. The courts are simply much less receptive to the Justice Department's opposition to mergers. Further, the changes in antitrust policy due to changes in the courts are likely to be more long lasting than changes due to the actions of a particular administration.

Christopher DeMuth responded to Feldstein's earlier question about how one can account for the successes and failures of economic thinking in influencing policy. He suggested that antitrust was the area of regulation where economic thinking has had the most practical influence—because, he believed, there is very little organized interest group politics in antitrust policy. It is hard to identify a group in the economy that has a large immediate stake in either a strengthening or a relaxing of merger policy. Thus, scholarly thinking has more influence in antitrust because it enjoys more free rein than in areas such as health and safety regulation. In the one area in which there *are* groups with a clear stake in government policy—the area of restrictive distribution systems—Baxter and other reformers have had the least success.

Reasoner agreed with DeMuth in part, but suggested also that the historical way of dealing with antitrust laws has been not to try to change them but to try to get around them. Attacking the sugar trust led to sugar subsidies and sugar quotas—effectively, government cartels that are far more efficient than private cartels. Similarly, the tobacco trust was attacked, and antitrust law cannot touch the kind of subsidies received by the tobacco industry today. In cases such as these, special interest groups have taken themselves beyond the influence of antitrust laws.

James Burnley wanted to set the historical record straight on two points. First, in 1983, when the act governing the Department of Transportation's role in merger regulation was being debated, Secretary Elizabeth Dole argued that Transportation should not have the oversight responsibility on airline mergers. The Justice Department did not take an active role in the debate, whereas the airline industry took particular interest in making sure the responsibility fell on Transportation, as in the end it did.

Second, only two or three of the mergers that were approved by the DOT were questioned at all by the Justice Department. One of those was the purchase of Eastern Airlines by Texas Air, which at the time still owned New York Air. This acquisition would have created a tremendous problem on the shuttle routes, and for this reason Transportation rejected the merger. The merger was approved only on resubmission of the application after New York Air had sold its shuttle service to Pan Am.

David Stockman wondered what the harm was in those mergers.

Burnley replied that, although the Northwest-Republic merger did not result in unforeseen problems in his view, the TWA-Ozark merger did create a problem in St. Louis because those two carriers controlled an overwhelming number of gates at St. Louis under very long-term leases. The department may not have fully understood the underlying facts regarding the St. Louis airport when they reviewed that merger. He suggested that there are alternatives available to assure competition in the St. Louis market, such as converting Scott Air Force base to commercial use.

Elizabeth Bailey noted that most of the discussion had focused on economic policy from 1980 to 1987. She opened the question of how policy had changed toward the end of the decade. One case of particular interest was the Justice Department's inquiry regarding scholarship setting by academic institutions.

Areeda suggested that the Justice Department's inquiry into *tuition* setting by academic institutions is sound policy. If they are fixing tuitions, that would be a violation of antitrust laws and detrimental to the country. On the scholarship side, he believed that scholarship fixing may be perfectly lawful under antitrust law. Areeda said that the inquiry is troubling because it appears that the government has pursued its investigation without first formulating a theory. They seem to believe that a theory will emerge only after they collect the facts, but it seems more efficient to do it the other way around.

More generally, Areeda argued that the present antitrust chief, Jim Rill, is a "sound pragmatist." Rill is sensitive to the economic reforms effected by the Reagan administration but also ready to consider alternatives—ready to think, for example, that perhaps there should be restraints on leasing airline computer reservation systems. Rill may be somewhat more rigorous in enforcing the merger guidelines than his predecessors had been, but overall there does not seem to have been a fundamental change in antitrust policy in the late 1980s.

Joskow concurred, adding that there had been three minor changes under Rill. First, the power in making decisions has shifted back toward the lawyers in the Justice Department and away from the economists, a shift that is consistent with their pursuing the case against colleges without an initial theory. Second, Jim Rill has been very sensitive to the problems with the state attorneys general and has been striving to mend relations with them. Third, the Justice Department is requiring merger applicants to supply much more information so that it can abide by the Merger Guidelines as they were written.

Reasoner argued that mergers in the United States have been driven by tax law. The government has created an arbitrage situation where one can change equity into debt and obtain tax advantages. The double taxation of corporate dividends is a great mistake because it biases corporate finance toward heavy debt, which can cripple the competitive staying power of U.S. companies, especially during recessions. The United States went through a period in which leveraged buyouts (LBOs) changed hundreds of millions of dollars from equity to debt, and, during this recession, the public is having to pay for that.

Lionel Olmer asked Baxter to comment on the role of the Justice Department in intervening on behalf of IBM with the European Community (EC) and to comment generally on the application of our antitrust laws outside domestic territory.

Baxter responded that the IBM situation arose from an EC requirement that IBM engage in "predisclosure." Predisclosure is a "nutty notion," originating in the 1970s, that large and successful companies that made products that were subject to competition in complementary markets had an obligation to predisclose technological changes in the central good. This predisclosure would allow the competitors of the complementary goods to be ready to meet the new product in the marketplace the day it was unveiled. Kodak, for example, had an obligation to predisclose new film technology so that competitive makers of cameras could have a headstart making cameras that used the new film. In the IBM case, the EC felt that IBM had an obligation to predisclose new technology with respect to CPUs in order to benefit the European manufacturers of peripheral equipment. This action was apparently prompted by the CEO of Memorex.

Areeda added that no court had adopted predisclosure yet, and *Baxter* concurred.

Litan noted that, while the courts and the legal profession have undergone a revolution in the adoption of economic analysis, the International Trade Commission's (ITC) decisions over the 1980s did not display a similar trend. Only a few commissioners applied economic reasoning in their decisions. Although the ITC considers many of the same issues, such as defining the relevant market, there are virtually no references to the antitrust revolution in the ITC literature.

Paula Stern agreed that different members of the International Trade Commission have displayed different tolerances for economic analysis. She noted that the ITC had heard presentations from the Federal Trade Commission and the Justice Department in the steel cases of the early 1980s. These presentations had failed to provide clear links, however, between the material presented and its implications for the ITC's decisions.

Stern asked for specific comment on the steel antitrust cases of the early 1980s, raising the question of whether different outcomes of the Justice Department's review of those cases would have been better for the industry.

Baxter recalled the LTV/Republic merger, which Secretary of Commerce Malcolm Baldrige had supported but which Baxter had opposed. About two weeks after Baxter left office, Baldrige prevailed, and the merger was approved. *William Niskanen* clarified that the most immediate action after Baxter left was a disapproval of the merger issued by Paul McGrath. The decision was later reversed after Baldrige and the president made public remarks critical of the first decision.

Martin Feldstein asked the discussants to address the rationale underlying the decision.

Baxter explained that, even if LTV was viewed as a failing firm, it was too big to be allowed to merge and form a larger company. Further, he argued, there were less offensive purchasers available.

Stockman noted the context of the LTV/Republic merger. It was approved in the spring of 1984, when there was a massive inflow of steel imports, both because the dollar was so high and in anticipation of protectionist trade policy. Steel imports represented 26 percent of the market, while the merging of LTV and Republic would have joined pieces holding 9 percent and 11 percent, respectively. Since that time, however, Republic LTV has been broken down into four companies, two of which are owned by the Japanese. Stockman asked what the long-term harm of the merger could be, given the context of such strong world competition.

Baxter responded that he had been urged by the White House to view steel as a world market, despite the likelihood of quotas being imposed. He had argued that the existence or importance of a world market depends on the amount of protectionism in place. For example, in a protected domestic market where quotas are determined as a percentage of domestic output, attempts by domestic producers to restrict output and raise price will simultaneously create a decrease in imports. In this situation, there is not a competitive world market.

Areeda added that now, ten years after the LTV merger, we know that it had no anticompetitive effects and that no market power was achieved, as demonstrated by the split-up of the company. But this does not mean that disapproving the merger would have been wrong at the time. For all kinds of decisions, the question is whether they are wise at the time they are made, so in antitrust one has to judge the market at the time a merger is proposed. If one believes that a merger consolidates a substantial part of the market or makes tacit coordination between oligopolists more likely, the government should prevent that. The legal standard says that the purpose of the antimerger statute is to prevent *potentially* dangerous transactions. The fact that a merger turns out all right does not necessarily bear on the wisdom of the initial decision.

Stockman countered that the outcome was predictable. At the time of the LTV/Republic merger decision, the steel market had 50 million tons of overcapacity, imports were large, and the domestic industry was unraveling. The structure of the industry at that time said that no possible market power could be accumulated or sustained.

Stockman said that, in his experience buying companies, he had looked at 200 potential acquisitions since 1987. Of the 200 companies, 175 claimed to have a market share of 45 percent or more, and this can be completely true depending on the way the market is defined: if you define the market as your product, you have a 100 percent market share. However, there is capital and technology today that can bear on almost any tradable goods market from around the world. Consequently, one cannot find a market where market power can be established and sustained for any appreciable period of time. He concluded that antitrust doctrine is obsolete.

Areeda said there was an element of truth in Stockman's argument. There is a great deal of competition and substitutability, so entry is not always blocked. Antitrust law is supposed to take these considerations into account, but a case-by-case review would really be needed to argue the point. His larger objection to Stockman's point was that Stockman comes close to saying that we don't need antitrust law because all markets "take care of themselves" in the long run. Areeda is not as confident that this happens, and, further, much injury can result before anticompetitive distortions are ultimately corrected.

Baxter agreed with Areeda and added that the right question is not whether entry is possible but whether the conditions of the industry make entry economically attractive. It really does not matter how contestable a market is if there are no profits there to attract new investment. Particularly in an industry like steel, which was in very serious financial difficulty, one was unlikely to see entry as a practical matter. Therefore, how easy it was to enter the steel industry under those circumstances was quite irrelevant.

Reasoner disagreed with Stockman, arguing that many companies do possess market power. *Niskanen* suggested that perhaps the proper test is not whether antitrust policy will do good but whether it is likely to do more good than harm. On that question, he believed, the jury is still out.

10 Trade Policy

1. J. David Richardson
2. Lionel H. Olmer
3. Paula Stern

1. J. David Richardson

U.S. Trade Policy in the 1980s: Turns—and Roads Not Taken

This paper is an assessment of turning points in U.S. trade policy during the 1980s, of their economic and political causes, and of whether there might have been other roads not taken. It is not a detailed political economic history[1] and is purposely selective in its treatment.

Section 10.1 describes the unfavorable U.S. trade policy environment of the 1980s and U.S. policy responses to it, emphasizing three significant new "tilts"—minilateralism, managed trade, and congressional activism. Section 10.2 assesses alternative courses of action, how outcomes might have differed,

The author is indebted to Robert E. Baldwin for sparking his enthusiasm for these topics over the years as well as for his detailed and insightful comments on a previous draft. He is also indebted to more than the usual number of commentators since in this case many of the following people provided answers to the "why?" questions that were part of the mandate for the paper. All deserve much credit: Raymond J. Ahearn, C. Michael Aho, Robert E. Baldwin, Thomas O. Bayard, C. Fred Bergsten, Geoffrey Carliner, William R. Cline, I. M. Destler, Geza Feketekuty, Martin Feldstein, Anne O. Krueger, Paul R. Krugman, Robert E. Litan, Keith E. Maskus, Allan Mendelowitz, Michael Mussa, Lionel Olmer, Alfred Reifman, Robert Rogowsky, Jeffrey J. Schott, Susan Schwab, Paula Stern, John W. Suomela, and Murray Weidenbaum.

1. Destler (1986) is the political/economic/historical Bible for 1980–86 and roots from the 1970s. Destler (1990) updates the earlier work. Pearson (1989) is a briefer but also comprehensive evaluation of the period 1980–88. See also still briefer treatments by Baldwin (1990), Deardorff (1989), Niskanen (1988, 137–54), and Vernon and Spar (1989, chap. 3).

and what the risks might have been. Section 10.3 briefly sizes the trade policy actions and alternatives described earlier.[2]

10.1   What Happened in the 1980s: A Review

There is a difference of opinion among commentators on U.S. trade policy in the 1980s. At one extreme is the "devil-made-me-do-it" camp. It believes that laudable trade policy intentions of the Reagan administration were overwhelmed by unfavorable circumstances. It grants that some of those circumstances were of the administration's own macroeconomic making yet observes that others were historical legacies and random bad luck. Niskanen's (1988, 137) view verges toward this camp: "Trade policy in the Reagan administration is best described as a strategic retreat. The consistent goal of the president was free trade, both in the United States and abroad. In response to domestic political pressure, however, the administration imposed more new restraints on trade than any administration since Hoover. A strategic retreat is regarded as the most difficult military maneuver and may be better than the most likely alternative, but it is not a satisfactory outcome." Another commentator has remarked similarly, "Unprecedented pressures breed unprecedented reactions."

At the other extreme is the "venality" camp. It turns the quotation on its head: "Unprincipled trade policy invites unprecedented trade policy pressures." Verging toward this point of view is Pearson (1989, 36, 65): "The record of the Reagan administration in resisting new import protection is weak. . . . [On the export side,] . . . the same administration that has taken a restrictive view of government's role in domestic unfair trade—for example, the antitrust area—has had few reservations about seeking out and challenging foreign unfair trade practices. The explanation would appear to be in a trade policy grounded in pragmatic politics, not in principle."

Regardless of camp, all commentators agree that environmental circumstances and policy intentions cohabit to produce policy responses. Deardorff (1989, 20–22), citing Baldwin (1982), describes this as the crossing of the demand for protection with its supply.

In that spirit, this section summarizes first the U.S. trade policy environment of the 1980s and then the U.S. trade policy responses.

10.1.1   Trade Policy Environments

The Historical Environment

The trade policy environment of the 1980s inherited and accentuated several legacies from the 1970s. Chief among them in the United States was growing

---

2. Members of the U.S. trade policy community have been extraordinarily helpful in preparing this assessment. Many are still active in the government. They are referred to below, without attribution, as "sources" or "commentators."

sensitivity to trade policy as domestic policy, not just foreign policy, and to the U.S. spillovers of industrial policy abroad, which was often perceived to be unfair.

Growing U.S. sensitivity to the domestic effects of trade policy reflected growing U.S. dependence on exports and imports, the decline in U.S. hegemonic and market power (see, among many others, Baldwin 1990, 10–12; and Richardson 1984, 1–2), and a decreasing need for trade policy to function as foreign policy as the cold war cooled. The average of goods and services exported and those imported stood at over 12 percent of U.S. gross national product in 1980: it had been just over 6 percent in 1970. But it showed almost no further rise in the 1980s, standing still at just over 12 percent in 1989.

The Organization of Petroleum Exporting Countries (OPEC) had shaken U.S.-led Western hegemony in the 1970s. It set the stage for macroeconomic policy reversal in the early 1980s as a result of its massive 1979–80 increase in contract oil prices. U.S. unemployment surged from 5.8 to 7.0 percent between 1979 and 1980, and inflation rose from 11.3 to 13.5 percent[3] with fears of further stagflationary aftershocks from OPEC's action. Macroeconomic policy was about to change radically, and, with it, trade policy.

OPEC's ideological and creditor support for developing-country industrialization also helped produce the first fruit of "newly industrializing country" (NIC) export success.[4] Industrial targeting and subsidies were growing, not only in the NICs, but in developed countries as well, as governments debated the merits of industrial policy and wrestled with structural change forced by energy prices and NIC success.[5] Sectoral surge and collapse spilled across borders as world trade continued to grow faster than world output during the 1970s.

U.S. trade policy in the 1970s was becoming more and more sensitive to perceptions of "unfair" trade. Both the Trade Act of 1974, authorizing U.S. participation in the Tokyo Round, and the Trade Agreements Act of 1979, implementing its agreements, facilitated the quest for "relief" from unfair trade practices abroad. Relief was delivered by various barriers to trade. By the 1980s, what had been sensitivity became certainty (see, among others, Baldwin 1990, 14–17; Hufbauer 1989, 125–28; or Pearson 1989, 72–75), and U.S. trade policy increasingly accepted the mandate of facilitating "free but fair" trade, not just free trade.[6]

The Tokyo Round itself had a strong core of fair trade activism, with its codes on dumping, subsidies, government procurement, and customs-valuation

---

3. This is the year-to-year change in the consumer price index for all items; the inflation rate for 1978 had been 7.7 percent.

4. See, e.g., the first comprehensive report on the phenomenon in OECD (1979).

5. A recent paper on the history of industrial subsidies in the OECD is Ford and Suyker (1990). On industrial policy, CBO (1983) is a useful survey.

6. Ronald Reagan in essence baptized the mandate in his "free but fair" speech in September 1985.

and import-licensing procedures. U.S. expectations for the success of the codes ranged from cautious optimism to skepticism in the early 1980s. But events were soon to overwhelm the impact of even the more successful codes,[7] with the result that the United States entered the 1980s not only suspicious of pervasive "unfair" trade but suspicious of betrayal too. The raw undercurrents were that codes should have ameliorated the inequities, but didn't; that our trading partners were not only unfair, but deceitful; that "once burned (by GATT agreements), twice shy." U.S. fair trade activism, born in the 1970s, was to reach adolescent self-confidence in the 1980s.[8]

The Economic Environment

The economic environment for U.S. trade policy in the 1980s was dominated by the dramatic decline and sluggish recovery of the U.S. balance of trade. The trade balance in turn was influenced by the sharp early and mid-1980s breaks in monetary, fiscal, and foreign exchange policies and by the shifting ideologies that prompted them. Also important, but secondary, were perceived changes in the structure of U.S. trade: apparent losses of competitive advantage in manufactures, especially high-technology manufactures; inadequate and dubious gains of competitive advantage in business services; increasing specialization on narrow product varieties; and outsourcing. A third economic influence toward the end of the period was the reacceleration of foreign direct investment in the United States, especially through takeovers.

The story of the U.S. trade balance in the 1980s is familiar, although involved. Its main features are best summarized in the paper on exchange rate policy by Jeffrey Frankel, although its deeper roots are in the companion papers on macroeconomic policies by Michael Mussa and James Poterba (all in this volume).

U.S. trade policy in the 1980s ended up a weak and unwilling handmaiden to macroeconomics. It was forced into trying to do what macroeconomic policy could or would not do and has been ultimately unsuccessful in the attempt. The trade balance deteriorated precipitously in the early 1980s, as shown in fig. 10.1. Pressures to protect devastated U.S. industries and regions (especially the industrial "Rust Belt" in the mid-Atlantic and Midwest states) reached feverish intensity. U.S. trade officials tried to diffuse these pressures and to bandage together a wounded protrade constituency by export-market-opening initiatives. But they were constantly fighting a rearguard action.[9] Protectionist and

---

7. Grieco (1990, esp. chaps. 3–5) is one of the most recent and comprehensive assessments of the Tokyo Round codes. See also Stern, Jackson, and Hoekman (1986) or Foster (1983).

8. As Pearson (1989, 72–75) remarks, it is curious that this legacy of the 1970s is almost entirely perception. There is no evidence that world trade had become any less fair on average during the 1970s or 1980s or less fair toward the United States. Nor is there any evidence that U.S. trade practices are fairer than those of its trading partners on average.

9. They were also fighting against the conclusion of most economic research that trade policies have unpredictable and only fairly small effects on the trade balance in the long run (after prices and exchange rates respond fully). For an early discussion of the point, see McCulloch and Rich-

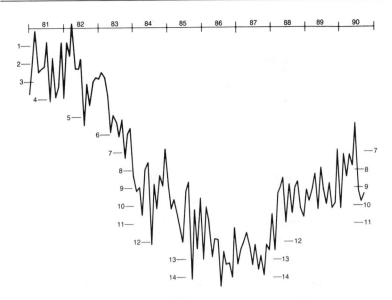

Fig. 10.1   The monthly U.S. trade balance, 1981–90 current dollar exports, f.a.s., less general imports, customs value, seasonally adjusted [except 1986])
Sources: U.S. Department of Commerce (1990, exhibit 2); and President of the United States (1990 and earlier issues, tables B-101–B-105).

market-opening pressures receded only mildly in the later 1980s as the trade balance itself was slow to recover in response to macroeconomic and exchange rate reversals, as shown also in fig. 10.1.[10]

Changing trade structure also played an important role, although its influence was hard to separate from trade balance. Perceptions of impending loss of production capability in manufactures buttressed the case for protecting autos, steel, semiconductor chips, and machine tools (discussed below). Export-promotion initiatives for high-technology products and services were buttressed by perceptions of unfair market blockage abroad and subsidies to local competitors. Figure 10.2 illustrates the plight of several familiar industries in the early 1980s. The import share shoots up for all, sometimes doubling in a mere four-year span. Export shares decline less precipitously (construction machinery and home appliances lose dramatically, however), but in almost every case fall.

---

ardson (1986). Although this was widely understood, its force was vitiated by the urgency of political pressures and the belief that short-run effects of protection and export promotion were favorable. Favorable to what? was a question rarely addressed. Not likely to unemployment rates, which declined steadily from 9.5 percent in 1982–83 to near 5 percent as the decade closed.

10. The real trade balance, purged of price effects, recovered much more quickly than the dollar trade balance in the late 1980s. Although this was well known, it could be quantitatively assessed only with a significant six to nine-month lag. Monthly figures, on which much of the trade policy community hung, became available on a price-adjusted basis only in late 1989.

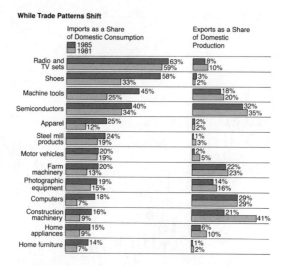

Fig. 10.2   Half-decade structure of U.S. trade balances, 1981–85
Source: Wall Street Journal, 27 October 1986, 1, 12 (original sources: U.S. Department of Commerce and National Association of Manufacturers).

Figure 10.3, however, shows how perceived structural shifts in U.S. trade over the entire 1980s were probably overstated. The high-technology manufacturing trade surplus has more than rebounded from its mid-1980s slump; it exceeds the surplus of the early 1980s. The trade surplus in capital goods has almost fully recovered its level of the early 1980s. Nonfood consumer goods, including autos, have been most sluggish to recover, yet even they show signs of partial restoration. The trade surplus in business services, largely high-technology services,[11] has indeed taken off, as perceptions suggested. But the structural shifts seem less significant a part of the trade policy environment at the end of the 1980s than they did in the middle.

Finally, table 10.1 documents the increased prominence of foreign direct investment in the U.S. economy.[12] Toward the end of the 1980s, this aspect of the economic environment directly influenced important provisions of the Omnibus Trade and Competitiveness Act of 1988. It also increased U.S. weight on TRIMs (trade-related investment measures) in the Uruguay Round negotiations.

A sense of even greater unfairness may be growing in the U.S. trade policy community as the 1990s begin. The United States is seen as having had virtual free trade in "corporate control," unlike its trading partners. Yet, in this view,

11. Business services include construction, engineering, architecture, consulting, brokerage, communications and reinsurance, management, professional and technical services, research and development assessments, and miscellaneous other services.
12. Deardorff (1989, 17–18) and many others argue that the threat of protectionist U.S. trade policy has contributed to the acceleration of direct investment in the United States.

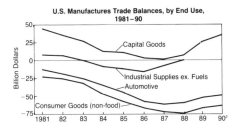

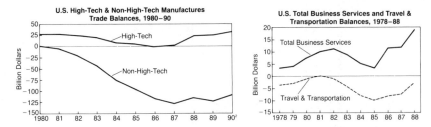

Fig. 10.3   Full-decade structure of U.S. trade balances (i.e., current-dollar exports less imports), 1980–90 (1990 data = [12/5] × [cumulative January–May 1990)

Sources: U.S. Department of Commerce (1989, figs. 3.3, 3.7, 5.3); U.S. Department of Commerce (1990, exhibits 3, 5, 11).

it is not clear how the U.S. national interest is served by allowing open market access to foreign direct investors here while their governments encumber U.S. investors abroad with barriers to entry and merger/takeover and with performance requirements concerning exports, imports, technology transfer, and local staffing/supplier relationships. The investment aspect of the trade policy environment of the 1980s is likely to be one of the decade's legacies to the 1990s.[13]

Ideologies, Institutions, Personalities

U.S. trade policy was also influenced by the personalities, institutions, and ideologies of the 1980s. This was true not only in the timing of trade policy feints and thrusts but in their direction and intensity as well. Three groups were involved (in descending importance): the executive branch, Congress, and academics.

In both the Reagan and the Bush administrations, three ideologies were con-

---

13. For example, Levinson (1987) and Reich (1990) have both observed the anomalies that can arise when U.S. protection and trade promotion policies benefit resident affiliates of foreign-owned firms, sometimes at the expense of overseas affiliates of U.S.-owned firms. Traditional policies toward dumping, subsidies, and import surges may become increasingly irrelevant if multinational ownership, interfirm joint ventures, and cross-penetration of markets continue to grow (see, e.g., "Some Big U.S. Companies" 1990).

Table 10.1   Role of Foreign Direct Investment (FDI) in the U.S. Economy (%), 1977–88

Measure	1977	1978	1979	1980	1981	1982	1983	1984	1985	1986	1987	1988
FDI stock ratio[a]	2.1	2.4	2.6	3.5	4.0	3.9	4.2	4.8	5.3	6.3	7.6	8.9
Foreign share of U.S. mfg.[b]	5.2	5.7	6.6	7.2	9.6	9.8	10.1	10.2	10.8	11.4	12.2	N.A.
Foreign share of U.S. employment[c]	1.7	1.9	2.2	2.6	3.0	3.1	3.2	3.3	3.3	3.4	3.5	N.A.
Foreign share of mfg. employment[d]	3.5	3.9	4.8	5.5	6.5	6.6	7.2	7.1	7.6	7.3	7.9	N.A.
Foreign share of GNP[e]	1.7	1.9	2.2	2.6	3.3	3.3	3.3	3.5	3.5	3.4	N.A.	N.A.
Foreign share of mfg. value added[f]	3.7	4.1	4.8	5.5	7.6	7.8	8.1	8.4	8.3	8.3	N.A.	N.A.

Source: Graham and Krugman (1989, table 1.2, p. 13).

Note: N.A. = base data not available.

[a]FDI stock ratio equals FDI stock as percentage of total net worth of nonfinancial corporations.

[b]Assets of foreign mfg. affiliates as percentage of assets of U.S. mfg. corporations (excluding petroleum refining).

[c]Employment of foreign affiliates as percentage of total U.S. employment.

[d]Employment of foreign mfg. affiliates as percentage of total U.S. employment.

[e]Output of foreign affiliates as percentage of total U.S. output.

[f]Mfg. value added of foreign affiliates as percentage of total U.S. mfg. value added.

tinually represented, but with varying degrees of influence: traditional liberal trade ideology, pragmatic political economy, and managed-trade activism. The Council of Economic Advisers most consistently embodied the first (as usual). The Office of the U.S. Trade Representative (USTR), the White House staff, and James Baker personally (no matter where housed) most consistently embodied the second (as usual). The Commerce Department most consistently embodied the third (as usual). Traditional liberal trade ideology seemed in ascendance very early in the 1980s, as it was reasonably consistent with the administration's ubiquitous promarket pressure.[14] But it was not very consistent either with the government's legal obligation for trade intervention in well-defined cases of injury or inequity or with the macroeconomic devolution that seemed at the time to be making such cases the rule and not the exception. When the GATT ministerial meeting of November 1982 (described below) produced only acrimony and meager results, traditional liberal trade ideology lost initiative and influence.[15] For a time, the vacuum was filled with first mild and then more ambitious experiments with managed trade (new voluntary restraint arrangements, new Section 301 initiatives, and the semiconductor agreement, described below). Martin Feldstein and George Shultz resisted these initiatives strongly from liberal trade perspectives and with persuasive arguments that the trade deficit was due to macroeconomic policies at home, not unfair trade policies abroad. Managed-trade proponents could claim no clear victories by 1985 as James Baker and the political economy realists exerted control.[16] The ongoing history of their experimental managed-trade agreements in the late 1980s has provided no strong support for managed-trade activism. Political economy realists have dominated trade policy in the executive branch since that time.

14. But it was far away from the "unilateral" free trade ideology voiced by David Stockman in his ruminations (1987, 168–69, 171): "Free trade is merely an extension of free enterprise; free markets don't stop at the border. But here was a cabinet officer [Drew Lewis] talking protectionism [auto import restrictions] in the White House, not two months into the administration. . . . Don Regan, who was a stout free trader, was as mad as I'd ever seen him. Steam was coming out of his ears. Murray Weidenbaum didn't show any steam, but he was upset, too. . . . Industrial policy [such as auto protection] therefore sought to use the subsidy, trade and legal powers of the state to sustain industries that could no longer sustain themselves. Industrial policy replaced the test of the marketplace with raw political power. It locked in obsolete labor and capital to unproductive use. It impoverished society. It was the antithesis of supply side." This extreme textbook view never held any ideological sway, even in the early Reagan administration.

15. William E. Brock as USTR was in any case an uneasy spokesman for liberal trade ideology. Besides the "brokering" nature of his office, he was not part of the ideological inner circle of the early Reagan team and was under lingering suspicion of pragmatism from his service as Republican national chairman. But no one else among the top advisers of the early Reagan administration had significant international vision or sensitivity, and even those with the most sensitivity underestimated the spillover of domestic policy into international competitiveness and the trade balance.

16. It is more accurate to suggest that they were influenced by congressional activism (described below) to exert control. Destler and Henning (1989, 104–7) describe the inherent inconsistency of laissez-faire ideology in both trade and the foreign exchange market, given the macroeconomic picture: "When the Congress forced it to choose, the Reagan Administration . . . preferred a regulated exchange market over regulated traded-goods markets" (p. 106).

To the extent that a 535-member, two-party body can be said to have a personality or an ideology, Congress tried to fill the executive branch vacuum of 1983–85. It began to take atypical initiative in trade policy developments. The initiative accelerated until 1985, when the dollar began declining, with the Plaza Agreement and monetary ease ratifying its decline. But the momentum of congressional trade policy activism continued through the 1988 passage of the Omnibus Trade and Competitiveness Act,[17] when Congress returned to its more passive and customary role as a sort of board of directors for the executive's management of trade policy. Congressional activism might be best characterized today as "in remission." It could rise again in the 1990s, especially in the absence of an unexpectedly attractive outcome to the Uruguay Round. This, too, may be a 1980s legacy to the 1990s.

Finally, academic personality and ideology at least mildly supported U.S. trade policy shifts of the 1980s. The growth of "strategic trade policy" research and perspective afforded politicians and lobbyists the chance in some cases to support their constituencies and self-interest intellectually.[18] More important, it undermined the moral force of traditional academic consensus on the near-unconditional merits of liberal trade policy. It held out for a more pragmatic approach, leaning presumptively toward liberal policies, but not unconditionally. In strategic trade policy perspectives, the grounds for policy activism overlapped substantially with antitrust and technology policy activism: trade protection/promotion in some cases where it might encourage innovation (e.g., by better protecting intellectual property) or in some cases where it might significantly vitiate injurious market power (e.g., by encouraging entry of new firms or by blocking predation on viable incumbent firms).

10.1.2   The Policy Responses

The U.S. trade policy response to these environmental influences and pressures in the 1980s was a two-part mix. One part was increased recourse to the normal channels of protection and promotion of market access. The second part was turns ("tilts" is more accurate) toward three qualitatively new emphases in U.S. post–World War II tradition.[19]

Table 10.2 summarizes the increased recourse to normal trade policy channels as the U.S. trade balance plummeted. Petitions for trade policy relief in 1981–85 almost doubled from their late 1970s averages, although the percentage that were successful remains fairly constant at 22 percent.[20] Actually, the

17. Ahearn and Reifman's (1984, 1986, 1988) chronicles are the best account of the ebb and flow described here.

18. "New Theory Backs Some Protectionism" was the headline of a September 1985 *New York Times* article. Of the many surveys of strategic trade policy perspectives, Krugman's (1987) and Levinson's (1988) are especially cogent and accessible. The approach assesses the case for and against active trade policy in a world of imperfect (instead of perfect) competition among firms and reactive (instead of passive) trading-partner governments.

19. Each of the turns, however, has antecedents and parallels in U.S. prewar tradition.

20. Deardorff's (1989, table 6) figures from John A. Jackson's trade action data base yield success rates of 22.2 percent in 1975–80 and 22.7 percent in 1981–85.

Table 10.2   **U.S. Use of Instruments of "Normal" Trade Policy Recourse**
(no. of cases filed)

	Period (annual) Averages			Early 1980s Accentuation				
	1975–80	1981–85	1986–88	1981	1982	1983	1984	1985
Fair trade recourse								
Protection against injury from *fair* trade (Section 201 cases)	7.5	2.4	2.7	2	1	2	5	2
Unfair trade recourse								
Protection against unfair *dumping* (Section 701 cases)	28.7	44.4	43.0	13	53	41	37	78
Protection against unfair *subsidies* (Section 701 cases)	19.2	37.0	10.7	17	100	20	12	36
Protection against unfair violations of *intellectual property* rights (Section 337 cases)	12.8	27.6	18.0	19	20	22	37	40
Action against *other* unfair trade practices (Section 301 cases)	2.7	4.4	18.0	2	8	1	7	4
Total unfair	63.4	113.4	76.0	51	181	84	93	158

Sources: Deardorff (1989, table 6 [relying on a trade-action data base maintained by John H. Jackson]; Grinols (1989, table 2); USITC (1988, 1989).

"success" rate was higher because some allegedly unsuccessful petitions (most dramatically the steel industry's 1984 election-year 201 petition) were granted through ad hoc managed-trade alternatives (described below). It is striking to see in table 10.2 how tightly the number of cases filed tracks the macroeconomic cycle, peaking at its trough in 1982. There is also a second peak in most series in 1984 or 1985 as the dollar soared still higher and the trade balance slumped still lower, even though strong macroeconomic performance had returned. Petitions then decelerate in 1986–88 (especially in 1988, not shown), as the dollar returns to earth and congressional trade policy initiative mounts. But the "success" rate doubles to 45 percent in the later period.

It is also striking to see the near total eclipse of "neutral" recourse to trade policy relief (Section 201 petitions) by unfair trade petitions that villainize trading partners. From 89 percent of all petitions filed in 1975–80, unfair trade petitions rise to 98 percent in 1981–85 and remain at 97 percent even afterward.

Accentuated trade policy activism against unfair practices abroad is not merely a U.S. phenomenon, however. Table 10.3 reveals nearly the same trends—accentuation and villainization—in Australia, Canada, and the European Community. What *was* perhaps new in the 1980s was that the United States became just "one of the gang" in its practice of trade policy.

"Becoming one of the gang" is also the way to characterize the first two of the three new tilts in U.S. trade policy during the 1980s. In the first, the United States turned toward more "minilateral" initiatives. Minilateral initiatives are

Table 10.3   U.S. and Foreign Use of "Normal" Trade Policy Recourse (no. of actions)

	Period (annual) Averages			Early 1980s Accentuation				
	1979–80	1981–85	1986–88	1981	1982	1983	1984	1985
United States								
Fair trade recourse[a]	3.0	4.6	2.7	6	1	7	6	3
Unfair trade recourse[b]	46.5	113.8	60.0	47	215	76	127	104
European Community								
Fair trade recourse[c]	.0	4.8	6.0	0	3	5	2	9
Unfair trade recourse[d]	40.5	46.2	36.3	48	59	46	43	35
Canada[e]								
Fair trade recourse	.0	.4	.0	1	1	0	0	0
Unfair trade recourse	28.0	41.2	78.7	23	73	39	33	38
Australia[e]								
Fair trade recourse	.0	.2	.0	0	0	1	0	0
Unfair trade recourse	58.0	68.8	32.7	49	80	87	62	66

Source: Messerlin (1990, table 1).

[a]Section 201 cases plus GATT Article XIX safeguard cases.

[b]Dumping, subsidies, and privately initiated 301 cases only.

[c]EC Regulation 288 cases plus GATT Article XIX safeguard cases.

[d]EC "new trade instrument" cases.

[e]Dumping, subsidies, and Australia's and Canada's 1979–80 averages represent 1980 figures only.

those that involve less than the full complement of trading partners. They include regional trade liberalization initiatives and "grievance minilaterals," such as the Structural Impediments Initiative with Japan. The essence of all minilateral arrangements is that they are preferential, or potentially so. The United States essentially began practicing in the 1980s what it preached against in the 1960s and 1970s: preferential trading arrangements, a much more typical aspect of European Community and British Commonwealth trade relations and of the generalized systems of preferences for developing countries. This new tilt is summarized in table 10.4 and discussed further below.

The United States turned next toward managed-trade initiatives in the 1980s, ranging from mild to moderate experimentation. Managed-trade initiatives insert government agencies into regular international market transactions as regulators or monitors. Among the milder managed-trade experiments were voluntary restraint arrangements on machine tools. The most thoroughgoing experiment was the semiconductor chip agreement with Japan. Although trade management is perceived in the United States to be "what our trading partners do," neither the allegation nor their alleged success at it is easy to demonstrate. It is arguable from U.S. experimentation in the 1980s that we do it "less well," but it is not clear whether this is vice or virtue. Managed-trade initiatives are summarized in table 10.5 and discussed further below.

Table 10.4   **U.S. "Minilateralism" in the 1980s**

Regional/preferential trade liberalization	*"Grievance" bilaterals/minilaterals*
Caribbean Basin Initiative (1984)	Section 301 activism after 1985
United States–Israel Free Trade Area (1985)	Market-oriented sector-selective (MOSS) negotiations with Japan (1985–86)
Canada–United States Free Trade Agreement (1988)	Structural Impediments Initiative with Japan (1989)

Table 10.5   **U.S. Managed-Trade Initiatives in the 1980s**

Mild initiatives	*Modest initiatives*
Voluntary restraint arrangements with Japan on automobiles (1981)	Voluntary restraint arrangements with principal suppliers of steel (1985–86)
Voluntary restraint arrangements with Japan and Taiwan on machine tools (1986)	Semiconductor Agreement with Japan (1986)

In the third tilt of U.S. trade policy in the 1980s, Congress became a more active and directive participant. The unique American separation of government powers has historically divided the initiatives most relevant to trade policy, assigning to the Congress initiative on taxation, including tariffs, and assigning to the executive branch initiative to make treaties (with congressional consent).

For fifty years, however, since the advent of the Trade Agreements Program, Congress ceded much of its broad trade policy initiative to the executive.[21] In the 1980s, Congress began reasserting itself into U.S. trade policy as an independent player. It became a much more active monitor and director of USTR and of the general management of trade policy by the executive branch. It became an initiator of significant trade policy legislation and not just the sounding board for and ornamentor of administration-initiated bills. Its accelerated activism (discussed below) is summarized in table 10.6 and enshrined in the Omnibus Trade and Competitiveness Act of 1988.

The Turn toward Minilateralism

The minilateral turn in U.S. trade policy in the 1980s has been the most enduring of the three "tilts." Although the turn toward managed trade began earlier in the decade, it was on hold in the later 1980s. Congressional activism surged in the mid-1980s and then decelerated in the wake of the 1988 trade bill and the commencement of Uruguay Round negotiations.

U.S. minilateralism was born in the aftermath of the GATT ministerial meetings of November 1982.[22] Ministerial meetings are traditionally called to begin

21. Congress has kept, naturally, its initiative to draft narrow, special protection bills when necessary. For discussion, see Baldwin (1985, chaps. 2, 4) or Destler (1986, chaps. 2, 4).
22. So, ironically, was the Uruguay Round of negotiations and the successful 1986 ministerial meeting that mandated it.

Table 10.6   **Growing Congressional Trade-Policy Activism prior to the 1988 Omnibus Bill**

Congress (years)	Destler (1986) Count[a]	Ahearn (1986) Count[b]
96th (1979–80)	62	1089
	. . .	. . .
97th (1981–82)	56	1150
	(−10)	(−6)
98th (1983–84)	57	1401
	(+2)	(+22)
99th (1985–86)	93[c]	1758[d]
	(+60)	(+25)

Source: Richardson (1988, table 3.6 [based on Destler (1986, 75–76) and Ahearn (1986)]).

Note: Figures given are number of trade bills introduced in various U.S. Congresses (and % change over previous Congress).

[a]Counts bills whose primary purpose was to restrict trade or benefit U.S. producers.

[b]Counts bills employing twenty trade-related terms, some to expand trade, some to protect, with various shades based on personal evaluation.

[c]Growth rate between January–September 1985 and January–September 1983 applied to number of bills introduced to 98th Congress: (49/30) × 57.

[d]1985 figure times 2.

each round of the multilateral trade negotiations for which the GATT has been renowned. The 1982 meeting was the first since 1973, the beginning of the Tokyo Round.

The 1982 meeting was largely a U.S. initiative. USTR officials had been working since the close of the Tokyo Round on an agenda for a new round. The agenda was sensibly made up of thorny "old chestnut" issues—agriculture and safeguards, especially—and "new issues" such as rules for rapidly expanding trade in business services and high-technology goods. The shape of this agenda had been presented and discussed at the annual OECD ministerial meetings for several years, but without any commitment to act or perhaps adequate U.S. consultation over the agenda itself. Yet the United States pressed quite hard to obtain such a commitment (for November 1982) at the July 1981 Ottawa economic summit (Rubin and Graham 1983, 11) of leaders of the largest seven industrial countries. Within the administration at the time, it seemed not only "natural" but supportive of the strong ideological thrust toward freer markets. Trading partners, however, clearly felt pressured, not coaxed. They were more now the equal of the United States and naturally sought consensus over being coerced.

In the event, the timing was at best inauspicious. Sixteen months' preparation was less than for the Tokyo Round, although the agenda was broader. Unknown to the leaders in mid-1981, the world was then at the portal of the deepest global recession since the Great Depression; November 1982 was approximately the trough!

The result was foot-dragging and acrimony of an intensity rarely seen even in these naturally intense ministerial meetings. The European Community was especially resistant to agricultural liberalization, India and other developing countries were dead set against services liberalization, and all accused the United States of ramming its agenda onto the table without adequate documentation, interpretation, persuasion, or quid pro quo. The meeting dissolved in bitter frustration after mandating further study of agricultural liberalization and sanctioning national studies of services, to be coordinated by the GATT.[23] A representative summary of the outcome is Rubin and Graham's (1983, 11): "It was a U.S. show from beginning to end. It represented the best and the worst of the American approach to such things—the best, because it was an earnest attempt to lead a faltering trading system and reluctant trading partners forward into important new areas; the worst, because it was too ambitious, and it raised among political constituencies unrealistic expectations that could not be met, leaving them disillusioned with GATT and determined to take corrective trade-restrictive actions in the 98th Congress."

U.S. trade policy officials were themselves "disillusioned with GATT" after this experience. While committed to ongoing liberalization, GATT rounds seemed a cumbersome and unpredictable vehicle. Reflective evaluation and opportunity seemed to recommend a two-handed approach that could be called *contingent multilateralism* or, more descriptively *multilateralism where possible, minilateralism where necessary.* The United States would continue to push for a new GATT round covering important old and new issues. But it would simultaneously respond to minilateral opportunities as a supplementary insurance policy against multilateral failure.[24]

Minilateral opportunities would of course include regional trade liberalization. The Trade and Tariff Act of 1984 included authorization for the president to negotiate bilateral free trade areas. But minilateralism would also include "grievance" negotiations, aimed at sensitizing trading partners to issues con-

---

23. Some commentators suggest that these studies were really what the United States wanted from the ministerial in the first place, not (yet) any ministerial commitment to a new multilateral round. If so, the 1982 ministerial would have been setting a new precedent for early involvement by ministers. And there is some indication (e.g., Aho and Aronson 1985) that the "study only" objective was plan B when it became clear early in 1982 that plan A would fail because of hostile trading partners and environments.

24. The change is visible between the president's 1982 and 1986 reports on the Trade Agreements Program. The 1982 report said, "The United States remains committed to the multilateral system of the GATT as the primary vehicle for the realization of its own interests and those of other trading nations. Thus, the United States gives the highest priority to the deliberations and negotiations to be conducted in the upcoming GATT Ministerial meeting" (p. 2). The 1986 report said, "The United States remains committed to GATT and the multilateral negotiation process. There are gains to be achieved through its discussions that cannot be achieved in other forums. . . . Nevertheless, multilateral negotiations are not an end in themselves. . . . America has decided to pursue trade liberalization opportunities wherever and whenever they exist, whether in a multilateral, plurilateral or bilateral context. . . . The purpose of this strategy is not to supplant but rather to supplement GATT. By providing examples of the types of agreements possible and benefits promised, American believes bilateral and plurilateral negotiations can serve as a useful step toward achieving a multilateral consensus" (p. 61).

cerning U.S. market access, especially in services, agriculture, and high-technology products. USTR officials first encouraged Section 301 petitions as a way of carrying out these "grievance minilaterals" and subsequently developed the market-oriented sector-selective (MOSS) approach to Japan over the period 1985–86.[25] The most elaborate of the grievance minilaterals, the Structural Impediments Initiatives (SII), is discussed below.

Out of the liberalizing minilateral spirit in the mid-1980s came the Caribbean Basin Initiative (CBI) of 1984, the United States–Israel Free Trade Area of 1985, and the Canada–United States Free Trade Agreement of 1989. Each successive regional initiative was more important than the previous one. The CBI was a tightly constrained "aid-through-(preferential)-trade" arrangement. The agreement with Israel was a long-standing foreign policy initiative on the congressional back burner that conveniently allowed the United States to signal to trading partners that it really was serious. But it also included liberalization provisions in services. The Canada–United States Agreement took more than three years to negotiate and was a GATT-defensible, across-the-board initiative between countries that were each other's dominant trading partner. Its innovations included liberalizing coverage of most services, trade-related investment matters (TRIMs), and some trade-related intellectual property (TRIPs) concerns in pharmaceuticals; innovative dispute-settlement institutions; and ongoing negotiations over subsidies. All the items were at the same time special concerns of the United States in the multilateral Uruguay Round.

The Bush administration continued the two-handed strategy of multilateralism and minilateralism. It was an active initiator in the Uruguay Round. It implemented the institutionalization of grievance bilaterals in the "Super 301," "Special 301," and telecommunications provisions of the 1988 trade act (described below). It actively encouraged Mexico in planning to authorize 1991 negotiation for a free trade area to encompass all three North American countries. And it publicly probed the potential for a hemispheric free trade area in its 1990 Enterprise for the Americas initiative.

The Turn toward Managed Trade

The United States turned toward managed trade in the early 1980s for automobiles, machine tools, steel, and semiconductor chips. Managed-trade initiatives for the first two covered substantial trade, yet were mild. They amounted to negotiated export restraint arrangements with varying degrees of supplier coverage. The managed-trade initiative for chips was, by contrast, more ambitious, involving target market shares beyond U.S. boundaries and other third-country practices. Export restraint arrangements in steel, of course, had roots in the 1970s and earlier but were expanded in the 1980s. Significant for the

---

25. These sectoral negotiations covered telecommunications, pharmaceutical, medical, and electronic equipment, and forest products (see Pearson 1989, 49; Destler 1986, 233–34; and Prestowitz 1989, 480–85).

same reason was U.S. tightening of textile/apparel quotas and rules of origin in 1983–84.[26]

Most important in the turn toward managed-trade experiments was the deterioration of the economic environment—the deep 1981–82 recession, the soaring 1980–85 dollar, and the slumping 1980–87 trade balance. Of secondary importance was the frustration of the 1982 GATT ministerial. This caused USTR William Brock to lose impetus and influence within the Reagan economic leadership. It was only natural for U.S. Commerce Department activists to find their position, agenda, and established business constituency enhanced.[27]

Managed-trade experimentation stabilized or diminished in the late 1980s, as the economic environment improved, as USTR became itself more aggressive and Congress more active, and as managed-trade experience was assessed to be mixed at best. Yet it remains dormant, rather than defeated, and could easily rise again with economic downturn, Uruguay Round failure, or election of a Democratic president in 1992.[28]

Voluntary export restraints (VRAs) are the mildest form of trade management, in which an importing country cajoles a supplier government into serving as an agent of the importer government. The agent government is charged with "managing" (moderating) the surge of supplies to the importer, whose government is in essence a passive manager, suggesting targets and monitoring the results. As is well known, VRAs are questionably compatible with GATT conventions because of their similarity to quantitative import barriers and selectivity (see Jackson 1988). Yet their political-economic features are in some ways attractive. They can compensate an exporting country's government and/or firms with implicit revenues from being able to raise prices on reduced sales. They are inherently temporary (degressive) since they invite a panoply of avoidance measures that gradually bleed away their effectiveness.[29] From these points of view, they are very similar to a selective, temporary safeguard with compensation. In essence that is what they have become, as virtually all countries have reduced their recourse to traditional fair trade import-relief remedies (see table 10.3 above).[30] The main liabilities of VRAs are their anticompetitive features: their blunting of incentives to compete on price or innovate to reduce

---

26. The only development in the 1980s cutting against the managed-trade grain was President Reagan's decision in 1981 not to renew orderly marketing agreements for footwear with Taiwan and South Korea.

27. Niskanen (1988, 298) quips that Malcolm Baldrige, Reagan's first Commerce secretary, "never met an import restraint that he did not like."

28. For recent statements of the case for managed trade—trade "by results, not rules"—see ACTPN (1989) or Tyson (1990).

29. Avoidance measures include foreign direct investment in the importing country, diversion of shipments through unrestrained third countries, quality upgrading or downgrading, and changes in the degree of fabrication.

30. The Reagan administration did grant escape-clause (Section 201) relief to four comparatively small industries: mushrooms, motorcycles, stainless steel, and wood shakes and shingles (Pearson 1989, 22–24).

costs; their invitation to supernational regulation and cartel-like market sharing among incumbent firms, often at the expense of new entrants (their discriminatory selectivity, sometimes alleged to be a liability, lasts only as long as the arrangements themselves are efficacious).[31]

Before the 1980s, the United States's own recourse to quantitative and managed-trade policies was small compared to its trading partners. During the 1980s, the United States ceased to be an outlier. Voluntary restraint arrangements for passenger cars and carbon steel were negotiated in 1981 and 1985–86, respectively. The auto VRA covered Japan only, but the steel VRAs initially covered nineteen countries and eventually more, nearly all important suppliers to the U.S. market. Each had in the background a failed escape-clause (Section 201) petition for relief from injury from fair trade. The International Trade Commission (ITC) turned down a petition for relief from Ford and the United Auto Workers in November 1980. Just before the 1984 election, President Reagan "turned down" an ITC recommendation for steel relief while in the same breath mandating the sweeping VRAs that, from the industry's point of view, were even better. The 1985–86 steel VRAs revised and expanded the coverage of VRAs negotiated with the European Community in 1982 after the U.S. industry had "delivered to the Commerce Department, on a single day, 494 boxes containing 3 million pages of documentation for 132 countervailing duty antidumping petitions, mainly against European exporters" (Destler 1990, 23–24).

Unlike the auto VRAs, the steel VRAs negotiated target market shares rather than a numerical limit and ultimately included all important suppliers. This virtually guarantees cartel-like behavior and closure of some of the more obvious VRA-avoidance channels. Auto VRAs ceased to bind in 1987–88, as Japanese quality upgrading and investment in "transplants" in the United States rebuilt and increased Japanese shares of auto sales without violating the trade barrier.[32] Steel VRAs, by contrast, were renewed with minor adjustments by President Bush in late 1989, but for two and a half years only, instead of five, and with a strong verbal commitment to negotiate—multilaterally—their complete phaseout in the interim.[33]

Machine tool VRAs were negotiated in 1986 after the Commerce Department ruled in 1985 that (fair trade) imports were presenting a threat to U.S. national security.[34] A 1983 petition on similar grounds had been rejected. Ma-

---

31. For example, small Japanese auto firms were likely losers from the U.S. voluntary restraint arrangements with Japan, in contrast to large firms. On the other hand, the same arrangements may have increased entry to the U.S. market by Korean and Taiwanese suppliers.

32. Assessments of the auto VRAs such as those of Collyns and Dunaway (1987) imply that U.S. consumers paid an extremely high price for temporary protection of the big three U.S. firms, which went more than originally hoped into higher prices and profits and less into volume, quality, employment, and wages. Sources suggest a distinct cooling of congressional support for the big three U.S. firms toward the end of the 1980s.

33. These negotiations are linked to the outcome of the Uruguay Round.

34. Section 232 of the Trade Act of 1962 is the national security route to relief from fair trade.

chine tool VRAs, like those for steel, set rigid market-share targets for imports. Like those for autos, however, they cover only certain suppliers—Japan and Taiwan. Germany and Switzerland explicitly refused to negotiate VRAs, so the United States very publicly "monitors" their exports as well as those of other suppliers. In this context, monitoring is to free trade roughly what parole is to a free ex-convict!

The 1986 Semiconductor Agreement with Japan was managed trade of a different color and deeper intensity. It consolidated the antidumping petitions of U.S. firms like Micron, competing with Japanese chip makers in sales to the U.S. market, and the market-access (Section 301) petitions of U.S. firms like Texas Instruments, competing through its Japanese operations with Japanese chip makers in sales in Japan (and elsewhere).[35] In an attempt to please all petitioners, the United States leaned on Japan to monitor (raise) its firms' chip prices in the United States and third-country markets and to work to allow U.S. firms a 20 percent share of the Japanese chip market by 1991. To the rest of the world this looked like classic cartel bullying. Third-country price maintenance/monitoring was for all purposes extraterritorial price fixing, especially heinous to countries that were heavy users of chips, but not producers.[36] Market-share insurance in the Japanese chip market was for all purposes preemptive market splitting against European and other producers.[37] The U.S. defense was that its chip makers' lives were on the line; here, if anywhere, was a classic case of predatory dumping along with predatory denial of market access; U.S. firms were the prey.

Whatever the merits of this defense, no commentators consider the Semiconductor Agreement a managed-trade success. In 1987, the United States retaliated against Japan for failing to enforce the agreement adequately, with some subsequent softening but not removal of the punitive retaliatory tariffs. U.S. market share in the Japanese market was in 1990 nowhere near 20 percent, and extreme volatility has characterized chip prices in Japan and chip availability in the United States and other markets.

In light of the experiments with managed trade, the 1980s closed with surprisingly supportive sentiment for it. Some, perhaps, springs from declining respect for U.S. private-sector management. The perception remains unproved and certainly at variance with the strong position of U.S. multinational firms in worldwide exports (see Kravis and Lipsey 1985, 1987). Nor does it seem convincing that public-sector management has risen in U.S. esteem (consider NASA, e.g.). The United States seems particularly ill equipped to embark on additional managed-trade experiments. Yet a strong coalition has formed for 1991 revision and renewal of the Semiconductor Agreement, and the prospects

35. For discussion, see Destler (1990, 34–38) and Prestowitz (1989, chap. 2).
36. Their situation is why the GATT insists that only an importer government has the right to decide whether to levy antidumping duties.
37. Europe subsequently negotiated its own semiconductor agreement with Japan, in a sort of metastasis of managed-trade activism.

for ending steel VRAs in 1992 have been dimmed by world recession and meager outcomes of the Uruguay Round.

The Turn toward Congressional Activism

The turn toward congressional activism in U.S. trade policy dates to the 1970s and even before. But the turn was much sharper during the first Reagan administration than at any previous time. Having set a new course, Congress turned no further after the Omnibus Trade and Competitiveness Act of 1988. The decade ended with Congress "back on the board of directors" instead of trying to manage trade policy, but committed to a much more active directorship than at any time in the postwar era.[38] Among other effects, congressional activism has added even more complexity to the traditional multivoice, multi-agency, multiconstituency U.S. approach to trade policy. Such complexity can indeed breed disarray, but it can also make U.S. government strategy options richer, increasing the credibility of threats toward recalcitrant trading partners and allowing recourse to good cop/bad cop tactics.

Congressional restiveness was aggravated by the deteriorating economic environment and the laissez-faire executive branch ideology of the early 1980s. Not only were constituents battered by a recession of record postwar severity, but traded-goods sectors and their host region in the industrial heartland were devastated by uncompetitive exchange rates and the $125 billion plunge in the trade balance, as seen in figures 10.1 and 10.2 above. The export-dependent protrade coalition shrank; the import-battered protectionist coalition mushroomed. Administration attacks on the Export-Import Bank and refusal to renew footwear relief seemed wholly wrongheaded on Capitol Hill. Administration crowing about the strong dollar ("America is back") and impenetrability to the sectoral fallout from its macroeconomic policy weapons only rubbed salt into the perceived wounds of Congress.

Congress's first activist reaction was the Trade and Tariff Act of 1984. The original version included many protectionist provisions, removed only after masterful persuasion by USTR William Brock, an ex-senator (see Niskanen 1988, 147–48). Important provisions of the bill that remained were negotiation authority for bilateral free trade areas, mandated reporting by USTR on overseas trade barriers, and authorization for USTR to become activist itself, not just reactive. Specifically, USTR was given the ability to "self-initiate" Section 301 negotiations to end unjustifiable, unreasonable, and discriminatory barriers to U.S. export market access.

Congress exploded in trade policy activity in early 1985 when the dollar soared to its February peak, when the self-initiating 301 still remained dormant, and when President Reagan nonchalantly agreed to end the auto VRA with Japan and transferred Brock to the Labor Department, leaving USTR

---

38. As Destler (1986, 1990) documents, Congress's desire is generally to have influence on and input into trade policy without having direct responsibility for policy outcomes.

leaderless for three months (see Destler 1986, 105–7; and Destler and Henning 1989, 38–40).[39] Senate Republicans, frightened and betrayed by shortcomings of their own leadership and (according to one source) chary of competitive initiative from the House of Representatives, began the process of drafting the legislation that became the 1988 Trade Bill. House and Senate Democrats actively promoted an import surcharge (an idea originating with Republican Senator John Danforth).

The revolution brought results—the administration finally heard. Clayton Yeutter, the new USTR, promised and began delivering more aggressive words and actions. USTR "self-initiated" four 301 cases in August and subsequently many more. A Trade Policy Task Force was formed to "seek and destroy" egregious foreign trade barriers. The Plaza Agreement provided coordinated government ratification for a weaker, more competitive dollar.

But the administration had lost the initiative on trade legislation to the Congress. The Omnibus Trade and Competitiveness Act of 1988 was three years in the making and the first congressionally initiated broad trade legislation since Smoot-Hawley in 1930.

What emerged at the end was an act that more than anything else embodies congressional commitment to vigilant monitoring of trade policy, to executive branch activism in pursuing unfair practices and enhancing market access abroad,[40] and to retaliation if necessary to prompt reluctant trading partners to negotiate in good faith (essentially Congress's "right to strike" if bargaining fails).

What also emerged was authorization for ambitious Uruguay Round negotiations and a stifling of the cascade of explicitly protectionist legislation enumerated in table 10.6 above. Almost all explicit protection was excised from the bill during protracted drafting by both houses, with input from a far more pragmatic second Reagan administration, and during the mammoth meetings of the 199-member conference committee.[41]

Admittedly, the final act contained a contingent arsenal. But almost all the most infamous weapons were aimed at trade liberalization. The best known of these, the "Super 301," "Special 301," and "Telecom 301" provisions mandate USTR designation of trading partners for liberalizing negotiation, with deadlines. Under Super 301, retaliation is mandated only for unjustifiable violations of previous trade agreements, not for "unreasonable" or "discriminatory" practices. And mandated retaliation can be easily short-circuited by acceptance of

---

39. Brock's transfer was a surprise even to him, according to most sources. It also sent an unsavory signal to the rest of the world since at that point Brock was the senior trade minister of the larger countries.

40. It was in this spirit that Congress strengthened the USTR's position in trade policy, insisting that she be the president's chief spokeswoman and adviser on trade, chair all trade policy advisory committees to the president, and have the right to attend all meetings where international trade is prominently discussed (see USITC 1989, 3).

41. Whether a leaner, tighter, non-Omnibus bill would have been possible is discussed in the next section.

GATT dispute settlement or when it would damage U.S. national security. Similar safety valves exist to avoid mandatory retaliation in other provisions as well.

After two years of experience, no retaliation seems likely to occur. Even India's refusal to negotiate after its May 1989 *and* April 1990 namings as a priority unfair trader under Super 301 seems likely to be ironed out under GATT auspices, as part of Uruguay Round bargaining, rather than prompting retaliation.[42]

But the arsenal is not toothless, of course. Significant Korean liberalization made it possible to avoid being named under Super 301. Brazilian liberalization saved it from being *re*-named in 1990 after its 1989 designation. And, although Japan refused to negotiate broad practices under Super 301 designation, it did consent to negotiate narrowly on wood products, supercomputers, and satellites.

Both the Japanese and the U.S. governments then agreed to assign the broad grievances to the face-saving Structural Impediments Initiative, which was explicitly decoupled from Section 301 proceedings. There U.S. grievance was matched with Japanese grievance, and attempts to exchange mutual remedial commitments were the outcome. This innovative device has the feel of "principal supplier" practice under conventional tariff multilaterals, but in that light it will be important for world trade policy stability to assure that commitments are most-favored-nation (MFN) equivalent, not preferential, as discussed below.[43]

An important liability of SII, however, is lack of congressional linkage. The SII negotiations were not explicitly authorized by Congress. Nor therefore will any U.S. implementing legislation to fulfill commitments to Japan be privileged with "fast-track" (yay or nay without amendment) treatment. In the 1990s, congressional activism may come into serious conflict with SII commitments.

Managed-trade activists, meanwhile, view the arsenal with hope for a different reason. If it fails to foment liberalization, the ensuing retaliation may be an ideal vehicle by which managed-trade activism can attain de facto legitimacy in U.S. policy.

Less prominently noted in the activist arsenal that Congress created are some additional powerful but dangerous weapons: potential scrutiny of foreign direct investment in the United States for threat to national security; potential denial of MFN extension of Uruguay Round agreements to industrial countries

---

42. In fact, if the Uruguay Round succeeds, then unilateral U.S. 301 cases would presumably become rarer. Services, investment, and intellectual property would all be vested with GATT rights, and improved GATT dispute settlement procedures might substitute for Section 301 initiatives. This is presumably the U.S. carrot or olive branch behind what the rest of the world sees as a club.

43. SII meetings will continue for two years to monitor progress and discuss matters relevant to problem areas already identified.

lacking full reciprocity; potential U.S. government procurement embargoes against countries that violate U.S. rights or discriminate against U.S. suppliers in their own procurement policy; and potential for a unilateral import surcharge to fund adjustment assistance programs if other countries do not agree to negotiate a uniform counterpart.[44]

Trading partners have naturally accused the U.S. government of "bullying" and "unilateralism." The emphasis on foreign offenses certainly does seem one-sided, but SII-style mutual grievance negotiations may redress that. Otherwise, it is not yet clear whether bullying and unilateralism is the right metaphor. Congressional and administration intent seems so far merely to be activism, the abandonment of historical passivism, "no more Mr. Nice Guy," "no more unhealthy enabling of foreign addiction to trade policy interventionism." The trade policy environment of the 1990s will no doubt shape the growth of the malleable features of the 1988 bill into mature and reasonable adults or monsters. A few disciplining features along these lines are discussed below.

10.2   Roads Not Taken

U.S. trade policy choices in the 1980s were clearly constrained by the unfavorable trade policy environments—the growing perception of unfair foreign practices, the macroeconomic decline of the early 1980s and even more enduring slump in the trade balance, and the ideological ferment of the first Reagan administration.

Yet alternatives were still possible to the choices made, and this section of the paper assesses some, starting with alternative strategies, then moving to alternative tactics. Among tactics, alternatives to the three important "tilts" in U.S. trade policy will be examined, then several tilts not taken (or dogs that did not bark).

10.2.1   Alternative Strategies?

With respect to trade policy strategy, it is worth repeating that this paper takes the macroeconomic environment and its underlying policy thrust as given. Had early 1980s macroeconomic policy been different, alternative trade policy strategies would have been more numerous than they were. Another way of saying this is that one of the most attractive alternative strategies for U.S. trade policy would have been a more sensitive appreciation in macroeconomic policy for the unhealthy fallout from the soaring dollar.[45] Trade policy's flanks were left dangerously exposed by the retreat of seasoned macroeconomic forces. Trade policy then had to retreat itself, with casualties along the way.

Given the macroeconomic environment, the first trade policy strategy to

---

44. For a detailed discussion of these and other provisions, see USITC (1989, 1–9).

45. For an extensive account of why early and frequent expressions of this view carried so little weight, see Destler and Henning (1989).

consider might be called "multilateral diversion." Multilateral diversion is a long-standing U.S. practice, involving more-or-less continuous rounds of multilateral trade negotiations that divert and delay the ever-present pressures for protection and promotion. Congress and the president can channel such pressures into the multilateral agenda and urge patience on petitioners "until the results of the round are in." The premise behind this strategy is captured by the familiar bicycle metaphor. If the bicycle of trade liberalization isn't moving forward continuously, it will fall victim to the gravity of protection.

In essence, multilateral diversion *was* the strategy of USTR Brock in 1981. But, for reasons described above, it failed and was replaced by eclectic tactics: "multilateral if possible; minilateral if necessary." To have continued to press along traditional lines after the GATT ministerial meetings of 1982 would have been politically suicidal, within the administration, in the eyes of Congress, and in public opinion.

The second alternative trade policy is the inverse of the first and might be called *consistency and insulation. Consistency* implies common approaches to trade policy petitions and cases, presumably by following U.S. administrative remedies closely. It could have been couched in the rhetoric of *law and order in trade policy. Insulation* implies ignoring GATT multilaterals and dispute settlement until more auspicious environments emerge than those of the early 1980s.[46] It is hard, however, to see that strategy dominating the tactical pragmatism actually practiced. Consistently might have implied the administration accepting more petitions (e.g., the escape-clause petitions of footwear in 1981 and copper in 1985) and pressing others to their logical conclusion (e.g., the massive number of steel petitions against dumping and subsidies in 1982). Although Congress might have been placated by such a strategy, trading partners in the recession of 1981–83 would almost surely have seen such rigidity as Smoot-Hawley revisited and retaliated (e.g., the EC in steel).

In the later 1980s, *sectoral minilateralism* is a third strategy that might have given the U.S. executive an initiative independent of Congress. Especially in the cases of steel and semiconductor chips, the U.S. government might have been instrumental in activating liberalizing negotiations among principal suppliers.[47] Given the issues involved in steel, the signatories of the Tokyo Round Subsidies Code might have been the logical charter group and, for parallel reasons, signatories of the Anti-dumping Code for chips. Such negotiations would of course have been GATT related, but also distinct in the same way the codes are distinct from the GATT. Naturally, such sectoral minilaterals could have been brought under the umbrella of a subsequent Uruguay Round, but

46. At least one source thought that the U.S. initiative for a 1982 GATT ministerial was unwise, but it is not clear whether he would have thought so without hindsight, e.g., early in 1981 when the initiative was planned.

47. The Bush administration illustrated the application of this strategy in its approach to shipbuilding in 1989, convincing U.S. shipbuilders to withdraw a Section 301 complaint and pressing simultaneously for OECD negotiations to reduce subsidies.

prior to that might have served to hold back the cartelizing forces of comprehensive steel VRAs and special semiconductor deals among big-country suppliers. The danger in this alternative is that liberalizing negotiations would become perverted by narrowly sectoral interests, and the results would be "MFAs for steel and chips"[48] instead of orderly progress toward market outcomes.

Finally, as a fourth alternative to the late 1980s Uruguay Round thrust, the maxi-minilateral strategy of negotiating an OECD Free Trade and Investment Area is worth consideration (see Hufbauer 1989, chap. 7). Proponents favored expansion of the negotiations to include a few prominent NICs and coverage that would have been just as comprehensive as the Uruguay Round—services, investment, dispute settlement. Proponents argued that the risk of failure would be less, as would temptations for accelerated U.S. "unilateralism."

This alternative strategy looks uncompelling at this time. Proponents did not anticipate the destructive importance of agriculture and services issues in the Uruguay Round negotiations—issues that would have splintered the OECD initiative as well. At least the Uruguay Round has succeeded (however tempestuously) at provoking the active initiative of the developing countries that would have been isolated under the OECD-centered proposal. So far there has been no acceleration of U.S. unilateralism, despite the doubtful prospects for the round. The OECD approach would probably have fared no better.

10.2.2   Alternative Tactics?

Beyond alternative trade policy strategies, were there tactical roads not taken? For sound reason or not?

Alternatives to Minilateralism?

U.S. minilateral tactics in the 1980s elicited considerable handwringing.[49] Regional liberalization has been alleged to undermine the GATT, and "grievance minilaterals" have been dismissed as unilateral bullying. Handwringing notwithstanding, the Uruguay Round was launched, and the United States has conducted its grievance initiatives judiciously and with retaliation only in the Semiconductor Agreement. Furthermore, many of its Section 301 initiatives have had the flavor of the long-respected tradition of a principal supplier bargaining bilaterally with a principal demander, only often on issues not explicitly covered by the GATT.

These observations suggest a supplementation of the U.S. approach that might be considered an alternative tactic. It would be to add MFN-equivalent application to all U.S. grievance minilaterals so that market-opening concessions would be made clearly available to all potential suppliers, not just to the

48. The phrase is Robert E. Baldwin's.
49. See, e.g., the contributions by Isaiah Frank, Anne O. Krueger, Gardner Patterson, and Martin Wolf to Schott (1989) and also Bhagwati (1988, 1989).

U.S. principals. Although this has been the U.S. practice in most cases, there have been exceptions, such as the late 1980s negotiation of access for U.S. firms alone to the Korean insurance market.[50]

Otherwise, grievance minilaterals between principal suppliers and demanders have the familiar advantages of involving the parties with the strongest commitment and, presumably, the best information. Bilateral approaches may often in fact be the most feasible approaches for complex new issues in services and foreign investment measures, involving sensitive cultural and institutional issues. That is, for example, why most tax treaties are bilateral, not multilateral.

Given the environment of the 1980s, it is hard to imagine other alternatives to minilateralism that would have maintained liberalizing impetus. This is not true of alternatives to the sharper of the U.S. turns toward managed trade.

Alternatives to Managed Trade?

One obvious alternative to the milder U.S. tilts toward managed trade would have been sanctioned administrative remedies. VRAs with Japan on autos, for example, could have been avoided by the introduction of legislation that altered the way the International Trade Commission defined *substantial cause* of serious injury. The auto industry could then presumably have resubmitted an escape-clause petition. In the event, the alternative to the auto VRA was a strict quota bill introduced by Senators John Danforth (R) and Lloyd Bentsen (D) that would presumably have attracted significant congressional support. Unlike the VRA, it might still be rigidly protecting U.S. automakers today.

Similarly for machine tools, temporary import relief could have been provided in principle on the statutory grounds that imports were threatening national security. Yet relief to a manufacturing industry on these grounds would have been unprecedented (oil had received such relief in the 1970s), and the persuasiveness of the case had already been undermined by its rejection three years previously. Since Germany and Switzerland would presumably have been unable to avoid barriers to their exports in this case, a GATT appeal and/or retaliation might well have been the result.

Yet, in the cases of both autos and machine tools, it is arguable that the mild, noncomprehensive VRAs supplied roughly the amount of temporary relief (until circumvented),[51] with compensation, that escape-clause or national security relief would have supplied. Thus, alternative tactics may boil down to essentially the same thing—except, of course, that the one chosen is at or beyond the fringe of accepted rules.

---

50. One commentator observed how tempting it is for the target country to offer a preferential concession only, which would be adequately valuable to the complaining country but not as costly for the target as an MFN-equivalent concession.

51. U.S. machine tool imports were 10 percent higher in 1988 than in 1986 as increased shipments from noncontrolled sources more than compensated for reduced shipments from Japan and Taiwan (see GATT 1990, 219–20, 254).

By contrast, the more aggressive managed-trade experiments in steel and semiconductors had arguable stronger anticompetitive effects. Here, most of the sanctioned administrative remedies were probably not feasible alternatives. Although steel could have been awarded escape-clause relief, any levying of significant antidumping and countervailing duties would likely have elicited European appeal to the GATT and/or retaliation. And semiconductor petitioners were divided between those who wanted protection in the U.S. market and those who wanted access to the Japanese market, with each potentially injured by the other's relief.[52]

Here a sensible alternative might have been sectoral minilateralism, as described above, and as George Bush essentially promised in his 1989 renewal of the steel VRAs for only two and a half years. In semiconductor chips, this would merely have involved inviting the EC, and perhaps Korea, to join the negotiations that the United States and Japan were carrying out anyway.

Alternatives to Congressional Activism?

Could there have been a kinder, gentler Omnibus Trade and Competitiveness Act of 1988? a leaner but not so mean nonomnibus act that would still have authorized Uruguay Round negotiations?

These questions are hard to answer because the effects of the 1988 act on U.S. trade policy are still not clear. In its short-run impact, the act has both enabled the Uruguay Round to proceed and provoked significant liberalization and promises of more from Brazil, Korea, Japan, and other countries. But the efficacy of the act's provisions in the medium and long run are not so clear. The Uruguay Round may deliver far less than it promised, if anything at all. And, after easy conquests of obvious inequities, the search for priority unfair practices and traders may provoke only acrimony and retaliation.

It seems likely that, if the Reagan administration had become activist a year or so earlier, it could have preempted congressional activism in trade legislation.[53] This would almost surely have produced a bill with more discretion and fewer mandated reports and deadlines. But it would still have been tough and possibly not as effective in encouraging concessions from trading partners. Congress is a better "bad cop" than any part of the executive branch.

Also, if the Reagan U.S. had initiated trade legislation sooner, it might have resulted in a slightly leaner bill because it would have choked off the "y'all come" flavor of congressional initiative.[54] But, in the late 1980s, there is almost no way to avoid the involvement of myriads of committees and subcommittees

52. Micron might have been disadvantaged by any competitive scale/cost advantage that Texas Instruments acquired by increasing its chip sales in Japan.

53. The administration did not submit its own draft of a trade bill until 1987, and it was then virtually ignored by a Congress intent on drafting its own, according to one source, who said, "They never opened the envelope."

54. One source reports being called by the chairman of a congressional committee, who said, "Every time there's a trade bill we pass; this time we want to play." The result was ultimately incorporated into the bill.

since the ambitious Uruguay Round agenda touches on the regulatory domain of virtually all.

Tilts Not Taken?

It is easy to forget several tactical tilts that were briefly considered, then resisted. Among these the most important were domestic content and import quota bills to protect the U.S. auto industry in the early 1980s; import quota bills to protect textiles, apparel, and footwear in the late 1980s; the import surcharge bill of 1985; and the proposal from the early 1980s to merge USTR and the Commerce Department into a Department of International Trade and Industry (DITI).

Each of these had the potential to become a significant and self-perpetuating shift in U.S. trade policy. The first two would have extended the scope of "special protection" beyond fibers and steel to autos and footwear, each a large U.S. industry in output and employment. The first was short-circuited by the auto VRAs, and the second was suppressed by presidential vetoes. A tilt toward explicit protectionism was consequently avoided, a tilt that would arguably have been as significant as minilateralism, managed trade, and congressional activism.

The thrust for an import surcharge was blunted by the Reagan administration's 1985 concessions, then essentially transformed to emerge as the Super 301 provision of the 1988 trade bill. Had the surcharge passed in its original form, it would have levied extra duties up to 25 percent on imports from partners with large trade surpluses. This might have made the Uruguay Round inconceivable and most likely would have delayed it. It would clearly have been an explicit violation of GATT tariff bindings and the most-favored-nation principle. Thus, it could have been interpreted as virtual abandonment of the GATT by the United States.[55]

Finally, had the United States weakened the multiagency tradition in trade policy and consolidated its administration under the DITI, this would almost certainly have accentuated the tilt toward managed trade and given that tilt more momentum than in fact it had in the late 1980s. Almost surely the tilt would have been so great that it would be better described as a turn toward industrial policy, a resurgence of Hamiltonian perspectives from the U.S. past!

With due allowance then for these tilts not taken, one might assess U.S. trade policy in the 1980s by saying that the traditional boat rocked, but did not capsize. I turn in the last section of the paper to a slightly more detailed assessment.

---

55. Unlike the U.S. import surcharge of 1971, it could not have been defended as a desperate, one-time signal that global negotiations were in order.

10.3 Effects and Assessment

U.S. trade policy in the 1980s seems on balance to have become mildly more restrictive. It has almost surely contributed to the stagnation in the ratio of U.S. trade to output, relative to its 1970s surge, and relative to the ongoing growth in the ratio for the world as a whole (see GATT 1989, 8). The future effects of particular turns and tilts of U.S. trade policy, however, vary.

Minilateral initiatives seem likely to continue and have the potential for effective liberalization. Regional liberalization is, on the basis of empirical evaluation, at least somewhat liberalizing. Trade war (as opposed to competition) among rival blocs seems possible in the name of economic security, yet unlikely. "Forced" bilateral and minilateral negotiations have the potential to be no more severe or undesirable than "forced" confrontation in any setting.

Managed-trade initiatives are more mixed. Mild, limited voluntary restraint arrangements have always come and gone on the international trading scene.[56] Their metastasis into MFA-like complexity is the exception, not the rule. But steel VRAs are not reassuring and may be the next exception. In general, there seems to be undue alarm over mild VRAs and undue nonchalance over the anticompetitive effects of sweeping managed-trade initiatives.

Trade policy activism on the part of the U.S. Congress and the executive branch will have uncertain outcomes, it seems. Like an arsenal of weapons, it can either keep the peace or terrorize. Much depends on who is in command.

On balance, then, of the three important turns in U.S. trade policy in the 1980s, one seems to have liberalizing potential, and the other two draw mixed assessments. In an economically healthy future, this nets to a mildly positive assessment and might ultimately be judged even more enthusiastically. If the 1990s environment, however, turns out to be unhealthy, then the dark potential of managed trade and congressional activism may overwhelm any positive aspects of minilateralism.

One alarming legacy of U.S. and European trade policy in the 1970s and the 1980s is the preoccupation with unfair practices and remedies. This has all the debilitating aspects of older "divorce for abuse only" cases, emphasizing the adversarial relationship and casting one part as devil and the other as angel. More promising, perhaps, is the cooler approach that deemphasizes conflict and reemphasizes the need for adjustment and potential for mutual gains from trade through negotiation over the policy skeletons that every government has in its closet. More promising perhaps is a road that traverses communication, then mediation, then, as a last resort, "no-fault divorce" when necessary. The trick is how to shape international institutions and domestic policies to

---

56. For an engaging history of how frequently these devices were used even in the "good old days" of GATT preeminence, see Patterson (1966).

these ends in an environment increasingly given to seeing selling and buying as a species of war and "economic security" as an end above economic prosperity.

References

Advisory Committee for Trade Policy and Negotiations to the United States Trade Representative (ACTPN). 1989. *Analysis of the U.S.–Japan trade problem.* Washington, D.C., February.

Ahearn, R. J. 1986. Protectionist legislation in 1985. Washington, D.C.: Congressional Research Service, Library of Congress. Typescript.

Ahearn, R. J., and A. Reifman. 1984. Trade policy making in the Congress. In *Recent issues and initiatives in U.S. trade policy,* ed. R. Baldwin. Conference report. Cambridge, Mass.: National Bureau of Economic Research.

———. 1986. U.S. trade policy: Congress sends a message. In *Current U.S. trade policy: Analysis, agenda, and administration,* ed. R. E. Baldwin and J. D. Richardson. Conference report. Cambridge, Mass.: National Bureau of Economic Research.

———. 1988. Trade legislation in 1987: Congress takes charge. In *Issues in the Uruguay Round.* Conference report. Cambridge, Mass.: National Bureau of Economic Research.

Aho, C. M., and J. D. Aronson. 1985. *Trade talks: America better listen!* New York: Council on Foreign Relations.

Baldwin, R. E. 1982. The political economy of protectionism. In *Import competition and response,* ed. J. Bhagwati. Chicago: University of Chicago Press.

———. 1985. *The political economy of U.S. import policy.* Cambridge, Mass.: M.I.T. Press.

———. 1990. U.S. trade policy, 1945–1988: From foreign policy to domestic policy. In *The direction of trade policy,* ed. C. S. Pearson and J. Riedel. Cambridge, Mass.: Blackwell.

Bhagwati, J. 1988. *Protectionism.* Cambridge, Mass.: MIT Press.

———. 1989. U.S. trade policy today. *World Economy* 12 (December): 439–79.

Collyns, C., and S. Dunaway. 1987. The case of Japanese automobile exports to the United States. *International Monetary Fund* Staff Papers 34 (March): 150–75.

Congressional Budget Office (CBO). 1983. *The Industrial policy debate.* Washington, D.C.

Deardorff, A. V. 1989. Trade policy of the Reagan years. Seminar Discussion Paper no. 239. Ann Arbor: University of Michigan, Department of Economics, Research Seminar in International Economics, 25 August.

Destler, I. M. 1986. *American trade politics: System under stress.* Washington, D.C.: Institute for International Economics; New York: Twentieth Century Fund.

———. 1990. United States trade policymaking in the eighties. Paper presented at the NBER conference Politics and Economics in the Eighties, Cambridge, Mass., 14–15 May.

Destler, I. M., and C. R. Henning. 1989. *Dollar politics: Exchange rate policy-making in the United States.* Washington, D.C.: Institute for International Economics.

Ford, R., and W. Suyker. 1990. Industrial subsidies in the OECD economies. Working Paper no. 74. Paris: Organization for Economic Cooperation and Development.

Foster, D. 1983. The MTN codes in the GATT ministerial. In *Managing trade relations in the 1980s: Issues involved in the GATT ministerial meeting of 1982,* ed. S. J. Rubin and T. R. Graham. Totowa, N.J.: Rowman & Allanheld.

General Agreement on Tariffs and Trade (GATT). 1989. *International trade 88–89.* Geneva.

———. 1990. *Trade policy review: United States.* Geneva.

Graham, E. M., and P. R. Krugman. 1989. *Foreign direct investment in the United States.* Washington, D.C.: Institute for International Economics.

Grieco, J. M. 1990. *Cooperation among nations: Europe, America, and non-tariff barriers to trade.* Ithaca, N.Y.: Cornell University Press.

Grinols, E. L. 1989. Procedural protectionism: The American trade bill and the new interventionist mode. *Weltwirtschaftliches Archiv* 125, no. 3:501–21.

Hufbauer, G. C. 1989. Background paper. In *The free trade debate: Reports of the Twentieth Century Fund Task Force on the Future of American Trade Policy.* New York: Priority Press.

Jackson, J. H. 1988. The GATT consistency of export restraint arrangements. *World Economy* 11 (December): 485–500.

Kravis, I. B., and R. E. Lipsey. 1985. The competitive position of U.S. manufacturing firms. *Banca Nazionale del Lavoro Quarterly Review* 153 (June): 127–54.

———. 1987. *Banca Nazionale del Lavoro Quarterly Review* 161 (June): 147–65.

Krugman, P. R. 1987. Is free trade passé?" *Journal of Economic Perspectives* 1 (Fall): 131–44.

Levinson, M. 1987. Asking for protection is asking for trouble. *Harvard Business Review* (July/August), 42–48.

———. 1988. Is strategic trade fair trade? *Across the Board* (June), 47–51.

McCulloch, R., and J. D. Richardson. 1986. U.S. trade and the dollar: Evaluating current policy options. In *Current U.S. trade policy: Analysis, agenda, and administration,* ed. R. E. Baldwin and J. D. Richardson. Conference report. Cambridge, Mass.: National Bureau of Economic Research.

Messerlin, P. A. 1990. Antidumping. Paper presented at the conference What Can be Achieved? Institute for International Economics, Washington, D.C., 25 June.

Niskanen, W. A. 1988. *Reaganomics: An insider's account of the policies and the people.* New York: Oxford University Press.

Organization for Economic Cooperation and Development (OECD). 1979. *The impact of the newly industrializing countries on production and trade in manufactures.* Report by the Secretary-General. Paris.

Patterson, G. 1966. *Discrimination in international trade: The policy issues, 1945–1965.* Princeton, N.J.: Princeton University Press.

Pearson, C. S. 1989. *Free trade, fair trade?* Lanham, Md.: University Press of America.

President of the United States. 1982. *Twenty-sixth annual report of the president of the United States on the trade agreements program, 1981–82.* Washington, D.C., November.

———. 1986. *Annual report of the president of the United States on the trade agreements program, 1984–85.* Washington, D.C., February.

———. 1990. *Economic report of the president.* Washington, D.C., February.

Prestowitz, C. V., Jr. 1989. *Trading places: How we are giving our future to Japan and how to reclaim it.* New York: Basic.

Reich, R. B. 1990. Who is us? *Harvard Business Review* (January–February), 53–64.

Richardson, J. D. 1984. Currents and cross-currents in the flow of U.S. trade policy. In *Recent issues and initiatives in U.S. trade policy,* ed. R. Baldwin. Conference report. Cambridge, Mass.: National Bureau of Economic Research.

———. 1988. Trade policy. In *International economic cooperation,* ed. M. Feldstein. Chicago: University of Chicago Press.

Rubin, S. J., and T. R. Graham, eds. 1983. *Managing trade relations in the 1980s: Issues involved in the GATT ministerial meeting of 1982.* Totowa, N.J.: Rowman & Allanheld.

Schott, J. J., ed. 1989. *Free trade areas and U.S. trade policy.* Washington, D.C.: Institute for International Economics.

Some big U.S. companies favor loosening anti-dumping laws. 1990. *Wall Street Journal,* 31 August, A2.

Stern, R. M., J. H. Jackson, and B. Hoekman. 1986. An assessment of the implementation and operation of the Tokyo Round codes. Discussion Paper no. 174. Ann Arbor: University of Michigan Research Seminar in International Economics.

Stockman, D. A. 1987. *The triumph of politics: The inside story of the Reagan revolution.* New York: Avon.

Tyson, L. 1990. Managed trade. In *An American trade strategy: Options for the 1990s,* ed. R. Z. Lawrence and C. L. Schultze. Washington, D.C.: Brookings.

U.S. Department of Commerce. 1989. *United States trade performance in 1988.* Washington, D.C.: International Trade Administration, September.

———. 1990. *U.S. merchandise trade: May 1990.* CB-90–130, FT-900 (90–05). Washington, D.C.: Bureau of the Census.

U.S. International Trade Commission (USITC). 1988. *Operation of the trade agreements program, 39th report, 1987.* Publication no. 2095.

———. 1989. *Operation of the trade agreements program, 40th report, 1988.* Publication no. 2208. Washington, D.C., July.

Vernon, R., and D. L. Spar. 1989. *Beyond globalism: Remaking American foreign economic policy.* New York: Macmillan.

2. *Lionel H. Olmer*

Considerations of domestic politics were rarely absent from trade policy debates, but they were not always controlling factors in reaching decisions; nor was the "threat" of strict enforcement of U.S. trade laws, or ideology, the compelling element. Sometimes it was one of these factors, sometimes another; but most often, it will surprise no one, a combination of all three determined the result.

What follows are some anecdotes about trade policy decisions with respect to steel, automobiles, export controls, and semiconductors. To my recollection, in none of these instances did any commitment to free trade principles appear to control the outcome. "Compromise"—between ideals and politics, often despite the economic analysis, or what common sense dictated, or obligations that existed under the General Agreement on Tariffs and Trade (GATT)—was the motive force that shaped decisions. Whether this was good or bad, effective or a failure, is, I suppose, about to be debated during this conference. And that makes it all the more worthwhile to be here.

My earliest recollection of how trade policy was formed in the first Reagan administration goes back to the beginning of 1981. As the new undersecretary for international trade in the Department of Commerce, a position created in

1979 and occupied by a Democratic appointee for a brief nine months, I had resolved quickly to review the matters within my responsibility and to straighten out several areas that I perceived needed attention.

First were antidumping and countervailing duty cases, functions only recently transferred from the Treasury Department (where they had historically resided until shifted to Commerce over the objection of the administration by the same act of Congress that created the undersecretary position). Petitions were not being processed within statutory time frames, and the U.S. business community made clear its dissatisfaction with the "foreign bias" in Treasury's processing of cases.

Second, controls on exports of civilian products and technology that could have military applications were excessive, and the policy seemed driven by the Pentagon's desire to impose economic hardship on the Soviet Union, the Eastern-bloc countries, and the People's Republic of China rather than to restrain the development of modern weapons systems. Ironically, the policy penalized American businessmen, alienated many of our friendly trading partners, and affected the Communist nations' military capabilities only marginally.

Third, the antiboycott law, which makes it a crime (in addition to a civil offense) to aid in the creation or maintenance of "secondary and tertiary" boycotts, had the U.S. businessman in a painful dilemma, sorely disadvantaged relative to his foreign competition and unable to get straight answers about or know in advance what the U.S. government's policy was. Even the provision of publicly held information, such as an annual report, could be deemed a response to a "boycott-related request" and subject a company to severe penalties.

Fourth, trade policy with Japan did not take account of what I believe should have been obvious to government officials: most important was Japan's compact with its private sector to become preeminent in high-technology industries, together with a pattern of excluding imports and any sizable foreign market presence.

Finally, there were over 2,000 civil servants employed by Commerce to promote exports who were based in forty-seven cities in the United States and about a hundred countries. They were unfocused, inadequately compensated, and, especially abroad, ordinarily had to function under the disdainful eye of U.S. embassy staff that little valued commercial work. Even with access to key foreign government officials and businessmen internationally and domestically, their utility was being hamstrung by Washington politics.

So there was a lot of work to be done, and, as I set out, I did not think in terms of "protectionism" or "free trade." I preferred characterizing the process as simply sensible and fair. To the extent possible, I believed that we should get the system of international rules to work effectively. To the extent that this was not possible, I thought that we should not shrink from intervening unilaterally. In the abstract, this approach met with no visible criticism from within the administration and with widespread approval by the private sector, from which I had just emerged. When applied in specific instances, however, I and the Commerce Department often became embroiled in controversy, sometimes savaged in the media and viewed by some elements of the administration as impediments to Reaganonomics.

One of the earliest decisions made by the new administration was to end the trigger-price mechanism (TPM). The TPM was the Carter administration's way of dealing with the U.S. steel industry's complaints of foreign dumping and government subsidization. Rather than impose duty penalties or quotas on imported steel, the TPM's approach was to have the Treasury Department (later the Commerce Department) calculate who was the world's low-cost producer and publicize the per ton landed price to the rest of the world's producers, who were told that so long as they sold above that level they would not be in danger of any unfair trade complaint being filed against them.

I became persuaded that the TPM was simply not working, that it was being circumvented easily by several foreign companies (with criminal fraud later proved against a few), and that the American companies—who had consented to withdraw unfair trade petitions in return for the TPM—were being victimized. Free trade ideology was not the basis for the decision to do away with the TPM, inasmuch as six months later we instituted an equally complicated, interventionist pact with the European Community (EC) that set precise quotas on a dozen or so products from the twelve member states.

In my mind, the TPM was a perfect example of the government attempting what it was not well equipped to do: to be effective, TPM would have required an army of trained, knowledgeable staff to monitor and enforce the program from hearth to end user. This, clearly, the government was not prepared to undertake.

What we promised the industry as an alternative to TPM was "strict enforcement of U.S. trade laws." Steel industry leaders were skeptical, to say the least, but, because they knew the system was not working, and with the goodwill and credibility that attaches to the beginning of a new administration, the industry went along. Additionally, I must also say, Secretary of Commerce Malcolm Baldrige had enormous credibility with the U.S. business community, from which he had only recently come, and with the steel industry in particular.

Well, we had our shot at totally unregulated steel trade, and it lasted roughly half a year. Overcapacity in Europe, most of it built with government funds, resulted in a huge surge of exports to the United States sold at prices that could not be matched by domestic companies. The companies were back with their trade cases ready to file again, and we knew that under U.S. law very severe dumping and countervailing duties were likely to be imposed. To follow our maxim of "strict enforcement" would have brought down governments in Europe because the EC's industrial policy openly acknowledged the payout of millions of dollars to inefficient steelmakers and the penalties would cripple their export prospects. So we negotiated a settlement of cases with the EC, giving it a percentage of our market, looked knowingly at Japan as if to say, "Don't dare take advantage of the absence of formal restraints with you," and kept our fingers crossed about the rest of the world. The White House and most others in the administration were opposed to the settlement—low regard for the steel industry probably was at the root of this attitude as much as was free trade ideology.

Congress played an enthusiastic role, but, despite the threat of legislated quotas, its influence was not dominant. There were several White House meetings with the president and members of the "Congressional Steel Caucus," and they encouraged the tilt toward a negotiated restraint agreement, but the dispositive element was the fact that our trade laws would severely disrupt U.S. relations with its most important allies.

Was this an example of protectionism? And, if so, would the free trade ideologues have preferred "strict enforcement of trade laws" whatever the consequences?

Actually, not only did the ideologues not want intervention, but they did not think much of U.S. trade laws or the means by which Commerce administered them! Indeed, early on, a proposal was briefly floated, very informally I might add, that the secretary should review unfair trade cases with an interagency group before taking final decisions. This suggestion was summarily dismissed and never appeared again.

Stuck with the law being the law and a secretary who would not tolerate encroachment, this deal with the EC was the best that could be achieved. And, because of the foreign policy implications, the State Department breathed a sigh of relief and lent encouragement to our efforts to gain administration acquiescence.

Of course, lines were drawn in the sand between the "black hats" and the "white hats" months before on the subject of automobiles. The decision to force the Japanese government "voluntarily" to impose mandatory quotas on its automobile industry was justified as an essential but temporary measure to give Detroit time (two years, with an option to renew for an additional third year) to "retool and become competitive." Whether this was a sincere belief held by anyone in the administration or the Congress, where a quota bill had been introduced on 5 February 1981, is debatable. The fact is that political pressures from the Hill, the industry, and organized labor were substantial, no one expressed any sympathy for what this might do to Japanese industry, and neither the bona fides nor the competence of Detroit was challenged with any discipline.

Domestic politics was everything in this calculus, with barely a passing glance as to the implications that a quota arrangement would have for the administration's trade policy during the next three and a half years. The restraint was imposed despite the absence of evidence of unfair trade or injury to the industry by reason of imports. Indeed, in 1980, the International Trade Commission had concluded that the U.S. automobile industry's problems stemmed primarily from the recession, its failure to shift production to smaller cars, and a public perception of poor quality.

My personal view, argued at the time with no success, was that restraints at the levels being discussed (1.68 million passenger cars) were not sufficiently low to make a large enough difference to Detroit and that the U.S. industry's claim that "two to three years was adequate to retool" rang hollow. Thus, I felt that we might have to pay a high price to the Japanese to get them to accede to our desires, in exchange for a decision that would not prove effective. Frankly, the weight of politics was so substantial as to quash the few who argued that a voluntary restraint agreement should be rejected on principle.

What to do about trade and competitiveness in high-technology products was an issue that involved politics, ideology, and U.S. trade laws. Moreover, in one respect or another, the Soviet Union, Communist China, Europe, and especially Japan were central to the development of these policies and were directly affected by the decisions that were taken or avoided.

The Soviet Union, China, and the European Community each had grievances against U.S. regulations and policies regarding technology transfer that served to limit the character and quantity of exports. Such policies hindered not merely East-West trade; because of the ingenious device known as "reexport controls," virtually every single destination, worldwide, became fair game since recipients of U.S. goods or technology had to keep informed of our restrictions and to abide by them before transferring the products elsewhere. Indeed, statistically, trade with friendly nations was affected by several orders of magnitude greater than was trade with Communist countries.

For years, the Pentagon's ideology prevented change except at the margin, despite overwhelming evidence that our policies hurt us more than they did the Soviets. Objections from our Western European allies were like cries in the wilderness. Sustained criticism from the business community was also of no avail. (Even today as we speak, as a matter of fact, negotiations in Paris between the United States and other members of the Coordinating Committee (COCOM) are almost as fractious as they were when the Soviet Union was characterized as the evil empire.) Changes did take place, to be sure, but only grudgingly, sparingly, and at a pace totally at odds with the growth and widespread availability of modern technology. Why?

My answer is that there was (and is) no single official responsible for technology transfer policy and that the issues are too voluminous and complicated to be "coordinated" in the White House. (Recently, a senior Defense Department official answered congressional criticism that President Bush's policy was not being implemented by responding on the record to the effect that "the President does not speak for the Pentagon.") Given the existing organization, and absent some truly overwhelming external motivations, policies regarding technology transfer are unlikely ever to be a seamless, rational web.

If "tech transfer" is too complicated for politicians, the determination of U.S. trade policy toward Japan is certainly too intricate for them, the business community, or, forgive me, economists. But it does have to be made—or does it?

Almost from the beginning of the first Reagan administration, those who argued that Japan was "different" and needed to be dealt with differently from other trading partners were labeled black hats, protectionists, and worse. Studies that revealed the extent to which U.S. technology leadership was lost or threatened were rejected as superficially based on market-share analysis and as transparent justification for the injection of government subsidization to compensate for what U.S. industry had failed to do for itself (see tables 10.7 and 10.8). In addition to the resistance of economists and ideologues, the grandest consideration of all, foreign policy, added further weight to the white hats of trade policy with respect to dealing with Japan.

Why and how did it change so drastically as to inspire the administration in 1986 to create a worldwide price cartel for semiconductors in the name of achieving fair trade with Japan? In largest part because the Commerce Department and the U.S. Trade Representative's Office had found the means of holding virtually everyone else in the administration at bay, through determinations of incredibly large dumping penalties against several Japanese semiconductor manufacturers and the existence of barriers to entry of American products. The alternative to the imposition of 150 percent duties in some cases, and the labeling of Japan as an unfair trading nation, was an agreement signed between the

Table 10.7   **MITI Assessment of U.S. and Japanese Technology (comparative standings)**

	1983		1988	
	Level of Technology	Technology Development Capability	Level of Technology	Technology Development Capability
Data base	U.S.	U.S.	U.S.	U.S.
Semiconductor memory devices	Equal	Equal	Japan	Japan
Computers	U.S.	Equal	Equal	Equal
VCRs	Japan	Japan	Japan	Japan
D-PBX	U.S.	U.S.	Equal	Japan
Microprocessors	Equal	Equal	Equal	Japan
Laser printers	U.S.	Equal	Equal	Japan
Copy machines	Equal	Equal	Equal	Japan
Assembly robots	Equal	Japan	Equal	Japan
CAD/CAM	U.S.	Equal	Equal	Japan
Communications satellites	U.S.	Equal	Equal	Equal
Photovoltaics	Japan	Equal	Japan	Japan
Aircraft engines	U.S.	U.S.	U.S.	Equal
Skyscrapers	U.S.	U.S.	Equal	Equal
Advanced composite materials	U.S.	U.S.	Equal	Equal
Fine ceramics	Equal	Japan	Japan	Japan

Source: MITI Trends and Future Tasks in Industrial Technology (1988), White Paper.

Table 10.8   **Declining U.S. Market Share in Technology-Based Industries (% of World Market)**

	1975	1980	1985	1988
Steel	16.2	14.2	11.1	11.6
Automobiles	27.0	20.6	26.1	23.2
Machine tools	17.6	18.2	12.5	6.7
Fiber optics	N.A.	73.0	59.2	41.9
Semiconductors	N.A.	60.0	49.0	36.0
DRAM	95.8	55.6	35.0	20.0
Supercomputers	N.A.	100.0	80.0	76.0

Source: Council on Competitiveness analysis of U.S. government and industry data.

Note: With the exception of DRAM, figures represent production in the United States as a percentage of world production. DRAM figures represent production of companies headquartered in North America as a percentage of world production. Fiber optic, semiconductor, DRAM, and supercomputer figures do not include the Soviet Union and the Eastern bloc in total world market. N.A. = not available.

two governments by which Japanese prices would be raised above levels that were to be set by the Commerce Department, quarterly, derived from on-site audits of the Japanese companies and their confidential records. The so-called fair market value, or floor price, as some preferred to call it, led to an immediate rise from $2.00 to $7.00 per chip.

Far from enhancing the competitiveness of U.S. manufacturers or punishing the Japanese, the agreement resulted in huge windfall profits for the latter (which has since been invested in even more modern plant facilities), increased costs for users of semiconductors such as the automobile, telecommunications, and computer industries, and the further reduction of worldwide market share in this sector for U.S. companies.

Would a more sympathetic policy toward high-tech and a tougher policy toward Japan earlier in the administration, a recognition that semiconductors are critically important to all technology-sensitive industries, have led to a different approach? My answer is maybe. Consider the following, in which the availability of "trade cases" with which to punish Japan and the 1986 decision on semiconductors are set in a larger context:

(a) The "competitiveness" craze had exploded on the Washington scene, and almost everyone wanted to be included in the debate and to appear helpful and concerned. Of course, Capitol Hill urged an industrial policy aimed at high technology in particular, while the administration deflected anything with a budgetary impact and volunteered strong rhetorical support.

(b) Rhetoric was not enough to restrain the body politic or U.S. industry. In fact, this was seen as a lack of empathy, and it enraged a broad spectrum of legislators and industry. This industry possessed enormous appeal, and its leadership without question represented the "best" that America had to offer in terms of scientific genius and entrepreneurial spirit.

(*c*) The uniqueness of semiconductors was recognized by government and manifested very clearly by the passage of the Semiconductor Chip Protection Act of 1984, a sui generis acknowledgement of the intellectual property rights inherent in the semiconductor design process.

(*d*) Japan was moving forward swiftly to replace the United States as the technology leader in the world; the National Science Foundation, a number of universities, and the publications emanating from Japan itself testified to this reality. It was simply no longer supportable to maintain that "market forces" could be relied on to reverse these trends.

(*e*) Japan's trade surplus with the United States had ballooned to $50+ billion dollars, and, because it resisted changing its import-restricting policies until forced, few voices rose to its defense.

Perhaps there was no realistic alternatives to the taking of strong measures against Japan, given the trade cases. Certainly, the administration was not prepared to launch a major industrial policy, as some Democratic forces urged. Yet it should have been possible to avoid a price cartel! (As it happens, the agreement with Japan expires next year, and, although significant modifications are being sought that would eliminate the price-fixing component, the U.S. high-tech community—joined [silently] by the Japanese companies who have profited more than anyone—is petitioning the administration to extend a number of its basic elements.)

For some time, the contemporary nature of international business, particularly manufacturing and especially the high-tech sector, has not been well understood by government officials. The degree to which U.S. imports derive from U.S. companies abroad or from U.S.-based subsidiaries of foreign corporations has largely escaped attention. In 1987, for example, the combination of these two categories amounted to nearly two-thirds of total U.S. imports. Nowhere is this growing trend more evident than in semiconductors and high-technology products generally. In 1985, when the U.S. industry supported the elimination of all tariffs on semiconductors trade with Japan, it did so, not in an ideological pursuit of free trade (as some in the administration seemed to believe), but because such an agreement would permit duty-free imports by U.S. companies from their foreign affiliates everywhere (since the agreement extended duty-free treatment to all countries on a most-favored-nation basis).

Next time around, and, it is to be hoped, before the administration commits itself, the new realities of international trade will be better understood, and concern for our high-tech future will not prove synonymous with establishment of worldwide cartels. But the making of trade policy is unlikely ever to be free of politics or consideration of U.S. foreign relations.

3. Paula Stern

Congress, the executive branch, and the U.S. International Trade Commission each play a role in shaping trade policy in our political system. Presidential leadership, however, is critical if the United States is to continue on the path of trade liberalization chartered in the 1930s and prevent domestic interest groups from taking over the trade policy process.[1] Using this criterion as a measure of success, the Reagan administration's trade policy deserves very low marks.[2] Notwithstanding free trade rhetoric, Ronald Reagan—currying political favor—was the most protectionist president since Herbert Hoover.[3]

By pursuing a macroeconomic mix of a loose fiscal policy and a tight monetary policy and ignoring the exchange rate effects of its macroeconomic policies in its first term, the Reagan administration generated unprecedented pressures for protection and responded to the pressures to the same degree. By treating only the trade symptoms with import protection, it pushed off the day that critics would squarely address the source of much of the problem and lost the chance to tackle the necessary sectoral adjustment challenges that lingered. Eventually, the day came in the second term to deal with the overvalued dollar. The Plaza Agreement of 22 September 1985 was a major departure in ex-

1. See historical discussion in Goldstein and Lenway (1989, 309). Specifically, they state, "In the mid-twentieth century, however, many congressional representatives and other policy-makers concluded that tariffs should no longer be used to shelter American industry from market forces. In 1934 when Congress surrendered its tariff-making authority, there was no consensus among congressmen that liberalization was necessary for the U.S. There was no recognition that overly protective tariffs had caused the Depression and therefore no longer served the nation's interests. Over the next two decades, however, both parties came to accept the view that lower trade barriers had brought prosperity to the U.S. Eisenhower, the first Republican President since Hoover, abandoned the traditional party position favoring high tariffs and accepted liberalization as a necessary component of foreign and domestic policy. This consensus about the validity of liberal trade principles and the inability of Congress to deal directly with constituent pressures led to the creation of rules and norms, our parametric variables, which define the more or less unquestioned context in which protectionism is debated and undertaken."

2. Keen academic observers of both Congress and the president have emphasized the predominant role that the president plays in influencing the outcome of sector-specific requests for protection. Goldstein and Lenway make this observation: "Our analysis further indicates that although presidents do not appear influential in our regression equations, they may ultimately be more important than the Congress in deciding which industries actually receive aid. Presidents have the power to modify and reject ITC decisions, and as noted above, they have regularly asserted their authority to overrule the ITC on decisions to protect industry. Even in cases in which the President agrees to accept the ITC's finding of injury, he often modifies the specific remedy. Further, the President has political influence, albeit indirect, through the appointment process. Presidential actions, however, are not reducible to partisan politics. Both Democratic and Republican presidents have used this power; all have favored free trade over protectionism. In short, variation in the use of presidential prerogatives appears not to be a function of party politics" (1989, 323).

3. According to Hufbauer, Berliner, and Elliot (1986, 20) "special protection" in the United States increased from 8 percent in 1975 to 22 percent in 1986. Correspondence between Gary Hufbauer and the author updates the figures through 1986. Hufbauer, Berliner, and Elliot define "special protection" as "exceptional restraints on imports, implemented through high tariffs, quota restraints, or other limitations that go well beyond normal tariff or border restrictions" (1986, 2).

change rate policy. However, by showing little leadership in trade and adjustment policy throughout the decade, the Reagan administration never effectively shaped a long-term adjustment policy to deal constructively with the protectionist pressures that were generated. Once it let the genie out of the bottle, it never really stuffed it back in.

David Stockman, the president's director of the Office of Management and Budget, summed up the Reagan administration's record on trade as follows: "And so the essence of the Reagan Administration's trade policy became clear: Espouse free trade, but find an excuse on every occasion to embrace the opposite. As time passed, [it] would find occasions aplenty" (Stockman 1986, 158).

The level of trade protection should not be the sole criterion to judge any administration's trade policy or even its import relief policies. Indeed, the deeper faults in the Reagan administration's record lay in its macroeconomic and exchange rate policies, which generated severe casualties in the tradable sector; in its choice of political—not legal—criteria to award import relief; and in its lack of long-term policies either to restore recipients of import relief to global competitiveness or to facilitate their adjustment into other, more promising industries.

The major trade development of the Reagan period was the series of record-breaking trade deficits. The tradable sector was the primary casualty of the Reagan era's superdollar exchange rate policy that derived from its macroeconomic policy mix. The record-breaking trade deficits of the 1980s fueled enormous protectionist pressures from U.S. interests that were directly hurt by the competitive buffeting from imported goods. These economic pressures, in turn, presented demands on the government for policies to deal with the mounting list of industries seeking import relief.

While macroeconomic policy generated unprecedented pressure for protectionism, to which the Reagan administration succumbed in its trade policy, there were times that the administration—for whatever calculus of political, economic, and legal reasons—chose not to raise tariffs or quotas in the face of an import relief petition. And there were important differences between Reagan's first and second administrations. His second administration abandoned its neglect of the dollar and coordinated with its trading partners in the Plaza Agreement of 22 September 1985 to depreciate the dollar. Moreover, in the second Reagan administration, the pressures from some industries to gain market access overseas eventually captured the attention of the new team of policymakers—Treasury Secretary James A. Baker III and U.S. Trade Representative Clayton Yeutter—which resulted in the first self-initiated Section 301 market-opening initiatives. Other important and constructive initiatives were taken by the Reagan administration during its eight years in office—most notably, the conclusion of negotiations for a U.S.-Canada Free Trade Agreement and the launching of the Uruguay Round of multilateral trade talks.[4] In short,

---

4. For further details, see Richardson's paper in this volume. Note, moreover, that neither Richardson's paper nor this one discusses export controls.

while the flawed efforts to deal with politically potent import pressures were not the sum total of the Reagan administration's trade policy, they colored practically every other trade issue at the time.

The Reagan administration's trade policy has left a burdensome legacy. By granting import relief in ways that exceeded its legal mandate or skirted conventional import regulatory practice, the White House legitimized efforts of others to use political muscle—not necessarily economic merit or legal criteria on "injury" or "unfair competition"—and opened the door wider for special interest pleading to replace national interest as the basis for making U.S. trade policy. Moreover, it opted for short-term political expediencies of import relief and rejected long-term constructive, competition-enhancing policies for import-affected industries, by greatly reducing, for example, displaced worker benefits under the Trade Adjustment Assistance program. By substituting protection for adjustment, it lost its chance to restore trade-affected industries and workers to health in the event that those protected industries that had been fundamentally crippled by the macroeconomic and exchange rate blows would eventually have their import relief crutch removed.

Today's economists, politicians, and media commentators are preoccupied with finding solutions to the problematic economic legacy left by the Reagan administration in the 1980s.[5] Most attention is presently devoted to the budget deficits amassed during this period, the causal role of which in trade deficits is not coincidental. The severe consequences of these are slowly being perceived by the average American and acknowledged by a growing number, including those who supported the administration's policies at the time.

Similarly in trade policy, the legacy of the Reagan administration haunts its successors. In spite of the fact that the U.S. trade deficit has declined 80 percent in volume terms from the third quarter of 1986 to the fourth quarter of 1990, the Reagan-era record-breaking trade deficits and ensuing protectionist pressures have bequeathed America and the world a legitimization of certain ideas and processes that the trading system is struggling with today.[6]

While protectionism—which rose as high as 22 percent of GNP in 1986 (Hufbauer, Berliner, and Elliot 1985, 20)—may presently be receding, the

---

5. For a recent expression, see Rowen (1990): "Instead of the Reagan promises, what the nation got was a series of budget deficits that more than doubled the national debt accumulated over the prior 20 years."

6. For example, "results-oriented" trade policy is a popular banner for today's interventionists in international markets, who contrast their approach to a multilaterally sanctioned, process-oriented, rules-based policy that the proponents claim has been asymmetrical and disadvantageous to the United States. The results-oriented managed traders even find themselves frustrated by the negligible results of bilateral negotiations that purport to open foreign markets by changing the rules. A results-oriented managed-trade approach tends to be bilateral, not multilateral, and attempts to achieve "trade results"—e.g., quantifiable quotas or market share—not changes in rules: "'Results-oriented' advocates measure success in terms of reductions in the U.S. bilateral deficit with Japan or increased market shares for specific sectors or industries in that country. The measure of success of the Reagan Administration's 'results' was not so much economic as political" (Tyson, in press).

Reagan administration's most lasting legacy may be not what it bequeathed but rather what it failed to leave behind. The Reagan administration's trade policy may have achieved short-term political objectives, but it neglected an important long-term trade policy objective: equipping American firms to compete better by improving their performance through adjustment strategies for both management and workers.[7] Thus, the cost of Reagan's trade policy to the consumer was high but the benefits to the producer and the nation fleeting.

The Rule-Oriented versus the Politics-as-Usual Systems

In the United States, there are two basic structures for dealing with trade complaints. The first structure is the *rule-oriented* system of settling trade disputes. Here, problems are resolved within the framework of legal standards. The second structure utilizes the *political* system. Relief can be sought from either Congress or the president. The Reagan administration's trade policies of the 1980s set into play actions resulting in the political system swamping the rule-oriented system, leaving behind a legacy—in terms of processes—that unfortunately the United States and the world will have to cope with economically, politically, legally, and diplomatically for decades to come.

The Rule-Oriented System

The rule-oriented system is designed to produce a particular foreordained outcome. When complainants allege unfair competition, the relevant statutes require investigations with relatively little room for political influence. Experts, evidence, data, and analyses play significant roles.[8]

Under the rule-oriented system, criteria are set, transparency prevails, and decisions made on the record are all sanctioned by multilateral covenants under the General Agreement on Tariffs and Trade (GATT). This is the basis for the trade laws administered by the International Trade Administration (ITA) of the Department of Commerce (DOC) and the U.S. International Trade Commission (ITC).

The ITC is an important part of the rule-oriented approach to settling trade disputes. An independent agency of the U.S. government, the ITC is equipped to shield Congress and the president—an instrument that is designed to yield swift, nonpolitical approaches to trade issues that would be difficult for elected officials to resolve (see Stern 1990).[9] At the ITC, all industries and countries—

7. According to David Stockman (1986, 156–57), the trade policy of the Reagan administration "sought to use the subsidy, trade, and legal powers of the state to sustain industries that could no longer sustain themselves. Industrial policy replaced the test of the marketplace with raw political power. It locked in obsolete labor and capital to unproductive use. It impoverished society."

8. For further elaboration, see Stern (1989, 1–2).

9. Note also the following: "We argue later that the autonomy of the ITC from short-term congressional preferences reflects a preference for liberal trade that is more fundamental than the need to respond to short-run constituency pressures for trade protection. We do not suggest that if

large and small—get their day in court. With the ITC anchoring the system, there is a reliance on expert opinion, and a definite procedure is apparent to all litigants.

Most investigations involve allegations of unfair and injurious competition from subsidized imports or dumped imports (imports sold at less than fair value) and are intended to yield "fair" pricing. Complaints are filed under antidumping and countervailing duty statutes (Title VII of the Tariff Act of 1930). The ITA rules on whether dumping or subsidization has in fact occurred as alleged. The ITC rules in a parallel investigation on whether a petitioning domestic industry is suffering "material" injury as a result of dumped or subsidized imports.

If the ITC and the DOC both make positive determinations, a dumping or countervailing duty is applied to remove the unfair advantage of the import. The level of the duty is determined by calculations by the DOC based on the margin of "unfair" activity it has found. Another arm of the executive branch, the Customs Service of the Department of Treasury, collects the duty. The ITC also pursues complaints against imports involving intellectual property rights disputes (patents, copyrights, and trademarks; Sec. 337 of Tariff Act of 1930). Its Section 201 escape clause cases combine elements of both the rule-oriented and the political system. Under Section 201, the ITC conducts investigations of fairly traded imports and sends a recommendation for action to the president, who may consider questions within the political realm before acting to limit imports (see Stern 1989).

The International Trade Commission was originally designed by progressives at the turn of the century to "take the tariff out of politics." [10] Changes in the law, particularly in 1975 and 1978, structured the agency to be even more independent of the political process and especially to be freer from White House influence. The ITC budget goes directly to Congress without passing the scrutiny of the Office of Management and Budget. The members of the commission are appointed to the quasi-judicial tribunal for nine years—one year longer than any president can sit in the White House. An appointee cannot be reappointed by the president, so decisions at the commission need never be made with the thought of pleasing or displeasing the White House or Capitol Hill. The chairmanship rotates between the parties, and the president may not designate either of his last two appointees to be chairman—again as a way

---

congressional preferences dramatically shifted, Congress could not reassess control" (Goldstein and Lenway 1989, 308).

10. The progressive participants at the turn of the century tried to "take the tariff out of politics" by establishing an independent, nonpartisan agency: "A Congress distrustful of the President can give more power to the Commission; a President who wishes to avoid congressional criticism can attempt to manipulate policy through the instrumentality of the Commission. . . . Both the executive and legislative branches can try to exploit the agency's theoretical impartiality in supporting their own views. Instead of taking the tariff out of politics, the result has been to draw the Tariff Commission into politics" (Dobson 1976, 81).

of insulating commission decisions from diplomatic pressures that might be transmitted through the White House.

It is no surprise, however, that, in a democracy such as the United States, the ITC is not entirely divorced from the political process. Congress—particularly chairmen of the Finance and Ways and Means committees—endeavors to influence the appointment process of commissioners and chairmen to the commission, which ultimately is decided by the president with the advice and consent of the Senate. The Reagan White House played "fast and loose" with the appointment process to try to tip the party balance and strengthen White House control over the commission through the timing and designation of members and the chairman to the agency. At least on one occasion Congress objected to White House manipulation of the rules for selecting members and designating the chairman, and the chairmanship eventually rotated as the statute had originally envisioned.

Furthermore, the fact that the ITC conducts its "unfair imports" investigations—of dumped and subsidized imports—in tandem with the ITA of the Department of Commerce suggests that the "rule-making" process itself is neither entirely mechanistic nor divorced from the political process. The ITA is part of the executive branch, which is ultimately headed by the highest elected official in the nation, the president. As shall be discussed in the case of semiconductors and lumber, the rules on "unfair imports" left room for judgment and discretionary behavior on the part of the decision makers who were political appointees in the Reagan administration and who thus were exposed to political pressure to read their mandate narrowly or broadly, depending on the situation.

The Politics-as-Usual System

In contrast to the rule-oriented system is the political system, where decision makers are elected officials who have to achieve policies that are politically palatable. Here, the decision makers are directly exposed to political muscle.[11]

The guidelines for the political approach to trade issues are obviously less clear. Both the Congress and the president can operate outside the confines of the formal trade laws. Congress passes new laws to supersede the old—if the president goes along with Congress and does not veto the legislative changes.

---

11. For a discussion of the multiple objectives that an elected official pursues in U.S. trade policy, see Stern (1978, p. xiii): "One may reasonably presume that the prospect of electoral impact drives politicians to take stands that a non-elected policy-maker would not take. Policy in the United States is the product of elected politicians, not simply the work of bureaucrats—even bureaucrats who are keenly aware of the American political scene. Elected politicians—in the Congress or White House—who act to shape foreign policy have other equally important objectives in mind. They must try to satisfy requirements at home, too" (see also pp. 196–97). See also the discussion in Goldstein and Lenway (1989, 305): "State policy is a function of the equilibrium which emerges from the efforts of those who want a protectionist policy and those who represent interest in free trade. Governments, composed of election-maximizing representatives, reflect the current amalgam of social pressures."

In the case of the Reagan administration, the White House took full advantage of the flexibility inherent in the political system to promote a free trade public image while simultaneously protecting many powerful industries claiming to suffer from international competition. Without the encumbrance of statutory standards such as the "serious injury" test in Section 201 or the "material injury" test in Title VII cases, the administration unilaterally decided what imports were "fair" and/or injurious in a number of significant trade cases. By legitimizing the unilateral interpretation of what constitutes "unfair" competition, the Reagan administration has opened the door for others to follow suit.

William Niskanen, one of three members of President Reagan's Council of Economic Advisers, frankly details the "breaches" in the Reagan administration's own objectives for its trade policy once the Reagan administration provided "an opening for a unilateral U.S. interpretation of what constitutes 'fair trade.'" Niskanen blames the breaches on "the combination of some 1980 campaign commitments, controversies with [sic] the administration, the long recession of 1981 and 1982, and the rapid increase in the real exchange rate." [12]

Congress and the Executive Branch

Trade policy in the political system of the United States is a good example of the separation of powers. Two branches of government—Congress and the executive—have claims on shaping trade policy outcomes, which naturally has led to a history of White House–Congress tension in the trade policy arena. In democratic America, both Congress and the president feel the pressure of domestic economic groups wanting protection from international competition (and/or help pushing past market barriers overseas). And cooperation and trust—important requirements for better trade performance—have not always characterized policy over the past three decades.

The history of the ITC is a paradigm of White House–Congress tensions in the trade policy area. The Tariff Commission, the forerunner of the ITC, was created in 1917 to give the Congress leverage with the White House in the

---

12. This is the quotation in its entirety: "The draft of this statement [the 8 July 1981 'Statement on U.S. Trade Policy'], prepared by the Office of the U.S. Trade Representative and the Commerce Department, described the objective as 'free and fair trade,' providing an opening for a unilateral U.S. interpretation of what constitutes 'fair' trade. A last-minute intervention by Treasury, OMB, and the CEA—the core of the free trade coalition in the cabinet—was the origin of the primary theme in the final statement. The statement developed five central policy components: (1) Restoration of strong non-inflationary economic growth; (2) reduction of U.S.-imposed disincentives to exports; (3) effective enforcement of U.S. trade laws and international agreements; (4) effective approach to industrial adjustment problems, with a primary emphasis on market forces; and (5) reduction of government barriers to the flow of trade and investment among nations, with strong emphasis upon improvements and extensions of international trade rules. For the conditions anticipated in mid-1981, these five elements would have been a satisfactory and sufficient statement of trade policy. The combination of some 1980 campaign commitments, controversies with the administration, the long recession of 1981 and 1982, and the rapid increase in the real exchange rate, however, led to numerous breaches of this policy by the administration" (Niskanen 1988, 138–39).

trade area. However, its creation also had a different—if not contradictory—purpose. The Tariff Commission was meant to create a buffer that would shield Congress (and ultimately the president) from a constant stream of petitions for trade protection. Congress wanted and still wants a strong voice in trade policy, but it recognizes that it needs political protection from all the specific demands of industries that before 1917 it had faced directly. Likewise, over the years, the presidency has also learned to use the ITC as a political "flak catcher."

Clearly, in a democracy, it is never possible to take the "tariff out of politics" entirely, but, as this paper argues, the Reagan administration did much to reverse the tendency in U.S. trade jurisprudence to make U.S. trade law more rule-oriented and less politicized.

The Reagan Administration's Macroeconomic Policies Fuel Protectionist Pressures, to Which It Succumbs

The administration of the Reagan era's macroeconomic policies—loose fiscal policy and tight monetary policy—fueled much of the protectionist animus that spread among the industrial and agricultural trade casualties of these policies. Interest rates had started to shoot up in the late 1970s, but their stinging effects continued in the early 1980s through the longest and deepest recession experienced by America in the postwar period. Among the strongest and loudest casualties were the heavily cyclical and heavily trade-affected auto and steel industries, whose international competitiveness had already been slipping in the 1970s.[13]

The strong dollar, caused largely by high interest rates, compounded the trade woes of American industry. While the strong dollar facilitated the financing of the U.S. fiscal deficit and helped fight inflation, it did so at the expense of the tradable sector in the economy. The superdollar was a super-headache, making the problems of declining competitiveness, which many American firms had been experiencing since the 1960s and 1970s, much worse and more apparent.[14] It made imports cheaper in the U.S. market and exports costlier overseas, exposing in the form of growing trade deficits the weaknesses that admittedly had already been developing at home. In short, U.S. industries and workers were rocked, and pressures for protection mounted.

By the mid-1980s, as U.S. industries staggered from the burden of a soaring

---

13. While serving on the International Trade Commission from 1978 through 1984, and as chairwoman from 1984 to 1986, I witnessed the increasing U.S. dependence on international trade through the increase in the caseload of the commission. The ITC caseload grew by 82 percent from recession year 1981 to recovery year 1983. In 1984, 203 cases were instituted, and the workload was growing at an annual rate of 26 percent. In the 1985 fiscal year, the ITC initiated 22 percent more investigations than in 1984 (see my speeches at Wender, Murase & White, 20 October 1984, and the National Economists Club, 12 November 1985).

14. The fact that the 1980–81 current account was in surplus masked the underlying deterioration of many of America's most prominent industries (see my speech to the Los Angeles Foreign Affairs Council, 8 November 1989; and also Stern and London [1990]).

dollar and burgeoning import competition and flat exports, the perception was rife that the administration was neither adequately nor consistently using its legal authority to defend U.S. trade interests that Congress had authorized in prior legislation.

The Reagan administration's positions on trade encouraged this perception by talking "free trade" for the general public but acting "protectionist" for specific industries. It opposed "protectionism" philosophically. It reveled in the rise of the dollar and appeared to disregard the impact of the superdollar on almost the whole U.S. manufacturing sector and on sectors of the agricultural economy exposed to foreign competition.

Ironically, the policy contradictions within the Reagan administration yielded results that it did not welcome. Its basic macroeconomic and dollar policy neglect made it impossible to realize their trade philosophy and rhetoric. Its antiprotectionist rhetoric disdained congressionally sanctioned trade remedies, yet the administration in fact expanded areas for executive action. At the same time that the Reagan team criticized and/or ignored the trade laws and adjustment programs developed by Congress over the years, it took the political lead in using so-called voluntary restraint agreements (VRAs) or orderly marketing arrangements (OMAs) negotiated with U.S. trading partners to achieve the same objectives. By using VRAs or OMAs, which were either outside the congressionally sanctioned list of trade remedies or outside the international system of rules, the president limited imports in a number of major sectors of the economy while reinforcing White House links with important constituency groups.

Automobiles

In 1979, the United Auto Workers and Ford Motor Corporation petitioned the ITC for import relief. At the same time, workers petitioned the Carter administration for trade adjustment assistance, and the Carter administration complied. Approximately $1 billion was paid to auto workers who lost their jobs because of imports. By mid-1981, Ronald Reagan had taken office, and he persuaded the Congress—the Senate being controlled by the Republican party—to eliminate funding for the worker displacement program. Instead, Reagan substituted protection for adjustment (see Lang 1991, 10–11).

In the automobile investigation, unfair trade was not even alleged. The ITC issued a negative Section 201 finding that imports were not the most important cause of serious injury. But the Reagan administration ignored the finding and the law. For the first and only time ever, a president chose to ignore the political shield that the ITC had provided and proceeded to provide protection for an industry found *not* injured by imports. The negative finding did not stop the petition. The Reagan administration, keeping a 1980 campaign pledge, negotiated a so-called voluntary restraint agreement (VRA) with Japan.

Japan announced a VRA in May 1981 in an atmosphere of increasing congressional support for automobile import quotas, domestic content legislation, and sectoral reciprocity in conducting trade relations. From Japan's point of view, it is not difficult to understand that it may have calculated that agreeing to the VRA might help fend off worse actions. But the Reagan administration's reasons are harder to defend.

Some have argued that Reagan had no choice but to bow to congressional pressure. However, in 1981, Reagan had been overwhelmingly elected and was still in his honeymoon period with the Congress. Had Congress pushed a quota or domestic content bill through both houses of Congress—something that never occurred—Reagan had the political clout to veto such legislation and sustain a veto override that would have required both houses of Congress to whip up a two-thirds margin to defeat the president.

In fact, contemporary sources now confirm that Reagan was determined to keep a campaign pledge to protect the automobile industry. David Stockman gives a lively account of the Cabinet Council meeting on Tuesday, 3 March, 1981, where Transportation Secretary Drew Lewis announced that "the time had come to 'keep faith with our campaign pledge' to restrict Japanese auto imports." Stockman's account throws sharp light on the Reagan choice:

> [Special Assistant to the President] Meese was trundling around the White House, doing what he did best: quietly pounding square pegs into round holes, convincing himself and the President that all we had to do to maintain our free trade position was to convince the Japanese "voluntarily" to restrict their own exports.
>
> Under the Meese formulation, our hands would be clean; the Japanese would do the dirty work to themselves. It was another case of not knowing the difference between campaigning and governing. In the latter what counts is outcomes, not positions.
>
> Thus, at a task force meeting on March 19 attended by the President, the scheme was laid on the table. Our ambassador to Japan, Mike Mansfield, would be instructed to "talk turkey" in private with the Japanese, and warn them of the building momentum on the Hill in favor of the Danforth auto quota bill. He could tell them that it was up to them: that if they wanted to head the bill off at the pass, they must impose export restrictions on themselves. Otherwise it would be done by the U.S. Congress.
>
> I hadn't yet given up the fight. So much depended on it. I told the President that if he was against the Danforth bill, then all he had to do was to signal, in no uncertain terms, that he would veto it. He would tell the Congress that the bill violated every free market principle we held.
>
> What's more, it would be a serious political mistake to grant special relief to one industry and region of the country. All that would do was encourage the fiercely parochial instincts of the Congress, the same ones that were already causing such havoc with our spending cuts.
>
> The President replied that he would not signal a veto in advance. My heart sank when I heard that. Studied silence on our part on the matter of this horrendous piece of legislation would itself be an unmistakable signal to the Japanese: unless they imposed their own "voluntary" restrictions, we would serve them up to the tender mercies of the auto belt politicians.

Sure enough, after Mansfield and [U.S. Trade Representative] Brock had held a few "consultations" with the Japanese, they did mysteriously "volunteer" to limit their auto exports to 1.68 million vehicles—right on the eve of Prime Minister Nakasone's visit in May. (Stockman 1986, 154–55, 157–58)

Reagan had decided to relegate regulatory issues such as protecting domestic industries to the lowest of his economic priorities, telling his chairman of the Council of Economic Advisers, Murray Weidenbaum, that political capital in the economic field would be reserved for budgetary battles.[15] But, no matter what priority he placed on trade regulation, the impact of his policy was measurable.

The voluntary restraint agreements with the Japanese auto industry that were in effect from 1980 through 1984 brought U.S. automakers some $9 billion in added revenue. But an ITC study in 1985 showed that Japan earned an extra $5 billion as well. The automobile experience gave us a new trade phenomenon. The Japanese renewed the VRA unilaterally for a fifth and again for a sixth year and so on. This is bilateralism degenerating into "monolateralism"—preemptive self-imposed protection for one's ailing trading partner (see Stern 1990a, 8).[16] Ironically, the quotas also intensified the competitive challenge to the Big Three U.S. automobile manufacturers by accelerating the foreign direct investment of Japanese manufacturers in the United States.

Steel

Another cavalier misuse of the law occurred in October 1984, one month before the presidential elections. The Reagan administration again ignored the ITC, this time dismissing a Section 201 affirmative finding of import injury on several categories of carbon steel. But, while the Reagan administration ignored the affirmative finding, its negotiators imposed VRAs with twenty-seven different countries, *expanding* the categories of steel to include specialty steel. The administration muddied the distinction between fair and unfair competition by justifying its quotas, which came in response to the ITC recommendation on a Section 201 fair competition petition for relief for the steel industry, as a necessary response to "unfair" import competition to steel.[17]

15. Students of protectionism have also noted that there is a general exaggeration of Congress's ability to influence the direction of policy. Specifically, Goldstein and Lenway state, "What is unusual is, given the extent to which trade policy has been politicized, the minimal role Congress plays in deciding the amount and form of aid to constituents. In retrospect, congressional activities appear to be far more symbolic than substantive" (1989, 304). See also Stern and Wechsler (1985) and Weidenbaum (1985).

16. Auctioning quotas would arguably minimize the cost of relief to the economy by transferring the quota rents from the foreign producers to the U.S. Treasury. It also provides a source of revenue for the administration of the quota. The revenue generated by auctioned quotas could also conceivably be dedicated to an adjustment program designed to assist genuinely those bearing the greatest burden of an industry's efforts to compete globally. For other arguments favoring auctioning quotas, see "Additional Remedy Views" (1985) and Bergsten et al. (1987).

17. The confusion sown by this decision is best appreciated by citing the official language describing it: "On September 18, 1984, the President announced he would not provide import

CEA member Niskanen (1988, 141–44) recalls the politics surrounding the administration's decision:

> Shortly after the cabinet meeting [in which the cabinet decided to ignore the recommendations made by the ITC], Brock held a press conference on the decision that was a masterpiece of blue smoke and mirrors. The first press reports, with one exception, reported that "Reagan rejects steel import curbs." Only Clyde Farnsworth of the *New York Times* saw through the blue smoke to recognize that the administration had substituted its own system of quotas for those recommended by the ITC, quoting a foreign steel official to the effect that "the administration is either lying to the steel industry or to the importers." . . . As was characteristic of the 1984 campaign, the administration was on both sides of this issue, articulating a policy of free trade and implementing an extensive set of new import quotas.

The actions of the administration with regard to the steel industry are representative of its consistent choice of political solutions over the use of the rule-oriented system. In this case, it submitted to the pressures of an industry and chose to ignore the established methods of import relief recommended by the ITC. The consequences were the same as in autos: import protection was given to one of the country's most politically influential industries in a way that deviated from congressionally sanctioned rules that call for temporary relief extended on a nondiscriminatory basis (see Stern 1990a, 8–9).

While the president was willing to grant import relief, he abhorred anything that could be labeled an *industrial policy*. The United Steel Workers wanted conditional relief to make sure that the steel companies would reinvest and modernize during the period of relief. So, at the urging of the steelworkers, Congress passed the Steel Import Stabilization Act requiring the reinvestment into modernization efforts of any cash flow derived from relief. The act also required the ITC and the USTR to monitor this reinvestment. Both Congress and the White House lined up on the side of import relief. The difference was that the Reagan administration seemed to be interested in the short-term political imperative to provide relief while Congress endeavored to force actions by management to encourage long-term adjustment.

---

relief under a section 201 petition filed by Bethlehem Steel Corporation and the United Steel Workers of America. The President determined such relief would not be in the national economic interest since it would raise steel prices, reduce jobs and undermine the domestic and international competitiveness of U.S. steel-consuming industries. At the same time, however, the President announced a program designed to handle the growing volume of unfairly trade steel imports entering the United States. The program's objectives included: avoiding global protection; offsetting the injurious effects of unfair trade practices and vigorously applying unfair trade laws; negotiating arrangements with countries whose exports have increased rapidly, excessively and unfairly; and giving the steel industry a period of relative stability to facilitate its restructuring and modernization" (*Annual Report . . . on the Trade Agreements Program* 1988).

The Second Reagan Administration

The rhetoric changed after the President's reelection. Rhetorically, *fair trade* replaced *free trade*. The "unfair" trade justification had debuted as a theme during the 1984 presidential campaign decision to forge VRAs for the steel industry. In the second Reagan administration, it became the cloak for new forms of import protection for other industries including lumber and semiconductors. Secretary Baker enunciated the rhetoric that characterized the second Reagan administration: "Nor have we neglected our responsibilities to fair trade—because without fair trade, public support for free trade would surely collapse. For the last several years, I think I can safely say, no Administration has worked harder than this one against subsidized imports and trade barriers abroad. President Reagan, in fact, has granted more import relief to U.S. industry than any of his predecessors in more than half a century."[18]

The White House responded to import petitions as it had in the first administration: when politically expedient. The freewheeling use of the trade laws also persisted into the second administration. But, whereas the "unfair" trade statutes that are on the books to counteract subsidized and dumped imports were eschewed in the first administration, the administration actually stretched its mandate by self-initiating or reopening previously closed investigations when political pressure to do so mounted.

Semiconductors

On 31 July 1986, President Reagan announced the Japan–United States Semiconductor Agreement. The semiconductor case led to a five-year bilateral pact with Japan signed 31 July 1986. The agreement covers pricing in the United States and third markets and an understanding on increasing U.S. market share in Japan. In return, the United States agreed to suspend a U.S. industry–initiated Section 301 market access case and two antidumping cases, including one case that the DOC self-initiated on dynamic random access memory (DRAM) covering 256 K and above semiconductor chips. In March 1987, the United States subsequently claimed that Japan had "breached its bilateral agreement on fair and equitable market access and 'dumped' Japanese semiconductors in the United States and third country markets," and the president increased duties to 100 percent ad valorem on $300 million worth of Japanese products, including color televisions, laptop computers, and hand-powered tools (see Stern 1990a, 11).

Lumber

In 1983, the Department of Commerce dismissed the original softwood lumber industry countervailing duty case on grounds that there was no countervailable subsidy. On 19 May 1986, the U.S. industry filed another complaint

---

18. From remarks by Secretary of the Treasury James A. Baker III to the Institute for International Economics, 14 September 1987.

against the Canadians. Under mounting pressure from industry and its representatives in Congress from the Northwest and the South, the Department of Commerce chose to take up the petition. The political pressure continued during the period of the investigation when lower-level bureaucrats at the DOC ordinarily calculate countervailing duty margins that dictate the duty level. During this stage of the investigation, top political appointees from the Department of Commerce made repeated appearances on the Hill both in open hearings and behind closed-door sessions.[19]

On 16 October 1986, the Department of Commerce imposed a preliminary countervailing duty of 15 percent on Canadian softwood lumber. On 30 December 1986, the United States and Canada settled by agreement the long-standing dispute over Canada's pricing practices. Canada agreed to implement a 15 percent tax on exports of softwood lumber, thereby neutralizing the effect of its lumber subsidies. In return, the U.S. lumber industry withdrew its countervailing duty petition, and the United States agreed to terminate the increased duty (while Canada got the revenues) (see Stern 1991a, 8).

Machine Tools

When the administration wanted to raise import barriers but lacked an "unfair" trade excuse, it resorted to actions not contemplated in the trade laws. In the spring of 1986, Secretary of Commerce Malcolm Baldrige rejected a petition from the National Machine Tool Builders Association to restrict imports, on national defense grounds. But, on 20 May 1986 the president announced that cutbacks would be sought as an inducement for the supplying nations—Taiwan, Japan, Switzerland, and West Germany—to cut back on their own. Baldrige likened the process to the steel VRAs (see Stern 1990a, 9).

Renewed Congressional Assertiveness in Trade Policy

The beginning of wisdom for the Reagan administration was the admission that its macroeconomic policies that yielded the superdollar had compounded the problem of restoring U.S. economic competitiveness, which had been slipping for decades. Once the president's reelection had been achieved, the administration in 1985 shifted policy course. In coordination with its chief trading partners, the United States achieved the Plaza Agreement in September 1985, which leaned on the dollar, already beginning to decline from its extraterrestrial heights. The hope was that a dollar depreciation would reduce the trade deficit. And the administration—in an unsuccessful attempt to eliminate the justification for Congress to enact new trade legislation—also began to pursue Section 301 market-access trade cases that heretofore had been ignored (see Stern 1990a, 12). The hope was that these actions would avert congressional action. So argued Secretary Baker, who justified the policy shift at the

---

19. From a conversation with former congressman Don Bonker (D-WA), 2 February 1991.

White House as a way to extract the sting from some of Congress's original legislative initiatives, including the Gephardt Amendment.[20]

But it was too little, too late. Congress had lost its confidence in the administration's ability to initiate trade policy effectively. As a result, the Omnibus Trade and Competitive Act of 1988 became the first congressionally initiated major trade bill since Smoot-Hawley half a century before.

This congressional preemption was precipitated by a number of basic beliefs held by the bipartisan majority of Congress. Impatience and disdain for the Reagan administration's trade policy underpinned the congressional assertion of power. But, even if the bill is interpreted as a repudiation of the Reagan administration's blend of rhetoric and action, Congress echoed the Reagan administration's explanations for America's trade problems (namely, "unfairness") and its solutions (namely, heavy reliance on protection). Consequently, at least one important theme in the trade bill was that "unfair" trade is a major cause of the U.S. trade deficit and of the problems experienced by the U.S. industrial sector (see Stern 1990b).

Legacies of the Reagan Era

Inadequate leadership in the 1980s has left the United States with a trade policy legacy that rewards industries that can bring political muscle to bear at both ends of Pennsylvania Avenue. Trade protection increased in the Reagan era, but the industries that received protection at significant cost have not adjusted to the point of catching up or surpassing their overseas competition.

There are other unintentional negative results of the legacy that flow from the above observation. By appearing to give low priority to trade regulation—particularly in its first term—and giving short shrift to trade remedies and adjustment that the law provided, the Reagan administration set into play movement among restive casualties of its 1980s economic policies to dismiss the legal framework for dealing with import competition—particularly Section 201—or at the most to use it to set the stage for a political assault on the White House.

The frequent references to "unfair" trade, as in the steel VRAs, to justify market intervention in spite of the fact that no unfair trade had been demonstrated have led to confused official and public thinking about the purpose of the trade laws. The administration relied on claims of "unfair" trade to support trade actions that ignored the mandated rules. The public has consequently been misled to believe that the major U.S. trade problem is the unfairness of

---

20. "The Gephardt amendment would trigger Presidential negotiations with major trade-surplus nations that exclude American goods or services" (Stern 1987). See also Wolf (1991, 1): "The Gephardt Amendment . . . would have required those countries that had a large bilateral trade deficit with the U.S. to reduce that deficit ten percent a year for three years. This proposal was found wanting, and Super 301 emerged as a more or less general set of guidelines to the President who retained ultimate discretion in its application."

our trading partners. In fact, despite hundreds of claims of "unfairness" from U.S. industry in the 1980s, "the volume of U.S. imports affected by antidumping and countervailing duty investigations as a share of total imports amounted to only two-tenths of one percent in 1987, four-tenths of one percent in 1988, and two-tenths of one percent during the first half of 1989."[21]

The public has also been given the false impression that protection, especially against unfairly traded goods, will solve a given industry's problems. In fact, very often an industry's most important problems are not unfair competition and may not even be overseas competition, whether fair or not. The source of the industry's problem may very well be internal and/or exacerbated by government rules that have unintended consequences for industry. Imports, therefore, may be more symptoms than causes of an industry's uncompetitive distress.[22]

By substituting political expediency for the use of the rule-oriented system, which establishes economic criteria for acting and employs tools that could be used to encourage positive and constructive adjustment, the scope and results of the actions were short term and limited. The industry—and the nation—missed out on the full opportunity of "providing temporary relief for an industry so that the industry will have sufficient time to adjust to the freer international competition," to borrow the language of Section 201 (19 U.S.C. 2251–53).

Altogether, the actions and the accompanying rhetoric—which often hid more than it revealed about the Reagan administration's trade political thinking—have contributed to the undermining of the intellectual support for the rule-oriented approach to trade policy, which had characterized every post–World War II administration's support for the GATT system.

Conclusion

The trade policies of the Reagan administration during the 1980s have left a legacy to the 1990s both in terms of results and in terms of processes. In the results category, consumer costs rose. And, while protected U.S. producers were able to increase profits (i.e., rents) and/or market share in the short term, the longer-term adjustments did not materialize. Lost was the opportunity to reap the long-term adjustment benefits that American industries require to respond to increasing international competition.[23]

21. From a statement by Ambassador Rufus H. Yerxa on the GATT trade policy review mechanism, Geneva, Switzerland (14 December 1989).

22. For elaboration of the concept of "unfairness" in U.S. trade law, see Stern (1989).

23. Having spent nine years (involved in over a thousand investigations) at the International Trade Commission examining the role of imports in the U.S. marketplace, I caution the reader to be very careful when crediting or blaming imports or import relief for how industry performs. Take the steel industry, e.g., which has had special trade protection in some form with only short lapses since 1968. How did Reagan's VRAs perform? For the first time since 1982, the industry reported profits in the first eight months of 1987. In the meantime, tens of thousands of workers

The legacies of protectionist actions with respect to the processes of trade policy will also have lasting effects. The politicization of the rule-oriented approach to trade policy and the retreat to unilateral protectionism diminished intellectual support for the rule-based multilateral system.[24] The public has been misled about the purpose of the trade laws and the use of protection when a claim of unfair trade is made. And greater congressional assertiveness in the trade policy arena has resulted from the inadequate use of the rule-oriented system by the president.

On the positive side, it is unlikely that any future administration will ever again engage in such neglect of exchange rate and trade issues. Nevertheless, the Reagan administration's neglect of the existing trade laws and rules has permanently saddled the United States with a political, economic, diplomatic, and legal legacy that George Bush, Reagan's successor, together with Congress, will have for years to come. The Uruguay Round of multilateral trade talks, the declining dollar, and bilateral talks with Japan—and others—are all helping manage the protectionist pressures that have been stirred up. Unfortunately, however, the United States now must deal with these problems in a recessionary environment that it had been spared for eight years. And recession naturally brings cries for more protection.

The best hope is that the United States might achieve measurable results in reducing barriers in the trading system, based on agreed-on rules with our trading partners. Such an approach would not pit results against rules but rather achieve a synthesis of the two.

---

lost their jobs, and plants closed forever. Did import relief help? Yes. Combined with the dollar decline, import relief helped firm prices and fetch profits. But it is noteworthy that most of the serious steps to adjust to the realities of international steel trade in the 1980s had taken place from 1980 to 1983, a period when the U.S. steel market was relatively open and U.S. steel producers were subject to import pressure. In contrast to its relative inactivity during the 1960s and 1970s, the steel industry had only just embarked on making some of the adjustments necessary to return it to a more competitive position in the steel market. Plant shutdowns by U.S. producers were more highly concentrated between 1982 and the first quarter of 1984. Because of world steel overcapacity during this period, these closures, primarily of less efficient facilities, were necessary adjustments. The shutdowns allowed the steel industry to focus future investment strategy on those facilities that were more efficient and had a better chance of competing in the world steel market.

Two years after the steel industry's VRAs were in effect, closures of outmoded excess capacity, new labor arrangements, reorganizations (involving mergers and employee buyouts), some modern technology, and an infusion of foreign investment occurred. Arguably, market forces had dictated those necessary changes before the VRAs. But trouble lurked under the good news. Capacity utilization had not exceeded 70 percent since 1981. Labor had not made all the needed changes. And the financial problems remained severe, as evinced by the Chapter 11 filing by the second largest producer, LTV.

By 1989, the steel producers were seeking five additional years of quota protection (see *Rebuilding American Manufacturing* 1989). At that time, the industry was running at full capacity, producers were more efficient, and the exchange rate of the dollar was 40–60 percent below its highs in 1985.

24. As noted at the outset, the administration did initiate the Uruguay Round. Thus, it bears repeating that, as with other administrations, there were internal contradictions in trade policy directions during the eight years of the Reagan administration.

References

Additional remedy views of Chairwoman Paula Stern. 1985. Footwear Investigation. Publication no. 1717. Washington, D.C.: U.S. International Trade Commission, July.

Annual Report of the President of the United States on the Trade Agreements Program, 1988. 1988. Washington, D.C., October.

Bergsten, C. Fred, et al. 1987. *Auction quotas and United states trade policy.* Publication no. 19. Washington, D.C.: Institute for International Economics, September.

Dobson, John M. 1976. *Two centuries of tariffs: The background and emergency of the U.S. International Trade Commission.* Washington, D.C.: U.S. Government Printing Office.

Goldstein, Judith, and Stefanie Ann Lenway. 1989. Interests or institutions: An inquiry into congressional-ITC relations. *International Studies Quarterly* 33 (September): 303–27.

Hufbauer, G., D. Berliner, and K. Elliott. 1986. *Trade protection in the United States: Thirty-one case studies.* Washington, D.C.: Institute for International Economics.

Lang, Jeffrey. 1991. United States trade laws in the context of the Uruguay Round. 20 March. University. Typescript.

Niskanen, William. 1988. *Reaganomics: An insider's account of the policies and the people.* New York: Oxford University Press.

Rebuilding American manufacturing in the 1990s: The case against steel VRAs. 1989. Washington, D.C.: Stern Group, February.

Rowen, Hobart. 1990. George Bush's illogical economics. *Washington Post,* 14 October, H1.

Stern, Paula. 1979. *Water's edge: Domestic politics and the making of American foreign policy.* Westport, Conn.: Greenwood.

———. 1987. Stop the trade bill hysteria. *New York Times,* 15 December.

———. 1989. Regulating U.S. trade and foreign investment. *University of Miami Inter-American Law Review* 21 (Fall): 1–15.

———. 1990a. Reaping the wind and sowing the whirlwind: Section 301 as a metaphor for congressional assertiveness in U.S. trade policy. *Boston University International Law Journal* 8, no. 1 (Spring): 1–19.

———. 1990b. The U.S. Congress is poised to reassert itself on trade again. *International Economy* 4 (June/July): 50–53.

Stern, Paula, and Paul A. London. 1990. Deficits in trade and leadership. *Washington Quarterly* 13 (Autumn): 105–17.

Stern, Paula, and Andrew Wechsler. 1985. Escape clause relief and recessions: An economic and legal look at Section 201. In *Law and trade issues of the Japanese economy: American and Japanese views.* Seattle: University of Washington Press.

Stockman, David. 1986. *The triumph of politics: How the Reagan revolution failed.* New York: Harper & Row.

Tyson, Laura D'Andrea. In press. *Managed and mismanaged trade: Lessons for U.S. trade policy in high-technology industries.* Washington, D.C.: Institute for International Economics.

Weidenbaum, Murray. 1985. A "Dutch uncle" talk on foreign trade. Center for the Study of American Business 16 (October).

Wolf, Ira. 1991. The U.S. Congress and America's Japan policy. *Hotel Okura News,* vol. 15, no. 2 (February).

Summary of Discussion

Murray Weidenbaum started the discussion by saying that, compared to the average member of Congress, everyone in the Reagan administration was a paragon of free trade. Strom Thurmond, for example, led the congressional delegation on textiles to the White House. As chairman of the Senate Judiciary Committee, he was working very hard to push through the Reagan administration's judicial appointments, so he had significant influence at the White House. The shoe delegation, on the other hand, was led by Senator Ted Kennedy, so protectionism for shoes was avoided. Weidenbaum felt that the first major free trade victory was letting the orderly marketing agreement on shoes expire.

William Niskanen thought that the major charge against the Reagan trade policy was that it had undermined the rule of law in international trade. Almost all the trade actions taken by the Reagan administration were inconsistent with GATT, which expressly prohibits quotas, and had no basis under U.S. law. These actions were instead private deals between other countries and the Commerce Department or the U.S. Trade Representative.

Niskanen noted that Congress passed no significant trade legislation until 1988. In fact, the trade law under which the United States operated until late 1988 had been established in the 1970s and earlier. But trade policy in the 1980s was consistent with neither these laws nor GATT, and that inconsistency has come back to haunt the United States now as it tries to reinforce the rule of law in international trade through the Uruguay Round. The United States "has spent the last decade building a record of going around and under and over that law," and the cost of the direct effects has been far less than the cost of undermining the rule of law in trade.

Phillip Areeda said that, when he worked in the White House under Eisenhower, some of his work was related to international trade. At that time, as he supposed was true in the 1980s, much executive branch activity was designed to preempt even worse decisions or activities by Congress.

Areeda believed that one way in which the 1980s differed from the 1950s is that protectionist sentiments were more at the fringe of American economic life in the 1950s. Some of the industries that requested protection at that time seemed quite insignificant, such as the violin-making industry and the clothes pin industry. Still, voluntary restraints on textiles also began in the 1950s and began on the assumption that, if the administration did not act, Congress would do something worse. The disastrous oil import restrictions adopted in the late 1950s were ostensibly to protect American national defense but were in fact just as politically based as other trade restrictions.

Overall, Areeda felt that the primary impulse of the executive branch since World War II has been in the direction of relatively unencumbered (although not perfectly free) trade. The various mechanisms of antidumping rules, national security restrictions, and the International Trade Commission (ITC) had been designed to contain the political heat as it erupts from time to time.

Stern had commented earlier that the Reagan administration had imposed certain trade restrictions without taking advantage of the political shield provided by the ITC. Areeda supposed that the administration had concluded that the ITC had not provided a sufficient shield. Although the ITC's determinations that certain industries had or had not been injured had been helpful to the administration, they may have been inadequate to deflect the political heat that arose in some cases.

Paula Stern responded that the president is a very powerful man. President Reagan *could* have vetoed any congressional legislation on automobiles, just as he later vetoed textile and footwear legislation. Reagan had made a campaign promise in 1980 to help autoworkers, however, even though the ITC's decision was still pending and he could have said, "Well, wait and see what the ITC is going to do." Stern argued that trade decisions had been highly political calculations and had much to do with the president's desire or willingness to check the Congress.

Weidenbaum added that there was a very deliberate presidential decision to expend political capital on issues of budget and taxes. Regulatory issues, such as this trade issue, fell into second place and did not receive as much attention.

William Baxter noted that trade is not a topic on which the administration turned to the Justice Department for advice. The Justice Department had "a seat at the table" that Baxter usually filled, but, although it repeatedly admonished the administration that its proposed actions were not authorized by the trade laws, nobody seemed to be much influenced by this reasoning. The administration split very consistently, with the same groups on the same sides on issue after issue; the legal questions were barely alluded to.

Martin Feldstein said that he had been shaken on the "rules versus discretion" issue when a delegation of Brazilian steel manufacturers *requested* a quota. They said that their potential buyers were unable to buy their product because of the risk of an ex post antidumping assessment and large legal fees. A quota, on the other hand, would provide them a safe harbor and enable them to import into the Untied States.

Jeffrey Frankel agreed that the enforcement of U.S. trade rules is quite unpredictable. Rules on antidumping and countervailing duties are sufficiently elastic that one can justify intervening or not intervening for almost any industry. Perhaps what is needed is a mechanism for settling international disputes, such as that being discussed in the Uruguay Round. With such a mechanism, the settlement of these disputes would be perceived internationally as being more fair and more predictable. The effectiveness of legal rules hinges on this perception, so the unpredictable enforcement of U.S. trade rules is undermining their use.

Charls Walker added that timely application of the rules is important in general and can be critical to the survival of small companies being hurt by unfair trading practices.

Feldstein then returned to the question of how the 1980s were different from earlier periods. Was the results-oriented approach new, as Stern had suggested? Have the industry-specific market-opening issues become more important in the last few years of negotiations, especially with the Japanese and the Koreans? Are these issues new to the 1980s, or did they already exist but are now presented in a slightly different form?

Stern responded that there was a fourth theme of the Omnibus Trade Act of 1988, which involved market opening. There was a realization that the United States needed to export its way out of its 1980s trade problems, so it needed to have open markets overseas. Particularly in the case of Japan, however, there was a certain unfairness in market access. In 1985, when the Reagan administration changed its views about the dollar, it also changed its views about Section 301 cases, cases that had largely been ignored until that time. Section 301 cases are petitions from industries saying that they have had trouble obtaining access to overseas markets. They are, in effect, "export-enhancement" petitions. In 1985, work was initiated on some 301 cases—perhaps in an effort to head off congressional legislation, Stern believed—but it was again a case of too little, too late.

David Richardson said that the Trade Act of 1988 gave the U.S. Trade Representative the right to initiate actions on Section 301 cases alone. It was the lack of executive action in this area from 1984 to 1985 that built pressure in Congress for further changes in trade policy.

Feldstein asked why trade policy turned to industry-specific market opening in the 1980s. He acknowledged that several earlier rounds of GATT negotiations had produced reciprocal reductions of tariffs across the board but noted that much attention is now focused on particular markets for particular products, such as plywood in Japan or cigarettes in Korea. Is there a history of such industry-specific efforts, and, if not, what caused that change in trade policy?

Niskanen responded that, as a consequence of the prior tariff negotiations, average tariffs had dropped substantially. During the 1980s, for example, the average tariff in Japan dropped to approximately 2 percent, as compared to 4 percent in the United States. Thus, tariffs are no longer the effective or marginal trade restraint; nontariff barriers are. Some of these other barriers are more difficult to negotiate on a multilateral basis, so pressure turned toward using other instruments, like Section 301, to reduce the barriers.

Feldstein concurred with Niskanen's explanation. He recalled that former Treasury Secretary Mike Blumenthal had once described an experience he had had as a trade negotiator. He had successfully negotiated substantial reductions in tariff rates in an earlier GATT round, and then he was told by the French negotiators that it was a waste of his effort because trade would now be restricted through administrative procedures to the same end as before. To accomplish any actual change, he would have to fight the battles in a new, more detailed arena.

Richardson said that there were precedents for market-opening, export-oriented negotiations. Certain Tokyo Round codes from the late 1970s had been viewed as devices for enhancing U.S. markets, specifically the government procurement code, the standards code, and the civil aircraft code. Of these, civil aircraft was a success, but the others were generally regarded as having had little effect. Those codes were rules oriented, so the American perception became that rules do not work as market-opening devices.

Thomas Enders suggested that what was different about the 1980s was that the international system had come under intolerable pressure when U.S. policy shifted toward fiscal ease and monetary tightness at the same time that Europe and Japan moved in the opposite direction. He felt that this pressure was much more severe than the pressures on trade in earlier decades and that it probably stimulated the great proliferation of administrative interferences with trade as well as the enormous complexity of the Trade Act of 1988. The question has now become whether these effects can be reversed.

Frankel noted the hypothesis that protectionist pressures are greater whenever the dollar is overvalued in real terms. The three most recent episodes of such an overvaluation were 1971–73, 1976–77, and 1981–85. Frankel suggested an alternative hypothesis that the trade deficit is a more important driving factor than the dollar itself.

Michael Mussa argued that, given the pressures that existed, U.S. trade policy in the 1980s was not all that bad. He noted that, since the turnaround in 1986, real U.S. exports have expanded by 60 percent. The U.S. manufacturing industry has recovered a great deal from the circumstances of the early 1980s despite the complaints of individual industries. And the Free Trade Agreement negotiated with Canada was an important accomplishment.

Further, while the Reagan administration did bend before the political winds, it was not totally lacking in backbone. Congress pushed consistently for even greater protection for the textile industry, and the administration vetoed those actions with equal consistency. Mussa thought that there may have been a political game at work there: Congress voted majorities almost equal to the amount required to override the president's veto, but not quite, and they therefore got credit with their textile constituents without having to fear that the "dirty deed" would be done.

The Omnibus Trade Bill is not all that bad either, given the pressures of the time. This is particularly due to the efforts of Senator Lloyd Bentsen and Representative Dan Rostenkowski, who prevented a lot of potentially damaging legislation from being included with the bill. Although Super 301 may be imperfect in some aspects, a reasonable job was done under the circumstances, and some specific trade actions taken under Section 301 have been very successful. Opening the Japanese market to beef and citrus, for example, has been a good thing for both countries. The important thing is to pick the right targets for trade policy changes: by and large, the trade representatives have done a good job of picking battles that can be won.

Finally, the administration's free trade rhetoric had an important impact around the world. Mexico moved away from a very protectionist trade policy toward a more open trade policy. There has been a similar trend in a wide variety of countries, and, in part, this can be attributed to the impact of U.S. free market rhetoric and the general orientation of the Reagan administration.

Russell Long put in a word on behalf of Congress. He pointed out that Congress and the public are not educated in the finer points of trade theory; consequently, they look at more direct issues. Someone in the domestic rice-producing industry, for example, might point to the fact that the Japanese pay about six times as much to produce rice but are unwilling to buy rice from U.S. producers. This raises the question, in their minds, of why the United States buys Japanese cars when they will not buy our rice. Members of Congress feel a responsibility to protect people, and sometimes that results in actions that do not agree with a more idealistic view of the situation.

William Poole raised the issue of whether industries that are granted relief ought to be required to give something in return. The problem with this approach is that many of these industries are declining permanently; they are at a comparative disadvantage. In the long run, nothing but protectionism will maintain these industries, so they cannot realistically be asked for much commitment in return for protection.

Feldstein agreed and added that those industries that will be viable in the long run will probably take steps to become more competitive anyway. Ford, for example, has become much more competitive in car manufacturing. But anybody could submit a seemingly convincing statement to the Commerce Department or the ITC explaining the thirty-two things they were going to do to shore up their industry and cut costs. It is hard to see how they could be held to this list except in the case of highly quantitative statements such as intended investment rates, for example.

David Stockman maintained that neither the auto nor the steel agreement was as bad as had been suggested. He discussed the auto import restrictions first, looking at both the process by which they were created and their consequences over the decade. There had been a great deal of pressure on the Hill to protect the auto industry, and in addition there was the Danforth bill. Perhaps that bill would have passed, but it could have been vetoed, and the veto certainly would have been sustained. There was a new secretary of Transportation, however, who believed that he was responsible for policy on cars, to the exclusion of the Commerce Department, which was responsible for commerce, and the ITC, which was in charge of trade. So the new secretary, Drew Lewis, "conspired with Ed Meese and others who wore their Adam Smith ties every day." They concluded that the Japanese should be induced to take responsibility for quotas themselves.

Thus, the Japanese were presented with an ultimatum: either they imposed a quota on themselves, voluntarily, or the administration would acquiesce to the Danforth bill, and it would be signed into law. Soon the White House received a phone call in which the president was informed that the Japanese had decided to take a statesmanlike course. So the president proceeded to a meeting of his Economic Policy Advisory Board and announced that the administration had gotten very lucky. They were not going to have to face the auto trade issue, as the Japanese had decided, surprisingly, to take action on their own.

The consequences of these shenanigans are the more interesting issue, Stockman argued. The "voluntary" restrictions created a tremendous scarcity of Japanese cars in the United States from 1981 to 1984. Until that time, it had not been clear that the Japanese would dominate the North American car industry. They were selling "econo-boxes" at the very low end of the market at a time when oil prices were $60.00 per barrel in today's dollars. The Japanese did not have a permanent foothold in the marketplace, and their dealer network was made up of retread used car dealers and worse.

In the early 1980s, however, the quota created monopoly rents, as Toyotas and Hondas were selling not at markdowns or with cash rebates but with huge premiums to the list price. The Japanese manufacturers allowed their dealers to keep these windfall profits, causing many failed Ford dealers to move over to Toyota, Honda, Nissan, Mazda, Mitsubishi, and so on. The infrastructure of the Japanese automobile distribution system was created during this period, giving the Japanese companies a permanent place in the auto market.

Japanese car sales rose to over 1 million each year, about the same as today. With sales at that level, with a permanent distribution system in place, and with the brand equity that had been created in their cars as a result of the early 1980s, the Japanese could then proceed with the next logical step—they made multibillion dollar capital investments to build state-of-the-art plants in the United States.

Stockman argued that this whole development was, paradoxically, enormously positive for the North American automobile industry. Millions of cars and trucks are now being built in North America with state-of-the-art technology and the best management practices in the world automobile industry. The white elephants of the car industry were forced to retire much faster than might otherwise have been the case. In the end, the apparent policy mistake of 1981 created, for the 1990s, a very strong 13–15 million unit per year North American automobile industry based on sparkling new plants.

In the case of steel, the administration had a strong political motivation for adopting protectionist measures—the negotiations on quotas were conducted only two months before the 1984 election because Drew Lewis had concluded that the Republicans would lose Pennsylvania without them. At the same time, there was concern that the solutions being developed by the Commerce Department were going to be worse and that the remedies responding to the large number of Section 201 cases at the ITC could have been even more damaging. Further, the industry had been demanding a 15 percent quota on all steel, which would have been very damaging to all the steel users in the U.S. economy. With a little finesse, the policymakers arrived at an 18.5 percent quota on finished steel with a big loophole for slab.

Although this new policy looked protectionist, U.S. Trade Representative

Bill Brock pronounced it a victory for free trade on the very next day. And, in most years, the steel quotas have not even been filled. The changes in the market probably would have occurred without the influence of the quotas, owing simply to movements of exchange rates, but passing the policy at the time may have prevented the application of more damaging solutions.

Weidenbaum pointed out that the Japanese auto producers shared rents with their dealers, as opposed to permitting the dealers to keep the entire excess. The increased corporate profits provided the funds used to develop higher-priced models such as the Infiniti and the Acura.

Stern wanted to clarify the distinction between dumping laws and the Section 201 cases she had discussed in the context of the auto and steel industries. Section 201 cases deal with fair trade, responding to injury complaints and basically allowing an industry breathing space for a predetermined amount of time. In 201 cases, the president has the power to adjust the ITC affirmative recommendation for import relief taking into account broader national economic and trade considerations. In contrast, the dumping law does not contemplate presidential exercise of discretion over the administration of the law, which tends to be highly technical but is often nevertheless controversial in its economic consequences.

Lionel Olmer remarked that not all the Reagan administration's trade policy interventions violated international law or the GATT. As Areeda mentioned, there is enormous flexibility permitted in the determinations made under those regulations. The steel agreement, for example, is totally consistent with U.S. obligations under GATT. Section 301, however, *is* inconsistent with GATT. The concept of fairness was enacted into law using the term *reciprocity,* which conveys some notion that there is a basic equity between the United States and its trading partners.

Olmer emphasized also that the European Community and Japan had conspired to allocate markets, including the United States, and that nothing had been done to stop them. This inaction had led to a perception of enormous unfairness in the American business community, building pressure for some changes in trade policy.

11 LDC Debt Policy

1. *Paul Krugman*
2. *Thomas O. Enders*
3. *William R. Rhodes*

1. *Paul Krugman*

U.S. Policy on Developing-Country Debt

U.S. policy on Third World debt was a major anomaly in the first Reagan administration. On taking office, that administration was strongly committed to the ideal of laissez-faire economic policies, suspicious of international economic coordination, and opposed to new forms of government intervention. Those administration officials who had strong views on the role of multilateral financial institutions such as the International Monetary Fund (IMF) and the World Bank—for example, Treasury Undersecretary Beryl Sprinkel—were sharply critical, arguing that, by providing an implicit safety net for both borrowing nations and lenders, these institutions encouraged irresponsible behavior. Initial administration policy called for limiting the resources and the role of both institutions and for a greater reliance on self-policing in international capital markets.

Yet, less than two years after taking office, the Reagan administration found itself at the center of an unprecedented piece of international financial coordination. This effort involved discreet but unmistakable coercion of private creditors, a key role for the previously scorned multilateral agencies, growing commitment of public resources, and eventually a de facto alliance between the U.S. government and some debtors to pressure banks into relinquishing their contractual rights. It is instructive to imagine how an administration economic official in 1981 would have viewed the Mexican debt reduction package of 1989, which in effect expropriated a large fraction of commercial bank claims, with partial compensation provided from official sources, that is, ultimately by creditor nation taxpayers. (Most estimates suggest that the banks did not lose and may have gained as a result, but that is not the issue.)

The question is how this policy emerged. How did a U.S. government that was ideologically committed to a hands-off financial policy, uninterested in international coordination, and convinced of the sanctity of property rights find itself leading a highly interventionist international effort that eventually came to center on debt forgiveness?

This paper examines the evolution of U.S. debt policy from the initial crisis through the 1989 Mexican plan, in an attempt to shed light on how and why policy decisions were made. It is important to emphasize that this paper is *not* primarily intended as an evaluation of the appropriateness or success of the policies followed: it will be evident that I have my own views about developing-country debt, but the main question here is why we did what we did, not what we should have done instead.

The paper is in three main sections. The first provides a brief history of debt policy, highlighting several crucial turning points. The second discusses conceptual issues in debt policy, reviewing the options that faced the U.S. government. The third is concerned with the actual process of policy-making. A brief final section asks whether the evident defects in the process of policy formation actually did much harm.

11.1   A Brief History of Debt Policy

Table 11.1 presents a selective chronology of the debt problem. Some of the events singled out are familiar turning points; others are singled out because, in retrospect, they can be seen as indicators of future trends. The chronology also mixes real-world events with statements and reports. Obviously, such events as the publication of Cline's (1983) study on debt prospects were not as

Table 11.1   A Debt Chronology

1982	August	Mexican weekend: onset of crisis
	November	Mexico reaches IMF agreement
1983	February	Rohatyn plan for debt reduction
	March	Cline study of debt prospects
	December	Alfonsin takes office in Argentina
1985	October	"Baker Plan" unveiled at Seoul
1986	June	Bradley Plan for debt reduction
1987	February	Brazilian debt moratorium
	May	Citibank reserves against LDC debt
	December	Mexico attempts to reduce debt via bond swap
1988	June	U.S. agrees to allow African debt reduction
1989	February	Riots in Venezuela
	March	Brady Plan
	September	Mexican debt reduction package

important as, say, the Brazilian debt moratorium (practical men are the slaves of defunct economists, not live and kicking ones), but the statements are useful indicators of the drift in ideas.

What the chronology alone cannot convey is a sense of the dynamics of the problem. Any partition of events is arbitrary, but I will identify five stages in policy:

1. A "firefighting" stage from August 1982 through most of that fall, as desperate efforts were made to mobilize enough financial resources to prevent a feared financial crisis:
2. A relatively calm period in 1983 and 1984 during which problem debtors were widely viewed as being on the road to recovery, under programs that had as their centerpiece "concerted lending" by private creditors;
3. As the concerted lending strategy came under widespread attack in 1985, a rethinking of that strategy that culminated in the Baker Plan—in essence, a reaffirmation of the concerted lending strategy's basic thrust, but with an increased role for official lending;
4. The "menu approach" period, a period from 1986 through 1988 in which there was widespread optimism that new financial techniques could substantially reduce debt burdens; and
5. The official U.S. acceptance of the idea of coordinated debt reduction in the so-called Brady Plan and a first effort at implementing that plan in Mexico.

Let us review these different stages.

11.1.1 Firefighting

Although it arguably should not have, the Mexican payments crisis of August 1982 took the U.S. government completely by surprise. Federal Reserve staffers had prepared a report in April warning of potential debt-service difficulties, but this report did not receive high-level attention. The U.S. government should not be especially faulted for this, however, since few outside the government saw the crisis coming either. The rapid spread of the crisis to other debtor countries, most importantly Brazil, also came as a surprise.

Ex ante, one might have expected some agonizing over appropriate government policy. Mexico and the other debtors who soon found themselves in difficulty primarily owed their money to private creditors. Thus, one might have supposed that a free market–oriented administration would treat the matter as a private affair, especially given statements by such officials as Undersecretary Sprinkel in opposition to the international rescue role of the IMF. Indeed, such was the inertia of policy positions that, at the Toronto IMF–World Bank meetings in September 1982, *after* the Mexican crisis broke, the United States was at odds with all other major nations in its opposition to any large increase in the IMF's resources.

In fact, however, with very little hesitation, the United States plunged into the provision of cash to Mexico. Substantial administrative creativity was displayed in releasing cash; most notably, an advance purchase by the Strategic Petroleum Reserve was used to funnel funds to Mexico via its state-owned oil company. The Mexican example then served as a model for Brazil, Venezuela, and other countries as they developed similar debt-servicing problems. Any and all financial resources to hand—swap lines, General Agreement to Borrow, Bank for International Settlements (BIS) loans—were pressed into service to avert an immediate default.

In retrospect, this emergency financing played the role of a bridge to the more organized process of rescheduling plus concerted lending. We should not, however, abuse hindsight in interpreting the policy at the time. As of the early fall of 1982, emergency lending was *not* viewed as a temporary measure leading to a prolonged process of workout. Instead, the situation was viewed as both more dangerous and less fundamental—more of a bank run than a basic problem of excessive debt. The U.S. economy was in a deepening recession at the time of the crisis, and there were widespread fears that Third World debt could trigger a 1931-style financial collapse. At the same time, it was generally expected that, if such a collapse were avoided, the crisis would blow over quickly: Treasury and Federal Reserve officials expected to see normal market access restored within months if not weeks.

By late fall 1982, this perspective had changed in both respects. An immediate financial crisis had been averted, and the growing signs of a rapid U.S. recovery were making officials breathe easier. On the other hand, the magnitude of the debt-servicing problem became increasingly apparent, and the short-term emergency mentality shifted to a medium-term perspective.

11.1.2 Concerted Lending

The Mexican debt agreement of November 1982, and the similar agreement reached by Brazil in February 1983, set the basic pattern of debt policy for the next several years.

The basic premise of this policy was that the problem of debtors was one of liquidity, not solvency. That is, while the debtors could not maintain normal debt service given their inability to attract new funds from international capital markets, they would eventually be able to grow out of their problems given a combination of recovery in the world economy and appropriate policies at home. The main idea of the policy was therefore to buy time. If enough debt service could be postponed, countries might be able to meet their remaining obligations by adopting austerity programs under IMF surveillance. As their export revenues grew, the countries would begin to look more creditworthy, and eventually they would resume normal access to credit markets.[1]

---

1. Official statements during this period generally stressed the need for policy reform, not just austerity. That is, one would not simply wait for growth; one would do something actually to encourage it. In practice, however, this was little more than lip service. Optimistic estimates of growth prospects were based on historical relations between OECD growth and LDC exports, not on hopes for success of innovative growth-oriented policy, while the IMF-imposed economic plans

Table 11.2   **Long-Term Bank Credit Commitments to Developing Countries ($billion)**

	Developing Countries		Western Hemisphere	
	Spontaneous	Concerted	Spontaneous	Concerted
1983	17.6	13.9	1.9	13.3
1984	12.7	16.5	.6	15.5
1985	13.8	2.2	.2	2.2
1986	14.7	8.1	.8	7.7
1987	14.1	2.3	.4	2.3
1988	11.8	5.7	1.2	5.2
1989	12.9	2.3	1.6	1.6

Source: IMF, *International Capital Markets: Developments and Prospects* (April 1990), table A22.

The normal method of postponing debt service is, of course, rescheduling of repayment of principal. It was generally believed, however, that this would not be sufficient—that the debtor countries could not in fact run trade surpluses large enough to cover all the interest on their debt. Thus, there had to be de facto relending of interest payments. This could have been accomplished via interest capitalization, but this option was opposed for a variety of reasons, described in the appendixes at the end of this paper. Instead, a more ad hoc approach was adopted in which existing creditors were rounded up to provide new loans the proceeds of which could be used to pay interest on existing debt. This procedure was widely referred to as "involuntary" lending but was more discreetly described as "concerted" lending in official documents.

Table 11.2 shows the role of concerted lending in the debt problem from 1983 to 1989. It shows long-term credit commitments by commercial banks to developing countries in general, and to Latin American countries in particular, and separates these commitments into "spontaneous" lending (i.e., normal voluntary lending) and concerted loans. Two points stand out. First, for the Latin American nations, essentially all bank credit since 1982 has taken the form of concerted lending. Second, the major period of such lending was 1983 and 1984. It dwindled to negligible sum in 1985, and despite occasional packages—for example, the sizable package negotiated by Mexico in 1986, after the combined effects of the 1985 earthquake and oil price collapse created a desperate need for cash—concerted lending ceased to play a major role.

It is also important for discussing the eventual abandonment of the concerted lending strategy to note that concerted lending was not identical either to net financing for developing countries or to the change in bank exposure. Bank exposure grew by less than the concerted lending numbers would suggest. To

emphasized stabilization rather than growth. Realistically, U.S. policy may be summarized as, "Get the debtors to run as big a trade surplus as they can, push the banks to relend the interest the countries can't pay, and wait for better conditions."

a limited extent, this was because of a variety of leakages—for example, repayment of principal on loans not covered by rescheduling agreements and contraction of short-term credit. After 1985, there was also a significant reduction in bank claims as a result of debt buy backs, swaps, etc. Meanwhile, bank credit was supplemented by official credit and some other capital flows, such as direct investment, while offset in part by capital flight.

Timing and coverage issues make an exact comparison difficult, but the rough comparisons shown in table 11.3 may be useful. From the end of 1982 to the end of 1985, concerted lending commitments totaled about $30 billion. However, the commercial bank debt of fifteen heavily indebted countries rose by only $22 billion, and this rise was nearly offset by a fall in other private debt. From the end of 1985 to the end of 1988, concerted lending commitments totaled approximately $15 billion; the change in bank claims was *minus* $1.5 billion, largely because about $14 billion in claims was canceled through buy backs and swaps.

Official financing nonetheless covered some debt service: the fifteen heavily indebted nations were able to finance a cumulative current account deficit of $17 billion in 1983–85 and of $35 billion in 1986–88. ("Financing" through arrears played a significant role in the latter period.)

In retrospect, it is apparent that the concerted lending strategy did not really function as advertised. It was initially envisioned that the brunt of the financing burden would in fact be borne by the commercial banks, with official finance playing a secondary role. In reality, this was true only at the very beginning— perhaps only in the first year. Thereafter, bank claims on problem debtors grew very slowly in nominal terms and thus declined both in real terms and a fortiori as a share of bank assets, while official creditors bore a steadily increasing share of the risk.

This risk shifting, which accelerated over time, would eventually be a key argument for the rethinking of debt strategy that culminated in the Brady Plan. In 1983–84, however, this was far in the future.

11.1.3   The Baker Plan

There was a kind of pause in the debt problem during 1984. Essentially, this pause was due to a temporary glut of cash in debtors' hands. Debtor trade

Table 11.3   **Financing of Fifteen Debtors ($billion)**

	1983–85	1986–88
Current account	−17.0	−35.3
Change in commercial bank debt	22.2	−1.5
Change in other debt to private creditors	−18.4	−1.8
Change in debt to official creditors	37.8	50.4
Long-term borrowing from official creditors	34.7	32.1

Source: IMF, *World Economic Outlook* (May 1990), tables A39, A42, A47.

adjustment proceeded much more rapidly than had been expected: the fifteen heavily indebted nations moved from a trade surplus of $4 billion in 1982 to $43 billion in 1984 and reduced their current account deficit from $51 billion to near zero. At the same time, the commitments from early rounds of concerted lending were disbursed. The result was that major debtors found themselves with swelling foreign exchange reserves and no immediate need for new financing.

During 1985, however, pressures began to build again. The debtor countries had achieved their rapid trade improvement overwhelmingly through import compression rather than export growth, and a counterpart to the import compression was a severe slump in output. As debtor countries attempted to reflate, they found that the foreign exchange constraint was once again binding, and complaints rose about the increasingly niggardly supply of bank finance.

At the same time, the prospects for a restoration of normal capital flows to problem debtors—an event that had initially been expected to occur within a few years—appeared to recede. In spite of a rapid economic recovery in the United States and a more modest one in the rest of the world, exports of developing countries did not show strong growth. Indeed, thanks to falling commodity prices, they actually fell in 1985. Thus, the ratio of debt to exports, widely watched as an indicator of creditworthiness, worsened instead of improving.

As a result, during the first half of 1985, there was a growing sense that a departure was needed in the debt strategy. A number of plans for debt reduction as opposed to further financing were circulated outside the U.S. government, and Preston Martin, the vice-chairman of the Federal Reserve, publicly called for debt reduction in June 1985. He was, however, reprimanded by Paul Volcker.

Instead, the U.S. government chose to emphasize a revitalization of the basic debt strategy of the previous two and a half years rather than a fundamental departure. In October 1985, at the Seoul IMF–World Bank meeting, Treasury Secretary Baker announced a program intended to expand financing for a group of heavily indebted countries—the "Baker 15," now a standard subcategory in IMF analyses.

Although hailed at the time as a major new initiative, the Baker Plan was quite conservative in that it did not change the basic premises of the previous strategy. Debt problems continued to be viewed as issues of liquidity rather than solvency, even though by 1985 it was no longer possible to attribute them to recession in the OECD nations. The United States remained firmly opposed to any debt package that involved debt reduction as opposed to a postponement of obligations. Indeed, until 1988, the United States refused even to allow other official creditors to offer unilateral debt forgiveness (which several European nations wanted to offer to desperate African nations), for fear that a damaging precedent would be set.

The main innovation of the Baker Plan was its call for a shift in the sources of official lending, with the World Bank now expected to play a much larger role, shifting away from its traditional project lending. Under the initial proposal, World Bank lending would still have played a secondary role to concerted lending by private creditors: the initial plan called for $9 billion of World Bank money and $20 billion from commercial banks over the next three years. In practice, as we have already seen, the Baker Plan had the effect of accelerating the shift of risk from the commercial banks to official creditors.

It is also important to see the Baker Plan in context. It came closely on the heels of the Plaza Accord to drive down the dollar. Both actions were seen as indicating a new U.S. willingness to engage in international policy coordination; in both cases it was widely expected that the initial actions would be only a forerunner to more extensive commitments. Thus, even though the sum of money proposed in the Baker Plan was modest even in prospect, the plan did temporarily dispel the sense that the debt strategy had run aground.

11.1.4 The Menu Approach

The renewed enthusiasm for a strategy of growing out of debt that followed the Baker Plan did not last very long. Among debtors, Peru and then Brazil tried a tactic of aggressive confrontation with their creditors. In the United States, however, policy discussion was dominated for much of 1986 and 1987 by hopes that market forces could be harnessed to alleviate the debt problem.

Mexico instituted the first debt-equity swap program in 1984, and Brazil and Chile followed in 1985; by 1986, Chile's program had assumed significant proportions relative to its debt, and it grew even larger in 1987. In essence, these programs allowed creditors to cash in their claims, provided that the proceeds were invested in the debtor country and that other restrictions were met. The main attraction of such swaps was the existence of a secondary market in debt at which claims on problem debtors traded at substantial discounts from par. A potential investor could therefore make the investment at lower cost by first acquiring debt on the secondary market, then convert that debt into local currency.

Initially, debt-equity swaps were viewed with enthusiasm both by U.S. financiers and by U.S. officials. They were seen as a double advantage: both canceling a part of the debt, and thus reducing the burden, and attracting direct investment as a new source of funds. Over time, it became clear that the advantages of such swaps had been overstated; the limitations of debt-equity conversions are reviewed in the appendixes at the end of this paper. For a time, however, debt-equity swaps were seen as demonstrating the possibility of alleviating and perhaps even solving the debt problem through market mechanisms. The idea was that, by offering creditors a "menu" of debt conversion alternatives, they could be induced both to cancel a significant fraction of debt and to supply a stream of additional financing.

Chile proved unique in its willingness to pursue debt-equity conversions on a large scale relative to debt. In spite of pressure both from the financial community and occasionally from the U.S. Treasury (which at times appeared to

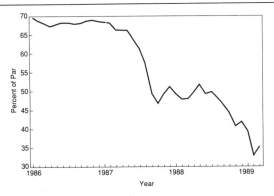

Fig. 11.1   Secondary market prices of LDC debt

view a willingness to facilitate debt-equity swaps as a key test of debtor-country virtue),[2] Mexico and other nations scaled back their programs because of budgetary issues. There remained a hope, however, that sophisticated financial engineering could still play a major helpful role. The attraction of such schemes grew in particular because of a market event: the collapse of secondary market prices.

As late as the beginning of 1987, the secondary market discounts on developing-country debt were moderate: the average discount for the heavily indebted nations (fig. 11.1) was only about 35 percent, and that for Mexico and Brazil was less. In February 1987, however, an increasingly frustrated Brazil declared a moratorium on debt service, leading to a general decline in secondary prices. In May 1987, Citibank announced that it was reserving against its developing-country claims, a move that was quickly matched by other creditors. In principle, reserving is an accounting measure that should have had little real effect, but in this case it apparently served as a signal that the debt problem was not improving, and secondary market prices crashed further, to an average of 40 percent or less of par.

Given the huge discounts on developing-country debt, it was natural to search for ways to capture that discount and pass at least part of it on to the debtor. A major effort along these lines was the Morgan-Mexico swap announced in December 1987. New bonds were issued and offered in exchange for existing debt. The new bonds were expected to sell at much lower discounts than commercial bank debt, partly because their principal was guaranteed by money placed in escrow at the U.S. Treasury, but also because Mexico attempted to convince its creditors that the new bonds would be treated as senior to the old debt. Thus, it was hoped that the debt swap would reduce overall debt.

2. The persistent faith of the U.S. Treasury in debt-equity swaps was demonstrated by press interviews given by Treasury Undersecretary David Mulford in the spring of 1989—by which time the severe difficulties of such swaps were generally understood—in which he argued that swaps could make a major contribution to the Brady Plan.

In practice, the discount on the new bonds was much higher than hoped; to a first approximation, Mexico did no better than it would have had it used the money placed in escrow to finance a straight buy back of debt for cash (see Lamdany 1988). While hopes were expressed that a second try would yield better results, in effect the disappointment with the Morgan-Mexico deal marked the end of optimism that a menu of clever financial packages could do much to resolve the debt problem (except, perhaps, at the U.S. Treasury, where the initial version of the Brady Plan seemed to presume that small official resources could be leveraged up into major debt relief).

11.1.5   The Brady Plan

By 1988, it was already clear that the Baker Plan, like the previous concerted lending strategy, was not working as advertised. With debt claims selling at 35 percent of par and debt-export ratios higher than they had been in 1982, it was no longer realistic to suppose that a return to normal market access was a reasonable target for the medium term. Any reconsideration of the strategy was, however, unwelcome for most of the year, for two reasons: the administration in general did not want publicly to abandon a widely touted policy before the election, and the secretary of the Treasury did not want to repudiate its own policy publicly. The United States was more willing than before to accept the idea of debt reduction in some circumstances. Notably, no objection was raised to the use of external resources to buy back and cancel much of Bolivia's debt, and, in September, the United States agreed that other official creditors could forgive African debt if they so desired (although the United States would not participate). However, any major change in U.S. policy was ruled out.

Following the election, however, an interagency group began serious discussion of debt strategy. According to accounts of participants, what this group found most alarming was not so much the generally disappointing results of the Baker Plan as the evident shifting of risk from private creditors to government and multilateral agencies. A chart that looked something like figure 11.2

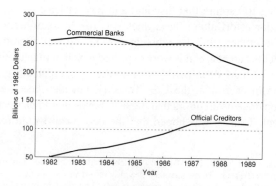

Fig. 11.2   Composition of "Baker 15" debt

was the subject of alarmed discussion. This figure shows claims on the "Baker 15" by private and public creditors, deflated by the U.S. CPI. Recall that both the initial concerted lending strategy and the Baker Plan were advertised as "bail-ins" rather than bailouts for banks; by late 1988, they were looking rather like bailouts after all.

Adding pressure for a change were serious riots in Venezuela following imposition of an austerity plan in February 1989. Although it was quickly noted that Venezuela was perhaps the least deserving of the debtor nations—more than 100 percent of its debt accumulation had been used to finance capital flight rather than investment—the riots reinforced a sense that something new had to be done.

Finally, in March 1989, the new Treasury secretary, Nicholas Brady, announced that the United States now favored a policy of debt reduction. The circumstances surrounding the Brady speech need further discussion and are revealing about the U.S. policy process; I return to these in the third section of the paper. For now, however, let us focus on the substance.

As initially presented, Brady's initiative had two somewhat contradictory features. On one side, for the first time Brady threw the support of the U.S. government behind the idea of seeking debt reduction rather than growing out of the debt problem. On the other hand, his speech emphasized the use of voluntary, market-based mechanisms to reduce debt. (Bankers were later to make a point of the fact that the word *voluntary* was used seven times in the speech).

The reason these features were somewhat contradictory was that it was difficult to envision any large-scale debt reduction within a voluntary framework. As initially presented, the Brady Plan seemed to envision the use of resources from creditor nations and multilateral institutions as sweeteners for financial engineering along the lines of the Morgan-Mexico plan. The results of that plan suggested, however, that such schemes would do little better than straight buy backs at reducing debt. A large debt reduction through buy backs, however, would be extremely expensive, even at the secondary market prices prevailing at the time of the announcement—and a buy back scheme would drive these prices up further. (Secondary prices of developing-country debt actually did rise by about a third in the two weeks following the Brady speech.)

Following Brady's speech, Treasury officials floated suggestions that a debt reduction on the order of 20 percent would be sought. Even though this seemed modest, the available resources at the World Bank plus other likely sources seemed inadequate to support voluntary debt reduction on that scale while at the same time continuing to meet debtors' financing gaps. And, if resources had been made available on the requisite scale, the benefits would have gone in large part to the creditors.

This raises some interesting questions about U.S. policy-making. Why did Brady make a proposal that was immediately seen by knowledgeable observers as infeasible? Was it simply an error, or was it a way of establishing a position for a subsequent, achievable policy? I will return to these questions below. The important point now, however, is to note the position that the Brady speech created. Essentially, the U.S. government had committed its prestige to achievement of significant debt reduction, but such debt reduction could not be achieved without either committing much larger resources or abandoning the principle that debt reduction would be voluntary.

Three alternatives thus presented themselves. The U.S. could forgo the goal of large-scale debt reduction, abandon the principle of voluntarism, or commit much larger amounts of money than Brady seemed to have envisioned. It is still too early to tell the full story, but in general the United States gave ground on all three fronts.

The reduction in the ambitions of the Brady Plan may best be seen by considering the case of Mexico, which was the first major beneficiary of the plan and arguably the country for whose benefit the plan was devised. In the end, after very intense negotiations, Mexico achieved a reduction in the present value of its debt of approximately $14 billion, or 14 percent. This was clearly insufficient to make much real difference in the Mexican situation, although it was enough to count as a political victory for the Salinas government that indirectly raised confidence. Mexico was unique in its situation, both as a model of reformist policy and as a vital interest of the United States that would receive special treatment in any case; thus, the modest size of the Mexican package implies that the Brady Plan as a whole will be even more modest.

Whether the principle of voluntarism has been abandoned is more controversial. As of the time of this writing, four debt reduction packages had been concluded subsequent to the Brady Plan—in Mexico, the Philippines, Costa Rica, and Venezuela. The Philippine plan was of minor size both relative to its debt burden and in dollar terms, while Costa Rica is of course a small nation. Thus, the two major debt reductions have been the Mexican and the Venezuelan, which essentially followed the Mexican model.

In the Mexican debt reduction, the idea of voluntary action was essentially abandoned. Mexican debt was converted into new instruments, and the agreement contained a paragraph stating that the conversion would explicitly constitute a new contract (a "novation"). This was taken to imply that the new contracts would not be subject to the sharing clauses originally contained in loan agreements and thus in effect that banks that refused to participate in the debt reduction would not be able to demand payment. So the only "voluntary" aspect of the debt reduction was the choice among several options offered to creditors: whether to receive bonds with reduced interest payments or lower face value or, alternatively, to offer new money.

As compensation for the forced debt reduction, banks were given guarantees of principal and partial guarantees on interest. Evaluating these guarantees is tricky, but most estimates suggest that the compensation per dollar of reduction in the present value of claims was well below the secondary market price of debt—perhaps 25 rather than 40 percent. At the same time, however, the debt reduction enhanced the value of remaining claims so that the market value of the debt after the reduction was little changed.

In the appendixes at the end of this paper, I argue that a Mexican-style debt reduction package, in which banks are given the choice of exiting at the initial secondary price or of providing new money, is in effect a way of ensuring that the bulk of the benefits of the commitment money from international financial institutions go to the country rather than to its creditors.

The Venezuela debt reduction was similar in form to the Mexican plan, in that a menu of options was offered; however, the terms were more generous.

The size of resources available for debt reduction is to some extent an arbitrary number. Initial estimates in the weeks following the Brady speech suggested that as little as $10 billion might be available. The current usual number suggested is $34 billion: $12 billion each from the World Bank and the IMF and another $10 billion from Japan.

So the outcome of the Brady Plan to date is two fairly modest debt reductions for large debtors—altogether the debt reduction attributable to "Brady Plan" initiatives has been perhaps 5 percent of the outstanding debt burden rather than 20 percent. The form of the major debt reductions, however, marked a fundamental change in procedure: essentially, bank claims were seized by a kind of international eminent domain rather than through a voluntary market transaction.

11.1.6   Observations

This brief history conveys two impressions. First, after the dramatic rescue operations of 1982 and 1983, the pace of events in debt policy seems remarkably slow. The failure of the concerted lending strategy to deliver significant increases in commercial bank exposure was apparent by mid-1984, yet there was no revision of the policy until October 1985, and the Baker Plan amounted to a reaffirmation rather than a change in course. Even more strikingly, the failure of the Baker Plan to yield either significant new private capital flows or any prospect of a return to creditworthiness was evident by mid-1987, with the Citibank provisioning and the collapse of secondary market prices. Yet the Brady Plan did not come until March 1989—and has moved forward at a very sluggish pace.

Second, after the 1982–83 response, U.S. policy has consistently been very cautious about departures from previous strategy—to an extent that seems to have surprised debtors and creditors alike. Thus, in 1985, there was widespread expectation of a major rethinking of debt policy; the Baker Plan was instead more of a continuation of existing policy, with only modest new resources proposed and much less actually delivered. In 1989, the Brady Plan was initially treated as a major departure in strategy, but it soon became clear that the United States was prepared neither to devote major new resources nor to back any radical demands for debt reduction on the part of the developing countries themselves.

The overall picture, then, is one of a U.S. policy on developing-country debt that has responded as little as possible, as late as possible—essentially a reactive policy. (This is not necessarily a bad thing.) Later in this paper I will try to account for this absence of initiative. First, however, it is necessary to review the options on debt policy: what the United States *might* have done.

11.2   Debt Policy Options

The theory of debt policy has been the subject of an excessive literature. This paper will not review that literature in any depth; many of the key concepts appear in the volumes edited by Sachs (1989) and by Frenkel, Dooley, and Wickham (1990). Instead, I want to focus on three key dimensions of choice in debt policy.

The first dimension of choice is that of how much to have a debt policy at all—of intervention versus laissez-faire. It was by no means necessary that the U.S. government intervene in the debt problem. Most of the debt of problem debtors was owed to private creditors, primarily commercial banks. These private creditors lent money voluntarily before 1983, charging premia over low-risk rates that reflected their own judgment of the risk entailed in such lending. Why should the U.S. government take any responsibility if these risky loans happened to go bad?

This is not as naive a question as it sounds. Before World War II, as Eichengreen and Portes (1989) have noted, the U.S. government paid little attention to defending the interests of its bondholders with claims on Third World debtors. Even in 1982–83, conservative critics of the emerging debt policy argued that, by intervening, the United States was reinforcing a moral hazard problem, in which banks would lend and/or countries borrow irresponsibly in the expectation of a bailout. Later, a different critique would arise from the left, claiming that the U.S. government's intervention had been detrimental to the interests of the debtors, deterring them from making a straightforward default.

On the other side, there are several rationales for intervention. The most widely discussed have been the following:

1. *Stability of the international financial system.* Relative to the size of the world economy, the debt problem is not especially large. The combined gross national products of the "Baker 15" amount to only about 4 percent of that of the OECD, the face value of their debt to only about 1 percent of OECD wealth, the interest on that debt to only about one-quarter of 1 percent of OECD GNP. The Third World debt problem nonetheless provoked considerable anxiety in 1982 because the debt was concentrated in the hands of large commercial banks, which are highly leveraged, so, even though the debt was small relative to the size of the OECD economy, it considerably exceeded the capital of money center banks. As a result, it was feared that the debt crisis could spiral into a collapse of the banking system. This created a perception

of urgency about government intervention that overrode what might otherwise have been caution in 1982–83.

2. *Free-rider problems.* A few months after the onset of the crisis, one began to hear from a number of quarters the argument that government action was necessary to induce creditors to act in their own interest; Cline's influential 1983 study was representative on this point. The argument ran as follows. Once a country was in trouble, it was in the interest of any individual creditor to halt lending and, indeed, to pull out as much money as possible. When all creditors tried to do this, however, they provoked a liquidity crisis that would without action have forced immediate default. Yet there was a perceived possibility that the debtor countries could return to solvency given a breathing space and that creditors as a group would be better off if they gave the country time. So there was a conflict between the interests of individual creditors and their collective interest. As a result, official arm-twisting to force creditors not just to reschedule but to increase their exposure was actually doing them a favor.

This argument also surfaced in a different form in later discussions of debt reduction, where it was argued that pure debt forgiveness might be in the collective but not the individual interest of the creditors. We return to this point below.

In either case, it is tricky to turn the free-rider argument into a case for commitment of official funds to the process, which as we have seen was the bulk of the financing after the first year or so. However, a few shaky grounds for official finance can be offered. To the extent that the United States and other governments might find themselves short of sticks with which to coerce banks into acting in their own interests, a carrot might have been necessary. Also, if coordination of creditors turns out to be difficult, official lending may be a second-best answer for protecting the value of claims that ultimately represent domestic wealth. Early analyses of the debt strategy emphasized concerted lending as the main solution to the free-rider problem, with official lending as a secondary lubricant. As we have seen, of course, this is not what happened.

3. *Other economic interests.* Aside from the financial stake in recapturing as much as possible of the value of bank claims, creditor country governments found themselves with some other economic interests, notably on the trade side. Since the trade adjustment forced by the debt crisis primarily took the form of import compression, the debt problem had a significant impact on industrial country exports. Arguably, then, this created a trade policy and/or macroeconomic interest in helping in a debt workout.

While the trade consequences of the debt problem were widely cited by reports prepared outside the government calling for more generous terms for the debtors, however, it is doubtful whether concern over these consequences played much role in actual policy. Notably, periods when debtor countries were running very large trade surpluses, as in 1984–85, and as a result did not immediately need much cash, were times of quiescence rather than urgency in U.S. debt policy.

4. *Political interests.* The last concern motivating the U.S. government in its departure from laissez-faire on debt was concern over the possible radicalizing effects of a confrontation between debtors and creditors. In particular, the United States could not ignore the possible effects of debt on Mexican politics. It was not unimportant that the crisis first broke in Mexico; it is doubtful that the U.S. response would have been as swift and decisive had, say, Brazil been the first major debtor to get into trouble. It is also no accident that the first major Brady Plan debt reduction also involved Mexico; as described below, Mexican President Salinas deliberately positioned himself so that a debt reduction package was essential to him politically and thus in such a way that the U.S. government had a compelling interest in making such a package happen.

I would argue that, in practice, U.S. policy has primarily been motivated by the first and last of these concerns: by the desire to protect financial stability and by worries over the political implications of debt. The economic case for coordination arguably *should* have been driving U.S. debt policy, and lip service was given to it as a principle; but, in practice, when either financial or political jitters were absent, U.S. debt policy tended to drift.

11.2.1   Financing versus Forgiving

Given a determination on the part of the U.S. government to do something about debt, what should it do? Should it seek to postpone debt service, giving the countries involved time to improve their situation, or should it seek to reduce the obligations of the countries permanently?

The conventional view is that it is appropriate to "finance" the debt, simply postponing debt service, if the country's problem is merely one of liquidity but that one should seek debt forgiveness if the country is insolvent. This is a useful way to ask what features of the country's situation should be examined, but it is ultimately inadequate as a way of posing the problem. The reason is that a country that was demonstrably solvent would not be illiquid: it would be able to borrow from confident creditors. Thus, a debt problem is prima facie evidence of at least a significant risk that the country is indeed insolvent.

Instead of a hard and fast distinction between liquidity and solvency, then, we should instead ask whether creditors are best served by maintaining the face value of their claims and playing for time or by reaching a settlement that reduces a country's obligations. There is by now a standard way of thinking about this issue, the "debt value curve" (illustrated in fig. 11.3).[3]

---

3. This curve, which I apparently first introduced (Krugman 1990), is often referred to as the "debt Laffer curve." I named it that to emphasize the theoretical possibility that reducing debt could actually increase expected repayment. It is probably better, however, to drop Laffer's name in order to deemphasize the question of whether countries are literally on the wrong side of the curve—which no major debtor can be confidently asserted to be. As it turns out, for Brady Plan issues it is more important to emphasize instead the fact that the curve may be fairly flat in the relevant range—which *is* borne out by the evidence.

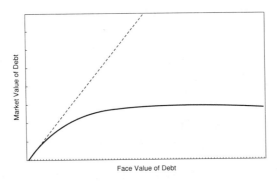

Fig. 11.3 The debt value curve

On the horizontal axis of figure 11.3, I show the face value of claims on a country, on the vertical axis the present value of expected payments (which will normally be close to the value of the debt on the secondary market). For low levels of debt, the face value will lie close to the forty-five-degree line since the country will almost always be able and willing to pay in full. For higher levels of debt, however, the expected payments will fall short of the face value to a steadily increasing extent. And it is at least possible that, at sufficiently high levels of debt, less is more: that a reduction in debt would actually increase the expected payments to creditors.

The reason for this potential downturn, if it happens, is that a debt burden so large that it is virtually unpayable acts like a heavy tax on an economy, both discouraging effective action on the part of the government and discouraging private investment.

When is it in the financial interest of creditors as a group to forgive debt? In principle, when the country is actually on the downward-sloping side of this curve. In this case, a lower debt burden will improve a country's prospects sufficiently to make the smaller face value of debt actually worth more.

Four points should be noted about this analysis. First, the simple fact that debt is worth considerably less on the secondary market than its face value is not a sufficient indicator that debt reduction is in the interests of creditors. There is a range of the debt value curve that lies well below the forty-five-degree line yet is still upward sloping. Underlying this observation is the point that a debt that *probably* will not be paid in full nonetheless *might* be paid; creditors who reduce their claims lose the possibility of benefiting from surprising good fortune.

Related to this point, it is by no means straightforward to evaluate just when debt reduction is in fact in creditors' interest. Estimates of the debt value curve, for example, by Claessens et al. (1990), suggest that some debtors may indeed be on the wrong side. But the largest debtors are not, and, in any case, these estimates are far from reliable and play no role thus far in practical discussion. The most that one can say with any confidence is that a country with a very low secondary market price is more likely to be on the wrong side than one whose debt sells at close to par. The sharp fall in secondary market prices in 1987 therefore made the case for debt reduction stronger but not conclusive.

Finally, note that any case for debt reduction is, like the case for lending to a troubled debtor, a collective rather than an individual one. Each creditor would benefit if all other creditors reduce their claims, but would prefer to maintain its own at full value. Thus, even when debt reduction is clearly in everyone's interest, no individual creditor may be willing to act.

On the whole, no convincing case has yet been made that debt forgiveness is in the financial interests of creditors—even though such an assertion was less implausible by early 1989 than a few years previously. This may, however, be a misleading way to pose the question because U.S. policy interests are not purely financial.

Suppose for a moment that, while private creditors are not convinced that debt reduction will actually raise the value of their claims, they do believe that the probability that the last dollar will be paid is low and that reducing the debt will at least somewhat increase the probability that what is left will be serviced. This amounts to a belief that the curve, if not downward sloping, is at any rate quite flat in the relevant range. In this case, creditors should be willing to agree to substantial debt reduction in return for modest compensation from official sources. And suppose that the U.S. government perceives other interests, say political, in promoting debt relief. Then a debt reduction deal will be attractive: a small expenditure of public money can buy large debt reduction, with non-economic benefits that outweigh the cost.

Note that this is a different case for officially sponsored debt reduction from the usual one. Most calls for debt relief are based on the assertion that the creditor nations have a compelling, urgent national interest in debt relief. Here, their interest need not be so overwhelming because the costs of debt reduction need not be large.

It is probably excessively charitable to think of the Brady Plan as being based on a clear appreciation of the likelihood that debt reduction could now be carried out cheaply, but in a vague way the sense that banks could be induced to forgive debt with modest incentives did underlie the U.S. change of policy. Unfortunately, the plan immediately ran into a difficulty: the difference between collective and individual costs of going along.

11.2.2   Voluntarism versus Collective Action

Suppose that it is decided to pursue debt reduction, using official resources to compensate creditors. How should this debt reduction be carried out?

One model would be to impose a concerted solution: each creditor must reduce its claims by some fraction (or exchange its claims for new claims with reduced debt service). Creditors might be offered some kind of compensation under such a model, but they would not be offered a choice.

An alternative, however, would be to induce creditors to reduce claims voluntarily, by offering them the option of cashing in their existing claims for new claims that promise reduced contractual debt service but are "enhanced" in some way, for example, by guarantee of principal and some interest.

The natural preference of a market-oriented administration is for the voluntary approach—and, indeed, in Brady's initial speech the word *voluntary* was used repeatedly. Within a few days, it was apparent, however, that such a voluntary approach would be prohibitively expensive, and the major debt reductions so far, in Mexico and Venezuela, have been essentially involuntary.

The problem with the voluntary approach is straightforward. To a first approximation, offering creditors "enhanced" securities is simply a sophisticated way of buying back debt. And the price at which debt can be bought back is likely to be much higher than the cost to creditors as a group of reducing debt by a single dollar. The reason is that the secondary price of debt represents the *average* value of debt, that is, the fraction of debt that is likely to be repaid, not the *marginal* value, the likelihood that the last dollar will be repaid—surely a much lower number.

Matters are even worse when a large buy back is announced because then the secondary price of debt will rise; the cost of the buy back will reflect the average value of debt *after* a debt reduction has increased the probability of repayment.

Figure 11.4 illustrates the point. It shows a debt value curve that does not turn down but that is fairly flat in the relevant range. D_2 is the face value of debt before debt reduction, D_1 the face value after. V_2 is the initial value of the debt on the secondary market and V_2/D_2 the initial secondary price, indicated by the broken line.

The value of the debt to creditors will fall as a result of debt reduction, but only modestly, from V_2 to V_1. Thus, one might hope that creditors could be induced to accept such a debt reduction in return for compensation of roughly $V_2 - V_1$. But, if creditors are asked but not required to sell their debt, the cost will be much higher. The reason is that no creditor will sell claims for a price less than the secondary price that will prevail after the debt reduction, V_1/D_1.

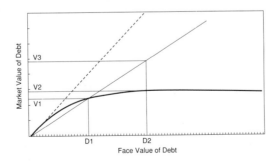

Fig. 11.4   Concerted vs. voluntary debt reduction

The value of the initial stock of debt at this higher secondary price is V_3. The required outlay to reduce debt by $D_2 - D_1$ will thus actually be $V_3 - V_1$—a much larger sum than would be needed simply to compensate creditors for their losses. The difference represents an extra cost to taxpayers, for the benefit of the private creditors.

While calculations based on estimated debt value curves should not be taken too seriously, they give some idea of the problem. If the 20 percent debt reduction number floated soon after the Brady speech were meant seriously, it would have required canceling some $90 billion in debt. Using the estimates of the debt value curve in Claessens et al. (1990), a buy back of this magnitude would have cost perhaps $40 billion in cash equivalent—considerably more than the resources available even given the sizable warchest now accumulated.[4] Yet the sum needed to compensate creditors would have been much smaller, on the order of $10 billion. The balance would represent a capital gain to creditors. For a larger debt reduction effort, the disparity would be even larger; Claessens et al. estimate that a $200 billion debt reduction would cost creditors about $25 billion but would cost $110 billion if achieved through buy backs.

Given this arithmetic, why did the initial Brady proposal stress voluntary debt reduction? One possible answer is lack of clear thinking: as described in the third section of this paper, the circumstances of the Brady Plan's formulation were sufficiently harried that sheer confusion probably played a role. Another answer is that Treasury staff still hoped that clever financial packaging could have a multiplier effect on public resources—that the lesson of the disappointing results of the Morgan-Mexico plan had not sunk in or been seen the same way at the U.S. Treasury as it had elsewhere.

In any case, in the first major test of the Brady Plan, in Mexico, the idea of using a voluntary approach was quickly shelved. Instead, as already described, a combination of legal maneuvering and pressure on banks was used to leave banks no option other than to participate in a debt reduction program.

By all accounts, however, the negotiations leading to the Mexico package were extremely difficult, leading to doubts about whether the U.S. government could achieve similar deals for other nations or would even be willing to try for countries of less strategic importance. (The Venezuelan deal may belie this expectation, but the arithmetic of that deal is still unclear at the time of writing.)

---

4. As noted above, official resources now available for debt reduction are typically estimated at around $34 billion. These resources are, however, available for loans and guarantees, not as cash. If the funds could be lent to finance cash buy backs without regard for the risk assumed by the World Bank and the IMF, they could still finance a considerable reduction in net debt: $34 billion if the buy back price is 50 percent, $51 billion if it is 40 percent. The international financial institutions have, however, been reluctant to engage in very large lending to finance buy backs, precisely because it would force them to assume too much risk—i.e., they prefer not to see the $34 billion lending authority as the equivalent of $17-$20 billion of simple cash outlays.

11.3   The Process of Policy Formation

Up to this point, I have described the policies followed by the U.S. government and provided a framework that tells us how such policies should be conducted. But what actually determined U.S. policy?

To state the obvious, policy-making did not at all resemble the textbook ideal in which the government is modeled as a single actor, well informed, who acts in the public interest. Policy was made through an interaction of a number of institutional players, not all of them inside the U.S. government proper; institutional priorities and to some extent personal ambitions were key motivations; and much policy-making took place in a fog of misconception and misinformation. In other words, debt policy was made in the real world.

11.3.1   The Players and Their Motivations

A key organizing principle for thinking about U.S. policy-making is the "turf theory," sometimes summarized as, "Where you stand depends on where you sit." That is, the U.S. government may be seen as consisting of a number of institutions such as the Federal Reserve, the Treasury department, and so on, each of which has a built-in predilection for certain kinds of policy, based less on ideology than on what serves the institution's interests; policy then emerges from the interaction of these agencies.

This way of thinking about policy can be either excessively cynical or not cynical enough: an official at, say, the State Department might support policies that run counter to the interests of State per se either out of conviction or, in the "revolving-door" system, because his longer-term career objectives lie elsewhere. Still, a turf-theory approach does seem to yield a useful view of debt policy.

Let us therefore review the main institutional players on debt policy.

The Federal Reserve

From 1982 until the resignation of Paul Volcker in 1987, there is little question that the Federal Reserve was the lead player in U.S. debt policy—in spite of occasional efforts to dislodge it, as described below. This Federal Reserve dominance resulted from several factors.

First, unlike counterparts at other institutions, Volcker himself took a sustained personal interest in the debt problem, regarding it as a central issue. (Indeed, one may even argue that his interest was excessive: what would have happened had he given equal attention to the savings and loan issue?) For example, at several points, Volcker personally intervened to put pressure on banks to go along with concerted lending packages. Volcker's concern with debt, according to Federal Reserve staffers, reflected a sense of history and an urgent desire to avoid repeating the 1930s as much as a specific concern with the immediate financial obligations.

Second, the Federal Reserve had a high degree of continuity of policy-making. Volcker, of course, served far longer than any of his counterpart Treasury secretaries. A similar or even greater disparity was visible at lower levels. Most visibly, Edwin Truman was second-in-command on international economic issues for the whole decade; although he receives little press attention, Truman is a legendary figure among insiders for his acumen and knowledge.

Third, by all accounts the Federal Reserve boasts a much more experienced and talented staff than any other agency can offer. At the crudest level, the Federal Reserve pay scale exceeds that of the executive branch. Perhaps more significant, the Federal Reserve is a highly professionalized and depoliticized organization, in which a civil service career can lead to very high-level positions; this is in contrast to the U.S. government paper, where positions down to deputy assistant secretary or even lower are now usually filled by short-term political appointees. These appointees are less knowledgeable than their Fed counterparts, and it is difficult to attract ambitious staff at lower levels when they are aware of a fairly low ceiling on their ambitions.

Fourth, traditional players in the policy game within the executive branch were unusually weak for much of the period 1982–89—even the Treasury, and other players much more so. I return to this issue below.

So for most of the 1980s the Federal Reserve played the most important role in setting U.S. debt policy. But what were its objectives?

Clearly, the overriding objective of the Federal Reserve was financial stability. The emergency rescue operations of 1982 were led by the Fed, at times in the face of reluctance by the Treasury, to prevent a potential banking crisis. The concerted lending strategy served the same function. The chief concern of the Federal Reserve was to head off country defaults that would force major banks into bankruptcy. In the initial period, this meant a preoccupation with maintaining the paper value of claims.

Concern over financial stability galvanized the Federal Reserve into action in 1982–83. But, as we saw, the pure financial stability issue faded in importance as banks increased their capital. What motivated the Federal Reserve after that point?

The answer is unclear. Some Federal Reserve staffers now concede privately that the policies of 1982–83—the push for new finance, the opposition to any move that would write down debt and thus threaten the financial system—became reflexive and that the Federal Reserve developed a bias toward new money as opposed to forgiveness more on the basis of habit than of analysis. Indeed, arguably, the advantage of continuity in personnel had the disadvantage that officials from Volcker on down remembered what they thought in 1982 all too well and were reluctant to propose policy changes that would prove their old opinions wrong.

The Treasury

Traditionally, the U.S. Treasury has been roughly coequal with the Federal Reserve in setting international economic policy. In the 1980s, however, the Treasury suffered from several disadvantages as a policy-making center.

First, as already suggested, the Treasury was notably lacking in experienced players at high levels. During the first Reagan administration, the highest officials at Treasury with *any* background or experience in international finance were at the deputy assistant secretary level. Nor were the high officials at Treasury widely regarded as quick learners: Federal Reserve officials were privately scornful of their counterparts' qualifications, and sources have reported at least one occasion in which the Fed's Truman publicly reprimanded senior Treasury officials for their ignorance.

This situation changed in some respects after 1985, when a new team including James Baker, Richard Darman, and David Mulford moved into the top positions at Treasury. Although none of these men had experience with international financial policy per se, they were much more highly regarded than their predecessors. However, the change in top personnel apparently did little to change the Treasury's growing weakness at staff level.

Part of this weakness was due to the general problems of the U.S. executive branch: low pay, lack of opportunities for promotion, and a gradual reduction in staffing. Press reports and conversations with sources confirm, however, that this structural problem was exacerbated by an attitude of disdain for staff work on the part of a series of Treasury officials, from Regan to Mulford.[5]

As a result, the Treasury suffered (and continues to suffer) from a lack of effective staff work, which makes policy initiative difficult. One Federal Reserve staffer asserts that "there's nobody at Treasury who can build a spreadsheet."

Nonetheless, by virtue of its institutional position, Treasury has been a major player on debt. What are its objectives? We may distinguish three levels of objective: administration, department, and personal.

Since the Treasury is an arm of the executive branch, it is of course responsive to directives from above. On the domestic side of Treasury, there was a strong conservative ideological mission among many appointees in the first half of the 1980s. On the international side, however, ideological crusading was relatively scarce. Especially after 1982–83, the basic international financial concern of the administration was apparent and clearly coincided with the Fed's objectives: preserve the stability of the financial system.

---

5. A widely reported anecdote bears repeating here. When Mexican finance minister Pedro Aspe arrived at a meeting with some of his own staff, Mulford demanded that they leave, saying, "What are your [expletive] numbers guys doing here?" The U.S.-trained Mexican team subsequently took considerable pleasure in referring to themselves as "[expletive] numbers guys". A confirming anecdote: soon after the signing of the Mexican debt reduction accord, Mulford rather smugly told an off-the-record meeting that the key to getting anywhere was to ignore the numbers.

At the other end of the spectrum, individual officials at Treasury inevitably have their own agendas—agendas that sometimes lead to conflict with the Federal Reserve. Most important is the understandable desire of high officials to play an active role in formulating policy and to be seen doing so. This is normal but in the case of debt policy had some peculiar results. Treasury officials were generally inexpert themselves and poorly staffed; this made it difficult for them to play a leading role in policy formulation and generally put the Fed in the driver's seat. Yet the Treasury officials chafed under this restraint and carried on a continual low-grade struggle to wrest control of issues away from the Fed.

We may illustrate this conflict with two examples; the major example, the formulation of the Brady Plan, is dealt with below.

First, throughout the post-1982 period, administration debt policy was at least in principle formulated within some kind of structure of interagency groups: a subset of the cabinet at the top, an assistant secretary–level group below, and staff-level interagency task forces or working groups below that. At no point was the Federal Reserve represented in these groups. This makes some constitutional sense since the Federal Reserve is not exactly part of the executive branch or, indeed, of the government. But, given the crucial role of the Fed in the actual policies, especially at staff level, the absence of even an observer status effectively gutted the process. The reason for Fed exclusion is generally acknowledged to be Treasury concern that the Fed would dominate the interagency process if it were allowed into the room.

Another example of the pressures generated by the desire of Treasury officials to play a more active policy role was the brief flurry of excitement generated by Secretary Regan in December 1982, when at a G-5 finance ministers meeting he suggested the need to create a new international institution to handle the debt problem. This suggestion generated a flurry of speculation about the apparent shift in U.S. policy and its reasons, but in fact the statement was undertaken on the secretary's own initiative, without any prior staff work at Treasury, let alone interagency consultation. Staffers at Treasury speculated privately at the time that Regan's statement had been motivated by the desire to play a more active role in the meeting.

The efforts of the Treasury in effect to grab hold of the ball reached a pinnacle in the case of the Brady Plan, but I return to that below.

The Rest of the U.S. Government

One of the surprising aspects of U.S. debt policy has been the virtual silence of arms of the U.S. government outside the Fed and the Treasury. Within the executive branch, one might have expected some role for the State Department; outside, one might have expected some role for Congress. In fact, neither materialized in any important way.

Traditionally, the State Department plays the role of resident internationalist inside the U.S. government—the advocate of measures that serve U.S. diplomatic and political interests even at some financial and/or economic cost. It might have been expected to advocate a soft-money policy, that is, more lending in the early stages of the debt problem, an earlier turn to debt forgiveness. In fact, it did not.

State's silence was apparently due to the effects of politics on the choice of personnel. George Shultz, as secretary, had surprisingly little interest in economic affairs. His undersecretary for economics was Allen Wallis, an economist with strong conservative credentials but little taste for policy formulation. And the assistant secretary for economics for most of the 1980s was Richard McCormick, a former aide to Jesse Helms who, despite earlier experience as a foreign service officer, showed little interest in usual State Department preoccupations.

Congress traditionally has little role in international financial (as opposed to trade) policy. The debt problem attracted the interest of a number of members, Senator Bill Bradley in particular. During the period between the Baker and the Brady plans, Bradley was perhaps the most visible advocate of debt reduction. The so-called Bradley Plan, unveiled in 1986, remained a benchmark for such plans until the Brady speech, and Bradley received advice from leading academic advocates of debt relief, such as Harvard's Jeffrey Sachs and MIT's Rudiger Dornbusch. Treasury officials were routinely grilled on debt issues by congressional committees, and some sources suggest that the pressure from Congress on Secretary Brady and especially on Undersecretary Mulford may have played a role in provoking the Brady Plan.

At no time, however, did Congress manage to find any direct lever for affecting debt policy. At no time in the 1980s did U.S. debt policy require enabling legislation.[6] Only by directly passing legislation forcing a change in debt strategy could Congress have had any impact on the policy, and this was never a serious prospect.

So the story of U.S. debt policy is overwhelmingly one of the Federal Reserve and the Treasury.

Outside Forces

The U.S. government played a leading role in determining debt strategy throughout the period 1982–89. To some extent this is surprising since U.S. banks accounted for less than 30 percent of the bank loans to problem debtors. However, there was no other independent player able to formulate an alternative.

That said, the role of two other key players needs to be recognized. These were the following:

1. *The banks.* The process of concerted lending led to the creation of bank advisory committees, effectively leading banks to speak with far more of a

---

6. Increases in IMF and World Bank resources did require legislation, and in principle Congress could have held them up as a way to exert pressure on debt policy. But, whether from lack of interest or concern over the damage that such a strategy would do, no confrontation occurred.

single voice than usual. In some ways, these bank advisory committees were more of a match for the Federal Reserve than the Treasury, in that key members—especially Citibank's William Rhodes, who remained chairman of the Mexican advisory committee throughout the period—both came to their positions with considerable expertise and remained in place for extended periods.

2. *The IMF.* During most of the 1980s, the IMF, like the Fed, was a highly professionalized institution under a strong leader. Arguably, the concerted lending strategy can be attributed at least as much to the IMF's Jacques deLarosiere and his staff as to Paul Volcker and his. The staff work that helped lead to the 1989 change in policy direction also was largely carried out at the IMF rather than the Fed or the Treasury.

The point for understanding U.S. debt policy in the 1980s is that the effective policy-making apparatus was not contained within the boundaries of the U.S. government. Senior staffers at the IMF had more impact on U.S. debt policy than senior staff at any U.S. agency except, and perhaps including, the Treasury.

11.3.2   The Rhythm of Policy

Action Forcing Events

Given this set of players, how was policy actually made? The best answer seems to be that policy was made as little as possible. The Federal Reserve's interest in the debt problem was a narrow one: it wanted to preserve financial stability, which it came to interpret as meaning preserving the face value of bank claims. It would initiate policies when this goal was threatened, but not otherwise.

The Treasury might have wanted to initiate policies aimed at broader interests, but it lacked the knowledge and staff to formulate any departure in policy. Therefore, like the Federal Reserve, it acted reactively. The result was that policy was very much driven by "action-forcing events"; absent such events, nothing much happened.

The first action-forcing event was, of course, the Mexican crisis and its spread to other debtors. The Treasury and the Fed, together with the IMF and the bank advisory committee, moved cooperatively to head off the crisis and put together the concerted lending strategy: an altogether remarkable response, even though it did not in the end work out as planned.

The Baker Plan does not at first sight appear to have responded to a similar event. However, the climate of dissatisfaction over the results of debt policy was significant by the fall of 1985; the United States (in general) and James Baker (in particular) were trying to establish a new regime of international cooperation, and it was very necessary for political reasons that the United States present some kind of plan at the Seoul meetings. If this sounds like a weak justification for a policy initiative, we must note that the Baker Plan was a weak policy initiative: cut through the favorable publicity, and one finds a modestly funded continuation of the existing strategy.

The reactive character of policy also appears in smaller responses. Concerted lending, as we saw, evaporated after 1983–84. No real effort was made to restart it, even after the announcement of the Baker Plan. When Mexico found itself in crisis in 1986 as a result of oil price collapse and earthquake, the Federal Reserve and the Treasury once again set to work rounding up banks for another round of lending.

The major change in policy in 1989, however, does not fit this description too well. What can we say about the genesis of the Brady Plan?

The Brady Plan

The genesis of the Brady Plan may be viewed in three quite different ways. All contain some truth.

One way to approach the creation of the plan is to note the real reasons why such a policy change made sense. Playing for time, and waiting for countries to return to normal access, no longer made much sense. The stronger capital positions of banks made concern over the financial repercussions of debt reduction less urgent. The decline in secondary market prices made debt reduction appear more feasible with limited resources. The evident shifting of risk away from banks and to official creditors was raising fears that the process was turning into a bailout. Arguably something like the Brady Plan was long overdue, and the Treasury was simply doing what it should have done before. The Federal Reserve, one may argue, was simply too committed to its opposition to debt reduction to appreciate the obvious; the Treasury, once the author of the Baker Plan was gone and the election was over, was not.

A second explanation, stressed by several officials inside and outside the U.S. government, focuses on the special relationship between the United States and Mexico. The Salinas government in Mexico decided quite early on that it needed a debt reduction, as much or more for domestic political reasons as for strictly economic ones. And the Salinas administration, with its remarkably aggressive reform efforts, was the best Mexican government the United States could hope to have. Thus, there was a strong U.S. policy interest in giving Salinas some highly visible reward. In a meeting between President-elect George Bush and Salinas in the fall of 1988, Mexico was essentially promised that something would be delivered; the Brady Plan may thus be seen as a way in which the United States provided a context in which it could do Mexico a favor.

The final, cynical view is to think of the Brady Plan as in large part a turf struggle within the U.S. government rather than a serious response to real policy concerns.

The actual process by which the Brady Plan emerged was certainly a peculiar one. First, the review of debt policy that provided the basis for the policy change was carried out, as usual, by an interagency group in which the Federal Reserve was not included. Second, according to a number of sources, at a certain point a special team was formed within Treasury, its activities kept secret even from the interagency group, to prepare a debt reduction plan. The number of staff was very small—three or four people—none of them with extensive background.

Third, Secretary Brady announced his conversion to the idea of debt reduction in a speech that was not cleared with other agencies (including the Fed) and was in effect presented to the White House as a fait accompli only shortly before delivery. Finally, when questions were raised about the conceptual basis of the plan (its reliance on voluntary debt reduction) and the size of the resources required, the understaffed Treasury reportedly did not at first turn to the Federal Reserve for staff support: it turned to the World Bank and the IMF. This makes some sense since the international financial institutions would serve as the prime source of finance for debt reduction packages, but the neglect of internal staff resources is odd.

In other words, while a good case can be made that the Treasury policy shift was a reasonable and indeed overdue response to changed circumstances and that it was also a deliberate foreign policy move aimed at Mexico, the actual process of the policy shift looks suspiciously like an effort by the Treasury, particularly by-now Undersecretary Mulford, to grasp control of the debt issue away from the Federal Reserve. In this it succeeded.

11.4   Evaluating U.S. Debt Policy

This paper is intended primarily as a descriptive rather than prescriptive exercise. Nonetheless, it is unavoidable that some evaluation be offered.

U.S. debt policy may be evaluated in two ways: as a process or by its results. It may seem that the latter always supersedes the former, that the proof of the pudding is in the eating. But the uncertainties of economics are too large to judge policymakers solely by their success. Not only may a good policy hit bad luck; officials may be right for the wrong reasons or wrong for the right ones. Without question, one of the ways that Paul Volcker earned his right to be regarded as one of history's great central bankers was by his decisive actions on debt in 1982–83, yet a respectable case can be made that the world would have been better off had the Fed had a weaker leader and had the debtors simply been allowed to go into open default, as they did in the 1930s. So we need to evaluate the process on its own terms, before asking whether the policies that emerged from it were actually more or less right.

The policy-making story described in this paper is a mixed one. The initial phase of U.S. debt policy was marked by a rare combination of intellectual clarity and decisiveness. After that point, the story is much less inspiring. As described above, policy was reactive rather than creative for most of the period

1983–88, intellectual confusion was rampant, especially over such issues as debt-equity swaps, and there was a preoccupation with the public relations aspects of policy as opposed to substance. The pettiness and amateurishness of the policy process leading up the Brady Plan are fairly hair raising. On the other hand, policy formulation was untainted by special interest politics (a brief flurry over James Baker's holdings of Citibank stock was silly) and the international diplomacy by which agreement was reached quite skilful.

What about the results? Was the policy actually a good one?

There are two overwhelming facts about the results of the debt crisis in the 1980s. First is that financial stability was maintained: there was no 1930s-style collapse. Second is that the economies of the debtor nations performed very badly: real GNP per capita in almost all highly indebted countries was lower in 1989 than it was in 1981.

The policy response of 1982–83 can fairly take credit for the preservation of stability. It is hard to see that any very different strategy could have been undertaken given what was known at the time; the actual strategy was implemented forcefully and bought time while the overall world economic and financial picture improved sharply.

The question is whether another policy could have brought faster growth. The U.S. government could have been more aggressive in seeking to mobilize bank capital after 1983, and it could have sought a Brady-style debt reduction plan two years earlier. Alternatively, the United States could have declared a victory and gone home, implicitly encouraging debtor countries to go into arrears. In either case, the resource transfers from debtors to creditors might have been smaller.

But would this have brought better economic performance? Many observers have contrasted the 1930s—during which many debtors defaulted, then went on to do reasonably well economically—with the almost universally dismal record of debtors in the 1980s. Eichengreen and Portes (1989) have also shown that, during the 1930s, countries that were willing to default early and massively did better than those that were not. However, in the 1980s, there was no visible correlation between the burden of debt service and economic success. So by selective use of evidence, it is possible to make either case. One may maintain, as Cline (1990) implicitly does, that growth in debtor countries would have collapsed whatever the debt strategy and that the fact that the financial system has remained intact despite the growth collapse represents a signal success for policy. Or one may argue, as so many critics have, that the "overhang" of debt that could not be eliminated because the preoccupation with financial stability acted as a major drag on growth.

The political economy point, however, is that it is hard to see how the essentially reactive U.S. policy could have evolved much differently. It is interesting as an economic counterfactual to ask what would have happened had, say, Felix Rohatyn's 1983 global debt reduction plan been put into effect in 1984; but it was never a serious political possibility.

Appendix A
Debt-Equity Swaps

Six years after Mexico introduced its debt-equity swap program, the economics of such swaps are still the source of considerable mystification. Most economists working on developing-country debt regard swaps with considerable suspicion, while many private-sector participants take their desirability as axiomatic. So it is worth taking some space to describe the issues.

In essence, in a debt-equity swap, an investor is allowed to redeem external dollar debt for local currency, on the condition that this currency be invested in an approved local asset. From the point of view of the investor, this is a more attractive proposition than simply exchanging dollars for local currency at the central bank because the debt can be acquired at a discount on the secondary market.

What does the country gain? It does *not* reduce its overall foreign liabilities, except to the extent that it charges investors a fee for the right to carry out the swap. Instead, it converts one kind of obligation, debt, to another, equity. The country also does *not* attract additional net foreign investment: when an investor pays for his investment with the country's own debt, as opposed to dollars, this does not provide any immediate increase in its ability to import.

The potential gain comes instead from the change in the nature of the foreign claim. Equity investments will produce a stream of repayments to foreigners that is delayed relative to debt service, which may be an advantage in a country short of liquidity; they shift some risk from domestic residents to foreigners; and the foreign investors may bring intangible benefits in terms of knowledge, competition, etc.

Against this potential gain may be set two potential costs. First, debt-equity swaps pose a fiscal problem. Essentially, they "unreschedule" debt, forcing governments to redeem debt immediately. While the redemption takes place in local currency, simply issuing the currency would be inflationary, so responsible governments must issue new domestic debt to soak up the issue of local currency. The problem is that the real interest rate on this domestic debt is usually much higher than that on the rescheduled foreign debt that it replaces, thus aggravating fiscal problems.

Second, in many cases, debt-equity swaps are used to finance investments that would have taken place in any case. They thus divert foreign exchange that would otherwise have arrived at the central bank into the secondary market, aggravating rather than helping the liquidity situation.

Most developing countries now appreciate these problems and have scaled back their debt-equity programs.

Appendix B
The Limited Menu Approach in Concerted Debt Reduction

Both the Mexican and the Venezuelan debt reduction packages offered creditors a choice: either accept a conversion of debt into a smaller claim backed by some enhancements, or provide new money. These schemes were intricate and are still the source of considerable dispute. However, it may be argued that, in principle, such a "limited menu" approach offers a neat way to reduce debt without providing capital gains to creditors. This argument is laid out formally by Diwan and Kletzer (1990); here, I summarize it briefly.

It helps to imagine a scheme considerably simpler than either of the actual debt reduction packages. Suppose that creditors are offered only two choices: to be bought back at the market price prevailing before the scheme was announced or to provide new money in some ratio to original claims. Suppose also for a moment that creditors are identical in their concerns and expectations.

The new money option has an obvious undesirable feature: the new money is lent at an expected loss. However, the debt reduction that results from the buy backs should lead to a rise in the secondary market price of debt, and, by choosing the new money option, a bank preserves its ability to benefit from this rise. Now, notice that, if a large number of banks choose the new money option, debt will not fall by much, and hence the secondary price will not rise much; this will make the new money option unattractive. Conversely, if few banks choose new money, the secondary price will rise considerably, and new money will be more attractive. If the right number of banks choose new money, the new money option will yield the same value as exit; and the fraction of banks choosing the new money option will tend to be such as to produce this result.

In the Mexican case, those banks that chose to reduce their claims were given new assets that were, according to the estimates of Diwan and Kletzer, worth about 42 percent of original face value. Those banks that chose the new money option were obliged to increase exposure by 25 percent, but they benefited from a rise in the price of their claims to about 52 percent of par. Each dollar lent was lent at an expected loss of $1 - .52 = .48$, for a total loss of $.25 \times .48 = .12$ per dollar of initial claims; but, by not accepting debt reduction, the new money banks realized a gain of $.52 - .42 = .10$ per dollar of claims. Within the limits of reasonable uncertainty, the new money and debt reduction options were roughly equivalent.

But notice that, in such a scheme, neither the new money nor the exiting banks gain from the buy back. The exiting banks receive the ex ante market price; the new money banks are no better off. Thus, the whole of any official resources provided go to benefit the country. In terms of figure 11.4, the debt reduction from D_2 to D_1 is achieved at the cost $V_2 - V_1$ rather than $V_3 - V_1$.

To the extent that banks differ in their preferences, the limited menu approach has the further advantage of offering some limited accommodation of these preferences.

The main problem with such a scheme is that it is difficult to predict how many banks will choose the new money option and thus how much official money will be needed. If the new money requirement is set too high, few banks will choose it, and the resources needed for buy backs may exceed the available funds. This in effect happened in the Mexican case, creating some serious headaches.

References

Claessens, S., I., Diwan, K., Froot, and P. Krugman. 1990. *Market-based debt reduction for developing countries: Principles and prospects.* Policy and Research Series, no. 16. Washington, D.C.: World Bank.

Cline, W. 1983. *International debt and the stability of the world economy.* Washington, D.C.: Institute for International Economics.

———. 1990. From Baker to Brady. In *Finance in the international economy,* ed. R. O'Brien and I. Iversen. Oxford: Oxford University Press.

Diwan, I., and K. Kletzer. 1990. Voluntary choices in concerted deals: Mechanics and attributes of the menu approach to LDC debt. Washington, D.C.: World Bank. Mimeo.

Eichengreen, B., and R. Portes. 1989. Dealing with debt: The 1930s and the 1980s. In *Dealing with the debt crisis,* ed. I. Husain and I. Diwan. Washington, D.C.: World Bank.

Frenkel, J., M. Dooley, and P. Wickham. 1990. *Analytical issues in debt.* Washington, D.C.: International Monetary Fund.

Krugman, P. 1990. Market-based debt reduction schemes. In *Analytical issues in debt,* ed. J. Frenkel et al. Washington, D.C.: International Monetary Fund.

Lamdany, R. 1988. Voluntary debt reduction operations: Bolivia, Mexico, and beyond. Discussion Paper no. 42. Washington, D.C.: World Bank.

Sachs, J., ed. 1989. *Developing country debt and economic performance.* Chicago: University of Chicago Press.

2. *Thomas O. Enders*

To put the debt crisis in focus, you can look at it from the point of view of the debtors, the commercial creditors, or the creditor governments.

If you are most Latin Americans, the 1980s have been, as they often say, a "lost decade." The whole continent has stagnated, been marginalized. Work available and income earned have fallen. You have been subject to some of the most extreme price rises in history. Violence and disorder in your neighborhood have grown explosively. You have watched the rich, already recipients of a disproportionate share of income, get richer.

If you are a commercial banker, it has been a mixed experience. You made good money up front, but since then you have been coerced by the U.S. government first to lend more, then to write down your claims. Many small debtors and one big one—Brazil—have recently paid you little or nothing. Although some countries are recovering and accessing the voluntary capital markets, the crisis is by no means over. But you have had time to build up capital and loss provisions. The gross flows these last years and the remaining values are well short of pre-1982 hopes, but they are not insubstantial.

If you are the U.S. government, you have given an uneven performance that is turning out well. As Paul Krugman reports, you failed to anticipate the crisis (with the exception of the chairman of the Federal Reserve and a few others). Then you misread it as due to the business cycle, not to a general crisis in the mercantilist growth model standard in Latin America and elsewhere. You got such things as financial engineering wrong and permitted one part of government to take initiatives to preempt others. But the things you feared didn't happen. The money-center banks didn't lose their capital. Latin America didn't throw itself into the arms of dictators of the Left or the Right but made breathtaking steps toward democracy. Instead of confronting Washington, the hemisphere sought its help, first to twist arms for involuntary lending, then to permit/stimulate a rise in official lending, then to force a write-down, and now to negotiate what may be the ultimate solution to the debt problem—North-South free trade. Moreover, you found that you could exercise a leadership role—the initial rescue, the Baker Plan, the Brady Plan, the Enterprise for the Americas Initiative—and relatively easily beat back sporadic attempts by the French or the Japanese to outbid you. And most of the time you did it with other people's money: from the commercial banks, from the multilateral agencies. Your policy was reactive, but that posture made you sought after in a way that you hadn't been since the Alliance for Progress or the Good Neighbor Policy. Indeed, out of the debt crisis there is emerging a remarkably close, confident, and fruitful North-South relationship.

Looked at as a historian might, the results of this debt crisis appear to be the reverse of those of the first debt crisis in the 1930s.

At that time, some countries defaulted early and massively. Few paid more than a few cents on the dollar (Argentina was the main exception). Much foreign investment was nationalized. No government (other than the Mexican) survived the decade. In many cases, military regimes replaced outward-looking, if elitist, republics. Everywhere a new growth strategy emerged that centered on import substitution, was hostile to foreign investment, and exalted state enterprise. The new model often created monopoly opportunities for local capitalists. Unable to tax the monopolies, the governments sought to offset ever wider income disparities by such populist measures as subsidies for food and basic services as well as artificial exchange rates for key imports.

Creditor governments intervened little to enforce bondholder claims, but the crisis set loose xenophobic and specifically anti-U.S. currents in a number of countries.

Thus, while most of the world learned the lesson from the 1930s that autarchy did not pay, Latin America concluded that reliance on foreign markets and capital did not pay.

Indeed, the new growth strategy proved spectacularly successful, yielding continent-wide growth of some 6 percent for three decades to 1980.

It was that record that again attracted massive flows of foreign capital to Latin America in the 1970s. And it was, of course, that record that desensitized bankers and governments to the risks. Had we been watching, we would have seen that foreign money was masking or aggravating the vulnerabilities of the Latin American growth model. Governments, never good at raising revenue, were relying more on borrowed money to cover expenses. Easy availability of resources was fostering ever greater misuse in essentially nonaccountable state enterprises. Local capitalists were exploiting artificial exchange rates to move huge amounts of capital out.

What we do not know, and must leave to future historians to decide, is whether the import-substitution growth strategy could have survived if Latin America had not borrowed so heavily in the 1970s, or if it had defaulted massively in the 1980s, or if creditors had listened to those few advocating early, large-scale forgiveness. Maybe the collapse would have taken longer, but I personally have no doubt that it was coming.

What is certain is that, just as the injection of foreign cash exaggerated the import-substitution model's weaknesses, the need to service the debt brought it under intolerable stress.

Governments with weak revenue bases had to acquire from their citizens the resources to service the debt. Most ended up doing it by printing money. There resulted a continent-wide inflation, in Argentina and Brazil at Weimar levels, in Mexico and Venezuela at lower but wholly unprecedented levels.

Once again, it will be for historians to determine what finally convinced first Mexico, then Argentina, Venezuela, and Brazil, to attempt the radical liberalizing reform of their economies. I think that it was the searing experience of inflation out of control coming on top of the failure of their systems to respond to the worldwide upswing in the mid-1980s and the failure of official and private creditors, taken together, to come up with net new resources. Radical reform then became the new politics of survival, notably for Mexico's Revolutionary Institutional party.

It would be comforting to think that the call for reform by the United States and other creditors, at first perfunctory, then with more feeling, had an impact. I doubt it. Rather—although it was not their intention to impose runaway in-

flation on Latin America—creditors did contribute to it and thus finally to
the start of serious reform. And, whatever you think of the financial engineering, when the new Salinas government, having already put through an aggressive liberalization program, turned to creditors for a dramatic gesture of
support, the fact that the United States responded with the Brady Plan was of
enormous importance in consolidating support for change within Mexico.

There remain some important questions.

The ultimate success of the reforms remains in doubt. Mexico, gratified by
high petroleum prices, fears a U.S. recession. Two-thirds of its exports are now
nonhydrocarbons. And the democratization of the Mexican state must someday be faced. Brazil's structural reforms, which each week bite deeper into one
of the few last remaining mercantalist economies, depend for their survival on
success in containing inflation. They, too, could fall victim to a world down-
swing. The debt crisis is unwinding, not over.

Second, as the continent moves toward open markets, the willingness of
Latin capitalists to recommit their resources to Latin development is still not
confirmed. So far only a small part of flight capital—which may be as much
as $150 billion—has returned. Interestingly, people who trade in official Latin
debt, as I do, have had little success in persuading Latin capitalists to invest
in it. But money is going into private investment as a new pattern emerges:
government credit is more or less permanently impaired, while private enterprise expands. To sustain growth, Latin America must attract much of the flight
money back.

Finally, what is done, or not done, in trade can be decisive. Latin America,
and thus the debt problem, stands to gain much from a successful Uruguay
Round. Free trade, first with Mexico, then with others, can be had only at the
cost of a major political fight in the United States. But it can be the ultimate
way out of the debt problem.

What do I think of U.S. policy on Latin American debt in the 1980s? It was
not foresighted or proactive, but it kept us engaged, moved us to respond at
critical junctures, and contributed to, rather than thwarted, the historic transformation now under way.

3. *William R. Rhodes*

The adage that hindsight is 20/20 is true only because of the corrective lenses
that time provides. While historians will have the final verdict on what transpired during the debt crisis, this is offered as a blow-by-blow account of
where the crisis started and where it is today from the viewpoint of a commercial banker who has been in the trenches. It is not my intention to get into the

causes of the crisis, but I will offer some general observations on the policies that were followed by the various parties involved, including the creditor governments, the debtor governments, the international financial institutions, and the commercial banks.

Before I get into the specifics, I would like to give you some background in both economic and political terms on Latin America—where the debt crisis hit the hardest. In looking at the past and the present in Latin America, it is important to understand that, during the decade of the 1980s, there occurred the most significant change from military governments to democracies in the history of the region. In other words, all during this very difficult economic period for Latin America, there was a move away from military government toward democracy. And, at the same time—particularly toward the end of the decade—there was a massive opening up of the economies to structural economic reform and privatization. Whether either or both of these two trends prove definitive or not, they need to be kept in mind when thinking about the 1980s and the future of Latin America. It is also interesting to note that what is going on now in Eastern and Central Europe has many similarities to the Latin American experience of the 1980s with the move toward democratic pluralism and economic reform.

Beginning in August 1982, when Mexico decided to call its creditor banks together at the New York Fed, the so-called debt bomb became an international financial crisis without precedent in modern history. Along with the social and political impact felt by tens of millions in the developing world and particularly in Latin America, it resulted in a profound change in the business of international banking. It posed fundamental strategic business questions to thousands of banks worldwide, many of which had only recently ventured into international lending in the late 1960s and 1970s, and certainly threatened the survival of many banking institutions, both large and small. In 1982 and 1983, many people were concerned about what the crisis would do to the international financial system itself.

Other countries certainly had experienced debt-servicing problems before. There were the problems of the 1920s and 1930s, and you can go back to Argentina and the Baring Brothers crisis of the late nineteenth century. Certainly, none of those earlier cases had debts the size of Mexico, Brazil, or Argentina in the 1980s. Thus, those of us who were approached by Mexico to work on the problem in August 1982 had no real road map to deal with anything of this size. However, given the stakes, we had to assume that the crisis could be managed.

Looking back, we had two goals. First and foremost was to prevent the collapse of the international financial system—obviously, the banking system. Second, the countries needed help to eventually return to the private capital markets in order to finance what former Treasury Secretary James Baker liked to call "sustained growth."

If greed often drives people apart, fear often drives them together, and certainly Mexico in August 1982 was an example of the latter. There quickly developed an unusual international working arrangement among competing commercial banks, bank regulators, international financial institutions, creditor countries, and many of the borrowing countries. On the basis of experiences with earlier restructurings in the 1970s (e.g., Nicaragua, Jamaica, Zaire, and Turkey), the commercial banks organized themselves into steering—or advisory—committees, with membership based on the size of exposure and geographic representation. These committees were organized in coordination with each of the debtor countries, and it is important to remember that they were not put together by the banks alone but were requested by the debtor countries themselves.

A major factor in this working arrangement at the beginning was the leadership of people like Paul Volcker at the Federal Reserve and Jacques de la Rosiere at the International Monetary Fund (IMF). A balanced and case-by-case approach was developed, recognizing the fact that each of the restructuring countries had its own particular and peculiar realities.

In the first phase of the crisis, commercial banks, of necessity, assembled short-term emergency financing packages. These involved restructurings to stretch out approximately two years of maturities over five to seven years and new money to meet the immediate cash needs of the borrower countries. The 1982–83 restructurings of Mexico, Argentina, and Brazil were set up along these lines. The countries, in turn, began to adjust their economic policies to reflect, belatedly, the changes that had been occurring over several years in the international economy.

The second phase looked beyond the countries' immediate needs with longer-term packages to buy time. The idea for this type of approach was first put on the table—again by Messrs. Volcker and de la Rosiere—in the late spring of 1984 at the International Monetary Conference in Philadelphia, attended by the chairmen of the world's largest commercial banks. I was asked to attend to represent the bank advisory committees. What emerged was an agreement that the IMF would institute enhanced surveillance or monitoring—something that has now long been forgotten. This meant that the IMF would monitor a country's economic performance over periods substantially longer than normally done under standby or extended fund arrangements and that this information would be made available to the commercial banks.

This allowed the banks to negotiate the first multiyear restructuring agreement (MYRA) with Mexico later in 1984. This stretched out for up to fourteen years all debt maturing over a six-year period, as opposed to the maximums mentioned earlier of seven years and two years. A more market-based approach started in 1984, when we negotiated a clause under which banks could convert debt into equity (the famous debt-equity swaps) as part of this same Mexican MYRA package.

This marked the beginning of the concept of debt reduction. Although unheralded, the "menu of options" approach began later that year, in a package negotiated with Argentina that allowed banks to allocate part of their new money commitment for trade or directly to clients in the country—something that we call *on lending*. In 1985, the Chilean package further enhanced the menu of options idea, by providing for a variety of debt-reduction programs, mostly debt-equity swaps. The result of these programs of debt reduction for Chile has been a total reduction of over 50 percent of its long- and medium-term debt.

Phase 3 was aimed at shifting the focus from short-term adjustment to longer-term growth. It reflected the philosophy—first expressed by Jesus Silva Herzog, the former secretary of finance for Mexico—that the only way out of the crisis for the developing world was to grow out of it. This phase followed Secretary Baker's decision that the U.S. Treasury should be more actively involved in the management of the debt than it had been under his predecessor, Don Regan.

In October 1985, at the IMF–World Bank meetings in Seoul, Secretary Baker announced his plan—the so-called Baker Plan—for world debt. Chief among the points was the emphasis on growth-oriented structural economic reforms by the borrower countries. In response to the countries' economic adjustments, the commercial banks were asked to continue to make available a prudent amount of new loans. What Baker suggested as prudent was $20 billion over three years. One of the major points of the plan was to bring the World Bank into the fray because the debt strategy up to this point had been dominated principally by the IMF and Baker was calling for major involvement of the World Bank in structural adjustment.

Although the Baker Plan is often attacked for not raising sufficient new money, Bill Cline of the Institute of International Economics, who has spent the last seven or eight years studying the debt crisis, estimates that banks disbursed over $13 billion in net new loans to the Baker countries over the three-year period envisioned. Although the $20 billion mark was not reached, this is as much a reflection on the inability of some of the countries to make the structural adjustments that were a prerequisite as it is a reflection on the commercial banks' unwillingness to lend in some cases.

Meanwhile, the role of the market increased with the Argentine agreement of 1987, when the list of options was substantially expanded. This is when you first started hearing about the menu of options. To the bankers involved it was old hat, but to Washington and to the Treasury it was something new on the table. What we did here was to have cofinancings with the World Bank, trade financing facilities, new money bonds, etc. What is often overlooked in this agreement is that this was the first time that we put on the table an exit bond with a fixed below-market interest rate in order to try to stimulate debt reduction. The Argentine exit bond, which was priced inadequately and lacked enhancements, was a failure. Only three banks took it. However, it helped set the stage for the next phase, which was voluntary debt reduction. That was in 1987—the same year Citibank raised its reserves. This action, in turn, stimulated similar action by many banks in the United States, the United Kingdom, and Canada. Obviously, the decision by Citibank was, to a great degree, stimulated by Brazil's declaration of a moratorium on its medium- and long-term debt. Although that was not the only reason, certainly it was a major one that encouraged Citicorp's chairman, John Reed, to go ahead with his reserving. This higher reserve gave banks greater flexibility to manage their loan portfolios through such debt-reduction options as exchanges of debt for equity and cash buybacks of debt.

Following within a few months was the so-called Morgan-Mexico deal, which was another attempt at debt reduction. As you will remember, it was an offer to banks to exchange loans for bonds at a discount, with principal collateralized by U.S. Treasury zero-coupon bonds. This later became the basis for the so-called Brady Plan. The Morgan-Mexico deal did not produce the results that some had hoped for, most importantly because only the principal was collateralized, not the interest. Instead of reducing the debt by $3–$4 billion, the deal reduced debt by only $1 billion; but this certainly was a milestone.

Although never fully implemented by Brazil, the medium-term financing package signed in September 1988 to bring Brazil out of its moratorium demonstrated for the first time that new money and voluntary debt reduction were not mutually exclusive. Both the banks and the countries were now looking toward voluntary debt reduction as a major part of these financial packages. The package itself contained $5.2 billion of new money. Unlike the earlier attempt in the Argentine deal, it was the first time that an exit bond was successfully put on the table with below-market interest rates (with 6 percent, twenty-five years, ten years' grace). Some hundred banks subscribed to a total of $1.1 billion of them. If the Brazilians had not initially restricted participation, we probably could have obtained two or three times that amount. One interesting highlight is that, although Brazil later suspended interest payments on its medium-term debt to commercial banks, it never stopped paying interest on its bonds.

This set the stage for the next event in March 1989, when Secretary Brady proposed voluntary debt reduction by commercial banks. I would emphasize commercial banks because he said nothing in his statement about official debt reduction by governments or the international financial institutions. This reduction of debt by commercial banks became the focus of the debt strategy in place of new money. Secretary Brady did mention, however, some six or seven times in his speech before the Bretton Woods Committee the idea that some new money flows were still necessary, but most people did not pick that point up, and it certainly was not emphasized. The Group of Seven subsequently met on several occasions after the speech to work out guidelines, and the IMF and the World Bank for the first time agreed to offer resources to back debt-reduction programs for countries with viable economic programs.

All this set the stage for the Mexican debt package, which was signed in

February 1990. This package included most of the debt-reduction techniques used earlier, such as debt-equity conversions, interest rate reduction, and principal reduction bonds. It also incorporated many of the new money techniques, including bonds, trade finance, and on-lending facilities. In addition, the package introduced two new techniques: collateralized interest for debt-reduction bonds and value recovery. These two innovations have since been incorporated into other packages, including the one for Venezuela.

Where are we now? What follows are a few brief highlights. A number of countries have implemented important economic reforms, including privatizations, and negotiated or completed agreements with their creditor banks. Mexico has put the debt crisis behind it and returned to the voluntary markets, and Chile and Venezuela should soon do likewise. Colombia and Uruguay are also close to regaining market access. However, two of the largest borrower countries—Brazil and Argentina—have yet to reach agreements with creditor banks and have built up large arrearages.

In reflecting on the events of the past ten years, there are some key points that should be mentioned. First, the strategy employed has proved successful, in that the debt problem no longer appears to be a systemic risk situation.

Second, a key decision taken early in the crisis was the so-called case-by-case, or country-by-country, approach, a decision that continues today. It is a decision that is supported by most of the debtor countries. The alternatives were the so-called global solutions, of which we have seen many. The global solutions have two drawbacks: they do not speak to the differing needs of each individual country, which is why the countries have not favored them, and they tend to be forced rather than voluntary, which is why the banks have not backed them. Each country situation is different, and each requires a tailored solution. Also, there was a feeling that this type of solution would impede the countries from eventually getting back to the voluntary capital markets. The case-by-case approach has been followed from the beginning and is certainly a mainstay of the Brady Plan.

Third, the advisory committee system, overall, has functioned well in representing the interests not only of the creditor banks but also of the borrowing countries themselves. The committees have served as an informational pipeline for the borrower governments, who otherwise would find it difficult—if not impossible—to negotiate with the thousand or so interested banks at any one time around the world. These committees will be dissolved as the countries return to the voluntary markets. However, the potential usefulness of the committees to a country was highlighted last year, when a number of commercial banks tried to get the Chilean government to dissolve its committee and the Chileans refused to do so. They wanted to use it one last time, in order to put a package on the table to assure Chile's return to the voluntary markets.

Fourth, although the commercial banks have been criticized for not being sufficiently supportive, I believe that they have generally met the financing needs of the restructuring countries with either new money or debt reduction, and certainly they have done so for those countries that have instituted viable economic reform programs. For example, since the Brady Plan was announced in March 1989, the banks have completed or arrived at preliminary packages with substantial debt reduction and/or new money for Mexico, the Philippines, Costa Rica, Morocco, Venezuela, Chile, and Uruguay, along with a refinancing for Colombia with a new money tranche. I think that the process has been flexible and has evolved over the years. For example, we have had the introduction of a longer-term menu of options through the voluntary debt-reduction mechanism, including debt-equity exchanges, cash buy backs, and interest and principal reduction bonds. I think that these innovations have bought time for the countries to institute the necessary structural economic reforms, including privatization.

One of the major conceptual errors from the beginning of the debt crisis was the idea that the countries were in a short-term liquidity situation and that all that was needed was short-term stabilization programs of eighteen to twenty-four months. The results of this view were programs that lasted a maximum of two to two and a half years. The countries often ignored the need simultaneously to make basic structural economic reforms, including privatizations, in order to lay the basis for investment and growth.

Many people did not understand the important point that, if the countries did not change basic structures and open up their economies and privatize, one stabilization program after another would end in failure. Certainly that was the case in Brazil, Argentina, and even with the initial programs in Mexico. As an example, Brazil had about seven letters of intent with the IMF over a four-year period. What you ended up with was a vicious cycle because the necessary economic structural changes were not being made.

Even in the case of Mexico, it was not until late 1985, under President de la Madrid, that the country finally decided to join GATT. At the same time, the government began putting in place the necessary mechanisms to reduce the role of the public sector through privatizations and the closing of a number of inefficient and money-losing state institutions, such as Fundidora Monterrey. I think that one of the hopeful things that we are seeing today is that most of the governments in Latin America are beginning to recognize that stabilization alone is not good enough, that you must have basic structural changes, including privatization.

I hope that the importance of structural reforms will not be lost on the countries of Eastern Europe. While Poland quickly initiated a courageous stabilization program to combat inflation, only recently did it begin its structural adjustment program centered around privatizations. The delay in adopting structural adjustments has made it difficult to create markets for labor and capital and has cost the country needed investment.

I am also concerned about the Brady Plan's emphasis on voluntary debt reduction alone, with little interest in new money flows from commercial banks. Debt-reduction programs, particularly those involving debt principal reduction, often encourage banks to end their lending relationships with the countries. However, in order to grow, there will still be a need for some flows of new money from at least a core group of banks—that is, if a country is pursuing its program of structural reform and privatization and is becoming competitive and creditworthy. Despite the skepticism of some that banks would not lend, even where there were proper conditions, examples of the willingness to lend new money are the recent agreement with Venezuela and, most important, the return of market access for Mexico.

A growing impediment to bank lending, however, is the substantial amount of overdue interest owed by some countries. These arrearages to commercial banks from restructuring countries worldwide amount to nearly $24 billion at the end of the third quarter of 1990, with Brazil and Argentina accounting for more than half. Arrearages undermine confidence in a country, not just among banks, but among other potential investors, local and foreign. Funds are not likely to flow to those countries that fail to regularize their financial obligations. Bank arrearages have also encouraged arrearages to the IMF and the World Bank. But I would put to you that part of the problem was in these institutions themselves because in many ways they encouraged the countries to use arrearages as a form of external finance. Certainly, there are those people who believe that that was implicit in the Brady initiative. I do not think that the secretary meant that. But it is only recently that the U.S. Treasury has come around to recognizing the importance of this issue, and, if you read the G-7 statement at the September 1990 IMF–World Bank meeting, you will see that they finally understood that the arrearage problem is a serious one.

The progression in the use of debt reduction also concerns me. It was first used by the commercial banks, then appeared as the focus of the Brady Plan, and then was proposed for President Bush's Americas Initiative. One of the dangers in this progression is that new money flows could be diminished or, in some cases, even halted. An interesting question, therefore, is, To what extent should debt reduction be viewed in the context of new money?

When we look back at this crisis, there is still one question that I believe needs further review. I am referring to the criticism directed toward the banks in the 1980s for overlending, by the regulators, and by officials of the international financial institutions, saying that banks did a poor job in the two recycling efforts of the 1970s. One could ask, however, where was the G-5, and the official sector in general? They were not prepared to lead the effort, so the commercial banks took it on. What would have happened if the major industrialized countries had decided to step in and head the recycling effort, using, among other things, the international financial institutions more actively than they did to achieve this goal? Under the circumstances, the banks did a reasonable job—perhaps not good enough in some cases—but nobody else stepped forward.

Summary of Discussion

Paul Krugman began the discussion by asking about the real effects of reserving. Reserving appears to an economist to be simply a relabeling of some of a bank's assets with no real consequences. In particular, a decision to increase reserves appears to have no impact on either the present or the future cash flow of the bank. Yet financial markets view decisions to reserve as important events. Why?

William Rhodes said that Citibank's 1987 decision to increase its reserves had been based on a recognition on their part that they had not seen the progress that they had hoped for since 1982. They had recognized that times had changed and wanted to be more flexible with their portfolio. This basic rationale had been somewhat lost in the theatrics of the press coverage, but Rhodes emphasized that Citibank had certainly not chosen to increase its reserves by so much in order to put other banks in a more difficult position.

Rhodes believed that Citibank's decision had had a large effect on the financial markets because of the bank's long-standing leadership role in international lending. Citibank was the largest international lender, so many people thought that Citibank's increase in reserves indicated a widespread recognition that American banks were underreserved and undercapitalized in the face of the LDC debt problem. Another possible effect of the reserving decision was that many developing countries wanted to reduce their own debt balances in line with the discounting of their debts on banks' balance sheets.

Martin Feldstein summarized Rhodes's description of reserving as a combination of a public admission of the seriousness of the LDC debt problem and a reaction by developing countries that they should pay the banks less money. But that combination should have lowered the value of Citibank stock, not raised it, as actually happened.

Rhodes said that Citibank had been quite surprised that the stock price had risen temporarily because they had expected it to fall themselves. In any case, however, the change in stock price had not been the focus of their attention.

Thomas Enders asserted that Citibank's reserving decision had involved a much more precise allocation of capital to the risks on its balance sheet. This effort to identify the bank's problems had been viewed by the market as an important step toward better management of the bank's assets, thus boosting the value of the stock.

William Poole offered another explanation for the rise in Citibank's stock price. At the time, the U.S. government had been coercing many banks into lending additional money to the developing countries, and banks with higher net worth were more likely to be coerced. When a bank transferred capital into its reserves, it became more difficult for the bank to be put into a position where it would have to put up—as the market saw it—good money after bad.

Rhodes said that this had not been a consideration for Citicorp because they had been the leaders in the effort to encourage new lending to the developing countries. He admitted that this issue may have played a role in other banks' subsequent reserving decisions.

Robert Litan maintained, however, that Poole correctly explained how the market had perceived Citibank's action.

Krugman then shifted the discussion to the Brady plan [named for Treasury Secretary Nicholas Brady]. Rhodes described the Brady plan as a *voluntary* debt-reduction plan, which is the way that Brady's original speech had described it. But the biggest Brady deal to date, involving Mexico, had not been a voluntary plan; although the creditors had had some choices, doing nothing had not been one of them.

Rhodes said that, although the Treasury Department had pushed the banks to participate in the Mexico plan, most of them had been prepared to participate anyway. One reason is that, unlike Brazil and Argentina, Mexico had never defaulted on its interest payments. A second reason is that Mexican President Carlos Salinas had been implementing a structural reform package that the banks had liked. So, although it had been possible for the banks to challenge the Treasury plan publicly, all but a few banks had believed that Mexico deserved support anyway.

Feldstein said that, of the five major changes in U.S. debt policy that Krugman had described in his paper, the introduction of the Brady Plan had been the most dramatic one. Feldstein wondered what had caused this change and whether the banks had been involved in the change before it was publicly announced.

Rhodes answered that an important motivation for the Brady plan had been the political situation in Mexico. President Salinas had emphasized to President Bush the importance of debt relief, and Mexican Finance Minister Pedro Aspe had visited Brady several times to make the same point. So it was Rhodes's understanding that the Brady Plan had not been just Brady's idea but had had the full backing of the president because of the situation in Mexico.

Rhodes continued that Treasury Undersecretary David Mulford and his staff had consulted with a few bankers before the public announcement, but not with very many. Rhodes said that he had spoken with Mulford before the announcement and had stressed two issues. First, he had argued that the debt reduction should be voluntary, not mandatory. He had thought that a mandatory plan would be of doubtful legality and would not induce the cooperation of the international banking community in the way that a voluntary plan would. Second, Rhodes had argued strongly that there should be a continuing flow of new money to countries that were creditworthy and were implementing appropriate economic reforms. Unfortunately, this issue did not receive much attention at the time, which the Treasury now regrets because they realize its importance.

Feldstein added that the Brady Plan had been developed at the Treasury Department with little input from either the rest of the executive branch or from the Federal Reserve. Feldstein also hypothesized that the introduction of the Brady Plan may have been due to a new Treasury secretary wanting to make his mark, not to any change in the fundamentals of the debt situation or in the thinking of other people at the Treasury Department.

Michael Mussa suggested that the introduction of the plan had been deferred until after the election, along with other bad news like the savings and loan disaster. *Feldstein* did not think that announcing the Brady Plan a year earlier would have cost any votes.

Charls Walker said that Brady had been scheduled to make a speech to the Bretton Woods meeting and that people had known in advance that it was supposed to be a major policy announcement. Thus, Brady had told the president that they could not back down from the plan at the last minute.

Rhodes believed that Mulford's views on debt reduction had in fact changed by the time of the Brady Plan, but he also agreed with Feldstein that Brady had wanted to take a fresh look at the problem when he became Treasury secretary. Rhodes reiterated, however, that the primary motivation for the plan had been the political situation in Mexico.

Enders added that, whatever the reason that the Treasury had decided to take some action on the LDC debt problem, the Brady plan was possibly the only approach that met the critical test of not requiring government money.

Litán turned the discussion to the origins of the LDC debt crisis. Rhodes said that, because the leading central banks and the international organizations had been playing no role in recycling petrodollars, the large commercial banks had had no choice but to do that recycling by lending funds to the less developed countries. This description made it sound as if the banks had made these loans out of a sense of civic obligation. It is also possible, Litan argued, that the U.S. government, and the Federal Reserve in particular, had coerced the banks into making these loans. Or maybe the banks had simply entered into LDC lending in search of higher profits. Litan asked to what extent the Fed had been encouraging the banks to recycle, taking a hands-off approach, or warning the banks to be careful about this kind of lending.

Rhodes said that the banks had not been coerced or pushed into making LDC loans. Citibank Chairman Walter Wriston and other leading international bankers had felt that this lending was somewhat of a crusade to help both the international financial system and the developing world, and the speeches of senior bankers during the 1970s had been replete with comments about the banks performing a needed public function because nobody else was doing it. Rhodes said that the U.S. government and many Western governments had praised the banks for their actions, but, in the end, it had been bankers' decisions to make those loans; no one had forced them.

William Taylor said that he did not know what the regulators' views about LDC lending had been in the early and mid-1970s but that, by the late 1970s, the banks were being cautioned about their overexposure in the developing countries.

Enders noted that the issue of recycling petrodollars had been a major preoccupation of the U.S. government in the early 1970s. He thought that there had been great applause for the banks' willingness to receive the deposits and invest them but that, despite this substantial encouragement, there had been no coercion.

Geoffrey Carliner alluded to Enders's previous assertion that the LDC debt crisis of the 1980s had worked out better than the debt crisis of the 1930s because of the involvement of the U.S. government. Was it a widely shared view that the crisis would not have been resolved as well if the government had taken a hands-off approach during the 1980s, as it had during the 1930s?

Rhodes discussed two reasons why the debt problems of the 1980s had been resolved in a better way than the debt problems of the 1930s. First, the Bretton Woods institutions had not existed in the 1930s. It had made a big difference in the 1980s to have an International Monetary Fund that could bring together debtors and creditors and provide useful information as well as money. Rhodes said that both Volcker and Jacques de la Rosiere had worried that, if the debt problem had not been managed promptly and with the help of the Bretton Woods institutions, a financial crisis could have ensued.

Second, the 1930s debt had been almost entirely in the form of bonds, while, by a "stroke of fortune," the 1980s debt had been almost entirely in the form of bank loans. The resulting concentration of creditors had made it possible to renegotiate the terms of the debt in ways that would have been impossible with a diffuse and anonymous group of bondholders.

Feldstein wondered whether the concentration of creditors really had been a stroke of good fortune. Because the loans were concentrated in the money center banks, a default on the debt could have triggered a true financial crisis. If the debt had been securitized, however, with bonds dispersed around the world in many separate portfolios, a default on the bonds would not have triggered a financial crisis. Feldstein said that a decline in the value of LDC debt of $100 billion would have represented only 2 percent of the value of the New York Stock Exchange. While this would have meant a significant loss to some bondholders, it would not have imperiled the financial system as a whole.

Rhodes responded that the ability of the debtor countries to buy time, which had been greatly facilitated by the debt being in the form of loans, had been important. *Taylor* added that the developing countries had been able to work out their loans, while they would have been forced to simply default on any bonds.

Feldstein wondered if the debtor countries would be able to reenter the financial markets more quickly because there had been workouts of the old debt rather than defaults on it. He added that the 1980s debt crisis might not have arisen at all if the debt had been in the form of bonds because the bonds would probably have paid fixed interest rates. Thus, the sharp increase in interest rates from 1979 to 1982 would have reduced the value of the outstanding bonds, but it would not have forced the developing countries to default on their payments.

Jeffrey Frankel said that the 1980s debt problem had been worsened by the widespread acceptance in the 1970s of the view that changes in inflation rates were reflected one for one in changes in short-term interest rates. If the interest rates on the debt had been linked to commodity prices rather than to other short-term interest rates, the debt problem would have been much less severe.

Krugman pointed out that economic growth in the Latin American debtor countries had been relatively strong in the 1930s in the face of a disastrous world economy but had been very poor in the 1980s with a fairly strong world economy. So it seemed bizarre to argue that there had been a better outcome to the 1980s debt crisis.

Rhodes responded that virtually none of the 1930s debtor counties had been able to return to the financial markets until after World War II, which showed the high cost of defaulting. He also believed that the decline in the value of LDC bonds in the early 1980s would have been much larger than the $100 billion mentioned by Feldstein. Finally, he thought that the actions of the money center banks had been the only realistic way to recycle petrodollars during the 1970s, especially considering that the G-5 countries in particular, and the official sector in general, were not prepared to lead the effort.

Enders contrasted the continued involvement of developing countries with financial institutions during the 1980s with the default and subsequent withdrawal of developing countries from world financial markets during the 1930s. He asserted that this continued involvement in the 1980s, made possible by the use of loans rather than bonds, had meant that pressures could build up within the developing countries that are now resulting in fundamental economic reforms.

William Niskanen said that most of the debt policies of the U.S. government had seemed designed to cost money to either American banks or American taxpayers. He asked whether it was clear that those policies had been on net beneficial.

Enders said that both the Federal Reserve and the Treasury Department had made substantial use of so-called swap lines at various points in the LDC debt crisis and that, if there had been defaults on those loans, there would have been real losses for American taxpayers. But the use of the swap lines had been very important—for example, they had played a critical role in the recent Mexican agreement—and in fact there had been no losses for taxpayers.

There had, of course, been great losses incurred by the banks, and the central question was whether those losses would have been larger or smaller without the involvement of the government. Enders believed that the actions of the government and of the international organizations had helped keep the banks engaged with the developing countries until the countries had been ready to undertake serious reform. In the end, this reform will give the banks an opportunity to recoup more of their original investment than if the debt problem had been left solely to market forces.

Enders added that Volcker and others in the Federal Reserve had had a stronger sense of the importance of the developing countries to the United States than had most other people. If there had been a different Fed chairman at that time, the history of the debt problem might have been quite different than it was.

Rhodes added that Volcker and de la Rosiere had been instrumental in "bringing order to a process that was being driven by fear." He thought that those two people in particular had been important catalysts in creating a global framework for dealing with the debt problem. After that framework had been set, however, he believed that it had been right to allow the banks and countries to negotiate between themselves.

Mussa argued that a key reason that the petrodollars had been recycled through the international banking system had been the perception of several parties that the governments of the developed countries would intervene to protect their interests. The people with funds to deposit had assumed that the governments would in some way guarantee the value of those deposits, and the bankers had assumed that the governments would help the banks collect on their outstanding loans. Mussa believed that this de facto intervention by the governments had represented a serious distortion of the international allocation of capital.

As for government intervention after the crisis began, Mussa conceded that there was an argument for government intervention to prevent a financial crisis. But he wondered whether an early default and an immediate writedown of banks' assets, as with creditors in a typical bankruptcy resolution, would have been preferable to the long, dragged-out process through which the same end had been achieved gradually.

Feldstein noted that some people in Washington had been suggesting a more lenient treatment of debtor countries well before the Brady plan had been adopted. Would it have been better if the Brady Plan had been adopted earlier, or was it right to wait until countries like Mexico had initiated significant economic reforms?

Enders responded that, if the U.S. government had produced more resources or induced more debt forgiveness at an earlier point in the crisis, it would have greatly eased the developing countries' short-term problems but also greatly prolonged them. Enders explained that, when the debt crisis began, he had been very worried that Latin America was a political tinderbox, and he thought that the Treasury and the Federal Reserve should have taken a more lenient position for foreign policy reasons. But, when the international institutions proposed a variety of sensible policy actions and made their loans conditional on policy performance in the usual way, very little changed in the debtor nations. In the end, fundamental economic reform was instituted only when the people had become desperate. In Mexico, for example, it was the runaway inflation that had ultimately persuaded the country to start the reform process. So more debt relief at an earlier time would simply have prolonged those countries' underlying economic problems.

Enders emphasized that he was not opposed to the small amount of aid that had been given at an early point in the crisis. In fact, he had been strongly in favor of making those resources available and of encouraging coordinated lending by the banks. He thought that it would actually have been damaging, however, to have made large quantities of aid available through an early Brady Plan.

Rhodes responded to several previous comments. First, he addressed the merits of an early Brady Plan, arguing that neither the banks nor the debtor nations would have benefited from it. In 1982, the banks did not have sufficient capital or reserves to cover the asset writedowns that were required for significant debt reduction. By 1989, they had increased their capital and reserves sufficiently to make the Brady plan possible. Also, Rhodes said that he shared Enders's view that the debtor countries had not started to implement basic structural reforms until 1985. Their previous reforms had consisted of a variety of short-term stabilization programs—based on adjusting the exchange rate in an attempt to build trade surpluses—that did not address their fundamental economic problems. When banks had tried to "prime the pump" for reform in Argentina by lending money in advance, Rhodes felt that it had actually exacerbated their problems.

Second, Rhodes said that, although he could not speak for any other banks, Citibank at least had not thought that the U.S. government was going to stand behind their loans to developing countries. If mistakes had been made, they were the bank's own mistakes and had not been made on the assumption that someone would bail them out. Rhodes said that he sometimes believes that commercial bankers are driven by fear, greed, and ignorance, but he hoped that some lessons had been learned in the 1980s. In fact, he thought that the future problem would be, not profligate bankers lending money to everybody, but rather a dearth of banks that lend to the developing world.

Enders concluded that the LDC debt story was ending reasonably well, although maybe for the wrong reasons. The U.S. government had not devoted a lot of resources to the problem, but, because major political upheavals had been avoided, there is a good chance of improved economic growth in Latin America.

12 Policy Toward the Aged

*1. David A. Wise and
   Richard G. Woodbury*
2. Rudolph Penner

1. *David A. Wise and Richard G. Woodbury*

American Economic Policy in the 1980s: Policies Affecting the Aged

The increasing proportion of older people in the United States and increasing life expectancy have given particular importance to the public policies that affect older Americans. Indeed, policies affecting the aged have been a major component of federal legislation throughout the 1980s. This paper considers aging legislation in the 1980s from an economic perspective, evaluating the motivations for legislative developments and the economic implications of the legislation enacted. A central goal is to relate the economic perspective on aging issues to the objectives and motivations expressed by policymakers in considering and enacting new legislation.

The discussion is organized around three major issues: (1) retirement and retirement income programs, including Social Security and private pension plans; (2) individual saving for retirement and the tax-incentive programs that encourage savings, such as Individual Retirement Accounts, Keogh plans, and 401(k) plans; and (3) the increasing cost of health care and the public programs

The authors benefited from comments by Victor Fuchs and Martin Feldstein on earlier drafts of the paper and from discussions, some quite extensive, with Lawrence Atkins, Robert Ball, Nathalie Cannon, Gary Christopherson, John Cogan, Elaine Fultz, Elma Henderson, Joseph Humphreys, David Koitz, Brian Lutz, Manuel Miranda, Don Muse, Judy Schuub, Theodore Totman, Christine Williams, and Karen Worth—all of whom were involved in the process of evaluating and developing aging legislation in the 1980s.

that reimburse health care expenses (particularly Medicare). Some significant federal policy changes were enacted in each of these areas in the 1980s, including Social Security reform (1983), new private pension plan regulations (various years), prohibition of mandatory retirement (1986), IRA restrictions (1981, 1986), Medicare reimbursement procedures (1983, 1989), and catastrophic medical insurance (1988, 1989).

The discussion of each issue begins with a description of the economic context in which the policy decisions are made. The changing age demographics of the U.S. population are particularly important since, even without the enactment of new legislation, they have an enormous effect on the cost and the effects of government programs. Other economic trends are important to the discussion of specific aging issues—such as younger retirement, low rates of personal saving, and high inflation for health care services.

Having developed an economic context for each issue, the legislation impinging on the issue and the motivation for the legislation is then reviewed. Finally, the motivation for the legislation (as expressed by policymakers) is contrasted with the economic description of the problem. For example, given the existing trend toward younger retirement in the United States, does Social Security legislation in the 1980s aggravate or moderate this trend? An attempt is made to judge the key factors that molded the final legislation and to contrast those factors with those reflected in economic analysis.

Several themes, none of which are new in this discussion, are important across legislation in all the areas. First, the budget deficit was an overriding concern throughout much of the 1980s, and this concern placed an important constraint not only on the legislation that was passed but also on the legislation that was considered. Second, who benefits and who loses is typically a more critical determinant of policy choice than the economist's "efficiency." Third, fairness and protection of rights have taken precedence over incentive effects of policies or the economic efficiency of the policies.

12.1   Retirement and Retirement Income

12.1.1   The Economic Issue

The American population is aging rapidly, and individuals are living longer, yet older Americans are leaving the labor force at younger and younger ages. Earlier departure from the labor force may have been made possible by and may be attributed to the introduction of Social Security and firm pension plans. These programs can lead to younger retirement for two reasons. First, these programs provide a means of support during retirement so that people can afford to retire. Of course, the major reason for retirement programs is to do just this. Second and more worrisome, the benefit structure of these programs includes financial incentives that encourage retirement and penalize work. Neither Social Security nor firm pension plans have been neutral with respect to the age at which individuals decide to retire. Rather, their provisions encourage early retirement and penalize continuing participation in the labor force.

According to a recent study, the labor force participation rates of men over sixty were essentially constant between 1870 and 1930 and then declined continuously thereafter (see Ransom and Sutch 1988). The data on labor force participation, based on the decennial censuses, are reproduced in figure 12.1. These census data also have been used to construct labor force participation rates by age group for men and women at ten year intervals, beginning in 1940 (see Sandefur and Tuma 1987). The rates for men fell in each age group. For example, 61.4 percent of men aged fifty-five and over were in the labor force in 1940; by 1970, the proportion had fallen to 52.7 percent; and, by 1990, only 39.4 percent of men in this age group were in the labor force. The participation rates of women aged fifty-five and over increased until 1970. Since 1970, however, even the participation rates for older women have fallen.

The decrease in labor force participation rates after 1930 roughly corresponds to the implementation of the Social Security program and federal tax incentives for private pension plans. Social Security was introduced under the Social Security Act of 1935. Company pensions were spurred by the Revenue Act of 1942, which granted tax incentives to firms to establish pension plans. The correlation between the introduction of these retirement policies and the change in labor force participation at older ages suggests that the policies may have induced younger retirement. Many researchers have pointed to the Social Security system's high benefit levels and work disincentives as a major contributor to the continuing trend toward early retirement, and a great deal of research has focused on the effect of Social Security on labor force participation. More recent research has identified similar but more pronounced work disincentives in most private pension plans. The discussion below explains the incentive effects inherent in the provisions of public and private plans, independent of the retirement wealth that they represent.

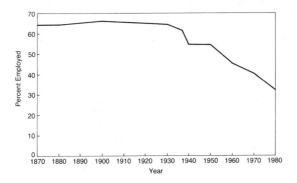

Fig. 12.1   Labor force participation of men over 60, 1870 to 1980

Social Security—Incentives

Social Security benefits are based on past individual earnings, although the benefit levels are a much larger proportion of the past earnings of low-wage workers than of high-wage workers.[1] The easiest way to understand the incentive effects of the benefit structure is to consider the compensation value of the Social Security program at different ages. The compensation value of the program is the incremental change in the present value of all future Social Security benefits that results from continued work—referred to as Social Security accrual. Work and retirement incentives are caused by the changes in Social Security accrual occurring at particular ages.

To exemplify these incentives, nominal wages by age and nominal Social Security accrual by age are shown in figure 12.2 for two representative workers, one a low-wage and the other a high-wage employee. Thus, the figure represents two forms of compensation: fig.12.2a nominal earnings by age and fig. 12.2b the increase in the entitlement to future Social Security benefits by age. Figure 12.2c shows Social Security accrual as a percentage of earnings. As shown, Social Security accrual is a small proportion of wage earnings for the high-wage worker but can be a significant proportion for the low-wage worker.

For the low-wage worker, Social Security accrual is about 6 percent of wage earnings at age fifty and increases to almost 10 percent at age sixty-two. However, if the low-wage worker continues to work from age sixty-two to age sixty-five, Social Security accrual becomes *negative*—negative 10 percent of the wage at age sixty-four, for example. The *loss* in the present value of future Social Security benefits is about 39 percent of wage earnings if the person continues to work after age sixty-five. This large reduction in the compensation value of the Social Security program at older ages encourages retirement at older ages. A similar (although less pronounced) pattern is apparent for the high-wage worker.

Firm Pensions—Incentives

Roughly three-quarters of all persons participating in private pension plans are enrolled in defined benefit plans where benefits are determined according

---

1. The initial benefit is based on nominal earnings indexed at age-sixty dollars using the Consumer Price Index (CPI). After retirement (receipt of benefits), the benefits are indexed to the CPI. The normal Social Security retirement age is sixty-five. But benefits can be taken as young as sixty-two, with the benefit amount actuarially reduced to reflect the increase in the expected number of retirement years over which benefits will be received. That is, if the benefit entitlement is not changed because of a change in earnings, the expected present value of future benefits is the same irrespective of the age, between sixty-two and sixty-five, at which the benefits are first received. After age sixty-five, however, the increase in the benefits is much less than actuarial. It is now 3 percent per year but was only 1 percent per year until 1981. Although the change from 1 percent to 3 percent was the result of a 1977 law, it applied to those who would be sixty-five in 1981 and later years.

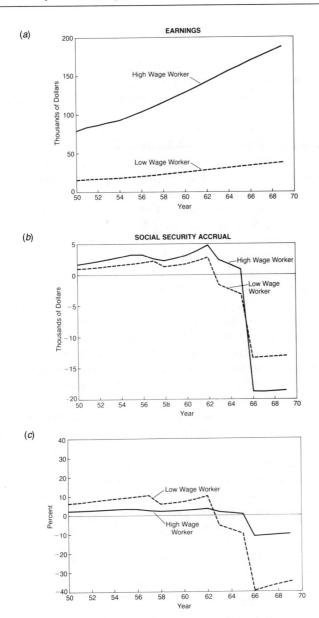

Fig. 12.2   (*a*) Employment earnings, representative low- and high-wage workers; (*b*) Social Security accrual, representative of low- and high-wage workers; (*c*) Real Social Security accrual as a percentage of real earnings, low- and high-wage workers

to a specified formula. The remainder are enrolled in plans where benefits are directly related to contributions made on behalf of the employee and to the performance of the plan's investment portfolio. Because most workers are covered by defined benefit plans, and because they are likely to have the greatest effects on labor market behavior, the discussion here emphasizes the incentive effects of this type of plan.

The incentive effects of defined benefit pension plans can be expressed in the same way as the incentive effects of Social Security—through the accrual of future pension benefits. The compensation value of a firm pension plan is the incremental change (or accrual) in the present value of all future pension benefits that results from continued work. Kotlikoff and Wise (1985, 1987) evaluated the retirement incentives inherent in a large number of firm plans. Figure 12.3 (taken from Kotlikoff and Wise [1987]) shows the average accrual rates (weighted by plan membership) for U.S. defined benefit plans with selected early and normal retirement ages. Pension accrual is represented as a percentage of wage compensation.[2]

Work and retirement incentives result from changes in the compensation value of the plans at particular ages. For example, consider the plans with early and normal retirement at age fifty-five, a plan stipulation that is common in the transportation industry. For these plans, the average decline in the rate of pension accrual at age fifty-five is equivalent to about 30 percent of wage earnings. The average decline in pension accrual at age sixty-five is equivalent to another 20 percent of wage earnings. This sharp decline in the compensation value of these plans creates a substantial retirement incentive.

A similar decrease in compensation value at older ages occurs in plans with different early and normal retirement ages. The more common plans with early retirement at age fifty-five and normal retirement at age sixty-five, for example, exhibit an increase in pension wealth accrual to age fifty-five, with a decline thereafter. Again, continued work past age sixty-five is associated with a substantial decrease in pension accrual—equivalent, on average, to approximately 20 percent of wage earnings. Thus, on the basis of industry-wide earnings profiles, continued employment with the plan sponsor after the age of early retirement and, in particular, after the age of normal retirement typically involves a substantial reduction in total annual compensation because of declines in pension wealth accrual.

Retirement Policies—Effects

Whether incentive effects like those described above have an effect on retirement decisions may be illustrated by considering the relation between pension

2. The data come from a random sample of approximately 2,500 plans from the Bureau of Labor Statistics Level of Benefits Survey. Similar calculations have been made by Lazear (1983) on the basis of the Bankers Trust Survey of large pension plans. For each plan, accrual rates are calculated assuming average wage-tenure profiles in the industry and occupation to which the plan pertains, based on current population survey data (see Kotlikoff and Wise 1985).

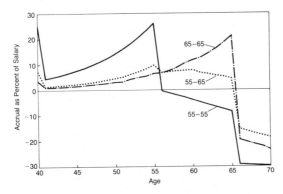

Fig. 12.3   Weighted average pension accrual as a percentage of wage earnings for percentage of earnings plans with ten-year cliff vesting, for selected early and normal retirement ages

plan provisions, Social Security provisions, and retirement in a firm. Kotlikoff and Wise (1989) have done that for a large Fortune 500 firm, showing a very strong relation between the economic incentives in the retirement policies and departure rates from the firm.

The proportion of the firm's employees who leave at each age beginning with age fifty is shown in table 12.1. The yearly departure rate (shown in the middle column) is the proportion of those employed at the beginning of the year that retires—more strictly speaking, leaves the firm—during the forthcoming year. About 3 percent of employees between ages fifty and fifty-four leave each year. The departure rate jumps to about 11 percent at age fifty-five. There is another jump at age sixty and again at ages sixty-two and sixty-five. The last column of the table ("cumulative departures") shows the proportion of employees working at fifty who *remain* at later subsequent ages. For example, only 21 percent remain until age sixty-two, only 5 percent until sixty-five.

The jumps in departure rates (at ages fifty-five, sixty, sixty-two, and sixty-five) coincide with the economic incentives in the firm's pension plan and in the Social Security program. Figure 12.4 shows wage earnings by age, pension accrual by age, and Social Security by age for a representative employee at the company. The compensation value of the plans changes discontinuously at certain specific ages. The discontinuities in compensation correspond directly with the jumps in departure rates from the firm.

The discontinuities are as follows. (1) By working until age fifty-five, the worker becomes eligible for early retirement benefits. Thus, there is a very large pension accrual at age fifty-five (shown as a large spike in the graph). This leads to a large increase in retirement at age fifty-five.[3] (2) Employees

---

3. To understand the potential importance of the early retirement benefits, suppose that, if it were not for this inducement, the departure rates would remain at 3 percent until age sixty instead of the 11 or 12 percent rates that are observed. Departure at 3 percent per year means that 14

Table 12.1   Yearly and Cumulative Departure Rates by age, for Employees with 11 or More Years of Service 1980

Age	Yearly Departure	Cumulative Departure
50	3	97
51	3	94
52	5	89
53	4	85
54	3	83
55	11	74
56	12	66
57	9	60
58	10	54
59	11	48
60	17	40
61	17	33
62	36	21
63	37	13
64	29	10
65	53	5

with thirty or more years of service can receive "full" unreduced retirement benefits at age sixty. The same "full" benefit formula is used for retirement in every year after age sixty. For these employees, there is a sharp decrease in the compensation value of the pension plan between ages sixty and sixty-one, equivalent to a wage cut of about 14 percent. Again, there is an increase in departure rates at age sixty, corresponding to this decrease in pension accrual. (3) Although there is no discontinuity in the compensation value of retirement programs at age sixty-two, workers first become eligible for Social Security benefits at age sixty-two, and this eligibility appears to induce a jump in retirement rates. (4) Social Security accruals increase up to age sixty-five (the normal retirement age) but fall sharply thereafter. After age sixty-five, Social Security accrual becomes negative, equivalent to about −$8,500 at age sixty-six.

In summary, possibly the most important economic trend among older Americans has been the dramatic reduction in their labor force participation. The trend toward earlier retirement is especially striking when viewed in the light of increasing life expectancy and the increasing proportion of the population that is old. The prospect is for a declining proportion of working people supporting an increasing proportion of retirees. In addition to this economic squeeze, economic analysis reveals that public and private pension provisions have themselves contributed to the decline in labor force participation. It seems apparent that the retirement income provided by Social Security and private

---

percent of those who were employed at fifty-five would have left before age sixty; at 11 percent per year, 44 percent would leave between fifty-five and fifty-nine.

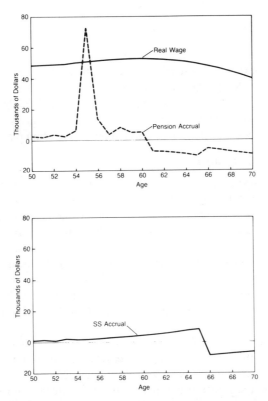

Fig. 12.4   Wage earnings, pension accrual, and Social Security accrual, representative person in Firm 1

pensions has allowed older workers to leave the labor force at younger and younger ages and still support themselves after retirement. Indeed, a principal intent of pensions is to allow just this. But Social Security and private pension provisions do not just provide for post-retirement income in a neutral fashion; they provide strong incentives to remain in the labor force until some age and then typically provide strong incentive to leave at some later age, often as young as fifty-five. Put another way, they penalize work by older employees.

Reversing the trend toward early retirement represents an important alternative for addressing the demographic transition. Additional labor supply of the elderly would relieve Social Security's finances as well as offset a potential shortage in the supply of labor relative to that of other productive factors. In addition, it is argued that, for many elderly people, prolonging their labor force participation would mean more fulfilling lives.

12.1.2   The Legislation

The most important retirement policy legislation in the 1980s pertains to Social Security reform and to the regulation of private pension plans. Although the discussion of the economic context emphasizes declining labor force participation and Social Security and private pension plan incentives to leave the labor force, the legislation in this area was motivated in large part by other concerns. In particular, the early retirement incentives inherent in Social Security and firm pension plan provisions were not the driving force for legislative change, although the legislation that resulted may be expected to have implications for retirement. Rather, the legislation was motivated first by the financial position of the Social Security system and second by a concern for protecting private pension benefits of workers covered by firm pension plans.

Social Security Legislation

Legislation enacted in 1983 made several major changes in the Social Security program. The fundamental motivation for the Social Security Act Amendments of 1983 was the pending bankruptcy of the Old Age and Survivor's Insurance (OASI) trust fund that supports the Social Security program.[4] Most of the debate on the legislation dealt with the mix of taxes versus benefit reductions and with how the burden of restoring the system to financial health should be distributed, rather than the work and retirement incentives of the Social Security program or the economic efficiency of the program. The legislation did, however, have potentially important implications for the labor force participation of older workers.

Congress had attempted to address the financial shortage in the Social Security program in 1977 by raising payroll tax rates. By 1980, however, because of lower than expected economic growth, it became apparent that the OASI trust fund would still face bankruptcy without additional reforms. Congressional consideration of Social Security reform began in 1981, although the final reform package was not enacted until the spring of 1983.

The positive spirit for reform that opened the 1981 legislative session ended abruptly with the introduction of a reform proposal from the administration. The two most controversial provisions of the administration proposal were to reduce the benefits of those retiring early from 80 percent of the normal (age sixty-five) benefit to 55 percent of the normal (age sixty-five) benefit and to impose a three-month delay in the annual cost-of-living adjustment. Congressional Democrats quickly framed the proposal as an effort by the administration to cut the Social Security program rather than to restore its financial health. Members of both parties expressed their opposition to at least parts of the administration proposal, and congressional Democrats vowed to prevent its enactment. Although the administration quickly stepped back from the details of the proposal, the momentum for Social Security reform within Congress was severely deterred.

This set the stage for the appointment of a fifteen-member bipartisan commission (known as the Greenspan Commission) to study the problem and to

---

4. The potential insolvency of the Social Security system is discussed in the paper by Jim Poterba in this volume.

submit a report by the end of 1982. The Social Security reform legislation enacted early in 1983 closely followed the recommendations of the Greenspan Commission. The key to the commission's success was in finding a compromise that could be accepted by the administration and by congressional leaders from both parties *before* being presented to the more politically charged legislative forum.

Many of the provisions of the legislation were closely related to the financial solvency of the system: either raising revenues or decreasing benefits. For example, the legislation delayed the cost-of-living adjustment in Social Security benefits by six months. The dates for previously scheduled payroll tax increases were advanced, gradually raising the rates (including both the employer and the employee contributions) from 13.4 percent to 15.02 percent. And up to 50 percent of Social Security benefits became taxable for higher-income individuals and couples.[5]

A number of other provisions potentially influence labor force participation among older workers. First, the rate of adjustment in Social Security benefits for delaying retirement after the normal retirement age will increase gradually from 3 percent per year of delayed retirement to 8 percent per year. On the basis of the economic incentives inherent in this change, one would expect more people to choose retirement at older ages. Once the new law is fully phased in (in 2008), the benefit that a person loses from postponing retirement for one year will be roughly offset by larger benefits over the years that they will be received. Thus, there should be no incentive to take the benefits at age sixty-five to avoid a loss in the present value of the benefits that will be received ultimately, as there is under the current 3 percent adjustment.

In describing the purpose of this provision, the House Ways and Means Committee explicitly stated its intent to encourage older workers to defer retirement. According to their report on the bill, "Your Committee continues to believe that it is desirable to provide incentives for individuals to remain in employment beyond normal retirement age. . . . This [legislation] will dramatically increase the amount by which the combined effects of (1) the reduction factors before age 65, (2) use of earnings after age 61 in the benefit computation and (3) the delayed retirement credit can result in higher benefits for workers who delay retirement."

A second part of the legislation that is likely to affect labor force participation is the change in the normal retirement age and in the amount of retirement benefits provided to those retiring before the normal retirement age. The age of eligibility for normal retirement benefits is to increase gradually from age sixty-five to age sixty-seven over the period from 2003 to 2027. Retirees will continue to be eligible for reduced Social Security benefits at age sixty-two,

---

5. The tax was imposed on individuals whose income (including half their Social Security benefits) exceeds $25,000 and married couples whose income (including half their Social Security benefits) exceeds $32,000.

but their early retirement benefits will be 70 percent of the normal benefit, rather than 80 percent as under previous law. Overall, the amount of the benefit for retiring at any age before age sixty-seven will be lower than the amount of the benefit that would have been received prior to the legislation.

The increase in the normal retirement age and the reduction in the amount of benefits received at each age before the normal retirement age will also tend to prolong labor force participation, especially among workers not covered by a firm pension plan. The strongest evidence for this expectation is the concentration of retirement at the current Social Security normal retirement age among persons who have not retired before then. In part, this concentration is probably due to a psychological incentive to retire at the "normal" retirement age that has nothing to do with economic incentives. But it must also be due to the economic incentives associated with the current benefit computation formulas.

A third provision of the legislation that is likely to affect labor force participation relates to the "earnings test." Prior to the 1983 legislation, Social Security beneficiaries under age seventy lost $1.00 in benefits for every $2.00 in earned income above the earnings limit (then $6,600). Beginning in 1990, these Social Security recipients lost $1.00 in benefits for every $3.00 in earned income above the limit (currently about $10,560). The apparent reason for this change was to reduce the perceived penalty[6] for work after retirement and thus to encourage labor force participation. Reducing the penalty for earned income also had the political advantage of giving something back to higher-income Social Security beneficiaries, who would now be subject to a tax on part of their Social Security income.

While the need to restore the Social Security system to financial solvency served as the primary catalyst for Social Security reform, economic analysis of the retirement incentives inherent in Social Security provisions seems to have had a significant impact on the composition of that reform. Some of the most important changes in the Social Security program were not cost saving but were implemented for other economic reasons. Social Security benefits for those with earned income above the specified earnings limit were increased, not decreased, as were the benefits for individuals choosing to delay retirement after the normal retirement age.

Economic analysis of Social Security has emphasized the work and retirement incentives associated with these provisions and thus may have been critical in informing Social Security reform in these areas. Economic analysis has tended to show, for example, that the earnings test discourages work among Social Security benefit recipients. The 1983 reform of the earnings test reduces

---

6. Although the tax on earnings above the limit tends to discourage work, the earnings are incorporated in the calculation of subsequent benefits. The increase in later benefits may approximately offset the large earnings tax, but the adjustment in later benefits is probably not understood or appreciated by the typical beneficiary or is too far removed from the present to matter. There has been a large concentration of earnings just at the limit, suggesting that, were it not for the tax, many persons would work more.

the magnitude of this work disincentive. Similarly, economic analysis tends to show that the small (3 percent per year) increase in Social Security benefits for delaying retirement beyond the normal retirement age encourages retirement at the normal retirement age of sixty-five. Again, the change in the benefit computation formula enacted in 1983 reduces the magnitude of this retirement incentive. A financial crisis provided the initiative for reform, but more comprehensive reform, not just financial restoration, was an important part of the legislative outcome.

Further revisions of the earnings test continue to be considered in Congress, with the primary motivation of reducing the work disincentive among Social Security recipients. According to Senator Bentsen, who introduced one bill easing the earnings test in 1989, "We can't afford to keep healthy and vigorous older Americans out of the work force. It's like keeping your best hitters on the bench." Legislation raising the earnings limit came very close to enactment in 1989. The House of Representatives approved a plan to raise the earnings limit to $9,720 in 1990 and to about $10,440 in 1991. The Senate Finance Committee approved a different plan, raising the earnings limit to about $11,700 in 1990 and about $14,500 in 1991. The Senate version would also have decreased the reduction in Social Security benefits to $1.00 for every $4.00 in earned income above the limit for the first $5,000 of earned income above the limit. The House earnings test provisions became part of the fiscal 1990 budget reconciliation bill. At the end of the 1989 session, almost all provisions of the budget reconciliation that did not reduce the deficit were categorically dropped.[7] Proposals to ease the earnings test are again being evaluated at the current time.

Regulation of Firm Pension Plans

The economic description of firm plans given above emphasizes their early retirement incentives. Most recent pension legislation, however, is directed toward plan "fairness" and toward the protection of "promised" benefits.

ERISA. To put the 1980s legislation in context, it is necessary to review the 1974 Employee Retirement Income Security Act (ERISA), which protects the pension benefits of most employees covered by private pension plans and continues to be the primary tool for government regulation of firm pension plans today. The ERISA legislation established minimum funding standards for pension plans and created the Pension Benefit Guarantee Corporation (PBGC), a federal agency responsible for insuring pension plans. Employers with defined benefit pension plans were required to pay a premium of $1.00 per worker to the PBGC for pension insurance. Both the creation of the PBGC and the pen-

---

7. Many bills were introduced in Congress that related to the earnings test. A bill to repeal the earnings test had two sponsors and 130 cosponsors. The bill that eventually passed the House was introduced by the chairman of the House Ways and Mean Subcommittee on Social Security. On the Senate side, there were several strong advocates for easing the earnings test. Legislation was introduced by the Finance Committee chairman and the Social Security Subcommittee chairman.

sion funding requirements were designed to assure that workers expecting pensions would not lose these expected benefits if the company experienced financial difficulties.

Congress was also concerned that companies were able to back out of their pension obligation when workers terminated their employment (either voluntarily or involuntarily) just before their retirement. An important characteristic of most defined benefit pension plans is the concentration in the accrual of pension benefit entitlements late in the working life, often referred to as "backloading." Since most of the value of pension plans accrues to workers approaching retirement age, companies can at least theoretically terminate workers just before taking on these large pension liabilities. Because pension backloading imposes the risk that workers will lose most of their pension benefits, limiting the backloading of pension benefit accrual was an important objective of ERISA as well as of subsequent legislation. Senator Bentsen expressed this concern in introducing ERISA to Congress: "There are instances where workers have not received pension benefits that they have earned through years of long hard labor. Their dreams of financial security after retirement have been shattered."

To limit the extent of pension backloading, ERISA stipulates that defined benefit pension accrual must satisfy *one of three* provisions. The first is a 3 percent rule requiring that a worker's accrued benefit must exceed his years of service times 3 percent of the normal retirement benefit he would have if he had begun service at the earliest possible age of participation and had remained with the firm until normal retirement. The second is a 133 percent rule requiring that future projected annual pension accrual not exceed 133 percent of current annual pension accrual. The third provision stipulates that the terminating worker's benefit not be less than his projected normal retirement benefit times the ratio of actual completed service to the service the worker would have if he had remained with the firm through early retirement.

While these provisions were designed to limit pension backloading, they were largely unsuccessful in this intent. First, each of these anti-backloading rules specifies that the projection of future normal retirement benefits and future pension accrual be determined by assuming that a worker's future wage equals his current wage. Accounting for wage inflation, however, future wages are likely to be much greater than current wages, and thus the real value of current accrual may be quite low. Even with a very modest rate of wage inflation, a pension plan that is significantly backloaded will meet at least one of the three anti-backloading provisions.

Second, pension plans are often backloaded through the early retirement provisions. The accrual rules specified by ERISA pertain to normal retirement benefits rather than early retirement benefits. Early retirement benefits that are larger than the actuarially fair adjustment of normal retirement benefits are apparently not restricted by the three anti-backloading rules in ERISA. Thus, for example, a firm would be free to structure its plan to have small normal retirement benefits (which satisfy one of the three ERISA rules) but substantial early retirement benefits. In this case, the large early retirement benefits might be structured with the accrual concentrated in the years just before the early retirement age rather than just before the normal retirement age. Again, a pension plan that is significantly backloaded at the early retirement age will meet at least one of ERISA's anti-backloading provisions, all of which apply to the benefit amounts at the normal retirement ago.

As the illustrations presented above demonstrate, the legislation appears to have been largely unsuccessful in limiting pension backloading. Thus, the economic implications of pension backloading are applicable to almost all defined benefit pension plans today. Backloaded pension plans encourage workers to continue working until they receive the backloaded benefits, and then to retire, once those benefits have been received and the rate of pension accrual declines. Thus, backloading decreases job mobility prior to the early or normal retirement ages and then increases retirement after the early or normal retirement ages.

The incentive effects of backloaded pension plans were not emphasized in the 1974 ERISA legislation. Congress was concerned about the risk associated with backloaded plans rather than the job mobility and retirement incentives associated with those plans. This may have been partly because the behavioral incentives of pension plans were not widely recognized at that time; only later did economic research direct attention to the potential importance of these incentives for job mobility and retirement.[8]

Legislation enacted in the 1980s. The emphasis of pension plan legislation in the 1980s was to promote "fairness" in the treatment of different workers, to protect the pension benefits of plan participants, and to prevent "abuses" of the tax advantages associated with pension plans. As in the 1974 consideration of ERISA, there was little emphasis in the 1980s on the work and retirement incentives inherent in the plans. In fact, very little of the pension legislation enacted in the 1980s is likely to have a significant effect on retirement behavior.

One exception may be a 1986 provision requiring that employers continue to provide service credit for their employees after the normal retirement age. Prior to 1986, companies could stop counting years of service, once their employees reached the normal retirement age. Since the new law enables employees to continue to accrue service credits, employees have more incentive to continue working until older ages. Despite the potential effect of this legislation on labor force participation, retirement incentives were not the primary motivation for this legislation. Instead, Congress was concerned about fair-

---

8. Even today, most companies with pension plans do not fully understand the work and retirement incentives associated with their plans. Companies tend to design their plans primarily to meet income replacement objectives rather than to influence retirement behavior (see Woodbury 1990).

ness—allowing older workers to accrue service credits in the same way that younger workers accrue service credits. In addition, driven by the political influence of organized labor, the legislation was intended to increase the retirement benefit levels of workers choosing to continue working at older ages.

Many other pieces of legislation were enacted in the 1980s to promote fairness in pension coverage. In 1984, Congress enacted the Retirement Equity Act, designed to provide greater pension coverage for women. The legislation was promoted largely by vice presidential candidate Geraldine Ferraro. In a hearing on the bill, Ferraro stated, "My proposed private pension reforms would require private pension systems to recognize the contribution women make to our economy and to take into account women's unique work patterns—patterns which revolve around childbearing and other family responsibilities." Prior to the legislation, many workers (particularly women) who left their jobs temporarily lost their credited years of service toward vesting and were required to accumulate a full ten years of service after returning to their jobs. The 1984 legislation lowered the age of pension plan participation from age twenty-five to age twenty-one, permitted employees to leave a job (for up to five years) without losing the credited years of service, and required that maternity or paternity leave not be counted as a break in service. The legislation also required companies to provide survivorship benefits to the spouses of employees who died prior to retirement eligibility.[9]

In 1986, congressional concern about the loss in pension benefits for mobile workers inspired a change in pension vesting rules. The 1986 legislation required that employees become fully vested in a company's pension plan after five years of employment (rather than ten years) or that vesting be phased in (20 percent per year) during the third through the seventh years of employment. The intent of the legislation was to increase pension coverage for workers leaving jobs before meeting the prior vesting rules. Because of backloading, however, the effect of the legislation on pension loss due to job mobility will be slight.

Also in 1986, Congress enacted several measures intended to reduce employer discrimination among different groups of employees. First, Congress imposed new regulations on the Social Security offset provisions used in many pension plans. Under the new law, benefit formulas that accounted for Social Security could not reduce an employee's pension by more than 50 percent. Second, Congress developed very detailed regulations that were designed to prevent discrimination in the provision of employee benefits. In general, the new rules ("Section 89") prohibited the provision of special employee benefits for highly compensated employees, unless those benefits were also provided to lower-compensated employees. Because companies expressed enormous

9. Prior to the legislation, companies were not obligated to provide survivorship benefits to the spouses of workers who died before becoming eligible for retirement. The 1984 legislation required companies to provide survivorship benefits to the spouses of all vested workers, regardless of their age at death.

dissatisfaction with the complexity of the "Section 89" rules, the rules were initially postponed and eventually were repealed in 1989.[10]

Also to protect pension benefits, Congress enacted several laws regulating the funding of pension plans and assuring the financial solvency of the PBGC. The financial condition of the PBGC was a concern throughout the 1980s, particularly after the bankruptcy of several large corporations.[11] The PBGC insurance premium was increased from $1.00 per worker to $2.60 per worker in 1977, to $8.50 per worker in 1986, and to $16.00 per worker in 1987. In 1987, a supplemental premium was also imposed on companies with underfunded plans. The supplemental premium was $6.00 per participant for every $1,000 of underfunding per participant (up to a maximum of $34.00). New pension funding requirements were enacted in 1987, setting specific pensions contribution rules for companies with underfunded pension plans. The intent of this legislation was to build up underfunded pension plans to full funding expeditiously, thereby reducing the potential risk of the PBGC.[12]

Finally, pension legislation in the 1980s was used to limit several perceived abuses in the tax advantages of pension programs. For example, legislation enacted in 1987 prohibited tax-deductible contributions to pension funds with assets exceeding 150 percent of current obligations. The intent of this provision was to prevent companies from using their pension funds to avoid tax liabilities rather than to provide for the retirement income of their retirees. Legislation enacted in 1986 imposed a 10 percent tax on pension payments in excess of $112,000 per year. Again, the intent of the legislation was to prevent the use of tax preferences for what were believed to be excessive pension benefits.

None of the pension legislation enacted in the 1980s was motivated by the declining labor force participation rates, and very few of the pension regulations enacted are likely to have any significant effect on labor force participation. In developing pension legislation in the 1980s, Congress attempted to promote fairness in pension coverage, to protect pension benefits for workers participating in pension plans, and to eliminate abuses in the tax advantages of pension programs.

Unresolved pension issues. Congress considered several other pension issues in the 1980s that were not fully resolved and that remain on the congressional

---

10. Although the concept behind Section 89 was simple, the rules themselves were quite complex. Companies have complained about their complexity since they were enacted in 1986. The original effective date for compliance with Section 89 was 1 January 1989. The effective date was immediately postponed to 1 October and then to 1 December. Section 89 was repealed in 1989.

11. The largest bankruptcies included Wheeling-Pittsburgh Steel Corp. ($500 million in pension obligations) in 1985, Allis Chalmers Corp. ($170 million in obligations) also in 1985, and LTV Corp. ($2.2 billion in obligations) in 1986.

12. Other retirement benefits were also addressed by legislation in the 1980s. A 1988 law protects the health and life insurance benefits of retired workers when their employer files for bankruptcy. Only a bankruptcy court could approve reductions in benefits and, even then, only after negotiating in good faith with an employee representative. This legislation was motivated by the loss of retirement benefits to steelworkers at LTV when the company filed for bankruptcy in 1986.

agenda. Even in these unresolved issues, there is very little concern about labor force participation or retirement incentives. One unresolved issue relates to pension portability. The motivation for legislation in this area is described in a report from the House Education and Labor Committee in 1988:

> Under current law, pension plan asset accumulations are increasingly being distributed at job termination and "cashed out" in the form of lump sum distributions of employees' entire pension plans interests. This is especially so in the case of defined contribution plans, although even defined benefit plans are increasingly taking on the form of cash accumulation accounts to be distributed upon termination of employment. . . . Studies demonstrate that the vast majority of pension plan lump sum distributions are used for current consumption and that few employees reinvest such amounts for retirement in individual retirement accounts or annuities.

The pension portability legislation proposed in 1988 would have allowed workers (or their employers) to transfer assets from an employer's pension plan to a tax-exempt retirement account (an IRA, for example) without paying any early withdrawal fees or taxes on those assets. Under current law, only the worker can make this transfer, and only the contributions made by the employer (not the employee contributions) could be transferred. Pension portability legislation was reported from the House Education and Labor Committee in 1987 and 1988 but was not enacted.

A second issue that received considerable attention in Congress in the 1980s relates to pension plan terminations and reversions. Congressional concern about the issue arose for several reasons. First, with the enormous rise in the stock market in the early 1980s, the value of many pension fund portfolios became very large relative to the discounted future value of the funds' future liabilities to retired employees. Many pension funds were significantly overfunded. Second, companies with overfunded plans were finding legal ways to remove excess assets from the pension funds to be used for nonpension purposes. Many in Congress were particularly concerned about the use of pension fund assets in corporate takeovers. In an increasing number of cases, the bidding company used the assets in the pension fund of the target company to help finance the acquisition. Third, many companies were terminating their pension plans to gain access to the overfunded assets and were not replacing the terminated plans with new pension plans.[13]

The frequency of plan terminations and "reversions" of the overfunded assets increased dramatically through the 1980s.[14] The use of pension fund

13. Under current law, companies can withdraw pension assets only by terminating the pension plan. After a plan termination, both active and retired employees are entitled to the retirement income that they have already accrued under the plan, but there is no further accrual after the termination. While most companies also replace their terminated pension plan with a new pension plan, about 27 percent of companies who terminated plans in 1987 offered no new plan, and about one-third of companies who terminated plans in 1988 offered no new plan.

14. Between 1980 and 1986, over 1,300 overfunded plans were terminated. These plans had provided pension benefits for over 1.6 million participants. Together, the terminated plans had

assets for nonpension purposes sparked a major political controversy over who owns (and who should own) these assets: the employers or the employee. Groups representing workers and retirees argued that the funds were the for the explicit purpose of providing retirement income for workers and that the workers should have at least part of the surplus assets. Groups representing businesses argued that the funds belonged to the employer and that it would be inappropriate for Congress to dictate how those funds are dispensed. While the assets legally seem to belong to the employer, the sentiment in Congress about who *should* own the assets has been mixed.

Congress came close to resolving the issue in 1987, with a compromise proposal to split surplus pension assets between workers, retirees, and the employer. This proposed legislation was never enacted. Instead, Congress enacted a series of bills that have been considered temporary while the issue is studied more carefully. In 1986, Congress enacted a 10 percent excise tax on surplus assets removed from pension funds. Legislation enacted in 1987 prevented companies from making tax-exempt contributions to a pension fund if the fund were already valued at over 150 percent of current obligations. In 1988, the excise tax on surplus assets removed from pension funds was raised to 15 percent.

Again, the concern in Congress was the provision and protection of employee benefits, not with the economic incentives associated with those benefits.

Mandatory Retirement

One area of legislation that impinged directly on retirement behavior was the increase in the mandatory retirement age from sixty-five to seventy enacted in 1978 and the complete prohibition of mandatory retirement enacted in 1986. Although both pieces of legislation were intended to limit or prevent forced retirements, they were not motivated by a general concern with reduced labor force participation among older workers. Rather, they were intended to prevent the inequitable treatment of older workers. President Reagan supported the legislation because he thought that older workers should not be forced to stop working when they reached a specified age. In enacting the legislation, however, Congress addressed age discrimination more broadly, modifying the Age Discrimination Act to prevent any employer discrimination on the basis of age. Representative Claude Pepper (the oldest member of Congress) was a particularly strong advocate of the legislation. According to Pepper, "This legislation is an important step in guaranteeing the elderly of this nation a fundamental civil right—the right to work as long as they are willing and able."

The legislation was strongly supported by senior citizen interest groups and opposed by business groups, who argued that it would disrupt labor turnover

---

pension fund assets of over $35 billion, of which about $20 billion was used for pension benefits and over $15 billion was taken by the companies for other purposes.

cycles, slow down the advancement of qualified workers, and result in fewer jobs for younger people. While the elimination of mandatory retirement enabled some workers to continue working past age seventy, the number of workers affected by this legislation is fairly small. Even when mandatory retirement was legal, few workers remained employed through age seventy, and only some of those working to age seventy were employed by firms with mandatory retirement policies.[15]

In summary, retirement policy legislation concentrated almost entirely on the protection of benefits and issues that were considered matters of fairness. Incentives for early retirement received almost no attention. Thus, for example, mandatory retirement was eliminated, but little attention was given to pension plan provisions that encourage early retirement. Only in the revisions of Social Security did labor force participation incentives receive serious consideration, and this was only incidental to the principle motivation to return the Social Security trust fund to solvency. The loss in pension benefits from job mobility would appear to be an important economic issue and one that might be expected to be the subject of congressional attention. The early retirement incentives of defined benefit pension plans might also have been the subject of legislative debate, although, in both cases, the appropriate legislative response is problematic, and possibly no strict regulation is best.

12.1.3   The Result

The reduction in the labor force participation of older workers and the trend toward earlier retirement has continued unabated for several decades, although it may have slowed in the late 1980s. The planned increase in the Social Security delayed retirement adjustment, the increase in the normal retirement age, and the reduction in the postretirement earnings tax rate might be expected to reduce the incentive to leave the labor force among workers who have not retired before age sixty-two. While new Social Security policies may induce some workers to continue working longer, the strong incentives that firm pensions provide for early retirement remain as they were. Indeed, firm pension plans typically provide incentive to retire much earlier than the normal retirement age for Social Security benefits (age sixty-five) and often earlier than Social Security's early retirement (age sixty-two). Although some companies are beginning to reevaluate the early retirement incentives associated with their policies, legislation in the 1980s has not affected the basic economic incentives of most pension plans.

15. In 1986, prior to the legislation, about 15.1 percent of people aged sixty-nine were in the labor force, and 10.6 percent of people aged seventy-one were in the labor force. (Thus, roughly 4.5 percent of seventy-one-year-olds had retired between ages sixty-nine and seventy-one—including both voluntary and mandatory retirements.) In 1989, with almost no employees subject to mandatory retirement, about 15.4 percent of people aged sixty-nine were in the labor force, and 12.0 percent of people aged seventy-one were in the labor force. (Thus, roughly 3.4 percent of seventy-one-year-olds had retired between ages sixty-nine and seventy-one—all voluntarily.)

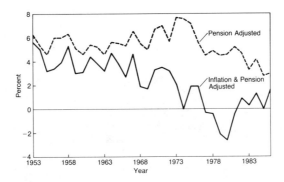

Fig. 12.5   Personal saving as a percentage of disposable private income, 1953–87

12.2   Personal Saving for Retirement

12.2.1   The Economic Issue

Personal saving in the United States has declined substantially as a fraction of personal income since the early 1950s, and a large proportion of families reach retirement age with little or no personal saving. Personal saving declined from between 3 and 6 percent of disposable private income in the 1950s to around 1 percent in the early 1980s, figures based on computations made by Summers and Carroll (1987) and reproduced in figure 12.5. These numbers are adjusted for inflation and exclude saving by employers through defined benefit pension plans.[16] Without the inflation adjustment, the downward trend begins only after 1973.

Aggregate saving rates of course reflect the wealth accumulation of all households, some of whom save very large amounts. Micro data show that a large fraction of families have almost no personal saving. On the basis of the recent Survey of Income and Program Participation (SIPP), Venti and Wise (1991) have computed the composition of total wealth for all households, for homeowners, and for renters in 1984. The results are summarized in figure 12.6. The amounts reflect median wealth by asset category. It is clear from figure 12.6a that most families approach retirement age with very little personal saving other than housing equity. Among households with heads aged sixty to sixty-five, the median amount of liquid wealth is only $6,600; the median value of housing equity is $43,000.[17] The majority of families rely heavily

16. The national income accounts include firm contributions to defined benefit pension plans under "personal saving." Inflation-adjusted saving is measured saving minus the inflation rate (the GNP deflator) times net interest-bearing assets.

17. Liquid wealth is broadly defined to include interest-earning assets held in banks and other institutions, mortgages held, money owed from sale of businesses, U.S. savings bonds, and checking accounts, equity in stocks, and mutual fund shares, less unsecured debt. Other wealth includes net equity in vehicles, business equity, and real estate equity (other than owned home).

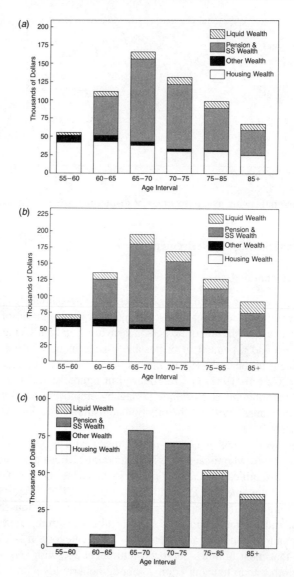

Fig. 12.6 (*a*) Median wealth by age and asset category, all households; (*b*) Median wealth by age and asset category, homeowners; (*c*) Median wealth by age and asset category, renters

on Social Security benefits for support after retirement and to a much more limited extent on the saving that is done for them by employers through defined benefit pension plans.

The Survey of Income and Program Participation data allow estimation of the value of Social Security and pension plan benefits only after the payments are received.[18] Thus, wealth in the form of Social Security and pensions is recorded only for persons who have begun to receive the payments.[19] Most persons have retired by sixty-five and thereafter are receiving the benefits to which they are entitled. About 59 percent of households with reference persons between sixty-five and seventy receive pension benefits; 89 percent receive Social Security benefits. The median of Social Security and pension wealth *combined* is $113,400 (the median of Social Security wealth is $83,700 and the median of pension wealth $11,200); the median of housing wealth is $38,000, and the median of liquid financial assets is only $10,000.[20]

In summary, the U.S. personal saving rate is currently the lowest of any industrialized country and has declined substantially since the 1950s. A large proportion of households have almost no personal saving, even as they approach retirement.

12.2.2 The Legislation

A series of legislative initiatives beginning in 1962 established and revised tax-advantaged saving programs. Initially, the legislative proposals were motivated by concerns for income security after retirement and for fairness in access to tax-advantaged saving programs. Later, legislation was motivated by the low observed national saving rates and by the tax cost of the programs at a time of large budget deficits. (These motivations of course have opposite implications for whether these tax advantages should be limited or extended.)

IRAs

Individual Retirement Accounts (IRAs) were first established in 1974 as part of the ERISA legislation. At that time, IRAs were limited to employees without firm pension plans and were intended to encourage these workers to save for retirement. IRAs were explicitly designed as a vehicle for retirement savings rather than savings more generally. The tax on the contribution and the interest were deferred until money was withdrawn from the account. According to a report from the House Ways and Means Committee, "Since the objective of the new provision is to encourage adequate provision for retire-

---

18. The SIPP data do not contain Social Security earnings histories (which determine Social Security benefits), nor do they contain detailed pension plan provisions.

19. Social Security benefits are indexed to inflation; private pension benefits typically are not. The present values of pension and Social Security are the discounted and survival weighted streams of income from each source received by the reference person and the spouse if present. Discounting is at 6 percent, and survival probabilities are calculated from mortality tables by sex. Payments from Social Security, military pensions, federal employee pensions, and the railroad retirement pension are assumed to be indexed at an annual rate of 4 percent. All other sources of pension income are not indexed in the wealth calculations.

20. The decline in Social Security and pension wealth with age is largely an artifact of declining life expectancy. The lower housing equity of older households is a cohort effect and does not reflect a reduction of housing equity as individual households age; in fact, housing equity increases on average as the elderly age; there is little change in housing equity even among families that move from one home to another.

ment needs, withdrawal of the retirement savings prior to age 591/2 will result in a penalty tax equal to 10 percent of the amount of the premature distribution."

The primary motivations for the legislation creating IRAs were to encourage income security after retirement and to impose greater equity in federal retirement policy. It was thought that workers without firm pension plans should have some of the tax advantages to prepare for retirement that workers received at companies with pension plans. This concern for fairness was expressed in the House Ways and Means Committee report recommending the passage of ERISA: "The committee believes that there is need on equity grounds to grant individuals who are not covered by any kind of qualified pension plan some of the tax advantages associated with such plans by providing them with a limited tax deduction for their retirement savings." Keogh plans had been established much earlier (1962) and were motivated by similar concerns about equity in retirement policy for the self-employed.

The Economic Recovery Act of 1981 extended the availability of IRAs to all employees.[21] Following the 1981 legislation, any employee with earnings above $2,000 could contribute $2,000 to an IRA each year. An employed person with a nonworking spouse could contribute $2,250, while a married couple who were both working could contribute $2,000 each. The 1981 IRA legislation was motivated in large part by the need to increase national saving as well as the desire to enhance the economic well-being of future retirees. The report of the Senate Finance Committee recommending passage of the bill states,

> The committee is concerned that the resources available to individuals who retire are often not adequate to avoid a substantial decrease from preretirement living standards. The committee believes that retirement savings by individuals can make an important contribution toward maintaining preretirement living standards and that the present level of individual savings is too often inadequate for this purpose. The committee understand that personal savings of individuals have recently declined in relation to personal disposable income (i.e., personal income after personal tax payments).

Over the next few years, IRAs became an immensely popular form of saving. Annual contributions grew from about $5 billion in 1981 to about $35 billion in 1984, accounting for about 20 percent of total personal saving.

Initial plans for tax reform contemplated substantial increases in the IRA limit. The 1984 Treasury Plan (see U.S. Department of the Treasury 1984), for example, called for an increase in the IRA limit for an employed person from $2,000 to $2,500 and an increase in the limit for a nonworking spouse from $250 to $2,500. Thus, the contribution limit for a husband and a nonworking spouse would have increased from $2,250 to $5,000. A Modified Treasury Plan would have increased the limit for an employed person from $2,000 to $2,500,

---

21. Indeed, even a self-employed person could have an IRA, but the contribution would be counted against the Keogh limit.

but the limit for a nonworking spouse would have increased to only $500. The so-called President's Plan would have left the limit for an employed person at $2,000 but would have raised the spousal limit to $2,000 (see U.S. President 1985). As tax reform legislation progressed through Congress, however, these proposals to expand IRAs were overshadowed by an alternative motivation—controlling the budget deficit.

Most of the subsequent congressional debate on IRAs seemed to be conditioned in large part by the tax cost of IRAs and the large budget deficit, which had become a widespread concern. In addition, two claims about IRAs themselves received considerable attention. The first was that IRAs were a benefit to the rich—that IRA savings were held primarily by wealthy people. The second was that IRAs produced no new saving. It was argued that funds were simply transferred from non-tax-advantaged savings accounts to IRA accounts or that IRA savings would have taken place anyway, even without the tax incentive. When this debate began, there was essentially no direct evidence on the saving effect of IRAs, yet Congress was exposed to pronouncements on both sides of the issue. The claims were based largely on personal anecdote and on the observation that aggregate personal saving had not increased. As shown above, the decline in personal savings (as measured by the national income accounts) that began in the early 1970s continued through the late 1980s.

Despite the lack of direct evidence, speculation on the savings effect of IRAs had a substantial effect on the legislation that was enacted. The first proposal put forth by the Senate Finance Committee was to eliminate entirely the IRA tax deduction. This proposal met with considerable public resistance. In the end, a compromise was reached that limited the IRA tax advantage for higher-income families who were covered by a firm pension plan. For persons with employer-provided pension plans, full tax-deductible IRA contributions were allowed only for individuals with income below $25,000 and couples with income below $40,000. Partial tax-deductible contributions would be allowed for individuals with incomes up to $35,000 and couples with incomes up to $50,000. No deduction was allowed for individuals with incomes above $35,000 and families with incomes above $50,000. However, the return on contributions continued to accrue tax free. The contribution limits were not changed. In recommending legislation limiting tax-deductible IRA contributions, the Senate Finance Committee made the following justification in its report to the full Senate:

> Since 1981, the expanded availability of IRAs has had no discernible impact on the level of aggregate personal savings. In addition . . . the committee believes that the wide availability of the option to make elective deferrals under cash or deferred arrangements [usually known as 401(k)s] and tax-sheltered annuities reduces the prior concern that individuals in employer-maintained plans should be able to save additional amounts for retirement on a discretionary basis.

Further, data have consistently shown that IRA utilization is quite low among lower-income taxpayers who may be the least likely to accumulate significant retirement saving in the absence of a specific tax provision. . . . The committee believes that those taxpayers for whom IRA utilization is the largest would generally have saved without regard to the tax incentives.

More substantial evidence on the savings effects of IRAs and the wealth of those benefiting form IRA contributions was introduced during the debate and has been further developed since the 1986 legislation. New analysis of IRA saving suggested that the net saving effect was substantial. In addition, it became clear that, although wealthier families were more likely to contribute to an IRA, the large majority of contributors were not wealthy.[22] Although this new evidence did not prevent the enactment of legislation limiting tax-deductible IRA contributions, it may have forestalled the much more extreme legislation first proposed by the Senate Finance Committee (to eliminate new IRA contributions altogether).

Possibly fewer than 40 percent of prior contributors were affected by the 1986 legislation, and, even for these families, only the up-front tax deduction was eliminated. Nevertheless, IRA contributions fell by over 50 percent between 1986 and 1987, the first year under the 1986 rules. Whereas over 15 percent of tax filers made contributions in 1986, only 7 percent contributed in 1987. The reporting of the tax reform act and the less intense promotion by financial institutions apparently left the widespread impression that the IRA had been eliminated. Indeed, a 1988 survey showed that about half of all persons who were in fact still eligible to contribute to an IRA thought that they were not (*IRA Reporter,* vol. 6, no. 9 [30 September 1988]).

Potential revisions of the IRA legislation have continued to be discussed to the present time. An overriding consideration has continued to be the effect of any proposal on the budget deficit. But the extent to which IRAs increase the saving rate and the extent to which they present an advantage to a broad spectrum of the population have been painted in different colors depending on the political circumstances. Whereas in 1986 the IRA was portrayed by some as a gift to the rich, in 1989 the IRA was put forth as a saving program that would increase saving and benefit individual savers over a broad spectrum of the population.

What had changed? In 1989, the administration was pressing for a capital gains tax reduction, arguing that at lower capital gains tax rate would increase national saving. The proposal to reduce capital gains taxes was being promoted at a time when the 1990 congressional budget resolution required a net *increase* in tax revenues by at least $5 billion. Senator Bentsen (the Democratic chairman of the Senate Finance Committee), in part at least to defeat the capital gains proposal, put forth an IRA proposal, appealing to the argument that the capital gains tax was a gift to the rich since only the wealthy owned stocks

22. For example, initial drafts of papers by Venti and Wise (1986, 1987) Wise (1987), and Summers and Carroll (1987) appeared during the spring of 1986.

and bonds. He argued that an expanded IRA would encourage more saving by the broad middle class rather than the rich. Indeed, the discussion revolved much more around who would gain from the savings incentive proposals rather than around what the effect of either would be on the economy overall. Who got the "tax break" was more important than aggregate saving and the potential benefit to the economy as a whole.

Under Bentsen's IRA proposal, those with incomes high enough to preclude a tax deduction for IRA contributions under current law would be allowed to deduct 50 percent of their IRA contributions up to the current limits ($2,000 for individuals, etc.). Both the capital gains proposal and the IRA proposal were politically popular, but it was unlikely that Congress could find enough additional revenues from other tax policy changes to pay for both the IRA expansion and the capital gains tax reduction—thus the opening to pit the IRA proposal against the capital gains tax reduction. Both could appeal to the need to increase the low rates of national saving, but the capital gains reduction could be classed as helping the rich, while now the IRA proposal could be characterized as helping everyone.

As the issue developed, Senator Roth introduced an alternative IRA proposal that became coupled with the proposal to reduce capital gains tax rates. Under Roth's proposal, the tax incentives associated with IRAs would be substantially altered, leading to increases in short-term tax revenue—and thus enabling the hoped-for cut in the capital gains tax—but decreases in longer-term tax revenue. Roth's plan would completely eliminate the tax deduction for IRA contributions (raising short-term tax revenue) but would allow both the principal and the interest earnings to be withdrawn tax free in retirement (causing long-term revenue losses). In addition, the plan could be used to save for the purchase of a first home and for college expenses. A key motivation for this structure was to avoid the up-front tax cost of the program. Under this arrangement, the tax cost would come later, when no tax would be levied on the IRA funds withdrawn. The inability of Congress to reach a compromise on the interrelated issues of capital gains tax rates and IRAs prevented legislation on either issue in 1989. In 1990 Bentsen reintroduced his IRA proposal, and the administration proposed a "back-ended" savings plan, similar to Roth's proposal in 1989. Although neither plan was enacted, legislation modifying IRAs continues to be evaluated.

In summary, the initial (1974) IRA legislation was intended to impose greater equity in federal retirement policy and to encourage retirement income security for people without firm pensions. The 1981 legislation that expanded the availability of IRA tax incentives was directly responsive to the low and declining national saving rate. The debate leading to the 1986 limitations on IRA contributions and the more recent discussion of other IRA revisions have been dominated by the tax cost of IRAs, the question of whether the benefits of IRAs devolve to the rich or to the poor, and the extent to which IRAs generate new saving. In general, the distribution of the tax benefits by income seemed to carry more weight than the potential effect on the economy at large through the saving effect.

401(k)s

These plans were formally established by the Revenue Act of 1978 but were not used much until the 1981 clarifying rules. The plans, also known as cash and deferred arrangements (CODAs), permit employees to contribute before-tax dollars to qualified retirement plans. Prior to the Tax Reform Act of 1986, the annual 401(k) contribution limit was $30,000. The 1986 legislation reduced the maximum employee contribution to $7,000 and also introduced nondiscrimination provisions to prevent plans from providing benefits exclusively to high-income employees. Employer contributions (subject to nondiscrimination rules) could still be as high as $30,000. Participants in 401(k) plans defer constructive realization of their contributions, thereby postponing their income tax liability. They also benefit from tax-free accumulation of the 401(k) investment, just as with IRAs, and may also obtain additional benefits if the employer matches part of their 401(k) contribution.[23]

As with Keogh plans (in 1962) and IRAs (in 1974), the 1978 legislation creating 401(k) plans was motivated by a concern for equity in federal retirement policy. Prior to 1978, companies with cash or deferred profit-sharing plans were not assured tax-advantaged treatment for these plans if employees had the option of taking their compensation as cash or as deferred benefits. According to the Senate Finance Committee report dealing with 401(k) plans, "The committee believes that the uncertainty caused by the present state of the law has created the need for a permanent solution which permits employers to establish new cash or deferred arrangements."

As with IRAs, the budget deficit dominated the discussion by 1986. Surprisingly, the net saving effect of 401(k) plans received little attention, even though the 401(k) plans can be thought of much like IRAs and their effect on savings is likely to be substantial. The lack of attention to the savings effect of 401(k) plans may be explained by the relatively low utilization of 401(k)s at that time. Utilization has increased enormously since then.

While the 1986 Tax Reform Act led to at least a temporary fall in IRA contributions, this has been partly offset by the rapid growth of 401(k) plan contributions. In 1983, total employment at firms with 401(k) plans totaled 7.1 million; by 1988, the number eligible to participate had increased to 27.5 million. The number of employees choosing to participate in these plans also has increased sharply, from 4.5 million in 1983, to 10.3 million in 1985, to 15.7 million in 1988. Most large firms now have 401(k) plans. A 1987 survey by Hewitt Associates, for example, found plans at 91 percent of the firms in the

---

23. In the Massachusetts Mutual (1988) survey, 57 percent of the firms offering 401(k) plans matched some fraction of an employee's contribution. A 1988 GAO study (U.S. General Accounting Office 1988) found that 51 percent of firms made some matching contribution.

Fortune 200. More recent adoption of 401(k) plans has been fastest at small firms: the Massachusetts Mutual (1988) survey shows an increase in the number of small firms offering these plans from 8 percent in 1984 to 36 percent in 1988.

For those eligible to participate in 401(k) plans, participation rates are much higher than the rates in other saving plans, including IRAs. Tabulations from the March 1988 Current Population Survey (CPS) suggest a utilization rate of nearly 57 percent, up from 38 percent in 1983. In contrast, about 15 percent of tax filers contributed to an IRA account; possibly 25 percent of tax filers have IRA accounts. The average annual contribution to 401(k) plans in 1988 was about $2,000.

In summary, like Keogh plans and IRAs, 401(k) plans were introduced primarily to provide greater equity in federal retirement policy and to encourage retirement saving. The $30,000 limit allowed a great deal of tax-advantaged saving, and the possibility of employer matching made the plan more advantageous than IRAs. But, unlike IRAs, individuals could contribute only after a plan had been established by their employer. Thus, the participation rate was at first low but has been expanding rapidly. Again, like IRAs, the program was cut back just as 401(k)s were gaining in popularity. But, unlike IRAs, the 401(k) limit is still high enough that only a small proportion of participants contribute at the current $7,000 employee limit.

12.2.3   The Result

Despite the increasing availability of tax-advantaged savings programs in the early and mid-1980s, this period had among the lowest rate of personal saving in U.S. history. This observation led many policymakers to conclude that tax-advantaged savings programs do little to increase savings behavior and thus had little positive social value. An increasing number of economic studies suggest just the opposite—retirement savings programs (such as IRAs and 401[k]s) have induced a great deal of savings that would not have occurred otherwise (see e.g., Venti and Wise 1986, 1987, 1990, 1991; and Feenburg and Skinner 1989). Indeed, savings rates would have been even lower in the 1980s without these programs.

Even ignoring the savings effect of IRAs and 401(k)s, the short-term tax cost of these programs at a time of large budget deficits led Congress to limit these programs rather than extend them. The decisions to cut back 401(k) contribution limits and IRA participation were motivated largely by the budget deficit. It seems, therefore, that the concerns about the budget deficit in the short run have taken precedence over long-run concerns for national saving. Indeed the long-run tax cost associated with either of the tax-advantaged saving programs is very small compared with the short-run tax costs that are motivating policy decisions.

12.3 Health Care

12.3.1 The Economic Issue

Health care costs have risen almost continuously as a proportion of GNP since the early 1960s, as shown in figure 12.7. Total national health care expenditures claimed a full 11.1 percent of GNP in 1987. Public expenditures on health care are rising, employer expenditures on health care are rising, and out-of-pocket consumer expenditures on health care are rising.

The increases in national health care expenditures have resulted from a number of factors, including the aging of the population (and the higher health care utilization rates of older people), an increasing number of health care procedures performed per patient, an increasing sophistication of health services for most illnesses, and high rates of inflation associated with health care services. Figure 12.8 shows the increase in medical care prices as compared with the increase in the general price level, as measured by the consumer price index.

The basic economic issue is how to provide health insurance while containing the expenditures induced by the insurance—the moral hazard problem. Because health care needs vary enormously across the population, and because these health care needs are typically unexpected, there is a natural role for health insurance. However, health insurance tends to increase the total use and cost of health care services. The greater use of health care is drive by both consumers of health care (who want to get healthy at the expense of insurers) and providers of health care (whose income depends on the provision of health care services).

The moral hazard problem arises because the cost of health care to the individual is lower than the total cost of the care. When people decide how much to spend on health care, they base their decisions on their own personal costs rather than the costs to society. Once the cost is covered by insurance—either

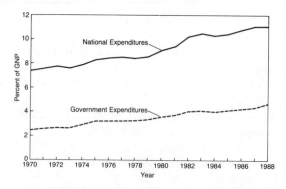

Fig. 12.7 **National health care expenditures and government health care expenditures, as a percentage of GNP**

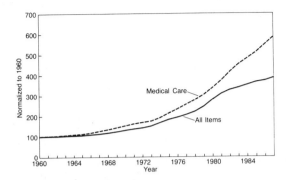

Fig. 12.8   Consumer price index, medical care and all items, normalized to 1960

through the government or through private insurance programs—the remaining personal costs of health care are small, so there is little incentive for patients to limit the use of health care. The moral hazard incentive is even more acute with health care than with other forms of insurance because the providers of health care (not just the patients) have an enormous influence on the amount and the composition of health care demanded. Like patients, health care providers have little incentive to economize on health care costs when they are fully reimbursed by health insurance.

Both economic research and legislative activity have been directed to containing the moral hazard effects of health insurance. On the demand side, one way to moderate the use of health care services is through deductibles and copayments. Since the recipients of health care services then pay at least part of the cost of their care, there is a greater incentive for them to limit these expenditures, by limiting either the extent of care of its cost. On the supply side, the use of health care services may be moderated through fixed reimbursement policies. If insurance companies (or the government) pay health care providers a fixed fee per patient (or per illness), then the providers will have a greater incentive to reduce the cost of care for their patients so that they can retain a larger share of that fee. Both the supply-side and the demand-side approaches are reflected in health care legislation in the 1980s.

12.3.2   The Legislation

The major themes of health care policy in the 1980s have been access, "catastrophic" insurance, and cost control. Two major health care policies were enacted by Congress. The first, in 1983, fundamentally changed the way the federal government reimburses hospitals for Medicare-covered services. The second, in 1988, expanded Medicare coverage for "catastrophic" medical care expenses. Owing to public dissatisfaction with the financing of catastrophic insurance, the new catastrophic coverage was almost totally repealed in 1989. These major legislative developments are discussed below.

Many other changes in health care policy were considered by Congress in the 1980s, including national health insurance, public long-term care insurance, and mandatory employer-provided health insurance. Owing to the enormous cost of health care services, the significant strain on the federal government budget throughout the 1980s, and opposition outside the government (from insurance companies, physicians, businesses, and others), none of these additional proposals has come close to gaining congressional approval.

Medicare Reimbursement

Controlling government expenditures on health care has been the single most important objective of health care legislation in the 1980s. Cost-control measures have been motivated by the large federal budget deficit, the escalating public expenditures on health care services (through both the Medicare and the Medicaid programs), and the rapid acceleration of health care costs generally. Cost-saving legislation was enacted almost every year throughout the 1980s, generally limiting the amount of reimbursement provided by the Medicare and Medicaid programs for hospital and physician services.

The most significant legislation took place in 1983, when the Medicare reimbursement procedure for hospital services underwent fundamental reform. Like Social Security reform (also in 1983), the reform of the Medicare program was inspired by a pending financial crisis. Medicare costs were rising rapidly, and the Hospital Insurance Trust Fund was projected to go bankrupt around 1987.

While the final composition of Medicare reform was developed and enacted in 1983, the background for the legislation took place a year earlier, when Congress placed new limitations on the amount of hospital reimbursement under Medicare. Under the 1982 legislation, hospital reimbursement would be limited to 110 percent of the average per-case cost among similar hospitals. During a phase-in period, the limit would be placed at 120 percent in 1983, 115 percent in 1984, and 110 percent thereafter. The 1982 legislation also limited the annual increase in reimbursements to the increase in an index of hospital wages and prices plus 1 percent.

As expected, the health care industry was not at all satisfied with the new limitations, arguing that the reimbursement limits did not adequately account for the legitimate differences among hospitals. Because of their dissatisfaction with the 1982 legislation, hospital officials were pleased to help develop and support the policy eventually implemented in 1983. In fact, anticipating that the 1982 limits would not be acceptable as a permanent hospital reimbursement policy, Congress had instructed the Department of Health and Human Services (HHS) to develop an alternative proposal for a "prospective" payment system for hospital reimbursement. The Medicare reform enacted by Congress in 1983 followed the framework of the proposal submitted by HHS.

Prior to the 1983 reform, Medicare reimbursements for health care services were cost based. Within certain guidelines, hospitals were reimbursed according to the costs incurred in providing health care services. Some believed that the cost-based Medicare reimbursement system was at least partially responsible for rising health care costs because there was little economic incentive for health care providers to control costs. The 1983 reform directly addressed this concern. The new reimbursement system provided a fixed fee for inpatient hospital services, regardless of the costs actually incurred in treatment. The amount of the fixed fee depended on the illness or the condition of the patient. Illnesses were categorized (and payments specified) for about 500 "diagnosis-related groups," or DRGs. The fixed DRG fees were intended to cover all hospital expenses in treating the illness or condition.

The intended effect of the Medicare reform was to create incentives for hospitals to decrease their health care costs. Under the old system, hospitals were reimbursed more when they incurred higher costs—creating an incentive for more extensive (and possibly excessive) treatments. Under the new reimbursement system, hospital payments were unrelated to costs. Any cost-saving measures would directly benefit the hospital because there would be no reduction in the predetermined reimbursement from Medicare.

Similar reimbursement limits have been placed on physicians at various times throughout the 1980s. Most recently (1989), Congress developed a reimbursement procedure based on a predetermined value of physicians' services. Prior to the 1989 legislation, Medicare reimbursed physicians for Medicare-covered services on the basis of the physicians' standard rates. Under the new system, physicians will be reimbursed according to a "resource-based relative value scale" (RBRVS). The RBRVS will specify a reimbursement rate for each type of service provided and will be based on the time, training, skill, and overhead costs associated with providing each service.

Both the 1983 reform of hospital reimbursement and the 1989 reform of physician reimbursement account for at least some of the behavioral incentives emphasized in economic research on health care issues. Prior to these reforms, attempts to control health care costs focused on the recipient of care rather than on the provider. Medicare policies contained (and still contain) deductibles and copayments that make the recipients of care at least partially responsible for the expenses incurred by their health care decisions. Even in the means-tested Medicaid program, Congress enacted legislation in 1982 that allows states to collect small deductibles ($1.00 or $2.00) from Medicaid patients so that the health care decisions of Medicaid patients are more cost conscious.

Both the 1983 and the 1989 reforms focused on the providers of care. The 1983 Medicare reform was intended to create cost-saving incentives for health care providers similar to the cost-saving incentives of patients when they face deductibles and copayments. Since profits under the DRG system are inversely related to costs, health care providers presumably would have a strong incentive to reduce costs. The 1989 Medicare reform was intended to control physician costs by imposing more control on their reimbursement rates. Both demand- and supply-side policies are likely to affect health care costs, although supply-side policies may be particularly effective because of the large role of health care providers in determining the choice of care for their patients.[24]

Catastrophic Health Insurance

The second major development in health care policy in the 1980s was the enactment of the Medicare Catastrophic Coverage Act in 1988 and its subsequent repeal in 1989. Congressional consideration of "catastrophic" health insurance was initiated by President Carter in the late 1970s and later by President Reagan in both his 1986 and his 1987 State of the Union addresses. Responding to Reagan's 1986 request, Secretary of Health and Human Services Otis Bowen released a report in November 1986 outlining a catastrophic health insurance plan. Secretary Bowen's initial proposal provided the basic framework for the legislation that was eventually enacted in 1988.

Bowen had recommended that a $2,000 annual limit be established on all out-of-pocket expenditures for Medicare-covered health care services and that this coverage be financed through a modest increase in the Medicare Part B insurance premium. The legislation actually enacted placed an annual limit of about $564 (1989) on out-of-pocket expenditures for hospital care and an annual limit of about $1,370 (1989) on out-of-pocket expenditures for all Medicare Part B services (including physician and other outpatient health care services). The limit would be increased each year so that 7 percent of Medicare beneficiaries would be expected to reach the limit. The final legislation also expanded the number and duration of health care services covered by Medicare, including an increase in skilled nursing home care from 100 to 150 days, elimination of the 210-day limit on coverage for hospice care, the addition of coverage for thirty days of home health care, the addition of coverage for eighty hours of respite care, and the provision of 80 percent insurance for prescription drug costs above a $600 deductible. After the phase-in period, the new benefit would be financed primarily by an increase in the monthly Part B premium from $24.80 to $35.00 and a supplemental premium imposed on all Medicare-covered individuals with an income tax liability above $150. Once phased in, the supplemental premium would be $42.00 for each $150 of annual income tax liability, up to a maximum premium of $1,050. About 60 percent of Medicare beneficiaries would pay no supplemental premium.

When the legislation was enacted in 1988, there was very little opposition to the concept of catastrophic health insurance (except among those who thought that catastrophic insurance was better left to private medical insurance policies), although opinions varied on the most desirable content of the legislation. The main lobbyists expressing an interest in catastrophic health insurance

---

24. However, demand-side policies may also be quite effective. For example, some anecdotal evidence suggests that one of the reasons that internists are paid less than surgeons is that a much larger proportion of the fees of internists is paid by the patient for office services for which the patient is likely to face a copayment or even the entire cost.

were the American Association of Retired Persons (AARP), which supported the legislation; the National Commission to Preserve Social Security and Medicare, which objected to the premium increases and the lack of coverage for long-term care services; and the Pharmaceutical Manufacturers Association (PMA), which opposed insurance for prescription drugs, worrying that insurance coverage would lead to price controls at a later date. When enacted in 1988, the Catastrophic Coverage Act was viewed by many as an excellent (landmark) change in public health policy.

Opinions changed dramatically in 1989, when the effect of the program's financing became more apparent. First, Medicare recipients who were subject to the income-based supplemental premium argued that an income-based premium was unfair. For the highest-income recipients, the supplemental premium added $1,050 to their annual health insurance costs. Second, Medicare recipients began paying higher premiums before becoming eligible for any additional health care benefits. This was also considered unfair. Third, about 3.3 million Medicare beneficiaries already received catastrophic insurance from employer-provided post retirement medical benefits. Under the catastrophic care legislation, these people faced higher Medicare premiums (especially those subject to the supplemental premiums) with no additional health care benefits. Responding to the public dissatisfaction, Congress repealed the catastrophic care laws in 1989.

National Health Insurance and Long-Term Care

Some members of Congress have expressed a strong interest in expanding health insurance coverage to include both more people and more health care services. In particular, there have been numerous legislative proposals for national health insurance and for public long-term care insurance. Because of the enormous cost of these proposals, no comprehensive health and long-term care policy reform was enacted in the 1980s.

Despite the cost, the financing of long-term health care is still widely considered to be one of the most important issues on the legislative agenda for the 1990s. Nursing home care and other forms of long-term care are paid for almost entirely by the recipient, until the recipient becomes eligible for means-tested Medicaid assistance. As a result, many older people are impoverished by long-term disabilities, and the financing of long-term care has developed as a major public concern. Several bills have been introduced in Congress that would provide at least some public insurance for long-term care services. Owing to the enormous cost of long-term care services, however, Congress has only initiated studies of long-term care needs and the financing of long-term care; it has not enacted any major long-term care legislation.

Limited long-term care legislation has been enacted in several areas, however. Congress enacted legislation in 1982 to provide Medicare coverage for hospice care (home health care and related services) to terminally ill patients. The 1982 legislation provided up the $4,200 in hospice care benefits; 1983 legislation raised the maximum benefit to $6,500; 1984 legislation raised the daily hospice care rate from $46.25 to $53.17; and the 1988 catastrophic care legislation eliminated the 210-day limit on coverage. The catastrophic care legislation also expanded Medicare coverage to include up to thirty days of home health care and up to eight hours of respite care (professional health and custodial care services to relieve informal caregivers). While the provisions of the catastrophic care legislation were repealed in 1989, those relating to long-term care are being evaluated again in 1990.

One component of the catastrophic care legislation relates to the Medicaid rules limiting "spousal impoverishment." Under previous Medicaid rules in most states, most of the income and assets of the married couple was used to determine Medicaid eligibility. As a result, both the institutionalized and the at-home spouse were often impoverished, before the institutionalized spouse became eligible for Medicaid assistance. Under the 1988 legislation, when one spouse enters a nursing home, the assets of the couple were to be divided between them (with no less than $12,000 and no more than $60,000 attributed to the at-home spouse). Only the assets of the institutionalized spouse are considered in determining Medicaid eligibility. In addition, the at-home spouse is entitled to a "maintenance needs allowance" from the income of both spouses. Once phased in in 1992, the maintenance needs allowance will be 150 percent of the federal poverty threshold for a two-person household up to $1,500 per month.

While long-term care seems to be a higher priority in Congress, various forms of national health insurance have also been discussed periodically. President Carter had been determined to enact a form of national health insurance during his presidency in the late 1970s. With the budgetary pressures of the 1980s, expectations about publicly provided national health insurance were replaced with the less ambitious catastrophic insurance proposals. An alternative approach to national health insurance received more attention later in the 1980s. This alternative would require all employers to provide health insurance for their employees.[25] Senator Kennedy was a leading proponent of mandated health benefits. The Senate Committee on Labor and Human Resources (which Kennedy chairs) reported a bill in 1988, but no legislation was enacted. Opponents of the bill, such as Senator Hatch, argued that the mandated benefits would reduce jobs and raise health care costs. The disagreement, where conflicting "economic" analyses provided the political ammunition, was in how much it would cost businesses and how many jobs would be lost.

---

25. Related legislation affecting employer-provided health insurance was enacted in 1982. Under this legislation, employers were required to provide the same health benefits for workers aged sixty-five to sixty-nine as were provided to younger employees. Medicare would pay only for the difference between these benefits and full Medicare benefits.

12.3.3   The Result

The objectives of health care legislation in the 1980s were to extend health insurance coverage and to control health care costs. Nonetheless, the 1980s have seen very little change in coverage and continued growth in national health care expenditures.

The Medicare reform enacted in 1983 was intended to create economic incentives for hospitals to reduce costs. While the composition of health care costs was affected by this legislation, total health care costs have continued to rise rapidly. The DRG system apparently led to a reduction in the average length of stay of hospital patients. Hospitals reduced costs by reducing the length of stay, and this apparently led to a reduction in fees paid to physicians through hospitals. The reduction in direct hospital reimbursement, however, was largely offset by an increase in outpatient physician fees paid through outpatient hospitals and offices. Total government expenditures on health care continue to increase, along with total national health care expenditures.

Efforts to extend health insurance coverage have also been largely ineffective. Proposals for national health insurance, public long-term care insurance, and employer-mandated health insurance were considered, but not enacted, in the 1980s. Catastrophic health insurance was enacted and then repealed. The distributional consequences of these proposals appear to have been the most significant factors preventing legislation in this area. Catastrophic care failed because higher-income elderly would pay more; employer-mandated insurance failed because employers would pay more; national health insurance and long-term care insurance failed because certain taxpayers would need to pay more to support the extended coverage. In fact, since even the "uninsured" have access to charity care, proposals to "expand" health care coverage seem to have more to do with distribution (who pays for the care) than coverage (who gets the care).

12.4   Conclusions and Discussion

Aging issues have been an important component of federal legislation throughout the 1980s. The legislation enacted was influenced by and will have consequences for economic behavior, income distribution, and "fairness." While economic analysis is most useful in understanding the behavioral implications of government policies, distribution and fairness were more often the dominant factors influencing aging legislation in the 1980s.

In some cases, such as Medicare reform, economic analysis has been central to the legislative debate on the issue. The intent of the prospective payment system of Medicare reimbursement was to create economic incentives for hospitals to reduce the cost of health care. Most health economics research had focused on the economic incentives among insured users of health care and reimbursed providers of health care. The results of this research were applied extensively in developing the 1983 Medicare reform legislation.

In other cases, economic analysis contributed extensively to the legislative debate but was not the central motivation for the legislation enacted. For example, Social Security reform was motivated by a projected financial shortage in the Social Security trust fund, and the legislation enacted was designed primarily to prevent this projected shortage. While not the central motivation for the reform, economic analysis was introduced and evaluated throughout the policy-making process, and the reforms enacted have important behavioral implications that were identified and evaluated through economic research. Some of the reforms enacted in 1983 decrease the work disincentives associated with prior Social Security policies and might be expected to defer retirement among workers not yet retired by age sixty-two.

In still other cases, such as IRA legislation, economic analysis was sought and considered, but its influence may have been diminished by conflicting views among economists. In 1981, when IRA eligibility was extended, most policymakers seemed to believe that IRAs would be an effective vehicle for promoting retirement saving. When IRA eligibility was limited in 1986, many believed that IRAs were not an effective means of increasing personal saving. The debate leading up to the 1986 legislation and the more recent debate on expanding IRAs have had vociferous advocates of both economic conclusions about the effects of IRAs on savings.

Finally, in some areas, such as private pension plan legislation, the issues addressed in Congress were outside the purview of central economic research. Changes in vesting rules, funding requirements, Social Security integration rules, pension insurance programs, survivorship benefits, nondiscrimination rules, and plan termination regulations were motivated by concerns about fairness or equity in the treatment of different employees and protection of pension benefits. Even the elimination of mandatory retirement was motivated by concerns about equity rather than the declining labor force participation of older workers. The work and retirement incentives associated with pension plans were rarely considered in the legislative debate, and they were scarcely affected by any of the 1980s pension legislation.

In almost all instances, members of Congress and their staff are exposed to a large amount of economic research before making any policy decisions. However, because almost no economic analysis is definitive, at least initially, the staff member must use individual judgment and intuition to evaluate this research. The more the conclusions of economic analysis differ, the greater the difficulty in making this evaluation, and the greater the role of intuition.

Economic research considers both efficiency and distributional issues. But, ultimately, concerns about distribution and fairness are typically more significant in influencing the legislative outcomes than even the most conclusive of analyses of the potential efficiency effects of alternative policies. Nonetheless, economists' warnings about the inefficiencies of potential policies and regulations may have warded off proposals that might otherwise have been enacted. And, in other cases—like the DRG legislation—efficiency arguments played a key role.

References

Congressional Quarterly Almanac. 1980–89. Washington, D.C.: Congressional Quarterly News Features.

Feenberg, Daniel, and Jonathan Skinner. 1989. Sources of IRA saving. In *Tax policy and the economy 3,* ed. L. Summers. Cambridge, Mass.: MIT Press.

Kotlikoff, Laurence J., and David A. Wise. 1985. Labor compensation and the structure of private pension plans: Evidence for contractual versus spot labor markets. In *Pensions, labor, and individual choice,* ed. D. Wise. Chicago: University of Chicago Press.

———. 1987. The incentive effects of private pension plans. In *Issues in pension economics,* ed. Z. Bodie, J. Shoven, and D. Wise. Chicago: University of Chicago Press.

———. 1989. Employee retirement behavior and a firm's pension plan. In *The economics of aging,* ed. D. Wise. Chicago: University of Chicago Press.

Lazear, Edward P. 1983. Pensions as severance pay. In *Financial aspects of the United States pension system,* ed. Z. Bodie and J. Shoven. Chicago: University of Chicago Press.

Ransom, Roger L., and Richard Sutch. 1988. The decline of retirement and the rise of efficiency wages: U.S. retirement patterns, 1870–1940. In *Issues in contemporary retirement,* ed. R. Ricardo-Campbell and E. Lazear. Stanford, Calif.: Hoover Institution.

Tuma, Nancy Brandon, and Gary D. Sandefur. 1988. Trends in the labor force activity of the aged in the United States, 1940–80. In *Issues in contemporary retirement,* ed. R. Ricardo-Campbell and E. Lazear. Stanford, Calif.: Hoover Institution.

Summers, Lawrence, and Chris Carroll. 1987. Why is U.S. national saving so low? *Brookings Papers on Economic Activity,* no. 2: 607–42.

U.S. Congress. 1974–89. *Congressional Record;* and various committee hearings and committee reports. Washington, D.C.

U.S. Department of Treasury. 1984. *Tax reform for fairness, simplicity, and economic growth.* Washington, D.C.: U.S. Government Printing Office.

U.S. General Accounting Office. 1988. *401(k) plans: incidence, provisions, and benefits.* Washington, D.C.

U.S. President. 1985. *The president's tax proposals to the Congress for fairness, growth, and simplicity.* Washington, D.C.: U.S. Government Printing Office, May.

Venti, Steven F., and David A. Wise. 1986. Tax-deferred accounts, constrained choice and estimation of individual saving. *Review of Economic Studies* 43: 579–601.

———. 1987. IRAs and saving. In *The effects of taxation on capital accumulation,* ed. M. Feldstein. Chicago: University of Chicago Press.

———. 1990. Have IRAs increased U.S. saving?: Evidence from consumer expenditure surveys. *Quarterly Journal of Economics* 105, no. 3 (August): 661–98.

———. 1991. The saving effect of tax-deferred retirement accounts: Evidence from SIPP. In *National saving and economic performance,* ed. B. Douglas Bernheim and John B. Shoven. Chicago: University of Chicago Press.

Wise, David A. 1987. Individual retirement accounts and saving. In *Taxes and capital formation,* ed. M. Feldstein. Chicago: University of Chicago Press.

Woodbury, Richard G. 1990. Why businesses design policies that induce retirement: An analysis of the retirement policy motivations at twenty large United States employers. Ph.D. diss., Economics Department, Harvard University.

2. *Rudolph Penner*

Federal government payments to the elderly population make all other civilian budget issues pale in relative importance. Spending on people over sixty-five now absorbs almost half of noninterest civilian spending, and the Congressional Budget Office (CBO) estimates that payments to the elderly will absorb some seventy cents of each additional dollar of noninterest civilian spending over the next five years.

Figures 12.9 and 12.10 show how important the two main elderly programs, Social Security and Medicare, are in the budget. Over the long run, the relative importance of defense has declined relative to GNP, and interest has increased, as has Social Security and Medicare. Since the late 1970s, everything else has declined, which, I believe, indicates a significant ideological shift away from the view that prevailed in earlier decades. Figure 12.10 compares Social Security and Medicare and all other types of civilian, noninterest spending and shows how rapidly Social Security and Medicare have grown, almost catching up to all other civilian noninterest spending in terms of importance.

While Social Security and Medicare are overwhelming in their importance, the elderly receive a disproportionate share of other benefits as well. Medicaid is very rapidly becoming an elderly program because of soaring nursing home costs. There are special housing subsidies for the elderly, SSI exists mainly for the poor elderly, the elderly get a disproportionate share of food stamps, and numerous nutrition programs are aimed at the elderly. In addition, civil service pensions and military pensions provide significant support to the elderly.

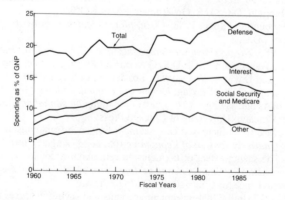

Fig. 12.9   Federal spending, by type of program, fiscal years 1960–89

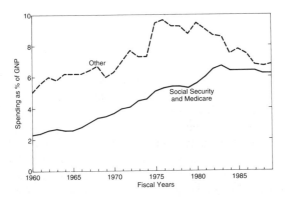

Fig. 12.10   Federal civilian noninterest spending, fiscal years 1960–89

Currently, Social Security is the most costly program focused on the elderly, although current projections suggest that without radical reform, Medicare will exceed it in size in the early twenty-first century. The OASDI program constitutes about 21 percent of total spending and about 34 percent of noninterest civilian spending.

The ordinary citizen obviously must take a very long view of the Social Security system. It affects us through our working life because of a large payroll tax burden, and it affects our expected well-being while retired. Because it is to some degree a substitute for intergenerational transfers, it probably also has significant effects on private transfers from parents to children and from children to parents. Given that you have to take a long view, I am a little tempted to begin my story in the 1880s, rather than the 1980s. We did have a fairly substantial social security program in the nineteenth century, called Civil War pensions. By some magic, almost everybody qualified. The demise of eligible veterans was one of many factors responsible for the establishment of Social Security. I have a feeling, however, that a three-hour history would not be much appreciated here.

However, the policies of the 1980s were very much a reaction to the policy changes of the late 1960s and early 1970s, and I think that it is necessary to look at those in some detail. The peak year of Vietnam defense spending was 1968, and defense spending continued to fall relative to GNP until the mid-1970s. About 70 percent of the fall in defense from the peak to the trough was absorbed by increases in the Medicare and Social Security programs. The problem was that we made permanent long-run promises to the elderly financed by a peace dividend that was, of course, temporary.

Changes in the Social Security replacement rate for the single retiree illustrate the growing generosity of the program. The average replacement rate is here defined as the benefit that a single person would get relative to his or her last year of income if the person earned the average wage for his or her whole working life. The replacement rate had eroded a bit in the early 1960s and was about 31.4 percent in 1965, but it was quickly raised to 42.3 percent by 1975. That is a before-tax replacement rate, and the after-tax rate would be considerably higher. Also, someone retiring with a dependent spouse gets an extra 50 percent.

But more important than the benefit increases during this period was the adoption of indexing in 1972. It represented a profound change in the philosophy of the system because indexing changed the definition of the entitlement. The nation said, not only that retirees are entitled to a certain nominal benefit, but also that they are going to be protected against inflation as well. Furthermore, the initial attempt to index was designed to go beyond CPI indexing and to provide a small real increase to each successive cohort of new retirees. In other words, the Congress tried to put the system on automatic pilot. Given the rates of inflation and real growth expected at the time, it was thought that the replacement rate would erode despite the small real increases expected with the new indexing system, so that Congress would have had the opportunity from time to time to be generous and give people a more substantial real increase.

The arithmetic of the indexing formula was faulty. When a surprising acceleration in inflation occurred, the formula was such (and I certainly will not try to explain it here) that the real increase in benefits increased as the inflation rate increased. The replacement rate began to soar, eventually going over 50 percent.

Ironically, indexing was first passed as a money-saving measure. I remember believing that it would, in fact, control costs. In the late 1960s, the Congress had to adjust benefits upward periodically because of the Vietnam-related acceleration of inflation. Every time they opened up the issue, which they often did just before an election, there was enormous political pressure to provide increases in excess of inflation. Indexing was seen as a discipline. It was supposed to constrain real benefit increases, and the Congress hoped that it would allow them to ignore Social Security for long periods of time.

With the benefit of hindsight, it now appears that the 1960s was a very unusual decade. There was unusually rapid economic growth, and in the early 1960s the elderly were among the poorest segment of the population. A serious social problem existed, and the nation thought that it had sufficient resources to solve it because it was forecast that rapid growth would last forever. It was not surprising, in retrospect, to see intense political pressure to spend some of the anticipated growth dividend on the elderly.

In the 1950s and the early 1960s, the needs were just as great, but the Congress did allow replacement rates to erode for long periods. I am very doubtful now that, in an unindexed system, the Congress would have compensated for the whole increase in the CPI in the late 1970s, when resources were more limited and real wages were eroding. Moreover, the CPI was upward biased during the period because of the flawed treatment of housing costs.

One of the themes in this conference asks how important economic analysis is to policy decisions. With regard to Social Security, Martha Derthick has written brilliantly on how that program evolved, and her main theme is that a coterie of experts surrounds the system and has significant power over policy changes. The system is so intricate that very few people understand it, but there is a small group of people, such as Robert Ball and Robert Myers and various other former actuaries and commissioners, who understand it well and who are advocates for the system. They have enormous influence with the Ways and Means Committee and the Senate Finance Committee because, in the 1970s, they were about the only people who understood the details of the system. So it was up to the technicians to develop an indexing system that replaced the flawed inflation indexing system that had been adopted in 1972, and I think that their choice was considered to be a technical matter, not a philosophical matter.

Their choice, nevertheless, changed the philosophy of the entitlement once again because they invented a system that attempted evermore to keep the replacement rate constant for newly retired persons at each segment of the income distribution. In other words, during people's working life, they would accumulate an entitlement that allowed them to share in the rewards of economic growth. Oddly enough, the philosophy was schizoid in that, as soon as you retired, you were just guaranteed a constant real payment, and you did not share in real growth unless Congress explicitly acted to increase real benefits.

I was working at the Office of Management and Budget (OMB) at the time that indexing reform was being considered, and I truly felt that nobody knew what was going on. I could not believe the proposed legislation when I read it. It indexed the benefit formula to wages, not to prices. I tried to create a fuss and ran head-on into the intricacies of the system. It was extraordinarily difficult to explain what was going on to any policymakers. I vividly remember our effort to prepare the presentation of different indexing options to the cabinet and to President Ford, and we corralled some very bright defense analysts, thinking that they would be a good example of the intelligent laymen that we were trying to convince and that we could explain the issues to them. We tried, and they did not know what we were talking about. We reformulated the presentation and tried it out on them again, and they seemed to understand it. But the next morning we asked them to explain it back, and none of them would have received 30 out of 100 on a test on it. I was not personally involved in the presentation to President Ford (I was at too low a level at the time), but somehow my name got associated with the presentation and, when I saw him several months after the end of his presidency, he said, "Don't try to explain double indexing to me again!"

It was very hard to make people understand the importance of the issue. The histories of policy developments (whether they be in Social Security or tax policy or whatever) are always written as though that is the only thing on the president's mind during a particular period. If you read Derthick's book about this indexing incident, it seems as though President Ford was considering little else for several weeks. In fact, he was very busy at the time preparing for an economic summit meeting in Puerto Rico, which he considered to be very important. I remember being frustrated because I saw the summit as a ceremonial occasion whereas the Social Security issue was worth hundreds of billions of dollars in present value terms.

As an aside, you might not think that the choice of wage over price indexing cost much because of the slow subsequent growth in real wages, but the Social Security Administration (SSA) uses its own index. For reasons that I do not understand, real wages have grown much faster using the index the SSA uses for the purposes of adjustment than you would believe looking at the Bureau of Labor Statistics (BLS) index for the average hourly wage.

President Ford eventually recommended wage indexing to the Congress, but it was not enacted before he left the presidency. President Carter could not possibly recommend something less generous than President Ford, although there was some debate over the issue within his administration.

Although the 1977 indexing reform was too generous in my view, the reform also took back a lot of the unintended increase in the replacement rate that had occurred under double indexing and that caused the famous problem of the notch baby. The new reforms were designed to put the Social Security system on automatic pilot, but all sorts of things went wrong. I have already mentioned some of them, including the upward bias in the CPI. But then the nation faced back-to-back recessions in 1980 and 1982, and the system was on the verge of technical bankruptcy.

The administration and the Congress set out to reform it once again, and the reformers faced a difficult task, given the difficult politics surrounding the system. The indexing prevented them from using inflation to erode benefits, and even real growth did not help because of the wage indexing of the benefit formula. So some of the entitlement had to be withdrawn, or else the taxes used to finance the system had to be increased significantly. Politicians dreaded that task, and, to shield themselves from blame, they appointed a commission led very skillfully by Alan Greenspan. I think that, if you talk to him, he will be very modest and say that he had a lot of good luck and that there were many times in the proceedings when it looked like the commission would fall apart. But, with the help of a subgroup of commission members from the Congress, they came forth with a major set of recommendations designed to finance the system for fifty years into the future.

That commission has often been used as a model for how we might solve the fiscal crisis, and, indeed, that thinking brought forth the unfortunate National Economic Commission in the late 1980s. I think that one thing that people do not realize about the Social Security crisis of 1983, however, is that it was tiny quantitatively. If you spend a penny more than you earn every year, you will go bankrupt eventually, and that was the type of situation that the Social Security trust fund faced at the time. All the commission recommendations, and some things that the Congress added later, amounted only to about 2 percent of payroll, or to about 1–1.5 percent of GNP. With the fiscal deficit problem, the gap, when the National Economic Commission was meeting, amounted to about 3 percent of GNP, and now it is about 5 or 6 percent of GNP. Consequently, it is a much more serious problem quantitatively. The Greenspan Commission had a much easier task. But still, I give them great credit for coming up with a reform. Most of the reforms were directed at increasing the revenue of the system: payroll taxes were raised, civil servants and others were brought into the system for the first time, the benefits of the more affluent were taxed for the first time, and a cost-of-living (COLA) benefit increase was delayed.

Some see the creation of the commission as a symptom of the lack of courage of politicians, but that ignores the fact that, when the commission's recommendations came to the Congress, the Congress went far beyond the commission in one very important respect. They put the system on an actuarially sound basis for seventy-five years by extending the normal retirement age. That is to say, the age at which full benefits are paid will eventually reach sixty-seven. Under this new approach, people are still allowed to retire as early as age sixty-two, but they suffer an actuarially appropriate reduction in their benefits relative to the full benefits at the new retirement age. This is a very clever way of achieving exactly what I was trying to achieve in the Ford administration by using CPI indexing rather than wage indexing. It implies a lower replacement rate at any specific age of retirement. However, when I talk to laymen, not many people know that falling replacement rates are going to occur in the early twenty-first century, and, whether the reform will survive when people figure it out, I do not know. The replacement rate for a single person retiring at age sixty-five is now a little over 42 percent, while, under this scheme and the assumptions of the actuary, it would decline to 36 percent at age sixty-five by 2030. During the debate on the retirement age, Senator Dole suggested, perhaps with tongue in cheek, that we should index the normal retirement age to life expectancy at age sixty-five. That might not be a bad idea.

The reforms of 1983 focused on Social Security and largely ignored Medicare. This came from focusing on the viability of the trust fund, and the Medicare trust fund at that moment was not in terrible shape, although it was clear that it would go broke eventually. But we could have saved quite a bit of money in the future by increasing the eligibility age for Medicare to the new normal retirement age for Social Security. There was some debate about that, but I gather that people thought that that just might be too tough to swallow at the same time as Social Security was being made less generous. So the eligibility age for Medicare remains at age sixty-five.

There is a continuing controversy over the so-called retirement test: the level of earnings at which you start to lose benefits. That has been made more lenient through time. There was also an important 1983 reform that increased the reward if you work past the normal retirement age. That increase in the reward will phase in very slowly and is not complete until 2007. The reform makes the retirement test less relevant. The reward for waiting for benefits is almost actuarially fair. If the retirement test was eliminated after 2007, some who choose to work longer might nevertheless wait for higher benefits when they do choose to retire.

Perhaps the most important policy event of the 1980s—and I am a little surprised that neither Charles Schultze nor David Stockman discussed this earlier with regard to budget policy—was a law that failed to pass in 1985. At that time, under the very courageous leadership of Senators Bob Dole and Peter Domenici, the Republicans in the Senate fashioned a major federal deficit reduction package, which included as one of its components a COLA reduction for Social Security. A dramatic fight occurred in the Senate—the Republican leadership managed to get a 49-49 tie vote by carrying Pete Wilson in on a stretcher to vote for the package, and Vice President Bush broke the tie, voting for the package. President Reagan, having first backed the package, then turned against it as Republicans in the House fled from the proposal in the face of complaints from the elderly. Speaker Tip O'Neill was also violently against it.

To me, that was a very important event. The proposed cut in Social Security was small, but in the subsequent campaign in 1986, wherever you went, you saw Democratic candidates running ads that the Republicans were against Social Security, and many Republicans, rightly or wrongly, blame that episode for the loss of the Senate in that year. If the package had passed, pensioners would have hardly noticed the cut in benefits, but, ever since that time, Social Security has been far off the bargaining table. The cliché is that it is the third rail of politics: "Touch it and you die." Even options as reasonable as taxing benefits as though they were private pensions are effectively off the table.

Turning to Medicare briefly, the new payment system for hospitals (the DRGs, or diagnosis-related groups) enacted in 1983 is very important. Oversimplifying somewhat, the reform took compensation for hospitals off a cost-plus basis and made it a fee for service. This changed incentives for the better and is saving a lot of money. There were many attempts in the 1980s to reduce payments to physicians by freezing their fees and doing other things, but they outgamed the system every time. Every time their fees were limited, they prescribed more procedures, so their income did not suffer. We now have yet another attempt at reform that promulgates a detailed fee structure with some similarities to the DRG approach used for hospitals. Figures 12.9 and 12.10 showed the growth of Social Security and Medicare slowing somewhat recently, and I believe that that is partly related to some of the curbs on Medicare payments. But, even if these reforms work in the long run, they obviously do not imply a fundamental change in the system. Once you stop cutting payments to providers, the system will just resume growing again at its former rate. And you cannot keep cutting providers year after year.

In conclusion, I think that the elderly have gotten off very easily during the budget wars of the 1980s, given that they get almost half the civilian noninterest budget. The record shows how extraordinarily difficult it is to deal with this powerful constituency. But there is only a very small chance of cutting the rate of growth of civilian noninterest spending in the long run if the nation does not renegotiate its social contract with the elderly. The problem gets very much more serious after 2005, when the baby boomers of the 1940s and 1950s begin to retire. We are sure to return to the issue again and again.

Summary of Discussion

David Stockman explained the events surrounding the unsuccessful 1981 proposals for Social Security reform. He said that a package had been proposed in May 1981 that fleshed out $44 billion in unidentified savings in the original 1981 budget. The plan was directed at structural reform of Social Security— it reduced the benefits received by early retirees and also removed a variety of "social policy add-ons" that had been instituted over time but did not qualify, in Stockman's view, as earned retirement benefits.

The plan was announced on 10 May. By 12 May it was being denounced by the Department of Health and Human Services as a White House plan, and by 15 May it was being advertised by the White House as the Social Security Administration's plan. On 20 May the Senate voted 93-0 against the plan, and that was the end of it.

Martin Feldstein believed that it was the focus on early retirees that had killed the plan. Rather than reducing benefits by 2 or 3 percent for the entire population of retirees, the plan said that sixty-two- to sixty-five-year-olds who were about to retire would face a 20 percent cut in benefits.

William Niskanen argued that the May 1981 Social Security proposal was the major domestic policy mistake of the Reagan administration. He believed that the central lesson of the proposal's failure was that short-term budget concerns often thwart more important structural reforms.

To illustrate this point, Niskanen recalled the genesis of the 1981 proposal. Robert Myers would not entertain any changes in the basic structure of Social Security, but he had recommended a variety of changes in peripheral features of the program. In particular, he had proposed a reduction in the benefits for early retirees from 80 percent of full retirement benefits to either 75 or 70 percent. When an administration task force was considering this issue in the spring of 1981, Stockman had proposed a more drastic cut to only 55 percent of full retirement benefits, effective at the beginning of 1982. The task force had then divided into two groups, with one more concerned about early budget savings and the other more interested in long-term reform. Niskanen had been a member of the latter group, which revived the recommendations of the Hsiao report, recommendations that Penner had tried to implement during the Ford administration and that economist Henry Aaron had pushed during the Carter administration. The crucial recommendation was to index the "bend points" in the benefit formula to prices rather than wages; over time, this would transform Social Security from a system that maintains relative incomes into one that maintains real incomes. The replacement rate (the ratio of benefits to preretirement earnings) would drop gradually, without reducing the real benefits of anyone who is currently retired or near retirement. This approach reduces spending by trillions of dollars in present discounted value, but it produces almost no savings in the first year or even over a five-year budget horizon. Niskanen believed that the task force did not give this proposal sufficient consideration because of this lack of short-run savings, but he stressed that the recommendation remains the most politically realistic proposal for substantive reform.

Stockman agreed with Niskanen's description of this debate, although he added that the administration's proposal had included some bend point reform. Stockman also argued that the Hsiao report made Social Security reform sound easier than it actually was. If the bend points were in fact indexed to prices, there would be no real return on workers' contributions to the program. Stockman asserted, therefore, that something must be added to the indexing formula to proxy for the average real asset return over time. He agreed that the current approach of indexing benefits to wages or productivity is clearly excessive.

Rudolph Penner noted that, even under the Hsiao report's recommendations, Congress could increase benefits at any time in order to provide a real return on workers' contributions. Penner had supported the Hsiao report, however, because he believed that such increases would be less generous than increases generated automatically from the growth in real wages.

Feldstein added that indexing the bend points to prices would cause the entire system to shrink over time in real terms, encouraging people to put more money into private savings and pensions.

Feldstein then shifted the discussion to the Social Security reforms of 1983. Those reforms entail future increases in the regular retirement age and thus represent a significant implicit reduction in benefits. The combination of delayed retirement and the expected increase in life expectancy will mean a decline in the replacement rate for sixty-five-year-olds from 42 percent today to 36 percent in 2012. Further, essentially all those benefits in 2012 will be taxed because the 1983 reforms also called for taxing all benefits above a quite high, but unindexed, threshold.

Stockman contrasted the political design of the successful 1983 reforms with that of the failed 1981 reforms. The 1983 plan was officially sponsored by a bipartisan commission led by Alan Greenspan, but it really had been negotiated by Speaker of the House Tip O'Neill, Senator Daniel Patrick Moynihan, Senator Bob Dole, Representative Dan Rostenkowski, and President Reagan. It was arranged that President Reagan and Tip O'Neill would make simultaneous announcements endorsing the package, thereby eliminating any possible stigma or blame. This approach had worked perfectly, and it presented a brilliant act of leadership in the face of a very large national problem.

Stockman noted, however, that the reforms included only one short-term benefit change—a six-month delay in the annual cost-of-living adjustment. In the year that this delay occurred, the inflation rate had fallen to only 3.8 percent, so the delay represented a 1.9 percent real reduction in benefits for the 36 million people then receiving Social Security. Although their benefits remained permanently lower as a result, the delay had no impact on the benefits to be received by future retirees. If this delay had been implemented in 1980, on the other hand, when the inflation rate was 12.6 percent, there would have been a 6.3 percent real, permanent reduction in benefits. Stockman added that the decision to delay the cost-of-living adjustment had been made by the commission but had not been publicly announced until later; the precise mechanism for the delay was determined by Congress.

James Tobin wondered whether reductions in Social Security benefits would lead to equal reductions in payroll taxes or to reductions in the budget deficit instead. He believed that these two ways of thinking about the relation of Social Security to the rest of the federal budget corresponded to two different views that one might have of the role of the Social Security program. One view is that Social Security is a very large transfer program, involving both a large part of federal taxes and a large part of federal spending. From this perspective, for example, Moynihan is correct that the United States is using payroll taxes as a way of financing general government needs. The other view is that Social Security is a retirement program, admittedly an "imperfect and awkward" one, in which one pays taxes in order to accumulate an entitlement to future benefits. If one thinks that workers are paying more into this plan than the benefits are worth to them, then one would reduce both benefits and taxes, and there would be no effect on the deficit.

Feldstein responded that the big difference between a private pension plan and Social Security is that, until recently, the Social Security program was accumulating no assets. Thus, Social Security was reducing national saving by substituting for the asset accumulation that otherwise would have occurred through private pensions or personal saving. The 1983 reforms were a partial response to this problem because they initiated the accumulation of surpluses in the Social Security trust fund. But he believed that the policy had been proposed in order to smooth the projected tax rate, not as a deliberate effort to raise national saving. Feldstein added that the system is still pay as you go over the next seventy-five years but involves a massive buildup of assets over current workers' lifetimes.

Penner said that he regarded Social Security as a transfer program, not a retirement program, because the redistribution goals of the system imply that the amount of taxes paid by an individual has little relation to the amount of benefits received. For someone retiring today, the ratio of the present value of benefits to taxes is quite high, computed at a 2 percent real discount rate, but for most single people starting to work today, and for more affluent married couples, the present value of benefits is projected to be quite a bit less than the present value of taxes. Thus, Penner saw great merit in Moynihan's proposal to cut the payroll tax and return to a more explicit pay-as-you-go system, but only if other taxes were increased so that the deficit would not rise. But he recognized that such tax increases were a "political dream" in the current environment.

Stockman added that the Social Security system involves enormous transfers between income classes as well as between generations. First, the benefit and contribution rules shift income from those who have higher lifetime earnings to those who have lower lifetime earnings. Second, and more important, the rules index everybody's early earnings to the cumulative productivity growth in the economy over the following forty years. So the system is designed to capture the economic growth over time for every cohort of retirees and to slightly shift income from the better off to the worse off. This is a public fiscal program, not a retirement program.

Michael Mussa said that the total benefits being provided to retirees by current taxpayers had increased substantially over time as a share of GNP. He thought that the critical question is, What is the expected present discounted value of the benefits that current retirees will receive from both Social Security and Medicare, as compared to the present discounted value of their contributions to those programs? Although Penner discussed the Social Security replacement rate for those currently retired, he did not compare the benefits from these programs to the benefits that those same contributions would have purchased in a private pension or health insurance plan.

Penner thought that most people retiring in the early twenty-first century will earn roughly a market rate of return on their and their employers' contributions to Social Security. In contrast, the real return for all people retiring before the late 1980s is highly positive. Penner then returned to the replacement rate concept to capture the income redistribution element of Social Security. A retiree with average lifetime earnings faces a 42 percent replacement rate today, while someone who earned the Social Security maximum throughout his or her life faces roughly a 25 percent replacement rate, and someone who always earned the minimum wage faces a 57 percent rate.

Feldstein returned to the rationale for the 1983 Social Security agreement. He asked to what extent the agreement had been viewed as a way of reducing the budget deficit by increasing revenue through the Social Security system rather than through an explicit increase in general taxes. Also, to what extent had it been seen as a way of balancing benefits and taxes over the seventy-five years of the actuaries' projections? And to what extent had it been viewed as a way to avoid big future tax increases because of a concern that future generations of workers would not agree to those tax increases?

Stockman said that the Greenspan Commission had been driven by two numbers. One was the short-run solvency target, which had been $167 billion from 1983 to 1990. The 1983 reforms dealt with this problem by accelerating taxes that were scheduled to take effect later anyway. Thus, the planned 1986 tax increase was moved to 1985, the 1990 increase to 1989, and there was a six-month delay in the cost-of-living adjustment. The other important number was the seventy-five-year projection of the trust fund balance, which estimated that benefits would exceed taxes by 1.9 percent of payroll. Stockman said that people had not viewed the 1983 reforms as changing the Social Security system from a pay-as-you-go basis to a fully funded plan with an accumulation of capital.

Charles Schultze pointed out, however, that Poterba's paper quotes Tip O'Neill as saying that the reforms *had* fundamentally changed the way that the system works. Schultze also explained two aspects of the Social Security benefit rules that had greatly distorted the system by 1983. First, the old measure of the CPI had overstated inflation by roughly 10 percent between 1971 and 1981. This overstatement led to permanently higher benefits for everyone who was retired at the time, although, as those people pass away, this issue will disappear. Second, and more systematically, the indexing formula for benefits guarantees the elderly an absolute standard of living after they retire. Thus, the elderly are unaffected by supply shocks that hurt the rest of the population. By 1982, this indexing formula may have benefits by roughly 4 percent above the level based on more reasonable indexing.

Geoffrey Carliner commented that the discussion had proceeded as if the elderly were a special interest group, like farmers or the oil and gas industry, who had been able to win a generous support program from the government. But, during this period of Social Security expansion, there had been huge decreases in poverty among the aged and widespread public support for the program. Carliner suggested that Social Security should be viewed not as a success story for a special interest group but rather as a program that is understood and liked by most people.

Penner agreed that there is enormously strong and widespread support for Social Security. The public choice theory of special interest groups is based on the idea of concentrated benefits and diffused costs, where some small group receives a benefit whose cost is diffused throughout society and is so small that no one objects. The elderly do not fit this definition of a special interest because they are a large group and the cost of Social Security is very apparent in everyone's paycheck. Further, when one talks about reducing Social Security benefits, most of the complaints come not from the elderly but from their children, who are concerned that, if the government pays less, they will have to pay more. And, when one suggests increasing the eligibility age for Medicaid along with the normal retirement age under Social Security, the complaints come from corporate benefit officers, who realize that they would have to pay more in medical benefits.

Penner argued, however, that some of the support for these programs is based on a misperception. A recent *Los Angeles Times* poll showed that a vast majority of the public thinks of the elderly as one of the country's neediest groups. But, when one looks at the income of the elderly and adjusts for household size, it is clear that their income has grown faster than everyone else's and has reached a higher average level. What this average obscures is that the young elderly are generally better off, and one can still find horror stories among the very old. So, when people think of the elderly, they tend to think of the very poor, although they are no more representative of the elderly than are the retired people playing golf in Palm Beach.

Stockman said that, before any taxes or transfers are counted, 53 percent of the elderly have incomes below the poverty level. But, including taxes, cash transfers like Social Security, and in-kind transfers, only 4 percent of the elderly live below the poverty line. So the combined effect of all government policies toward the aged is to take a population that is 50 percent poor and make it 4 percent poor. This role for the government is now built into the fabric of U.S. society, so the aged are not a special interest group, and these policies will never be fundamentally changed.

Feldstein responded that people's private income during retirement is not independent of the fact that they can count on Social Security. *Stockman* emphasized that one cannot go back to 1935 and restart the world by telling everybody to do more private saving.

David Wise asked about the political power of the elderly. Did the expansion of Social Security in the 1970s arise from that political power, or did it result from the peace dividend as the Vietnam War was ending? It was Wise's impression that the Social Security expansion was essentially unrelated to the increasing portion of the population that was old or to the lobbying of the American Association of Retired Persons (AARP).

Penner admitted that payroll taxes had been increased to match the increase in benefits at the same time that the end of the Vietnam surtax was reducing income taxes. He was uncertain whether that huge increase in benefits and payroll taxes would have been possible without the peace dividend and accompanying income tax cut.

More generally, he believed that the elderly are extremely powerful politically but that it would be impossible for them to capture such a large share of GNP without the strong support of most of the rest of the population. Polls suggest that even the youngest workers strongly support Social Security, even though some of them do not believe that the program will exist when they retire.

Feldstein added that, when he had gone to Washington as chairman of the Council of Economic Advisers, he had thought that he had arrived in Washington at *the* moment when Social Security benefits were likely to be cut. But, even when the Greenspan Commission was searching for ways to return the system to solvency, there were no votes for significant reductions in benefits.

Wise said that it was natural that taking benefits away would be very hard, but he was still curious about the politics surrounding the increases in benefits in the 1970s.

Stockman said that the political power of the elderly and of the AARP had developed in the 1980s out of a fear of Social Security benefit reductions. He did not think that the elderly had played a large role in the earlier expansion of Social Security; rather, he believed that the expansion of the program (and its design more generally) had been the work of an unusually small priesthood of technicians. Prior to 1970, the Social Security actuaries had not included inflation in their work because people did not believe that inflation was a permanent part of the system. When inflation was first included in the seventy-five-year projections in the 1970s, the priesthood had made a number of decisions about bend points, indexing, and so on. One decision was to tie future benefits to the total growth of the economy, in the form of wage indexing of the bend points. When this rule became part of the expectations of the elderly population (with one correction of the technical error that caused double indexing in 1977), the elderly lobby was able to prevent the rule from being changed. But the elderly did not push the expansion through; the priesthood did.

Charls Walker turned to the role of commissions in resolving difficult public policy problems. He believed that the success of the Greenspan Commission showed that well-constructed commissions are sometimes able to deal with issues that weak congressional leadership cannot. He argued that the inability of the National Economic Commission to resolve the budget deficit problem was due not to an inherent failing of commissions but instead to particular circumstances at the time. When the tax issue arose during the presidential campaign, George Bush should have said that Congress had chosen a distinguished group of Americans to devise a solution and that he would listen to what they proposed before making up his mind. But when Bush said to "read his lips," he had committed himself to a course of action that precluded acceptance of the commission's ideas.

Feldstein returned to a central theme of the conference, namely, the role of economic analysis in the making of economic policy. He argued that economic analysis had played almost no role in the macroeconomic aspects of Social Security reform—determining the appropriate buildup of the trust fund—except in the almost trivial sense of having enough money in the fund to pay the future bills. But on the microeconomic aspects of reform—the retirement test on earnings and the delay in the retirement age—the economic analysis about the extent to which Social Security distorts retirement decisions had apparently gotten through to policymakers, and the reforms embodied the kinds of changes for which economists had been pressing.

Penner believed that the 1983 reforms that increased the reward for working beyond the normal retirement age had been motivated by a strong sense of fairness as well as by the economic analysis of possible distortions to people's retirement decisions. Penner found it hard to believe that the retirement test actually is very important to work effort because there is a strong trend toward early retirement anyway. He suspected, however, that many of the elderly who work do not report that fact to the government.

Feldstein said that, when all the approved changes are fully phased in, they will eliminate any differential in the present value of benefits based on whether one retires early, at the regular age, or late. *Wise* added that, given the elimination of this differential, the major effect of the reforms on labor force participation would come from changing the early retirement age, not from changing the normal retirement age.

Paul Joskow raised the issue of Medicare. The introduction of diagnostic related groups (DRGs) in 1983 seemed to be a good example of the use of economic analysis in policy-making. The idea had come from people who studied regulation, and it had been designed to promote fundamental changes in the health care system. The effects had not been as large as people would like, and they may not be as long lasting, but, as a consequence of the government buying medical care in a different and more sensible way, even private insurers have changed their approach to reimbursing health care providers. Joskow asked Penner whether policymakers at the time had perceived the introduction of DRGs as a significant event in terms of health care provisions and financing or whether it had been viewed as just a way of balancing the books?

Penner responded that this had been a clear case of a policy analyst's dream coming true. Even the strongest advocates of this reform, however, were very concerned that the system might find some way around the new rules, and that has yet to be proved one way or the other. But he had found the first reports of the effectiveness of the reform very encouraging because it appeared that a lot of money had been saved without significantly lowering the quality of patient care.

Biographies

This list shows affiliations as of the time of the conference as well as previous government service.

Alberto Alesina
Assistant Professor of Economics, Harvard University
Faculty Research Fellow, National Bureau of Economic
   Research

Phillip Areeda
Professor of Law, Harvard University School of Law
Counsel to President Ford (1974–75)

Elizabeth Bailey
Visiting Scholar, Yale University
Professor of Economics, Industrial Administration and
   Public Policy, Carnegie Mellon University
Commissioner, Civil Aeronautics Board (1977–83)

William F. Baxter
Professor of Law, Stanford University School of Law
Assistant Attorney General (1981–83)

C. Fred Bergsten
Director, Institute for International Economics
Assistant Secretary of the Treasury (1977–81)

James Burnley
Partner, Shaw, Pittman, Potts & Trowbridge
Secretary of Transportation (1987–90)

Geoffrey Carliner
Executive Director, National Bureau of Economic
   Research
Senior Staff Economist, Council of Economic Advisers
   (1980–84)

Christopher DeMuth   President, American Enterprise Institute
Administrator of Information and Regulatory Affairs,
Office of Management and Budget (1981–84)

Douglas W. Elmendorf Assistant Professor of Economics, Harvard University

Thomas O. Enders   Managing Director, International Corporate Finance,
Salomon Brothers
Ambassador to Spain (1983–86)
Assistant Secretary of State for Inter-American Affairs
(1981–83)

Martin Feldstein   Professor of Economics, Harvard University
President and Chief Executive Officer, National Bureau
of Economic Research
Chairman, Council of Economic Advisers (1982–84)

Jeffrey A. Frankel   Professor of Economics, University of California,
Berkeley
Research Associate, National Bureau of Economic
Research
Senior Staff Economist, Council of Economic Advisers
(1983–84)

Don Fullerton   Professor of Economics, University of Virginia
Research Associate, National Bureau of Economic
Research
Deputy Assistant Secretary of the Treasury (1985–87)

William M. Isaac   Managing Director and Chief Executive Officer, Secura
Group
Chairman, Federal Deposit Insurance Corporation
(1981–85)

Paul L. Joskow   Professor of Economics, Massachusetts Institute of
Technology
Research Associate, National Bureau of Economic
Research
Public Member, Administrative Conference of the United
States (1980–82)
Member, National Committee for the Revision of
Antitrust Laws (1978)

Paul Krugman   Professor of Economics, Massachusetts Institute of
Technology
Research Associate, National Bureau of Economic
Research
Senior Staff Economist, Council of Economic Advisers
(1982–83)

Robert E. Litan	Senior Fellow, Brookings Institution Senior Staff Economist, Council of Economic Advisers (1977–79)
Russell B. Long	Long Law Firm United States Senator (1948–87)
Michael Mussa	Professor of Business, University of Chicago Member, Council of Economic Advisers (1986–88)
William A. Niskanen	Chairman, CATO Institute Member, Council of Economic Advisers (1981–85)
Roger G. Noll	Professor of Economics, Stanford University Senior Staff Economist, Council of Economic Advisers (1967–69)
Lionel H. Olmer	Partner, Paul, Weiss, Rifkind, Wharton and Garrison Undersecretary of International Trade, Department of Commerce (1981–85)
Rudolph Penner	Senior Fellow, Urban Institute Director, Congressional Budget Office (1983–87)
William Poole	Professor of Economics, Brown University Research Associate, National Bureau of Economic Research Member, Council of Economic Advisers (1982–85)
James M. Poterba	Professor of Economics, Massachusetts Institute of Technology Research Associate, National Bureau of Economic Research
Harry M. Reasoner	Partner, Vinson & Elkins Chairman, Antitrust Section of the American Bar Association (1989–90)
William R. Rhodes	Senior Executive-International, Citibank, N.A. Group Executive Chairman, Restructuring Committee (1986–90)
J. David Richardson	Professor of Economics, Syracuse University Research Associate, National Bureau of Economic Research Lecturer, Foreign Service Institute, Department of State (1985–) Visiting Scholar, Federal Reserve Board (1978)

Charles Schultze	Director of Economic Studies, Brookings Institution Chairman, Council of Economic Advisers (1977–81) Director, Office of Management and Budget (1965–67)
Paula Stern	President, The Stern Group Fellow, Foreign Policy Institute, Johns Hopkins University Chairman, International Trade Commission (1984–86)
David Stockman	Partner, Blackstone Group Director, Office of Management and Budget (1981–85) Member, United States Congress (1977–81)
William Taylor	Staff Director, Division of Banking, Supervision and Regulation, Federal Reserve Board
James Tobin	Professor of Economics, Yale University Member, Council of Economic Advisers (1961–62)
W. Kip Viscusi	Professor of Economics, Duke University Deputy Director, President's Council on Wage and Price Stability (1979–80)
Paul A. Volcker	Chairman, J. D. Wolfensohn Company Chairman, Federal Reserve Board (1979–87)
Charls E. Walker	Charls E. Walker Associates Undersecretary of the Treasury (1969–72)
Murray Weidenbaum	Director, Center for the Study of American Business, Washington University Chairman, Council of Economic Advisers (1981–82)
David A. Wise	Professor of Economics, Harvard University Research Associate, National Bureau of Economic Research
Richard G. Woodbury	Doctoral Candidate, Harvard University

Contributors

Alberto Alesina
Department of Economics
Harvard University
Cambridge, MA 02138

Phillip Areeda
Harvard Law School
Langdell Hall West
Cambridge, MA 02138

Elizabeth Bailey
Carnegie Mellon University, GSIA
Frew & Tech Streets
Room 226
Pittsburgh, PA 15213

William F. Baxter
Stanford Law School
Stanford University
Palo Alto, CA 94305

C. Fred Bergsten
Institute for International Economics
11 Dupont Circle, NW
Washington, DC 20036

James Burnley
Shaw, Pittman, Potts & Trowbridge
2300 N Street, NW
Washington, DC 20037

Geoffrey Carliner
National Bureau of Economic Research
1050 Massachusetts Avenue
Cambridge, MA 02138

Christopher DeMuth
American Enterprise Institute
1150 17th Street, NW
Washington, DC 20036

Douglas W. Elmendorf
National Bureau of Economic Research
1050 Massachusetts Avenue
Cambridge, MA 02138

Thomas O. Enders
Salomon Brothers, Inc.
125 Broad Street, 14th Floor
New York, NY 10004

Martin Feldstein
National Bureau of Economic Research
1050 Massachusetts Avenue
Cambridge, MA 02138

Jeffrey A. Frankel
Department of Economics
University of California
Evans Hall
Berkeley, CA 94720

Don Fullerton
Department of Economics
University of Virginia
Rouss Hall
Charlottesville, VA 22901

William M. Isaac
Secura Group
3 Lafayette Center
1155 21st. NW Suite 850
Washington, DC 20036

Paul L. Joskow
Department of Economics
MIT E52-2808
50 Memorial Drive
Cambridge, MA 02139

Paul Krugman
Department of Economics
MIT E52-383
50 Memorial Drive
Cambridge, MA 02139

Robert E. Litan
The Brookings Institution
1775 Massachusetts Avenue, NW
Washington, DC 20036

Russell B. Long
Long Law Firm
1455 Pennsylvania Avenue, NW
Suite 975
Washington, DC 20004

Michael Mussa
Graduate School of Business
University of Chicago
1101 East 58th Street
Chicago, IL 60637

William A. Niskanen
The CATO Institute
224 2nd Street, SE
Washington, DC 20003

Roger G. Noll
Department of Economics
Stanford University
Stanford, CA 94305

Lionel H. Olmer
Paul, Weiss, Rifkind, Wharton and
  Garrison
1615 L Street, NW
Suite 1300
Washington, DC 20036

Rudolph Penner
The Urban Institute
2100 M Street, NW
Washington, DC 20037

William Poole
Department of Economics
Brown University
Providence, RI 02912

James M. Poterba
Department of Economics
MIT E52-350
50 Memorial Drive
Cambridge, MA 02139

Harry M. Reasoner
Vinson & Elkins
3300 First City Tower
1001 Fannin
Houston, TX 77002

William R. Rhodes
Citibank
399 Park Avenue
New York, NY 10043

J. David Richardson
Department of Economics
202 Maxwell Hall
Syracuse University
Syracuse, NY 13244

Charles Schultze
The Brookings Institution
1775 Massachusetts Avenue
Washington, DC 20036

Paula Stern
The Stern Group
1133 Connecticut Avenue, NW Suite
  1000
Washington, DC 20036

David Stockman
Blackstone Group
345 Park Avenue, 31st Floor
New York, NY 10154

William Taylor
Passed away on August 20, 1992

James Tobin
Cowles Foundation
Yale University
30 Hillhouse Ave.
New Haven, CT 06520

W. Kip Viscusi
Department of Economics
Duke University
Durham, NC 27706

Paul A. Volcker
J. D. Wolfensohn Company, Inc.
599 Lexington Avenue, 40th Floor
New York, NY 10022

Charls E. Walker
Charls Walker Association
1730 Pennsylvania Avenue, NW
  Suite 200
Washington, DC 20006

Murray Weidenbaum
Center for the Study of American
  Business
Washington University
St. Louis, MO 63130

David A. Wise
National Bureau of Economic Research
1050 Massachusetts Avenue
Cambridge, MA 02138

Richard G. Woodbury
National Bureau of Economic Research
1050 Massachusetts Avenue
Cambridge, MA 02138

Name Index

Subject Index

Accelerated Cost Recovery System (ACRS): introduction in 1981 ERTA legislation, 247; opposition to and support for depreciation levels, 180–81; in 1981 tax legislation, 172

ACRS. *See* Accelerated Cost Recovery System (ACRS)

Act to Regulate Commerce of 1887, 404–5

ADR. *See* Asset Depreciation Range (ADR)

Age Discrimination Act of 1986, 759–60

Agricultural marketing orders, 506

Agricultural sector: regulatory change in Reagan Administration, 442; response to exchange rate policy, 323–24

Airline Deregulation Act of 1978, 380, 394

Airline industry: deregulation in, 391–404; effects of deregulation, 394–99; regulatory changes in, 380–82; safety record with deregulation, 403–4

American Conference of Governmental Industrial Hygienists (ACGIH), 485

American Telephone and Telegraph Company (AT&T): antitrust suit against, 443, 593–96, 601–4; postreform performance, 419–24; regulation of, 409, 411; with settlement of antitrust action (1982), 414–15. *See also* Western Electric

Anti-inflation policy: of Federal Reserve, 6, 66, 152; impact on savings and loans,

526–32; Reagan administration assistance to, 162

Antitrust action: against AT&T (1949, 1974), 412, 414–15, 593–96, 600–605; against IBM, 605–6, 623; in intellectual property cases, 606–9; in LTV/Republic merger, 624; merger guidelines, 608–12, 621; against monopolies, 597–98; in predatory pricing, 596–97, 621

Antitrust laws: attempts to remake, 616–17; decline of private enforcement of, 617

Antitrust policy: amicus program, 612–14; federal court system produces, 599; players in, 575–78; role of courts and judges in enforcement of, 575–78; states' role in, 575, 618–19; on vertical integration, 593–98

Arab-Israeli War (1973), 87

Asset Depreciation Range (ADR), 172, 215

Automobile industry: Carter regulatory reform efforts, 474; effect of U.S. trade policy on, 689–90; protection for, 674–76; Reagan regulatory reform measures, 474–78; safety regulations, 498–99; safety regulations of, 513–14

Baker-Miyazawa yen/dollar agreement, 306

Baker Plan, 696–98, 700, 703, 716–17, 728

Balanced Budget Act, 266–67